GunDigest 2014

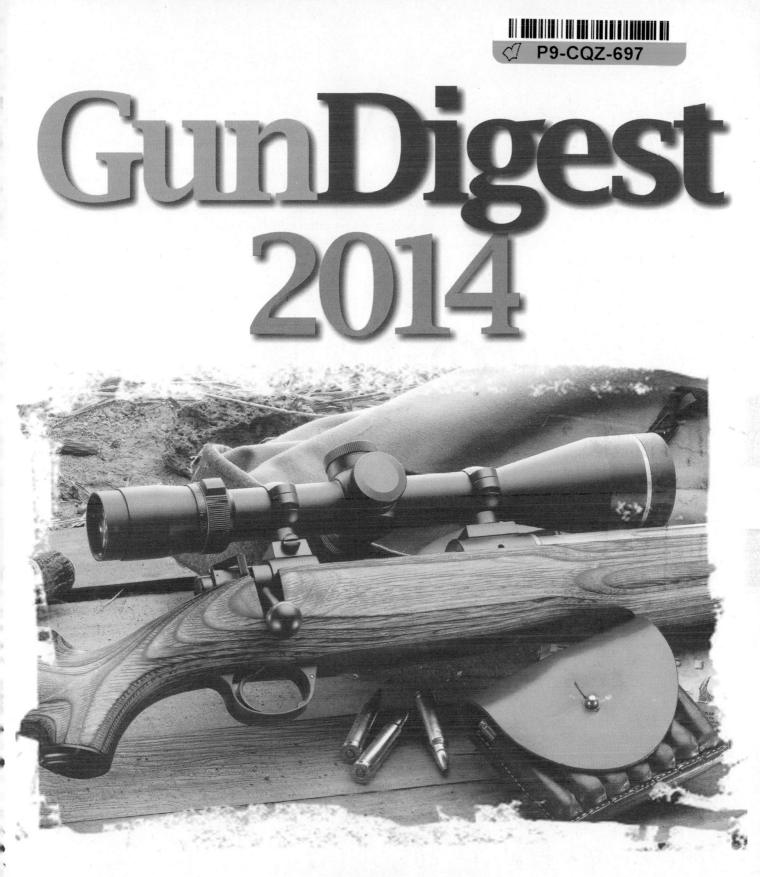

Edited by
JERRY LEE

Published by

Gun Digest® Books, an imprint of F+W Media, Inc.
Krause Publications · 700 East State Street · Iola, WI 54990-0001
715-445-2214 · 888-457-2873
www.krausebooks.com

To order books or other products call toll-free 1-800-258-0929
or visit us online at **www.gundigeststore.com**

CAUTION: Technical data presented here, particularly technical data on handloading and on firearms adjustment and alteration, inevitably reflects individual experience with particular equipment and components under specific circumstances the reader cannot duplicate exactly. Such data presentations therefore should be used for guidance only and with caution. Gun Digest Books accepts no responsibility for results obtained using these data.

ISSN 0072-9043

ISBN 13: 978-1-4402-3542-9
ISBN 10: 1-4402-3542-2

Cover & Design by Tom Nelsen

Edited by Jerry Lee & Jennifer L.S. Pearsall

Printed in the United States of America

John T. Amber
LITERARY AWARD

It's our pleasure to announce that Tom Caceci is the recipient of the 32nd Annual John T. Amber Literary Award. The award is presented in recognition of his excellent story, "The Hillsville Courthouse Tragedy," which was published in last year's 67th Edition of *Gun Digest*. Tom's detailed account told of a gun battle that took place in a courtroom in the southwest Virginia town of Hillsville, in 1912, following a guilty verdict in a murder trial. The shootout took the lives of a judge, a sheriff, an attorney, and a member of the jury and was a national news story at the time.

Tom Caceci has been involved in hunting, shooting, and gun collecting for more than 50 years. He's a native of New York City, and, in his teenage years (long before the restrictive laws of today), New York was home to many fine gun shops where Tom spent his Saturday afternoons, whenever he could. This included the greatest one of all, the famous Gun Room at the original Abercrombie & Fitch department store, where an awe-struck 14-year-old wasn't allowed to touch anything, but could dream of someday owning and using one of the gorgeous guns on display.

We asked Tom to tell us about himself and his interest in firearms.

"I like to combine my interest in history and my fascination with the technical aspects of firearms development to write about famous guns and historical events. My collecting interests include Webley revolvers and Lee-Enfield rifles, and I'm also fascinated by guns of the 'transitional' era between muzzleloaders and guns using fixed ammunition.

"The major historical events of the years between 1875 and 1939—the close of the American frontier, the ascendance of the United States to the status of a major world power, and tensions in Europe that led to major wars— all were accompanied by revolutionary changes in firearms technology. Those events were the testing ground for new ideas and new operating principles. The design challenges of the times were met by geniuses like John Moses Browning and J.D. Pederson, and the products of their workshops were used by good men and bad, for both good and for evil. Firearms and their use are threads woven into the fabric of our nation. I hope my writing on historical subjects helps to convey some sense of connection between prior times and our own.

"In 2010, I put my love of history and of larger-than-life characters together with my passion for African hunting, to produce a piece in the 2011 *Gun Digest* about an H&H double rifle President Roosevelt took on his famous 1909 safari, 'T.R.'s Big (Fire) Stick.'

"In southwest Virginia, the story of the Hillsville courthouse tragedy is well known, and, so, it was a natural subject for me to write about, with its drama, colorful characters, pathos and, of course, the classic guns used in the event."

Tom bought his first hunting license at the age of 13 and has been as active as he could be in the field ever since, having hunted large and small game on four continents so far, much of it using "traditional" blackpowder rifles. He took a fine warthog in Namibia with a T/C .54 a couple of years ago.

Tom is a Benefactor Member of the NRA, first becoming a member of the organization nearly half a century ago. He obtained his first NRA Instructor certification, in 1968, and is currently certified in several shooting disciplines. As an active member of a local shooting club, he has provided many hours of instruction to new shooters and hunters over the 26 years he's lived in southwest Virginia, where he is also a Master Hunter Education Instructor with the Virginia Department of Game and Inland Fisheries' Outdoors Education program. Tom is also a Charter Member of the Professional Outdoors Media Association, and he has a website devoted to hunting, shooting, and gun collecting in Virginia's New River Valley.

Tom served in the United States Air Force, from 1969 to 1975, including a year in Vietnam. Following military service, he attended graduate school at Georgetown University, and today he is a professor of Basic Sciences at the Virginia-Maryland Regional College of Veterinary Medicine. Before moving to Virginia, in 1987, he spent five years teaching at Texas A&M's veterinary school. Tom says his work in veterinary education has allowed him to write articles that draw on a knowledge of animal structure and physiology, as it applies to large and small game.

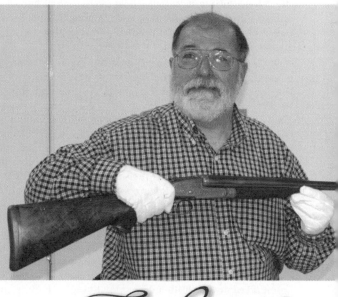

Tom Caceci

The late Dan Shideler recruited Tom to be a Contributing Editor for the *Standard Catalog of Firearms*, in 2007, to do a piece on an interesting offshoot of firearms technology, the "humane killer" used by veterinarians. When Dan took over *Gun Digest*, Tom continued to write for him. For a couple years he covered the SHOT Show, reporting on new developments in air guns. In addition to *Gun Digest* and the *Standard Catalog*, Tom has long been a writer for *Magnum*, the most widely circulated hunting and shooting publication in South Africa, and for *African Outfitter* and *Safari & Hunting Magazine*.

We asked Tom about his future writing plans. He said, "I've been a teacher pretty much my entire adult life. Writing for popular publications about the things I love is a way of continuing to teach, even as I wind down my working career. Young people are the future of the shooting sports, and I want to do whatever I can to give them a sense of history, as well as passing on the importance of firearms, shooting, and hunting as part of the mainstream of American life."

Congratulations Tom Caceci, recipient of the John T. Amber Literary Award! Well deserved!

WELCOME
to the 2014 Edition of *Gun Digest*!

Welcome to the 68th Edition of the World's Greatest Gun Book! Once again we've assembled a group of some of the best writers in the field to share their knowledge and opinions on firearms and their uses. Among the bylines are many that are familiar to regular readers of this publication, and, as always, we like to introduce a few new writers.

Jim Wilson is new to *Gun Digest*, but his name is probably a familiar one to most readers. In this edition he explores the concept of the back-up gun and the idea that, if you need to carry a gun, you probably need to carry two. Wilson is currently seen in the pages of *American Rifleman* and his face is known to viewers of several shooting-related TV programs produced by the NRA and aired on the Outdoor Channel. He also is a senior field editor for NRA Publications. Sheriff Jim's writings previously have appeared in *Guns & Ammo, Petersen's Handguns, Handloader,* and *Shooting Times.* Some of his readers may also know that he is a popular entertainer on the cowboy music circuit, who has recorded several CDs of classic and modern songs about the Great American West. Wilson spent 30 years as a peace officer is Texas, serving as the elected sheriff of Crockett County, down near the Rio Grande. I asked him for a comment on his career, and he said, "I have spent all of my adult life making my living with guns, and it's been a mighty good life."

Also among those new to *Gun Digest* is Denys Beauchemin, who gives us a very complete introduction to F-Class high-power shooting. This fast-growing sport involves long-range shooting, with scopes and from the prone position, making it popular with hunters. The "F" in F-Class is in honor of George "Farky" Farquharson, the Canadian shooter who originated the discipline. Denys Beauchemin is a software engineer in his day job and has been shooting competitively on and off for 30 years in IPSC, Ful-bore, Palma, Service Rifle and, most recently, F-class, where he has attained the classifications of Mid-Range High Master and Long Range Expert, all in F-TR. He is active in his club in South Texas, serving as the Long Range Match Director, herding cats, and welcoming new shooters to the discipline. Denys has been writing technical articles for many years and has recently started writing about shooting and competition for the general public. He likes to caution new competitors with, "Beware, competitive shooting can be very addictive, and you will be amazed at how accurate you can become."

Another new byline in this edition is that of Buck Pope. For many years, he has planned his "someday" rifle, a custom gun made to his very own needs and specifications. Buck tells the story of his Prescott Stalking Rifle in this edition. He is fortunate to live in Prescott, Arizona, a beautiful little city that is home to many companies and individuals in the firearms industry. Among them are several craftsmen involved in the creation of custom rifles, such as Pope's Prescott Stalking Rifle. After retiring from General Motors Corporation almost 20 years ago, Buck started his second career as an outdoor writer and is a regular contributor to several publications. He has been an avid hunter and involved with guns and shooting all if his life. Over the years he has hunted a large variety of big game and has also worked as a guide in Alaska, Wyoming, and New Mexico.

Highlights Of This Edition

Just what is a "magnum" rifle cartridge? The definition has certainly changed over the years. Back in the '50s, a magnum cartridge had to have a belt and the name had to include "H&H," "Weatherby," or "Norma." Since those days, many new calibers have come on the scene, including various magnums, some that have been successful and some not. Jon Sundra gives us an in-depth look at the winners and losers, including the great saga of the short-magnums.

There are several reports in this 68th Edition that are devoted to some of the more significant models in rifle history. Phil Schreier profiles Teddy Roosevelt's long association with Winchester lever-actions, including the Model 1895. Phil is Senior Curator at the NRA's National Firearms Museum and has some exceptional photos in his story. Our buddy Phil appears with Museum Director, Jim Supica, on the TV show, *Guns & Gold*, Monday nights on the Sportsman's Channel.

Paul Scarlata tells a well-researched story of the Ross, the unique straight-pull action rifle that became entangled in Canadian politics in the first decade of the last century. There have been many rumors, myths, and mysteries surrounding this controversial battle rifle over the years, and Scarlata provides some provocative insights.

Terry Wieland gives us a superb story on what he calls the world's finest production rifle, the Mannlicher-Schoenauer. He makes a strong case for that opinion by giving his story the title, "In a Class By Itself." From the early 1900s through the 1960s, the various M/S models set the standard for what a quality "gentleman's rifle" should be. To this day, there are many who agree that the workmanship of these fine rifles and carbines is unsurpassed.

For almost half a century now, Winchester aficionados have been comparing the pre-'64 Model 70 to the later versions. Wayne van Zwoll examines the evolution of the "rifleman's rifle," including the good and the bad changes along the way and how the current model stacks up with the original. In his report, he also dares to suggest that reader's forget the pre-'64.

Is the wildcat cartridge a dying breed? With more than 130 factory centerfire calibers currently being loaded, do we need more? You can always find someone who will answer in the affirmative, and that gives gun writers something to write about. Larry Sterett takes on the subject and provides an excellent look at the history of wildcats in his article on the care and feeding of same.

On the military side, Gary Paul Johnston, a retired law enforcement officer who has been writing about guns for many years, compares two battle rifles of the mid-twentieth century, the M14 and the FN-FAL. Both designs came about not long after World War II, and there is some interesting history that Gary shares in his story with his great title, "Old Soldiers Never Die, They Just Get Upgraded." Also, we have an excellent report by Corey Graff on the Remington M24 Sniper Rifle.

Turning to handguns, John Taffin has been a fan of Ruger single-action revolvers since they first appeared on the scene in the 1950s, back when John was a teenager. He has tinkered, modified, and customized many a Ruger since then, and now he shares those experiences in this edition. Taffin probably knows as much about single-actions as any gun writer around today. He is author of several fine books on the subject including *Single Action Sixguns* and *Book of the .44*, both from Gun Digest Books.

If you were going to pick a handgun cartridge that most represented the twentieth century, which one would it be? Frank W. James gives his vote to the original magnum, the .357, and tells you why within these pages. About to enter its ninth decade, there is still a place for this versatile cartridge in any handgun battery.

Jim Dickson gives us a nostalgic look at some of the pocket guns of another time, back 100 years or so, long before there were many laws pertaining to concealed carry. Bob Campbell reminds us that it's almost always a good idea to use a holster if you are carrying a handgun, and makes some sensible recommendations for various situations.

For shotgunners, Terry Wieland tells the story of one of the lesser-known English gun makers, E.M. Reilly. (A tip readers will learn is that you never know what you will find in a chicken barn.) Brad Fitzpatrick takes a look at the top guns and loads for waterfowl, and Nick Hahn remembers the Breda autoloader. Fitzpatrick reviews the Browning Model 725 Citori, and it's not a Citori like the others that came before it.

Other highlights of this issue—and I don't have the space to cover them all—include the story on the wonderful little Winchester Model 1903 and 63 .22 auto-loading rifles by C. Rodney James, Rick Hacker's photo essay "Bullets and Blades," and our annual review by Tom Turpin on the high-grade custom guns most of us can only dream about. Plus, you will learn all about two major companies in the industry and the people who run them—Hodgdon and Norma.

Industry Update

Since our last edition was published, the firearms industry has gone through several shockwaves. Tragic events like the shootings in Aurora, Colorado, and Newtown, Connecticut, have brought demands for stricter gun control back into the headlines. Efforts to pass "assault rifle" bans and magazine capacity limits so far have failed to get very far, at least at the national level. A bill requiring broader background checks narrowly failed to pass in the Democrat-controlled Senate and, at our press time, it appeared the legislation would soon be reintroduced.

All the talk about new gun control legislation has, predictably, led to increased demand for virtually all types of firearms, and ARs and other military-style models in particular. Lawrence Keane, NSSF Senior VP and General Counsel commented that it is "… like 1994, all over again." The results are inventory shortages of both guns and ammunition in virtually every gun store in America. How long this will last is anyone's guess. It is important for readers of *Gun Digest* to realize that the MSRPs (manufacturer's suggested retail prices), shown in our catalog section at the back of the book, may not be the actual asking or selling prices at your neighborhood gun store. The basic laws of supply and demand have resulted in higher prices in many instances, especially for AR-style models.

On the positive side of the state of the industry, the 2013 SHOT Show once again set an attendance record, with more than 62,000 attendees. More than 1,600 industry companies exhibited their guns, ammo, and related products at the January show in Las Vegas, including about 100 new exhibitors. Exact figures were not available, but the National Shooting Sports Foundation (NSSF), reported record sales at the SHOT Show, obviously spurred by the continuing threat of more restrictive gun legislation.

Sincerely, Jerry Lee

About the covers

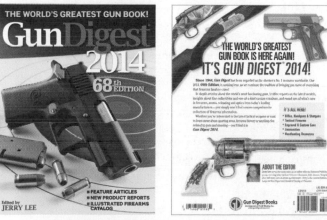

FRONT COVER:

The concealed-carry category continues to play a dominant role in today's handgun market, and Colt's new polymer-frame Mustang XSP is perfect for the job. Like other members of the Mustang series, the XSP is chambered for the .380 ACP round. While similar to the alloy-frame Mustang Pocketlite, the XSP has new features including an accessory rail, ambidextrous safety, and grips molded into the frame. Weighing less than 12 ounces, the XSP takes concealed carry to a new level.

BACK COVER:

On our back cover is a Remington Model 700 SPS "Bone Collector" special edition rifle, Beretta's popular 686 Silver Pigeon O/U, and from Colt, the old and the new: a modern concealed-carry 1911, the New Agent, and a Custom Shop Single Action Army engraved by George Spring, Colt Engraver for 37 years.

Gun Digest Staff

EDITORS
Jerry Lee
Jennifer L.S. Pearsall

CONTRIBUTING EDITORS

Holt Bodinson: Ammunition, Ballistics & Components; Web Directory
John Haviland: Shotguns
Gary Paul Johnston: Handguns/Autoloaders
Jeff Quinn: Handguns/Revolvers
Wm. Hovey Smith: Blackpowder
Tom Tabor: Optics

Tom Turpin: Custom and Engraved Guns
Wayne van Zwoll: Rifles

TESTFIRES

GunDigest 2014

TABLE OF CONTENTS

Getting Past The Old
MODEL 70

We'd plowed through waist-deep snow ramped steep up against a mountain thick with alder and devil's club. We'd pulled our way up through those alders, then clawed over iced rock without looking down. Three hours and a thousand vertical feet later, we'd pretty much run out of steam. The wall of opaque, battleship-gray that blocked the southwest horizon now obscured lowlands much closer. It had no top. This storm would dump tons of snow on our corner of Alaska.

"One more hour." That would put us at two o'clock, with three hours of light for a downhill dash. My partners nodded.

An hour later, clouds towering and snow driving in, we gave the slope one more look.

"There!"

I saw the billy a second later, scrambled forward, and flopped against a snowy rock. The goat, moving off, was a step from gone when my bullet struck. I cycled the Model 70 and fired again. And again. Despite the withering impacts of

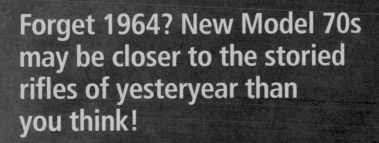

One of the first M70s in .325 WSM got this goat for Wayne, on the cusp of an Alaska storm.

Forget 1964? New Model 70s may be closer to the storied rifles of yesteryear than you think!

Fetching and functional, this Jack O'Connor Tribute rifle is a specially stocked Featherweight.

BY Wayne van Zwoll

200-grain soft-points from my .325 WSM, the billy inched toward the cliff. The last round in my magazine felled him at the brink.

Skinning the goat and packing our loads off the mountain, we suffered the brunt of the storm. At midnight, we reached the road. Morning would break on two feet of new snow.

Some game is still taken the old-fashioned way, and some rifles are still built as they were before the Alaska Highway. I could have taken an early Model 70 on that hunt—but the new version worked fine.

Pick up a 70 shipped in 1937, the year of the model's introduction, and you'll see features and craftsmanship absent on current production rifles. Such change has long plagued our industry, which counters the criticism with improved design. A late model may not show the machining and woodworking talents of early rifles, but it is less costly to build, functions as well as (or better) than its forebears, and meets the needs of contemporary shooters.

You can trace this defense of progress to the 1850s. Oliver Winchester, a shirt merchant, had nothing to do with the design of the Jennings rifle that would evolve, between 1849 and 1873, into the cornerstone of a dynasty. The relatively weak action of the Model 1873 didn't stop it from becoming "the gun that won the West." It fed reliably and held lots of rounds in its magazine—and they were cartridges that also chambered in Colt's 1873 revolvers.

When John Browning sold Winchester a larger and stronger action that worked the same way, it became a hit with hunters. The Model 1886 wasn't as handy in the saddle as the '73, but .45-70 ammunition gave it muscle for bears, elk, and moose. Teddy Roosevelt's exploits in the West and in Africa helped popularize the '86 and, later, the box-fed 1895. At the turn of the century, Winchester lever rifles were the best a sportsman could buy.

By that time, Winchester engineers had already recognized the merit of Paul Mauser's turnbolt action. Adoption of the Krag (over Arthur Savage's splendid lever-action), as the U.S. service rifle, and development of smokeless propellants, in the 1890s, triggered a new trend. Charles Newton's brilliantly designed rifles didn't get the attention they deserved, but they illustrated a change in thinking that would steer rifle design on a new path. The future belonged to bolt-actions.

Winchester failed in its first attempts to convert the lever-action faithful. Its .45-70 Hotchkiss was dropped before 1900, shortly after introduction. The Lee Straight Pull, unveiled in 1897, survived just six years. During World War I, Winchester manufactured Pattern 14 and Model 1917 Enfield rifles for British and American troops, an experience that would catalyze company efforts to develop a bolt-action hunting rifle. By 1922, Winchester designers had critically reviewed the Lee, the Hotchkiss, and the Enfield. Soon, blueprints for a new Winchester rifle were approved. Three years later, the Model 54 appeared.

The 54's coned breech derived from the 1903 Springfield's, but its receiver,

The rifle that started it all, Winchester's Model 54. Introduced in 1925, it was replaced by the M70, in 1937.

This rifle, from the 1940s, has an early stamp. The first Model 70 barrels were the same as those on the M54s.

bolt, extractor, and safety mirrored Mauser design. The ejector, patterned after Newton's, eliminated the need for a slotted locking lug. The action cocked on opening and was strong enough to bottle .30-06 pressures. While the safety proved awkward to use under a scope, few shooters of that day owned scopes.

The 54's nickel steel barrel was gracefully contoured. Its slim, continental-style stock had a sharp comb, schnabel fore-end tip, and "shotgun" butt. Weighing 7¾ pounds, a Model 54 listed for little more than you'd spend to refurbish a military rifle, and much less than the cost of a Sedgley or Griffin & Howe sporter.

Modest price, intelligent design, and the Winchester name all gave the 54 a boost at market. But pivotal to the rifle's success was its chambering of a new Winchester cartridge. Designed for the 54, the .270 was essentially a .30-06 necked down and loaded to over 3,100 fps. The 130-grain bullet flew faster and flatter than any from an '06. Jack O'Connor would praise the .270; hunters snapped it up.

But the 54's time in the sun was short. The U.S. stock market collapse put Winchester Repeating Arms into a tailspin. By 1931, the firm was in receivership. On December 22 of that year, it was bought by Western Cartridge Company. Still, Western's management, under the leadership of John Olin, decided to keep the Model 54. T.C. Johnson and his staff refined the rifle they'd engineered and, in 1931, equipped it with a beefier "NRA" stock. A year later, they added a speed lock for the .22 Hornet (a chambering that didn't appear until 1933).

Initially offered only in .270 and .30-06, the 54 added eight other chamberings. These were, in order of increasing rarity, the .22 Hornet, .30-30, .250 Savage, 7mm Mauser, .257 Roberts, .220 Swift, 7.65mm Mauser, and 9mm Mauser. Ten versions of the 54 included target and sniper configurations. In 1936, its final full year of production, the Model 54 ranged in price from $59.75 to $111.

The 54's main weakness was its trigger, which, like military triggers of the day, also served as the bolt stop. Competitive shooters balked. While hunters were content to fight the mushy trigger,

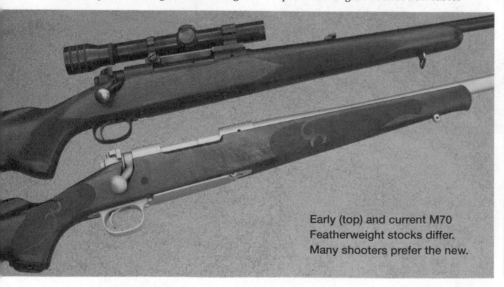

Early (top) and current M70 Featherweight stocks differ. Many shooters prefer the new.

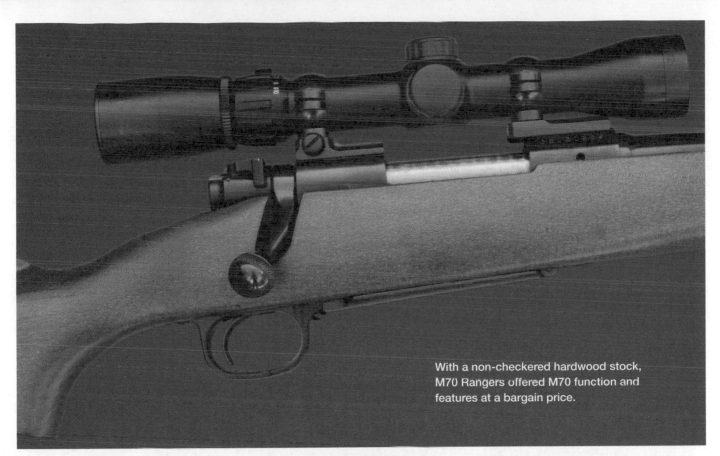

With a non-checkered hardwood stock, M70 Rangers offered M70 function and features at a bargain price.

they didn't appreciate the high-swing Mauser-type safety, as it precluded low scope mounting. The Model 54 was also not drilled for bases, and the use of optical sights was clearly increasing. Other liabilities included the speed lock, which didn't work as well as predicted, and there was poor provision for handling gas in the event of case rupture.

Cataloged and available through 1941, the Winchester 54 took a back seat its last five years. Of 52,029 Model 54s shipped, 49,009 had been boxed by the end of 1936. Authorization for work on a new bolt-action rifle, the Model 70, was given December 29, 1934.

Development of the 70 took a long time, for three reasons. First, the 54 still sold well. Secondly, the Depression had drained many shooters of disposable income. Finally, the Marksman stock designed for the Model 70 target rifle had yet to prove itself on the 54 (whose metal had about the same footprint). When the U.S. economy warmed up and competitive riflemen began to warm to the new stock, Winchester started building 70s. On January 20, 1936, the first receivers got serial numbers. On January 1, 1937, when the Model 70 was officially released, 2,238 rifles were ready to ship. You could buy one for $61.25.

Though the 70's barrel and receiver looked like the 54's, the trigger was a vast improvement. A separate sear allows for precise adjustment in take-up, weight, and over-travel. The bolt stop, pivoting on the trigger pin, was also separate and operated through a slot at the rear of the left lug race. On rifles chambered for .30-06 and longer cartridges, the bolt stop arrested the

left lug. For shorter rounds, a bolt stop extension fitted to the extractor collar limited bolt throw. Three extensions were used, for cartridges the length of the .220 Swift, the .250 Savage, and the .22 Hornet.

Old (1947), left, and new (2012) Model 70s are distinct, but still have much in common.

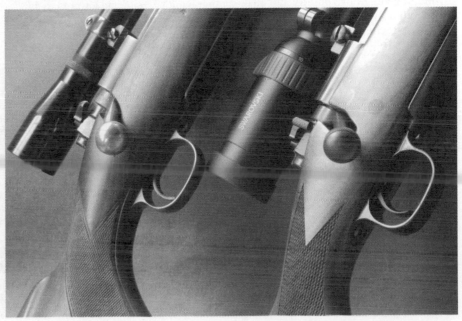

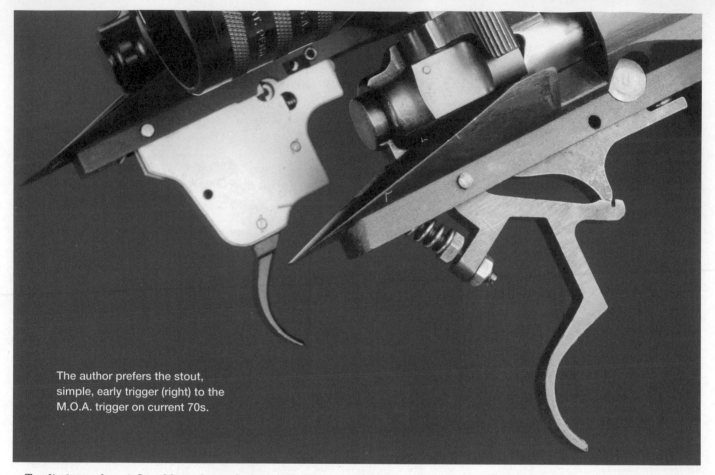

The author prefers the stout, simple, early trigger (right) to the M.O.A. trigger on current 70s.

To eliminate the misfires blamed on the Model 54's speed lock, firing pin travel on the Model 70 was extended by an increment of $1/16$-inch. To augment the 54's bolt head gas ports, Winchester put a hole in the right side of the 70 receiver ring. The first M70 safety was a small tab atop the bolt shroud. It swung horizontally. Because it was unhandy to manipulate under a scope, Winchester moved it, four years later, to the side of the shroud.

A middle detent prevented striker fall, but permitted bolt operation.

The Model 70 had three guard screws, but instead of the 54's stamped, fixed magazine cover and guard, the 70 wore a machined floorplate hinged at the front and secured by a spring-loaded plunger set into the machined trigger guard. The bolt handle, swept and lowered to 45 degrees, acted as a safety lug. A cut in the receiver became the abutment; the stock was also notched. A square bolt

shoulder precluded low scope mounting and was later eliminated.

The Model 70 of 1937 lured hunters with its fine trigger, low-slung safety, and aggressive Mauser extractor that controlled cartridge feed. It had a comfortable stock, an accurate barrel, and a receiver that, though not "magnum-length" by strict definition, would cycle the longest cartridges. The 70 was, in fact, bored from the start for the .300 and .375 H&H Magnums, rounds

The Model 70 Ranger featured push feed. This bolt is from a .223 built in the 1990s.

Early bolts (left) show machining marks. Current 70s look cleaner, thanks to CNC tooling.

that wouldn't fit Springfield or military Mausers without extensive alterations. Besides those cigar-size numbers, early 70s chambered the Hornet, Swift, .250-3000, .257 Roberts, .270, 7x57, and .30-06. Between 1941 and 1963, nine more chamberings appeared; however, only eight were cataloged. Winchester "Gun Salesman Handbooks" of 1947 included the .300 Savage, offered until 1954.

Of the eight cartridges added, the .35 Remington appeared first, in 1941. It vanished from the list after only a year, but a few sold into the early 1950s. Intended to replace the 54's 9mm Mauser, the .35 Remington hull had too small a shoulder to hold against the powerful blow of the M70 striker. Its short life in this rifle made .35s rare. Painfully, I recall the ill-omened day when I failed to buy a .35 Remington Model 70. Condition: like new. Price: $400.

A third tier of Model 70 cartridges arrived in the 1950s and early '60s. They were all Winchester rounds: the .243, .264 Magnum, .308, .300 Magnum, .338 Magnum, .358, and .458 Magnum. Their late introduction precluded a large manufacturing run before the rifle's redesign, in 1963. Of 581,471 Model 70s built before that change, 208,218 were .30-06s and 122,323 were .270s. The .35 Remington and .300 Savage had production totals of only 404 and 362, respectively. The .308 and .358 were cataloged only in Featherweights. Special-order 70s (13,283 between 1936 and 1963) included other, unusual chamberings.

Eventually, pre-'64 Model 70s would sell in 29 basic styles and 48 sub-configurations. These don't include variations in small parts or subtle design changes. Super Grade 70s had special stocks and a floorplate stamp, but no distinctive metalwork. They were made throughout pre-'64 production. Pre-war rifles with the top safety also had a "cloverleaf" tang, changed in the late '40s to a spatulate shape that actually hid the tang proper. (Close inletting of the early tang could result in stock splits from recoil; a generous gap was unsightly.) The receiver bridge, first matted and undrilled, was later left smooth and drilled for scope mounts. Bolt knobs were solid at the outset, hollowed in the mid-1950s. Changes in the bolt sleeve, bolt stop, and other components were largely phased in quietly. Late M70 stocks got higher combs, for scope accommodation. Checkering quality deteriorated over time; diamond size increased, panels got smaller.

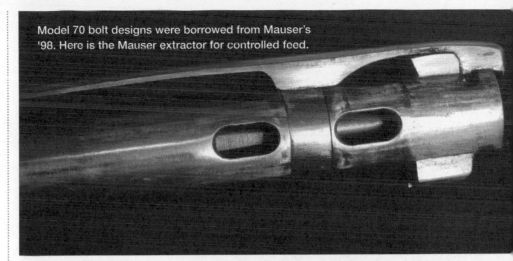

Model 70 bolt designs were borrowed from Mauser's '98. Here is the Mauser extractor for controlled feed.

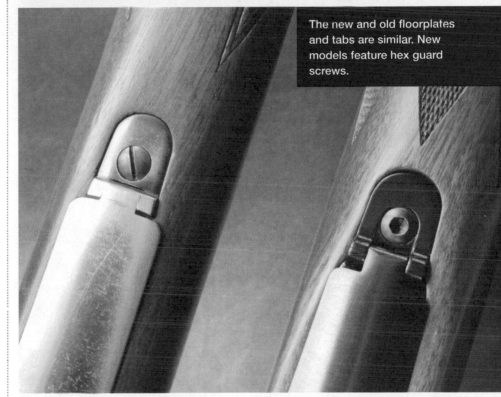

The new and old floorplates and tabs are similar. New models feature hex guard screws.

So popular it became known as "the rifleman's rifle," Winchester's Model 70 was less attractive to company accountants. In 1960, number-crunchers at New Haven decided they could make more money by revamping the rifle. Two years later, engineers had identified 50 changes. These were implemented, in 1963. On October 1 of that year, serial number 700,000 was stamped on the first "new" Model 70.

Some of the cost-saving changes escaped notice, but those that drew attention *incensed* shooters. The stock wasn't checkered; stamping machines now produced dark, crude cavities at gripping surfaces. The free-floating barrel wallowed in a gap big enough to swallow car keys. A tiny hook extractor replaced the beefy Mauser claw. Machined-steel bottom metal was supplanted by aluminum, solid action pins by roll pins, the bolt stop's coil spring by music wire. A painted red cocking indicator stuck out like a tongue from under the bolt shroud. The shooting press pounced, accusing Winchester of both insulting its customers and ignoring its legacy. The price of pre-'64 Model 70s vaulted; new rifles languished on dealer racks.

After the shock wore off (and Remington pulled several furlongs ahead with its new Model 700, released in 1962), Winchester retrenched. In 1966, an anti-

Rifle maker Patrick Holehan built this lovely sporter on the author's early Model 70 action.

The late John Nosler adored M70s. Here he is with one of his favorite custom 70s in .280.

bind device smoothed bolt operation on all 70s. In 1972, the XTR model appeared, with more attractive, better fitted wood and machine-cut checkering. A redesigned Featherweight stock got rave reviews, in 1980. About then, the company began to resurrect the pre-'64 Model 70. But this wasn't to be done overnight. Indeed, it would take a decade.

"The extractor is one of our proposed changes," engineer Ed Vartanian told me at the time. "But the original, controlled-feed version will add $16 to the cost of building a rifle."

Winchester wisely bit the bullet on that one, reintroducing the Mauser-style claw as the defining feature of a new Classic series, in the 1980s. A short action was unveiled in 1984, a major improvement, as earlier 70s, from the tiny Hornet to the .375 H&H, had been built on one receiver! (Magazine inserts and bolt stop extensions had taken up the slack.) Soon thereafter, the firm introduced synthetic stocks on a 70 Winlite. These McMillan stocks were comfortable to shoot and well adapted to scopes. Winlites lasted from 1986 to 1990. Less fetching polymer stocks followed, as did detachable box magazines. Winchester cataloged DBMs in push-feed and Classic rifles during the early '90s, but has since dropped the option.

In 1986, at Safari Club International's annual convention, a rifle built by Arizona gunmaker David Miller went to

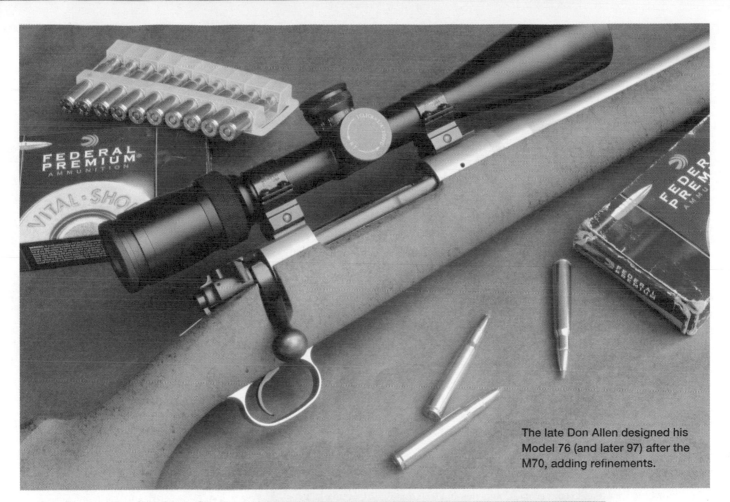

The late Don Allen designed his Model 76 (and later 97) after the M70, adding refinements.

auction. Fine wood and workmanship, with Lynton McKenzie's engraving, contributed to the $201,000 winning bid—the highest price then recorded for a modern sporter. But the "Leopard" rifle, the last in a series of "Big Five" rifles SCI had commissioned, had been built on a *new* Model 70 action! By then, Winchester had married the Mauser claw of the old M70 with the anti-bind device of the new to produce a superior hybrid. The pre-'64's bolt lump was gone. Less effective than the new extractor-ring block in redirecting wayward gas, it couldn't match the anti-bind feature as an aid to bolt cycling.

In 1991, Winchester built its new .30-06 Super Grade around this controlled-feed action. It would gradually supplant the push-feed mechanism in all 70s. While early M70 claws were designed to chamber rounds from the magazine only, the improved version also snapped over single rounds fed by hand. In 1995, Winchester offered it on 10 versions of the Model 70, including synthetic-stocked rifles and those of stainless steel (first used in M70s in 1991). All-steel components were held to closer tolerances than were possible

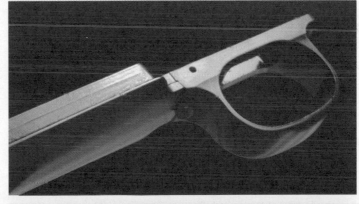

One-piece bottom metal on new M70s is an improvement; early rifles had separate guards.

This floorplate is from a 1950s Model 70. Later a Custom Shop rifle, a Super Grade is now cataloged.

before the advent of CNC. A run of low-priced, push-feed Model 70 Ranger rifles appeared—and died—during the '90s. I bought a handful, wish I'd bought more. They had well-finished hardwood stocks and nicely polished steel. They came in .223, .243, .270, .30-06, and 7mm Remington Magnum.

Between 1999 and 2006, Winchester leaned heavily on synthetic stocks, hawking the Stealth and Shadow series in various versions, and chamberings that included the WSM (Winchester Short Magnum) and WSSM (Winchester Super Short Magnum) rounds. They featured "controlled round push feed." The bolt

face boasted a three-quarter shroud that permitted a cartridge to slide up into the extractor, as on early 70s. But *this* extractor was pinned to the right-hand lug. Small and cheap, it has since been discontinued.

Jack O'Connor's Choice

No one liked Model 70s better than Jack O'Connor. The famous gun writer's pair of Featherweight .270s, stocked by Al Biesen, got world-wide exposure on his many big-game hunts. In 2006, Jack's son, Bradford, proposed a tribute rifle.

"The 'Number Two' came to mind," he said. That's the Featherweight Jack originally had built as a backup. But it shot so well, it became his first pick. In 2009, Brad renewed efforts for the special rifle, enlisting Tony Caligiuri, a Director of the Jack O'Connor Hunting Heritage and Education Center, in Lewiston, Idaho. Winchester product manager, Glenn Hatt, instantly approved. Brad also credits the Center's administrator, Darrell Inman, and Jack's long-time friend Hank Kaufman, who joined with rifle enthusiast and O'Connor historian Buck Buckner early on to establish the Center. Roger Biesen, who builds rifles in the shop where his father crafted O'Connor's, helped, too.

"Brad loaned us the original Number Two rifle," Glenn told me. "CAD and CNC equipment gave us a close match to the Biesen stock. We made some concessions to trim cost." Completed in 2011, this is still a remarkable Model 70, handsome and functional. Disparities: checkering doesn't equal Biesen's hand-cut panels, and it doesn't wrap the grip. Al's strong, rounded, low-fluted comb nose was discarded in favor of the standard Winchester profile. The engraved steel grip cap, also standard stock, is smaller than on the Number Two, because Jack preferred a slight swell at the grip terminus. His .270s also wore steel butt-plates; the Tribute rifle has a Decelerator pad.

"First pick was a lipped Neidner plate," conceded Glenn Hatt. "But that would have been costly to fit."

The walnut (AA Claro or French) boasts a low-luster gloss, but instead of a traditional linseed-oil finish, Winchester gets that look with more durable urethane. Winchester also installed the M.O.A trigger, knurled bolt knob, and one-piece bottom metal of current 70s. The floorplate is tastefully engraved with the image of a ram. Jack O'Connor's signature, in a subdued silver hue, graces the trigger guard. The 22-inch barrel is of ordinary Featherweight profile, with hammer-forged rifling. Winchester guarantees one-inch three-shot groups with factory ammunition.

A 500-rifle run of high-grade Custom Tributes sold out right away. Winchester put no lid on the number of standard Tributes, but stopped manufacture at the end of 2012, as announced. Prices: $2,600 for the Custom, $2,000 for the standard rifle. Six percent of sales goes to operation of the Jack O'Connor Hunting Heritage and Education Center in Lewiston.

As the twenty-first century began, Winchester's Custom Shop produced rifles with fine stocks of maple and walnut, in Continental, Mannlicher, and Safari Express configurations. But the New Haven factory, in which 20,000 workers had toiled during the Second World War, would not survive the decade. Even at my first visit in the '80s, as Winchester struggled on under Olin's umbrella, the great brick structure harbored mostly ghosts. Oil-soaked hardwood creaked hollowly in empty rooms. Small cells kept alive by workers in soiled aprons gave up modest stacks of completed rifles. The building that had undergirded the Allied war machine and served generations of sportsmen gasped with the echoes of solitary footfalls and the clink and whir of machinery pre-dating Truman. In March 2006, the New Haven plant closed. Union contracts had driven annual losses "into seven figures." With its closing, Winchester's Model 70 also died, 70 years after its debut, behind windows stained by decades of industrial soot, under skylights blackened to foil the Luftwaffe.

No Model 70 enthusiast thought the rifle would die. Even as the company broke the sad news, its Belgian parent, which also owns Browning, was turning out rifles on Model 70 actions at the Fabrique Nationale factory, in Columbia, South Carolina. These were built for military and law enforcement use. In short order, though, the plant tooled up to produce sporting rifles, too, on the latest controlled-feed action. Alas, the original trigger, unscathed by the 1963 and subsequent revisions, gave way to a new "M.O.A." trigger. Winchester claims "zero take-up, zero creep, and zero overtravel." I've used it successfully. But, in my view, it doesn't trump the original.

Now Winchester lists 11 Model 70 rifles, stainless and chrome moly. Six wear walnut stocks, five synthetic. All have one-piece steel bottom metal and black, Pachmayr Decelerator recoil pads. The Super Grade is a handsome rifle indeed. The Sporter and Featherweight, too, have well-polished steel and nicely cut-checkered walnut. The Alaskan, new this year in .375, is particularly fetching. The first Alaskan came along in 1958, chambered for the then-new

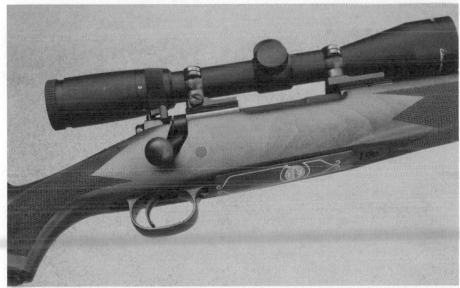

ABOVE: Wayne fired this group with a current 70 Alaskan. "Better accuracy than from early .338s."

LEFT: Winchester has built special 70s for special markets. This .264 Magnum went to Cabela's.

.338 Winchester Magnum. Its thick red pad and 25-inch "egg-lump" barrel distinguished it from other 70s. Last year, the .338 Magnum joined the .30-06 and .300 Winchester in the current Alaskan.

This rifle has the walnut stock and long barrel of the original. Its recoil pad is black. I snatched up a sample as soon as it became available. Though cosmetic detailing left me disappointed, the rifle

cycled smoothly and shot much better than early Alaskans I'd carried. Most of all, it looks and feels like a *hunting* rifle—lean and carnivorous, but, at the same time, elegant. It's honest and solid and unmistakably a Model 70. You can't look at it without snugging the butt to your shoulder.

Winchester's accountants still ponder profits. But they've evidently learned that, no matter how much money you save in manufacturing, you don't profit if rifles don't sell. The newest Model 70s, priced from $760 to $1,420, are selling well, I hear.

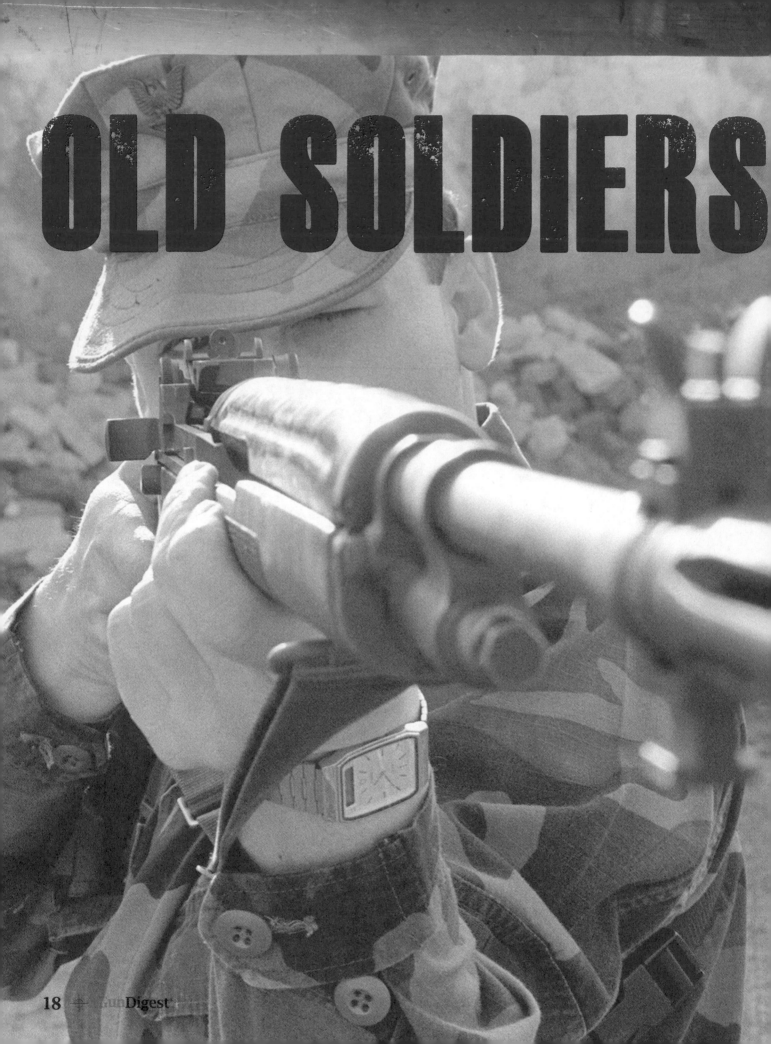

OLD SOLDIERS

NEVER DIE,
THEY JUST GET UPGRADED

BY **Gary Paul Johnston**

The amazing longevity of the FAL and the M14!

In the history of military rifles, some have seen more service than others. The reasons include wars lost and won, with arms destroyed, technological advances rendering earlier designs obsolete, politics, etc. Particularly affected have been contemporary battle rifles from the mid-twentieth century to the present, the most significant cases in point being the FN-FAL, the U.S. M14, and their semi-automatic ilks.

Born of the experiences of World War II, the FN-FAL and the U.S. M14 rifles came not from vacuums, but from parent rifles that had few things in common, one from what was still called the "Old World," and one from the New. These parent rifles were the U.S. Cal. .30 M1 (Garand) and the Belgian FN-49 (SAFN), both of which were conceived in the latter part of the 1930s.

Designed by John C. Garand, of Springfield Arsenal, the rifle that became the M1 was a semi-automatic turn-bolt design operating by long-stroke gas piston. Using an en bloc clip inserted into (and ejecting from) the top of the magazine, this clip first held 10 rounds of 2.76 Pedersen cartridges and, later, eight rounds of .30-06. Garand's rifle was adopted, in 1939, as the U.S. Rifle, Cal. .30 M1 and was America's main battle rifle (MBR) through World War II, Korea, and beyond.

The brainchild of Dieudonne Saive, of Fabrique Nationale (FN), Belgium, it was no coincidence that the rifle that was to become the FN-49 bore a striking resemblance to the Soviet SVT-38 (Tokarev) rifle. It used a similar short-stroke gas piston operation and a rear tilt (or prop) bolt, with right side cocking and a detachable, 10-round box magazine. Saive's prototype was put on hold, in 1939, when the Germans invaded Poland. With the Nazi invasion of Belgium, in 1940, Saive fled to England, where he continued work on his design at Britain's Royal Small Arms Factory. There he stayed until 1944, when he returned to FN to finish his design. In 1947, the rifle was designated the FN-49. It went on to be adopted by at least nine countries, mostly in caliber .30-06 (7.62x63mm).

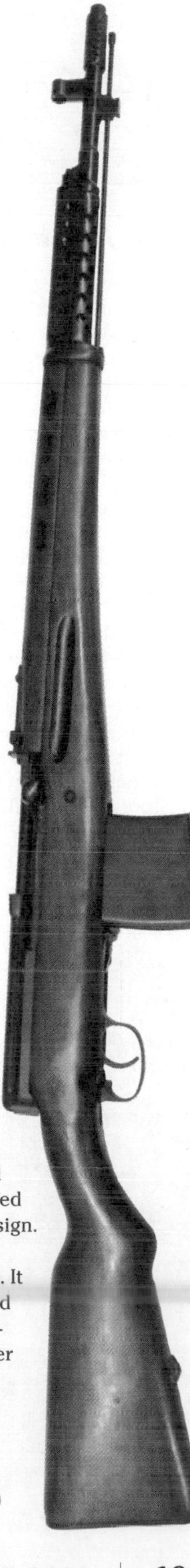

The predecessor to the FN-FAL, the FN-49, was based on the Soviet Tokarev.

The U.S. M1 (Garand) rifle is the father of the U.S. M14 Rifle.

Fusil Automatique Legere

Although the pre-WWII U.S. .276 Pedersen cartridge was never adopted, intermediate-size cartridges were widely experimented with in Europe during the same period, with two being adopted during the war. One was the German 7.92x33mm (Kurz), the other the Soviet 7.62x41mm (M43), later the 7.62x39mm. Following the war, Siave and Ernest Vervier, of FN, began work on a new rifle based on the FN-49, but in the configuration derived from several rifles that had emerged during the war. These rifles used a separate pistol grip, had a buttstock more in line with the barrel and a detachable 20-round magazine, and possessed selective fire capability. One extremely popular feature of the new rifle that evolved, one the FN-49 had not offered, was a non-reciprocating charging handle on the left side, a feature much like that of the U.S. Browning Automatic Rifle. The addition of this handle meant the operator did not have to remove the strong hand from the fire control group to charge the rifle. This also also works for left-handed users, albeit with a little more work on their part, by rolling the rifle over to the right.

First chambered for the 7.92x33mm (Kurz) cartridge, the new rifle was prototyped in 1947 and called the "FN Fusil Automatique Legere" (Rifle Automatic Light) or FAL. It drew great interest from Britain, which had developed the .280 British intermediate cartridge. FN continued development of its new rifle and, in 1950, the latest version was tested by the British.

Meanwhile, following WWII, continuing work in progress on the M1 rifle had been undertaken by the U.S. Military via the Light Rifle Program, and Springfield was at the helm. With more than a dozen variations of the M1 and other designs tested, a new cartridge was developed from the .300 Savage cartridge case. The slightly longer cartridge fell in between the .300 Savage and the .30-06, and the .30 Light Rifle Cartridge, soon to become the 7.62x51mm NATO, was adopted by the U.S. Military in 1954.

The "Right Arm of Freedom"

Tested in conjunction with the new cartridge was the near final development of the Light Rifle Program, a refined prototype variation of the M1 rifle called the T-44. However, the fly in Springfield's ointment was the latest of several outside entries into the Light Rifle competition. This one was a special version of the already popular FN-FAL, but in 7.62x51mm. Like the model being tested (and later adopted) by Canada, this one had a charger guide in the top cover. Designated the T-48, a small number was made for testing by the U.S. company Harrington & Richardson. The T-48 performed superbly, but, in the end, politics won and, in 1957, the T-44 was adopted as the U.S. Rifle, 7.62mm M14. Nevertheless, the FN-FAL was adopted by no less than 99 countries worldwide and was manufactured by nine of them. As such, it became known as "The Right Arm of Freedom."

While the M14 and the FAL retain some of the characteristics of their parent rifles, the M1 and the FN-49, they also share a few things in common. In addition to using the same cartridge, both the M14 and the FAL use "swing-in" 20-round box magazines and are of short-stroke piston operation. (In the M14, the operating rod takes the place of a bolt carrier and travels the full operating stroke of the bolt, providing the advantage of a long-stroke piston.) Both rifles are also capable of selective fire, a questionable decision for any battle rifle firing the 7.62x51mm NATO cartridge.

The differences in the two are somewhat greater. As with their parent rifles, a major design difference lies in the locking systems of the two rifles. The M14 uses the M1's front locking, rotating two-lug bolt, whereas the FAL uses a rear-locking (Tokarev/FN-49) tilt bolt.

This U.S. soldier demonstrates his Mk 14 Mod 0 to Afghan townsmen.

Above the Wagal Valley, in Afghanistan's Nuristan Province, this U.S. soldier goes prone with his Mk 14 Mod 0 M14 sniper rifle.

Although the M14 rifle was designed with an integral receiver base for the mounting of optics, the FAL was not, though variations of its sheet metal receiver cover were designed to host optical sights with some success. Scope mounts were also designed for the M14 rifle, but, keeping with its role as a "light rifle," most were made of aircraft alloy and suffered under the recoil. Even mounts of steel did not hold up well with the single screw that held them in place.

The SCHV Craze

Not long after the adoption of the M14 rifle, the Small Caliber High Velocity program that swept the U.S. Continental Army Command (CONARC) overtook the new U.S. Military rifle with the .223 Remington (5.56x45mm) cartridge and the AR-15 rifle designed with it. The catalyst for this was the Vietnam War, with its relatively close-range battle engagements; there were other perceived advantages, and the AR-15 was adopted as the U.S. Rifle, 5.56mm M16, in 1963. By 1964, five years after it was begun,

production of the M14 rifle had ended with a total of 1,376,031, and the rifle was given reserve status with all branches of the U.S. Military (with the exception of the U.S. Navy where it remains standard issue).

This U.S. soldier uses cross-sticks to aim his Mk 14 Mod 0, in Afghanistan.

Despite being replaced, within the U.S. Army, special versions of the M14 were retained during the Vietnam War for sniping. Based on the M14 National Match rifles developed for competition, in 1959, such rifles had their M14 designation ground off the receiver and were then hand stenciled "XM21." Fitted with special new optical sight systems and sound suppressors, these rifles proved invaluable in Vietnam.

Subsequent to the Vietnam War, a joint program within the Army and Navy was initiated to further develop the XM21 rifle, in spite of opposition by the Clinton Administration, which was responsible for the destruction and liquidation of hundreds of thousands of the rifles. Using a then-revolutionary steel bedding system, the improved XM21 was called the XM25. While the XM25 program divided, with the Army and Navy going in separate directions, the rifles are still in use by the U.S. Navy SEALS in several configurations.

DSA, Inc.

Despite the growing popularity of the 5.56x45mm NATO cartridge and the lightweight M16 rifle throughout much of the world, the FAL continued to prevail, especially regionally, where engagements were at distances much farther than those encountered in lush jungle environments. In addition, the FAL's superb reputation for reliability and ergonomics, as well as the economics of the countries that issued it, helped sustain its favor. While many of these countries have since adopted one of the new 5.56mm NATO rifles that continue to emerge, they have also retained their FAL's, repairing and rebuilding them as necessary, as well as upgrading them.

With FN no longer producing the FAL and few of its licensees producing spare parts for it, one of the few sources for repairs and upgrades of the rifle comes from the only company that still manufactures it, DSA, Inc., of Illinois. Literally taking the FAL into the twenty-first century, this longstanding company designs and produces no less than 16 FAL rifle models, from 11-inch barreled CQB guns to a 19-inch barreled long-range precision Special Purpose Rifle, all in 7.62x51mm NAT0).

Of all its accomplishments, one of DSA's greatest has been in extending the life of the FAL via a state-of-the art scope base/top cover that guarantees POA/POI when properly mated with high quality rings, optics, and ammunition. This scope base provides the rifle with unlimited optical mounting capabilities. DSA also offers Mil-Spec-1913 short and long rail handguard systems for the FAL, in addition to an almost an endless number of bipods, sights, vertical foregrips, Para-folding and standard stocks, and other parts, including 40mm M203 grenade launchers to law enforcement agencies. (dsarms.com)

The M1A

In spite of the politics and long delay in the adoption of the M14 rifle, it proved to be an excellent weapon, and the early, albeit short-lived, development of a semi-automatic-only model for competition led to an almost identical commercial semi-automatic version called the M1A. It

is now made by Springfield Armory, also of Illinois, which obtained the Springfield name after the original factory closed. Using a new receiver with original M14 components, the Springfield M1A accepts all M14 accessories. Springfield offers several models of the M1A, including the standard 20-inch barreled version, a National Match rifle, an 18-inch barreled Squad Rifle, a 16-inch barreled Tactical Carbine, and a long-range precision version (springfieldarmory.com).

In addition to Springfield Armory, Smith Enterprises, of Arizona, manufactures new, forged, selective fire M14 and semi-automatic M1A receivers, bolts, match grade barrels, gas cylinder operating rods, and dozens of other parts and accessories, all of the highest quality. Smith Enterprises also rebuilds M14 sniper rifles for various special units of the U.S. Military, where the company's M14 Scope Mount is in wide use. (smithenterprise.com).

The Middle East

In the wake of the Western world's involvement in Iraq, Afghanistan, and other war zones, the need for a rifle and cartridge system more suitable for long-range engagements has become painfully apparent. U.S. personnel have, as contractors, on many occasions, been seen using both FAL and M1A rifles, and an increasing number of M14 rifles have been returned to duty by the U.S. Military, for the same reason. Of particular interest are those that have been rebuilt as long-range precision rifles. The most notable of these is the MK 14 Mod 0.

SAGE International

Designed and produced by SAGE International, of Michigan, the heart of the MK 14 Mod 0 is an aircraft alloy chassis (stock). Made to the most stringent specifications, this chassis is CNC machined to fit to perfection the Mil-Spec M14 receiver, as well as its commercial counterpart. After removing the issue stock and handguard, the operating rod guide is also removed from the barrel and replaced with a new guide that also anchors the barrel to the stock. This literally makes the rifle and chassis one piece. Using machine hex bolts, an equally rigid top rail handguard mounts to the stock, which also comes with Mil-Std-1913 rail sections on both sides and bottom.

This U.S. Army sniper goes kneeling to aim his Mk 14 Mod 0 (SAGE), in Afghanistan.

SAGE M14/M1A chassis are offered with dual-rail extending stock, M4 tube stock, M16 fixed stock, fully adjustable sniper stock, and commercial stock systems, all with a black hard-anodized finish. Just added is a special SAGE multi-cam type pattern finish, and all of SAGE's M14/M1A chassis will accept a new, dual cam-lever cantilever rail that bridges the rear of the top rail to the charger guide on the receiver. This new rail extension will accommodate any optical system. The SAGE MK 14 Mod 0 and the newer EBR version accepting a Mil-Std "slider" stock are now in wide use with the U.S. Military and growing. (sageinternationalltd.com)

Here, a late version of the SAGE EBR is seen with 16-inch barrel, rail extension, Magpul buttstock, and Leupold MR/T sniper scope.

VLTOR Weapon Systems

Yet another stock upgrade for the M14/M1A rifle is that from VLTOR Weapon Systems, of Arizona. Called the M14/M1A Modstock System, it starts with a high-quality U.S. Military synthetic M14 stock. VLTOR then removes the rear portion in order to interface its fully adjustable aircraft alloy back plate with M4 tube, with which any of VLTOR's MOD-Stock butt stocks can then be furnished.

In place of the standard handguard, VLTOR offers its M14/M1A Rail System. Consisting of a full-length Mil-Spec-1913 top rail, this handguard rigidly anchors to the operating rod guide and als to the rear of the barrel and scope base via two hardened bolts. Another mounting block replaces the charger guide and provides a platform on which the rear of the top rail anchors. This M14/M1A Rail System is

A U.S. Navy SEAL practices with the SAGE Gray Mk 14 Mod 0 stock made for the Navy.

The latest version of the SAGE MK 14 Mod 0 stock comes in digital camouflage. It was fielded in early 2013.

This 16-inch SAGE EBR is equipped with a laser designator, Gemtech titanium Sandstorm Suppressor, and GripPod with SureFire G2 Light. Also seen is the new Bushnell HDMR Tactical Elite Scope with H59 Horus Reticle, in a 3.5-21x50mm on a 34mm tube.

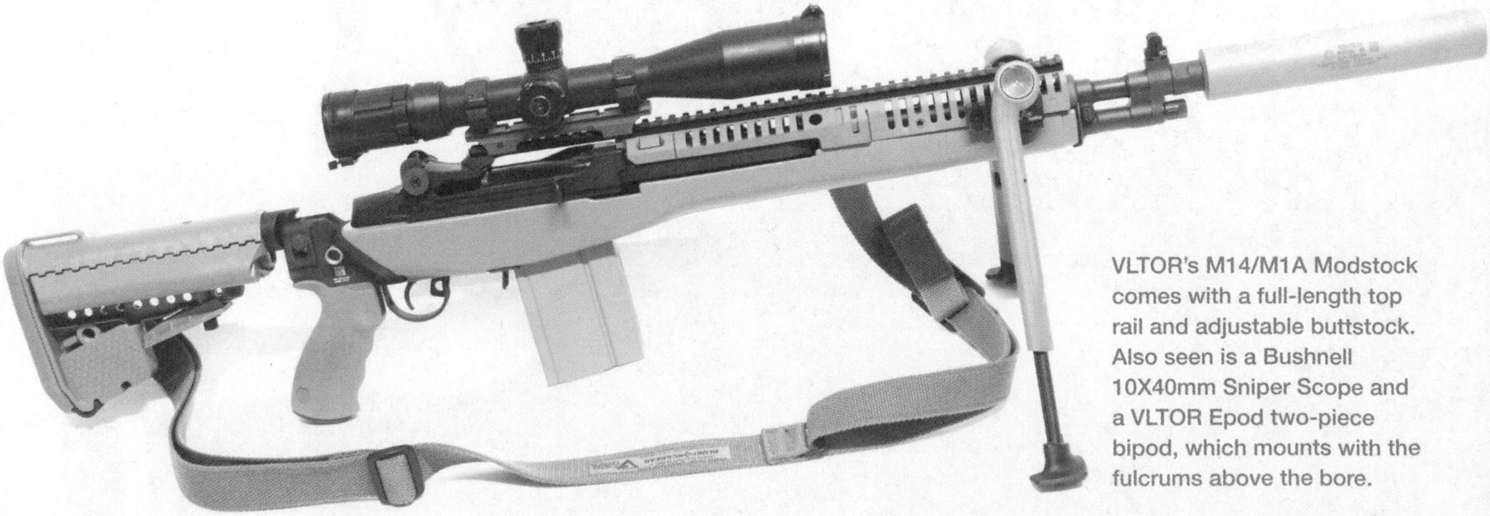

VLTOR's M14/M1A Modstock comes with a full-length top rail and adjustable buttstock. Also seen is a Bushnell 10X40mm Sniper Scope and a VLTOR Epod two-piece bipod, which mounts with the fulcrums above the bore.

an option on M1A rifles manufactured by Springfield Armory, while the entire MOD-stock and top rail system is available to the military, law enforcement, and others. (vltor.com)

Magazines

Although, as mentioned, both the M14 and the FAL came with 20-round double-column magazines, magazines of 10 rounds also exist, and even five-round magazines are made. However, there is another option, and this is a single-column 50-round rotary magazine from XS-Products. Made completely of steel and aluminum, the X-14 and X-FAL .308 50-round magazines are ceramic coated to never need lubrication, and they weigh just 4.9 pounds loaded. (xproducts.com)

The Future

Almost 60 years since it was first adopted, the FAL is no longer the standard issue battle rifle of 99 countries, but it remains in use with more than a half-dozen. With or without the new DSA upgrades, we can expect to see the FAL in service for a long time.

The U.S. M14 rifle was made for the U.S. by Springfield Armory, Winchester, Harrington & Richardson, and Thompson-Ramo-Wooldridge, Inc. (TRW). In addition, after M14 production ceased in the U.S., all M14 tooling at TRW was given to the Republic of China/Taiwan, where it was produced for that country. The M14 was also reverse-engineered by Red China for clandestine use by guerillas in the Philippines and elsewhere. Hundreds of thousands of M14 rifles were given to at least a dozen countries, including South Korea, Israel, Jordan, Chile, Turkey, and Greece. In addition to the current special purpose variations by SAGE and VLTOR, it has existed in more than a dozen variations as used by the U.S. Military, including a special bullpup version, the G2, designed by AWC Systems Technology, and McMillan Rifle Company, of Arizona.

In spite of a new crop of 7.62x51mm NATO sniper rifles being fielded by the U.S. Military, M14 rifles are being rebuilt and upgraded at an equal pace, but why? The main reason is stopping power. While the 5.56mm NATO rifles will reach out to 600 yards and beyond, by the time the get there they have about the same effectiveness of a .22 Long Rifle bullet; the post-Vietnam theaters in which most armies are now fighting call for a more powerful, longer-range battle rifle. The 7.62x51mm NATO cartridge fills that requirement. It and the M14 and FAL rifles that use it will be with us for years to come.

For CQB work, DSA's SA58 FAL OSW Rifle is hard to beat. It is seen here with an Aimpoint Comp M3 Red Dot optic and an ACE adjustable stock.

THE WINCHESTER MODEL 1895s OF
THEODORE ROOSEVELT

BY Philip Schreier, Senior Curator, National Firearms Museum

The wagon load of guns, ammo and parts from Winchester Repeating Arms Co. numbered 15 crates in total.
Photo courtesy Theodore Roosevelt Collection, Harvard College Library

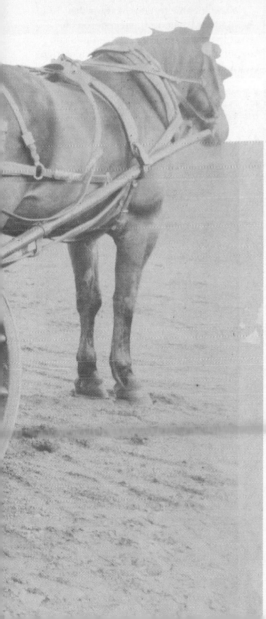

> *"A cool man with a rifle, if he has mastered his weapon, need fear no foe."*—Theodore Roosevelt, *Through the Brazilian Wilderness (1914)*

Of all the figures in history to have given their patronage to a firearm, perhaps none are so well known as the twenty-sixth President of the United States, Theodore Roosevelt. He was a human dynamo. He was the youngest President to ever hold office. He was an avid hunter, a Nobel Prize winner, a wildlife conservationist, a war hero who earned the Medal of Honor, a Life Member of the National Rifle Association, the author of 39 books and 150,000 personal letters, a father of six, and the most gun-savvy man to ever occupy the White House. When it came to gun knowledge and shooting skill, no chief executive, now or then, was or has been his peer.

When it came to firearms, he wrote a number of times that his favorite was the Winchester. From his first, a Model 1876 he ordered when he was 22 years old, to his favorite Model 1895, last used on a river exploration just scant years before his death at the age of 60, Roosevelt's Winchesters are now legendary and priceless pieces of Americana.

Roosevelt, who was fond of exquisite goods, had within his economic means the ability to own any rifle manufactured during the period. Fine English doubles were considered the apex of the sporting world, yet Roosevelt chose an American classic—or, perhaps, the rifles he chose helped make *them* classics. Roosevelt's poor eyesight may have been a mitigating factor in his fondness for the arms of Oliver Winchester and the Winchester Repeating Arms Co. He was fond of saying that "I don't know how to shoot well, but I know how to shoot often."

No gun of the period shot more often—some models were capable of holding as many as 16 cartridges—or as reliably as did the Winchester. Roosevelt no doubt enjoyed the capability of having plenty of ammunition in the gun, as well as having a firearm that could easily bring each successive round into battery, with effortless ease and remarkable reliability. To a man whose shooting skills were severely hampered by his eyesight—nearsightedness and, later, blindness in one eye—the fact that a Winchester could be sighted and fired and fired again without having to remove the gun from his shoulder would have been a welcome feature for this "Bull Moose" of a man.

Roosevelt's deeds with his Winchesters are certainly the stuff of legend. You could hardly be expected to find a more colorful figure so strongly linked to something that is now, and in no small measure due to his patronage, considered a household word and so instantly recognizable.

It is unknown to this author as to when T.R. first acquired or fired a Winchester Model 1895, but it is well known that he took one with him to Cuba, during the Spanish American War of 1898. An 1895 saddle ring carbine (SRC), serial number 7588, was shipped to him in San Antonio, Texas, on May 21, 1898. It was not U.S. Ordnance marked, as some have speculated, but was chambered in .30 Government, which is .30-40 Krag,

T.R.'s Saddle Ring Carbine as carried by tennis champion Bob Wrenn during the Battles of Kettle and San Juan Hill. *Photo courtesy T.R. Birthplace National Historic Site, NPS*

using today's nomenclature. It has all the standard factory features of an SRC, with the exception that it is missing the top fore-end wood. The gun has no special features, unusual for a Roosevelt Winchester.

In T.R.'s *The Rough Riders* (1899), he writes about how his 1895 was used during the campaign in Cuba:

[Wrenn] had joined us late and we could not get him a Krag carbine; so I had given him my Winchester, which carried the government cartridge; and he was mustered out he carried it home in triumph, to the envy of his fellows, who themselves had to surrender their beloved rifles.

The "Wrenn" Roosevelt spoke of was Trooper Robert D. Wrenn (1873-1925) of Company A. Bob Wrenn was the U.S. singles tennis champion four times before the war and on the U.S. Davis Cup team in 1903. He had been a quarterback on the Harvard football squad and was one of the first inductees into the International Tennis Hall of Fame. This famous Model 1895 carbine eventually found its way into the Theodore Roosevelt Birthplace National Historic Site collection, in Manhattan. It was loaned to the National Firearms Museum's 2012-2013 exhibit, "Theodore Roosevelt; Trappings of an Icon."

T.R. also mentions the use of 1895 SRC's early in *The Rough Riders*. He wrote:

Our arms were the regular cavalry carbine, the "Krag," a splendid weapon, and the revolver. A few carried their favorite Winchester, using, of course, the new model, which took the government cartridge.

He is undoubtedly writing about the 1895 as the "new model which took the government cartridge." It is unknown how many Troopers of the 1st USV carried their "favorite" Winchesters into Cuba with them.

When it came to Winchester rifles, T.R. heaped praise upon them generously. His biggest and best-publicized hunting expedition was the one he made to Africa with son Kermit in 1909-1910. Prior to the

T.R. personally inspected each crate before they were loaded onto the *S.S. Hamburg* for the trip to Africa. *Photo courtesy Theodore Roosevelt Collection, Harvard College Library*

public announcement of his trip, Roosevelt's personal secretary, William Loeb, sent the following letter to Winchester:

To: The Winchester Repeating Arms Company

From: William Loeb, Jr., Secretary to the President.

Date: July 16, 1908

Gentlemen:

The president is going to Africa … . He probably has all the rifles he needs but his son has not. Before deciding what he will buy, the president would like to see your catalog … . Will you send your catalog to the President at Oyster Bay? … .

Signed: Loeb

This simple letter started a chain of events that resulted in dozens of exchanges via wire and mail over the next seven months, concerning the rifles and equipment needed for the great expedition to Africa. Far from just wanting a few rifles for Kermit to have on the safari, Roosevelt ended up having 15 wooden crates full of Winchester rifles, thousands of rounds of ammunition, and spare parts for his expedition shipped by Winchester to his waiting steamer, the *S.S. Hamburg.* On March 23, 1909, less than three weeks after William Howard Taft succeeded him into the White House, he set sail for Africa. Of the rifles, he chose the 1895 lever-action in .30-03 U.S., as well as in .405 Win., to be the highlighted arms.

T.R.'s correspondence with Winchester's second vice president, Winchester Bennett (1877-1953), a grandson of Oliver Winchester, was voluminous and often times abrasive. This was due, in part, because the President was confused as to the various calibers of some of his own guns. He started off by asking Winchester to make up some 1895s for the African safari stocked and sighted identically to a Model 1894 of Kermit's. Additionally, he sent along his custom Springfield M-1903, serial number 6000, and asked that they see to the recent problems he was having getting the gun to shoot accurately. It turns out that he had failed to notice that his Springfield was chambered in .30 GVMT (or .30-03) and not the .30-06 that was, by 1908, the new .30 GVMT round.

T.R. with one of the nine Lions he shot during the safari. Ever present is his 1895 in .405. *Photo courtesy Theodore Roosevelt Collection, Harvard College Library*

Throughout the numerous letters that flew between New Haven and Washington, Roosevelt kept making inquiries as to the practicality of taking his beloved Model 1886 rifle. He wrote:

Have you any data on how this .45-70 will do on African buffalo and Rhino for instance? … As I have said to you, I do not want to use any one of our American guns for any game for which it is unsuited, because there will be a good deal of attention attracted to this trip and I want to be sure that it comes out all right.

In keeping with his reputation for being the consummate outdoorsman and conservationist, Roosevelt was sincerely concerned that the ammunition he would be using would be of enough power and performance so as not to be inhumane to the game he was stalking. In another letter regarding his M-1886, he wrote:

I herewith send you my .45-70 rifle. Really I cannot make my mind act to take this rifle with me on my African trip. It is handy as a knife and fork, and it shoots just where I want it to. I have never had a

rifle I was as fond of, or felt as confidant of … ."

Eventually, he decided to leave it at home and relied solely on the Winchester Model 1895s, his Springfield M-1903, and a Holland & Holland gifted to him by friends in England. Still, he was well aware that his safari would garner much press attention and wished to be shown as the champion of an American gun, rather than an English gun. He wrote to Winchester:

As you know, I have always used your rifles and I am using them now instead of the English rifles which my English friends are giving to me, because it is a matter of pride with me to use an American rifle. Now I don't want to have any slip-up.

To be sure, Winchester expended much in the way of time and resources to make sure every gun was perfect and acceptable to the President. Guns were shipped back and forth for testing and trials. Special Silver's gun pads were ordered from overseas to T.R.'s personal specifications. Bennett must

In any moment of decision, the best thing you can do is the right thing, the next best thing is the wrong thing, and the worst thing you can do is nothing.

—Theodore Roosevelt

LEFT- Kermit Roosevelt and one of the eight lions he took during the year-long safari. *Photo courtesy Theodore Roosevelt Collection, Harvard College Library*

RIGHT- T.R. with a female lion taken for the Smithsonian Institution's Museum of Natural History. *Photo courtesy Theodore Roosevelt Collection, Harvard College Library*

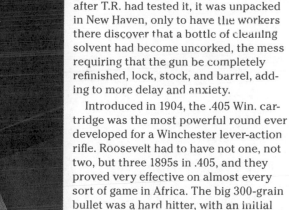

TOP: Thought to be a presentation M-1895 from T.R. to General Leonard Wood, in 1899.

BOTTOM: An 1895 takedown in .405 that belonged to General Theodore Roosevelt, Jr. This rifle was used on his and Kermit's 1928 safari into China. *NRA Staff photo*

have been in a state of near panic every time a new letter from the White House arrived. Once, when one of the rifles that had been sent back to Winchester after T.R. had tested it, it was unpacked in New Haven, only to have the workers there discover that a bottle of cleaning solvent had become uncorked, the mess requiring that the gun be completely refinished, lock, stock, and barrel, adding to more delay and anxiety.

Introduced in 1904, the .405 Win. cartridge was the most powerful round ever developed for a Winchester lever-action rifle. Roosevelt had to have not one, not two, but three 1895s in .405, and they proved very effective on almost every sort of game in Africa. The big 300-grain bullet was a hard hitter, with an initial muzzle velocity of more than 2,230 fps.

In perhaps the best presidential endorsement of any product ever, Roosevelt wrote in *Scribner's Magazine*:

The Winchester .405 is, at least for me personally, the medicine gun for lions.

Previously, in his book, *Hunting Trips of a Ranchman* (1885) Roosevelt had written:

The Winchester, stocked and sighted to suit myself, is by all odds the best weapon I ever had, and I now use it almost exclusively ... .

The Roosevelt safari lasted nearly one calendar year. Over 5,000 specimens of African flora and fauna were collected for the Smithsonian Institution. Many of them are still on exhibit in The Kenneth E. Behring Family Hall of Mammals, at the National Museum of Natural History. For Theodore and Kermit, they were able to personally record taking 17 lions, 11 elephants, 20 rhinos, eight hippos, nine giraffes, and 10 Cape buffaloes. Of the effectiveness of the M-1895s, T.R. wrote:

The Winchester and the Springfield were the weapons one of which I always carried in my own hand and for any ordinary game. I much preferred them to any other rifles. The Winchester did admirably with lions, giraffes, elands and smaller game and as will be seen, with hippos. For heavy game like rhinoceroses and buffaloes I found that for me personally the heavy Holland was unquestionably the proper weapon. But in writing this I wish most distinctly to assert my full knowledge of the fact that

the choice of a rifle is almost as much a matter of personal idiosyncrasy as the choice of a friend. The above must be taken as merely the expression of my personal preferences. It will doubtless arouse as much objection among the ultra champions of one type of gun as among the ultra champions of another. The truth is that any good modern rifle is good enough. The determining factor is the man behind the gun.

He added:

I never left camp on foot or horseback for any distance no matter how short without carrying one of the repeating rifles and when on a hunt my two gun bearers carried one the other magazine rifle and one the double barrelled Holland.

As to the astonishing size of the animals collected for the museum, Roosevelt wrote:

Kermit and I kept about a dozen trophies for ourselves otherwise we shot nothing that was not used either as a museum specimen or for meat, usually for both purposes. We were in hunting grounds practically as good as any that have ever existed but we did not kill a tenth nor a hundredth part of what we might have killed had we been willing. The mere size of the bag indicates little as to a man's prowess as a hunter and almost nothing as to the interest or value of his achievement.

With the successful completion of the safari and the collection of articles written for *Scribner's Magazine*, as well as his best selling book *African Game Trails* (1910), he created a sensation for the Winchester M-1895 that lasts to this day. The .405 was discontinued in 1932. But rifles chambered in "Teddy's" caliber continue to bring a high premium over examples that are chambered in a round still readily available. In 2000, Winchester announced the reintroduction of the Browning 1895 in .405 caliber, demonstrating that the spirit of "Big Medicine" is still alive and well.

Africa would not be the last time Roosevelt would have the chance to use the 1895 on wild game. In 1914, T.R.,

Detail shots of the T.R./Bob Wrenn M-1895 SRC used in Cuba. *Photo courtesy T.R. Birthplace National Historic Site, NPS*

again accompanied by his son Kermit, set off for the Brazilian wilderness to explore one of the last great unknowns of geography in this hemisphere. Along with two curators/naturalists from the American Museum of Natural History in New York, as well as Father John Zahm and Col. Cândido Rondon of the Brazilian Army, the Roosevelt expedition set off, in early 1914, to find the source of *Rio da Dúvida*, the River of Doubt, a 1,000-mile tributary of the mighty Amazon. The Roosevelts arrived in South America in early December 1913, and, after numerous appearances, public speeches, and semi-official state visits, the former President, who preferred to be called "Colonel" Roosevelt, set off on the river exploration on February 27, 1914. Of their complement of firearms, Roosevelt wrote:

MANUFACTURED BY THE WINCHESTER REPEATING ARMS CO.
NEW HAVEN. CONN. U. S. A. PAT. NOV. 5. 95. NOV. 12. 95. AUG. 17. 97.

For arms the naturalists took 16-bore shotguns, one of Cherrie's having a rifle barrel underneath. The firearms for the rest of the party were supplied by Kermit and myself, including my Springfield rifle, Kermit's two Winchesters, a 405 and 30-40, the Fox 12-gauge shotgun, and another 16-gauge gun, and a couple of revolvers, a Colt and a Smith & Wesson.

The two referenced Winchesters were undoubtedly two M-1895s from the African safari of 1909-1910. Here, T.R. continues to reference the .30-caliber 1895 as being in .30-40, when it was settled in 1908 that the .30-caliber M-1895's were to be in .30-03, matching the M-1903 Springfield serial-number 6000 that he was so fond of.

Before they actually set off on the expedition, T.R. and Kermit went on a jaguar hunt. T.R. wrote:

… [W]e saw him, a huge male, up in the branches of a great fig-tree. A bullet behind the shoulder, from Kermit's 405 Winchester, brought him dead to the ground. He was heavier than the very big male horse-killing cougar I shot in Colorado, whose skull Hart Merriam reported as the biggest he had ever seen; he was very nearly double the weight of any of the male African leopards we shot; he was nearly or quite the weight of the smallest of the adult African lionesses we shot while in Africa.

Quite the endorsement for the killing power of the .405!

The jaguar was skinned and the hide was later converted into a rug and given to William Lindsay White, son of William

Allen White, a newspaper editor from Emporia, Kansas, and a close personal friend of Roosevelt. It is currently on display at the Red Rocks State Historic Site, in Emporia. As for the exploration into the unknown wilderness, T.R. wrote:

We were still wholly unable to tell where we were going or what lay ahead of us. We could not tell whether or not we would meet hostile Indians, although no one of us ever went ten yards from camp without his rifle. We had no idea how much time the trip would take. We had entered a land of unknown possibilities.

Tragedy struck the expedition when Kermit and a beloved guide were caught in sudden white water rapids. Their canoe capsized, drowning the guide and almost killing Kermit. From T*hrough The Brazilian Wilderness*:

Kermit clutched his rifle, his favorite 405 Winchester with which he had done most of his hunting both in Africa and America, and climbed on the bottom of the upset boat. In a minute he was swept into the second series of rapids, and whirled away from the rolling boat, losing his rifle. The water beat his helmet down over his head and face and drove him beneath the surface; and when he rose at last he was almost drowned, his breath and strength almost spent.

Such was the fate of one of the three .405 M-1895s that had seen so much hard use in Africa. During another tragic incident, one of the guides murdered another guide and fled the camp. Roosevelt grabbed his M-1895 and rushed into the jungle to apprehend the criminal, who was never found. In

the appendix to *Through The Brazilian Wilderness*, T.R. wrote:

Too much emphasis cannot be placed upon the need of being provided with good weapons. After the loss of all our arms in the rapids we secured four poor, rusty rifles which proved of no value.

T.R. summed up the importance of the expedition, writing:

We put upon the map a river some fifteen hundred kilometers in length, of which the upper course was not merely utterly unknown to, but unguessed at by, anybody; while the lower course, although known for years to a few rubbermen, was utterly unknown to cartographers. It is the chief affluent of the Madeira, which is itself the chief affluent of the Amazon.

The *Rio da Dúvida* is now known as Rio Roosevelt, a lasting testament to the legendary exploits of the hardiest of all of our chief executives. The expedition to Brazil almost cost the 57-year-old Rough Rider his life. He nearly died of malaria and fever and, at one point, begged Kermit to leave him behind. Eventually, his fever broke; he was barely able to walk out of the wilderness in May, having lost over 30 pounds during his ordeal. For T.R., the trip to Brazil would be his last great adventure. When asked by his wife, Edith, why he was taking on such an endeavor at his age, he replied, "It's my last chance to be a boy."

The outspoken proponent of the strenuous life died in his bed at his beloved Sagamore Hill, on January 6, 1919, at the age of 60. "The old lion is dead" was the text of the telegram that Archie

Close-ups and detail shots of Dr. Edmund Heller's Winchester 1895. Heller represented the Smithsonian Institution during the safari. *Photo courtesy Smithsonian Institution National Museum of American History*

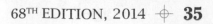

The 1st United States Volunteer Cavalry (The Rough Riders) atop San Juan Hill, July 1898. Theodore Roosevelt would call his actions that morning "my crowded hour." The events that day guaranteed him a chance at the presidency and eventually earned him the Medal of Honor.

Roosevelt cabled to his brothers Ted and Kermit. Vice President Thomas R. Marshall said, "Death had to take Roosevelt sleeping, for if he had been awake, there would have been a fight."

The story of Roosevelt's Winchester 1895s did not die with him. Ted Junior and Kermit formed two expeditions through Asia, bringing back countless specimens for the Field Museum of Chicago.

In 1924, after Ted lost his race for the Governorship of New York, he and Kermit decided they wanted to organize an expedition through Asia, for the purposes of scientific achievement. They approached Stanley Field, the president of Chicago's prestigious Field Museum, and museum director Davies about sponsoring the expedition in a manner similar to what Andrew Carnegie and the Smithsonian Institution had done for the African expedition of 1909. Field and Davies received the needed funding from science enthusiast James Simpson. The trip would focus on exploring the Pamirs, Turkestan, and the Tian Shan Mountains. In May 1925, the James Simpson-Roosevelt-Field Museum Expedition embarked for the Himalayas. This expedition would be the first to acquire a collection of wildlife from this region, for an American museum. By the end of their journey, they had collected over 2,000 specimens of small mammals, birds, and reptiles, along with 70 large mammals, including *Ovis Poli*, the great wild sheep now known as the Marco Polo sheep.

In their 1926 book, *East of the Sun and West of the Moon*, the Roosevelt brothers wrote:

First of all, of course, the question of rifles came up. Originally we intended to take .405 Winchesters, [M-1895s] but though the smashing power of this arm is very great, the trajectory is hardly flat enough for long-range shooting. For this reason we left these rifles in Kashmir for use on our return to India. For central Asia we decided upon two .375 Hoffman arms and two sporting model Springfields.

It is unknown to this author whether or not the M-1895s were used later on in the expedition, once they returned to India, and what game they may have taken with them.

In 1928, the two brothers, citing wanderlust, approached the Field Museum again, this time with a plan to travel through uncharted territory in Indo-China to hunt the giant panda, a feat never before accomplished by a Westerner. Stanley Field found them the proper funding again, this time by introducing them to a generous patron of the museum, William V. Kelley. Kelley was immediately open to the plan, and the Kelley-Roosevelt-Field Museum Expedition was established.

The Kelley-Roosevelt-Field Museum Expedition set out in 1928 and collected 40 big mammals, 2,000 small mammals, and 6,000 birds and reptiles, which included the first giant panda ever taken by a Westerner. Pandas had only been known in the West since 1869, and no live specimens were ever seen in the United States until the World's Fair of 1939. The hide of the panda the Roosevelts took in 1928-1929 was the first ever displayed in an American museum and, to this day, is still on display at the Field Museum, in Chicago. Only one known photograph of the panda was taken, by Kermit, with his brother Ted posing with a guide who has Ted's rifle slung over his back. Family history records the rifle as Ted's M-1895 in .405, a takedown model with a crescent buttstock. This rifle was passed to Ted's daughter Grace McMillan, whose husband used the rifle for many years on his own hunting trips. It was sold at auction, in 1993, following Ms. McMillan's death, and is now loaned and on display at the National Firearms Museum, in Fairfax, Virginia.

Unfortunately for firearms enthusiasts, Ted and Kermit did not record their two Asian safaris with the same attention to detail that their father used when recounting the firearms inventory on his numerous hunting expeditions. There is little to quote from their two books on the effectiveness of the Winchester M-1895. The displays at the Field Museum will have to speak for the rifles themselves.

To Winchester enthusiasts, and to all gun and hunting devotees, Roosevelt will forever be a heroic figure—the perfect example of the responsible hunter, sportsman, and shooter. He was an authentic statesman who knew, understood, and loved firearms. He comprehended what firearms represent not only to a free society, but to the future of conservation and the sustained use of natural resources.

NOTE: *This article is excerpted from the forthcoming book,* The Winchester Model 1895-The Last of the Classic Lever Action Rifles, *by Edmund Lewis and Rob Kassab.*

Bullets &

by Rick Hacker

There is a great correlation between guns and knives. After all, not only are they are both made with steel, either can be used with equal effectiveness for defense, offense, or recreation. While the knife certainly emerged first in the chronology of weaponry, once firearms came upon the scene, it was soon common for men who were serious about their survival to carry both. Today they still do, and chances are pretty good that, if you own one, you also own

the other, whether it's a boot knife to back up your carry gun, a sheath knife to skin what your rifle has brought down, or a pocket knife that adds to the versatility of your .22 rimfire.

By that same token, certain guns just seem to naturally inspire specific knives as kindred spirits. And while there is no absolute—indeed, the choice of a gun or knife is a very individualistic thing—I do have a few personal favorites I consider to be classic bullet and blade pairings.

& Blades

Starting Out At Any Age

Shooting and hunting memories usually begin with a .22 rifle and a W.R. Case pocket knife, two classics that have been produced since the late nineteenth century. The Marlin Model 39 lever-action started out as the Model 1897 and was so accurate it became a favorite of trick shooter Annie Oakley. In 1939, it was revamped with thicker stock contours and renamed the Model 39, which is still in the line as the Golden 39A, the world's longest reigning rifle still in production. Able to handle .22 Short, Long, and Long Rifle cartridges interchangeably, it can be taken down in minutes, using nothing but a coin. Small wonder more than 2,200,000 of these versatile .22s have been made to date, including this Model 39 TD Take Down from the 1980s, before the push button safety and hammer block were introduced. Of course, any boy or man with a Marlin 39 has to have a Case folder, in this case (and I mean that literally), an amber bone, medium-sized Texas Jack knife with clip and pen knife blades, or, for bigger chores, a three-bladed large Stockman with yellow synthetic handles. That's really all you need for an autumn day afield after rabbits or squirrels

Concealed Carry

The Kimber Ultra-Carry II, with its steel slide, aluminum frame, match grade three-inch barrel, and seven-round magazine is, perhaps, the ultimate carry gun, especially in the hard-hitting .45 ACP (a 9mm is also offered). The Ultra-Carry's versatility is amplified in this stainless steel version, which features a satin silver finish on the frame. I fired a perfect score with this little pistol right out of the box. The only thing I did was replace the black rubber grips with Kimber's checkered rosewood, which look better and anchor the gun just as well in my hand. Of course, being a cigar smoker, the perfect pocket blade for this pocket pistol is the new Famars Sigaro Automatic pin-less sidelock, available in blue, red, white, gray, or black aluminum panels. A push of the button on either side of the slabs opens and locks a two-inch tanto or clip-point blade (a golf divot or bottle opener are also available). The real attraction for me is the round cut-out, which neatly slices the cap of a cigar, when the blades are closed.

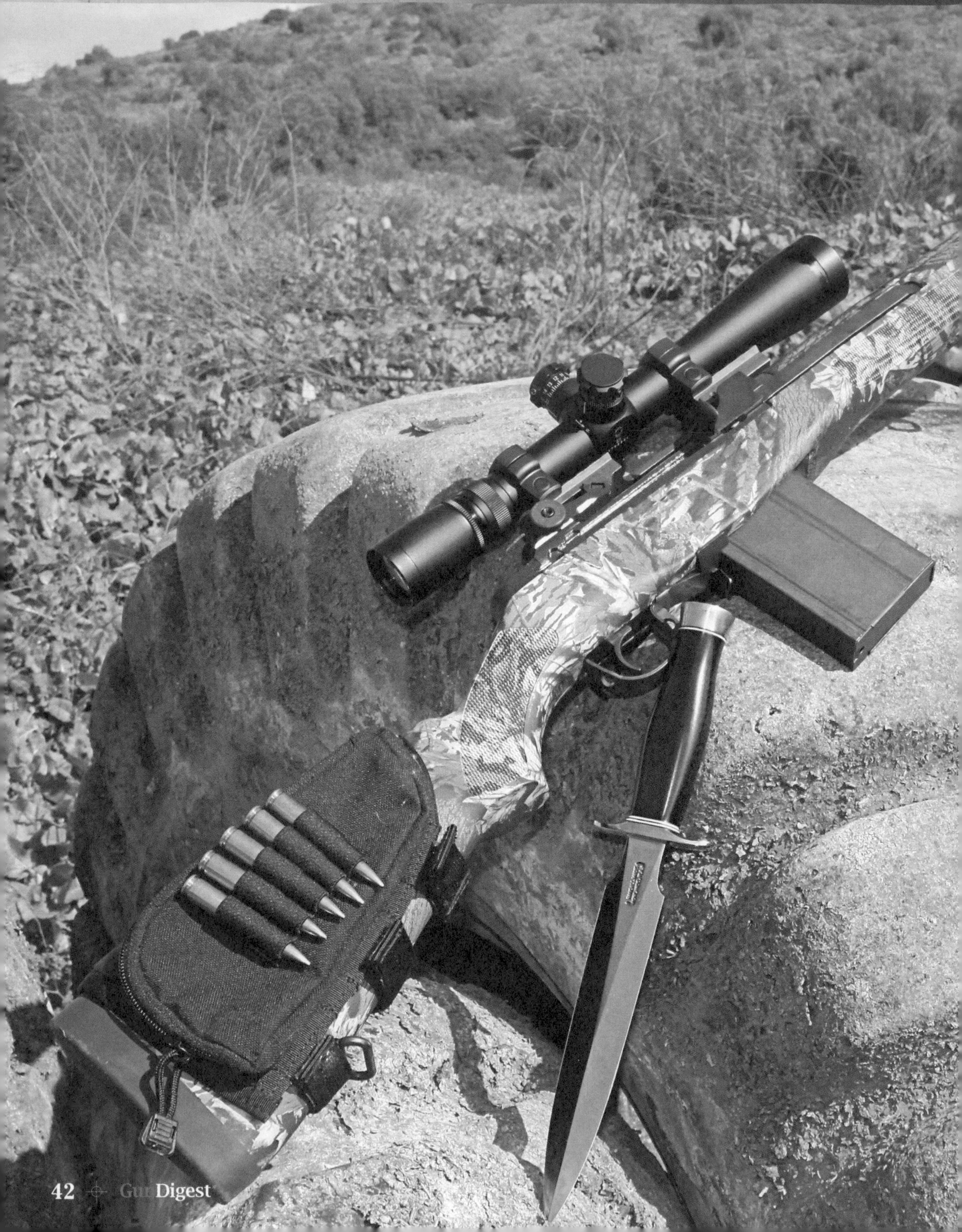

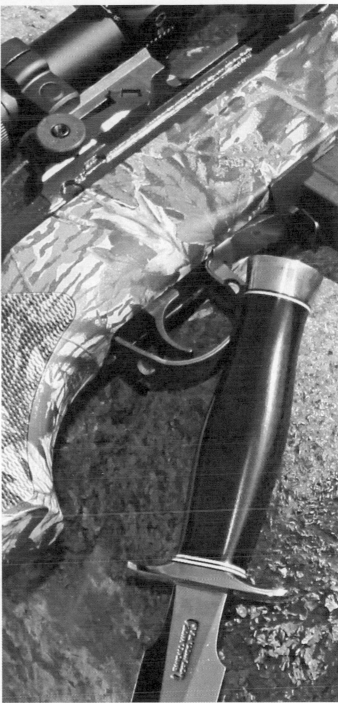

Tactical Twosome

This Springfield Scout Squad Rifle is outfitted with a factory Mossy Oak camo stock and an aftermarket Blackhawk Ammo cheek pad. It is topped off with Springfield's fourth generation scope mount and a Leupold 3.5x10x Mark IV Tactical scope. Its perfect battle partner for close-in work is a Randall Model 2 fighting stiletto with a U.S. Special Forces Airborne-inspired maroon Micarta handle and a brass buttcap to even out the balance of its eight-inch blade. (www.randallknives.com)

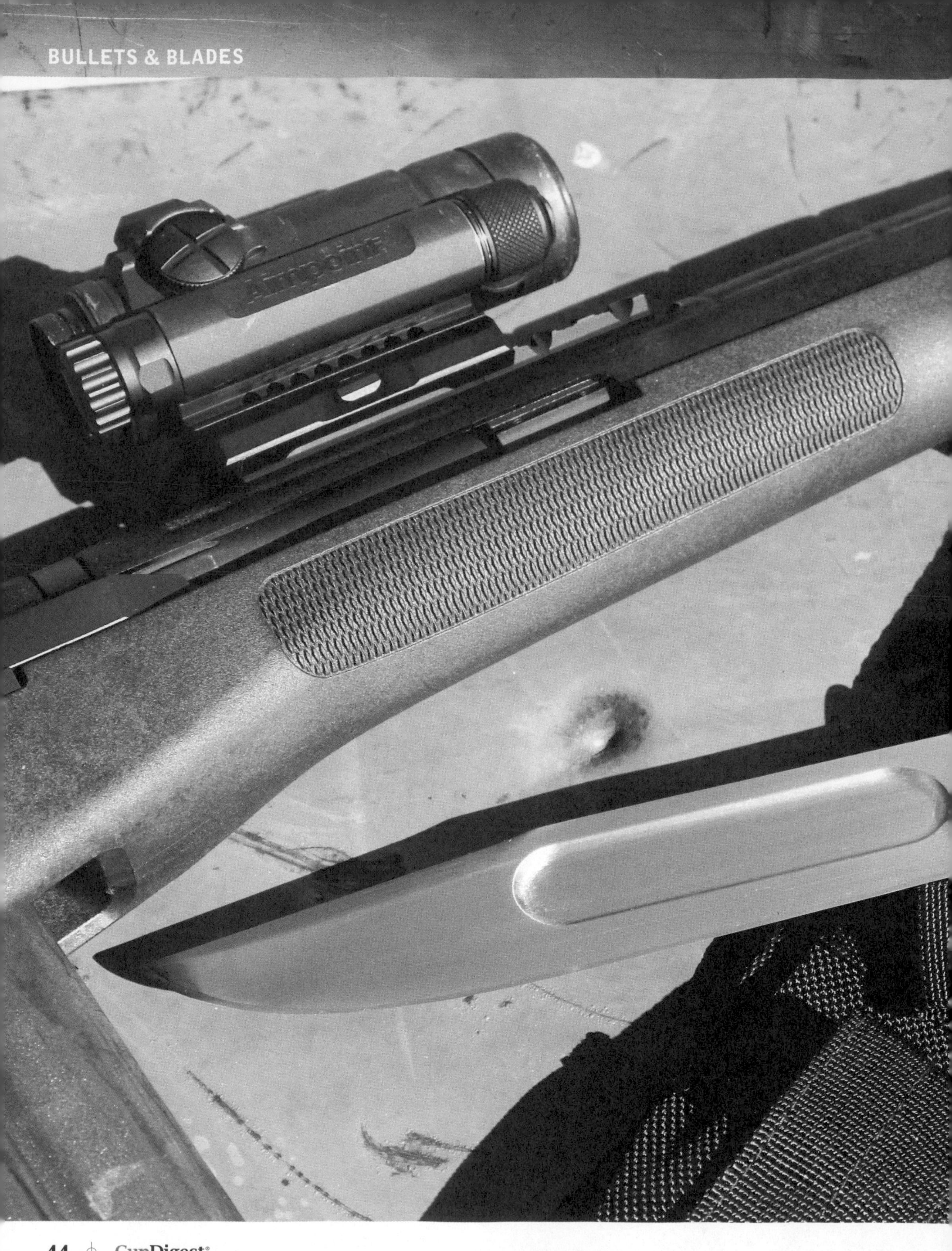
Aimpoint

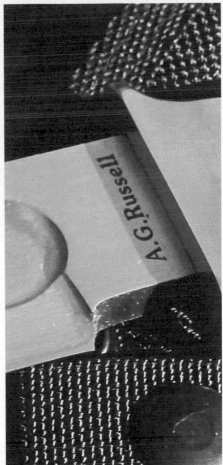

Ready For Your Close-Up (Encounter)

The Springfield Armory 16¼-inch barreled SOCOM version of the M1A is one of the most popular rifles in the law enforcement community. This one cranks things up a notch, outfitted with an M14/M1A tritium front sight, a forward-mounted Picatinny rail, and an Aimpoint CompM4 with night vision compatibility. Yet even with all of this technology, the knife of choice is a highly refined melding of a 1930s design and a nineteenth-century Bowie, the A. G. Russell Field Knife 2, with a nylon sheath that features a pouch that will accommodate a pistol magazine; a leather sheath is optional. The knife itself is made in Taiwan, sports a 7⅛-inch clip-point blade of AUS-10 steel, and features a dramatic blood groove. Its black Micarta handle and stainless steel hilt add to the Field Knife's all-weather durability and, if shipped to a military address, A.G. Russell (www.agrussell.com) offers a 25-percent discount.

Hunting Partners

The late gun writer Jack O'Connor called the Winchester Model 70 "The rifleman's rifle," and though he was referring to this famous bolt-action in .270 chambering, the same gun in .30-06 is no less deserving of the title. In fact, this particular .30-06 Model 70 was made in 1948 and was originally purchased by the father of one of my old high school buddies. After having taken numerous deer, moose, and elk, I acquired it and replaced the vintage Redfield Widefield scope with its TV-screen ocular and objective lenses, with a Leupold Vari-XIII 2.5x8x optic, which continues to serve the old rifle well. My long-time hunting knife is a Randall No. 4 Big Game and Skinner, which (while not wishing to date myself), I ordered, in 1965, from the late Bo Randall. With its seven-inch blade and stag horn handle, it was the first custom knife I ever bought—I had to wait two years for the knife to be made and delivered. It has since acquired a deep and luxurious patina that reminds me of many a past hunt, and although the blade has been sharpened and resharpened numerous times, thus affecting its collectability, that really doesn't matter, because I can't envision ever selling it. By that same token, the currently made, traditionally styled Case Hunter, with its five-inch clip blade, "Crow's Beak" butt cap, and leather handle, holds the promise of creating its own memories.

Military Might

It was thought that nothing could replace the Government Model 1911A1, but, in 1985, the 9mm Beretta M9—the military version of the current civilian M92FS did just that. At least officially. Although I am a big fan of the 1911, I gained new respect for the Beretta and its 15-round stacked magazine, both single- and double-action operation, and one-handed decocking capabilities. Moreover, during government testing, the M9 fired 17,500 rounds without a single malfunction, far surpassing the Army's 5,000-round requirement. Plus, it is reasonably accurate and, when stoked with some of the new self-defense 9mm ammo now on the market, such as Federal 124-grain Hydra-Shok or Hornady's 115-grain Critical Defense loads, the M9 more than fulfills its U.S. Army classification of being a "close personal-defense weapon." I increased the gun's close-range effectiveness by outfitting it with Crimson Trace LG-402M laser grips. Then I matched it up with a Randall No. 1 All-Purpose Fighting Knife, the blade that the late Bo Randall originally made for WWII G.I.s and which his company still makes for our boys in the sandbox—except that I ordered this version with sawteeth on its eight-inch blade (the tip of the top cutting edge is sharpened), a Commando-shaped leather handle, and a brass butt cap with wrist thong. As one individual said, upon seeing me use this knife for the first time, "That's one mean looking cutting machine!"

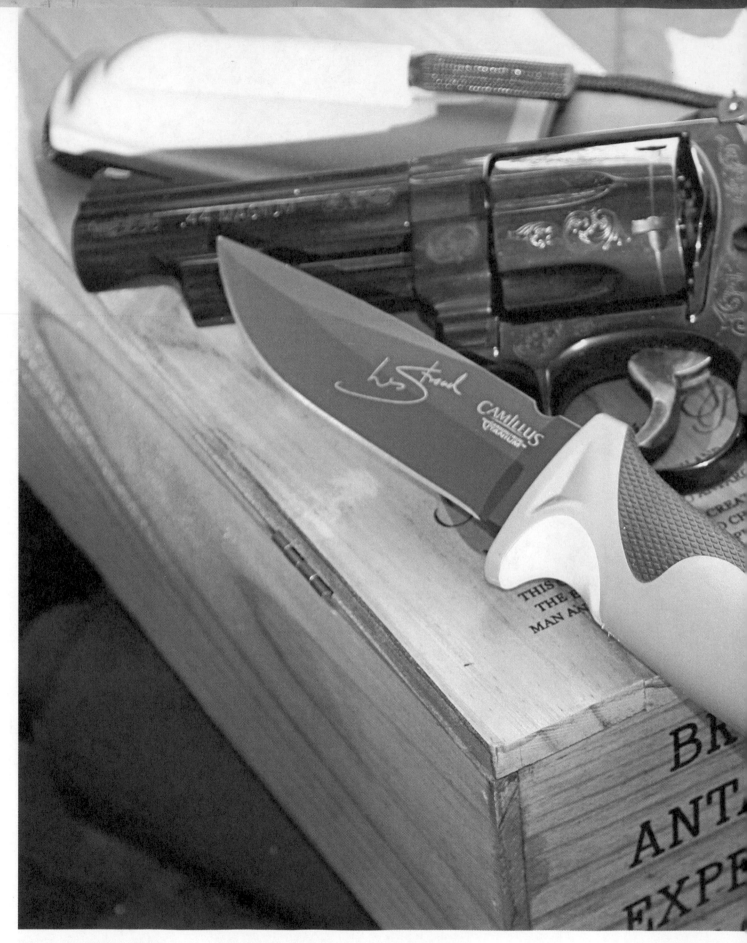

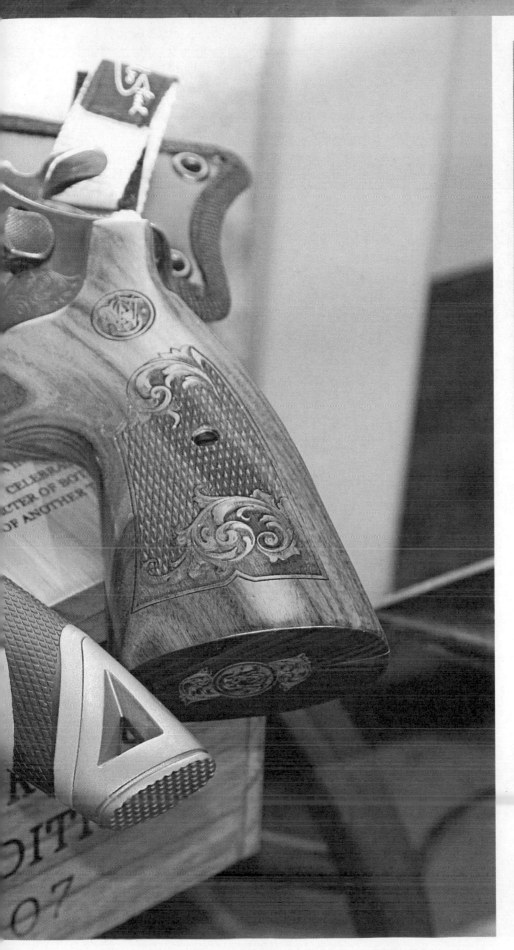

Survival of the Fittest

I have long considered the Smith & Wesson Model 29, especially with a four-inch barrel, one of the best all-around survival handguns. It is compact enough to carry in a backpack or holster, yet has plenty of power to get you out of most dangerous encounters with two- or four-legged adversaries. In addition, the recoil of the .44 Magnum, while stout, allows a much faster recovery time than that of more powerful calibers. For milder shooting requirements, such as bagging small to medium-sized game for camp meat, you can switch to .44 Specials. This factory laser-engraved Model 29 Classic is a perfect example of combining beauty with brawn. By the same token, the Camillus Les Stroud S.K. Arctic knife takes the basic survival knife to a new level, with its titanium-bonded, 440 stainless steel drop-point blade and ergonomically shaped handle with knurled steel pommel. What's more, the hard nylon sheath contains a fire starter and has a mesh trail map pocket on the back. This all comes with a sheet of Les Stroud's survival tips, which you might want to read before strapping this blade—and your gun—on your hip.

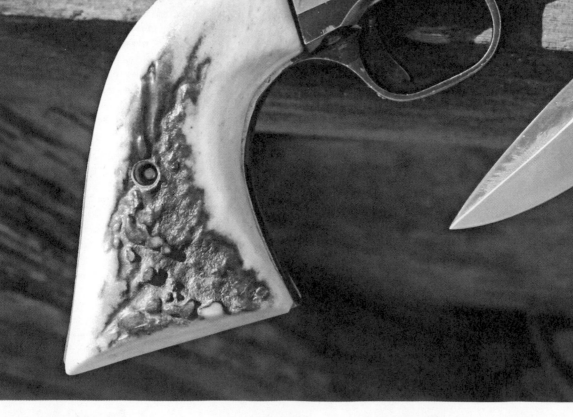

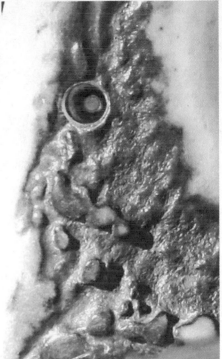

Frontier Favorites

There is, perhaps, no more famous, recognizable, and collectable revolver in the world than the Colt Single Action Army. It was the Army's first .45-caliber sidearm and, ever since its government adoption, in 1873, has gone on to achieve immortality not just on the American western frontier, but in western motion pictures and television programs. Indeed, one cannot say "western movies" without thinking of the Model P, as it was officially known at the factory. With a few brief interruptions caused, in part, by World War II and retooling, the Peacemaker is still in production and has enjoyed renewed interest, thanks to the sports of fast draw, cowboy action shooting, and hunting, not to mention collecting. This 1958-era Second Generation .45 Colt with a 5½-inch barrel features aftermarket two-piece stag grips. In the 1995 movie *Tombstone*—now a cult classic—the character of Doc Holliday made the SAA synonymous with the gambler's dirk or boot knife. Like the Colt Peacemaker, this uncataloged Randall Gambler, with its four-inch, top-sharpened blade, Ivorite handle, and domed brass butt cap is a perfect example of a nineteenth-century classic still being made today.

THE SECOND GUN

Why You Should Carry A Backup Gun

BY **Jim Wilson**

Backup guns have been carried by American lawmen and citizens, virtually since the beginning of firearms history. Though accounts vary, James Butler "Wild Bill" Hickok (1837-1876) may have used a derringer to end the life of Phil Coe, while Hickok was an officer, in Abilene, Kansas. Going out into the street to check on the sound of gunshots, Hickok came face to face with Coe, who already had a gun in his hand. Reportedly, Hickok relied on a derringer, carried in his coat pocket, when Coe fired a shot his way.

Another early lawman who believed in backup guns was Texas Ranger Capt. Frank Hamer (1884-1955). Hamer's primary handgun was an engraved Colt single action called "Old Lucky," which he carried in the waistband of his trousers. In October 1917, Hamer was the target of an assassination attempt, in Sweetwater, Texas. Wounded in his strong-side shoulder, Hamer drew a Smith & Wesson .44 Special from a shoulder holster and stopped the fight. Years later, in 1934, Hamer was part of the team that ended the careers of Clyde Barrow and Bonnie Parker. Still carrying Old Lucky, Hamer relied on a Colt 1911 in .38 Super, for backup. Today, savvy defensive handgunners, lawmen, and civilians alike continue the practice of carrying a backup gun, as part of their daily regimen.

In modern times, the backup gun has been carried in deep concealment, ready and waiting to allow the defensive shooter to stay in the fight. One of the main uses for the backup gun is when the primary handgun has been hit by an attacker's bullet and rendered useless. Untrained shooters often aim at the thing they are most concerned about and, in many cases, that is the handgun. This very thing happened to one of the FBI agents involved in a famous shootout with Miami bank robbers, in 1986, when his auto loading pistol was taken out of commission by incoming fire. The middle of a fierce gunfight is no place to be holding an inoperative handgun, so transitioning to a backup may just save your life.

Another use for the backup gun is when the primary gun runs dry. It is extremely difficult to count the number of rounds one has fired, when there are bullets flying all around. We generally know that we are out of ammo when the auto's slide locks to the rear or the revolver hammer clicks on an empty chamber.

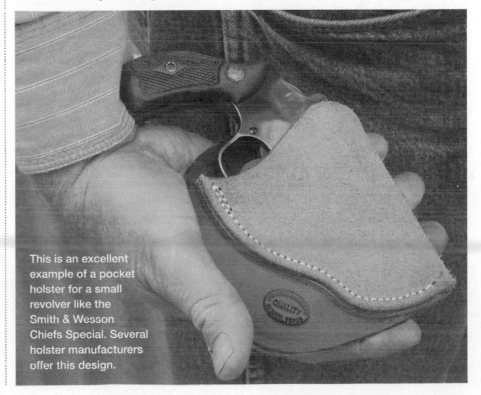

This is an excellent example of a pocket holster for a small revolver like the Smith & Wesson Chiefs Special. Several holster manufacturers offer this design.

While a speed reload may be the solution, there can be times when it is more advisable to transition to another gun. Carrying a backup gun provides the option to resolve a particular problem in more than one way.

Experiencing a jam or malfunction in the primary handgun is another reason to consider the backup gun. For our purposes here, a malfunction is a problem that can be resolved with the hands, while a jam is something that needs tools to fix. (In the case of a jam, the gun will probably need to go to a gunsmith to get it back in working order.) Malfunctions such as a stovepipe or failure to feed may be cleared fairly quickly, if the shooter has practiced the proper clearance drills. However, resolving a double-feed situation takes much longer. In revolvers, a cartridge case slipping under the extractor can take quite some time to clear, as is the case when the extractor rod has backed out. Again, one should know how to clear the various malfunctions common to their handgun, but a backup gun provides another option to dealing directly with the problem.

As in Frank Hamer's case, the defensive shooter may also be wounded in the strong-side arm or hand, making it difficult to use the primary handgun.

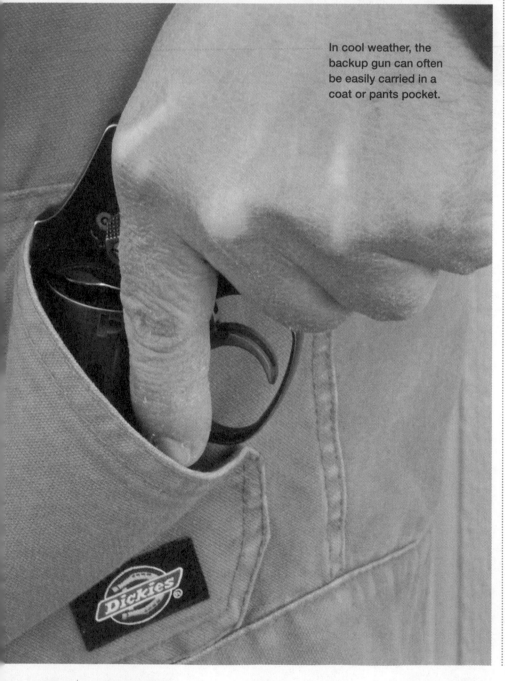

In cool weather, the backup gun can often be easily carried in a coat or pants pocket.

You could also be using your strong-side hand to hold onto something or ward off a physical attack. This makes the backup gun even more valuable, especially when it can be easily accessed by the support hand, or, as in Hickok's case, the backup gun may serve as a surprise, allowing one to take control of the situation.

Years ago, as a young patrol officer, I learned the value of carrying a backup gun that was accessible to my support hand. In warm weather, a Smith & Wesson Model 60 snub-nose .38, the hammer spur removed, rode in my otherwise empty left pant pocket. In cold weather, the little revolver was at home in the left-hand pocket of my Tuffy jacket.

Making a traffic stop, I could approach the vehicle with my left hand casually in my pocket. If the driver was an honest citizen, which was usually the case, he or she never knew that I had my hand on a gun. This practice was especially valuable when responding to domestic violence calls, as those can turn nasty in a hurry. Although I never had to use my backup gun in a fight, its presence and quick appearance kept trouble from escalating on several occasions.

Choosing a backup gun to fit a person's specific needs has never been easier. There was a time, in the not too distant past, when the only selections consisted of a few small .38 Special revolvers and a handful of small auto-loaders generally chambered for .32 ACP or .380 ACP. Thanks to an increased interest in personal-defense and modern technology, that has all changed. Polymer construction has allowed for some very small pistols, and modern technology allows us to have 9mm, .45 ACP and .357 Magnum backup guns of a diminutive size that was formerly only dreamed of. The police officer and armed citizen can now carry a backup gun that is small and lightweight enough to be comfortable, yet one that still packs a significant payload.

The ammunition companies haven't been asleep on the job, either. Advanced bullet designs have increased the defensive performance of handgun loads, so that a .32 or .380 auto, if that is your choice, are not to be taken lightly.

Today, there are so many good backup guns available that it is virtually impossible to list all of the suitable candidates. Instead, let's look at some of the characteristics that all good backup guns should possess.

The first important characteristic of a backup gun should be reliability. It must function. And it must function reliably

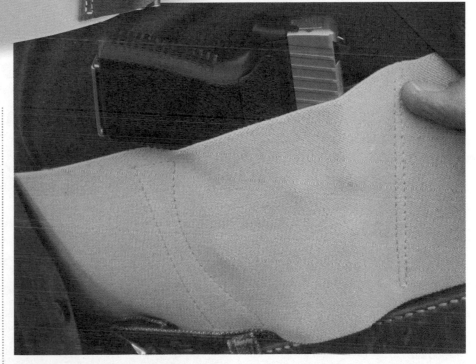

Galco's Belly Band offers a sensible way to comfortably carry a compact revolver or semi-auto. It is shown here with both a Smith & Wesson Model 442 and a Kahr PM9.

with the ammunition chosen. Fortunately, most handguns from reputable manufacturers will meet this test. Care should be taken with auto pistols to test each magazine, too. The garbage can is the place for any magazine that doesn't work. Using quality magazines, quality ammunition, and keeping the pistol properly cleaned and lubricated will go a long way towards insuring reliability.

I still carry a five-shot revolver as backup, because of the reliability issue, though I will also freely admit that part of my choice is due to familiarity. Still, the double-action revolver is about as reliable a gun as man is capable of creating, and it will stand more neglect than the average auto pistol. However, today that is more a matter of splitting hairs, thanks to the increased reliability of the modern semi-auto.

The backup gun should be small and lightweight enough that it can be comfortably worn throughout the waking hours of the day. While any defensive handgun should be comfort*ing* instead of comfort*able*, if it is too heavy, a person will start looking for excuses to leave it behind—you're only running down to the corner store for a loaf of bread. What could possibly happen?

The backup gun should be powerful enough to reliably stop an attack. For most of us, that means it should be .38

Special, 9mm, or larger (although a good argument can be made for the .380 and .32 autos with modern defensive ammunition). We often hear the argument that any handgun caliber will kill a man, when the bullet is properly placed. But we are not concerned with killing, nor are we concerned with the fact that an attacker hit with a .22 will die in a few hours or days. We are concerned with stopping an attack as quickly and efficiently as possible.

The smart person will carry the most powerful handgun that he or she can shoot quickly and accurately and conceal effectively. The task of the backup

gun is to save your life. Don't skimp and expect a little dog to do a big dog's job.

Throughout my years as a peace officer and an armed citizen, I have carried backup guns in just about every conceivable location on my person. Some were good and some were not so good. I finally found what works for me, but let's look at some of the various carry techniques and examine their pros and cons.

I've always worn cowboy boots and, years ago, got the idea of a boot-top holster. It seemed like the smart idea to put my .38 snubby in one of those in-the-pants holster that has the little metal belt clip; I could just clip the whole rig

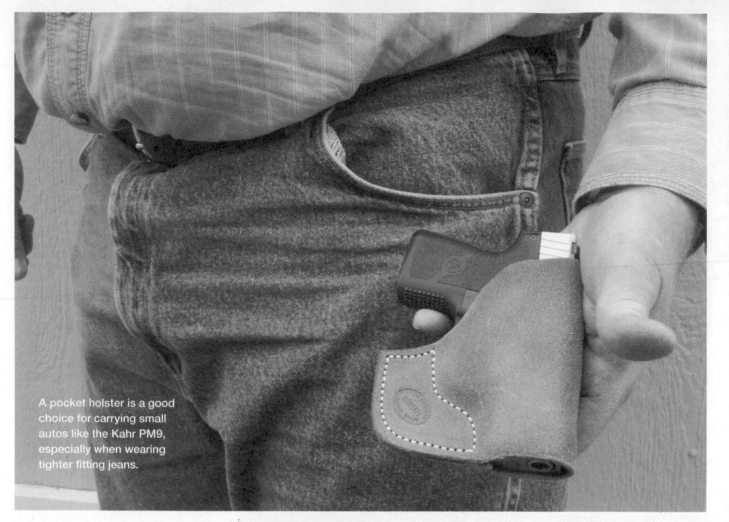

A pocket holster is a good choice for carrying small autos like the Kahr PM9, especially when wearing tighter fitting jeans.

into the top of my boot. It was concealable and fairly secure, so much so that I just couldn't believe that everybody who wore boots wasn't doing it.

Then came the day when, off duty and armed only with my boot-top backup gun, I was asked to help locate a drunk who was armed with a pistol and wandering around the downtown business district. Naturally, it fell my luck to walk around the corner of a building and come nose to nose with the miscreant. His pistol was in his pocket and his hand was on it. My pistol might as well have been in the gun case at home. The solution, fortunately, did not end up in gunfire, but it sure required a lot of physical exertion and some Band-Aids.

While there are a lot of ankle holsters on the market, I can't help but see them in the same light as my boot-top rig. Ankle holsters are comfortable to wear and will conceal a small pistol quite nicely. But getting to them is the problem. Drawing from an ankle holster requires one to either kneel or to stand on one leg during the draw. Neither posi-

With the support hand in the pocket on the backup gun, an LEO can approach a traffic violator, ready, but not obvious.

tion is a good place to be in the middle of a gunfight.

I think a far better choice is to carry the backup gun somewhere around the mid-line of the body. Pocket carry makes a lot of sense, assuming one is not wearing tight jeans. The pocket chosen for carrying the backup gun should be empty of everything else; you sure don't want to make your draw and find your key ring hanging from the pistol's rear sight.

Numerous holster companies offer some excellent choices in pocket holsters. I prefer the leather ones manufactured with the rough side of the leather on the outside. This creates a bit of friction between the holster and the pocket lining during the draw and allows the holster to remain in the pocket.

Another good carry method for backup guns is to carry in the waistband, under the shirt. Several companies offer elastic bands that fit around the waist and have an integral holster for the small handgun. If you're into western wear, a snap-button shirt will speed up your draw considerably. If not, lower buttons can be fastened to the front tab of the shirt so that it appears to be buttoned, while Velcro strips that have been sewn on actually close the shirtfront. Either way, the shirtfront can be quickly ripped open to access the backup gun.

Several companies are now making T-shirts that have pistol pockets on either side, just under the armpit. These can be quite comfortable, but one still has to find a way to get the shirt front open quickly. In a similar vein, law enforcement officers will find some manufacturers making holsters that can be fastened to the side tabs of the ballistic vest worn under the uniform shirt.

Being the individuals we are, it is important to experiment with various backup guns and carry techniques to find what works for you and fits your needs. The important thing to remember is that the backup holster should hold the gun securely and be fairly readily accessible.

It is also critically important to practice getting the gun into play. Drawing from deep concealment is not nearly as easy as drawing from a belt rig. Nor is it anywhere near as quick. Regular practice, several times a week, will help smooth out the pistol presentation and increase one's speed.

The same can be said of practicing with the backup gun. A while back, I was part of a three-day defensive pistol course. Two days were devoted to training with the service pistol, while

The author is not in favor of the boot-top or ankle holster. One does not want to be kneeling or standing on one foot when a fight goes down.

one day was given over to shooting the backup gun. The first two days went great, and you could tell folks knew what they were doing and had been practicing. The third day, with the backup guns, went straight to hell. I've never seen so much fumbling and so many poor scores. Small handguns are simply more difficult to shoot accurately, and this group had clearly not been practicing with their backup guns. No range day should be complete unless there is some practicing with the backup gun. One must not only practice getting the gun into action as quickly

as possible, one must also determine his effective range with the diminutive pistols. Practice doesn't make perfect; only perfect practice makes perfect.

Backup guns can truly be a lifesaver, if the policeman and armed citizen will take the time to select a gun that works for them, suitable defensive ammunition, and an effective carry method. Then, all that is lacking is to practice, practice, practice. And then you have to carry them with you. I like to call backup guns "always guns," because they should always be on you. Your life may depend on it.

In a Class by Itself

BY Terry Wieland

An early Model 1908 in original, pristine condition. The quality and workmanship glow through like a halo.

The Mannlicher-Schönauer was the world's finest production rifle.

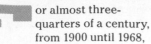

For almost three-quarters of a century, from 1900 until 1968, Mannlicher-Schönauer sporters set a standard of excellence unexcelled by any other production rifle. The Mannlicher was a first-rate design, with many features that have never been matched, produced in one of the world's best arms-making facilities by some of the worlds finest gunmakers. The Austrian Arms Factory at Steyr was in the business of supplying weapons not only to the Austro-Hungarian Empire, but also to other countries; for decades, Steyr, with its Mannlicher rifles, competed with Mauser for military contracts around the world.

The commercial Mannlicher grew out of one of these contracts, the Greek military design of 1903. It, in turn, grew from the 1888 German Commission rifle, the work of several different designers, including Ferdinand Ritter von Mannlicher and Otto Schönauer.

Mannlicher was one of history's greatest firearms designers, with 150 patents to his credit, many of which were far ahead of their time. He was involved in the initial "German Commission" design, and Steyr received a contract to produce some of those rifles for the Germany Army. When Steyr began work on the design that was to become the Greek military Mannlicher, it was natural the company would start with the Commission rifle.

The Commission bolt-action was smooth, strong, and reliable, but it needed a sophisticated magazine and feeding system. Otto Schönauer, the director of the plant at Steyr, had been working on a rotary magazine since 1885, and he combined with designer Antonin Spitalsky to perfect the system. They were not the only ones studying this approach; in the United States, Arthur W. Savage was following the same line and had patented a rotary magazine as early as 1893.

In the late 1800s, as repeating rifles using smallbore cartridges became the standard military arm, developing a magazine system that was durable and reliable was as important in rifle design as the action itself. For this reason, several hyphenated rifle names from that era give credit to the magazine designer; James Paris Lee, for example, designed the Lee-Enfield detachable box magazine. The tubular magazine used in lever- and early bolt-actions had several drawbacks, and some sort of container beneath the action was the usual alternative.

The rotary magazine's advantage over the box used by Paul Mauser was that it was very precise and could be tailored to an individual cartridge to ensure exact alignment with the feeding ramp, giving smooth, flawless functioning. The disadvantages were that it required greater skill to produce and was expensive.

Mannlicher, who had patented methods of clip-feeding rifles, was brought

A Model 1908 stock (left) compared with the Monte Carlo of the Model 1956. The 1956 stock is the best the author has ever seen for accommodating both iron sights and a rifle scope.

in to assist in adapting clip-feeding to the Schönauer design and to develop a method for removing the rotary magazine for maintenance. Almost certainly, Mannlicher also applied his expertise to ensuring the rifle as a whole functioned perfectly. The resulting Greek Mannlicher was chambered for the 6.5x54 M-S military cartridge loaded with a long, slim, 160-grain bullet having a muzzle velocity of 2,223 feet per second.

The Mannlicher-Schönauer Model 1903 commercial sporter incorporated the action and cartridge of the Greek rifle, but there the resemblance ended. The M1903 was given a 17½-inch barrel and was stocked to the muzzle—the *stützen* design known to this day as a "Mannlicher stock." Really a carbine designed for the mountain hunting of Austria, the stock had a cheekpiece and sling swivels, and it was light, compact, and designed for accurate shooting under tough conditions.

With its long bullet's high sectional density, the 6.5x54 M-S gave excellent penetration. Ivory hunter W.D.M. "Karamoja" Bell used one to kill hundreds of elephants, usually by stalking close and placing his bullets precisely in the brain. Other famous hunters who used the "little Mannlicher," as they came to be known, included professional hunter Werner von Alvensleben, who, shooting in Mozambique, killed more than a thousand Cape buffalo with one, and American Charles Sheldon, who hunted mountain sheep and killed dozens of grizzlies with a 6.5x54.

Made to the highest standards of Austrian craftsmanship, the rifle became renowned for its quality. Because it was expensive, it also became known as a "gentleman's rifle." Ernest Hemingway later put Mannlichers in the hands of some of his fictional characters, notably Margot Macomber.

From its introduction, in 1903, until 1914, Mannlicher rifles were retailed by all the great English gunmakers. In 1906, Charles Lancaster sold two Mannlichers to Sir Charles Ross, inventor of the straight-pull Ross rifle. In 1907, Frederick Courteney Selous ordered one custom-made in .375 (the original short case .375, not the 1912 magnum) from Holland & Holland. Purdey, Boss, Daniel Fraser—all offered Mannlicher rifles finely finished and cased, as befitted a London gun. These magnificent specimens command high prices at auction today.

Generally speaking, however, the English preferred to work with Mauser actions, because they could be adapted to their own proprietary cartridges. Mannlichers were available in their own chamberings and it was difficult to alter them to anything else. The M1903, on the other hand, was chambered only for the 6.5x54 M-S and every function was precisely tailored to and for that specific cartridge. This approach, while requiring painstaking work, paid off in superb feeding and absolute reliability that Mauser could only dream of. The drawback was its lack of flexibility. To introduce a

Comparing Monte Carlos: Top is a Mannlicher Model 1956, a Model 1908, and below is a Schultz & Larsen in the Weatherby style of the 1960s.

new chambering meant reworking every component and dimension of the magazine well. (Many years later, in the 1960s, exasperated by feeding problems with Mauser rifles and box magazines, professional hunter Terry Irwin ordered a custom Mannlicher from Austria, that rifle chambered for the .458 Winchester Magnum. Once he received his Mannlicher, he wrote that he never had another feeding problem.)

In 1905, Steyr introduced a second model, the M1905, chambered for the 9x56 Mannlicher-Schönauer; a third, the M1908, was chambered for the 8x56, and the series was completed, in 1910, with a rifle in 9.5x57. The latter three cartridges all used a case slightly longer than the original 6.5x54.

Such specialization of rifle and cartridge was required, because the spools of the rotary magazine were sculpted to cradle each round and hold it firmly, preventing any movement under recoil. As the spool rotates, the cartridges act like roller bearings, presenting minimal resistance and moving into exact position for feeding into the chamber.

The magazine is unloaded by depressing the spring-loaded cartridge stop via a small, knurled button on the flat of the receiver. It is not necessary to cycle each cartridge through the chamber or remove the magazine.

The cartridge stop was precisely fitted to accommodate cartridge cases of exactly one diameter. Because of this precision, it is not possible to simply re-chamber a Mannlicher to a different cartridge. Even adapting an 8x56 to the more common (and almost indistinguishable) 8x57 Mauser is a difficult task, one involving altering the width of the magazine box, as well as the cartridge stop. Writer and gunsmith Frank de Haas once undertook to convert a Mannlicher, re-barreling it to .308 Winchester. He wrote that it was not worth the trouble.

From the Model 1905 on, the barrels were 20 inches, with some additional cosmetic changes, alterations to the shape of the pistol grip and the checkering pattern, for example, and slight changes to the distinctive "butter knife" bolt handle. But, essentially, the 1903, 1905, 1908, and 1910 are the same rifle, differentiated only by their chamberings. Because of this, these rifles do not have caliber markings; you can determine the caliber by looking at the model designation engraved on the receiver ring.

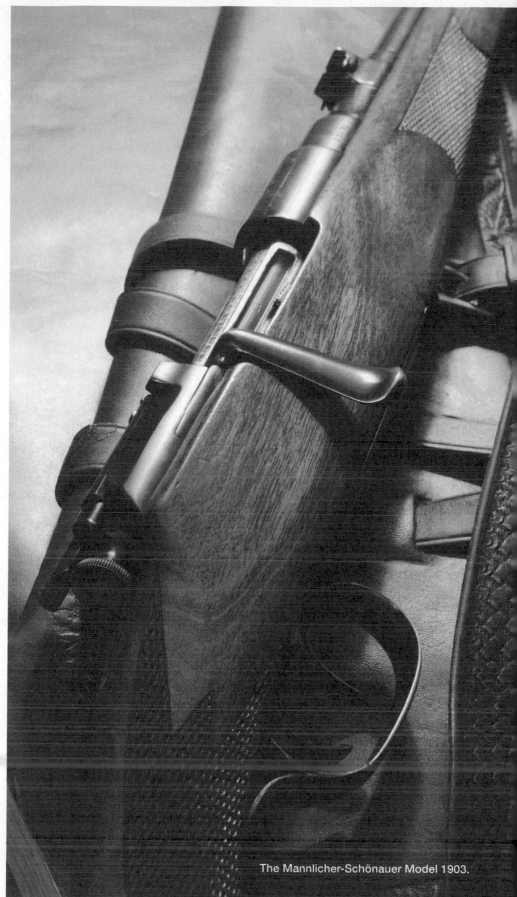

The Mannlicher-Schönauer Model 1903.

The author with a Model 1956. The Monte Carlo, although rather outlandish in appearance, works like a charm, much like the exaggerated cheekpieces found on 1900-era *schützen* (schuetzen) rifles.

After the Great War, as Austria slowly recovered and Steyr returned to commercial gun making, further modifications were made to allow the rifles to be offered in many different chamberings. This is reflected by the range of rifles imported to the U.S. and offered for sale by Stoeger Arms, Steyr's American importer. Then, in 1925, Steyr lengthened the action to allow the use of cartridges such as the 6.5x68. From that point, commercial Mannlichers were available in many popular chamberings.

If one were to make a generalization regarding Mauser rifles versus Mannlichers, it would be this: Mauser's commercial rifles were civilianized military weapons, whereas the Mannlicher was a quality commercial rifle adapted to military use. Without exception, factory Mannlichers are more finely finished than commercial Mausers and, in some ways, a Mannlicher is of a more sophisticated design.

Two particular features of the Mannlicher stand out as unique among production rifles: the rotary magazine and the trigger group. The Schönauer rotary magazine makes the Mauser box seem crude by comparison. It is a self-contained unit with a spring-powered spool whose tension increases as cartridges are fed into the magazine. It can be removed from the rifle for cleaning and further dismantled and reassembled without tools. There is a spring-loaded catch that locks the floorplate in place when it is in the rifle; this catch is depressed using anything handy—the tip of a cartridge, usually—and the floorplate is rotated out of two grooves, one at each end, that hold its lips firmly. The box then slides out. This is easy and convenient, yet there is no way the magazine can open accidentally.

The spindle can also be removed from its housing without tools. The spindle is so closely sculpted to fit its cartridge that, with the magazine out of the rifle, you can place a cartridge in the top cradle and it will rest there, seemingly in defiance of gravity.

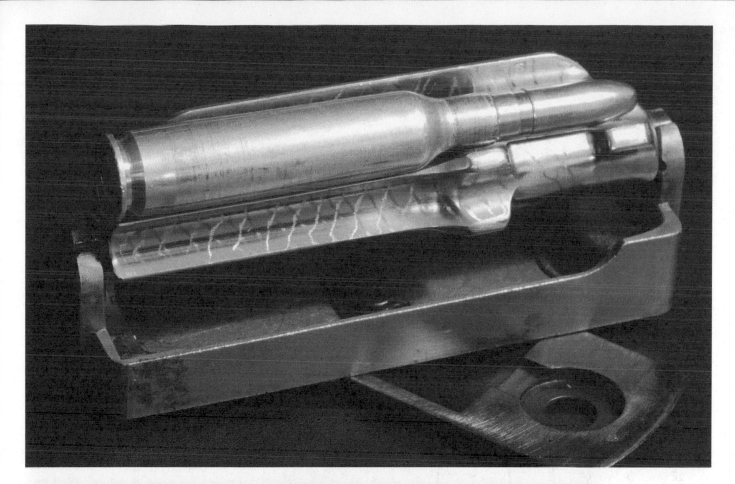

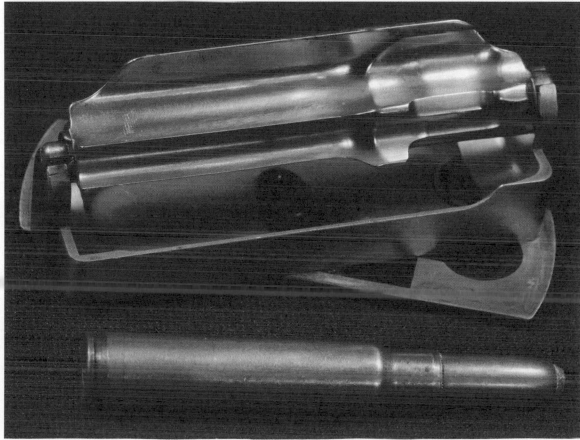

ABOVE: A 6.5x54 rotary magazine, cradling a cartridge. The fins of the spindle were sculpted to fit the exact cartridge for which the rifle was chambered. (Note: the engraving on this spindle is not original.)

LEFT: The rotary magazine, removed from a Model 1908. The spool is sculpted to fit the 8x56 Mannlicher-Schönauer cartridge. The spool can be lifted out of its cradle, without tools, for cleaning and lubrication.

The famous Model 1903. The machine turning is not original.

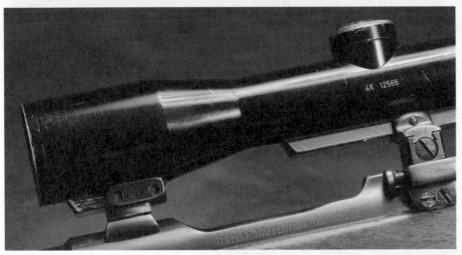

ABOVE: A Model 1908 with a typical claw mount.

The trigger assembly is every bit as ingenious. The trigger guard is held in place by a lip at the front and one screw on the tang. Remove that screw and the guard lifts away. The trigger group, as a unit, has a similar lip, with the rear held in place by a stout guard screw.

Originally, commercial rifles were fitted with double set triggers; later, single triggers were offered. The trigger groups are interchangeable, without special fitting. A hunter could have two trigger groups for his rifle, either to be used as a spare or for different purposes. Lift one out, drop the other in, replace the trigger guard, and you are ready to go.

The sear of the striker is fitted with a roller to smooth the trigger pull as it lifts the sear. The workmanship and finish on the mechanism is comparable to that found on the internal workings of a London double. The forward trigger trips the sear and can be released in the conventional manner, but it is heavy—usually about six pounds. It can be set to a "hair" release by pulling the rear trigger until it clicks. If the shooter decides not to shoot, the trigger can be un-set by pulling the rear trigger back and holding it, then pressing the forward trigger. This operation, Stoeger cautioned, should be practiced with an unloaded rifle before attempting it with a round in the chamber. Better still, the bolt can be opened while you do it; in later models, it can be done with the auxiliary safety on. The relative release-weights for both triggers is adjusted by means of a tiny screw positioned between them.

After the Great War, the United States became an increasingly important mar-

RIGHT: Leupold's Adjusto mount on a Model 1903.

A Pachmayr Lo-Swing scope mount on a Model 1950 in .270 Winchester.

kct. To increase their appeal, Steyr offered Mannlicher rifles in a greater array of calibers. These were listed in Stoeger catalogs and the *Shooter's Bible*, along with schematics and explanations of how the magazine and triggers functioned.

Each magazine was carefully fitted to its particular cartridge, just as the originals had been. As long as European labor was cheap, the additional work did not add unduly to the cost, but the Mannlicher's reputation as a gentleman's rifle and the fact that they had never been inexpensive to begin with put them out of reach of the average person. Still, Stoeger sold enough of them between the wars to justify their importation, and Western Cartridge and others offered ammunition in the standard Mannlicher calibers. Production was not resumed until 1950, after the Second World War, at which time Steyr introduced the modified Model 1950.

One difficulty the Mannlicher action possesses, with its split bridge and bolt handle placed forward of the bridge, is in mounting a rifle scope; in the 1950s, this had become an increasingly important factor in sporting rifles. Early Mannlichers were often fitted at the factory with claw mounts and a scope like a Kahles or Zeiss, but such an arrangement is a custom proposition.

The Mannlicher's information was always engraved on the receiver ring, as with this Model 1908.

When it became necessary to include the caliber, it was engraved on the receiver ring, along with patent information and the model designation.

From left: Model
1903, Model 1903
rifle with long barrel,
Model 1908, and
Model 1956.

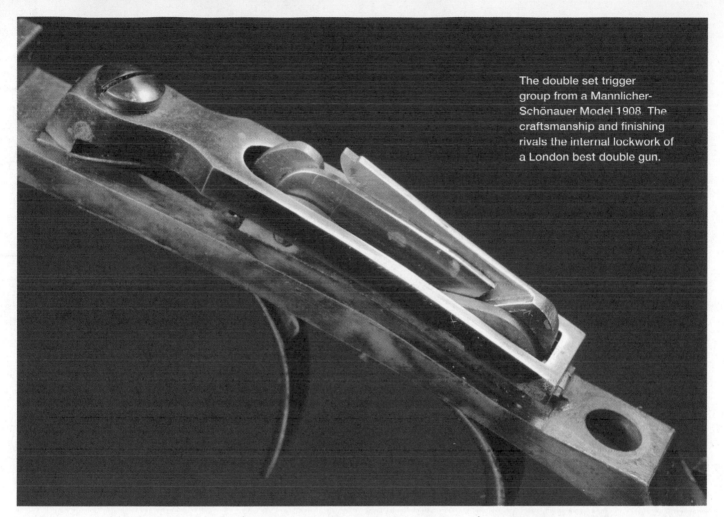

The double set trigger group from a Mannlicher-Schönauer Model 1908. The craftsmanship and finishing rivals the internal lockwork of a London best double gun.

In the post-war years, various scope manufacturers designed their own mounts for the Mannlicher-Schönauer, including Leupold, Griffin & Howe, Pachmayr, Redfield, and Paul Jaeger.

At the same time, Steyr changed its models. Gone were the old 1903 *et al*, replaced by models with designations such as the 1950, 1952, 1956, MC, and MCA. Traditionally, model and caliber were engraved on the receiver ring, and this continued even as the receiver ring was covered up or removed by installing a scope mount. This can create difficulties identifying models.

Although Steyr continued to offer the traditional stützen carbine, it added a rifle configuration with a 24-inch barrel and conventional stock. These were often fitted with a single trigger.

The most obvious changes in the different models appeared in the stock shape, notably the sculpting of the cheekpiece and the reduction of drop, as Mannlicher attempted to make its rifles more compatible with rifle scopes. The stock shape evolved through the 1950s and '60s, with the Model 56 having one

of the best of all stock designs, of any manufacturer, for use with iron sights and detachable scopes. It had a high rollover comb with a dished cheekpiece that allowed the head to move up and down comfortably. Whether this design was too expensive or simply failed to catch on, it was replaced in later models by a conventional Monte Carlo design.

Other changes included a swept-back butter-knife bolt handle, polished and left in the white, rather than blued. There was also a modernized bolt release and a progression of different safety mechanisms. The original two-position wing safety on the bolt shroud rotates up and over. Because it is an integral part of the bolt, this safety was left in place, but an auxiliary safety was added for scope use, first to the right of the shroud above the trigger guard, like a Weatherby or Remington Model 700, then, after 1964, on the tang like a shotgun. The wing safety, when "on," locks the bolt closed as well as blocks the trigger. The auxiliary safety does not lock the bolt.

From 1950 until it was discontinued in 1968, the Mannlicher-Schönauer

was offered in an array of models and model numbers, with both rifle and carbine configurations. The rifles from 1903 through 1910, if unaltered and in good condition, command high prices, whereas the later models are less attractive, especially if they have been fitted with scope mounts or otherwise altered. Prices for excellent Mannlichers are considerably less than those for commercial Mausers.

The early 1970s were a watershed for the global arms industry, with Browning ceasing production at FN in Belgium, Steyr discontinuing the Mannlicher, and Weatherby moving production from Germany to Japan. All were due to rising costs in Europe that made high-quality, European-made firearms uneconomic. Still, while some makers compromised, cutting corners and offering products that were noticeably inferior, Steyr did not. As a result, any Mannlicher you can find is a fine and finely made rifle. It is one of the world's great—and, in recent years, under-appreciated—sporting rifles.

U.S. ARMY

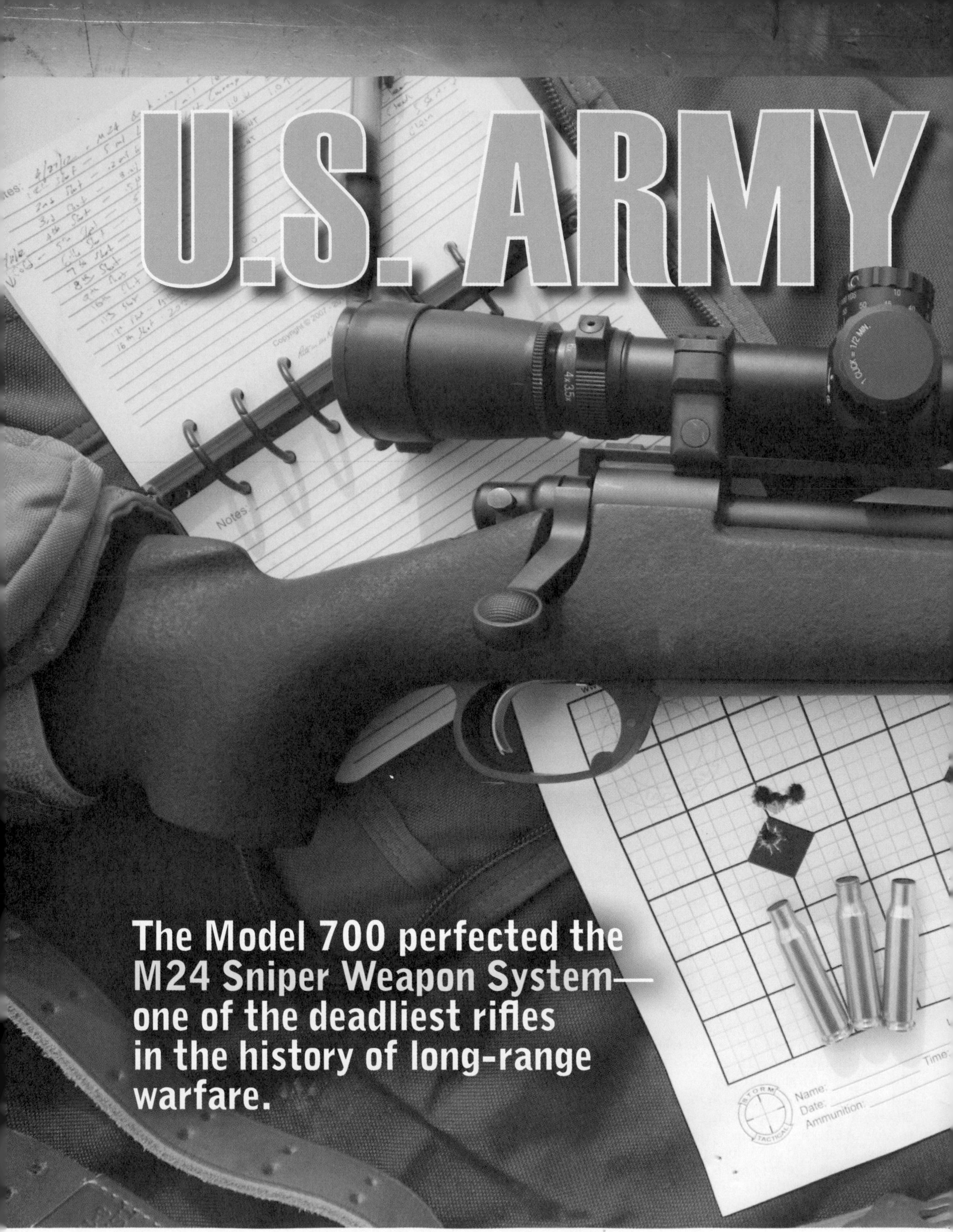

The Model 700 perfected the M24 Sniper Weapon System— one of the deadliest rifles in the history of long-range warfare.

M24 SNIPER RIFLE

BY **Corey Graff**

Kneeling down at roadside's edge, an insurgent works frantically, while two armed men pile out of a car and stand guard with AK-47s. They're up to no good, in plain view now, in the pre-dawn light. A cloud of dust from the vehicle's sudden stop floats aloft on morning thermals, the day's first mirage in a half-value crosswind.

An Army sniper and his spotter are watching.

"Range me."

The IED had to be placed quickly, but he wasn't going to be fast enough.

"Send it."

And the crack of a rifle.

Before the improvised explosive—a hidden deathtrap for American troops or local children, whoever happened by one first—can be set, the terrorist is turned inside out, buckling over. Two seconds later, the sound of the distant shot, fired from some 900 yards out, echoes like the sharp crack of a whip through the mountainous valley. The Army sniper racks the bolt for another shot, but the mission is over; the caravan of terror speeds away.

Though the above account is ficticious, it is based on documented U.S. Military operations in Afghanastin. Point being, the U.S. Army is there and there's hell to pay on the enemy's side, because with them is the M24 sniper rifle.

For the enemy, the sniper rifle is a horrible contraption, pure death from afar. It was the culmination of more than four centuries of perfected tools and tactics used by the *sharfscützen*, or sharpshooter—or "sniper," as the fine lads are called in these latter times. This rifle could deliver precision fire on enemy targets at 800 meters and beyond, was highly adjustable to fit any soldier, built on a field-proven and reliable action, and was, for those who would come to love this rifle in battle, built like a little Sherman tank. Between 1962, when the Remington Model 700 was first introduced, and 1988, when the U.S. Army settled on a new rifle for its sniper program, the design was truly perfected. It was the M24.

Indeed, the rifles procured by the U.S. military from the 1960s onward reflect a renewed focus on marksmanship training. There were other players in the field, of course. By 1966, when the Marine Corps M40 rifle was adopted (which were made in the Remington Custom shop from 40X Target Rifles),

The M24 is just as comfortable on the 1,000-yard range as it is in deer camp. It's a solid, accurate rifle platform that's not too bulky to carry into the woods on opening day.

The H-S Precision stock on the M24 is fully adjustable for length of pull, but height must be customized by adding after-market products. This stock pack from Triad Tactical worked perfectly for me.

the mold was cast, but it would be nearly two decades before the Army would settle on its requirements. While the Army's initial stab at a sniper training school was launched in 1955, it wasn't until 1984 that the U.S. Army Special Warfare Center (SWC), at Fort Bragg, established the Special Forces Sniper School (known as the Special Operations Target Interdiction Course,

or SOTIC). With a brand new school, the Army needed a rifle.

Up to that period, Army snipers had used a hodgepodge of weapons—the M21, M40-A1, Winchester Model 70, Parker Hale 1200TX, and French FR-F1, to name but a few. But planners needed standardization—and a centerpiece for their new training curriculum. Surely the government's Armament Research

Development and Engineering Center, in New Jersey, was looking back on the success of the M40, when Remington's proposal got the nod. The arms maker invested heavily into materials, testing, and workmanship and could not only hand the Army a rifle that met all its requirements, but also one that could boast of attaining levels of performance never before seen in a sniper rifle.

"Improvements in steel manufacture and barrel construction mean that the M24 shows no appreciable falloff in accuracy after 10,000 rounds," reports Martin Pegler in *Out of Nowhere: A History of the Military Sniper*, "which is a considerable improvement over the expected 500-round life of the British SMLE of the First World War."

The system was commissioned on July 15, 1998, with a $12,087,430 defense contract going to Remington Arms, the complete order to be fulfilled by February 27, 2010. What made the M24 project interesting is that Remington had never before undertaken a production sniping rifle. When the guns were finally delivered (the first batch on December 20, 1988), the cost was $4,995 each—but being fully tooled up for production meant "Big Green" was able to drop per gun cost to $3,900.

It surely is not your granddaddy's Model 700. The M24 was built on the Remington 700 long action, with the

The Leupold Mark 4 M3 optic features 1 MOA elevation knobs (.5 MOA windage) and a 40mm objective lens. While there are scopes out there with finer adjustments, the M3 is one of the fastest scopes when it comes to dialing in elevation out to 1,000 yards. While it reflects military long-range shooting doctrine so prevalent in the mid 1980s, the scope still works today.

The GA Precision U.S. Army M24 is a stocky, super-accurate sniper rifle chambered in 7.62 NATO.

original intent to chamber it in .30-06, but also with the option (thanks to influence from Special Forces), to later re-chamber it for .300 Win. Mag. However, at that time, there was a lack of military-grade .30-06 in the supply chain. That fact, combined with the need to standardize, meant most M24s were actually chambered in 7.62x51mm NATO, which is how they tended to remain.

The gun is 43 inches long overall, with a 24-inch 416R stainless steel barrel in a 1:11¼ twist. The barrel bore itself is interesting, because it is machined with a five-land/five-groove design (5-R). As a result, no two lands are directly across from one another. Additionally, the lands themselves are cut to 65 degrees, as opposed to conventional 90 degrees. This design was intended to reduce fouling and extend barrel life, both desirable attributes in the military's various operational environments.

This specialized bolt-action has an internal magazine feed design, one within an HS-Precision stock (PST-011). The stock's length of pull is adjustable by more than two inches. Adjustment is via a distinctive knob, knurled and lockable, which sits between the recoil pad and butt stock.

The whole thing comes as a complete deployment-ready package: the Army would later designate it as the M24 SWS, or Sniper Weapon System. It is comprised of a massive Hardigg case, a Leupold Mark 4 M3 10x scope, cleaning accessories, M1903 leather sling, Harris bi-pod and Redfield Palma Match or OK Weber aperture-style sights. The gun can be readily identified by its distinctive front and rear sight post. The SOTIC Committee first approached Leupold to build a scope to replace the Redfields then in use. That's when the M3 Ultra (today available as the Leupold Mark 4 M3) was born, a fixed 10x optic with Mil-Dot reticle and 42mm objective lens.

As good as it was, the M24 actually had a strange and somewhat rocky start. Initially, planners had worked with McMillan, which had given them a rifle with a large, bulky, prone stock. The reason for this was that, in the early days, the developers had been looking more for a training tool to teach prone shooting, rather than a completed sniper rifle outfit. But there were bedding issues in the early McMillans, and an H-S Precision-stocked weapon was brought in for testing by 1985.

The M24's ultimate fate hinged on a 1,000-yard shot. As told in *Sniper* magazine, Brig. Gen. James Guest attended

The 24-inch stainless barrel of the M24 is a heavy tube, tapering down to .920-inch. Its muzzle is crowned and the barrel comes tapped for the OK Weber front sight post.

Even someone with very little long-range shooting experience can make hits at extreme ranges with the M24. That's due in part to its inherent accuracy, excellent trigger, and familiar Remington Model 700 feel.

This group was shot at 550 yards—all dead center hits on an IDPA target. There is some debate about whether a 10X optic is sufficient for long-range shooting, but, in the history of long-range warfare, that magnification is more than triple that used by snipers in World War II.

Due to its overall heft and mild-mannered cartridge (.308 Winchester), recoil on the M24 is very tame. In the Army's final competition phase, it was actually the Remington that beat out the Steyr, by retaining accuracy while being shot all afternoon under the hot Georgia sun.

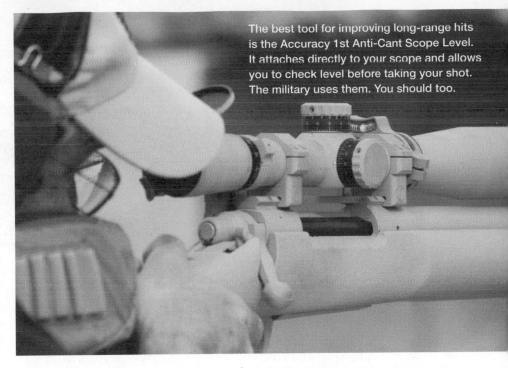

The best tool for improving long-range hits is the Accuracy 1st Anti-Cant Scope Level. It attaches directly to your scope and allows you to check level before taking your shot. The military uses them. You should too.

a test firing not far from Fort Bragg, in 1985, and decided to do some shooting for himself. After less-than-stellar groups were fired from the M-21, he got down behind the M24 prototype.

According to the account of that day, the General's first shot smashed the X-ring, after which he stood up and said, "Buy it." That same General later testified before Congress about the problems with the M-21s, and it was he who secured the program its official funding to proceed. Had the General's first shot landed off-mark, the outcome of this interesting firearm's history could have turned out much differently.

Funding secured, the caliber discussions began. With its long action, the .300 Winchester Magnum was a top contender to make the M24 a 1,000-yard and beyond gun, but other ideas were floated, in particular, the .338-416 and the early incarnation of the .338 Lapua Magnum.

Refinements to the M24 continued through 1986 and 1987, at which time the Army got completely involved in the program. The internal debate over cartridge chambering at this stage in the game had been narrowed down to the 7.62 NATO or .300 Win. Mag.; the big .338s were off the table, because shooters voiced concerns over excessive recoil. The Army settled on the 7.62, but those closest to the program made sure to keep the long action for future re-chambering to .300 Win. Mag., when logistics over ammunition could be worked out. It is unknown how many

M24s are chambered in .300 Win. Mag.

Before final approval, the guns needed to be evaluated under field stress, so the Army Special Operations devised a competition, in the summer of 1987, to put M24 contenders from two prospective commercial suppliers, Steyr and Remington, to the test. Both were excellent samples of the platform, but the Steyr's cold hammer-forged barrel reportedly began to shift point of impact, as things heated up. The stock also warped. By contrast, the Remington shot consistently, making the decision an easy one. By the end of 1988, the Army had its sniper rifle, and instructors at SOTIC had a gun for their program. Remington would continue to supply Big Army with the new M24s through February 2010, ultimately producing 2,500 rifles over the life of the contract.

Five years before Remington's fulfillment came to an end, Knight's Armament Company had been awarded an Army contract to replace the M24 with its M110, a semi-automatic weapons system. That change had been influenced by Special Forces snipers operating, since 2001, in the Middle East. The advantage of the long-range semi-auto option quickly gained popularity with soldiers and, in 2008, the first Army unit went into battle, in Afghanistan, armed with M110s. Still, the fate of the M24 wasn't completely doomed, because the military finally came back around to the idea of the Remington 700 long action upon which it was built and the

excellent .300 Win. Mag. cartridge. This line of thinking was also influenced by Middle East operations, where the .300 Win. Mag. was providing sniper teams a much more suitable gun at the 1,200-yard range, yet with the 1 MOA or better accuracy of the M24 platform (as opposed to the .50 BMG and its 2.5 MOA accuracy).

Not unlike the international popularity of the prolific Mauser 98, albeit on a much smaller scale, other countries took notice of the M24. The Afghan military and at least seven other countries, including Iraq, Brazil, Georgia, and Japan,

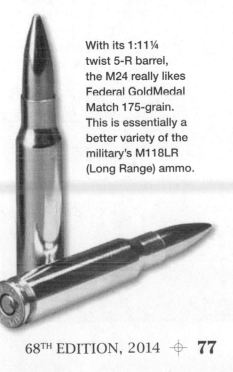

With its 1:11¼ twist 5-R barrel, the M24 really likes Federal GoldMedal Match 175-grain. This is essentially a better variety of the military's M118LR (Long Range) ammo.

The Ever-Evolving M24

now use the rifle, and various police agencies and S.W.A.T. teams in the U.S. have adopted the once military-only gun for domestic law enforcement operations.

The military's shifting doctrine are the winds of change that continue to shape the M24 and its role in the field to this day. The classic design approved in 1988 is still available from Remington and is in use by the military in more or less its original configuration. But variants have also crept into the picture in the M24A1, M24A2, and M24E1/XM2010.

The M24A1 and M24A2 are basically refined versions of the original, with a slightly different M40XB-style stock, detachable five-round magazine, modular accessory rail (for night vision), and a suppressor. The A1 is a 7.62 NATO gun, the A2 the .300 Win. Mag. version, and both are outfitted with Leupold's Mark 4 M3 LR/T 3.5-10x variable scope.

The M24E1, or XM2010, is an entirely different animal. It bears nary a resemblance to the M24 designed by the SOTIC back at Fort Bragg in the late '80s. It is indeed chambered for .300 Win. Mag., making it an effective 1,000-yard-plus weapon. Its 10-inch suppressor is said to reduce muzzle flash by 98 percent, recoil by 60 percent, and sound by 32 percent. The Remington Arms Chassis System (RACS) is a space-age looking thing, the ultimate adjustable folding stock. Like the M24A2, it has a detachable magazine, but its optics are actually more robust; the gun is outfitted with the Leupold 6.5-20x50mm variable-power first focal plane scope. An estimated 3,600 elite XM2010s were to be created, either from upgraded M24s or newly produced.

A U.S. Army sniper team from Jalalabad Provincial Reconstruction Team (PRT) and his M24 SWS scans the horizon, after reports of suspicious activity along the hilltops near Dur Baba, Afghanistan, October 19, 2006, and after a medical civic-action project was conducted.

Civilian M24s Today

Today, if you're a civilian shooter and want an M24 reproduction, you basically have three options: a gun can be custom built by a gunsmith or you can order one from one of the two firms that offer them in their regular lineups, those being Texas Brigade Armory and GA Precision.

I turned to GA Precision. The firm regularly turns out this rifle for civilian shooters, but expect to pay premium prices. You do get what you pay for—a

The latest rendition of the M24 is the XM2010. This space age-looking rifle is built on the M24's original Model 700 long action, but is chambered for .300 Win. Mag. It features a fully adjustable and folding stock known as the Remington Arms Chassis System (RACS), suppressor, and magazine. The optics have also been upgraded to the Leupold 6.5-20x50mm variable power first focal plane scope.

The M24 Sniper Weapon System (SWS) contains the rifle, a 1903 leather sling, cleaning accessories, front and rear iron sights, and the Leupold Mark 4 scope and accessories, all in a tough Hardigg case.

The M24A2 sniper rifle has a few refinements over the original M24, including a five-round detachable box magazine, one-piece modular accessory rail (for night vision), and a variable power Leupold optic.

The current Remington M24 sniper rifle is still made by Remington Defense and is pretty much the same gun produced in 1988.

rifle that'll cut a ragged hole all day. I didn't attempt to replicate all the military's specs, but chose, instead, to make mine "sport scale." For example, instead of the Leupold fixed 10x scope, I installed a Leupold Mark 4 LR/T M3 3.5-10x40mm optic, which I have been able to verify was used by the Army on some M24s. I also went with the variable version, because I specifically wanted the Tactical Milling Reticle (TMR), an option not available on the standard fixed power.

While I did install a standard six-to-nine-inch swivel Harris bi-pod, the added Phoenix Tactical Podclaws improve purchase, reduce felt recoil, and allow me to consistently "load the bipod." Also added was a KMW Pod-Loc, for added control on the bi-pod's swivel feature.

Shooting the M24

The rifle shoots about as good as you'd expect a Mil-Spec sniper rifle to shoot: darn near perfect. The gun weighs about 14 pounds with optics, and the adjustable stock allows me to achieve perfect length of pull and eye relief. The trigger action is smooth and crisp, but not excessively light, about three pounds, nine ounces, according to the Lyman Trigger Pull Gauge (www.brownells.com).

The Leupold Mark 4 scope sits extremely low, thanks to high-quality steel rings and the M24 base from Badger Ordnance. A Triad Tactical Stock Pack raises the eye to the ideal height.

A 20-round initial barrel break-in was shot from the bench, using .308 Win.

Federal Gold Medal 175-grain MatchKing ammo. Groups were good to start with, about 1 MOA, but, as the barrel broke in and came to life, those groups shrunk down to about .37-inch at 100 yards. This is the sort of accuracy for which the M24 platform, and the GA Precision guns in particular, are known.

Out on the 500-meter range, the rifle's sub-MOA accuracy really makes the difference. While the rifle is not as long or bulky as some, particularly those with the A-3 or A-4 stocks, it is a little tank of a rifle and sits rock steady, even in a substantial wind. The stock is chunky, just about the perfect size for providing a solid platform, but it's also very maneuverable in the field. Shooting the 175-grain Sierras makes this an effective 1,000-yard rifle. At 550 yards, the gun shot a little two-inch group, dead-center on a white IDPA target.

More shooting at much longer distances remains to be done. Until then, my initial impression of the GA Precision US Army M24 is that this is truly the king of the Model 700s; for the long-range shooter or the military gun collector, it's the best of both worlds.

Conclusion

If the Remington Model 700 is the greatest bolt-action rifle conceived during the last century, then the M24 is the very best of the Model 700s. From the collective minds of the Army's best marksmen, all aspects of the rifle, from the trigger, stock, and scope to the lands inside the barrel, were developed and refined with clockwork precision

for durability and ease of use by sniper school students in the classroom and on the battlefield. Indeed, it was the M24's deadly accuracy that the enemy would come to fear wherever the gun and the men who use it are deployed.

GA Precision
U.S. Army M-24 Specs

Caliber: 308 Win / 7.62 NATO / .300 Win. Magnum

Action: Remington 700 long action

Barrel Type: 1:11¼ twist, 5-R, stainless steel

Barrel Length: 24 inches

Stock: H-S Precision, M-24 stock

Trigger Guard: Steel M-24 trigger guard

Finish: Matte black

www.gaprecision.com

Bibliography

U.S. Department of Defense, Office of the Assistant Secretary of Defense (Public Affairs) Contracts. DefenseLink: Contracts for Wednesday, July 16, 2008

Pegler, Martin, Out of Nowhere: A History of the Military Sniper, Osprey Publishing, Elms Court, Chapel Way, Botley, Oxford OX2 9LP, United Kingdom

Beckstrand, Tom, Shooting Times, Sniper, Intermedia Outdoors, 512 7th Ave., 11th Floor, New York, NY 10018

Bacon, Lance, Army Times, Gannett Government Media, 6883 Commercial Dr.

Springfield, Va. 22159-0500, Apr 25, 2011

BY Jon R. Sundra

MAGNUM, SHMAGNUM!

What is and isn't a "magnum" isn't as simple as it once was.

All rifle cartridges belong to one of four cartridge-length families (l. to r.): true "magnum," as represented here by the .375 H&H; "standard" length, as dictated by the '98 Mauser and represented here by the .300 Win. Magnum (which was once referred to as a "short magnum"); "short," as in the 2.8-inch WSM family; and "super short," which is already obsolete, because no major rifle manufacturer chambers for them.

Back in the Jurassic era, when I was a budding gun weenie, I pretty much knew what a magnum was, and so did everybody else who was into guns. Back then—I'm talking the mid-1950s—there was little mystery as to what was and wasn't a magnum. We had the .300 and .375 H&H that had been around since 1912 and 1925, respectively, the Weatherby line, and the .308 and .358 Norma Magnums. However, all were proprietary cartridges and, of those, only the two H&H rounds were loaded and only by Winchester, which, along with Remington, were the only major sources of generally available factory ammunition. Moreover, the rifles chambered for any of the aforementioned rounds were either custom jobs or limited production guns. The bottom line to all this is that, in 1955, there was not a single magnum cartridge of American origin being offered in a production-grade rifle from any of our major domestic gun manufacturers.

What really started the Magnum Era here in America was the appearance of the .458 Win. Magnum, in 1956, followed two years later by the .264 Win. and .338 Win. Magnums. Finally, we had "our own" magnums, and they were just like all the others in that they were based on the ubiquitous H&H belted case. Yes, the ammo was a little more expensive, as were the domestic production rifles chambered for them, but not to where they were out of the financial reach of Joe Average.

Before going any further, let's try to establish what actually was meant when we used the term "magnum," back in those days. The consensus definition was that any cartridge officially designated as a "magnum" provided ballistic performance that was appreciably better than that which theretofore had been considered the standard, if you will, for a particular caliber. Of course, there have been plenty of exceptions to that rule since, and we'll get into them, but, for now, let's use that as our definition.

A classic example is the .30-06. It has set the standard for "standard" .30-caliber performance ever since its inception, in 1906, and a very high standard it was. It wasn't until the introduction of the .300 Win. Magnum, in 1963, that the "magnum" was set for that caliber. Now granted, the existing .300 H&H was superior, and the .300 Weatherby even more so, but neither was a mainstream commercial cartridge, nor were the rifles chambered for them, and that, after all, has to be our criteria here—generally available and affordable production rifles and ammunition from the two industry giants, Remington and Winchester.

A few years earlier, in 1955, the .243 Win. and .244 Rem. were introduced, establishing both a brand new bore size

and the performance standard for the caliber, because both were virtually identical ballistically and there were no other existing cartridges of that caliber. Actually, they were preceded by the 6mm Lee Navy of the 1890s, but very few commercial sporting rifles were chambered for that round, and production of it had ceased in 1935. For all intents and purposes, then, the .243 and .244 cartridges set the 6mm performance standard.

The appearance of the .270 Win., in 1925, set up a situation similar to that of the 6mms in that it established a new bore size. With no other commercial rounds to compete with, the .270 Win. set the bar for the .277-caliber. (That bar, of course, was shattered by the .270 Wthby. Magnum, but, again, that was (is) a proprietary cartridge, so that doesn't count in the context of this article.) It would be quite some time before a mainstream rifle/cartridge would set the magnum standard for this caliber.

In the 7mm bore size, it was not until 1957 that we had an American commercial cartridge, that one in the form of the .280 Remington. Prior to its appearance, the only round that had achieved

even a modicum of popularity here was the 7x57 Mauser, and that was found virtually only all in surplus military and custom built rifles. It was the .280 Rem., then, that set the performance standard for the 7mm, a standard that was eclipsed five years later, in 1962, with the introduction of the 7mm Rem. Magnum.

The same can be said of the 6.5mm. There were several European and Japanese military 6.5s, but, here in the States, the most popular by far was the 6.5x55 Swedish version, and, again, it was in surplus military rifles in various stages of customization. It was blown out of the water by the .264 Win. Magnum.

Just to recap thus far, in 1963, we had five homegrown magnums: the .264, .300, .338, and .458 Winchesters and the 7mm Remington. All five, as well as all the other proprietary magnums already enumerated, were based on the H&H case and varied only in length and shoulder configuration. It was all so simple back then, all so black and white, as to what was a magnum and what wasn't.

It all began to change, in 1960, with the introduction of the .256 Win. Magnum, a cartridge based on a necked-down .357

Here we have (l. to r.) the .256 Winchester Magnum (which isn't), and the .257 Roberts, which set the performance standard for the caliber until Remington adopted the .25-06, in 1969. Compared to the Roberts, it offers true magnum performance, which makes the .257 Weatherby a super magnum.

Magnum pistol round designed exclusively for the Ruger Hawkeye handgun. But long before the Hawkeye went into production, Marlin chambered for the round in its Model 62 Levermatic rifle, so it was listed as a *rifle* cartridge and, as such, it was hardly a magnum. In those days, the .257 Roberts set the .25-caliber performance standard. In those days, too, the .25-06 was one of the most popular wildcat cartridges, and if ever there was a magnum that wasn't labeled as such, it was the .25-06, which ran circles around the .257 Roberts.

By 1965, the belted H&H case had became so synonymous with "magnum" that, if a cartridge didn't have a belt, many questioned its qualifications. Then came the .350 and 6.5 Rem. Magnums, which really confused the issue. Because the .300 and .375 H&Hs were full-length magnums requiring action/magazine lengths greater than standard (as set by the '98 Mauser), the Winchester and Remington magnums were based on shortened H&H cases to where overall cartridge lengths did not exceed the 3.34

Compared to the nickel-cased 7mm and .300 Win. Short Magnums, the Remington SAUM equivalents didn't offer anything the Winchester rounds didn't, and the WSM case had more capacity.

Winchester's Super Short Magnums, shown here with their respective ballistic competitors. For the .22 WSSM it was the .22-250 Rem., for the .243 WSSM it was the .243 Win., and in the .25 WSSM it was the .25-06. In 6mm and .25, neither WSSM offered any ballistic advantage, yet were still designated as "magnums."

RIGHT: Lazzeroni's Short Action Magnums predated the Winchester .300 WSM (at left) by several years. None of the Lazzeroni cartridges carried the "magnum" suffix, yet all qualified.

BELOW: What constituted a magnum in 1963 was sharply defined, as represented here by (l. to r.), the .264 Win., 7mm Rem., .300 Win., .338 Win., and .458 Win. These five cartridges constituted the entire non-proprietary magnum family.

inches of a Mauser-length magazine. You see, back in those days, there were still tens of thousands of rifles being built on military and commercial Mauser actions, so, for a new cartridge, magnum or otherwise, to have a chance at commercial success, it had to be short enough to fit Mauser actions (i.e., .30-06-length). As a result, the Winchester magnum family, along with the 7mm Rem., were designated as "short magnums." But, with the introduction of the .350 and 6.5 Rem. Magnums, these rounds were based on yet even shorter versions of the H&H case to an overall cartridge length of 2.8 inches, so they would cycle through Remington's short action.

So now we had short magnums and short short magnums! Further confusing the situation was the fact that neither the .350 nor the 6.5 Rem. Magnums were true magnums. Winchester's .264 ran circles around Remington's 6.5, and the same held true for the .350 compared to the .358 Norma. Even the wildcat .35 Whelen, based on the beltless .30-06 case, bested the .350 (though not by a lot).

From the 1970s to the mid-'80s, it was fairly quiet, as far as new commercial belted magnums went, but that's because wildcatters now had increasing access to readily available supplies of newly manufactured .404 Jeffery cases. Introduced in 1910, the .404 goes back even further than the belted H&H case. Not only was the Jeffery hull as long as the .300/.375 H&H, it was fatter and, thus, held about 20-percent more powder. Moreover, it didn't have a belt which, from the handloading standpoint, made it more desirable, because it made controlling headspace easier. It also had a rebated rim. In other words, even though its body was fatter than the H&H, its rim diameter was the same, so it would fit a conventional magnum bolt face without alteration.

First out with an entire line of proprietary cartridges based on the Jeffery case was Don Allen, founder of Dakota Arms. His line consisted of six cartridges ranging from 7mm to .416, all based on full-length and shortened versions of the .404. All Dakota cartridges provided performance superior to their belted H&H equivalents.

Not to be outdone, it was John Lazzeroni, in the early '90s, who came out with not one, but three lines of beltless magnum cartridges, one based on a full-length .404 Jeffery, one based on the even larger .416 Rigby hull, and one on a unique case of John's own design (and which are, essentially, what the Ruger Compact Magnums are based on, only slightly shortened). One of John's lines was called "Short Action Magnums," and these were designed accordingly, as to overall cartridge length.

As it turned out, John was a bit too optimistic with his hopes for the market

The author took this large Vancouver Island Black bear with a .350 Rem. Magnum, a cartridge that, along with its sibling, the 6.5 Rem. Magnum, caused a lot of confusion as to what a "short magnum" was. They did not offer magnum ballistics and were shorter than what had previously been considered short magnums

The introduction of Winchester's Short Magnum family, starting in 2001, redefined the term (l. to r.): .270, 7mm, .300, and .325.

This nice muley buck was taken by Sundra using the ill-fated 7mm Rem. Short Action Ultra Mag, which, along with its sibling, the .300 SAUM, are now obsolete.

To fit the 2.8-inch magazines that dictate the newer definition of "short magnum," bullets must be deeply seated. Shown here are bullets of 150, 160, and 175 grains in the 7mm WSM. This is not what you'd call optimizing available powder capacity.

for his expensive rifles and ammunition, and the Lazzeroni cartridge line today has been drastically reduced to but a few calibers. Nevertheless, the interest generated by his and Don Allen's Dakota line of proprietary cartridges did not go unnoticed by our mainstream American gun and ammo manufacturers and, in 1999, we had the introduction of the .300 Remington Ultra Mag. *Finally*, we had a generally available cartridge that upped the performance bar set 50 years before by the .300 Win. Magnum, and it was a full-length magnum cartridge requiring a magnum-length action. Soon thereafter, Remington added 7mm, .375, and .416 versions to the Ultra Mag line.

Winchester went the other direction, in 2001, with its introduction of the .300 Win. Short Magnum, and perhaps no other cartridge since the 7mm Rem. generated more interest on the part of manufacturers and consumers alike. In fact, it caused so much excitement in the firearms media that Remington couldn't stand being on the sidelines; within six months of Winchester rolling out its .300 WSM, Remington countered mid-year with its own .300 and 7mm Short Action Ultra Mags. Neither offered any ballistic advantage over the Winchester versions, nor did they best the old 7mm Rem. and .300 Win. Magnums. In fact, the only thing either line had going for it was the fact that they matched belted magnum ballistics in cartridges and rifles that were about a half-inch shorter and a couple ounces lighter in weight.

The old definition of short magnum that had been used to describe the Winchester and Remington belted magnums of the 1950s and '60s was out the window. Now a "short magnum" meant something else.

Winchester's .300 WSM was quickly followed by a .270, a 7mm, and a .325 version. They have been reasonably successful, particularly the .300 and the .270. The same can be said of Remington's Ultra Mags, which, in all four cases, raised the magnum performance bar for their respective calibers. Unfortunately, for Remington, its SAUMs did not offer any advantage over the WSMs, which had arrived first. The market simply couldn't support two lines of short magnums and, within five years, both were dropped from the Remington 700 and Model Seven lines.

On the heels of its success with the .300 WSM, Winchester decided that, if short was better, *super*-short would also sell. Thus, in 2002, it introduced the .223

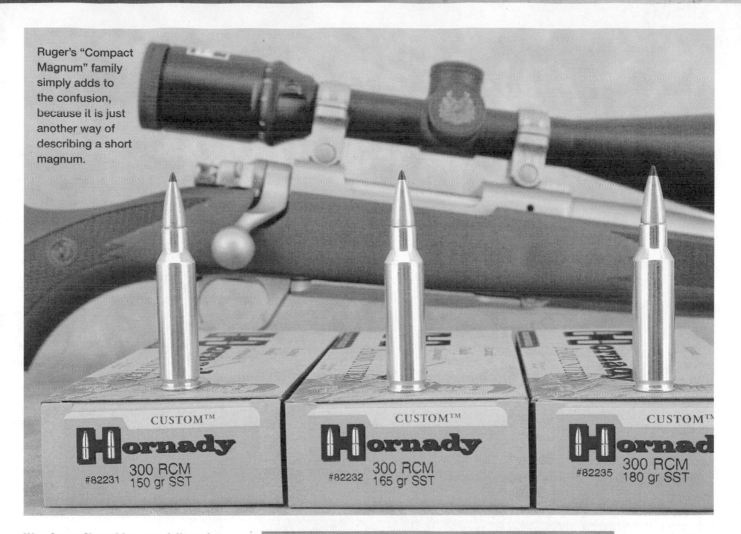

Ruger's "Compact Magnum" family simply adds to the confusion, because it is just another way of describing a short magnum.

CUSTOM™ **Hornady** 300 RCM #82231 150 gr SST

CUSTOM™ **Hornady** 300 RCM #82232 165 gr SST

CUSTOM™ **Hornady** 300 RCM #82235 180 gr SST

Win. Super Short Magnum, followed, in 2004, by a .243 and a .25-caliber version. But Winchester had miscalculated—big time. Not only did no other rifle manufacturer adopt the chamberings, but Browning and Winchester both went through the added expense of developing special super-short actions to accommodate the squat rounds. By 2010, all three calibers had been dropped from the Winchester and Browning rifle lineups.

The bottom line to all this is that there are now super magnums, magnums, magnums that aren't, and cartridges that qualify ballistically as magnums, but are not labeled as such. Further confusing the issue is that Ruger, Thompson/Center, Marlin, and Federal have, in the past five years, also developed proprietary cartridges of their own. Clearly, what is and what isn't a magnum these days is nowhere nearly as sharply defined as it used to be. But, in the end, even with the demise of a good number of relatively new cartridges, we still have twice as many to choose from as we did just a couple of decades ago. And that's good!

Among the biggest anomalies in cartridge nomenclature are the 6.5 and .350 Remington Magnums, because they blurred the lines of what was a "short magnum." Moreover, neither could quite match the wildcat 6.5-06 and .35 Whelen, at right, respectively, neither of which had a belt.

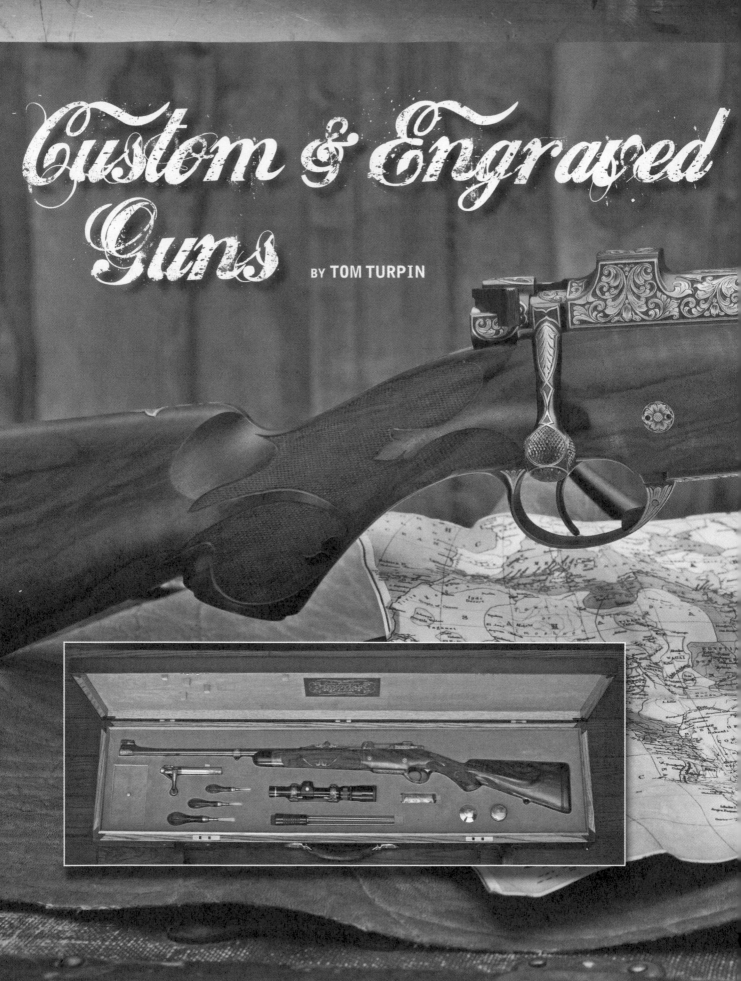

Custom & Engraved Guns

BY **TOM TURPIN**

Our Annual Look at Some of the Most Drool-Worthy Firearms Out There

Dubber–Bolliger

This unusual project is the result of a collaborative effort between two masters of their crafts, John Bolliger's Mountain Riflery and Master Engraver Mike Dubber. Bolliger started with a MAS 45 French training rifle, still new and in Cosmoline. Apparently, these rifles were manufactured from 1945 to 1947 at the French MAS factory, using liberated Germany equipment from the Mauser plant. A few of these rifles were imported into the U.S., in the 1980s, of which this was apparently one.

At any rate, the magnificent rifle in the photos started as one of these military style training rifles, and one made in France, no less! Talk about lipstick on a pig! I would need a full-blown feature-length article to even begin describing the alterations done for this project. Since we don't have that luxury, it suffices to say that extensive modifications have been made and leave it at that. It can be accurately stated that about everything you see in the photos is custom made. Mike Dubber did his usual masterful job of adorning the rifle with his wonderful engraving. "Superb" is the first word that comes to mind. Peter Wermer built the lovely oak and leather trunk case.

Photos by Eric Gordon

Al Biesen

The rifle shown here is a pretty unique piece of craftsmanship and history. Not only is it exceptionally well crafted, and by one of our early and best custom makers, it was made for one of our best outdoor writers of all time. The craftsman was Al Biesen and the writer was Jack O'Connor. Anyone who read much of O'Connor's writings knows that, up until the big factory changes made in 1964, his favorite rifles were based on Winchester Model 70 components. He was not the least impressed with Winchester's changes.

This rifle, O'Connor's final custom rifle, was built on a much-modified Ruger M77 rifle chambered for, of all things, the .280 Remington cartridge. My guess is the changes in rifles and cartridges were intended to show his displeasure to Winchester. Alas, the grim reaper intervened, and O'Connor never saw the rifle. It was completed in the early '80s, a couple years after O'Connor's passing.

Al Biesen is now in his ninth decade. At his advanced age, he's no longer able to craft his wonderful rifles, but his son Roger is, and his granddaughter Paula Biesen-Malicki is engraving them.

Many thanks to the owner of this lovely rifle, Henry Kaufman, for allowing me to photograph this important piece of hunting and custom rifle history.

Photo by Tom Turpin

Goudy-Evans

Veteran custom stock maker Gary Goudy has been turning out wonderful custom stocks for a lot of years now. Most went out the door, as soon as they were finished, to his salivating customers awaiting their arrivals. You know the old story about the Cobbler's kids' shoes? Well, with all the work turning out customer guns, Gary never had a lot of time left over to work on any for himself. But several years ago, he made a huge swap with the late Don Allen of Dakota Arms. He traded a goodly number of fine walnut gun stock blanks for the making of a Dakota Traveler rifle with two barrels, a couple Dakota Legend shotguns imported from Italy, and perhaps another item or two.

Now, quite a few years later, the Traveler is finished. Dakota Arms did the metalwork on the rifle. The stock work is by Gary, of course, and eighty-four-year-old Bob Evans adorned the rifle with his elegant blackthorn scroll and inlay work.

The rifle barrels are chambered for two Dakota proprietary cartridges, the .375 Dakota and the 7mm Dakota. The rifle will shoot ½ MOA three-shot groups (or better), with either barrel attached. Gary's plan is to do a lot of hunting with this rifle, and this ensemble is ready to go anywhere in the world and successfully hunt most anything.

Photo by Tom Turpin

James Anderson

The client for this lovely rifle provided a Mexican Mauser action and a presumably German-made octagon barrel with integral rib to Louisiana gunmaker Dave Christman, who performed the exquisite metalwork on the rifle. The take-off barrel, while expertly machined, had been chambered for the .243 Winchester cartridge, not a chambering the client either wanted or needed. Therefore, Jim DuBell's Clearwater Reboring took on the task of making the original barrel into a 6.5mm (.264). The refreshed bore was then re-chambered for the .260 Remington cartridge.

James Anderson crafted the lovely stock from a nice piece of walnut, including a great point pattern checkering job at 24 lines per inch and a mullered border. He then did all the finish work. All the craftsmen working on this lovely rifle are members of the ACGG.

I've added a photo of the client's nice buck taken with the rifle, showing that fine custom rifles are used for hunting and are not just "safe queens."

Photo by James Anderson

Dave Norin

Dave Norin is pretty much a one-stop shop for custom gun work. About the only thing he doesn't do in his Illinois shop is engraving—at least I don't think he does. He can arrange such artistry, though. He does about everything else in-house.

One great skill I feel is tremendously underrated is fine metalwork. Everyone with the least understanding of a custom gun can a see and appreciate a beautiful custom stock made from a blank of fantastic walnut and then finely checkered. Equally impressive work, and even more so to the informed, is the metal of the custom job, which is usually hidden and, thus, often unappreciated. While Dave does everything well, I wanted to showcase what really good metalwork looks like when not covered up by the rest of the gun. Shown here is a Mauser action that Dave has worked over. The action is now ready for barreling and a

good handcrafted stock. Also shown is an example of how Dave installs a sling swivel stud. Please note that the screw slots are properly timed, pointing fore and aft. This is the way it should be done.

Photos courtesy of Dave Norin

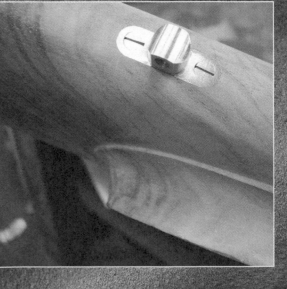

Steven Dodd Hughes

Steven Dodd Hughes has been earning a living making custom guns for a long time. I've known him for more than 20 years, and he was doing it when I met him. Early on in his gun making career, he decided he wanted no part of the bolt-action rifle-making clan. Instead, he decided to concentrate on single-shot rifles, lever-action rifles, and double-barrel shotguns. If he has made anything other than those since I've known him, I'm unaware of it. Steve is also a writer and an excellent photographer.

Shown here is an example of his current work. He started the project with a Hagn falling-block action, which he recontoured, including the lever and the trigger. Ralf Martini did the octagon barrel with integral full-length rib, quarter rib, and front sight base. Martini also fitted and chambered the barrel for the .280 Remington cartridge. Hughes then crafted the lovely stock from a very good stick of English walnut and checkered it 25 lines per inch in a pleasing point pattern with beveled borders. Finally, it was turned over to Diane Scalese for her outstanding rose and scroll engraving pattern. The result of all this artistry speaks for itself.

Photo by Steven Dodd Hughes

Glen Morovits

The single-shot rifle shown here is the work of Butch Searcy, who manufactured the barreled action, and Glen Morovits, who took the Searcy components, modified them to suit his client's wishes, and turned them into a lovely custom rifle. Morovits did all the work on the rifle, with the exception of the case coloring, which West River Rifle Co., in Sturgis, South Dakota, performed. Glen used a really nice stick of English walnut with lots of figure and wonderful color to fashion the stock. He added an ebony fore-end tip, a leather covered recoil pad, and a well-done point checkering pattern with a mullered border. The rifle is chambered for perhaps the best all around cartridge out there, the .30-06.

Photos by James Anderson

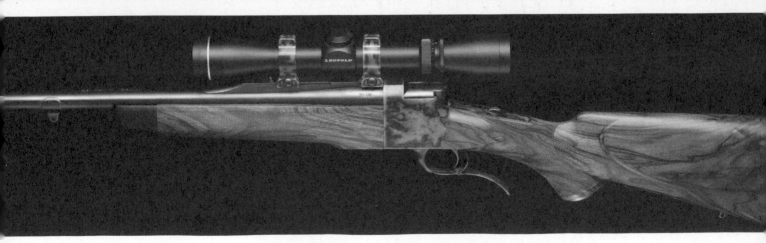

Lee Griffiths

Master FEGA engraver Lee Griffiths has a number of distinguishing characteristics to his persona. He is simply not content doing tiny English scrollwork, though he can do so as well as anyone. Rather, he likes to tell a story in his engraving. Thank goodness he didn't take up writing.

Anyway, he delights in formulating a story within his engraving patterns. And so it is with the photo of the 90-percent finished frame of a Browning

.22 RF semi-auto shown here. I asked Lee how he decided on the theme of this engraving job. He told me that, since the little Browning had a long and narrow frame, the scene had to fit in this space. The first thing he thought of was a train. From train it went to train robbery, all depicted on the other side of the little Browning. On the side shown are the aftereffects of the train robbery. Well, you can use your own imagination. Look forward to next year when I'll attempt to show the completed piece and, in the infamous words of Paul Harvey, "the rest of the story."

Photo by Sam Welch

Joe Smithson

Joe Smithson is one of the rising stars in the custom gun business. There are, to my knowledge, no limits on his talents. Even Jerry Fisher thinks he's great, and Jerry doesn't like or approve of anyone. I'm exaggerating, but only slightly. Joe is about as close to a protégé as Jerry has ever had. Shown here is a rifle that Joe built, starting with a Granite Mountain Arms standard-length action. Chambered for the .275 Rigby, it will get the job done on all game up to and including moose. Joe's styling is decidedly English, and there is nothing wrong with that. Of special note is the grip cap compartment, which contains covers for the scope mount base recesses, for use when a scope is not mounted on the rifle. Joe's bases are milled into the receiver and when the scope is off, these covers snap into the recesses, making for a very clean receiver His QD scope mounting system is superb.

Photos by Steven Dodd Hughes

Diane Scalese

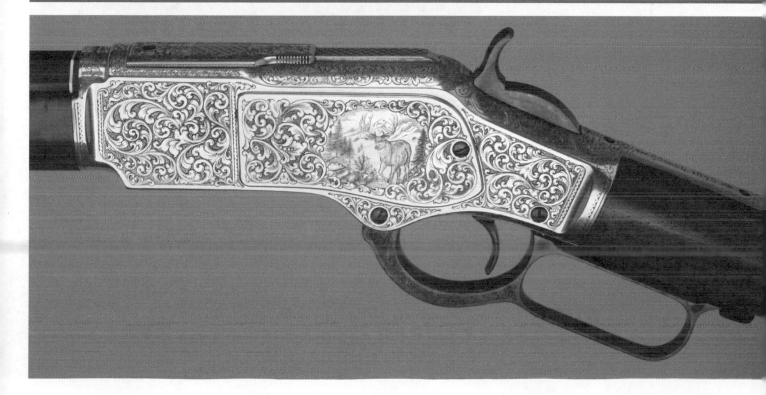

Diane Scalese began engraving around the mid-1980s, starting with bits, buckles, and spurs. Living in Montana, where these items, along with saddle silver and other jewelry, are in demand, it was only logical and natural that she progressed into engraving fine firearms. These days, she's a Master Engraver in the Firearms Engraver's Guild of America (FEGA), and has also been awarded the title of Engraver of the Year by the Academy of Western Artists. Her favorite engraving style is the traditional Western bright cut, but she is very capable in many different styles. The Winchester Model 1873 shown here is typical of her work these days. Lovely work by a lovely and gracious lady.

Photo by Steven Dodd Hughes

Heilmann-Reece

Gun maker Steve Heilmann and engraver Denis Reece have collaborated on several projects the last few years. Shown here is just such an endeavour. Its parentage is hardly recognizable, but it is a Winchester Model 63 that Steve Heilmann has extensively altered. It now has a quarter rib and shotgun trigger guard, the forearm has been substantially changed, and the trigger system completely reworked. While Steve was at it, he removed the factory plunger and installed a cocking piece on the bolt. It now features a tang safety, as well as a trap door buttplate. With the metalwork complete, Steve selected a fantastic stick of Turkish walnut for the stock. Denis Reece then executed the engraving and extensive inlay work, using 24-karat gold and platinum for raw materials. This is one fabulous rimfire rifle.

Photos by Mustafa Bilal, Turks Head Productions

Reto Buehler

Starting with a Granite Mountain Arms left-hand Mauser action, a custom contour Pac-Nor barrel, and a super fancy stick of Turkish walnut as the primary raw materials, Swiss-born and -trained custom gun maker Reto Buehler created this fantastic rifle. After moving around a bit, Reto established Buehler Custom Sporting Arms, in 2005, and hasn't looked back since. The rifle shown here is representative of the superb work he is doing today. Although European trained and very capable of turning out high-quality, Teutonic-styled arms, he mostly builds his rifles showing a very heavy influence from pre-war, best-quality English rifles. The one shown here reflects substantial influence from pre-war H&H rifles. Buehler did all the wood and metalwork on this fine rifle. Chambered for the .416 Rigby cartridge, it's ready for Africa.

Photo by Tom Alexander

D'Arcy Echols

D'Arcy Echols & Company is a two-man shop composed of D'Arcy and his team member, Brian Bingham. Together, they craft some of the finest custom bolt-action rifles on the planet. They essentially produce two models, the Legend and the full-blown custom Classic. The Legend is a top-quality synthetic stocked rifle fabricated using Winchester Classic actions and a synthetic stock designed by Echols and made exclusively for him by McMillan. The Legend is about as close to perfection as one is apt to find in a synthetic stocked hunting rifle.

Then there is the full custom job, where the sky and the pocketbook are about the only limits. Shown here is a fine example of this latter model. For this .375 H&H, Echols used a New Haven-manufactured Winchester Model 70 Classic action and a Krieger CM barrel as the key components. He added a set of Blackburn bottom metal (trigger guard bow and floorplate), at his client's request. They then machined a magazine box and follower precisely fitted for the .375 H&H cartridge. They also made the sights and bases for Echols last remaining set of Burgess QD scope rings. The peep sight and front sight blade fit snugly into the Jerry Fisher grip cap fitted to the stock. Echols stocked the rifle in a nice stick of thin-shelled walnut and checkered it in his standard point pattern. The finished rifle will shoot three-shot groups, using 350-grain Woodleigh bullets, both FMJ and SN, into .6 MOA at 100 yards.

The owner, Mr. Peter Treboldi, believes in hunting with his fine rifles and used the rifle on the magnificent lion shown.

Lion photo courtesy of Mr. Peter Treboldi. All other photos by Kevin Dilley.

Lisa Tomlin

I first learned of Lisa Tomlin in the mid- to late-1980s. A dear friend of mine, the late Ray Diehl, loved fine custom guns as much as I do, and he asked me one day if I knew of Lisa, before showing me photos of some fine engraving she had done for him. Her work was exquisite. I met her at an SCI convention not long after that and have kept in touch since. She has come a long way in the intervening years, and she was great to begin with. These days she can boast of having done presentation pieces for kings, presidents, and prime ministers, as well as many lesser mortals. A Southern belle from Virginia, she's still turning out her lovely work from her Virginia shop. Over the years, a good bit of her artistry has been devoted to fantastic custom knives by the best of our makers. I've included an example she did on a Joe Kious Persian folding knife. Joe is one of the icons in the custom knife arena. Also included is an example of her work on a John Rigby double rifle and a Winchester Model 53 lever-action rifle.

Photos courtesy of Lisa Tomlin

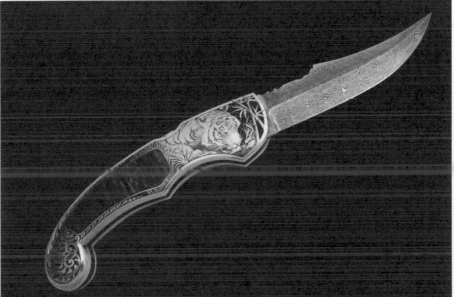

Dave Wesbrook

Dave Wesbrook is a professional stock maker, a book author, and a professional photographer. His iconic book *Professional Stockmaking* was recently reprinted by Wolfe Publishing Co. and is once again available after a few years out of print. In the book, Wesbrook preaches what he practices! The rifle shown here is an example of his artistry in wood. The rifle is a G33/40 small-ring Mauser action on which another icon in the business, Ted Blackburn, did all the metalwork; better known for his bottom metal sets and Mauser triggers that he manufactured and sold for many years, Ted is also a superb metalsmith. Wesbrook then stocked the rifle is a super stick of *Juglans regia* (thin-shelled walnut), in his classical style. It is clean, seemingly simple, and everything is in the right place in the right amount. Just doesn't get any better than this.

Photo by David L. Wesbrook

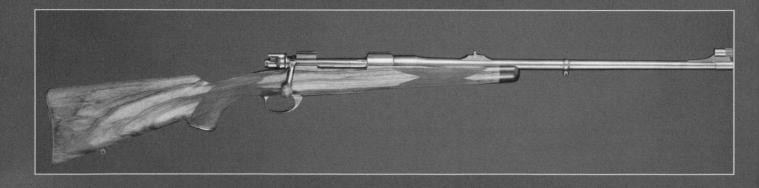

Sam Welch

One of our best and most versatile engravers is Sam Welch. Sam started engraving as a hobby and is largely self taught. Early in his engraving career, he had the good fortune of having engraver Ray Viramontez as his neighbor. Viramontez tutored him in the finer points of engraving techniques and some of the tricks of the trade. Sam can and does engrave about anything that is engraveable. The three photos shown here were selected to show his versatility. There is an engraved guitar, a custom knife, and a set of false sideplates for a Fox shotgun. Engraved knives and guns are normal fare, but I've only seen one engraved guitar and engraved Model A Ford! Sam did them both.

Photos by Sam Welch

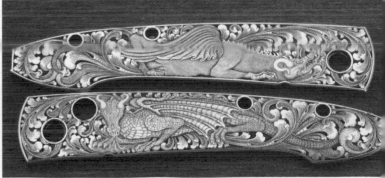

Lofgren – Hochstrat Rifle

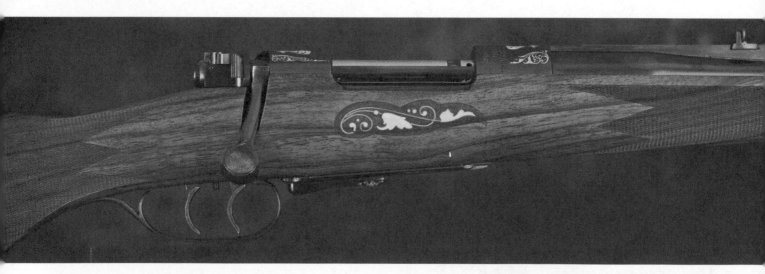

Al Lofgren mostly specializes in custom work with a Germanic flair—at least most of his work that I've seen has a definite Teutonic styling. The example shown here certainly follows that theme. Al started the project with a Mauser 94-96 action, often called a Swedish Mauser. It is a small ring, intermediate-length action. He made a few, as he calls them, "crazy changes," to the top tang and bottom metal and then sent it off to Dave Norin for the majority of the metalwork, including installing and chamber-ing a new barrel for the .250 Savage cartridge. It then went to Brian Hochstrat for his meticulous engraving and gold inlay, also showing a Germanic flair. The pronghorn inlay is composed of white gold, yellow gold, and platinum, just as an example. Al then did all the stock work, carving, and ivory inlays. Dave Norin did the finish work on the rifle.

Photo by Doug Markusic

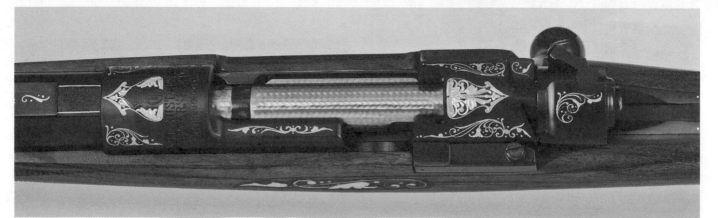

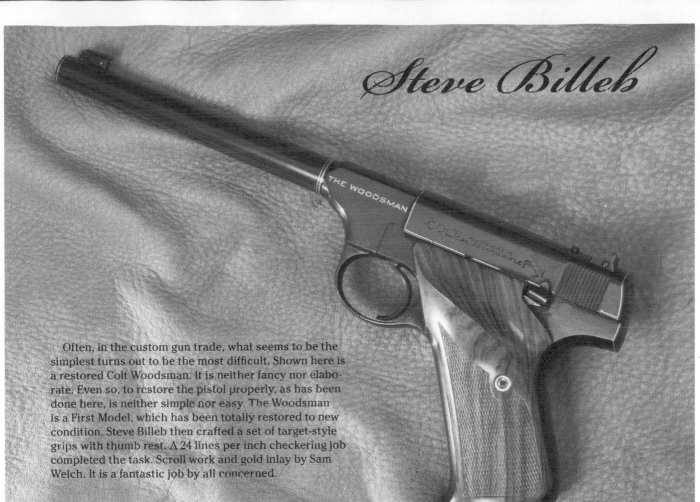

Steve Billeb

Often, in the custom gun trade, what seems to be the simplest turns out to be the most difficult. Shown here is a restored Colt Woodsman. It is neither fancy nor elaborate. Even so, to restore the pistol properly, as has been done here, is neither simple nor easy. The Woodsman is a First Model, which has been totally restored to new condition. Steve Billeb then crafted a set of target-style grips with thumb rest. A 24 lines per inch checkering job completed the task. Scroll work and gold inlay by Sam Welch. It is a fantastic job by all concerned.

Photos by Tom Alexander

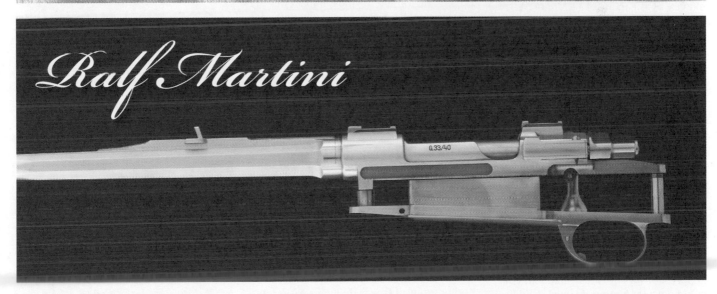

Ralf Martini

German-born Canadian Ralf Martini can do it all. Well, I've not seen any of his engraving, nor do I know that he has tried that difficult talent, but, in metalsmithing and stockmaking, there is none better. He can and does build rifles the way they should be built. I am not going to showcase a completed rifle this year from Ralf. Rather, I'm going to emphasize the difficult, largely unappreciated, and often unnoticed talent of metalsmithing.

The accompanying photos show a G33/40 that Ralf did all the metalwork on, and it is, in a word, superb. I am a big fan of the small ring G33/40 action, and the one shown here is a good as it gets. Ralf could put it under my Christmas tree anytime.

Photo by David L. Wesbrook

Cute Little .300s

BY **Patrick Sweeney**

As a way of leaading into the reviews of the various .300s of the smaller than .308 size, I figured I'd give you a bit of background and overview.

A long time ago, there was this crusty old guy by the name of J.D. Jones. A prolific inventor, he and Larry Kelly of Mag-na-Port fame used handguns to slay just about every critter than walked, swam, flew, and slithered across the globe. Actually, back then, J.D. wasn't old, but he certainly was of firm opinion.

The workshop of J.D. is SSK Industries, where he made many wondrous things. After he designed handgun cartridges so big and powerful that no sane individual would shoot them, he turned his attention to certain aspects of rifles, in particular, how to make them quiet.

Now, for most inventors, the obvious way to make a rifle quiet is to put a "can" on it. A suppressor. A silencer, for those who haven't gotten caught up in the language. J.D. decided that, while a suppressor was obviously needed, you could get a lot further if you started first with a cartridge that didn't produce as much of the stuff you needed to silence. Clearly, this leads us to the lowly .22 LR, so quiet that further suppressing it produces awe-inspiring levels of quietness. However, not everyone is impressed by the .22 LR, even while being shot by it.

Something more robust was called for. J.D. wanted to do several things:

- He wanted a cartridge that would require the least modification of an existing rifle design.
- He wanted the most impact he could get, at the lowest sound level.
- He wanted the least fabrication of components. If at all possible, everything should be an off-the-shelf item.
- He wanted it compact. A super-quiet rifle the size of a belt-fed machine gun was stupid.

The most common firearm in military use at the time (and still, really), was the M16. This was before the M4, so a shorter, carbine version of the M16 would have been a Colt Commando or one of the carbines Colt had made. So, starting with the M16/AR-15, J.D. got to work. Going to a bigger cartridge case was not an option, as there were no bolts other than the 5.56-diameter bolt-face bolts extant. J.D. was doing his research in the early 1980s, and Colt didn't come out with the Lightweight Sporter in 7.62x39 until 1993.

Not wanting to make new bolts, he used the existing one. The problem with the .223/5.56 was velocity. To gain that velocity, the case uses a bunch of

Accurate. Deadly. Dependable.

Accurate? Of course it is accurate No one makes inaccurate ammo or rifles any more. The market won't stand for it.

While the base starting point of the Whisper and others was the .221, the best way to get it is as factory brass. No need to cut and re-form your own brass.

powder (relatively speaking), and pushes a light bullet very fast. Could he use a heavier bullet? Not unless he went to a larger diameter. Bigger means a shorter case, in this instance, a good thing. As he went larger and larger, he had to get shorter and shorter. Finally, at .308-inch bullet diameter, he struck on the combo: take the existing .221 Fireball case, neck it up to .308-inch bullet diameter, and make the whole thing short enough to fit into an AR-15/M16 magazine. Which is kind of like telling Rembrandt "You need to make the backgrounds a bit darker, to bring out the subjects."

There were problems and details to sort out. There's still enough case capacity to boost regular .308 bullets supersonic. Subsonic bullets of 150 grains don't do anything a suppressed 9mm already did. So, he kept boosting bullet weight. This led to further problems. You see, longer bullets end up with the ogive (the curved nose portion of the bullet), rubbing on and being crabbed by an

internal stiffening rib of the AR mag. So, he had to be careful of overall length.

The end result was impressive. A 220-grain subsonic bullet, launched out of a suppressed AR, was impressively quiet. How quiet? I watched my friend Ned Christiansen shooting a .300 Whisper (the name J.D. gave his cartridge), AR with a can on it. This was at Second Chance, and he was plinking on the LRPF falling plate bowling pins on the back range. For a while, the only sounds were the empties hitting the ground, the syrupy sound of the bolt shuffling back and forth, and the bullets smacking onto the timber glacis in front of the pin racks. Once he found the point of impact (to call the trajectory of the 220s "rainbow" is to say that rainbows are relatively flat), the plates went down with more noise than any other step in the process.

The initial reaction many have is, "So what, a .45 ACP fires a 230 subsonic, why this?" Simple: a .45 ACP carbine is not a trivial thing to manage. Let's assume

you wanted to do it (as an individual or a law enforcement agency, even perhaps the US military), where would you go? A Thompson? A quick search turns up Dealer Samples (only another Class III dealer can buy one) for $7,000, and a beautiful Colt 1921 for only $30,000. Ouch. And that's a common .45 SMG.

Converting an AR (perhaps now the most common rifle in America), is an incredible hassle. First of all, you have to make it a blowback, and then you have to decide what kind of magazine you're going to modify the receiver to accept. I had an excellent .45 ACP carbine made by Olympic Arms, and I regretted selling it almost as soon as it left my hands.

To convert an AR to .300 Whisper takes but one part: the barrel. Oh, you can modify everything else if you want, but the barrel is the only required part. The result is an interesting hammer with which to quietly strike down the bad guys. A 220 at 950 fps is not exactly the hammer of Thor, but it is plenty good enough to settle accounts. It is pretty close to what a .45 ACP, hot-loaded or +P, would do, out of a handgun. However, there is a bonus. I found this out when testing Hornady 208-grain A-Max ammo in ballistic gelatin, from an S&W M&P15 in .300 Whisper. The .45 ACP, and its standard 230 round-nosed jacketed bullet, will penetrate through two blocks of ballistic gelatin (over 32 inches) in a dead straight line. It will create a permanent wound cavity of, you guessed it, .451-inch in diameter.

The twist rate on the .300 Whisper is 1:10, the standard rate for all .308-inch rifles. It is spectacularly unsuited to keeping bullets point first at the subsonic velocities the .300 Whisper pushes them. As a result, the bullets are unstable, and they go end for end soon after entering the ballistic gelatin. In fact, they go end for end for end. I was using large, rifle-sized blocks, and the extra (eight inches square on the receiving end, instead of six inches for handguns), allowed me to collect many sample bullets. They had flipped over twice, and at the 20-inch depth of gelatin range, were attempting to exit the blocks by the sides. The bullets were undamaged, and except for the rifling marks on them, could be loaded and fired again.

So, a quick calculation: .308-inch bullet, A-Max length, (carry the two ...), comes out to having nearly twice the surface area when going sideways as a standard 230 hardball going sharper

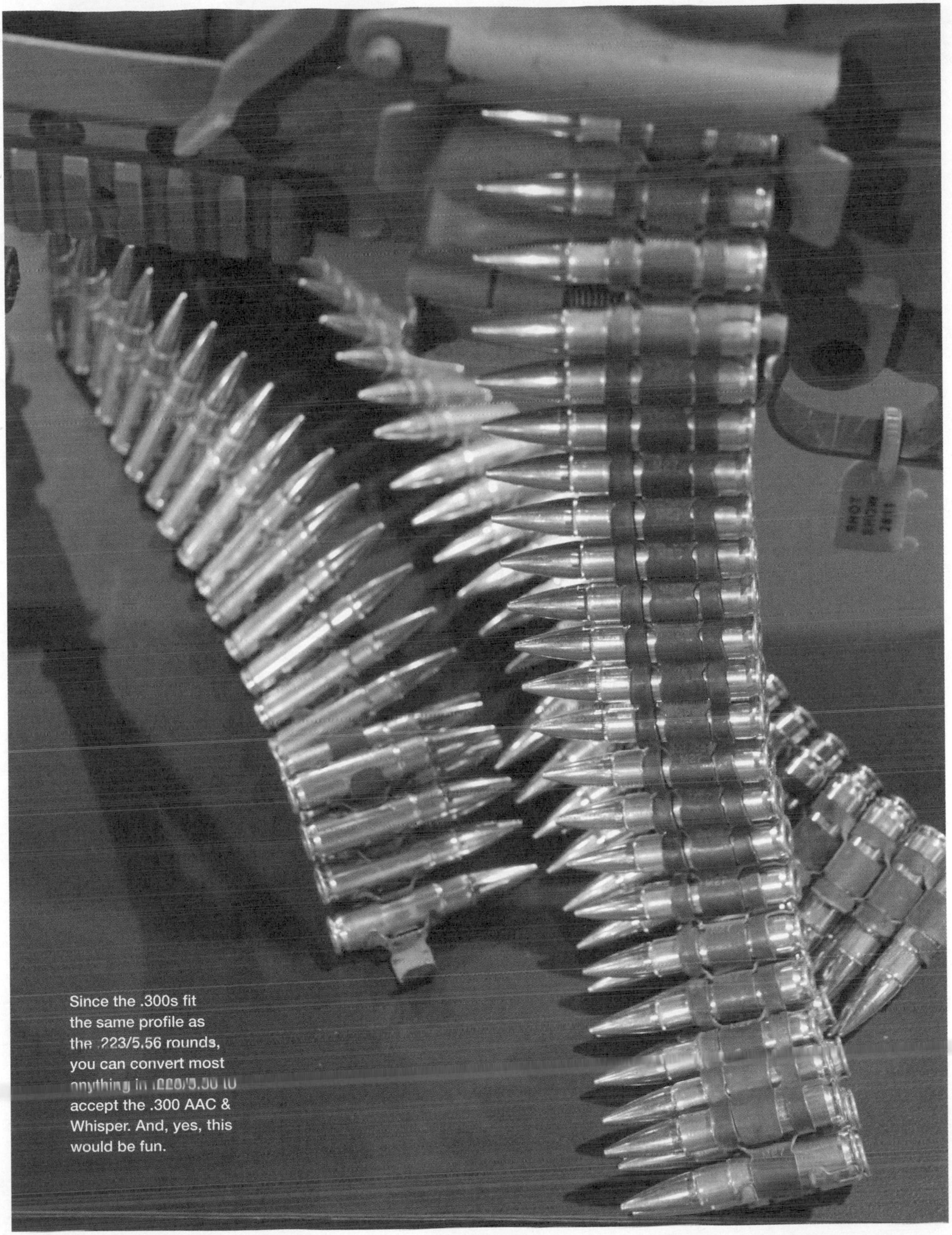

Since the .300s fit
the same profile as
the .223/5.56 rounds,
you can convert most
anything in .223/5.56 to
accept the .300 AAC &
Whisper. And, yes, this
would be fun.

The elegant thing about the .300s is that they use the standard AR-10 thread pattern for flash hider and suppressor mounts.

end first. A .308-inch bullet, going sideways, has got to hurt.

As the project progressed, using .221 Fireball brass turned out to not be such a good idea. It meant being at the mercy of the supply of .221 Fireball brass, not a common brass, not easily found or even regularly produced. So, J.D. had brass made. It was easy enough to do a bit of experimenting and work out the exact length to cut .223/5.56 brass to and then neck it down (by the time it was that short, it was full-body case diameter) to .308-inch. Double bonus! Not only was the Whisper on a common rifle, needing but a barrel, the shooters of the regular caliber were prodigious in creating once-fired brass to be cut down to .300 Whisper.

Life was good, but there was the small matter of making it a standard item.

The group that sets the dimensional standards for ammunition in the United States is SAAMI—the Small Arms and

Ammunition Manufacturing Institute. SAAMI (pronounced "Sammy") does not *invent* anything. It simply acts as the clearinghouse of record for the dimensions, pressures, etc., of a caliber and its chamber. Members can propose cartridges. Accepted cartridges get named by those proposing them. Once accepted, the dimensions are in the realm of "freeware" in the software industry. Anyone can make it, but, if they make bad ammo they'll go out of business, regardless the product being something SAAMI has approved.

If you want to get your whiz-bang cartridge SAAMI-approved, you have to have a member of SAAMI bring it up at one of the semi-annual meetings. Of course, if you don't, you can control who makes it and who gets to call their product by your name and charge a licensing fee. So, "in" and its it free for anyone, "not in" and you can make it

your own product and recoup some of your R&D investment.

J.D. decided to keep it for his own, and that caused some problems over time. Anyone could make a similar product and call it what they wanted, but, if you had someone else do it, you had to be sure you made your own brass, and re-loaded to fit your own rifle. There was no interchangeability between makers. (The downside of proprietary cartridges.)

Then, Steve Hornady at Hornady ammo put .300 Whisper into full, public production. He got it approved by C.I.P., the European standards organization, and offered two loads: a supersonic 110-grain V-Max and a 208 subsonic A-Max. To back it up, Smith & Wesson started offering its M&P15 in .300 Whisper. All it takes is a new barrel, right?

Now, at this point, it is worth taking a slight sidestep to look at super- versus.

Along with its uppers and barrels, AAC offers suppressors. Actually, it made suppressors long before it started making things .300.

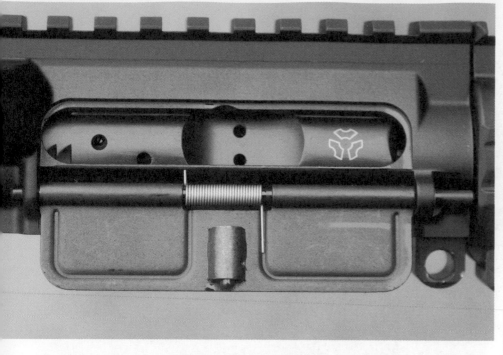

If you are converting an AR to one of the .300s, the only thing you need different is the barrel. Bolt, carrier, upper, accessories, all are the same.

subsonic. Depending on the altitude and density, air temperature, and even humidity, the speed of sound is roughly around 1,120 fps. Above that, you get the supersonic "crack" of the bullet creating a shockwave. Below that, you just get the normal muzzle blast and bullet passage.

To get a 110-, 125-, or 150-grain bullet to go supersonic, in the case of Whisper, requires powders of a particular burn rate range. To merely boot 200-plus-grain bullets to subsonic takes powders in a different range. To make them as efficient as possible, J.D. Jones' approach was to load the best powder for that application, and he made his barrels to accommodate that. His barrels have a switchable gas block for high and low. You'll want to turn the setting from one to the other, if you use his approach or his ammo.

Hornady was not so keen on that, and it created ammo so that the gun would work with the ammo commingled. The two loads will eject their brass to two different angles and distances, but they both work.

From the originator, J.D. Jones, you have a bunch more choices in bullets. He makes some bullets you'd expect to have microchips in them, they are so high-tech. How about a heavyweight subsonic with a turned-brass bullet notched to create petals? The bullet not only overturns, it breaks off the petals

and generally acts like a miniature food processor set on "frappé." This leads us to the next step.

.300 AAC Blackout

Advanced Armament Company is a suppressor company that also makes rifles. It was bought by the same company that owns Remington and subsequently folded into the family. Its work on a subsonic cartridge was going on as this happened, and one of the aspects of the corporate purchase was a delay in getting the new cartridge product

out. But it is out now, as the .300 AAC Blackout, made by Remington.

The big controversy when the Blackout was unveiled centered around the cry "They stole J.D.'s design!" With all due respect, I have to look at it from the perspective of an engineer, gunsmith and reloader. Given the constraints the magazine imposes, the limits the bullets intended to be used put on case design, and the need to make the resultant cartridge as simple a conversion as possible, I'm not sure you could come up with anything else. If you think you can, give it a try. The cries should not have been "They ripped off J.D.," but, rather, "J.D. was so clever, you can't improve on it, even if you start with a clean sheet of paper."

The guys at AAC started from scratch, worked the details for all they were worth, and produced the .300 AAC Black out. As this was going on, the company was being bought, and the resulting work had a serendipitous outcome; since Remington was now a fellow organization in the overall company, it simply (or at least, as simply as these things can happen) had Remington apply to SAAMI for cartridge recognition. Remington makes the ammo to the specs as laid down before the SAAMI acceptance board, AAC makes the uppers and rifles, and everyone is happy.

That said, there are dimensional differences between the .300 AAC Blackout and the .300 Whisper. They are, however, quite minor, and you could use reloading dies for either with the other and not notice a thing. As long as the dies are adjusted to work in your rifle, you will be fine. In fact, rifle makers who

The barrels you can get in .300 (either type) will have fast twists. Where a .308 Winchester would have a 1:10 twist, the .300 AAC and Whisper have 1:8, 1:7½, or 1:7 twists.

are not in one or another camp will, in many cases, mark their products as being able to use both cartridges interchangeably. However, if you have fine-tuned your loading dies to work with any and all .300 brass that happens by, you may find your ammo may not work in other shooters' rifles. If you are in the habit of swapping ammo with other shooters, that could be a problem. If not, you're good to go. Ideally, if you are going to have both in inventory, you'd use Whisper dies with Whisper brass and feed them through your Whisper rifle, ditto for the .300 AAC Blackout.

Final note: As with Hornady, Remington also compromised on the powders it uses, so that either load will work in your rifle.

Testing

I had two rifles and two extra uppers with which to test the ammo. One rifle was built by me using a barrel from J.D. Jones and chambered in .300 Whisper. The other is a complete rifle from S&W, its M&P15 in .300 Whisper and done up in the latest camo finish for hunters. The first upper comes from CMMG, chambered in .300 AAC Blackout, and the second upper is an AAC product, chambered in (what else?) .300 AAC Blackout.

The SSK barrel is a 16-inch long, medium weight stainless steel and has a two-position gas block, for supersonic and subsonic loads. The twist is 1:7½, a common twist in this application. It came with a bare muzzle, which is fine, if you are simply plinking, as the Whisper has absolutely no chance whatsoever of producing muzzle flash, unless you put the round through a barrel more appropriate for a handgun, say six or seven inches. Still, I like flash hiders on my rifles, I don't live in California and I can have them. I can also have suppressors, so I had Surefire send me a suppressor

adapter/flash hider, and, when my .30 can makes it through the paperwork song and dance routine, I'll be able to install it.

I had a spare Stag upper on the shelf, so, with the SSK barrel, I installed a Vltor CASV-MT handguard, as I find I like the light weight and how the contours of the tube fit my hands. However, in order to access the two-position gas block, I had to drill through the top rail of the CASV-MT. Once that was done and I did a little trimming inside the Vltor handguard to clear the argument between the gas block and internal stiffening ribs of the Vltor handguard, things went together like strawberry jam and peanut butter in a sandwich.

The lower is one JP Enterprises sent as a test drone and had John Paul's excellent trigger already installed. I simply slapped the Stag-uppered SSK barrel top half onto the JP lower and went to work. While I was testing the setup, Hi-Lux

This Surefire .308 suppressor is efficient for a .308. For anything in the .300s, it is a veritable vacuum cleaner of a can.

Recoil? What recoil? The .300 in any guise is a low-shove round and perfect for new deer hunters or those who have trouble with recoil.

sent me one of its 1-4x scopes; since the .300 Whisper is not at all a long-range cartridge, a 1-4x with a wide field of view is very useful. In a LaRue mount, it goes on or off quickly, if I need to I change to iron sights easily.

It was with this setup that I ran into the first unusual situation with the Whisper, one I should have remembered from watching Ned on the back range of Second Chance: point of impact. The Hornady 110s and 208s did not hit near each other, except on the 25-yard zero target. The trajectories are so different, you really have to know which your rifle is zeroed for and where it is zeroed. With a 5.56 rifle, you can establish a 25-yard zero, refine it at 100, and be ready to go with any bullet or load (at least for people-shooting) out to 300 yards. With the Whisper, you can be a foot apart in point of impact at 100 yards. Just keep that in mind.

The S&W M&P15 comes in one of the latest camo patterns: RealTree APG. Well, the upper, lower, and pistol grip are done in RealTree. The barrel and stock are not. Interestingly, the lower of the M&P15 in

.300 Whisper has the triggerguard as an integral part of the lower, not the winter triggerguard of the Mil-Spec models.

The barrel is medium-weight and has a twist of 1:7½. That's to stabilize the heavyweights while not over-spinning the lighter bullets. The M&P15 receiver is a flat-top upper, but, rather than install yet another optic, I simply bolted on Midwest Industries' folding iron sights. The result is a handy carbine that weighs a bit less than 6½ pounds, less than a Winchester 94 saddle ring carbine in .30-30. With a five-round magazine, it is the handiest thing to hunt with, and you can hunt with it everywhere. Well, almost. Pennsylvania is off limits, as it doesn't allow you to hunt with a self-loading rifle. Buzzkills.

Where I did accuracy testing with the SSK-barreled upper at 100 yards (due to the optics), I limited myself to 50 yards with the iron sights on the S&W.

Uppers

The CMMG .300 Blackout upper is available in either a free-float handguard

or an M4 handguard. The free-float model comes without sights, while the M4 has the front sight. (It has to, that's where the gas system starts.) Barrels are 16 inches long with a 1:8 twist. The muzzle is threaded ⅝x24, the standard .30 AR muzzle threading, so you can put any .30-caliber flash hider (but not a .223/5.56 one) on the end. Or, you can install a flash hider/suppressor adapter, if you wish. If you have all the parts you need, then CMMG can simply ship you a barrel, to be assembled at your end into a working upper or carbine.

The upper CMMG sent to me differs from the items shown on the company's web page, in that the one sent me has the M4-type front sight, "F" marked for the correct height with which to use a BUIS, but an aluminum free-float handguard. The handguard, as a non-railed, is a very slim tube with stabilizing tabs on it to keep it properly oriented with the upper. CMMG shipped it to me with soft rubber panels on it, but it would be a simple matter to unbolt the panels, bolt on rails where needed and, if you really had to have the rubber, trim them and bolt them back on. Even with the rubber panels, the handguard is very slim and, with gloves on, it does not become this sewer pipe-sized object (as so many railed handguards feel like) you're trying to hold on to.

The CMMG offers its .300 AAC Blackout uppers in two gas systems: the pistol- or carbine-length system. The carbine is the same as your basic AR-15/M4 and it is meant for the supersonic loads. You may or may not be able to get subsonic loads to work with the carbine setup, as gas pressure has dropped markedly by the time the bullet gets to the gas port in a carbine design. At least .300 gas pressure. Conversely, if you opt for the pistol-length gas system, your supersonic loads may work the system excessively hard, what with the extra gas pressure provided by the supersonic loadings; even more so if you use supersonic loads in a pistol gas-length setup and put a suppressor on the end. CMMG puts a chart on the web page, next to each of the .300 AAC Blackout uppers pages, so you can keep track of this.

I would opt for the pistol-length gas system only if I was going to use the upper solely for subsonic loads and mostly with a suppressor attached. Otherwise, I'd go for the carbine-length system hands down.

CMMG also treats its barrels with a proprietary treatment that increases hardness and wear- and corrosion-resistance. The acronym WASP indicates that this particular barrel had been given the treatment. There is a lot of research going on these days, looking for something

to replace hard-chrome plating of the bore. WASP is one approach and, so far, appears to be a good one.

AAC, Advanced Armament Corp., sent an upper built with one of its barrels and with the superb Knight's railed URX-II handguard system on it. The URX-II sent was a mid-length, which, combined with a carbine-length barrel, creates a nicely-balanced look to an AR. (We all know that looks are the most important thing, right?) The URX-II also has a front sight on it. If you didn't know it was there, you might not get around to using it, so well hidden is it that I would not be surprised to see someone with a URX-II installed on their rifle and a flip-up front sight bolted to the rail. You see, the URX front sight looks like it is just another section of rail. Press the lock button and you can pivot the sight up. It isn't spring-loaded, perhaps the one trick Knight's missed here. Probably something the end users didn't want. In re-reading this, I realized that asking why the front sight isn't spring-loaded is kind of like asking why the latest Lamborghini doesn't have cup holders. Once up, the sight locks in the up position and you'll need to press the locking button to unlock it and fold it down. The front sight assembly also has a knurled wheel in it, for elevation adjustments. As convenient as it is, it is something I'd definitely paint in, to mark the zero location.

In consulting the Knight's catalog and web page, I notice that the URX II is listed as a Knight's part, but you cannot order it from the web page. Hmm. AAC lays hands on a part Knight's reserves

for their own builds. I can see this upper hanging around Gun Abuse Central for some time.

The barrel is a mid-weight profile, although, with the .30 hole down the middle instead of a .22, it weighs less than a regular AR of that profile, and it is made with a twist of 1:7, just a bit faster than the others. It also had the AAC fast-attach flash hider, which can accept one of its suppressors. Alas, the time constraints of this book precluded acquiring a suppressor to test on the upper. (We will have to address suppressors in *Gun Digest Book of the AR-15 Volume 5*, I think.)

The flat top upper is AAC marked, and the carrier (parkerized) has a logo on it. All the upper needs is a rear sight or optics, and a lower to park it on.

Ballistic Gelatin

This was the really fun part, as I got to use handgun-sized blocks and not the "chunks of the pyramids" rifle-sized blocks. Rifles usually require the 8x8x36-inch blocks and, even then, they have to be tied down. If we try to use the handgun blocks (6x6x16), the rifles usually explode them, throwing chunks of ballistic gelatin across the range. Or, they leap off of the table so much that they thrash themselves to pieces in the dust, dirt and gravel of the range floor, making it really tough to do a proper autopsy.

The report and recoil from any of these loads is mild, to say the least. The lighter bullets are snappier and

The .300 conversion is so low-profile that you can't tell (this is the CMMG .300), unless you look at the barrel markings.

would make excellent deer hunting loads for those who want to use the modern sporting rifle come November. A 110-grain to 125-grain bullet, designed for deer, at the velocities these rifles can produce, is plenty good enough to slay any whitetail that has ever walked the planet.

With a zero an inch and a half high at 100 yards, you're going to be within an inch and a half of point of aim out to 200, which is essentially point blank zero for most deer hunting. In the hands of a new shooter, posted in a blind with clear instructions as to what is "too far," you can count on the rifle doing its job.

Slapping the lightweights into ballistic gelatin produces the usual results. You get an expanded or fragmented bullet, a foot of penetration, and impressively shredded gelatin. If you have a deer hunting bullet you prefer and you know it works the way you want in the velocity ranges the .300s can produce, load it and have a blast. Just be sure to shoot enough to be sure it feeds reliably in your rifle. It would be a real shame to load up a big batch, only to find it doesn't feed all that well. If your gun club won't let you shoot rounds from the magazine (I've heard of such places, but I would never join a club that was so Neanderthal-ic), you may just have to find a place where you can.

The subsonic ammunition is what is really interesting. At subsonic velocities, the bullets are far too tough to expand, fragment, or otherwise de- form. They may as well be lathe-turned solids, as far as what the speed and gelatin can combine to do. As a result, and due to the inability to spin the bul- lets fast enough—you'd have to have a rifling twist so quick you couldn't force the bullets down the bore, to stabilize them in gelatin—the bullets swap end for end. As they overturn, they begin to veer off the axis of impact. In some cases (especially the 208-grain A-Max in .300 Whisper), they will swap ends twice, and those all try to exit the sides of the gel blocks at the 20-inch depth. On one hand, a 200-grain bullet going subsonic isn't much more on paper than a .45 ACP, but that bullet going sideways is going to leave a mark.

Just as an aside, there is a category of competition in USPSA matches that some clubs allow: Pistol Caliber Carbine. The match entry is for rifles chambered in pistol calibers, typically 9mm or .45, and you shoot the same stages and course as do the handgun

shooters. The typical shooter will be running an AR in 9mm, on the same cardboard and steel targets as the handgun shooters. It is not unusual for a "C"-class handgun shooter, hosing a course with a 9mm AR, to post times and scores that an "A"-class Open shooter would be happy with.

A bit of quick testing showed me that the heavyweight subsonic loads are not abusive to falling steel plates or poppers. They are right on par with .38 Super major or .45 ACP loads and don't cause dents or craters. (Now, if your club uses cheap steel, you may have a problem, but, then, you'll have a problem the first time someone shows up with a .38 Super at Major, running 125-grain bullets, as well.) Plus, you could even load your own to create special match loads; a 150-grain soft- point or fmj (whatever is cheapest) at about 900 fps, which, with the right powder, would run your .300 just fine.

As reliable as a properly tuned 9mm AR can be, the .300 is going to be more reliable, and you also have the muscle memory of the same-sized magazines to handle as you'd be doing in the club match later that month: 3-Gun.

Bill Wilson

Okay, you all know Bill Wilson, right? Premier 1911 pistolsmith, competitor, inventor, and purveyor of primo 1911 custom guns and parts for same. Well, in due time, Bill decided to semi-retire, and he moved from the business in Berryville, Arkansas, to a place even more wild and remote. There he found his little piece of paradise was afflicted with the same ailment from which so many places now suffer: hogs. Members of the porcine family are, in many ways, like people. They are smart, adaptable, omnivorous, and family oriented. For a while, it was a common business prac- tice for ranches to import big pigs, feral hogs, and non-native species (well, they are all non-native to the Americas, but here we mean non-native in a twentieth century sense), for hunting preserves.

Pigs escape, hunting preserves go out of business, and the pigs from regular pig ranches have escapees, as well. Stir them all together and mix in modern agribusiness and what do you get? A burgeoning population of pigs. In some locales, they are so numerous they are not just annoyances to farmers, but real financial hazards. Bill Wilson soon finds that his location is one subject to

regular rapacious attention from the piggish set.

The first thought for most of us would be, "What 1911 works best here?" Alas, none. Since they have already been shot at, repeatedly, the pigs are often noc- turnal and travel in packs. You do not go out in the darkness after "The Pig" with just a handgun, when there can be a family of tuskers waiting in the wings to stomp, tusk, and thrash you. You may not come back. Bill starts with one of his custom AR-15s, but finds that, while 5.56 is good enough in a military context, it is not so good when you're trying to smack all of a group. So, he looks at the .300, at that time the Whisper, as the Blackout was still being developed. What he found was useful, but not the best for his needs. He had no need whatsoever for subsonic loads. Since the feral hogs he was shooting were not game animals, they were not covered by nor protected by the DNR regs he had to work under. So he could use a suppressor and even night vision optics as aids to shooting them. (If you think that sounds like more fun that should be allowed and really want to have a go at it, welcome to the club.)

With a "can," the subsonic loads be- come less important. But the supersonic loads were not all they could be. So, Bill changed the cartridge. He kept the maxi- mum overall length—he had to. But, since he was going with bullets on the lighter end, the 110- and 125-grain hunting bul- lets, he could move the shoulder forward to better hold those bullets and also gain case capacity. Where a 110-grain bullet in the Whisper/Blackout can be going right around 2,300 fps, the 7.62x40 Wilson can boost that same bullet to nearly 2,400 fps out of a 16-inch barrel, and over 2,500 fps out of a 20-inch barrel.

As with the Whisper/Blackout, you can make your brass from cut down .223/5.56 empties. You can't just neck up the .221 Fireball, as it is too short, but that isn't really an option for a lot of people. Since the various .300s have been unveiled, .300 Whisper and .300 Blackout brass are both far more com- mon than .221 Fireball ever was. Or, you just buy ammo and dies from Wilson Combat and follow the loading data it's generated for your use.

Now, the 7.62x40 Wilson, just like the Whisper and Blackout, can be yours simply by replacing the barrel from a .223/5.56 rifle. And, as you'd expect, Wil- son Combat offers a host of barrel options for your shooting pleasure. However, there is one slight hitch in the situation; magazines. You see, when Bill decided to move the shoulder forward, he ran into (literally) the forward vertical stiffening rib in the AR magazine. Now, if you are just working up loads and aren't planning on wholesale harvesting of porkers by moonlight, an occasional malfunction in standard magazines is no big deal. The Wilson folks tell me that, using standard magazines, you'll lose a couple rounds of capacity due to the uneven stacking and the crowded bullet tips being pinched in towards the centerline.

On USGI magazines, removing the stiffening rib pretty much destroys the structural integrity of the magazine tube. But, once again in the modern era, polymer comes to the rescue. Wilson teamed up with Lancer to produce a version of the new L5 magazine just for the 7.62x40. What it did was simple; Lancer removed the stiffening/feed guide rib on the inside that caused the problems. You can get a full 20 rounds into a 20-round 7.62x40-marked magazine.

Now, just because Bill Wilson didn't intend for his cartridge to be used in the subsonic role, doesn't mean you can't make it do that. If you have a 7.62x40 Wilson and want to shoot subsonic, you can do it, but it won't be as easy as the others. The neck/shoulder location on the case will make seating heavy bullets problematic and, since the barrel is meant for supersonic and the gas port drilled to a size for that, you may find it tough to find a powder to run the gun reliably in subsonic. This will only be made more difficult if you eschew the use of heavyweights for subsonic work, and try to make USPSA pepper-popper-safe loads with 125-grain bullets. Still, shooters being shooters, someone out there is going to try, and succeed.

As I mentioned, Wilson has dies. You can't use the other .300 dies to reload the Wilson, nor vice-versa.

The extra velocity does not come without a price. You'll have a bit more recoil, and you will have to use a smidge more powder to make those velocities, but that is it. And, if you are in a locale where the .223/5.56 is not approved for hunting, you can hunt with your AR.

Ammunition

To start with, we have the original: SSK industries. J.D. Jones makes some loads that are not just specialized, but work in ways you have to scratch your

When Remington makes something, you know you can get lots and lots of it.

head over. Are these meant for use against platinum-plated space squids, when our alien overlords send in their interplanetary jannisaries to enforce their edicts? I mean, subsonic, pre-fragmented loads, saboted penetrators, expanding bullets (a neat trick with subsonic loads), and more. If you need ammo a bit more standard, you can go to CorBon, which makes and has made .300 Whisper for many years. It can offer you 125-grain and 220-grain self-defense loads, as well as a 150-grain hunting load.

The big news that started a lot of this is the Hornady line. Big Red offers two loads: its 110 V-Max bullet in a supersonic loading, and the 208-grain A-Max subsonic. The V-Max performs as you'd expect, with penetration and fragmentation, and would be a good choice on whitetail, as long as you aren't trying to bust them through the shoulder. The 208 A-Max is for having fun and removing sentries. Okay, not much of that these days, at least not stateside, so it is the quietest, funnest load Hornady makes.

In .300 Blackout, Remington loads a 115-grain fmj, your basic plinking load and 7.62x39 equivalent, as well as a 155 open-tip match and a subsonic 220 open-tip match bullet.

For the 7.62x40, Wilson Combat is loading 110- and 125-grain bullets.

Of course, if you do your own reloading, you can use any bullet that will fit the case and magazine and feed properly. I'd suggest you pay close attention to the existing loading data, as the small case is not very forgiving of "experimental" reloading.

CorBon makes superb hunting loads, and, if you need something for defense, this would be a good one to choose.

Starting with the 220-grain subsonic, Remington now makes a 115-grain UMC load for practice and plinking.

Hornady has been making .300 Whisper for a long time, but now it offers it as a factory brand.

Benelli Super Black Eagle II

TODAY'S TOP WATERFOWL Guns & Loads

BY **Brad Fitzpatrick**

Benelli Super Vinci

On average, America's million-plus waterfowl hunters spend over 13 million days in the field annually and generate more than $900 million in funds that directly impact both migratory birds and other species of wildlife. Duck and goose hunting is big business, and firearms, accessories, and ammunition companies have taken note of this, providing purpose-built products.

What follows are my picks of the best shotguns and ammunition choices for hunting waterfowl, from springing teal in September to snows and speckled geese late in the year. Today's crop of guns and loads means hunters can go afield with confidence in their hunting equipment and, no matter what type of waterfowl you're chasing, you'll be able to find just what you're looking for.

Benelli

Benelli's M2 and Super Black Eagle semi-autos have a solid reputation among waterfowlers who appreciate the simplicity and reliability of the company's Inertia-Driven system. Recently, the more radically styled Vinci and 3½-inch Super Vinci semi-autos have been added to the Benelli lineup, and both guns met with immediate success. Employing a patented In-Line Inertia-Driven system, the Vinci and Super Vinci are built to last for thousands of rounds, and the company has incorporated the popular ComforTech plus system to reduce felt recoil, as well as including Crio choke tubes for better patterns. In addition, Benelli still offers its popular Nova and Super Nova pump guns, a more economical option for those who don't mind shucking their own shells. (www.benelliusa.com)

Beretta

Beretta, the world's oldest firearms maker, has certainly kept up with the times, offering some of the most innovative shotguns and premium features that are exclusive to the brand. Beretta's A400 line is still a popular shotgun

Benelli Super Vinci

Beretta A400 Xtrme Unico

among waterfowlers, thanks in part to features like the Blink gas system, which is extremely fast and ultra-reliable, Beretta's Aqua Technology that prevents corrosion of both internal and external parts, and the Kick-Off system that reduces recoil up to 60 percent over other comparable shotguns. The more budget-wise A300 semi-autos represent "best buys" in the shotgun world, combining features like a self-cleaning rotating gas system that has proven to be reliable for thousands of rounds, and a lightweight aluminum receiver with a hard anodized finish. The A300 and A400 are available in either black or camo finishes. (www.berettausa.com)

Browning

Browning has long been synonymous with waterfowl guns, and the company is still at the leading edge of the industry. It currently offers four different semi-autos designed for waterfowling, one pump, and an over/under built duck-blind tough. For those hunters requiring extra punch for big birds, the Gold 10-gauge is available in three camo patterns, including Mossy Oak's new Shadow Grass Blades. The BPS pump is also available in 10-gauge in a variety of finishes. Browning offers an extensive line of 12- and 20-gauge BPS pumps in a wide variety of camo patterns. The bottom-eject BPS is a favorite among Southpaws, because it works equally well for both left- and right-handed shooters.

The popular Silver and Maxus gas-operated guns remain in Browning's lineup, with the addition of new models sporting the Shadow Grass Blades camo pattern. Traditionalists will appreciate the reengineered A5, which incorporates a modern recoil-operated action. For those who prefer stack-barrels, the radical-looking Cynergy over/under is a natural choice and is available in several camo patterns. All Browning guns include Inflex Technology recoil reduction. (www.browning.com)

Escort

Escort shotguns, which have been introduced by Legacy Sports International, are gaining popularity among waterfowlers, because they offer a lot of innovative features and capability at a reasonable price. The company's Extreme Magnum Semi-Auto is available in both 3- and

Browning A5

Browning Cynergy

Escort Extreme
Magnum

3½-inch versions and a variety of camo finishes. The Extreme Magnum action uses the company's SMART Valve gas regulating piston for reliability across a wide number of loads. The gun also includes such features as a magazine cutoff, soft touch textured inserts, HIVIZ MagniSight fiber optic system, a nickel/chrome moly-lined barrel, and extended waterfowl chokes. Also, Escort offers its budget-priced pump shotgun in basic black, with stock adjustment shims and a receiver drilled and dovetailed for mounting optics, all with an MSRP below $400. (www.legacysports.com)

Franchi

Franchi relied on parent company Benelli for the Inertia-Driven action on the its new Affinity semi-autos. The Affinity is available in both 12- and 20-gauge in black synthetic and Realtree MAX-4 and APG patterns, and there is a compact version built to fit smaller-framed shooters. Shims come standard, to adjust the stock to the shooter's dimensions, and three choke tubes are also standard, although Franchi offers additional extended tubes, some with names like "Pass" and "Decoy" designed for specific waterfowling situations. The trigger assembly on the Affinity drops out by punching a single pin, and the lightweight receiver keeps weight to a minimum. Franchi's slim fore-end makes it one of the best handling shotguns on

Franchi Affinity

FIVE GREAT DUCK HUNTING DESTINATIONS

Kentucky—Western Kentucky has lots of birds passing through during the season, but the region receives less waterfowling pressure than Arkansas and Tennessee. The areas around Lake Barkley and Kentucky Lake are prime locations, with plenty of public land, or, if you choose a guided hunt, check out Winghaven Lodge. (www.winghavenlodge.com)

Maine—Maine's sea duck hunting is some of the best in the nation. This is one of the best places to take an eider, scoter, or old squaw. Coastal Maine draws lots of attention, and the best guides know where to connect with large numbers of sea ducks on cold water late in the fall. Be prepared for low temps and red-hot duck hunting in Maine. (www.maineseaduck.com)

Wisconsin—If you're looking for a bull canvasback, Wisconsin is your best bet, as the Upper Mississippi is a stronghold for these birds during fall migration. But the Upper Mississippi is also a great place for a mixed bag hunt, as you can expect to see mallards, goldeneye, bluebills, pintail, and others. This is one of the best areas in the entire Mississippi flyway to hunt, and the wide variety of species that might come into the decoys makes this a prime waterfowl destination. (www.hideawayhollowoutfitters.com)

Texas—The Gulf Coast of Texas is one of the premier spots in the nation for a mixed bag hunt. In late winter, there are lots of ducks around. Near the barrier island of Matagorda, which runs almost 40 miles along the coastline, you can expect to get your limit of redheads each day, and you'll also encounter pintails, widgeon, gadwall, teal, shovelers, and snow and speckled geese. (www.bayflatslodge.com)

Alaska—Alaska's Aleutian Islands are formidable and the weather can be unpredictable at any time of year. But, for hard-core duck hunters, the possibility of taking such rarities as king eider, Pacific eider, harlequin ducks, Aleutian teal, and Eurasian wigeon makes the possibility of bad weather seem inconsequential. (www.alaskaduckhuntingguides.com)

Stoeger P350

the market, and the reliability of the Inertia System means that the Affinity will keep firing time and time again, even under the worst conditions. (www.franchiusa.com)

Ithaca

Ithaca is one of the most respected names in American shotguns. After a hiatus from the firearms landscape a few years back, it is again producing guns in Sandusky, Ohio. One of those guns is the Model 37 Waterfowl pump. Protected with a black synthetic stock and Perma-Guard finish, the Ithaca is tough enough to withstand the absolute worst conditions. The bottom-feed design prevents muck and debris from entering the chamber, and I think the Ithaca's trigger is among the best in the industry. The M37 Waterfowl is a modern take on an American classic and is available in both 12- and 20-gauge variants with either 28- or 30-inch barrels. (www.ithacagun.com)

Mossberg

Ask most hunters what comes to mind when you talk about Mossberg, and many will utter a single word: tough. Mossberg's

original 500 pump shotgun is a classic waterfowl tool, revered for its durability and price point. Today, waterfowlers who also happen to be pump-gun lovers can take heart in knowing that Mossberg doesn't rest on past successes, but is instead expanding its waterfowl offerings. Currently, Mossberg offers its 500 Waterfowl, 535 Waterfowl, and 835 Waterfowl shotguns, as well as the Bantam pumps designed for smaller shooters. On the semi-auto side, the company offers its 930 and 935 models in waterfowl variants.

Mossberg's latest development is its FLEX system, which allows the shooter to change stocks, forearms, and barrels on their pumps, providing the ultimate level of versatility and reinventing the concept of the "do-all" pump. The company is also offering a new, patented recoil reduction system to help make its guns easier to manage and more comfortable to shoot, even with the heaviest loads. (www.mossberg.com)

Remington

Remington's 870 pump has been in production for more than 60 years, and there's a very good reason for that. The

870 is not only time-tested, for many shotgunners it was the first (and perhaps only) shotgun they picked up. The 870 has fans worldwide, and over its 60 years has been available in dozens of configurations. The current 870 is available with a variety of camo finishes and also in a 3½ inch version for those who prefer extreme shotgunning capabilities. Remington's semi-auto lineup contains both the 1100 and the 11-87 gas guns, though in more limited configurations. The Versa Max is now the company's flagship semi-auto gun, incorporating Remington's Versaport gas system that reliably cycles a variety of load weights and that reduces recoil. The self-cleaning system has proven to be quite reliable, and the Versa Max offers many waterfowler-friendly touches, like easy to grip over-molded surfaces and an oversized safety and trigger guard that makes it easier to shoot the gun while wearing gloves. (www.remington.com)

Stoeger

A favorite brand among shooters who appreciate great value, the most economical of Stoeger's waterfowl guns is the P-350 pump gun. But don't confuse inexpensive with cheap. Stoeger guns

Mossberg 835 with recoil reduction system

THE LONG AND SHORT OF IT: RECOIL VERSUS INERTIA

Many shotgunners have opinions about recoil guns and Intertia-Driven guns, but few understand what makes these two action types different.

Understand that both inertia guns and recoil guns rely on the rearward energy produced by the shell being fired to work the action. The traditional recoil operated semi-autos like the Browning A-5 and the Franchi 48AL, though, should technically be referred to as long recoil operation shotguns. According to Jens Krogh of Franchi, on these long operation recoil systems, "The barrel recoils back into the chamber with the bolt and ejects the spent load." This means the barrel and the bolt are attached and move backwards as one; the spent shell is extracted and ejected after the bolt unlocks.

The Stoeger model 3500 bolt assembly includes an inertia spring and rotating locking head, two features that distinguish the bolt as an integral part of an Inertia Driven System.

The Intertia-Driven system (or, more technically, the short recoil operation system) that Benelli made famous acts in a somewhat similar fashion, though the barrel of an inertia-driven gun does not travel backwards. Instead, there is a coil spring that sits just behind the rotating bolt head. When this spring is compressed under the force of recoil, the bolt head travels rearward until the spring is compressed, and then the recoil spring allows the bolt to travel rearward and remove the shell from the chamber.

Both systems rely on the energy produced when the gun is fired. Unlike gas operated systems, which rely on the energy of gases produced by the shot, recoil operated systems don't use gaskets or O-rings. However, modern technology has made gas systems much cleaner and more effective.

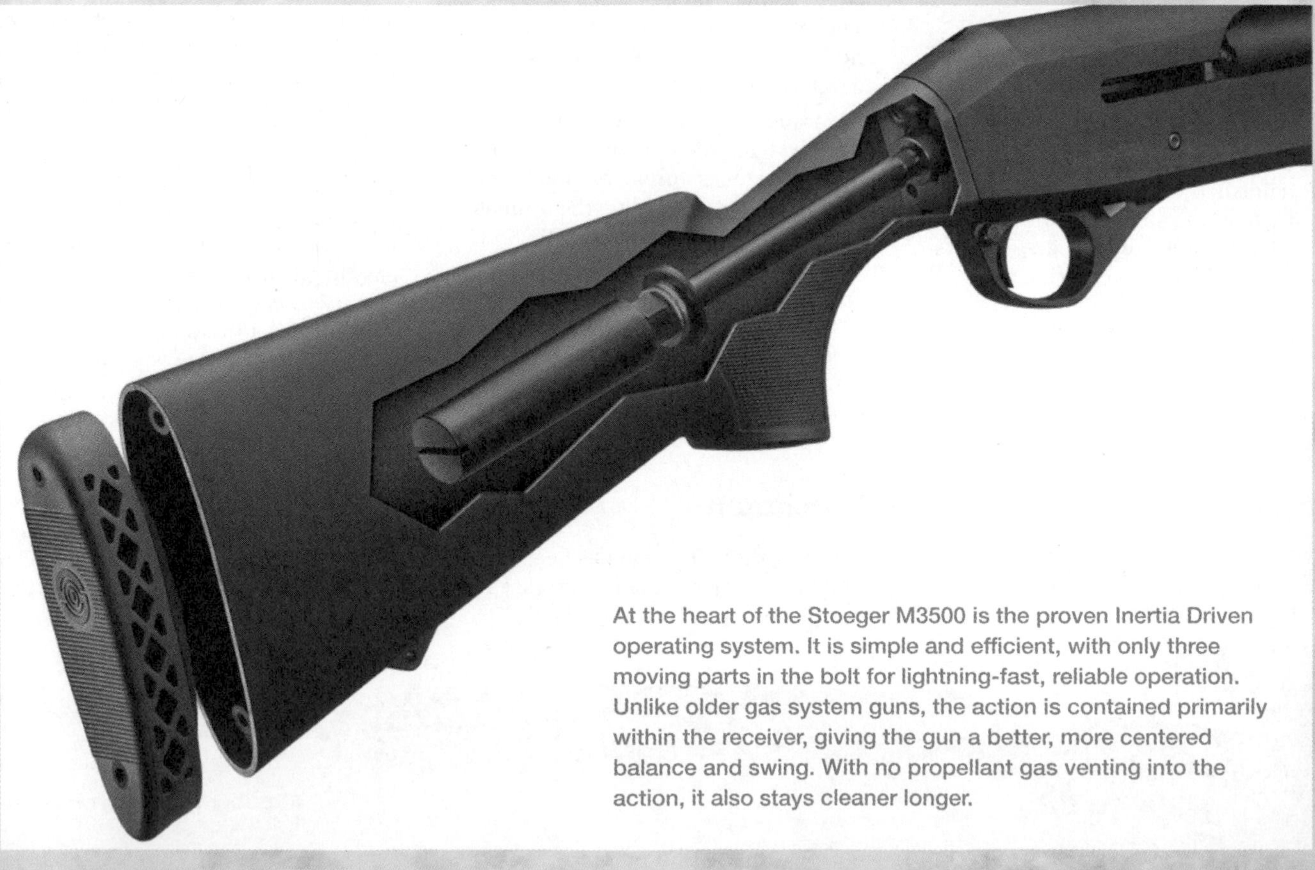

At the heart of the Stoeger M3500 is the proven Inertia Driven operating system. It is simple and efficient, with only three moving parts in the bolt for lightning-fast, reliable operation. Unlike older gas system guns, the action is contained primarily within the receiver, giving the gun a better, more centered balance and swing. With no propellant gas venting into the action, it also stays cleaner longer.

Winchester SX3

are well-built and robust. The P-350 is available in Realtree MAX-4 and APG.

The company's Model 3000 (3-inch) and Model 3500 (3½-inch) semi-autos set a new standard in affordable reliability and are Intertia-Driven gun. These models offer adjustable stock shims, textured grip surfaces, red bead optics for rapid target acquisition, and a variety of camo patterns. There's also an optional 13-ounce mercury recoil reduction system. (www.stoegerindustries.com)

Winchester

Winchester shotguns have been in duck blinds a long, long time. Today, Winchester offers some of the finest scatterguns around. Perhaps best known for the venerable Model 12, Winchester now offers an updated pump gun, the SXP. Available in both Realtree MAX-4 camo patterns and Black Shadow synthetic versions, SXPs are chambered in both 3- and 3½-inch versions to cover everything from honkers to greenheads

and woodies reliably. The SX3 semi-auto line also continues to impress hunters, thanks to its dependable Active Valve gas system that feeds a wide range of shells, while the Quadra-Vent ports expel gas to reduce fouling. (www.winchester-guns.com)

New Ammunition

Federal's Black Cloud ammo is a favorite among waterfowlers, because it offers consistent patterns, thanks in large part to the rear-braking Flitecontrol wad, as well as the Flitestopper shot, which increases the lethality of steel. Also available is Black Cloud Close Range for shots in heavy timber, the honker hunter will want to check out the Snow Goose line of Black Cloud ammo.

With a velocity of 1,700 fps, the new Hypersonic steel loads from Remington produce devastating results and improve upon the lethality of non-toxic shot through increased energy. Remington claims these loads move shot so fast you can shorten your lead on crossing targets up to 11 percent, or eight inches at 40 yards!

Winchester's Blind Side waterfowl loads are in a class by themselves. First, the shot isn't round, it's hexahedronal — six-sided, or dice-shaped. This squared-off shape allows for less wasted space in the shell and, thus, a heavier payload. The wad is also a work of art, a full-length, one-piece unit that lacks separate petals. Just after exiting the muzzle, diamond-shaped plastic cutouts in the sides of the wad open like petals, acting as a brake for the wad and sending the shot string onward in a nice, dense, duck-killing pattern.

Classic .22 Semi-Auto Rifles
of the 20th Century, the 63 and the 1903

BY **C. Rodney James**

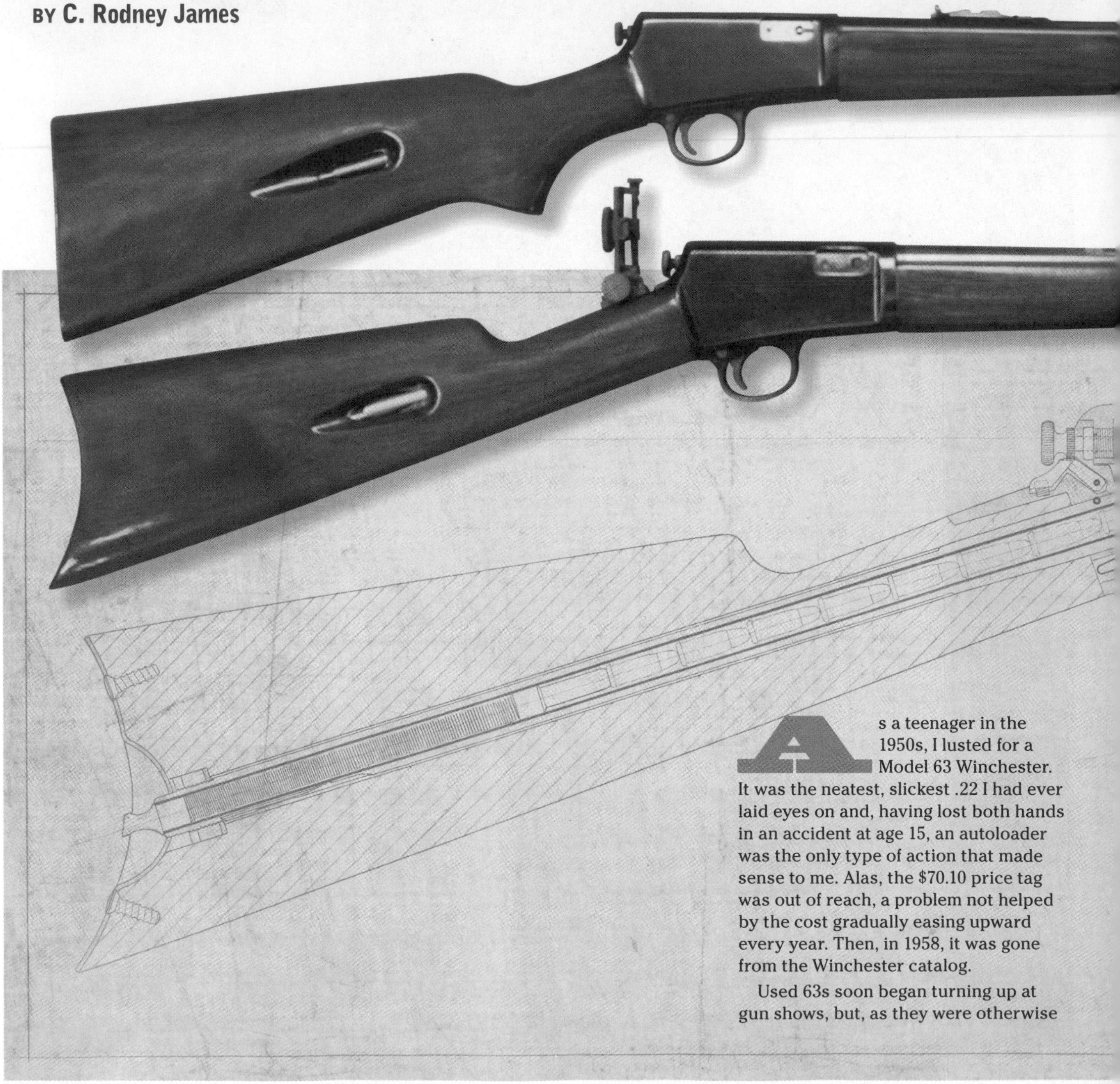

As a teenager in the 1950s, I lusted for a Model 63 Winchester. It was the neatest, slickest .22 I had ever laid eyes on and, having lost both hands in an accident at age 15, an autoloader was the only type of action that made sense to me. Alas, the $70.10 price tag was out of reach, a problem not helped by the cost gradually easing upward every year. Then, in 1958, it was gone from the Winchester catalog.

Used 63s soon began turning up at gun shows, but, as they were otherwise

ter's

*The Winchester
Repeating Arms Company
was the world's first
to create and market
an autoloading rifle.*

An original patent drawing for the
M-1903, dated 1901. The M-63 is
identical in all important aspects.

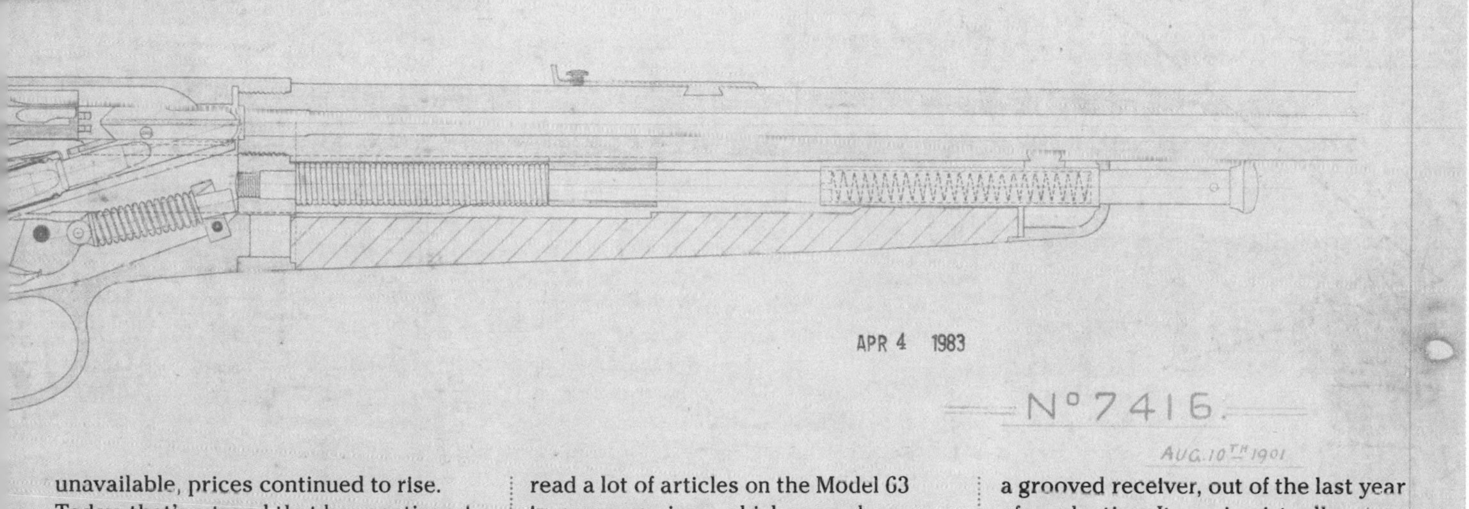

APR 4   1983

N° 7416.

AUG. 10TH 1901

SHEET-2

unavailable, prices continued to rise. Today, that's a trend that has continued on to levels approaching stratospheric, as collectors got heavily into the game.

I went through a bunch of autoloaders through the '50s and well into the '70s, looking for a full-sized .22 rifle that was accurate without being a bullet-chewer and a jammer. Now, total production of the 63s was under 200,000. None of my shooting buddies owned one, so I'd never had the opportunity to even try one. Still, there remained that itch to find out how well one actually shot. I'd

read a lot of articles on the Model 63 in gun magazines, which were always full of praise for the rifle—then again, they were full of praise for just about everything. In between those flowery sentences rhapsodizing on glowing walnut stocks, deep and lustrous blue finishes, and seamless wood-to-metal fit, I kept looking for function and accuracy data. This never got past "good" and "about 1½ inches" at 50 yards.

Flash forward to the age of geezerdom. A gun writer buddy was selling a friend's collection, and there it was, a 63 with

a grooved receiver, out of the last year of production. It was in virtually mint condition. The price he quoted as "a bargain," $1,000, verged on astonishing to my mind, but the old lust overcame the sticker shock with the rationalization that I could likely get my money back in a resale if I didn't like it.

The Winchester Repeating Arms Company was the world's first to create and market an autoloading rifle. Plans for autoloaders dated from the 1890s. Things came apart, however, when the relationship between Winchester and

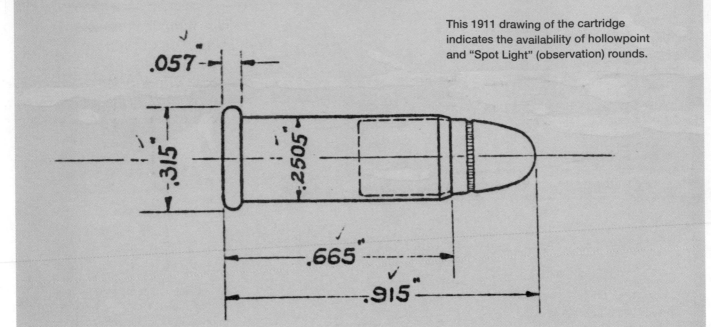

MAX. SIZES.

This 1911 drawing of the cartridge indicates the availability of hollowpoint and "Spot Light" (observation) rounds.

John Browning ended with Winchester's refusal to pay royalties on a per-gun basis and Browning decamping to Belgium.

Designing autoloaders that didn't infringe on Browning's patents (as written by Winchester before the breakup), fell to Thomas Crossly Johnson, Winchester's top in-house engineer. Johnson proved up to the job, with his creation of the Model 1903. Using a proven spring-

T.C. Johnson, the designer of the M-03 and M-63, among other successful and popular Winchester rifles and shotguns.

balanced technology that had worked in low-powered handguns, the Model 1903 featured a proprietary cartridge, the .22 Winchester Automatic. It was loaded with smokeless powder to ensure minimal fouling, and had an inside-lubricated bullet set deep in a cartridge that would move smoothly through a tubular magazine in the rear stock. This latter was also a proven system dating from the Civil War Spencer rifle.

The blowback system has been the basis for every .22 autoloading rifle for more than 100 years. While Winchester management undoubtedly wished to chamber the new autoloader in the popular .22 LR caliber, it knew that, in spite of clear instructions not to, users would fire blackpowder and semi-smokeless ammunition in their rifles, then complain (bitterly) when their '03s gummed up after a magazine's worth of cartridges.

The nifty little '03 rifle quickly became popular as a small-game "snapshooting" rifle—just the thing with which one could pick off a squirrel from a tree branch, stop a running rabbit, or nail a woodchuck heading for his hole. Because of the easy, two-piece takedown of the rifle, accomplished by the removal of a single screw in the receiver, the compact '03 (overall 36½ inches, 20-inch barrel, 1:14 twist, 5½ pounds), also gained favor with trappers and wilderness hunters as a handy camp rifle. Cocking and loading worked from a simple pull and release on

the plunger under the barrel. It offered a nearly instant followup shot without the shooter losing his sight picture during the operation of a more manual feeding action. To quote the advertising for the Savage automatic pistol of that same era, "10 shots quick!"

The '03 became an instant favorite with Winchester's top exhibition shooter, Adolph Topperwein. Topperwein, who had begun his professional career as a cartoonist, created, as part of his act, the art of "bullet drawing"—hammering out 450 .22-caliber 45-grain slugs to create dot by dot images of Buffalo Bill, an Indian chief in full war bonnet, and other popular characters of the day. He also laid down the gauntlet (as it were), shooting at 72,500 2½-inch wooden blocks thrown 30 feet in the air, with only nine misses. This 1907 record stood for more than 50 years.

The original 45-grain bullet had a velocity of 950 fps. It was quiet and would penetrate far more deeply than the softer, lighter .22 Long Rifle (see Table 1). It was offered in a hollowpoint and an explosive "Spot Light" round. In the early 1930s, velocity was stepped up to 1,050 fps. Gun writer Henry Stebbins described the '03's ability for killing dangerous game with head shots, quoting a New York sporting goods dealer talking about taking a young bull moose, "I shot him in the forehead and I don't think he even heard the gun go off."[1]

An '03 becomes the talisman of Jack Pathurst, tough guy novelist in Jack London's ripping 1914 yarn of the sea, *The Mutiny of the Elsinore*. Pathurst rescues the beautiful captain's daughter, Margaret West, using his trusty Winchester to hold a gang of mutinous cutthroats at bay. (The book was made into a film twice, in 1920 and, again, in 1939.)

The '03 was officially made until 1932. A "clean-up" of parts produced additional rifles to 1936, with a total production of 114,962. Improvements in rimfire ammunition from non-corrosive priming and high-speed loadings (introduced in 1930), gave impetus to converting the '03 from its Winchester .22 Automatic cartridge to .22 Long Rifle. There are no records as to who was in charge of this operation, though T.C. Johnson likely made it one of his final projects. Johnson held 124 patents, started work in 1885, and remained at his post until his death, in 1934, a company man to the end.

The improved Model 1903 was dubbed the Model 63 and came on the market in 1934. The original 20-inch barrel was replaced by a heavier 23-inch barrel, in 1936. In spite of the Great Depression, the rifle achieved rapid fame as the highest quality (and most expensive), .22 autoloader on the market. This status remained until 1958, when it was replaced with a series of—well, perhaps the word "junk" is a little too caustic for some, but it pretty well sums up the autoloaders that followed.

Production of the 63 totaled 174,692, not counting some later runs made for Winchester in Japan (they had a bunny engraved on the receiver), and knockoffs made by Taurus. The Model 63 was the last forged steel, machined parts, high-grade, walnut-stocked, smallbore autoloader.

Unable to afford a model 63, I once found a 1903 at a gun show that was in nice shape and had a reasonable price. I figured this was about as close to the 63 as I would ever get. The ammunition for the '03 got discontinued about five minutes after I bought the rifle, so I began a sweep through old-time gun and hardware stores, acquiring what I could stockpile before the collectors got there.

For the '03, the ammunition choice is expensive (thank you, Mr. Collector). The .22 Win. Auto ammo was discontinued around 1980. I believe Remington was the last supplier. If you can find some at a reasonable price, be sure to get the non-corrosive product. About 10 years ago, The Old Western Scrounger cut a deal with Industrias Tecnos, of Mexico, for a special run of this ammunition. The headstamp is "OWS" for Old Western Scrounger. OWS was recently bought by Navy Arms/Gibbs Rifle Co., and the most recent information I received is that an additional production run is on the way. We hope so! Collector boxes of this stuff are going for about $50. The previous run sold for around $13. The current run I was told will be "under $20 a box." In all my scrounging, I have yet to find even a partial box of hollowpoints, let alone Spot Light.

When it comes to fodder for the Model 63, the good news is that it's .22 Long Rifle. The not so good news is you will

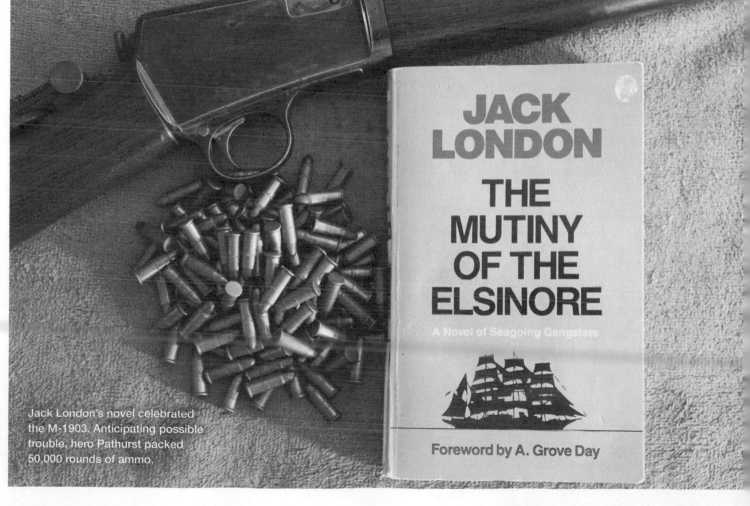

Jack London's novel celebrated the M-1903. Anticipating possible trouble, hero Pathurst packed 50,000 rounds of ammo.

JACK LONDON

THE MUTINY OF THE ELSINORE

A Novel of Seagoing Gangsters

Foreword by A. Grove Day

WESTERN RIFLE CARTRIDGES—SPECIFICATIONS AND BALLISTICS

The following tables represent standard velocity, energy, and trajectory figures as adopted by the Sporting Arms and Ammunition Manufacturers' Institute.

ALL CARTRIDGES LOADED WITH SMOKELESS POWDER

LOAD No.	PRIMER No.	CARTRIDGE	Wgt. Grs.	BULLET Type	Muzzle	VELOCITY 100 Yds.	200 Yds.	300 Yds.	ENERGY Muzzle	100 Yds.	200 Yds.	300 Yds.	MID-RANGE TRAJECTORY 100 Yds.	200 Yds.	300 Yds
K1201R	.....	B.B. CAP	18	Lubaloy	780	570	.....	.....	24	13	.....	.....	.....	.....	
K1202R	.....	C. B. CAP Greased	29	Lubaloy	720	605	.....	.....	33	24	.....	.....	.....	.....	
K1211R	.....	22 Short KANT-SPLASH Greased	26	Synthetic	970	.....	.....	.....	.....	.....	.....	.....	.....		
K1208R	.....	22 Short SUPER-X Wax Coated	29	Lubaloy	1,130	925	.....	.....	82	55	.....	.....	4.1	.....	
K1209R	.....	22 Short H.P. SUPER-X Wax Coated	27	Lubaloy	1,155	925	.....	.....	80	51	.....	.....	4.1	.....	
K1262R	.....	22 Short XPERT Greased	29	Lead	1,030	860	.....	.....	68	48	.....	.....	5.1	.....	
K1216R	.....	22 Long SUPER-X Wax Coated	29	Lubaloy	1,275	1,020	.....	.....	122	67	.....	.....	3.2	.....	
K1225R	.....	22 Long Rifle SUPER-X Wax Coated	40	Lubaloy	1,375	1,080	.....	.....	168	104	.....	.....	2.9	.....	
K1226R	.....	22 Long Rifle H.P. SUPER-X Wax Coated	37	Lubaloy	1,400	1,075	.....	.....	161	95	.....	.....	3.0	.....	
K1268R	.....	22 Long Rifle Shot SUPER-X		No. 12 Shot	.....	.....	.....	.....	.....	.....	.....	.....	.....	.....	
K1264R	.....	22 Long Rifle XPERT Greased	40	Lead	1,180	995	.....	.....	124	88	.....	.....	3.8	.....	
K1267R	.....	22 Long Rifle SUPER-MATCH MARK II Gr.	40	Lead	1,160	985	.....	.....	120	86	.....	.....	3.8	.....	
K1234R	.....	22 W.R.F. (22 Rem. Spl.) SUPER-X In. Lub.	45	Lubaloy	1,450	1,110	.....	.....	210	123	.....	.....	2.7	.....	
K1236R	.....	22 Winchester Automatic Inside Lub.	45	Lubaloy	1,055	930	.....	.....	111	86	.....	.....	4.6	.....	..

Page Fifty-five

Ammunition handbooks from the 1930s and '40s listed the .22 LR high-speed cartridge at a much higher velocity than in later years. Loads were toned down in the '50s, again in the 1980s.

need to figure out what will work in your gun. Here's a little history lesson.

The Model 63 was designed for Winchester/Western Super Speed and Super-X Long Rifle; it's stamped right there on the barrel. The first high-speed LR ammunition came out in 1930. A look at those old ammunition handbooks and listing ballistic data, and you'll find the 40-grain high-speed LR solid listed at 1,375 fps and the 37-grain hollowpoint at 1,400!

Did they really go that fast? I put this question to an engineer/representative of a major ammunition company. He prefaced his remarks with something about bovine manure, which he tempered with statements regarding advertising, pointing out that the methods of measuring bullet velocities were nowhere near as precise then as they are now. Furthermore, about 25 years ago, U.S. ammunition companies made an agreement, supported by SAAMI, to standardize the velocities of high-speed .22 LR ammunition at 1,235 fps for the 40-grain solid, and 1,260 fps for the 36-grain hollowpoint. Some years ago, I chronographed Super-X 40-grain ammunition dating from the 1930s, 1960s, and 1990s. The averages were 1,269, 1,236, and 1,184 fps, respectively.

While the early claims don't hold up, there is a difference. When I tried some of the old pre-1941 Super-X in my M-63, it ran and grouped quite well, with the exception of one squib and one burst head. Still, not bad for 75- to 80-year-old ammunition stored in unknown conditions. A current box of Super-X had one stoppage from an under-loaded cartridge. A similar experience occurred with current Remington high-velocity hollowpoints. Expect variations from lot to lot of ammunition, and also rifle to rifle. I have read of some 63s working with standard velocity ammo.[2]

For functional reliability, the heavy recoil spring of the M-63 does best with the faster product. I experienced no stoppages with Winchester Power Point, CCI Velocitor, or Stinger (the Stingers ran perfectly). Interestingly, some Remington Pistol Match functioned without a hitch. The Stingers turned in good groups despite a good breeze; these were from an exceptionally good lot. See Table 2.

The Model 63 is an excellent rifle once you get to know it. The tubular magazine is easy to load and also quick when you get used to it. The feeding mechanism is precise and gentle. There is no bullet damage, the bane of so many, many .22 LR autoloaders and devastating to accuracy.

The Model 63 is clearly marked for use with high-velocity ammunition.

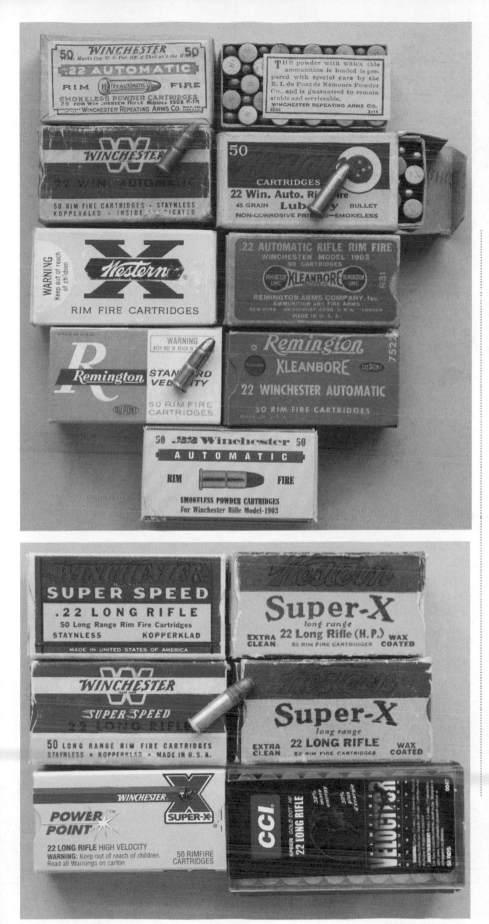

Ammunition for the Model 1903 is hard to find. The top dates from about 1915 and is both highly collectable and very corrosive. Various designs from the 1930s on down contain shootable, non-corrosive ammunition. Beware of loose ammo. Copper-colored cases may or may not be non-corrosive. Those with copper-plated bullets are okay, but plain lead is a maybe. If the report is very soft, expect corrosive priming and clean accordingly. OWS (bottom) is the only current product.

A really slick feature is the rifle's single-shot, drop-in loading. Open the bolt, drop in a cartridge, release the plunger under the barrel, and the cartridge is chambered without a scratch. The trigger pull is heavy, about 5¼ pounds. The let-off, though, is crisp, so the combination is something to get used to. The rifle is, according to a number of owners and users, including former *Gun Digest* editor Ken Warner and Brett Boyd, editor of *The Single Shot Exchange* magazine, one of the best balanced, nicest handling rifles ever.

The takedown of the rifle, as it is with the Model 1903, occurs by removing the takedown screw at the rear of the receiver. The two halves are then separated by hinging them apart, much like opening a break-open shotgun. Locking the bolt open is done by pressing the operating plunger under the barrel, then turning the end-cap to the right a quarter turn to lock it. With pressure from the heavy recoil spring, though, this is nearly impossible. I discovered that less skin and fewer tears are shed by opening the action and inserting a small piece of softwood (maybe 1⅛-inch wide) into the ejection port to hold the bolt open. With the pressure thus relieved, turning the plunger to the right to lock it open is relatively easy.

The rifle must be cleaned from the muzzle. This should be done with a plastic-coated rod. After studying the many pages and photos in the disassembly/assembly book from the publisher of the book you are reading, my advice is to stop here, unless you possess the skills and tools of a gunsmith. Here's why.

The old Super-X and Super Speed Long Rifle were hotter than our current loads. If they're in good condition, they work fine. Unfortunately, collectors are after this stuff, too. Velocitor and Power Point equal or better the earlier velocity performance.

Takedown is relatively easy. Use of a 1 1/8- by ¼-inch piece of softwood makes it easier to lock open the 63.

Both the '03 and 63 have the same tubular magazine in the stock, with a small locking lug that locks the tube securely with a slight turn to the right. Loading is through the port in the stock.

The plunger operating sleeve spring serves to stop plunger rattle and isn't really necessary to function. If you try to remove it, you will likely wreck it trying to get it back in. A heavier, shorter spring placed too much pressure on the fore-end tip, making it very difficult to reattach. You have been warned.

TABLE 1.

Comparative penetration in ½-inch pine plywood at 25 yards with no spaces between slabs. Rifles: Winchester M-52 .22 LR, Winchester M-1903 .22 Winchester Auto.

RIFLE	LOAD	PENETRATION
M-52	CCI Mini Mag	2.2"
	Ccl Mini Mag HP	1.8"
	CCI Stinger	1.5"
	Remington HV	1.9"
	Remington Viper	1.9"
	Western Super-X	1.7"
	Western Super-X HP	1.8"
M-1903	Winchester Auto RP	2.7"
	Remington Win. Auto	1.3"

Note: The round-point M-1903 bullet shows little expansion, while the flat-point style will expand in a hard target such as wood.

TABLE 2.

Accuracy of various .22 LR ammunition at 50 yards. Rifle: Winchester M-63 with a Burris 4X Mini scope. Two-point sandbag rest, three five-shot groups.

LOAD	GROUP 1	GROUP 2	GROUP 3	AVERAGE
Remington Pistol Match	1.4"	1.3"	0.5"	1.0"
Remington HV HP	1.0"	1.6"	0.9"	1.1"
CCI Velocitor HP	1.3"	1.5"	2.1"	1.6"
CCI Mini Mag HP	1.5"	2.0"	1.9"	1.8"
CCI Stinger HP	1.6"	1.5"	0.5"	1.2"
W/W Super-X HP (ca 1930-40)	1.3"	1.0"	1.0"	1.1"
W/W Super-X HP(current)	1.6"	1.9"	1.6"	1.7"
W/W Power Point HP	1.4"	1.4"	1.1"	1.3"

Overall average for 120 shots 1.35".

Note: The Pistol Match was tried, since similar ammunition performed well in semi-auto rifles. It did so here, as well. This is a hunting rifle, so I saw little point in testing solids, which are pretty useless for anything other than practice.

M-1903 Rifle, tang peep sight, 50 yards, same conditions.

OWS (Old Western Scrounger)

22 Winchester Automatic	2.2"	2.5"	2.9"	

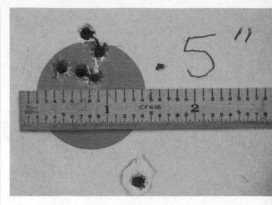

When the wind dropped, groups closed up, as did these five Stingers.

Within the hollow tube of the operating plunger is a very thin and soft coil spring. Removing the plunger releases this spring. Getting the spring back in, in its original and intended shape, is close to impossible. The spring in mine was bent into uselessness. Fortunately, the only function of this spring is to place slight, forward pressure on the plunger to keep it from rattling. The spring in my '03 disappeared long ago, and the plunger rattles a bit. Minus this spring, my 63 actually doesn't rattle and is also otherwise fine.

Aside from the plunger spring, a previous amateur gun plumber had reinserted the firing pin upside down. This broke it and also burred the chamber. New pin, burr removed, no problem. Will dry firing with the pin in the proper position burr the chamber? I don't know and I'm not about to experiment. Count your shots.

To de-cock the rifle, pull the plunger, moving the bolt fully to the rear. Allow the bolt to move forward a quarter-inch by pulling the trigger. When you hear a click, indicating release of the sear, allow the bolt to go fully forward. The spring is released.

To conclude, I have owned and shot a few autoloaders that were equally reliable, perhaps two that were gentle with ammunition, and one that is a shade more accurate. The Model 63 was built to last—no sintered metal, no alloys, no plastic (except the fore-end tip on the last version). In the final analysis, the M-63 possesses that element best summed up in the word "class."

FOOTNOTES:

[1] Henry Stebbins, *Small Game and Varmint Rifles*, A.S. Barnes 1947, p 11.

[2] Henry Stebbins, *Rifles A Modern Encyclopedia*, The Stackpole Company, 1958, p. 57-58.

The .500 Nitro Express
is enjoying a revival,
thanks, in part, to
Norma's fine PH ammo.

The
norma
Story

BY **Wayne van Zwoll**

**Renowned for
Weatherby ammo
and best-quality
brass, Sweden's
famous firm is
fielding some
exciting new loads.**

oose are easy to hide, you just need a big place.

Like Scandinavian forest. We'd not seen many moose. On the third day, an old-fashioned drive launched one bull ahead of the beaters. He galloped from thick conifers into a logged block that left him exposed for 300 yards. Mistake. Two riflemen, firing from stands proven by a decade of drives, tagged the big animal.

"Retrieving a moose in this terrain is hard work," said Kenneth, one of my Swedish hosts. "So we have a machine."

The tracked vehicle has no operator platform, rather a long hand-bar, such as on a small forklift, affords steering. A four-cycle engine, scarcely bigger than a lawn mower's, powers the tracks. Expertly, Kenneth maneuvered the machine off its trailer, then led it, a low-geared mechanical dog, over rocks, logs, and hummocks and through logging trash and willow clumps. It crawled up vertical mud. Only when a track met a rain-slick upright stump did Kenneth have to reverse it and snake the device around the obstacle.

The moose lay in a swale. Its coat had great chunks torn from it, the hair lying all about.

Established in 1895, Norma didn't build a factory until 1911. World War II boosted its fortunes.

"The dog gets its reward," explained Amund, Kenneth's son. His Norwegian elkhound had the shape, color, and features of a husky, but a trimmer profile. Released during a drive or by a handler hunting an area alone, the dog, working singly or, at most, as one of a pair to cover more ground, canvases the forest for scent. "It will try to pick up scent in the air," said Amund. "But these dogs can also ground-trail." When one spots a moose, it barks. The moose usually isn't much concerned and will often stand. The hunter/handler then moves in. If the

Floor to ceiling, Norma's Åmotfor's plant is clean and technologically advanced.

moose sees, hears, or smells the man, it will run off. On drives, the handler may barge ahead, pushing the moose toward standers. Hunting alone with a dog, he sneaks towards the moose for the shot.

After some wrestling, with help from a winch on the machine, we pulled the carcass onto the machine's steel platform, where the weight would add traction. Long legs dragged behind as the seat-less ATV chugged up the brushy hill, saving us many arduous trips with backpacks.

Moose populations have declined in much of Sweden over the last couple decades. Wolves, once hunted to near extermination, are now protected. "Some foresters would like to see still fewer moose," Kenneth told me, "even where tree damage is negligible." Moose quotas include cows and calves, though some hunters decline shots at cows. When a hunter sees a cow with a calf, he is expected to kill the calf first, taking cows only when unaccompanied by young.

Though hunting tactics and traditions in Scandinavia differ from those in North America, makers of hunting ammunition have many of the same goals. Indeed, Norma, Sweden's premier ammo firm, has had a foot in both markets since it began manufacturing Weatherby's cartridges more than 50 years ago.

"It's from an opera by Bellini," explained Torbjörn Lindskog. He is speaking of the Norma name. It dates to the company's birth, in 1895. Seven years later, the workforce was still just one employee tending two machines in a modest ammunition shop in Åmotfors.

By 1906, the cords binding Norway and Sweden had unraveled. Norway's bonanza in offshore oil was still decades from discovery, and the country had little wealth. Sweden, however, soon succeeded with various industries. In 1911, Norma built a factory. During subsequent decades, the firm prospered, its fortunes enhanced by World War II. New structures grew up around the plant. In 1940, the company added 10 buildings, and, two years later, Norma's workforce had grown to 800.

"Nils Kavle exploited strong demand for munitions," recalled Torbjörn, now the firm's CEO. "But not until 1950 did Norma export hunting cartridges."

Following the predictable post-war sag in military orders, Norma cultivated the sporting market. By 1965, it had 420 employees on the payroll, producing more than 40 million cartridges. The next year, 530 people punched in at the Åmotfors plant, rolling out 64 million rounds.

In 1975, Hasselfors Burks AB bought Norma, and, four years later, the company became a subsidiary of FFV. In 1990, ownership was assumed by Dynamit Nobel AG. Production slowed, and by the mid-1990s the payroll had been reduced to 175 workers. Concurrently, automation was boosting efficiency. At century's end, 135 employees were turning out 25 million cartridges, plus an equal number of cases and bullets. Then, in 2002, RUAG of Switzerland assumed control of Norma. Production reached 23 million cartridges in 70 chamberings. A decade later, output topped 30 million rounds in 106 different chamberings!

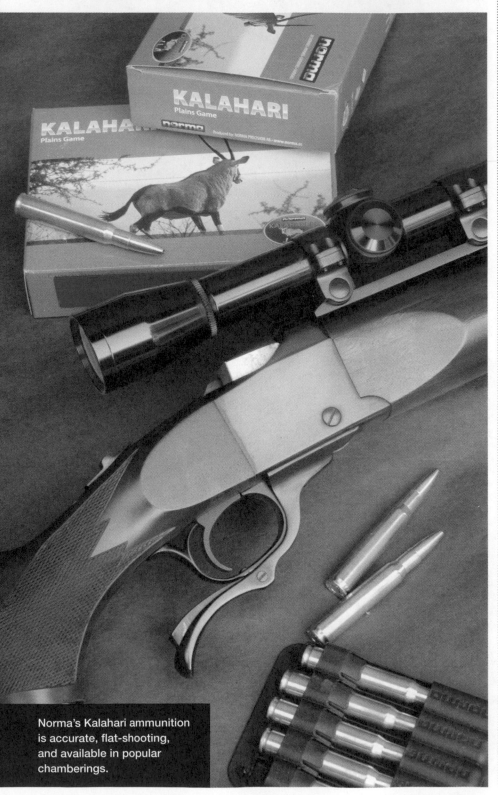

Norma's Kalahari ammunition is accurate, flat-shooting, and available in popular chamberings.

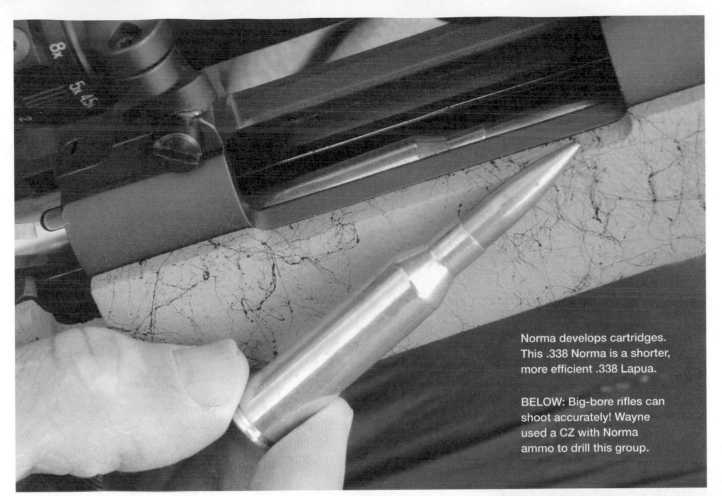

Norma develops cartridges. This .338 Norma is a shorter, more efficient .338 Lapua.

BELOW: Big-bore rifles can shoot accurately! Wayne used a CZ with Norma ammo to drill this group.

In an interview with Torbjörn a few years ago, I found that, excluding Finland, Norma owned 70 percent of the ammunition market in Scandinavia. It served 30 percent of the European market, mainly in France, Germany, and Spain. A quarter of its annual production stayed in Sweden, and another 25 percent landed in the U.S. Just over half was hunting ammo, while about 17 percent went to target shooters. Then, Norma's catalog listed 275 loads in chamberings from .223 to .470 Nitro Express. Rimfire ammo sales accounted for just two percent of revenues. A line of pistol ammunition had been all but dropped to keep focus on rifle ammo and Norma's own bullets. Jörgen Sandström, now in charge of sales, tells me those figures have changed little, but that Norma has strengthened marketing efforts Stateside and vigorously pursues development of so-called niche products, those bullets and ammunition for specific purposes and customers.

Torbjörn has told me that some rifle rounds are quite difficult to manufacture.

"The 7x57R, for example. But it sells well. A lot of Swedish hunters use it in drillings. Another rimmed cartridge, the .303 British, is costly to make. Still, the SMLE is a famous rifle; many survive in countries that buy from us."

In Scandinavia, the 6.5x55 has long been the firm's best-selling cartridge. It is required for rifle competition there, and it's the most popular Swedish hunting cartridge. But demand for this round has been diluted, of late, by popular U.S. cartridges. Two Swedes accompanying me on a moose hunt I attended last fall carried rifles in .338 and .300 Winchester. As in North America, the shooting public in northern Europe is aging, which means it is shooting less.

"Our average customer is 58 years old," Torb told me.

In 1975, Norma manufactured 11 million 6.5x55 rounds for target shooting alone. Though the factory can produce 75,000 cases per shift, demand for target ammo won't now absorb that level of output. Norma still delivers 25 million rounds of target ammunition each year, twice as much as RWS or Lapua. By way of comparison, Winchester, Remington, and Federal each sell between 120 and 160 million target rounds annually.

Norma's PH ammunition fuels rifles like Wayne's CZ 550 Magnum in .416 Rigby.

buys .338 Lapua sniper cartridges from Norma. Research and development under Christer Larsson and Don Heath bring a steady stream of new loads to hunters. Barnes, Hornady, Nosler, Swift, and Woodleigh supply millions of hunting bullets for Norma's own ammunition and for that branded by Weatherby.

"One of our most important corporate relationships began in the 1940s, with Roy Weatherby," said Torbjörn. Currently, Norma produces more than 70 loads in 13 chamberings for Weatherby. A more recent, equally important partnership between Norma and Nosler put the Partition, Ballistic Tip, and AccuBond bullets in Norma's catalog, along with the superb Swift A-Frame and Scirocco and the Barnes TSX.

Norma's own bullets include the Vulkan, introduced in 1980. The jacket of this easily upset deer bullet is inverted over a slight depression at the tip. The Alaska, a traditional soft-nose with lots of lead exposed, dates to the 1940s and comes in diameters .264 to .366. Use it for medium-size game at modest ranges. Ditto Norma's Soft Point, which is a bit more streamlined and listed for .22- to .30-caliber rounds. Norma Plastic Tip bullets have a polymer ball, not a pointed insert, up front. Evidently the ball's main purpose is to protect the bullet from deformation. For elk, moose, and big bears, Norma once had a TXP dual-core bullet that, in cross section, resembled the Nosler Partition, but had a bonded front core; the Oryx has supplanted it. This bonded-core bullet has much in common with Federal's fine Trophy Bonded. I've used it on several tough animals, with excellent results. Weight retention often exceeds 90 percent.

Norma uses Bofors powders, under the Normal labels of 200, 201, 203B, 204, MRP, MRP2, and URP. There's also Norma Match 1211 and 1214. About 80 percent of primers in the company's ammo come from RWS, with some from Hirtenberger and Federal.

"The Federal 215 is especially good in big cases with slow powders," Torbjörn noted. "Weatherby specifies the Hirtenberger 1204."

Besides adding modern American cartridges like the .300 WSM to its ammunition stable, Norma has launched special lines, most notably the PH. The Professional Hunter series features Woodleigh solid and soft-nose bullets in 12 classic and contemporary safari rounds: .375 Flanged, .375 H&H, .404 Jeffery, .416 Remington, .416 Rigby, .500/416

Built in 1967, Norma's main plant has been continually updated. But, as recently as a decade ago, many of Norma's 6.5x55 match cartridges came off a 1928 machine loading 210 rounds a minute. Still, this hardware yields fine ammunition.

"Quality control is key," says Jörgen. International rifle champions—from Switzerland, Norway, Slovenia, and elsewhere, as well as from Sweden—favor Norma cartridges. At one CISM World Championships, Norma 6mm BR ammo

claimed 11 of the 12 top medals!

The care lavished on target ammo is not forsaken in hunting cartridges. Norma buys its raw material from the best sources—Diehl for brass and copper, Sala Bly and SM for lead—and components from RWS and Bofors to assemble ammunition world-renowned for its uniformity. Norma has filled OEM contracts for 14 well-known companies, including Dakota, Federal, Winchester, Weatherby, RWS, Blaser, Sako, CorBon, and Hirtenberger. The Dutch Army

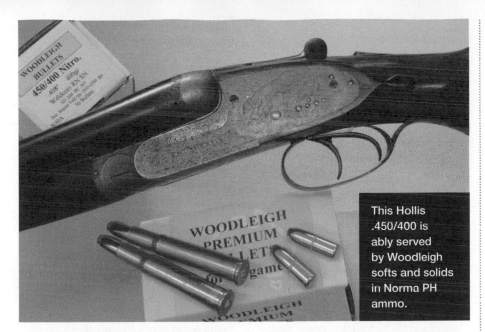

This Hollis .450/400 is ably served by Woodleigh softs and solids in Norma PH ammo.

NE, .450 Rigby, .458 Lott, .470 NE, .500 Jeffery, .500 NE, and .505 Gibbs. Those intended for double rifles are loaded to traditional pressures and velocities. Woodleigh bullets are acknowledged as being among the best available for heavy game. I used a Woodleigh solid in a PH load to shoot an elephant a few seasons back. The .375 bullet struck between the eyes and came to rest in the animal's flank. You'll also find Norma's own solid (brass) bullets, outside the PH line, loaded in most of these chamberings, plus 9.3x62, .416 Taylor, and .458 Winchester.

Most recently, Norma has trotted out its Kalahari cartridges, with a new, solid-copper, tapered-heel hollowpoint whose nose is scored to encourage fragmenting. The shank is designed to shatter bones, and penetrate to leave a blood trail. Treated with a proprietary coating to reduce fouling, flat-flying Kalahari bullets appear only in specially labeled Norma ammunition in .270 Winchester, .270 WSM, 7x64, .280, 7mm Remington Magnum, .308, .30-06, .300 Winchester Magnum, and .300 WSM. Those I've fired from the bench have turned in exceptional accuracy, like the Norma rounds I packed to Norway years ago … .

Climbing above treeline 100 miles from the fjords, we hunted to 4,500 feet, a couple thousand feet above the valley floors. Water from snow melt and springs glistened in silver ropes over smooth, gray rocks. The strands converged into thundering falls that cascaded into rolling green pastures below, where shepherd cottages of mustard-hue and the ubiquitous Swedish-red would be buried in winter. By October, the sheep would be trucked out, leaving the reindeer.

The first day of our hunt delivered freezing fog, then a bitter wind that, oddly enough, didn't clear it. We couldn't glass. My hosts boiled coffee on a fire started with pitch pine from their backpacks. They laughed at jokes told in a language I didn't know. It was a long day.

The next morning, we awoke to cobalt skies and a bright sun that made wet heather sparkle. Not long into our climb, we spied a group of reindeer with one fine bull. I scrambled to a rise and readied the Sako. But the wind betrayed us, and they fled. At 400 yards, they paused. I thought the range too great.

Luck was with us, though, because shortly we spotted another group high on a rim. At Kenneth's urging, I crossed a broad valley, then struggled up a headwall. The animals were on the move by the time I saw them again, but I'd made the correct call, angling windward. The front of the herd passed through my scope field at 80 yards, the bull protected by other bodies. When, briefly, this river of reindeer parted, I swung the .30-06 and fired. The bull crumpled.

Visit Norma's spotless factory floor, and you'll find a curious mix of wartime presses chugging smoothly in the shadow of CNC machines. Norma buys cups from which to make most of its cartridge cases, but it imports discs for magnums.

"There are two draws after the initial cup," Torbjörn bellowed over the hum and clang of the machines during my tour last autumn. "Then we anneal the brass, draw it a third time, trim, prepunch the primer pocket to ensure the strength of the head, and send it to the header, which cuts an extractor groove. Necking comes next, then the flash-hole finishing." Some holes at Norma are punched, some drilled.

The factory's loading room likewise complements new technology, with lovely old machines that still deliver uniform, accurate cartridges to be buffed and boxed like so many gems. Together, the loading machines hold no more than 20 kilograms of powder—44 pounds. Propellant storage is in the ceiling, with drop tubes feeding the machines.

"Lapua had a serious fire, in 1977," explained an engineer. "We've isolated the powder magazine from the workers. A fire here would be survivable."

Any visit to Norma must include the shooting tunnels, which boast the latest

Kenneth Skoglund (left), huntmaster, marksman, and ammo guru, chats with a colleague afield.

Don Heath, formerly a Zimbabwe PH, brings years of field experience to Norma R&D.

Wayne killed this bull with a Norma Oryx from a Krieghoff double in .375 Flanged.

electronic ballistic equipment. Twenty firing points span 30-, 50-, and two 100-yard ranges. Pelleted rubber aprons allow for bullet recovery. To measure penetration, Norma uses gelatin.

Then there's the gun vault. It's really a huge underground chamber chock full of firearms, many of which you'll find nowhere else.

"We need at least one rifle for each chambering, of course," Christer Larsson once pointed out.

The wall racks hold more than 200 rifles, many discontinued, and some in such condition as to drive a collector mad. Military weapons include Broom-handle Mauser pistols, Thompson sub-machine guns, plus items in truly short supply these days, like a Navy M-16.

Norma remains an unusual company, a major munitions firm nestled in the forest and staffed by people of rural heritage. It draws its own brass, but loads American rounds with American bullets for sale in America and gets a 20-percent subsidy from the Swedish government for capital investment. Norma's name is known to every shooting enthusiast Stateside and is highly regarded by them. The only fly in this ointment: Norma ammunition and propellants have not always been readily available.

"That's a situation we hope to correct," said Marketing Director Lennart Falk. Clearing the path of marketing roadblocks remains a top priority at Norma. "We're committed to improving the flow of product to the U.S." Torbjörn, who's well read and fond of pithy truisms, told me, "Chesty Puller once said that paperwork will ruin an army. He was right."

Torbjörn Lindskög's plan is to retire in 2013. He has proven himself a far-sighted and capable executive at Norma.

"Our fortunes depend on the international economy," he emphasized, when last we talked, "and on who controls Norma. We're in the dream business. People want what we make, but few

Norma Man

Like many long-time Norma employees, Kenneth Skoglund is a keen shooter. Norwegian-born and still living in Norway a short drive from Åmotfors, Kenneth was 15 years on his country's Olympic team in running boar events. He competes with fellow Scandinavians in local running moose matches and was among the first shooters to try two post reticles to build in lead with standard-velocity rounds, rather than employ a single reticle with high-speed cartridges. He has used a Mauser M59 in 6.5x55—the original smokeless round for the Swedish military.

"For 300-meter shooting, I like a 130-grain VLD load at 800 meters per second (about 2,600 fps). It bucks the wind better than most 7.62 (.308) bullets. For unknown distances from 150 to 600 meters, I prefer a 130-grain bullet at 900 meters per second."

In that event, each of 20 shooters on the team fires from prone and kneeling. Running moose matches are popular, partly because they satisfy government requirements for practice.

"To get a hunting license in Norway, you must fire at least 15 shots in training each year, then qualify with a five-shot group in a 25-centimeter circle (about 10 inches) from any position."

A Norma machinist before taking on his sales job, Kenneth grew up on a small farm, helping his father log with horses. He now owns 200 acres of forest, part of a 1,250-acre hunting preserve managed for moose. Though he still favors the 6.5x55 for competition and has good things to say about the .30-06, he has turned to the .338 Winchester Magnum for most of his big game hunting.

customers need it. Our first task is to keep their dreams alive."

The distant barking rang hollow over the lake. Amund and I hurried through the forest toward it. The last quarter mile, we throttled our step; the litter made fast travel noisy. But we couldn't count on the bull standing much longer, and the afternoon was slipping away.

Amund at my shoulder, I closed to within 50 steps, then straightened from my stoop, bringing the rifle up alongside the spruce shielding me. The thick conifers revealed nothing. But even big animals escape notice when still. I didn't dare raise the binocular. Then, like a picture puzzle that suddenly makes sense, an ear twitched. A cow was looking me in the eye! More detail—that patch of young conifers, no bigger than a parking spot, held four moose! The biomass shifted. A paddle blinked through a slit. The bull's neck vanished, when my red dot bounced in recoil. Mayhem! The drum roll of hoof beats faded quickly, as I dashed forward over windfall. The bull lay quiet, felled by the Norma soft-nose from a borrowed Krieghoff double in .375 Flanged.

The CIP

The CIP, or Commission Internationale Permanente pour l'Epreuve des Armes, was founded, in 1916, in Belgium, to regulate rifle manufacture. This organization also sets ammunition standards for its 14 member countries.

"Sweden is not a member," said Karl-Erik Backman, who has supervised Norma's quality assurance operations. "But we must have CIP approval to export to member countries." He added that Weatherby specifies its own pressure ceilings. The energetic performance of those cartridges is due partly to their design, but also to the strength of the Mark V action. "Of course, cartridges that might be used in old military rifles can't be loaded so ambitiously." CIP conducts firearms and ammunition proof tests at its own facilities.

The CIP's counterpart in the U.S. is SAAMI, or the Sporting Arms and Ammunition Manufacturers Institute. Cartridge dimensions and pressures are official, when SAAMI nods.

Rifles influence pressures.

"In the 1990s, some 7mm Remington Magnum rifles with three-degree throats showed signs of excessive pressure," Karl-Eric recalled. "So we had to ease back on the loads." Such events can trigger long-lasting changes in manufacture. Some improve the ammunition. "Our job is to produce safe, uniform ammunition—but efficiently," he said. "We try to limit scrap to three percent for cases and bullets, one percent for cartridges."

Norma has loaded Weatherby ammunition for decades. Wayne shot this with an old Mark V.

THE .357 M

A Twentieth Century Handgun and Cartridge

BY Frank W. James

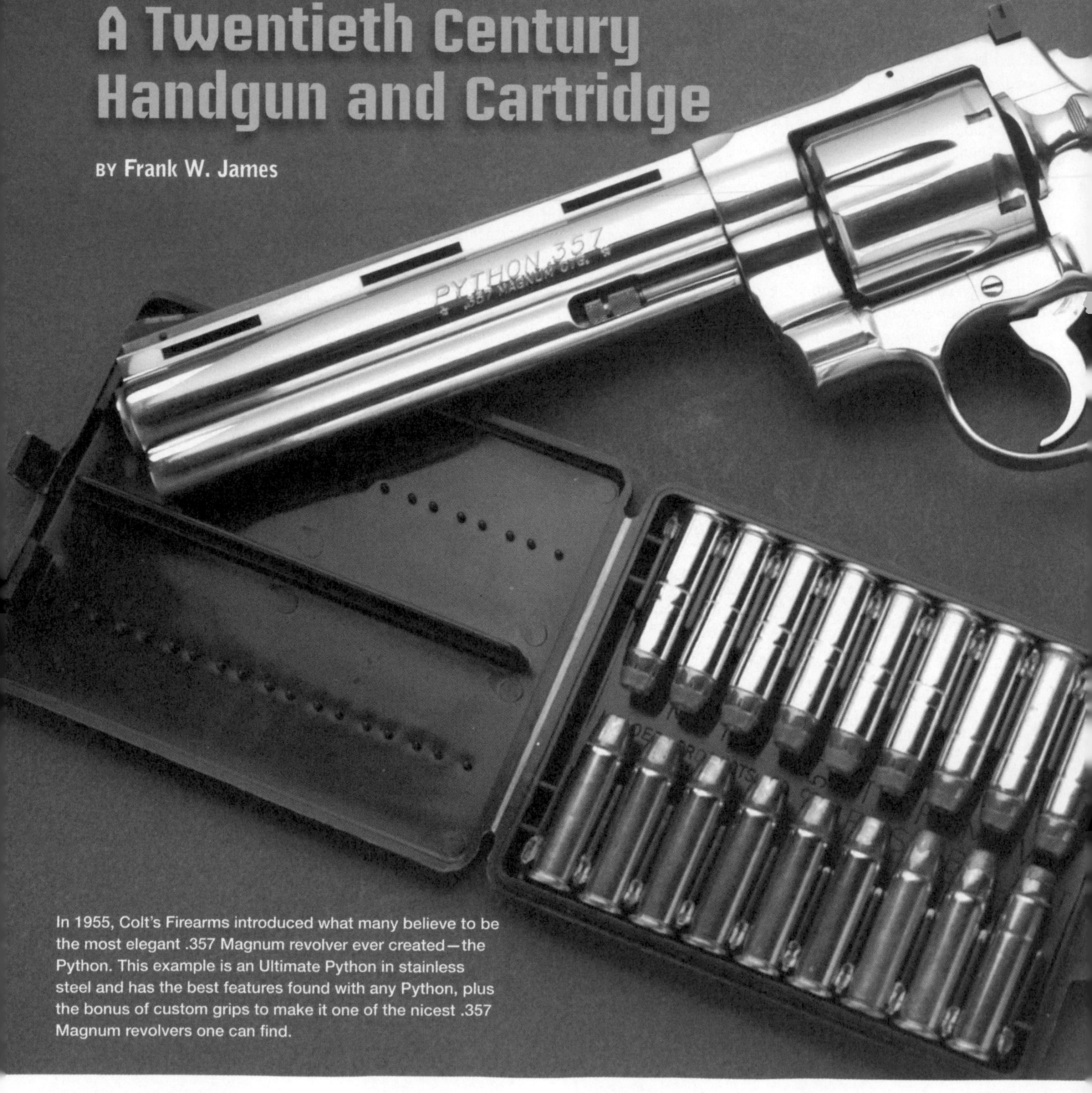

In 1955, Colt's Firearms introduced what many believe to be the most elegant .357 Magnum revolver ever created—the Python. This example is an Ultimate Python in stainless steel and has the best features found with any Python, plus the bonus of custom grips to make it one of the nicest .357 Magnum revolvers one can find.

MAGNUM,

At the time of its introduction, the .357 Magnum was, in fact, the most powerful handgun round in production.

Forty years ago, one handgun caliber dominated all others, regardless the intended application. It didn't matter whether it was used by law enforcement, for self-defense, the relatively new sport of handgun hunting for whitetail deer, or for just plain fun and plinking—the most popular handgun at the time was a revolver chambered for the .357 Magnum.

The adoption by the United States military of the 9mm Beretta, in 1985, changed things dramatically for both revolver shooters and devotees of the beloved 1911 .45, as both law enforcement agencies and civilian consumers stampeded to a variety of semi-auto pistols in 9x19mm caliber. These guns held far more rounds in reserve than did the six-shot .357 Magnum or the 7+1 1911 .45, but, for a major part of the 20th century, the .357 Magnum held sway. Many experts feel that, even today, if the firearms world had not witnessed the tidal surge move to semi-autos during the 1980s, the .357 Magnum would still be the most popular handgun caliber out there.

Origins

The .357 Magnum cartridge was introduced, in 1935, by Smith & Wesson, but Winchester Ammunition worked directly with S&W to bring it to market. Major Douglas B. Wesson and Phil Sharp were responsible for much of the final developmental work, although it is noted in several historical records

The Smith & Wesson Model 386 utilized a lightweight frame with a six-inch barrel to create a .357 Magnum revolver that employed some of the most advanced technology available in the twenty-first century.

A steel spring shield is positioned above the barrel on the Smith & Wesson Model 386, to prevent damage to the top strap of this revolver from the gas escaping through the barrel/cylinder gap.

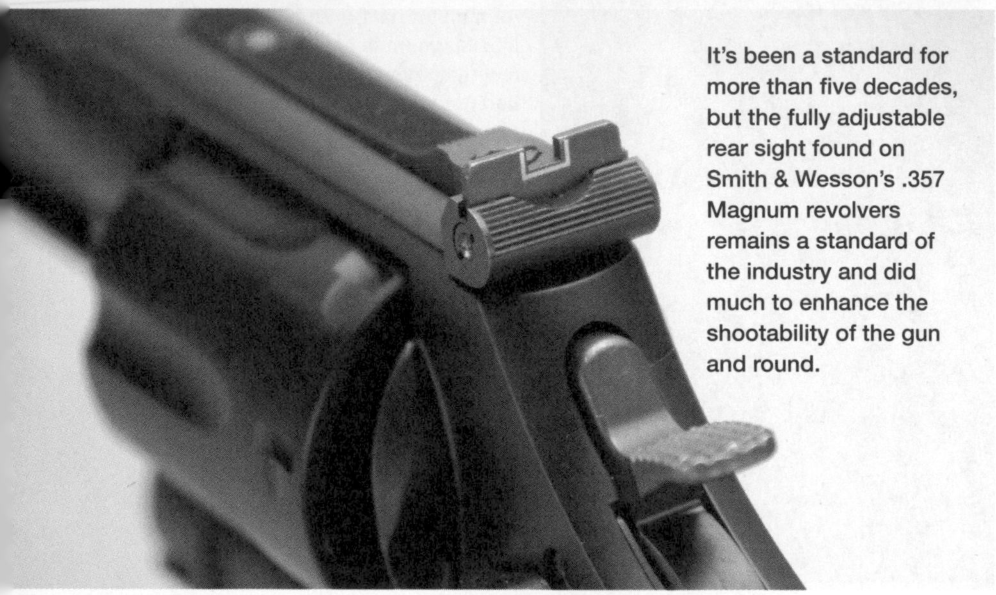

It's been a standard for more than five decades, but the fully adjustable rear sight found on Smith & Wesson's .357 Magnum revolvers remains a standard of the industry and did much to enhance the shootability of the gun and round.

WINCHESTER

357 MAGNUM
125 GR. JACKETED HOLLOW PT.
X3576P

that both authorities consulted with Elmer Keith, because of his experience in developing heavy bullet loads with higher than normal muzzle velocities for the .38-44 cartridge. The .38-44 had been an attempt to develop a more powerful cartridge than the standard police .38 Special. Smith & Wesson, prior to the introduction of the .357 Magnum, even made a heavy-frame revolver that was nominally a .38 Special revolver, but it was referred to as the ".38-44."

At the time of its introduction, the .357 Magnum was, in fact, the most powerful handgun round in production. The original load chronographed 1,510 fps with a 158-grain bullet out of an 8¾-inch barrel. It certainly wasn't the first attempt to create a powerful handgun cartridge. Other startups had come before it. The most notable was that by an Englishman, H. W. Gabbet-Fairfax, who'd developed, around 1900, a self-loading pistol employing a cartridge called the 9mm Mars. It had a reported muzzle velocity of 1,607 fps with a bullet weight of 156 grains. But the British military rejected it after trials, and neither the gun nor that cartridge ever achieved commercial success.

Smith & Wesson chambered its heaviest revolver frame (later known as the N-frame) for it. The revolver was a special order item introduced during the height of the Great Depression. Each revolver was registered with the factory and came with a certificate designating this registration. The Smith & Wesson "Registered Magnum" and its cartridge soon acquired a mystique that created a following among legendary lawmen (J. Edgar Hoover received Registration No. 1), military generals (one of General George S. Patton, Jr.'s famous ivory revolvers was Registered Magnum No. 506), and high-profile Hollywood movie actors (a Registered Magnum supposedly belonging to Clark Gable sold at a high-end gun auction in 2012).

Originally, Smith & Wesson felt the round should be fired through the 8¾-inch barrel, but because the early .357 Magnum Registered revolvers were all

LEFT: It was the lightweight bullet loads in the .357 Magnum that really established the round's reputation as a stopper in lethal-force encounters between law enforcement officers and armed criminals. This success carried over to the civilian self-defense market and made the .357 one of the popular cartridges of the twentieth century.

Smith & Wesson has produced a wide range of .357 Magnum revolvers in stainless steel. First introduced in the mid-1960s, the use of corrosion-resistant material, together with the caliber, helped make this one of the more popular self-defense cartridges in history.

custom orders, they had been made with a wide variety of individual character-istics. These revolvers have been found with 23 different barrel lengths, as well as a number of non-cataloged sight and grip combinations.

.357 Advantages

The designation ".357" refers to the bore diameter, which is also the bore diameter of the less powerful and older .38 Special cartridge. The .38 Special was introduced in 1902, also by Smith & Wesson, to provide a .38-caliber handgun cartridge that was more powerful and effective than any of the previously seen .38-caliber rounds such as the .38 S&W, the .38 Short Colt, and the .38 Long Colt. The latter had served briefly as the standard service handgun round of the military services and was blamed, in large part, for its many failures to stop antago-nists during the Spanish-American War and the insurrection in the Philippines.

The .38 Special was initially loaded with a 158-grain round-nose lead bullet and it had a muzzle velocity of 855 fps out of a standard service-length revolver barrel. While proving extremely popular with American law enforcement, the .38

Even though it has a large frame, it doesn't mean it can't have a short barrel and extra-capacity cylinder. This Model 327 from Smith & Wesson sports a short barrel and an eight-shot cylinder in .357 Magnum.

Special also experienced criticisms for failures to stop armed bad guys, particu-larly during the more violent episodes of the 1930s. These criticisms are what lead to, first, the development of .38-44 rounds (.38-caliber loads meant for use in a .44-sized revolver frame), and then, ultimately, to the .357 Magnum.

Still, by the late 1940s and early 1950s, the .38 Special was the dominant handgun service round in American law enforcement. This popularity was due to its inherent accuracy and relatively easy recoil ,and, with its straight-walled case, it was an easy round for the recreational shooter to reload.

When the designers created the .357 Magnum, they took the existing .38 Special case and simply lengthened it by 1/10-inch, mostly to prevent chambering of this new, more powerful, far higher chamber pressured round from being loaded in the older, weaker guns of .38 Special design. The bullet diameter, naturally, is the same for both the .38 Special and the .357 Magnum. For training or practice purposes, this meant the .38 Special round could be safely loaded and fired in any cylinder chambered for the .357 Magnum; that was and is probably the greatest asset of any .357 Magnum handgun, its versatility across both rounds.

My First .357

I acquired my first .357 Magnum while I was a lowly college student. Money

was extremely scarce. It was during the mid-1960s, the Vietnam War was on, and finding a brand new .357 Magnum Smith & Wesson was virtually a search for the Holy Grail, because so many of the guns being made during that time were committed to law enforcement agencies. Having worked every extra hour I could get during a summer between semesters, I was determined to reward myself with the purchase of a new and powerful handgun. It would be the fourth handgun I would ever own, the first two being .22 rimfires the third a like-new Smith & Wesson Model 10 in .38 Special.

I wanted a .357 Magnum because I knew I wouldn't have to buy new ammo. I could use the ammo I already had, the .38 Special ammunition, and keep reloading the same cases, using the same projectiles and, after readjustment, the same reloading dies. For a college kid

counting his pennies, this caliber and gun combination made a whole lot of sense.

Just before I had to return to school, I put out the word that I was looking for a .357. I was working as a meat cutter at a large supermarket, and the night security consisted of city cops. A couple of these cops asked around and, finally, they told me to head down to a big sporting goods store outside the city of Indianapolis, as that was the only one known to have anything such as I wanted in stock.

I walked up to the counter after finding the place, and the older gentleman behind the counter asked what he could do for me?

"I would like to buy a Smith & Wesson .357," I stated flatly.

He paused and looked to his right, then slowly to his left. Without saying a word, he reached under the counter and pulled out a blue box with silver lettering on top that said "SMITH & WESSON." It was the only one he had.

The clerk's name was Sherm, and he explained the store kept the Smith & Wesson .357s out of sight because they didn't want police officers to spot them. If an officer did, then the store had to sell them at a police discount and, with the demand so high, they wanted to sell to law enforcement only on an agency order, with everything else sold at full retail.

I had wanted a Model 19 with a four-inch barrel, but, after weeks of searching, I knew that wasn't going to happen. So, when Sherm opened the box and I saw the deep blue finish of that six-inch barrel Model 27, I knew I was in love. It cost me $143 plus $2.86 tax. I still have this gun!

Later on, a last minute trip out west to visit a cousin in San Francisco that same summer, I stopped at P.O. Ackley's shop, in Utah, and purchased a set of diamond centered-checkered goncalo alves target grips to replace the Magna-style grips that had come with it. A few years later, I would trade with an acquaintance the narrow hammer and trigger on my Model 27 for the wide hammer and trigger that were on his Model 29, and that is pretty much the way the gun has remained for the 45 years I've owned it.

In a way, this particular .357 Magnum is something of a nostalgic revolver, one like those seen back in the 1930s, where the barrels were cut back and the grips shortened so they could be carried comfortably in a pants pocket. The difference here is the enhanced capacity of the cylinder and its chambering—.357 Magnum!

Shooting the .357

Over the years since that first purchase, I've owned a large number of .357 Magnum revolvers, and if there is one characteristic of this gun and caliber combination that can be universally said, it is the fact that they are accurate. I think I may have scrounged up enough loose change to purchase one 50-round box of .357 Magnum cartridges when I got that first one, but, by and large, most rounds I fired that first year were heavy .38 Special handloads.

I started casting my own bullets, because I was always looking for a way to shoot more for less. At the time, Elmer Keith was one of the foremost handgun writers in print, and he constantly promoted a cast bullet of his design every time he mentioned the .357 Magnum. It was made by Lyman, and the mould was No. 358429. I ordered a two-cavity mould and was soon producing my own cast bullets that I sized at .358-inch. Depending upon the mixture and ratio of tin to lead, this bullet normally casts up at 168 grains in the typical Keith-style bullet having a relatively long nose, flat meplat, and wide grease groove. Later, I would obtain a four-cavity mould for this bullet and, over the decades since, I have shot literally thousands upon thousands of these bullets through .357 Magnum handguns. I still say this bullet,

loaded in either a .38 Special case or a .357 Magnum case, with just about any decent charge and corresponding .357 Magnum revolver, will yield one of the most satisfying and accurate handgun/ammo combinations available—even today in this age of plastic frame pistols and enhanced magazine capacities.

I should mention I discovered that Elmer must have used this load and caliber on larger stuff than I did initially, mostly, I suspect, because it would really penetrate. I've shot raccoons, red foxes, coyotes, and a number of whitetail deer, and I have to say that only on the deer did I feel this load worked as Elmer advertised. Everything else it just flat sailed through as if each of the creatures were a sheet of paper. That was fine if the bullet hit vital organs in its passage through, but, if it didn't, then I wound up looking rather foolish in front of my friends.

It was the introduction of lightweight jacketed hollowpoint bullets (125- to 140-grain) and high-velocity loads that really gained the .357 Magnum the respect it so richly deserved in law enforcement and self-defense circles during the 1970s. It has that same respect today.

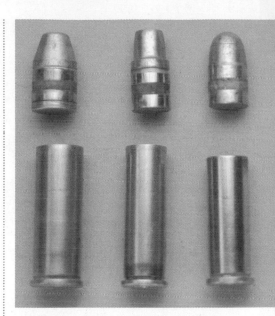

The rounds represented here are three of the author's favorites. From left is a .41 Magnum with a cast truncated cone gas check bullet. Next is the .357 Magnum with the Keith 168-grain Lyman No. 358429 SWC bullet and, on the right, a typical, 158-grain lead round-nose bullet for the .38 Special case.

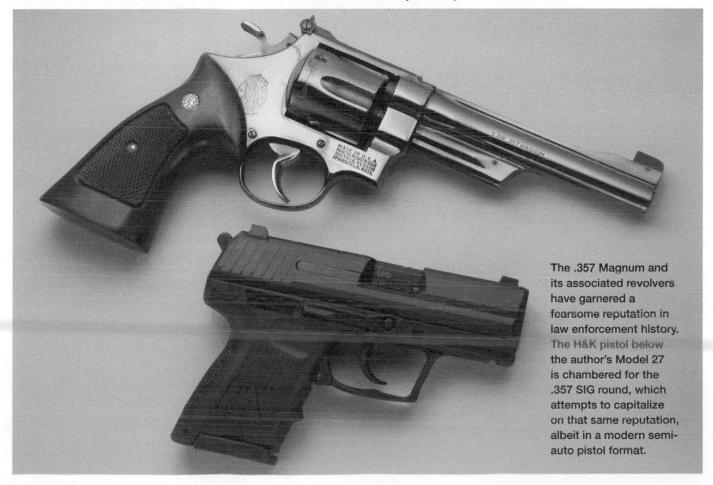

The .357 Magnum and its associated revolvers have garnered a fearsome reputation in law enforcement history. The H&K pistol below the author's Model 27 is chambered for the .357 SIG round, which attempts to capitalize on that same reputation, albeit in a modern semi-auto pistol format.

This L-frame Mountain Gun from Smith & Wesson features a four-inch barrel and a seven-shot cylinder, and is chambered for the .357 Magnum cartridge. It represents an advancement, in terms of construction and size, over the original .357 Magnum revolvers.

The Mateba is a twenty-first century design chambered for the .357 Magnum round. Unlike most conventional designs, this revolver fires the bottom chamber on the cylinder, so as to provide the shooter with a lower bore axis and increased control.

On the left, a .357 Magnum handload employing the Keith 168-grain cast SWC. On the right, the round many believe is its equal, the factory .357 SIG round with a 125-grain bullet. The author feels the .357 SIG round is a good one with lightweight bullets, but lacks the case capacity to work well with heavier bullets.

I discovered these same loads worked far better at stopping varmints on our farms than had the previous loads that employed Elmer's cast bullets. I know that sounds like heresy to some, but it was an observation I learned through experience on our farm fields and not the square target-shooting range.

The .357 Expands

In the 1950s, the cartridge's popularity grew when manufacturers other than Smith & Wesson began chambering revolvers for it. Colt's started the ball rolling, when it introduced the Colt .357 Magnum, in 1953, a heavy-frame, double-action, swing-out cylinder revolver with either a four- or six-inch barrel length. Later, the large New Service revolver was chambered for the round, but, then, in 1955, Colt's started producing what many feel is the most elegant .357 Magnum ever made—the Python.

Smith & Wesson would continue promotion of the round, but the next thing it introduced was a medium-frame gun (the K-frame) that was known far and wide as the Combat Magnum or, simply, the Model 19. Add another decade or more, and a host of other manufacturers would come out with their own service-style .357 Magnum revolvers, including the Ruger GP-100 that proved to be a popular alternative for those seeking a .357 Magnum from someone other than S&W or Colt's.

A Lasting Legacy

Perhaps the greatest legacy this cartridge established was its legendary reputation for ending a gunfight with its first solid hit. With relatively lightweight projectiles loaded above 1,250 fps, the round achieved a reputation that remains even to this day. Of course, the downside to these same effective loads was a fearsome muzzle blast and, if the gun was light enough, considerable felt recoil. Just about any .357 Magnum revolver with full-power loads requires a dedicated individual to master it and, for some, that simply wasn't in the cards. This certainly was a factor in the move, now more three decades ago, away from revolvers and toward semi-auto pistols.

The .357 SIG round that is chambered in many law enforcement semi-auto pistols capitalizes on the success of the .357 Magnum, if for no other reason than the use of ".357" in its name. In reality, the .357 SIG employs bullets of .355-inch diameter. It is a good self-defense/law enforcement round, when loaded with bullets weighing 125 grains or less, but it lacks the case capacity to duplicate the performance and terminal ballistics that so characterized the .357 Magnum over the decades, when it was loaded with heavier bullets. This is true even though the .357 SIG is offered in a modern pistol with more than twice the ammunition capacity of a six-shot revolver.

The .357 Magnum and its revolvers are not as popular today as they were 40 years ago, but the inherent traits of power, penetration, accuracy, and simple economics remain for those willing to explore one of the twentieth century's greatest handgun rounds. It certainly has proven itself in many different endeavors, and still holds potential for those willing to work with it.

Part of Smith & Wesson's Night Guard series of self-defense revolvers, this Model 386 sports a short barrel, a seven-shot cylinder, and a .357 Magnum chambering.

This retired police-duty Smith & Wesson Model 66 with a four-inch barrel in .357 Magnum is representative of what many in law enforcement thought was the ideal service revolver during the 1960s and 1970s.

The author's Model 27, with an 8³⁄₈-inch barrel and custom grips, is an expression of his appreciation for this gun and cartridge. The original Registered .357 Magnums from Smith & Wesson were supposed to have 8¾-inch barrels, but 23 different barrel lengths have been documented as shipped by the factory prior to World War II.

The E.M. Reilly
fully restored, in its
original case.

A MAN—AND GUNS—OF SUBSTANCE

REILLY

OF OXFORD STREET

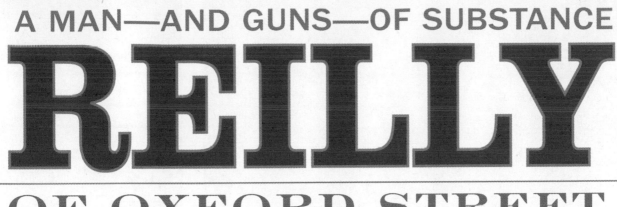

BY **Terry Wieland**

For one tumultuous century—1814 to 1914—London was the world's major center of firearms development. No other city was home to such a range of innovations, from Manton's exquisite flintlocks to Purdey's express rifle to the refinement of game guns and the development of the Nitro Express cartridges.

The histories of Manton, Lancaster, Boss, and Holland & Holland are well known and documented. What is less known is the story of the substrata of London businesses and companies that were an important part of the gun trade, but whose names faded, even as their products lived on.

As well as genuine London gun makers like Lancaster and Woodward, there were companies that had guns made in the trade and then put their own names on them—William Evans, for example. Others were gun retailers, selling new and used guns, but having some custom guns made to special order, usually in Birmingham. These included C.B. Vaughan (Guns) Ltd., of the Strand, and E.M. Reilly & Co.

Edward Michael Reilly was the son of Joseph Reilly, a jeweler who had a shop in Holborn, just east of Mayfair, as early as 1816, and was later listed as a gunsmith in the same district. In 1848, Edward parted from his father and opened a shop of his own on Oxford Street, very close to James Purdey.

There has been considerable confusion about Reilly's exact relationship with Purdey, because of their street numbers. These numbers changed several times between 1850 and 1900 due to renumbering, and depending on the source you consult, you may find both Reilly and Purdey occupying No. 315 Oxford. This has led some to conclude they were connected. They were not. Indeed, anything but.

Purdey was an inventor and a fine gun maker catering to the highest levels of the trade—princes, dukes, and other wealthy men—making bespoke guns and rifles to order. Reilly was a retailer, buying and selling and putting his name on guns and rifles that were manufactured in Birmingham, largely by W&C Scott, Webley, and other gun makers to the trade.

The sheer volume of business, as indicated by their serial numbers, gives an idea of how they worked. Purdey went into business in 1820 and, by 1880, was issuing serial numbers in the 10,000 range. Reilly started in 1848 and, by 1880, had reached serial number 20,000. Both were substantial companies.

The earliest known Reilly serial number is No. 254, belonging to a percussion pistol, circa 1840. Apparently, Edward took over his father's serial numbering system, for his numbers, from 1848, begin at 8400.

Little is known about E.M. Reilly the man. No photographs exist, and no journalist seems ever to have visited his premises, as did writers for *The Field* or *Land and Water* at the shops of Boss, Woodward, and Charles Lancaster.

An incident from 1866 may shed some light. On May 29, James Purdey wrote to his Oxford Street neighbor, protesting, in strong terms, a sales pitch, delivered by one of Reilly's employees, in which he intimated that a particular gun had been proved for them by Purdey, while another gun was half the price because it lacked the famous name. James Purdey stated that he did not make guns for other companies, period, and would Mr. Reilly kindly ensure that nothing like this happened again?

If Purdey catered to the upper classes, E.M. Reilly was purveyor to a different sort of client. These included army officers going out to India or the colonies, civil servants, middle-class men who liked shooting but were not into the big money, and younger sons on their way to Africa to make their way in the world as hunters or farmers.

Is there anything more graceful than a London game gun?

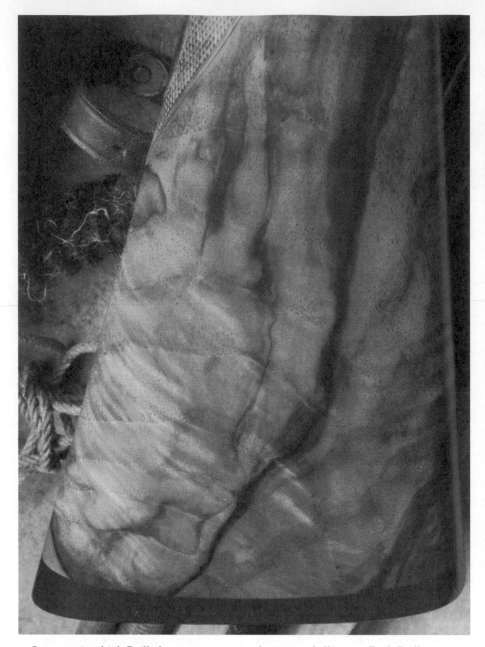

LEFT: Cleansed of old oil, with a stock extension of German rubber, the checkering recut, and with a London oil finish, the Reilly's French walnut stock is mouthwatering.

RIGHT: The screw-grip treble-bite. Note the slight slant to the step of the rib extension. The lever cams the barrels down, as it closes over the interrupted thread of the step.

One area in which Reilly became prominent was the raffish world of live pigeon shooting, a competition driven largely by gambling. Boss and Stephen Grant, among others, were also prominent makers of pigeon guns, but their names ceased to appear on the lists of winners in the newspapers, because those names were paid for, along with the type of gunpowder used. As gun makers like Boss and Grant ceased to need the publicity, they did without the expense. E.M. Reilly stuck with it, sending a representative to each meet to ensure the payments were made and that his name was listed should they win.

There is a wide range of guns still extant bearing the E.M. Reilly name, from horse pistols to Nitro Express rifles and shotguns of all types. Each Reilly gun presents its own puzzle to be deciphered from its features, serial number, patents related to it, and proofmarks.

I first encountered the Reilly name in 2004, when I bought an old shotgun that had been found in the rafters of a henhouse in southern Ontario. It had lain there, wrapped in burlap, for 30 years. The stock was battered and stained black with oil, but the metal was good. Its story was sketchy. The owner had died in 1975, and no one had been able to find his shotgun, until the owner's widow put the farm up for sale 30 years later and the buildings were cleared out.

History prior to this explained that the late owner's father had brought the gun to Canada, from Scotland, where he had inherited it from his father, who'd been a gamekeeper. The conclusion was that the gun had been a gift from the landowner to his gamekeeper—and a very nice gift it was, for it was as fine a boxlock as ever came out of London. Fitted with Damascus barrels, the gun was proofed for blackpowder. In the 1920s, the gamekeeper or his son had a set of fluid-steel barrels fitted to the gun by George Coster, a gun maker in Glasgow; that fact was easy to establish, since Coster was only in business at that address for a couple years. The gun arrived in Canada with both sets of barrels, but was probably used with the fluid-steel barrels from that point on.

The gun's serial number, 30456, suggests it was made around 1887, but some of its features indicate it was produced

somewhat later. At first glance, it appears to be a Webley screw-grip treble-bite boxlock, a fairly common (and usually very high quality) action used for both rifles and shotguns. However, delving more deeply, and with the assistance of books old and new, a different story emerges. The central character of that story is not Philip Webley, but a Birmingham action filer named Thomas Brain.

Thomas Brain first appears in 1877, in Geoffrey Boothroyd's *Directory of British Gun makers*, as an out-worker to the trade, located on Weaman Street, in the heart of the gun quarter. He was one of that tribe of highly inventive skilled gun makers who preferred to work on their own, inventing new mechanisms in between applying their skills to piece work for others. There

were many such men, and their names appear on individual features that later became famous, two examples being Henry Jones and the underlever, and Charles Harvey and his fore-end latch.

Thomas Brain worked with T.W. Webley on several developments, and 1882 patent No. 3053 for the Webley screw-grip treble-bite action was filed in the names of both men. Five years later, Brain filed another patent, No. 10487, in his own name. It covered a number of features—it was one of those "grab-bag" patents, to save money—including a method of attaching barrels with a monobloc, an improved screw-grip treble-bite, and a selective ejector.

Beretta is generally credited with inventing, or at least first using, a monobloc

for attaching barrels, in 1903, but the Brain patent predates this by 16 years. The difference between the two approaches is that Brain used a threaded barrel, while Beretta employed a friction fit.

Patent No. 10487 was accompanied by a detailed schematic drawing showing the complete internal mechanism, from the safety catch through to the coiled ejector springs. If one had set out to draw my E.M. Reilly gun, it could not have been more exact.

According to Crudgington & Baker, 1887 was the watershed year for ejector patterns and patents, and Brain's "patent ejector," was one of them.

The question is, did Thomas Brain build the entire gun for E.M. Reilly, or did

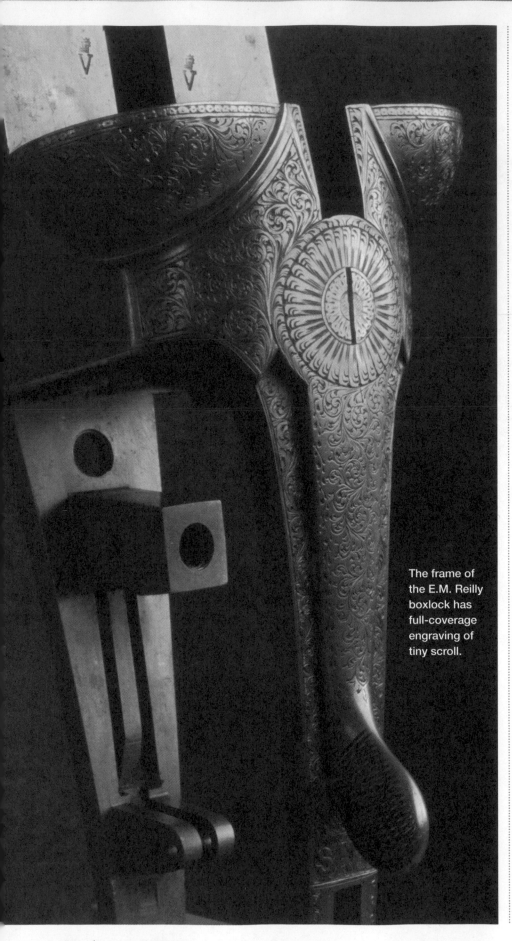

The frame of the E.M. Reilly boxlock has full-coverage engraving of tiny scroll.

he send the barreled action in the white to Reilly in London for Reilly to have it proofed at the London Proof House and stocked by a London out-worker? There are no marks to indicate either, but, since Brain was a metal man, I suspect the gun was stocked in London.

Unusual for that age, Reilly paid close attention to the quality of French walnut he put on his guns. A few other London gun makers were particularly noted for fine wood—Woodward and Boss spring to mind—but most paid it scant attention beyond ensuring walnut blanks had the correct grain for strength and attractive figure and color.

When I first acquired the Reilly, I expected to have it restocked. The butt was short, made for a left-handed shooter, and was so battered and oil soaked it looked unsalvageable. I reckoned with the skills of Edwin von Atzigen, my Swiss local gun maker. By holding the stock at an angle to the light, we could see some figure under the discoloration. Edy believed it could be saved. Eighteen months later, I saw the stock. Edy had lengthened it to my dimensions using a piece of hard, black, German rubber (which looks and behaves like the finest ebony), and bent it to the right degree of cast-off. Hidden beneath the oil, which he had drawn out slowly and patiently by a method he will not divulge, lay the most gorgeous piece of French walnut I have ever seen.

The balance of the restoration was fairly straightforward. Edy recut the checkering on the stock and reshaped the panels behind the fences. He then reconstructed the fore-end, where oil had rotted the wood, cutting out a small wedge of walnut and inserting an ebony diamond in which to set a new escutcheon. He filed a new steel escutcheon and steel fore-end cap, which we sent to Sam Welch, who engraved them with scroll to match the action. Finally, Edy recut the checkering on the fore-end and applied a London oil finish.

The original Damascus barrels were in excellent condition, and Edy refitted the fore-end to work with them, rather than Coster's 1925 fluid-steel replacements, which we relegated to back-up status. With the 30-inch Damascus barrels, the gun weighs six pounds, four ounces, and handles like a wand.

* * *

With this background, you can imagine my reaction when, five years later, I found an old gun collecting dust on the rag-bag shelf at Puglisi's Gun Emporium,

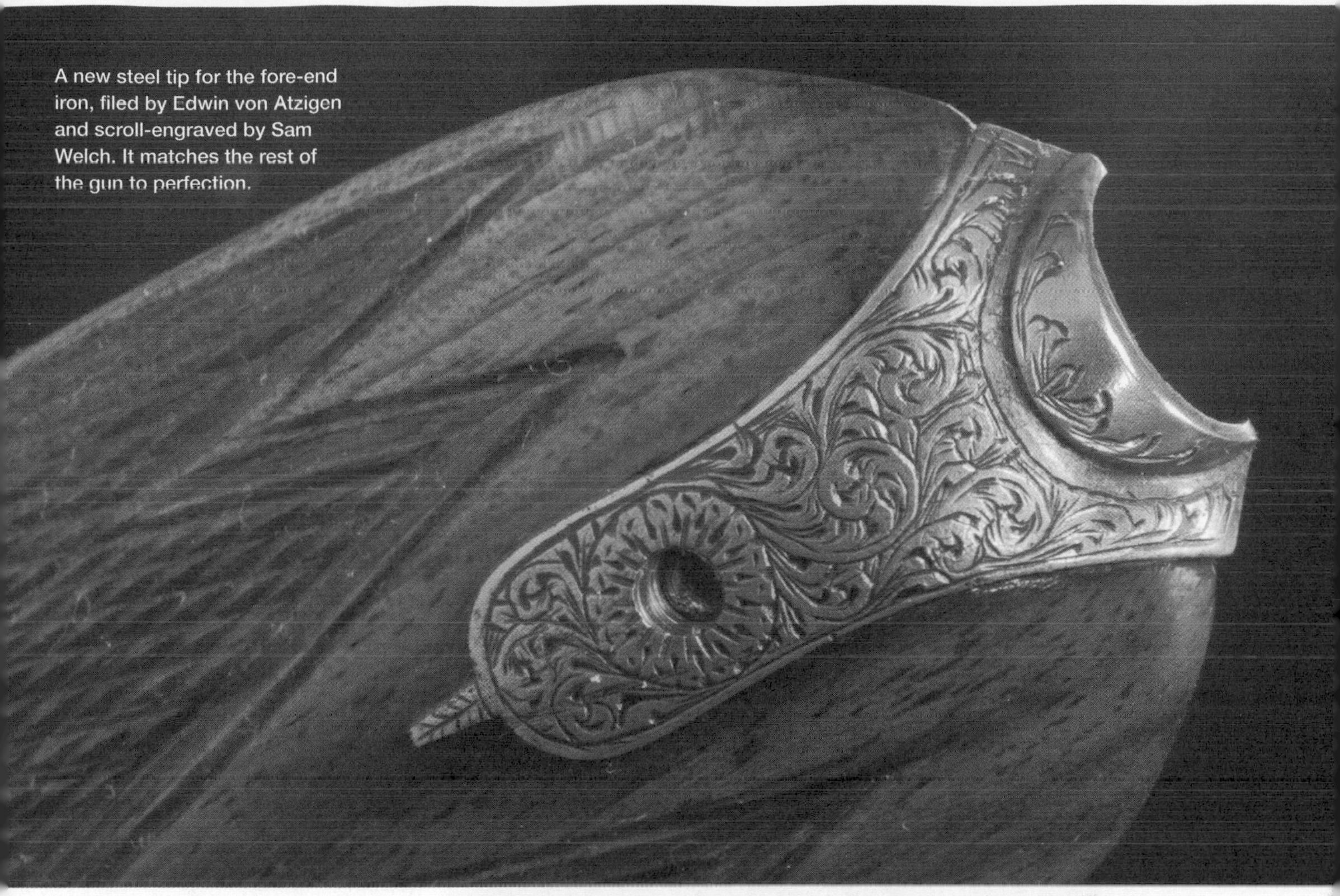

A new steel tip for the fore-end iron, filed by Edwin von Atzigen and scroll-engraved by Sam Welch. It matches the rest of the gun to perfection.

in Duluth. It was a strange and inexplicable beast, which was why John Puglisi had stuck a $950 price tag on it, to be sold "as is."

It was a 20-gauge hammer gun, but that barely begins to describe it. The barrels were only 24 inches long, with very thick walls, hence it was quite heavy at seven pounds, three ounces. It had a Jones underlever and various other features, including sling eyes and a wide, filed rib that more properly belonged on a double rifle than a shotgun. It was missing the original, sculpted, ebony fore-end tip, and someone had hot-blued the action. It was, overall, a mess.

The only thing John knew about it was that he had acquired the gun from a Duluth bartender, who'd traded for it with a mate off one of the Great Lakes freighters. That sounded suitably romantic. It said "E.M. Reilly" on the rib and looked like it needed a good home.

It would take too long to tell, in detail, the process of research and elimination that led to my final conclusions about the gun. We'll go straight to the result.

Edwin von Atzigen cut away some rotted wood from around the fore-end escutcheon, replaced it with an ebony diamond, and fitted a new diamond escutcheon. It was later engraved by Sam Welch to match the original scroll.

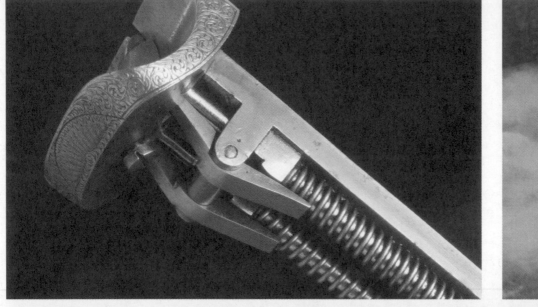

The E.M. Reilly's Damascus barrels are perfectly sound, and its 2⅝-inch chambers are quite happy with Baschieri & Pellagri High Pheasant loads. In its restored state, the gun handles like a wand and shoots beautifully.

TOP LEFT: Thomas Brain's patent ejector, in beautiful condition, even after 120 years.
TOP MIDDLE: The author with the E.M. Reilly 20-bore hammer gun, shooting blackpowder and ball.
TOP RIGHT: Thomas Brain's initials and patent number stamped on the standing breech. The patent covered improvements to the original screw-grip treble-bite patent of 1882, owned jointly with T.W. Webley, as well as a cocking system and ejectors.

The little gun did, in fact, begin life as a double rifle, a .577 Snider double, made in 1874. It was proofed for blackpowder and marked "26," indicating a 26-bore, or .577-caliber. It has Stanton's rebounding hammers, and the only fully "snap" Jones underlever I have ever seen. Usually, a Jones is moved back into place by hand after the barrels are raised; some later models snap the lever part-way over, but this one snaps it all the way, like a top- or sidelever, making it quicker to reload and shoot again.

With 24-inch barrels and chambered for what was then the British Army military cartridge, one can only speculate for whom it was made in 1874, and where it went from there. The Khyber Pass? A Royal Navy officer on the China Sea? The Zulu Wars? We'll never know. More's the pity.

At some stage in its life, the veteran was handed over to a skilled gunsmith who bored out the .577 barrels to make it a 20-bore shotgun. Probably, this was due to corrosion. The original iron sights were removed and blanks were fitted into the dovetails on the rib and engraved to match. At some point, alas, the action was given a glossy, 1960s hot-blue job too tacky for words. The stock, already discolored, was further disfigured with varnish.

The restoration of Reilly No. 16341 took considerably less time than had No. 30456. Gun maker Bill Dowtin sculpted a new ebony fore-end tip, refinished the stock in oil, and removed the hot blue, leaving the action a dull grey that's ready to age gracefully. Once again, the stock was a surprise. I'd known it was good, but I couldn't have known just how good. It's not in the class of my other Reilly, but it's a piece of French walnut that would make your mouth water if you saw it on a new gun today.

*　*　*

In its heyday, in the 1880s, Reilly was a substantial company. Along with its fashionable address on Oxford Street, E.M. Reilly & Co. (as it had become known by that time), had a shop in Paris, on the Rue Scribe. An 1884 advertisement makes reference to the company's "private shooting grounds" and lists pigeon shooting medals from Paris, Rome, and Belgium. Sir Samuel Baker and Frederick Courteney Selous both took E.M. Reilly guns to Africa and mentioned them in their books.

In 1899, Edward took over the surviving business of his father. There is no explanation for what had happened in the meantime, but the effect of this was to confuse the whole serial numbering

The Reilly puts its two 350-grain lead balls a few inches apart at 15 yards, using only the bead as a sight. It has not lost its double-rifle instincts.

Made in 1874, likely destined for the Khyber Pass or the Zulu Wars, the Reilly was originally a .577 Snider double rifle. Who knows where it has been and what it has seen?

situation for both companies. As a result, one can fix dates using the serial numbers only in a very general way.

In 1917, E.M. Reilly was taken over by Charles Riggs & Co., a dealer in shooting accoutrements. Such was Reilly's prestige, however, that Riggs continued to use the Reilly name right up until its own demise, in 1942.

Today, the E.M. Reilly name is owned by Charlie Pfleger of Hill Rod & Gun, in Bozeman, Montana, a dealer in vintage double guns and gun cases. He doesn't plan to have any guns made under the Reilly name. Just owning the rights is fun, and it gives him a connection to that extraordinary era in London when a unique generation of gun makers made history.

CUSTOM RUGER SIXGUNS

The Author Looks Back More than Six Decades of Custom Single-Actions

BY **John Taffin**

Some sixguns can only be had from the hands of skilled custom sixgunsmiths. From top left clockwise: John Gallagher .41 Magnum on a .357 Blackhawk three-screw frame, Hamilton Bowen .41 Special on a .357 Blackhawk three-screw flattop frame, and John Gallagher's .41 Special Single-Six.

In the 1920s and 1930s, between the two World Wars, King Gunsight Company did a brisk business customizing Colt and Smith & Wesson revolvers with such offerings as full barrel ribs, adjustable rear sights, specially shaped hammers, and short actions. Elmer Keith, writing for the *American Rifleman*, often featured stories and pictures of his custom Colt Single Actions. He related how Pennsylvania gunsmith Harold Croft traveled by train all the way out to Durkee, Oregon, where Keith had a small ranch, to show him four custom Colt Single Actions he had designed. They were numbered 1, 2, 3, and 4. Keith liked what he saw and incorporated many of Croft's ideas with his own to come up with the now famous Keith No. 5. This beautiful single-action, along with several others, is now displayed at the Elmer Keith Museum, in the Boise, Idaho, Cabela's store.

The King Gunsight Co. is long gone, but many of its ideas, as well as Keith's, were eventually found in factory produced sixguns. Keith's No. 5 was a 5½-inch barreled .44 Special with adjustable sights, a Bisley Model hammer and trigger, and what is now known as the No. 5 grip frame consisting of a Bisley backstrap and a Single Action Army trigger guard. A close look at today's Free-dom Arms grip frames and the current Ruger Bisley Model grip frame reveals the influence of Keith's No. 5 design. He also led the way with adjustable sights and flattop frames on Colt Single Actions, features that can also be seen today on Ruger Single Sixes and Blackhawks, Freedom Arms Model 83s and Model 97s, and the Colt New Frontier.

The Colt Single Action was frequently used for customizing, but just prior to WWII, it was dropped from production with an announcement that it would never be seen again. As a kid in the 1950s, I often gazed upon and lusted over pictures of Keith's custom single-actions. Not only did they appear in his magazine articles, but also in his book *Sixguns*, which arrived in 1955. By the time this definitive work was published, a new manufacturer was offering single-actions: Sturm, Ruger & Co.

Bill Ruger entered the firearms business, in 1949, with his Standard Model .22 semi-automatic pistol. At the same time, the new medium of television was filling much of its airtime with old Western movies. This stirred up a demand for single-action sixguns and, in 1953, Ruger stepped into the void with the Single-Six. It looked like a Colt, operated like a Colt, and had a grip frame identical to the Colt. However, the rest of this great little sixgun was different. It was downsized from the Colt version, the action was powered by nearly unbreakable coil springs instead of flat springs, and the chambering was in .22 rimfire, making it economical to operate. The Single-Six sold for $63.25 at a time when used Colt revolvers were bringing more than $100.

The original Single-Six had a 5½-inch barrel, a drift-adjustable rear sight and, instead of the beautifully contoured loading gate found on the Colts, there was a flat gate. In fact, collectors now refer to these early .22 Rugers as "flat gates." It wasn't long before other manufacturers started offering properly shaped replacement loading gates, and soon some sixgunners were getting adjustable rear sights and ramp front sights. The age of customizing a new single-action had arrived.

In 1955, the .22 Single-Six was joined by the .357 Blackhawk, complete with a heavy topstrap and adjustable sights, and then, one year later, the .44 Magnum Blackhawk was introduced. The original .357 Blackhawk was the same basic size as the Colt Single Action, while the .44 version was made slightly larger so as to better contain the pressure of the bigger cartridge. In *Sixguns*, Elmer Keith stated that the .357 Blackhawk would soon be chambered in both .44 Special

The author shooting the Harton Custom Ruger .44 Special.

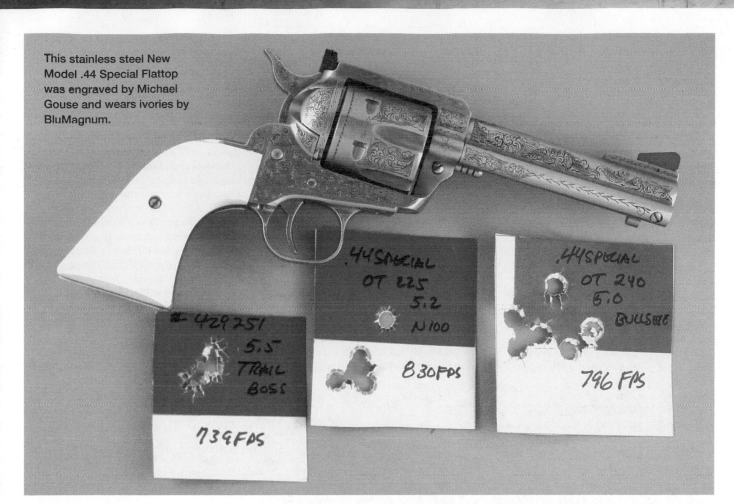

This stainless steel New Model .44 Special Flattop was engraved by Michael Gouse and wears ivories by BluMagnum.

Targets (handwritten notes):

#-429251
5.5
TRAIL
BOSS
739 FPS

.44 SPECIAL
OT 225
5.2
N100
830 FPS

.44 SPECIAL
OT 240
5.0
BULLSEYE
796 FPS

and .45 Colt. However, the arrival of the .44 Magnum changed all that, and we got a slightly larger gun chambered in that new cartridge instead. The .45 Colt Blackhawk would not arrive until the early 1970s, and it would use the same frame and cylinder size as the .44 Magnum. Once in a while, progress actually works and, today, the original .357-sized Blackhawk Flattop is offered chambered in both .45 Colt and .44 Special, albeit with the New Model action.

DIY Single-Actions

My adventures in customizing Ruger single-actions began by fitting a properly contoured loading gate to my .22 Single-Six. When the .357 Blackhawk arrived, I couldn't see anything that needed to be done to what was already a perfect sixgun. The .44 Magnum Blackhawk followed this same theme, except for its 6½-inch barrel. To me a 6½-inch barrel looks great on a double-action sixgun, such as the Smith & Wesson 1950 Target or original .44 Magnum, but it seems to be out of place on a single-action. I had a local gunsmith cut the barrel of my

.44 Magnum Blackhawk to a length even with the ejector rod. What my hunting companions dubbed the "Bear Buster" became one of my most carried sixguns—in fact, you could call it the first of my many "Perfect Packin' Pistols."

Later on I would send the Bear Buster off to Ruger to have a 7½-inch barrel installed so the shorter .44 barrel could be used for another project (more on this later). About the same time, my Super Blackhawk went off to Larry Kelly at Mag-Na-Port to be turned into another Perfect Packin' Pistol. The barrel was cut to 4¾ inches and Mag-Na-Ported, and the entire gun was finished in a nickel looking Mag-Na-Loy. This same basic gun was soon offered by Mag-Na-Port as the Predator model. I replaced the Super Blackhawk grip frame with a stainless steel version from the Ruger Old Army, and now, more than 40 years later, it remains one of my favorite Perfect Packin' Pistols.

Customizing the Ruger single-action really falls into two categories: those touches easily accomplished by virtually anyone (if I can do it, anyone can); and those extensive alterations requiring the services of an expert revolver-smith. The

modern era of customizing Ruger single-actions really began more than 40 years ago, with an article in *Shooting Times* by Skeeter Skelton, in which he talked of converting .357 Magnum revolvers, three-screw Rugers, and Smith & Wesson N-frames to .44 Special. At that time, it was virtually impossible to find a .44 Special sixgun, but Skeeter led the way, starting a process that is still going strong and has resulted in companies such as Colt's Manufacturing Co., LLC, Freedom Arms, Ruger, and USFA offering .44 Special single-actions. Those of us who consider the .44 Special as "Very Special," owe a deep debt of gratitude to Skeeter.

Let's first look at what we as individuals can do to customize our prize Ruger single-actions. Ruger's first .44 Magnum Blackhawk, the Flat Top, had the same grip frame as the Colt Single Action Army. This grip frame, dating all the way back to 1851, when it was on the Colt Navy, handled recoil with standard cartridges very well. However, there was nothing standard about the .44 Magnum round.

I was 17 when I purchased the Ruger, that purchase made mainly because of the reputation of the grip frame for handling recoil. It didn't work with the .44 Magnum! Firing the first shot resulted in the hammer digging into the back of my hand and drawing blood. Over the years I learned to handle .44 Magnum recoil (and more), but I was certainly intimidated as a teenager.

In 1959, Ruger sought to improve its .44 Magnum with the introduction of the Super Blackhawk. They added weight with a 7½-inch barrel, a non-fluted cylinder, and an all-steel grip frame; the original Blackhawk version was of aluminum alloy. Ruger also changed the shape of the grip frame from the smallish 1851 Navy Colt to the larger Colt Dragoon-style of 1848, complete with a square-backed trigger guard. While most shooters felt the Super Blackhawk was a great improvement, I did not. That square-backed trigger guard hammered the knuckle of my middle finger every time I shot it and today, after 50 years and a lot of pounding on my knuckle

from many different revolvers, even .44 Specials in the Super Blackhawk nail me. So I am back to using the original .44 Blackhawk XR3 grip frame and have even installed it on .45 Blackhawks to replace the later XR3-RED grip frame, which allows too much room between the back of the trigger guard and the front strap.

After more than 50 years of shooting single-action sixguns, I proclaim the Ruger Bisley Model grip frame as the best ever for handling heavy recoil. In the past, I have turned a pair of .45 Colt 4⅝-inch Blackhawks, one blue and the other stainless, into Bisley Models simply by swapping out grip frames, grips, hammers, and triggers from Bisley Vaquero Models. Bisley Model parts have also been installed on a .44 Magnum and a five-shot .45 Colt, again, making recoil much easier to handle.

As close to perfection as it is, the Bisley Model can be made even more user-friendly by slightly round-butting it.

I am not a fan of extreme round-butted grip frames, but I do like to take the sharp edges off the front and the back of the butt. This probably does more to cut down on felt recoil than anything else and can certainly be done to standard grip frames.

Swapping hammers is something else that most of us can handle ourselves, with the result being a better handling sixgun. In the past, I have added Super Blackhawk hammers to standard Blackhawks. After I had my local gunsmith alter five Ruger New Model Bisley hammers, I was able to basically drop them into five New Model Flattop Blackhawks. From time to time, David Clements offers Bisley Model hammers that easily drop in to three-screw Blackhawks. I have two of these, one each on a .45 and a .41 Magnum Blackhawk, and both dropped in without any fitting required.

Ruger's New Vaquero harkens back to the days of the original .357 Blackhawk in

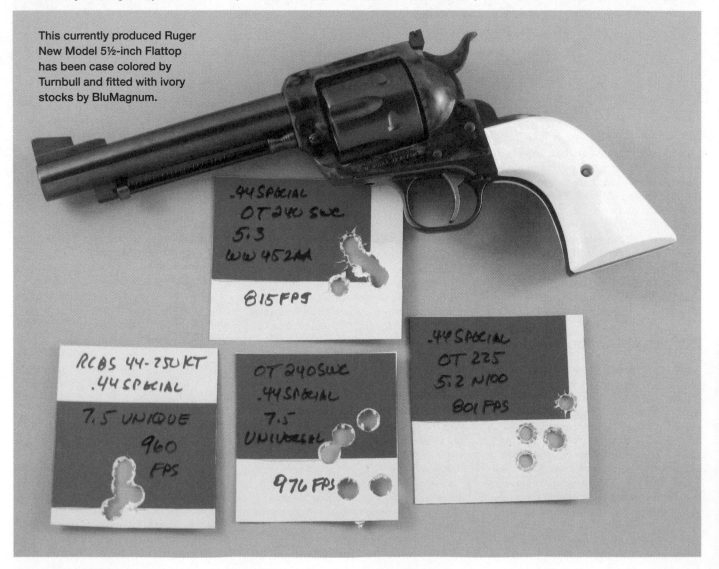

This currently produced Ruger New Model 5½-inch Flattop has been case colored by Turnbull and fitted with ivory stocks by BluMagnum.

All of these Rugers started life with longer barrels that have been cut to an easier packing 5½ inches. From top left clockwise: .22 Super Single-Six, .41 Magnum, .45 Colt, .44 Magnum Flattop, and .357 Magnum.

that it is the same size as the Colt Single Action. It is a great sixgun for outdoor use. However, the hammer profile is all wrong, at least for me. Supposedly, it was designed to make it easier for Cowboy Action shooters to reach, but the result is just about the ugliest hammer ever put on a sixgun. I have replaced mine with standard Blackhawk hammers, as well as Ruger Montado hammers. When a sixgun looks good, I have a much better chance of shooting it well.

While they are not something most of us can easily make ourselves, there are many craftsmen who offer custom grips for Ruger single-actions. Those I have used for helping raise my pet Rugers above the ordinary include Eagle, Hogue, Precision Pro, Roy Fishpaw, BluMagnum, Herrett's, Cary Chapman, Larry Caudill, Scott Kolar, and the late Charles Able, these companies and craftsmen using materials such as exotic woods, stag, ivory, and buffalo bone. BluMagnum and Herrett's offer wood stocks that fill in behind the trigger guard area and make

shooting .44 Magnum and heavy .45 Colt loads a lot more pleasant.

After reading Skeeter's article on converting three-screw Ruger .357 Blackhawks to .44 Special, I sent off a 6½-inch Ruger .357 to a fellow in the Northeast to convert it. He re-chambered the cylinder, cut the barrel back to 5½-inch, and then reamed it and installed a .44 barrel liner. When I got it back, I could see it was a very slow twist barrel, and the 'smith apparently had used a liner made for the .444 Marlin rifle. It would only shoot well with full-house .44 Special Keith loads. I wanted something more versatile, so I removed the previously mentioned cut-down barrel from my original .44 Magnum Blackhawk and sent the custom .44 Special off to Trapper Gun, in Michigan. The folks there installed the barrel and beautifully blued the entire sixgun, except for the grip frame, which I polished out, and it now wears very creamy ivory grips. It was my first, but certainly not my last, .44 Special Perfect Packin' Pistol. Long before Ruger was offering a

10-inch barreled Super Blackhawk, I had Trapper build me such a sixgun complete with a satin nickel finish. It was a prized hunting handgun even before Ruger began offering the stainless steel 10½-inch Super Blackhawk.

There are some who would say I have more custom Rugers than I need. Maybe so, if we go by regular standards. However, I am driven by a special need. My father was killed before I was a year old. The only thing I have that belonged to him is a broken pocket watch and a belt buckle. His father died before I was born, and I have nothing that belonged to him, nothing to remind me of who he was. I cannot let this happen with my kids and grandkids. Right now I have 17 people to whom I want to leave a legacy of my life; three kids and their spouses and eight grandkids, three of whom are now married. When the other five marry, I will have 22 people—not counting any great grandkids who may arrive while I'm still here—to leave gun stuff to. I want to make sure they each get plenty.

Customized Ruger Vaqueros: .45 Colt Vaquero with four-inch barrel, new front sight, Super Blackhawk Hammer, brass grip frame with stocks by Larry Caudill; and a .357 Magnum New Vaquero with Freedom Arms front sight, Bisley hammer, and stocks by Larry Caudill.

Ruger single-actions are basically great sixguns. Questions often arise on the Internet, especially to the effect of "I just bought a new Ruger, so what do I have to do to make it shoot?" Well, the only thing necessary to make it shoot is to load the cylinder and pull the hammer back. Most could benefit from a qualified gunsmith's trigger job, but it's not absolutely necessary. In fact, I mostly perform a "Taffin Instant Trigger Job" and go.

Custom Sixguns Makers and Shakers

Not only are Ruger single-actions good basic guns, they are also excellent platforms for building custom sixguns. With large-framed Rugers, one can go from eight-shot cylinders in such little cartridges as the .25 Flea, up to and including five-shot cylinders in the big .500 calibers. Let's take a look at some of the gunsmiths who specialize in custom-izing Ruger single-actions and whose work I have personally experienced. Space constraints will prevent me from covering everyone who is doing excellent work, so I will start chronologically with the first three custom gunsmiths who built Rugers for me back in the 1980s and then go alphabetically.

I first met John Linebaugh more than 30 years ago, when he was building heavy-duty .45 Colt sixguns. He sent me one of his first examples, which I wrote up, and we have been friends ever since. With the coming of the Ruger Bisley Model, John had a grip frame that allowed shooters to handle really heavy loads and, from there, he went on to create his .500 Linebaugh, which uses a .348 Winchester case cut to 1.4 inches. He then followed it with the .475 Linebaugh using cut-down .45-70 brass. Five-shot cylinders were built to utilize the frame window of the Ruger to the maximum, the geometry of the action was changed to handle five shots instead of six, and new barrels were fitted.

The Linebaugh cartridges are extremely powerful and made possible, for most of us, only because of the Bisley Model grip frame. More than 25 years ago, John built me a 5½-inch .500 using a Ruger Bisley Model .357 Magnum as the platform. Ivory Micarta grips were added. This is one of John's first .500s and, today, it is still as tight as it was when it left his shop in Cody. John specializes in packable sixguns—"old-school" sixguns, as he calls them—guns easy to carry on

Custom Ruger .44s from left to right: Original Flattop cut to 4¾ inches; a fully customized Super Blackhawk by Mag-Na-Port; and a current production .44 Special New Model fitted with a Bisley hammer, taller front sight, and Ruger Rosewood stocks.

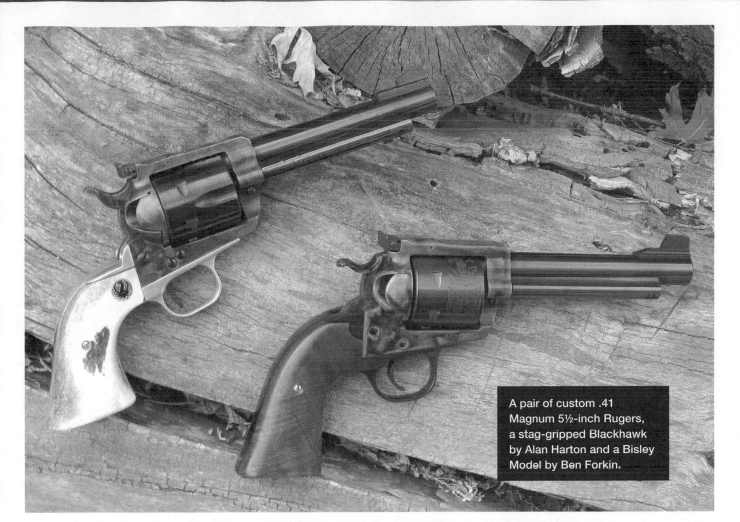

A pair of custom .41 Magnum 5½-inch Rugers, a stag-gripped Blackhawk by Alan Harton and a Bisley Model by Ben Forkin.

the hip all day and then placed under a pillow at night. He believes in sixguns that are big on performance, but not ungainly in size.

When I saw a small ad for .44 Special sixguns from Andy Norvath, I knew I had to get in touch with him. He sent me a pair of .44 Specials for testing, one on a Ruger three-screw .357 Blackhawk and the other a converted Model 92 Winchester carbines. I was so impressed with his work I sent off one of my own three-screw .357 Blackhawks to him with instructions to make something a little different. We went with a four-inch barrel and a round-butted grip frame, and this became the first of several "L'il Guns." When I wrote it up in *American Handgunner*, I got a call from Hollywood wanting to use it in a movie. I wasn't about to let it go, but I told them how they could have their own made up, and Andy wound up making guns for the movie, as well as personal guns for the two stars. Back at the Taffin homestead, Tedd Adamovich of BluMagnum fitted mine with custom stocks and also engraved it for me. A few years ago, Andy sent me another

.44 Special custom Ruger for testing and evaluation. This one was made with a 5½-inch barrel cut from an S&W full rib Model 29 .44 Magnum barrel. The hammer he created is the most beautiful you will ever see on a single-action sixgun. It never went back to him. Instead, he got a check.

The original .44 Magnum was the first of my L'il Guns, but certainly not the last. Over the years, Andy has built up five small-caliber sixguns for me. Three of these are .22 Single-Sixes, all with short barrels and slightly rounded grip frames. One is blue, one is stainless steel, and the third has a Bisley grip frame. The other two little L'il Guns are .32 Magnums, one blue and the other stainless. All are destined to make five of my grandkids extremely happy.

The first revolver-smith to do extensive big-bore custom revolvers for me on Ruger three-screw .357 Blackhawks was Hamilton Bowen. I kept him busy during the 1980s, as he built a matched pair of blued 4⅝-inch .44 Specials with stag grips polished to remove the heavy bark, and a Long Range .44 Special with

a 7½-inch barrel. The latter is especially attractive, with its blued finish, polished aluminum grip frame, and black Micarta grips. Needless to say, it shoots as well as it looks. My "Beater Bowen" is a .44 Special built on a hundred-dollar Ruger .357 three-screw Blackhawk that, finish-wise, had definitely seen better days. Rather than spend a lot of money polishing and bringing it back to bright blue, I had it bead blasted and finished in a matte blue. It gets its name from the fact that any of the kids or grandkids can borrow it and not have to worry about scratching it or hurting it in any way. When the going was rough and I was much younger, this is the .44 Special I would put on my belt.

Back in the mid-'00s, Hamilton and I put our heads together to come up with a sixgun chambered in the cartridge that never was but should have been, the .41 Special. That round is simply the .41 Magnum cut to .44 Special length. Hamilton first chambered it for me in a 5½-inch Colt, and this was followed with a four-inch S&W Model 586. However, his supreme effort with the .41 Special was

None of these .45 Colt Rugers started life as Bisley Models. The two on the right were fitted with Bisley Model parts by the author, and those on the left by Jim Stroh.

built on a Ruger .357 Magnum Old Model. This one also has a 4⅝-inch barrel, but, instead of the all blue finish, the frame and hammer have been beautifully case colored. BluMagnum fashioned a pair of exquisite walnut stocks, the wood of which came from the scrap barrel at Dakota Arms.

Hamilton literally wrote the book on custom revolvers, and it is aptly called *The Custom Revolver*. It is highly entertaining and informative and answers just about every question anyone could ever have about custom sixguns.

My good friend Robert G. Baer, of Texas, does professional work, but he is not a professional gunsmith. Bob does what he likes, starting with Old Model .357 Blackhawks and Marlin lever guns. He especially likes small sixguns that are easy to pocket or pack. Many of Bob's ideas are now routinely used by a lot of sixgun 'smiths. Some of the most notable are lightweight guns, rounded butts, and lanyard rings. The latter makes a lot of sense on an outdoorsman's gun, to prevent loss under any circumstance.

Several years ago, an old model three-screw .357 Ruger Blackhawk of mine was turned over to Bob, with instructions to simply build me a special gun, his choice of style and caliber. Since he already knew of my fondness for the .44

Special, that's the direction he went. The bright polished aluminum grip frame is round-butted. The aluminum ejector rod housing is also polished bright, while the rest of this sixgun is finished in a very hard nickel plating. To aid in the

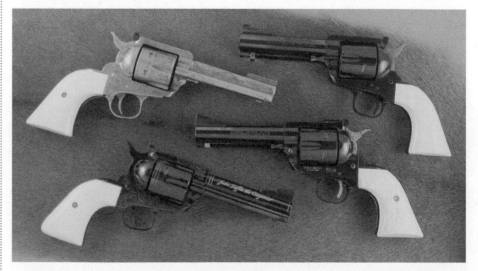

All of these short-barreled .44 Rugers now wear ivory stocks. From top left: Ruger Super Blackhawk by Mag-Na-Port; Skeeter Skelton Special by Bill Grover; Taffin's first custom .44 Special finished by Trapper Gun; and Gary Reeder's El Diablo.

project, gunsmith Keith DeHart expertly re-chambered the cylinder and furnished the 3¼-inch barrel. The total package is 30 ounces, very easy to pack.

Other special custom touches include a shortened base pin head, and a thinned ejector rod head with an offset recess in the bottom of the housing so the housing doesn't have to be removed to remove the base pin. The hammer spur has been slightly lowered, broadened, and checkered, the top strap has been tapered on both sides, and the front edges of the cylinder have been beveled. Another really special custom touch is a very slight offset at the back edge of each chamber, so one can remove fired cartridges with a thumbnail. Of course, the entire action has been smoothed.

Sixguns are very personal, and to identify this as my very personal sixgun, special markings on this .44 Special include my initials "JAT" on the front of the frame, while in front of the trigger guard on the bottom of the frame you'll find "RGB", "01 SS SPL." The RGB is for Robert G. Baer, and the SS is for Skeeter Skelton, who inspired us all in so many ways. Short-barreled sixguns are not the easiest for me to shoot, but this little .44 will do one-inch groups at 20 yards, using 240-grain LaserCast bullets over 5.0 grains of Bullseye at just under 800 fps. That makes it a Pleasantly Powerful Perfect Packin' Pistol.

I earlier mentioned Elmer Keith's No. 5 S.A.A. with a grip frame made by mating a Colt Bisley Model backstrap with an SAA trigger guard. David Clements brings this idea up to date, by fashioning a No. 5 grip frame for a custom Ruger .44 Special. Just as with Keith's No. 5, this one has a 5½-inch barrel, as well as beautifully crafted walnut stocks by Larry Caudill. Add a Bisley Model hammer, case coloring of the hammer and the frame, and the result is an exceptionally beautiful sixgun, which, like just about every custom .44 Special Ruger, shoots the way it should.

A second Clements .44 Special was made up on a .357 Ruger three-screw by using a Colt New Frontier barrel. The barrel threads on the first and second generation Colt Single Actions are 20 tpi, but, for some reason, Colt went with 24 tpi with its third generation run. This just happens to be the same thread pattern as used in Ruger single-actions, so the barrels mate up nicely with the Ruger frame.

David installed the 4¾-inch Colt barrel along with a Colt ejector housing and rod

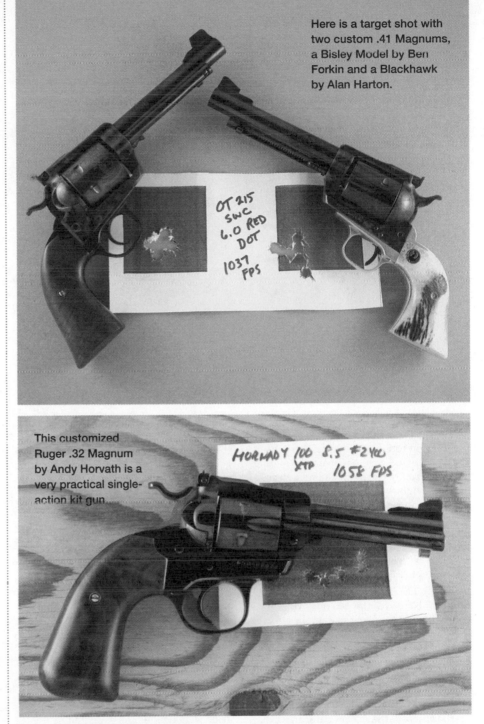

Here is a target shot with two custom .41 Magnums, a Bisley Model by Ben Forkin and a Blackhawk by Alan Harton.

This customized Ruger .32 Magnum by Andy Horvath is a very practical single-action kit gun.

and converted the original cylinder to .44 Special, then had a second furnished cylinder became a .44-40, making this a dual-purpose sixgun. The adjustable sights make it easy to transfer from one cartridge point of impact to the other. This sixgun is also all blue with a polished grip frame, and stocks by Larry Caudill.

When I wanted something a little different, namely a custom Ruger not chambered in .44 Special, I turned to

Brian Cosby. Brian is a do-it-all custom gunsmith who especially appreciates single-actions and lever guns. He can take some of the most abused old firearms and restore them to perfection. My old .44-40 Winchester 1873 was totally re-worked by Cosby. The barrel, with more than 100 years of wear and black-powder corrosion, was lined to bring it back to perfection. I've seen a pair of well-worn .32-20 Colt Single Actions Brian was able to bring back by lining the

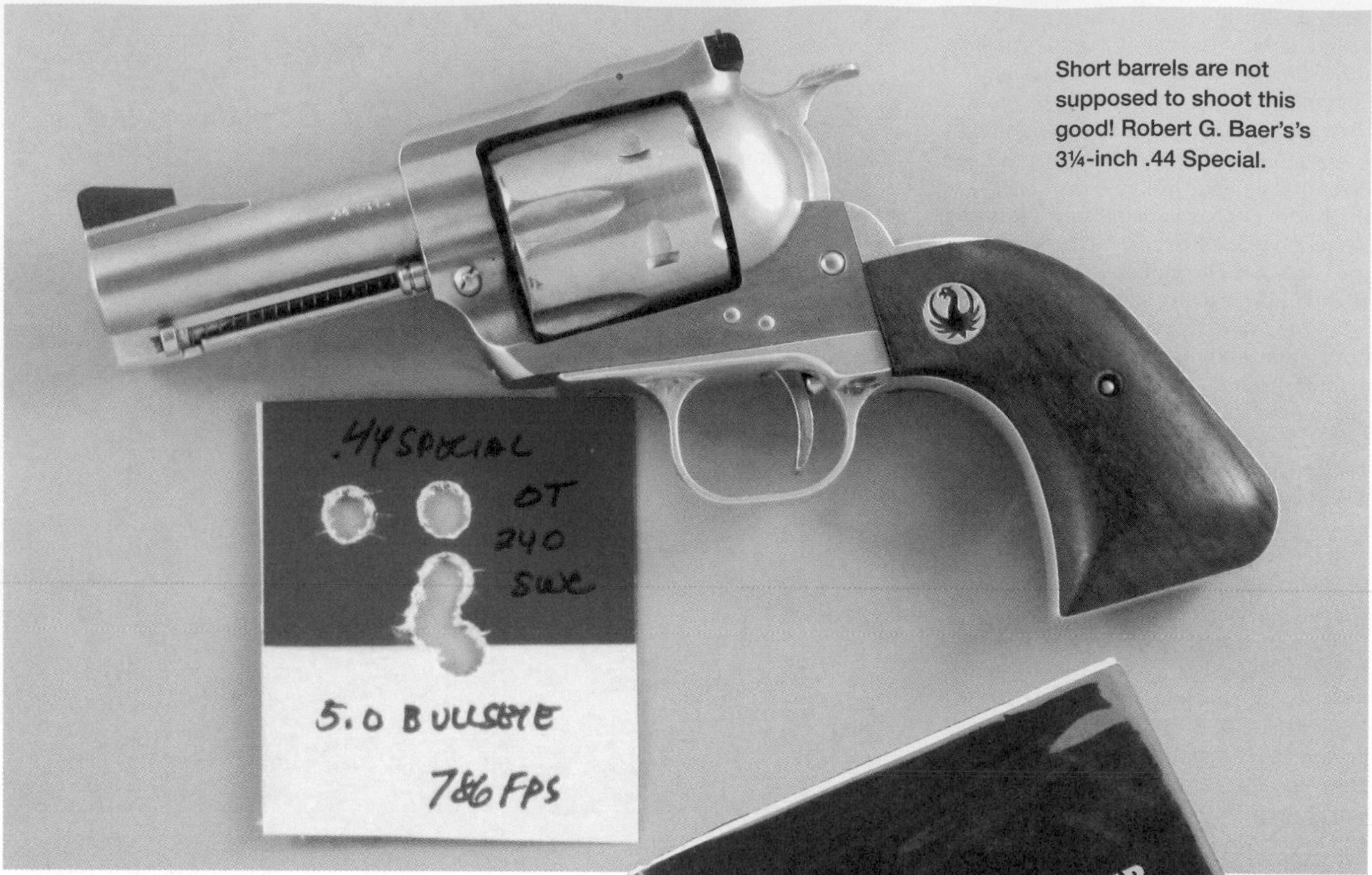

Short barrels are not supposed to shoot this good! Robert G. Baer's 3¼-inch .44 Special.

Hamilton Bowen's book provides a resting place for this beautifully crafted .41 Special with stocks by BluMagnum.

barrels and totally refinishing the exterior in blue and case hardening, resulting in two virtually worn out single-actions being brought back from the grave to be used for another 100 years. It isn't always possible to find replacement barrels properly marked, but, by lining the original barrel, the markings are maintained and you get a new bore.

When a local gun shop went out of business, I bought all of its third generation Colt New Frontier barrels. Most were either .44 Special, .44-40, or .45 Colt. I used the first 4¾-inch .44-40 barrel on the above-mentioned Clements sixgun, and now I turned to Brian, sending him a 7½-inch .44-40 barrel and a Ruger Old Model .357 Blackhawk for building a .44-40. The cylinder was re-chambered, the action smoothed, tuned, and tightened, and the entire gun was refinished. The result is an easy handling, good shooting .44 WCF. Since the barrel dimensions of Colt New Frontier barrels for the .44 Special and .44-40 are the same, a second cylinder converted to .44 Special will someday be added.

When Ruger brought out the Bisley Model, in the mid-1980s, I bought all four chamberings—.357 Magnum, .44 Magnum, .45 Colt, and .41 Magnum. Although they are all good shooters, as I've gotten older, I've decided to turn the last three into Perfect Packin' Pistols. These all had 7½-inch barrels, so they were sent to Ben Forkin to have them shortened to 5½ inches, with new front sights installed along with Bowen rear sights, the actions tuned, and frames and hammers case colored. Each of these guns had been fitted with walnut stocks by the late Charles Able, so no custom grips were needed. As expected with anything by Ben, all three sixguns turned out beautifully, and I shoot them much more than I ever did when they had longer barrels.

Speaking of barrels, I sent three more Rugers off to Ben, along with new barrels. Two of the sixguns were standard Old Model .357 Blackhawk Rugers. For converting them to .44 Special, we went with a 5½-inch Colt New Frontier barrel and a new, unfired Ruger original Flattop 6½-inch barrel, which was also trimmed back to 5½ inches. Both mainframes were beautifully case colored, and the latter was fitted with a new front sight. The results are two excellent Perfect Packin' Pistols.

For the third .44 Special, I took a

A very special Special is this David Clements custom with a No. 5 grip frame. Stocks are by Larry Caudill.

.44 SPECIAL
RCBS
44-250 KT
7.5 UNIQUE

988 FPS

44 SPECIAL
OT 225 RNFP
5.5 452AA

876 FPS

.44 SPECIAL
OT 240 SWC
7.5 UNIVERSAL

1001 FPS

different path. With the arrival of the production Ruger .44 Special Flattop New Model, it is no longer necessary to start with a .357 Magnum, if one is happy with the New Model action, as opposed to the Old Model geometry. I was one who did not care for the New Model, back in 1972. However, I have changed my mind and now find them exceptionally convenient for loading, unloading, and especially for carrying six rounds safely. So Ben received one of the New Model .44 Specials, fitted it with a 7½-inch Colt New Frontier barrel, case colored the frame and hammer, and then I fitted it with a pair of Ruger checkered rosewood stocks which, unfortunately, are no longer available from Ruger.

The first sixgun John Gallagher ever built for me was several years ago, and it is my "Big Little Sixgun." Actually, it's a big sixgun shooting a small cartridge. To build a premier custom .32-20, Gallagher started with a Ruger New Model Blackhawk that is built on the same frame as the Super Blackhawk. John basically used only the frame and grip frame. The cylinder is a custom built, eight-shot .32-20, which is made oversized to completely fill the frame window. It matches up with a slightly tapered barrel with a deeply crowned muzzle. The front sight is a serrated ramp style, which is mated up with a Hamilton Bowen rear sight. Instead of the conventional hammer, this custom Blackhawk has a Super Blackhawk hammer and a creep-free trigger set at 3½ pounds. The mainframe is color case hardened and the balance

A pair of John Gallagher 4-inch .44 Specials on a New Model Flat-Top .357 and an Old Model Three-Screw.

A heavy-barreled Ruger .44 Special Target Model by Jack Huntington. The spalted maple stocks are by Cary Chapman.

of the gun is beautifully blued. I added a pair of stag grips with a black eagle Ruger medallion, and the combination is exceptionally attractive.

At the opposite end of the spectrum is Gallagher's "Little Big Sixgun," which shoots a relatively big cartridge from a small frame—the .41 Special in a Single-Six. As stated earlier, the .41 Special is nothing more than the .41 Magnum trimmed to .44 Special length. This mild wildcat has become popular enough that properly headstamped brass, though expensive, is available. I normally load a 215-grain bullet at 900 to 1,100 fps, or about where I load 250-grain bullets in the .44 Special. Gallagher came up with the idea of making a really little gun to shoot the .41 Special by starting with a Ruger three-screw Single-Six; a New Model will not work, as the enlarging of the loading port area to accept larger cartridges cuts into the transfer bar safety.

Gallagher reset the firing pin to center-fire, then built a custom five-shot cylinder that fills out the frame window and matched it up with a four-inch .41 barrel. The top of the frame has been rounded off on both sides, as well as the front, and the rear sight was set in a dovetail and matched up with a slightly sloping and serrated front sight. The steel grip frame is from a Ruger Old Army, the

trigger pull is 2½ pounds, and the base pin is a Belt Mountain knurled pin with a locking set screw. The little sixgun has been finished in high polished blue, except for the top of the frame, which is matte blue to reduce glare.

Gallagher not only works in steel, he also does an excellent job with wood, and this .41 Special wears perfectly shaped and fitted exotic wood grips. With the Oregon Trail 215-grain SWC running from 680 to 800 fps, it gives mild recoil and excellent accuracy.

John Gallagher has built me two Perfect Packin' Pistols. They are both chambered in .44 Special with four-inch barrels and are excellent little sixguns. However, they are definitely not twins. The first one started life as an Old Model .357 Blackhawk. Gallagher took a different route with this one, using a custom over-sized cylinder to completely fill out the frame window and allow for recessed case heads, this last a very nice custom touch. The barrel is four inches, and the rear sight is a custom Bowen with the top of the frame serrated on both sides of the sight assembly. The front sight is a ramp style with a serrated blade, and the ramp is nicely contoured and blended into the barrel. The hammer is from a Super Blackhawk, and both the ejector rod housing and grip frame are

steel, making this an all-steel .44. Other custom touches include scalloping out the reloading gate and the corresponding recoil shield on the left side, as well as removing metal, or "stepping down," the frame on both sides in front of the trigger guard.

The second Gallagher Perfect Packin' Pistol started life as a Ruger 50th Anniversary .357 Flat Top. The grip frame is the same size and shape as the original, which had been changed in 1962. For whatever reason, the original grip frame feels better and handles recoil much better for me than the Old Model. For this .44 Special, Gallagher re-chambered the original cylinder, fitted a Bisley Model hammer, and melted the corners of the rear sight and top strap. Except for maintaining the original width of the frame in front of the trigger guard, the rest of this .44 Special has the same touches as the Old Model version, including a deep blue finish.

The late Bill Grover, of Texas Longhorn Arms, was instrumental, along with Bob Baer, in building the "Skeeter Gun," as they call it, the .44 Special that was Skeeter Skelton's last sixgun. Its serial number is SS1, and I now have SS4. My particular SS4 started life as a .357 Magnum Ruger Flattop Blackhawk from the 1950s that had been re-blued by Ruger. Grover and I worked out this

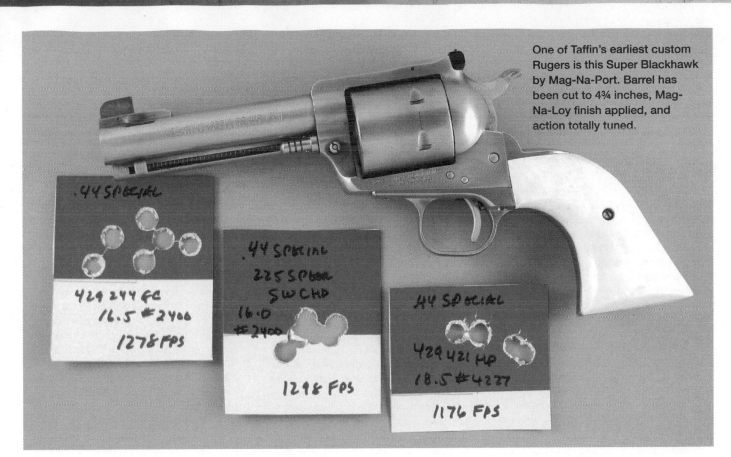

One of Taffin's earliest custom Rugers is this Super Blackhawk by Mag-Na-Port. Barrel has been cut to 4¾ inches, Mag-Na-Loy finish applied, and action totally tuned.

project together. The cylinder was rechambered to .44 Special, tightly to allow the use of .429-inch diameter bullets, but kept to minimum dimensions for long case life. The barrel/cylinder gap was set at .0025-inch. The Ruger XR3 grip frame and steel ejector housing were held back for use on the other .44 Special that Grover was building. In their place, he fitted steel Colt parts, a Colt backstrap, trigger guard, and ejector rod housing, along with a Bullseye ejector rod head. The stocks are heart-stopping, creamy, one-piece ivories by BluMagnum. The front sight is a TLA Number Five, bold, flat, and black, and a Number Five base pin with a large, easy to grasp head installed. The finish is high polish blue, and the gun is marked "SKEETER SKELTON .44 SPECIAL" on the left side of the barrel and "TEXAS LONGHORN ARMS INC, RICHMOND TEXAS" on the top strap. The serial number, SS4, is marked in the same three places as the original Colt.

The second sixgun .44 Special style from Grover was built with a 7½-inch barrel, using a cut-down 10½-inch Ruger Super Blackhawk barrel. The XR3 grip frame of the SS4 now resides on this sixgun, along with rosewood stocks by Charles Able. This long-range sixgun to compliment the SS4 packin' pistol also

wears a Number Five front sight and a Number Five base pin. The cylinder has also been beveled with the barrel/cylinder gap set at .0025-inch. The top of the frame reads "TEXAS LONGHORN ARMS, INC. RICHMOND TEXAS" and the left side of this barrel is marked "44 SPECIAL." Serial number is JT1, and it is also marked in three places, as with the SS4 sixgun.

To most sixgun 'smiths, I send a fairly good specimen to use as a basis for building a custom sixgun. Alan Harton was not treated so kindly, as I sent him a real dog of a gun. Today, a decent Flattop from 1955 to 1962 will run $600 or more, while Old Models from 1963 to 1972 command prices in excess of $400. The 4⅝-inch Old Model I sent to Harton cost me $100. It was originally purchased as a beater sixgun. The action was loose and the finish basically gone (actually, the finish could be called "early pitting"). The rest of the condition did not make any difference, as Alan would basically discard everything except the frame and the cylinder. Even so, it would be a challenge.

Alan was up to the challenge in spades, and the result is one of most beautiful sixguns I own. It is inspired and loosely based on Elmer Keith's No. 5 SAA, which Keith had built in the 1920s.

Mine is a .44 Special, just as his was, and it has a 5½-inch barrel, adjustable sights, No. 5-styled grip frame, a No. 5 locking base pin, case colored frame and hammer, and ivory stocks. The 5½-inch octagonal barrel sets this particular .44 aside as one very special Special. To come up with the barrel, Harton started with a Douglas barrel blank and machined it to shape. The left side is marked ".44 SPECIAL" and the top is inscribed "SINGLE ACTION SERVICE."

The grip frame, hammer and trigger have all been replaced with Bisley-style parts, with the trigger coming from Dave Clements. The original hammer was used, but it was greatly altered. The standard hammer spur was removed and a Bisley-style spur expertly welded into place and polished. The grip frame was then trued up to be perfectly square before fitting beautifully creamy milky grips of elephant ivory that fit my hand perfectly. The factory rear sight was replaced by a Bowen adjustable rear sight, the frame, loading gate, and hammer were all case hardened by Doug Turnbull, and the balance of the sixgun has been blued.

My second Harton custom Ruger is simply a good sixgun made into a Perfect Packin' Pistol. The .41 Magnum has been playing catch-up with shooters ever since it was introduced, in 1964. This is unfortunate, as it is an excellent cartridge. When I came into a standard Ruger three-screw .41 Magnum with a 6½-inch barrel, I saw how easily it could be made into a PPP with minimal expense. It was turned over to Alan, who shortened the barrel to 5½ inches, case colored the frame, bright polished the aluminum grip frame, and expertly fitted stag grips with a Ruger medallion.

Jack Huntington specializes in custom Rugers, including those chambered in cartridges of his own design. Shortly after the 50th Anniversary .357 Flattop was introduced, I talked to Jack about doing a custom sixgun. I learned long ago that good things happen when you turn revolver-smiths loose, as they certainly know more about building great guns than I do. A 50th Anniversary .357 was sent to Jack with only one stipulation: He could do anything he wanted to except change the shape of the grip frame. Just like the original, this Flattop's grip frame is identical to the Colt Single Action, making it extremely comfortable for shooting the loads of 250-grain bullet up to 1,000 fps muzzle velocity.

Almost every six-gunsmith builds a custom .44 Special Ruger as a Perfect Packin' Pistol, but Jack took a different direction. The cylinder was converted to .44 Special, the action was totally tuned and tightened—so far nothing unusual. However, instead of a standard 4⅝-, 5½-, or 7½-inch barrel, Jack chose a 6½-inch barrel in a heavy persuasion. Instead of the usual ramp style easy in-and-out of the holster front sight, Jack fitted a square post on the base. This may very well be a one of a kind Target Model Ruger .44 Special. Normally, I would choose one of the standard barrel lengths over the 6½-inch version; I always wondered why Bill Ruger went with this in his original .357 and .44 Magnum Blackhawks, as well as with the .22 Single-Six and the .41 Magnum, but then did *not* use it with the .45 Colt or .30 Carbine (and only very rarely with the Super Blackhawk).

I believe this barrel length is better suited to double-action sixguns. However, by using a heavy barrel and real target sights, Jack has given me an excellent shooting sixgun that balances perfectly for target shooting. That barrel just seems to hang the right way for offhand shooting, and with the proper holster design, such as a pancake or shoulder holster that prevents the front sight from digging into the leather, it can also certainly be used for hunting.

One of the first companies to specialize in customizing Rugers was Mag-Na-Port, whose main enterprise was porting barrels to reduce muzzle flip. Larry Kelly's company soon evolved into a full custom shop. I have already mentioned the Predator, based on a special gun it built up for me way too many years ago. Larry Kelly was first and foremost a handgun hunter. In fact, he could be called the handgun hunter's handgun hunter. Not only did he hunt all over the world, he also established the Handgun Hunters Hall Of Fame and Museum. Kelly hunted with handguns he had personally customized, his favorite being the Stalker. This model was built on a Super Blackhawk with an 8⅜-inch barrel, hand-honed action, Velvet Hone finish, sling swivels, deep muzzle crown, and a Leupold scope. Larry took virtually everything, including elephant, rhino, and lion with his .44 Magnum Ruger Stalker. After a long series of heart problems, Larry is now gone from us, but his son Ken aptly carries on the tradition of providing beautifully customized Ruger single-actions, as well as others.

A man I have often looked to when I needed barrels for projects is Gary Reeder. Gary probably customizes more Ruger single-actions than any other

These three Ruger New Model .44 Special Flattops were customized by Gary Reeder.

Two custom .45 Colt Rugers by Jim Stroh. The top sixgun is a five-shot, heavy-duty .45 Colt on a New Model .44 Magnum frame, while the bottom gun started life as a three-screw .357 Magnum and is now a standard duty .45 Colt with a Colt New Frontier barrel.

gunsmith in the business, offering not only traditional cartridges in Rugers, but also several of his GNR series of cartridges such as the .356 GNR. This is a .41 Magnum necked down to take .357 Magnum bullets, which results in a standard-length cartridge equivalent to the .357 Maximum/Super Mag. Gary was supplied with a 7½-inch Ruger Bisley Model in .357 Magnum, plus an extra cylinder, so I could have both cartridges. No one can outdo him when it comes to bluing, and this Bisley Model now wears Gary's Black Chromex finish, a slightly round butted grip frame, and a few gold accents, including my name.

After the .44 Special Flattop Blackhawk became a standard offering from Ruger, I purchased three of them and sent them to Gary, first checking to see if he had the barrels I needed. In fact, I had him send me two .44 Magnum Super Blackhawk barrels, a 7½-inch and a 10½-inch, which I had my local sixgun 'smith install after removing the ugly liability warning on the side of the barrel. I wanted to make sure they would shoot before we went to the trouble of refinishing them. They shot fine, and off they went to Gary to be totally refinished in Black Chromex and have "The Sixgunner" marked on each barrel. They are excellent shooting .44 Specials. What of the third .44 Special Ruger? This one became an El Diablo. Barrel length is 4⅝-inch and has the same

finish and embellishments as the longer barrel .44s, and the grip frame is slightly rounded and fitted with ivory Corian stocks. I think this is the most beautiful sixgun package Gary offers.

The project for a second trio started when a friend in Texas located not one, but two of the hard to find .32 Magnum Bisley Model Rugers, one with adjustable sights and the other with the standard rear sight. Both of these were turned over to Gary to be finished just like the .44s, but they now wear custom 7½-inch barrels. While I was in my local gun shop, Buckhorn, arranging for these .32 Magnums to be shipped, what should I find but a 4⅝-inch .32 Ruger Single-Six. I immediately decided to make the .32 pair into a trio, so it also went off to Gary Reeder. It now wears a 9½-inch barrel, along with a brass grip frame. Whatever your needs or wants, when it comes to customizing Ruger single-actions (or double-actions, for that matter), if it is safe, Gary can do it.

We've mostly been talking about custom .44 Specials and a few others, but, when it comes to .45s, I turn to Jim Stroh. Jim is a master metalsmith and has come up with two totally different Rugers in .45 Colt. When I was doing long-range silhouetting regularly, one of my most-used guns was a 10½-inch Super Blackhawk. When I quit shooting long-range silhouettes, this sixgun went off to Jim, who turned it into a heavy-duty

.45 Colt with a five-shot cylinder and a 5½-inch barrel with interchangeable front sight blades for different level .45 Colt loads. He also fitted it with a Bisley Model grip frame, hammer, and trigger. It is the ultimate, do it all .45 Colt sixgun, handling everything from standard loads up to those just under the .454 Casull. It is also very special to me for the fact it wears scrimshawed ivory Micarta grips by the late Charles Able.

My second .45 Colt from Jim Stroh is totally different and is for standard loads only. Starting with a three-screw .357 Blackhawk, Jim converted the cylinder to .45 Colt and fitted a 7½-inch New Frontier barrel I supplied to him. The action, of course, was totally tuned, and the alloy grip frame polished bright. This is an everyday working gun for everyday .45 Colt working loads. With a 260-grain bullet at 900 fps, it can certainly handle more than 90 percent of my sixgunning chores.

One last note on customizing Ruger single-actions. One of the characteristics of the Colt Single Action that has set it apart from other sixguns is the case colored/hardened frame. I have seen several times in print the statement that Ruger frames cannot be case hardened. A look at some of the pictures in this article will attest to the fact this is definitely not true. Ruger frames and hammers can be as beautifully case colored/-hardened as the finest Colt.

HODGDON
—AMERICAN FAMILY, AMERICAN ENTREPRENEUR

BY **Steve Gash**

Hodgdon's new modern office complex is a welcome addition of space for the growing company.

The Hodgdon name is recognized by almost every shooter. Whether one handloads for cartridge arms or shoots muzzleloaders, the company has products specifically tailored for virtually every shooting application. To appreciate the historical importance and impact of Hodgdon in America, we really need to look at two similar entities, distinct, yet intertwined.

Hodgdon is known as "The Gunpowder People," and for good reason. The company supplies handloaders and ammunition manufacturers with a comprehensive assortment of propellants for all sorts of firearms, and is always coming up with innovative products to fill yet another reloading niche. It's a corporate kaleidoscope, where new reloading combinations are continually forming, much to the delight of shooters. Plus, comprehensive loading data for its products are available from the company, free for the asking.

There's another equally important facet of Hodgdon. The Hodgdon family includes not only those folks who are related to the company's founder, Brewster (Bruce) Eltinge Hodgdon, but also the employees of the company, who are considered part of the family—kin and kith.

While Bruce was always interested in shooting, he swerved into the powder business in a roundabout way. Rumor has it that, around the start of World War II, Bruce was talking with a friend who lamented that the government had burned tons of leftover gunpowder after World War I, simply because there was no market for it. Bruce surmised that a

(left) Hodgdon's president and CEO, Tom Shepherd, and COO Tim Vaitekunas discuss business in the new office building. (right) This sign greets visitors to the remote Herington, Kansas, facility.

similar situation might exist after World War II. He also figured there would be a demand, so he started investigating just what he'd have to do to buy surplus gunpowder from the government. On November 26, 1947, using his life insurance policy as collateral, he borrowed the princely sum of $1,500 from his bank. After cutting through seeming miles of red tape, he found himself the owner of 50,000 pounds of surplus 4895. Now what?

Bruce wasn't really sure whether there were enough reloaders who would buy it.

Recall that, in those days, right after the war, returning GIs were busy building homes and families and didn't have a lot of spare cash to spend on guns and ammo. Further, handloading was still in its infancy. Many shooters regarded the practice as dangerous alchemy, and ammunition companies did nothing to dissuade people from that notion; handloaders were competition.

Nevertheless, Bruce persevered. He moved an old boxcar to a rented farm field to store the powder, placed a one-inch ad in *American Rifleman*, and

waited. Fortunately, he was right about the demand, and the orders came. A 150-pound keg of 4895 sold for all of $30, plus shipping. And, so, in 1947, an American icon was born. In 1952, B.E. Hodgdon, Incorporated, was formed. As for the $1,500 note? Bruce paid it off on February 11, 1948, just 76 days after the loan had been obtained.

When the supply of government surplus powders ran out, the company turned to newly manufactured propellants ranging from smokeless to blackpowder and its substitutes, all with

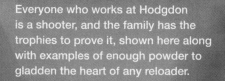

Everyone who works at Hodgdon is a shooter, and the family has the trophies to prove it, shown here along with examples of enough powder to gladden the heart of any reloader.

Several members of the Hodgdon management team gather around a bust of founder Bruce Hodgdon in the new digs. From left: Tim Vaitekunas, COO, Chris Hodgdon, Marketing and Sales, Ron Reiber, Chief Ballistician, and Bob Hodgdon, Bruce's son and Chris' dad—and obviously a fan of Gun Digest!

unique features tailored to specific uses. The company ventured into various retail businesses, too, but these were ultimately sold so the firm could concentrate on its core business, propellants.

In 1947, Hodgdon bought what was then rural land and built a new office building, where it remained for 65 years. However, as the decades rolled on, a residential/commercial city evolved around them and, as the company grew, it needed more space.

In August 2011, Hodgdon bought a new and vacant building in Shawnee, Kansas, about eight miles from the original offices. The move was completed in April 2012. The new digs provide 9,000 square feet, compared to 3,500 in the original building, a welcome addition for the thriving entity.

Today, Hodgdon has three facilities. The main office, as noted, the packaging and distribution plant in Herington, Kansas, and the Goex Black Powder Co. in Doyline, Louisiana. There are 16 employees at the main office, about 45 to 50 in Herington, and about 30 at Goex. It is important to note that the Hodgdon company is family owned, but is not family run. A board of 11 directors provides the leadership, but only four are mem-

Hodgdon's influence on American life even reached the space shuttle. Hodgdon H4227 powder was used to blow the explosive bolts to help separate the SRB (solid booster rocket) from the space shuttle Atlantis, two minutes after liftoff.

bers of the Hodgdon family. In fact, the company has strict protocols that must be followed before a family member can be considered for a managerial position in the company.

Shortly after the move, *Gun Digest* was granted exclusive access to Hodgdon's new offices and the manufacturing and packaging facility. My friend Chris Hodgdon, Bruce's grandson, graciously took time out of his busy schedule to show off the new space and squire me to the Herington plant for what was to be a fascinating glimpse into a unique and modern industrial complex.

The new offices are beautifully appointed and include a mini-museum of artifacts from the company's history. Each bibelot brought forth a flood of recollections to this long-time reloader. A highlight of the visit was chatting with Bob Hodgdon (Chris's dad), CEO Tom Shepherd, and COO Tim Vaitekunus. I also managed to trap Ron Reiber, Hodgdon's chief ballistic wizard, and picked his fertile mind for kernels of reloading lore. But we had to move on, so Chris and I piled into an SUV for the trip to Herington, about 130 miles to the west.

Hodgdon moved certain operations to this rural facility, in 1978, after a disastrous fire that destroyed its Pyrodex plant. The Herington complex started life as a military training base. Today, it is a marvel of industrial efficiency and economy. It is virtually self-contained and has no discharges—everything reusable is recycled, including powder drums, cardboard boxes, and even metal cuttings from the ballistics lab. It is indeed environmentally friendly. As good a thing as that is, the overriding concern at the plant is safety. Chris said their goal is for "every employee to go home to their family at night."

The sprawling complex has three basic functions. First, it is where smokeless powders are received from various manufacturers and re-packaged into the cans and jugs with which handloaders

Chris Hodgdon, left, and the author, with the granite slab engraved with the Hodgdon name and logo that has stood in front of the company's original offices for decades.

HODGDON POWDER CO

are all familiar. Second, this is where the blackpowder substitutes Pyrodex, Triple Seven, and White Hots are made. A third, separate building holds the sophisticated ballistics lab, where load data are developed.

Hodgdon doesn't manufacturer any smokeless powders at Herington, rather each powder is made to Hodgdon's exacting specifications by outside vendors. The propellants are received in 40- to 82-pound drums, are fed robotically into large hoppers, and then measured into smaller containers. As a safety measure, the hoppers and metering devices are on one side of a substantial wall and the operator is on the other side.

Every hunting family has its heirlooms, and Hodgdon is no exception. Here, Chris shows the author his Grandfather Bruce's Browning 12-gauge A-5, handed down to his grandson.

Additionally, only a certain amount of a given powder can be present at a loading magazine at a time.

Just before packaging, the lot number of the powder is keyed into a computer and a huge roll of pre-printed labels is fed into a printer that applies the lot number to the labels. This is an important step; this documentation will be checked frequently, as the containers make their way through the plant.

Special safety measures are taken at powder packaging. The operator places a limited number of empty labeled cans on a specially designed turntable that rotates them to the other side of a blast-proof wall. There, a precisely calibrated powder measure fills the containers, then the turntable rotates them back to the operator's side of the wall for capping. Numerous large copper ground wires are present on all equipment, as a safety measure.

Get this: every can or jug is individually weighed to make sure it contains the full stated amount. I asked Distribution and Packaging Manager David Johnson what their tolerance was for weights.

"From minus-zero percent to plus 1.5 percent," he said. "We'd rather give away some powder than cheat the customer," he added, matter-of-factly.

Next, Dave explained the lot number that appears on every can. "The first number is the size of the can, either one, four, or eight pounds. The next six numbers are the date, and the last three are the manufacturer's actual lot number. For example, '1120512123' means it is a one-pound can, packed on December 5, 2012, and the manufacturer's lot number is 123."

Each lot of powder is tracked from receipt to final packaging, and the lot number and powder type are double-checked by two people before it can leave the packaging area. If a container says H-4895 on it, you can rest assured that's what is in the can. There can be no mix-ups here.

Of course, of special interest to this reloading writer was the ballistics lab. I could only drool at the sophisticated equipment used to develop pressure-tested load data for Hodgdon products. The inventory of components—cases, and bullets, in addition to powders—was truly mind-boggling.

A sight to make any handloader swoon. This is just part of the Hodgdon ballistics lab's inventory of brass and bullets for load development.

Each cartridge requires its own pressure barrel and attendant electronic transducer; dozens of barrels adorned the walls. I asked Rick Basore, Production and Planning Manager, how much a pressure barrel costs. "About $3,500 each," he said. Plus, there's the technician's time required to calibrate and test each system, load the test rounds, and do statistical analyses on the results before it's ready for use by reloaders. This expensive work is especially impressive, when you consider that Hodgdon provides data for more than 5,000 loads free on its Loading Center website.

The manufacturer of Hodgdon's muzzleloading products at Herington is especially impressive, with the emphasis on safety and efficiency. The mixing of ingredients is accomplished in a separate building, and only a relatively small amount of an individual powder is present at any given time.

Hodgdon is involved in community outreach and holds reloading classes in this well-equipped classroom. Here it's shown set up here for shotshells.

For added safety, an expert production manager is discretely isolated in another building, and every nuance is directed via a series of computers and a bank of closed-circuit TV monitors that show every activity in the mixing bunker—it is otherworldly. The finished loose powders are then either packed for distribution or shunted to another building, where a uniquely designed press produces the muzzleloading pellets with which many readers are familiar. Interestingly, every employee is responsible for the individual product they make. They take care of and treat their pellet presses like they're their own cars; it's not a "rental car" approach, but rather one that's a unique approach to quality control.

The Hodgdon company and family represent values that are the bedrock of America—industry, hard work, and personal responsibility. In spite of trials and tribulations, Hodgdon continues to operate its company and its family as it always has. Part of the company's mission statement reads, "We deal with integrity and honesty, reflecting that people are more important than dollars." This is not idle chatter. Here's but one example.

A valued long-time employee we'll call "Bill" served in a job that involved repetitive bending and stooping. Bill developed problems with his knees, and his job caused him considerable discomfort. The company could have laid off Bill, but that's not the way Hodgdon treats "family." Instead, Bill was transferred to a different job where he doesn't have to bend and stoop, and one that still contributes to production. Since plant employees are already "cross-trained," this was a smooth transition.

Indeed, every employee I met was totally invested in the enterprise. Many have reached retirement age, but have chosen to stay on. After all, one does not retire from one's family.

The Hodgdon Company has been in business for more than six decades and supplies a total of 58 powders. Let us hope that 60 years hence, this fine old firm continues to prosperously serve shooters and the country. Bruce Hodgdon represented quintessential America, and his legacy is aptly maintained by his extended family of relatives and dedicated employees. So, as we celebrate Bruce's accomplishments, we must also soberly recognize that we'll probably not see his likes again.

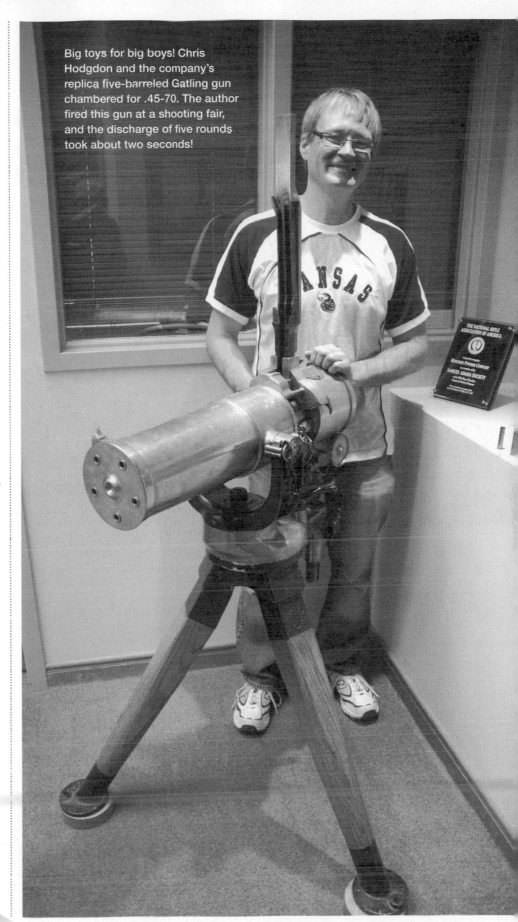

Big toys for big boys! Chris Hodgdon and the company's replica five-barreled Gatling gun chambered for .45-70. The author fired this gun at a shooting fair, and the discharge of five rounds took about two seconds!

THE REMARKABLE ROSS

BY Paul Scarlata, Photos by Paul Budde & Becky Leavitt (unless otherwise indicated)

Canadian Ross Straight-Pull Military Rifles: "If at first you don't succeed, try, try ... try again!"

It is disheartening to realize that the average American has little real knowledge of our northern neighbor Canada, a country with which we share so many historical, cultural, and economic ties. Canada has been a good neighbor, a staunch ally, and one of our largest trading partners.

Even lesser known is the country's proud military heritage. With her rather modest population, Canada has never been able to support a large military, but Canadian soldiers have fought with distinction all over the world. American veterans of our Revolution and the War of 1812 could speak from firsthand experience of the fighting qualities of the Canadian frontier scouts and militiamen.

In the late 1860s, Canadian militiamen repelled several incursions into Ontario by armed Irish-American extremists, the Fenians, many of them veterans of the Union and Confederate armies. The year 1885 saw the militia and North West Mounted Police suppressing a widescale uprising by the mixed-race Métis and Native Americans in the North-West Rebellion.

That same year saw Canadian troops serving with British forces in the Sudan. They also fought in the Second Anglo-Boer War (1899-1902), where their marksmanship, horsemanship, and veldt craft proved the equal of their Afrikaner foes. The also earned an enviable reputation in the trenches of the Western Front, during the First World War.

World War II again saw "Canucks" in action, with Dominion forces fighting Nazis, in Europe. They formed joint units with American troops in Italy, and later assisted U.S. forces in the recapture of the Aleutian Islands from the Japanese. During the post-war years, they maintained occupation troops in Germany, and provided a contingent to the UN forces during the Korean conflict.

Canadian units served alongside U.S. forces during the Gulf War, in Somalia, and, more recently, in Afghanistan. In the latter conflict, Canuck snipers have garnered much attention for impressive feats of long-range marksmanship.

It is perhaps ironic that, despite this proud record, the Canadian military's biggest claim to fame (at least from the viewpoint of military and firearms historians), is that they fielded one of the most controversial (disliked?) shoulder weapons ever seen on a battlefield, the Ross Straight-Pull Rifle.

Webster defines perseverance as the "determination to persist; to maintain an effort; refusal to give in." While some may view this characteristic as commendable, it can also lead to obstinacy, intractability, and the expenditure of a great deal of time, effort, and money, all to little purpose. Throughout history, a number of firearms designers have had this adjective connected with their names, as they persisted in attempting to improve upon a design whose obvious faults would have convinced more practical persons to give up. It can be fairly argued that the most notable member

The author test-firing from an MTM K-Zone rest.

of the clique was the Scottish-Canadian rifle designer, Sir Charles Ross.

Born in Scotland, on April 4, 1872, Charles Henry Augustus Frederick Lockhart Ross was the Ninth Baronet of Balnagown. His family was one of the wealthiest in Great Britain, but, unlike the bon vivant scions of many noble families, Sir Charles displayed a practical bent and had a variety of interests, eventually becoming an accomplished engineer, agricultural expert, and businessman.[1]

Ross was an accomplished outdoorsman, big-game hunter, fisherman, and renowned rifle shot. His interest in firearms, combined with his mechanical proclivities and engineering studies, led to his patenting a rifle, in 1893, while still a student at Eton. But, while Sir Charles possessed obvious talents as an engineer and businessman, he displayed two less well-regarded traits. He tended to be impatient; when he wanted something done, he wanted it done yesterday. He also would not abide criticism of his inventions, often failing to recognize their

shortcomings. Despite these traits, his commanding personality—and wealth—usually resulted in him getting things his way. Once his inventive genius was set upon the task of developing a new repeating rifle, there was no stopping him.

I don't know if it was the water or the mountain air, but, for some reason, all the well-known nineteenth century straight-pull rifles were invented by men who hailed from either the Alpine regions of central Europe, or the Scottish highlands: Ferdinand von Mannlicher, Oberst Rudolph Schmidt, James Paris Lee, and Sir Charles Ross. While all are well known, only those rifles developed by Mannlicher can be considered truly successful, with large numbers seeing service with Central European, Balkan, South American, and Asian armies, from 1886 into the early 1950s. Schmidt's rifle was adopted by Europe's most neutral nation, Switzerland, and, thus, never saw combat service. Lee's M1895 rifle was adopted by the U.S. Navy and Marine Corps., but was replaced after a mere six years in service. Still, it

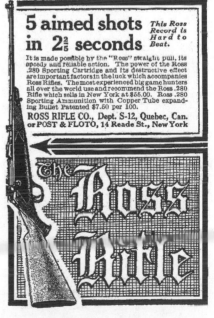

5 aimed shots in 2⅖ seconds *This Ross Record is Hard to Beat.*

It is made possible by the "Ross" straight pull, its speedy and reliable action. The power of the Ross .280 Sporting Cartridge and its destructive effect are important factors in the luck which accompanies Ross Rifles. The most experienced big game hunters all over the world use and recommend the Ross .280 Rifle which sells in New York at $55.00. Ross .280 Sporting Ammunition with Copper Tube expanding Bullet Patented $7.50 per 100.

ROSS RIFLE CO., Dept. S-12, Quebec, Can. or POST & FLOTO, 14 Reade St., New York

The Ross Rifle

This pre-WWI advertisement sings the praises of the Ross as a hunting and target rifle.

was Ross' weapon that became the most controversial of the straight-pull genre, gaining both international acclaim on the target range and condemnation in the trenches of the Western Front.

In 1897, Ross obtained a patent for a design that was influenced by his contemporary, Mannlicher. THis gun displayed strong similarities to the Österreichische-Repetier-Gewehr M.95.

The bolt was composed of two pieces, a hollow sleeve with the bolt handle at its rear, and a shaft that was inserted into the front of the sleeve, which had dual lugs that locked into mortises in the receiver. On the shaft were a series of opposed helical ribs that mated with grooves in the sleeve. When the bolt handle was pulled to the rear, the ribs, moving in the grooves, caused the shaft to rotate, unlocking the lugs and allowing it to be pulled to the rear, extracting and ejecting the spent cartridge case. Pushing the bolt forward chambered the next round from the magazine and rotated the shaft to the locked position. Bolt binding was prevented by ribs on the outside of the sleeve moving in grooves in the receiver. Ross' Model 1897 rifle used a unique hinged hammer-sear that struck a spring-loaded firing pin, which extended out into the hollowed-out bolt.

Lack of interest by British gun makers led to Ross arranging for two U.S. companies, Billings & Spencer and Frank Mossberg Company, to produce parts and complete rifles to his design. He arranged for the firm of Charles Lancaster to assemble rifles in England, using American-made actions, but barreled and stocked to British tastes.

In 1900, Ross improved the design to use a "normal" firing pin and mainspring, which was compressed by the forward movement of the bolt. U.S. patents for this and other improvements were held by his American agent, Joseph A. Bennett.

Both the Model 1897 and 1900 Ross rifles used magazines that were copied from Mannlicher. The magazine body extended below the stock and was loaded with a packet (clip) of five cartridges that remained in and functioned as an integral part of the magazine. After the last round was chambered, the clip fell out of an opening in the bottom of the magazine body.

As was to be expected of a man of his social position, during the Second Anglo-Boer War (1899-1902) Ross served as a lieutenant with the Seaforth Highlanders, and from 1904 to 1913 as a reserve Captain with the Lovat Scouts Yeomanry.[2] In fact, it was Britain's imperialistic conquest of the hard fighting Afrikaners that provided the impetus Sir Charles was seeking with which to promote his rifle as a military weapon. Canada, as a part of the British Empire, had traditionally used British-pattern military weapons. In the late nineteenth century, all the world's powers were racing to reequip their armies with the new smallbore, smokeless powder repeating rifles, but, as Canada had no neighbors with hostile intentions, it was viewed as a "safe" colony and, thus, was at the end of the pipeline, when it came to obtaining supplies of new weapons. While most armies were using these newer repeating rifles, Canadian militia forces were still equipped with single-shot, blackpowder Martini-Henry and Snider rifles.

When Canadian troops left to serve in South Africa, the government in Ottawa requested that Britain provide Canada with the new .303 Lee-Enfield rifles. Instead, they received Martini-Enfields re-barreled to .303. The British government not forthcoming, the Canadians attempted to place orders with private firms in England for 15,000 Mark I Lee-Enfields, only to have this overruled by the War Department, which claimed that British army demands took priority.

The Canadian government then attempted to interest the Birmingham Small Arms Company (BSA) in setting up a rifle factory in Canada, but its efforts proved fruitless. As it was with most nations at the time, Canada was experiencing a surge of nationalism, and members of Parliament opined that Canada should not have to depend upon foreign sources for its military armament. After repeated entreaties to Great Britain were ignored, the Minister of Militia, Sir Frederick Borden, told the government that Canada had no alternative but to build its own rifles. Enter Sir Charles Ross.

With his business acumen, Sir Charles saw the Canadians' dilemma as a perfect opportunity to market his rifle.

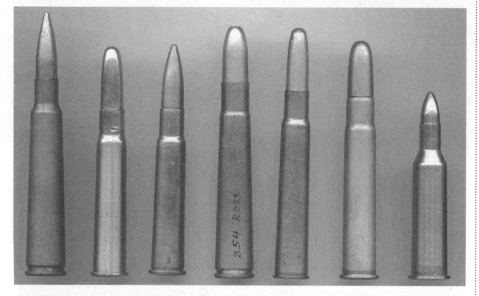

Ross military, target, and sporting rifles were chambered for the following cartridges (L to R): .280 Ross, .303 Mark VI, .303 Mark VII, .354 Ross, .35 Winchester, .375-303 Nitro Express, and the 6.35x54R Soviet Running Deer cartridge. (Lou Behling photo)

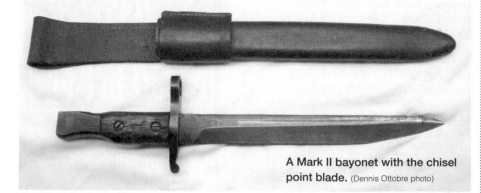

A Mark II bayonet with the chisel point blade. (Dennis Ottobre photo)

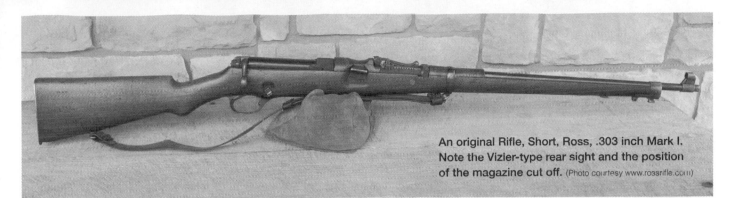

An original Rifle, Short, Ross, .303 inch Mark I. Note the Vizler-type rear sight and the position of the magazine cut off. (Photo courtesy www.rossrifle.com)

The Mark I pioneered the doughnut-shaped bolt handle. Note the knurled cocking piece and sliding safety on the bolt handle.

A meeting was arranged and a military version of his Model 1900 rifle was demonstrated, followed by Sir Charles offering to set up a factory in Canada to produce rifles—at his own expense!

This was too good a deal for the Canadian government to pass up, and a militia committee was established to test the Ross rifle. Initial tests of a tool room sample rifle were disappointing because, while the rifle proved accurate and had a higher rate of fire than the Lee-Enfield, it failed the excessive proof and endurance trials. Ross claimed this was due to the poor quality of the Canadian-manufactured .303 cartridges, but, with his usual dogged determination, he set about rectifying the problems and adopting the changes the committee suggested. After another series of trials, the improved Rifle, Ross, .303 inch, Mark I was officially adopted in April 1902.

In March 1903, the Canadian government signed a contract with Ross for 12,000 rifles, to be followed by 10,000 rifles annually for the next five years. That same year, construction began on the $500,000 Ross Rifle Factory, in Quebec City. In August 1905, the first rifles were actually delivered, these going to units of the Royal North West Mounted Police.

The early Ross factory Mark I rifles were assembled with some parts imported from Mossberg and Billings & Spencer, resulting in an outcry from the opposition Conservative party about the "all-Canadian-made rifle that was promised us." But Ross also had supporters among the Conservatives, including General Sir Samuel Hughes, who dominated his party's military affairs. Sir Sam, as he was known, was a brash and bull-headed man—a kindred spirit of Ross it would seem—and there was no changing his mind once it was made up. A fellow Boer War veteran and noted marksman, he was suitably impressed by the rifles long-range accuracy and became Ross' staunchest supporter.

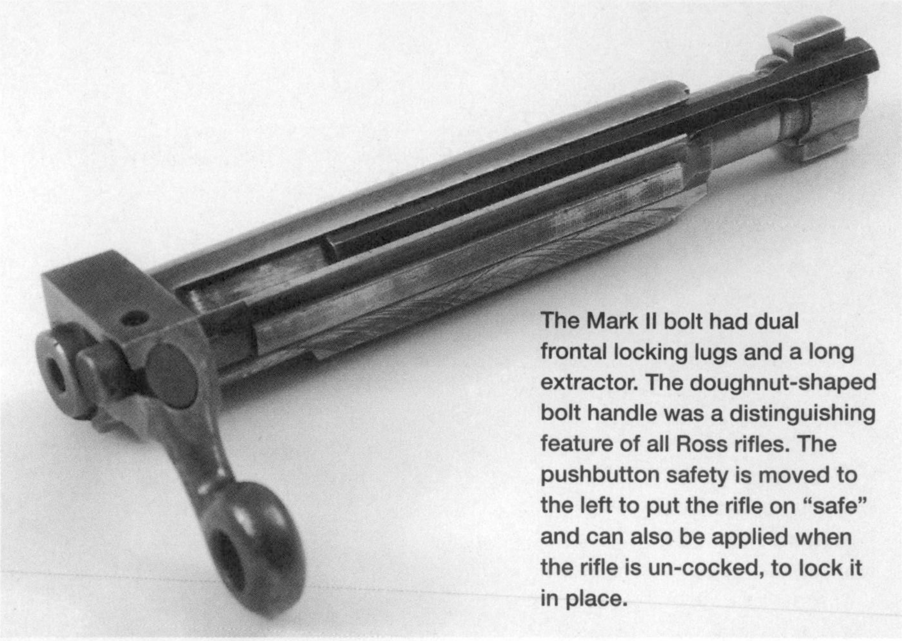

The Mark II bolt had dual frontal locking lugs and a long extractor. The doughnut-shaped bolt handle was a distinguishing feature of all Ross rifles. The pushbutton safety is moved to the left to put the rifle on "safe" and can also be applied when the rifle is un-cocked, to lock it in place.

In 1911, when the Conservatives won control of the government, Sir Sam was appointed Minister of Militia, a post he would hold until 1916.[3] Till the very end he remained an ardent believer in Sir Charles' rifle and personally saw to it that the Quebec factory continued to receive government orders.

At a time when the British army was going to the shorter No. 1 Lee-Enfield (SMLE), and the U.S. had adopted the handy M1903 Springfield, the Canadians opted for a traditional long-barreled infantry rifle, although the Mark 1's slim, walnut, pistol grip stock kept its weight down to a very manageable eight pounds.

After its straight-pull bolt, the Mark 1's most distinctive feature was the Harris Controlled Platform Magazine, a box magazine that was manually loaded through the open action. A long lever with a finger-actuated depressor on the

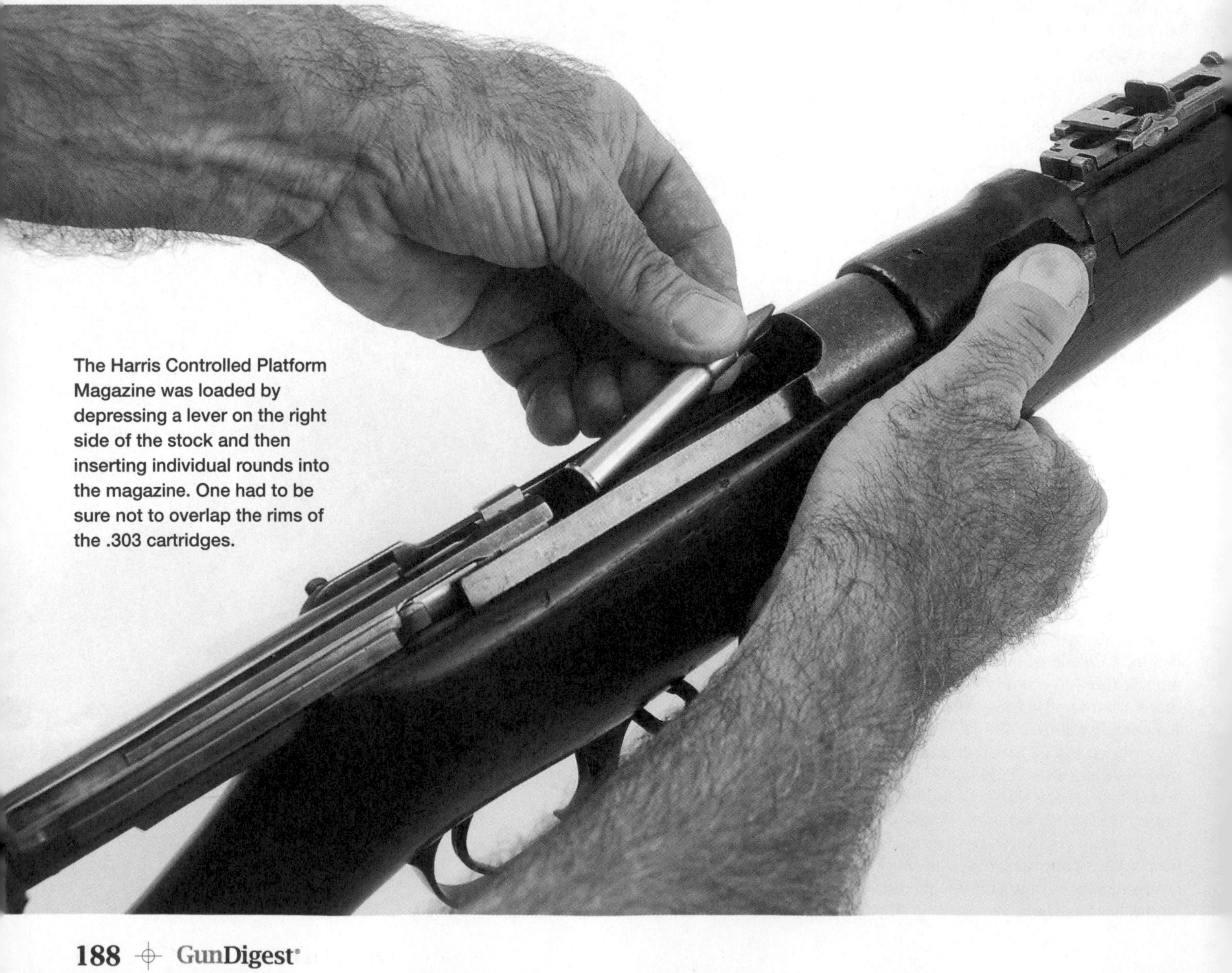

The Harris Controlled Platform Magazine was loaded by depressing a lever on the right side of the stock and then inserting individual rounds into the magazine. One had to be sure not to overlap the rims of the .303 cartridges.

right side of the stock was attached to the magazine follower. Pushing it down depressed the follower, allowing five loose rounds to be loaded into the magazine. When released, the follower would spring back up, so rounds could be chambered by the forward-moving bolt. A magazine cutoff lever was located above the right side of the trigger guard. Why this system was used, when charger-loaded Mauser and Enfield magazines were already in wide use, is anyone's guess.

Specifications: Rifle, Ross, .303 inch, Mark I	
Caliber	.303 Mark VI
Overall length	48.6 inches
Barrel length	28 inches
Weight (unloaded)	8.03 pounds
Magazine capacity	five rounds
Front sight:	hooded blade
Rear sight:	fold up leaf, adj. to 2,200 yds.
Bayonet	knife-style with a 10-inch blade

According to bayonet collector Dennis Ottobre (www.e-bayonet.com), there are two different Ross bayonets, the Mark I and Mark II (often incorrectly referred to as M1905 and M1910). The Mark I had a smaller-diameter muzzle ring than the Mark II, and the two were not interchangeable. Both were originally produced with a "fat" blade profile and later had the blade profile changed to a "chisel point," so as to improve penetration.

During this period, Sir Charles attempted to interest the British army in his rifle. But he received short shift from the army, despite a repeat of his offer to bankroll building a factory to produce his rifles. Returning to Canada, Ross found himself embroiled in the first—but not the last—controversy over the new rifle.

With field service, numerous shortcomings came to the fore, and these peaked in August 1906, when a RNWMP constable, Sgt. Major W.J. Bowdridge, was blinded in his right eye, when part of his Mark I bolt assembly was blown back into his face during target practice. This incident prompted the Force Commander to withdraw all Ross rifles from service and return them to the factory.

Complaints about Militia-issue rifle receivers bursting became numerous, enough that a special commission was appointed to investigate. It suggested re-

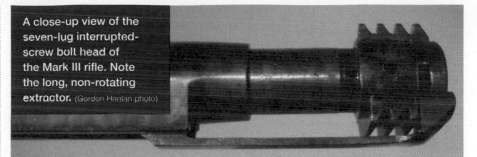

A close-up view of the seven-lug interrupted-screw bolt head of the Mark III rifle. Note the long, non-rotating extractor. (Gordon Hanlan photo)

ABOVE: This was the type of sight originally fitted to Mark II rifles. (courtesy www.rossrifle.com)

This view shows the open-notch battle sight, offset charger guide, distinctive bolt handle, and safety lever. (Gordon Hanlan photo)

designing the bolt to cock on opening, not closing, modification of the bolt stop and extractor, relocating the cutoff lever inside the trigger guard, and the installation of a more rugged rear sight. The resulting rifle, the Mark II, was a temporary fix at best, because, as soon as a problem was corrected, a new one seemed to arise. With each new modification to the basic rifle, a star (*) was added to the model designation. Thus the Mark II*, Mark II**, Mark II***, Mark II****, and Mark II***** followed each other in rapid succession, each differing from the other to some minor or major degree.

The most obvious changes were the rear sights. The fold-up leaf was replaced by a tangent, which was replaced by a

This pre-WWI Canadian soldier is armed with a Mk. II rifle. (Photo courtesy Barry DeLong)

Sir Samuel Hughes was the Ross rifle's most influential, and stubborn, supporter.

Corporal Francis Pegahmagabow, an Ojibwa Indian from Ontario, was the most effective sniper of World War I, credited with killing 378 Germans and capturing 300. He is shown here with a Ross Mark III rifle that armorers had modified by shortening the forearm.

Lang Vizier-style, then a ramp/tangent and, finally, two other types of fold-up leaf sights. Other changes included extractors, safeties (levers or push buttons), cutoff levers, barrel bands, stronger stocks, and 30½-inch barrels (Mk. II**). There was even a short-lived Mark II carbine, intended for mounted units and fitted with a 26-inch barrel. But Sir Sam firmly believed that accuracy required a long barrel, and that was the end to that.

In 1909, Sir Sam pressured the RNWMP into purchasing 1,000 Ross Mark II* rifles. It appears they were only used for training purposes at the Regina Depot, while most constables in the field continued to use M1876 Winchesters and various "Long" Lee-Enfield rifles.

In the best traditions of parliamentary democracy, the opposition Conservative Party had a field day over the continuing inability of the Liberal government to sort out the problems with the Ross. Once the euphoria of its 1911 electoral victory had subsided, the Conservatives discovered—much to their chagrin—that, along with the normal political spoils, they had inherited the Ross! Of course, with Sir Sam running interference, it was possible for them to deflect much of the criticism that continued to be heaped upon the army's rifle. Of even more help was that despite its shortcomings as a military weapon, in the intervening years, the Ross rifle had come to dominate international competition. Indeed, when teamed up with the new high-performance .280 Ross cartridge, the Mark II** rifle had proven itself the long-range champion of the day. At the 1909 Bisley Shoot, it scored so many successes that its praises were sung in newspapers and gun periodicals on both sides of the Atlantic.

With its pride damaged, the British National Rifle Association questioned whether the Ross truly qualified as a "service rifle," being it was chambered for a non-regulation cartridge and sported special sights. Once again, Sir Sam came to the rescue, browbeating the Canadian Department of Militia and Defense into declaring the Ross .280 rifle an "issue weapon to the Canadian forces." The .280 Mark II** rifle went on to chalk up an impressive record of wins in various international competitions during the pre-war years.

In addition to military and target rifles, the Quebec factory also offered sporting rifles chambered for the .280 Ross, .303 British, .354 Ross-Ely, .35 Winchester, and .375-303 Nitro Express. The .280 rifles,

in particular, became the darlings of a devoted clique of British and American sportsmen. There was a steady stream of accolades in the firearms press of the day.

Despite its winning ways on the target range, eventually, Sir Sam had to admit that the situation had become too chaotic to be allowed to continue. The government requested Ross redesign his rifle in an attempt to iron out all of the bugs and so silence, once and for all, the embarrassing criticism that continued to be heaped upon it. Meanwhile, an attempt was made to camouflage the continuing problems and incessant modifications necessary to keep the Ross in service.

In 1912, the Department of Militia and Defense declared the Mark II** rifle fitted with the 30½-inch barrel as the Rifle, Ross, .303 inch, Mark II and the *standard* rifle of the Canadian armed forces. Those Mark II*** and Mark II***** rifle with 28-inch barrels were referred to as the Rifle, Short, Ross, .303 inch, Mark II, while all others, regardless their level of modification, were relegated to the status of Rifle, Ross, Short, .303 inch, Ross Mark I.

Specifications: Rifle, Ross, .303 inch, Mark II (formerly Mark II**)	
Caliber	.303 Mark VI
Overall length	51 inches
Barrel length	28.5 inches
Weight (unloaded)	8.04 pounds
Magazine capacity	five rounds
Front sight:	hooded blade
Rear sight:	fold up leaf, adj. to 2,200 yds.
Bayonet	knife-style with a 10-inch blade

It's been said the success of the Ross rifle in competition caused Sir Charles' attention to be diverted away from the battlefield and towards the target range. The rifle designed as a replacement for the Mark II displayed all those characteristics he felt necessary in a long-range match rifle, more so than a military weapon. He also attempted to convince Canadian authorities—unsuccessfully—to replace the .303 with the .280 Ross.

While Sir Sam was loath to discard the Empire's official rifle cartridge, to no one's surprise, he found the new rifle to his liking. Adopted in the summer of 1911, the

Rifle, Ross, .303 inch, Mark III (sometimes referred to as the M10) differed radically from its predecessors, the most obvious of these changes concerning the bolt, magazine, and rear sight.

Specifications: Rifle, Ross, .303 inch, Mark III	
Caliber	.303 Mark VI
Overall length	50.6 in.
Barrel length	30.5 in.
Weight (unloaded)	9.85 lbs.
Magazine capacity	five rounds, charger loaded
Front sight:	hooded blade
Rear sight:	fixed open battle sights for 600 & 1,000 yards, fold up leaf with aperture adj. from 200 to 1,200 yards
Bayonet	knife-style with a 10-inch blade

The new rifle utilized a "triple-thread interrupted screw double-bearing cam bolt head." In layman's terms, the simple and rugged double locking lugs on the bolt were replaced with an interrupted screw system with seven small lugs. In theory, this provided much stronger breech locking, which was not actually necessary with the .303 cartridge. But it was more difficult to manufacture, clean, and maintain these all important considerations of a military weapon.

An easier to manufacture, squared-off, slab-sided receiver was used that was rather homely, when compared to the finely machined Mark II receiver. A single-column magazine extended down past the stock and was loaded with standard Lee-Enfield five-round chargers.

The rear sight, similar to those on Ross target rifles, was mounted on the receiver, providing a longer sight radius. It had a "U"-notch battle sight set for 600 yards, a fold-up leaf with another "U"-notch battle sight set for 1,000 yards, and an aperture finely adjustable by micrometer from 200 to 1,200 yards and for windage. A thumb piece on the left side of the receiver did double duty as both a magazine cutoff and bolt release. The Mark III was fitted with a 30½-inch barrel and a more robust stock, increasing weight by almost two pounds.

When chambered for the .280 Ross, the new Mark III Target Rifle lived up to the reputation for long-range accuracy its Mark II predecessor had established. In fact, after sweeping its way to successive victories at both Bisley and Camp Perry, in 1913, the American National Rifle Association rewrote its service rifle rules to *exclude* the Ross.

In spite of these "improvements," the Mark III rifle possessed one unforgivable trait: The bolt could be assembled in such a way that the bolt shaft did not rotate upon being closed. It does not take much imagination to visualize what occurred, when a rifle with an unlocked bolt was fired. Ross did not consider this a problem for well-trained troops or target shooters, but, with the hastily raised units typical of the Great War, it would be the beginning of the end for the Ross rifle.

Continuing production problems resulted in the Ross Rifle Company falling behind its scheduled delivery of rifles, leading to more acrimonious debate in Parliament that was stilled only by the outbreak of the Great War. In fact, the first contingent of the Canadian Expeditionary Force (CEF) to arrive in England was armed with Mark II rifles, though these were replaced with Mark IIIs before the troops left for France. Apparently, no Mark II rifles were used in combat on the Western Front.

While the Mark III has proved much more accurate than the No. 1 Mk. III Lee-Enfield carried by the rest of the Empire's troops, once it was exposed to the rigors of combat, the Ross was plagued with a series of problems, the most damning, after the bolt assembly problem, being persistent jamming. It appeared that the bolt provided insufficient initial extraction, especially when the rifle became hot or the chamber was dirty. In an attempt to mollify continuing criticism, Sir Charles again blamed the issue ammunition and suggested all soldiers be issued a cleaning stick, so they could swab out their rifle chambers periodically—no mean feat with battalions of Huns charging down upon you!

Those Canadian politicians and journalists who were already well versed at assailing the Ross and its backers had a field day, as reports came back from Flanders of Canadian troops being forced to kick open the bolts of their rifles or use entrenching tools to hammer them free. Despite orders from Sir Sam forbidding the practice, Canucks in the trenches began throwing away their Ross rifles and replacing them with any Lee-Enfield they could beg, borrow, trade for, or steal. Reportedly, Canadian troops showed a great aptitude for the latter.

Sir Sam's defense of the Ross rifle in Parliament began to verge upon desperation, but he remained loyal to the end, even predicting that his career would stand or fall on the Ross rifle.

A new outcry arose in Parliament, in late 1915, when it was learned that Sir Charles had signed a contract to supply the British army, then desperate for weapons, with 100,000 rifles. This resulted in the last of Ross' military designs, the Mark IIIB, which differed from the Canadian rifle in that it used a Pattern 14-style front and rear sight—the latter with triangular guards—and a more substantial forearm. The government's opponents in Parliament asked how Ross could sell rifles to Britain, when he could not produce sufficient numbers for Canadian forces. The situation was further exacerbated, when it was discovered Ross had tendered a similar offer to the Imperial Russian government.

Canadian armorers in France eventually overcame the bolt assembly problem by the simple expedient of installing a rivet or screw in the sleeve, preventing incorrect assembly. But the jamming problem had by then reached epidemic proportions, resulting in an official investigation by Maj. R.M. Blair, Assistant Inspector of Small Arms for Canadian Ordnance. Careful tests and examination of malfunctioning rifles led to the determination that the culprit was the bolt stop. When the bolt was pulled to the rear, the rearmost bolt lug thread came into violent contact with the bolt stop, and its rear edge soon became burred or cracked. When the bolt was thrust forward, the deformed lug tended to jam in its receiver mortise. Continued operation, especially during rapid fire, exacerbated the situation, until the bolt could no longer be opened.

The remedy actually proved simple enough: Increasing the diameter of the bolt stop at the area of impact halved the stress at each blow and stopped deformation of the lug thread. While the modification would have been simple enough to perform on rifles in the field, Canadian troops had lost all faith in the Ross, with many ignoring orders to turn in "liberated" Lee-Enfields and resume using the much-distrusted Mark III.

Orders came from Ottawa, albeit somewhat quietly, to begin rearming Canadian troops with No. 1 Mk. III rifles and, by September 1916, no Ross rifles remained in frontline service. True to his earlier

A typical 100-yard group measuring slightly over three inches in size.

prediction, Sir Samuel Hughes was asked to tender his resignation shortly afterwards, and all further Canadian contracts for Ross rifles were cancelled.

The Quebec factory continued to produce Mark IIIB rifles to fulfill the British order, eventually delivering some 66,500 before the contract was cancelled, in March 1917. That same month, the Canadian government expropriated the Ross Rifle Company, paying Sir Charles two million dollars. Such a return on his initial investment once again confirmed his reputation as an astute businessman.[4] Plans to convert the factory to production of Pattern 14 Enfield rifles and M1911 pistols were cancelled by the Armistice.

Despite the scandal it created, the Ross rifle continued to soldier on. A number of Mark IIIs, some in .280-caliber, were equipped with Warney & Swasey prismatic and Winchester A5 telescopic sights and used by Canadian snipers—a task for which they earned an enviable reputation as the best snipers of WWI.[5] Aside from their use as sniper rifles, British contract Mark IIIB Ross rifles were used for training and issued to the Royal Navy, Royal Marines, and the Royal Flying Corps so as to free up additional No. 1 Mk. III Lee-Enfield rifles for front line units.

After the war, the British became involved in the Russian civil war and supplied large amounts of military equipment, including Ross Mk. III and IIIB rifles, to Lithuanian, Latvian, and

Estonian nationalist forces fighting the Bolsheviks in the Baltic region. Many of these remained in service with the Baltic republics until they were occupied by the USSR, in 1940.

When the United States entered the war on the Allied side, in 1917, they, too, found themselves short of rifles. Among other non-standard models, they purchased 20,000 Mark II*** Ross rifles from Canada, for use as training rifles by the U.S. Army. About half were provided to the New York State National Guard, while a small number went to the U.S. Junior Naval Reserve. U.S.-issue Ross rifles can be identified by the Ordnance Department's "flaming bomb" symbol and "U.S." stamped on the stock behind the trigger guard.[6]

Reportedly, many of the Mark II rifles sold to the U.S. Army have "LC" marked on the receiver, which stands for "Large Chamber." This was done at the regimental level, in both Canada and England, after it was found that out-of-spec .303 ammunition was causing difficult extraction, the cause a result of Canadian Politicians steering lucrative contracts to companies with little or no experience manufacturing ammunition.[7] To correct this problem, armorers were instructed to ream out the chambers and then mark the receivers with "LC" on Mark IIs and "E" (Enlarged) on Mark IIIs. It appears the U.S. Army shortened and re-chambered barrels on some of

the LC-marked rifles it received (much as was done on the M1903 Springfield rifle after the adoption of the .30-06 cartridge).

During the inter-war years, the Ross faded into obscurity, except for a few still seen on the rifle range. But, with the outbreak of World War II, the old Ross was recalled to the colors (excuse me, "colours"). Once again desperate for rifles, the British issued those Mark IIIBs they still had in storage and additional Mark IIIs provided by Canada to the Home Guard, until they were replaced with Pattern 14 Enfield and U.S. Model 1917 rifles. Some ex-Home Guard Ross rifles were then transferred to the merchant marine.

On this side of the Atlantic, the Royal Canadian Navy, the Veterans Guard of Canada, coastal artillery, militia, and training centers all used Mark III rifles until local production of the No. 4 Lee-Enfield caught up to demand.[8]

A few of the British Mark IIIB rifles supplied to the former Baltic republics turned up in Finland during the Winter War (1939-1940), in that nation's heroic fight against the USSR's unwarranted aggression. Others rifles that had been confiscated when the USSR annexed the Baltic republics were used by Soviet Peoples Militia, during the desperate battles around Leningrad and Moscow. Some Mark IIIs were reportedly included in military aid shipments from Canada. Last, it has been reported that, in the immediate post-war years, Britain supplied some Mark III rifles to Luxembourg's la Gendarmerie Grand-Ducale, although they were replaced in less than a year with Lee-Enfields.[9]

Footnotes

1 At one point, in an attempt to evade the United Kingdom's taxation on the income from his arms manufacturing activities, Ross declared his Scotland estates to be a territory of the United States of America. This led to his being branded an outlaw for a time by the British Government.

2 During the Boer War Ross equipped some members of his unit with of his straight-pull rifle at his own expense. He reported that they performed with complete satisfaction.

3 Sir Sam's regular attempts to promote and appoint officers based upon patronage and Canadian nativism instead of ability not only created tension and jealousy between units but negatively affected the early performance of the Canadian Expeditionary Force in France. (http://en.wikipedia.org/wiki/Sam_Hughes)

4 Sir Charles relocated to the United States where he worked briefly as a small arms advisor. He eventually retired to St. Petersburg, Florida where he avidly pursued deep sea fishing until his death at the age of 70.

5 Cpl. Francis Pegahmagabow, an Ojibwa Indian, from Ontario is credited with killing 378 Germans and capturing 300. He was the most highly decorated Native American soldier in Canadian history.

6 Canfield, Bruce N. U.S. Infantry Weapons of the First World War. Andrew Mowbray Publishers, 2000. Pages 88 – 90 & 128.

7 Experienced Canadian riflemen were known to shift through ammunition to find that made by the Dominion Arsenal in Canada which was known to be of a higher quality.

8 A paramilitary unit who provided security at important military installations and prisoner of war camps.

9 http://en.wikipedia.org/wiki/Ross_rifle

THE 7.62X39 RUSSIAN SHORT

A Misunderstood but Effective Mid-range Centerfire Round Proves Itself Down Under.

BY **L.P. Brezny**

It was early September, when my feet hit the ground at the airport in Brisbane, Australia. After depositing about a full pound of paper work on a customs officer's desk and getting the third degree for the next half hour as to why I was bringing deadly tools into the country, I was finally granted my required papers and allowed to tote a lightweight, turn-bolt, four-shot Model 85 Zastava Mauser into this strict, urban, non-hunting, and clearly dictated anti-gun state. If my writing makes me seem a bit rattled, it's because I hunt Australia often. In fact, I've done so about three times in the last 18 months. But, in even that short period of time, the gun regulations for non-residents have gotten stricter and, because of that, I have considered just buying a rifle, sending it south, and leaving it with the good folks at the cattle station I hunt most often, when I venture down under. The problem with that plan, however, is that each time I head for Australia, I have a task before me that always includes using a new offering, such as a bullet, complete cartridge, or a new rifle that requires a detailed field review.

On this trip, one of the most common cartridges and rifle type used across this massive continent turns out to be the 7.62x39mm, also known as the Russian Short or .30 Russian short (this to help differentiate it from the 7.62x54 Russian round, known as the .30 Russian Long), as chambered in a nice, Serbian-built Mauser rifle. I had been doing a great deal of work accurizing the basic AK-47 the previous year and, as such, had crossed tracks with just about every known factory load and more than several handloads offered for the famous so-called "assault cartridge" of Russia. Wanting to push for better down-range performance, I'd gone on a search for a turn-bolt rifle chambered in the legendary cartridge. Even though the 7.62x39 in the SKS and AK-47 has not had the best reputation in the accuracy department, my previous shooting of it back home, in South Dakota, had indicated that further review of this cool little round was in order. The AK project had convinced me that this was not an inaccurate round at all. In fact, when pressed to work by way of a good rifle, quality sights, and a proper fitting stock, the Russian Short .30-caliber tended to stand quite tall, as an option for taking on kangaroo, hogs, or deer Down Under.

When my mates up at the cattle station, near Toowomba, got wind of my project cartridge and rifle, they were quick to muster up by way of their own gun shop operation at Hyper Fire, in the town of Crows Nest Queens Land, a new CZ 527 bolt-action in 7.62x39. As it was to turn out, that wasn't such a hard thing to do Down Under, thanks to the popularity associated with this rather inexpensive and available round.

A Subsistence Rifle Cartridge

Back home in South Dakota, and much as it is with the cattle station folks in Australia, the 7.62x39 is a fairly popular round among those brush-busting swamp hunters in the middle of the state, or with the jack pine savages who cut trails in the deep pine foothills of the massive Black Hills region in the western portion of the state. I got an early education as to this fact, being an Eastern tenderfoot at the time, when local hunters came to me requesting some help in selecting cartridges and sometimes even a deer rifle, only to learn in each case they were thinking about buying an SKS, a used Ruger M-77, or an old Ruger Mini 30 carbine chambered in the Russian Short, with

A range of ammunition was taken afield for hogs. All have soft-point bullets, selected to get the job done with the 7.62x39 Russian Short.

which they could put meat on the table all winter long.

Times were changing then, in terms of rifle prices and cost per round of ammunition. Folks who lived off the land and didn't have a pile of money seemed to have discovered, much like my Aussie blokes, that this very well designed, basic cartridge could be used for mere pennies on the dollar, versus the cost of the high-end cannons carried by most hunters.

Thinking back, I can't count the number of walrus, African big game, and other related critters I've seen both in person and on film taken by way of the 7.62x39 cartridge. With its tapered case wall and short length, it is a dream to handload, extracts like warm butter and, when paired with the 123- through 125-grain bullet that's designed for the case and volume of propellant, the round generates positive ballistics.

I have never agreed with the writers who say this is a close relative of the .30-30 Winchester or a smaller version of the .308 Winchester. The 7.62x39 is in a class by itself. Designed as a machine gun round to function flawlessly in the AK-47 and other rifles, regardless conditions or wear and tear on the firearm, it is a battle round turned game taker and home-, ranch-, or farm-defense tool when necessary. In the past few years, it seems like everyone is trying to dance around this cartridge and come up with a new military round; enter the new Remington .30-caliber, for instance. As the final icing on this ballistic cake, check out the 6mm PPC, perhaps the best benchrest round ever produced. Its parent case? Why it's the 7.62x39 Russian Short. Small wonder how that happened, isn't it?

Into the Field

Now that I have made my case for this cartridge, it's about time to measure the success (or possible failure) of the round. So, back to Australia and day one of hog hunting in the Outback. In terms of the first animal downed with the 7.62x39, the credit goes to a young lady. Her name is Anne Fallon, and she is the mate of Mike Groth, the fellow who runs the Hyper Fire gun shop. Anne had just started hunting, after taking some shooting lessons from Mike on the range at Glenelg. She had elected to take on the CZ 527 in 7.62x39 in a Serbian soft-nose 123-grain (.308-diameter

My partner and stock station owner Scott Withey, with a dusted-off porker. Scott was shooting the CZ 527.

) cartridge dubbed the "Highland AX." This ammo is very common among the Russian Short shooters down there, and after she was given the assignment to drop a young doe kangaroo for camp meat, there was just about no question in my mind as to how effective the cartridge was on a 100-pound or so target.

A kangaroo was located. Anne missed the straight-on vitals as the kangaroo faced her, but she had caught enough of the upper chest area so as to distribute the energy from the 123-grain soft-nose bullet across the critter's lung/heart area, ending its escape in short order. This 123-grain soft-nose bullet was reaching velocities exceeding 2,200 fps

at the 75-yard range at which Anne took the doe.

First Pig Down

With Scott Withey, my partner and friend at the wheel of his 4x4 utility vehicle, we rolled across the endless space that makes up Glenelg Station, the cattle station Scott had set up for guest hunters, and also as a thriving stock operation in its own right. While I didn't get lead on target, Mike's son did by way of his .308 Winchester. Anne pulled up on a good boar hog, too, but missed him. It was not until midday,

'Roo on the lookout. You'll never go hungry in the bush, as long as you have ammo.

and a lunchtime split from the team that saw Scott and I hunting alone, that our luck changed.

While starting up a steep rise with the 4x4, we spotted five good hogs about 200 yards downrange. Easing up the ridge on foot, we both opened up with the 7.62x39 Russian Shorts, managing to hit one good-sized sow right off. Scott was shooting some of my Remington 125-grain PSP fodder that I had hauled along for testing, and I was using my Sierra MatchKing 125-grain handloads, so it was difficult to say who hit what part of that sow that far out. Nevertheless, it can be stated clearly that even while not well hit, and with a bullet a bit far back, the big sow was stopped cold, rendered unable to escape a second Sierra MatchKing at half the distance that I next delivered to her upper body. That lung shot hit with a sharp crack, letting the air out of her in short order, and the 130-pound critter dropped on the spot.

It should be pointed out at this point that the rifles and paired loads we were shooting were all .308-diameter rounds and rifle bores. The 7.62x39 can be found in rifles with bore diameters of .311, which, according to some experts, can result in less

The author took this running boar in timber at close range.

then stellar accuracy when crossed up with the wrong bullets. Since the Model 85 Zestava measures out to a true .308-caliber, I stayed with both handloaded bullets and factory fodder that matched this calibration. (I did not evaluate the .311-bore bullets and rifles, as most of these .311 calibrations are found in the AK-47, which played no part in this ballistics overview.)

Scott and I walked over another ridge with care and slowly approached the crest of the hill, then glassed a marsh area below. We knew that at least two big boar tuskers were somewhere down in that long snake grass bog. Scott, being far more Australian snake savvy then I, went deep into the swampy cut, while I stayed high on the ridge and a bit ahead of him, covering each open spot a pig could cross during an escape attempt. I had chambered a mixed bag of Sierra hand-loads and Remington SPS cartridges in the Mauser's box magazine, and when Scott crossed over into the second patch of high grass, the first boar emerged out of the grass and into a clearing about 160 yards downrange. It was shooting time in a flash, and with a swinging motion and a press of the trigger, a 125-grain bullet went straight through the big pig's front shoulders. About the same time, Scott turned loose a round and sent in a second slug that went the full length of the boar's body. A second later, two more hogs appeared, and this time I pushed a bullet mid-body through the first pig, then administered a second round that went though a small, three-inch tree before completely penetrating the body of the pig at the lungs; that bullet was out of one of my Sierra MatchKing handloads, a choice I'd made because Sierras have always been known to hold together well. Many elk hunters swear by them. All I can say is that the high-numbered ballistic coefficient and well-made MatchKing is a handloader's dream applied to the 7.62x39. This bullet was stacking up an impressive series of hard-hitting kills.

We got off a number of clear shots over the next several days of pig shooting and, as such, I was clearly able to draw a very clear picture as to the net effect of the Russian Short round. Thanks need to go to the folks at Remington who offered up both full metal jacket ammo for zeroing and practice, as well as SPS pointed lead loads that dropped a significant number of pigs and some other camp meat. While hunting almost a full month at the Cape, in Queensland, and at Glenelg Station, I had a clear opportunity to really get this cartridge and rifle on a pile of warm targets.

The Drawbacks

While the Russian Short has many advantages, it also has a few problems. The 7.62x39 is not even close to being an all-around cartridge for big game. This is a medium-range cartridge, so push it too far and the ballistics start to fall apart. Why is this an issue? Because the major amount of game and varmints are taken well inside 250 yards, even when shooting over-the-top cartridges. Remember, 250 yards is two and one-half football fields. Put the last deer, coyote, or boar hog you killed in your mind's eye. Be honest, how far away was it?

One limitation to distance work is the lack of the 7.62x39's ability to buck the wind. I noticed this during the testing of many different brands of ammunition back in South Dakota. Shooting the Sierra MatchKing boat-tail 125-grain helped reduce wind drift, as did shooting Russian Army high-velocity 123-grain pills. It seems like nothing can be handloaded that gets close to the muzzle velocity of the Russian Army AK-47 rounds. That's too bad, because velocity at 2,587 fps with the high BC bullet would result in additional performance levels.

Another drawback is that there are no heavy bolt-action 7.62x39 rifles in production today that match a mid-size target or benchrest system. My carbine-like Model 85 comes in at a weight of six pounds with a scope, that gun having a 22-inch barrel. The CZ 527 is much the same as the Serbian Mauser, and even the M-77 in a Ruger turn-bolt—when one can be found—is still well under the weight, barrel thickness, and general accuracy of a good benchrest rifle.

If I continue to work with the Russian short, I tend to think I will eventually gravitate to a Remington 40X or one like it as an action, and with a medium-heavy target barrel, and have that barreled action custom stocked by Charlie Sisk, my gunsmith friend at Sisk Rifles, in Texas.

Can the rifle become a sub-MOA system? I'm not sure about that, but currently, with a light rifle, I have put two rounds though one rough hole; I've always sent a third a bit wide and opened any group to a bit over an inch. Even at that, the field work illustrated with the Mauser indicates that the total system can get the job done on targets, when kept inside the 250-yard mark.

South Dakota Wrap

After pounding the daylights out of grass rats and a few other odds and ends on the stream beds back home in South Dakota, the rifle and cartridge were turned toward whitetail deer in the wide Missouri foothills of the central part of the state. The pile of dead pigs Down Under had clearly shown this cartridge was a winner, along with its positive reputation among ranchers as a low-cost meat rifle in the gun rack of a pickup. But I still wanted to see for myself how it performed against the big whitetails common in the north-central part of the my home state. Ammunition selection was, without question, my own handloaded fodder by way of that Sierra MatchKing 125-grain pill, 27 grains of Reloader 7, and a Small Rifle primer set in once-fired Remington brass. As a secondary round, the Russian Golden Bear 123-gain soft-nose with a muzzle velocity of 2,600 fps was also hauled into the field.

My hunting partner Jerome Besler, who had taken to the Russian Short, managed to drop a good buck with the Golden Bear. During a mid-season local whitetail hunt, I also took a two-year-old 4x4 whitetail, mine with a well-placed Sierra MatchKing bullet at a range of 123 yards. The double-lung hit took the deer cleanly, and it traveled just a short 20 yards before folding up like a wet rag.

In summary, I believe the 7.62x39 Russian Short tends to be undersold in the face of other modern centerfire cartridges. It shouldn't be. When taken to task, It is a solid performer and an affordable alternative to other cartridges out there today.

CARTRIDGE: 7.62x39mm							
Bullet: 125 grains • Ballistic Coefficient: .2720 • Zero: 175 yards • Sight over bore: 1.5 inches							
RANGE (YARDS)	IMPACT (LOS-IN)	DEFL.	VEL (FPS)	TIME (SEC)	ENERGY (FT-LBS)	DROP (IN)	30MPH-LEAD (FEET)
0	-1.5	0.0	2452	0.0000	1669.2	0.0	0.0
25	0.0	0.1	2374	0.0311	1564.4	-0.2	1.4
50	1.1	0.4	2297	0.0632	1464.8	-0.8	2.8
75	1.9	0.8	2222	0.0964	1370.1	-1.7	4.2
100	2.1	1.5	2147	0.1307	1280.3	-3.2	5.8
125	1.9	2.3	2075	0.1663	1195.1	-5.1	7.3
150	1.2	3.4	2004	0.2031	1114.5	-7.5	8.9
175	0.0	4.8	1934	0.2412	1038.3	-10.4	10.6
200	-1.8	6.3	1866	0.2807	966.4	-13.9	12.3
225	-4.3	8.1	1799	0.3216	898.6	-18.1	14.2
250	-7.4	10.2	1734	0.3641	835.0	-22.9	16.0
275	-11.2	12.6	1671	0.4081	775.4	-28.4	18.0
300	-15.8	15.3	1610	0.4538	719.7	-34.8	20.0
325	-21.3	18.2	1551	0.5013	667.9	-42.0	22.1
350	-27.7	21.5	1494	0.5506	619.7	-50.1	24.2
375	-35.0	25.2	1439	0.6017	575.3	-59.2	26.5
400	-43.4	29.1	1387	0.6548	534.3	-69.3	28.8

A good holster
is an essential
part of a plan
for carrying a
handgun.

BY **Robert K. Campbell**

What You Should
Know About
HOLSTERS

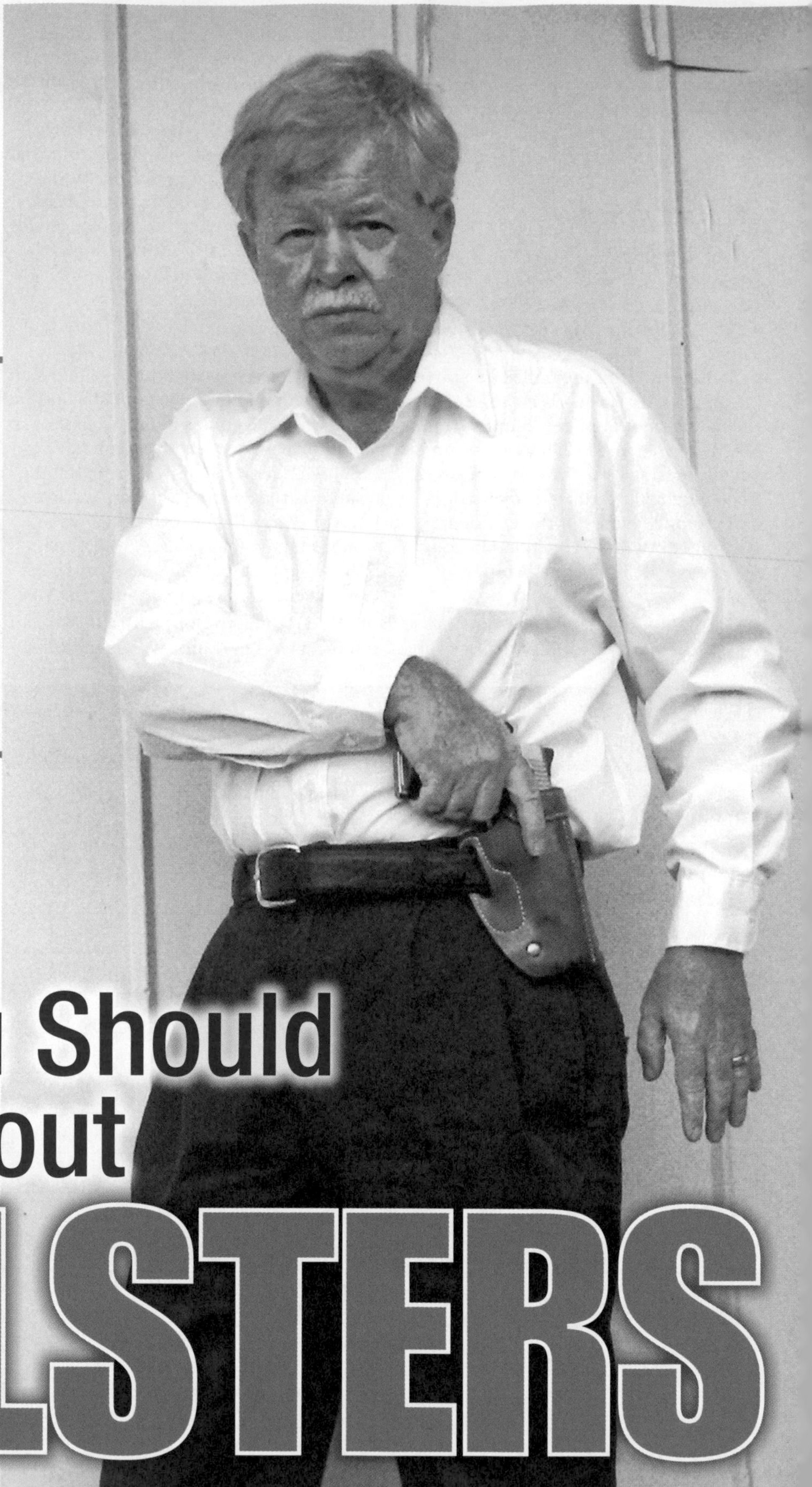

The great advantage of the handgun over the long gun is that the handgun is portable and concealable. As such, you should be armed at all times to meet an unexpected threat. Ideally, you should have on hand a number of holsters for wear with both casual and professional garments, dependent upon the situation and the weather. After carrying a handgun for most of the past 40 years, I have formed a number of opinions based upon fact and experience. There is no one answer for everyone, but there should be an answer for each individual.

Some effort is required to find the right holster, but no matter what the choice, there is always an acclimation period. Some handguns are more ergonomic than others, but few are completely devoid of sharp edges. A quality holster goes a long way towards making carrying a defensive handgun bearable. There are many choices, and some are readily available. Blackhawk, DeSantis, and Galco are among the best-known and most reliable mass-produced holsters.

There are fine holsters that are custom made and that might be said to be examples of the maker's art. These are not inexpensive and often take weeks, if not months, to obtain. Still, while the concepts of inexpensive and high quality don't always go together, there are good holsters offering a balance of value and cost.

My choice in defensive handguns is based on many years of practical experience. Having been in the wrong place at the wrong time more than once, and having written quite a few reports concerning shootings and other mayhem, I am aware of the relative wound potential of different handguns. I prefer the .45 ACP and the .357 Magnum. The .38 Special and 9mm+P are also realistic minimum calibers. While a number of handguns in these calibers are reasonably compact,

TOP: Galco's Double Time is representative of the present consumer-driven holster market—it's versatile, affordable and capable. The inside-the-waistband option makes for excellent concealment.

BOTTOM: When the Double Time is worn as an OWB holster, concealment is compromised, but speed is greater.

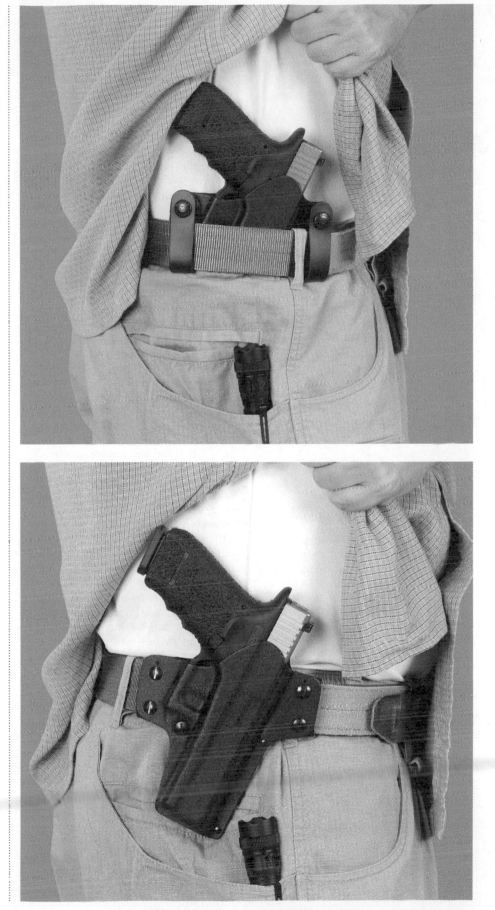

This is the Galco Royal Guard, an excellent design available off the rack.

I'll always lean towards one that is manageable and accurate. Concealing a serious defensive handgun under lightweight garments can be problematic. If the handgun is short and compact, an outside-the-waistband (OWB) holster under a sport shirt will work fine, but, for most of us, the inside-the-waistband holster (IWB) is superior.

Your covering garment is important. I have adopted a Kakadu sport shirt for much of my concealment needs. This shirt is made of Gravel canvas and has a leather collar. I admit it is stylish, but it also conceals a holster well without printing the outline of it for the world to see. Under this garment or a heavy T-shirt, the IWB holster will conceal a pistol the size of a Commander .45 or Glock M23 without undue difficulty. It is true that the grip angle is compromised with an IWB holster, but, with practice, the speed of gun draw and presentation is acceptable.

Among the most proven IWB types is the Galco Royal Guard. It offers good

retention, something I know from experience. While field-testing this model some years ago as a law enforcement officer, I was in a struggle that resulted in a headlong tumble. The Royal Guard held my handgun throughout the tussle. It offers a top blend of speed and retention by means of its excellent design and execution. Constructed of high-quality leather, the Royal Guard is well stitched, with a solid spine and reinforced holster mouth.

Leather is attractive, but these days, Kydex, a thermoplastic resin, is a more popular holster material. (Do not confuse Kydex with ordinary cheap plastic, which isn't durable enough for the rigors of concealed carry.) There are tradeoffs inherent in Kydex, but there are also advantages. One of the biggest pluses is that the material is maintenance-free and impervious to solvents or moisture. A tradeoff, if it can be called one, is that a leather holster maintains security on the long bearing surfaces of the pistol, while the Kydex holster keeps its grip primarily on the muzzle and trigger guard area.

Of the downsides? Some say Kydex will wear the finish off a pistol quickly, but so does properly fitted leather. Plainly said, a service pistol will become worn if used. If you are not willing to accept wear on your pistol, you may not practice on a regular basis and your gun might as well be a "safe queen." Too, some say there is a distinctive sound when the handgun is draw from a Kydex holster, but this sound is no louder than the "swoosh" of a tightly fitted leather holster; it is simply different. The bottom line is that Kydex is long wearing, sometimes less expensive, and often as fast as leather.

The custom holster option is always a good one, if you have the time and funds to obtain one. Among the most respected shops—and in this case, respect means legendary—is Milt Sparks (www.miltsparks.com). The original Milt Sparks Summer Special, designed by Bruce Nelson, remains the classic concealed carry holster. My personal example has survived more than a decade of constant use. The holster rides correctly and offers both good retention and the trademark reinforced holstering welt for ease of re-holstering. It just doesn't get any better.

There are a number of new holster types that have gained popularity during the past decade. In some cases, though, the final verdict has yet to be read. The hybrids that mate Kydex to a leather backing for comfort are popular and relatively inexpensive, but the draw angle

is seldom as good as a purpose-designed leather or Kydex IWB. Still, the hybrids are convincing many shooters to carry a gun in a holster instead of thrusting it into the waistband. That's a good thing, because carrying a handgun without a holster is a very bad idea; the handgun could easily become lost, and, in the case of a Glock or a cocked-and-locked 1911, a gun stuffed inside your pants is idiocy.

Another class of holster gaining favor is the combination OWB/IWB holster. Typically, this is a belt holster with conventional belt loops, as well as additional apertures in order to attach to belt loops for inside the waistband carry. Some come across better than others, and the ones designed primarily for IWB carry usually work the best. Among the newest and best designed is the Galco Double Time. It is designed to allow the user to carry the holster on the strong-side position, but also wear it inside the trousers when more concealment is needed.

When it comes to custom holsters of this OWB/IWB type, Luke Adams crafts a first-class combination (www.adamsholsters.com), with the emphasis on IWBs. It takes a few minutes to switch the belt loops, but, once accomplished, either configuration is sturdy and reliable. This type of holster is not only versatile, it's less expensive than purchasing two holsters. Just be certain that the holster is viable for you in each role.

I have emphasized the superiority of the IWB for concealed carry and all-around use, but, just the same, there should be a good reason for leaving the strong-side belt holster behind. If a covering jacket is long enough to conceal the OWB holster, the gun is fast into action and less likely to become entangled in your covering garments. As an example, the tuckable, under-the-shirt variation of the IWB offers good concealment, but isn't high on my list for comfort or draw speed. The standard, low-riding IWB is well suited to most of my concealment needs, and I usually deploy a Commander or even a full-size .45 1911 pistol.

Holster materials that are gaining attention are exotic skins. Crocodile, alligator, ostrich, and sharkskin are popular. Elephant skin is among the most attractive and long wearing. Various snakeskins are also popular, but are not as rugged as sharkskin. A good sharkskin holster locked into a sharkskin belt is as rigid and reliable a rig as you can ask for. D.M. Bullard (www.dmbullardleather.com) sharkskin holsters take scuffs and

The Lucas Adams convertible holster offers brilliant options and real versatility. Its well-designed, quick-change components allow the holster to be used as an IWB or OWB. It is among the few that work equally well in either position. Molded in sharkskin, it is rigid and offers excellent draw speed.

bumps better than cow or horse leather. It may take a wait of several weeks for a custom product, and they are more expensive than the average holster, but they last a lifetime.

There are a number of alternative carry types that will serve many well. As an example, the crossdraw holster is a good option for those who are seated behind a desk or driving most of the day. The crossdraw has been criticized as slow on the draw and accessible to a gun grabber, but those who understand it beg to differ. When properly executed, the crossdraw is brilliantly fast for addressing a threat that originates from the weak side; the shooter blades himself to the target, and the pistol is scooped out

of the holster as the shooter goes into a Weaver stance. If the shooter is constantly aware of the holster and keeps their weak-side arm near it, retention tactics are available that make the crossdraw more secure than most would imagine. Yes, the crossdraw is a poor choice for open carry or uniformed police use, but it's a good choice for concealed carry in many other scenarios. The crossdraw done poorly is a terror. Done correctly, it is a jewel.

This holster, from D.M. Bullard, is well made of good material and offers the correct tilt for concealed carry and the concealed draw. If you cannot tolerate an IWB, this is as good as it gets.

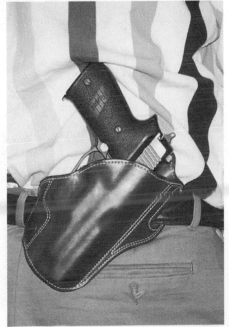

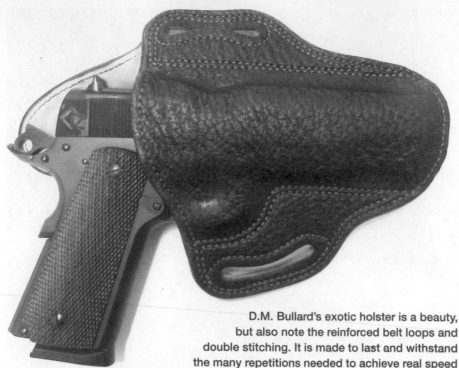

D.M. Bullard's exotic holster is a beauty, but also note the reinforced belt loops and double stitching. It is made to last and withstand the many repetitions needed to achieve real speed and smoothness in practice.

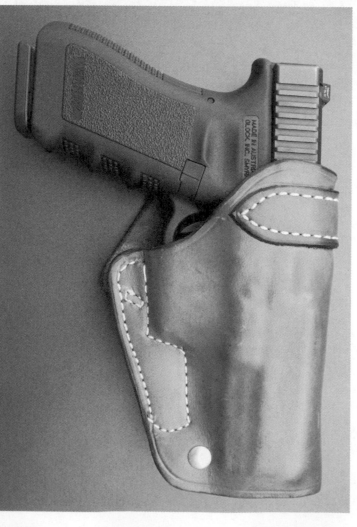

The Ted Blocker crossdraw has earned the "classic" title, because it continues to work well with modern handguns. With practice, it is versatile and fast into action.

Ted Blocker (www.tedblockerholsters.com) offers a classic crossdraw holster. I have tested quite a few, but none perform as well as the Blocker. The Ted Blocker X 16 is a classic design well worth your consideration.

Many concealed carry shooters cannot wait months to obtain a custom-grade holster. Others are on a fixed budget that demands service-grade gear at a fair price. Among the leaders in affordable gear is BLACKHAWK! (www.blackhawk.com). These holsters are found on the shelf of dedicated gun shops and pawn shops alike. There are also a number of "express leather" lines that offer good quality, top-grain leather that are only perhaps not as tightly molded as the top of the line. This allows the consumer to quickly obtain a decent quality holster at a fair price. Among other makers offering good quality gear at a fair price is Jedco (www.jedcoleather.com). This designer offers well turned-out leather with surprisingly good basketweave work. The company use quality leather, and the fitting and stitching are good.

Old Faithful Holsters (oldfaithfulholsters.com) offers an unusual deal, a partially finished holster that you assemble yourself. This allows some custom variation on the angle and cant and a significant savings in a tuckable type holster. I've used several of these kits and found they offer a good value, while allowing the user to choose the exact cant (degree or angle) that suits them best.

Women's Holsters

Women are obtaining and carrying firearms more than ever. At my training company, I've conducted any number of all-female classes, and not always by intent (sometimes it was simply groups of friends and co-workers signed up who all happened to be women). Those choosing holsters for female shooters must take into account the shorter torso and high waist of women. You cannot simply take a holster, mold it in pink leather, and expect a female to be able to use it well. Fortunately, there are a number of makers who understand the needs of female shooters. The Kydex rigs from Garage Works Holsters (www.garageworksholsters.com) appear simple, but represent considerable effort in design and execution. This holster rides high and with a good draw angle.

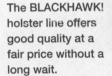

The BLACKHAWK! holster line offers good quality at a fair price without a long wait.

Above: The hybrid tuckable holster is very popular, due to its affordability and function. Crossbreed popularized the type, and it has been widely successful.

Left: Two classics, the author's 1958 Colt Commander and a well-worn Milt Sparks Summer Special holster. The snaps and loops are solid and the holstering welt is as new. The sewn-in sight track isn't wallowed out, nor has the holster lost its shape. Buy quality and buy once.

For women shooters and their higher waistlines, the IWB is particularly difficult, because it is a strain to reach behind the hip and grip the gun effectively. But a short pistol and an IWB holster work well for the appendix carry. One maker who understands the needs of female shooters is Cerisse Wilson (www.soterialeather.com). They are well made of good material, and while Cerisse offers excellent gear for both men and women, she creates some of the finest female-specific gear around. I have obtained a pair for my significant other, one an easy on-and-off holster and the other an inside-the-waistband type. These holsters, molded for the Pretty Girl's SIG, are flawless. Most impressive? Despite the obvious skill and craftsmanship seen in these holsters, their maker is not yet 30 years old.

There are many options in concealed carry, and all cannot be covered in this report. The reader must consider their own experience and individual needs. Whichever carry mode and gear you choose, go with the best quality you can afford, practice the draw, and consider the likely scenarios. The holster is part of a plan that includes the handgun and ammunition selection, but the part between the ears matters most of all. Train hard, know your gear, and stay safe.

THE PRESCOTT
STALKING

BY Buck Pope, Photos by Tom Douglass

RIFLE

Realizing the dream of a "someday" rifle

Nothing dresses up a fine custom rifle better than quality optics by Swarovski (scope) and Zeiss (binoculars).

nyone who has hunted for any length of time has mentally built a "someday" rifle. Sitting long hours in the blind or spending days behind the wheel driving to hunts frees the mind to dream, to design. Eventually, as our "someday" gun gets closer to reality, we create parameters. How much can we spend? What are we going to hunt with it and where?

My someday gun has become a rifle that would work on North American elk and moose and that would also be competent on larger African plains game. Both applications require a rugged, dependable rifle in a caliber that has adequate killing power for any and all game that might be found.

Since retiring almost 20 years ago, I've been working on my someday gun and, as I live in Prescott, Arizona, there is a lot of inspiration around me. Located in north-central Arizona, Prescott is a mountain town with an incredible history and was the original state capitol. The city has a population of almost 40,000 and sits a mile high. An amazing thing about Prescott is the concentration of gun-related businesses here, both in town and the surrounding area. It is one of the strongest gun communities found anywhere in the West.

The gun community got its start just after World War II. Several of the post-war pioneers were men such as Fred Wells (Wells Sport Store), Bill Atkinson, Paul Marquardt (A&M Precision), Guncraft Associates, Jack Ashearst (a barrel maker), and Lester Womach (gunsmith and barrel maker), along with several gun writers such as Jim Carmichel, Rick Jamison, and Al Miller, all of whom have all lived in Prescott at one time or another.

Over the years, more gun businesses came to be: The Rifle Ranch (Jim Wilkinson), Jeff Cooper (Gunsite), and Bill Ruger (Sturm, Ruger & Co.). Ruger had a ranch southwest of town and built his plant in Prescott, a concern still going strong today. Others located in Prescott are Wolfe Publishing (Don Polacek), along with Davidson's Guns, J&G Sales, Classic Barrel & Gunwork (Danny Pedersen), Gunsite (Buzz Mills), RMS Custom Gunsmithig (Robert Szweda), and Kelly Arms (Tim Putman). There are also several gun engravers in the community, such as Rachael Wells, Ka'imiloa Chrisman, and Mark Swanson.

Then there is Yavapai College, host to one of the top gunsmithing schools in the country and managed by Al Lohr.

There are also two shooting facilities, Prescott Sportsman's Club and the Trap and Skeet Range. In Prescott and the close surrounding area there are well over a dozen retail gun dealers. The list goes on. It is a dynamic community. But back to the someday gun.

Caliber

One of my first priorities was to select the caliber. I had heard about a certain cartridge off and on for years

and have several friends who have hunted big game with it. After much consideration, the chambering decided upon was the .338-06 A-Square, a round that goes back to the days of Elmer Keith. In fact, Keith, Charles O'Neil, and Don Hopkins developed it at the tail end of World War II, naming their wildcat the .333 OKH.

In the early days, it was hampered by limited bullet selection. Today, there is a large number of quality projectiles available in the bore size. The .333 OKH/.338 A-Square is, basically, a .30-06

Springfield necked up to .338 diameter with a 17.5-degree shoulder. In 1998, A-Square standardized this cartridge, and it is now commercially loaded by several manufacturers.

Ballistic comparison to the garden variety .338 Winchester Magnum load shows it to be about an 85-percent performance level. The beauty of this cartridge, compared to its magnum brother, is the considerably lower recoil and the reduced muzzle blast, even with a shorter barrel and lighter rifle. This cartridge allows you to shoot bullet weights fairly close to

The graceful cheekpiece and all the stock work were done by Tim Putman.

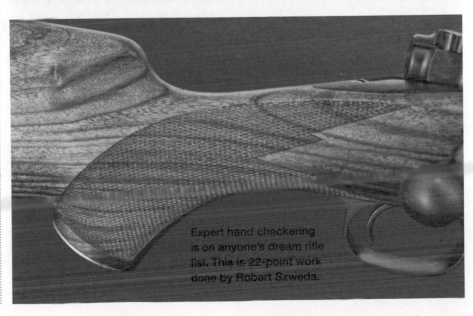

The barrel is topped with a solid rib that becomes the ramp for the front sight.

the .338 Win. Magnum, and the effect on heavy game is similar.

My interests lay with three bullet weights, the 210-, 225-, and 250-grain. Having hunted and guided in Alaska with the .338 Win. Mag., I am well aware of the performance this bullet diameter and weights have going for it. As more than 90 percent of our big game is taken under 200 yards, the mass and energy of .338s make them ideal for the hard hitting needed for larger, tougher game species. It's also a good bet for those more ferocious critters that show up to help share in the cleanup.

Expert hand checkering is on anyone's dream rifle list. This is 22-point work done by Robert Szweda.

The grizzly grip cap was the work of Ka'imiloa Chrisman.

Components

I selected a Winchester Model 70 Pre-'64 action I'd taken from a .30-06 I had purchased years before. The Pre-'64 Winchester is my personal favorite bolt-action and it is one is quite familiar to custom rifle makers.

Barrel maker Danny Pedersen and I decided on a 24-inch custom octagon barrel with a tight, 1:9 twist and a solid rib. I had seen several vintage, early '20s custom Mausers in Wells Sport Store and very much liked the design. Pedersen is known for custom cut-rifled barrels and is one of only six left who make them this way.

The Pre-'64 has one of the most dependable and simplest trigger designs ever made, and I saw no need to replace it. The trigger pull was adjusted to break at three pounds, something that, over the years, I've found to be ideal for a hunting rifle.

A chunk of English walnut seemed to reach out to me from Tim Putman's inventory of stock blanks. I've become a big fan of English walnut and I was hoping the finished piece would have the grain structure the outside had promised. I wasn't disappointed. Putman cut out the stock using a pattern from Robert Szweda's inventory. When finished, the stock would have a one-inch, solid red Pachmayr Decelerator recoil pad and an old-school ebony fore-end tip.

The Pedersen barrel's solid rib included a raised front sight ramp and front sling swivel. This allowed for open irons. The rear sight is a classic express design ideal for the rifle. The front sight is a typical white bead very similar to Winchester's original sights found on pre-'64s. Dovetail cuts were made to fit both front and rear.

Optics

On the initial build, I used a beautiful Leupold VX6 2-12x42mm mounted in Talley quick-detachable rings. The scope and rings were anchored to the receiver by custom two-piece bases made by Gila River Gun Works. By the time the project was completed, a high-end Swarovski Z6i 1.7-10x42mm had serendipitously become available. This scope featured a 30mm tube and illuminated 4AI reticule. I couldn't pass it up and mounted this ideal optic, using another set of Talley rings on the Gila bases.

Finish and Fit

The receiver had a coarse bead-blast finish to mimic the appearance of an original pre-'64. The barrel had a fine bead-blast finish to it, and this was done prior to a matte bluing of the entire barreled action. The bottom metal is a Williams one-piece steel floorplate, and it was also matte blued. As a bit of a cosmetic upgrade, we decided to jewel the bolt.

The stock was finished using multiple coats of Pilkington Spirits Stain to reach its final desired satin finish. The barreled action was then fiberglass-fitted to the stock. A point-to-point checkering pattern was selected for a custom checkering job. In another custom touch, we took a metal grip cap and had a grizzly bear engraved on it. I might add, all the various components such as metal grip cap, bottom metal, stock finishing, and others were selected from Brownells.

Proof's in the Pudding

The components were completed, assembled, and bore-sighted. It not only looked great, but it was a perfect fit for my size and arm length. My someday rifle had become a well-balanced instrument that comes up perfectly to my cheek and shoulder—a natural pointer and one that did not require a trip to London.

How does it shoot? Accuracy requirements were pretty standard for our age of perfect ammunition, rifling, bedding, and optics: minute of angle or less three-shot groups at 100 yards.

Everyone involved felt this rifle should be capable of producing half-inch groups, once it was broken in. The rifle certainly met these requirements early, with rested groups ranging from .5- to .875-inch at 100 yards. It particularly likes the Hornady 225-grain Interlock bullet, an ideal weight for this caliber.

During the course of its building, my "someday gun" had become a genuine community project, a Prescott rifle. This team effort brought together five master craftsmen, all performing at the peak of their skills: Ka'imiloa Chrisman (engraver), Greg Bardsley (gunsmith), Danny Pedersen (barrel maker), Tim Putman (stock and rifle maker), and Robert Szweda (stock checkering).

In addition to its excellent accuracy, my rifle is a classically handsome and practical big-game rifle, the result of the best talents this high-desert town has to offer. It is truly The Prescott Stalking Rifle.

Sources

Greg Bardsley
Gunsmith / rifle builder.
g.bardsley@yahoo.com
Cell 785-554-3725

Ka'imiloa Chrisman
Chrisman & Chrisman Engravers
kaimilon@earthlink.net
928-639-4683; 928-202-8411

Danny Pedersen
Classic Barrel & Gunworks
www.cutrifle.com
928-772-4060

Tim Putman
Kelly Arms LLC
www.kellyarmsllc.com
928-710-8231

Robert Szweda
R.M.S. Custom Gunsmithing
www.customstockmaker.com
928-772-7626

Gila River Gun Works
www.michaelsherz.com
208-241-2718

Leupold & Stevens
www.leupold.com
Toll free 1-800-leupold

Talley Mfg. Co.
www.talleyrings.com
803-854-5700

The Care and Feeding of
WILDCATS

BY Larry Sterett

Still Filling a Need in Today's Cartridge Lineup, or a Dying Breed?

Left to right: .30-06 Winchester Silvertip, .360 Howell, .340 Howell, .300 Howell, .270 Howell, and 7mm Howell. Developed by noted editor Ken Howell, this line of cartridges features a sharp shoulder and a case body with little taper, providing the cartridges with maximum powder capacity.

Left to right: .30-06, .30 ICL Caribou, 6.5mm-257 or 6.5mm Spence, .300 ICL Grizzly Cub, .25-06, .227-303 Savage, 7mm Gradle (based on the .348 Winchester case with the rim removed and new extractor groove turned), and the .228 Ackley Magnum.

Left to right: 6mm Page, designed by shooting editor Warren Page, .242 Wallack, designed by author and editor Bob Wallack, .228 Ackley Belted Ackley Express, and .242 Ackley Belted Express. These Belted Express cases were based on the .30-06 case with a new belt swaged on in the manner of some small British cartridges.

ccording to the generally accepted definition, a wildcat cartridge is one that has never been commercially loaded by a company in the ammunition business. If a cartridge has been commercially loaded and later discontinued, it becomes an obsolete commercial cartridge, even if it began life as a wildcat. Thus, the .219 Zipper and the .256 Newton, both of which were commercially loaded by Western Cartridge Company up to and shortly after World War II, are not wildcats, but commercially obsolete. (Western's successor, Winchester Ammunition, has not loaded either cartridge in decades, although a special run is always a possibility.)

In the *Ammo Encyclopedia 4th Edition*, author Michael Bussard defines a wildcat cartridge as "an experimental cartridge design created from a standard parent cartridge by individual experimenters seeking to improve ballistic performance or adapt the cartridge to meet specific requirements." Such a cartridge might embody changes in some or all of the case features: case length, body taper, shoulder location, shoulder angle, neck length, neck diameter, and rim diameter. This fits well with this writer's story on what became the .338 Lapua in the 1986 edition of *Gun Digest*. What was being wildcatted as a possible new sniper cartridge—something it did eventually become— also became an excellent hunting cartridge for big game.

What was the first wildcat cartridge? Good question. It might have been the .577-450 Martini Henry, prior to it being adopted by the British military. Some of the early .577 Snider cartridges utilized a wrapped sheet-brass case attached to a steel base and, later, so did some of the first .577-450 cases. In the U.S., wildcat

Left to right: The 6mm PPC originated as a wildcat, but is now available as a limited factory load; the .475 Wildey was a wildcat, but is also a limited factory load (although reported .400 and .357 Wildey rounds are probably still wildcats); the .502 Sabre is based on the .50 AE case with rebated rim, and it and the .44 AutoMag (to its right) have seen limited factory loading.

Left to right: A commercial .44 Remington Magnum cartridge for comparison with the .357 Grizzly wildcat, available in the L.A.R. Grizzly auto-loading pistol.

Left to right: A commercial .44 Remington Magnum for comparison; .44 AutoMag; .41 Auto-Mag (sometimes called the .41 Lee Jurras); .357 Auto Mag; and the .30 or .308 AutoMag, all designed for the power-house AutoMag pistol.

The .44 AutoMag cartridge achieved commercial loading in Mexico, but the others were custom loaded or, as with most wildcats, handloaded by the owner. All four cartridges were excellent for hunting whitetail-sized game.

A few of the J.D. Jones line of wildcats, at least one of which is now commercially loaded by CorBon and Hornady, and possibly others. Left to right: .30 Mini Whisper on a 7.63mm Mauser case; .300 Whisper on the .221 Fireball case; the .338 Whisper on the 7mm BR case; the 7mm Whisper on the .221 Remington case; the .458 Whisper on the .458 Winchester Magnum case; and a different .458 Whisper, also on the .458 Winchester Magnum case. All these cartridges are loaded to subsonic velocities.

Some great cartridges for the M1911 pistol, left to right: .45 Super, .45 J-Mag, .38-45 (The .38-45 Clerke and .38-45 JDJ are similar.). Next is an unloaded .38 Casull case and a factory loaded .400 CorBon. The J-Mag cases are formed from cut, trimmed, and sized 7.62mm NATO cases, to provide head strength.

cartridges appeared shortly after the first solid-head centerfire cases came into use. A number of early .22- and .25-caliber wildcats were based on the .30-40 Krag case. (The 6mm Lee-Navy cartridge didn't survive long commercially or militarily, but it did serve as the basis for what became the .220 Swift, which is still with us today, following a brief lapse in the post-World War II period.)

Over the years, a number of wildcat cartridges have moved to the commercial production stage, the latest being the .17 Hornet, which is based on the .22 Hornet case. The .22 Hornet was a wildcat prior to its introduction by Winchester and, in fact, the ammunition was available for some time prior to the introduction of commercial rifles so chambered. Other wildcats that achieved commercial success include the .25 Roberts, which became the .257 Remington-Roberts; the .22-250 Varminter, which became the .22-250 Remington; the ..25-06 Niedner High Power Special that became the .25-06 Remington; the .17-223, which became the .17 Remington; and the .35-06 that later achieved fame as the .35 Whelen. In fact, there were at least three or four or more different .25-06 wildcat designs being toted by various gunsmiths in the 1930 to 1950 era, including the Griffin & Howe .25 High Power Special, the Whelen .25 High Power, and the .25 Gibbs. Today, it should be noted that the Remington Arms Company has tended to be receptive to commercializing wildcats.

When the .250-3000 cartridge was introduced by Savage, it was with the 87-grain bullet, in order to achieve the desired 3,000 fps velocity. The standard .25-06 Niedner, based on the .30-06 case, could achieve 3,345 fps with an 87-grain bullet ahead of 54 grains of IMR 4350 powder, and just over 3,300 fps with the same bullet of ahead of 45 grains of IMR 4320. Blowing out the shoulder and reducing the body taper via re-chambering to an .25-06 Ackley Improved design permits an increase in the velocity of the 87-grain bullet, as reported by ballistician Bob Hutton. Ahead of 52 grains of IMR 3031 powder, the 87-grain bullet could achieve 3,600 fps, while switching to 62 grains of IMR 4350 could break the 3,850 mark. The .25 Gibbs, which represents about the maximum in case capacity for the .25-06 design, has been reported as moving the 87-grain bullet out at 3,800 fps ahead of 63 grains of IMR 4831.

Why do we need wildcats? At one time there were distinct gaps in rifle and handgun cartridge lines. Many cartridges were needed to do jobs none of the then-available cartridges were capable of doing. Today, most of those gaps have been filled with commercially loaded cartridges, and it's fair to say there's at least one cartridge suitable for the taking of any small- or big-game species found on the planet. Yet new wildcat cartridges are being developed each year. It may be a cartridge for 1,000-yard shooting, varmint hunting, a more compact design for carrying on a mountain sheep or goat hunt, or any one of a dozen other reasons—such as just to have something new.

Wildcat cartridges tend to be oriented toward rifle use, although there have been a good number of wildcat handgun cartridges. Until roughly the post-Vietnam War era, most rifles for wildcat cartridges were built on Krag, M1903 Springfield, M1917 Enfield, or '98 Mauser actions, with some on single-shot Winchester actions, and fewer still on single-shot Stevens actions. A few other military rifle actions have been used, including the Japanese Arisaka, Russian M1891 Mosin-Nagant, Remington Rolling Block (in several models, with the M1902 version being the best choice), the Greek Mannlicher, British Lee-Enfield, and the list goes on. It seems to have a lot to do with availability.

For a number of years following World War II, many American veterans wanting a good deer rifle and, having little cash, they had their souvenir Japanese Arisaka 6.5mm rifles converted. No surplus 6.5mm Japanese ammunition was readily available, and commercial ammunition in this caliber wasn't being loaded. The solution was to have a gunsmith re-chamber the rifle with a .257 Roberts reamer, with the neck opened to accept 6.5mm (.256-inch) bullets. The result was a good cartridge for deer-size game. It was known as the 6.5-257, and sometimes the 6.5mm Spence Special after a Mr. George Spence, who claimed to have been an original producer. Loaded with 42 grains of IMR 3031 powder behind an 87-grain bullet, the 6.5-257 could reach nearly 3,200 fps. With the heavier 120-grain bullet and 47 grains of IMR 4831, it could top 2,600 fps.

Another excellent cartridge for the Arisaka conversion, though one requiring some action work to feed properly, was the .260 AAR (some say it stands for "All Around Rifle"), developed by the Apex Rifle Company. Featuring a sharp shoulder and blown-out case, this cartridge

can be thought of as an Improved .257 Roberts with the neck expanded to hold 6.5mm bullets. With 51.5 grains of IMR 4350, a 120-grain bullet could be pushed out the muzzle at 3,160 fps, topping the great .256 Newton. The .256 Newton was commercially loaded by the Western Cartridge Company, and possibly others, prior to World War II, with a 129-grain bullet at 3,100 fps. Handloaded with 54.5 grains of IMR 4350, the Newton can push a 120-grain bullet out at 2,955 fps.

In Australia and Canada, with lots of

Left to right: A .22 Long Rifle rimfire cartridge for comparison; 5.7 MMJ or Spitfire, designed by Melvin Johnson for possible military or law enforcement use; 4.8x36mm; 4.7mm; 5.7x28mm; 4.3x45mm; 4.8x36mm; and 5.45x35mm. These last cartridges are not wildcats, per se, but experimental or prototypes for possible military use.

Lee-Enfield and M1914 Enfield rifles available after World War II, it was not surprising to find wildcat cartridges being developed based on the .303 British case. In Canada, many of the wildcat designs were the work of G.B. Crandall, W.B. Elliott, and Ellwood Epps, all Ontario residents. The .25-303 Elliott moved a 100-grain .250 bullet out the barrel at 3,200 fps, or about the same as the Arisaka converted to handle the .260 AAR. (There were actually two Elliotts producing wildcat cartridges about the same time, except the second,

Left to right: .500 Cyrus, .375 Barnes Supreme, .423 Buhmiller, .475 Ackley Magnum, .333 Belted OKH, .450 Smith Magnum, .350 Smith Magnum, and .476 Rhino. While most were designed for use in bolt-action rifles, the .476 Rhino is for use on an AR-10 platform, as is the .500 Phantom.

Left to right: The .288 Barnes Supreme, 7mm Gradle, Thirty Smith, .300 ICL Grizzly, .30-06 (for comparison), .300 ICL Grizzly Cub, .14 Hornet, .950 JDJ. This last cartridge is the largest wildcat in the current J.D. Jones line.

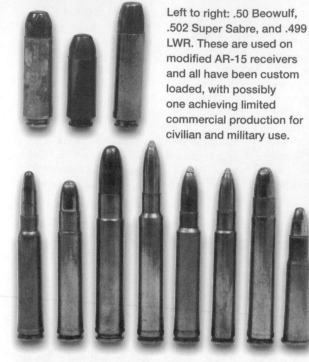

Left to right: .50 Beowulf, .502 Super Sabre, and .499 LWR. These are used on modified AR-15 receivers and all have been custom loaded, with possibly one achieving limited commercial production for civilian and military use.

Left to right: .333 Havoc, .429 Magnalaska Sr., .500 Buhmiller, .358 Barnes Supreme, .358 Barnes-Johnson Express, .35 Brown-Whelen (an Improved .35 Whelen), .429 Magnalaska Super, and 9.3x53R Finnish (factory wildcat for converted M91 Mosin-Nagant rifles). Buhmiller has a line of big-bore wildcats that he field-tested in Africa, culling elephants. Most were excellent, but there was not enough demand to make commercial production of these cartridges a reality.

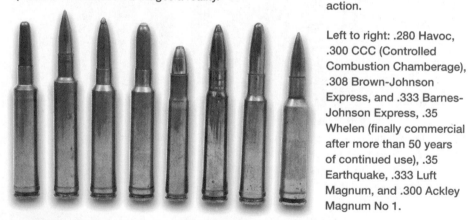

Left to right: .228 Ackley Magnum, .22 CCC, 6.5-250 Savage (for use in re-barreled M99 Savage rifles), .224 ICL Marmot, .224 ICL Benchrester, .400 Casull (based on the .44 Magnum case), and .400 Casull No. 2 (based on .454 Casull case). These last two wildcats were designed for use in single-action revolvers.

Left to right: A .50 BMG for comparison; custom loaded .416 Barrett; .50 Spotter (this round was a military load for spotting recoilless rifle rounds some decades back, but is now a sporting wildcat favored by some 1,000-yard target shooters as being almost as good as the .50 BMG cartridge.); .408 Cheyenne Tech, a wildcat that has achieved at least custom-loaded status; and the .500 Phantom. The Phantom is one of the largest cartridges that can function through a modified AR-10 action.

Left to right: .280 Havoc, .300 CCC (Controlled Combustion Chamberage), .308 Brown-Johnson Express, and .333 Barnes-Johnson Express, .35 Whelen (finally commercial after more than 50 years of continued use), .35 Earthquake, .333 Luft Magnum, and .300 Ackley Magnum No 1.

O.H. Elliott, tended toward the use of the .405 Winchester case as the basis for his designs.) The Epps line of cartridges included a .25, 6.5mm, .270, and possibly one or two other calibers, all based on the .303 British case. The Crandall .303-B .22 Varmint-R cartridge, developed in 1941, could move its .22 projectiles past the 4,000 fps mark from a 30-inch barrel, according to published date. Using 37 grains of IMR 4320 would push a 50-grain Sisk bullet out the muzzle at a chronographed 4,129 fps, while 39 grains of the same powder would move a 40-grain bullet at 4,320 fps. Not too shabby.

The 6.5-303 Elliott cartridge featured a double-shoulder design, but whether it was ever fully developed or not isn't known. In the early 1940s, P.O. Ackley produced at least one double-shoulder wildcat that he called the .228-300 Double-Jointed Magnum, a creation based on the .300 H&H Magnum case. The first shoulder was formed on the lower portion of the case, a half-inch above the base. From this point, the case was straight-walled for 1¾ inches, where the second shoulder was then formed to handle the 70-grain .228-inch bullets. Using a duplex load, Ackley figured he'd pushed the 70-grain bullet past the 4,000 fps mark. A couple decades later, the George L. Herter firm published loading data in its loading manual for four double-shoulder cartridges. Both shoulders were located in the conventional necking area of the cases, much like stair steps from the body diameter to the neck diameter. This writer has never seen one of the Herter double-shoulder cases, nor located shooting data pertaining to these cartridges—loading data, yes, shooting data, no.

Every so often, a factory rifle is chambered for a wildcat cartridge, when factory ammunition is not available. Three or so decades back, the firm of Harrington & Richardson chambered one of its bolt-action Mauser rifles for the .17-223 cartridge—a wildcat—but discontinued it in favor of the .17 Remington cartridge, when commercialized factory ammunition became available. Another wildcat cartridge for which rifles are chambered, but for which ammunition must be handloaded, is the 6mm Remington International developed by Remington engineer Mike Walker. The cartridge is based on the .250-3000 Savage case, and Remington chambers its 40-XB rifle for it in its Custom Shop.

A less common wildcat is what has been called the "factory wildcat," that being a cartridge that is commercially loaded, but for which no commercial rifle is or has been chambered. At least five such wildcats exist in Finland, with four of them designed to make use of surplus Mosin-Nagant M1891-series rifles. These four include the 6.3x53R, 7x53R, 8.2x53R, and 9.3x53R, all using the standard 7.62x54R Russian case. The surplus rifles are re-barreled or re-bored and re-chambered and a new deer, moose, etc., rifle is born. The other Finnish factory cartridge is the 7x54 Finnish, based on the 6.5x55 Swedish case necked up and shortened one millimeter. With a 120-grain Hornady bullet, a velocity of over 2,800 fps is possible using 41.7 grains of N135 VihtaVuori powder. The 9.3x53R cartridge could be handloaded with a 255-grain bullet to a velocity of 2,330 fps using 51.1 grains of N140 powder.

The majority of wildcat rifle cartridges have been designed for use in bolt-action rifles, but the other action types—pump, lever, and semi-auto—have not been forgotten entirely. The .35 Whelen was tried in a pump-action rifle prior to such a rifle being commercially available. The lever-actions received a bit more attention, with some of the Model 71 Winchesters in .348 Winchester being given an Improved chamber. With the return of the Model 71 by Browning in the late 1980s, a number of wildcat cartridges based on the .348 case came about. Even some of the older Model 1886 and Model 71 rifles have been re-barreled. In addition to the .348 Ackley Improved, a couple of the most popular wildcats for this rifle include the .450 Alaskan and the .50 Alaskan. The .450 Alaskan, originated by Harold Johnson of Cooper's Landing, is much the same as .450-348 Ackley Improved, and a 300-grain Nosler Partition can be pushed to over 2,100 fps ahead of 55 grains of H-4198, and 66 grains of H-322 will push a 400-grain Speer or Barnes bullet to the 2,000 fps neighborhood. The "Big 50," or .50 Alaskan, can be handloaded to nearly 2,000 fps with a 450-grain Barnes bullet ahead of 59 grains of RL-7 powder or 55 grains of IMR-4198.

A couple other wildcat cartridges used in Model 71/M1886 rifles include the .375 Alaskan and the .416-348 Ackley Improved. Most of the wildcats intended for use in the Model 71 are big bores needing rounded or flat-tip bullets to feed safely through the gun's tubular magazine. However, back 75 years, there was at least one smaller wildcat, the Seegert-Wilson .30-348 (S-W .30-348). Cast lead bullets

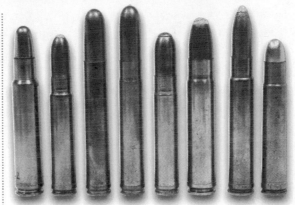

Left to right: .423 Buhmiller Magnum, .404 Barnes-Johnson Magnum, .475 Barnes Supreme, .450 Barnes Supreme, .450 Barnes-Johnson Express, .500 Buhmiller, .404 Barnes Supreme, and the .423 OKH.

The Rocky Gibbs line is based on sharp-shouldered, blown-out .30-06 cases. Rocky also did some work on the front or forward of the ignition flash-tube, in a few of his designs. Left to right: 8mm, .30, 7mm, .270, 6.5mm, and .25. The .25-06 Gibbs was about a hot as any .25-06 wildcat, and the 8mm Gibbs in an altered '98 Mauser was definitely a "poor man's magnum."

Left to right: The .400 CorBon is not a wildcat, being loaded by CorBon, but is shown here for comparison. Another commercial round is the 7.62x25mm Tokarev, which is nearly identical to the 7.63mm Mauser. The following are for use in auto-pistols or single-shot handguns, and most serve no purpose, other than being different. Left to right: .30-380 ACP, .357 SIG (for comparison), 9mm based on 7mm Mauser case, .30 Parabell, (which doesn't do anything the regular 7.65mm Luger (Parabellum) does with regular factory ammo), .22-7.65 or .22-32ACP, and the .22 Mite or Flea based on the .25 ACP base.

Left to right: .338 Lapua factory load, .300 Pegasus, .416 Chapuis, .338 Excaliber, and 7mm STW. All five cartridges were wildcats at one time, with the three in the middle being developed by A-Square, which also loads ammunition in these calibers. The STW (Shooting Times Westerner) is also available commercially.

Left to right: .303 British military round, .303 ICL Buttress, .260 AAR, 6.5-257, and 7mm-06. The .303 ICL Buttress provides the .303 British with a bit more oomph, and the .260 AAR (All Around Rifle) was a bit better than the .260 Remington—but the Remington round is available as a factory load.

or jacketed flat-tip bullets designed for .30-30 Winchester use would need to be loaded, if the cartridge was used in a Model 71 conversion.

The Model 99 Savage lever-action rifle was chambered for a range of commercial cartridges, from the .22 Hi-Power to the .358 Winchester. In addition, there were at least two wildcat cartridge designed for use in the Model 99's rotary magazine, the first being the .270 Titus. Both were based on the .300 Savage case necked down to .277- or .284-inch bullets. They served the need of those M99 shooters wanting something in power between that of the .250-3000 Savage and the .300 Savage.

Until the AR-15 came along, wildcat cartridges for use in auto-loading rifles were relatively rare. This may have been due to the lack of suitable auto-loading actions, although at least one was tried on the recoil-operated Johnson action, and possibly some Improved chambers on the Remington and Winchester actions exist. The AR-10 and AR-15 actions have been used for a variety of wildcats up to at least the .502 Super Sabre. Every major manufacturer has probably toyed with the possibility of putting its own special caliber on the AR platform, but those using the .223/5.56x45mm NATO case require the least amount of work on the upper receiver.

The M1 Carbine has been given the wildcat treatment in at least four calibers, the .17-30 Carbine (.17 Pee Wee or .17 Schuetz), 5.7 MMJ (.22 Carbine, .22 Schuetz, .22 Oresky, .22 Casull), .375 Shannon, and the .375-38/40 Rimless. The last two require some major work on the M1 Carbine action and represent about the maximum the action can handle. It is possible a .20 Carbine wildcat exists, but this shooter is not aware of any.

Over the past century, a number of popular wildcat cartridge lines have been developed. The Weatherby cartridges were wildcats at one time, until commercial ammunition began to be loaded. Today, the only Weatherby cartridge still a wildcat is the .220 Rocket. Its cases can be created by fire-forming .220 Swift cartridges in a Rocket-chambered rifle. According to the late Roy Weatherby, the Rocket could provide minute-of-angle accuracy with a 55-grain bullet at 4,100 fps and safe pressures. A maximum load of IMR 4064 at 45 grains pushed a 55-grain bullet to 4,188 fps, but the use of a 48- or 50-grain bullet would top that.

The mid-twentieth century saw a good bit of wildcatting, in particular, large-capacity cases necked down to handle

The Littlest Wildcat

What's the smallest-caliber wildcat available? Supposedly it is the .50 BMG case necked down to hold a bronze phonograph needle of the type used to play the 78 rpm records of yesteryear. A source for brass photograph needles is unlikely, rifling a barrel bore of approximately 0.039-inch is questionable, and what powder to use poses another problem. The smallest wildcat caliber realistically reported upon is the .10 Eichelberger Dart, and the smallest large-capacity wildcat reported might be the .22 Eargesplitten Loudenboomer. This last cartridge is the .378 Weatherby Magnum case necked down to handle .224-inch bullets. This cartridge had a sharp, 40-degree shoulder and was produced in the 1960s by P.O. Ackley for Robert Hutton of the *Guns & Ammo* staff. Loaded with 105 grains of H570 powder, Ackley achieved 4,600 fps with a 50-grain bullet, and Mr. Hutton may have bettered this figure.

The smallest caliber wildcats this shooter has worked with are the .14 Walker and the .14 Hornet. Recoil with both cartridges was almost non-existent, and velocities of over 4,000 fps were achieved, but maintaining such speeds and accuracy were not practical due to the heat generated. Bullet weights for the .14 Walker and the .14 Hornet included 15-, 17-, 18-, and 20-grain sizes and, while it was possible to achieve 4,330 fps using 17.5 grains of IMR3031 powder behind the 15-grain bullet, the slightly heavier bullets were more accurate. With a 17-grain bullet, 15.5 grains of H4198 produced a velocity of just over 4,100 fps. The results on ground squirrels were spectacular.

various weights of .222- to .228-inch bullets in attempts to reach the 4,000 fps mark. Entire lines of wildcat cartridges were developed, with some of the better known being those by P.O. Ackley, C.C.C. (Controlled Combustion Chamberage) by Hollywood Gun Shop, Harvey A. Donaldson, PMVF (Powell-Miler-Venturi-Freebored), Barnes-Johnson, Gibbs, ICL, and many more. Anyone who spends much time shooting rifles and/or handguns will eventually attempt to build or have built to specifications his or her idea of the perfect wildcat. Even this shooter has a couple of each, rifle and handgun, wildcat cartridges. The 8mm Havoc was designed to provide more oomph to surplus 8mm rifles, and my .429 Havoc was designed to make the Remington Model 600 action a bit more useful. My two handgun wildcat cartridges were designed for use on the Model 1911 action and consist of a .400 and a .22, both bottlenecked.

The major wildcat cartridge designer of the mid-twentieth century was probably P.O. Ackley, with more than 40 designs bearing his name, from the .17 Ackley Hornet to the .475 Ackley Magnum. Many of these wildcats were Improved versions of regular factory loads, such as the .218 Ackley Improved Bee and .30-06 Ackley

Improved, while others were Improved versions of other wildcats such as the .30-348 Ackley Improved and the .35 Ackley Improved Whelen.

For the last portion of the twentieth century and the first part of the twenty-first, the most prominent wildcatter has to be J.D. Jones, with more than 55 different cartridges, from the .226 JDJ to the .950 JDJ, to his credit. Many of the JDJ cartridges, such as the .375 JDJ and the .270 JDJ, have gained a following among hunters, and at least one, the .300 Whisper, has attained commercial status, now commercially loaded by Sturgis Ammo (CorBon) and Hornady, and under a different name by a couple other firms.

Wildcat handgun cartridges are fewer in number than those for rifle users, although the introduction of the Thompson/Center Contender and Remington XP-100 single-shot pistols prompted an increase of such cartridges. Single-shot pistols are ideal for wildcats, with auto-loaders and revolvers being less so, partially due to overall length, available cases, and headspacing problems. Back in the 1970s, Elgin Gates, then president of the IHMSA (International Handgun Metallic Shooters Association), designed a whole line of short bottleneck cartridges for use in the Remington XP-100 single-shot pistol. These IHMSA cartridges were based on a shortened .300 Savage case blown out and given a new shoulder. Preformed brass was available, and the only alteration to the XP-100 was to re-barrel the pistol and have the bolt face opened for larger case head.

When it comes to wildcats and pistols, the Model 1911 pistol served as the basis for the .38-45 Clerke and similar wildcats, plus the .45 Super and a few other hyped-up .45s. There was also a .40-45 cartridge. (The .400 CorBon is factory loaded and, hence, not a wildcat.) The .44 AutoMag was in its heydey in the 1970s, and there were three or four wildcats designed around it, including the .357 and .41 AutoMags (.41 Jurras) and there may have been a .375 AutoMag. These smaller calibers usually needed a nine-inch barrel to achieve velocity. A couple other big auto-loaders were the LAR Grizzly and the Wildey, both chambered for the .45 Winchester Magnum cartridge. The Grizzly was also available for a .357 wildcat, the Wildey for a .475 design.

Revolvers and wildcats have a problem. Bottleneck cartridges have a tendency to freeze in the cylinder, putting the revolver out of operation. This killed the .256 Winchester; the revolvers Colt's advertised in this chambering were never produced, Smith & Wesson never apparently climbed on this wagon, and Ruger produced only a single-shot pistol.

One of the best wildcat cartridges for revolvers was the .357 Bain & Davis. Developed by Keith Davis, it consisted of the .44 Magnum case necked down to hold .357-caliber bullets. With a lightweight bullet, a muzzle of 2,000 fps could be obtained using Unique powder, but a better load consisted of 18 grains of No. 2400 behind a 148-grain bullet for a velocity in the 1,400-fps range. The late Elgin Gates also designed a couple other IHMSA cartridges, both rimmed. One, the 7mm/.375 Super Mag, was a bottlenecked cartridge for use in single-shot pistols, such as the T/C Contender, but the other, the .445 Super Mag, was intended for use in large-frame Dan Wesson revolvers. The .445 could also be used in single-shot pistols and was capable of moving a 240-grain bullet over 1,900 fps ahead of 43 grains of AA-1680 powder, (with a C.U.P. of 48,900).

Other wildcat revolver and pistol wildcat loads have been developed, including the .44 Magnum necked down to .22 and .30-caliber, but a sharp bottleneck case, as previously mentioned, tends to

Left to right: The .25 Souper, based on the .308 Winchester case, made a big splash in the 1950s, prior to the introduction of the .243 Winchester; the .30 Herrett, based on shortened .30-30 Winchester cases, was an ideal whitetail load for handgunners, when used in the T/C Contender pistol; a .22/30-30 loaded round not yet fire-formed; this .227-6.5x54 wildcat was designed for use in re-barreled surplus M-S Greek rifles available some years back and were ideal in the rotary magazine; .220 Swift Improved with minimum body taper and ICL/CCC style shoulder; .220 Rocket, one of Roy Weatherby's first wildcats and still a good one; regular .220 Swift rounds could be fired in the Rocket chamber to provide a fire-formed Rocket case for handloading.

Left to right: 7.62x25mm Tokarev, .22x24mm Spitnek, .22 TCM as loaded by Rock Island Armory, 9x25mm Dillon as loaded by Double Tap, 9mm-7.65 Swiss, and the .35 or .357 Herrett. The 9x25mm Dillon was a wildcat for many years, but Double Tap has given it new life. The Herrett, originated by those of the handgun stock fame, is an excellent choice for use in the T/C Contender pistol.

Left to right: .17 Remington factory load, .17/222 Magnum, .17/222 Ackley, .17 Javelina, .17 A&M Bee, .17/.25-20 Ackley Improved, .14 Walker Hornet, .14 Walker based on the .221 Fireball case, and the .14 double-shouldered Spitter (the Spitter is not worth the effort).

Left to right: A regular 5.56mm (.223) NATO round, regular 7.62mm (.308) NATO blank, and the .14 double-shoulder Spitter. The 7.62mm blank is simply to show what a double-shoulder 6mm or 6.5mm wildcat might look like, but with the neck shortened at least by half.

Left to right: .17 Remington factory load, .17-222 Magnum, .17 A&M Bee, Ackley .17 Bee Improved, .17-222 Ackley, .17-223 H&R, .17 Javelina, .14 Walker Hornet, and .14 Walker based on the .221 Fireball case.

Left to right: .300 Mt. Shasta; unloaded PMVF case to illustrate shoulder shape; .257 Weatherby Magnum to illustrate shoulder shape; 7.62mm NATO blank to illustrate possible double-shoulder concept; and the .14 double-shoulder or DS Spitter.

Left to right: .334 Lee Magnum (note the rebated rim of this pre-1950s wildcat), .30-06 for comparison, .288 Barnes Supreme, .338 Xtreme, 7mm Mashburn Super Magnum, .308 Barnes Supreme, and .333 Barnes Supreme.

Left to right: The 8mm-06, the original "poor man's magnum" following World War II; this second one somehow escaped designation, but the shoulder on this .30-06 case is about as sharp as is possible to obtain; .300 Mt. Shasta; .375 Whelen; .30-06 for comparison; 7mm Sharps intended for use in the single-shot Colt Sharps rifle of the 1970s; and the .300 Apex Super. The Sharps was based on the 9.3x74R case, and there was reportedly a .22 Sharps for use with 100-grain bullets.

create set-back problems in the cylinder, and a long sloping shoulder, such as on the Remington .22 Jet, cuts the powder capacity.

Shooters looking for wildcat loading dies should check with Huntington Die Specialties (www.huntingtons.com). The founder of the firm, the late Fred Huntington of RCBS fame, was a wildcatter in his own right, with a number of great Rockchucker cartridges to his credit. His son runs the operation now, and this firm has more loading dies than any other this shooter knows about. Plus, they can probably turn out any die set required, if provided with three fired cases of the wildcat in question. Huntington is also a good source of unprimed brass in some wildcat calibers, as is Quality Cartridge (www.qual-cart.com), which specializes in the production of new brass for obsolete rounds, such as the .30 Newton, as well as wildcats. Another possible source for a few of the more popular wildcats is Hayley's Custom Ammunition (no website or e-mail available for this Seymour, Texas, business, but the phone number is 940-888-3352).

There are many wildcat cartridges, good and not so good, that have not been mentioned in this article. Few wildcats obtain legitimate status, and there aren't many today that provide an advantage over available factory ammunition. Too, no longer are there many gaps in the line of factory cartridges available (and each year that gap lessens). Currently, we have factory loads in .17, .22, 24, 25, 27, .28 30, .31, 32, .33, .35, .36, .40, .41, .45, .48, and .50 calibers, depending on whether you consider bore or groove sizes, and there are a number of others to fill any gaps. Wildcats are not a dying breed, and they will continue to be with us. Some will become popular, while most will exist only in a few sporting arms of the originator. Either way, it's a realm worth exploring.

NOTE: The loading data appearing in this article should not be taken as being recommended. It is only what has been achieved. Different rifles, primers, cartridge case brands, bullet seating depths, and neck sizing dies all having bearing on the end result.

Left to right: .300 Apex, .375 Whelen, .333 CCC, .340 Brushcutter, .270 Titus (designed to function in the Savage M99 magazine), .300 Luft Short Magnum, .264 Clark Magnum, (Kenneth Clark is more remembered for his .224 Clark, which used 80-grain bullets.), 6.5-257 Roberts, .300 Apex Super, and the .300 Mt. Shasta.

BY **Jim Thompson**

GUNS ONLINE

Avoiding the Quicksand, Pitfalls, and Nervous Breakdowns of Buying and Selling Guns Online.

Over the course of about eight years, I purchased and sold about 40 Bulgarian Makarovs, but this shot is the captured history of a small error. There is brown leather chaff in the thumb grooves of the slide. This was sometimes interpreted as rust. It's a fine, honest photo, but I had to retake the picture, after using a toothbrush and pipe cleaner to get the leather out of the striations on both sides. The pistol was then kept wrapped in sheet plastic and shipped that way.

This discussion is not a rule book for online auctions. Each site will have its own, but, whether one is buyer or a seller, there are some "rules of the road" more imperative than the protocols and terms of service of particular sites.

The first unwritten construct is "Stay on the road!" That is, one is there to buy or sell or both, and any frustrated schoolteacher buried deep in one's DNA is never going to be very productive in the world of commerce. It is imperative to use and impart knowledge on the merchandise in question, but the very instant that process or any similar impulse becomes a goal, then the meaningful goals of enterprise are being defeated.

Way back in the '70s, long before home computers, cell phones, and the Internet, there was a buy-and-sell circular/newspaper for camera buffs and photographers called *Shutterbug Ads*. Prefacing all the classified listings was an admonition to readers. I no longer have a copy, but it was a priceless piece of logic and psychology that we all know, and only a few refuse to acknowledge. It went something like this:

There are some people to whom commerce is an incomprehensible Gordian knot. Everything bought or sold is an abstract confusion of hatreds, paranoia, conspiracies, and problems. These folks work hard to make their own lives and those of everyone with whom they do business an endless misery. Every transaction to the chronic malcontent is studded with "buyer's remorse" and/or "seller's regret," and unreliable to deranged information/ misinformation/disinformation is used to further fuel a complex of problems entirely self-generated. If you are one of them, you've heard about it. It is strongly suggested if that is so, you not even endeavor to do business here. We will not brook your problems or support your delusions, fantasies, and hatred.

I was never able to find out if that language (and my version may be somewhat stronger than the original), originated with Glenn Patch, the original publisher, but, in those days, I was a commercial and sometime portrait photographer doing large-format work for markets all over the planet, and I needed to buy optics, even cameras sometimes, for specific jobs, then get rid of them quickly, and a national market was required to do so efficiently. I couldn't do it in a town of 50,000, and I doubt it would've worked even in New York City. But it did work nationally.

That brings me to Rule No. 2 of avoiding problems in any arena of commerce, and that is "Do not try to do business with those whose agenda has nothing to do with yours."

Very early on, before beginning my own online commerce adventures, I was advised by an old hand who had sold collector's items on eBay for years, that, "Anyone who seems crazy, just presume he is. If his question is deranged, is based on false information he got from

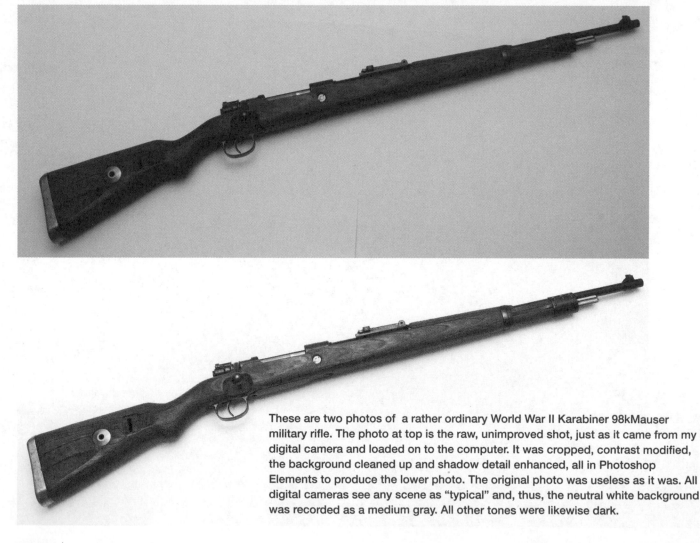

These are two photos of a rather ordinary World War II Karabiner 98kMauser military rifle. The photo at top is the raw, unimproved shot, just as it came from my digital camera and loaded on to the computer. It was cropped, contrast modified, the background cleaned up and shadow detail enhanced, all in Photoshop Elements to produce the lower photo. The original photo was useless as it was. All digital cameras see any scene as "typical" and, thus, the neutral white background was recorded as a medium gray. All other tones were likewise dark.

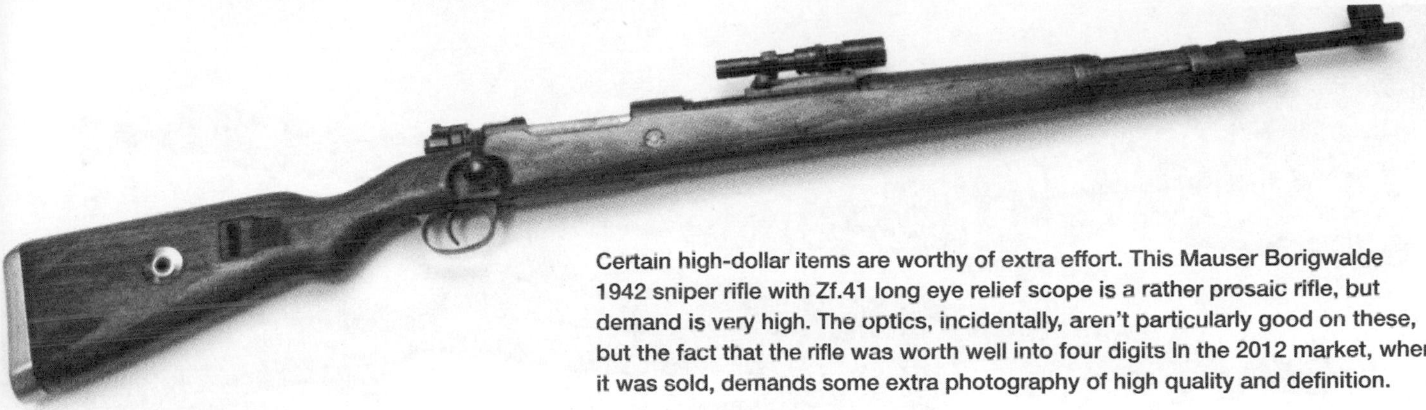

Certain high-dollar items are worthy of extra effort. This Mauser Borigwalde 1942 sniper rifle with Zf.41 long eye relief scope is a rather prosaic rifle, but demand is very high. The optics, incidentally, aren't particularly good on these, but the fact that the rifle was worth well into four digits in the 2012 market, when it was sold, demands some extra photography of high quality and definition.

some other fool, or is offensive, block him as a bidder, block his e-mail if you can and, if it's far-out enough to be threatening, report it to the web administrators at the auction site or forum. Mostly, the message services are for expediting sales and, if it's an attack, especially a crazy one, he should be banned!" This is a prudent policy.

By the way, none of this is anything new. Gun shows harbor many of the same "aisle experts," who pontificate on subjects about which they know little to nothing and who can be relied upon to produce nothing but confusion and anger (though sometimes we can get a laugh from them, too). For the most part, they are not customers, sellers, or even potentially so, and it is often downright dangerous to do business with such

folks. Those of us old enough to remember encountered them 50 years ago and more. The only difference is that, in the current electronics age, they aren't close enough to hit and have the additional protection of anonymity. In other words, a few "mouth cruisers" will attack just to attack. Others are looking for responses via e-mail and would be more than glad to inflict more balderdash or even malicious viruses upon their victims.

Still, the advantages of online buying and selling are such that entering the arena is productive, and it can be fun. I haven't been to a gun show in four years, and can't now think of a reason to go. Nor have I been to an old-fashioned, in-person auction for about six years (frankly, most of what I have seen change hands at such events in half a century in

this business has been overpriced and, often, mis-described).

Just as with gun shows and live auctions, a key rule to self-protection as a buyer or seller online is very simple. Call it Rule No. 3, or knowing that "avoiding the 'valid' literature of the items that interest you is always going to benefit you." This is the old "knowledge is power" cliché come home to roost.

The first corollary of this rule should be obvious: The stuff one hears casually, whether online, in bars, from winos sleeping in gutters, or phony baloney "experts" at gun shows, is worth a great deal less than what is paid for it. The only way to know what's real and what's not is if the genuine experts verify that snippet you think you know. Second, of course, and especially if you're selling expensive items, remember to admit you actually don't know that of which you are not sure.

A case in point. Recently, I had a very nice L.C. Smith 10-gauge (circa 1890), consigned to me by a retired friend. It was a Number 3 engraved. It took months of snooping and digging to verify the engraving pattern. During that time, I got several e-mails from "experts" telling

While they're a sort of boogie man to some of the anti-gun crowd, Chinese semiautomatic AK-47 clones from the pre-ban era are very valuable. This mint, unfired specimen, with box and instructions, went for several thousand dollars, in early 2012.

Small nuances, such as the unusual sights on this Swedish Model 1896 club target rifle, have to be emphasized and photographed in detail to sell effectively in the electronic arena.

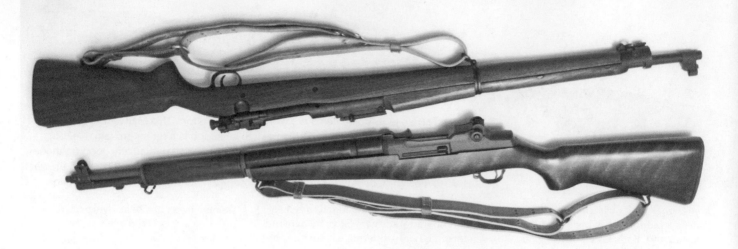

This Springfield M1 Garand and Remington Model 1903 were sold at the same time, on the same auction site. Neither was original, as both had many late match features added by first-quality civilian 'smiths. This is the same photo below, but the contrast was suppressed to match the other photography. Both rifles, while in some ways historic, would find their real market with shooters, and such an auction should specify that.

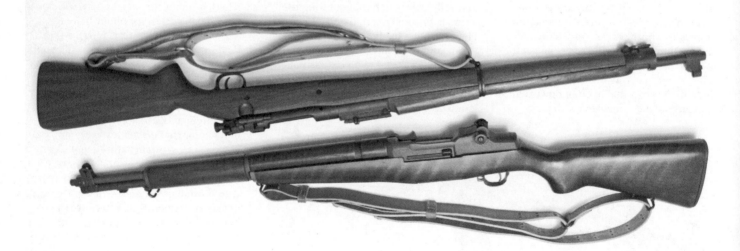

me it was misidentified. They were wrong. From several of the country's leading Smith collectors, I had verified the engraving pattern, basic features, markings, and so on. Only 90 of these guns were ever made, but the barrel was an odd length. The experts saw the photos and were about evenly divided. Two said they were "pretty sure," based upon several detailed muzzle shots, that it was a custom-length gun. Two said that, while it didn't seem to have been cut by an amateur, it was most likely not a factory job, either. I included all the photos, sold it on Auction Arms (now called GunAuction.com), and, basically,

stated flatly that the buyer should draw his own conclusions about the barrel length, because I didn't know.

The best literature in my research of this gun proved to be an e-mailed scanned copy of an 1890 catalog, very kindly sent to me by a collector who did so out of pure magnanimity. It listed the standard lengths, then said, at the bottom, that a customer could order "any desired length" in the Number Three.

This example could reasonably constitute the second corollary to Rule No. 3, that being, "If you don't know what you don't know, don't just admit it, say it in so many words!"

There's a third corollary, closely related, that makes for good seller's auctions and which helps buyers sort out the pieces and the information: "If you're aware of a rumor that seems to have some credibility or creates some interest, it is often wise to pass it on as amusing chit-chat, but be sure to identify it as a rumor." Sometimes, these things prove, in the long run, to be hogwash or hyperbole. Other times, they are proven to be correct. Most often, they live on as what amounts to gun gossip.

The same goes for the undocumented tales that often accompany individual firearms. As this is written, my online

Unusual combinations require explanation. This is an authentic U.S. Model of 905E1 bayonet with two scabbards, one genuine, but with an added tip gusset, the other a rather nice reproduction. In the copy, I had to explain that I needed the bayonet for a book photo, but it had to look as it might have in 1943 or so, and the gusset was a later strengthening addition. Interestingly, the shot finally selected didn't use the scabbard at all. Notice the use of type text right on the graphics. A surprising percentage of shoppers online do not read auctions, but will read the captions right on the photo frames.

original scabbard

original
bayonet in
replica scabbard

array of firearms across 47 auctions includes a German K98k that was supposedly an escapee with its soldier or Volkspolizei trooper, from East Germany, back in the 1950s or early 1960s. If it had arrived carrying a post-1985 import mark, I'd have never even relayed these tidbits. However, the very dark oxide finish is like those on rifles and some handguns that came out of East Germany, when that nation ceased to exist in the early '90s. So, too, is the oddly detailed renumbering system used on the parts details. Though I cannot verify the yarn, and even though it is not in any way used to inflate the price, it is passed forward as another sort of rumor in the auction.

Most of these details are much simpler with pieces that are solely shooters. Right now, among the guns I have at auction, are a Ruger M77 and an EAA Baikal 7x57R/12-gauge over/under, as well as a number of sheerly practical handguns.

Whether shooters' or collectors' items, and including parts, there's a fourth rule that ought to be observed by sellers and intensely watched for by potential purchasers: "If there's a stamped proof mark, inspector's mark, serial number, or other detail that even

might be important, photograph it and include it in the auction. This can make a rather large difference. I just sold several Winchester-marked M1 Garand clips for $25 to $40 each, and the "WRA" stamping is what distinguished mine from the more mundane types, typically worth, at this writing, about a dollar each.

There are folks with elaborate tales used to justify the exclusion or obscuration of serial numbers. Some sellers, likewise, avoid showing various other markings. Thing is, if one is interested

in doing business, the serial number is the only way to establish the background of a piece, and that includes date of manufacture, whether stolen or not and, in some cases, its actual history. Our U.S. government-issue M1 Garands, as an example, end their numbering sequence not far beyond six million. Those with numbers over seven million are cast-receiver clones made by the commercial firm Springfield Armory, Incorporated, and have never seen military service of any kind. The

Essential markings must be shown on original pieces. This very thin, light stamping is on a wartime Enfield Number 4 Mark I, from 1942.

This is a cleaned up, generic shot of a duo-code, World War II BRNO/Waffenfabrik Brunn K98k rifle. But even this shot shows some small reflection from my walnut cabinet in the butt plate area, and some viewers might construe that as rust—which is a good reason to avoid as much in the way of extraneous reflection as possible in auction photography. With very expensive items, I often tent the camera area with white carding or sheets.

real U.S. Armory, of course, was in Massachusetts, whereas Springfield Armory, Inc., is located in Illinois.

I've been utilizing online auctions for more than five years on two sites, Auction Arms (gunauction.com) and GunBroker. As of the day this summary is composed, I have more than 1,200 A+ positive feedbacks—just on those two! These are true auction sites. There are others I have used, and there is also GunsAmerica, which is a flat-price firearms dealing site. On the two sites I use most regularly, I have a grand total of three neutral and two negative feedbacks.

Feedback makes the system run. Neither site will even admonish individuals for false or misleading feedback, which, of course, also involves the buyer's remorse (or buyer's embarrassment) kinds of comments so common to those who are pathologically incapable of following the rules. Those who do this to me are blocked instantly and, for the record, I always file complaints, even knowing nothing will be done based upon one

complaint to me. Ultimately, two of these parties were banned from the auction sites in question as chronic troublemakers and one as an out-and-out charlatan.

I got my first Federal Firearms License about 1967. I've had my current one since about 1985. On modern firearms transactions, individuals without FFLs must usually receive a firearm through a licensed dealer. Collectors may acquire a Curios and Relics license, which is not a full dealer's license, but does imbue them with some shipping and receiving latitude. Anyone can buy or sell on an auction site, though with those legal loopholes and local laws properly satisfied. Some FFL dealers will not accept firearm shipments from individuals outside their areas. The law allows them to do so, if ID and so on is provided, but many have been burned, in various ways, by untrustworthy individuals.

Online gun auctions are very much like live auctions having an audience and bidders, wherein the website becomes the auctioneer. Some sellers

will use a hidden reserve as a minimum binding bid. No one I know personally will bid on a reserve auction or even ask a seller a question. This is learned fairly early. A very few sellers are experimenters of dubious virtue who will set a downright absurd reserve, simply to see if there is someone on the planet foolish enough to pay it. Some will attempt to haggle, if the reserve is not met. Others will reduce the reserve somewhat and move on. A very few—basically, opportunists—will simply fold their auctions and look for suckers elsewhere.

Most auctions feature a fixed minimum bid, wherein lower figures will not even be recorded. Most commonly, these are accompanied by a "buy it now" price. If a bidder opts for the "buy it now," the auction is over, that bidder has won, and a billing can thus be sent.

When a "buy it now" price is not listed, once a minimum bid has been placed, the auction will continue for its stated period, usually seven or 14 days

This all-steel, original wartime P.38 was shown with a reproduction German World War II, Nazi era Kriegsmarine Model 1935 helmet, partly for eye appeal and window dressing, but also because it allowed the manipulation of the pistol to stand up against a dark object, at an angle, which is always a more interesting photo than a straight-on "mug shot." As always, it is necessary to specify that only the pistol is for sale.

Unusual inclusions in an auction need to be explained, in both text and graphics. This Remington M1903 sported a brand new barrel and a CMP-supplied C Target stock and wood, a more commodious arrangement than the scant or straight stocks. The sling was a correct style, but reproduction leather unit, appropriately marked.

and running from Sunday to Sunday (Sunday is the biggest day for closures in the online auction business). The highest bidder at the approximate end is the winner. One has to say "approximate end," because the biggest players in the industry both have rules whereby a bid extends an auction briefly, usually for 15 minutes, so that lurking potential bidders can counter.

A couple years ago, I had a splendid Browning Hi-Power, a premium Model of 1935 up for bid. On the auction system on GunBroker, I could determine it had more than 30 "watchers." It was on for many weeks. Finally, just before close and after more than a month, someone made a minimum bid. However, the sale didn't actually end until the next morning, with far beyond 20 bids at exactly the "buy it now" price.

In that respect, if possible, it is prudent to adjust the bidding dollar interval to higher figures, when a venue allows that control. If this isn't done, in some circumstances, a bid of a mere 50 cents more will be acceptable, and an auction goes on way too long for most sellers.

The big trick for a buyer is always getting in that first bid; the number of watchers means very, very little. It is not uncommon to note as many as 30 watchers on an item with no bidding activity for months, which is why most sellers put their items on automatic renewal mode. Many watchers are window shopping, some are competitors, some are folks hoping their ship comes in, and a few are just hoping a seller might reduce the minimum bid price.

Most adventurous of the sellers are the penny and dollar auction participants. They literally allow binding bids for as little as one cent. And many of them do it on all their merchandise. I

think this may take more courage than I have, but I recently tracked a Navy Luger Model of 1906 that caught my eye, and it got a very high number of bids, winding up selling for about $3,000. Then, checking the Auction Arms site for penny auctions, I realized most everything the Luger's seller had posted went for about normal wholesale or above, sometimes far above, and their close rate was much better than mine. Over time, I may dip my toe in that arena, but doing it the very first time is going to take a lot of fortitude.

For 20 years, I was a firearms writer. Now retired, this stuff is at once a hobby and a business. My areas of interest as a writer primarily involved military firearms, but also extended to western firearms, commercial Lugers, and target rifles. I've always been a shooter first, everything else second. My first book, from Paladin, in 1989, was *Machine Guns: A Pictorial, Practical and Tactical History*. In 1998, there was *The Complete M1 Garand*. In college, I learned to do hard research with original sources,

and while I neither do nor much enjoy dry, dull, industrial histories, I used to gobble them up like ice cream on a hot day. If one means to enter either end of the online firearms commerce business, even as a hobby, that kind of "hobbyist and student as the boss" is about the only way it can be done. On the selling side, profits are usually not high, but the nightmare of dealing with a completely untrained and uninformed general public is considerably reduced. In my experiences dealing with laymen face to face, selling merchandise that is really the province of the specialist can only be described as annoying and frustrating. Yes, in the online venues, on the buying end, savings can be substantial, though such deals are intermittent. Call this Rule No. 5, and another that applies to everyone: "If you can't do it properly and by the rules, better to not even try!"

There's a sixth rule that you can use to quickly figure out what your car or firearm might cost if you had to build it up out of loose parts: "The sum of the sold parts is a whole lot more money than

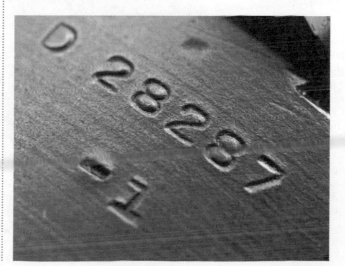

Another detail shot, well under an inch in real area, showing the original detail parts number marking on a very early M1 Garand bolt. Since it is the marking that defines the age of the gun, not showing them is not merely an error, it is a virtual guarantee a serious collector won't touch it.

the sold assembly by itself." Yup! That $9 extractor, $75 bolt, the springs—they all add up. Keep in mind that, if one wishes to become a parts merchant, it's necessary to be able to state whether an item is in working condition, and your statement had best be reliable and correct, because all auction sites have provisions for returning defective items that are not listed as such. Startlingly, both on my own and by consignment from others, I have sold old and even rusted parts, honestly and in detail presented, and satisfied the customers who purchased them. Whether they were doing visual restorations, figured they could restore the items, or simply found damaged miscellany amusing, I do not know. There is always the dim possibility they were treasures I somehow failed to interpret properly. If so, for me there was either profit involved or the need to recapture the space the item consumed, so there are few, if any, second thoughts.

The seventh and final rule is the biggest and most vital, and the one without adherence to which everything else eventually fails. It's dead simple and very plain: "Photography is everything!"

I had been a practicing photographer for almost 40 years, when I put together my first online auctions. I did them on film, scanned to JPEG files on my computer, and stormed ahead. I did have some misconceptions, at the time I started. For the life of me, I could not understand why an overall configuration shot of a firearm was necessary, especially with a rifle, which requires a long vertical shot, is often hard to light, and which, reduced (especially by Gun-Broker), offers very little detail. Frankly, I still think such photos are overrated. After all, what person about to buy a $2,000 competition-quality M1 Garand has no idea what the overall rifle looks like? However, within hours of posting my first auction, I had several e-mails inquiring what the whole rifle looked like. I had included individual shots of both sides, every single parts marking, bolt and sight details, and even a shot of the buttplate, for crying out loud! Right or wrong, I had overall configuration shots on the auction within an hour and have not failed to use them since.

While the photography in the auctions is not as demanding as the double-trucked photo spreads I did for magazine ads back in the '70s, I still apply a lot of the same principles.

A white or neutral-gray background is easiest to use for most subject matter

and casts no color-distorting reflections. I do sometimes use red, blue, green, or camouflaged backgrounds, but, to eliminate color spillover, usually separate the item from its background.

I use bounced studio flash—not on-camera flash, which is the most useless lighting for this stuff—with about four heads, for most items. This is soft, portrait-like lighting that casts very soft shadows, which I very rarely remove. (There is no such thing as photography without shadows, by the way.)

Tungsten incandescent flood lighting has many drawbacks, of which the heat generated and potential fire and burn issues are just a couple. Hard reflection control is best done with a polarizing filter, and one can even drape polarizing material over the lights for nearly absolute control. Camera stores and their professionals will generally have good advice on lighting and close-up photography that will be very, very helpful.

I would have been content to stay with film, save that during one of my first winters back in the Midwest, I got very annoyed with driving to the photo finisher, then driving back to pay my money and pick up the work a second time. Too,

with as many as a dozen consignment items coming in a typical week, there was a pretty substantial photo finishing bill involved. One particularly ugly set of trips in very heavy snow convinced me to go digital, and the money saved going forward allowed me to purchase PhotoShop Elements 8, my current photo editing software. (It's good I did, because I immediately discovered my digital camera is convinced that all subject matter is "average" and, thus, photos against my white background are often underexposed. The camera, you see, is convinced that big white hunk of paper is very bright and darkens down the entire frame to compensate.)

Some beginners do their work outdoors, in shade, to avoid the whole studio setup, but that has disadvantages of its own. Working in sunlight generates hard shadows and reflections, especially with nickeled, stainless, or high-polished blue surfaces. Years ago, editing an article for a gun magazine, I wondered what the "blue stuff" was on a nice old Colt Single Action. It was the sky! I didn't bother with it on the transparency back

Rough textures, damage, pitting, missing parts, and so on need to be illustrated. This rare WIN-13 M1 Garand receiver still has strong markings, but shows evidence of corrosion on the outside surfaces. Not to show this would have resulted in a very angry response from any purchaser, and rightly so. Somewhat unusually, and the reverse of common encounters, the rifle was very clean in the areas under the wood, and even the bottom of the trigger housing was free from pitting.

This shot of a near-mint Enfield Model of 1914 in .303 is a useful lead shot, and it isn't just about the color. It at least strongly implies that the rifle has been fired.

then, since it was a very small detail that, in the end, didn't matter. But the online auction seller is prudent to present his treasures as objectively as possible, and extraneous reflections and backgrounds can only detract.

The key rule in photography of this type is to get close, followed shortly by get closer. My auctions for firearms typically include 15 to 40 photos; on high-dollar items, 60 or 70 is not uncommon. With rare exceptions, every shot goes through editing to enhance the images and eliminate background flaws, color cast, and just generally present the most complete and honest image of the merchandise that can be shown in the space provided.

By the way, both big auction sites "shrink" your images, but it is singularly unwise to shoot at low pixel levels. Shooting at 1 MG or better is not strictly necessary, and half that (500 kb) will provide suitable images. But 100 kb will show on GunBroker not much bigger than a postage stamp, and it's a picture that, for practical purposes, is not worth taking. Auction Arms shrinks images much less; for certain commercial items with a lot of detail, I will often use that site, simply because the picture can be more reliably read. The photos with this article should provide some illustration of the difference between raw and edited images. Lousy photos are lousy photos and are often regarded as a form of deception, so using yours in their unedited form is singularly unwise.

To purchasers, a little advice: on an expensive item, where there are too few pictures, lousy photos, and not much visual information, don't bother asking for more. It may be an attempt to deny information or deceive, but it's more likely the seller simply doesn't care enough to develop good images and, therefore, there is no point bidding.

To sellers, this wisdom: If the pictures aren't bright and sharp, big enough, or plentiful enough, there can be a world of apathy or hurt just around the corner.

Acquiring photo software and learning how to use it is absolutely essential, if online auction selling is to be a major part of one's hobby or income. It is a money-making tool that very quickly pays for itself. There is some free photo software out there that will allow cropping, which is very important, and some lightening and darkening, but most of it is very slow to use and limiting. I have not used all of them, but all I have used were far too rudimentary. Remember, an online seller is competing with professionals and manufacturers, who have seasoned professionals taking their firearms photos.

More than five years ago now, I took my first big consignment, and the seller saw the auction online. "Why so many pictures?" he asked.

"I have to show everything I can," I responded.

"It isn't necessary!"

That was a few hours before the flashy M1 sold later that day for about $1,500, the "buy it now" price. The same consignee now says, "There is no such thing as too many photos!" I am inclined to agree.

There are some ethical considerations that aren't rules, just mechanisms used to sort things out. For example, many of us consider it unethical, in response to potential bidders using the message systems to request "extra photos," to furnish shots that are not ultimately put in the auction. In fact, the last couple dozen such requests I have gotten were asking for photos that were already in the auction, and in some numbers—some people don't know how to scroll down! Others don't wait for all the photos to load. And guess what? If you send them a 2 MG file, they won't know how to read that, either, since it will more than fill up the screen (if they can figure out how to open it).

I was heartened a couple years ago, when a friend was looking at one of my guns, took it under a stronger light, but still couldn't see all the inspector's marks he was attempting to view. He then signed on his computer and looked at the auction.

"You know," he said, "I can see it better online than I can in person!"

That, of course, is the way the whole thing is supposed to work.

SAFETY FIRST

*"There's a popular misconception—
often stated in training courses!—
that says, 'Autoloaders have
safeties, revolvers don't,' which
is certainly incorrect."*

— But Whose Safety?

BY **Tom Caceci**

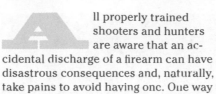

ll properly trained shooters and hunters are aware that an accidental discharge of a firearm can have disastrous consequences and, naturally, take pains to avoid having one. One way to do this is to equip a gun with some sort of disabling device. This is especially important in the case of handguns, whose ergonomics are such that picking one up more or less immediately puts it into "firing mode."

Most (though not all) autoloading handguns are equipped with a manual safety of some kind that has to be positively disengaged or put "off" by the shooter before the handgun can be fired, but there's a popular misconception— often stated in training courses!—that says, "Autoloaders have safeties, revolvers don't," which is certainly incorrect. While most revolvers[1] lack a manual safety device, revolvers that do have them have been around for quite a long time; it's by no means unusual to encounter a mechanical safety catch on revolvers, especially some made in Europe well into the twentieth century.

Some years ago, I purchased a revolver of the "constabulary" type. A prototypical "constabulary" has a saw-handle grip and is a solid frame, gate-loading double-action with a swinging under-barrel ejector rod. The best ex-ample is the Webley Metropolitan Police used by the British constabulary (hence the generic name for similar guns), a design widely copied by Continental gun makers. Constabularies usually have a lanyard ring, as well, consistent with European police practices.

Many Continental constabularies were made for export, and many were issued to police forces. Mine was made in Belgium and is in the 9.4mm "Dutch Service" caliber. Externally, it is virtually identical in appearance to guns marked "Maastricht" that are known to have been issued to Dutch police forces. Internally, it differs considerably.

When I received it, the action seemed to be completely inoperable. Neither the trigger nor the hammer budged, no matter how hard I pulled. Thinking the internal lockwork was frozen with rust, I took off the grip, and there I saw the answer to one question, but encountered an even more fascinating one, namely, "What have I got *here*?"

The lanyard swivel is not (as most are) free rotating. It is, instead, attached to the lower end of a long rod that passes through a boss cast into the frame. This rod is located behind the hammer pivot in such a way that, when elevated to a certain position, it completely blocks the hammer's movement. When the lanyard swivel is

By all outward appearances, a garden-variety Continental "constabulary" style revolver: a gate loading, solid frame, double action with s swinging ejector rod. These revolvers are fairly close copies of the popular Webley Metropolitan Police revolver, but the scooped cylinder flutes identify it as a Continental product. Such flutes are typical of Belgian, French, and German guns; this one was made in Belgium.

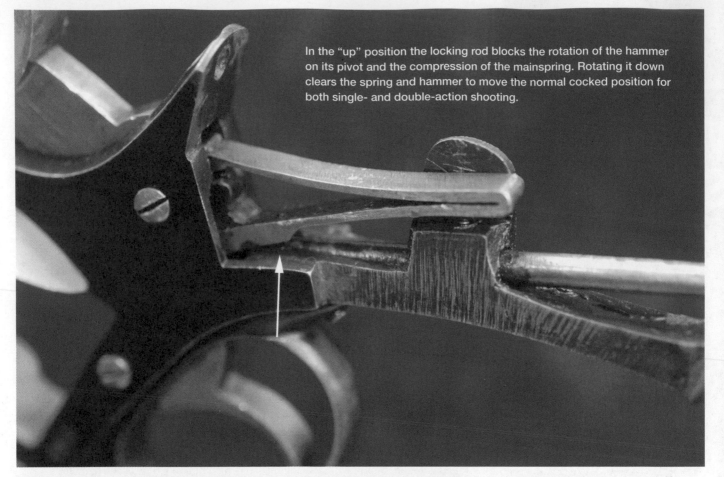

In the "up" position the locking rod blocks the rotation of the hammer on its pivot and the compression of the mainspring. Rotating it down clears the spring and hammer to move the normal cocked position for both single- and double-action shooting.

The "Crown-over-ELG" proof mark was introduced in 1894 and indicates a gun that meets German proof standards, probably to facilitate export to other countries in Europe. The inspector stamps match those on the barrel.

rotated half a turncounter-clockwise, the rod moves down and out of the way of the hammer and the action then works smoothly. When rotated the same amount clockwise, the rod moves up behind the hammer and tightly locks the entire action. The rod has a helical groove machined into it that slides over a small stud concealed inside the boss. Turning the lanyard ring thus imparts a screw-type motion and operates the mechanism. The total movement is perhaps a quarter-inch from the bottom position to the top. It's a little cumbersome, perhaps, but about as positive a safety device as could be imagined.

To all outward appearances, the gun is an ordinary Continental Constabulary, but that safety is unique, in my experience. Constabularies with safeties usually have those safeties mounted somewhere on the frame, and they often work simply by blocking the cylinder's

The "Crown-over-R" mark was introduced in 1894 and is used on firearms with rifles barrels. The accompanying stamp is a Belgian inspector's mark.

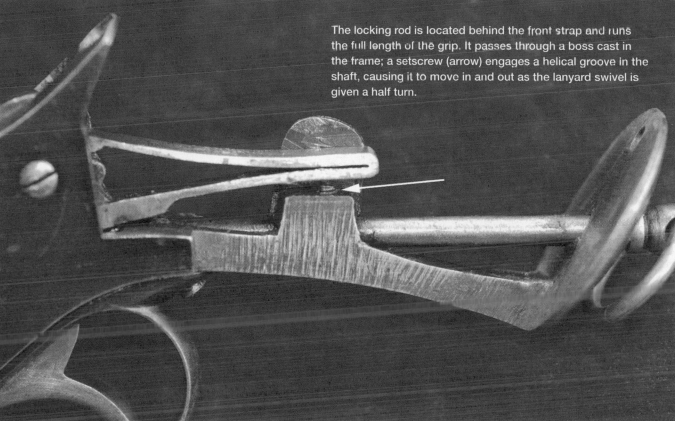

The locking rod is located behind the front strap and runs the full length of the grip. It passes through a boss cast in the frame; a setscrew (arrow) engages a helical groove in the shaft, causing it to move in and out as the lanyard swivel is given a half turn.

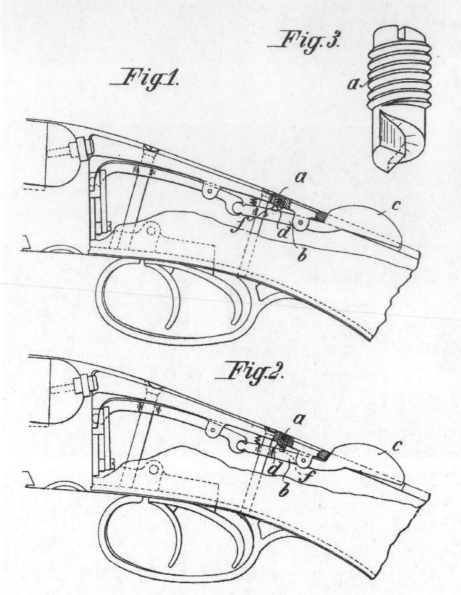

These figures from Tambour's patent #20,373 of 1905 clearly show a "helical screw" being used to block the firing mechanism, along with a grip safety that can be locked by it. Many of Tambour's other patents have this combination of a blocking bar and a grip safety.

In all, Tambour held more than 40 patents issued between 1899 and 1925, all but one dealing with firearms safeties. Since he usually described himself as "… a subject of his Majesty the Emperor Franz Josef" and was therefore probably born in Austria-Hungary, a letter to the Vienna State Archives elicited the information that he was born July 17, 1857, in Lemburg. The official record describes his occupation as *waffentechniker* (a "weapon technician") and gives some details of his places of residence through April 1930. No date of death has been established, but I believe he may have died about that time.

I continued to search old records, contact collectors, and haunt gun shows and auction sites looking for a similar revolver, but came up with nothing that resembled the safety on my revolver. Well, *nearly* nothing. Then I found U.S. Patent #2,945,316, issued in July of 1960 to Lester F. Mulno and assigned to his employer, Harrington & Richardson of Worcester, Massachusetts.

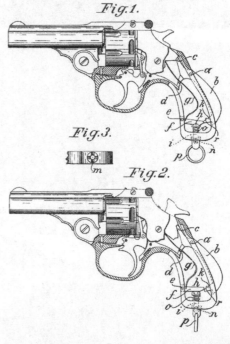

Tambour's Austrian patent #36388, dated 1909, is the closest thing in the records to the safety on my Constabulary. It lacks the rising rod, and instead uses the lanyard ring to block the grip safety; a typical Tambour design.

rotation; if the lockwork is blocked, the safety lever is on the left side of the frame convenient to the shooter's thumb. Examples of this sort of side-mounted safety are easy to find.

Never having encountered a safety that worked the way this one did, I wrote to several noted collectors and major collector's magazines to ask about its origins, but was met with shrugs or the reply that "It's probably a removable ejector rod," which it most certainly is not. So I went on a hunt to see what I could find in old patent records. I knew a

device like this had to be the subject of a patent.

A day or two at the National Firearms Museums Library, where I was courteously granted access to a voluminous book of firearms patents from all over the world, showed me several safeties that were similar, but all differing in some essential characteristic. These old patents, however, had one thing in common: they were almost all the product of the mind of one Joseph Tambour, originally of Vienna, Austria, later of Nanterre, France.

H&R briefly marketed a variant of its "Guardsman" revolver employing the Mulno device, which bears an eerie resemblance to the safety on my revolver and works in exactly the same way. A rod in the grip rotates in a screw-type motion, rising up to block the movement of the internal lock parts. Mulno's version incorporates a key-activated lock to control the movement of the rod, rather than a lanyard swivel. Mulno actually cited Tambour's Austrian patent #20,373, issued in June of 1905—in fact the only patent he referenced—but nowhere in the text is the relationship of the two devices explained.

Mulno's claims for his device could be applied to my gun:

10. [a] ... releasable locking means carried by said frame comprising a threaded locking member *movable toward and away from said firing member* ... **engageable with [the] firing member so as to hold it in a position such that it cannot fire.**

11. [a] ... releasable locking means for positively obstructing movement of the firing means ... *comprising a rotatable threaded locking member within the frame and movable toward and away from locking engagement with the firing means*

12. [a] ... releasable locking means ... comprising *a threaded locking member carried by the firearm and movable toward and away from said firing member, the locking member having an inner end portion engageable with the firing member,* **to lock said firing member against firing movement ...** *the locking member has a steep pitch thread so that approximately, a single rotation of the locking member is sufficient to move the locking member between locking and release position.* **... the threaded engagement ... with the ... frame is provided by** *a pin disposed in the frame generally transverse to the axis of rotation of the locking member and intersecting the thread groove thereof.*

Mulno's design (and the safety on my revolver) bears an even closer resemblance to another of Tambour's

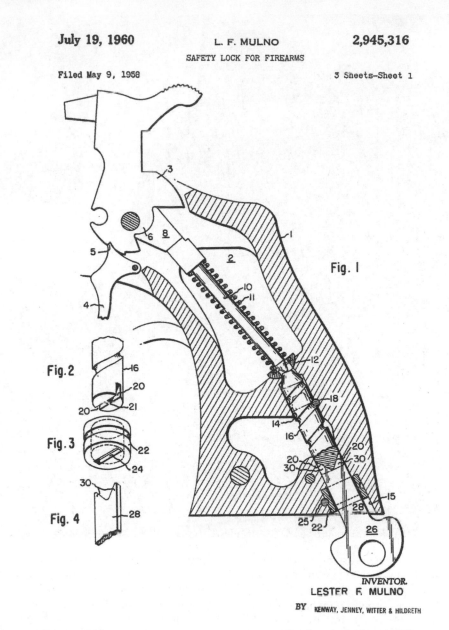

July 19, 1960   L. F. MULNO   2,945,316
SAFETY LOCK FOR FIREARMS

Filed May 9, 1958   3 Sheets—Sheet 1

Fig. 1

Fig. 2

Fig. 3

Fig. 4

INVENTOR.
LESTER F. MULNO
BY KENWAY, JENNEY, WITTER & HILDRETH

Lester Mulno's 1960 patent closely resembles some of Tambour's designs. H&R Guardsman revolvers were made with this device, but are very uncommon.

Austrian patents, #36388, issued in February 1909, a drawing from which clearly shows a screw-in lanyard loop attached to a helical screw that rises to block the grip safety that controls the firing mechanism of a revolver. Add the rising rod and eliminate the grip safety, and it would be identical to mine. Mulno must have been aware of this patent, but makes no reference to it.

Based on the research I've done, I have to conclude that the safety mechanism on my constabulary is a Tambour design. There are simply too many similarities to his other patents for it to be the work of some other inventor,

although it's possible that someone who worked with Tambour might have come up with the idea. But the inability to locate any patent that exactly corresponds raises a couple questions.

Could this odd revolver be a tool room prototype incorporating a new safety mechanism? It has no indication of the maker, none whatever. It does have Liege proof marks on the cylinder face, Belgian inspector's marks on the barrel, and a laconic "253" hand-stamped on the left side of the frame. A half-dozen companies in Belgium could have made it, but there is no way to know which one. Another question is whom Tambour

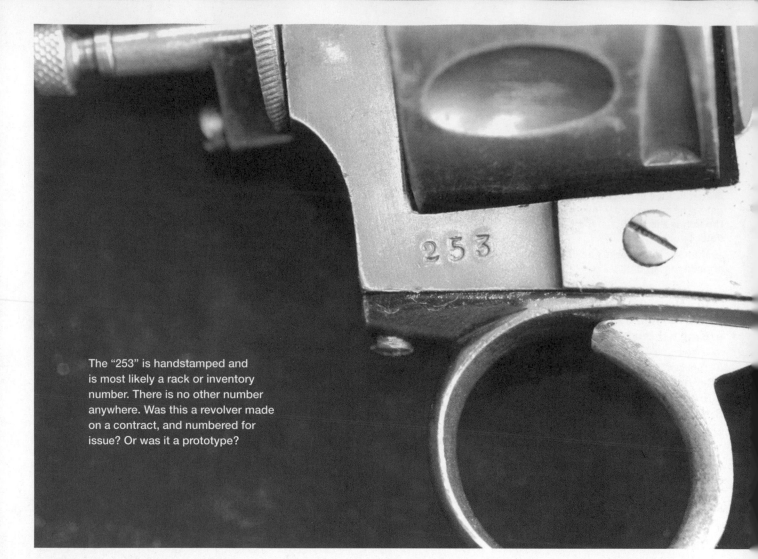

The "253" is handstamped and is most likely a rack or inventory number. There is no other number anywhere. Was this a revolver made on a contract, and numbered for issue? Or was it a prototype?

might have been working for. Unlike Lester Mulno's patents, Tambour's have no indication of an assignee.

The Liege proof is one that was first used in 1894; the "Crown over R" mark indicates a rifled barrel and went into use in 1894, as well. Thus, the gun cannot be older than 1894, but could be significantly newer. Constabularies were made well into the 1920s, as the design was very popular.

The "253," which is clearly stamped with individual numeral dies, I believe to be a rack or inventory number, not a serial number. If this assumption is correct, given that the caliber is that used by Dutch *civilian* police forces, could it have been part of an order sold to some municipality, or one of a number of guns used in "field trials"?

Was it made for export? If so, where to? Belgian makers enjoyed a worldwide market, but probably not in the reaches of the Dutch colonial empire. The Dutch used a somewhat longer version of

the 9.4 round, which implies that this revolver was not intended for use in the East Indies, but rather in Europe. The arms-making capabilities of the Dutch were rather limited, and they are known to have contracted with the sizeable Belgian arms industry for their needs.

Was Tambour planning to file yet another patent to cover this safety device, but perhaps died before he could do so? Was Mulno aware of this safety mechanism when he designed his own?

Some of the frustrating aspects of arms collecting is that often the people who can answer specific questions are no longer with us, and records usually don't exist. Tambour died long ago. Mr. Mulno died in the early 1990s. Luckily, the U.S. Patent Office database, as well as the European equivalent, are searchable on line, but H&R is out of business. Its successors have no old records, and access to copies of old factory records turned in to the BATFE require a request under the Freedom of Information Act.

This can take years to be granted. (And while this might indicate how many "Guardsman" guns were made with the Mulno device—it can't have been very many—it probably wouldn't shed much light on how and where Mulno got his ideas.)

I have looked for years for another example of a gun with such a safety, contacting many collectors and high-end auction sites, but have found nothing like it. On occasion someone says, "Oh, yes, I've seen one like that," but if, in fact, another example exists, I've been unable to locate it for examination. If any of *Gun Digest's* readership knows of such a gun, and/or where I can find an H&R Guardsman with the Mulno lock, I would very much appreciate having the information. I can be contacted through the editor's office at any time and extend thanks to the community of gun collectors for any help you can provide.

Looking back at the concealed carry guns of another era.

YESTERDAY'S
Pocket Pistols & Bedside Guns

BY **Jim Dickson**

The late nineteenth and early twentieth centuriey were times when many people carried a gun and weren't afraid to use one to defend themselves, their family, and their property. The pistols they used tended to be small, top-break .32s and .38s, with an increasing number of .32 autos coming into use as the twentieth century progressed.

Today, guns of this type are often dismissed with a flippant, "We have better guns today. Get something more modern." They also had better guns back in the

nineteeth century. The fast-pointing .45 Colt Single Action Army and the New Service double-action were unsurpassed as gun-fighting revolvers and, in 1911, the ultimate fighting pistol, the Colt M1911 .45 automatic came on the scene. Yet most people chose a small pocket pistol because, like today, it was something that could easily be carried. By day, these guns rode in a discrete holster or a pocket or purse. At night, it was the bedside table.

While the Colt .45s tamed the frontier, the ubiquitous .32s and .38 S&W revolvers were the guns that tamed the cities

and small towns and made it safe for you to take your family for a stroll along the boulevard. Most of these guns were carried or kept in a bedside table more than they were shot, and many have survived to today in serviceable condition. These are worth a second look by today's users.

The top of the line for most buyers was the compact, five-shot, top-break revolver. It ejected and reloaded faster than a swing-out cylinder gun and was easy to carry. The .32 S&W and .32 S&W Long were very popular cartridge choices, because they gave off less noise and

Loading a S&W .38 top-break revolver is fast and easy. This was one of their selling points.

Breaking it open quickly ejects the empty cases. Nothing here to befuddle users already under stress from an emergency.

The .32 was considered the smallest caliber suitable for a defensive gun and, as today, some people were uncomfortable with it. The next tier up was the .38 S&W. That gun was proportionately larger, but still a handy size, and the noise and recoil were comfortable for a woman or child to handle. (In those days, children were expected to pick up a gun and defend the family if they found themselves in that position.)

The .32 and .38 top-break revolvers could be had in both hammer and hammerless versions. A high percentage of these guns were carried in pockets, and it didn't take long for folks to find out how easy it was to hang a sharp hammer spur on a pocket lining. For this reason, the hammerless models were popular for those who preferred pocket carry.

Colt's, Smith & Wesson, Harrington & Richardson, Hopkins & Allen, and a host of others made fine top-break revolvers in an era when it seemed that American shooters couldn't get enough of them. While Smith & Wesson maintained the lion's share of the market, the Iver Johnson "Owlhead" pistols equaled them in workmanship, fit, and finish, while surpassing them in design. Called an Owlhead because of the owl trademark set in the top of the grips, the Iver Johnson had simpler, more robust parts and coil springs, and their famous "hammer the hammer" hammer-block safety that prevented the gun from firing if it was dropped on its hammer.

The semi-automatic pistol began to make its presence felt at the turn of the twentieth century. The fine-pointing Colt Model 1903 auto was the modern invention of the hour. It held more ammo then the small revolvers, was easier to conceal, and remains one of the finest pocket automatics of all time even today.

All these guns can keep all their shots in a Campbell's soup can at 25 yards. That's good enough practical accuracy then and now. I

n preparation for this article, an assortment of these century-old and older handguns were fired at that ever popular target. The earliest model was an 1880 Smith & Wesson Baby Russian top-break spur-trigger single-action chambered in .38 S&W. Well worn and lightly pitted inside and out, with no original finish on it for probably 100 years, it still delivered gilt-edge accuracy, putting all its shots "plumb center" with the greatest of ease. It pointed fast, and anyone on the wrong end of it in a gunfight then or now would be in trouble.

recoil than the bigger guns, and because the ammunition was very affordable. The .32s were considered more reliable than the .22 rimfire, which was sometimes prone to misfire, and they also had twice the stopping power of a .22.

How effective were these choices? A typical example of the period was when my aunt Lily woke up to find a burglar entering her bedroom window. One shot from her .32 S&W Long top-break revolver, and the burglar grunted as the bullet hit, fell back out of the window, and ran away. It would take an awfully fanatical attacker to keep climbing

through a window, when someone was firing at you, even with a .32.

The .32 S&W Long became a very popular police cartridge for a time in this country, until it was replaced by the .38 Special. In 1896, New York Police Commissioner Theodore Roosevelt standardized the Colt .32 New Police revolver for the NYPD, and many other police departments followed his lead. Smith & Wesson even named one of its swing-out cylinder revolvers the .32 Regulation Police, to fight for a share of the police market.

The guns test-fired were, left and right: Savage .32 and Colt .32 semi-autos. Top to bottom: 1880 Smith & Wesson single-action spur trigger in .38 S&W; a later Smith & Wesson double-action .38 S&W; a .32 S&W double-action; and an Iver Johnson .38 S&W Owlhead double-action.

When the chips are down, I would prefer this old relic to some of the more modern guns I have fired over the years. Recoil was negligible, and it was very pleasant to shoot. The little Smith proved that accuracy can be found in places you would not expect to find it.

Like several other guns profiled in the article, it required a bit of repair before returning to duty. Gunsmith Ken Lundquist, at Tucker Guns, in Tucker, Georgia, had to replace a sideplate screw, knock a dent out of a chamber, free a sticking hand spring, and repair a shattered gutta-percha grip. Still, not bad for a gun that has seen hard use for well over a century.

A later sample of a Smith & Wesson top-break double-action revolver had a mint bore and almost perfect original nickel plating, but it could not improve on the accuracy of its predecessor. It was very efficient at fast double-action shooting. J. Henry Fitzgerald was one of the great exhibition shooters with a pistol, in the early years of the twentieth century. His comments in his book *Shooting* are as pertinent today as they were in the 1930s. Fitz believed that drawing and firing a double action revolver should be one motion. He said that your life was in little danger until the criminal got within 15 feet of you, and that 90 percent of police shootings are within 10 feet and last less than

An 1880 Smith & Wesson single-action .38 S&W model 1½.

The Iver Johnson Owlhead .38 was so called because of the owl logo at the top of the grips.

1880 S&W single-action spur trigger revolver with turn-of-the-century-style holster.

S&W single- and double-action revolvers.

two seconds. These vintage guns shine within these parameters.

A top-break Iver Johnson Owlhead .38 S&W double-action revolver in very good condition was also fired extensively. It was easy to see why there were stories in the old days of farmers shooting foxes and other predator with guns like this. It is fast, accurate, and easy to hit with, and it is also a lot of fun to shoot. Ken Lundquist also had to work on this gun to get it ready for testing, including freeing the bolt spring, which was impeded in operation by 100 years of crud.

The Owlhead's hammer-block safety and coil springs made it the safest and most reliable of the top-break revolvers of its day. It carried a low price without sacrificing quality, which contributed greatly to its popularity. Iver Johnson designed the gun to be easy to build, with a solid frame (no expensive side-plate), and simple robust parts intended for easy mass production, thereby enabling it to be extraordinarily competitive in price. In its day, the Owlhead came to represent the average man's pistol; huge numbers were sold.

A .32 Smith & Wesson top-break in our group of handguns had seen the most use. This was a rare example of a bore worn down by lead bullets to where it is almost a smoothbore. It was inoperable when received and was a problem getting back into service because of all the parts that had to be replaced. This worn-out wonder still managed to shoot accurately enough at gunfighting ranges of 10 to 15 feet for any defensive use. Perfectly scaled for the .32 cartridge size, it was a most diminutive piece, so light one could easily forget they were carrying it. Of course, that was the idea.

All four of these revolvers have grips that are small for my hand, but that did not interfere with accurate shooting. Recoil was so little that, if the back of a trigger guard or spur bumped a knuckle, there was no discomfort. I found that a two-finger grip with the little finger below the bottom of the grip gave better control and pointing, especially on the three double-actions.

These little guns all share the top-break revolver's ease of removing the cylinder for cleaning. Just break the gun open, lift the top latch, and spin the cylinder while pulling it back out of the gun. It sure is more convenient to clean than a swing-out cylinder gun, especially if you are cleaning with hot soapy water, as was mandated by the use of the blackpowder and corrosive primers of the day.

An early Smith & Wesson Hand Ejector swing-out cylinder model in .32 S&W Long was the final revolver fired. This gun wore the early grips of a S&W top-break revolver and was the property of a distinguished Chinese doctor of traditional Asian medicine. An extremely small man, it fit him quite perfectly. Sometimes, that is the most important thing in selecting a firearm. This very early example of a modern swing-out cylinder Smith & Wesson was in very good condition and looked much like a miniature Military & Police .38 Special revolver. It was very accurate and a joy to shoot.

An early Colt M1903 .32 Pocket auto that is more than 100 years old also proved to be a delight to fire. I wish I'd had more ammo, as I didn't want to stop shooting it. The .32 ACP with a full metal jacketed bullet has enormous penetrating power, as evidenced by the damage to Archduke Ferdinand's automobile, in 1914. His assasination caused his father, Emperor Franz Joseph of Austria-Hungary, to declare war on Serbia, which mushroomed into WWI.

It's easy to understand why this gun was always so popular. The hand-filling grip is comfortable and houses a magazine that holds eight rounds—quite an improvement over a five-shot revolver. It packs comfortably and well concealed in a Strong Leather Company pancake holster. This pistol has always been noted for its concealability, but the modern pancake holster design takes it into the twenty-first century in style. (I have used the pancake holster ever since it was first invented and have never found a better design for police or civilian carry.) There are smaller .32 autos today, but they aren't as much fun to shoot or as accurate; some are also a lot harder to take apart and put back together.

A Savage .32 that was tested is a scaled-down version of the Savage .45 that gave the Colt M1911 a run for its money in the U.S. Army acceptance trials. Putting it into shooting condition required a new barrel and magazine, but it was well worth it, for the little gun performed beautifully. Like the old Savage ads said, "Aims as easy as pointing your finger" and "If Grandma can handle it, so can you!" The Savage sports an extractor that pivots out 90 degrees for easy cleaning, once the bolt is out. This is a very desireable feature every

The S&W Safety Hammerless .38 was also called a Lemon Squeezer, because of its grip safety. It's a fine fighting pocket pistol.
(Photographed at Tucker Guns)

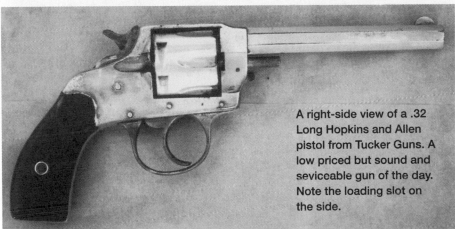

A right-side view of a .32 Long Hopkins and Allen pistol from Tucker Guns. A low priced but sound and seviceable gun of the day. Note the loading slot on the side.

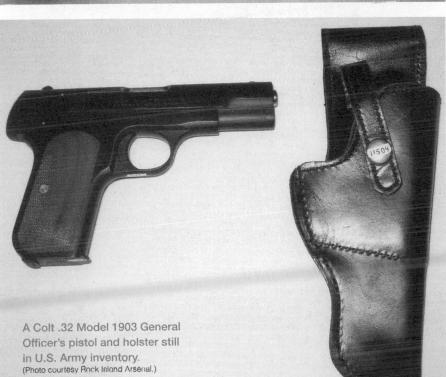

A Colt .32 Model 1903 General Officer's pistol and holster still in U.S. Army inventory.
(Photo courtesy Rock Island Arsenal.)

automatic should have, and the rest of the gun is also unusually accessible for cleaning.

Both the Colt and the Savage .32s had distinguished military careers, with 17,000 Colts bought by the U.S. in WWII, and 27,000 Savage .32s purchased by France and 1,200 by Portugal in WWI. The Colt 1903 and 1908 (.380) models became the pistols that were issued to Army generals, as well as serving with the OSS and the U.S. Navy.

In the course of the shooting tests for this article, 650 rounds were fired. The breakdown was 250 rounds of Winchester .38 S&W 145-grain LRN; 150 rounds of Winchester .32 Long 98-grain LRN; 50 rounds of Remington .32 Long 98-grain LRN; 50 rounds of Georgia Arms .32 Long loaded with an 85-grain Hornady jacketed hollowpoint; 50 rounds of Remington .32 S&W short 88-grain LRN; 50 rounds of BVAC .32 ACP FMJ; and 50 rounds of Remington .32 ACP 72-grain FMJ.

All this shooting got a pile of guns filthy fast. They make non-corrosive primers, so why can't they make something that doesn't get guns so dirty? Oh well, modern gun cleaning products have come a long way from the G.I. bore cleaner and gun oils of the two World Wars, Korea, and Vietnam.

I was very thankful to have a supply of Shooter's Choice bore cleaner, lead remover, and gun oil, as I faced a monumental cleaning chore. These products worked infinitely faster than previous bore cleaners; we never had anything that would take out lead like this new lead remover, and believe me, I had a *lot* of lead to take out of some of these guns. At least one of them had not been cleaned since the 1930s, and those that didn't have plenty of lead already in the bore got a fresh chance to stock up with all this shooting.

Two legendary .32 autos: Top, a Colt 1903 Pocket Model M, and bottom, a Savage Model 1907.

Another Colt 1903 Pocket Hammer .38 auto semi-automatic pistol. Total production of this civilian model was approximately 26,000 between 1903 and 1929, with this pistol having been manufactured in 1922.
(Photo courtesy Rock Island Arsenal.)

Finally, modern gun oil, with its extreme hot and cold service ranges, made the old, dry lock work of some of the guns work perform like greased lightning.

Shooting these old guns reinforced the fact that they are marvelously efficient at what they were designed for. They are fun to shoot, easy to hit with, and first-rate defensive weapons. They are not manstoppers, but a study of contemporary American shootings produces few cases of fanatical attackers compared to those who are quickly stopped once shot. This would not hold true in other times and places, and most people know to pack a .45 if they want stopping power. These guns were meant to be carried "just in case" and were small enough not to be left behind. They were easy enough to master and instill confidence in their owners. There is a lot to be said for that and these guns today.

Using an LMT Monolith in .308 Win. and equipped with his D-760 night scope, the author shot this feral hog, while patrolling at night on a large ranch in northeast Texas. His thermal imaging goggles used to find this animal are hanging from his neck in this photo.

FERAL HOGS,
Night Vision, and the Right Rifle

BY **Frank W. James**

The shooting world and the firearms community is hearing more and more about feral hogs. To the uninformed, a number of questions are raised, but the truth is that this invasive species is a pestilence and a scourge for both agriculture and urban communities. Feral hogs are descended from domestic swine, Eurasian wild boars, and hybrids of both. Their numbers are increasing and they're making their presence known in some of the most unlikely places. One thing is for sure, they are not going away.

The attraction for firearms owners wanting to hunt these animals is that few states have a regulated season. That means you don't really "hunt" feral hogs, because shooters participate in the unregulated control of their population numbers.

There are two big negatives, when it comes to feral hogs. The first is that they are, essentially, the animal world's version of a plow. They use their snouts to dig, rooting up vast amounts of vegetation and soil, which farmers and ranchers have learned can ruin prime crop and pastureland over the course of a single evening. They can quite literally destroy a municipal golf course in a matter of hours.

The second negative is that feral hogs are intelligent, possibly the most intelligent free-roaming animal in North

The author has worked with the EOTech Model 556 and feels it is an excellent red-dot aiming system. A night vision scope like the PVS-14 can be mounted behind the EOTech for effective nighttime engagement of feral hogs.

America and, as a result, they learn, both individually and as a group. (As an aside, a group of free-ranging feral hogs is called a "sounder.")

Feral hogs range from Florida to California, but the state with the biggest problem is Texas. Texas AgriLife Extension wildlife specialist Dr. Billy Higginbotham estimates the increase in feral hog numbers, in Texas, is approximately 18 to 20 percent annually. According to studies, Texas has between 1.9 million and possibly up to a high of 3.4 million feral hogs roaming over approximately 79 percent of the state. Some estimates point towards the possibility of as many as four million feral hogs nationwide, but the truth is no one really knows how many there are.

Feral pigs breed and multiply at an exponential rate. While female domestic swine can be sexually mature at six months of age, Higginbotham believes that most feral sows are 13 months of age when they have their first litter consisting, on average, of 5.6 piglets. He believes a sow will average 1.5 litters per year, but, if left unchecked, any population of feral hogs can double in number in as short as five years.

Understanding the Problem

I was born and raised on a purebred hog farm in northwestern Indiana, so I have some understanding of hogs, their habits, and the level of their intelligence. There is one thing I'm convinced of and that is this problem can't be solved with two or three guys with rifles driving around at night in a four-wheel-drive pickup with a $30 spotlight.

All swine possess a keen sense of hearing and smell. Most sounders have learned the hazards of foraging during daylight hours and tend to be active nocturnally. In the depth of winter, when food is scarce, you can usually bump into the occasional sounder out feeding during the mid-afternoon hours, but most feral hog sounders have become nocturnal out of necessity. This requires the use of technology that was formerly found only with military and special operations forces.

I use both night vision equipment and thermal imagining equipment, because even a red lens on a visible light spotlight is enough to spook and drive off these wary animals, even from a great distance.

My Night Vision Recommendations

The ITT PVS-14 monocular night vision device is, in my experience, the gold standard of night vision devices

The author has used rifles and carbines chambered for the 6.8SPC round extensively and feels it is an extremely effective round for feral hogs if the engagement distances are kept to less than 250 yards.

Steve Snyder sights in the Night Optics D-760 night vision scope during daylight hours. As such, the front cover is closed to keep from burning the nighttime image intensifier. The cover has a small pinhole that permits daylight sighting in. The rifle is a Remington R-1 in 7mm-08 caliber.

and a great tool for anyone to start with if they are interested in working with night vision. Besides its outstanding clarity and brilliance, it is also one of the most versatile designs on the market for civilian users. (It should be mentioned that Litton Industries makes a PVS-14 for military users.)

Essentially, these devices are light amplifiers and, as such, are made with an image intensifier tube, a somewhat waterproof housing, and a mounting system. Many are also equipped with an infrared illuminator for use when the night is as dark as the inside of a cow. Most of these night vision devices are characterized by generations. The PVS-14 I've worked with for several years now

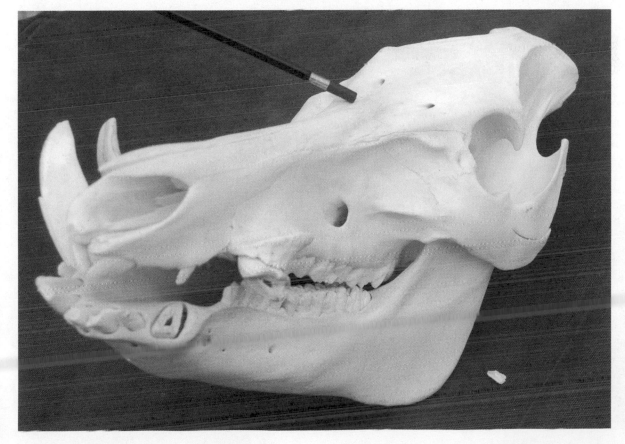

The author learned, to his chagrin, that the front sloped bone of a hog's skull can almost act like armor when struck with a straight-on shot. He used a .264 LBC to complete such a shot. The hog, while initially knocked down, soon got up and ran away.

is a third generation night scope. Its light amplification is somewhere between 30,000 to 50,000 times that of natural light, depending upon conditions.

The big advantage to the PVS-14 is that it can be used for nighttime scouting, navigation and, when mounted with the appropriate sighting system, as a no-artificial lighting-supported sighting device. It all depends on how you set it up. GG&G makes a throw-lever quick detach mount that can be mounted on the Picatinny rail of the firearm, and which also has a ring with a lug that fits into this mount for the front of the PVS-14. Multiple mounts enable the same PVS-14 unit to be moved from one rifle to another. None of this affects the zero of a rifle, as the

PVS-14 does not contain the aiming point. The big benefit to all this is that it takes only seconds to change the monocular's usage or role.

I've found you have to be careful about what sighting system you use in combination with the PVS-14. Conventional scopes simply won't work, because they require too much light, but good quality red dot sights are another matter. I've worked with a military-grade Aimpoint,

the model 556 EoTech, and the ACOG. The first two were easy in that the PVS-14 mounts behind the sight, while the ACOG requires it be mounted in front of the ACOG. I've found the combination of this sight and the PVS-14 is good to about 100 yards, with a fingernail moon. Activation of the built-in infrared illuminator adds definition to what you're seeing through the optics, but it doesn't really add any range extension.

The author feels the ITT-produced PVS-14, a third generation night vision optic, is the Gold Standard of such devices, because it is so versatile. It can be used in conjunction with a weapons sight, or it can be used for scouting terrain in the dark of night or for simple navigation.

One of the secrets to the ersatility of the PVS-14 is its ability to be quickly mounted and dismounted from its host weapon through the use of GG&G's quick-detach mount, which consists of a Picatinny rail mount and a lug on the ring mounted to the front of the PVS-14.

The NIVI-Systems UTAM-32 is a thermal imaging weapons sight the author has used in control of feral hogs. This sight has 320x240 resolution and features a quick-detach base.

The Best Tool for Scouting

As good as the PVS-14 and even the much larger D-760 night scope/weapons sight are, the best tool for scouting an area for feral hogs is a thermal imaging scope. I've worked with a wide range of them, including what I consider to be the ultimate, in terms of clarity and range. These are the thermal imaging scopes sold by Jager Pro and Rod Pinkston, of Columbus, Georgia.

Thermal imaging scopes are expensive, and those high price tags call into question their utility. But, if their cost can be surmounted, it is impossible to beat them for finding feral hogs, even under the worst conditions. All you have to do is drive slowly down a farm lane, all the lights out and keeping absolutely quiet—which means no valve-clattering diesel engines or squeaky shocks—while scanning the forward 270 degrees of terrain. Most thermal imaging systems operate off a white-is-hot and black-is-cold type of display. (There are color thermal imaging systems out there, but I haven't worked with them.) With the black and white viewers, the heat of the animal comes stark white against a black background. It's almost impossible to miss, even when moving at 15 mph, as you stand in the back of a pickup truck on the darkest of nights.

Rifle Calibers

I've used many calibers over the years to control feral hog populations in Texas, Oklahoma, and Georgia. In listing them in the paragraphs that follow, it should be noted that the hunt location is important, as it relates to the available food sources. In those states that farm

The author and his partners found the Remington R-1 rifle in 7mm-08 to be an accurate rifle for use against feral hogs. When using Remington's 140-grain JSP load, they discovered that none of the hogs shot with this combination rifle and ammo had a round exit.

peanuts, a high-quality, easily digestible protein, feral hogs usually are larger at a younger age, as they thrive on high-quality protein. In areas where food is more difficult to find—say Oklahoma, during the winter, where the short winter wheat is the only freely available food source—they are usually smaller and lighter in weight.

I believe that, in terms of pure ballistic efficiency, it is extremely hard to beat the .308 Winchester round, when it comes to effectiveness on feral hogs, even the largest examples. Rod Pinkston, of Jager Pro, relies on a factory 180-grain partition load, while I like the 165-grain ballistic tip available from a number of ammunition manufacturers. I prefer my pick over the heavier round, simply because it flies better at long range.

An example, and I only did this once, but it was in front of witnesses, so I feel I can write about it. During a mid-afternoon scouting expedition in Oklahoma, some years back, I set up and then killed a feral hog with one shot at a distance estimated by the ranch guide to be over 530 yards. The rifle was my Remington Model 700 Tactical with the 20-inch barrel, a Leupold scope, Harris bipod, and the ballistic tip 165-grain Remington factory load.

That instance aside, I've also had a great deal of success with a JP Enterprises LRP-07 rifle in .308 equipped with a Night Optics D-760 night vision scope. I used that combination to down a really big hog in northeast Texas, under the darkest of conditions, at 2:30 a.m. As we patrolled, I picked up the hog from a long way out with my Night Optics thermal imaging glasses (they look like PVS-7 goggles, but they're thermal), and I squeezed the shoulder of the jeep driver to give him the silent signal to stop. The wind was in our favor. I handed the thermal glasses to the driver and picked up the animal in the night vision scope. After watching him move

around for quite a while, he hesitated, stopped, and turned as if he knew we were there. That's when I busted him with one round. He dropped at the shot, the distance approximately 275 yards. The ranch guide estimated the hog's weight to be over 250 pounds.

Another caliber I've used, this in an AR-10-style rifle, is the 7mm-08. The rifle was a Remington R-1 and the ammunition was Remington's 140-grain JSP load, an extremely accurate combination it turned out. My control partner Steve Snyder used this rifle and load to kill a large boar at more than 200 yards. Unfortunately, about half the time, multiple hits were required to anchor the target animal. One odd aspect of this combination is that we never witnessed complete through-and-through body shot. Every fired round was a hit, but not one of the bullets exited the hogs. Another minus? The JP Enterprises LRP-07 rifle is also very long, and that's a big negative, when working out of the top of a Jeep Wrangler with a roll bar.

In an effort to find something shorter, lighter in weight, and handier in the

The author has used suppressed rifles, like this "Frankenstein" AR-15 in .300 Whisper. As shown here, it is equipped with the D-760 night vision scope, an SSK suppressor, and a Harris bipod. The .300 Whisper load is subsonic and features a 240-grain Sierra Match .30-caliber projectile.

The longest kill shot the author has ever made was accomplished, in front of witnesses, when he killed this feral hog with one shot at a distance estimated by the ranch guide to be over 530 yards. The rifle is a Remington Model 700 Tactical, with a Leupold scope and a Harris bipod. The load was Remington's 165-grain ballistic tip in .308 Winchester.

This feral hog was shot by the author's son during daylight hours, with his lever-action Marlin 1894 in .41 Magnum. This, too, was a one-shot kill, but the engagement distance was around 100 yards.

confines of the Jeep's roll bar, I started working with an AR-15 in 6.8SPC some years ago. I like the round, but it, too, has limitations. Under 250 yards, I feel the .68SPC is an extremely effective round on feral hogs, and I can say that after using it to take more than two-dozen hogs over the years. But once the range goes beyond that distance, the results are iffy, certainly not as predictable as they are at shorter ranges.

Many feel the 6.5 Grendel is a better alternative to the 6.8SPC. In my efforts to research that cartridge, Les Baer sold me one of his rifles in .264 LBC, which is, essentially, the same round. Unfortunately, I've only had an opportunity to use it on one hog, and that situation was more of an embarrassment than anything else.

We were patrolling during daylight hours, in Oklahoma, and had stopped to examine some tracks. The ranch guide looked up and grabbed me by the shoulder, while pointing slightly behind us and to my left. Approximately 75 yards distant was a large hog looking me square in the eye. I raised the rifle, centered the crosshairs right between his eyes, and slowly pressed the trigger. He dropped like a bag of wet laundry. I turned to say, "I think he's DRT (dead right there)," when the guide started to

say, "Yeah … No! He's gone!"

And he was! He'd jumped up and run behind a small mound, which, fortunately, put him in the sights of Steve Snyder, who was armed with an AR-15 in .50 Beowulf. Steve fired. The hog did a complete somersault, but then got to his feet and disappeared in the puckerbrush. We never saw him again, not even over the following days, as we looked for sign or a carcass.

What happened to my shot? After examining the skull of a large feral hog, it's easy to see how any straight-on shot could be deflected by the sloped, armor-like bone of the hog's skull above the eyes. That is not meant as a criticism of the 6.5 Grendel round, nor a recommendation, just an explanation of my single experience with it while working hog control.

Probably the most popular round used for hog control is the .223 Rem., because so many AR-15s and other semi-autos in this caliber are available. My feeling is it is not a good cartridge to use for hog control, except when working at extremely close distances, like those seen when shooting from a helicopter, a practice legal in Texas. Otherwise, it is a poor choice—with one exception. The Black Hills 77-grain Sierra bullet load will, in most cases and with a single

hit, somersault and ground feral hogs, even when they've been on the run. With other loads, though, I feel this caliber is simply too light for the task at hand.

The Future

Due to their out-of-control reproduction rate, feral hogs will continue to become more than just a nuisance invasive species in the years ahead. Unlike prairie dogs, which are confined to mostly desolate areas, feral hogs are continually moving into more urban areas. The threats and property damage from these creatures will continue to increase and, regardless what anyone says, the only viable and effective control technique is lethal force.

For the shooter, this offers the possibility of new sport. There are those who prefer to perform this task solely during the daylight hours, but, for those interested in nighttime control, the costs of night vision and thermal imagining equipment is constantly decreasing as the technology matures. Night or day, though, one thing's for sure. Those states afflicted with this pestilence are not going to run out of feral hogs at any point in the foreseeable future.

So You Want To Shoot
F-CLASS?
Are you ready for this fast-growing discipline?

BY **Denys P. Beauchemin**

igh Power F-Class is arguably the fastest growing competitive shooting discipline, and while its allure is real, many people are somewhat mystified by its requirements. Some common questions are: What does it take to become competitive in F-class? How does one acquire a suitable rifle? What kind of accuracy is required?

To put things into perspective, it's only proper that we look at the genesis of F-Class. This discipline first started in Canada, at the end of the last century, when an aging full-bore competitor from Kamloops, British Columbia, by the name of George "Farky" Farquharson (the eponymous shooter of F-class), successfully petitioned the DCRA (Dominion of Canada Rifle Association) for permission to shoot alongside other competitors, using a rifle scope on top of his target rifle to compensate for aging eyes, as well as a bipod to assist his frail arms in holding the rifle steady. The discipline spread like wildfire around the world and eventually got divided into two classes: F-Open and F-TR (Target Rifle).

In 2007, the NRA sanctioned F-class with its two sub-classes, and also sanctioned the use of its new F-class target centers. The NRA High Power rules were revised to define and incorporate the F-Open and F-TR disciplines, and the NRA started issuing classifications for the F-class shooters in two different categories; Mid-Range (MR—300, 500, and 600 yards), and Long Range (LR — 800, 900, and 1,000 yards).

The difference between F-TR and F-Open is chiefly about three items. F-Open can be any caliber up to .35, whereas F-TR allows the use of only unadulterated .223 Remington and .308 Winchester ammunition. F-Open allows the use of front rests not attached to the rifle, whereas F-TR uses attached bipods. Finally, F-Open rifles have a weight limit of 10 kilos (22 pounds) for rifle and scope, and F-TR has a weight limit of 8.25 kilos (18.18 pounds) including scope, bipod, and sling, if the latter is also used. There are a few other restrictions, such as a three-inch width for the fore-end on the F-Open rifle, but the preceding are the big ones.

As an F-TR shooter, I will highlight the areas where there is a difference between the two classes, but, apart from the initial setup, the differences are few when it comes to shooting at the target. Also, I'll walk you through a typical match so that, after reading this article, you should have a good idea if F-class is for you.

The first choice you need to make is whether to shoot in F-Open or F-TR. As a general rule, F-Open makes it easier to attain a higher LR (long range) F-class rating, because the calibers used are more suited to long-range precision shooting than .223 or .308. Some people consider F-Open to be somewhat of an armaments race and, in many ways, it is.

If you decide on F-Open, the next selection is the caliber. The current favorite for LR is the .284/7mm in various chamberings: .280 Remington, .284 Winchester, .284 Walker, etc. The erstwhile favorite was the .264/6.5mm in a .284 Winchester cartridge, the 6.5-284 Norma. If you are going to compete in LR (800 to 1,000 yards), these are the calibers to consider. If you intend to shoot only in MR (300 to

The firing line during Team Match at the 2012 F-Class Nationals. The author, seated with a white shirt, is monitoring his teammate's progress, using his spotting scope.

600 yards) a .243/6mm is very competitive. Whichever caliber you select, you will need to decide on the chambering and, in order to fit in with the crowd, the headstamp of your chosen case should have three digits, no less than three consonants (more is better), and include the letter X; this will be a handloading proposition, but more on this later.

If you opt for F-TR, your cartridge choice, as I've explained, is simple: there's .223 Remington or .308 Winchester. No improvements to the cases are allowed, so get the Ackley Improveds and such out of your mind. I have competed at 1,000 yards with a .223 using long, 80-grain bullets, but I switched to a .308 with long-for-caliber bullets a few years back and have not regretted the move. Shooting a .223

is very pleasant, but, when the wind blows, the 80-grainers simply do not hold a candle to the long and heavy .308s. For mid-range (MR), the .223 can be a fearsome competitor and, again, it's ever so pleasant to shoot. F-TR competitors usually have lower scores than top-end F-Open competitors, but that's not a hard and fast rule, especially at MR. Regardless, the big matches have separate trophies and awards for both classes, but the NRA rates all F-class shooters along the same lines, making no distinction between F-TR and F-Open.

The Rifle

Let's say you've decided you want to shoot F-TR, because you have a nice,

heavy-barreled .223 or .308 rifle that shoots lights out, sub-MOA, all day long, as long as you do your part. You have a Harris bipod, and the rifle is topped by a 12X scope. I think that is an excellent idea, but probably for different reasons than you would expect.

The way I see it, you aren't going to waste any money up front. Instead, you will show up at a competition and experience first-hand what it's like. The good thing about using old Thor's Hammer, or Daisy or whatever you call your rifle, is that you will observe a few things that will help you in your quest and not make you spend tons of money just to get to the first match. There will be plenty to learn and lots of time to upgrade your equipment, if you decide you want to continue.

The author's latest F-TR rifle on its first outing for load development. Notice the one-piece cleaning rod and the bore guide. The syringe near the ammo box is used to apply a special grease at various points on the bolt.

The author and his rifle with the NRA Whittington Center's George Tubb range as backdrop. The author favors large hats with wide brims in the New Mexico sun.

Among the first observations you will make is that the targets are small and far away, so more scope magnification would be nice, and the reticle should not wipe out the 10- and X-rings. Also, the 15- or 20-round matches heat up the barrel, and you may experience point-of-impact shift, which can be disconcerting during a string. If you're shooting LR, you may be wondering if that miss was due to ammo, marksmanship, or conditions. It could be all three.

I am currently on my third F-TR rifle, and while the first two where production rifles I'd had re-barreled with long, top of the line, heavy barrels, my most recent one was built to my exact specifications for long-range competition. My first rifle was an AR-15, to which I fitted a 26-inch Krieger Varmatch barrel with a .920-inch overall diameter (OD). I still use this rifle for MR competitions, using 80-grain bullets, and I have attained High Master at that distance with it. It is amazingly precise and just a joy to shoot. At long range, however, the 80-grain bullets are toys for the conditions. If the wind was calm they're fine, but calm days are rare at long range.

My second rifle was an old Ruger M77, to which I had fitted a phenomenal 32-inch Broughton 7.9-contour barrel. I also changed the stock to a Boyd's and the trigger to a Timney, so the only Ruger component left is the action. That rifle did very well for me, and I still keep it as my backup in big matches.

My current rifle is made up of premium components that were assembled by a competition gunsmith. The action

is a Stolle Panda F-class, right-hand, right-bolt, micro-port and no ejector from Kelbly's. The trigger is a Jewell, the one-ounce version with no safety and no bolt release. The stock is the laminate F-TR model from Precision Rifle and Tool, with the three-way adjustable buttplate and the Anschütz rail underneath the fore-end. Scope rings are from Kelbly's and are mounted on the integrated 20 MOA rib on the receiver. The scope is a Nightforce NXS 12-42X56mm with 1/8 MOA adjustments and an NP-2DD reticle. The barrel is a Krieger 32-inch 1:11 twist stainless steel barrel with a medium-heavy Palma contour.

Designing an F-TR rifle is a budget game; you always want the heaviest, longest barrel you can get, but you are limited by the weight restrictions of the F-class game. The last thing you want is to show up at a big match and find out your rifle is over the 18.18-pound limit. Once you have all the component weights figured out (including the rifle, scope, rings, and the bipod), you can then play around with the barrel contour and length to get close to but not over the limit. Know that fluting isn't really a good idea, because it reduces the rigidity of the barrel, as well as the quantity of heat sink material (i.e., the barrel steel). I wanted the 32-inch length in order to get as much muzzle velocity as possible without having to go over maximum on my loads, and I was willing to sacrifice some contour (but no fluting). You do want the barrel bead blasted, because that really does promote cooling.

My target weight was 17 pounds, 12 ounces, so as to provide some leeway in case of a bad scale somewhere or a mistake in my calculations. As it is, the total rifle weigh comes to 17 pounds and 8.5 ounces. The stock is five pounds, including finish and pillar bedding; the action is 1.9; the trigger is 0.15; the rings are 0.25; the bipod is 1.96; the scope is 2.13; and the anti-cant device is 0.1-pound. The barrel worked out to be 6.15 pounds after chambering and prep.

The Ammo

Whichever discipline you elect to shoot, the ammo you will use will most probably be handloaded, especially for the LR portion. In .223 or .308, there simply is no factory-loaded ammo that will allow you to be competitive and, when you shoot 60 to 80 rounds a day in a match, any factory ammo would be expensive. In F-Open, the repertoire of superb bullets is just too great and ever

changing, so handloading really is the only option.

The bullet selection should be one of the main determinants in the barrel specifications. For example, I selected the very long, 180-grain .308 JLKLBT bullet, so I opted for the 1:11-twist barrel detailed above. Handloading for competition is all about maintaining consistency—in everything. I buy components in large quantities: 2,000

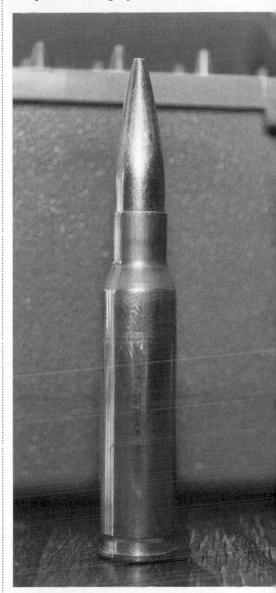

Cartridge case life management is part of the competitor's life. This Lapua case is on its eighth loading and is still going strong. Full-length resized for every load and tumbled clean and annealed, these steps keep the case usable and consistent. Primer pocket expansion is usually the determining factor in the life of the case. The bullet is a .308-caliber 180-grain JLK LBT from Swampworks.com.

Name:	300 MR		500 MR		600 MR		800/900/1000 LR	
	MR63FC	MR-63	MR65FC	MR-65	MR1FC	MR-1	LRFC	LR
X-Ring	1.42	2.85	2.50	5.00	3.00	6.00	5.0	10.00
10-Ring	2.85	5.85	5.00	10.00	6.00	12.00	10.0	20.00
9-Ring	5.85	8.85	10.00	15.00	12.00	18.00	20.0	30.00
8-Ring	8.85	11.85	15.00	20.00	18.00	24.00	30.0	44.00
7-Ring	11.85	17.85	20.00	25.00	24.00	36.00	44.0	60.00
6-Ring	17.85	23.85	25.00	30.00	36.00	48.00	60.0	72X72
5-Ring	23.85	29.85	30.00	36.00	48.00	60.00	72X72	

bullets, 16 pounds of powder, 5,000 primers, etc. I bought 500 pieces of Lapua brass, all with the same lot number, and I organized these cases in five MTM ammo boxes onto which I record and keep track of the life of the brass.

The cases from the same box will stay together for their useful life, but I rotate through the boxes in turn, so as to use them all at the same rate. I always have cases prepped, ready for powder loading and bullet seating, and I try to load a few days before a match. Only in instances of big matches do I load several hundred rounds.

After an entire box has been fired, I full-length resize each case using a bushing die, then tumble clean and prime. Every other load, I anneal the cases using my Giraud annealer, and every fifth load I trim the cases and then chamfer and deburr the mouths. I have been using the same load for several years, always using the same components of Varget powder and Russian primers. This load-to-load consistency allows me to shoot a match using cartridges in multiple boxes, as they are all loaded the same way and fired in sequence.

Targets and NRA Classifications

There are four main targets for F-class, depending on the distance. The targets all consist of concentric rings that make up the aiming black, and then a few more outside the black. The targets are based on the regular High Power targets, with an additional X-ring. In essence, they are the same targets, but with the point value pushed in by a factor of one for all rings.

The grid shown at the top of the page depicts the diameter of the rings for the various targets (distances). The target names ending in FC are the F-class

targets, and the values given are in inches. A hit that does not fall within a ring at 300 to 600 yards is considered a miss. Hitting the LRFC target will get you a minimum of five points. The dark area in the grid denotes the ring is part of the aiming black.

A match will be 15 or 20 rounds for scores, with a maximum score of 150 or 200. A competition or tournament will consist of multiple matches at various distances. For instance, a Mid-Range tournament could consist of a match at 300, 500, and 600 yards, and an LR tournament could be made up of a match at 800, 900, and 1,000 yards. If the tournament is sanctioned by the NRA, the scores will be turned in to the organization and recorded for each shooter. When the shooter has accumulated a minimum of 120 scored rounds in a sanctioned match, the NRA will calculate the shooter's rating and issue a card with the earned classification. As the shooter progresses and additional scores are turned in, this classification will go up accordingly. The classifications are as follows:

- Marksman: 91.5%
- Sharpshooter: 91.5%
- Expert: 94.0%
- Master: 96.5%
- High Master: 98.0%

In a match with a maximum score of 200, a score less than 183 (91.5%) is considered Marksman level; between 183 and 187 it's a Sharpshooter score; between 188 and 192 it's an Expert

Right: This is what the impact berm looks like at NRA's Whittington Center in Raton, New Mexico, site of the F-class nationals in 2012 and 2013.

score; between 193 and 195 it's a Master score; and 196 (98%) and above is a High Master Score.

At the Match

Let me now share what it's really like to shoot F-Class. A week before a match, I set aside some time to load ammo, if I do not have enough on hand. For a 60-round match (3x20) with limited sighter rounds, I need a minimum of 70 rounds; if sighter rounds are *un*limited, I load another box of 100 rounds. I make sure I have Gatorade, water bottles, and snacks on hand, because there is usually nothing to eat or drink at the range.

The night before a match, I go to bed early, because I have to get up at 5:00 a.m. the day of the match. While driving to the range, I observer the conditions, meaning I look at whatever flags I see along the way. I know we shoot due north at the range, so I want to see where the wind will be coming from, and also if I can discern any cycle to it.

At the range, I park as close to the firing line as possible and then register and pay the match fee, $15 where I am a member. I put my name on the proper sheet for F-TR and my classification for the distance, "Expert for LR," and get my scorecard. Next, I enter my information on the scorecard and I put it in my clipboard. I unload my equipment from the vehicle and assemble it all in one spot. I take my rifle out of its case, making sure the empty chamber indicator (ECI) is inserted, and I place it in one of the rifle racks near where I will be shooting.

Once registration closes, the match director does the squadding for the

match, with three shooters per firing point. Once that's done, there is a safety briefing; it's important to listen and understand the safety rules. There may also be some announcements for upcoming matches and special events, and then the squadding assignments are announced or handed out. I put my assigned relay and firing point info on my scorecards. This match happens to have three relays and 10 firing points. I am on relay No. 1, so I will be firing first. As relay No. 3 drives to the pits to setup the targets, relay No. 1 shooters can bring their equipment, minus rifles, to the firing line.

I survey the firing point to make sure there is no junk on it and check for fire ants. Then I put down my rubber mat at the position I want, square to the target line. The rest of my position will be set relative to the mat. Next, I put down my shooting mat with just a hint of an angle from the rubber mat and slip the front edge of the shooting mat under the rubber mat. I put the rear rest down on the shooting mat at the same place every time. Next, I set up the tripod for my spotting scope right next to where I will be lying down. I then place the elbow pad to the right and slightly behind the rear rest. Finally, my ammo box and notepad go in front of the elbow pad and on the shooting mat.

While waiting for prep time, I adjust my spotting scope so that I have a good view of the entire range, and I look at the flags out on the range. If the wind is steady from a specific direction, I will probably put an appropriate amount of windage on the spotting scope. If not, I will leave the windage alone for the time being.

Eventually, the match director will declare the pits to be sealed. This means everyone who is supposed to be in the pits at this time is present and accounted for and no one can come out of the pits until they are declared unsealed by the match director. Firing time now approaches. I hand my scorecard to the relay No. 2 shooter for my firing point, then remind him that I will tell him when I am going for record and that I want to hear score value and round number for every shot.

The match director will instruct the relay to bring their rifles to the line, with the ECI still inserted. Prep time will start shortly. I fetch my rifle from the rack and place it with the bipod legs on the rubber mat and the stock in the rear rest.

If the sun is going to interfere in any way during the next 30 minutes, I put on my shooting hat with the long bill and side flaps. I don my hearing protection and get down alongside my rifle. I adjust the bipod so that I have the scope's reticle pointed where the target will be. During these preparations, the match director will announce the start of prep time. This is a three-minute period in which the targets will appear and I make my final adjustments to the bipod and general position. I want to be lying alongside the rifle, with my legs straight back. I make sure I can transition to my spotting scope easily and that everything is comfortable. During prep time, you can remove the ECI from the rifle and play with the trigger, but woe to the competitor who shoots a round downrange during prep time; he can be disqualified or get a big fat 0 for his first shot for record.

While I am adjusting my position, my scorer is setting up next to me on a little stool, along with his spotting scope and my scorecard. He is close to me, so I can hear him and don't have to look around to find him during the match. I remove the bolt on the first match, put the ECI next to my ammo box, and look down the bore to make sure there are no surprises. Then I reinsert the bolt and adjust the cheekpiece's elevation screw.

"Preparation time has ended," announces the match director, as the targets go down in the pits. "This is match No. 1, relay No. 1. You will have 30 minutes for unlimited sighters and 20 rounds for records. With one round, load. Ready on the left? Ready on the right? All ready on the firing line! Time will begin and you may fire when your targets appear."

The match director starts the clock and the targets come up. I usually do not fire right away. Instead, I observe what is happening on other targets. I want to see if people are going right or left, are they doing so as a whole, and by how much. I don't know what the others on the line have put in for correction, but I do know that most people will aim their first shot dead center and correct from there. For the first match of the day, I usually shoot

five sighter rounds to bring the barrel to temperature and foul it after the cleaning it got after the last outing. If I have decided I want windage on the scope, I put it in before my first sighter; no need to help the other guy get a read from your sighter shot. If the conditions are calm, I take aim and fire dead center. In the subsequent matches, I limit myself to two sighter shots, even if the format is unlimited sighters, because the big matches usually have two sighters after the first match of the day.

During the sighter period, I want to get the elevation set properly. At long range, that elevation setting can change from day to day, and even match to match during the same day. I am also looking for what I think is the proper hold for windage and identifying which specific flags I want to rely on for the match. When I feel I have the proper scope adjustment and wind offset or five shots downrange, whichever is more, I tell my scorer I am going for record and wait for him to acknowledge.

During the "for record" period, I keep track of the conditions, the flags and mirage, if any, so I can fire in similar conditions as much as possible. My left

arm is tucked underneath me, with my left hand grabbing the rear bag. The rifle is in contact with my shoulder, firmly, but not too firmly; I don't want the rifle to smack me in the shoulder every time, because it's going to be a long day, but I don't want to transmit every body tremor to the rifle, either.

My right hand does everything else: loads the cartridge, closes the bolt, pulls the trigger, opens the bolt, plucks out the fired case and puts it in the ammo box, makes notes on a card if needed, and I repeat all of this 19 times. I drive the rifle with the left hand using the bag. I do not "load" the bipod, rather I let this expensive, sophisticated tool do its work supporting the rifle and letting it glide back into my shoulder while riding the bag. Because the rifle is so heavy, the recoil energy is just 9.5 ft-lbs, but, since I am also shooting prone, there is not much give. After a day of 70 rounds, I know I have been shooting, though I am not in any real pain. This is important, because heavy recoil and pain will lead to flinching, I don't care who you are.

As I fire each round, the scorer observes the target and, when it comes

back up, he calls out the score for that shot along with the round count—"X, 12 on," for example. When I get ready to fire the last round, the scorer will announce "final round going in." After I fire the last round, I put in the ECI and call safe. If I forget the ECI, the scorer will remind me to put it in. The final round is scored and the target is put back up. The scorer will call out the final shot's value, add up the scores, and sign the card before presenting it to me to sign. The card is then turned in to the match officials, as I remove my equipment from the line.

In the Pits

It's my turn, now, to go to the pits and pull the target for the other shooters on my firing point. When I get to my target, I bring it to half-mast to indicate it is manned. At some point, the match director will announce that the pits are sealed. There is usually a pit boss, or a loud speaker over which the pit commands are issued. When prep time starts, we all bring our targets all the way up. Then we wait. At the end of the three-minute prep time, we bring the targets down to half-

The author's first F-TR rifle, an Armalite M15T with a 26-inch Krieger barrel, Magpul PRS stock and Weaver T-36 scope on the Sinclair Gen2 bipod. That is a Bob Sled under the rifle, the best device for single load of an AR with 100-percent bolt open. There's nothing worse than trying to cycle the action in prone position during a match.

mast and stand by them. I make sure my hearing protection is on correctly.

The targets come up on the order to raise them and, within a few seconds, the first rounds come down. The bullets are surprisingly loud, and you'll hear the sonic crack for each one. The noise level indicates how fast the bullet is coming in. If it's loud and sharp, the bullet is solidly supersonic, but if it's soft, the bullet is barely supersonic. If there is an impact berm, I watch that spot to detect the impact of the bullet and get an idea of where on the target the hole will be. Once I see the splash in the dirt, I bring the target down right away and look for the hole.

If the shooter is good and has the conditions down, it's easy to score their target. Any other way and you are looking for a very small hole on a 36 square-foot target dominated by a big black disk in the middle. Once I find the hole, I move the shot indicator from the prior hole to the new hole, put a paster on the newly vacated hole, and start pushing the target back up as I move the scoring disk (if needed). With a good shooter, I can service a target in under eight seconds from the time I detect the

impact. The shooters appreciate fast pit service, especially if the conditions are stable for a bit. Indeed, sometimes, as soon as the target is back up, the next shot is coming down. It is my duty as a target puller to provide the fastest, most accurate and fair service possible. When the firing is complete, I clean up the target, removing all scoring implements from it and pasting the last hole.

Scoring the Line

When pit duty is complete, the firing line is made safe, the pits are declared unsealed, and I return to the line to assume my duty as scorer for the other shooter on my firing point. The next person to shoot brings his equipment to the line as prep time approaches. I make sure I have his card and that it's filled out, and then I set up a little seat near him and focus my spotting scope on the target. During prep time, I make sure I see the target properly and keep an eye on my shooter to make sure he does not slip a cartridge in the rifle at this time. It has happened, and I have caught it in time, saving embarrassment and lost points or worse.

When prep time ends, I usually wish my shooter good luck and remind him of the target number by saying something like, "Target 10, good luck, Sam." When his first shot goes downrange, I observe the target and make sure it goes down. It takes about 1.5 seconds for the bullet to get to the target, and a few seconds of reaction time, but if the target does not go down within five seconds, I call for a mark on the target: "Mark target 10!" When the target comes back up, "Sighter one is an eight." When the shooter announces he is now going for record, I respond back to him "Target 10, going for record." From that point on, I just go with "nine, seven on," score and round count. I do remind the shooter when he is loading the last round and also to put in his ECI after the last round is fired. I add up the score, sign the card, and have him sign it. Then I turn in the card to a match official and I get ready to shoot next.

There are variations on the above procedures, depending on the venue. Some matches will have 15 rounds for record and limit you to two sighters after the first match of the day. Other matches will start at 800 yards for the first match, 900 yards for the second match, and finish off at 1,000 yards for the last match of the day. It pays to know the course of fire before the day starts, so there are no surprises.

The author in action, ready to take a shot. During the match, only the right hand moves to load the rifle and pull the trigger. The left hand is squeezing the rear bag.

Being Competitive

In the age of the Internet, there are numerous discussion sites where people discuss all aspects of shooting, and this is a great way to get some pointers and related information, if you can wade through the chaff of nonsensical and off-topic posts. One question that comes up frequently, in one variation or another, is something along the lines of "What does it take to be competitive in F-class?"

The answer is simple: experience. Experience will help you figure out the equipment you need to grow your marksmanship skills to reach your goal. There is nothing magical about the sport, and there are no magic combinations or

"must-have" gadgets that enable you to avoid experience. Sure, there are bullets that perform better at long range, and a quality scope will not give you a headache or cause eyestrain, but everybody figures out these things.

At some point, and it's sooner rather than later, it all comes down to the shooter. Most people would rather spend time in the loading room fussing over each individual case or spend money getting the very latest rifle scope, bipod, rear rest, etc., than learn to read the conditions. But reading and understanding the conditions is really what it's all about, and that only comes with experience.

There are many good books on the subject. Get them, read them, and understand them and that will be a

good start. But be warned, there are days when I can read the conditions and the score shows it. I think I have this thing nailed and I am pleased with myself. But that's ephemeral, because all too often, at the next match I try to read the conditions and discover the book is printed in classical Greek. I have learned a lot over the past several years of competition and I will share now with you, for the first time ever, the three rules for success in a match.

- **Rule No. 1:** Show up at a match with all your equipment.
- **Rule No. 2:** Finish the match.
- **Rule No. 3:** Screw up less than the other competitors.

A winning team with experience, who can read "classical Greek"—The Long Shots, 2012 F-Open National Team champions. Back row, left to right: Mark Walker, Ken Dickerman, David Gosnell. Front row: Coach Michelle Gallagher, who detects condition changes that elude mere mortals, and team Captain David Bailey. He is also the 2012 National F-Open champion. Trophies and medals aplenty for this bunch.

I believe competition shooting has helped me improve my marksmanship a great deal. While everyone likes to believe he or she is a great shot, there is nothing like showing up at a competition to have that belief adjusted rapidly. But along with that dose of reality you'll get served, know that the camaraderie among competitors is something that has to be seen to be believed—*everyone* is happy to talk about their equipment and load in detail, and they all will readily share observations on the conditions during the match. It's almost as if everybody *wants* everybody else to do well.

About the Author: Denys Beauchemin has been competing in F-Class for several years now and currently holds High Master mid-range and Expert long-range classifications, all earned shooting F-TR. Married with children and grandchildren, in real life he is an old software engineer who has published numerous articles in that field over the decades.

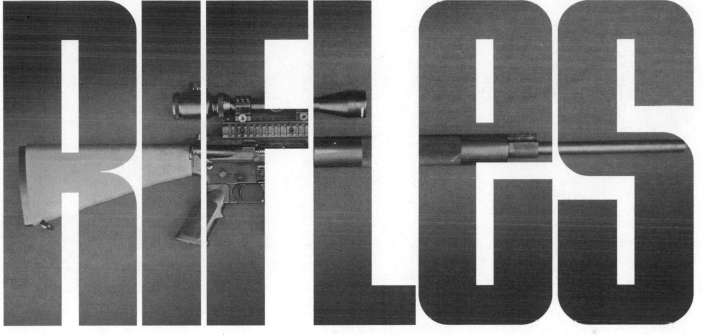

RIFLES

BY Wayne van Zwoll

In the first of our annual Reports from the Field, Wayne van Zwoll covers the new crop of rifles hitting dealers' shelves this year.

ANSCHÜTZ ADDS .17S.

Its Match 54 rimfire competition series has won many International and Olympic championships, and Anschütz has not refined the more affordable Model 64. The latest of the type is a walnut-stocked 1517 in .17 HMR. A conservatively styled stock distinguishes this box-fed bolt gun (and the 1516 in .22 WMR). Available with single- or two-stage trigger—the latter with a movable blade and weight adjustment to six ounces—the 1517 weighs 6.4 pounds with its .22-inch barrel.

The new Model 1727 sporting rifle is a straight-pull repeater in .17 HMR. As with actions on .22 Anschütz biathlon rifles, you open the 1727 with a tap of your index finger, close it quick as a wink with your thumb. Lock time is just .4-millisecond. The detachable box magazine holds four rounds. Having competed with Anschütz target rifles, I tested its first bolt-action .17 HMRs. Surely this walnut-stocked .17, with its two-stage, 1.2-pound trigger, will drill one-hole groups at 50 meters! (www. anschuetz-sport.com)

BLASER'S R8: THUMBHOLE AND LEATHER

It has a telescoping, radial-head bolt you can cycle with a flick of your hand. Like its predecessor the R93, the R8's bolt head locks by forcing a collet into

The new Anschütz Model 1727 sporting rifle is a straight-pull repeater in .17 HMR.

a circumferential groove in the barrel shank. But the R8 breech is stronger, because the locking angle is steeper. A bushing slips into the collet's center during lock-up, for additional support. The R8 has held pressures of 210,000 psi.

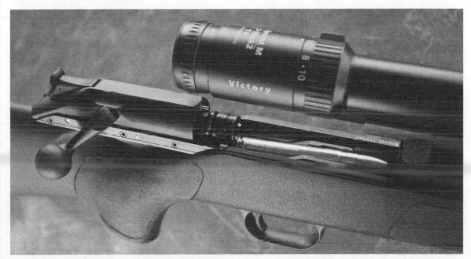

The Blaser R93 (here) and the new R8 both use an expanding collet to lock the straight-pull bolt.

A thumb-switch shoved forward cocks the rifle. To de-cock, push again, but down slightly, and ease the switch back. You can carry a loaded R8 safely until it's cocked.

Stateside, R8s come with a trigger pull of 2.5 pounds. This excellent trigger is tucked into a detachable single-stack magazine. You can top load without removing the box. Squeeze the release tabs on either side of the trigger, and the box and trigger group drop into your hand. The assembly can't release accidentally from the rifle; in place, it does not rattle. The R8 is chambered for myriad cartridges, .223 to .500 Jeffery. Barrels and bolts are easy to change.

Plasma nitriding on the R8 barrel hikes surface hardness. Saddle scope rings fit so precisely you can remove and replace a scope without losing zero. I didn't believe that until, after firing at a 600-yard target, I yanked the Zeiss scope. Re-mounting it on the barrel, I resumed shooting—the bullets hit center!

The R8's stock, walnut or synthetic, is straight combed, with cast-off at toe, heel, and grip. The Turkish walnut comes in several grades. For 2013, Blaser added the thumbhole stock announced mid-year 2012. You can now specify leather gripping surfaces—an unlikely but classy and functional touch—and Blaser is working on a left-hand version. While I like traditional profiles, I must say the R8's thumbhole stock has clean, attractive detailing, a good feel. It's not clubby. I used one in a .30-06 last fall. It carried more comfortably than I expected, and I shot well with it. A bull elk fell to that R8. (www.blaser-usa.com)

BROWNING: ANOTHER A-BOLT

In the wake of Browning's High Power rifle, the Browning A-Bolt was itself superseded by the A-Bolt II, then the X-Bolt with its rotary magazine, bolt-unlock button, and four-screw platform for scope bases. The "II" has since been dropped. Not so the Boss device, which serves as a brake and barrel tuning tool. All A-Bolts except the Target and Eclipse versions feature the Boss, as well as a CR accessory for shooters annoyed by a brake's blast. The A-Bolt III, new this year, is "an A-Bolt with cost-saving features to bring list price below $600," says Browning's Paul Thompson. These days, that's where the money is. (www.browning.com)

Blaser's R8 now offers a thumbhole stock (add leather, if you like!). It worked for Wayne.

CZ BORES THE 527 FOR .17 HORNET, ADDS 455V

Besides its stout, Mauser-style 550 mechanism, barreled from .243 to the .505 Gibbs, CZ markets the daintier 527 action for the likes of the .223. Mine is in .221 Fireball. You can get a 527 in .22 Hornet or .204 Ruger, too. Now CZ has added the .17 Hornet, recently loaded by Hornady with a 20-grain V-Max bullet to 3,650 fps. Available in American and Varmint versions, the .17 Hornet traces the arc of 55-grain bullets in the .223. The 527 comes in full- and synthetic-stocked, including European variations. There's even a Carbine in .223 and 7.62x39.

Two years ago, CZ announced it would "consolidate all the receivers currently used in the 452 line into a common platform that would allow for easy barrel changes." The adjustable trigger, CZ assured us, would remain. So, too, hammer-forged barrels and receivers machined from steel billets. The first 455 was the American. Chambered to the .22 Long Rifle and .17 HMR, it wore a conservative black walnut stock checkered fore and aft. It weighed six pounds with its 22½-inch barrel, felt good and shot well. Soon thereafter, I took in a new 455, the

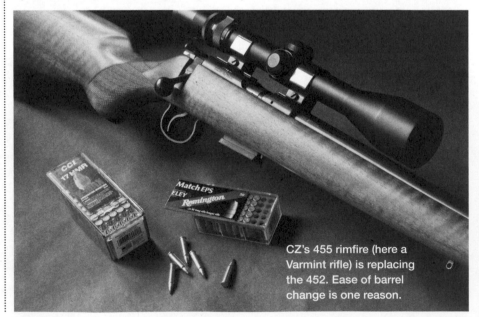

CZ's 455 rimfire (here a Varmint rifle) is replacing the 452. Ease of barrel change is one reason.

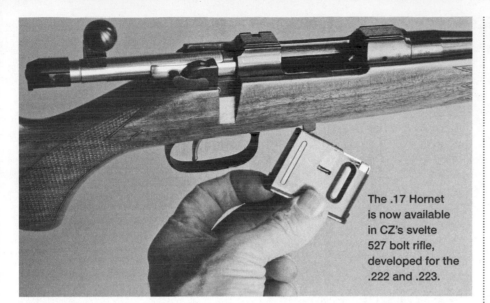

The .17 Hornet is now available in CZ's svelte 527 bolt rifle, developed for the .222 and .223.

Varmint model. At a glance, you can't tell it from its 452/453 predecessor and, from the receiver back, it seems the same as the 455 American. But the fore-end is longer and uncheckered. It is not, praise be, a fore-end common to other varmint rifles; it does not feel like a toaster. It fills your hand, but does not overwhelm it. The barrel is short (20½ inches) and stiff; the muzzle mikes .864. (The .22 LR gets no ballistic advantage from barrels longer than 16 inches.) While the .17 HMR can use a little more length, it doesn't need 24, or even 22, inches.

Twin extractors and a mechanical ejector cycle cartridges from the five-shot, detachable polymer box. Because the 455V is a switch-barrel rifle, the magazine well must accommodate the long box for .22 WMR and .17 HMR rounds. A filler block pairs with .22 LR magazines. Fire control: a clean 3½-pound trigger and two-position thumb safety.

My first five-shot 50-yard group with accurate Eley Match ammo stayed under half an inch. I followed with Remington/Eley Match EPS, then Remington Mohawk high-speed solids and Winchester Power Point high-speed hollowpoints, all 40 grains in weight. I also fired Federal Game-Shok 31-grain hollowpoint ammo. My biggest group measured an even inch; averages ran from .6 (Eley) to .9 for three five-shot groups! Feeding was a tad rough at first, but smoothed out during the session. No failures to fire or eject.

Then, with a couple of supplied L-wrenches, I pulled the .22 rimfire barrel and replaced it with one in .17 HMR. Easy. With two types of ammunition, CZ's 455V printed even tighter groups than it had with the .22 barrel. Hornady and

CCI .17 HMR loads with 17-grain jacketed hollowpoints at 2,550 fps nipped half-inch groups. Hornadys drilled a .3-inch knot. The action cycled more eagerly than with .22 rounds—predictably, given differences in profile between the two cartridges. Retail Price: $456 (.22 LR); extra .17 HMR barrel $149. (www.cz-usa.com)

COOPER'S PETITE MODEL 51

Announced in 2011, Cooper's Model 56 (magnum) bolt rifle has much in common with its Model 52 (long-action) and 54 (short-action) forebears. Now there's a Model 51, smallest of the quartet. Like the others, it's stocked in hand-checkered walnut (there are polymers, if you choose), with steel grip cap, Decelerator pad, and one-piece bottom metal. All owe a great deal to the Models 57 rimfire and 38 centerfire .22 rifles designed by Dan Cooper after he left Kimber to start his own rifle firm in Montana's Bitterroot Valley. Detachable box feed "is much harder to guarantee than you'd think," Dan told me, when the 52 was still a blueprint. But the slick cycling, straight stack 50-series bolt-actions are sunrise reliable and smooth. Dan has since relinquished company reins to Hugo Vivero, who owns the Wilson barrel company that supplies Cooper barrels. Ian, Hugo's son, is an engineer at Cooper.

Each Cooper centerfire starts as a block of steel. Blanks are meticulously machined, each three-lug bolt finished to slide like a piston. The Sako-style extractor works opposite a bolt face plunger ejector. The serrated bolt release and two-position thumb safety are small and neatly inlet. The safety doesn't lock

the bolt. A thick-walled stainless steel magazine fits almost flush; a tidy forward latch drops it into your hand. A modest ejection port keeps the receiver stiff for top accuracy, but it's open enough to permit single feed. Shaped on CNC machines, stocks are hand-bedded. Barrels float, but the gap is so thin you'd think it a press fit. Cooper triggers adjust from 1½ to five pounds. Talley or Leupold scope bases are included.

Accuracy? I don't have a 51 yet—they won't be available until later this year—but my .270 Model 52 cut a .6-inch group with its first magazine of Remington factory loads. A Model 54 in .250 delivered a .35 cluster with my handloads. Six .308 Norma loads I tried in a Model 56 averaged 1¼ inches. The best, a TSX from Safari Arms, Ltd., printed a .6-inch group while clocking 3,001 fps over my Oehler 35. (www.cooperfirearms.com)

DAKOTA OUTFITTER AND PH: PROFESSIONAL GRADE!

In 1984, Don and Norma Allen founded Dakota Arms in Sturgis, South Dakota, to pursue Don's dream of reviving the Winchester Model 70. The Model 76 is still the firm's flagship. The subsequent round-bottom Model 97 costs less, but it has all the refinements of the 76 that matter. When I requested a 97 Outfitter

The author fires a Dakota Outfitter. The big-bore PH is similar, with drop-box and barrel swivel.

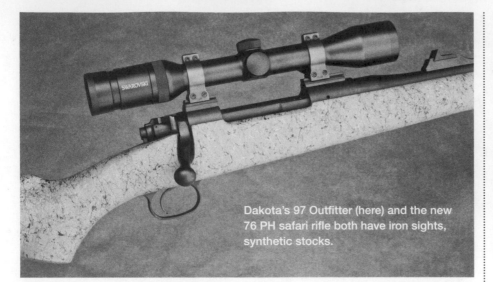

Dakota's 97 Outfitter (here) and the new 76 PH safari rifle both have iron sights, synthetic stocks.

in .30-06 for a mountain goat hunt, Richard Spruill didn't quibble. "Scoped and zeroed?" he asked. Lest you think this special treatment for a gun scribe begging a loan, I must add that zeroing is a routine service at Dakota. And it's free.

If you've been numbed by the mediocrity of most contemporary bolt rifles, you might expect one from South Dakota to mimic the rest. I actually expected more. "We try not to build mediocre guns," Don Allen told me 30 years ago. The 97's button rifled Douglas barrel secures a thick, washer-style recoil lug. Choose right- or left-hand in two action lengths, for cartridges to 2.80 and 3.60 inches OAL. The CeraKoted stainless action is glass- and pillar-bedded to a carbon-fiber/fiberglass stock. Dakota detailing shows throughout, from the seamless fit of its two-screw swivel studs to the silky slide of the bolt. Stock fill (weight, balance) is tailored to each rifle's use and chambering. I like the blind magazine.

The test rifle shot 10 of 12 loads into 1½ inches or less, with Norma-loaded AccuBonds chiseling a ⅝-inch group. A new bullet, Federal's 165 Trophy Copper, came in at a minute of angle.

The Outfitter is one of four configurations of the Model 97. Dakota's 97 and 76 bolts come from identical blanks.

"There's one small difference in the finished bolts," says Ward Dobler, who manages the Dakota shop. "It's the cams. The 97's extraction cam costs less to make and more closely resembles the 1898 Mauser's. Cam travel and cycling effort are the same."

Both bolts control cartridges with a Mauser-style extractor in breeching that derives more from the Mauser than from the 70. Both have an M70-type mechani-

cal ejector and three-position safety, and Dakota's folding-arm bolt release that vanishes into the bridge. Don Allen echoed my thinking when he said the Winchester Model 70 trigger "was the best ever designed for a hunting rifle." He adopted it for Dakota 76s and 97s.

Despite its catalog moniker, the Outfitter is not a takedown rifle.

"We do relieve the front of the lug recess for easy stock removal," says Dobler. "But the barrel is screwed on in normal fashion. One of our retailers thought 'Take Down' a catchy name, but the 76 Traveler is Dakota's only real takedown."

You can specify any reasonable barrel length, but 23 inches is standard for short actions, 25 inches for long. Unlike its siblings, the synthetic-stocked Long Range Hunter and All-Weather, and walnut-stocked Deluxe 97s, the Outfitter

comes with iron sights (on a nicely sculpted rear island and a long ramp). The shallow notch and gold bead line up just below the optical axis of a low scope. Don't want irons? Say so! Each Outfitter comes with Talley bases.

Dakota's newest Model 76, the PH (Professional Hunter), is a big-bore version of the Outfitter, for when you *must* stop the action. This businesslike rifle still has Dakota touches, the sculptured tang and blind guard screw hole. It features iron sights and a quarter-rib, barrel-mounted swivel stud and a deep magazine. Metal is CeraKoted matte black and pillar-bedded to a conservatively styled synthetic stock. "It's like the African and the Safari, without wood," says Richard Spruill.

The African has Dakota's biggest bolt and receiver. Bored to .404 Jeffery, .416 Rigby, .450 Rigby, and .450 Dakota, it features a deep magazine that holds three .450s, four .404s and .416s. The fore-stock houses an 11-ounce mercury recoil. The Safari boasts somewhat trimmer lines and lacks the recoil device. It's barreled to long belted magnums: the .375 H&H (four rounds in the stack), .416 Remington and .458 Lott (three). Both rifles have banded swivel studs and front sights on 23-inch chrome-moly barrels.

The PH is a dangerous-game rifle with the same action sizes, capacities, and chamberings as the African and Safari. Hand-laid carbon-fiber stocks are on the same patterns. They're pillar bedded, without a kick-reducer. The 23-inch barrels are CeraKoted stainless steel, with quarter-rib and a fiber optic bead on the front ramp. Sleek, muscular lines give the new PH pick-me-up appeal. As with the

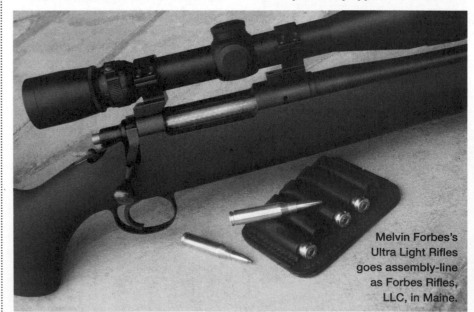

Melvin Forbes's Ultra Light Rifles goes assembly-line as Forbes Rifles, LLC, in Maine.

synthetic-stocked Outfitter that I recently took to the mountains, bedding surfaces are mirror-smooth. Stock-to-steel fit is skin-close. Expect the bolt on Dakota's PH to move like a race-car piston, the trigger to break with the snap of an icicle. The PH feels lighter than it looks, thanks to fine balance. Listing for $7,995, this potent Model 76 combines reliable design, exquisite detailing, and first-cabin components. (www.dakotaarms.com)

FORBES RIFLES ON A PRODUCTION LINE?

Melvin Forbes is Ultra Light Arms. His svelte bolt-actions, tailored to specific cartridge sizes and fitted with synthetic stocks that weigh less than a pound, delight hunters who walk far. ULA rifles shoot better than their feathery heft suggests. Fit and finish are top drawer.

To make these semi-custom rifles more affordable, Melvin has helped launch Forbes Rifles, LLC, in Maine, far from his West Virginia shop. The new company builds rifles on Melvin's design and the 24B action, in .25-06, .270, .280 and .30-06, with the 6.5x55 and .35 Whelen due by mid-year 2013. E.R. Shaw supplies barrels. Left-hand versions are available on request. Stainless and short-action Forbes rifles should follow. Melvin will still produce ULA rifles to custom order. (www.forbesriflellc.com)

HEYM SHEDS WEIGHT, BULK

Chambered for rounds as big as the .416 Rigby, Heym rifles, on square-bridge Magnum Mauser-style actions, feed with legendary reliability. Twin-lug lockup and a controlled feed claw complement the three-position safety and adjustable trigger. Recently, without fanfare, these powerful rifles got sleek, conservatively shaped stocks of handsome walnut. I shouldered one at the Dallas SCI Show, in January. My eye fell naturally in line with the iron sights on elegant rib and ramp. A barrel-mounted swivel stud and deep but not bulbous magazine box hint of the muscle in this trim new Heym. You can order custom features, but, even in Spartan form, Heym sporters stand out in any crowd. Rifles this good aren't cheap—and won't get cheaper! (www.heymusa.com)

JARRETT RIFLES NOW IN WOOD

Kenny Jarrett is stepping out. Not away from the accuracy that made his "beanfield" rifles lethal at yonder forest's edge, but back to tradition. The precisely machined actions and barrels manufactured at his South Carolina shop are now available in hand-checkered walnut stocks, as well as his hand-laid synthetics. Actions in the new Prestige Series are secured in a stout 6061 aluminum bedding block, epoxied in place. The block (chassis) surrounds the magazine well. The action is pillar bedded; the barrel floats.

"We tried many sealants and finishes to make this stock absolutely waterproof," Kenny tells me. "We got there with multiple coats over an epoxy base that seals wood 3/16-inch deep. I've submersed these stocks for days with no measurable change in weight." No water up-take!

Jarrett's new walnut-stocked rifles feature the long, slim grips I favor. Choose standard or Prince of Wales (round-knob) design. A straight grip is also available. Comb and fore-end are "American classic" in profile. (www.jarrettrifles.com)

LEGACY SPORTS, FROM AUSTRIA

Howa, Escort, Puma, Citadel—all are brands marketed by Legacy Sports International. Now the Nevada-based company also counts Austrian-made ISSC rifles (and pistols) among its firearms. New for 2013 are the ISSC SPA (Straight-Pull Action) rimfires. These rifles feature 20-inch "German Match" barrels and 10-shot detachable box magazines. Choose a high comb walnut "hunter" stock or a straight comb synthetic option. There's also a Target SPA rifle with a fully adjustable stock. Weighing in at just under eight pounds, the new ISSC rimfires are chambered in .22 LR, .22 WMR, and .17 HMR. Price: $499 for the synthetic model, $599 for the walnut, and $699 for the Target. (www.legacysports.com)

LYMAN MODEL OF 1878

Known for its handloading, bullet casting, and blackpowder supplies, Lyman offers gunsmithing tools and Pachmayr grips, as well. It has now teamed with Pedersoli to produce high-quality replica firearms faithful to the originals. For 2013, there's the Model of 1878 Sharps in .45-70, complete with Lyman tang and globe sights and a double set trigger. The checkered pistol grip stock has a steel-capped shotgun butt and ebony fore-end tip. Receiver and sideplates are laser engraved. The Model of 1878 follows a scaled down, Sharps-style Ideal Model in .22 Hornet and .38-55. I've found my Ideal (.38-55) well finished and silky smooth in operation. It shoots accurately with Black Hills Cowboy Action ammunition and evokes the romance of times we'll not see again. (www.lymanproducts.com)

MCMILLAN MOUNTAIN EXTREME —FOR THE LONGEST SHOT

For 2013, McMillan has announced a new Mountain Extreme stable configured for long shooting. These synthetic-stocked rifles feature McMillan's G30 long action and are barreled and throated for leggy cartridges using VLD bullets. The lightweight Alpine is chambered in 6.5x284. The Yukon, a bit heavier, comes in several borings, from 7mm Ultra Mag to .338 Lapua. Ditto the

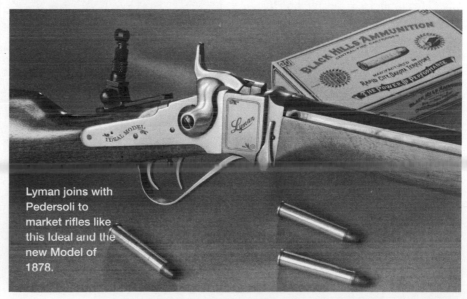

Lyman joins with Pedersoli to market rifles like this Ideal and the new Model of 1878.

Kelly McMillan fires a G30 in .404. His 2013 offerings: new long-range and modular rifles.

Denali, with a longer, heavier barrel and an adjustable "tactical" stock. All Mountain Extreme rifles wear muzzle brakes.

The Arizona firm has also introduced a modular bolt-action rifle, with a futuristic, military look. The Alias features steel and synthetic components in three basic versions. Each has a closely fitted bolt in a tubular receiver with an Anschütz trigger. The 10½-pound CS5, most compact of the trio, has what McMillan calls an "urban rifle" profile. Its 12½-inch .308 barrel has a 1:8 twist to stabilize 200-grain subsonic and 175-grain supersonic loads. It wears a suppressor. An 11½-pound STAR (Standard Tactical Application Rifle) with 18- to 24-inch barrel (rifled 1:11 in .308), also comes in 6.5x47 Lapua and 6.5 Creedmoor. The Target Competition model has a 24- to 30-inch barrel, weighs 12 pounds, and boasts six chamberings. All Alias rifles have adjustable stocks more comfortable than they look. They're designed to control recoil and muzzle flip. McMillan offers a full custom option for shooters who want to mix and match components. (www.mcmillanusa.com)

MORE MUSCLE FROM MONTANA

Montana Rifle Company has announced new AVR (American Vantage Rifle) and XVR (Xtreme Vantage Rifle) models that resemble the ASR and XWR (walnut and synthetic stocks)—"but with stiffer barrels, iron sights," says Jeff Sipe. "The AVR also comes in stainless." Chamberings: .35 Whelen, .375 Ruger,

.375 H&H, .416 Remington, .416 Ruger, .458 Lott, .458 Winchester. Said Sipe, "The new offerings fill a gap in the Montana line between Safari rifles and traditional sporters for deer and elk."

They're built in-house on Montana's own Winchester 70-style actions, with barrels from The Montana Rifleman next door in Kalispell. Brian Sipe, Jeff's father, started both businesses and supplies barrels to several firearms firms. The AVR rifle lists for $1279, the AVR SS for $1309, the XVR for $1399. (www.montanarifleco.com)

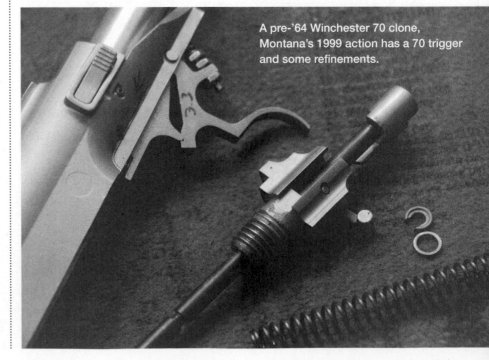

A pre-'64 Winchester 70 clone, Montana's 1999 action has a 70 trigger and some refinements.

REMINGTON REVISITS ENTRY-LEVEL RIFLES

The Model 783, Remington's new centerfire rifle for 2013, features a twin-lug bolt that rides in a cylindrical receiver wedded to its 22-inch button rifled barrel with a barrel nut. Fed by a detachable box magazine, the rifle is pillar bedded to an injection-molded synthetic stock with integral swivel studs and a SuperCell recoil pad. The seven-pound 783 has an adjustable trigger and two-position safety. Chambered for the .270, .308, .30-06, and 7mm Remington Magnum with 24-inch barrel. $451.10. (www.remington.com)

CULLING RUGER'S NO. 1: TWEAKING THE 77

"We list more chamberings in the No. 1 rifle than are practical to stock," Ruger's Ken Jorgensen told me last year. "So, beginning in 2013, we're offering just one per variation." The No. 1 Light Sporter is bored to .222 Remington this year, the Medium Sporter to .45-70. The Tropical comes in .375 H&H, the International in 7x57, and the Varminter in 6.5x284. Next year, that slate will change. Ken points out that special editions for distributors remain. The elegant dropping block No. 1 debuted in 1967 at $265—when new Ford Mustangs listed for $2,700.

Since its reemergence as the new, trim Hawkeye, Ruger's Model 77 has shown many faces. The latest is a comely, walnut-stocked African, with Express-style sights, barrel-band swivel, and a radial-port muzzle brake you can replace with an equal-weight solid sleeve when hunting, to protect your ears; point of impact shouldn't shift. Available in .300 and .338 Winchester, .375 Ruger (also in left-hand) and .416 Ruger, these are chrome-moly rifles with the Mauser-type extractor of all Hawkeyes. A new, stainless 77 Magnum Hunter in .300 Winchester wears the same brake and a synthetic stock, comes with no sights.

A year after the 77 Scout Rifle appeared at the SHOT Show, it is still Ruger's best-selling Model 77. The short, box-fed .308s are "going out the door as fast as we can make 'em," says one Ruger salesman. For 2013, the Scout is available with an 18-inch stainless barrel, in addition to the 16¾-inch chrome-moly original. The new version also has a stainless receiver. Hewing closely to the lines of the rifle made famous by Jeff Cooper, this Ruger features iron sights and a rail for an IER (intermediate eye relief) scope. A nimble hunting rifle, it doubles as a survival tool and home-defense gun. "In fact, many people buying Scout rifles own no other firearms," says Ken Jorgensen. "They're not enthusiasts. They want one versatile, reliable rifle. They like how the Scout looks and feels." (www.ruger.com)

SAKOS FOR SOUTHPAWS

When the Sako Model 85 replaced the 75, hunters noted few changes. But the Model 85 action now appears in several distinctive rifles. The stainless/laminated Kodiak ranks among my favorite .375s. In my view, it has the best iron sights on any production rifle, plus an outstanding trigger and magazine design. For 2013, Sako extends its left-hand Model 85 to the S or short action. While the modestly priced Tikka T3, made in the Sako plant, continues to give the Model 85 stiff competition, and the Sako Bear series is a head turner. Newest in this line is the quick-handling Arctos—marketed in Europe as the Grizzly, go figure! At this writing, there are only two Arctos rifles Stateside. I'm chasing one. (www.berettausa.com)

SAVAGE B. MAG: 4½ POUNDS OF LIGHTNING

Not since Charles Newton produced the .250-3000 for Savage, in 1913, has the company leaned so unexpectedly on a new, fast-stepping cartridge "from outside." And it is building a rifle specifically for the round! The B.MAG chambers the just-announced .17 Winchester Super Magnum, a rimfire cartridge that spits 20-grain bullets downrange at 3,000 fps. Combining rimfire and centerfire features, this 4½-pound, synthetic-stocked rifle has an eight-round rotary magazine. The B. MAG's rear-locking bolt cocks on closing and headspaces like a centerfire rifle. Savage claims the action is stronger than its slender lines suggest. You can shoot this rifle accurately, too, thanks to its AccuTrigger. Retailing for $349, the B. MAG reaches dealer shelves during the second quarter of 2013. (www.savagearms.com)

SHILOH SHARPS: ANOTHER PAGE FROM THE PAST

Shiloh Sharps, the small, central Montana company that builds historically faithful Sharps rifles, is out with a new one. The 1877 Model, dutifully detailed after the last significant Sharps, is scheduled for christening this summer. "Right now, we're still building the first one," Shiloh's crew told me in January. I expect the 1877 Model will be worth the wait—and that many orders have already been placed. Shiloh's 1874 line now includes a dozen models of military, sporting, and target rifles for blackpowder cartridges from .38-55 to .50-110, and offers a plethora of authentic accessories, including tang and globe sights, and several grades of walnut for its custom-built rifles. (www.shilohrifle.com)

SMITH & WESSON'S POTENT M&P 10 RIFLE

Though S&W uses a gas-piston mechanism in some of its M&P (Military & Police) 15s, it chose to equip the new M&P 10 .308 AR rifle with the traditional, direct-impingement action standard on most of its .223s.

"A piston keeps the action cleaner and cooler," Bill Booth explained, "because gas and debris don't reach the

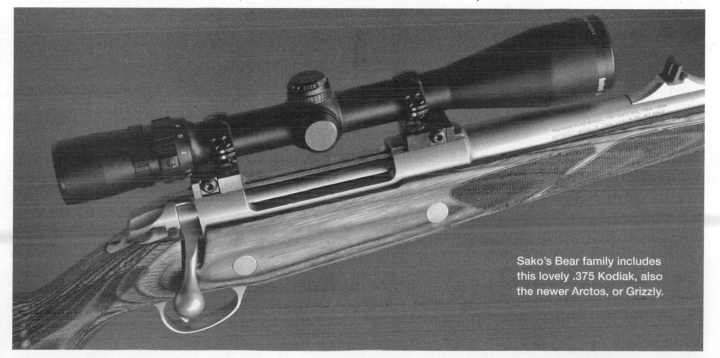

Sako's Bear family includes this lovely .375 Kodiak, also the newer Arctos, or Grizzly.

This Steyr SBS is almost as sleek as a 1952 M-S. It's more accurate. Ditto the new MS 12.

carrier. But you shouldn't notice any difference unless you're firing almost non-stop for many minutes. Direct-impingement actions are simpler; they've cycled reliably under very grim conditions."

The M&P 10 has a mid-length system. Gas key, bolt carrier, and firing pin are chrome-plated. The trigger is adjusted to break at just over six pounds. A five-shot magazine comes with the eight-pound civilian rifle. The 7¾-pound LE (Law Enforcement) version gets a 20-shot box. S&W installed ambidextrous controls—safety, bolt catch, and magazine release all appear on both sides of the lightweight 7075 T6 alloy receiver. Thoughtfully, engineers made the safety bar slightly shorter on the right-hand side, so as not to interfere with the trigger hand. Lefties can reverse the bar, to put the long lever on the right.

An integral Picatinny rail distinguishes this rifle as a flat-top, and the rail on the gas block up front is properly milled to the same height. The M&P 10 has a shell deflector and a forward assist, like its .223 siblings. While 16-inch barrels are standard on the M&P 15, the new 10 has a smooth, medium-weight 18-inch tube. It's a useful length. The blast from a shorter .308 barrel can rattle your belfry, and bullet speeds drop substantially. The LE version has a lighter barrel, bumped up at the muzzle, behind a flash-hider.

Rifled 1:10, the barrel is made of 4140 chrome-moly steel. Melanite finish

"bonds to the steel in such a way that the two materials become one," according to Bill Booth, "so you needn't fret about rust, inside or out." Melanite nixes that even better than chrome plating.

The civilian M&P 10 wears a fixed A-2 Magpul stock with an integral sling slot and holes for toe supports. You can replace this butt (in RealTree camo, to match the metal) with the six-position (black) stock of the LE rifle. Smith & Wesson lists the M&P 10 at just under $1,800. Of course, the mechanism can handle many short-action rifle cartridges, but, for now, it's barreled only to .308. Demand will surely outstrip supply for some time. (www.smith-wesson.com)

STEYR: NEW RIFLES FROM AN OLD PLACE

The lithe profile, sinewy and graceful, of the full-stocked 1952 Mannlicher-Schoenauer, with its split bridge and butter-knife bolt, are no more. Even in my youth, such rifles were very costly, more so than a Model 70 Winchester or a Remington 700.

"We tried to bring back those lines," said Oliver Bauer. He handed me the newest Steyr bolt rifle, the SM 12 (Steyr Mannicher Model 12). Introduced in 2012 but just now available, this rifle does have a taut, sleek, almost carnivorous look. Still, the bolt handle doesn't hug the stock as on early Mannlichers, and the lock-up differs. The bridge is solid. But the slim fore-end nestles

deep in my hand. "This action is stronger, the barrel more accurate," Oliver declared. The bolt has two pairs of opposing lugs, a recessed face with plunger ejector. The barrel retains a visible twist imparted by hammer forging.

The tang switch is not a safety, as on the earlier Steyr SBS. Instead, it's a cocking mechanism, so you can safely carry the SM 12 with a chambered cartridge. A couple other European firms have adapted this idea to double rifles and straight-pull bolt guns. "But their strong springs can resist weak or cold hands," said Oliver. The Steyr's new switch moves like a safety. To decock, press forward and down. The striker protrudes slightly when cocked, so you can check it with a glance or a touch. At just over two pounds, the clean-breaking trigger is light enough for most shooters, but you can set it (with a forward nudge) to release at 12 ounces.

The MS 12 stock is of open-grained walnut, with a modest rise to the comb and a "double-flame" cheek-piece with crisp edges. The grip is tight, but comfortable. Checkering has been replaced by "scaled" panels that are functional, if not as attractive. There's a thin black rubber butt-pad.

The MS 12 is chambered for 10 popular cartridges, .243 to .300 Winchester and including European favorites like the 6.5x55, 8x68, and 9.3x62. Choose the standard polymer magazine or stamped steel. The rifle weighs 7¼ pounds with its 22-inch barrel. Add eight ounces for magnums with 24½-inch barrels. The front is adjustable for elevation, the rear for windage. I've not yet range-tested the MS 12, but can vouch for Steyr accuracy. From the bench, an SBS carbine in 9.3x62 and a rifle in .270 WSM routinely drill sub-minute groups. Steyr's new MS 12 lists for $3,200.

Also new this year is the Duett, a hinged-breech, hammerless, boxlock combination gun. Bored for 3-inch 12-gauge shells below and your choice of eight rifle cartridges above, the 23½-inch, cold hammer-forged barrels can be regulated with a screw at the muzzles. "We adjust them so a rifle bullet and a shotgun slug shoot to the iron sights at 50 meters," explained Ernst Reichmayr, co-owner of Steyr. The Duett also comes with an 11mm scope mount rail. Each of the two triggers has a pull weight of 3½ pounds. The mechanism is cocked by a tang-mounted cocking switch that slides forward (and back to de-cock) easily. In my view, the barrel lever is a tad long, contacting my big thumb on the switch.

Scaled panels help you grip the Duett's walnut stock, crisply contoured in European style. Nicely fitted to the metal, it puts my eye in line with the iron sights. In fact, the most appealing virtue of this 6½-pound combination gun may be its handling. Though a combination gun can't match the lean look of a smallbore shotgun or a rifle, the Duett does feel svelte. It meets my cheek on its own and has a nose for the target. Weight-between-the-hands balance is part of it. Credit, also, the modest barrel length, a short breech, and excellent stock design. Magic or just intelligent engineering, this gun points itself.

You can choose from five levels of engraving on the Duett's false sideplates. That embellishment and wood quality affect price. The standard Duett lists for $2,850, with rifle chamberings .223, .243, .308, 7x65R, .30-06, .30R Blaser, 8x57, and 9.3x74R. If, like me, you recall the ubiquitous Savage Model 24 of the 1960s, the .22/.410 that started many a youngster hunting cottontails, you owe yourself a few minutes with the versatile, nimble Steyr Duett. (www.steyrarms.com)

SURGEON'S SCALPEL

A few years back, when I visited Preston Pritchett and his one employee, he'd just started building super-accurate sniper-style rifles under the Surgeon shingle. All-steel components were fashioned in his modest but well-equipped shop, in rural Oklahoma. They still are, though Pritchett's business has grown, as long-range shooters, police, military marksmen, and even hunters have discovered the remarkable precision of a Surgeon. The first group I fired with a "Remedy" in .338 Lapua measured ¼-inch! A newer "Scalpel" in .223 gave me similar eye-popping results, with less recoil. Surgeon rifles aren't cheap, but if you want bullets to cut one hole, you'll get on Preston Pritchett's list. I'm there, for a mid-weight sporter in .260 Remington. (www.surgeonrifles.com)

T/C DOWNSIZES THE VENTURE

Following its move to Smith & Wesson's factory in Springfield, Thompson/Center has enjoyed steady demand for its accurate, modestly-priced Venture bolt rifle. Now there's a short-stocked, short-barreled Venture that makes handling and shooting easier for shooters of small build. The Venture's low-lift, three-lug bolt and stiff receiver, plus T/C's famous 5-R rifling, are a proven recipe for tight groups. My .270 punches ¾-inch knots! All Ventures

Surgeon rifles aren't sleek, but they are accurate, no matter what you feed them.

wear synthetic stocks. Incidentally, the more costly T/C Icon is having a tough time competing with the Venture at market. Word is that the Icon will soon be phased out. (www.tcarms.com)

TRADITIONS STRIKER-FIRED MUZZLELOADER

The hinged-breech, in-line design of Traditions muzzleloaders has been proven by blackpowder buffs. The mechanism comes in myriad guises, with blued steel and CeraKoted models, pistol grip and thumbhole stocks, and various sight options. All feature convenient front-of-the-guard latch levers. Until now, all had exposed hammers, but a new hammerless version appeared at January's SHOT Show. This striker-fired Vortek rifle has a sliding cocking switch on the tang; not a safety, the switch cocks the rifle, so you can carry it safely loaded. To uncock, press a recessed button and ease the switch back.

The new Vortek has a 28-inch, .50-caliber, chrome-moly barrel rifled 1:28. Get it with or without iron sights. The one-piece 209 Accelerator Breech Plug allows use of loose powder or pellets. Synthetic stocks come with black or camo finish. A button releases the butt-pad so you can store "possibles" in the stock cavity. More hinged-breech, bolt-action, and in-line muzzleloaders, with "Classic" side-hammer, wood-stocked rifles, appear in the 2013 catalog. Scopes and muzzleloading accessories too! (www.traditionsfirearms.com)

WEATHERBY COMES HOME

The Weatherby story dates to the Depression. Roy spent most of his childhood working in Kansas farm fields and earned his first BB gun by peddling garden seed on foot. Later, employed at Southwestern Bell, he took night classes from the University of Wichita. In 1937, the young man and his wife, Camilla, headed for California. He started an insurance business, then ordered a lathe and a drill press from Sears and started building rifles on surplus military actions in his basement shop. By 1945, Roy had designed several of his signature Weatherby Magnum cartridges. Based on .300 H&H brass, they had more powder capacity. Radiused shoulders distinguished them from other wildcats. Soon, Roy left his insurance job and hitched his fortunes to the rifle business. He courted heroes, industry giants, and film stars as customers: Elmer Keith and Jack O'Connor, Jimmy Doolittle, Gary Cooper, and Roy Rog-

ers. The young rifle maker caught the eye of Texas oil man and big-game hunter Herb Klein, who floated him a big loan.

Roy's first store opened in 1945, on Long Beach Boulevard in the Los Angeles area. A move came shortly after Weatherby's (later Weatherby), Inc. was founded, in 1949. The new Firestone Boulevard address in Southgate would be Weatherby's headquarters and retail outlet for more than 40 years. In 1957, Roy and company engineer Fred Jennie developed the Mark V rifle action to replace the Danish Shultz & Larsen, one of few big enough for Weatherby's .378 Magnum. It had a fully adjustable trigger, 54-degree bolt life, and terrific strength in lock-up. The Mark V, with its distinctive profile, nine-lug breeching, and rakish Claro stocks, came to define the company and symbolize the globe-trotting hunter's lifestyle.

Roy Weatherby died in 1988, but son, Ed, has continued to grow the company and to diversify its line of rifles. The Vanguard, on the sturdy Howa action, has earned a big following as an economical alternative to the Mark V. The recently upgraded Vanguard Series 2 features a three-position safety and adjustable two-stage trigger. It's guaranteed to punch minute-of-angle groups. Choose walnut or

Bold colors and patterns adorn the Weatherby X rifles designed to entice young shooters.

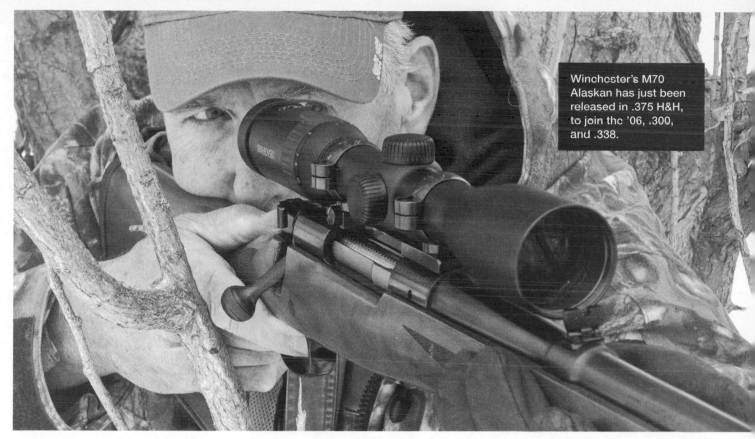

Winchester's M70 Alaskan has just been released in .375 H&H, to join the '06, .300, and .338.

synthetic stock, internal or detachable box magazine. The Back Country, my favorite in the Series 2 line, returns, in 2013, in .240, .257, and .300 Weatherby Magnums, as well as .270, .30-06, and .300 Winchester.

The long-barreled AccuMark has sold briskly to the Mark V faithful who like to shoot far. This year a Range Certified AccuMark debuts, its floorplate so marked. Minute-of-angle accuracy is the bar. The AccuMark's fluted stainless barrel floats in a hand-laminated synthetic stock with T-6 alloy bedding plate. Chambered for all Weatherby big-game rounds to .338-378, the rifle also comes in .270, .308, .30-06, 7mm Remington, and .300 Winchester Magnums—and .338 Lapua! Price: $2,400 ($2,700 for the .30-378, .338-378, .338 Lapua). Left-hand rifles are available in .257, .300, and .30-378.

The Weatherby X brand covers a new line of rifles (and shotguns), with graphics and dimensions for young shooters. So unlike the main Weatherby line that it has its own catalog, Weatherby X rifles, on Vanguard (Howa) actions, feature names like Hog Reaper and Whitetail Bonz. Bold colors in arresting patterns distinguish their synthetic stocks. "The exclusivity of the Weatherby X line, with its cosmetic tilt to young shooters,

targets a market we all want to reach," says the company's Mike Schwiebert. (www.weatherby.com)

WINCHESTER M70 ALASKAN RETURNS, AND THE TIMELESS '73

The Model 70 Alaskan debuted in 1958, chambered for the then-new .338 Winchester Magnum cartridge. With its thick red recoil pad and 25-inch "egg-lump" barrel, the Alaskan was easy to recognize. Though Winchester has chambered the M70 in .338 for 55 years now, it didn't bring the Alaskan name back until recently.

In mid-2012 the .338 Magnum joined the .30-06 and .300 Winchester in a resurrected Alaskan. The rifle has the walnut stock and long barrel of the original, plus the Mauser-style extractor that again graces all M70s. Trigger, checkering, and one-piece bottom metal differ from the early model. The recoil pad is black. But, in the important aspects, this latest .338 lives up to its name. For 2013, Winchester will chamber its handsome Alaskan in .375 H&H.

"The gun that won the West" has also returned to Winchester's corral, albeit with some changes since its debut 140

years ago. Built in the Miroku plant that has produced high-quality, replica lever-actions for Winchester and Browning (the 1892, 1886, and M71 among them), the 1873 Short Rifle is true in profile to the original. But a firing pin striker block adds the predictable "margin of safety." A brass carrier block kicks empties away from your eye. The straight-grip walnut stock wears a crescent butt and a steel fore-end cap. Equipped with semi-buckhorn rear and Marble gold bead front sights, the '73's 20-inch round barrel is chambered in .357 Magnum. You can use .38 Special ammo, too, of course. The full-length magazine, secured by an under-barrel ring, holds 10 .357 cartridges or 11 .38s. Winchester's new 1873 Short Rifle weighs 7¼ pounds and retails for $1,300.

This year, Winchester adds a Carbine to its Model 94 series, re-introduced after the New Haven plant closed, in 2006. The Carbine features angled ejection, a tang safety, and a carbine-style steel buttplate. The 20-inch barrel is chambered in .30-30 and .38-55. Barrel bands fasten the seven-shot, full-length magazine. All four Model 94s are drilled and tapped for scope mounts. (www.winchesterguns.com)

NEW SH

Benelli's M2 20-Gauge

BY JOHN HAVILAND

The continual number of new shotgun models is amazing, especially considering they originated from essentially the same shotshells that have been around for about 150 years. At least rifles have a constant flow of new cartridges, and handguns an occasional new round as impetus for new guns. But shotgun manufacturers must constantly develop niche markets and then tailor their guns to fit. That creativity works, as shotguns are being purchased at a record rate. Let's see what's in store this year.

Benelli

Benelli's 20-gauge M2 lefty autoloader is available with a black synthetic stock with GripTight, an over-coating bonded to the stock and fore-end that is weather resistant and provides a sure grip. Three optional combs for height adjustment are available for the ComforTech stock, and a set of stock shims is standard, to adjust drop and cast. A gel recoil pad has three optional pads: a short one providing a 14-inch length of pull (LOP); medium for 14½; and a long pad providing a 14¾ LOP. Choke tubes include Cylinder (C), Improved Cylinder (IC), Modified (M), Improved Modified (IM) and Full (F).

The M2 Field Compact in 12- and 20-gauge is designed for small-

The Remington Sportsman VERSA MAX took this North Carolina cottontail rabbit. The Sportsman is the plain version of Remington's VERSA MAX.

OTGUNS

This ruffed grouse was taken with a Browning PS Micro Midas pump .410-bore.

Browning A-5. Mossy Oak Shadow Grass

Browning Maxus Sporting

Browning Maxus Ultimate

statured shooters with a 13¹/₈-inch LOP, a ComforTech gel butt pad, and a set of shims for adjusting the stock drop and cast. The Compact 12-gauge has a 26-inch barrel, the 20-gauge a 24-inch tube.

Benelli has improved a couple of its autoloaders. The Montefeltro's style has always included a walnut stock. The 12-gauge Montefeltro Synthetic retains the gun's lines, but with a slim, synthetic stock. At the heart of the Vinci Speed-

Bolt is a tungsten inset in its bolt that helps the action cycle faster and shoot loads as light as an ounce of shot. The QuadraFit stock allows easy adjustment of heel drop, cast, comb height, and LOP.

Browning

Browning has added features to its guns that include new camouflage patterns, weight-saving aluminum receivers, engraving, micro guns that

fit smaller-statured shooters, and new choke tubes. The A-5, MAXUS, and Silver autoloaders and BPS 10- and 12-gauge pumps are now concealed in Mossy Oak Shadow Grass Blade camo. The 725 Feather 12-gauge over/under has an aluminum receiver, with a steel breech face and hinge and a weight of 6½ pounds, as compared to the 725 Field's 7.4 pounds and its steel receiver. The Citori 725 Sporting now also comes with a comb adjustable for height.

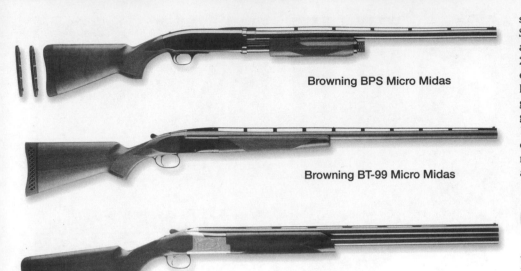

Browning BPS Micro Midas

Browning BT-99 Micro Midas

Browning Citori 725 Feather

The stocks and fore-ends have been scaled down on the BT-99 Micro Midas 12-gauge and BPS Micro Midas pumps. The 12-gauge BT-99's stock has a 13-inch LOP and a slim fore-end. The BPS Micro Midas pump also has a 13-inch LOP and the stock wears an Inflex Technology recoil pad. Two ¼-inch stock spacers are included to lengthen the pull as the shooter matures. The BPS Micro comes in 12-, 20-, and 28-gauge and .410-bore.

The Maxus autoloader Ultimate and Sporting Golden Clays wear a satin nickel-finished receiver with laser engraving. The Ultimate pictures pheasants on the right side of the receiver and mallards on the left. The Golden Clays displays a game bird transforming into a clay target.

To accompany those guns into the waterfowl blind are Invector-Plus Dirty Bird choke tubes designed to shoot steel shot, especially Winchester's Blind Side ammunition. The Long Range tube produces a 70-percent pattern, the Medium Range a 60-percent pattern, and the Close Range a 30-percent pattern.

CZ-USA

CZ has refined a few of its guns with a steel receiver, adjustable stocks or barrel sets, and three new 12-gauge pumps ready for waterfowl or the walking dead.

The 612 Home Defense is a plain pump with an 18½-inch Cylinder-bore barrel and a black synthetic stock. The 612 Wildfowl is designed for turkey or waterfowl hunters, wrapped in camouflage, with a Modified choke for nontoxic shot and an Extra-Full turkey choke. For those concerned about a zombie uprising, the 612 Horde Control pump features a vertical grip stock, ghost ring rear sight, and fiber dot front.

An Adjustable Length Stock (ALS) has been added to the CZ 712 autoloader to allow changing LOP with the push of a button. Comb height can also be set at three positions via a screw adjustment. The ALS has an easily removed magazine plug.

The CZ Sporter Standard Grade over/under is designed for sporting clays, with single-selectable trigger, a Monte Carlo stock with an adjustable comb, and a right-hand palm swell. This competition gun is available with 30- or 32-inch barrels and six stainless

steel extended choke tubes. The Super Scroll Combo Set over/under is built on a 20-gauge frame, with 30-inch 20- and 28-gauge barrel sets and fore-ends for each. Hand-engraved scrollwork embellishes the receiver, sideplates, trigger guard, and mono-block. Five chokes per gauge are included. The Upland Sterling 12-gauge over/under has a steel, instead of aluminum, receiver. The Turkish walnut stock features stippling on the grip and fore-end, rather than checkering.

Legacy Sports International

Legacy has added two camo patterns to its Escort Youth and one to its Ladies Escort 20-gauge semi-auto shotguns. The Youth guns are covered with Realtree MAX4 or AP camo, the Ladies with Moon Shine Muddy Girl camo, a pink/black/silver/white pattern. The guns have a 13-inch length of pull, FAST loading system, SMART Valve cycling system, and magazine cut-off for single round loading. The Youth barrel is 22 inches, the Ladies 26 inches. Both have a ventilated rib with a fiber optic front sight and IC, M, and F choke tubes.

The Escort Supreme 20 autoloader is available in right- and left-hand models, with a Turkish walnut stock and fore-end. With a retail price of $619, the Supreme 20 has a nickel-lined bore, a magazine cut-off for single round loading, and Skeet, IC, M, IM, and F choke tubes. Sling swivel studs are standard, as well as extra stock shims for a custom fit.

Franchi

Franchi's new over/under Aspire has a color case hardened round receiver that blends with an oil-finished walnut stock sporting a thin wrist and slim fore-end. The Aspire's hammers cock when the action breaks open, and the automatic safety is integrated with a barrel selector. There are 28-inch barrels in 28-gauge or .410-bore; the sighting plane rib is a 6mm vent-style with a fiber optic front sight. The Aspire weighs 5.8 pounds and comes with C, IC, M, IM, and F choke tubes.

Franchi's Affinity Sporting Inertia Driven 12-gauge semi-auto features a brushed nickel anodized receiver.

CZ 612 HCP

Franchi Aspire

The synthetic stock has a slender grip and fore-end that help keep its weight to a feather, under seven pounds. The Sporting's 30-inch barrel sports a stepped, ventilated rib, red fiber optic front sight, and a set of IC, M, and F extended choke tubes.

Recoil pads of three different thicknesses offer the option of a 14½, 14¼, or 15-inch LOPs. Stock drop and cast are set with a shim kit. The Affinity Sporting handles loads from 1⅛-ounce to 3-inch magnums.

The Affinity Compact is a 5½-pound 20-gauge version of the Affinity. The Compact has a slim fore-end and stock with a 12⅜-inch LOP. Supplied spacers can be added to increase LOP to 13⅜ inches, and a shim kit allows four adjustments of stock drop and cast. The Compact's 26-inch barrel and synthetic stock and fore-end are covered with Realtree Max-4 camo.

Mossberg

Mossberg has partnered with compound bow maker Mathews to develop one of three parts to a new Recoil Reduction System included on seven Mossberg pump-action shotguns. The Mathews part of the system is the Harmonic Damper wheel, similar to the one Mathews puts on its bows to diminish limb and string vibrations. On the Mossberg shotguns, the wheel is positioned in the center of the stock, slightly forward of the recoil pad. Mossberg says the Damper "interrupts the recoil wave, while weights floating in an internal elastomer wheel absorb recoil vibrations." Low- and high-profile comb inserts and a new recoil pad are the other two parts of the system. The comb inserts are a wide two inches and attach to the stock with an Allen screw.

The low comb was just the right height to keep my cheek tight on the comb and my head erect, while aiming with the fiber optic sights on a

Mossberg Model 835 Ulti-Mag Turkey 12-gauge. The high insert raised the comb about 1½ inches, which would be the right height for a tight cheek weld, when aiming with a scope or red dot sight. A spongy and ventilated recoil pad caps off the stock.

I've shot several loads through a Model 835 Ulti-Mag Turkey 12 gauge with the Recoil Reduction System. The system fairly well soaked up the kick of regular 1⅛-ounce field loads. However, there was a substantial amount of kick generated by Winchester 3-inch 12-gauge turkey loads firing 1¾ ounces of shot. That's just the law of physics with any shotgun shooting a hat-full of powder and shot.

To determine if the Recoil Reduction System had softened the blow of those turkey loads, I also shot them through a Remington 870 Express pump with a hard rubber recoil pad. From the sitting position, the kick from three of those shells fired through the Remington made my teeth ache and my shoulder throb. Comparing the recoil of the two guns, the Recoil Reduction System did reduce recoil by the 20 percent Mossberg claims. The Damper wheel and recoil pad removed the sting of the recoil, and the thick comb allowed me to keep my head erect and cheek tight on the comb, preventing whiplash. The Mossberg Recoil Reduction System is

available on 835 Ulti-Mag and 535 ATS Turkey and Waterfowl 12-gauge 3½-inch pump guns, the Model 500 12-gauge 3-inch pump Field/Deer Two-Barrel Combo, and a special-purpose Tactical 6-Shot model.

Mossberg has also added two new finishes to some of its guns. Mossy Oak Shadow Grass Blades camouflage is available on six Waterfowl 12-gauge guns. They include the 835 Ulti-Mag, 535 ATS and 500 pumps, and 935 Magnum and 930 auto-loaders. Each gun has a 28-inch vent rib barrel with interchangeable ACCU-CHOKE F, M, and IC chokes tubes, as well as a front fiber optic bead and sling swivel studs. The 930 Special Purpose SPX 8-Shot is also covered with Coyote Tan finish.

Mossberg has greatly expanded its offerings of 20-gauge guns. The Mossberg line of Maverick 88 pumps is now available in a Youth 20-gauge with a 12-inch LOP, combined with a 22-inch barrel wearing a front bead sight. The Youth has the interchangeable ACCU-CHOKE system and comes equipped with a Modified tube. The Model 500 Cruiser/Persuader 8-Shot pump and SA-20 Field/Tactical auto-loader have a fixed Cylinder bore on their compact 20-inch barrels, ghost ring aperture sight, and a fiber optic winged front sight. The exposed metalwork has a non-reflective matte blue finish, while

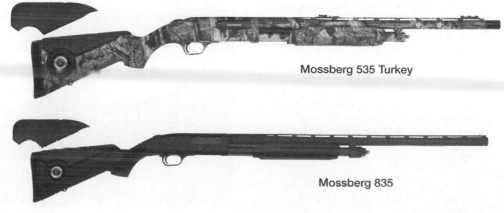

Mossberg 535 Turkey

Mossberg 835

Mossberg Silver II

Mossberg Maverick Youth

synthetic stocks and fore-ends feature a matte black finish. A receiver-mounted Picatinny rail provides for the addition of optics, while the magazine cap tri-rail allows for the attachment of accessories or lights. Completing these tactical shotguns are an eight-shot total round capacity, ambidextrous top-mounted safety, and sling swivel studs. The Model 500 8-Shot Bantam has a 13-inch LOP and a six-position adjustable stock.

The 500 FLEX Slugster 12-gauge pump continues Mossberg's FLEX system of three connectors that allow switching stocks, fore-ends, and recoil pads to address a variety of shooting situations, without the use of any tools. The Slugster has a four-position adjustable FLEX hunting stock in Mossy Oak camouflage that has two LOP adjustments and low and high comb inserts. The matte blue finish on the metalwork, sling swivel studs, and a six-round shell capacity complete the list of standard features.

Since Mossberg's Silver Reserve line was introduced, in 2005, the guns have grown into the Silver Reserve II, with 14 models of over/under design and four side-by-sides. The Silver Reserve II guns are available in 12-, 20-, and 28-gauge and .410-bore. All models feature checkered black walnut stocks and fore-ends, blued barrels, and polished silver-finished receivers with wrap-around engraving. Chrome-plated chambers and bores and tang-mounted safety/barrel selectors are standard. Choke tubes include C, IC, M, IM, and F for 12-, 20-, and 28-gauge and fixed chokes of M and F for the .410-bore.

Remington

Remington has expanded the utility of its VERSA MAX autoloader 12-gauge

The Mossberg Recoil Reduction System with the Mathews Harmonic Damper wheel helped soften the recoil of stout, 3-inch magnum turkey loads.

with a plain version, one for big-game, and a third for blasting the "reanimated dead." A special Model 1100 is also available to celebrate its fiftieth anniversary, and there is a new variation of its tactical 870 pump.

I shot targets and hunted waterfowl and pheasants last season with a VERSA MAX, and it never hiccupped once. But I pretty much left the Modified choke in the gun, never used the stock shim or LOP kit, or took off the barrel to store the gun in its hard case. The Sportsman is a gun for VERSA

MAX shooters like me, because this stripped-down version lacks all those extras and gets a $375 price tag. I shot the Sportsman with Remington Game Loads of an ounce of No. 7½ at 1,290 fps during a rabbit hunt in North Carolina, and the gun cycled every one of the shells. Several hundred Remington Target loads with an ounce of 7½ also cycled through the gun.

If I ever want to hunt big game with the Sportsman, Remington is now selling a 25-inch barrel with rifle sights. The VERSA MAX Zombie is designed

This is the left side of the receiver of the Remington Model 1100 50th Anniversary Limited Edition.

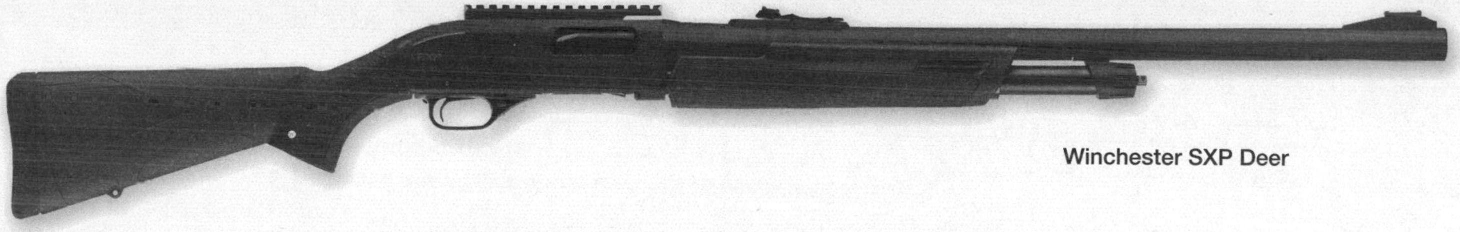

Winchester SXP Deer

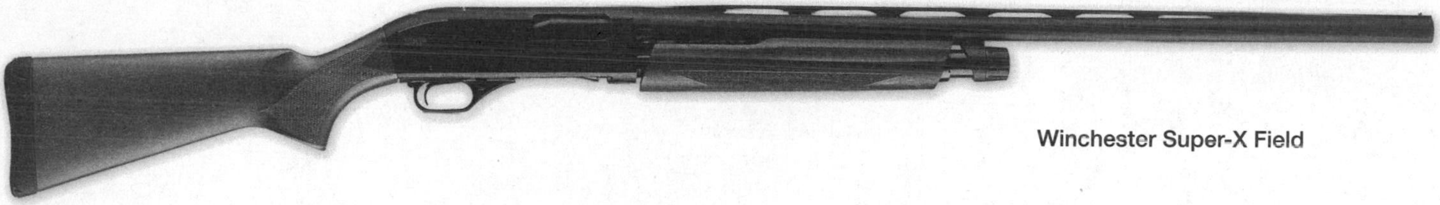

Winchester Super-X Field

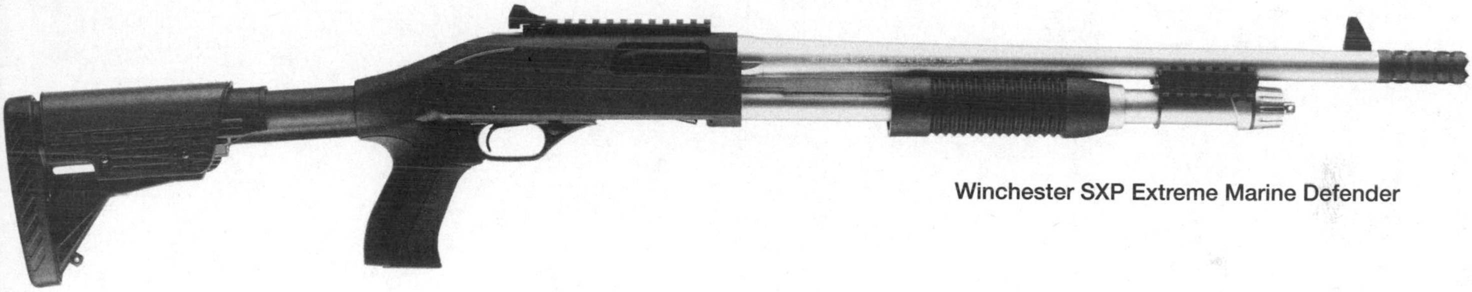

Winchester SXP Extreme Marine Defender

for 3-Gun shooting and zombie slayers. It has a 22-inch barrel with ProBore Tactical choke tube, Picatinny receiver, barrel clamp rails, and magazine extension that holds eight rounds.

The Model 1100 50th Anniversary Limited Edition features a machine-cut engraved receiver with a gold fill of birds and bird dogs similar to the two-millionth Model 1100 on display at Remington's Ilion, New York, museum. In addition, the receiver is numbered with a commemorative 1963 serial number prefix. The limited edition 12-gauge gun features a B-grade walnut stock with white diamond grip cap and white line spacers, and comes standard with a 28-inch vent rib barrel.

The Model 870 Express Tactical now has a Magpul SGA stock and MOE fore-end. The stock has spacers for LOP adjustment, a SuperCell recoil pad, and comb risers for use with optics and raised sights. The fore-end has an extended length and front and rear hand stops.

Stoeger

Stoeger is all about value, and its Model 3000 Waterfowl 12-gauge Inertia Driven autoloader costs about half as much as similar guns from its sister companies Franchi and Benelli. The Model 3000 Waterfowl has a synthetic stock and fore-end of black, Realtree APG, or Max-4 camo. Its 26- or 28-inch barrel has a red bar front sight and IC, M, and Extra Full turkey choke tubes. A shim kit is included to adjust stock drop, and the receiver is drilled and tapped to accept a Weaver-style optics base.

The Stoeger Longfowler 12-gauge guns hark back to waterfowling days of a century past. The Longfowler side-by-side and over/under models have walnut stocks and fore-ends that match, along with matte blued 30-inch barrels and receiver. Hardware includes a tang-mounted automatic safety, extended IC and M choke tubes, and a ventilated rib, with a front brass bead on the Longfowler over/under.

Winchester

Winchester has added a new camo pattern to a couple of its guns and worked over its Super X pumps. The Super X autoloader Waterfowl and Super X pump (SXP) Waterfowl 12-gauges have been covered with Mossy Oak Shadow Grass Blades camo. New SXPs include the Field with a checkered satin finished stock and fore-end and soft recoil pad. The diameter of the 12-gauge chrome-lined bore is a wide .742-inch, and it's backed by a three-inch chamber and IC, M, and F choke tubes. Black chrome protects the bolt and other metal parts. The trigger assembly drops out for easy maintenance.

The SXP Black Shadow Deer has a fully rifled 22-inch barrel, TRUGLO fiber optic front sight, and adjustable rear sight. A Picatinny rail on the receiver allows mounting of electronic and optical sights. The SXP Marine Defender has hard chrome plating on its barrel and magazine tube, chamber, and bore for protection from salt spray. The front brass bead can be covered with a bracket that holds a TRUGLO fiber optic pipe front sight. The Extreme Defender has an ATI Gunstocks vertical grip on a black composite stock, and its 18-inch barrel has a door breecher choke tube. A rear ghost ring sight is integrated into a Picatinny scope base, and an optional side-mounted Picatinny rail attaches lasers and lights.

In addition to its new Deluxe National Standard and Jones Deluxe variations, Cabot has added a totally new model called the American Joe. With unique engraving, this full-house custom beauty comes with special American flag grips.

Semi-Auto Pistols

BY **GARY PAUL JOHNSTON**

Beginning around 1,300 years ago, the first guns appeared, the prototypes of today's shotguns, handguns, and rifles. The etymology of the word "pistol," which arrived about the year 1550, is vague, but may have come from similar sounding words in German, Russian, and French, which referred to a small pipe or flute. Whatever the case, the term was applied to any and all handguns until the mid-nineteenth century, when the term "revolving pistol" came into use so as to differentiate between the (then modern) revolver and the handguns that did not have a revolving cylinder.

At the end of the nineteenth century, with the advent of the self-loading, magazine-fed pistol, revolvers began to be simply called revolvers, leaving all other handguns to be called pistols, the latter usually with an adjective in front, i.e., single-shot, double-barrel, and that newfangled one, the self-loading pistol. When, soon after, fully automatic pistols arrived on the scene, a more descriptive term emerged to categorize those

pistols that fired only one shot for each press on the trigger, and that term was "semi-automatic." Today, these guns are more commonly referred to as pistols with the term "semi-automatic" being generally understood.

All self-loading pistols (and other arms of semi-automatic mechanism), are gas operated, but how the gas is used further describes particular operations. The vast majority of today's semi-automatic pistols operate by simple blowback or short recoil.

In blowback, the breech is not mechanically locked, such as happens in .22 rimfire and .25, .32, and .380 centerfire pistols. Rather, it is only the mass of the slide and other recoiling parts and spring pressure that slows the opening of the breech until the bullet has left the muzzle.

Most pistols of larger calibers use a mechanical lock to keep the breech closed for a longer time after the gun is fired. In the vast majority, this operation is called "short recoil." As a subset, the type known as "Browning short recoil"

is the most common, with the more simplified versions referred to as "modified Browning short recoil." A few other pistols use "rotating barrel short recoil," such as is found with some European models. In any case, the barrel and slide (or bolt) recoil together for only a short distance before being unlocked, with kinetic energy completing the rearward travel of the slide. Although there are others, blowback and short recoil operating systems will remain the most common in semi-automatic pistols for the foreseeable future.

Various types of fire are used in semi-automatic pistols to include single-action-only, double-action-only, first shot double-action with successive shots single-action (DA/SA), and these can be hammer or striker fired. What's more, various safeties can be found that work automatically, manually, or both. None of these modes seems to be in preference over the others, but the revival of manual safeties is apparent.

The main materials used in semi-automatic pistols continue to be steel, aircraft quality aluminum, and polymer, with the last having taken a quantum leap in popularity since the success of the Glock pistol introduced three decades ago. We can expect to see this trend in pistols to continue, but let's look at some of the new ones for 2013.

ARMSCOR/ROCK ISLAND ARMORY

New for 2013 is a compact hi-capacity version of Armscor's 22 TCM (Tauson Craig Micromag), a variant of the model 1911 pistol that's chambered for an ultra high-velocity .22-caliber centerfire cartridge made from a necked-down 9mm case. Called the 22 TCM MS 1911 VZ, the new pistol is a Commander-sized compact with full-house features, including adjustable sights, and it has a frame rail for mounting lights and lasers. Also offered is a 9mm barrel to convert the gun to use the 9x19mm cartridge.

From Rock Island comes the TAC II, a five-inch 1911 in 10mm with a host of custom features. (www.us.armscor.com)

BOBERG

Boberg Arms has introduced its XR9 S, a variation of the company's XR9, but in two-tone, with a stainless steel slide and a black anodized receiver. Billed as the world's most powerful 9mm compact pistol, the XR9 is a hair over five inches long, with a 3¼-inch barrel and a 7+1 capacity of 9x19mm +P ammunition. The secret of the XR9 S is its unique feeding system, with the slide extracting rounds from the chamber and the rear of the magazine at the same time. (www.bobergarms.com)

CZ

CZ's new entry for 2013 is the P-09 Duty. A full-size version of the polymer frame P-07, the P-09 Duty has a capacity of 19+1 rounds of 9x19mm ammunition and used an Omega system and ambidextrous decocking levers that can be converted to thumb safeties with parts supplied. Three interchangeable backstraps come with the gun, and a 1913 frame rail is part of the package. Also new are variations of the CZ75 and CZ97 models. (www.czusa.com)

CABOT GUN COMPANY

The Cabot Gun Company's 2013 offerings include deluxe versions in its Jones and National Standard 1911 pistols, both of which sport two-micron mirror hand polishing, Novak Adjustable Sights, and deep double blue in the case of the Jones Deluxe. The Jones Deluxe features Sonoran Desert ironwood grips, while the National Standard Deluxe comes with polished mammoth ivory stocks. Cabot's totally new pistol is the "American Joe," a gorgeous 1911 inspired by rock star Joe Ferris and with unique engraving designed by him. This 420 stainless steel beauty features 20 lines per inch checkering on the frontstrap, three-dot Novak Adjustable Sights, alloy tri-star trigger, and custom designed aluminum American flag grips. (www.cabotguncompany.com)

CARACAL USA

Caracal's new pistol for 2013 is a .40-caliber with a 4.1-inch barrel and a 14-round magazine. Noted for sitting

Above: Firing Armscor's .22 TCM powerhouse cartridge in a new compact version of the company's 1911, it gets furnished with a 9x19mm conversion barrel.

Right: Complementing the longer Boberg XR9, this new micro-compact is one of the smallest 9x19mm pistols in the world.

CZ's new P-09 pistol is loaded with the right features, including ambidextrous controls.

extremely low in the hand, the Caracal is a double-action-only handgun from which most will find muzzle flip easier to control. (www.caracalusa.com)

CENTURY ARMS

Just announced from Century Arms are its newly imported GP K100 Mk7 and P1 Mk7 9x19mm pistols. Being issued to the Slovakian military, these pistols are from the Czech Republic. They employ 4140 steel components, a steel-reinforced, polymer GF-30 frame, and incorporate a rotating barrel locking system with a DA/SA firing mode and totally ambidextrous controls. Four interchangeable grip inserts ensure a fit for almost any hand. Measuring just under eight inches long, the full-size K100 Mk7 weighs 1.8 pounds, while the 7.4-inch P1 Mk7 tips the scale at 1.7. Both come with two 15-round magazines. (www.centuryarms.com)

COLT'S MFG. COMPANY, LLC

The big news from Colt is the winning of the U.S. Marine Corps contract for the new 1911 pistol. Called the "CQBP M45," this pistol is based on the Colt Rail Gun. Packed with features normally reserved for full-house custom 1911 pistols, this one comes with a unique reinforced frame rail, front and rear slide grasping grooves, a dual recoil spring/buffer system, Novak LoMount Night Sights, a desert tan finish, Wilson seven-round magazines, and G10 grips. On the left side of the slide are

the letters, U.S.M.C. The Colt Custom Shop is also offering a beautiful, exact recreation of the Colt Model of 1911, as made in 1912. (www.coltsmfg.com)

CYLINDER & SLIDE

Adding to its series of turn of the century-styled pistols is Cylinder & Slide's new/old inside-hammer C&L Automatic, complete with outside extractor and grip safety. A limited edition in .45 ACP, this pistol has characteristics of the Model 1905 Colt and its 1902 sibling in .38 Colt, but does not use the "parallel ruler" system of locking. C&L's not so limited new pistol is the .45 1911 Trident, a full-house gun with a ported slide, Novak adjustable sights, and much more. (www.cylinder-slide.com)

FNH-USA

Last year, FNH-USA introduced the FNS-9. A double-action 9mm polymer frame pistol, with a 17+1 capacity magazine, it was accompanied by the FNS-40 in, of course, .40 S&W. This year, FNH-USA introduces the FNS Combination Kit, which allows the user of either to switch caliber to the other. The kit includes a slide, barrel, spring, and magazine and comes in a soft-sided Cordura case. As an aside, the FNS-9 won the NRA's coveted NRA 2013 Golden Bullseye Award. (www.fnhusa.com)

GLOCK

The exciting news from Glock for 2013 is the new .45 ACP G30S Compact. Weighing just over 22 ounces, the G30S amounts to a G36 slide on a 30SF frame. Holding 10 rounds of .45 ACP ammunition, the G30S has a barrel just 3.78 inches long, with a total length under seven inches. The G30S even has a short frame rail, is comfortable in the hand, and is easy to conceal. With a muzzle velocity of 787 fps, this little .45 should prove formidable. (www.glock.com)

HECKLER & KOCH

This year, H&K offers a Compact Tactical Pistol for commercial sale. Based on the U.S. military H&K candidate pistol, this one has virtually all the same features, including a threaded barrel, interchangeable grip panels, and eight- or 10-round magazines. With an overall length of 7.91 inches, the H&K .45 Compact Tactical has a barrel 4.57

Glock's new G30S is the company's smallest .45 yet and holds 10+1 rounds of .45 ACP.

inches long and a weight of 1.82 pounds. A Mil-Spec frame rail is also standard. (www.hk.com)

KAHR ARMS

Kahr's new pistols for 2013 include the 380 CW, a micro-compact pistol with Kahr's super smooth double-action and an excellent grip just aggressive enough to hold onto. Also new is a Kahr P40, now with the welcome addition of an external thumb safety, and the same with night sights. (www.kahrarms.com)

KIMBER AMERICA

Kimber introduced several new superb pistols this year. They are the all black 9mm SOLO DC (Deep Cover), with DLC self-lubricating finishes, night sights, and optional laser grips. The new smooth 3-Gun .45 ACP Master Carry Series 1911 comes with a black slide and as a stainless frame Master Custom, or alloy frames on Master Pro and Ultra models, and all three have rounded heels (butts) and laser grips. Last, but far from least, is Kimber's new match grade Warrior SOC (Special Operations Capable). A five-inch rail gun designed for optimum performance under the worst conditions, the Warrior SOC comes with a Crimson Trace Rail Master Laser and tan and green KimPro II finish on the slide and frame, plus all of Kimber's custom grade 1911 features and beautiful G10 grips with a lanyard ring. (www.kimberamerica.com)

LION-HEART

A brand new company, Lion-Heart Industries, of Washington, is importing a unique new 9mm alloy frame variation of a system that made headlines three decades ago in the FN-Fast Action Pistol. Called the LH9, the gun resembles the S&W Model 59 (it will use M59 magazines), but has many changes, including its two-part hammer. With slide-cocking grooves fore and aft, the LH9 has a large, undercut trigger guard, external thumb safeties, and aggressive grips. Inside is a standard DA/SA system, but the gun can also be carried cocked and locked. Lastly, the cocked (outer) hammer can be pushed forward under a kickstand-type motion, where it and the trigger will remain. By pulling the trigger back about ³/₈-inch, the trigger and (outer) hammer overcome the détente and return to single-action, ready to be

Right: The FNS-9 (here) and FNS-40 from FNH-USA, introduced last year, is now offered with a combination kit that allows conversion from one caliber to the other.

Below: Kahr Arms' new 380CW is a great DA .380 ACP micro pocket pistol with an equally great trigger.

Below: Lion-Heart is a new company offering a 9mm pistol family with a unique firing system of DA/SA, SA cocked and locked, and hammer down semi-cocked. It is based on the FN-Fast Action pistol. A .40-caliber version is planned.

Left: Offered in 9mm, Para USA's Elite LS Hunter comes with a six-inch barrel, a frame rail, and fully adjustable sights.

Left: One of Para USA's many new three-inch Agent 1911s, this .45 ACP Executive Agent comes with a rounded butt and seven-round magazine.

Left: Para USA's Black Ops Combat .45 comes ready for tactical use, with a threaded muzzle and a frame rail.

Left: With a polished blue finish and rosewood grips, Remington's Carry 1911 .45 was meant for serious concealment.

fired. Or it can be manually returned forward. An LH9C (compact) and LH9R (rail) are also now being offered. (www.lionheartindustries.com)

EAGLE IMPORTS/METRO ARMS

From Eagle Imports/MAC come several new 1911 pistols, everything from concealed carry models to tactical types to competition guns. One meant for personal protection is the new .45 ACP BOBCUT, a Commander-style pistol with a rounded butt. Offered in stainless and blue, this gun comes with a number of custom features, including adjustable combat sights. Aimed at competition, the SPS Vista is a five-inch 1911 with a compensator, optical sight mounting system, adjustable sights, a 21-round capacity, and much more. Vista calibers include 9x19mm and .38 Super. (www.metroarms.com)

PARA USA

Para USA's 2013 1911 lineup can be described as nothing less than astounding, with 45 new models ranging from its new three-inch Executive Agent series (SA and LDA) to the PRO series, the Long Slide Hunter, and the revamped BlackOps models. One of the most appealing of this last is the BlackOps Recon, a tactical five-inch 1911 with frame rail, threaded muzzle, and extra high XS sights. (www.parausa.com)

REMINGTON

Remington's R1 1911 line continues to grow with the R1S, a stainless steel R1, high polished blue R1 Carry, and the R1 Enhanced with threaded muzzle, frame rail, and lots of custom tactical extras. (www.remington.com)

ROBAR

In addition to rendering the Glock pistol hardly recognizable, thanks to excellent forward slide cocking grooves, custom trigger, match accuracy, tritium combat sights, a tactical gripping surface, and other frame modifications, Robar now offers a simple grip angle conversion package with three inserts to force existing Glock pistols to point more naturally in different sized hands. (www.robarguns.com)

RUGER

Ruger introduced the new SR1911 Commander-style 1911 .45 pistol for 2013. With a 4.25-inch barrel, this new all stainless pistol measures eight inches overall, and tips the scale at 36.4 ounces, with all other features the same as its bigger SR45 brother. Also big news is Ruger's

Top: Remington's new Threaded Enhanced R1 .45 comes with a threaded stainless steel barrel, a frame rail, and XS High Sights. Above: Remington's new R1S is the company's R1 .45 1911 in all stainless steel.

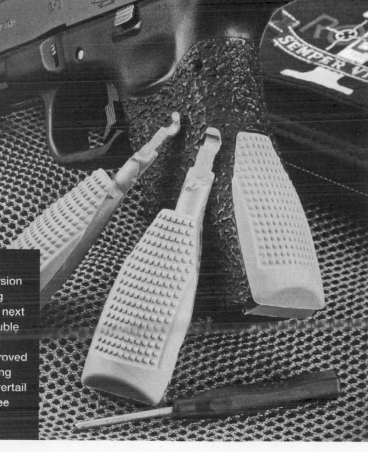

Robar's new Glock conversion takes existing pistols to the next level with double slide cocking grooves, improved sights, gripping surface, beavertail tang, and three backstraps.

LC380 pistol, a 7+1 round, six-inch pocket pistol with a 3.2-inch barrel at a hair over 17 ounces, but we're not done. Ruger also added an SR45 to that line. A polymer frame duty grade 10+ 1 .45 ACP, this one has a 4½-inch barrel and weighs just 30.2 ounces. Finally is a 22/45 family, with black hard-anodized upper receivers, and Mark III pistols with special target grips. (www.ruger.com)

SCCY

This year, SCCY has introduced the CPX-2, an all-black version of the CPX-1. A 9mm pocket pistol, the CPX-2 is a double-action-only weighing just five ounces with a 3.1-inch barrel and an overall length of 5.7 inches. With no external manual safety, the CPX-1 and CPX-2 pistols operate much like a double-action revolver, but with a capacity of 10+1 rounds. (www.sccy.com)

SIG SAUER

The days of SIG Sauer offering only a handful or two of semi-automatic pistols are long gone. Even those new for 2013 number far more than we could hope to illustrate here, but the two shown are showstoppers. In the 1911 world, SIG's new Spartan Model is a sight to behold. A tribute to that renowned group of warriors, this pistol is a full-house .45

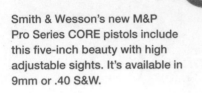

Smith & Wesson's new M&P Pro Series CORE pistols include this five-inch beauty with high adjustable sights. It's available in 9mm or .40 S&W.

The new Sphinx is an ultra-modern DAO 9mm with a combination alloy and polymer frame.

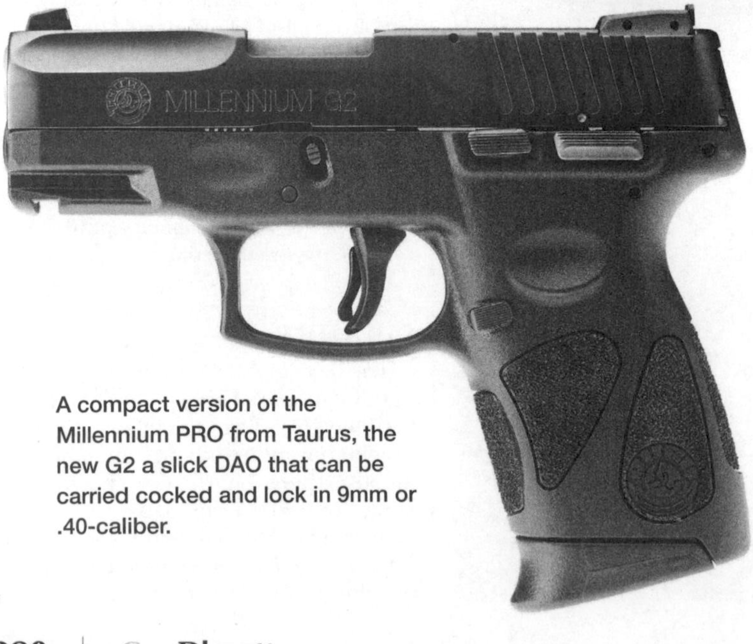

A compact version of the Millennium PRO from Taurus, the new G2 a slick DAO that can be carried cocked and lock in 9mm or .40-caliber.

ACP 1911 with an oil-rubbed Nitron finish and the words "Come and get them" in Greek inlaid with 24-karat gold. The same is seen on the Hogue Spartan Grips. The other new SIG pistol seen here is the P226 Elite SAO, a single-action, cocked and locked 9mm pistol with a beavertail tang, an accessory rail, and undercut trigger guard. It is an ideal choice in a duty 9mm. (www.sigsauer.com)

SMITH & WESSON

New 2013 pistols from Smith & Wesson include three versions of its also new Competition Optics Ready Equipment (C.O.R.E.) family of 9mm and .40 S&W semi-autos. Based on the S&W M&P plat-form, these Performance Center pistols are filled with enhancements to win in competition, including the use of a wide variety of optical sights. Included are 9mm and .40-caliber full-length models and a .40-caliber Compact.

Equally impressive are two new S&W Performance Center 1911 pistols, a five-inch barreled gun and a 4¼-inch model with a rounded butt, both with stainless steel slides and Scandium alloy frames. Featuring a fully adjustable rear sight and Novak LoMount Sights, respectively, these 1911s are packed with custom features including 30 lines per inch checkered front straps, ported lightening slide cuts, and beautiful G-10 grips. (www.smith-wesson.com)

SPHINX

The latest from this family of pistols is the 9mm Compact. Using the same CNC manufacturing as the Standard Model Sphinx, the Compact also employs a full-length, aircraft quality upper frame sec-tion, which is joined with a lower grip section made of glass-filled polymer. A DA/SA pistol, the Sphinx 9mm Compact, is hammer-fired with a decocker and has six internal safeties. It is 7½ inches long with a 3.7-inch barrel and weighs jut 27.5 ounces. A 15+1 magazine is standard, as are three backstraps and a frame frail. A threaded barrel is optional. (www.sphinxarms.com)

STI

Adding more 1911 pistols for 2013, STI has introduced two new series of three guns each. The Duty 1 and the Tactical SS families each come with five-, four-, and three-inch barrel models.

STEYR USA

Steyr now offers the latest and longest version of its Model M Pistol. Called the L9-A1, the new Steyr is about a ½-inch longer than the standard version and has a 17+1 capacity in 9mm, 12+1 in .40-caliber. Also new In this model is a loaded chamber indicator at the rear that can be felt while the pistol is holstered, a magazine release that is easily reversible from left to right, and front slide cocking grooves. The L9-A1 also comes with Steyr's instant locking mechanism, an all-steel frame module with full-length slide rails, and two sight options. (www.steyrusa.com)

TAURUS

The big news this year from Taurus is its Millennium G2. An updated version of the Taurus Millennium Pro, this 22-ounce compact pistol is a hair over six inches with a 3¼-inch barrel, and is offered in 9mm and .40 S&W, holding 12+1 and 10+1 rounds, respectively. Operating by double- and single-action, the Millennium G2 comes with high-profile adjustable sights, an aggressive grip texture, and a frame rail. As with others in this Taurus family, it can be carried cocked and locked via a subtle thumb safety. (www.taurususa.com)

USELTON ARMS

Uselton's new Commander-sized 1911 pistol is lighter than most, because of the Explosively Bonded Metal technology it uses. Initially aiming this system at the 1911 market, Uselton permanently bonds 303 stainless steel rails to aircraft aluminum or titanium alloy for strong and super smooth operation, while reducing the weight from 40 to 60 percent. The single frame gets made of two metals by explosive welding at the billet stage, having all precision machining operations done thereafter. The result is a frame that is far lighter than a steel frame, while still maintaining the strength and operating smoothness of steel. (www.useltonarms.com)

WALTHER

Walther's new pistols include the 9mm PPQM2 Series and the PPK/S .22. Upgraded from the existing PPQ pistols, the striker-fired Walther PPQM2 features a frame rail, ambidextrous magazine and slide releases, a tactical grip surface, and backstrap inserts for

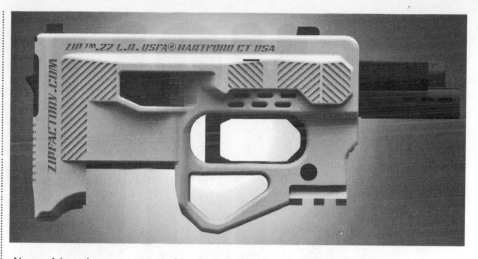

Above: A brand new company with a brand new pistol is ZIP Factory, which introduced the ZIP, a radical, modular .22 LR pistol system that uses Ruger 10/22 magazines.

Right: The newest PPK/S from Walther blends the iconic PPK design with the fun and cost savings of the .22 LR.

Left: The latest from Walther includes the PPQ Navy, a 15+1 9mm DAO pistol with fully ambidextrous controls and a threaded muzzle.

different hand sizes. A PPQ M2 Navy Model has also been added, this one with a threaded barrel. The PPK/S .22 is the traditional .22-caliber PPK in stainless steel. (www.waltheramerica.com)

ZIP FACTORY

A new pistol from an equally new factory is the primarily polymer ZIP .22, a totally out-of-the-box design with almost unlimited modularity. Looking like nothing you have seen short of Star Wars, the 5½-inch barreled ZIP .22 can be a pistol, an auxiliary under-barrel arm on an AR platform, or a survival SBR, all in one, and, yes, it can also be suppressed. Of simple blowback operation, the under-a-pound ZIP .22 will accept any Ruger 10/22 magazine and will shoot any .22 Long Rifle cartridge. A pistol of the future, it is manufactured by the company previously known mainly for it's fine single-action revolvers, U.S. Fire Arms. (www.usfirearms.com).

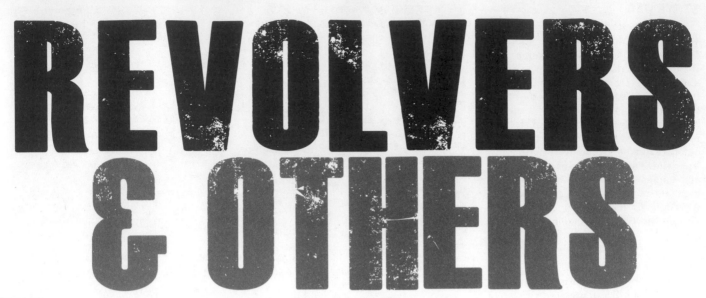

REVOLVERS & OTHERS

BY **Jeff Quinn**

As I hammer out this year's section of *Gun Digest* that covers the world of revolvers, many of our nation's leaders are working diligently to strip away from us our right to own firearms. Their activities are a mixed blessing for the gun industry. Firearms makers are running at full capacity, and it is not just the manufacturers of semi-automatic weapons struggling to keep pace with the demand created by the jeopardy of losing our Constitutional rights. Makers of revolvers and derringers are also running wide open, as more and more people who have never owned a gun are now choosing to enter the market, and those who already own guns are buying more.

For this year, we are seeing the introduction of a few new variations in the revolver market. The fastest-growing segment of the revolver and derringer market is geared towards defensive weapons. Both revolvers and derringers chambered for the .45 Colt/.410 shotshell combination are selling really well, as many people are coming to see the advantages of such a weapon for up close and personal-defense.

While on the national level and in a couple of our more liberal states gun rights are being threatened and infringed upon, still more and more jurisdictions now allow for concealed carry. In those jurisdictions, the drop in the crime rate reflects that trend. While most criminals are stupid, they are also street-wise, and knowing that a potential victim might be armed, they will usually go for an easier target.

The selection of suitable handguns to carry concealed seems to grow more everyday. Most gun manufacturers have one or several handguns that are small enough, light enough, and powerful enough for comfortable concealed carry, and holster makers are building some high-quality gear in which to carry the chosen weapons.

While many choose a semi-automatic weapon for concealed carry, the compact revolver still holds its own, with many knowledgeable citizens recognizing the advantages of a reliable revolver as a last-ditch fighting gun. While revolvers can break, it is a rare occurrence with a quality weapon. Of course, you've never heard of a revolver having a failure to feed or a cartridge case hang up halfway through its ejection cycle, for the obvious reasons. Another plus is that a revolver does not leave your empty brass lying on the ground, covered with your fingerprints, which may or may not cause a problem, depending upon the circumstances and location. Many of us choose revolvers for personal-defense for all these

The author with a Ruger Super Redhawk in .45 Colt

reasons and, while there are some good semi-autos that are used for hunting, most handgun hunters choose either a revolver or a quality single-shot, for their accuracy, power, and reliability.

Here, we're going to take a look at some of the better offerings in revolvers, derringers, and single-shot pistols available today. While modern revolvers now have capacities from five to 12 rounds in their cylinders, many do not feel at all under-gunned with a high-quality derringer that carries but two rounds of big-bore firepower. The mini-revolvers chambered for the .22 rimfire cartridges are also more popular than ever.

AMERICAN DERRINGER

American Derringer has been around for more than three decades now, and it makes quality derringers chambered for some serious cartridges well-suited for defense, whether from venomous snakes or other close-range vermin, or when applied for defense in a social situation that has turned sour. These derringers are relatively flat in profile, carry well concealed, and offer two quick shots when needed. Many chamberings are available, including .22 LR, .22 Magnum, .32 H&R Magnum, .38 Special, .357 Magnum, 9mm Luger, .40 S&W, 10mm Auto, .44 Special, .44-40, .45 ACP, .45 Colt, and .45 Colt/.410 shotshell.

AMERICAN WESTERN ARMS

AWA is best known for its line of 1873 single-action revolvers, which are excellent Colt's replicas. Offered in the most popular chamberings and barrel lengths, the AWA line consists of its Classic revolvers, made very much like the sixguns of the late nineteenth century, and its Ultimate series, with upgraded coil springs and various stock options. AWA has also added an octagon-barreled version of the 1873. These revolvers have a reputation for smooth actions and quality production. AWA also has its pump-action, tubular magazine Lightning bolt handgun, similar to the lever-action Mare's Leg style pistols on the market, but using a sliding forearm to cycle the action.

BERETTA

Beretta has been cranking out some very good looking Old West-style firearms for a few years now, since its corporate acquisition of Uberti. Building upon the quality firearms produced by that firm, Beretta markets its Single Action Army replicas with some high-grade finishes like a brilliant carbona-type blue, along with authentic looking case coloring and an antique finish that makes the gun appear to be an original gun from the late nineteenth century. Beretta adds a transfer bar safety system to its revolvers, which allows the firearm to be carried fully loaded with a live cartridge under the hammer, unlike the original 1873 single-action, which should be safely carried with an empty chamber under the hammer. Beretta offers not only the 1873 Single Action Army style, but a modified Bisley style sixgun, as well. One of my personal favorites is the Stampede Marshall, which has a Thunderer-style bird's head grip frame. Beretta revolvers are chambered for either the .357 Magnum or .45 Colt cartridge.

BOND ARMS

Bond Arms has been producing high-quality two-shot derringers for several years now and seems to have reached the apex in derringer design. Its derringers are often regarded as the best money can buy, and Bond offers an extensive variety of chamberings, from .22 LR up through .45 Colt/.410 shotshell, and covering many popular cartridges in between. Bond derringers are built primarily of stainless steel and exhibit first-class craftsmanship built upon quality materials. My personal favorite is the Snake Slayer. I have one I carry often. Besides its intended use against venomous reptiles, it is also a fine personal-defense arm for use against carjackers and other two-legged predators. Loaded with 000 buckshot or Winchester's new PDX1 buck and bird-shot load, it would be a very effective close-range defensive weapon.

The Bond Arms derringers offer a lot of versatility, with the barrels being interchangeable, so one can switch calibers as needed. Bond has recently changed the design of its hammer and trigger, resulting in a much better feel for many shooters. Bond Arms also offers some high-quality leather holsters in which to carry its derringers. I particularly like the horizontal driving holster. It is ideal to wear while riding in a vehicle, ATV, or on a motorcycle, as it places the handgun within easy reach for a fast and comfortable draw. The Bond derringers are all made in Texas, and are arguably the finest of their type ever built.

CHARTER ARMS

Charter Arms built its reputation upon providing useful gun designs that are affordable for the common man. I have many times relied upon a Charter revolver for various needs, mostly a .38 Special that rides in a boot or pocket for protection, or at other times

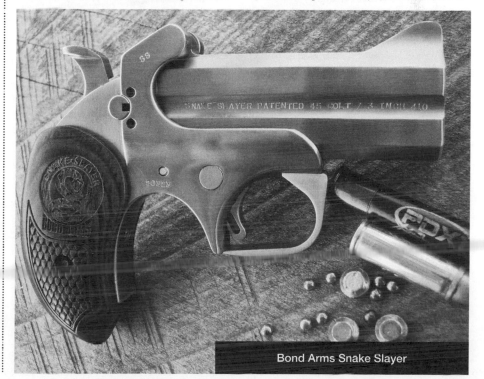

Bond Arms Snake Slayer

packed in the handy little Pathfinder rimfire variation as a trail gun, while I bum around in the woods. The Charter revolvers are available in blued steel or stainless, and more recently the company has added alloy frames to the lineup for those who want to carry the lightest possible package. Charter also has many different finishes available on its aluminum-framed revolvers. These are made in a variety of colors, and the pink finish has proven to be extremely popular with women in Charter's Pink Lady five-shot .38.

In addition to its small and medium-bore revolvers, Charter still builds the legendary .44 Special Bulldog five-shot revolvers. These powerful belly guns fill a needed niche in the market, as they have for the past few decades. The Bulldog is lightweight and easy to conceal, yet carries five .44 Special rounds. Recoil is stiff with heavy loads, but not really painful. These blued or stainless steel revolvers are not much bigger than a compact .38 Special, but pack a more powerful punch.

In addition to its popular .38 Special and .44 Special revolvers, Charter still has the Pathfinder rimfire line in .22 LR or .22 Magnum, along with revolvers chambered for the .32 H&R Magnum, .327 Federal Magnum, and .357 Magnum. Charter also makes a true left-handed snubnose revolver called the Southpaw. The Southpaw is a mirror image of the standard revolver design, but the cylinder latch is on the right side; the cylinder swings out to the right, as well. Charter currently lists 70 variations of its compact revolvers, suiting just about anyone looking for a reliable revolver.

CHIAPPA

The Chiappa Rhino is a very unique sixgun that fires its cartridges from the bottom of the cylinder, resulting in a lower bore axis in relation to the shooter's hand and, thus, greatly reduced muzzle jump upon firing. Much like the Mateba in design, the Rhino is more compact. I have had the opportunity to fire one on several occasions, and its feel and handling are like no other. Available with various barrel lengths, the Rhino appears to be well crafted of quality materials. It certainly has a very unconventional appearance, but feels really good in my hand and does exhibit much less muzzle jump than does a conventional revolver of like chambering.

CIMARRON FIREARMS

Cimarron Firearms, in Fredericksburg, Texas, has been at the forefront of marketing quality replicas of Old West-style rifles and handguns for many years, focusing its efforts upon some of the best quality firearms available. Of interest here is its extensive line of authentically reproduced, historic sixguns. Cimarron has not only 1873 Single Action Army replicas, the company also delves into the lesser known but historic firearms of the nineteenth century. There are replicas of most of the major players in the cap-and-ball sixgun business of that era, such as the Walker, Dragoon, and Army and Navy guns, as well as the Remington, and even the Leech & Rigdon guns. Cimarron covers the transition from cap-and-ball to cartridge, with its conversion revolvers and the 1872 Colt replica. The company also

markets the Remington 1875 and 1890 cartridge revolvers, and a variety of the Smith & Wesson break-open sixguns like the Russian and Schofield models.

Besides these authentic single-action replicas, Cimarron has a selection of two-shot derringers. They are small and easily concealed and chambered for the .22 LR and Magnum rimfire cartridges, as well as .32 H&R Magnum and. 38 Special.

The .22 LR and .22 Magnum Plinkerton revolvers are priced to get most anyone into the single-action revolver game. These guns are built from a non-ferrous alloy, but have steel-lined chambers and barrel. They shoot surprisingly well. When I first handled the Plinkerton and looked at the low price, I wasn't expecting much in the way of performance, but was surprised to find the sixgun was both reliable and accurate.

COBRA

Cobra Firearms, of Utah, manufactures some small and reliable two-shot single-action derringers. These compact guns are made in .22 LR, .22 Magnum, .38 Special, 9mm Luger, .25 Auto, .32 Auto, .380 Auto, and .32 H&R magnum. The Titan model is built of stainless steel and is offered in 9mm Luger or .45 Colt/.410 shotshell. These derringers are available in a variety of colors, and each sells at an affordable price. Cobra also has its line of Shadow +P-rated, five-shot .38 Special revolvers. These revolvers have a concealed hammer and look very much like a Smith & Wesson model 642. They have stainless cylinders and barrels and an aluminum frame, for a weight of 15 ounces.

COLT'S MFG. CO., LLC

Colt has been producing revolvers for more than 175 years, now. In fact, if it were not for Sam Colt, we might not have revolvers. His first successful design, the Paterson, set the stage for all revolvers that have followed. That design, though it worked pretty well, was delicate and underpowered, but it led to the big Walker Colt, which packed a lot of punch and set the company on its way to success. Through the years, Colt has produced some very good revolver designs, but today makes only single-actions, those being the Single Action Army and New Frontier. The SAA is probably the most recognized

Colt New Frontier

handgun in the world and is certainly the most copied revolver design ever produced. Colt still produces the SAA, and the latest sixguns it's been shipping for the past few years are as good as any Colt has ever produced. Available in three barrel lengths—4¾, 5½, and 7½ inches—the Single Action Army is chambered in a choice of .357 Magnum or .45 Colt, with other calibers available through the Custom Shop. The SAA is available in blued/case-hardened or nickel finishes. Through the Colt Custom Shop, many options are available, such as non-standard barrel lengths and hand engraving.

Colt's adjustable sight New Frontier in production again, after being absent from the line for a few years. The New Frontier revolver was originally introduced by Colt, in 1961, and was a very special sixgun, similar to the Single Action Army, but with a flat-topped frame and fully adjustable rear sight. With its deep bluing on the barrel, trigger guard, cylinder, and grip frame contrasting nicely with the case-hardened frame, the New Frontier is a very elegant and useful single-action sixgun. The New Frontiers are offered chambered in either .44 Special or .45 Colt, in the same barrel lengths as the SAA.

EUROPEAN AMERICAN ARMORY

EAA produces the double-action Windicator revolver chambered for the .38 Special cartridge with an alloy frame, or an all-steel .357 Magnum version. These revolvers are compact and feature a synthetic rubber grip and a business-like matte blue finish, with a choice of two- or four-inch barrels. EAA's line of Single Action Army replica revolvers are called the Bounty Hunters. These sixguns are available chambered for the .22 LR and Magnum cartridges and come with an alloy frame and a choice of six- or eight-shot cylinders. Larger centerfire sixguns are chambered for the .357 and .44 Magnums, as well as the .45 Colt.

These centerfire sixguns are built with all-steel frames in a choice of nickeled, blued, or case-hardened finishes. They have the traditional half-cock loading feature, but with a modern transfer bar safety action that permits carrying the guns fully loaded.

FREEDOM ARMS

Freedom Arms, of Freedom, Wyoming, is best known for its fine, sturdy, and super-accurate revolvers. A Freedom Arms revolver is tough. It is built to very close tolerances, but can also take a lot of abuse. Chambered for such powerful rounds as the .454 Casull, .475 Linebaugh, and .500 Wyoming Express, these revolvers will withstand a lot more punishment than most shooters can endure. They are meticulously fitted and finished to perfection. The chambers in the cylinder are precisely aligned with the bore, and every detail of these firearms follows the same precise standard of quality.

The large-frame Model 83 is the flagship of the Freedom Arms line and is chambered for the aforementioned cartridges, as well as the .22 LR and the .357, .41, and .44 Magnums. They are available with either fixed or adjustable sights, and the adjustable sight guns will also accept a variety of scope mounts.

The Model 97 is Freedom's compact single-action revolver. Built to the same tight tolerances as the Model 83, the Model 97 is a bit handier to carry all day. It is chambered for the .17 HMR and .22 LR or Magnum rimfires, as well as the .327 Federal, .357 Magnum, .41 Magnum, .44 Special, and .45 Colt centerfire cartridges. In addition to these, the Model 97 is also available in Freedom Arms own .224-32 cartridge, which is a fast-stepping .22 centerfire based on the .327 Federal cartridge case.

There have been several very good single-shot pistols on the market for years, but the one from Freedom Arms is the only one built like a Freedom Arms revolver. I've fired a couple

chambered in the 6.5x55 and 6.5 JDJ (non-standard) cartridges, as well as one chambered for the .375 Winchester. Current chamberings offered are the .223 Remington, 6.5 Swede, 7mm BR, 7mm-08, .308 Winchester, .357 Magnum, .357 Maximum, .338 Federal, .375 Winchester, .260 Remington, .454 Casull, and .45-70 Government. Standard barrel lengths are 10, 15, or 16 inches, depending upon the caliber chosen, but non-standard lengths are available for a nominal cost.

What makes this single-shot so comfortable to shoot is the single-action revolver grip style. Shooting the pistol allows the gun to recoil comfortably, with none of the pain to the hands that's encountered with other single-shots. The barrels are interchangeable, with extra fitted barrels available from Freedom Arms, allowing the shooter to switch among any of the available barrel and caliber options all on one frame. The Model 2008 weighs in around four pounds, depending upon barrel and caliber chosen. The barrel is drilled for a Freedom Arms scope mount, and the scope stays with the barrel, allowing the exchange of the barrels without affecting the sight adjustment.

HEIZER DEFENSE

The Heizer Double-Tap two-shot pistol is on hold at the time of this writing, but the company is working on getting production set up very soon for this unique pistol.

HENRY REPEATING ARMS

Henry Repeating Arms is well known for its American-made rifles, and it now has its version of a Mare's Leg lever-action pistol in production, chambered for the .22 LR cartridge. These are a very affordable alternative, both to own and to shoot, compared to the centerfire lever-action pistols available. Made like other Henry firearms, these pistols are very reliable and easy to operate.

Henry Repeating Arms Mare's Leg

LEGACY SPORTS

Legacy Sports is best known for its Howa and Puma rifles, but it also has an entry into the popular Mare's Leg market, with its Bounty Hunter Model 92 lever-action pistol. The Bounty Hunter resembles a sawed-off Model 92 lever-action rifle, but is built from the start as a pistol, so it needs no special NFA tax stamp. It can be purchased just like any other pistol and has become quite popular for its nostalgic appeal, as well as its reliable function and accuracy. Legacy also markets a couple good holster rigs for the Mare's Leg, these made by Bob Mernickle exclusively for Legacy Sports. The holster and belt combo is a beautiful rig and a necessary addition to the Bounty Hunter, completing the nostalgic package.

Legacy has a series of 1873 Colt replica sixguns called the Puma Westerners. These are reliable and well-built sixguns, chambered for the .357 Magnum, .44 WCF, and .45 Colt cartridges, with 4¾-, 5½-, or 7½-inch barrels. They are offered with a blued and case hardened finish with walnut grips, nickel finish with walnut grips, or with a stainless finish and white synthetic ivory grips. The Puma family also includes a line of very affordable single-action replica sixguns chambered for the .22 LR and .22 Magnum cartridges.

MAGNUM RESEARCH

Magnum Research, of Minneapolis, has been producing its quality BFR revolvers for many years now. These robust single-actions are built for hunting the largest, most dangerous game on the planet. Now owned by Kahr, Magnum Research continues to build these quality handguns, which are chambered for powerful rounds such as the .44, .454, .460, and .500, as well as rifle cartridges like the .45-70 Government. The BFR is also available chambered for the popular .45 Colt/.410-bore shotshell combination, which offers a lot of versatility in a handgun.

NORTH AMERICAN ARMS

The North American Arms mini-revolvers are well established in the market place, having been in production for a long time now, but today they seem more popular than ever. These little five-shooters are more often than not bought as deep-concealment handguns. The lightweight firearms are small enough to fit into most any pocket and are handy enough to always be with you, no matter what the attire or climate. Chambered for the .22 Short, .22 LR, or .22 Magnum cartridges, these little jewels are easy to carry and surprisingly accurate within their intended range. The newest is called the Sidewinder, which features a swing-out cylinder, a new feature in an NAA revolver. The Sidewinder is quicker to load and unload than the other revolvers in the NAA line and is a dandy little revolver to carry when nothing larger can be concealed, or as a backup to a primary sidearm.

ROSSI

Rossi still has its line of reliable and affordable revolvers chambered for the .38 Special and .357 Magnum cartridges. These are available in both blued carbon steel and stainless steel. The very popular Rossi Ranch Hand is a lever-action Mare's Leg resembling a sawed-off Winchester Model 92 carbine and is available in .357 Magnum, .44 WCF (.44-40), and .45 Colt. These are slick-operating pistols, and while not as concealable as Rossi's revolvers, are a lot of fun to shoot.

RUGER

Sturm, Ruger & Company builds some of the strongest and most reliable revolvers available today. Starting back in 1953, with the Single-Six rimfire revolvers, Ruger built upon the single-action line to include the Blackhawk and Super Blackhawk centerfire sixguns. For a short time, there was a single-shot pistol that resembled the Blackhawk. Called the Hawkeye, it was chambered for the .256 Winchester Magnum cartridge and used a unique rotating breech block. That one is long gone, and the Hawkeye is quickly scarfed up by collectors, when they appear for sale today. However, the Single-Six and Blackhawk lines are still running strong, and new for this year is a dandy little version of the Bearcat rimfire revolver, the Shopkeeper. It is a stainless steel Bearcat with a bird's head grip and a three-inch barrel. The Shopkeeper also has a unique button head base pin, and a crescent ejector rod button that allows the easy removal of the cylinder, without having to remove the ejector rod housing. It is a fun little sixgun that carries on the hip easily, serving as a wonderful little plinker or trail gun.

Joining the popular Single-Ten .22 LR revolver introduced last year, the new Single-Nine is the .22 Magnum version of that reliable handgun and, as the name implies, holds nine rounds of .22 Magnum ammunition.

The GP-100 has proven itself for many years, selling in large numbers since its introduction, in 1986, and continues on with no major changes, serving as one of the best double-action .357 Magnum revolvers on the market. Moving up in size a bit is the Ruger Redhawk, cham-

North American Arms Sidewinder

bered for the .44 Magnum and .45 Colt cartridges. The Redhawk is bull-strong and as reliable as an anvil. Though it has been around for more than 30 years, I have never seen a worn-out Redhawk. They can withstand a lifetime of shooting and never miss a beat.

At the top of the heap, at least in size, is the Super Redhawk, chambered for the .44 Magnum and the .454 Casull cartridges, as well as Ruger's own .480 Ruger. The .454 can also chamber and fire .45 Colt cartridges and is a very versatile handgun. Built for hunting, the Super Redhawk comes supplied with scope mounts and is a superb choice for hunting large game with teeth and claws.

At the other end of the size scale, Ruger introduced the polymer-framed LCR five-shot .38 Special revolver a few years ago, and it has met with great success. Newest of the LCR chambering is the .22 Magnum, which offers good penetration with very little recoil.

SMITH & WESSON

Smith & Wesson has been in the revolver business for more than 150 years. No longer producing any single-action revolvers, S&W is probably the most prolific producer of double-action revolvers in the world. From the .22 LR up through the formidable .500 Smith & Wesson Magnum, with only a couple of exceptions, if a revolver cartridge exists, chances are S&W has at least one revolver chambered for it.

The small, five-shot J-frame .38 Special revolvers are some of the most popular self-defense guns ever produced, and remain so today. The Model 642 is probably the best-selling revolver in the S&W line. It is a compact, reliable, five-shot revolver with a concealed hammer and a lightweight frame. One is easily slipped into the pocket, where it rides comfortably day in and day out, ready for action when needed. While not the first choice of a handgun I'd take if headed for a fight, I often carry a lightweight .38 Smith in my pocket. It can simply be placed there and forgotten, but is always ready should an unpleasant social conflict need resolution.

Moving up in size, the S&W K- and L-frame revolvers are the mainstay of the Smith & Wesson duty line. These revolvers have served well for generations of sixgun users, both for defense and hunting.

The larger N-frame guns are the epitome of what a Smith & Wesson

Top: Ruger Bearcat Shopkeeper

Middle: Ruger Bisley Super .44 Magnum

Left: Ruger LCR .22 Magnum

revolver should be. The classic Models 27 and 29 are back in the lineup, beautiful and functional examples of the timeless double-action revolver. Large but well-balanced, these .357 and .44 Magnum sixguns define the double-action revolver to many shooters, with crisp single-action trigger pulls and butter-smooth double-action take-ups, they are reliable and accurate.

Moving up again in size to the X-frame, we find the most powerful double-action revolvers ever produced. The .460 and .500 S&W Magnums are at the upper limits of what most would ever consider possible in a handheld revolver. Several years ago, the .44 Magnum was considered to be the upper limit of what could be handled in a revolver, but, today, it pales in comparison to the power of the .460 and .500 Magnums. These big S&W Magnums are powerful enough to take any game animal on earth.

TAURUS

Taurus USA imports what are still probably the hottest-selling revolvers on the planet in the many iterations of the Taurus Judge. Folks have really taken to these versatile handguns. They are available in all-steel or lightweight versions, with two, three, or six-inch barrels, depending upon the model chosen. Available chambered for the 2½- or three-inch .410 shotshells (including slugs), they'll also chamber the .45 Colt cartridge. These are

formidable close-range defensive weapons. I really like the .410 personal-defense loads sold by Winchester, Hornady, and Federal. These loads are tailor made for the Judge series of handguns and are very effective for "social work." My personal favorite of the Taurus Judge line is the Public Defender, which has a short barrel and a polymer frame, making for a relatively lightweight and compact package.

Taurus has many different revolvers available for concealed carry, target shooting, or hunting, from small, lightweight pocket revolvers up through the .454 Raging Bull. Its small-frame snubnose revolvers are available chambered for the .22 LR, .22 Magnum, .32 H&R, .327 Federal, .38 Special, and .357 Magnum calibers. They are available in blued, nickel, or stainless finishes, mostly with fixed sights, but a couple have fully adjustable rear sights. Duty-sized four- and six-inch .357 Magnum revolvers are still in production, with many models available. The Raging series of hunting handguns chamber powerful cartridges like the .44 Magnum and. .454 Casull and are good choices for dangerous game.

TAYLOR'S & COMPANY

Taylor's is an importer of nostalgic replica firearms and has some very good handgun offerings. Its 1873 Colt SAA replicas consistently display qual-

Taurus Judge 451

Taurus SF 380

ity workmanship and smooth actions. Taylor's has several variations of both cartridge and cap-and-ball revolvers, including Remington- and Smith & Wesson-pattern firearms. They also have bird's head and open-top sixguns, and all exhibit excellent fit and finish.

THOMPSON/CENTER

Thompson/Center is responsible for making the single-shot hunting pistol popular. Starting with the Contender model decades ago, T/C pistols have evolved into the Encore and Contender G2 designs, though both are really just improvements and refinements of the original Contender. They are offered in just about any chambering one would want, from .22 Long Rifle up through powerful rifle cartridges such as the .45-70 Government, as well as all the magnum handgun cartridges, including the .460 and .500 S&W Magnums. Thompson/Center offers wooden and synthetic stocks and a variety of barrel lengths. The barrels are interchangeable within the same frame group, and these hand-rifles come pre-drilled for scope mounts.

UBERTI

Uberti Firearms has been producing quality replicas of nineteenth-century

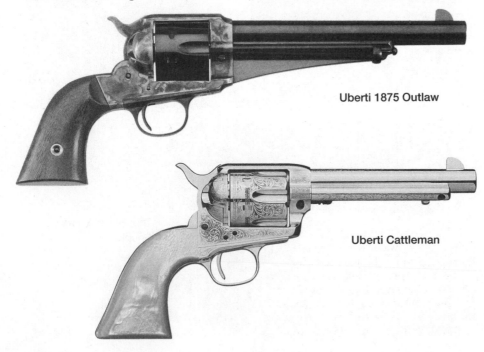

Uberti 1875 Outlaw

Uberti Cattleman

American firearms for decades. While manufacturing replica rifles and handguns for other companies such as Beretta (Uberti's parent company) and Cimarron, Uberti also markets its own line of replica firearms and has a variety of revolvers.

The Cattleman series replicates the Colt Single Action Army design and includes the Callahan Model chambered for .44 Magnum. This Magnum is offered with original-style fixed sights or as a flat-top style with adjustable target sights. In addition to the Callahan, Uberti has three 1873-style sixguns chambered for the .45 Colt, .357 Magnum, and .44 WCF (.44-40) cartridges. Finish options run from a standard blued/case hardened to nickel and even a bright charcoal blue finish.

The Uberti Stallion is a slightly scaled-down version of the Single Action Army and is chambered in a choice of six-shot .22 LR or .38 Special, or a 10-shot .22 LR. There are also Bisley and bird's head grip models. Uberti has fans of the old Remington revolvers covered, too, with its Outlaw, Police, and Frontier models that replicate the 1875 and 1890 Remington revolvers.

Uberti has several variations of the S&W top-break revolver, including the Number 3 Second Model and the Russian, in both nickel and blued finishes, as well as fully hand engraved models. These are available in .38 Special, .44 Russian, and .45 Colt chamberings.

Last, Uberti has not forgotten the fans of the early cap-and-ball sixguns, offering authentic replicas of the Colt and Remington cap-and-ball revolvers.

U.S. FIRE ARMS

USFA of Hartford, Connecticut, for many years has manufactured some very good examples of what a quality single-action revolver should be, but it saddens me to report the company is no longer in the revolver business, leaving Colt as the sole U.S. maker of the true Single Action Army revolvers.

CUSTOM CRAFTSMEN

Along with the manufacturers of quality revolvers, single-shots, and derringers listed above, there are several very good gunsmiths in the U.S. gifted at building high-quality revolvers for those who demand the very best.

David Clement's JQ Special

Dustin Linebaugh's Custom Ruger Vaquero .500

Dustin Linebaugh's Custom .500 I-Frame Redhawk

Starting with a base gun, such as a Ruger Blackhawk or Redhawk, these talented gunsmiths can and do build remarkable examples of the gunmaker's art, with limits upon what can be achieved dictated only by imagine and the customer's wealth. Craftsmen such as David Clements, Hamilton Bowen,

Jim Stroh, Ben Forkin, Alan Harton, John and Dustin Linebaugh, and others create, modify, and blueprint revolvers to the customer's specifications. If a revolver exists only in your mind, chances are very good that one of these men can build it for you.

The author bathed in early morning light on a North Carolina swan hunt, on Bodie Island.

MUZZLE LOADERS

BY WM. HOVEY SMITH

Muzzleloading manufacturers have continued to make significant improvements to their products. CVA has upgraded the mechanisms of its popular Optima rifles and pistols, new fouling and rust-resistant coatings have been applied by Knight Rifles, and several companies have produced lighter-weight guns using advanced materials.

Self-Defense Guns

It's bad if you're an old guy and have only one ball and lose it. It's worse if you also have a loose screw, and it's terrible if you are a young blunderbuss out to kill its first big game and suffer both afflictions. These were among the events that occurred, as I attempted to use nineteenth-century self-defense guns in the field.

A large variety of blackpowder guns were used for self-defense, including some patterns that now appear strange to modern users; man's inventive instincts provided not only the ancestors to the modern revolvers and derringers, but also items like the Duckfoot pistol and blunderbuss.

Field testing was possible, because kit guns were available for the three-barreled Duckfoot pistol from Dixie Gun Works, and Sportsman's Guide offered a new blunderbuss made by Traditions. Obtaining sample revolvers was a simpler process. The Italian firm of Pietta has sold a 5½-inch barreled version of its 1858 .44-caliber Remington revolver for years, and I was always attracted to Uberti's 5½-inch .36-caliber 1862 Pocket Police imported by Cimarron. I

chose these revolvers as representative civilian guns. Davide Pedersoli also introduced a replica .45-caliber Derringer last year, and I borrowed one of these from Dixie Gun Works.

I am a hunter. If I am going to own a gun, I likely will hunt with it, although I could not conceive of hunts for the derringer and Duckfoot pistols. However, the blunderbuss and revolvers went into the woods with me.

DAVIDE PEDERSOLI DERRINGER

When tried against a "zombie" pizza deliveryman target, the derringer, loaded with 20 grains of GOEX FFFg blackpowder and a patched round ball, shot one foot high and six inches left at 10 yards. Compensating, I managed to put five shots in the target's head zone using a two-handed hold. This load

The Duckfoot pistol with its three splayed barrels was more useful as a gun of intimidation than as a practical arm.

developed 433 fps and had 53 ft-lbs of energy, similar to the .41 rimfire used in the Remington Double Derringer.

THE DUCKFOOT PISTOL

Such guns were made during the late 1700s and early 1800s and sold to sea captains who might have to face down a mutinous crew. The pistol's barrels were splayed like a duck's three toes and, so, the name stuck. This is a pistol-sized variety of the volley gun, which has multiple barrels that are simultaneously discharged.

I shot the gun with its recommended load of 12 grains of FFFg blackpowder and patched .350 round balls loaded in each barrel. The Duckfoot was/is best used against a single opponent at ranges of less than 10 yards with the barrels held vertically, so that an adversary might be caught by all three balls. This would not be instantly disabling, but could surprise one to the extent that you might escape. The Duckfoot was more effective as a weapon of intimidation; in past centuries, even a small-diameter round ball in the body's midsection meant a lingering death.

I fired this gun loaded with a total of 33.6 grains of GOEX FFFg, and a combined weight of 192 grains of lead flying from its three barrels. At 10 yards, no hits registered on a target that was three feet high and nine feet long. Cutting the range in half and holding the barrels vertically, two shots hit the target, those hits having about a foot of vertical displacement. One word of caution is needed here, about shooting low-powered pistol loads: balls may return to hit the shooter if the projectile impacts a hard object or wood plank. Always shoot these guns against a soft backstop.

CIVILIAN PERCUSSION REVOLVERS

Remington's 5¾-inch 1858 .44 revolver and Colt's 5½-inch 1862 Pocket Police offer, respectively, six and five rapid-fire shots that have the potential of being more precisely aimed than those from the Duckfoot, and either of these guns is better suited for holster carry. My Pocket Police could not be contained in any but the largest pocket. It had the advantage of weighing a pound less than the Remington .44.

Initial shooting revealed a poorly fitted barrel wedge in the Uberti-made Pocket Police, and the gun was returned to Cimarron Arms for repair. No problems were found with the Traditions (Pietta) .44. I widened the narrow rear sight with a Dremel tool and lowered the front site for more precise shot placement. After initial shooting with 37 grains of GOEX FFFg blackpowder and a .454 round ball that produced 160 ft-lbs of muzzle energy (about the same as a .38 Special), it was time to take it hunting.

The gun's first use was as a back-up pistol in conjunction with CVA's .50-caliber Optima pistol. A shot with

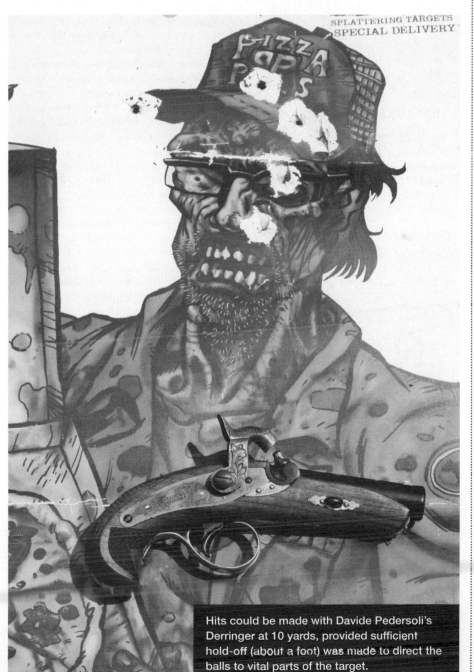

Hits could be made with Davide Pedersoli's Derringer at 10 yards, provided sufficient hold-off (about a foot) was made to direct the balls to vital parts of the target.

the Optima brought a 60- to 70-pound doe down at 50 yards. This was a spine shot, but the animal stood up. While still in my treestand, I fired five shots with the Remington at the moving deer. Three hit. One was in the rear flank, one clipped the back of the spine, and another hit behind the shoulder and passed through both lungs. I found the ball under the doe's skin, where it had penetrated about 10 inches.

My area's island deer are small, with the record deer weighing 132 pounds. Although the short-barreled replica revolver did kill the deer, I prefer to hunt with loads that can produce 400 to 500 ft-lbs of energy from longer-barreled revolvers. I consider loads from the short-barreled Remington replica suitable only for emergency use on wounded deer, or for shots at point-blank range. Check state regulations before hunting with a muzzleloading revolver.

The load from the Pocket Police is potentially useful as a small-game load, but the revolver shot eight inches high and left at 10 yards, impossible to hit squirrels, with that kind of accuracy. The Pocket Police shot Kaido Ojamma's heavier Keith-type revolver bullets so

high they hit my chronograph screen, and I gave up on the gun.

My preference for muzzleloading revolvers for hunting is that they have longer barrels, adjustable sights, non-reflective finishes, and use Hodgon's Triple Se7en powder. A stainless steel 12-inch barreled version of the Remington 1858 with adjustable sights is sold by Cabela's as the Buffalo Revolver. After having a matte black nitride finish applied by H&M Metal Processing, this gun was used to take 130- and 70-pound hogs from Georgia's Cumberland Island, with single shots from a treestand position at about 40 yards. The new finish made the pistol non-reflective and protected the gun from the corrosion caused by the load of 42.5 grains of Hodgdon's Triple Se7en and .454 round ball, which developed 395 ft-lbs.

SPORTSMAN'S GUIDE BLUNDERBUSS

The blunderbuss was an interesting self-defense gun, whose development peaked in the early 1800s. The distinctive belled muzzle aided rapid loading, but did little to scatter the shot. Mostly,

these guns were made as short-barreled flintlocks that could be easily handled by sailors or coachmen.

Naval blunderbusses were not often equipped with ramrods. During a fight on a crowded ship deck, there was no time or place to reload. There was more of a possibility that multiple shots might be fired by coachmen, and their guns were sometime equipped with attached ramrods that would be less likely to be lost. The more complex also had spring-loaded bayonets.

Blunderbusses were made in all sizes, from pistols up to guns intended to be mounted on walls or small boats and that might have two-inch bores and swivel mounts. Although some large blunderbusses had shoulder stocks, they could not be shoulder-fired; even the more usual 10- and 12-gauge guns were fired from the hip. Some guns had tapered bores, while others were of uniform caliber, except for the enlarged muzzle.

I did the initial shooting at a POMA outdoor writers' conference in Tunica, Mississippi. The load I used was 70 grains of Hodgdon's Triple Se7en, a hand-cut thin cardboard wad, a charge of about 30 grains by volume of Cream of Wheat uncooked cereal, another wad, No. 8 lead shot and 12, .177 air rifle pellets, and an over-top card wad.

Even though the blunderbuss had only a .54-caliber 16-inch barrel, it patterned fairly well (although hits were about a foot high). For small game, I used a load of mixed No. 6 and No. 8 shot to thicken the pattern. To date, I have taken eight squirrels with this gun.

This gun shoots as you would expect a Cylinder-bored "29-gauge" to shoot. At 10 yards, it gave an even pattern, but that quickly thinned as the range increased. Because of the small bore, non-deforming

The author shooting the Sportsman's Guide blunderbuss at Tunica, Mississippi.

Right: This impressive shot pattern at 10 yards demonstrated that the .54-caliber blunderbuss could kill close-range game.

hard shot larger than .25-caliber can bridge across the bore and not seat firmly on the powder. Thus, such shot should be used with a buffer. When I loaded lead air rifle shot, I dropped them down the barrel one by one and layered them in with Cream of Wheat.

As a hunter, my question was, "Could this gun be used to kill game?" The first obstacle was to raise the comb so that I could hit closer to the point of aim. After that adjustment, I felt confident enough to use the gun in the field and ended up taking five squirrels with it. So, yes, a person could have used this gun to take small game, provided he raised the comb, worked up a good load of smallish shot, and could get close to his target. The No. 6 shot penetrated the squirrels' hides, broke bones, and passed deep into the body; No. 7 shot is not common, but would probably be the optimum size for squirrels. For doves and quail, No. 8 would be the best choice. Always take a secondary tool, like a .22 pistol, for killing wounded squirrels.

The big-game load with the gun was 80 grains of Hodgdon's Triple Se7en powder, a cardboard wad, 20 grains of Cream of Wheat filler, another card wad, a .535 round ball and, after losing a ball from the barrel, an over-ball wad. This load developed 465 ft-lbs of muzzle energy, which I thought would be adequate for small deer and hogs. On a hunt on Georgia's Ossabaw Island, the ball apparently dropped from the barrel, resulting in my shooting at a deer with a blank charge. A month later, on Cumberland Island, I failed to hit a big hog at 20 yards, when the barrel retaining screw fell from the gun. This was disappointing, as the gun shoots four-inch groups at that range.

This blunderbuss with a one-ounce weight of combined No. 2 steel shot and No. 4 HeviShot was deployed to down a swan on North Carolina's Bodie Island.

Great fun was had by all, when shooting the Sportsman's Guide blunderbuss at a writers conference.

The blunderbuss and the author went on 10 deer and hog hunts, but, because of ill luck, did not make a kill. This deer died of unknown causes and was found on one of the author's hunts.

Load Table

Gun	Powder	Bullet	Velocity	Muzzle Energy
Blunderbuss	80 gr. 777	220 gr. .535 r.b.*	975 ft./sec.	465 ft-lbs
.44 Pietta	37 gr. GOEX FFFg	137 gr. .454 r.b.**	725 ft./sec.	160 ft-lbs.
.44 Pietta	40 gr. 777	137 gr. .454 r.b.	737 ft./sec.	165 ft-lbs
.44 Pietta Buffalo	42.5 gr. 777	137 gr. .454 r.b.	1139 ft./sec.	395 ft-lbs
.36 New Pol.	23 gr. GOEX FFFg	81 gr. .375 r.b.	644 ft./sec.	75 ft-lbs
.36 New Pol.	25 gr. 777	81 gr. .375 r.b.	694 ft./sec.	87 ft-lbs
.38 Special***	Win.	Win. 110 gr. Silvertip HP	818 ft./sec.	163 ft-lbs

* Loaded without patch.
** .451 Round balls are generally recommended for most .44 percussion revolvers, but I like the tighter seals provided by the .451-diameter balls in this Pietta revolver.
*** Fired from Taurus two-inch barreled revolver.

The charge broke the bird's wing, but the bird had to be killed with followup shots from a cartridge gun.

If you had nothing else, the blunderbuss could be used as a self-defense and hunting gun, but most contemporary rifles and larger-caliber single-shot smoothbores would have been better choices as hunting guns.

New Guns and Products

CVA (BPI INDUSTRIES)

CVA's Accura rifle has employed a premium trigger group that enhanced the gun's shootability, and this technology has been applied to the new Optima V2. The result is an easier to open gun with a better trigger. A quick-detachable breech plug, relieved muzzle, and a palm-saver ramrod make the new V2 a very user-friendly firearm.

The Wolf, CVA's entry-level muzzleloading rifle, will be offered in stainless steel with black and camo-finished stocks that enhance this gun's appeal. Optional shorter stocks are available for all of CVA's drop-barrel rifles, to accommodate young and smaller shooters.

CVA also introduced its new Scout centerfire rifles chambered in standard and compact models for the .35 Whelen, .35 Remington, and .44 Remington Magnum, which are legal for Louisiana's and Mississippi's muzzleloading seasons. There is also a Scout pistol that is identical to the Optima, except that it is chambered for .243 Winchester, .357 Magnum, and .44 Remington Magnum cartridges.

I hunted with the .50-caliber Optima pistol. That gun took a deer at 50 yards using two of Hodgdon's White Hot pellets (100-grain blackpowder equivalent), and a 295-grain PowerBelt bullet. This load produced a hard ridge of powder in the bore, making it difficult to reload. I used this gun with its factory-equipped red dot sight and hit the deer a little

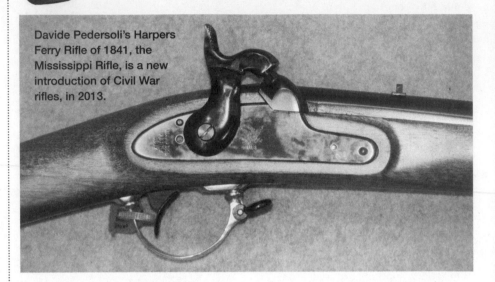

The Optima V2 pistol and rifle have an improved trigger-opening assembly for 2013, which makes these guns even easier to shoot.

Davide Pedersoli's Harpers Ferry Rifle of 1841, the Mississippi Rifle, is a new introduction of Civil War rifles, in 2013.

high. I feel that a scope would have allowed better shot placement.

Cleaning the all-stainless gun was easy, as the fouling was quickly dissolved and little of it had escaped into the breech. Using black and loose powders left primer blow-by fouling on the breech face and barrel. By using a thin-bladed screwdriver with a "U"-shaped end, I could extract the firing pin for cleaning.

DAVIDE PEDERSOLI

Continuing with its replications of rifles from the Civil War, this Italian company introduced the Harper's Ferry model of 1841, popularly known as the "Mississippi Rifle," in both .54 and .58 calibers. This rifle is distinguished by a brass patchbox, which was dropped on later military rifles. The replica gun has a production date of 1847, inspectors' marks on the stock, and the Italian proof marks are hidden under the barrel.

KNIGHT RIFLES

The new owners of Knight Rifles continue to upgrade their bolt-action guns with a six-pound, .50-caliber Ultra-Lite using a Kevlar stock. This rifle is guaranteed to shoot two-inch groups at 100 yards. Knight also uses a Dynatek ceramic coating for interior and exterior finishes, which is so slick that the "crud ring" resulting from using pelletized powders will not form.

CVA's Apex in .35 and larger calibers fired from single-shot rifles is now legal during blackpowder seasons in Mississippi and Louisiana.

KNIGHT
AMERICA'S MUZZLELOADER

The new Kevlar-stocked Knight Ultra-Lite is being hefted by a potential customer at the SHOT Show.

Traditions' (Pietta) Sheriff's Model .44-caliber Remington 1858 revolver made a save by putting one of five shots through the lungs of a wounded, but escaping, deer.

Turkey hunters will be pleased that Knight's outstanding TK-2000 Turkey Gun and accessories are still available, as are the entry-priced Bighorn and Littlehorn striker-fired rifles.

TRADITIONS

A sliding cocking mechanism is used on Traditions' new Vortek Strikefire. This large button is pushed forward to cock the hammerless gun. The Strikefire is decocked by pressing a release button on top of the sliding cocker, or by opening the gun. Other improvements include weight reduction via a hollow stock that also offers water-resistant storage. The gun, without scope, weighs 6.2 pounds, and the gun is also available with exposed ignition for use in Washington, Idaho, and Oregon.

Weight reduction is also found in the Ultralight versions of the hammer-fired Vortek and Pursuit drop-barrel rifles. Traditions' entry-level drop-barrel rifle is the Buckstalker, which has a 24-inch barrel, accelerator breech plug, relieved

muzzle, CeraKote finish, and optional shorter stocks for younger shooters.

The bolt-action Evolution muzzleloading rifle, which includes breech plugs for No. 11, musket caps, and 209 primers, is new for 2013. This gun also has a CeraKote finish and relieved muzzle.

Remaining in the line are the Vortek .50-caliber muzzleloading pistol and the traditional side-hammer flintlock and percussion rifles, pistols, and table-top cannon. This company has sold muzzleloading revolvers made by Pietta and, in 2013, introduced Colt Peacemaker revolvers in .22 LR, .357 Magnum, .44-40, and .44 Remington Magnum.

GOEX'S OLD EYNSFORD

Hodgdon, GOEX's parent company, reports that production from its Louisiana plant, which suffered an explosion two years ago, can now resupply the civilian market for blackpowders. A new powder, Old Eynsford, will be available in mid-2013. This is a premium powder that,

according to Chris Hodgdon, will produce about 50-fps higher velocities in many rifles. It may be used in all muzzleloaders and blackpowder cartridges. Initially, it will be available in 1½ F, FF, and FFF.

PERFORMANCE COATINGS AND FINISHES

An interior barrel coating of Dynamic Finishes will produce a permanent, super-slick interior barrel coating on muzzleloading barrels. The coating is applied to the inside of a clean barrel, and the gun is then shot as usual. After treatment, pelletized powders will no longer leave a "crud ring" in the barrel. This is the same coating used by Knight Rifles, and this version can be applied by the consumer.

A matte black nitride finish by H&M Coatings of Akron, Ohio, was heat-impregnated into the metal of my bright-polished stainless steel Pietta revolver, which is sold by Cabela's as its "Buffalo" model. This metal treatment is often used on guns, does not change the parts' dimensions, and worked well on my pistol.

HARD TO FIND CASES

Charles F. "Buzz" Huntington is a one-stop source for obsolete brass. He has brass for the Sharps rifles, the .577 Snyder, .577/.450 British Martini, and hundreds of other cartridges.

Hodgdon's new Old Eynsford blackpowder from GOEX is a more potent blackpowder for muzzleloading and cartridge use and is designed to compete with the very expensive Swiss blackpowders.

ammunition, Ballistics and Components

BY HOLT BODINSON

In spite of the launch of exciting new cartridges like the .17 Winchester Super Magnum, the .22 TCM, and dozens of new loads by the major ammunition companies, it's been a tough year for active shooters. Dealer inventories of ammunition, cases, powder, bullets, and primers dried up overnight. Bricks of .22 Long Rifle were priced as high as $88 on the gun show circuit. Hopefully, we'll get back to normal soon, but, in the mean time, handloading is certainly going to get a big boost.

Southwick Associates is the go-to national polling company, when the subjects are hunting, fishing, or shooting. The company has an enviable track record, when it comes to measuring the pulse of the shooting public and analyzing the brands of equipment it buys. Southwick's latest surveys provide some interesting data about us and our buying preferences, especially when it comes to ammunition and reloading. For example:

- The top rifle ammunition is Remington (21.4 percent of all purchases)
- The top handgun ammunition is Winchester (17.9 percent of all purchases)
- The top shotgun ammunition is Winchester (32.1 percent of all purchases)
- The top powder brand is Hodgdon (40.7 percent of all purchases)

- The top bullet brand is Hornady (34.0 percent of all purchases)
- The top primer brand is CCI (40.3 percent of all purchases)
- The top shot brand is Lawrence (30.2 percent of all purchases)
- The top reloading press brand is Lee Precision (37.9 percent of all purchases)
- The top reloading die brand is Lee Precision (38.3 percent of all purchases)

The Southwick survey also determined that one out of four shooters is already a handloader and that 86 percent of the respondents indicated that saving money was their primary motivating force, while improving accuracy was a close second.

ALLEGIANCE AMMUNITION

Using a compressed powdered-metal core in its projectiles, Allegiance has developed a series of target-specific defensive loads in 9mm, .40 S&W, and .45 ACP. Allegiance bullets are designed to deliver maximum energy to the target, while eliminating over-penetration or ricochets. One of the com-

pany's unique offerings is a 4.6x30mm round designed for the H&K MP7, featuring either a 30-grain powdered-core bullet or a 40-grain FMJ. (www.allegianceammunition.com)

ALLIANT POWDER

Alliant has a new pistol powder named BE-86. BE-86 has a burn rate similar to Unique, but meters better and has a flash suppressant added to its chemistry. Alliant indicates that BE-86 is a high-energy powder and a versatile propellant in a variety of handgun calibers. Could this new *wunderkind* replace the stalwart Unique? Could be! Alliant has also just published a new *Reloader's Guide* for handgun, rifle, and shotgun ammunition. (www.alliantpowder.com)

ARMSCOR

Martin Tuason, President of Armscor Precision International and Rock Island Armory, is introducing the new .22 TCM cartridge in both a 1911-style, semi-auto pistol and a bolt-action rifle. The .22 TCM—Tuason

Alliant's BE-86 pistol powder measures freely and moderates flash.

Armscor's hot .22 TCM cartridge will be chambered in both pistols and rifles.

Craig Magnum—is a short centerfire cartridge looking much like a 9mm Luger cartridge necked down to .22. In fact, the 1911-style pistol is available as a dual-caliber model for the 9mm and the .22 TCM. The squat little cartridge generates 2,000 fps with a 40-grain JHP bullet in the pistol, and 2,800 fps in the rifle. Armscor is making the ammunition in the United States, and the current price is only $24.95 for 50 rounds. Unfortunately, as we go to print, the Armscor engineers are still computing downrange ballistics data for the new cartridge. As soon as that's available, the data will be posted on the Armscor website. Lee loading dies, factory brass, and bullets are already in the retail pipeline, so shop the web. (www.armscor.com)

BALLISTIC PRODUCTS

This is the national one-stop store for anything to do with reloading shotshells—hulls, wads, shot, slugs, primers, powder, and common and specialized tools. You name it, it has it. The prices are simply great, too. More importantly, over the years, Ballistic Products has developed its own series of remarkable reloading manuals for various shotshell applications. There is a general shotshell load encyclopedia entitled *Advantages Manual*, followed by a series of specialty manuals with titles like *The Sixteen Gauge Manual, Small Bore Manual (24, 28, 32 & 410), Dove and Pigeon Load Manual*, and *Status of Steel Manual*. Its literature doesn't end there, though, because the company also offers a page full of $1.99 brochures with titles like "English Style Game Loads," "Subsonic

Loads," "Small Bore Non-Toxic Loads," "Hypersteel Loads," and "28-Gauge Low Pressure Loads." For shotgunners, Ballistic Products is a treasure of a company. (www.ballisticproducts.com)

BARNES

Attention long-range hunters! There's a new 129-grain .270 bullet in Barnes' Long Range X (LRX) line, which features polymer tipped, all-copper hunting bullets similar to the Tipped Triple-Shock, but with higher ballistic coefficients (BCs), due to extended ogives and boattails. Makes you want to go buy a .270 Weatherby Magnum and go hunting (or, maybe, just crawl 100 yards closer).

Best known for its advanced bullet designs, Barnes has gone on to develop several premium lines of rifle and handgun ammunition featuring the company's most successful all-copper bullets. New this year is its TAC-XP line of handgun ammunition, optimized for the concealed carry, home-defense, and law enforcement communities. The TAC-XP all-copper hollowpoint bullet is a proven performer. It penetrates any mix of materials without deviating from its intended course, expands rapidly, and retains nearly 100 percent of its original weight. Being lighter than conventional lead-core bullets, the all-copper TAC-XP generates less recoil, facilitating quicker recovery time for follow-up shots. Also, since most defensive events occur under low light conditions, the powder loaded in the

TAC-XP has been selected to produce minimum muzzle-flash. Currently available in the new line are an 80-grain .380 ACP, 115-grain 9mm, 140-grain .40 S&W, and a 185-grain .45 ACP. There are also several new loadings in the VOR-TX rifle ammunition line: a 50-grain TSX Rem. .22-250, 120-grain TTSX .260 Rem., 140-grain TTSX .280 Rem., and a 180-grain TTSX in the .300 Weatherby. (www.barnesbullets.com)

BERGER

Bringing the ballistic benefits of its famous VLD bullet to hunting designs, Berger is introducing a Classic Hunter Hybrid and an Elite Hunter Hybrid. The "Hybrid" concept blends two ogives: a secant ogive at the nose for higher BCs, and a tangent ogive at the body for less critical seating depths. The Classic Hunter is available in a 95-grain 6mm, 130-grain .270, 168-grain 7mm, and 168- and 185-grain .308s, designed to be shot in factory rifles with normal magazine length. The Elite Hunter in 250- and 300-grain .338 features an extra-long Hybrid nose for the highest possible BCs and is designed for custom rifles with extended length magazines. (www.bergerbullets.com)

BERRY'S

With a complete caliber bullet line based on copper-plated precision lead cores, Berry's is introducing a 185-grain HP .45 ACP bullet. Great bullets at very attractive prices. (www.berrymfg.com)

There's a new 129-grain .270 bullet in Barnes' family of Long Range X bullets.

The Remington .22-250, .260, and .280, plus the .300 Weatherby, have been added to Barnes' premium VOR-TX ammunition line.

Loaded with all-copper HPs, Barnes' TAC-XP ammunition is optimized for self-defense.

Black Hills' "optimized" 5.56 load featuring a Barnes 62-grain TSX bullet at 3,000 fps.

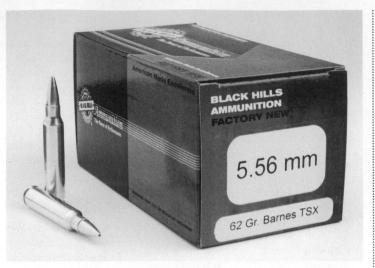

Black Hills' deadly accurate hunting load features a 150-grain SST bullet at 2,450 fps.

BLACK HILLS AMMUNITION

To the credit of Jeff and Kristi Hoffman, Black Hills Ammunition is celebrating its thirtieth anniversary this year. Black Hills is one of those great success stories in the ammunition business and, today, the company produces what many consider to be the most consistently accurate ammunition in the world, using only the highest quality and precision-gauged components available. In fact, each—yes, each—round is hand inspected before it walks out the door.

While filling the most stringent military contracts, Black Hills is always looking after the consumer by offering its most popular loads in either new brass, or recycled brass under its less expensive remanufactured label. There are three new loading in the lineup this year. First is an optimized 5.56 featuring the fast-opening, 62-grain Barnes TSX bullet at 3,000 fps and suitable for use in rifles with a 1:9 or faster twist. Next is a .308 Win. cartridge that gets a Hornady 150-grain

SST bullet at 2,450 fps for minute-of-angle hunting performance. Finally, there's a 178-grain A-MAX bullet at 2,550 fps for long-range competition and sniping applications. (www.black-hills.com)

BULLET PROOF SAMPLES

Tired of buying a box of 100 bullets only to discover your rifle won't group them? Bullet Proof Samples has a better idea—low-cost packs of 12 bullets in a variety of calibers from the leading bullet manufacturers. Why 12? It gives the shooter a chance to shoot four, three-shot groups. (www.bulletproofsamples.com)

CCI

The good ol' boys have taken the Quiet-22 Long Rifle round and given it a 40-grain HP that segments into three projectiles upon impact. It's now "Deadly Quiet" and would make quite the load for the squirrel woods. And, if you're a professional gator hunter and you appear in the History Channel's *Swamp People* series, you just might get your mug on a box of your favorite 'gator rounds. Troy Landry did this year, showing his face on CCI's bulk packs of .22 LR Mini-Mag and .22 WMR Maxi-Mag. (www.cci-ammunition.com)

D DUPLEKS

Following on the successful introduction of its steel-polymer, composite 12-gauge slug, D Dupleks has extended the design to the smaller gauges, specifically the 28, 20, and .410. If you're a slug gunner, these are some of the highest-tech projectiles ever offered. (www.ddupleks.com)

DILLON

Always coming up with innovative tooling for the reloader, Dillon is introducing its .50 BMG primer pocket swager, which can easily be converted into an off-the-machine primer seater. It's a neat combination tool that has been needed in the big .50-caliber circuit. (www.bluepress.com)

Right: Troy Landry of *Swamp People* thinks CCI rimfire is ideal for 'gator hunting. Far right: CCI's "Quiet" .22 LR now offers the option of a segmented hollowpoint.

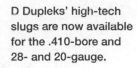

D Dupleks' high-tech slugs are now available for the .410-bore and 28- and 20-gauge.

Federal's MSR label is optimized for the shorter barrels of the AR-15 and AR-10.

FEDERAL

Loading Woodleigh's radical looking, Hydrostatically Stabilized, homogenous copper alloy solids in its dangerous game Premium Safari line is quite a coup for Federal. Available in calibers from the .370 Sako Magnum to the .500 Nitro Express, it is a versatile bullet that combines the qualities of a soft-point and a solid to create a massive and deep wound channel upon impact, making it equally useful for both plains game and dangerous game. It's not cheap, running from $123.95 to $314.95 a box, but it's still the cheapest part of the safari.

Also released this year is the premium Personal Defense HST

Below: Federal now offers Woodleigh's versatile solids in its Premium Safari line. Right: Federal's HST personal-defense load is designed to penetrate multiple barriers.

label. Offered as a bonded hollowpoint in the 9mm Luger, .40 S&W, and .45 Auto, the new bullet is designed not to plug up while passing through a variety of barriers.

The modern sporting rifle gets a lift this year, with a series of tailored loads under the Fusion label. Optimized for peak performance in the 16-inch barrel of an AR-15 or the 20-inch barrel of the AR-10, the new MSR loads include a 62-grain .223, 115-grain 6.8 SPC, 150-grain .308, and a 185-grain .338 Federal. Also new, under the Fusion label, is a 300-grain loading for the .50 Action Express.

Federal's TruBall slug loads have an enviable record of being some of the most consistently accurate on the market. This year, the three-inch 12- and 20-gauge rounds get a TruBall. The 20-gauge load features a ¾-ounce slug at 1,750 fps, the 12-gauge a one-ounce slug at 1,750 fps. (www.federalpremium.com)

FIOCCHI

Fiocchi reports it is running all out just to supply what it already offers. There is one new product, however, the 50-round Canned Heat canisters of 55- and 62-grain .223s. Canned Heat ammunition is packed in a sealed can with a desiccant added. The can also comes with a removable plastic top that acts as a sealing lid, once the can has been opened. Great stuff for your bug-out bag. (www.fiocchiusa.com)

Federal's deadly TruBall slug is now available in the three-inch 20-gauge.

Hornady's Critical Defense line now includes .32 NAA, .32 H&R, and .30 Carbine.

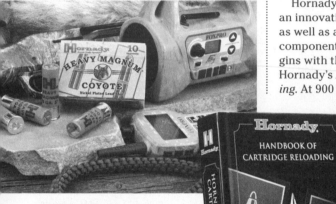

Varmint hunters will appreciate Hornady's 1½-ounce loads of BBs and 00 buck.

FORSTER PRODUCTS

The first Forster product I ever bought was a Forster 35 model airplane engine. It was quite a piece of precision machinery and was quickly followed by a Forster case trimmer, which I still use. The trimmer, too, was/is a beautifully machined product, and that's where Forster excels. Its products are well designed and precision crafted. New this year is a simple set of tooling that gives you precise headspace and seating data on the cartridges you're reloading. The versatile tooling is named the Datum Dial Ammunition Measurement System. The advantage of the Forster system is that it's versatile, measuring a wide variety of calibers without additional gauges. (www.forsterproducts.com)

HEVI-SHOT

Speed Ball is the name of Hevi-Shot's new waterfowling shell. It combines separate layers of copper-plated steel shot and Hevi-Shot. At the base of the shot column is an elastomeric ball that accelerates the shot column, while controlling pressures. The new shell is available as a three-inch 12-gauge with 1¼ ounces of BB or Nos. 1, 3, or 5 at 1,635 fps. A 3½-inch shell is also available with a payload of 1½ ounces of the same shot sizes, but at a velocity of 1,650 fps. Hevi-Shot claims the patterns delivered by Speed Ball out to 60 yards best those of straight Hevi-Shot shells. (www.hevishot.com)

HORNADY

Hornady occupies a unique niche as an innovative ammunition manufacturer, as well as a major supplier of reloading components and tooling. This year begins with the release of the *9th Edition* of Hornady's *Handbook of Cartridge Reloading*. At 900 pages, it's a comprehensive reference that includes several new cartridge additions, specifically the .17 Hornet, .327 Fed. Magnum, .356 Win., 5.56 NATO, .416 Barrett, and the .505 Gibbs. Hornady's newest bullets, the MonoFlex, NTX, GMX, and FTX are added, and new powders like CFE 223, Power Pro Varmint, and AR-Comp appear in the tables. The editorial comments by Hornady's staff, which address some of the handloading peculiarities of certain cartridges, are unique and invaluable.

If it seems a little dim and shadowy around your reloading tools, you'll love Hornady's new adhesive-backed Lock-N-Load Light Strip of LEDs

Hornady's latest 900-page manual covers new cartridges and new powders.

The .17 Hornet zips right along, with a copper/tin core bullet at 3,870 fps.

The new SST Lite shotgun slug load reduces recoil up to 30 percent.

that runs off any 110v outlet. Also new, cleaning cases, parts, or even a complete 16-inch AR upper got a whole lot easier with Hornady's release of a temperature-controlled nine-liter Hot Tub Sonic Cleaner. One of the nice design features of the self-contained unit is that one can segregate items to be cleaned, by inserting small, 1.7-liter tanks into the main tank. Hornady offers two sonic cleaning solutions, one for gun parts and one for cartridge cases.

There are six new bullets in the Hornady lineup this year: a 123-grain 6.5mm SST, 125-grain .308 SST, 180-grain 8mm GMX, 300-grain 9.3mm DGS, 250-grain 9.3mm GMX, and a 250-grain .375 GMX. If you own a S&W Governor or a Taurus Judge, there's also a new Critical Defense .410 cartridge loaded with two .35-caliber balls topped by a .41-caliber FTX slug. For My Lady's .38 Special, there's a reduced recoil loading, consisting of a 90-grain bullet featuring a pink Flex Tip. Part of the proceeds from the sale of this Critical Defense Lite ammunition will help fund breast cancer research.

Speaking of the Critical Defense line, it has been expanded with the addition of new loads for the .32 NAA, .32 H&R (.327 Federal), and .30 Carbine. The Critical Duty line, which is designed to pass FBI barrier protocols, is expanded with the addition of a .45 Auto +P cartridge featuring a 220-grain FlexLock bullet. Varmint hunters will like Hornady's new three-inch 12-gauge Heavy Magnum Coyote loads delivering 1½ ounces of either BBs or 00 buck, and a fast, 15.5-grain compressed copper and tin core bullet for the .17 Hornet at a muzzle velocity of 3,870 fps.

Finally, Hornady is introducing an extensive line of competitively priced big-game ammunition under the "American Whitetail" label. These feature the company's traditional InterLock bullets in calibers ranging from the .243 Win. to the .300 Win. Mag. (www.hornady.com)

HODGDON

Is this the end of copper fouling? Hodgdon's new CFE 223 spherical powder is revolutionizing handloading. It not only eliminates copper fouling, it seems to *de-foul* barrels with existing copper fouling. The chemistry is based on research undertaken for the military to develop a propellant that would stop copper fouling in rapid-firing small arms. The ingredients in CFE 223 convert deposited copper into an oxide that gets blown out the barrel with the next shot. It also leaves a film inside the barrel that reduces further copper-to-steel adhesion. The nice thing about CFE 223 is that it is usable in calibers ranging from the .17 Remington to the .375 H&H and delivers top velocities. Read all about it in Hodgdon's must-have *2013 Annual Reloading Manual*, which contains over 5,000 loads. (www.hodgdon.com)

HUNTINGTON

Looking for 8mm Nambu cases or .280 Ross bullets or Woodleigh's radical Hydrostatically Stabilized big-game bul-

Shop Huntington for Woodleigh's Hydrostatically Stabilized solids.

lets? Then be sure to visit the Huntington store, which thrives on supplying the hardest to find items, as well as the complete lines of RCBS reloading tools and parts. (www.huntingtons.com)

KENT CARTRIDGE

Known for its high-quality shotgun ammunition, Kent has just released its first slug load. Named the 10 Point Precision Slug, it's a three-inch 12-gauge one-ounce rifled slug with an attached base wad. Rated with a muzzle velocity of 1,850 fps, it is designed for both smoothbore and rifled barrels.

A new waterfowl specialty load called TealSteel features 1¼ ounces of No. 5 steel shot at 1,350 fps. Kent found that reducing the velocity of this load slightly improved patterning performance. (www.kentgamebore.com)

LAPUA

At the request of competitive rimfire marksmen, Lapua has opened a Rimfire Service Center in Mesa, Arizona. Here, in a 100-meter test tunnel, competitive rimfire shooters and teams can come and test various types of Lapua rimfire match ammunition, as well as particular lots, before buying a season's supply. Competitive shooters can also send in their rifles or pistols to the Service Center to be tested and matched with the most accurate type and lot of Lapua ammunition. Lapua's competitive Scenar line of bullets has earned an enviable reputation for accuracy. This year the line is being extended to include 120- and 136-grain Scenars in 6.5mm, and 155-, 175-, and 220-grain Scenars in .308-caliber.

There's a new free *11th Edition VihtaVuori Reloading Guide* available this year. Also, in celebration of its ninetieth anniversary, Lapua has set up a new interactive website at www.lapua.com/en/90/main.html, which even includes a biathlon shooting game. (www.lapua.com)

LEE PRECISION

Earning the top spot for reloading tool sales, Lee Precision has just released the *2nd Edition* of *Richard Lee's Modern Reloading* book. Lee offers a different slant on many aspects of precision reloading, which makes for interesting reading. (www.leeprecision.com)

LEHIGH DEFENSE

This is a new line of defensive and hunting ammunition, which makes use of pre-fractured solid copper or brass bullets formed with a deep hollowpoint. Upon impact, the bullet fractures, creating multiple wound channels, while the solid base acts as a penetrator. The company also layers multiple projectiles inside a case to deliver several impacts on the target. (www.lehighdefense.com)

LIGHTFIELD

Lightfield has been on the cutting edge of non-lethal shotgun ammunition for years. This year it is offering a variety of wildlife control ammunition in 12-gauge, loaded with rubber buckshot, .73-caliber rubber balls, and .73-caliber rubber slugs. Just the thing for that old tomcat on the back fence. (www.lightfieldlesslethal.com)

LYMAN PRODUCTS

If you're into bullet casting, take note: Lyman has just unveiled a 25-pound capacity, bottom-pour melting furnace with a key pad-controlled digital thermal management system. Additionally, there are two new touch screen-controlled powder dispensing systems this year: a Gen5, which is normal sized, and a Gen6, which is reduced in size for tighter spaces. There are also two new touch screen electronic scales: the Accu-Touch 2000, with a powder dribbler that can be mounted right on the scale, and the Micro-Touch 1500, a compact scale. Either model will run on a 9V battery or AC.

Lyman has a new hand- or drill-powered case trimming system, that accepts any brand of shell holder and is controlled by caliber-specific pilots. Improving on a classic design, there's also a new hand-priming tool that accepts any popular brand of shell holder. The large and small primer punches are built right into the large and small primer trays, so changing primer sizes is simply a matter of swapping out the trays. Pretty neat! (www.lymanproducts.com)

MCMILLAN GROUP INTERNATIONAL

Best known for its fiberglass stocks and tactical and hunting rifles, McMillan has announced it is getting into the ammunition business this year.

There will be four lines released: African Dangerous Game, Tactical, Extreme Velocity, and Precision. Bullet brands that will be loaded include Berger, North Fork and Barnes TSX/TTSX. (www.mcmillanusa.com)

NOSLER

The new 857-page *Nosler Reloading Guide 7* is a doozy, crammed full of invaluable technical advice and highlighted graphics that jump right off the page and indicating the most accurate powder for the bullet weight fired. There's even a "Classic, Wildcat and Obsolete Cartridge" chapter that covers oldies but goodies like the .225 Winchester and the .358 Norma Magnum.

There's a new bullet in the Nosler stable—the AccuBond-LR, with the "LR" standing for "Long Range." With its long ogive, boat-tail, and polymer tip, the AccuBond-LR offers the highest BC of any bonded bullet. The new bullet will be loaded in the Nosler Trophy Grade line.

One of the prominent new ammunition lines introduced this year is Nosler Defense. Both rifle and handgun ammunition will be offered loaded with Nosler's Bonded Performance bullets. There's also a new Match Grade Handgun line that upgrades the 9mm, .40 S&W, and .45 ACP cartridges with Custom Competition and Sporting handgun bullets.

Four new loads have been added to the Match Grade rifle line: a 6.5 Creedmoor, 6.5-284 Norma, .300 AAC Blackout, and the .338 Lapua. The Trophy Grade line has a dozen or more new loads and, in the Nosler Safari line, there are two new loadings for the increasingly popular .375 Ruger.

Fifty-caliber in-line muzzleloading hunters can look forward to a new sabot round this year that features a 300-grain .458-caliber Ballistic Tip stuffed in a .50-caliber sabot. Some interesting new varmint loads are being released, with a 110-grain FB-tipped bullet in the .300 Blackout (2,150 fps) and .308 Win. (3,150 fps), as well as a 35-grain tipped bullet in the .22 Hornet (3,000 fps). New brass by Nosler this year includes the 6.5 Grendel, 6.5 Creedmoor, .300 AAC Blackout, and .375 Ruger. (www.nosler.com)

PIERCE MUNITIONS

Having introduced the Ted Nugent Hi-Performance line of rifle and handgun ammunition last year, Pierce's newest product for 2013 is the Ted Nugent American Defender line of handgun ammunition, featuring Sierra hollowpoints and low-flash powders. Pierce is also fielding a rubber bullet line of cartridges for crowd control. (www.piercemunitions.com)

PMC

Building on its 5.56 X-TAC line, PMC has created the X-TAC MATCH line, featuring Sierra match bullets in the .223 Rem. and .308 Win., and a solid brass match-grade projectile in the .50 BMG. Retail PMC products this year will be available packed in Mil-Spec metal ammo cans and vacuum-sealed battle packs. (www.pmcammo.com)

POLYCASE

PolyCase is a new company focused on building ammunition using polymer cases reinforced with aluminum heads and primer pockets. The only caliber available at this time is the .380 ACP. The PolyCase .380 round is loaded with a 90-grain XTP HP or 90-grain Uni-Cor HP at 880 fps, and a 95-grain JHP or 100-grain plated RN at 875 fps. Plans are in the works for 9mm and .45 ACP PolyCase ammunition. (www.polycaseammunition.com)

RCBS

The RCBS Universal Case Prep Center has been around for a number of years. It has been a great design for repetitive trimming chores, but required the user to change out a series of case head plates for various cartridges. Frankly, it was a pain in the neck and, more often than not, you misplaced a plate or two somewhere in your shop. No more! The Prep Center has been improved with a universal case holder that accepts case heads measuring .25- to .625-inch, plus the Center will now accommodate cases .72-inch to 3.375 inches in length.

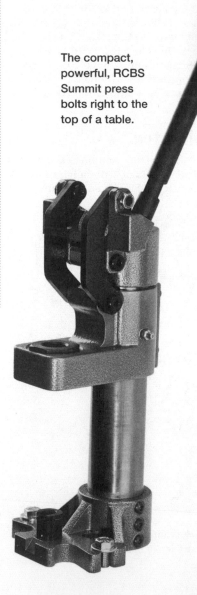

The compact, powerful, RCBS Summit press bolts right to the top of a table.

PMC's X-TAC MATCH line features Sierra match grade bullets.

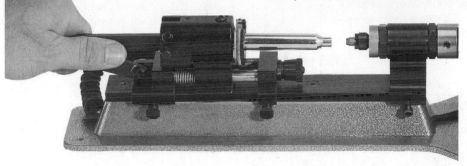

The RCBS Case Prep system now incorporates a universal case holder.

125-grain .30 Rem. AR, 150-grain .30-30 Win., 168-grain .308 Win., 150-grain .30-06, and 275-grain .450 Bushmaster.

Remington's introduction of the HyperSonic shotshell was revolutionary, and the concept has now been carried over to the centerfire rifle line and coupled with the loading of the Core Lokt Ultra Bonded big-game bullets. Examples of the new HyperSonic/Ultra Bonded line include a 62-grain .223 (3,262 fps), 140-grain .270 Win. (2,973 fps), 150-grain .308 Win. (2,924 fps), and 180-grain .300 Win. Mag. (3,122 fps).

RCBS is introducing a very interesting new press. Named the Summit, the compact, ambidextrous press can be bolted down anywhere on the top of a table. It features a two-inch-diameter ram and, in operation, the die comes down to the case, rather than the case being raised into the die. Access to the open front of the press is simply great, and there is a 4½-inch operating window for larger cartridges. The Summit even features a Zerk fitting for lubrication and accepts bushings for one-inch die bodies.

New dies this year include the .300 AAC Blackout and the .17 Hornady Hornet, and RCBS also has an ultra-sonic case cleaner. (www.rcbs.com)

REDDING

Redding has established itself as a premium source of innovative, precision loading dies and presses. One of the most interesting new products is a bullet seating micrometer stem that can replace the standard seating plug on any Redding die with a ½-20 thread and can be moved from one seating die to another. The micrometer seating stem is available for either standard bullet shapes or the increasingly popular VLD designs. Additional new products being offered this year include micro-adjustable taper crimp dies, a .45-70 FTX crimping die, competition seat and die sets for the .17 Hornet, and Master Hunter die sets that contain a standard full-length sizing die and a competition-grade, micro-adjustable seating die. (www.redding-reloading.com)

REMINGTON

With an estimated six million feral hogs roaming the fields and forests of the United States, it's Hog Hammer time at Remington. What was needed for this game animal was a tough bullet that could punch through their armor-like plate, while hanging together and still expanding. Remington chose the solid performing Barnes TSX bullet, with a dose of flash-suppressed propellant for low light or night hunting. There are some interesting cartridges and loads, specifically a 62-grain .223, 110-grain .300 Blackout,

The hammer in Remington's Hog Hammer is the Barnes TSX bullet.

Top: Redding seating die owners can retrofit their dies with a micrometer head.

Bottom: Redding has developed a much-needed adjustable taper crimp die.

Here's a cool idea for S&W Guardian and Taurus Judge owners. Package together 10 .45 Colt cartridges loaded with the Golden Saber 230-grain bullet, and 10 2½-inch .410 shotshells loaded with four pellets of 000 buckshot. Remington calls it the new Ultimate Defense Combination Pack. Indeed it is.

Zipping through FBI Barrier Test protocol is Remington's new Golden Saber Black Belt law enforcement ammunition. The new Black Belt bullet is a hollow-point constructed with a brass jacket and lead core. It has a slight hourglass shape and a very prominent reinforcing belt that locks the core and the jacket together. It's available in 9mm Luger, .40 S&W, and .45 ACP.

Speaking of new handgun ammunition, Remington is introducing two new lines with distinct consumer packaging. The High Terminal Performance (HTP) line in 9mm Luger, .380 ACP, .38 Special, .357 Mag., .40 S&W, .41 Mag., .44 Mag., and .45 ACP features JHP, Lead HP, SJHP, and SP bullets. The other new line, Target Pistol and Revolver loaded with Lead

Remington has added +/-200 fps to new loads in its Hypersonic series.

Below: Remington's Golden Saber Black Belt ammo meets the FBI's barrier protocol tests.

Remington's High Terminal Performance line is for self-defense use.

Above: For the popular .45/.410 revolvers, Remington combines .45 Colt and .410 shotshells in one package.

Below: For high-volume buckshot users, Remington is offering 25- and 100-round bulk packs.

SWC, Lead WC, and Lead RN bullets, will be available for the .32 S&W, .32 S&W Long, .38 S&W, .38 Special, .38 Short Colt, .357 Mag., .44 Special, and .45 Colt.

Finally, for high-use buckshot shooters, Remington is offering 25- and 100-round value packs of 2¾-inch 12-gauge 00 buck. (www.remington.com)

SIERRA BULLETS

The .375-caliber has a long history as an outstanding game caliber. Sierra just changed that, with the introduction of a 350-grain .375-caliber HPBT MatchKing target bullet with a whopping BC of 0.805! Just as a point of comparison, the 300-grain .338-caliber MatchKing, a very popular long-range sniping bullet, has a BC of only 0.768. There will be some great sniping cartridges developed around the new .375 MatchKing, and it may make in-roads in the 1,000-yard benchrest circuit.

If you like the 6.5mm, and who doesn't, Sierra has launched a new 130-grain HPBT GameKing for the hunting community. It will prove to be a great big-game bullet for the 6.5x55, .260 Rem., 6.5 Creedmoor, 6.5-284 Norma, and .264 Win. Mag. For 7mm fans, there's a new 140-grain HPBT GameKing.

One of the most interesting developments at Sierra that didn't get the fanfare it deserves is the redesign of the .308-caliber 155-grain HPBT PALMA MatchKing. The old PALMA MatchKing is still cataloged, but the difference between the old bullet and the new is in their ballistic coefficients. The old had a BC of 0.450. The new 0.504, which equals the BC of the 175-grain MatchKing. For .308 Win. competitors and snipers, the new PALMA bullet is sure to fly super-sonic and stable out to 1,000 yards and beyond. Sierra has a great tech support team available all day for shooters at (800) 223-8799, as well as an extensive lines of bullets, ballistic programs, how-to videos, and reloading manuals on its website. (www.sierrabullets.com)

SILVER STATE ARMORY

Want some brass? Silver State, which specializes in tactical ammunition, particularly for the 6.8mm SPC, is now drawing brass in a variety of calibers. New cases available this year include the .22-250, 6.5-284, 7mm-08, and .300 AAC Blackout. The existing brass line includes some hard to find cases like the 6mm PPC and the 6.8mm SPC. (www.ssarmory.com)

SPEER BULLETS

Speer just released its Reloading Manual #14. One of this manual's great attributes is reduced load recipes for most car-

Sierra's new 130-grain HPBT GameKing is ideal for 6.5mm shooters.

Weatherby (introduces value-grade .240 Wtby. loads, featuring Norma SP spitzers.

tridges—just the thing for pleasant practice and for times when powder supplies are in short supply. (www.speer-bullets.com)

WEATHERBY

Weatherby is bringing down the cost of shooting. "For some hunting and shooting applications, you don't need the performance or the cost of a premium grade bullet," said company President, Ed Weatherby. With a suggested retail price of $43 a box, Weatherby is marketing a value-grade load for the .240 Weatherby, consisting of a 100-grain Norma spitzer soft-point. (www.weatherby.com)

Winchester's .17 Super Magnum towers over the .17 HMR in size and performance.

WINCHESTER AMMUNITION

There's nothing like a brand new cartridge to invigorate the shooting community. Winchester's announcement that it was fielding a completely new .17-caliber rimfire varmint cartridge, followed by an-

nouncements from Savage and Browning that they would be chambering rifles for it, really shook up the rimfire world.

The .17 Winchester Super Magnum is indeed sensational, with a 20-grain polymer bullet clocking 3,000 fps and 25-grain polymer tip at 2,600 fps. The case is derived from the common .27-caliber powder-activated tool cartridge used in the construction industry. In performance, the .17 Winchester Super Magnum offers a flatter trajectory and higher energy and retained velocity than either the .17 HMR or the .22 Win. Mag. With the 20-grain bullet zeroed at 100 yards, there is only a four-inch drop at 200 yards. The new round is certainly the new magnum champ of the rimfire world.

It's been a long time since Winchester fielded a shotgun tracer round. The 12-gauge AA TrAAcker features a colored wad that actually tracks the shot string, making it visible to the shooter or coach. The secret to the wad's stable, tracking flight is a post incorporated into the wad that retains 1/8-ounce of No. 7 or 8 shot, thus acting as ballast. There's a fluorescent orange-colored wad for increased

Winchester now offers an AccuBond CT bullet and a Sierra MatchKing in the .338 Lapua.

Winchester's Blind Side shotshell is now faster and also available as a pheasant load.

Winchester's TrAAcker tracer ammunition is an ideal teaching tool.

The TrAAcker's secret is its wad that retains 1/8-ounce of shot for stability in flight.

visibility on overcast days or when shooting against a dark background like trees, and a black-colored wad for clear skies. The TrAAcker is available in the 2¾-inch 12-gauge with No. 7 or 8 shot and at two velocity levels, 1,145 fps and 1,250 fps.

The exotic Blind Side waterfowling shotshell, featuring hex-shaped shot, just got its velocity kicked up to 1,675 fps in the 12-gauge three- and 3½-inch shells. This year the Blind Side design goes upland, as a pheasant load with 12-gauge 2¾-inch and three-inch shells loaded with No. 5 shot at 1,400 fps.

The .338 Lapua, developed as a long-range sniper round, has gone mainstream in the hunting world. Winchester has cooked up a dandy new hunting load featuring a 250-grain AccuBond CT at 2,900 fps, as well as a new target load based on a 300-grain Sierra MatchKing at 2,650 fps.

Varmints beware! Winchester's successful VarmintX line now features a new, sleek, polymer-tipped bullet optimized for explosive long-range performance. It's available in .204 Ruger, .223 Rem., .22-250 Rem., and .243 Winchester.

The innovative PDX1 Defender ammunition line, designed to provide only 15 inches of penetration on a human torso, has been expanded with the addition of a 120-grain, split-core bullet in the widely popular 7.62x39 cartridge at 2,365 fps.

Do you have an iPhone, iPad, iPod or other social media device? If so, Winchester has a free download for you. It's the complete Winchester Ballistics Calculator program for rimfire, centerfire rifle, handgun, and slug loads. It's also available as a Windows 8 app. (www.winchester.com)

NEW OPTICS

BY Tom Tabor

It is truly a rare thing today to see a rifle that doesn't have a scope mounted on it. Rifle scopes have become so commonplace, I'm confident when I say some shooters today may have never sighted down a rifle barrel that possessed only iron sights. The reason for this is a simple one. Our scopes today have become so dependable, reliable, and of such high quality that, in most situations, a shooter would be a fool for not taking advantage of them.

Technological advances have been made in all areas of these products, including the types and styles of the reticles. Today, a shooter can choose anything as simple and basic as a crosshair design on up to those with multiple aiming points that allow the shooter to compensate for bullet drop and wind drift. We now have various style of dots and other configurations, programmable designs to specifically match the shooter's ammunition and load, a variety of illuminated reticles, or any combinations of these. In some cases, the manufacturers have even merged rangefinding technology into the scopes, to make those longer shots a tad easier to pull off.

One of the great innovations of our time is the recent breakthrough by the optic engineers that has allowed them to shatter the once-believed "impervious" 3x barrier in variable power magnification. For decades, variable power scopes have been commonly available primarily in magnification ranges like 2-7x, 3-9x and 4-12x, all in (approximate) multiples of three, but it has been only recently that manufacturers have been able to penetrate the 3x boundaries, thereby expanding their scopes' versatility. Now, a much broader range of magnifications is frequently encountered, such as 2-12x, 5-25x, 4.5-30x, and 15-55x, and with these new choices comes much more flexibility of use and incredible advantages for virtually all types of shooting disciplines.

The benefits of optical sights certainly aren't limited to only rifle applications. Today, many handgun and shotgun shooters have discovered that they, too, can improve their shooting performance through the use of various telescopic and dot-style sights—and no one should ignore the equally important improvements that have been made in other shooting related optical products, the spotting scopes, binoculars, and rangefinders.

In this relatively short report, it would not be possible to cover all the technological advances that have recently taken place in this field. I can only hope to whet the appetite and encourage you to dive deeper into those products to get a better understanding of what is now available.

An Alpen Apex XP (Xtreme Performance) 6-24x50mm rifle scope.

ALPEN

Alpen has recently expanded its Teton family of binoculars to include an ED HD (Extra Low Dispersion High Definition) design. This system helps to enhance the binoculars light-gathering capabilities and is now available in the Alpen 10x42, 10x50, and the newly designed 15x50 models. These Teton models come with a fully multi-coated BaK4 phase lens, long eye relief for eyeglass wearers, and twist-up eyecups, and they are hermetically sealed, making them fully water- and fog-proof.

Also new is Aplen's WBDC-TACT reticle, now available in the Apex XP (Xtreme Performance) 6-24x50mm and Model 4058 rifle scopes. This new crosshair design incorporates multiple aiming points, for both trajectory compensation and wind drift. The Apex XP rifles scopes are shock-tested to magnum level recoils of 1,000g's, come with fully multi-coated lenses, and are guaranteed to be waterproof, fog-proof, and shockproof.

Hunters and shooters are typically hard on products they use in the field and, for that reason, warranties are an important consideration, when purchasing any optical product. Alpen clearly

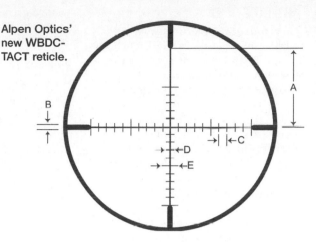

Alpen Optics' new WBDC-TACT reticle.

Model #4058 WBDC-TACT Reticle Subtentions (Inches at 100 Yards Distance)			
	6X	10X	16X	24X
A	40	24	15	10
B	2	1.2	.8	.5
C	4	2.5	1.5	1
D	4	2.5	1.5	1
E	8	5	3	2

At 50 yards distance multiply each value by .5
At 150 yards distance multiply each value by 1.5
At 200 yards distance multiply each value by 2
At 300 yards distance multiply each value by 3

excels in this area with its "Bulletproof/No Blame/No fault/No Problem Lifetime Warranty" on all items carrying the Alpen name. (www.alpenoptics.com)

BUSHNELL

For more than six decades, Bushnell has brought us an excellent selection of optic offerings, and that continues to this day. It was the first company to offer binoculars that possessed laser-ranging capabilities at under a grand. Now the company's new Fusion One-Mile Laser Range-Finder binocular

A Bushnell Elite Tactical 4.5-30x50mm XRS featuring a first focal plane G2DMR reticle.

Bushnell Fusion One Mile Laser Range Finder Binocular.

carries that technology one step further, with ranging capabilities from 10 yards all the way out to a full mile (1,760 yards). Three models are available: 8x32mm, 10x42mm, and 12x50mm. The benefits don't stop there. They also have built-in Angle Range Compensation (ARC), important to both archers and firearm shooters. In addition, the Variable Sight-In Distance (VSI) allows shooters to receive holdover data based on 100-, 150-, 200-, or 300-yard zeros. The MSRPs for the Fusion One Mile binoculars run from $999.99 up to $1,299.99, depending upon model.

Bushnell's new rugged and lightweight G-Force 1300 ARC laser rangefinder comes with a host of favorable features and the ability to range reflective targets out to 1,300 yards, trees and the like up to about 900 yards, and deer-size critters out to 500 yards. It comes with 6x magnification and Angle Range Compensation (ARC) technology for precise shooting adjustments. In addition, like the Fusion One-Mile binoculars, the 1300 ARC has been enhanced with VSI technology for rifle shooters, which allows them to program the hold-over/bullet-drop information.

Bushnell hasn't ignored the modern sporting rifle shooters. It's now offering a new series of rifle scopes specifically intended for use on AR-type rifles. These range from a 1-4x24mm version for close target acquisitions up to a 4.5-18x40mm model designed for extended range use. There are three bullet drop compensation (BDC) reticles to choose from. MSRPs range from $149.99 up to $299.99. Also intended for the tactical shooter is a precision long-range rifle scope, the Bushnell Elite Tactical 4.5-30x50mm XRS, featuring a first focal plan G2DMR reticle in a package that is only 14.4 inches long. The Elite Tactical comes with an estimated retail price of $2,149.99. (www.bushnell.com)

HI-LUX

In recent years, there's been a considerable upsurge in interest in both original, historic firearms and their modern reproductions, particularly those used in the days of the Old West. Some of this allure is surely due to the cowboy action competitions that are popular worldwide, but some shooters are simply drawn to these firearms as a way of recapturing the phenomenal excitement of that historic era. Several companies have capitalized on that interest by offering some great modern reproductions, especially in the form of various Winchester lever-action rifles and carbines. But, if you're like me and find a scope preferable to iron sights,

hanging a modern optic on one of these rifles simply doesn't look right and, due to the top ejection design of the Winchesters, a scope cannot be mounted directly over the top of the receiver.

The older-style, short, Wm. Malcolm scopes and mounting system now available from Hi-Lux Optics has the potential to solve both these problems. Hi Lux's Malcolm-series scopes are of the late 1880s and early 1890s vintage design and provide a nice match to these historic rifles. They come with a ¾-inch diameter steel main tube and are available in either a 3x or a 6x model. The company has also developed scope mounting systems that offset the scopes just enough to avoid the problems associated with the Winchester top ejection. The

mounts for the Winchester 1873 and 1876 models require no drilling or tapping of the receivers. Instead, the rear sight dovetail cut is utilized for the front mounting, while the rear mount requires the removal of the receiver sliding dust cover, which is then replaced with a bevel-edged rail-style mount. MSRPs run $299 for the 3x and $325 for the 6x. (www.hi-luxoptics.com)

KONUS

For more than 30 years, Konus has been providing shooters with high-quality optics at reasonable prices. For worldwide distribution, Konus is headquartered out of Verona, Italy, but, here in the U.S., Konus USA handles distribution from its facility in Miami, Florida. The company offers a wide variety of products for the American sportsman, including rifle scopes, electronic dot sights, spotting scopes, binoculars, and more. This year, Konus is offering a brand new line of compact tactical scopes that have been equipped with a dual illumination (red/blue) ballistic reticle. These T-30 series rifle scopes have ¼ MOA finger adjustable reticles, a fast-focus ocular lens, waterproof/fog-proof/shockproof construction, and a multi-coated (green) lens for optimum light transmission. The compact design of the T-30 3-9x40mm comes with enhanced resolution and a beefier, stronger frame at an MSRP of $379.99. The compact 44mm objective of the T-30 3-12x44mm provides 120 percent more light gathering capacity than that of the 40mm and carries an MSRP of $439.99.

For the shooter looking for more magnification without additional weight, the M-30 10-40x52mm might be just the ticket. This new scope comes with a dual illumination Mil Dot engraved reticle, 30mm main tube, lockable tactical turrets that are resettable to zero, a side parallax wheel, and anti-canting level bubble. All of this is in a one-piece construction, nitrogen purged unit complete with flip-up lens covers and a detachable sunshade. The M-30 10-40x52mm is available at a MSRP of $749.99.

Konus also produces a non-magnified dot-style sight, the Konus Sight Pro TR. This sight comes with a choice of four reticle patterns, tactical adjustments, tactical turrets that are resettable to zero, and dual mounting capabilities to fit either standard Weaver-style Picatinny rails or the smallbore bases commonly found on rimfire rifles.

Hi-Lux Short Malcolm 3 scope on a Winchester Model 1876.

Hi-Lux Short 6x Malcolm scope on a Winchester Model 92.

Konus Optics T-30
3-9x40mm scope.

Konus Optics
Sight Pro TR.

Konus Optics M-30
10-40x52mm scope.

Leupold's Ultimateslam 3-9x40mm
muzzleloader scope, which incorporates
both the FireDot illumination and the
SA.B.R. (Sabot Ballistic Reticle).

combinations. Two models are available, the Geovid 8x42 HD-B carrying a MSRP of $2,945, and the Geovid 10x42 HD-B for $2995. (www.leica-camera.com)

LEUPOLD & STEVENS

Leupold is frequently on the cutting edge of new optical product designs. A couple years ago, the company developed the illuminated FireDot technology. Finding the design to be very popular with shooters, the company is now making it available in a wider selection of its products. Leupold is also expanding its VX-6 CDS (Custom Dial System) scopes to include three new offerings, all possessing side-focus adjustment and 30mm main tubes. This includes a new 3-18x50mm model and two illuminated-models, a 3-18x44mm and a 3-18x50mm. The Leupold CDS technology allows the turrets to be

This unique design allows the user to convert the sight bases from one size to another by reversing a couple parts in the base of the unit. MSRP for the Sight Pro TR is $219.99.

The Konus Pro Series products are unique in a couple different ways. The reticles have been laser engraved for extra strength and durability and, for those shooters looking for optics that are safe to use on pellet guns, any of the Pro Series products are designed to handle the double recoil vibrations inherent to those tools. (www.konusscopes.com)

Leica's Geovid
HD-B 3D
10x42 laser
rangefinder
binocular.

LEICA

Leica's new Geovid HD-B 42 laser rangefinder binocular enables users to add or create their own custom ballistics. The newly developed ABC (Advanced Ballistic Compensation) system provides the proper aim point for the shooter through the use of Leica's Geovid HD-B's integrated ballistic processor. That's a mouthful, but, with one touch of the button, the bino provides the shooter with accurate information for the correct holdover, turret adjustment, or the drop-down reticle aiming point. In order to produce those calculations, the angle, temperature, and air pressure are all taken into account. Twelve ballistic curves, representing most of the trajectories of modern hunting cartridges, are already programmed into the system, but, through the use of an integrated micro-SD card slot, the hunter can program and save personal ballistic data information on specific cartridge/rifle

tailored by Leupold's custom shop to specifically match the ballistics of whatever cartridge, ammunition, and sight-in details the shooter prefers. These scopes incorporate Leupold Quantum Optical System and second-generation fog-/waterproof technology, and are backed by Leupold's Full Lifetime Guarantee and Golden Ring Electronics Warranty.

For today's modern muzzleloader shooters, Leupold has released a new Ultimateslam 3-9x40mm riflescope, which incorporates both the FireDot illumination and the SA.B.R. (SAbot Ballistics Reticle). This scope comes with a long list of modern innovations. A few include the Quantum Optical System, featuring lead-free, precision ground and polished lenses and Leupold's exclusive Multicoat 4 lens coatings for increased light transmission and clarity. (www.leupold.com)

MEOPTA

Meopta is a U.S. family owned, multinational company with facilities in both the U.S. and Europe. Meopta USA

Tom mounted a Leupold VX-6 2-12x42mm on his custom-built .17 Mach IV chambered rifles and found it to be a perfect choice for varmint shooting.

recently released four new MeoPro rifle scope models, all made in America and built on one-inch tubes. All MeoPro models feature the company's TO2 (Twilight Optimized Optics) system for enhanced light transmission. Two models of the MeoPro 3.5-10x44mm are available, one equipped with the company's RedZone (RZ) illuminated reticle system and

one without. In addition, there's a new 3-9x50mm and the fixed-power 6x42mm. The MSRP ranges from $599.99 for the MeoPro 6x42mm model, up to $959.99 for the MeoPro 3.5-10x44mm (RZ).

From Meopta's Czech Republic headquarters comes a new addition to its flagship MeoStar line of rifle scopes, the MeoStar 3-12x56mm RGD DualZone

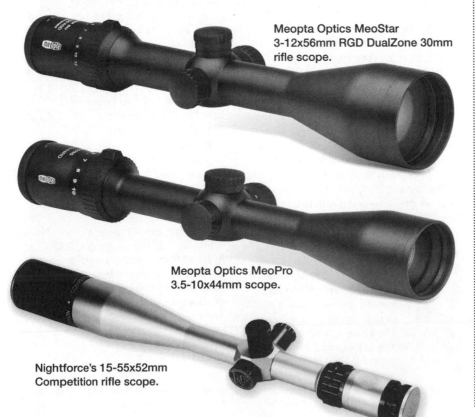

Meopta Optics MeoStar 3-12x56mm RGD DualZone 30mm rifle scope.

Meopta Optics MeoPro 3.5-10x44mm scope.

Nightforce's 15-55x52mm Competition rifle scope.

30mm. This scope is equipped with Meopta's DualZone red/green illuminated reticle system, making it a great choice for hunters faced with rapidly changing light situations. (www.meoptasportsoptics.com/us)

NIGHTFORCE

Nightforce's U.S. facility is located in the small town of Orofino, Idaho, where it supplies both sporting and tactical-style rifle scopes. Prior to any Nightforce scope leaving the facility, it is checked and inspected anywhere from 70 to 130 different points to ensure that, when the scopes arrive at the dealership, they are problem free and operationally perfect. Pre-production scopes are tested for 24 hours in a pressure tank simulating 100 feet of water, in order to ensure complete waterproof integrity. Thermal stability is checked by exposing the scopes to temperatures ranging from -80 degrees up to 160 degrees F over a span of one hour, and impact testing is conducted at 1,250g.

This year, Nightforce is offering an entirely new product, the 5-25x56mm ATACR (Advanced Tactical Riflescope). This is the first Nightforce rifle scope to be built on a 34mm main tube. It features ED glass, for improved light transmission, a brighter image, and overall better contrast. This scope is available with the MOAR or the Mil-R proprietary illuminated reticle design.

Another Nightforce model new this year is the company's 15-55x52mm Competition, which also comes with ED glass and zoom capabilities all the way up to 55x. It has .125 MOA reticle adjustments (5 MOA/rotation) and a full 65 total MOA elevation and windage travel adjustments. Available in either an all-black finish or as a silver/black two-tone, the scope has a modest weight of 27.4-ounces. (nightforceoptics.com)

NIKON

Nikon's new Monarch 3 rifle scope line has now become the largest series within the Nikon family. With five different reticles and eight different magnifications choices, these scopes have the ability to cover a broad and diverse range of shooting and hunting applications. The Monarch 3 scopes are designed and engineered to provide the theoretical maximum amount of light transmission for clear and sharp sight pictures when natural light is in scarce supply, and they are optimized for use with Nikon Spot

Nikon Monarch 3
6-24x50mm rifle scope.

On Ballistic Match Technology. The BDC reticle provides precise aiming points specifically geared to match the shooter's ammunition and load at specific ranges. Spot On can be purchased for iPhone, iPad, and Android users, or utilized for free at nikonhunting.com/spoton. MSRP ranges from a low of $279.95 for the 1-4x20 models up to $689.95 for the 6-24x50 scopes. (www.nikonhunting.com)

Pentax RD Mini Waterproof Dot Sight.

PENTAX

Pentax is now offering a waterproof mini red-dot (RD) sight in the company's Gameseeker sport optic series. This moderately priced optic comes equipped with a 5 MOA dot, intended to match a wide range of shooting applications, and is adjustable to seven brightness settings. Power comes from a single CR2032 battery that can provide 72 hours of continuous usage. The mini RD is constructed of rigid and durable aluminum, nitrogen filled and waterproof. Its objective lens is 20mm, and the unit comes equipped with Weaver-style mounts. Sighting adjustments are made at a rate of ½ MOA per click for both windage and elevation. At only 4.4 ounces and 2.7 inches long, this is truly a compact sight that can be used in a wide variety applications. MSRP for the RD Mini is $99.00. (www.pentaximaging.com/sport-optics)

PULSAR

The new Pulsar Expert LRF 8x40 Range Finder Binocular utilizes Porro prism optical system technology. This unit was designed to be lightweight, yet rugged enough to handle the harshest environments, even the ability to operate at extreme temperatures ranging from -22 degrees up to 113 degrees F. When compared to the more typical LCD units, the on-screen data input system of the Expert LRF is said to encourage a lower loss of light. The easy to operate controls make this binocular an effective tool for hunters, as well as for military and police spotters, where there's a need to quickly relay critical information back to a shooter. MSRP for the Expert LRF Range Finder Binoculars is $879.99. (www.pulsarnightvisionusa.com)

REDFIELD

It wasn't that long ago that I thought we'd lost the Redfield brand of optics forever. Fortunately, in 2008, Leupold & Stevens purchased the production rights to the bankrupted optics division of Redfield and, about two years later, began resurrecting the Redfield name. Since that time, the Redfield products have steadily increased. This year, the latest of these is a rifle scope called the Battlezone, specifically targeted at the fast-growing tactical market. While this scope has many of the inherent features such shooters are looking for, it is much more than simply a tactical scope. I personally believe any shooter would find many of the features in the Battlezone to their liking.

At the heart of the Battlezone is its built-in Bullet Drop Compensation System (BDC), which has been specifically calibrated to match the trajectory of a .223 Remington cartridge loaded with a 55-grain bullet and traveling from the muzzle at the typical speed of 3,100 fps. Redfield also includes a second BDC turret dial calibrated at the factory to match a .308 Winchester 168-grain bullet possessing a muzzle velocity of 2,650 fps. By simply switching around these turret dials, the shooter has a tailored ballistic reticle to match either cartridge.

Redfield's Bullet Drop Compensation System (BDC) reticle in the Battlezone tactical rifle scope.

Sightmark's new Mini Shot Pro Spec Reflex Sight.

Trijicon's new TARS (Tactical Advanced Riflescopes) MOA reticle (Model 101) is a versatile, 3-15x variable scope built on an aircraft-grade aluminum 34mm main-tube body that possesses a 50mm objective and an illuminated reticle.

I had the opportunity to test a Battlezone 3-9x42mm scope and found many of its features to my liking. For example, the reticle adjustment dials were sharp and precise in their movements. With each click of the dial comes an audible snap, assuring the user that the new setting has been locked securely in place. The horizontal and vertical reticle markings have been set in 2 MOA increments, and the reticle adjustment dials are resettable to zero by pulling up on the dial, turning it to the desired setting, then pushing it back down into place.

Currently, the Battlezone scope is available only in one model, the 3-9x42mm, but the company will be adding a 2-7x34mm model with the ballistics preset for the typical .22 LR.

SIGHTMARK

The compact size of Sightmark's new Mini Shot Pro Spec Reflex Sight helps to expand the shooter's field of view and encourages shooting with both eyes open. It features five brightness settings and double-paned glass. The Mini Shot Pro Reflex comes with either red or green reticles and features a front-mounted digital on/off switch, making activation easy for either a right- or left-hand shooter. The design includes two locking screws that help to keep the windage and elevation adjustments locked in place when used on heavy recoiling firearms. The Mini Shot Pro Reflex can be mounted and used on rifles, shotguns, or pistols, comes with its own removable base, or it can be mounted directly to a Weaver/Picatinny rail. Pistol mounts are also available and sold separately. (www.sightmark.com)

SWAROVSKI

When it comes to overall quality, many sportsmen feel there is no better choice than those products being built by the Austrian-based Swarovski. In many

cases, the products produced under the Swarovski name have become the standard other manufacturers are frequently judged against. Continuing with that high standard of quality, Swarovski is now offering an ergonomics-friendly line of very high-powered ATX/STX spotting scopes. This new design has conveniently placed the zoom and focusing rings right next to each other, allowing the user to intuitively and quickly make those adjustments with a single hand, while keeping an eye glued to the eyepiece. This reinvented design includes 65mm, 85mm, and 95mm models, with magnification capabilities of 25-60x, 25-60x, and 30-70x, respectively, as well as two eyepiece module (angled or straight) choices. I personally had an opportunity to test both the ATX 25-60x and 30-70x models and found them to be of unbelievably high quality, with clear precision even when adjusted to the highest magnification levels.

Swarovski has also announced a new reticle for the company's Z6(i) rifle scopes, called the 4W. This is a windcompensating reticle designed to work in conjunction with its Ballistic Turret (BT). This allows the shooter to dial in the correct elevation and compensate for the wind drift through the use of the vertical marks of the reticle, which have been positioned in 2 MOA increments. (www.swarovskioptik.us)

TRIJICON

I personally believe the new Trijicon TARS (Tactical Advanced Riflescopes) should be considered the flagship scope of the Trijicon rifle scope line. This is a versatile 3-15x variable magnification scope built on an aircraft-grade aluminum 34mm main tube body that

possesses a 50mm objective and an LED illuminated-reticle powered by a single CR2032 battery. The TARS are designed and intended for use as tactical optics or for sporting use and would be right at home for military and police applications, as well as benchrest competition, varmint shooting, or big-game hunting. The side-mounted parallax dial provides focusing capabilities all the way to out to infinity or as close as 10 feet. Each unit comes equipped with removable flip-up range caps and a sunshade. There are four reticle choices to select from, an intuitive MOA reticle (Model 101), JW Mil square (103), and two duplex versions (102 & 104). All are located in the first focal plane to help ensure sub-tension values remain constant across the magnification range. (www.trijiconoptics.com)

VORTEX

American-owned, Wisconsin-based Vortex Optics has several new offerings

The author used his Swarovski's 25-60x65mm to look over a herd of elk.

The author tries out Trijicon's new TARS scope on the range.

for hunters and shooters. The company's new Razor HD Gen II 1-6x24 rifle scope was specifically designed for short- to medium-range tactical shooting. The HD (High-Density) extra-low dispersion glass is fully coated on all air-to-glass surfaces with Vortex's proprietary XR antireflective coatings, and to protect the exterior glass surfaces from scratching and damage from oils and salts, they have been coated with Vortex's own ArmorTek. The 30mm aircraft-grade aluminum body is built to withstand abusive handling and is designed with an ultra-low mounting profile. The zero-resettable turrets offer a full 50-MOA range of adjustments, and Vortex's exclusive JM-1 BDC reticle can be set to custom match the exact ballistics of a particular cartridge by coordinating it with the Vortex's LRBC ballistics program. A daylight-illuminated center dot provides the shooter with red dot sight functionality and ultimate close-quarters versatility. The illumination is accessed and activated via a locking dial

positioned on the left side of the turret housing, which comes with 11 intensity settings and an "off "setting located between each of those setting levels. The scope is O-ring sealed and purged with inert argon gas to ensure fog- and waterproof capabilities.

The Vortex Crossfire binoculars have recently undergone a facelift both internally and externally, with the introduction of the Crossfire II series.

Two models are currently available, an 8x42, which carries a MRSP of $189, and a 10x42 model for $199.

The across the board warranty on Vortex products is certainly worth consideration. With the exception of loss, theft, or deliberate damage, the company will repair or replace any of its products that become damaged or defective, at no charge to the customer. Vortex says it doesn't matter how it happened, whose fault it was, or where the product was purchased, Vortex will take the necessary steps to make it right for the customer. (www.vortexoptics.com)

WEAVER

Weaver has been a leader for many decades, when it comes to moderately priced, high-quality rifle scopes. Many of us older shooters have fond memories of the 4x ¾-inch Weaver scope that sat proudly atop our old-time .22 LR rifles. I still have one of those, mounted on my now antique Winchester Model 69A bolt-action .22, and it is still functioning as perfectly as it did when I first bought it nearly five decades ago. But even though those old-time Weavers were good in their era, the company has come a long way from those early years. Now owned and operated by ATK (Alliant Techsystems), the company has moved into the twenty-

Weaver's Grand Slam 2-8x36mm.

The author used his Weaver Grand Slam 4-10x42mm Model 800310, mounted on his custom built .300 Win. Mag., to take this fine mule deer buck.

Vortex's new Razor HD Gen II 1-6x24mm rifle scope.

For shooting prairie dogs and marmots, the Weaver Grand Slam 6-20x40mm AO/DLPV Model 800469 worked perfectly, when mounted on a .22-250 rifle built by Cooper Firearms of Montana.

Weaver's Micro Dot Sight.

first century in a big way. The flagship is the Grand Slam series, and recently these scopes have undergone a complete transformation inside and out. Possibly the most noteworthy of those changes is the high-precision Micro-Trac Adjustment System, which helps to ensure repeatable adjustments of the reticles.

The company's moderately priced line of Kaspa scopes has now been expanded to include models specifically intended for shotgun and muzzleloader use. From turkeys to whitetails, there are three new 1-4x24mm models equipped with the reticle choices of Dual-X, turkey, or slug/muzzleloader. The MSRP for those new scopes run from $329.99 up to $359.99. Also within the Kaspa line is a new scope specifically intended for tactical use, the Tactical 1-4x24mm. This scope comes with an illuminated reticle, 30mm main tube, multi-coated lens for enhanced clarity, nitrogen purging to lessen the possibility of internal fogging, and a compact design permitting a low-profile mounting. MSRP for this Weaver is $329.99.

In recent years, micro dot-style sights have become very popular, particularly for shotgun, AR, and handgun use, and Weaver's new Micro Dot not only fits those applications very well, it carries a MSRP of only $108.45. This non-magnification sight comes with unlimited eye relief, adjustable brightness, and is easily mounted on many firearm designs.

Not to be left out in the boresight arena, Weaver has also developed a magnetically mounted boresighter that can be used on most firearms for only $41.49 MSRP. (www.weaveroptics.com)

ZEISS

Zeiss' new Conquest HD5 series of

Zeiss' new German-made Conquest 32mm binocular.

compact rifle scopes is being built specifically with hunters in mind and possesses a full 5x variable range of magnification. Designed, engineered, and assembled in Germany, these compact one-inch main tube scopes come with a ¼ MOA adjustments and are available in three models, 2-10x42mm, 3-15x42mm, and 5-25x50mm, all of which have a wide variety of reticle choices. They come with an updated ergonomic turret design, new ballistic lockable turrets, and rubberized magnification rings with finer adjustments than those on the previous versions. In addition, optical enhancements have been coupled with traditional features, such as the Carl Zeiss' proprietary T* lens coatings for better light transmission, and LotuTex water-repellant lens coatings to enhance protection. MSRPs run from $889 for the 2-10x42mm Z-Plex and up to $1,194 for the 5-25x50mm.

Zeiss also has expanded the Conquest HD binocular line to include a couple new lightweight, extremely durable choices of an 8x32 and 10x32. Like the Zeiss 42mm Conquest HD models, these 32mm units feature the same German-made quality and advanced HD lenses, but in a smaller and lighter weight body. The compact, entry-level premium binoculars feature a sleek, ergonomic design and a rugged, lightweight, magnesium body that is both water- and fog-proof. The HD 8x32 carries a MSRP of $944.43 and the HD 10x32 runs $999.99 (www.zeiss.com/sports)

***

At no other time in our history have we had such a large selection of extremely high-quality, shooting-related optical products. Whether you are looking for a scope to mount on one of your firearms, a binocular to aid you while hunting, or a spotting scope to evaluate horn quality or locate your shots on a range target, you can be assured there is a newly designed product out there to precisely fit your needs. Quality coupled with favorable prices is what most of us are looking for, and, today, I am quite confident that, with a little research and shopping around, you can find precisely the best product for your purposes.

The REMINGTON MODEL 721

SEVEN DECADES OF RELIABILITY

BY **Chris Libby**

That sunny spring morning in 1961, Maurice Libby drank his coffee and looked out the window of his camp, which overlooked the Saco River and Hiram Dam, in Oxford County, Maine. Maurice, age 52, was the older brother of famous Maine guide Arthur Libby, who regularly guided national celebrities such as baseball legend Ted Williams on fishing and hunting trips. Maurice had taught Arthur everything he knew about hunting and fishing. The only reason Maurice himself didn't guide was that guiding, unlike the Central Maine Power Company where he was employed, didn't pay regularly or provide benefits and a retirement pension.

Maurice glanced up on the face of a nearby mountain, as he did every morning while he sipped his coffee, but this morning he noticed movement. *Bear!* In a clearing halfway up, there was a black bear. A calf at a nearby farm had recently been attacked and killed, presumably by a bear. Maurice grabbed his coat and ran to the gun rack.

First Maurice grabbed his old, faithful, 10-gauge single-barrel Harrington & Richardson shotgun and a handful of paper Remington Shur Shot buckshot shells, but, on second thought,

Maurice's Model 721 .270 is still taking game with deadly precision, in its seventh decade of use. The author and his son Clint harvested this Maine doe at 140 yards.

The Remington 721 featured the strongest action on the market, due to Remington's "three rings of steel," which are still found on the Model 700 today.

In 1961, the year Maurice shot the charging bear, *Gun Digest* was still in its early years and celebrating its 15th Anniversary with a Deluxe Edition.

with deep regrets over misidentifying the young bears and ending their lives. But he had no regrets over choosing the fast-handling Remington that morning.

Maurice continued to use the Remington .270 for hunting whitetail deer, fox, and woodchucks. In the late 1960s, when he retired from the Central Maine Power Company and relocated to Florida, he took his Remington with him and used it for hunting wild hogs, and also as his home-defense weapon.

In 1949, a gallon of gasoline cost 27 cents. In the same year that Maurice's rifle was manufactured and purchased, the suggested retail price was $79.95. The Remington 721A (long-action, offered in .270 Winchester, .30-06, and .300 Magnum) and 722A (short-action, offered in .257 Roberts and .300 Savage), were first offered to the public in 1948 and were intended to compete directly against Winchester's famous Model 70. The 721/722 was a well-built, accurate rifle that offered shooters and hunters great value in the post-WWII era. The Winchester Model 70, which, along with the .270 cartridge had received widespread praise from the gun writer Jack O'Connor, had, in 1949, an MSRP of $106, almost a third higher

returned it to the rack. Then he grabbed his rifle, a tack-driving Remington Model 721 in .270 Winchester that wore a Weaver 4X scope. Armed with the Remington and a pocket full of cartridges, Maurice lit his cigar and headed out, knowing he had a long, vigorous stalk ahead of him.

Some time later, reaching the clearing high up on the mountainside, he approached cautiously, searching for the bear. He glassed the tree line about 80 yards away and spotted it, partially hidden in the branches, high up in a maple tree. Maurice aimed the rifle and fired. The bear was hit, but instead of falling it shifted itself, moving around behind the trunk. When it reappeared around the other side of the tree, the second 130-grain bullet struck, this time tumbling the bear to the ground. Then, as Maurice watched in confusion, a second bear on the other side of the tree trunk also fell to the ground! Only then did Maurice realize that he had shot two yearlings out of the tree, the distance, shadows, and branches giving the illusion of a single adult bear. He was overcome with sadness as he realized his mistake.

As the outdoorsman crossed the clearing and approached the fallen bears, he heard the sound of something running behind him, crashing through brush. Maurice turned and saw his worst fears unfolding before him. A large bear, obviously the mother of the two cubs, was charging at him full bore. In one fluid movement, Maurice worked the bolt action, ejecting the empty and charging a fresh round into the chamber, as the rifle was brought his shoulder. The rifle exploded for a third time, and the enraged bear crumpled and rolled to a stop, less than 15 yards from where Maurice was standing. His heart racing with adrenaline, the hunter quickly worked the bolt again, chambering the fourth round, but it was unnecessary. The bear was dead.

Maurice, my paternal grandfather, told me that story in the late 1970s. He credited his familiarity with bolt actions, gained from post WWI-era training in the Maine Army National Guard with the 1903A3 Springfield, and the fast, reliable, and strong action of the Remington 721 with saving his life. As an ethical sportsman, Maurice was haunted

This 1940 photo shows the author's grandfather Maurice Libby holding his H&R 10-gauge, along with a Maine buck and his two sons, Stan Libby (l) and Calvin Libby (r).

than the price of a Remington 721.

Remington Arms Company, which has been around since 1816, had a brilliant young design engineer named Mike Walker, who developed the 721/722. This gun later evolved into the model 725 and, finally, the famous Model 700. The 721 was a demonstrable improvement over Remington's Model 30, which was, essentially, a sporting version of the 1917 Enfield. The 721/722 was not only lighter than the Model 30, it was stronger, more accurate, and had a custom trigger pull.

Remington's famous "three rings of steel" provided strength (as added insurance against case rupture), unlike that of any other rifle offered at that time. A 360-degree encirclement of solid steel surrounded the case head in three rings that were comprised of the bolt, barrel, and receiver. The barrel was made from ordnance steel and quickly gained a reputation for its deadly accuracy. Although the basic 721/722(A), was offered with a plain walnut stock and blind magazine, the new Remington bolt-action rifles quickly became very desirable to American hunters, surpassing the competition by a wide margin due to their superb accuracy, durability, fast handling, and competitive price. Remington was also the first arms manufacturer to utilize bar stock for the receiver and bolt, which, from a manufacturing perspective, is cheaper and less time-consuming to produce than the forging process used by Winchester and the producers of Mauser-design rifles. With lower production costs derived from more efficient manufacturing process, Remington could make a profit and sell a quality product for less than the competition could. Under Mike Walker's supervision, the model 721/722 quickly propelled Remington into first place in the global production and sales of bolt-action rifles.

The Walker trigger system is crisp, with no travel or creep, and lends itself to superb MOA accuracy, hence the Model 700's popularity since its inception, in 1962, among competition shooters and hunters, as well as with police and military sniper units. Despite highly subjective media reports to the contrary, if properly maintained and not altered by non-factory persons, Remington states the Model 700 series trigger and safety systems are safe (this, of course, in no way negates the user's need to practice safe gun handling and muzzle control). In

The Model 721 (right), although quite plain in appearance, was the father of the Model 700 (left), shown here in the BDL version. The action and trigger systems are nearly identical.

response to tampering by non-qualified individuals—which, along with unsafe and reckless gun handling has unfortunately resulted in lethal accidents and litigation—Remington now epoxies the screws. Remington has produced more than five million Model 700s in all its variations, and that's not counting the early Model 721/722/725 models.

In 1979, despite his lifetime of fitness and strength training, Maurice's affinity for alcohol and cigars finally took their toll, and he passed away. The rifle was left to my Uncle Calvin, who, in 2002, gave the rifle to me. The years of hard use, neglect, and the Florida humidity had not been kind to the old rifle, and a thick layer of rust covered the barrel, action, and scope. Though the stock looked like it had been used as a canoe paddle, the action and bore, once scrubbed out with a brass brush and a liberal dose of Hoppes No. 9, was good. The Remington and the old Weaver 4X, sighted in by my Grandfather when he'd bought the rifle in 1949, was still shooting MOA, using bullets from the last box of Winchester .270 130-grain Silvertips he had purchased.

The old 721, now well into its eighth decade, is still being used to take game. This past November, despite previously bagging a Florida wild hog and a deer in Maine with my favorite bow, a 1968 50-pound Bear Kodiak Hunter recurve, I still possessed an unused deer tag. Although most of my hunting these days is done with a bow, with room in the freezer, it's time to get serious.

Maurice's old .270 and Weaver scope, shooting Remington 130-grain Core-Lokts, made shooting a doe at 140 yards seem easy. My seven-year-old son was with me, and he proudly carried the unloaded rifle, as I dragged the deer out of the field.

It was dark, as we journeyed home, and I had the strange feeling that we were not alone. Perhaps my grandfather's spirit was there, traveling alongside us and pleased that his descendants were still using his cherished rifle. It may have been my imagination, but I could have sworn I could smell the faint aroma of cigar smoke in that cold November air.

THOMPSON/CENTER'S

The exterior design of the Thompson/Center Dimension rifle is unique and distinctive.

Many shooters naturally think in terms of utility diversity when purchasing a new rifle. It only makes good sense to select a cartridge that can be used effectively for a variety of shooting and hunting applications. For example, a .243 can be used for hunting such critters as deer, antelope, and hogs and, in some instances, it can even double as a varmint and predator cartridge. On the other hand, if your focus is on larger animals, a .300 Win. Mag. has the ability to be effective on game as large as elk and moose, but it can also be used for deer, bear, and antelope. But, while there is a certain amount of flexibility built into many cartridges, no single caliber can do it all, and that is where the diversity built into the Thompson/Center Dimension (www.tcarms.com and www.dimensionrifle.com), comes into play.

The platform/switch-barrel concept utilized by T/C essentially allows the shooter to have one rifle that can be used for everything from shooting tiny ground squirrels all the way up to the largest of North American game animals.

By simply switching out a few parts, you could be shooting ground squirrels one minute with a .204 Ruger, and five minutes later your rifle could easily be converted into a .300 Winchester Magnum ready for a Canada moose.

Currently, there are 10 cartridge choices available in the T/C Dimension line, which have been divided into four series identified as "A" through "D." If your desired cartridges all fall within the same series of calibers, the

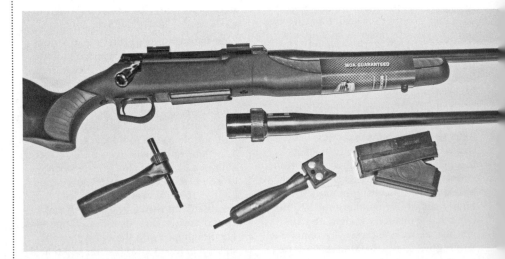

As long as the T/C Dimension calibers fall within the same cartridge series, all that's needed to change calibers is an additional barrel, magazine assembly, and the tools supplied by Thompson/Center.

DIMENSION

Versatility and Accuracy

BY Tom Tabor

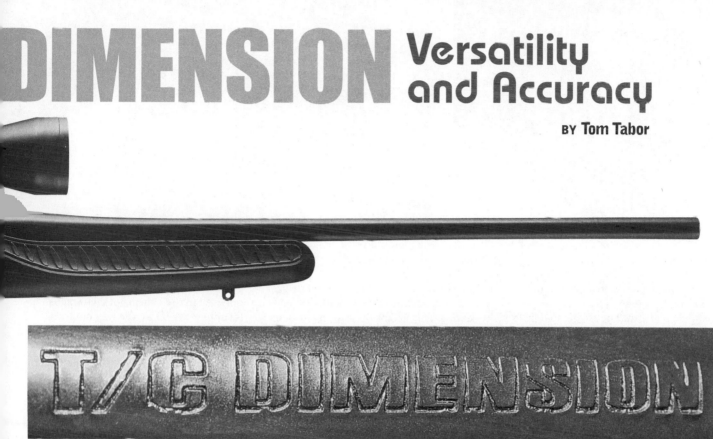

only parts needed for a conversion to a different cartridge is a barrel and a magazine assembly. On other hand, if your cartridges fall outside of a series grouping, it will be necessary to also purchase a bolt.

The flexibility and unique design features of the T/C Dimension rifle don't end with only the ability to change cartridges. The length of pull (LOP) of the Dimension stock can be changed from 12½ inches to 13½ inches by simply adding or removing a series of spacers located between the buttstock and the recoil pad. The barrels are free-floated, allowing for a range of different barrel diameters to be installed without the need of any stock modifications. The actions are pillar bedded to encourage a higher degree of accuracy, and the barrel muzzles have been cut with target style crowns. All T/C Dimension rifles come with three-shot removable magazines, but the overall capacity can be increased to four by feeding an additional cartridge directly into the chamber. The shooter-adjustable Dimension trigger can be set anywhere from 3½ to five pounds of pull. My own test rifle came from

The Dimension .22-250 worked out perfectly for Wyoming prairie dog shooting, and many of this nuisance species lost their lives because of it.

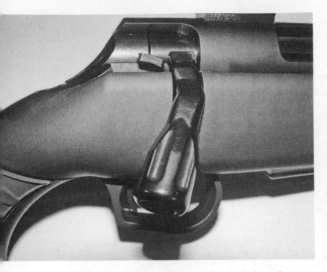

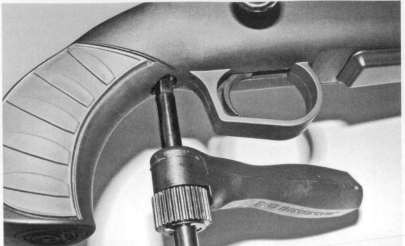

The Thompson/Center Dimension bolt handle comes in a tactical styling.

The multi-purpose T/C torque wrench is used to provide the exact amount of tension needed on the stock bolts.

the factory set at a conservative and pleasant 3.37 pounds (derived from a five-pull average). The trigger had little detectable creep in its movements, and the let off was both sharp and crisp. The short, 60-degree, LOC (Locking Optimized Components), three-lug fluted bolt lift makes cycling a bit quicker, when intense shooting action is called for. For protection against the elements, the

barrels, receiver, bolt handle, and trigger mechanism all receive a Weather Shield coating. This makes them as impervious to adverse weather conditions as is realistically possible.

My first real exposure to the T/C Dimension rifle came in the form of a Wyoming prairie dog shoot, where I shot a .22-250 topped with a Weaver 4-20x50mm Tactical model scope. Over three days

of shooting, a substantial number of dogs fell to the charms of the Dimension, including one hit all the way out to 560 yards. I came away so impressed with the rifle and its switch-barrel concept that I ordered one of my own for further testing and evaluation.

Like the one I'd shot for prairie dogs, the new rifle was also chambered for .22-250, but I added a second barrel

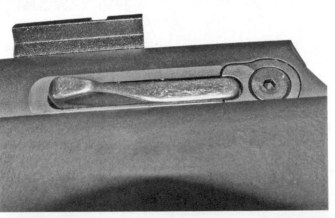

The Dimension bolt release is located on the left side of the receiver.

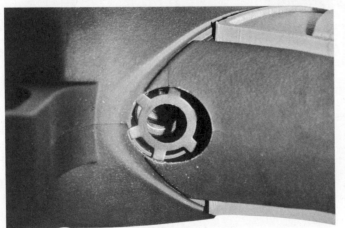

The stock mounting bolts are Allen-headed, but designed specifically to match the T/C torque tools.

A bit of class is the T/C logo molded into the pistol grip cap.

The rear mounting bolt is pillar bedded for enhanced accuracy.

and magazine assembly for the .308 Winchester. To me, this seemed to be the perfect combination for the shooter looking for a rifle that could be used for varmint and predator shooting and still be effective on deer-sized game animals.

When the rifle arrived, I mounted one of Leupold's new VX-6 CDS 3-18x44mm scopes on the rifle and, with the .22-250 barrel in place, I headed out back to my

rifle range to see how it would perform on paper. Two factory-loads were shot, Federal Premium ammo loaded with 43-grain Speer TNT Green bullets, and Hornady Varmint Express loaded with 40-grain V-Max bullets. Both loads produced similarly sized groups, but, as is common when switching manufacturers or load types, the cartridges printed to slightly different spots on paper at 100 yards.

After several days of .22-250 shooting, which produced many very respectable groups, I decided to convert the rifle over to .308 Winchester, leaving the Leupold scope in place. For the .308 ammunition, I shot two different Hornady factory loads, Superformance with 150-grain InterBond bullets, and Hornady Custom loaded with 165-grain BTSP bullets. As expected, the two calibers shot to different points on paper, but I also found considerable variation in the impact points between the 150- and 165-grain .308 loads. The results of all the range shooting, in both calibers, can be found on the chart "Thompson/Center Dimension Accuracy Testing."

About the time I was doing my testing, my wife still had a mule deer doe tag left. We figured a nice fat muley doe would "eat real good" over the coming winter months. So, with the .308 barrel in place on the T/C Dimension, the crosshairs got settled on a likely candidate standing slightly quartered to the shot of about 200 yards. Shooting the Hornady Custom 165-grain factory loads, the bullet entered a little further behind the shoulder than we would have preferred, most likely a result of underestimating the wind velocity. Hearing the bullet making its contact, we then watched the doe break into a full-speed run that carried her down a steep canyon wall and up the other side. After a run of about 250 yards, I began to think that a second shot would likely be needed, but, as the crosshairs were settled for the second time on her shoulder, she began to stumble, finally going over backwards, dead as a doornail, as the preverbal saying goes.

The T/C Dimension trigger is shooter-adjustable from 3½ to five pounds.

A Dimension rifle chambered in .204 Ruger, .223 Remington, or .22-250 Remington would be the perfect match for critters like prairie dogs.

Thompson/Center Dimension Accuracy Testing

.22-250 Remington

Cartridges	Best 3-Shot Group	Average 3-Shot Group
Federal Premium loaded with 43-grain Speer TNT Green Bullets	$^{15}/_{16}$"	$1^1/_8$"
Hornady Varmint Express™ loaded with 40-grain V-Max Bullets	$^{13}/_{16}$"	$1^1/_8$"

.308 Winchester

Cartridges	Best 3-Shot Group	Average 3-Shot Group
Hornady Superformance loaded with 150-grain InterBond™ Bullets	$1^1/_2$"	$2^9/_{16}$"
Hornady Custom loaded with 165-grain BTSP Bullets	$^7/_8$"	$1^7/_8$"

Thompson/Center Dimension Rifle Series

Series	Caliber Choices
A	.204 Ruger
A	.223 Remington
B	.22-250 Remington
B	.243 Winchester
B	7mm-08 Remington
B	.308 Winchester
C	.270 Winchester
C	.30-06 Springfield
D	7mm Remington Magnum
D	.300 Winchester Magnum

Because the first bullet had entered a little further back than ideal, due at least in part by the slight angle the doe had been standing at, the bullet had only taken out a single rib and one lung before exiting. Likely this was the reason for the fairly long run before the doe succumbed.

Making the caliber conversion on the Dimension rifle is really an easy proposition, when using the two T/C LOC hand tools, which universally fit all the Dimension rifles. These are extremely well thought-out tools. The LOC leverage tool's primary purpose is to hold the barrel. The LOC torque tool is used to loosen or tighten the torque collar connecting the barrel to the action, and on the opposite end there's an Allen wrench that can be used for initially tightening the stock bolts. Following that, the LOC torque tool can be used for the final precision tightening, and it provides the exact amount of torque for both the barrel collar and the stock bolts. Once you understand the procedure required to make the caliber conversion, the whole process of switching calibers is easy and trouble free and can usually be accomplished in less than five minutes. (There are a couple instructional videos available on YouTube that may be beneficial to a prospective new Dimension owner, including this one: www.youtube.com/watch?feature=player_embedded&v=XUa68KbuBeY.)

Possibly the most common Dimension rifle/scope setup would be to leave the scope mounted on the rifle action when the barrels are switched around, though no one should expect the bullet impact point to remain the same after switching the barrels and calibers. Still, there are a couple ways to get around having to sight in the rifle each and every time the barrels are switched. The Thompson/Center method would be to purchase the optional LOC Bridge Scope Mount Accessory and use it for mounting the scope. Doing so keeps the scope dedicated and attached to the barrel. Obviously, that would mean the shooter would have a scope for each barrel. Another method would be to mount the scope using quick detachable scope rings. But, like the T/C LOC Bridge Mount method, this would also make it necessary to have a scope for each barrel. I like quick release scope mount systems so well that I have these on practically all my rifles. In most cases, I use either Leupold QRW or Warne Maxima Quick Detach rings, but there are other brands available.

Throughout the range testing and hunting, I found the ammunition fed perfectly and smoothly from the detachable magazine into the chamber, and the empties ejected without any sign of a problem. The magazine slipped in and out easily each time, and the barrel cooled very quickly, due to its heavily floated stock design. The trigger seemed great, as well. Overall, I found the Dimension performed all its duties flawlessly as a varmint rifle for prairie dogs, on the range, and as a deer rifle.

For waterfowlers, the Breda was available in 10-gauge and in 12-gauge 3-inch magnum models. These guns weighed from 7½ pounds in 12-gauge, up to 8½ pounds in 10-gauge.

The Unique BREDA

This autoloading shotgun had features like no other.

BY **Nick Hahn**

There is no doubt that the grand old Browning Automatic Five, variously called the Auto Five, A-5, or just the plain ol' Browning Automatic, is the progenitor of all semi-auto shotguns. That includes the current crop of high-tech, gas-operated or inertia-operated autoloaders. Regardless the make or model, without question, there will be something, maybe very small, that was originally developed by John Browning for the enduring Auto-5. The most obvious parts are the bolt handle and the bolt release/shell carrier button, which were under Browning patent and caused all sorts of headaches for those gun makers, most notably

Winchester, that did not want to pay Browning for the rights.

Following the introduction of Browning's successful design, all subsequent autoloaders on the market were copies or were made under Browning license. Of course, there were gun designers busily working on new ideas—inertia, short recoil, floating chamber, gas, and other variations. German gun maker Walther even fooled around with a toggle-action autoloader that worked on the same principle as the Luger pistol. Italy probably had more gun makers working with new autoloading shotgun designs than did any other country. The Benelli inertia system so popular today was already in existence in the 1930s, in Italy, as the unique and very expensive Cosmi. Still other companies kept tinkering with new systems, and there were some that took the established Browning design and tried to improve or simplify it. None of these new designs were commercially successful at first.

The end of World War II appears to have been a watershed of sorts for semi-automatic shotgun designs. Shortly after the end of the war, Remington came out with the 11-48, a streamlined version of the Browning design that was simplified and made with many stamped parts to cut costs. In Italy, at the same time, Luigi Franchi had designed a lightweight autoloader that was, like the Remington, a modernized and simplified version of the Browning. There was also another unique autoloader based on Browning's system that came out of Italy, this one in 1946. It was made by a giant industrial

outfit known as Breda Meccanica Bresciana, a company that had made machine guns, airplanes, and tanks during the war.

The Breda autoloader, which appeared in the U.S. in the early 1950s, was an exceptionally well made, long-recoil

When Speed & Perfect Balance Really Count

BREDA
Mark II
skeet or trap autoloader

The skeet gun designed and manufactured for the American Shooter. The Breda Special Skeet Gun.

Here is the gun to help speed up your sighting and shooting. Perfectly balanced and light weight. The Breda Special Skeet Gun has semi fancy stock and forend of exact skeet design and dimensions. It comes equipped with a Special Skeet bore, 26" barrel. Simmons Deluxe Ventilated Rib and Simmons Glow Worm Front Sight. The Breda Mark II Special Trap Gun is available in both 12 and 20 gauges.

$210.00

DAKIN

This 1960s magazine ad was done by the Dakin Corporation, the Breda importer at the time.

operated, Browning-type shotgun. Its distinguishing features were that it could be completely disassembled without tools, and all parts were machined and polished. In short, the Breda was one of the best-finished autoloaders on the market, when it appeared. Additionally, it was light; only Franchi could

claim a lighter gun. The balance and the handling qualities were very good, and it was advertised as being a perfect autoloader for upland gunning.

Although the Breda utilized Browning's old long-recoil system, it was definitely a modernized version. It was made screw-less and also had interchangeable chokes—the original "extended" choke tubes. Breda's choke-tube system was called Quick-Choke, and the tubes, uniquely, screwed onto the *outside* of the barrel.

Bredas may have been imported in small numbers early on, but it was first imported in large numbers by Continental Arms, in the 1950s. Later, it was handled by Dakin Gun Company and, finally, by Charles Daly, in the late 1960s.

Just what made the Breda autoloader so special? As stated, it was an improved and modernized version of the Browning. Comparing the two, it can be seen that the disassembly of the Auto-5 requires screwdrivers of at least two sizes. Then there was the angular receiver profile of the A-5, which isn't the most attractive to some. Too, even in its Light Twelve model, the Browning was not the lightest around. For the European market, FN made some A-5s with alloy receivers and called them "Superlights," in an attempt to recapture part of the market it was losing to Franchi and Breda, but these guns were never imported into the U.S.

In contrast, the Breda could be completely disassembled without tools (all internal parts interlocked with each other), thus eliminating the need for

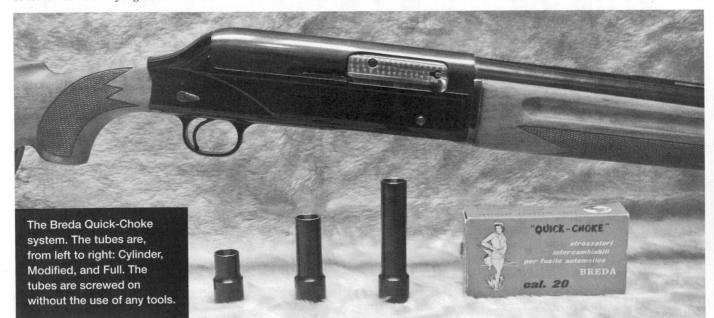

The Breda Quick-Choke system. The tubes are, from left to right: Cylinder, Modified, and Full. The tubes are screwed on without the use of any tools.

"QUICK-CHOKE"
strozzatori intercambiabili per fucile automatico
BREDA
cal. 20

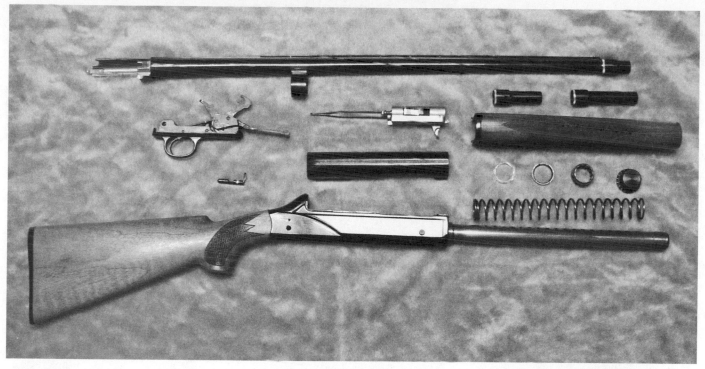

screws. The receiver was attractively sculpted, rounded, and streamlined, unlike the sharp angular silhouette of the Browning. Additionally, the Breda weighed less than the Browning, and the buttstock (at least on the 20-gauge model), could be adjusted for cast, pitch, and drop. Finally, It had interchangeable Quick-Chokes.

Despite these pluses, there were several things that kept Breda from becoming popular in the U.S. The first was Its availability. Although the model

The high-grade Breda autoloaders and their pricing in the early 1960s.

was imported over the years by several different companies, it was never widely distributed, and advertising was not as widespread or aggressive as it was for Browning and other popular brands. A second problem was the price, which was higher than most comparable shotguns. In 1959, the Breda autoloader with a ventilated rib cost $189, while a Browning A-5 Light Twelve with a vent rib was $154. Today, that may not seem like much of a difference, but, in 1959, the $35 difference could get you enough ammunition to last a couple seasons, or even procure a second, inexpensive shotgun.

Although the price was eventually lowered to make it more competitive with other autoloaders, that change came too late. The damage had been done. The smart marketing strategy is to initially price an item low and capture the market first. Breda importers had failed to do that, It is unfortunate that the Breda never met success in the U.S. Elsewhere, especially in Europe, it is still considered to be a premier autoloader, even though It is no longer in production.

The Breda autoloader, like Its progenitor, the Browning A-5, left its mark with other makers and can be considered a pioneer in several areas. The Benelli receiver owes much to the Breda. That company's two-part receiver, like the one on the Super Black Eagle and Super Sport, first appeared on the Breda. The takedown of the Benelli trigger group, which is held in place by a single pin,

The Breda was the only autoloading shotgun made that could be disassembled without the use of screwdrivers or other tools. All the parts are interlocking and do not require screws.

rather than the two of most other guns, is also borrowed from Breda. (Breda's trigger group is held in place by the "L"-shaped safety).

In an era when fairly open pistol grips, such as Browning's round knob semi-pistol type, were popular, Breda chose to go the other way. Breda used a close, full pistol grip with a tight radius, something that now appears to be standard on the various Berettas, Benellis, and other modern autoloaders. Like the Breda, most makers also now offer autoloaders with buttstocks that are adjustable for cast and drop, and you would have a hard time finding one that does not have a choke tube system.

Some say the Breda is an example of an over-engineered gun; no one has attempted, in recent years, to make a gun mechanism with interlocking parts that can be disassembled without tools. Whatever the case, in its day, it was, without a doubt, one of the finest autoloaders available. If you find one in the used gun rack, take a close look at it. You'd be hard pressed to find such fine workmanship on today's autoloading shotguns, and it still makes an outstanding upland gun.

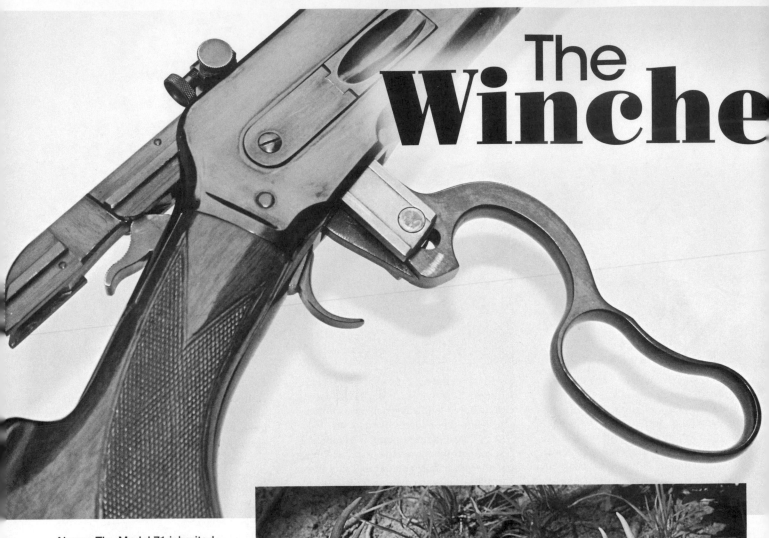

The Winche

Above: The Model 71 inherited its rugged action from the John Browning-designed Model 1886. Notice the twin locking lugs on either side of the lever.

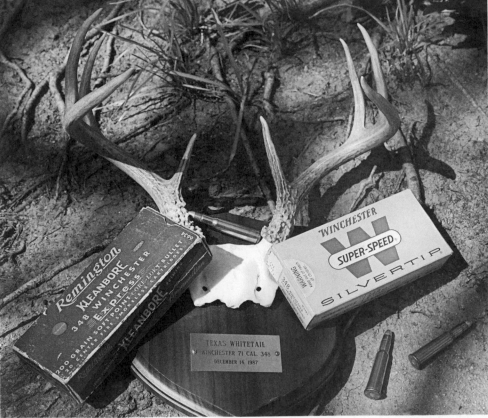

Right: Remington and Winchester were the only companies that loaded .348 ammo for the Model 71. This vintage Winchester box still has the original price tag of $6.17.

 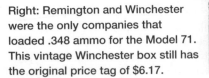

ster Model 71

The Ultimate Close-Range Big-Game Lever-Action

BY **Rick Hacker**

I will never forget the first time I laid eyes on that well-proportioned, full-figured form, sunlight and shadows highlighting every crevice and curve. It was more than love at first sight. It was closer to lust, slightly tempered with respect.

I'm talking, of course, about the Winchester Model 71, a big-game lever-action that was next of kin to the Winchester Model 1886, an equally muscular lever gun favored by serious late-nineteenth and early twentieth century hunters. The Model 71, in turn, was the only gun ever to be factory chambered for the .348 Winchester Centerfire, a big-game cartridge that descended from the .33 Winchester and, before that, the even older .50-110 blackpowder round, both of which had once found fame in the Model 1886.

The Winchester 1886 was the first lever-action repeater designed by the versatile John Moses Browning for Winchester Repeating Arms, thereby assuring that company's continued domination of the lever-action market. Subsequent Browning-designed lever guns were to eventually include the Model 1892 (which was really a scaled-down Model 1886), plus the Models 1894 and 1895. But it was Browning's 1886 that started it all and, in the guise of its alter ego, the Model 71, ended up outlasting all other Winchester lever-

Hacker's Model 71 has taken numerous game over the years, in weather ranging from hot and humid to sleet and snow. He dropped this Texas whitetail at a range of slightly more than 200 yards.

actions (recent reintroductions aside), with the exception of the Model 94.

Although Winchester had a winner with the Model 1873, "The Gun That Won The West" was chambered for what I refer to as the holy trinity of Colt-compatible revolver cartridges, the .44-40, .38-40, and .32-20 that, from a practical standpoint, were hardly suitable for the hard-to-kill big-game animals of the West. The New Haven company's attempt to break into the

camps of elk, moose, and brown bear hunters with the subsequent Model 1876, which was essentially a beefed-up Winchester 1873 designed to handle heftier cartridges, fell slightly short of expectations; the toggle link action inherited from the Model 73 was neither long enough nor strong enough to chamber the most popular hunting cartridge of the day, the .45-70 Government.

John Browning solved all of that by creating an entirely new action, which

The Winchester 71 was made from 1935 until 1958, with a total of 47,254 guns produced.

featured vertically sliding twin locking lugs that channeled up through either side of a fortress-like receiver and firmly anchored the bolt. Not only was the action as smooth as warm butter and solid as a Wells Fargo strongbox, the rifle was massive enough to chamber the .45-70 round, as well as other popular big-game cartridges, including the .38-56, .45-90, and the .50-110 Express. Rifles, carbines, and even muskets were produced and, as it was with most Winchesters, a number of special order options including half magazines and checkered stocks were available.

The Model 1886 proved to be extremely popular, with no less an authority than Theodore Roosevelt even wanting to take his engraved 86 on his famous African safari, in 1909, until Winchester people convinced him to settle on their newer Model 1895, which they were much more eager to promote. Otherwise, upon Roosevelt's return from the Dark Continent, he might very well have proclaimed the Winchester 1886 to be his "big medicine gun for lions," rather than the Model 95. But, in fact, it was just that type of insightful corporate thinking, with Winchester executives looking to the future, that set the stage for the makeover of the Model 1886 a few decades later.

By the early 1920s, the big-game hunting scene was starting to change. With World War I doughboys returning home after having experienced firsthand the long-range effectiveness of the Model 1903, and with a wave of custom gun makers converting thousands of war surplus Springfields into hunting rifles, bolt-actions were rapidly overtaking many of the older lever-actions in popularity.

In 1931, Winchester discontinued the Model 95, leaving only three lever guns in its line. They were the Models 1892 and 1894, which were suitable for medium-sized game at best, and the Model 1886, which, in essence, was its only true big-game lever-action. At this point, the hefty Winchester 86 was catalogued only in .33 Winchester and .45-70. Yet Winchester was not about to abandon the lever-action big-game market, as there was still a sizeable group of knowledgeable outdoorsmen who preferred the lever-action rifle because of its smooth, jam-proof action, its ergonomic balance, and its ruggedness.

Winchester had managed to achieve some moderate success by tweaking the Model 86 into a sporterized Light Weight takedown version with a tapered barrel and a four-round, three-quarters-length magazine. The company even came out with a .45-70 W.H.V. (Winchester High Velocity) cartridge with a 300-grain soft-point bullet to augment the standard 405-grain slug. The Model 86, although mechanically one of the strongest lever-actions ever built, clearly needed a makeover to appeal to a new generation of hunters. Thus, in 1935, with almost 160,000 Model 1886 rifles produced, the legendary gun was discontinued. Then, on November 2 that same year, a new legend was born: the Model 71.

As an aside, unlike the Model 1886, the numerical designation of the Model 71 had nothing to do with the year it was made. Instead, it reflected a new numbering system the company had adopted. For example, in 1935, Winchester's bolt-action Model 54 had been updated as the Model 70. As the next rifle to be introduced after that, the

updated Model 1886 was designated the Model 71.

The new Model 71 had many features previously available only on special order guns. It featured a checkered pistol grip stock with a grip cap, plus detachable sling swivels, along with a four-round, three-quarters magazine reminiscent of the Light Weight. A checkered beavertail forearm added to the rifle's muscular countenance, and a checkered steel buttplate replaced the older shoulder-thumping crescent curve. A factory rubber recoil pad was offered as an extra-cost option, and there was a choice of either a Lyman 22K semi-buckhorn open rear sight or an A-98 bolt-mounted peep sight. Later post-war versions omitted the sometimes disconcerting bolt-mounted peep and replaced it with a Lyman No. 56 peep fitted to their receivers.

The Model 71's improvements were more than cosmetic. For one, the metallurgy now consisted of Winchester's proprietary chrome molybdenum Proof Steel forgings originally developed for John Olin's no-holds-barred Model 21 shotgun. Moreover, the old flat springs of the 1886 were replaced with coil springs, and the entire action was simplified and strengthened without compromising its super-slick feel. With a 24-inch barrel topped off with a hooded ramp front sight and coming in at eight pounds, the Model 71 was truly the ultimate lever-action for a serious big-game hunter. In addition, from January 6, 1936, until 1947, a lower-priced, un-checkered variant without a grip cap and sporting a 20-inch barrel was offered, which collectors now call the Model 71 Carbine. The checkered version has become the Deluxe Model.

Collectors also call Model 71s up to approximately serial number 15,000 and having tangs measuring $3^7/_8$ inches in length "long tang" models, while later guns, up to the end of production and with tangs measuring $2^7/_8$ inches, have been dubbed "short tang" models.

Although a few of the initial guns were actually chambered with overrun .45-70 and .33 Winchester barrels, the Model 71 is primarily known for the cartridge created for it, the .348 Winchester. That round was designed to replace the earlier .33 Winchester, .45-70, .35 Winchester, and .405 Winchester numbers. The .348 is basically an Improved .33 Winchester. Initially offered by both Remington and Winchester in 150-, 220-, and 250-grain loadings, it was capable of taking anything that inhabited the North American continent, although effective range was limited to about 200 yards.

Frankly, the 150-grain slug left a lot to be desired, while the 250-grainer was all a woods hunter could wish for, as long as he didn't mind the extra recoil. Unfortunately, after 1962, only the 200-grain cartridge remained and, thankfully, is still available from Winchester in a factory Silvertip loading. A few companies, such as Buffalo Bore, offer a 250-grain cartridge, while Barnes Bullets provides 150-, 200-, and 250-grain slugs, plus a 220-grain variation. Thus, between cartridge and rifle, the Model 71 was really the only lever-action an American hunter needed.

This, then, was the rifle I now saw, sitting in a used gun rack of the no longer existing Pony Express Sports Shop on Ventura Boulevard, in Encino, California, once a favored Saturday haven for drooling young gun guys like myself. Specifically, it was a Deluxe "short tang" model made in 1948. Of course, this event, my happening up on this gun, took place back in the early 1970s, and the Model 71, with 47,254 rifles having been produced, had been out of production since 1958. Ironically, that was the year I discovered the Model 71 in an *American Rifleman* article bemoaning the discontinuance of what Winchester had once rightfully called "The Universal Big-Game Rifle." In its obituary, the writer had referred to the Model 71 as "businesslike," an apt description that I recalled a few years later, when I began my gun writing career.

With both a hunter's eye and a collector's scrutiny, I noted the Model 71 had been professionally restored (no worry about damaging an original finish,

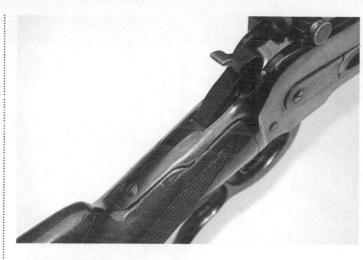

Hacker's Model 71 is the "short tang" Deluxe version.

For hunting with his Model 71, the author prefers to remove the aperture of the Lyman No. 56 peep and simply sight through the larger opening.

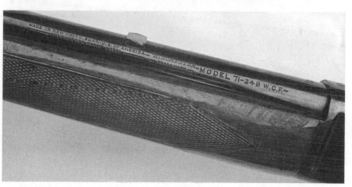

The Model 71 was the only factory rifle ever to be chambered for the .348 Winchester cartridge.

I rationalized), had a receiver-mounted factory Lyman No. 56 peep sight, and an aftermarket Noshoc rubber recoil pad. I picked it up, worked the action, sighted down the barrel, and bought it for $125.

After numerous hunts over the decades, in weather that has ranged from hot and humid to sleet and snow, I have since put a few marks and nicks on the gun's finish, which many still think is original. In fact, during one Colorado deer hunt, I was berated by my guide for taking such a fine collector's piece into the woods. No matter. Most of my kills have been made with a single 200-grain

.348 Winchester factory loaded bullet. And whenever I shoulder my Model 71, I am instantly transported back to a time before my time, where it is always autumn, tomorrow is opening day of whatever big-game season it happens to be, and I've got the best rifle in camp.

The fact that Browning offered a limited run of Model 71 rifles and carbines back in 1986, and that, in 2013, almost 80 years after it was introduced, Winchester again cataloged the Model 71, tells me that this is indeed—and perhaps always will be—the ultimate big-game lever-action.

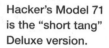

THE COLT MODEL 1903

The Colt Model 1903 in .32 ACP dates from the turn of the previous century, when many folks carried a gun for personal protection. Its light weight and comfortable ergonomics made it a very popular model.

BY **Steve Gash**

The approach to what we now call a "carry gun" was much different a generation ago. In those halcyon days, most folks tucked a neat little break-action revolver in their waistband or dropped a slim semi-auto in their pocket and went about their business. No one thought this was a menace to civil society. Such practices didn't evoke mass hysteria in the media, nor were they considered dangerous by anyone, except crooks.

The choice of defensive calibers was also much different then. It was determined not only by the petite size of the typical handgun, but also because high-powered antibiotics had not yet become widely available, and someone shot with anything, even a .22, had a good chance of getting a serious infection and heading to their last roundup.

It is within this cultural context that we assess the Colt Model 1903 semi-automatic. It is a typical example of the period's armament that, even today, fits *Gun Digest's* honored definition of "One Good Gun."

The M-1903 was designed by none other than John M. Browning and is the culmination of a series of pistols launched in 1896. Browning gave Colt the exclusive right to manufacturer pistols of his design and market them, not only

in the United States, but in Great Britain and Ireland, as well. A similar agreement was executed between Browning and Belgium's Fabrique Nationale (FN), in 1897, for Europe, but excluded the three countries noted above. The understanding was that Colt would make locked-breech guns and FN would manufacture blowback guns. While this convoluted arrangement evolved into several models on both sides of the pond in .32, 9mm, and .38 calibers, this geographical manufacturing dichotomy would later become significant in the popularity of the M-1903.

By 1900, Colt needed a sales success and petitioned Browning to allow them to make a blowback design. FN had introduced the .32 Automatic Colt Pistol (ACP) cartridge, in 1899, in its 1899/1900 pistol. Browning acquiesced, cut a very lucrative deal with Colt, and slightly modified the gun's design. Thus, in 1902, Colt started production of the Colt Automatic Pistol, Pocket Model (factory designation Model M). The gun went on sale in August of that year and was a huge hit. It was also called the Hammerless Pocket Model; of course, it wasn't truly hammerless, as the hammer was simply concealed in the frame. The M-1903 has a manual safety on the left side of the frame and was the first gun to be offered with a grip safety. All edges and corners were rounded and smoothed so that it was indeed easy to slip onto one's pocket, hence the model's moniker.

The Colt M-1903 is a marvel of simplicity. It is a straight blowback, single-action design with a fixed barrel, and operation is simple forward. A loaded magazine holding up to eight rounds is inserted into the butt, the slide then retracted and released. This cocks the internal hammer, chambers a round from the magazine, and then the arm is ready to fire. The manual safety can be applied at this point for pocket or holster carry.

Upon firing, the slide moves back, the fired case is ejected, and what Colt called the "retractor spring" on its guide beneath the barrel returns the slide into battery, stripping the next cartridge in line off the top of the single-stack magazine. The slide does not remain locked open after the last shot.

Disassembly is likewise easy and straight forward. Remove the magazine and make sure the chamber is empty. Pull the slide back to cock the hammer and release. Move the slide back until the takedown arrow on the left front of the slide is even with the front edge of the frame, and rotate the barrel to the left. The slide with the barrel can then be pulled forward and off the frame, and then the retractor spring and its guide may then be removed, if desired. To remove the barrel from the frame, turn it back to its original position and pull the barrel out of the slide. Reassembly is basically in the reverse order, but you have to turn the barrel ever so slightly to get the slide back far enough to lock the barrel lugs into their corresponding cuts in the frame.

I stumbled across my Model 1903 via a multi-item trade with a good friend

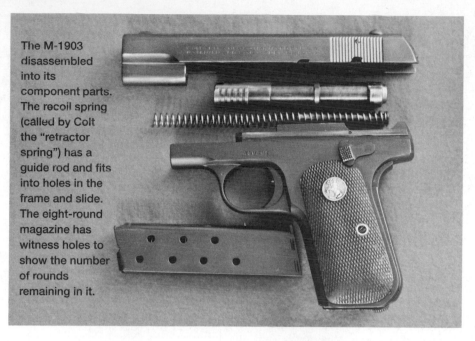

The M-1903 disassembled into its component parts. The recoil spring (called by Colt the "retractor spring") has a guide rod and fits into holes in the frame and slide. The eight-round magazine has witness holes to show the number of rounds remaining in it.

The M-1903 was designed by John M. Browning and is a single-action blowback with an eight-round magazine in the grip. A thumb safety on the left side of the frame and a grip safety made the arm relatively safe for pocket to carry.

who always seems to have something interesting with which to tempt the unsuspecting gun writer. Being a handloader at heart, the clincher was that the gun came with a huge jar containing hundreds of once-fired .32 ACP cases!

While my M-1003 is a quaint little gun, it is obviously somewhat of an amalgamation. Five major variations (some say four) of the M-1903 were made over its production life from 1903 to 1946, with a total of about 572,215 .32s produced. In 1908, a version chambered for the .380 ACP was introduced, known as the Model 1908. This resulted in the production of another 138,010 guns. (M-1908s in .380

could be easily converted to .32 ACP, but not vice versa.) My .32 ACP is a "Type III" specimen, made from 1910 to 1926, with some 363,046 guns being produced in that period. The Type III guns eliminated the barrel bushing and magazine safety of earlier versions. The minutiae of the numerous design changes over all the production periods have delighted Colt collectors for decades.

My gun's magazine is original, marked "CAL 32 COLT," but its spring has lost its zip and the last round or two sometimes fails to feed. Not to worry. If a gun has a spring problem, there's only one place to call: Wolff Gun Springs. This company

The barrel is fixed to the frame and does not move during the firing sequence. Six lugs atop the barrel, which Colt called "transverse ribs," mesh with corresponding recesses in the frame. The cut below the ribs is for the extractor.

makes every spring for the M1903 (and M1908), so I ordered a "Pistol Service Pak" (stock no. 69082). In addition to a five-percent extra-power magazine spring, this kit includes recoil, firing pin, and extractor springs. I installed the magazine spring, and presto, the little gun now functions as good as new. (I'll get to the other springs later.)

The serial number of my gun is 430501, indicating it was made in 1923. It has been nicely refinished with a uniform satin Parkerized finish reminiscent of Type V military guns. Might this mean that it was factory-refinished during the military production period? I don't know, but it's an interesting historical speculation on the "if this gun could talk" theme.

A hint of very light pitting is barely visible under the new finish at the right front of the slide and at the top of the frame above the trigger guard. The rifling is pretty sharp, but the bore is a bit frosty. There is a slight bulge in the barrel about mid-way; obviously, at some point there was a barrel obstruction (perhaps a stuck bullet?), when a round was fired. Thankfully, functioning and accuracy seem unaffected. I have

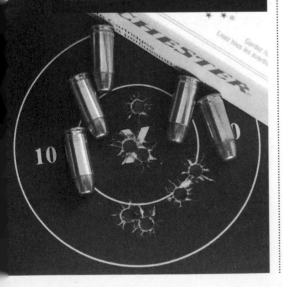

Winchester's 71-grain FMJ-FP delivered acceptable accuracy, but, for centered groups, I had to aim a little to the left.

Specifications

Model:	Colt Pocket Hammerless Model 1903
Type:	Internal hammer, semi-automatic, single-action pistol, blowback
Patent Dates:	April 20, 1897; December 22, 1903
Year of Manufacture:	1923, Model M, Type III (mfg. 1910-1923)
Caliber:	.32 Automatic Colt Pistol (7.65mm Browning)
Capacity:	8+1
Barrel length:	3¾
Overall length:	6¾ inches
Overall width:	¾-inch
Overall height:	4½ inches
Weight:	24 ounces (with empty magazine)
Safeties:	Slide lock safety, disconnector safety, and grip safety
Sights:	Fixed
Finish:	Bright blue or Parkerized, depending on model
Stocks:	Checkered hard rubber or checkered walnut
Manufacturer:	Colt Patent Firearms Mgf. Co., Hartford, Conn. U.S.A.

searched for a new replacement barrel, but to no avail.

In addition to the finish, my pistol's stocks are not original. Guns made in 1923 had checkered hard rubber stocks. In 1924, they were changed to checkered walnut with medallions, one on each side, featuring the rampant colts oriented so that they faced forward on both sides. In other words, there were two different medallions. In 1926, one medallion was used on both panels, so that the colts face left on both sides. This dates the stocks on my gun to that year or later.

While virtually all cartridges for semi-auto pistols are rimless, the .32 ACP (known in Europe as the 7.65 Browning Short), a truly unique round, is actually semi-rimmed. What rim there is, is a puny protrusion only .021-inch larger in diameter than the case ahead of the extractor groove. Nevertheless, the round headspaces on the case mouth, just as do other semi-auto rounds. A curious quirk is that, with its tiny rim, the .32 ACP can actually be fired in most .32 revolvers, in a pinch.

Ballistics of the .32 ACP are lackluster. The standard 71-grain FMJ bullet at a nominal 900 fps produces only 129 ft-lbs of energy. To put this in perspective, at handgun velocities, the 40-grain .22 LR has about 72 ft-lbs, the 50-grain .22 WMR has 126, and the .25 ACP (ironically, introduced three years after the .32 ACP) has 64 ft-lbs of muzzle energy. However, remember the earlier admonition about infection? You still didn't want to get shot with any of them!

S.A.A.M.I. maximum average pressure (MAP) for the .32 ACP is only 20,500 psi, out of deference to the relatively weak blowback pistols that are over 100 years old. The round must still see some use, as almost all the major manufacturers make factory loads, including the traditional 71-grain FMJ bullet, plus some new expanding types from Federal, Speer,

32 ACP Range Results
Colt M-1903, 3¾-inch barrel

Ammo Brand, Load Number, and COL	Bullet Wt. and Listed velocity (fps)	Recorded Velocity (fps)	SD (fps)	Muzzle Energy (ft-lbs)	Accuracy (inches)
Winchester FMJ-FP load #Q4255 COL – .912-inch	71 grains /905 fps	869	19	119	3 1/8
Hornady XTP-HP load #90062 COL = .902-inch	60 grains/ 1,000 fps	851	45	96	2½
Federal Premium PD HydraShok HP, load #P32HS1 COL = .899-inch	65 grains /950 fps	888	31	114	2½
Federal American Eagle FMJ, load #AE32AP, COL = .969-inch	71 grains /900 fps	822	11	107	2¾
CCI Blazer FMJ, load #3503 COL = .997-inch	71 grains/ 900 fps	848	19	113	2½
Aquila FMJ-RN (no load #) COL = .9608-inch	71 grains/ (no velocity listed)	920	6	134	1 3/8

Notes: *All loads tested at 15 yards from a sandbag rest. Accuracy is the average of at least two, five-shot groups. Velocities were measured with an Oehler M-35P with the first screen 10 feet from the gun's muzzle.*

Abbreviations: *COL, cartridge overall length; FMJ, full metal jacket; RN, round nose; FP, flat point; XTP, eXtreme Terminal Performance; HP, hollowpoint; PD, personal defense.*

and Hornady. I gathered up as many of these rounds as I could and headed to the range. The results are shown in the accompanying table.

The little M-1903 was really fun to shoot, mild of voice, and recoil was downright pleasant. Groups were fired at 10 yards and were in the 2½- to three-inch range. Never mind that the point of impact and point of aim didn't exactly coincide. At this defensive distance, it was well within minute-of-bad-guy.

Velocities of the 71-grain loads are rated at 900 to 905 fps, but only the Aquila ammo (which does not list a velocity) beat this, at 920 fps. The Winchester, CCI Blazer, and Federal American Eagle 71-grain loads were 869, 848, and 822 fps, respectively. Hornady's 60-grain XTP-HP, rated at 1,000 fps, clocked 851 fps. This dropped muzzle energy to 96 ft-lbs. The Federal HydraShok fared a little better at 888 fps and 114 ft-lbs. Be aware, however, that some guns refuse to cycle with these lightweight bullets, so, if you decide to use them, be sure and check for reliability with them.

Actually, if a stalwart citizen carries a .32 ACP pistol for personal defense these days, a good argument can be made for the use of ammo with 71-grain FMJ bullets. Penetration would be considerably better than the 60- and 65-grain hollowpoints, and, at these pedestrian velocities, their expansion may be a sometimes thing. Lastly, and although this is a minor point, the muzzle energy of the FMJ loads is about 12-percent greater than with the HPs.

The .32 ACP is one of the most popular cartridges ever designed and, even today, new pistol models chambered for it are available. But the little gun still does what it was designed to do and continues to command considerable interest from shooters, collectors, and historians alike. In the M-1903 and the .32 ACP, we have a classic example from an era that had a different approach and mindset to the concepts of personal safety. Thus, as long as law-abiding citizens are allowed to defend themselves with firearms against law-breakers, the Colt M-1903 will maintain its status as One Good Gun.

The W.C. Wolff Company can supply exact replacement springs for almost any rifle, shotgun, or handgun. Here are new springs for the M-1903 Colt 32 ACP, from left: extractor, firing pin, and recoil springs. The magazine and its old spring are at right.

RUGER'S ECONOMY-
AMERICAN

The Ruger American Rifle was tested by the author on his private rifle range, at 100 yards.

-PRICED RIFLE

BY Tom Tabor

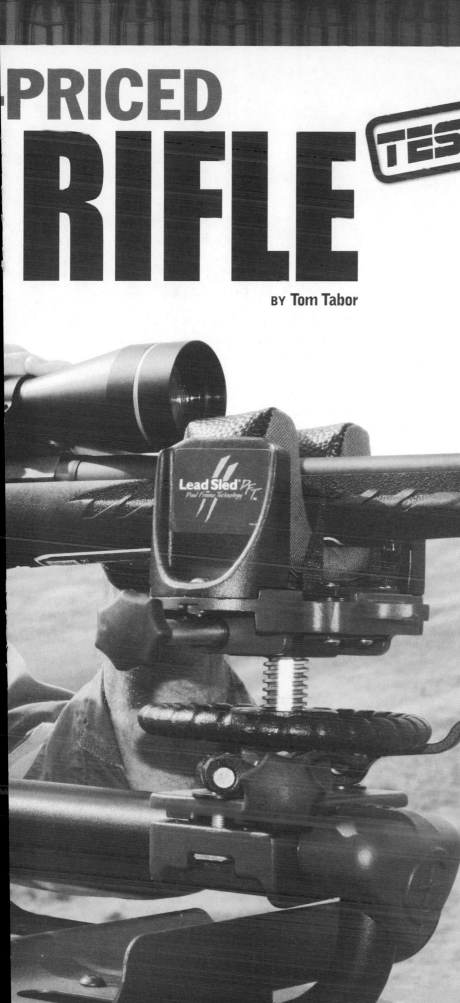

The quality of our firearms today has never been better, and our firearms manufacturers should take pride in that accomplishment. Unfortunately, improvements in quality frequently are accompanied by increases in manufacturing costs, and that almost always translates into higher costs to the consumer. A couple decades ago, you may have been able to purchase a new centerfire rifle of very good quality for about $500, but, today, that same model rifle may now carry a price tag of double that amount or more. The good news is that Sturm, Ruger & Company, one of America's largest and most respected gunmakers, has taken action to curb that trend with the introduction of its Ruger American Rifle.

This is a very good quality and accurate centerfire that is 100-percent American made and available in .22-250 Remington, .243 Winchester, .270 Winchester, 7mm-08 Remington, .308 Winchester, and .30-06 Springfield. Possibly best of all, the Ruger American Rifle carries an MSRP of only $449 and, with a little shopping around, it's likely you can trim that price down even lower.

I was anxious to see an American firsthand and finally obtained one chambered in one of my favorite calibers, the .243 Winchester. I've always felt the .243 was a great cartridge, but it has been made even better, in recent years, due to an insurgence of terrific, high-performing new bullet weights and styles. Now, by simply switching from a 100-grain big-game style of bullet to a 55-grain high-fragmenting design, the .243 can be easily transformed from a very effective killer of whitetail deer to a high-performance round for coyotes, prairie dogs, and jackrabbits.

Salient Features

Like many people, when I encounter what appears on the surface to be a bargain-priced item, a few ol' clichés immediately jump to mind, like, "You don't get something for nothing," or "You get what you pay for." So, understandably, I was a bit skeptical, when I first saw

The Ruger American Rifle, chambered in .243 Winchester, would be an excellent low-cost choice for hunting species like whitetails, as well as smaller game.

the advertisements touting the price of the new Ruger American. But, once I had an opportunity to personally look one over and even dirty its bore, that cautious skepticism vanished as quickly as a whitetail can be swallowed up in a brushy creek bottom.

While some compromises clearly have been made by the Ruger engineers in order to keep the end price down, in my mind, those concessions resulted in little to no affect on the actual performance of the rifle. And, aside from its favorable price, there are a number of unique attributes that are important to consider.

Topping the list of important attributes, each rifle comes equipped with Ruger's new Marksman Adjustable Trigger (RMA), which can be easily adjusted without the assistance of a gunsmith. My rifle came from the factory set with a trigger pull weight of

four pounds, five ounces (on a five-pull average), but I later adjusted it down to what seemed to be the minimum for that particular trigger, a reasonable and light 3½ pounds. Adjusting the trigger is as easy as pulling the stock off and turning a single Allen-headed adjustment screw located directly in the front of the trigger housing.

Outwardly, the Ruger trigger appears similar to Savage Arms' AccuTrigger, but it differs internally somewhat. Like the AccuTrigger, the RMA possesses a tiny, spring-loaded lever-like projection in front of the trigger that must be compressed before the rifle is allowed to fire. The inherent advantage in this type of trigger design is its ability to be set to fairly light pull weights, while still maintaining a high degree of safety from accidental discharges. In the case of my test rifle, I found the RMA trigger to be

relatively crisp, with little or no creep, and easy to get use to.

The Ruger American Rifle comes with a black synthetic stock equipped with what Ruger calls its Power Bedding system. Two stainless steel V-Blocks help to ensure proper positioning and consistent alignment of the barreled action to the stock. One of these blocks is located in front of the trigger assembly, the other in front of the magazine. This mounting system, along with a contact-free floated barrel, helps to improve the shooting accuracy of the rifle.

Ruger deviated from the usual method of welding the bolt handle to the body of the bolt. Instead, the metal of the one-piece handle passes through a hole in the side of the bolt, interlocking the two pieces together. The bolt lugs and the bolt body are machined from a single piece of steel. Coupled with dual cocking

The three locking bolt lugs and bolt body are machined from a single piece of steel.

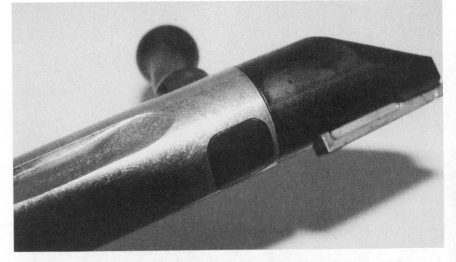

Rather than welding the bolt handle to the side of the bolt, in the case of the American Rifle, the metal of the handle projects through a hole in the side of the bolt, interlocking the two parts together.

cams and three locking lugs located on the face of the bolt, this helps to provide a higher degree of strength and integrity to the action. The bolt handle is positioned low and has a short 70-degree throw, a design that makes it easier for a shooter to cycle cartridges while the rifle remains on the shoulder. It also allows the scope to be mounted low to the action and barrel. The barrel, by the way, was hammer forged and free-floated, and the receiver came drilled and tapped for scope bases, which were included and installed on the rifle. These are the typical two-piece Weaver style that fits a wide variety of scope rings.

While the vast majority of centerfire magazines store their cartridges in a type of "Z" pattern, the American utilizes a rotary design, much like the one Ruger uses for its rimfire rifles. I must admit, I was a little disappointed to find that the magazine was entirely made of plastic, rather than metal, but I suppose that is one of the compromises necessary to keep down the overall cost of the rifle. Nevertheless, the magazine functioned flawlessly, feeding the cartridges into the chamber smoothly and perfectly every time. The magazine snapped in and out very easily, which is not always the case with some modern-day rifles. The magazine held three .243 cartridges, and a fourth could be fed directly into the chamber.

With the empty American weighing a mere 6¼ pounds, I would clearly place it in the class of a lightweight walk-about rifle. All six calibers come with a 22-inch barrel. There is also a Compact Model in .243, .308, and 7mm-08 with an 18-inch barrel and 12½-inch LOP, intended primarily for young shooters. The barrel of the .243 was very sleek and trim, with the muzzle measuring only .575-inch in diameter. It had a 1:9 right-hand twist and came with a target style crown. The entire rifle, both stock and metal, was nicely finished in a moderately fine-textured matte blue/black. The stock came with a recoil pad and sling swivel studs installed, and the pistol grip and forearm were attractively textured to produce a non-slip surface, even when wet. Rather than possessing the typical removable trigger guard, the trigger guard was actually a molded part of the synthetic stock.

Range Testing

I was anxious to see how the Ruger American Rifle would perform on the range and quickly mounted one of

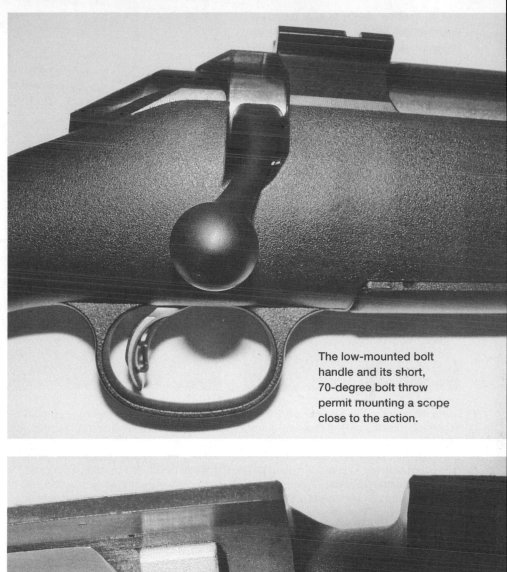

The low-mounted bolt handle and its short, 70-degree bolt throw permit mounting a scope close to the action.

Ruger's Power Bedding system consists of two stainless steel bedding V-Blocks. Shown here is the rearmost block. The other block is identical and located just ahead of the magazine housing.

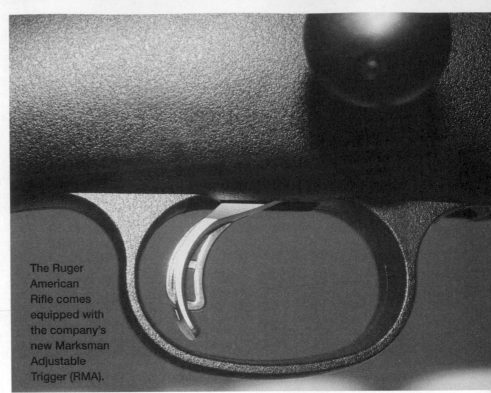

Below: Another unique feature found on the American Rifle is its cocked indicator. Shown here as a piece of un-blued metal located behind the bolt, it warns the shooter the rifle is in the cocked position.

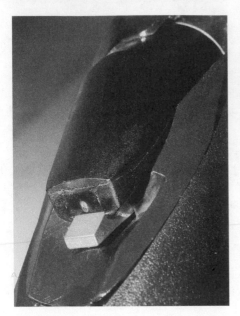

The Ruger American Rifle comes equipped with the company's new Marksman Adjustable Trigger (RMA).

Leupold's newer VX-R 3-9x50mmFireDot scopes on it, using a set of Leupold 30mm QRW (quick release) rings. This is a fairly big scope that possesses a substantially large front bell, but, due to the American's design, including the short 70-degree bolt throw and the low mount of the bolt handle, the scope mounted up perfectly, even with the lowest rings Leupold offers.

Whenever I'm doing a review of a firearm, I like to challenge the gun by shooting a wide variety of loads. I believe this kind of testing produces a more thorough evaluation and understanding of the firearm's overall capabilities. Some rifles are naturally inclined to shoot a particular bullet weight better than another. This is partially due to the rifling twist rate of the barrel, but other factors are also influential, so covering a broad spectrum of bullet weights and styles produces a more comprehensive picture of what a particular rifle may or may not like when it comes to accuracy. In this case, even though the American had a preference for some loads over others, it wasn't overly finicky about what I put down its bore. The most accurate groups came from my own handloads with 55-grain Nosler solid-base bullets, but it also shot the handloaded 87-grain Hornady V-Max loads nearly as accurately. When it came to the factory loads, the Hornady Superformance 58-grain V-Max loads slightly outperformed the others, but all of the factory-loaded cartridges produced very acceptable groups. For a complete look at how all the ammunition performed, I would encourage the reader to peruse the accompanying accuracy chart.

Conclusion

No one should expect the Ruger American Rifle to be on an even keel with rifles in the class of a finely crafted Dakota, Cooper, or Blaser, all of which demand prices multiple times higher than the American. Clearly, in order to keep the price down, Ruger made some construction and design compromises. Only you can determine whether those concessions are justifiable in lieu of a high price tag. In

55 gm Nosler S. B.

This excellent, three-shot 100-yard group was shot using the author's handloads consisting of Nosler 55-grain solid-base bullets backed by 43 grains of Hodgdon Varget powder.

Ruger American Rifle Accuracy Testing
.243 Winchester 100-yard 3-shot groups

Handloads				
Ammo	Powder	Best Group	Worst Group	Average Group
55-grain Nosler Solid Base	Varget - 43.0-grains	1/4"	1-1/4"	15/16"
87-grain Hornady V-Max	Alliant AL15	1/2"	1-1/4"	15/16"

Factory Loads			
Ammo	Best Group	Worst Group	Average Group
Hornady Superformance loaded with 80-grain GMX®	1-3/8"	1-7/8"	1-1/2"
Hornady Superformance loaded with 95-grain SST®	1-1/2"	2-5/8"	1-13/16"
Hornady Superformance loaded with 58-grain V-Max®	11/16"	1"	13/16"
Federal Premium loaded with 95-grain Nosler Ballistic Tips	1-5/8"	2"	1-5/8"
Federal Premium Vital-Shok loaded with 100-grain Nosler Partition	7/8"	1-15/16"	1-9/16"
Federal Fusion 95-grain	1-3/8"	2-1/2"	1-3/4"
Barnes Vor-Tx loaded with 80-grain Tipped TSX Boattails	1-3/16"	2-7/16"	1-3/4"

Note: All groups were shot off the bench at 100-yards and were comprised of 3-shots each. The handload data shown here is presented merely as an illustration of the potential of this particular test rifle. While the handloaded ammunition was felt to be safe in this particular firearm, they may not be safe in other firearms, even those of like construction. The author assumes no liability or responsibility for such use. For load data, you must consult the handloading guides published by the component manufacturers and never exceed those deemed to be maximum loads.

my opinion, I found the American to be a very appealing and serviceable rifle available in a price range that most shooters could easily work into their family budget. I was particularly pleased with the fact that the Ruger American Rifle is 100-percent American-made. With so many of our products coming out of China and other, less-desirable third-world countries

these days, many guns of which lack in overall quality, I find this rifle's origin an extremely comforting characteristic. I was also impressed with the American's out-of-box accuracy and the fact it didn't seem to be finicky when it came to shooting different types of the ammunition. Few rifles would perform any better, no matter what the price tag read.

In future years, I believe the Ruger American Rifle will turn out to be an overwhelming success story for the company. If that happens, it might encourage other manufacturers to follow suit with their own well-built, low-cost rifle models. We'll just have to wait to see if they take the hint. In the meantime, if you have a

One of the most accurate of the factory cartridges was the Hornady Superformance loaded with 58-grain V-Max. This three-shot 100-yard group was typical of the groups shot with this ammunition.

This nicely formed three-shot cloverleaf group was shot at 100 yards using Federal Premium loads with 100-grain Nosler Partition bullets, further demonstrating this rifle versatility.

TEST FIRE

RUGER SR40

BY Steve Gash

The SR40 has an accessory rail for the attachment of essential accessories, such as a high-intensity light, a laser sight, or even this pistol bayonet from LaserLyte.

Sturm, Ruger & Co. has been on the cutting edge of firearms design for decades, and not by chance, either. A Ruger design engineer was once asked why a certain gun turned out the way it had. The engineer just shrugged and said, "Because that's the way Bill [Ruger] wanted it." In addition to the innovative .22 semi-automatic pistol that launched it all, to the ubiquitous 10-22 rifle, the classy M-77 bolt-action sporters that festoon gun safes everywhere, and the sumptuously elegant No. 1 falling block single shot, Ruger can scratch almost any shooter's itch.

A troubling development for gun haters has been the virulent outbreak of freedom across the fruited plain. This has spawned a host of specially designed, lightweight, polymer-framed semi-auto pistols for home- and self-defense. There usually isn't much "me-

too-ism" from Ruger, but the company has recently developed a good variety of such arms. The initial model was the SR9 in 9mm Luger, which was quickly followed by a Compact SR9c. More recently, the SR40 and SR40c were introduced in the super-popular .40 Smith & Wesson cartridge. This makes a lot of sense, since many justifiably think any defensive caliber ought to begin with a "4."

Both frame sizes have their place, depending on the intended use. The compact models shave about .64-inch off the barrel and 3.1 ounces off the weight of the standard models. This is not to say the standard models are big. They're not, but they are a bit larger than the compacts. All four versions have a coordinated set of synergetic features that produce a comfortable, efficient, and reliable shooting system.

The Ruger SR40 is striker-fired and offers a host of unique features,

exceptional reliability, great ergonomics, and excellent accuracy. (I might mention that it is also modestly priced, with an MSRP of only $525.) The SR40 features a glass-filled nylon grip frame. The pistol fits my hand like a glove, and—praise be—its angle is exactly the same as a 1911, important to those of us trained on the old .45. When I raise the SR40 to shooting position, the sights are pointed right at the target.

The trigger has a trigger safety lever that prevents firing unless the trigger is completely pulled. An ambidextrous manual safety is also provided at the rear of the slide, which not only prevents firing, but also locks the slide. Its use is not required because, like most other DAO pistols, the gun is completely safe until the shooter picks it up and pulls the trigger. A flat loaded-chamber indicator, another safety feature, is on the top of the slide at the rear of the ejection port and sticks up when a round is loaded in the chamber.

The trigger pull on my test-fire sample was seven pounds, one ounce. It was a bit gritty at first, but, after a few break in rounds, it smoothed right up. To me, it felt like a highly tuned revolver—just as a DAO pistol is supposed to—first shot to last. Additionally, the SR40 uses a unique link-less system to lock and unlock the barrel that differs from those pistols in the Ruger P-series. Movement of the slide fore and aft is slick and quick. Combined with a grip frame that is extremely strong, lightweight, and very pleasing to the hand, felt recoil seems moderated. I also liked that the molded-in checkering on the grips, backstrap, and front of the grip, which provide a good handhold without sand-papering off your skin when firing.

The trim little pistol weighs a mere 27.2 ounces with an empty magazine.

Loaded with 15 rounds, it tips the scales at 36.4 ounces. The 4.1-inch barrel has six grooves with a 1:16 right-hand twist. Slides are made of either alloy or stainless steel, depending on finish. My test gun had the stainless slide, and I can report that it had a lustrous and uniformly brushed finish that is very attractive. A black nitride version is also available.

Another nice feature is the reversible backstrap. The pistol comes with the arched side out, but, if you prefer a flat backstrap (as you'd find with the original M-1911), just push out a little pin, turn the backstrap over, and reinstall. It takes all of about 30 seconds, if you go really slow.

The magazine release is ambidextrous. Thankfully, when it is pressed from either side, the magazine is instantly launched out of the grip like it's jet propelled. Insertion of a magazine is slick and effortless. The gun, by the way,

is shipped in a hard plastic case with two 15-round magazines.

The SR40 has a magazine disconnect system that prevents firing if the magazine is removed. The gun will "snap" with the magazine removed, but it won't fire with a live round in the chamber. Also, the trigger pull is not the same with the magazine removed as when firing a loaded gun. Importantly, the owner's manual specifically cautions that dry-firing a SR series pistol without a magazine "may result in damage or unnecessary wear to the magazine disconnect mechanism and/or striker," and may get you exiled to the Gulag. In other words, don't do it. The SR40 can be dry-fired without damage to the pistol, when an empty magazine is in place.

An accessory rail is provided at the bottom front of the grip frame, to which the user can hang all manner of accoutrements like a laser sight, high-intensity light, or a pistol bayonet. Up top, it

The SR40 is a comfortably sized pistol that comes with two 15-round magazines and a handy loading tool.

The SR40 sub-assemblies: the frame, barrel/slide/recoil spring, and magazine.

BELOW: The SR40 trigger features a safety lever that must be activated for the gun to fire. Note the right-side button for the ambidextrous magazine release.

Field striping the SR40 is a snap. With the recoil spring and its guide removed, the barrel slips right out for easy cleaning.

seems to be an article of faith that all defensive pistols have fixed sights, never mind that they don't always hit where they look and you can't change them, but guess what? The SR40 has excellent three-dot sights with a fully adjustable rear. There's a click-adjustment screw for elevation and a set screw that must be loosened to drift the sight for windage. The rear sight adjustment worked like a charm, and it stayed put. Another revelation is that the width of the rear-sight notch is actually wide enough to see light on either side of the front sight. Both sights are dovetailed in place, so fussbudgets can install after-market replacements, if desired.

Field striping the pistol for cleaning is a breeze. First, make sure the pistol is unloaded, then lock the slide back and remove the magazine. Push the ejector down and forward—you can't fieldstrip the pistol unless you do—then remove the takedown pin assembly and, while holding the slide, release the slide stop and ease the slide off the grip frame. Remove the guide-rod assembly and its spring, then remove the barrel. Reassembly is in reverse order. After the takedown pin is replaced and the slide is still locked back, the ejector then must be pushed up to its original position. This can be done either with your finger or simply by inserting the magazine back in place.

On the test range, the SR40 was accurate and reliable. I tested 13 factory loads and 20 handloads (see the results in the table). Mercifully, there was none of the "first shot out of the group" nonsense so common to many semi-autos. Reliability is absolutely paramount in any defensive pistol, and there was not one failure to feed, fire, or eject with any of hundreds of rounds I tested. Also, it was a lot of fun to shoot. Like Goldilocks said, "It's not too small or too big, it's just right."

Overall accuracy of the SR40 was excellent. With either factory ammo or selected handloads, groups averaged from two to three inches for five shots at 20 yards from a rest; 10 loads handily beat two inches. This is outstanding accuracy for any defensive pistol.

Several loads with new "wonder" bullets offer an optimum combination of penetration and expansion, even through clothing or other barriers—essential for self-defense or law enforcement work—and muzzle energies exceeded 400 ft-bs. The two mid-weight Hornady 155-grain loads were powerhouses, with the Custom XTP load registering a sizzling 1,152 fps and 457 ft-lbs of muzzle

energy, and the TAP/FPD version close behind at 1,098 fps and 415 ft-lbs. The various 180-grain loads clocked about 900 to 980 fps, and the SR40 favored the Hornady 180-grain Custom XTPs and Winchester's economical USA JHPs. A bonus with all these rounds was the SR40's excellent adjustable rear sight, which made switching loads easy. It was tough picking a "best" load, but I finally settled on the Hornady Custom XTP

load, because of its excellent accuracy and a crunching 457 ft-lbs of muzzle energy.

Handloading the .40 S&W is easy, and all bullets tested shot well with at least one load. All it took was a little experimentation. Conventional wisdom holds that the small .40 S&W case and powder charges don't call for magnum primers, but this has not been my experience. I have loaded thousands of rounds of

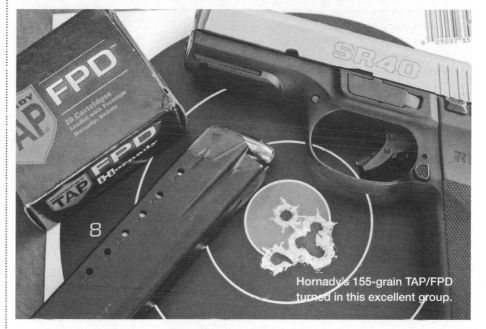

Hornady's 155-grain TAP/FPD turned in this excellent group.

Range Results, Ruger SR40 .40 S&W
Factory Loads

Factory Load & Bullet Type	Bullet Weight (gr.)	Listed Velocity (fps)	Average Velocity (fps)	Muzzle Energy (ft-lbs)	SD (fps)	Average Accuracy (inches)
Federal American Eagle FMJ	180	1,000	922	340	4	2.12
CCI Blazer FMJ	180	1,000	942	355	13	1.93
Speer Gold Dot GDHP	180	1,025	979	383	11	2.36
Winchester USA FMJ	180	1,020	883	312	6	2.72
Winchester SXT	180	1,010	894	320	10	2.03
Winchester USA JHP	180	1,010	951	362	13	2.09
CorBon DPX Barnes XBP	140	1,200	1,126	394	3	1.67
Hornady TAP/FPD	155	1,180	1,098	415	10	2.64
Hornady TAP/FPD	180	950	952	362	12	2.48
Hornady Custom XTP	155	1,180	1,152	457	3	2.83
Hornady Custom XTP	180	950	897	322	20	2.01
Hornady Critical Defense FTX	165	1,045	1,074	423	11	1.96
Winchester PDX1 Bonded JHP	180	1,025	1,032	426	12	2.09

RIGHT: Highly visible three-dot sights adorn the SR40 slide. The front sight is dovetailed and is, thus, easily replaceable, if desired.

The rear sight is likewise held in a dovetail and is drift-adjustable for windage, click-adjustable for elevation. It provides a clean sight picture for fast, accurate shooting.

HANDLOADS

Powder	Powder Charge (grains)	Bullet Brand, Weight (grains) & Type	Average Velocity (fps)	SD (fps)	Muzzle Energy (ft-lbs)	Average Accuracy (inches)
Power Pistol	8.0	Hornady 155 XTP	1,133	8	442	2.42
Titegroup	5.6	Hornady 155 XTP	1,077	14	399	1.77
Silhouette	7.1	Hornady 155 XTP	1,031	6	366	2.89
AutoComp	6.7	Sierra 165 JHC	1,062	22	413	1.81
VihtaVuori N350	7.1	Sierra 165 JHC	1,056	6	409	2.00
WSF	6.4	Sierra 165 JHC	1,023	5	384	1.77
Power Pistol	7.4	Sierra 165 JHC	1,053	8	406	1.53
True Blue	7.0	Sierra 165 JHC	971	17	346	2.40
True Blue	6.4	Sierra 180 JHC	884	11	312	2.41
AutoComp	6.3	Sierra 180 JHC	1,009	4	407	2.39
VihtaVuori N350	6.5	Sierra 180 JHC	982	13	386	2.50
Power Pistol	6.8	Sierra 180 JHC	980	11	384	2.51
Blue Dot	8.2	Sierra 180 JHC	974	21	379	2.67
Longshot	7.2	Hornady 180 XTP	1,086	10	456	1.73
SR-4765	6.3	Hornady 180 XTP	904	26	327	2.28
True Blue	6.4	Hornady 180 XTP	927	5	344	2.11
AutoComp	6.3	Hornady 180 XTP	997	6	397	1.81
AutoComp	5.0	Hornady 200 XTP	828	4	304	2.40
Longshot	5.7	Hornady 200 XTP	894	11	355	1.30
VihtaVuori 3N38	7.1	Hornady 200 XTP	864	16	332	2.46

NOTES: A Ruger SR40 semi-auto pistol with a 4.1-inch barrel was used for all testing. Velocities were measured with an Oehler Model 35P chronograph with the front screen 10 feet from the muzzle. Accuracy is the average of three five-shot groups at 20 yards from a Caldwell Matrix rest. Range temperatures were 48° to 66° F. Mixed-brand cases and CCI-550 primers were used for all loads. Cartridge overall length was 1.125 inches. Neither the author nor Gun Digest/F&W Media are liable for the suggested handloads listed here. ALL handloaders should consult their reloading manuals and gun manufacturers for appropriate handloading information.

ABBREVIATIONS: FMJ, full metal jacket; GDHP, Gold Dot Hollow Point; XPB, X Pistol Bullet; JHP, Jacketed Hollow Point; SXT, Supreme Expansion Technology; TAP/FPD, Tactical Application Police/For Personal Defense; XTP eXtreme Terminal Performance; JHC, Jacketed Hollow Cavity.

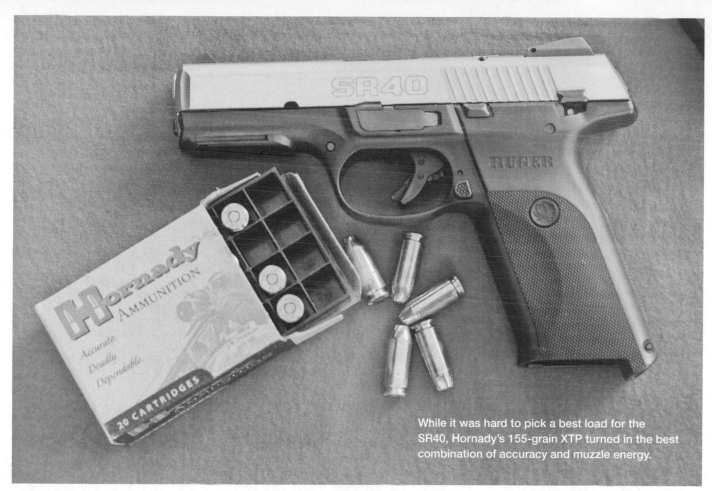

While it was hard to pick a best load for the SR40, Hornady's 155-grain XTP turned in the best combination of accuracy and muzzle energy.

.40 S&W for IPSC-type competition, and am convinced that hotter caps equal lower standard deviations in velocities and better accuracy than standard primers, so I used CCI-550 primers for all handloads shown in the table. Another technique that really improves handload reliability is the use of a Lee Carbide Factory Crimp Die. This innovative product resizes the complete round after it's loaded and assures it will chamber in any gun of that caliber.

I liked the performance of this pistol so much, I broke Gun Writer Rule No. 2*—"Never Buy Test Guns"—and sent Ruger a check. The SR40 is now my regular carry gun around the farm. Its user-friendly ergonomics, quality construction, excellent accuracy, total reliability, and modest price make it worth a look for anyone considering a self-defense handgun—or just a neat auto pistol for lots of shooting fun.

*Just so you know, Gun Writer Rule No. 1 is "Always Tell The Truth."

The SR40 gives the term "drop-free magazine" a whole new meaning. Pressing either magazine release button causes the magazine to be instantly ejected from the gun.

Ruger SR40 Specifications

Type: Striker-fired, semi-automatic, DAO pistol

Caliber/Gauge: .40 Smith & Wesson

Capacity: 15+1, two 15-round flush-fit magazines provided; 10-round versions available

Barrel length: 4.14 inches, 1:16 right-hand twist six grooves

Weight: 27.2 ounces (with empty magazine)

Overall length: 7.55 inches

Overall width: 1.27 inches

Sights: Fully adjustable three-dot sights

Finish: Brushed stainless steel (tested) or black nitride alloy steel slide; glass-filled nylon frame

Stocks: Nylon, integral with grip frame

MSRP: $529

Contact: Sturm, Ruger & Co., Inc. (www.ruger.com)

The S&W Model 647 comes fully equipped with both a bi-pod and a red dot/green dot sight.

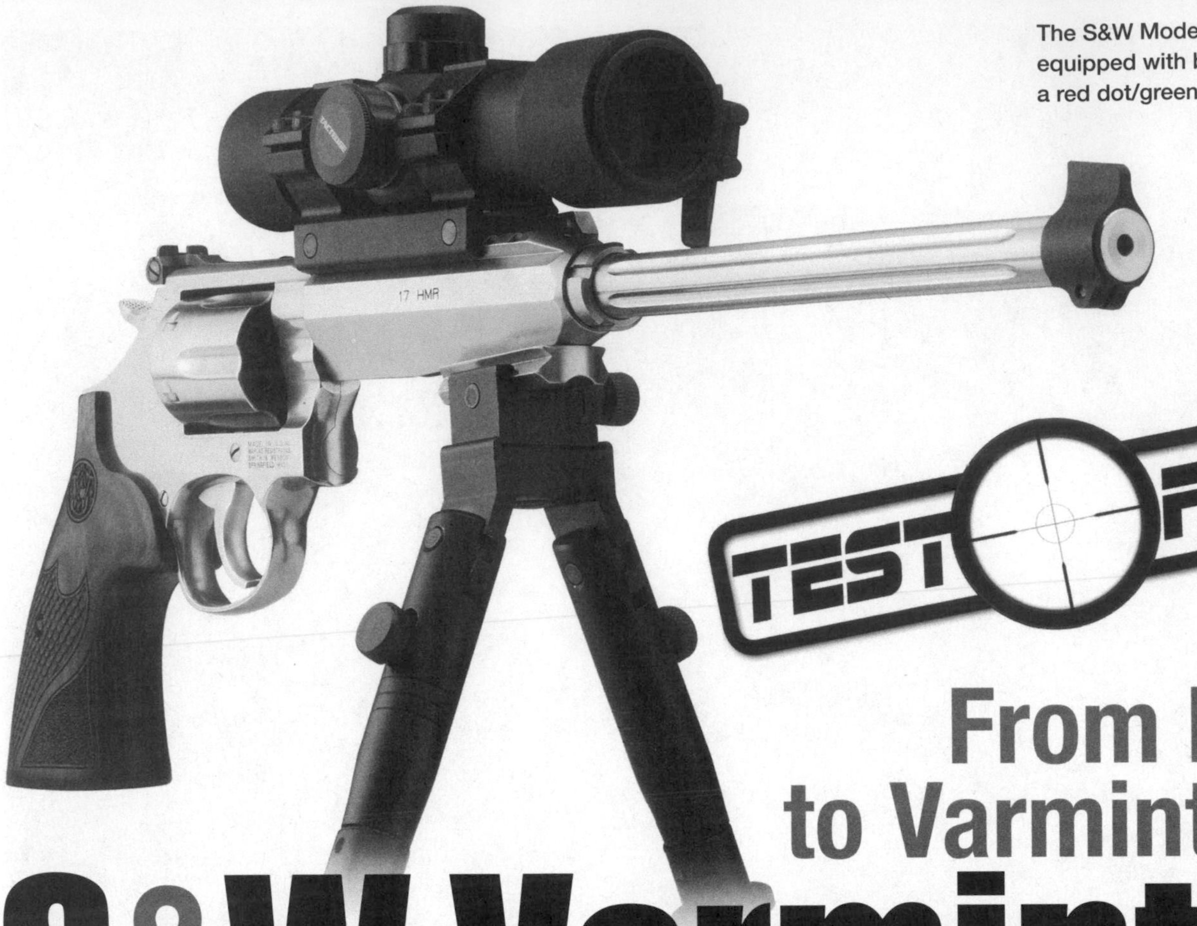

TEST FIRE

From Hand to Varmint—the S&W Varminter

BY Tom Tabor

For more than a century and a half, Smith & Wesson has been turning out handguns of impeccable and noteworthy quality, in a wide variety of designs. But, to me, the company's historical bread and butter has always been firmly rooted in the fine double-action revolvers it produces. Continuing today in that same vein of wheelgun excellence is the company's new Model 647 Varminter. This is a stainless double-action revolver specifically designed for shooters like me, who sometimes like to help rid the planet of vermin or hunt small game. The Varminter is a six-shot wheelgun chambered in the very popular .17 HMR rimfire cartridge, making it a great match for small game, whether that comes in the form of pest species or eatable critters.

Testing the Varminter, I found it to be both attractive to the eye and functionally perfect in its operation and makeup. Its 12-inch barrel has been distinctively designed in a combination of round fluted and modified hexagonal shapes. The iron sights are the typical low-mounted adjustable notched blade in the rear and what S&W calls a ramp sight in the front; I would, however, characterize the front sight as more of a non-ramp blade style. Both sights care in a matte blue finish, adding a bit of contrast to the general stainless appearance of the Varminter.

For most shooting applications, the iron sights are only for supplemental use. Intended for primary use, a Picatinny-style rail has been machined directly into the rearmost portion of the barrel, which allows the shooter the flexibility of mounting a wide variety of different shooting optics; S&W includes a red dot/green dot sight with every Varminter purchase. For steadiness of shooting, the company also saw fit to include a removable bi-pod, which mounts to a dovetail appendage on the bottom of the barrel.

My first exposure to the Model 647 Varminter happened at a prairie dog shoot outside the almost non-existent town of Grand Encampment, Wyoming. There I joined forces with several other gun writers and firearm enthusiasts, in an attempt to reduce the area's overwhelming infestation of prairie dogs and, at the same time, get a better handle on the performance of the Varminter.

Because of the typical longer range shooting often encountered on the open prairies, we felt it best to swap out the red dot/green dot optical sight for a scope possessing a bit of magnification. In this case, I chose a Weaver 1.5-4x20mm handgun scope. This combination worked out perfectly, I'm sure to the dismay of the local prairie dogs population in the area. All of Weaver's handgun scopes are built in Japan, which, in my mind, is certainly

The Varminter worked as well on small game like this cottontail as it did on prairie dogs.

a noteworthy advantage. The Japanese have a long and well-established reputation for constructing some of the best optics in the world, and this particular Weaver lived up to that standing. The Weaver came with a gloss blue finish and a Dual-X reticle. While it is common to set rifle scopes to be parallax-free at 150 yards, the Weaver handgun scopes are all adjusted to 50 yards. I think this is optimum for a handgun scope, particularly for this type of shooting application.

Overall, the combination of the .17 HMR Varminter handgun, the Weaver 1.5-4x20mm scope, and Hornady ammunition produced great results on the prairie dogs. I believe if a shooter would equip both a moderately powered handgun scope and the red dot/green dot sight that comes supplied with the Varminter with quick release rings, it would make an absolute perfect shooting/hunting combination. Doing so would provide the versatility needed to match just about every possible shooting situation imaginable. The open sights would be fine for shooting offhand at very close range, and, when needed, the red dot/green dot sight would provide a little more precision in

The muzzle of the Varminter is cut with a target crown for enhanced protection from damage and to improve accuracy.

Even though Smith & Wesson calls the front sight a "ramp sight," Tom feels it is better characterized as a bladed, non-ramp style.

The machined-in Picatinny-style rail mounting system makes installing and switching around optics easy and effortless.

bullet placement. Finally, for longer range shooting, the scope could be quickly mounted and employed. Plus, switching back and forth from one sighting option to another would be as easy as turning a couple levers, all without the need to re-zero on the range. Several companies are making quick release scope rings that can be used in conjunction with the Varminter's Picatinny rail base. A few examples that come to mind are Leupold's QRW, Warne's Maxima Quick

Detach, or Weaver's Grand Slam Lever Lok Quick Release System. All are great products that will consistently return the same point of bullet impact each and every time the optics are removed and remounted.

Another favorable attribute of the S&W Varminter is the dovetail base located on the bottom of the rearmost portion of the barrel. This works perfectly for mounting the bi-pod that comes with the Varminter. Depending

upon which way you position the bi-pod, the legs will either fold forward or to the rear, and procuring each position is as easy as loosening the locking nut on each individual leg, followed by moving the nut downward. This releases the catch that locks the leg in position, permitting it to be folded out of the way. I'm thinking this same dovetail base appendage could also be utilized for a light for night shooting, or maybe even for a laser sight.

A longer tripod, like this Vanguard Pro T68, provides the ability to get the bullet trajectory above the natural ground cover.

The Weaver 1.5-4x20mm scope just seemed to match the S&W Varminter perfectly, when it came to shooting prairie dogs.

Having an overall length of 17 inches and weighting 54 ounces, I would characterize the Varminter as a moderately large handgun. However, even with this amount of bulk, I found that the moderate recoil from the little .17 HMR cartridges still prohibited me from watching the bullet impact its target through the lens of the Weaver scope.

Like most modern S&W revolvers, the six-shot cylinder swings out the left side of the frame and rotates in a counterclockwise manner. As is always the case with double-action revolvers, the trigger pull was much heavier when it was shot double-action. Because of this, I found shooting it in single-action more conducive to accurate shot placement. Doing so simply allowed me to place my shots a bit more accurately both on the prairie dogs and, later, on the range. When shot as a double-action, the trigger pull measured a full 11.31 pounds, but, when shot as a single-action, the pull weight came in at a modest five-pull average of 3.875 pounds.

For strength and durability, the trigger, trigger-stop, and hammer have all been chromed, and the action comes from the S&W Performance Center fully tuned. I found the cylinder snapped in and out of place effortlessly and its movements to be very smooth. The empty cases were ejected easily and with little resistance.

The grips on the Varminter were both eye catching and functional. Made from some exotic type of hardwood, possibly rosewood, Smith & Wesson has combined the attractiveness of the black-and-red-grained wood with a pleasant blend of checking and texturing. To top that off, the S&W logo has been etched into the top of each grip panel. The grips weren't overly large, but they seem to fit my average-sized hand very nicely. They were designed to expose the metal on the back of the revolver frame, but wrapped around and made contact with each other in the front.

Field shooting of any firearm provides a great testing platform with which to judge a product's performance. Doing so puts a strain on the gun's capabilities, but I also like to expose most firearms to the less hostile conditions found on the firing range. This more controlled environment can add another facet to an overall evaluation. So, upon returning from Wyoming, I headed out back to my private range to see how the Varminter would perform on paper targets.

For this area of the evaluation I shot Federal V-Shok loaded with 17-grain Speer TNT spitzer bullets; Remington Premier Magnum loaded with 17-grain Accu-Tip V Boattails; and Hornady cartridges loaded with 17-grain V-Max bullets. All three types of ammo produced amazingly similar, five-shot 50-yard groups. The smallest group was produced with the Hornady ammo, which measured a respectable 1¹/₈ inches. Nevertheless, the Remington and Federal cartridges weren't far behind, with both shooting nicely shaped 1¼-inch groups.

Once I'd established the accuracy capabilities of the Varminter, I couldn't resist turning my sights in the direction of my brightly colored Champion Duraseal swinging silhouette prairie dog targets

The combination of checkering, texturing, and the S&W logo carved directly into the wraparound grips adds significantly to the beauty of the Varminter.

located a full 100 yards downrange. I wouldn't try to convince anyone that I hit those tiny swingers with every shot, but I will say I sent them spinning on a fairly routine basis.

The new Smith & Wesson Model 647 Varminter may not be every shooter's handgun. It certainly wasn't designed to be a defensive weapon (even though I'm thinking it would probably work fine in that capacity), but, when it comes to varmint killing potential, small-game hunting, wreaking havoc with silhouettes, or simply economical fun plinking on the range, I believe you would be hard-pressed to find a better handgun anywhere. Clearly, the Varminter demonstrates the quality of craftsmanship that Smith & Wesson has become famous for. MSRP for the Varminter, including the red/dot-green/dot sight and the bi-pod: $1,299.

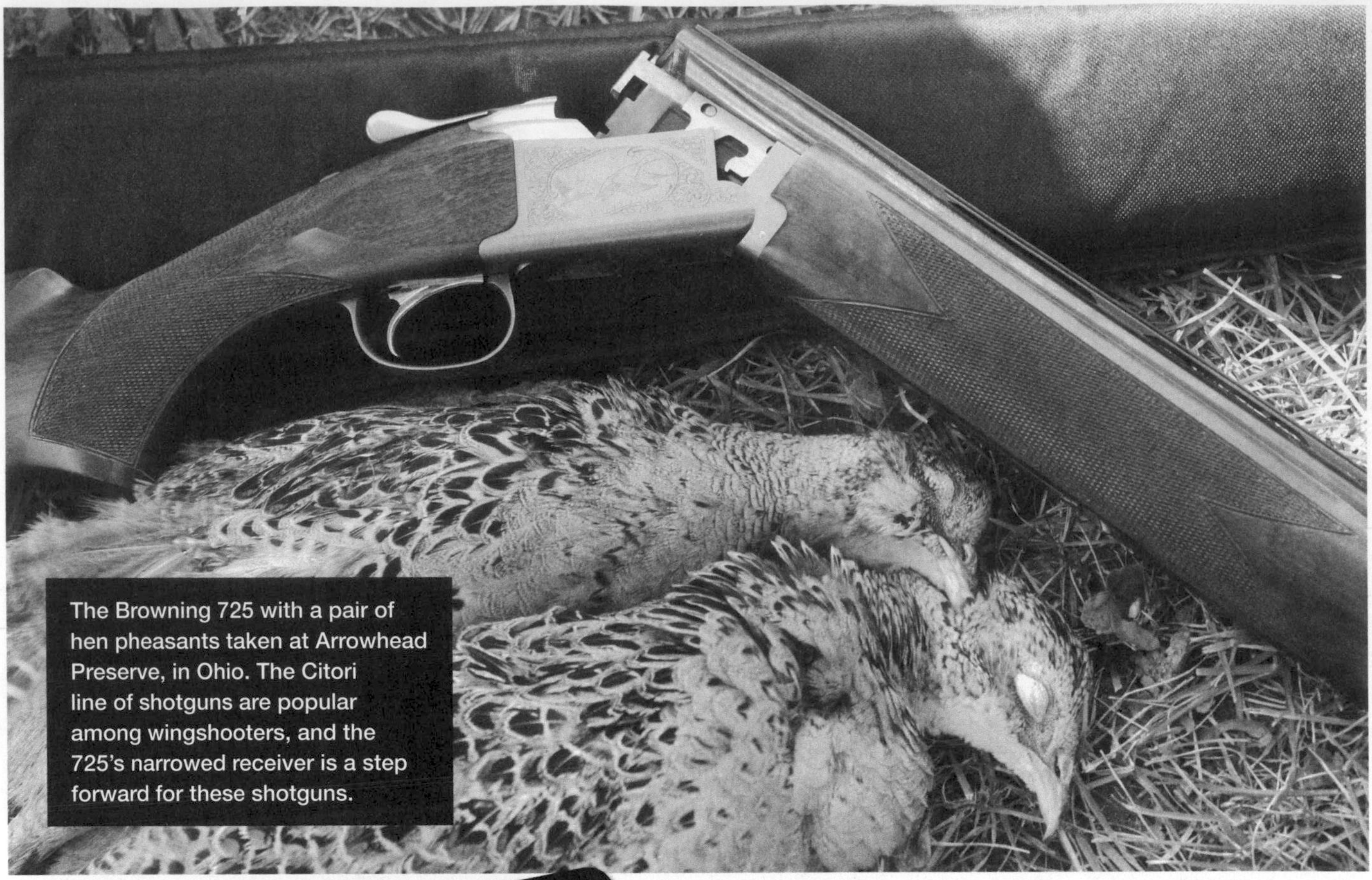

The Browning 725 with a pair of hen pheasants taken at Arrowhead Preserve, in Ohio. The Citori line of shotguns are popular among wingshooters, and the 725's narrowed receiver is a step forward for these shotguns.

TEST FIRE

THE BROWNING 725

America's Favorite Over/Under Gets an Overhaul.

BY **Brad Fitzpatrick**

here are some shotguns that are simply beyond reproach. Iconic guns usually attain this status because millions of them have been sold or because it's hard to find anyone who has anything bad to say about them. The Winchester Model 12 was such a gun, in its time the go-to pump gun for quail, doves, ducks, and everything else. The Remington 870 also classifies as an iconic American shotgun, and it seems that everyone has a fondness for Big Green's legendary scattergun. I think Parker's double guns fit in that category, as well as Remington's venerated 1100 semi-auto. Winchester's Model 21 side-by-side certainly shares the honor, too.

Gun designer John Moses Browning developed a number of iconic guns, including the Browning Superposed over/under, a gun that has become the standard by which all other stack-barrels are judged. Until that point, the viability of an over/under shotgun was questionable. Side-by-sides were already popular, pumps guns were selling well,

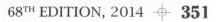

Steve Taylor with an Ohio pheasant taken with the 725. Browning's new Citori is a first-rate field gun that will also perform dutifully on the clays course. For the dedicated competition shooter, sporting clays models with and without adjustable combs are available.

The 725's steel receiver has a silver nitride finish and high-relief engraving. A duck adorns the right side of the field model, and a pheasant appears on the left. The receiver is narrower than older models, thanks to a smaller diameter full-length hinge pin.

Browning's new FireLite mechanical triggers are among the best found on any shotgun. Breaking at just under four pounds, FireLite triggers make it easy to shoot the 725 well.

and Browning's own semi-auto A-5 was a hit. Would American hunter and shooters buy into the concept of two vertical barrels? The answer was yes, and Browning's design was poised to revolutionize the shotgun industry.

Browning over/unders, whether they were the original Superposed guns (in production off and on from 1931 until 1960), or the more recent Citori line, have been an overwhelming success. In 2008, Browning produced its millionth Citori, a major milestone for any gun. That the Citori has always been priced higher than most field guns speaks volumes to the commitment shotgunners have to the world's most famous stack-barrel design.

It's not easy to improve on a classic, and any change to an iconic product is bound to bring with it some level of criticism. There certainly have been changes in Browning's line of over/unders during the past 82 years, but the overall appearance and function of the guns has remained largely unchanged. Sure, they've gone through a series of aesthetic and nomenclature changes—the Model 325 gave way to the 425, the 425 begat the 525, then the 625, and so forth. There were upgrades and tweaks along the way, both cosmetic and mechanical, but the formula remained much the same.

Then came the 725.

The 725 doesn't represent a radical revolution in either form or function, and many shooters would have a hard time telling the current 725 apart from its varied predecessors. Browning realized long ago that the Superposed/Citori line appealed to the purist, and it is

unlikely we'll see any dramatic changes or avant garde styling details on any new version of the company's storied stack-barrel in the near future. But there are changes to this latest model, some of which are minor—and some of which are significant.

The most striking change can't be seen while examining the smooth lines of the new 725. The most telling difference between it and all the Browning over/unders that came before lies within, specifically within the trigger assembly. Browning has always relied on inertia triggers for its Citoris, which means the recoil energy generated by the first shot cocks the firing pin for the second barrel. On the 725, the traditional inertia trigger has been replaced by a mechanical trigger, which does not rely on the first barrel firing to fire the second. In addition, Browning incorporated its new FireLite trigger into the design of the 725. This is truly an evolutionary step forward for the Citori line. The quality of triggers in centerfire rifles has improved vastly over the last decade, but very few companies boast that they offer light, crisp, clean triggers in their shotguns. The new FireLite system breaks at under four pounds, for both trigger pulls, without any creep, and the new Browning trigger is as good or better than anything short of high-end competition shotguns. It may go unnoticed by the casual shooter, but experienced shotgunners will appreciate the new trigger.

The other major alteration to the 725 has to do with the depth of the action. Since John Browning's original Superposed version, Browning guns have had deep actions, due in part to large, full-length hinge pins. The design was robust and durable, but many shooters preferred the sleeker, thinner, Italian guns like those of Beretta and Fausti, with their low-profile boxlock actions. The 725 was Browning's first attempt to narrow the storied action, and even though the company shaved less than 3/16-inch from the vertical depth of the 725 by reducing the size of the hinge pin, it looks much sleeker. The pistol grip contour has changed slightly, too, and is now canted rearward. The result is a gun that feels livelier and more connected to the shooter. The overall look of the gun is less paunchy than with previous models.

Other styling changes are far more subtle, but, to the Citori purist, these changes will immediately stand out.

Family ties. The gun in front is a 1930s Superposed with double triggers. The 725 bears many similar features. The main aesthetic differences are the depth of the action, the shape of the toplever, and the finish. Browning has produced quality over/unders for 80 years, so there's no need to make dramatic changes.

First, the action release lever on the top of the gun is radically different that the model that has been standard on Browning Citori guns since production began. Citoris have traditionally had a more rounded knob on their top levers than other shotguns, but the new 725 has a longer knob that stretches farther along the tang and is vertically shorter than traditional lever knobs. It's a minor detail, yes, but the Browning fans I shot with recognized it immediately.

Browning has never tried to make its Citori guns look gaudy or radical. You won't find any faux-gold game birds on the action, and scrolling has been kept to an austere but classy minimum. The new 725 Field bears traditional game scene engravings on each side of the receiver; a duck adorns the right side and a pheasant can be seen on the left. The engraving is very good quality. Likewise, the oil-finished grade II/III walnut stock is nicely figured, and the dark wood stands in sharp contrast to the silver nitride receiver.

As it is with its predecessors, the 725's receiver is steel and not aluminum. The overall weight of my test gun with

The fore-end of the 725 might be called a semi-schnabel style. It's comfortable and allows the shooter to point the gun well. This pointing ability is aided by gun's excellent balance.

28-inch barrels was 7 1/3 pounds. The fore-end appears to be a hybridization of the style found on the company's classic Lightning, and the schnabel style preferred by the sport shooting crowd. Regardless, the hands falls naturally in place and the grip is secure. The Inflex recoil pad is the same version found on other Browning guns like the Maxus and does a fine job minimizing recoil.

When the 725 Citori that I was to test for this article arrived, I pieced it together and was immediately impressed by its sleek lines and obvious build qual-

ity. The changes aren't radical, but I will say that I believe that those in action contour were indeed needed and well executed on the new gun. Even a 3/16-inch reduction in action depth brings the shooter's hands noticeably closer to the center of the gun, and the overall feel and handling of the 725 is better than with previous models. It isn't enough of a change to send purists into fits of rage, but it is effective and noticeable.

Browning guns are favorites in competitive skeet and sporting clays circles, and I believe the new 725 won't miss a step in

The combination of a lower-profile receiver, superb trigger, and better recoil pad complement the already robust and reliable design of the 725. It isn't cheap, but it is a well-built American shotgun that will last for many, many years.

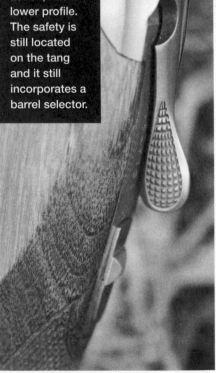

The toplever shape, like the action, has a lower profile. The safety is still located on the tang and it still incorporates a barrel selector.

the competition world; though the version I tested was a field gun, the DNA is there for a quality competition gun. The balance point is just ahead of the receiver, meaning the weight is evenly distributed between the hands. The field gun wears white front and mid-beads and includes the company's new Invector DS thin-walled choke tubes, which are designed to seal out gases and residue that gum up other tubes and make them difficult to remove after excessive shooting. The 725 seemed to pattern consistently, which helps the shooter break more clays and drop more birds.

I took the Model 725 afield and spent a day hunting ringnecks in Ohio, and it performed as expected. I'd shot several rounds of trap with the gun not long before and found the gun to be responsive, easy to shoulder, swing, and shoot. There was no difference when I hunted pheasants and, when a bird rose up in front of me, I shouldered the 725, swung the large white bead ahead of the rooster's beak, and pressed the trigger as I passed the bird. The trigger broke cleanly, and the pheasant cupped its wings, falling just ahead of the English setter hot in pursuit. Over the course of

Specifications
Browning 725 Citori Over/Under Shotgun

Caliber/Gauge: 12-gauge

Barrel length: 28 inches

Weight: 7.3 pounds

Overall length: 45¾ inches

Finish: Silver nitride receiver; blued barrels

Stock: Grade II/III oil-finish walnut

Triggers: Mechanical, 3.8 pounds

MSRP: $2,469.99

Contact: Browning www.browning.com

the day, I had a couple of more chances at birds, and the 725 worked its magic each time.

It's always dangerous to mess with a successful recipe, but Browning made the wise decision to address the issues that hunters and shooters carped about, with regards to their world-beating over/under. The result is an even better Citori, which is saying a lot, because the previous version wasn't too shabby.

Looking for a really good feeling sub-compact in the luxury pistol department? This may be your gun.

The HK P2000 SK

BY **Mark Kakkuri**

TEST FIRE

uns have a certain feel about them. And because of that, I have certain feelings about guns. Some guns feel chunky and plasticky and gimmicky. These guns make me feel like trying my hand at plastic surgery in order to trim them up or tone them down. Some guns feel heavy and stiff. These guns make me feel like giving them a massage to help them loosen up a bit. Some guns feel thin—functional but not outright durable. These guns I am afraid to shoot, let alone carry for self-defense. Guns like these I want to wrap in duct tape to help keep them together.

Not all guns have a bad feel. In fact, some feel just right in terms of fit and finish, functionality or how they fire. You can tell much about a gun's feel just by hefting it in your hand. You can tell much more, however, after a session at the range. Sometimes you're surprised by how a gun feels after shooting, but most often the range time simply confirms the suspicions you had before shooting it.

No surprise, there's lots of subjectivity in this matter of determining how a gun feels. It might be impossible to fully quantify, but I'm going to give it a shot.

The Heckler & Koch P2000 SK felt good when I first tried it out. Not in a nonspecific way but truly and functionally. Since HK is one of the premier firearms designers and manufacturers in the world, this came as no surprise. Frankly, with a retail price of $983, we're in the luxury class of handguns, so it had better be outstanding.

In-the-Hand Performance

A sub-compact pistol available in 9mm, .40 and .357 SIG, the P2000 SK feels good when I'm just holding it in my hand—remarkably good in fact. I'm not just talking about how I heft the pistol and appreciate the ergonomics or the balance. It's more than those. For example, the simple action of removing the magazine, a downward push on the ambidextrous magazine release, feels sure and confident. There's no mush in the controls. You won't eject the magazine on accident. When you do want the magazine to drop, it springs out perfectly. Put the magazine in and it seats perfectly. No extra push needed. No wondering whether it's fully seated.

With the magazine out, the simple action of pulling the slide back to check for an empty chamber demonstrates superbly engineered, mechanically perfect motions, noises and feels. Dry-fire it and the trigger stroke, a light double action known as the law enforcement modification (LEM), feels perfect, even as it is a bit longer than most trigger strokes. Yet it is smooth, sure and consistent and one of the best I've ever felt.

Besides shooting the P2000 SK, which I will address shortly, the other action worth mentioning is the loading of the magazines. Pushing in nine .40 caliber rounds revealed just the right amount of resistance from the spring under the follower. Loading rounds seven and eight and nine showed no classic signs of fight.

On-the-Range Performance

Shooting the P2000 SK was pure joy because the gun got out of the way of the shooting experience, so to speak. In other words, all the mechanisms worked together so well, so smoothly, that nothing stood out during the range session. I just squeezed the trigger, again and again, and the HK sent every round down range, right on target.

The balance was superb and the sights were easy to acquire, shot after shot. But the best part of shooting the P2000 SK was the LEM trigger. More than just a double action-only trigger, the HK LEM trigger incorporates a 7.3- to 8.5-pound pull in an action that combines a precocked striker with a double action hammer. So it's double action-only but it's light and smooth, with just slightly increasing pressure required as it travels back. You'll see the hammer move back and fall with every stroke. It doesn't jerk, grab or stutter in its travel. If a round fails to fire, the LEM trigger system allows for second and third strike capability, though I never needed it.

The LEM trigger felt much lighter than the advertised 7.3- to 8.5-pound pull, but I attribute that to the ultra-smooth trigger travel. Even with its gradually increasing resistance, I couldn't discern by feel if the trigger was nearing its breaking point; when the HK fired it surprised me every time but I was never unprepared for it. Indeed, after a while I could tell when the gun was about fire because it was always when my finger pulled the trigger back to exactly the same point. Shooting quickly—about two rounds per second—was remarkably easy, intuitive and fun.

Notice that I haven't yet mentioned recoil. That's because recoil on this handgun, while present, is aptly managed by the mechanical recoil reduction system—a dual captive recoil spring and polymer bushing. The system works so well in absorbing recoil that you have to actively think about the recoil in order to remember it's there.

The P2000SK (subcompact) is similar to slightly larger P2000 model and combines characteristics of the elements of the HK USP Compact pistol. It is available in 9 mm, .40 S&W, and .357 Sig with an MSRP of $983.

HK P2000 SK

Caliber:	9mm, .40 S&W, .357
Capacity:	10+1, 9+1
Frame:	polymer
Slide:	steel
Sights:	3-dot
Trigger:	single-action/double-action LEM/CDA trigger system
Barrel:	3.26 in., polygonal cold-hammerforged
Length:	6.41 in.
Height:	4.55 in.
Weight:	1.5 lb.
Options:	modular grip accessory
SRP:	$983
Website:	www.hk-usa.com

The combination of the HK's balance, ergonomics, LEM trigger and recoil absorption system worked in harmony with the three-dot sights, allowing for easy follow up shots. It was easier to shoot this gun faster and more accurately than most others I have fired.

Additional Features

HK includes a modular grip accessory to increase the depth of the stocks. My medium-to-large sized hands enjoyed the P2000 SK's stock in its standard configuration so much I didn't bother with the extra piece. Some might prefer flush magazine baseplates, especially for concealed carry, instead of the two included nine-round magazines that feature a baseplate with a pronounced lip. I actually liked how these felt.

All the controls on the HK are ambidextrous. I'm a right-hander so I would right thumb the slide release on the left side of the slide but use my right middle finger to push the magazine release on the right side of the trigger guard. The P2000 SK also featured a tactical rail for lights and lasers. For a carry pistol, I found this to be a bit superfluous and would have preferred a skinnier dust cover and slide.

I have to admit, prior to shooting the HK P2000SK I was skeptical that the $983 retail price was justified. Sure, I knew of HK's reputation for excellence, durability, reliability and accuracy. But once I experienced it first hand, the luxury price of this sub-compact pistol seemed more tenable. I just had to feel it for myself.

Mark Kakkuri is a freelance writer in Oxford, Mich. You can follow him on Twitter @markkakkuri.

Mossberg's New 20-Gauge Defensive Guns

BY Doug Howlett

Two new Model 500s offer the ultimate mix between ease-of-use and reliable performance no matter a homeowner's shooting skill level.

The Model 500 8-Shot 20-gauge with six-position adjustable stock is a versatile home defense option with a length of pull that varies between just under 11 inches to nearly 15 inches. The MSRP is $606.

Want to start a good debate among your fellow shooters? Just toss out the question: What is the best type of firearm for home defense? You'll likely get as many answers firing back at you as different people in the room, and for the most part, most of the opinions will be (at least partially) valid.

Certainly, those among the concealed-carry contingent will advocate the same sidearm they tote in public and practice with at the range, citing the familiarity developed with the handgun of their preference—revolver vs. semi-auto, 1911 vs. Glock, 9mm vs. 380 vs. .45 vs. you name it is a whole other argument—and this group of avid shooters makes a great point. Modern rifle fans will definitely dig versatility and the visual intimidation factor of an AR. Compact when outfitted with a collapsible stock or in a carbine configuration and rigged with a tactical white light or laser sights and able to feed ample rounds in an extreme defensive situation (of course, isn't any defensive situation extreme?), it's hard to argue against their choice. And of course, citing the minimized likelihood of pass-through shots in walls and

shot patterns that reduce the absolute necessity for the precise aim of a single projectile, scattergun fans will espouse the benefits of the shotgun as the ultimate defensive gun. To a point they're absolutely correct as well.

From that latter option, I imagine there have been more than a few non-gun owning couples that have strolled into a gun shop in search of a firearm they can use for self-defense, particularly to put the woman's mind at ease when the husband may be away, only to roll home with a hard-kicking 12-gauge that after the first shooting session, will leave the woman thinking, "No way!" A local gunsmith friend of mine encountered just such an elderly couple who were looking to unload their recently purchased 12-gauge for that very reason.

My buddy suggested instead of giving up their hopes for defensive peace of mind, that they try a lighter 20-gauge. The kick is minimal, the guns are typically lighter and easier for smaller stature shooters to handle, yet available loads still deliver plenty of close-range knockdown mixed with mid-range aim forgiveness. Let's be honest. Most people who are not avid shooters, but still want a gun for home

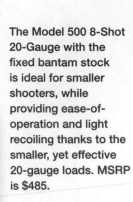

The Model 500 8-Shot 20-Gauge with the fixed bantam stock is ideal for smaller shooters, while providing ease-of-operation and light recoiling thanks to the smaller, yet effective 20-gauge loads. MSRP is $485.

SEMI-AUTOS UPDATED

Want to soften that 20-gauge recoil even more? Package it into an autoloading shotgun for rapid shot cycling and less punch to the shoulder. For 2013, Mossberg International has updated their SA-20 line with a full-length pistol grip stock model with mag cap tri-rails and a standard synthetic stock model with mag cap tri-rails. Both front cap rails allow for the mounting of lights, lasers or other attachments, while the ghost ring aperture site is also mounted with a receiver-top Picatinny rail for a red-dot or other sight attachment. Both models have a six-round capacity and retail for less than $530.

– Doug Howlett

defense, are not going to practice as often as they should—if more than once or twice—and are going to require a gun that is easy to operate in an unnerving situation and offer a little insurance against an unsteady aim. In fact, it might help if the gun is visually intimidating and maybe even generates a universally understood, blood-chilling sound as it is taken to battery. That alone can sometimes mitigate a situation before a shot ever even has to be fired. Enter the 20-gauge tactical pump shotgun—two new models of which hit store shelves in 2013 courtesy of North Haven, Ct., gunmaker Mossberg.

Mossberg is already the largest selling shotgun brand in the United States with more than 40 worldwide military contracts largely built around providing reliable, yet affordable tactical scatterguns for use by soldiers and even many law enforcement personnel. That alone is a ringing endorsement for the average homeowner.

New Model 500s

Recognizing the increasing value of the 20-gauge to the growing self-defense consumer, Mossberg (www.mossberg.com) introduced two new Mossberg 500 eight-shot pump actions. The guns are chambered to handle 2¾- or 3-inch shells and function on nonbinding twin-action bars for a positive lock-up

and smooth feeding. The compact 20-inch barrel is a fixed cylinder bore for rapid shot expansion in the typically short distances common to defensive situations. Aiming is aided by a ghost ring rear aperture sight and single-post front. For both concealment and ease-of-care, metalwork is finished in a nonreflective matte blue finish while the stocks and forends are made of a durable synthetic plastic in a matte black finish. The safety is the traditional ambidextrous Mossberg rear tang safety, and the guns come with swivel studs already mounted for easy sling attachment.

The Model 500 8-Shot Bantam has a shortened 13-inch length-of-pull fixed stock, ideal for smaller stature shooters, while the other model is a Model 500 8-Shot with a six-position adjustable stock and vertical pistol grip for a more tactical look and broader shooter versatility. The length of pull on the adjustable stock model ranges between 10¾ inches and 145/8 inches. The shotguns weigh 6 pounds and 6¾ pounds respectively with the suggested retail price on the fixed-stock model set at $485 and the collapsible stock model going for $606. Both guns boast the features and performance most homeowners seek in an easy-to-use tactical shotgun and will provide the peace of mind that should it ever be needed—by anyone in the house—it will deliver as promised.

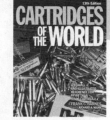

BY **John Haviland**

SAAMI

SPORTING ARMS & AMMUNITION MANUFACTURERS INSTITUTE

American shooters and hunters can buy a box of .30-06 cartridges produced by Federal, Hornady, or other ammunition manufacturers and fire them confidently and safely in rifles produced by Remington, Ruger, or other firearm makers. That reliable interchangeability of ammunition is entirely the result of the work of the Sporting Arms and Ammunition Manufacturers' Institute, Inc. (SAAMI), which is an association of the nation's leading manufacturers of firearms, ammunition, and components.

Decades ago, that wasn't the case. At the turn of the last century and into the 1920s, the American firearms and ammunition industry was shifting from an era of cartridges loaded with blackpowder to an increasing number of new cartridges loaded with smokeless propellants. Confusion with cartridge names was common. For example, the .40-60 Winchester and the .40-60 Marlin are different cartridges. However, the .40-65 Winchester and .40-60 Marlin are interchangeable and both can be fired in the same rifle. Perhaps the low pressures generated by blackpowder were a bit more forgiving of firing a cartridge that failed to conform to a rifle chamber, but the higher pressures generated by smokeless powders were not.

Factory-loaded cartridges of the same cartridge designation, such as these .458 Winchester rounds, are within SAAMI specifications and are therefore interchangeable in a variety of firearms for that given cartridge, no matter which American company produces the cartridges.

"Back then, there were really no safety or reliability standards," said Rick Patterson, the managing director of SAAMI. "One company's cartridges might work in their firearms, but not even fit in another company's gun chambered for the same cartridge! Essentially, everyone was wildcatting."

To rectify the problem, SAAMI was founded, in 1926, at the request of the Federal Government, its mission to create and coordinate firearm and ammunition industry standards for cartridge interchangeability, safety, reliability, and quality. Because firearms and ammunition are not regulated by the U.S. Consumer Product Safety Commission, SAAMI is a voluntary safety association comprised of the nation's leading manufacturers of sporting firearms, ammunition, and cartridge components. SAAMI members include firearms companies like Browning, Colt's, Marlin, Mossberg, Remington, Ruger, Savage, and Smith & Wesson, and ammunition manufacturers like Federal, Hornady, and Olin-Winchester.

When a company submits a new cartridge for SAAMI approval, it must provide quite a bit of data about the cartridge to start the acceptance process. Data includes cartridge and chamber dimensions, bullet diameter, and maximum average pressure limits, among other information.

"All members of the SAMMI Technical Committee go through the information with a fine-toothed comb, to make sure there are no errors," Patterson said. "From there, the information goes to Ammunition Committee for review to make sure, among other things, the cartridge differs from other established cartridges, and then it goes on to the Firearms Committee to make sure the cartridge works

BOTTOM RIGHT: American ammunition companies make dozens and dozens of different styles of .22 Long Rifle cartridges. All of them, though, will fit and fire in a variety of .22 LR firearms from full-sized rifles on down to handguns like this Colt Woodsman.

BOTTOM LEFT: When a shooter chambers a factory cartridge like this 7mm Remington Magnum in his rifle he can thank SAAMI that it will chamber and fire safely.

.223 Remington cartridges are manufactured by a variety companies, they all fit and fire safely in firearms chambered for the .223. merican shooters can thank SAAMI for that.

in firearms." Finally, a Joint Committee of the three sub-committees gives final approval to the cartridge. All this review may take up to six months.

"Once approved, the sponsoring company provides ammunition for the approved cartridge for use in our reference ammunition program," Patterson explained. "That ammunition is then fired in the test labs of different compa-

nies to calibrate their testing equipment, so that everyone's testing equipment is calibrated the same." (SAAMI recognizes two pressure measuring systems. The preferred is the piezoelectric transducer system, where pressure is measured in pounds per square inch (psi). The other and older system is the copper crusher method, where pressure is expressed in copper units of pressure (CUP).

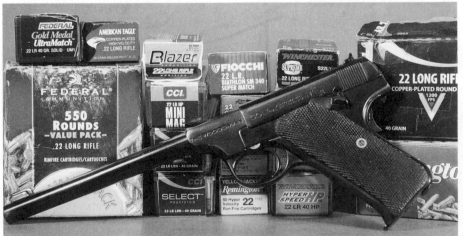

SAAMI specifications require factory-loaded cartridges to meet specific case and bullet dimensions (right). SAAMI specifications also helped standardize such old cartridges as the .220 Swift (bottom).

These cartridge approval committees, and other SAAMI committees, are made up of volunteers from SAAMI member employees.

"We have only three full-time employees," Patterson said, "but, we have 150 volunteers from member companies, and many consultants."

SAAMI does not test propellants used by handloaders to reload cartridges and shotshells.

"Really, our only guidelines for propellants are that they do not exceed the maximum average pressure for a particular cartridge," Patterson said. "That leaves a lot of innovative room to come up with a better cartridge design."

Nor does SAMMI test firearms.

"We only proof ammunition, as in 'here are the dimensions and the maximum average pressure at which it is loaded.' That provides lots of room for innovation on the part of the firearm manufacturer to come up with any firearm that will handle the cartridge and work safely within its pressure limits."

That lack of firearm testing is one of many differences between SAAMI and its European counterpart, the Permanent International Commission for Firearm Testing (CIP). CIP is an international organization comprised of 14 mainly European countries made up of a gathering of national proof houses sponsored by those countries' governments.

"How should I say this in a politically correct way?" Patterson posed to me when we spoke. "Europe has socialized medicine, so those governments figure they will end up footing the bill for the mistakes people make with all products, including firearms, so they figure they might as well have a hand in safeguarding firearms and ammunition."

Before a civilian firearm is sold in any of the CIP member countries, it is tested for safety in one of the proof houses by firing higher than normal pressure, or "proof," loads. Firearms that pass the test are stamped with a proof mark specific to that proof house. Ammunition is also tested at regular intervals, to ensure it meets pressure guidelines.

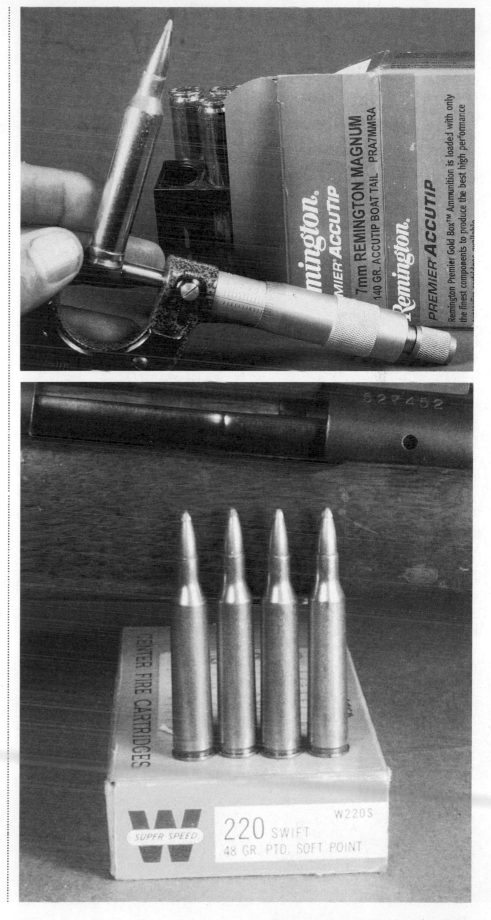

Pressure testing requires a properly chambered pressure barrel for every cartridge tested. Here are just a few of the pressure test barrels at the Western Powders laboratory.

"In the United States system, the government doesn't have such a stake in such things as they do in Europe. But we do have a legal system that assesses high punitive penalties and financial awards." said Patterson. "SAAMI approval of a cartridge provides consumers with a measure of confidence that, not only will the cartridge fit firearms chambered for it, but will fire safely. SAAMI endorsement of a cartridge also provides manufacturers with some legal and liability protection, because they can point to the fact it was loaded to SAMMI specifications."

Several of SAMMI's committees also have their hats in the political ring. The Legal and Legislative Affairs Committee tracks the development of state and federal product liability laws and legislation that may impact the design, manufacture, and sale of firearms, ammunition, and propellants by SAAMI member companies. The Committee actively represents SAAMI members in Washington, D.C., before Congress, the Executive Branch, the Bureau of Alcohol, Tobacco, Firearms, and Explosives, the Federal Bureau of Investigation's National Instant Criminal Background Check System, and other federal regulatory agencies.

"We're always willing to provide technical information, because we wouldn't want any politician to make decisions in a void of accurate technical information," Patterson said.

According to SAAMI's website, the Legal and Legislative Affairs Committee also monitors state legislative proposals. For example, the Committee played a leading role in defeating several California bills, including bullet serialization and firearms micro-stamping legislation that, while well-intentioned, were neither realistic nor workable. Had these bills passed, they would have had disastrous consequence for law enforcement, citizens, and SAAMI member companies alike.

The Committee is proactive, too, working to advance legislation consistent with SAAMI's mission. For example, the Committee worked together with a strong coalition of business groups, shooting sports organizations, and

RIGHT: This device measures pressure via the copper crusher system. A pressure barrel is inserted and a small cylinder of copper is positioned over the cartridge case. The pressure generated in the chamber then crushes the copper cylinder.

the conservation community to win passage in Congress of the Protection of Lawful Commerce in Arms, a law that blocks "junk" lawsuits that would blame firearm manufactures for the actions of criminals.

The Environmental Committee, meanwhile, examines environmental issues affecting the shooting sports by analyzing and collecting data and offering policy proposals to regulatory agencies and the shooting public. Responding to concerns about lead and lead mobility at shooting ranges, for example, SAAMI commissioned E.A. Engineering, Science and Technology, Inc., to prepare a literature search on the issue.

The SAAMI Logistics and Regulatory Affairs Committee (SLARAC) works to shape the constantly evolving transportation and storage regulations, both international and domestic, so that SAAMI products can be distributed economically, securely, and safely throughout the world. SLARAC works closely with domestic and international regulatory bodies. Nationally, this involves the Federal Departments of Commerce, State, Transportation, Labor, Homeland Security, and Justice.

The SLARC produces much information that is readily available to any shooter, range, shooting club, or law enforcement agency that is interested. SLARAC brochures include "Lead Mobility, Small Arms Ammunition (Properties & Recommendations for Storage & Handling)," "Smokeless Powder (Properties & Storage)," "Sporting Ammunition Primers (Properties, Handling & Storage for Handloading)," and "Sporting Firearms (Safe Handling Considerations and Shipping Guidelines for Interstate Transportation)," SAAMI also publishes informational and firearms safety pamphlets like "A Century of Success in Reducing Firearms Accidents," "A Responsible Approach to Firearms Safety," and "Unsafe Firearm-Ammunition Combinations."

Of most interest to shooters and hunters are SAAMI's books that detail industry standards for centerfire pistol and revolver and rifle cartridges, rimfire cartridges, and shotshells. These books, such as Centerfire Pistol & Revolver and

Rimfire, include explanations of pressure measuring systems, velocity versus barrel length data, cartridge maximum average pressure, and detailed cartridge and chamber drawings with minimum and maximum dimensions.

For example, the .357 Magnum has a maximum average pressure of 35,000 pounds per square inch firing 125-grain jacketed soft-point bullets at 1,475 fps from a four-inch ventilated barrel. Conversely, the .22 Long Rifle standard velocity load shooting a 40-grain solid lead bullet has a velocity of 1,135 fps with a maximum average pressure of 24,000 psi. Interestingly, the chamber drawings in the Rimfire book show a .22 LR match chamber is .1875-inch shorter than the .22 Long Rifle sporting chamber. No matter, though, because all .22 LR cartridges will fit and fire safely in all .22 LR chambers. Shooters can thank SAAMI for that positive interchangeability of all brands of .22 rimfires and, for that matter, all other cartridges in their appropriate chambers. Not only that, SAAMI safeguards shooters' rights by keeping an eye on the political climate and backdoor attempts to limit the sale of firearms and ammunition.

In short, SAAMI is the organization that dictates the standards for ammunition manufacture. Conformity to SAAMI

specifications, however, is not mandatory. A lot of small, custom ammunition manufacturers do not verify there ammunition meets SAAMI standards. This does not mean the ammunition they produce isn't safe, just that it has not been verified to meet SAAMI specs.

An example would be companies like Buffalo Bore, which offers "Heavy"

BELOW: These itty bitty copper cylinders are used in the copper crusher pressure measuring system. The shorter cylinder on the left has been crushed during the testing process and will be measured to determine the amount of pressure that compressed it.

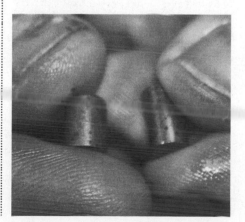

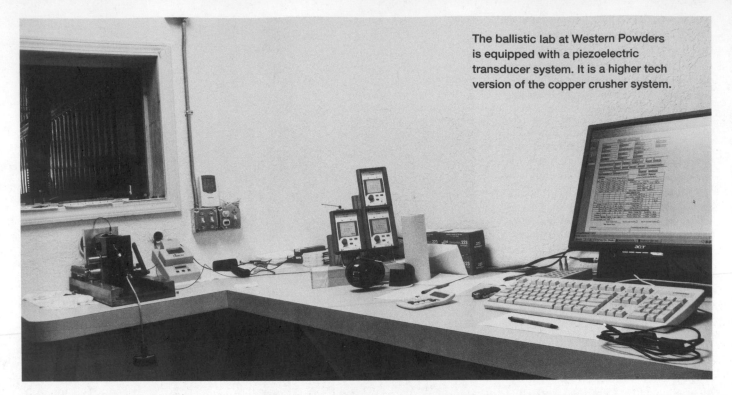

The ballistic lab at Western Powders is equipped with a piezoelectric transducer system. It is a higher tech version of the copper crusher system.

loads for the .45-70, .35 Remington, and other cartridges (their creation a response, in part, to the ongoing popularity of cowboy action shooting and the modern guns of the sport that can handle the increased pressures of these rounds). Generally, these companies post warnings on their ammunition boxes to keep these higher pressure loads from being fired in the weaker firearms (such as first and second generation Colt SAAs and other older and antique firearms), that cause SAAMI to limit maximum operating pressures in the first place.

Some shooters will actually complain that SAAMI limits the performance of cartridges with these lower pressure limits. The .257 Roberts and the 7mm Mauser are perfect examples. With maximum average operating pressures of 54,000 and 51,000, respectively, both cartridges are indeed hindered. However, there are so many older rifles of questionable integrity chambered for either one of these cartridges that these limits are what keep shooters safe. (In

modern bolt-action rifles, both the .257 Roberts and the 7mm Mauser can be safely loaded to pressures equivalent to more modern sporting cartridges like the .243 Winchester and the 7mm-08 Remington.) Taken in that light, it should

be easy to see that SAAMI is indeed on the side of shooters, and it is an organization imperative to all, hobbiests, competitors, hunters, and all other shooters, that this book is about.

These cartridge and chamber schematics found on the following four pages are for the .22 LR, .357 Magnum, .30-06, and 12-gauge 2 ¾-inch are actual SAAMI drawings. These are the schematics used by ammunition and firearms manufacturers when they create ammunition or cut chambers in firearms for these cartridges. Note the minimum and maximum measurements. This explains some of the variance between listed cartridge dimensions in this volume and those that might be obtained when measuring actual cartridges. SAAMI has drawings like this for every SAAMI-approved cartridge. These drawings contain a great deal more information than is presented for each cartridge in this volume, which is intended to offer a basic guide to cartridge identification and history. You can visit the SAAMI web site, www.saami.org, to view drawings for all SAAMI-approved cartridges. (Schematics Courtesy of SAAMI.)

Click HERE to return to the
Table of Contents

S A A M I

SPORTING ARMS AND AMMUNITION MANUFACTURERS' INSTITUTE, INC.

Since 1926

MAXIMUM CARTRIDGE / MINIMUM CHAMBER

22 LONG RIFLE - SPORTING

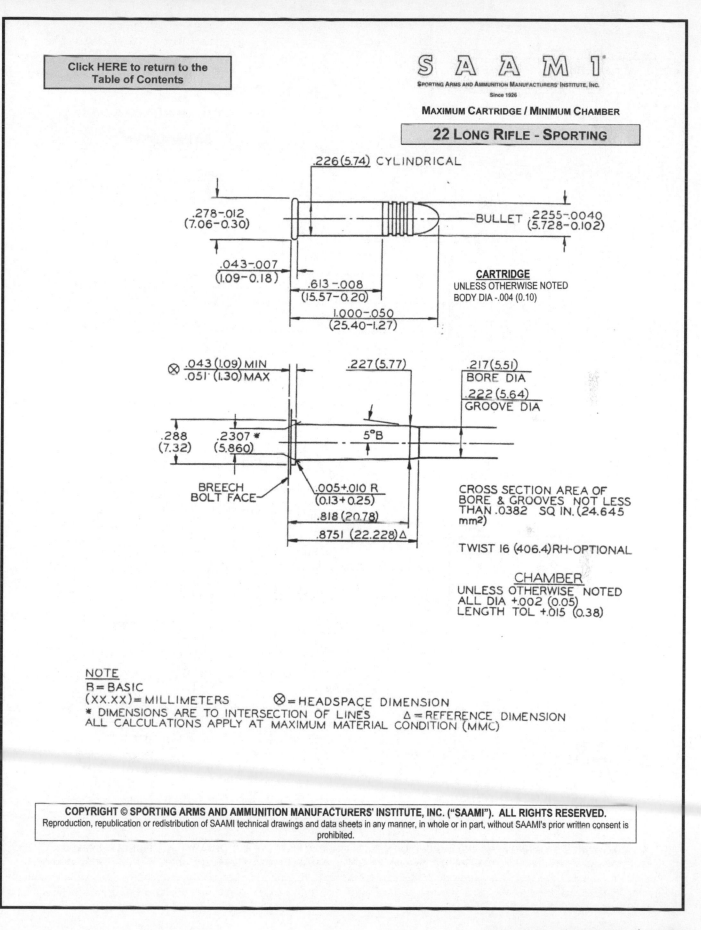

.226 (5.74) CYLINDRICAL

.278-.012
(7.06-0.30)

BULLET .2255-.0040
(5.728-0.102)

.043-.007
(1.09-0.18)

.613-.008
(15.57-0.20)

1.000-.050
(25.40-1.27)

CARTRIDGE
UNLESS OTHERWISE NOTED
BODY DIA -.004 (0.10)

⊗ .043 (1.09) MIN
.051 (1.30) MAX

.227 (5.77)

.217 (5.51)
BORE DIA
.222 (5.64)
GROOVE DIA

.288
(7.32)

.2307 *
(5.860)

5°B

BREECH
BOLT FACE

.005+.010 R
(0.13+0.25)

.818 (20.78)

.8751 (22.228) Δ

CROSS SECTION AREA OF
BORE & GROOVES NOT LESS
THAN .0382 SQ IN. (24.645
mm2)

TWIST 16 (406.4) RH-OPTIONAL

CHAMBER
UNLESS OTHERWISE NOTED
ALL DIA +.002 (0.05)
LENGTH TOL +.015 (0.38)

NOTE
B = BASIC
(XX.XX) = MILLIMETERS   ⊗ = HEADSPACE DIMENSION
* DIMENSIONS ARE TO INTERSECTION OF LINES   Δ = REFERENCE DIMENSION
ALL CALCULATIONS APPLY AT MAXIMUM MATERIAL CONDITION (MMC)

Click HERE to return to the
Table of Contents

SAAMI

SPORTING ARMS AND AMMUNITION MANUFACTURERS' INSTITUTE, INC.

Since 1926

MAXIMUM CARTRIDGE / MINIMUM CHAMBER

357 MAGNUM

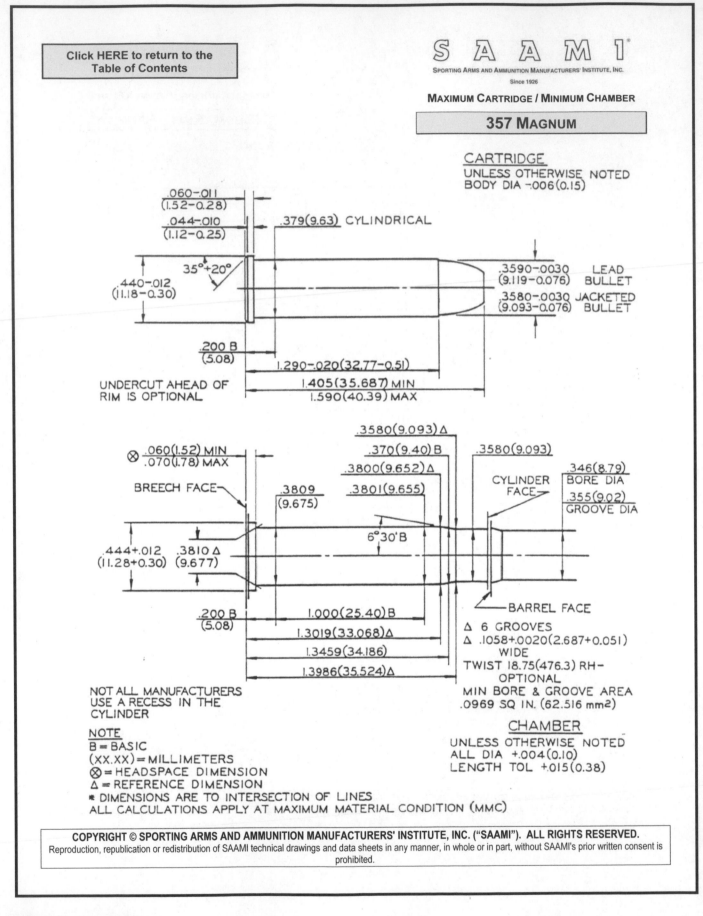

CARTRIDGE
UNLESS OTHERWISE NOTED
BODY DIA -.006(0.15)

.060-.011
(1.52-0.28)

.044-.010
(1.12-0.25)

.379(9.63) CYLINDRICAL

35°+20°

.440-.012
(11.18-0.30)

.3590-0030 LEAD
(9.119-0.076) BULLET

.3580-0030 JACKETED
(9.093-0.076) BULLET

.200 B
(5.08)

1.290-.020(32.77-0.51)

1.405(35.687) MIN
1.590(40.39) MAX

UNDERCUT AHEAD OF
RIM IS OPTIONAL

⊗ .060(1.52) MIN
.070(1.78) MAX

BREECH FACE

.3580(9.093)Δ
.370(9.40)B
.3800(9.652)Δ
.3801(9.655)

.3580(9.093)

CYLINDER
FACE

.346(8.79)
BORE DIA
.355(9.02)
GROOVE DIA

.3809
(9.675)

6°30'B

.444+.012
(11.28+0.30)

.3810 Δ
(9.677)

BARREL FACE

.200 B
(5.08)

1.000(25.40)B

1.3019(33.068)Δ

1.3459(34.186)

1.3986(35.524)Δ

Δ 6 GROOVES
Δ .1058+.0020(2.687+0.051)
WIDE
TWIST 18.75(476.3) RH-
OPTIONAL
MIN BORE & GROOVE AREA
.0969 SQ IN. (62.516 mm2)

NOT ALL MANUFACTURERS
USE A RECESS IN THE
CYLINDER

NOTE
B = BASIC
(XX.XX) = MILLIMETERS
⊗ = HEADSPACE DIMENSION
Δ = REFERENCE DIMENSION
* DIMENSIONS ARE TO INTERSECTION OF LINES
ALL CALCULATIONS APPLY AT MAXIMUM MATERIAL CONDITION (MMC)

CHAMBER
UNLESS OTHERWISE NOTED
ALL DIA +.004(0.10)
LENGTH TOL +.015(0.38)

Click HERE to return to the
Table of Contents

SAAMI
SPORTING ARMS AND AMMUNITION MANUFACTURERS' INSTITUTE, INC.
Since 1926

MAXIMUM CARTRIDGE / MINIMUM CHAMBER

30-06 SPRINGFIELD

CARTRIDGE
UNLESS OTHERWISE NOTED
BODY DIA -.008 (0.20)

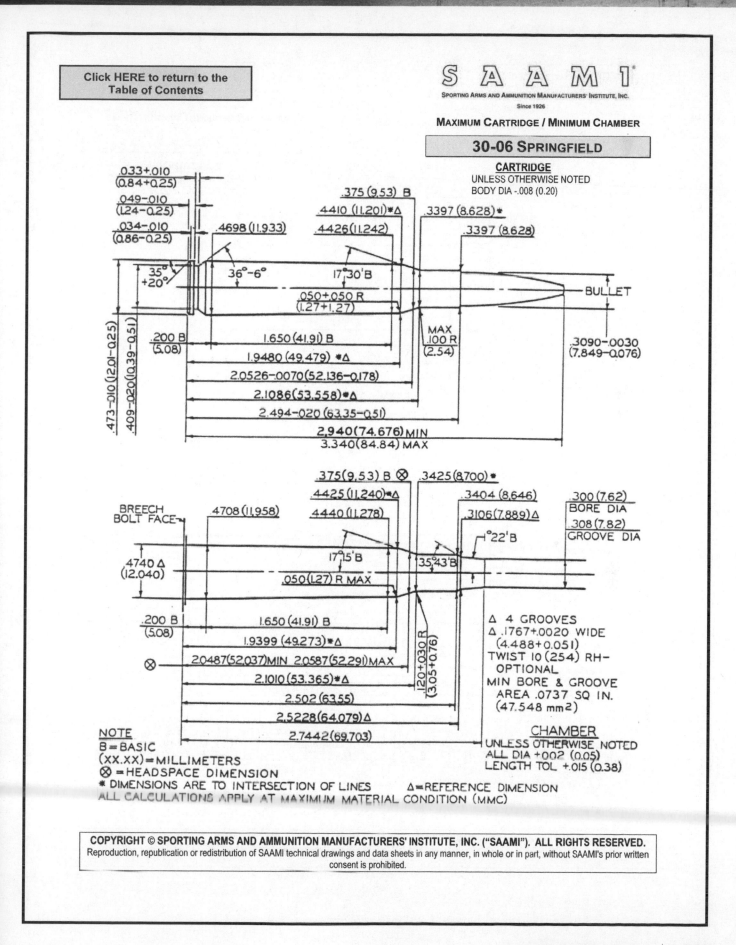

NOTE
B = BASIC
(XX.XX) = MILLIMETERS
⊗ = HEADSPACE DIMENSION
* DIMENSIONS ARE TO INTERSECTION OF LINES   △ = REFERENCE DIMENSION
ALL CALCULATIONS APPLY AT MAXIMUM MATERIAL CONDITION (MMC)

△ 4 GROOVES
△ .1767+.0020 WIDE
(4.488+0.051)
TWIST 10 (254) RH-
OPTIONAL
MIN BORE & GROOVE
AREA .0737 SQ IN.
(47.548 mm2)

CHAMBER
UNLESS OTHERWISE NOTED
ALL DIA +.002 (0.05)
LENGTH TOL +.015 (0.38)

Click HERE to return to the Table of Contents

SAAMI
SPORTING ARMS AND AMMUNITION MANUFACTURERS' INSTITUTE, INC.
Since 1926

MAXIMUM CARTRIDGE / MINIMUM CHAMBER

12-GAUGE – 2¾"

CARTRIDGE
UNLESS OTHERWISE NOTED
LENGTH TOL -.250 (6.35)

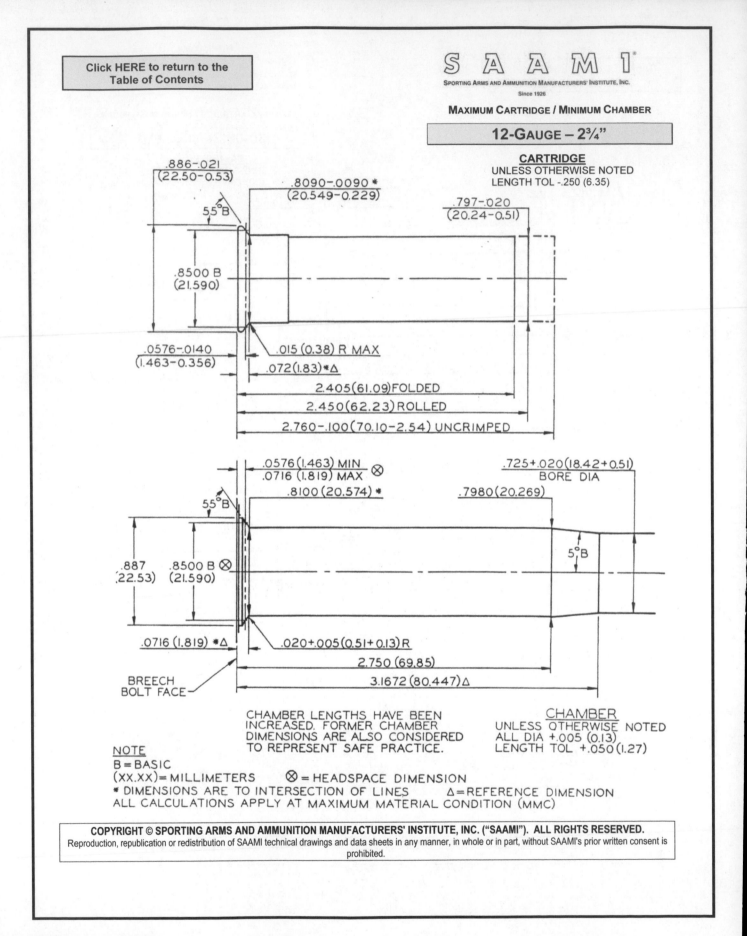

.886–.021
(22.50–0.53)

.8090–.0090 *
(20.549–0.229)

55°B

.797–.020
(20.24–0.51)

.8500 B
(21.590)

.0576–.0140
(1.463–0.356)

.015 (0.38) R MAX

.072 (1.83) *△

2.405 (61.09) FOLDED

2.450 (62.23) ROLLED

2.760–.100 (70.10–2.54) UNCRIMPED

.0576 (1.463) MIN ⊗
.0716 (1.819) MAX ⊗

.8100 (20.574) *

.725+.020 (18.42+0.51)
BORE DIA

.7980 (20.269)

55°B

.887
(22.53)

.8500 B ⊗
(21.590)

5°B

.0716 (1.819) *△

.020+.005 (0.51+0.13) R

2.750 (69.85)

3.1672 (80.447) △

BREECH
BOLT FACE

CHAMBER LENGTHS HAVE BEEN
INCREASED. FORMER CHAMBER
DIMENSIONS ARE ALSO CONSIDERED
TO REPRESENT SAFE PRACTICE.

CHAMBER
UNLESS OTHERWISE NOTED
ALL DIA +.005 (0.13)
LENGTH TOL +.050 (1.27)

NOTE
B = BASIC
(XX.XX) = MILLIMETERS   ⊗ = HEADSPACE DIMENSION
* DIMENSIONS ARE TO INTERSECTION OF LINES   △ = REFERENCE DIMENSION
ALL CALCULATIONS APPLY AT MAXIMUM MATERIAL CONDITION (MMC)

Many manufacturers do not supply suggested retail prices. Others did not get their pricing to us before press time. All pricing can vary dependent on the exact brand and style of ammo selected and/or the retail outlet from which you make your purchase. Pricing has been rounded to the nearest dollar and represents our best estimate of average pricing.

An * after the cartridge means these loads are available with Nosler Partition or Swift A-Frame bullets. Listed pricing may or may not reflect this bullet type.

** = these are packed 50 to box, all others are 20 to box. Wea. Mag.= Weatherby Magnum. Spfd. = Springfield. A-Sq. = A-Square. N.E.=Nitro Express.

Cartridge	Bullet Wgt. Grs.	VELOCITY (fps)					ENERGY (ft. lbs.)					TRAJ. (in.)				Est. Price/box
		Muzzle	100 yds.	200 yds.	300 yds.	400 yds.	Muzzle	100 yds.	200 yds.	300 yds.	400 yds.	100 yds.	200 yds.	300 yds.	400 yds.	
17, 22																
17 Hornet	15.5	3860	2924	2159	1531	1108	513	294	160	81	42	1.4	0.0	-9.1	-33.7	NA
17 Hornet	20	3650	3078	2574	2122	1721	592	421	294	200	131	1.10	0.0	-6.4	-20.6	NA
17 Remington Fireball	20	4000	3380	2840	2360	1930	710	507	358	247	165	1.6	1.5	-2.8	-13.5	NA
17 Remington Fireball	25	3850	3280	2780	2330	1925	823	507	429	301	206	0.9	0.0	-5.4	NA	NA
17 Remington	25	4040	3284	2644	2086	1606	906	599	388	242	143	+2.0	+1.7	-4.0	-17.0	$17
204 Ruger (Fed)	32 Green	4030	3320	2710	2170	1710	1155	780	520	335	205	0.9	0.0	-5.7	-19.1	NA
204 Ruger	32	4225	3632	3114	2652	2234	1268	937	689	500	355	.6	0.0	-4.2	-13.4	NA
204 Ruger	40	3900	3451	3046	2677	2336	1351	1058	824	636	485	.7	0.0	-4.5	-13.9	NA
204 Ruger	45	3625	3188	2792	2428	2093	1313	1015	778	589	438	1.0	0.0	-5.5	-16.9	NA
5.45x39mm	60	2810	2495	2201	1927	1677	1052	829	645	445	374	1.0	0.0	-9.2	-27.7	NA
221 Fireball	50	2800	2137	1580	1180	988	870	507	277	155	109	+0.0	-7.0	-28.0	0.0	$14
22 Hornet (Fed)	30 Green	3150	2150	1300	990	830	660	310	130	65	45	0.0	-6.6	-32.7	NA	NA
22 Hornet	34	3050	2132	1415	1017	852	700	343	151	78	55	+0.0	-6.6	-15.5	-29.9	NA
22 Hornet	35	3100	2278	1601	1135	929	747	403	199	100	67	+2.75	0.0	-16.9	-60.4	NA
22 Hornet	45	2690	2042	1502	1128	948	723	417	225	127	90	+0.0	-7.7	-31.0	0.0	$27**
218 Bee	46	2760	2102	1550	1155	961	788	451	245	136	94	+0.0	-7.2	-29.0	0.0	$46**
222 RFM	35	3760	3125	2574	2085	1656	1099	759	515	338	213	1.0	0.0	-6.3	-20.8	NA
222 Remington	40	3600	3117	2673	2269	1911	1151	863	634	457	324	+1.07	0.0	-6.13	-18.9	NA
222 Remington	50	3140	2602	2123	1700	1350	1094	752	500	321	202	+2.0	-0.4	-11.0	-33.0	$11
222 Remington	55	3020	2562	2147	1773	1451	1114	801	563	384	257	+2.0	-0.4	-11.0	-33.0	$12
22 PPC	52	3400	2930	2510	2130	NA	1335	990	730	525	NA	+2.0	1.4	-5.0	0.0	NA
223 Remington	40	3650	3010	2450	1950	1530	1185	805	535	340	265	+1.0	0.0	-6.0	-22.0	$14
223 Remington	40	3800	3305	2845	2424	2044	1282	970	719	522	371	0.84	0.0	-5.34	-16.6	NA
223 Remington (Rem)	45 Green	3550	2911	2355	1865	1451	1259	847	554	347	210	2.5	2.3	-4.3	-21.1	NA
223 Remington	50	3300	2874	2484	2130	1809	1209	917	685	504	363	1.37	0.0	-7.05	-21.8	NA
223 Remington	52/53	3330	2882	2477	2106	1770	1305	978	722	522	369	+2.0	+0.6	-6.5	-21.5	$14
223 Remington (Win)	55 Green	3240	2747	2304	1905	1554	1282	921	648	443	295	1.9	0.0	-8.5	-26.7	NA
223 Remington	55	3240	2748	2305	1906	1556	1282	922	649	444	296	+2.0	-0.2	-9.0	-27.0	$12
223 Remington	60	3100	2712	2355	2026	1726	1280	979	739	547	397	+2.0	+0.2	-8.0	-24.7	$16
223 Remington	62	3000	2700	2410	2150	1900	1240	1000	800	635	495	1.60	0.0	-7.7	-22.8	NA
223 Remington	64	3020	2621	2256	1920	1619	1296	977	723	524	373	+2.0	0.0	-9.3	-23.0	$14
223 Remington	69	3000	2720	2460	2210	1980	1380	1135	925	750	600	+2.0	+0.8	-5.8	-17.5	$15
223 Remington	75	2790	2554	2330	2119	1926	1296	1086	904	747	617	2.37	0.0	-8.75	-25.1	NA
223 Rem. Super Match	75	2930	2694	2470	2257	2055	1429	1209	1016	848	703	1.20	0.0	-6.9	-20.7	NA
223 Remington	77	2750	2584	2354	2169	1992	1293	1110	948	804	679	1.93	0.0	-8.2	-23.8	NA
223 WSSM	55	3850	3438	3064	2721	2402	1810	1444	1147	904	704	0.7	0.0	-4.4	-13.6	NA
223 WSSM	64	3600	3144	2732	2356	2011	1841	1404	1061	789	574	1.0	0.0	-5.7	-17.7	NA
222 Rem. Mag.	55	3240	2748	2305	1906	1556	1282	922	649	444	296	+2.0	-0.2	-9.0	-27.0	$14
225 Winchester	55	3570	3066	2616	2208	1838	1556	1148	830	606	412	+2.0	+1.0	-5.0	-20.0	$19
224 Wea. Mag.	55	3650	3192	2780	2403	2057	1627	1244	943	705	516	+2.0	+1.2	-4.0	-17.0	$32
22-250 Rem.	40	4000	3320	2720	2200	1740	1420	980	660	430	265	+2.0	+1.8	-3.0	-16.0	$14
22-250 Rem.	45 Green	4000	3293	2690	2159	1696	1598	1084	723	466	287	1.7	1.7	-3.2	-15.7	NA
22-250 Rem.	50	3725	3264	2641	2455	2103	1540	1183	896	669	491	0.89	0.0	-5.23	-16.3	NA
22-250 Rem.	52/55	3680	3137	2656	2222	1832	1654	1201	861	603	410	+2.0	+1.3	-4.0	-17.0	$13
22-250 Rem.	60	3600	3195	2826	2485	2169	1727	1360	1064	823	627	+2.0	+2.0	-2.4	-12.3	$19
220 Swift	40	4200	3678	3190	2739	2329	1566	1201	904	666	482	+0.51	0.0	-4.0	-12.9	NA
220 Swift	50	3780	3158	2617	2135	1710	1586	1107	760	506	325	+2.0	+1.4	-4.4	-17.9	$20
220 Swift	50	3850	3396	2970	2576	2215	1645	1280	979	736	545	0.74	0.0	-4.84	-15.1	NA
220 Swift	55	3800	3370	2990	2630	2310	1765	1390	1090	850	650	0.8	0.0	-4.7	-14.4	NA
220 Swift	55	3650	3194	2772	2384	2035	1627	1246	939	694	506	+2.0	+2.0	-2.6	-13.4	$19
220 Swift	60	3600	3199	2824	2475	2156	1727	1364	1063	816	619	+2.0	+1.6	-4.1	-13.1	$19
22 Savage H.P.	71	2790	2340	1930	1570	1280	1225	860	585	390	190	+2.0	-1.0	-10.4	-35.7	NA
6mm (24)																
6mm BR Rem.	100	2550	2310	2083	1870	1671	1444	1185	963	776	620	+2.5	-0.6	-11.8	0.0	$22
6mm Norma BR	107	2022	2667	2517	2372	2229	1893	1690	1506	1337	1181	+1.73	0.0	-7.24	-20.6	NA
6mm PPC	70	3140	2750	2400	2070	NA	1535	1175	895	665	NA	+2.0	+1.4	-5.0	0.0	NA
243 Winchester	55	4025	3597	3209	2853	2525	1978	1579	1257	994	779	+0.6	0.0	-4.0	-12.2	NA
243 Winchester	60	3600	3110	2660	2260	1890	1725	1285	945	680	475	+2.0	+1.8	-3.3	-15.5	$17
243 Winchester	70	3400	3040	2700	2390	2100	1795	1435	1135	890	685	1.1	0.0	-5.9	-18.0	NA
243 Winchester	75/80	3350	2955	2593	2259	1951	1993	1551	1194	906	676	+2.0	+0.9	-5.0	-19.0	$16
243 W. Superformance	80	3425	3080	2760	2463	2184	2083	1684	1353	1077	847	1.1	0.0	-5.7	-17.1	NA
243 Winchester	85	3320	3070	2830	2600	2380	2080	1770	1510	1280	1070	+2.0	+1.2	-4.0	-14.0	$18
243 Winchester	90	3120	2871	2635	2411	2199	1946	1647	1388	1162	966	1.4	0.0	-6.4	-18.0	NA
243 Winchester*	100	2960	2697	2449	2215	1993	1945	1615	1332	1089	882	+2.5	+1.2	-6.0	-20.0	$16
243 Winchester	105	2920	2689	2470	2261	2062	1988	1686	1422	1192	992	+2.5	+1.6	-5.0	-18.4	$21
243 Light Mag.	100	3100	2839	2592	2358	2138	2133	1790	1491	1235	1014	+1.5	0.0	-6.8	-19.8	NA
243 WSSM	55	4060	3628	3237	2880	2550	2013	1607	1280	1013	794	0.6	0.0	-3.9	-12.0	NA
243 WSSM	95	3250	3000	2763	2538	2325	2258	1898	1610	1359	1140	1.2	0.0	-5.7	-16.9	NA
243 WSSM	100	3110	2838	2583	2341	2112	2147	1789	1481	1217	991	1.4	0.0	-6.6	-19.7	NA
6mm Remington	80	3470	3064	2694	2352	2036	2139	1667	1289	982	736	+2.0	+1.1	-5.0	-17.0	$16
6mm R. Superformance	95	3235	2955	2692	2443	3309	2207	1841	1528	1259	1028	1.2	0.0	-6.1	-18.0	NA
6mm Remington	100	3100	2829	2573	2332	2104	2133	1777	1470	1207	983	+2.5	+1.6	-5.0	-17.0	$16
6mm Remington	105	3060	2822	2596	2381	2177	2105	1788	1512	1270	1059	+2.5	+1.1	-3.3	-15.0	$21

Cartridge	Bullet Wgt. Grs.	VELOCITY (fps)					ENERGY (ft. lbs.)					TRAJ. (in.)				Est. Price/box
		Muzzle	100 yds.	200 yds.	300 yds.	400 yds.	Muzzle	100 yds.	200 yds.	300 yds.	400 yds.	100 yds.	200 yds.	300 yds.	400 yds.	
240 Wea. Mag.	87	3500	3202	2924	2663	2416	2366	1980	1651	1370	1127	+2.0	+2.0	-2.0	-12.0	$32
240 Wea. Mag.	100	3395	3106	2835	2581	2339	2559	2142	1785	1478	1215	+2.5	+2.8	-2.0	-11.0	$43
25-20 Win.	86	1460	1194	1030	931	858	407	272	203	165	141	0.0	-23.5	0.0	0.0	$32**
25-35 Win.	117	2230	1866	1545	1282	1097	1292	904	620	427	313	+2.5	-4.2	-26.0	0.0	$24
250 Savage	100	2820	2504	2210	1936	1684	1765	1392	1084	832	630	+2.5	+0.4	-9.0	-28.0	$17
257 Roberts	100	2980	2661	2363	2085	1827	1972	1572	1240	965	741	+2.5	-0.8	-5.2	-21.6	$20
257 Roberts+P	117	2780	2411	2071	1761	1488	2009	1511	1115	806	576	+2.5	-0.2	-10.2	-32.6	$18
257 R. Superformance	117	2946	2705	2478	2265	2057	2253	1901	1595	1329	1099	1.1	0.0	-5.7	-17.1	NA
257 Roberts+P	120	2780	2560	2360	2160	1970	2060	1750	1480	1240	1030	+2.5	+1.2	-6.4	-23.6	$22
257 Roberts	122	2600	2331	2078	1842	1625	1831	1472	1169	919	715	+2.5	0.0	-10.6	-31.4	$21
25-06 Rem.	87	3440	2995	2591	2222	1884	2286	1733	1297	954	686	+2.0	+1.1	-2.5	-14.4	$17
25-06 Rem.	90	3440	3043	2680	2344	2034	2364	1850	1435	1098	827	+2.0	+1.8	-3.3	-15.6	$17
25-06 Rem.	100	3230	2893	2580	2287	2014	2316	1858	1478	1161	901	+2.0	+0.8	-5.7	-18.9	$17
25-06 Rem.	117	2990	2770	2570	2370	2190	2320	2000	1715	1465	1246	+2.5	+1.0	-7.9	-26.6	$19
25-06 R. Superformance	117	3110	2861	2626	2403	2191	2512	2127	1792	1500	1246	1.4	0.0	-6.4	-18.9	NA
25-06 Rem.*	120	2990	2730	2484	2252	2032	2382	1985	1644	1351	1100	+2.5	+1.2	-5.3	-19.6	$17
25-06 Rem.	122	2930	2706	2492	2289	2095	2325	1983	1683	1419	1189	+2.5	+1.8	-4.5	-17.5	$23
25 WSSM	85	3470	3156	2863	2589	2331	2273	1880	1548	1266	1026	1.0	0.0	-5.2	-15.7	NA
25 WSSM	115	3060	2844	2639	2442	2254	2392	2066	1778	1523	1398	1.4	0.0	-6.4	-18.6	NA
25 WSSM	120	2990	2717	2459	2216	1987	2383	1967	1612	1309	1053	1.6	0.0	-7.4	-21.8	NA
257 Wea. Mag.	87	3825	3456	3118	2805	2513	2826	2308	1870	1520	1220	+2.0	+2.7	-0.3	-7.6	$32
257 Wea. Mag.	100	3555	3237	2941	2665	2404	2806	2326	1920	1576	1283	+2.5	+3.2	0.0	-8.0	$32
257 Scramjet	100	3745	3450	3173	2912	2666	3114	2643	2235	1883	1578	+2.1	+2.77	0.0	-6.93	NA

6.5

6.5x47 Lapua	123	2887	NA	2554	NA	2244	2285	NA	1788	NA	1380	NA	4.53	0.0	-10.7	NA
6.5x50mm Jap.	139	2360	2160	1970	1790	1620	1720	1440	1195	985	810	+2.5	-1.0	-13.5	0.0	NA
6.5x50mm Jap.	156	2070	1830	1610	1430	1260	1475	1155	900	695	550	+2.5	-4.0	-23.8	0.0	NA
6.5x52mm Car.	139	2580	2360	2160	1970	1790	2045	1725	1440	1195	985	+2.5	0.0	-9.9	-29.0	NA
6.5x52mm Car.	156	2430	2170	1930	1700	1500	2045	1630	1285	1005	780	+2.5	-1.0	-13.9	0.0	NA
6.5x52mm Carcano	160	2250	1963	1700	1467	1271	1798	1369	1027	764	574	+3.8	0.0	-15.9	-48.1	NA
6.5x55mm Swe.	93	2625	2350	2090	1850	1630	1425	1140	905	705	550	2.4	0.0	-10.3	-31.1	NA
6.5x55mm Swe.	123	2750	2570	2400	2240	2080	2065	1810	1580	1370	1185	1.9	0.0	-7.9	-22.9	NA
6.5x55mm Swe.	140	2550	NA	NA	NA	NA	2020	NA	NA	NA	NA	0.0	0.0	0.0	0.0	$18
6.5x55mm Swe.*	139/140	2850	2640	2440	2250	2070	2525	2170	1855	1575	1330	+2.5	+1.6	-5.4	-18.9	$18
6.5x55mm Swe.	156	2650	2370	2110	1870	1650	2425	1950	1550	1215	945	+2.5	0.0	-10.3	-30.6	NA
260 Remington	125	2875	2669	2473	2285	2105	2294	1977	1697	1449	1230	1.71	0.0	-7.4	-21.4	NA
260 Remington	140	2750	2544	2347	2158	1979	2351	2011	1712	1448	1217	+2.2	0.0	-8.6	-24.6	NA
6.5 Creedmoor	120	3020	2815	2619	2430	2251	2430	2111	1827	1574	1350	1.4	0.0	-6.5	-18.9	NA
6.5 C. Superformance	129	2950	2756	2570	2392	2221	2492	2175	1892	1639	1417	1.5	0.0	-6.8	-19.7	NA
6.5 Creedmoor	140	2820	2654	2494	2339	2190	2472	2179	1915	1679	1467	1.7	0.0	-7.2	-20.6	NA
6.5-284 Norma	142	3025	2890	2758	2631	2507	2886	2634	2400	2183	1982	1.13	0.0	-5.7	-16.4	NA
6.71 (264) Phantom	120	3150	2929	2718	2517	2325	2645	2286	1969	1698	1440	+1.3	0.0	-6.0	-17.5	NA
6.5 Rem. Mag.	120	3210	2905	2621	2353	2102	2745	2248	1830	1475	1177	+2.5	+1.7	-4.1	-16.3	Disc.
264 Win. Mag.	140	3030	2782	2548	2326	2114	2854	2406	2018	1682	1389	+2.5	+1.4	-5.1	-18.0	$24
6.71 (264) Blackbird	140	3480	3261	3053	2855	2665	3766	3307	2899	2534	2208	+2.4	+3.1	0.0	-7.4	NA
6.8 REM SPC	110	2570	2338	2118	1910	1716	1613	1335	1095	891	719	2.4	0.0	-6.3	-20.8	NA
6.8mm Rem.	115	2775	2472	2190	1926	1683	1966	1561	1224	947	723	+2.1	0.0	-3.7	-9.4	NA

27

270 Winchester	100	3430	3021	2649	2305	1988	2612	2027	1557	1179	877	+2.0	+1.0	-4.9	-17.5	$17
270 Win. (Rem.)	115	2710	2482	2265	2059	NA	1875	1485	1161	896	NA	0.0	4.8	-17.3	0.0	NA
270 Winchester	130	3060	2776	2510	2259	2022	2702	2225	1818	1472	1180	+2.5	+1.4	-5.3	-18.2	$17
270 Win. Supreme	130	3150	2881	2628	2388	2161	2865	2396	1993	1646	1348	1.3	0.0	-6.4	-18.9	NA
270 W. Superformance	130	3200	2984	2788	2582	2393	2955	2570	2228	1924	1653	1.2	0.0	-5.7	-16.7	NA
270 Winchester	135	3000	2780	2570	2369	2178	2697	2315	1979	1682	1421	+2.5	+1.4	-6.0	-17.6	$23
270 Winchester*	140	2940	2700	2480	2260	2060	2685	2270	1905	1590	1315	+2.5	+1.8	-4.6	-17.9	$20
270 Winchester*	150	2850	2585	2336	2100	1879	2705	2226	1817	1468	1175	+2.5	+1.2	-6.5	-22.0	$17
270 Win. Supreme	150	2930	2693	2468	2254	2051	2860	2416	2030	1693	1402	1.7	0.0	-7.4	-21.6	NA
270 WSM	130	3275	3041	2820	2609	2408	3096	2669	2295	1564	1673	1.1	0.0	-5.5	-16.1	NA
270 WSM	140	3125	2865	2619	2386	2165	3035	2559	2132	1769	1457	1.4	0.0	-6.5	-19.0	NA
270 WSM	150	3120	2923	2734	2554	2380	3242	2845	2490	2172	1886	1.3	0.0	-5.9	-17.2	NA
270 Wea. Mag.	100	3760	3380	3033	2712	2412	3139	2537	2042	1633	1292	+2.0	+2.4	-1.2	-10.1	$32
270 Wea. Mag.	130	3375	3119	2878	2649	2432	3287	2808	2390	2026	1707	+2.5	-2.9	-0.9	-9.9	$32
270 Wea. Mag.*	150	3245	3036	2837	2647	2465	3507	3070	2681	2334	2023	+2.5	+2.6	-1.8	-11.4	$47

7mm

7mm BR	140	2216	2012	1821	1643	1481	1525	1259	1031	839	681	+2.0	-3.7	-20.0	0.0	$23
7mm Mauser*	139/140	2660	2435	2221	2018	1827	2199	1843	1533	1266	1037	+2.5	0.0	-9.6	-27.7	$17

Cartridge	Bullet Wgt. Grs.	VELOCITY (fps)					ENERGY (ft. lbs.)					TRAJ. (in.)				Est. Price/box
		Muzzle	100 yds.	200 yds.	300 yds.	400 yds.	Muzzle	100 yds.	200 yds.	300 yds.	400 yds.	100 yds.	200 yds.	300 yds.	400 yds.	
7mm Mauser	154	2690	2490	2300	2120	1940	2475	2120	1810	1530	1285	+2.5	+0.8	-7.5	-23.5	$17
7mm Mauser	175	2440	2137	1857	1603	1382	2313	1774	1340	998	742	+2.5	-1.7	-16.1	0.0	$17
7x30 Waters	120	2700	2300	1930	1600	1330	1940	1405	990	685	470	+2.5	-0.2	-12.3	0.0	$18
7mm-08 Rem.	120	3000	2725	2467	2223	1992	2398	1979	1621	1316	1058	+2.0	0.0	-7.6	-22.3	$18
7mm-08 Rem.*	140	2860	2625	2402	2189	1988	2542	2142	1793	1490	1228	+2.5	+0.8	-6.9	-21.9	$18
7mm-08 Rem.	154	2715	2510	2315	2128	1950	2520	2155	1832	1548	1300	+2.5	+1.0	-7.0	-22.7	$23
7-08 R. Superformance	139	2950	2857	2571	2390	2222	2686	2345	2040	1768	1524	1.5	0.0	-6.8	-19.7	NA
7x64mm Bren.	140						Not Yet Announced									$17
7x64mm Bren.	154	2820	2610	2420	2230	2050	2720	2335	1995	1695	1430	+2.5	+1.4	-5.7	-19.9	NA
7x64mm Bren.*	160	2850	2669	2495	2327	2166	2885	2530	2211	1924	1667	+2.5	+1.6	-4.8	-17.8	$24
7x64mm Bren.	175						Not Yet Announced									$17
284 Winchester	150	2860	2595	2344	2108	1886	2724	2243	1830	1480	1185	+2.5	+0.8	-7.3	-23.2	$24
280 R. Superformance	139	3090	2890	2699	2516	2341	2946	2578	2249	1954	1691	1.3	0.0	-6.1	-17.7	NA
280 Remington	140	3000	2758	2528	2309	2102	2797	2363	1986	1657	1373	+2.5	+1.4	-5.2	-18.3	$17
280 Remington*	150	2890	2624	2373	2135	1912	2781	2293	1875	1518	1217	+2.5	+0.8	-7.1	-22.6	$17
280 Remington	160	2840	2637	2442	2556	2078	2066	2471	2120	1809	1535	+2.5	+0.8	-6.7	-21.0	$20
280 Remington	165	2820	2510	2220	1950	1701	2913	2308	1805	1393	1060	+2.5	+0.4	-8.8	-26.5	$17
7x61mm S&H Sup.	154	3060	2720	2400	2100	1820	3200	2520	1965	1505	1135	+2.5	+1.8	-5.0	-19.8	NA
7mm Dakota	160	3200	3001	2811	2630	2455	3637	3200	2808	2456	2140	+2.1	+1.9	-2.8	-12.5	NA
7mm Rem. Mag. (Rem.)	140	2710	2482	2265	2059	NA	2283	1915	1595	1310	NA	0.0	-4.5	-1.57	0.0	NA
7mm Rem. Mag.*	139/140	3150	2930	2710	2510	2320	3085	2660	2290	1960	1670	+2.5	+2.4	-2.4	-12.7	$21
7 R.M. Superformance	139	3240	3033	2836	2648	2467	3239	2839	2482	2163	1877	1.1	0.0	-5.5	-15.9	NA
7mm Rem. Mag.	150/154	3110	2830	2568	2320	2085	3221	2667	2196	1792	1448	+2.5	+1.6	-4.6	-16.5	$21
7mm Rem. Mag.*	160/162	2950	2730	2520	2320	2120	3090	2650	2250	1910	1600	+2.5	+1.8	-4.4	-17.8	$34
7 R.M. Superformance	154	3100	2914	2736	2565	2401	3286	2904	2560	2250	1970	1.3	0.0	-5.9	-17.2	NA
7mm Rem. Mag.	165	2900	2699	2507	2324	2147	3081	2669	2303	1978	1689	+2.5	+1.2	-5.9	-19.0	$28
7mm Rem Mag.	175	2860	2645	2440	2244	2057	3178	2718	2313	1956	1644	+2.5	+1.0	-6.5	-20.7	$21
7mm Rem. SA ULTRA MAG	140	3175	2934	2707	2490	2283	3033	2676	2277	1927	1620	1.3	0.0	-6	-17.7	NA
7mm Rem. SA ULTRA MAG	150	3110	2828	2563	2313	2077	3221	2663	2188	1782	1437	2.5	2.1	-3.6	-15.8	NA
7mm Rem. SA ULTRA MAG	160	2960	2762	2572	2390	2215	3112	2709	2350	2029	1743	2.6	2.2	-3.6	-15.4	NA
7mm Rem. WSM	140	3225	3008	2801	2603	2414	3233	2812	2438	2106	1812	1.2	0.0	-5.6	-16.4	NA
7mm Rem. WSM	160	2990	2744	2512	2081	1883	3176	2675	2241	1864	1538	1.6	0.0	-7.1	-20.8	NA
7mm Wea. Mag.	140	3225	2970	2729	2501	2283	3233	2741	2315	1943	1621	+2.5	+2.0	-3.2	-14.0	$35
7mm Wea. Mag.	154	3260	3023	2799	2586	2382	3539	3044	2609	2227	1890	+2.5	+2.8	-1.5	-10.8	$32
7mm Wea. Mag.*	160	3200	3004	2816	2637	2464	3637	3205	2817	2469	2156	+2.5	+2.7	-1.5	-10.6	$47
7mm Wea. Mag.	165	2950	2747	2553	2367	2189	3188	2765	2388	2053	1756	+2.5	+1.8	-4.2	-16.4	$43
7mm Wea. Mag.	175	2910	2693	2486	2288	2098	3293	2810	2401	2033	1711	+2.5	+1.2	-5.9	-19.4	$35
7.21(.284) Tomahawk	140	3300	3118	2943	2774	2612	3386	3022	2693	2393	2122	2.3	3.2	0.0	-7.7	NA
7mm STW	140	3325	3064	2818	2585	2364	3436	2918	2468	2077	1737	+2.3	+1.8	-3.0	-13.1	NA
7mm STW Supreme	160	3150	2894	2652	2422	2204	3526	2976	2499	2085	1727	1.3	0.0	-6.3	-18.5	NA
7mm Rem. Ultra Mag.	140	3425	3184	2956	2740	2534	3646	3151	2715	2333	1995	1.7	1.6	-2.6	-11.4	NA
7mm Firehawk	140	3625	3373	3135	2909	2695	4084	3536	3054	2631	2258	+2.2	+2.9	0.0	-7.03	NA
7.21 (.284) Firebird	140	3750	3522	3306	3101	2905	4372	3857	3399	2990	2625	1.6	2.4	0.0	-6.0	NA

30

Cartridge	Bullet Wgt. Grs.	Muzzle	100 yds.	200 yds.	300 yds.	400 yds.	Muzzle	100 yds.	200 yds.	300 yds.	400 yds.	100 yds.	200 yds.	300 yds.	400 yds.	Est. Price/box
30 Carbine	110	1990	1567	1236	1035	923	977	600	373	262	208	0.0	-13.5	0.0	0.0	$28**
300 Whisper	110	2375	2094	1834	1597	NA	1378	1071	822	623	NA	3.2	0.0	-13.6	NA	NA
300 Whisper	208	1020	988	959	NA	NA	480	451	422	NA	NA	0.0	-34.10	NA	NA	NA
303 Savage	190	1890	1612	1327	1183	1055	1507	1096	794	591	469	+2.5	-7.6	0.0	0.0	$24
30 Remington	170	2120	1822	1555	1328	1153	1696	1253	913	666	502	+2.5	-4.7	-26.3	0.0	$20
7.62x39mm Rus.	123/125	2300	2030	1780	1550	1350	1445	1125	860	655	500	+2.5	-2.0	-17.5	0.0	$13
30-30 Win.	55	3400	2693	2085	1570	1187	1412	886	521	301	172	+2.0	0.0	-10.2	-35.0	$18
30-30 Win.	125	2570	2090	1660	1320	1080	1830	1210	770	480	320	-2.0	-2.6	-19.9	0.0	$13
30-30 Win.	150	2390	2040	1723	1447	1225	1902	1386	989	697	499	0.0	-7.5	-27.0	-63.0	NA
30-30 Win. Supreme	150	2480	2095	1747	1446	1209	2049	1462	1017	697	487	0.0	-6.5	-24.5	0.0	NA
30-30 Win.	160	2300	1997	1719	1473	1268	1879	1416	1050	771	571	+2.5	-2.9	-20.2	0.0	$18
30-30 Win. Lever Evolution	160	2400	2150	1916	1699	NA	2046	1643	1304	1025	NA	3.0	0.2	-12.1	NA	NA
30-30 PMC Cowboy	170	1300	1198	1121			638	474				0.0	-27.0	NA	NA	NA
30-30 Win.*	170	2200	1895	1619	1381	1191	1827	1355	989	720	535	+2.5	-5.8	-23.6	0.0	$13
300 Savage	150	2630	2354	2094	1853	1631	2303	1845	1462	1143	886	+2.5	-0.4	-10.1	-30.7	$17
300 Savage	180	2350	2137	1935	1754	1570	2207	1825	1496	1217	985	+2.5	-1.6	-15.2	0.0	$17
30-40 Krag	180	2430	2213	2007	1813	1632	2360	1957	1610	1314	1064	+2.5	-1.4	-13.8	0.0	$18
7.65x53mm Arg.	180	2590	2390	2200	2010	1830	2685	2280	1925	1615	1345	+2.5	0.0	-27.6	0.0	NA
7.5x53mm Argentine	150	2785	2519	2269	2032	1814	2583	2113	1714	1376	1096	+2.0	0.0	-8.8	-25.5	NA
308 Marlin Express	160	2660	2430	2226	2026	1836	2513	2111	1761	1457	1197	3.0	1.7	-6.7	-23.5	NA
307 Winchester	150	2760	2321	1924	1575	1289	2530	1795	1233	826	554	+2.5	-1.5	-13.6	0.0	Disc.

Cartridge	Bullet Wgt. Grs.	VELOCITY (fps)					ENERGY (ft. lbs.)					TRAJ. (in.)				Est. Price/box
		Muzzle	100 yds.	200 yds.	300 yds.	400 yds.	Muzzle	100 yds.	200 yds.	300 yds.	400 yds.	100 yds.	200 yds.	300 yds.	400 yds.	
7.5x55 Swiss	180	2650	2450	2250	2060	1880	2805	2390	2020	1700	1415	+2.5	+0.6	-8.1	-24.9	NA
7.5x55mm Swiss	165	2720	2515	2319	2132	1954	2710	2317	1970	1665	1398	+2.0	0.0	-8.5	-24.6	NA
30 Remington AR	123/125	2800	2465	2154	1867	1606	2176	1686	1288	967	716	2.1	0.0	-9.7	-29.4	NA
308 Winchester	55	3770	3215	2726	2286	1888	1735	1262	907	638	435	-2.0	+1.4	-3.8	-15.8	$22
308 Win. PDX1	120	2850	2497	2171	NA	NA	2164	1662	1256	NA	NA	0.0	-2.8	NA	NA	NA
308 Winchester	150	2820	2533	2263	2009	1774	2648	2137	1705	1344	1048	+2.5	+0.4	-8.5	-26.1	$17
308 W. Superformance	150	3000	2772	2555	2348	1962	2997	2558	2173	1836	1540	1.5	0.0	-6.9	-20.0	NA
308 Winchester	165	2700	2440	2194	1963	1748	2670	2180	1763	1411	1199	+2.5	0.0	-9.7	-28.5	$20
308 Winchester	168	2680	2493	2314	2143	1979	2678	2318	1998	1713	1460	+2.5	0.0	-8.9	-25.3	$18
308 Win. Super Match	168	2870	2647	2462	2284	2114	3008	2613	2261	1946	1667	1.7	0.0	-7.5	-21.6	NA
308 Win. (Fed.)	170	2000	1740	1510	NA	NA	1510	1145	860	NA	NA	0.0	0.0	0.0	0.0	NA
308 Winchester	178	2620	2415	2220	2034	1857	2713	2306	1948	1635	1363	+2.5	0.0	-9.6	-27.6	$23
308 Win. Super Match	178	2780	2609	2444	2285	2132	3054	2690	2361	2064	1797	1.8	0.0	-7.6	-21.9	NA
308 Winchester*	180	2620	2393	2178	1974	1782	2743	2288	1896	1557	1269	+2.5	-0.2	-10.2	-28.5	$17
30-06 Spfd.	55	4080	3485	2965	2502	2083	2033	1483	1074	764	530	+2.0	+1.9	-2.1	-11.7	$22
30-06 Spfd. (Rem.)	125	2660	2335	2034	1757	NA	1964	1513	1148	856	NA	0.0	-5.2	-18.9	0.0	NA
30-06 Spfd.	125	3140	2780	2447	2138	1853	2736	2145	1662	1279	953	+2.0	+1.0	-6.2	-21.0	$17
30-06 Spfd.	150	2910	2617	2342	2083	1853	2820	2281	1827	1445	1135	+2.5	+0.8	-7.2	-23.4	$17
30-06 Superformance	150	3080	2848	2617	2417	2216	3159	2700	2298	1945	1636	1.4	0.0	-6.4	-18.9	NA
30-06 Spfd.	152	2910	2654	2413	2184	1968	2858	2378	1965	1610	1307	+2.5	+1.0	-6.6	-21.3	$23
30-06 Spfd.*	165	2800	2534	2283	2047	1825	2872	2352	1909	1534	1220	+2.5	+0.4	-8.4	-25.5	$17
30-06 Spfd.	168	2710	2522	2346	2169	2003	2739	2372	2045	1754	1497	+2.5	+0.4	-8.0	-23.5	$18
30-06 Spfd. (Fed.)	170	2000	1740	1510	NA	NA	1510	1145	860	NA	NA	0.0	0.0	0.0	0.0	NA
30-06 Spfd.	178	2720	2511	2311	2121	1939	2924	2491	2111	1777	1486	+2.5	+0.4	-8.2	-24.6	$23
30-06 Spfd.*	180	2700	2469	2250	2042	1846	2913	2436	2023	1666	1362	-2.5	0.0	-9.3	-27.0	$17
30-06 Superformance	180	2820	2630	2447	2272	2104	3178	2764	2393	2063	1769	1.8	0.0	-7.6	-21.9	NA
30-06 Spfd.	220	2410	2130	1870	1632	1422	2837	2216	1708	1301	988	+2.5	-1.7	-18.0	0.0	$17
30-06 High Energy	180	2880	2690	2500	2320	2150	3315	2880	2495	2150	1845	+1.7	0.0	-7.2	-21.0	NA
30 T/C Superformance	150	3000	2772	2555	2348	2151	2997	2558	2173	1836	1540	1.5	0.0	-6.9	-20.0	NA
30 T/C Superformance	165	2850	2644	2447	2258	2078	2975	2560	2193	1868	1582	1.7	0.0	-7.6	-22.0	NA
300 Rem SA Ultra Mag	150	3200	2901	2622	2359	2112	3410	2803	2290	1854	1485	1.3	0.0	-6.4	-19.1	NA
300 Rem SA Ultra Mag	165	3075	2792	2527	2276	2040	3464	2856	2339	1898	1525	1.5	0.0	-7	-20.7	NA
300 Rem SA Ultra Mag	180	2960	2761	2571	2389	2214	3501	3047	2642	2280	1959	2.6	2.2	-3.6	-15.4	NA
7.82 (308) Patriot	150	3250	2999	2762	2537	2323	3519	2997	2542	2145	1798	+1.2	0.0	-5.8	-16.9	NA
300 RCM Superformance	150	3310	3065	2833	2613	2404	3648	3128	2673	2274	1924	1.1	0.0	-5.4	-16.0	NA
300 RCM Superformance	165	3185	2964	2753	2552	2360	3716	3217	2776	2386	2040	1.2	0.0	-5.8	-17.0	NA
300 RCM Superformance	180	3040	2840	2649	2466	2290	3693	3223	2804	2430	2096	1.4	0.0	-6.4	-18.5	NA
300 WSM	150	3300	3061	2834	2619	2414	3628	3121	2676	2285	1941	1.1	0.0	-5.4	-15.9	NA
300 WSM	180	2970	2741	2524	2317	2120	3526	3005	2547	2147	1797	1.6	0.0	-7.0	-20.5	NA
300 WSM	180	3010	2923	2734	2554	2380	3242	2845	2490	2172	1886	1.3	0	-5.9	-17.2	NA
308 Norma Mag.	180	3020	2820	2630	2440	2270	3645	3175	2755	2385	2050	+2.5	+2.0	-3.5	-14.8	NA
300 Dakota	200	3000	2824	2656	2493	2336	3996	3542	3131	2760	2423	+2.2	+1.5	-4.0	-15.2	NA
300 H&H Magnum*	180	2880	2640	2412	2196	1990	3315	2785	2325	1927	1583	+2.5	+0.8	-6.8	-21.7	$24
300 H&H Magnum	220	2550	2267	2002	1757	NA	3167	2510	1958	1508	NA	-2.5	-0.4	-12.0	0.0	NA
300 Win. Mag.	150	3290	2951	2636	2342	2068	3605	2900	2314	1827	1424	+2.5	+1.9	-3.8	-15.8	$22
300 WM Superformance	150	3400	3150	2914	2690	2477	3850	3304	2817	2409	2043	1.0	0.0	-5.1	-15.0	NA
300 Win. Mag.	165	3100	2877	2665	2462	2269	3522	3033	2603	2221	1897	+2.5	+2.4	-3.0	-16.9	$24
300 Win. Mag.	178	2900	2760	2568	2375	2191	3509	3030	2606	2230	1897	+2.5	+1.4	-5.0	-17.6	$29
300 WM Super Match	178	2960	2770	2587	2412	2243	3462	3031	2645	2298	1988	1.5	0.0	-6.7	-19.4	NA
300 Win. Mag.*	180	2960	2745	2540	2344	2157	3501	3011	2578	2196	1859	+2.5	+1.2	-5.5	-18.5	$22
300 WM Superformance	180	3130	2927	2732	2546	2366	3917	3424	2983	2589	2238	1.3	0.0	-5.9	-17.3	NA
300 Win. Mag.	190	2885	1691	2506	2327	2156	3511	3055	2648	2285	1961	+2.5	+1.2	-5.7	-19.0	$26
300 Win. Mag.*	200	2825	2595	2376	2167	1970	3545	2991	2508	2086	1742	-2.5	+1.6	-4.7	-17.2	$36
300 Win. Mag.	220	2680	2448	2228	2020	1823	3508	2927	2424	1993	1623	+2.5	0.0	-9.5	-27.5	$23
300 Rem. Ultra Mag.	150	3450	3208	2980	2762	2556	3964	3427	2956	2541	2175	1.7	1.5	-2.6	-11.2	NA
300 Rem. Ultra Mag.	150	2910	2686	2473	2279	2077	2820	2403	2037	1716	1436	1.7	0.0	-7.4	-21.5	NA
300 Rem. Ultra Mag.	180	3250	3037	2834	2640	2454	4221	3686	3201	2786	2407	2.4	0.0	-3.0	-12.7	NA
300 Rem. Ultra Mag.	180	2960	2774	2505	2294	2093	3501	2971	2508	2103	1751	2.7	2.2	-3.8	-16.4	NA
300 Rem. Ultra Mag.	200	3032	2791	2562	2345	2138	4083	3459	2916	2442	2030	1.5	0.0	-6.8	-19.9	NA
300 Wea. Mag.	100	3900	3441	3038	2652	2305	3714	2891	2239	1717	1297	+2.0	+2.6	-0.6	-8.7	$32
300 Wea. Mag.	150	3600	3307	3033	2776	2533	4316	3642	3064	2566	2137	+2.5	+3.2	0.0	-8.1	$32
300 Wea. Mag.	165	3450	3210	3000	2792	2593	4360	3796	3297	2855	2464	+2.5	+3.2	0.0	-7.8	NA
300 Wea. Mag.	178	3120	2902	2695	2497	2308	3847	3329	2870	2464	2104	+2.5	-1.7	-3.6	-14.7	$43
300 Wea. Mag.	180	3330	3110	2910	2710	2520	4430	3875	3375	2935	2540	+1.0	0.0	-5.2	-15.1	NA
300 Wea. Mag.	190	3030	2830	2638	2455	2279	3873	3378	2936	2542	2190	+2.5	+1.6	-4.3	-16.0	$38
300 Wea. Mag.	220	2850	2541	2283	1964	1736	3967	3155	2480	1922	1471	+2.5	+0.4	-8.5	-26.4	$35

Cartridge	Bullet Wgt. Grs.	VELOCITY (fps)					ENERGY (ft. lbs.)					TRAJ. (in.)				Est. Price/box
		Muzzle	100 yds.	200 yds.	300 yds.	400 yds.	Muzzle	100 yds.	200 yds.	300 yds.	400 yds.	100 yds.	200 yds.	300 yds.	400 yds.	
300 Pegasus	180	3500	3319	3145	2978	2817	4896	4401	3953	3544	3172	+2.28	+2.89	0.0	-6.79	NA
31																
32-20 Win.	100	1210	1021	913	834	769	325	231	185	154	131	0.0	-32.3	0.0	0.0	$23**
303 British	180	2460	2124	1817	1542	1311	2418	1803	1319	950	687	+2.5	-1.8	-16.8	0.0	$18
303 Light Mag.	150	2830	2570	2325	2094	1884	2667	2199	1800	1461	1185	+2.0	0.0	-8.4	-24.0	NA
7.62x54mm Rus.	146	2950	2730	2520	2320	NA	2820	2415	2055	1740	NA	+2.5	+2.0	-4.4	-17.7	NA
7.62x54mm Rus.	180	2580	2370	2180	2000	1820	2650	2250	1900	1500	1100	+2.5	0.0	-9.8	-28.5	NA
7.7x58mm Jap.	150	2640	2399	2170	1954	1752	2321	1916	1568	1271	1022	+2.3	0.0	-9.7	28.5	NA
7.7x58mm Jap.	180	2500	2300	2100	1920	1750	2490	2105	1770	1475	1225	+2.5	0.0	-10.4	30.2	NA
8mm																
8x56 R	205	2400	2188	1987	1797	1621	2621	2178	1796	1470	1196	+2.9	0.0	-11.7	-34.3	NA
8x57mm JS Mau.	165	2850	2520	2210	1930	1670	2965	2330	1795	1360	1015	+2.5	+1.0	-7.7	0.0	NA
32 Win. Special	165	2410	2145	1897	1669	NA	2128	1685	1318	1020	NA	2.0	0.0	-13.0	-19.9	NA
32 Win. Special	170	2250	1921	1626	1372	1175	1911	1393	998	710	521	+2.5	-3.5	-22.9	0.0	$14
8mm Mauser	170	2360	1969	1622	1333	1123	2102	1464	993	671	476	+2.5	-3.1	-22.2	0.0	$18
325 WSM	180	3060	2841	2632	2432	2242	3743	3226	2769	2365	2009	+1.4	0.0	-6.4	-18.7	NA
325 WSM	200	2950	2753	2565	2384	2210	3866	3367	2922	2524	2170	+1.5	0.0	-6.8	-19.8	NA
325 WSM	220	2840	2605	2382	2169	1968	3941	3316	2772	2300	1893	+1.8	0.0	-8.0	-23.3	NA
8mm Rem. Mag.	185	3080	2761	2464	2186	1927	3896	3131	2494	1963	1525	+2.5	+1.4	-5.5	-19.7	$30
8mm Rem. Mag.	220	2830	2581	2346	2123	1913	3912	3254	2688	2201	1787	+2.5	+0.6	-7.6	-23.5	Disc.
33																
338 Federal	180	2830	2590	2350	2130	1930	3200	2670	2215	1820	1480	1.8	0.0	-8.2	-23.9	NA
338 Marlin Express	200	2565	2365	2174	1992	1820	2922	2484	2099	1762	1471	3.0	1.2	-7.9	-25.9	NA
338 Federal	185	2750	2550	2350	2160	1980	3105	2660	2265	1920	1615	1.9	0.0	-8.3	-24.1	NA
338 Federal	210	2630	2410	2200	2010	1820	3225	2710	2265	1880	1545	2.3	0.0	-9.4	-27.3	NA
338 Federal MSR	185	2680	2460	2230	2020	1820	2950	2460	2035	1670	1360	2.2	0.0	-9.2	-26.8	NA
338-06	200	2750	2553	2364	2184	2011	3358	2894	2482	2118	1796	+1.9	0.0	-8.22	-23.6	NA
330 Dakota	250	2900	2719	2545	2378	2217	4668	4103	3595	3138	2727	+2.3	+1.3	-5.0	-17.5	NA
338 Lapua	250	2963	2795	2640	2493	NA	4842	4341	3881	3458	NA	+1.9	0.0	-7.9	0.0	NA
338 RCM Superformance	185	2980	2755	2542	2338	2143	3647	3118	2653	2242	1887	1.5	0.0	-6.9	-20.3	NA
338 RCM Superformance	200	2950	2744	2547	2358	2177	3846	3342	2879	2468	2104	1.6	0.0	-6.9	-20.1	NA
338 RCM Superformance	225	2750	2575	2407	2245	2089	3778	3313	2894	2518	2180	1.9	0.0	-7.9	-22.7	NA
338 WM Superformance	185	3080	2850	2632	2424	2226	3896	3337	2845	2413	2034	1.4	0.0	-6.4	-18.8	NA
338 Win. Mag.*	210	2830	2590	2370	2150	1940	3735	3130	2610	2155	1760	+2.5	+1.4	-6.0	-20.9	$33
338 Win. Mag.*	225	2785	2517	2266	2029	1808	3871	3165	2565	2057	1633	+2.5	+0.4	-8.5	-25.9	$27
338 WM Superformance	225	2840	2758	2582	2414	2252	4318	3798	3331	2911	2533	1.5	0.0	-6.8	-19.5	NA
338 Win. Mag.	230	2780	2573	2375	2186	2005	3940	3382	2881	2441	2054	+2.5	+1.2	-6.3	-21.0	$40
338 Win. Mag.*	250	2660	2456	2261	2075	1898	3927	3348	2837	2389	1999	+2.5	+0.2	-9.0	-26.2	$27
338 Ultra Mag.	250	2860	2645	2440	2244	2057	4540	3882	3303	2794	2347	1.7	0.0	-7.6	-22.1	NA
338 Lapua Match	250	2900	2760	2625	2494	2366	4668	4229	3825	3452	3108	1.5	0.0	-6.6	-18.8	NA
338 Lapua Match	285	2745	2623	2504	2388	2275	4768	4352	3966	3608	3275	1.8	0.0	-7.3	-20.8	NA
8.59(.338) Galaxy	200	3100	2899	2707	2524	2347	4269	3734	3256	2829	2446	3	3.8	0.0	-9.3	NA
340 Wea. Mag.*	210	3250	2991	2746	2515	2295	4924	4170	3516	2948	2455	+2.5	+1.9	-1.8	-11.8	$56
340 Wea. Mag.*	250	3000	2806	2621	2443	2272	4995	4371	3812	3311	2864	+2.5	+2.0	-3.5	-14.8	$56
338 A-Square	250	3120	2799	2500	2220	1958	5403	4348	3469	2736	2128	+2.5	+2.7	-1.5	-10.5	NA
338-378 Wea. Mag.	225	3180	2974	2778	2591	2410	5052	4420	3856	3353	2902	3.1	3.8	0.0	-8.9	NA
338 Titan	225	3230	3010	2800	2600	2409	5211	4524	3916	3377	2898	+3.07	+3.8	0.0	-8.95	NA
338 Excalibur	200	3600	3361	3134	2920	2715	5755	5015	4363	3785	3274	+2.23	+2.87	0.0	-6.99	NA
338 Excalibur	250	3250	2922	2618	2333	2066	5863	4740	3804	3021	2370	+1.3	0.0	-6.35	-19.2	NA
34, 35																
348 Winchester	200	2520	2215	1931	1672	1443	2820	2178	1656	1241	925	+2.5	-1.4	-14.7	0.0	$42
357 Magnum	158	1830	1427	1138	980	883	1175	715	454	337	274	0.0	-16.2	-33.1	0.0	$25**
35 Remington	150	2300	1874	1506	1218	1039	1762	1169	755	494	359	+2.5	-4.1	-26.3	0.0	$16
35 Remington	200	2080	1698	1376	1140	1001	1921	1280	841	577	445	+2.5	-6.3	-17.1	-33.6	$16
35 Rem. Lever Evolution	200	2225	1963	1721	1503	NA	2198	1711	1315	1003	NA	3.0	-1.3	-17.5	NA	NA
356 Winchester	200	2400	2114	1797	1517	1284	2688	1985	1434	1022	732	+2.5	-1.8	-15.1	0.0	$31
356 Winchester	250	2160	1911	1682	1476	1299	2591	2028	1571	1210	937	+2.5	-3.7	-22.2	0.0	$31
358 Winchester	200	2490	2171	1876	1619	1379	2753	2093	1563	1151	844	+0.6	-1.6	-15.6	0.0	$31
358 STA	275	2850	2562	2292	2039	NA	4958	4009	3208	2539	NA	+1.9	0.0	-8.6	0.0	NA
350 Rem. Mag.	200	2710	2410	2130	1870	1631	3261	2579	2014	1553	1181	+2.5	-0.2	-10.0	-30.1	$33
35 Whelen	200	2675	2378	2100	1842	1606	3177	2510	1958	1506	1145	+2.5	-0.2	-10.3	-31.1	$20
35 Whelen	225	2500	2300	2110	1930	1770	3120	2650	2235	1870	1560	+2.6	0.0	-10.2	-29.9	NA
35 Whelen	250	2400	2197	2005	1823	1652	3197	2680	2230	1844	1515	+2.5	-1.2	-13.7	0.0	$20
358 Norma Mag.	250	2800	2510	2230	1970	1730	4350	3480	2750	2145	1655	+2.5	+1.0	-7.6	-25.2	NA
358 STA	275	2850	2562	229*2	2039	1764	4959	4009	3208	2539	1899	+1.9	0.0	-8.58	-26.1	NA
9.3mm																
9.3x57mm Mau.	286	2070	1810	1590	1390	1110	2710	2090	1600	1220	955	+2.5	-2.6	-22.5	0.0	NA

Cartridge	Bullet Wgt. Grs.	VELOCITY (fps)					ENERGY (ft. lbs.)					TRAJ. (in.)				Est. Price/box
		Muzzle	100 yds.	200 yds.	300 yds.	400 yds.	Muzzle	100 yds.	200 yds.	300 yds.	400 yds.	100 yds.	200 yds.	300 yds.	400 yds.	
370 Sako Mag.	286	3550	2370	2200	2040	2880	4130	3570	3075	2630	2240	2.4	0.0	-9.5	-27.2	NA
9.3x64mm	286	2700	2505	2318	2139	1968	4629	3984	3411	2906	2460	+2.5	+2.7	-4.5	-19.2	NA
9.3x74Rmm	286	2360	2136	1924	1727	1545	3536	2896	2351	1893	1516	0.0	-6.1	-21.7	-49.0	NA
375																
375 Winchester	200	2200	1841	1526	1268	1089	2150	1506	1034	714	527	+2.5	-4.0	-26.2	0.0	$27
375 Winchester	250	1900	1647	1424	1239	1103	2005	1506	1126	852	676	+2.5	-6.9	-33.3	0.0	$27
376 Steyr	225	2600	2331	2078	1842	1625	3377	2714	2157	1694	1319	2.5	0.0	-10.6	-31.4	NA
376 Steyr	270	2600	2372	2156	1951	1759	4052	3373	2787	2283	1855	2.3	0.0	-9.9	-28.9	NA
375 Dakota	300	2600	2316	2051	1804	1579	4502	3573	2800	2167	1661	+2.4	0.0	-11.0	-32.7	NA
375 N.E. 2-1/2"	270	2000	1740	1507	1310	NA	2398	1815	1362	1026	NA	+2.5	-6.0	-30.0	NA	NA
375 Flanged	300	2450	2150	1886	1640	NA	3998	3102	2369	1790	NA	+2.5	-2.4	-17.0	0.0	NA
375 Ruger	270	2840	2600	2372	2156	1951	4835	4052	3373	2786	2283	1.8	0.0	-8.0	-23.6	NA
375 Ruger	300	2660	2344	2050	1780	1536	4713	3660	2800	2110	1572	2.4	0.0	-10.8	-32.6	NA
375 H&H Magnum	250	2670	2450	2240	2040	1850	3955	3335	2790	2315	1905	+2.5	-0.4	-10.2	-28.4	NA
375 H&H Magnum	270	2690	2420	2166	1928	1707	4337	3510	2812	2228	1747	+2.5	0.0	-10.0	-29.4	$28
375 H&H Magnum*	300	2530	2245	1979	1733	1512	4263	3357	2608	2001	1523	+2.5	-1.0	-10.5	-33.6	$28
375 H&H Hvy. Mag.	270	2870	2628	2399	2182	1976	4937	4141	3451	2150	1845	+1.7	0.0	-7.2	-21.0	NA
375 H&H Hvy. Mag.	300	2705	2386	2090	1816	1568	4873	3793	2908	2195	1637	+2.3	0.0	-10.4	-31.4	NA
375 Rem. Ultra Mag.	270	2900	2558	2241	1947	1678	5041	3922	3010	2272	1689	1.9	2.7	-8.9	-27.0	NA
375 Rem. Ultra Mag.	300	2760	2505	2263	2035	1822	5073	4178	3412	2759	2210	2.0	0.0	-8.8	-26.1	NA
375 Wea. Mag.	300	2700	2420	2157	1911	1685	4856	3901	3100	2432	1891	+2.5	-.04	-10.7	0.0	NA
378 Wea. Mag.	270	3180	2976	2781	2594	2415	6062	5308	4635	4034	3495	+2.5	+2.6	-1.8	-11.3	$71
378 Wea. Mag.	300	2929	2576	2252	1952	1680	5698	4419	3379	2538	1881	+2.5	+1.2	-7.0	-24.5	$77
375 A-Square	300	2920	2626	2351	2093	1850	5679	4594	3681	2917	2281	+2.5	+1.4	-6.0	-21.0	NA
38-40 Win.	180	1160	999	901	827	764	538	399	324	273	233	0.0	-33.9	0.0	0.0	$42**
40, 41																
400 A-Square DPM	400	2400	2146	1909	1689	NA	5116	2092	3236	2533	NA	2.98	0.0	-10.0	NA	NA
400 A-Square DPM	170	2980	2463	2001	1598	NA	3352	2289	1512	964	NA	2.16	0.0	-11.1	NA	NA
408 CheyTac	419	2850	2752	2657	2562	2470	7551	7048	6565	6108	5675	-1.02	0.0	1.9	4.2	NA
405 Win.	300	2200	1851	1545	1296		3224	2282	1589	1119		4.6	0.0	-19.5	0.0	NA
450/400-3"	400	2050	1815	1595	1402	NA	3732	2924	2259	1746	NA	0.0	NA	-33.4	NA	NA
416 Ruger	400	2400	2151	1917	1700	NA	5116	4109	3264	2568	NA	0.0	-6.0	-21.6	0.0	NA
416 Dakota	400	2450	2294	2143	1998	1859	5330	4671	4077	3544	3068	+2.5	-0.2	-10.5	-29.4	NA
416 Taylor	400	2350	2117	1896	1693	NA	4905	3980	3194	2547	NA	+2.5	-1.2	15.0	0.0	NA
416 Hoffman	400	2380	2145	1923	1718	1529	5031	4087	3285	2620	2077	+2.5	-1.0	-14.1	0.0	NA
416 Rigby	350	2600	2449	2303	2162	2026	5253	4661	4122	3632	3189	+2.5	-1.8	-10.2	-26.0	NA
416 Rigby	400	2370	2210	2050	1900	NA	4990	4315	3720	3185	NA	+2.5	-0.7	-12.1	0.0	NA
416 Rigby	410	2370	2110	1870	1640	NA	5115	4050	3165	2455	NA	+2.5	-2.4	-17.3	0.0	$110
416 Rem. Mag.*	350	2520	2270	2034	1814	1611	4935	4004	3216	2557	2017	+2.5	-0.8	-12.6	-35.0	$82
416 Wea. Mag.*	400	2700	2397	2115	1852	1613	6474	5104	3971	3047	2310	+2.5	0.0	-10.1	-30.4	$96
10.57 (416) Meteor	400	2730	2532	2342	2161	1987	6621	5695	4874	4147	3508	+1.9	0.0	-8.3	-24.0	NA
404 Jeffrey	400	2150	1924	1716	1525	NA	4105	3289	2614	2064	NA	+2.5	-4.0	-22.1	0.0	NA
425, 44																
425 Express	400	2400	2160	1934	1725	NA	5115	4145	3322	2641	NA	+2.5	-1.0	-14.0	0.0	NA
44-40 Win.	200	1190	1006	900	822	756	629	449	360	300	254	0.0	-33.3	0.0	0.0	$36**
44 Rem. Mag.	210	1920	1477	1155	982	880	1719	1017	622	450	361	0.0	-17.6	0.0	0.0	$14
44 Rem. Mag.	240	1760	1380	1114	970	878	1650	1015	661	501	411	0.0	-17.6	0.0	0.0	$13
444 Marlin	240	2350	1815	1377	1087	941	2942	1753	1001	630	472	+2.5	-15.1	-31.0	0.0	$22
444 Marlin	265	2120	1733	1405	1160	1012	2644	1768	1162	791	603	+2.5	-6.0	-32.2	0.0	Disc.
444 Mar. Lever Evolution	265	2325	1971	1652	1380	NA	3180	2285	1606	1120	NA	3.0	-1.4	-18.6	NA	NA
444 Mar. Superformance	265	2400	1976	1603	1298	NA	3389	2298	1512	991	NA	4.1	0.0	-17.8	NA	NA
45																
45-70 Govt.	300	1810	1497	1244	1073	969	2182	1492	1031	767	625	0.0	-14.8	0.0	0.0	$21
45-70 Govt. Supreme	300	1880	1558	1292	1103	988	2355	1616	1112	811	651	0.0	-12.9	-46.0	-105.0	NA
45-70 Lever Evolution	325	2050	1729	1450	1225	NA	3032	2158	1516	1083	NA	3.0	-4.1	-27.8	NA	NA
45-70 Govt. CorBon	350	1800	1526	1296			2519	1810	1307			0.0	-14.6	0.0	0.0	NA
45-70 Govt.	405	1330	1168	1055	977	918	1590	1227	1001	858	758	0.0	-24.6	0.0	0.0	$21
45-70 Govt. PMC Cowboy	405	1550	1193				1639	1280				0.0	-23.9	0.0	0.0	NA
45-70 Govt. Garrett	415	1850					3150					3.0	-7.0	0.0	0.0	NA
45-70 Govt. Garrett	530	1550	1343	1178	1062	982	2828	2123	1633	1327	1135	0.0	-17.8	0.0	0.0	NA
450 Bushmaster	250	2200	1831	1508	1480	1073	2686	1860	1262	864	639	0.0	-9.0	-33.5	0.0	NA
450 Marlin	350	2100	1774	1488	1254	1089	3427	2446	1720	1222	922	0.0	-9.7	-35.2	0.0	NA
450 Mar. Lever Evolution	325	2225	1887	1585	1331	NA	3572	2569	1813	1278	NA	3.0	-2.2	-21.3	NA	NA
457 Wild West Magnum	350	2150	1718	1348	NA	NA	3645	2293	1413	NA	NA	0.0	-10.5	NA	NA	NA

Cartridge	Bullet Wgt. Grs.	VELOCITY (fps)					ENERGY (ft. lbs.)					TRAJ. (in.)				Est. Price/box
		Muzzle	100 yds.	200 yds.	300 yds.	400 yds.	Muzzle	100 yds.	200 yds.	300 yds.	400 yds.	100 yds.	200 yds.	300 yds.	400 yds.	
458 Win. Magnum	400	2380	2170	1960	1770	NA	5030	4165	3415	2785	NA	+2.5	-0.4	-13.4	0.0	$73
458 Win. Magnum	465	2220	1999	1791	1601	NA	5088	4127	3312	2646	NA	+2.5	-2.0	-17.7	0.0	NA
458 Win. Magnum	500	2040	1823	1623	1442	1237	4620	3689	2924	2308	1839	+2.5	-3.5	-22.0	0.0	$61
458 Win. Magnum	510	2040	1770	1527	1319	1157	4712	3547	2640	1970	1516	+2.5	-4.1	25.0	0.0	$41
450 N.E. 3-1/4"	465	2190	1970	1765	1577	NA	4952	4009	3216	2567	NA	+2.5	-3.0	-20.0	0.0	NA
450 N.E. 3-1/4"	500	2150	1920	1708	1514	NA	5132	4093	3238	2544	NA	+2.5	-4.0	-22.9	0.0	NA
450 No. 2	465	2190	1970	1765	1577	NA	4952	4009	3216	2567	NA	+2.5	-3.0	-20.0	0.0	NA
450 No. 2	500	2150	1920	1708	1514	NA	5132	4093	3238	2544	NA	+2.5	-4.0	-22.9	0.0	NA
458 Lott	465	2380	2150	1932	1730	NA	5848	4773	3855	3091	NA	+2.5	-1.0	-14.0	0.0	NA
458 Lott	500	2300	2062	1838	1633	NA	5873	4719	3748	2960	NA	+2.5	-1.6	-16.4	0.0	NA
450 Ackley Mag.	465	2400	2169	1950	1747	NA	5947	4857	3927	3150	NA	+2.5	-1.0	-13.7	0.0	NA
450 Ackley Mag.	500	2320	2081	1855	1649	NA	5975	4085	3820	3018	NA	+2.5	-1.2	-15.0	0.0	NA
460 Short A-Sq.	500	2420	2175	1943	1729	NA	6501	5250	4193	3319	NA	+2.5	-0.8	-12.8	0.0	NA
460 Wea. Mag.	500	2700	2404	2128	1869	1635	8092	6416	5026	3878	2969	+2.5	+0.6	-8.9	-28.0	$72
475																
500/465 N.E.	480	2150	1917	1703	1507	NA	4926	3917	3089	2419	NA	+2.5	-4.0	-22.2	0.0	NA
470 Rigby	500	2150	1940	1740	1560	NA	5130	4170	3360	2695	NA	+2.5	-2.8	-19.4	0.0	NA
470 Nitro Ex.	480	2190	1954	1735	1536	NA	5111	4070	3210	2515	NA	+2.5	-3.5	-20.8	0.0	NA
470 Nitro Ex.	500	2150	1890	1650	1440	1270	5130	3965	3040	2310	1790	+2.5	-4.3	-24.0	0.0	$177
475 No. 2	500	2200	1955	1728	1522	NA	5375	4243	3316	2573	NA	+2.5	-3.2	-20.9	0.0	NA
50, 58																
50 Alaskan	450	2000	1729	1492	NA	NA	3997	2987	2224	NA	NA	0.0	-11.25	NA	NA	NA
505 Gibbs	525	2300	2063	1840	1637	NA	6166	4922	3948	3122	NA	+2.5	-3.0	-18.0	0.0	NA
500 N.E.-3"	570	2150	1928	1722	1533	NA	5850	4703	3752	2975	NA	+2.5	-3.7	-22.0	0.0	NA
500 N.E.-3"	600	2150	1927	1721	1531	NA	6158	4947	3944	3124	NA	+2.5	-4.0	-22.0	0.0	NA
495 A-Square	570	2350	2117	1896	1693	NA	5850	4703	3752	2975	NA	+2.5	-1.0	-14.5	0.0	NA
495 A-Square	600	2280	2050	1833	1635	NA	6925	5598	4478	3562	NA	+2.5	-2.0	-17.0	0.0	NA
500 A-Square	600	2380	2144	1922	1766	NA	7546	6126	4920	3922	NA	+2.5	-3.0	-17.0	0.0	NA
500 A Square	707	2250	2040	1841	1567	NA	7947	6530	5318	4311	NA	+2.5	-2.0	-17.0	0.0	NA
500 BMG PMC	660	3080	2854	2639	2444	2248	13688	500 yd. zero				+3.1	+3.9	+4.7	+2.8	NA
577 Nitro Ex.	750	2050	1793	1562	1360	NA	6990	5356	4065	3079	NA	+2.5	-5.0	-26.0	0.0	NA
577 Tyrannosaur	750	2400	2141	1898	1675	NA	9591	7633	5996	4671	NA	+3.0	0.0	-12.9	0.0	NA
600, 700																
600 N.E.	900	1950	1680	1452	NA	NA	7596	5634	4212	NA	NA	+5.6	0.0	0.0	0.0	NA
700 N.E.	1200	1900	1676	1472	NA	NA	9618	7480	5774	NA	NA	+5.7	0.0	0.0	0.0	NA
50 BMG																
50 BMG Match	750	2820	2728	2637	2549	2462	13241	12388	11580	10815	10090	1.5	0.0	-6.5	-18.3	NA

Notes: Blanks are available in 32 S&W, 38 S&W and 38 Special. "V" after barrel length indicates test barrel was vented to produce ballistics similar to a revolver with a normal barrel-to-cylinder gap. Ammo prices are per 50 rounds except when marked with an ** which signifies a 20 round box; *** signifies a 25-round box. Not all loads are available from all ammo manufacturers. Listed loads are those made by Remington, Winchester, Federal, and others. DISC. is a discontinued load. Prices are rounded to the nearest whole dollar and will vary with brand and retail outlet. † = new bullet weight this year; "c" indicates a change in data.

Cartridge	Bullet Wgt. Grs.	VELOCITY (fps)			ENERGY (ft. lbs.)			Mid-Range Traj. (in.)		Bbl. Lgth. (in).	Est. Price/ box
		Muzzle	50 yds.	100 yds.	Muzzle	50 yds.	100 yds.	50 yds.	100 yds.		
22, 25											
221 Rem. Fireball	50	2650	2380	2130	780	630	505	0.2	0.8	10.5"	$15
25 Automatic	35	900	813	742	63	51	43	NA	NA	2"	$18
25 Automatic	45	815	730	655	65	55	40	1.8	7.7	2"	$21
25 Automatic	50	760	705	660	65	55	50	2.0	8.7	2"	$17
30											
7.5mm Swiss	107	1010	NA	NA	240	NA	NA	NA	NA	NA	NEW
7.62mmTokarev	87	1390	NA	NA	365	NA	NA	0.6	NA	4.5"	NA
7.62 Nagant	97	790	NA	NA	134	NA	NA	NA	NA	NA	NEW
7.63 Mauser	88	1440	NA	NA	405	NA	NA	NA	NA	NA	NEW
30 Luger	93†	1220	1110	1040	305	255	225	0.9	3.5	4.5"	$34
30 Carbine	110	1790	1600	1430	785	625	500	0.4	1.7	10"	$28
30-357 AeT	123	1992	NA	NA	1084	NA	NA	NA	NA	10"	NA
32											
32 NAA	80	1000	933	880	178	155	137	NA	NA	4"	NA
32 S&W	88	680	645	610	90	80	75	2.5	10.5	3"	$17
32 S&W Long	98	705	670	635	115	100	90	2.3	10.5	4"	$17
32 Short Colt	80	745	665	590	100	80	60	2.2	9.9	4"	$19
32 H&R	80	1150	1039	963	235	192	165	NA	NA	4"	NA
32 H&R Magnum	85	1100	1020	930	230	195	165	1.0	4.3	4.5"	$21
32 H&R Magnum	95	1030	940	900	225	190	170	1.1	4.7	4.5"	$19
327 Federal Magnum	85	1400	1220	1090	370	280	225	NA	NA	4-V	NA
327 Federal Magnum	100	1500	1320	1180	500	390	310	-0.2	-4.50	4-V	NA
32 Automatic	60	970	895	835	125	105	95	1.3	5.4	4"	$22
32 Automatic	60	1000	917	849	133	112	96			4"	NA
32 Automatic	65	950	890	830	130	115	100	1.3	5.6	NA	NA
32 Automatic	71	905	855	810	130	115	95	1.4	5.8	4"	$19
8mm Lebel Pistol	111	850	NA	NA	180	NA	NA	NA	NA	NA	NEW
8mm Steyr	112	1080	NA	NA	290	NA	NA	NA	NA	NA	NEW
8mm Gasser	126	850	NA	NA	200	NA	NA	NA	NA	NA	NEW
9mm, 38											
380 Automatic	60	1130	960	NA	170	120	NA	1.0	NA	NA	NA
380 Automatic	85/88	990	920	870	190	165	145	1.2	5.1	4"	$20
380 Automatic	90	1000	890	800	200	160	130	1.2	5.5	3.75"	$10
380 Automatic	95/100	955	865	785	190	160	130	1.4	5.9	4"	$20
38 Super Auto +P	115	1300	1145	1040	430	335	275	0.7	3.3	5"	$26
38 Super Auto +P	125/130	1215	1100	1015	425	350	300	0.8	3.6	5"	$26
38 Super Auto +P	147	1100	1050	1000	395	355	325	0.9	4.0	5"	NA
9x18mm Makarov	95	1000	930	874	211	182	161	NA	NA	4"	NEW
9x18mm Ultra	100	1050	NA	NA	240	NA	NA	NA	NA	NA	NEW
9x21	124	1150	1050	980	365	305	265	NA	NA	4"	NA
9x23mm Largo	124	1190	1055	966	390	306	257	0.7	3.7	4"	NA
9x23mm Win.	125	1450	1249	1103	583	433	338	0.6	2.8	NA	NA
9mm Steyr	115	1180	NA	NA	350	NA	NA	NA	NA	NA	NEW
9mm Luger	88	1500	1190	1010	440	275	200	0.6	3.1	4"	$24
9mm Luger	90	1360	1112	978	370	247	191	NA	NA	4"	$26
9mm Luger	95	1300	1140	1010	350	275	215	0.8	3.4	4"	NA
9mm Luger	100	1180	1080	NA	305	255	NA	0.9	NA	4"	NA
9mm Luger Guard Dog	105	1230	1070	970	355	265	220	NA	NA	4"	NA
9mm Luger	115	1155	1045	970	340	280	240	0.9	3.9	4"	$21
9mm Luger	123/125	1110	1030	970	340	290	260	1.0	4.0	4"	$23
9mm Luger	140	935	890	850	270	245	225	1.3	5.5	4"	$23
9mm Luger	147	990	940	900	320	290	265	1.1	4.9	4"	$26
9mm Luger +P	90	1475	NA	NA	437	NA	NA	NA	NA	NA	NA
9mm Luger +P	115	1250	1113	1019	399	316	265	0.8	3.5	4"	$27
9mm Federal	115	1280	1130	1040	420	330	280	0.7	3.3	4"V	$24
9mm Luger Vector	115	1155	1047	971	341	280	241	NA	NA	4"	NA
9mm Luger +P	124	1180	1089	1021	384	327	287	0.8	3.8	4"	NA
38											
38 S&W	146	685	650	620	150	135	125	2.4	10.0	4"	$19
38 Short Colt	125	730	685	645	150	130	115	2.2	9.4	6"	$19
39 Special	100	950	900	NA	200	180	NA	1.3	NA	4"V	NA
38 Special	110	945	895	850	220	195	175	1.3	5.4	4"V	$23
38 Special	110	945	895	850	220	195	175	1.3	5.4	4"V	$23

Notes: Blanks are available in 32 S&W, 38 S&W and 38 Special. "V" after barrel length indicates test barrel was vented to produce ballistics similar to a revolver with a normal barrel-to-cylinder gap. Ammo prices are per 50 rounds except when marked with an ** which signifies a 20 round box; *** signifies a 25-round box. Not all loads are available from all ammo manufacturers. Listed loads are those made by Remington, Winchester, Federal, and others. DISC. is a discontinued load.

Prices are rounded to the nearest whole dollar and will vary with brand and retail outlet. † = new bullet weight this year; "c" indicates a change in data.

Cartridge	Bullet Wgt. Grs.	VELOCITY (fps)			ENERGY (ft. lbs.)			Mid-Range Traj. (in.)		Bbl. Lgth. (in).	Est. Price/box
		Muzzle	50 yds.	100 yds.	Muzzle	50 yds.	100 yds.	50 yds.	100 yds.		
38 Special	130	775	745	710	175	160	120	1.9	7.9	4"V	$22
38 Special Cowboy	140	800	767	735	199	183	168			7.5" V	NA
38 (Multi-Ball)	140	830	730	505	215	130	80	2.0	10.6	4"V	$10**
38 Special	148	710	635	565	165	130	105	2.4	10.6	4"V	$17
38 Special	158	755	725	690	200	185	170	2.0	8.3	4"V	$18
38 Special +P	95	1175	1045	960	290	230	195	0.9	3.9	4"V	$23
38 Special +P	110	995	925	870	240	210	185	1.2	5.1	4"V	$23
38 Special +P	125	975	929	885	264	238	218	1	5.2	4"	NA
38 Special +P	125	945	900	860	250	225	205	1.3	5.4	4"V	#23
38 Special +P	129	945	910	870	255	235	215	1.3	5.3	4"V	$11
38 Special +P	130	925	887	852	247	227	210	1.3	5.50	4"V	NA
38 Special +P	147/150(c)	884	NA	NA	264	NA	NA	NA	NA	4"V	$27
38 Special +P	158	890	855	825	280	255	240	1.4	6.0	4"V	$20

357

Cartridge	Bullet Wgt. Grs.	Muzzle	50 yds.	100 yds.	Muzzle	50 yds.	100 yds.	50 yds.	100 yds.	Bbl. Lgth. (in).	Est. Price/box
357 SIG	115	1520	NA	NA	593	NA	NA	NA	NA	NA	NA
357 SIG	124	1450	NA	NA	578	NA	NA	NA	NA	NA	NA
357 SIG	125	1350	1190	1080	510	395	325	0.7	3.1	4"	NA
357 SIG	150	1130	1030	970	420	355	310	0.9	4.0	NA	NA
356 TSW	115	1520	NA	NA	593	NA	NA	NA	NA	NA	NA
356 TSW	124	1450	NA	NA	578	NA	NA	NA	NA	NA	NA
356 TSW	135	1280	1120	1010	490	375	310	0.8	3.5	NA	NA
356 TSW	147	1220	1120	1040	485	410	355	0.8	3.5	5"	NA
357 Mag., Super Clean	105	1650									NA
357 Magnum	110	1295	1095	975	410	290	230	0.8	3.5	4"V	$25
357 (Med.Vel.)	125	1220	1075	985	415	315	270	0.8	3.7	4"V	$25
357 Magnum	125	1450	1240	1090	585	425	330	0.6	2.8	4"V	$25
357 (Multi-Ball)	140	1155	830	665	420	215	135	1.2	6.4	4"V	$11**
357 Magnum	140	1360	1195	1075	575	445	360	0.7	3.0	4"V	$25
357 Magnum FlexTip	140	1440	1274	1143	644	504	406	NA	NA	NA	NA
357 Magnum	145	1290	1155	1060	535	430	360	0.8	3.5	4"V	$26
357 Magnum	150/158	1235	1105	1015	535	430	360	0.8	3.5	4"V	$25
357 Mag. Cowboy	158	800	761	725	225	203	185				NA
357 Magnum	165	1290	1189	1108	610	518	450	0.7	3.1	8-3/8"	NA
357 Magnum	180	1145	1055	985	525	445	390	0.9	3.9	4"V	$25
357 Magnum	180	1180	1088	1020	557	473	416	0.8	3.6	8"V	NA
357 Mag. CorBon FA	180	1650	1512	1386	1088	913	767	1.66	0.0		NA
357 Mag. CorBon	200	1200	1123	1061	640	560	500	3.19	0.0		NA
357 Rem. Maximum	158	1825	1590	1380	1170	886	670	0.4	1.7	10.5"	$14**

40, 10mm

Cartridge	Bullet Wgt. Grs.	Muzzle	50 yds.	100 yds.	Muzzle	50 yds.	100 yds.	50 yds.	100 yds.	Bbl. Lgth. (in).	Est. Price/box
40 S&W	135	1140	1070	NA	390	345	NA	0.9	NA	4"	NA
40 S&W Guard Dog	135	1200	1040	940	430	325	265	NA	NA	4"	NA
40 S&W	155	1140	1026	958	447	362	309	0.9	4.1	4"	$14***
40 S&W	165	1150	NA	NA	485	NA	NA	NA	NA	4"	$18***
40 S&W	180	985	936	893	388	350	319	1.4	5.0	4"	$14***
40 S&W	180	1015	960	914	412	368	334	1.3	4.5	4"	NA
400 Cor-Bon	135	1450	NA	NA	630	NA	NA	NA	NA	5"	NA
10mm Automatic	155	1125	1046	986	436	377	335	0.9	3.9	5"	$26
10mm Automatic	170	1340	1165	1145	680	510	415	0.7	3.2	5"	$31
10mm Automatic	175	1290	1140	1035	650	505	420	0.7	3.3	5.5"	$11**
10mm Auto. (FBI)	180	950	905	865	361	327	299	1.5	5.4	4"	$10**
10mm Automatic	180	1030	970	920	425	375	340	1.1	4.7	5"	$16**
10mm Auto H.V.	180†	1240	1124	1037	618	504	430	0.8	3.4	5"	$27
10mm Automatic	200	1160	1070	1010	495	510	430	0.9	3.8	5"	$14**
10.4mm Italian	177	950	NA	NA	360	NA	NA	NA	NA	NA	NEW
41 Action Exp.	180	1000	947	903	400	359	326	0.5	4.2	5"	$13**
41 Rem. Magnum	170	1420	1165	1015	760	515	390	0.7	3.2	4"V	$33
41 Rem. Magnum	175	1250	1120	1030	605	490	410	0.8	3.4	4"V	$14**
41 (Med. Vel.)	210	965	900	840	435	375	330	1.3	5.4	4"V	$30
41 Rem. Magnum	210	1300	1160	1060	790	630	535	0.7	3.2	4"V	$33
41 Rem. Magnum	240	1250	1151	1075	833	706	616	0.8	3.3	6.5V	NA

44

Cartridge	Bullet Wgt. Grs.	Muzzle	50 yds.	100 yds.	Muzzle	50 yds.	100 yds.	50 yds.	100 yds.	Bbl. Lgth. (in).	Est. Price/box
44 S&W Russian	247	780	NA	NA	335	NA	NA	NA	NA	NA	NA
44 Special FTX	165	900	848	802	297	263	235	NA	NA	2.5"	NA
44 S&W Special	180	980	NA	NA	383	NA	NA	NA	NA	6.5"	NA

Notes: Blanks are available in 32 S&W, 38 S&W and 38 Special. "V" after barrel length indicates test barrel was vented to produce ballistics similar to a revolver with a normal barrel-to-cylinder gap. Ammo prices are per 50 rounds except when marked with an ** which signifies a 20 round box; *** signifies a 25-round box. Not all loads are available from all ammo manufacturers. Listed loads are those made by Remington, Winchester, Federal, and others. DISC. is a discontinued load.
Prices are rounded to the nearest whole dollar and will vary with brand and retail outlet. † = new bullet weight this year; "c" indicates a change in data.

Cartridge	Bullet Wgt. Grs.	VELOCITY (fps)			ENERGY (ft. lbs.)			Mid-Range Traj. (in.)		Bbl. Lgth. (in).	Est. Price/ box
		Muzzle	50 yds.	100 yds.	Muzzle	50 yds.	100 yds.	50 yds.	100 yds.		
44 S&W Special	180	1000	935	882	400	350	311	NA	NA	7.5"V	NA
44 S&W Special	200†	875	825	780	340	302	270	1.2	6.0	6"	$13**
44 S&W Special	200	1035	940	865	475	390	335	1.1	4.9	6.5"	$13**
44 S&W Special	240/246	755	725	695	310	285	265	2.0	8.3	6.5"	$26
44-40 Win. Cowboy	225	750	723	695	281	261	242				NA
44 Rem. Magnum	180	1610	1365	1175	1035	745	550	0.5	2.3	4"V	$18**
44 Rem. Magnum	200	1400	1192	1053	870	630	492	0.6	NA	6.5"	$20
44 Rem. Magnum	210	1495	1310	1165	1040	805	635	0.6	2.5	6.5"	$18**
44 Rem. Mag. FlexTip	225	1410	1240	1111	993	768	617	NA	NA	NA	NA
44 (Med. Vel.)	240	1000	945	900	535	475	435	1.1	4.8	6.5"	$17
44 R.M. (Jacketed)	240	1180	1080	1010	740	625	545	0.9	3.7	4"V	$18**
44 R.M. (Lead)	240	1350	1185	1070	970	750	610	0.7	3.1	4"V	$29
44 Rem. Magnum	250	1180	1100	1040	775	670	600	0.8	3.6	6.5"V	$21
44 Rem. Magnum	250	1250	1148	1070	867	732	635	0.8	3.3	6.5"V	NA
44 Rem. Magnum	275	1235	1142	1070	931	797	699	0.8	3.3	6.5"	NA
44 Rem. Magnum	300	1200	1100	1026	959	806	702	NA	NA	7.5"	$17
44 Rem. Magnum	330	1385	1297	1220	1406	1234	1090	1.83	0.00	NA	NA
440 CorBon	260	1700	1544	1403	1669	1377	1136	1.58	NA	10"	NA

45, 50

Cartridge	Bullet Wgt. Grs.	Muzzle	50 yds.	100 yds.	Muzzle	50 yds.	100 yds.	50 yds.	100 yds.	Bbl. Lgth. (in).	Est. Price/ box
450 Short Colt/450 Revolver	226	830	NA	NA	350	NA	NA	NA	NA	NA	NEW
45 S&W Schofield	180	730	NA	NA	213	NA	NA	NA	NA	NA	NA
45 S&W Schofield	230	730	NA	NA	272	NA	NA	NA	NA	NA	NA
45 G.A.P.	185	1090	970	890	490	385	320	1.0	4.7	5"	NA
45 G.A.P.	230	880	842	NA	396	363	NA	NA	NA	NA	NA
45 Automatic	165	1030	930	NA	385	315	NA	1.2	NA	5"	NA
45 Automatic Guard Dog	165	1140	1030	950	475	390	335	NA	NA	5"	NA
45 Automatic	185	1000	940	890	410	360	325	1.1	4.9	5"	$28
45 Auto. (Match)	185	770	705	650	245	204	175	2.0	8.7	5"	$28
45 Auto. (Match)	200	940	890	840	392	352	312	2.0	8.6	5"	$20
45 Automatic	200	975	917	860	421	372	328	1.4	5.0	5"	$18
45 Automatic	230	830	800	675	355	325	300	1.6	6.8	5"	$27
45 Automatic	230	880	846	816	396	366	340	1.5	6.1	5"	NA
45 Automatic +P	165	1250	NA	NA	573	NA	NA	NA	NA	NA	NA
45 Automatic +P	185	1140	1040	970	535	445	385	0.9	4.0	5"	$31
45 Automatic +P	200	1055	982	925	494	428	380	NA	NA	5"	NA
45 Super	185	1300	1190	1108	694	582	504	NA	NA	5"	NA
45 Win. Magnum	230	1400	1230	1105	1000	775	635	0.6	2.8	5"	$14**
45 Win. Magnum	260	1250	1137	1053	902	746	640	0.8	3.3	5"	$16**
45 Win. Mag. CorBon	320	1150	1080	1025	940	830	747	3.47			NA
455 Webley MKII	262	850	NA	NA	420	NA	NA	NA	NA	NA	NA
45 Colt FTX	185	920	870	826	348	311	280	NA	NA	3"V	NA
45 Colt	200	1000	938	889	444	391	351	1.3	4.8	5.5"	$21
45 Colt	225	960	890	830	460	395	345	1.3	5.5	5.5"	$22
45 Colt + P CorBon	265	1350	1225	1126	1073	884	746	2.65	0.0		NA
45 Colt + P CorBon	300	1300	1197	1114	1126	956	827	2.78	0.0		NA
45 Colt	250/255	860	820	780	410	375	340	1.6	6.6	5.5"	$27
454 Casull	250	1300	1151	1047	938	735	608	0.7	3.2	7.5"V	NA
454 Casull	260	1800	1577	1381	1871	1436	1101	0.4	1.8	7.5"V	NA
454 Casull	300	1625	1451	1308	1759	1413	1141	0.5	2.0	7.5"V	NA
454 Casull CorBon	360	1500	1387	1286	1800	1640	1323	2.01	0.0		NA
460 S&W	200	2300	2042	1801	2350	1851	1441	0	-1.60	NA	NA
460 S&W	260	2000	1788	1592	2309	1845	1464	NA	NA	7.5"V	NA
460 S&W	250	1450	1267	1127	1167	891	705	NA	NA	8.375-V	NA
460 S&W	250	1900	1640	1412	2004	1494	1106	0	-2.75	NA	NA
460 S&W	300	1750	1510	1300	2040	1510	1125	NA	NA	8.4-V	NA
460 S&W	395	1550	1389	1249	2108	1691	1369	0	-4.00	NA	NA
475 Linebaugh	400	1350	1217	1119	1618	1315	1112	NA	NA	NA	NA
480 Ruger	325	1350	1191	1076	1315	1023	835	2.6	0.0	7.5"	NA
50 Action Exp.	325	1400	1209	1075	1414	1055	835	0.2	2.3	6"	$24**
500 S&W	275	1665	1392	1183	1693	1184	854	1.5	NA	8.375	NA
500 S&W	325	1800	1560	1350	2340	1755	1315	NA	NA	8.4-V	NA
500 S&W	350	1400	1231	1106	1523	1178	951	NA	NA	10"	NA
500 S&W	400	1675	1472	1299	2493	1926	1499	1.3	NA	8.375	NA
500 S&W	440	1625	1367	1169	2581	1825	1337	1.6	NA	8.375	NA
500 S&W	500	1425	1281	1164	2254	1823	1505	NA	NA	10"	NA

RIMFIRE AMMUNITION BALLISTICS & PRICES

Note: The actual ballistics obtained with your firearm can vary considerably from the advertised ballistics.
Also, ballistics can vary from lot to lot with the same brand and type load.

Cartridge	Bullet Wt. Grs.	Velocity (fps) 22-1/2" Bbl.		Energy (ft. lbs.) 22-1/2" Bbl.		Mid-Range Traj. (in.)	Muzzle Velocity
		Muzzle	100 yds.	Muzzle	100 yds.	100 yds.	6" Bbl.
17 Aguila	20	1850	1267	NA	NA	NA	NA
17 Hornady Mach 2	15.5	2050	1450	149	75	NA	NA
17 Hornady Mach 2	17	2100	1530	166	88	0.7	NA
17 HMR Lead Free	15.5	2550	1901	NA	NA	.90	NA
17 HMR TNT Green	16	2500	1642	222	96	NA	NA
17 HMR	17	2550	1902	245	136	NA	NA
17 HMR	20	2375	1776	250	140	NA	NA
17 Win. Super Mag.	20 Tipped	3000	2504	400	278	0.0	NA
17 Win. Super Mag.	20 JHP	3000	2309	400	237	0.0	NA
17 Win. Super Mag.	25 Tipped	2600	2230	375	276	0.0	NA
5mm Rem. Rimfire Mag.	30	2300	1669	352	188	NA	24
22 Short Blank	—	—	—	—	—	—	—
22 Short CB	29	727	610	33	24	NA	706
22 Short Target	29	830	695	44	31	6.8	786
22 Short HP	27	1164	920	81	50	4.3	1077
22 Colibri	20	375	183	6	1	NA	NA
22 Super Colibri	20	500	441	11	9	NA	NA
22 Long CB	29	727	610	33	24	NA	706
22 Long HV	29	1180	946	90	57	4.1	1031
22 LR Pistol Match	40	1070	890	100	70	4.6	940
22 LR Shrt. Range Green	21	1650	912	127	NA	NA	NA
CCI Quiet 22 LR	40	710	640	45	36	NA	NA
22 LR Sub Sonic HP	38	1050	901	93	69	4.7	NA
22 LR Segmented HP	40	1050	897	98	72	NA	NA
22 LR Standard Velocity	40	1070	890	100	70	4.6	940
22 LR AutoMatch	40	1200	990	130	85	NA	NA
22 LR HV	40	1255	1016	140	92	3.6	1060
22 LR Silhoutte	42	1220	1003	139	94	3.6	1025
22 SSS	60	950	802	120	86	NA	NA
22 LR HV HP	40	1280	1001	146	89	3.5	1085
22 Velocitor GDHP	40	1435	0	0	0	NA	NA
22 LR Segmented HP	37	1435	1080	169	96	2.9	NA
22 LR Hyper HP	32/33/34	1500	1075	165	85	2.8	NA
22 LR Expediter	32	1640	NA	191	NA	NA	NA
22 LR Stinger HP	32	1640	1132	191	91	2.6	1395
22 LR Lead Free	30	1650	NA	181	NA	NA	NA
22 LR Hyper Vel	30	1750	1191	204	93	NA	NA
22 LR Shot #12	31	950	NA	NA	NA	NA	NA
22 WRF LFN	45	1300	1015	169	103	3	NA
22 Win. Mag. Lead Free	28	2200	NA	301	NA	NA	NA
22 Win. Mag.	30	2200	1373	322	127	1.4	1610
22 Win. Mag. V-Max BT	33	2000	1495	293	164	0.60	NA
22 Win. Mag. JHP	34	2120	1435	338	155	1.4	NA
22 Win. Mag. JHP	40	1910	1326	324	156	1.7	1480
22 Win. Mag. FMJ	40	1910	1326	324	156	1.7	1480
22 Win. Mag. Dyna Point	45	1550	1147	240	131	2.60	NA
22 Win. Mag. JHP	50	1650	1280	300	180	1.3	NA
22 Win. Mag. Shot #11	52	1000	—	NA	—	—	NA

NOTES: * = 10 rounds per box. ** = 5 rounds per box. Pricing variations and number of rounds per box can occur with type and brand of ammunition.
Listed pricing is the average nominal cost for load style and box quantity shown. Not every brand is available in all shot size variations.
Some manufacturers do not provide suggested list prices. All prices rounded to nearest whole dollar.
The price you pay will vary dependent upon outlet of purchase. # = new load spec this year; "C" indicates a change in data.

Dram Equiv.	Shot Ozs.	Load Style	Shot Sizes	Brands	Avg. Price/box	Velocity (fps)
10 Gauge 3-1/2" Magnum						
Max	2-3/8	magnum blend	5, 6, 7	Hevi-shot	NA	1200
4-1/2	2-1/4	premium	BB, 2, 4, 5, 6	Win., Fed., Rem.	$33	1205
Max	2	premium	4, 5, 6	Fed., Win.	NA	1300
4-1/4	2	high velocity	BB, 2, 4	Rem.	$22	1210
Max	18 pellets	premium	00 buck	Fed., Win.	$7**	1100
Max	1-7/8	Bismuth	BB, 2, 4	Bis.	NA	1225
Max	1-3/4	high density	BB, 2	Rem.	NA	1300
4-1/4	1-3/4	steel	TT, T, BBB, BB, 1, 2, 3	Win., Rem.	$27	1260
Mag	1-5/8	steel	T, BBB, BB, 2	Win.	$27	1285
Max	1-5/8	Bismuth	BB, 2, 4	Bismuth	NA	1375
Max	1-1/2	hypersonic	BBB, BB, 2	Rem.	NA	1700
Max	1-1/2	heavy metal	BB, 2, 3, 4	Hevi-Shot	NA	1500
Max	1-1/2	steel	T, BBB, BB, 1, 2, 3	Fed.	NA	1450
Max	1-3/8	steel	T, BBB, BB, 1, 2, 3	Fed., Rem.	NA	1500
Max	1-3/8	steel	T, BBB, BB, 2	Fed., Win.	NA	1450
Max	1-3/4	slug, rifled	slug	Fed.	NA	1280
Max	24 pellets	Buckshot	1 Buck	Fed.	NA	1100
Max	54 pellets	Super-X	4 Buck	Win.	NA	1150
12 Gauge 3-1/2" Magnum						
Max	2-1/4	premium	4, 5, 6	Fed., Rem., Win.	$13*	1150
Max	2	Lead	4, 5, 6	Fed.	NA	1300
Max	2	Copper plated turkey	4, 5	Rem.	NA	1300
Max	18 pellets	premium	00 buck	Fed., Win., Rem.	$7**	1100
Max	1-7/8	Wingmaster HD	4, 6	Rem.	NA	1225
Max	1-7/8	heavyweight	5, 6	Fed.	NA	1300
Max	1-3/4	high density	BB, 2, 4, 6	Rem.		1300
Max	1-7/8	Bismuth	BB, 2, 4	Bis.	NA	1225
Max	1-5/8	blind side	Hex, 1, 3	Win.	NA	1400
Max	1-5/8	Hevi-shot	T	Hevi-shot	NA	1350
Max	1-5/8	Wingmaster HD	T	Rem.	NA	1350
Max	1-5/8	high density	BB, 2	Fed.	NA	1450
Max	1-5/8	Blind side	Hex, BB, 2	Win.	NA	1400
Max	1-3/8	Heavyweight	2, 4, 6	Fed.	NA	1450
Max	1-3/8	steel	T, BBB, BB, 2, 4	Fed., Win., Rem.	NA	1450
Max	1-1/2	FS steel	BBB, BB, 2	Fed.	NA	1500
Max	1-1/2	Supreme H-V	BBB, BB, 2, 3	Win.	NA	1475
Max	1-3/8	H-speed steel	BB, 2	Rem.	NA	1550
Max	1-1/4	Steel	BB, 2	Win.	NA	1625
Max	24 pellets	Premium	1 Buck	Fed.	NA	1100
Max	54 pellets	Super-X	4 Buck	Win.	NA	1050
12 Gauge 3" Magnum						
4	2	premium	BB, 2, 4, 5, 6	Win., Fed., Rem.	$9*	1175
4	1-7/8	premium	BB, 2, 4, 6	Win., Fed., Rem.	$19	1210
4	1-7/8	duplex	4x6	Rem.	$9*	1210

Dram Equiv.	Shot Ozs.	Load Style	Shot Sizes	Brands	Avg. Price/box	Velocity (fps)
12 Gauge 3" Magnum (cont.)						
Max	1-3/4	turkey	4, 5, 6	Fed., Fio., Win., Rem.	NA	1300
Max	1-3/4	high density	BB, 2, 4	Rem.	NA	1450
Max	1-5/8	high density	BB, 2	Fed.	NA	1450
Max	1-5/8	Wingmaster HD	4, 6	Rem.	NA	1227
Max	1-5/8	high velocity	4, 5, 6	Fed.	NA	1350
4	1-5/8	premium	2, 4, 5, 6	Win., Fed., Rem.	$18	1290
Max	1-1/2	Wingmaster HD	T	Rem.	NA	1300
Max	1-1/2	Hevi-shot	T	Hevi-shot	NA	1300
Max	1-1/2	high density	BB, 2, 4	Rem.	NA	1300
Max	1-1/2	slug	slug	Bren.	NA	1604
Max	1-5/8	Bismuth	BB, 2, 4, 5, 6	Bis.	NA	1250
4	24 pellets	buffered	1 buck	Win., Fed., Rem.	$5**	1040
4	15 pellets	buffered	00 buck	Win., Fed., Rem.	$6**	1210
4	10 pellets	buffered	000 buck	Win., Fed., Rem.	$6**	1225
4	41 pellets	buffered	4 buck	Win., Fed., Rem.	$6**	1210
Max	1-3/8	heavyweight	5, 6	Fed.	NA	1300
Max	1-3/8	high density	B, 2, 4, 6	Rem. Win.	NA	1450
Max	1-3/8	slug	slug	Bren.	NA	1476
Max	1-3/8	blind side	Hex, 1, 3, 5	Win.	NA	1400
Max	1-1/4	slug, rifled	slug	Fed.	NA	1600
Max	1-3/16	saboted slug	copper slug	Rem.	NA	1500
Max	7/8	slug, rifled	slug	Rem.	NA	1875
Max	1-1/8	low recoil	BB	Fed.	NA	850
Max	1-1/8	steel	BB, 2, 3, 4	Fed., Win., Rem.	NA	1550
Max	1-1/16	high density	2, 4	Win.	NA	1400
Max	1	steel	4, 6	Fed.	NA	1330
Max	1-3/8	buckhammer	slug	Rem.	NA	1500
Max	1	TruBall slug	slug	Fed.	NA	1700
Max	1	slug, rifled	slug, magnum	Win., Rem.	$5**	1760
Max	1	saboted slug	slug	Rem., Win., Fed.	$10**	1550
Max	385 grs.	partition gold	slug	Win.	NA	2000
Max	1-1/8	Rackmaster	slug	Win.	NA	1700
Max	300 grs.	XP3	slug	Win.	NA	2100
3-5/8	1-3/8	steel	BBB, BB, 1, 2, 3, 4	Win., Fed., Rem.	$19	1275
Max	1-1/8	snow goose FS	BB, 2, 3, 4	Fed.	NA	1635
Max	1-1/8	steel	BB, 2, 4	Rem.	NA	1500
Max	1-1/8	steel	T, BBB, BB, 2, 4, 5, 6	Fed., Win.	NA	1450
Max	1-1/8	steel	BB, 2	Fed.	NA	1400
Max	1-1/8	FS lead	3, 4	Fed.	NA	1600
Max	1-3/8	Blind side	Hex, BB, 2	Win.	NA	1400
4	1-1/4	steel	T, BBB, BB, 1, 2, 3, 4, 6	Win., Fed., Rem.	$18	1400
Max	1-1/4	FS steel	BBB, BB, 2	Fed.	NA	1450

NOTES: * = 10 rounds per box. ** = 5 rounds per box. Pricing variations and number of rounds per box can occur with type and brand of ammunition. Listed pricing is the average nominal cost for load style and box quantity shown. Not every brand is available in all shot size variations. Some manufacturers do not provide suggested list prices. All prices rounded to nearest whole dollar. The price you pay will vary dependent upon outlet of purchase. # = new load spec this year; "C" indicates a change in data.

Dram Equiv.	Shot Ozs.	Load Style	Shot Sizes	Brands	Avg. Price/box	Velocity (fps)
12 Gauge 2-3/4"						
Max	1-5/8	magnum	4, 5, 6	Win., Fed.	$8*	1250
Max	1-3/0	load	4, 5, 6	Fiocchi	NA	1485
Max	1-3/8	turkey	4, 5, 6	Fio.	NA	1250
Max	1-3/8	steel	4, 5, 6	Fed.	NA	1400
Max	1-3/0	Bismuth	BB, 2, 4, 5, 6	Bis.	NA	1300
3-3/4	1-1/2	magnum	BB, 2, 4, 5, 6	Win., Fed., Rem.	$16	1260
Max	1-1/4	blind side	Hex, 2, 5	Win.	NA	1400
Max	1-1/4	Supreme H-V	4, 5, 6, 7-1/2	Win. Rem.	NA	1400
3-3/4	1-1/4	high velocity	BB, 2, 4, 5, 6, 7-1/2, 8, 9	Win., Fed., Rem., Fio.	$13	1330
Max	1-1/4	high density	B, 2, 4	Win.	NA	1450
Max	1-1/4	high density	4, 6	Rem.	NA	1325
3-1/4	1-1/4	standard velocity	6, 7-1/2, 8, 9	Win., Fed., Rem., Fio.	$11	1220
Max	1-1/8	Hevi-shot	5	Hevi-shot	NA	1350
3-1/4	1-1/8	standard velocity	4, 6, 7-1/2, 8, 9	Win., Fed., Rem., Fio.	$9	1255
Max	1-1/8	steel	2, 4	Rem.	NA	1390
Max	1	steel	BB, 2	Fed.	NA	1450
3-1/4	1	standard velocity	6, 7-1/2, 8	Rem., Fed., Fio., Win.	$6	1290
3-1/4	1-1/4	target	7-1/2, 8, 9	Win., Fed., Rem.	$10	1220
3	1-1/8	spreader	7-1/2, 8, 8-1/2, 9	Flo.	NA	1200
3	1-1/8	target	7-1/2, 8, 9, 7-1/2x8	Win., Fed., Rem., Fio.	$7	1200
2-3/4	1-1/8	target	7-1/2, 8, 8-1/2, 9, 7-1/2x8	Win., Fed., Rem., Fio.	$7	1145
2-3/4	1-1/8	low recoil	7-1/2, 8	Rem.	NA	1145
2-1/2	26 grams	low recoil	8	Win.	NA	980
2-1/4	1-1/8	target	7-1/2, 8, 8-1/2, 9	Rem., Fed.	$7	1080
Max	1	spreader	7-1/2, 8, 8-1/2, 9	Fio.	NA	1300
3-1/4	28 grams (1 oz)	target	7-1/2, 8, 9	Win., Fed., Rem., Fio.	$8	1290
3	1	target	7-1/2, 8, 8-1/2, 9	Win., Fio.	NA	1235
2-3/4	1	target	7-1/2, 8, 8-1/2, 9	Fed., Rem., Fio.	NA	1180
3-1/4	24 grams	target	7-1/2, 8, 9	Fed., Win., Fio.	NA	1325
3	7/8	light	8	Fio.	NA	1200
3-3/4	8 pellets	buffered	000 buck	Win., Fed., Rem.	$4**	1325
4	12 pellets	premium	00 buck	Win., Fed., Rem.	$5**	1290
3-3/4	9 pellets	buffered	00 buck	Win., Fed., Rem., Fio.	$19	1325
3-3/4	12 pellets	buffered	0 buck	Win., Fed., Rem.	$4**	1275
4	20 pellets	buffered	1 buck	Win., Fed., Rem.	$4**	1075
3-3/4	16 pellets	buffered	1 buck	Win., Fed., Rem.	$4**	1250
4	34 pellets	premium	4 buck	Fed., Rem.	$5**	1250
3-3/4	27 pellets	buffered	4 buck	Win., Fed., Rem., Fio.	$4**	1325

Dram Equiv.	Shot Ozs.	Load Style	Shot Sizes	Brands	Avg. Price/box	Velocity (fps)
12 Gauge 2-3/4" (cont.)						
		PDX1	1 oz. slug, 3-00 buck	Win.	NA	1150
Max	1 oz	segmenting, slug	slug	Win.	NA	1600
Max	1	saboted slug	slug	Win., Fed., Rem.	$10**	1450
Max	1-1/4	slug, rifled	slug	Fed.	NA	1520
Max	1-1/4	slug	slug	Lightfield		1440
Max	1-1/4	saboted slug	attached sabot	Rem.	NA	1550
Max	1	slug, rifled	slug, magnum	Rem., Fio.	$5**	1680
Max	1	slug, rifled	slug	Win., Fed., Rem.	$4**	1610
Max	1	sabot slug	slug	Sauvestre		1640
Max	7/8	slug, rifled	slug	Rem.	NA	1800
Max	400	plat. tip	sabot slug	Win.	NA	1700
Max	385 grains	Partition Gold Slug	slug	Win.	NA	1900
Max	385 grains	Core-Lokt bonded	sabot slug	Rem.	NA	1900
Max	325 grains	Barnes Sabot	slug	Fed.	NA	1900
Max	300 grains	SST Slug	sabot slug	Hornady	NA	2050
Max	3/4	Tracer	#8 + tracer	Fio.	NA	1150
Max	130 grains	Less Lethal	.73 rubber slug	Lightfield	NA	600
Max	3/4	non-toxic	zinc slug	Win.	NA	NA
3	1-1/8	steel target	6-1/2, 7	Rem.	NA	1200
2-3/4	1-1/8	steel target	7	Rem.	NA	1145
3	1#	steel	7	Win.	$11	1235
3-1/2	1-1/4	steel	T, BBB, BB, 1, 2, 3, 4, 5, 6	Win., Fed., Rem.	$18	1275
3-3/4	1-1/8	steel	BB, 1, 2, 3, 4, 5, 6	Win., Fed., Rem., Fio.	$16	1365
3-3/4	1	steel	2, 3, 4, 5, 6, 7	Win., Fed., Rem., Fio.	$13	1390
Max	7/8	steel	7	Fio.	NA	1440
16 Gauge 2-3/4"						
3-1/4	1-1/4	magnum	2, 4, 6	Fed., Rem.	$16	1260
3-1/4	1-1/8	high velocity	4, 6, 7-1/2	Win., Fed., Rem., Fio.	$12	1295
Max	1-1/8	Bismuth	4, 5	Bis.	NA	1200
2-3/4	1-1/8	standard velocity	6, 7-1/2, 8	Fed., Rem., Fio.	$0	1185
2-1/2	1	dove	6, 7-1/2, 8, 9	Fio., Win.	NA	1165
2-3/4	1		6, 7-1/2, 8	Fio.	NA	1200
Max	15/16	steel	2, 4	Fed., Rem.	NA	1300
Max	7/8	steel	2, 4	Win.	$16	1300
3	12 pellets	buffered	1 buck	Win., Fed., Rem.	$4**	1225
Max	4/5	slug, rifled	slug	Win., Fed., Rem.	$4**	1570
Max	.92	sabot slug	slug	Sauvestre	NA	1560

NOTES: * = 10 rounds per box. ** = 5 rounds per box. Pricing variations and number of rounds per box can occur with type and brand of ammunition.
Listed pricing is the average nominal cost for load style and box quantity shown. Not every brand is available in all shot size variations.
Some manufacturers do not provide suggested list prices. All prices rounded to nearest whole dollar.
The price you pay will vary dependent upon outlet of purchase. # = new load spec this year; "C" indicates a change in data.

Dram Equiv.	Shot Ozs.	Load Style	Shot Sizes	Brands	Avg. Price/ box	Velocity (fps)
20 Gauge 3" Magnum						
3	1-1/4	premium	2, 4, 5, 6, 7-1/2	Win., Fed., Rem.	$15	1185
Max	1-1/4	Wingmaster HD	4, 6	Rem.	NA	1185
3	1-1/4	turkey	4, 6	Fio.	NA	1200
Max	1-1/4	Hevi-shot	2, 4, 6	Hevi-shot	NA	1250
Max	1-1/8	high density	4, 6	Rem.	NA	1300
Max	18 pellets	buck shot	2 buck	Fed.	NA	1200
Max	24 pellets	buffered	3 buck	Win.	$5**	1150
2-3/4	20 pellets	buck	3 buck	Rem.	$4**	1200
Max	1	hypersonic	2, 3, 4	Rem.	NA	Rem.
3-1/4	1	steel	1, 2, 3, 4, 5, 6	Win., Fed., Rem.	$15	1330
Max	1	blind side	Hex, 2, 5	Win.	NA	1300
Max	7/8	steel	2, 4	Win.	NA	1300
Max	7/8	FS lead	3, 4	Fed.	NA	1500
Max	1-1/16	high density	2, 4	Win.	NA	1400
Max	1-1/16	Bismuth	2, 4, 5, 6	Bismuth	NA	1250
Mag	5/8	saboted slug	275 gr.	Fed.	NA	1900
Max	3/4	TruBall slug	slug	Fed.	NA	1700
20 Gauge 2-3/4"						
2-3/4	1-1/8	magnum	4, 6, 7-1/2	Win., Fed., Rem.	$14	1175
2-3/4	1	high velocity	4, 5, 6, 7-1/2, 8, 9	Win., Fed., Rem., Fio.	$12	1220
Max	1	Bismuth	4, 6	Bis.	NA	1200
Max	1	Hevi-shot	5	Hevi-shot	NA	1250
Max	1	Supreme H-V	4, 6, 7-1/2	Win. Rem.	NA	1300
Max	1	FS lead	4, 5, 6	Fed.	NA	1350
Max	7/8	Steel	2, 3, 4	Fio.	NA	1500
2-1/2	1	standard velocity	6, 7-1/2, 8	Win., Rem., Fed., Fio.	$6	1165
2-1/2	7/8	clays	8	Rem.	NA	1200
2-1/2	7/8	promotional	6, 7-1/2, 8	Win., Rem., Fio.	$6	1210
2-1/2	1	target	8, 9	Win., Rem.	$8	1165
Max	7/8	clays	7-1/2, 8	Win.	NA	1275
2-1/2	7/8	target	8, 9	Win., Fed., Rem.	$8	1200
Max	3/4	steel	2, 4	Rem.	NA	1425
2-1/2	7/8	steel - target	7	Rem.	NA	1200
1-1/2	7/8	low recoil	8	Win.	NA	980
Max	1	buckhammer	slug	Rem.	NA	1500
Max	5/8	Saboted Slug	Copper Slug	Rem.	NA	1500
Max	20 pellets	buffered	3 buck	Win., Fed.	$4	1200
Max	5/8	slug, saboted	slug	Win.,	$9**	1400
2-3/4	5/8	slug, rifled	slug	Rem.	$4**	1580
Max	3/4	saboted slug	copper slug	Fed., Rem.	NA	1450
Max	3/4	slug, rifled	slug	Win., Fed., Rem., Fio.	$4**	1570
Max	.9	sabot slug	slug	Sauvestre		1480
Max	260 grains	Partition Gold Slug	slug	Win.	NA	1900
Max	260 grains	Core-Lokt Ultra	slug	Rem.	NA	1900

Dram Equiv.	Shot Ozs.	Load Style	Shot Sizes	Brands	Avg. Price/ box	Velocity (fps)
20 Gauge 2-3/4" (cont.)						
Max	260 grains	saboted slug	platinum tip	Win.	NA	1700
Max	3/4	steel	2, 3, 4, 6	Win., Fed., Rem.	$14	1425
Max	250 grains	SST slug	slug	Hornady	NA	1800
Max	1/2	rifled, slug	slug	Rem.	NA	1800
Max	67 grains	Less lethal	2/.60 rubber balls	Lightfield	NA	900
28 Gauge 3"						
Max	7/8	tundra tungsten	4, 5, 6	Fiocchi	NA	TBD
28 Gauge 2-3/4"						
2	1	high velocity	6, 7-1/2, 8	Win.	$12	1125
2-1/4	3/4	high velocity	6, 7-1/2, 8, 9	Win., Fed., Rem., Fio.	$11	1295
2	3/4	target	8, 9	Win., Fed., Rem.	$9	1200
Max	3/4	sporting clays	7-1/2, 8-1/2	Win.	NA	1300
Max	5/8	Bismuth	4, 6	Bis.	NA	1250
Max	5/8	steel	6, 7	NA	NA	1300
Max	5/8	slug		Bren.	NA	1450
410 Bore 3"						
Max	11/16	high velocity	4, 5, 6, 7-1/2, 8, 9	Win., Fed., Rem., Fio.	$10	1135
Max	9/16	Bismuth	4	Bis.	NA	1175
Max	3/8	steel	6	NA	NA	1400
		judge	5 pellets 000 Buck	Fed.	NA	960
		judge	9 pellets #4 Buck	Fed.	NA	1100
Max	Mixed	Per. Defense	3DD/12BB	Win.	NA	750
410 Bore 2-1/2"						
Max	1/2	high velocity	4, 6, 7-1/2	Win., Fed., Rem.	$9	1245
Max	1/5	slug, rifled	slug	Win., Fed., Rem.	$4**	1815
1-1/2	1/2	target	8, 8-1/2, 9	Win., Fed., Rem., Fio.	$8	1200
Max	1/2	sporting clays	7-1/2, 8, 8-1/2	Win.	NA	1300
Max		Buckshot	5-000 Buck	Win.	NA	1135
		judge	12-bb's, 3 disks	Win.	NA	TBD
Max	Mixed	Per. Defense	4DD/16BB	Win.	NA	750
Max	42 grains	Less lethal	4/.41 rubber balls	Lightfield	NA	1150

ACCU-TEK AT-380 II ACP

Caliber: 380 ACP, 6-shot magazine. **Barrel:** 2.8. **Weight:** 23.5 oz. **Length:** 6.125 overall. **Grips:** Textured black composition. **Sights:** Blade front, rear adjustable for windage. **Features:** Made from 17-4 stainless steel, has an exposed hammer, manual firing-pin safety block and trigger disconnect. Magazine release located on the bottom of the grip. American made, lifetime warranty. Comes with two 6-round stainless steel magazines and a California-approved cable lock. Introduced 2006. Made in U.S.A. by Excel Industries.
Price: Satin stainless $275.00

ACCU-TEK HC-380

Simlar to AT-380 II except has a 13-round magazine.
Price: $314.00

ACCU-TEK LT-380

Simlar to AT-380 II except has a lightweight aluminum frame. **Weight:** 15 ounces.
Price: $308.00

AKDAL GHOST SERIES

Caliber: 9x19mm 15-round double stacked magazine. **Barrel:** 4.45. **Weight:** 29.10 oz. **Length:** 7.5 overall. **Grips:** Polymer black polycoat. **Sights:** Fixed, open type with notched rear sight dovetailed into the slide. Adjustable sight also available. **Features:** Compact single action pre-cocked, semiautomatic pistol with short recoil operation and locking breech. It uses modified Browning-type locking, in which barrel engages the slide with single lug, entering the ejection window. Pistol also has no manual safeties; instead, it has automatic trigger and firing pin safeties. The polymer frame features removable backstraps (of different sizes), and an integral accessory Picatinny rail below the barrel.
Price: $499.00

AMERICAN CLASSIC 1911-A1

1911-style semiauto pistol chambered in .45 ACP. Features include 7+1 capacity, walnut grips, 5-inch barrel, blued or hard-chromed steel frame, checkered wood grips, drift adjustable sights. A .22 LR version is also available.
Price: $564.00

AMERICAN CLASSIC COMMANDER

1911-style semiauto pistol chambered in .45 ACP. Features include 7+1 capacity, checkered mahogany grips, 4.25-inch barrel, blued or hard-chromed steel frame, drift adjustable sights.
Price: $600.00

ARMALITE AR-24

Caliber: 9mm Para., 10- or 15-shot magazine. **Barrel:** 4.671, 6 groove, right-hand cut rifling. **Weight:** 34.9 oz. **Length:** 8.27 overall. **Grips:** Black polymer. **Sights:** Dovetail front, fixed rear, 3-dot luminous design. **Features:** Machined slide, frame and barrel. Serrations on forestrap and backstrap, external thumb safety and internal firing pin box, half cock. Two 15-round magazines, pistol case, pistol lock, manual and cleaning brushes. Manganese phosphate finish. Compact comes with two 13-round magazines, 3.89 barrel, weighs 33.4 oz. Made in U.S.A. by ArmaLite.
Price: AR-24 Full Size $550.00
Price: AR-24K Compact $550.00

ARMSCOR/ROCK ISLAND ARMORY 1911A1-45 FS GI

1911-style semiauto pistol chambered in .45 ACP (8 rounds), 9mm Parabellum, .38 Super (9 rounds). Features include checkered plastic or hardwood grips, 5-inch barrel, parkerized steel frame and slide, drift adjustable sights.
Price: $500.00

ARMSCOR/ROCK ISLAND ARMORY 1911A1-45 CS GI

1911-style Officer's-size semiauto pistol chambered in .45 ACP. Features plain hardwood grips, 3.5-inch barrel, parkerized steel frame and slide, drift adjustable sights.
Price: $500.00

ARMSCOR/ROCK ISLAND ARMORY 1911A2-.22 TCM

Caliber: .22 TCM, 17-round magazine. **Barrel:** 5 inches. **Weight:**

36 oz. **Length:** 8.5 inches. **Grips:** Polymer. **Sights:** Adjustable rear. **Features:** Chambered for high velocity .22 TCM rimfire cartridge.
Price: $660.00

ARMSCOR/ROCK ISLAND ARMORY
1911 TACTICAL II FS
Caliber: 10mm, 8-round magazine. **Barrel:** 5 inches. **Weight:** 40 oz. **Length:** 8.5 inches. **Grips:** VZ G10. **Sights:** Fiber optic front, adjustable rear. **Features:** Parkerized finish, comes with two magazines, lock and lockable hard case. Accessory rail available.
Price: $660.00

ARMSCOR/ROCK ISLAND ARMORY
MAP1 & MAPP1
Caliber: 9mm, 16-round magazine. Browning short recoil action style pistols with: integrated front sight; Snag-free rear sight (police standard); Tanfoglio barrel; Single & double-action trigger; automatic safety on firing pin & manual on rear lever; standard hammer; side extractor; standard or Ambidextrous rear safety; combat slide stop; parkerized finish for nickel steel parts; polymer frame with accessory rail.
Price: $400.00

ARMSCOR/ROCK ISLAND ARMORY XT22
Caliber: .22 LR, 15-round magazine std. **Barrel:** 5 **Weight:** 38 oz. The XT-22 is a combat 1911 .22 pistol. Unlike most .22 1911 conversions, this pistol is built as a complete gun. Designed for durability, it is the only .22 1911 with a forged 4140 steel slide and the only .22 1911 with a one piece 4140 chrome moly barrel. Available soon.
Price: ....(pre-order) $473.99

AUTO-ORDNANCE TA5
Caliber: 45 ACP, 30-round stick magazine (standard), 50- or 100-round drum magazine optional. **Barrel:** 10.5", finned. **Weight:** 6.5 lbs. **Length:** 25" overall. **Features:** Semi-auto pistol patterned after Thompson Model 1927 semi-auto carbine. Horizontal vertical foregrip, aluminum receiver, top cocking knob, grooved walnut pistolgrip.
Price: $1,143.00

AUTO-ORDNANCE 1911A1
Caliber: 45 ACP, 7-shot magazine. **Barrel:** 5. **Weight:** 39 oz. **Length:** 8.5 overall. **Grips:** Brown checkered plastic with medallion. **Sights:** Blade front, rear drift-adjustable for windage. **Features:** Same specs as 1911A1 military guns-parts interchangeable. Frame and slide blued; each radius has non-glare finish. Introduced 2002. Made in U.S.A. by Kahr Arms.

Price: 1911PKZSE Parkerized, plastic grips $627.00
Price: 1911PKZSEW Parkerized..$662.00
Price: 1911PKZMA Parkerized, Mass. Compliant (2008) $627.00

BAER H.C. 40
Caliber: 40 S&W, 18-shot magazine. **Barrel:** 5. **Weight:** 37 oz. **Length:** 8.5 overall. **Grips:** Wood. **Sights:** Low-mount adjustable rear sight with hidden rear leaf, dovetail front sight. **Features:** Double-stack Caspian frame, beavertail grip safety, ambidextrous thumb safety, 40 S&W match barrel with supported chamber, match stainless steel barrel bushing, lowered and flared ejection port, extended ejector, match trigger fitted, integral mag well, bead blast blue finish on lower, polished sides on slide. Introduced 2008. Made in U.S.A. by Les Baer Custom, Inc.
Price: $2,960.00

BAER 1911 BOSS .45
Caliber: .45 ACP, 8+1 capacity. **Barrel:** 5. **Weight:** 37 oz. **Length:** 8.5 overall. **Grips:** Premium Checkered Cocobolo Grips. **Sights:**

Low-Mount LBC Adj Sight, Red Fiber Optic Front. **Features:** Speed Trgr, Beveled Mag Well, Rounded for Tactical. Rear cocking serrations on the slide, Baer fiber optic front sight (red), flat mainspring housing, checkered at 20 lpi, extended combat safety, Special tactical package, chromed complete lower, blued slide, (2) 8-round premium magazines.
Price: $2,109.00

BAER 1911 CUSTOM CARRY
Caliber: 45 ACP, 7- or 10-shot magazine. **Barrel:** 5. **Weight:** 37 oz. **Length:** 8.5 overall. **Grips:** Checkered walnut. **Sights:** Baer improved ramp-style dovetailed front, Novak low-mount rear. **Features:** Baer forged NM frame, slide and barrel with stainless bushing. Baer speed trigger with 4-lb. pull. Partial listing shown. Made in U.S.A. by Les Baer Custom, Inc.
Price: Custom Carry 5, blued $1,995.00
Price: Custom Carry 5, stainless $2,120.00
Price: Custom Carry 4 Commanche length, blued $1,995.00
Price: Custom Carry 4 Commanche length, stainless $2,120.00

BAER 1911 ULTIMATE RECON
Caliber: 45 ACP, 7- or 10-shot magazine. **Barrel:** 5. **Weight:** 37 oz. **Length:** 8.5 overall. **Grips:** Checkered cocobolo. **Sights:** Baer Improved ramp-style dovetailed front, Novak low-mount rear. **Features:** NM Caspian frame, slide and barrel with stainless bushing. Baer speed trigger with 4-lb. pull. Includes integral Picatinny rail and Sure-Fire X-200 light. Made in U.S.A. by Les Baer Custom, Inc. Introduced 2006.
Price: Bead blast blued $3,070.00
Price: Bead blast chrome $3,390.00

BAER 1911 PREMIER II
Caliber: 38 Super, 400 Cor-Bon, 45 ACP, 7- or 10-shot magazine. **Barrel:** 5. **Weight:** 37 oz. **Length:** 8.5 overall. **Grips:** Checkered rosewood, double diamond pattern. **Sights:** Baer dovetailed front, low-mount Bo-Mar rear with hidden leaf. **Features:** Baer NM forged steel frame and barrel with stainless bushing, deluxe Commander hammer and sear, beavertail grip safety with pad, extended ambidextrous safety; flat mainspring housing; 30 lpi checkered front strap. Made in U.S.A. by Les Baer Custom, Inc.
Price: 5 45 ACP $1,790.00

Price: 5 400 Cor-Bon $1,890.00
Price: 5 38 Super $2,070.00
Price: 6 45 ACP, 400 Cor-Bon, 38 Super, from.................$1,990.00
Price: Super-Tac, 45 ACP, 400 Cor-Bon, 38 Super, from $2,280.00

BAER 1911 S.R.P.
Caliber: 45 ACP. **Barrel:** 5. **Weight:** 37 oz. **Length:** 8.5 overall. **Grips:** Checkered walnut. **Sights:** Trijicon night sights. **Features:** Similar to the F.B.I. contract gun except uses Baer forged steel frame. Has Baer match barrel with supported chamber, complete tactical action. Has Baer Ultra Coat finish. Introduced 1996. Made in U.S.A. by Les Baer Custom, Inc.
Price: Government or Commanche length $2,590.00

BAER 1911 STINGER
Caliber: 45 ACP, 7-round magazine. **Barrel:** 5. **Weight:** 34 oz. **Length:** 8.5 overall. **Grips:** Checkered cocobolo. **Sights:** Baer dovetailed front, low-mount Bo-Mar rear with hidden leaf. **Features:** Baer NM frame. Baer Commanche slide, Officer's style grip frame, beveled mag well. Made in U.S.A. by Les Baer Custom, Inc.
Price: Blued $1,890.00
Price: Stainless $1,970.00

BAER 1911 PROWLER III
Caliber: 45 ACP, 8-round magazine. **Barrel:** 5. **Weight:** 34 oz. **Length:** 8.5 overall. **Grips:** Checkered cocobolo. **Sights:** Baer dovetailed front, low-mount Bo-Mar rear with hidden leaf. **Features:** Similar to Premier II with tapered cone stub weight, rounded corners. Made in U.S.A. by Les Baer Custom, Inc.
Price: Blued $2,580.00

BERETTA 85FS CHEETAH
Caliber: 9x19 15-round double stack magazine. **Barrel:** 4.45. **Weight:** 29.10 oz. **Length:** 7.5 overall. **Grips:** Plastic and Wood. **Sights:** Standard 3-dot system. Notched rear sight is dovetailed to slide. Blade front sight is integral with slide. **Features:** An open slide design that increases the reliability of the firearm. The frame is made from an aluminum alloy that delivers the strength and durability of steel – but with 65% less weight. The automatic firing pin block (FS models) prevents the gun from firing in case of inadvertent drops or strikes against hard surfaces. Available in nickel finish.
Price: Standard (black) finish..............................$770.00
Price: Nickel finish $830.00

BERETTA M92/96 A1 SERIES
Caliber: 9mm, 15-round magazine; .40 S&W, 12 rounds (M06 A1) **Barrel:** 4.9 inches. **Weight:** 33-34 oz. **Length:** 8.5 inches. **Sights:** Fiber optic front, adjustable rear. **Features:** Same as other models in 92/96 family except for addition of accessory rail.
Price: $725.00

BERETTA MODEL 92FS
Caliber: 9mm Para., 10-shot magazine. **Barrel:** 4.9. **Weight:** 34 oz. **Length:** 8.5 overall. **Grips:** Checkered black plastic. **Sights:** Blade front, rear adjustable for windage. Tritium night sights available. **Features:** Double action. Extractor acts as chamber loaded indicator, squared trigger guard, grooved front and backstraps, inertia firing pin. Matte or blued finish. Introduced 1977. Made in U.S.A.
Price: With plastic grips $650.00

BERETTA 92FS

in 9mm Para. and 14/10 in 40 S&W). Removable hammer unit. American made by Beretta. Introduced 2005.
Price: $600.00
Price: 45 ACP $650.00

BERETTA MODEL 80 CHEETAH SERIES DA
Caliber: 380 ACP, 10-shot magazine (M84); 8-shot (M85); 22 LR, 7-shot (M87). **Barrel:** 3.82. **Weight:** About 23 oz. (M84/85); 20.8 oz. (M87). **Length:** 6.8 overall. **Grips:** Glossy black plastic (wood optional at extra cost). **Sights:** Fixed front, drift-adjustable rear. **Features:** Double action, quick takedown, convenient magazine release. Introduced 1977. Made in U.S.A.
Price: Model 84 Cheetah, plastic grips $650.00

BERETTA MODEL 21 BOBCAT
Caliber: 22 LR or 25 ACP. Both double action. **Barrel:** 2.4. **Weight:** 11.5 oz.; 11.8 oz. **Length:** 4.9 overall. **Grips:** Plastic. **Features:** Available in nickel, matte, engraved or blue finish. Introduced in 1985.
Price: Bobcat, 22 or 25, blue $335.00
Price: Bobcat, 22, Inox $420.00
Price: Bobcat, 22 or 25, matte $335.00

BERETTA MODEL 3032 TOMCAT
Caliber: 32 ACP, 7-shot magazine. **Barrel:** 2.45. **Weight:** 14.5 oz. **Length:** 5 overall. **Grips:** Checkered black plastic. **Sights:** Blade front, drift-adjustable rear. **Features:** Double action with exposed hammer; tip-up barrel for direct loading/unloading; thumb safety; polished or matte blue finish. Made in U.S.A. Introduced 1996.
Price: Matte $435.00
Price: Inox $555.00

BERETTA MODEL U22 NEOS
Caliber: 22 LR, 10-shot magazine. **Barrel:** 4.5; 6. **Weight:** 32 oz.; 36 oz. **Length:** 8.8; 10.3. **Sights:** Target.
Features: Integral rail for standard scope mounts, light, perfectly weighted, 100 percent American made by Beretta.
Price: $250.00
Price: Inox $350.00

BERETTA MODEL PX4 STORM
Caliber: 9mm Para., 40 S&W. **Capacity:** 17 (9mm Para.); 14 (40 S&W). **Barrel:** 4. **Weight:** 27.5 oz. **Grips:** Black checkered w/3 interchangeable backstraps. **Sights:** 3-dot system coated in Superluminova; removable front and rear sights. **Features:** DA/SA, manual safety/hammer decocking lever (ambi) and automatic firing pin block safety. Picatinny rail. Comes with two magazines (17/10

BERETTA MODEL PX4 STORM SUB-COMPACT
Caliber: 9mm, 40 S&W. **Capacity:** 13 (9mm); 10 (40 S&W). **Barrel:** 3. **Weight:** 26.1 oz. **Length:** 6.2" overall. **Grips:** NA. **Sights:** NA.
Features: Ambidextrous manual safety lever, interchangeable backstraps included, lock breech and tilt barrel system, stainless steel barrel, Picatinny rail.
Price: $600.00

BERETTA MODEL M9
Caliber: 9mm Para. **Capacity:** 15. **Barrel:** 4.9. **Weight:** 32.2-35.3 oz. **Grips:** Plastic. **Sights:** Dot and post, low profile, windage adjustable rear. **Features:** DA/SA, forged aluminum alloy frame, delayed locking-bolt system, manual safety doubles as decocking lever, combat-style trigger guard, loaded chamber indicator. Comes with two magazines (15/10). American made by Beretta. Introduced 2005.
Price: $650.00

BERETTA MODEL M9A1
Caliber: 9mm Para. **Capacity:** 15. **Barrel:** 4.9. **Weight:** 32.2-35.3 oz. **Grips:** Plastic. **Sights:** Dot and post, low profile, windage adjustable

Prices given are believed to be accurate at time of publication however, many factors affect retail pricing so exact prices are not possible.

rear. **Features:** Same as M9, but also includes Integral Mil-Std-1913 Picatinny rail, has checkered frontstrap and backstrap. Comes with two magazines (15/10). American made by Beretta. Introduced 2005.

Price: $750.00

overall. **Features:** Otherwise similar to Thunder 45 Ultra Compact. 380 DLX has 9-round capacity. 380 Concealed Carry has 8 round capacity. Imported from Argentina by Eagle Imports, Inc.

Price: Thunder 380 Matte $310.00
Price: Thunder 380 Satin Nickel $336.00
Price: Thunder 380 Blue DLX $332.00
Price: Thunder 380 Matte CC (2006) $315.00

BERETTA NANO

Caliber: 9mm Para. Six-shot magazine. **Barrel:** 3.07". **Weight:** 17.7 oz. **Length:** 5.7" overall. **Grips:** Polymer. Sights: 3-dot low profile. **Features:** Double-action only, striker fired. Replaceable grip frames.

Price: $475.00

BERSA THUNDER 9 ULTRA COMPACT/40 SERIES

Caliber: 9mm Para., 40 S&W. **Barrel:** 3.5. **Weight:** 24.5 oz. **Length:** 6.6 overall. **Features:** Otherwise similar to Thunder 45 Ultra Compact. 9mm Para. High Capacity model has 17-round capacity. 40 High Capacity model has 13-round capacity. Imported from Argentina by Eagle Imports, Inc.

Price: Thunder 9mm Para. Matte $402.00
Price: Thunder 40 High Capacity Satin Nickel . . $419.00

BERSA THUNDER 45 ULTRA COMPACT

Caliber: 45 ACP. **Barrel:** 3.6. **Weight:** 27 oz. **Length:** 6.7 overall. **Grips:** Anatomically designed polymer. **Sights:** White outline rear. **Features:** Double action; firing pin safeties, integral locking system. Available in matte, satin nickel, gold, or duo-tone. Introduced 2003. Imported from Argentina by Eagle Imports, Inc.

Price: Thunder 45, matte blue $402.00
Price: Thunder 45, stainless $480.00
Price: Thunder 45, satin nickel $445.00

BOBERG XR9-S

Caliber: 9mm, 7-round magazine. **Barrel:** 3.35 inches. XR9-L has 4.2 inch barrel. **Weight:** 17.4 oz. **Length:** 5.1 inches, 5.95 (XR9-L). **Sights:** Fixed low profile. **Features:** Unique rotating barrel, locked-breech operation, with "pull-push" feeding system utilizing a claw-type loader attached to the slide to pull rounds from the magazine.

Price: $1,349.00
Price: (XR-9L)..$1,399.00

BERSA THUNDER 380 SERIES

Caliber: 380 ACP, 7 rounds **Barrel:** 3.5. **Weight:** 23 oz. **Length:** 6.6

BROWNING 1911-22 COMPACT

Caliber: .22 L.R.,10-round magazine. **Barrel:** 3.625. **Weight:** 15

Prices given are believed to be accurate at time of publication however, many factors affect retail pricing so exact prices are not possible.

68TH EDITION, 2014 ⟡ **387**

oz. **Length:** 6.5 overall. **Grips:** Brown composite. **Sights:** Fixed. **Features:** Slide is machined aluminum with alloy frame and matte blue finish. Blowback action and single action trigger with manual thumb and grip safetys. Works, feels and functions just like a full size 1911. It is simply scaled down and chambered in the best of all practice rounds: 22 LR. for focus on the fundamentals.
Price: **$600.00**

BROWNING 1911-22 A1

Caliber: .22 L.R.,10-round magazine. **Barrel:** 4.25. **Weight:** 16 oz. **Length:** 7.0625 overall. **Grips:** Brown composite. **Sights:** Fixed. **Features:** Slide is machined aluminum with alloy frame and matte blue finish. Blowback action and single action trigger with manual thumb and grip safetys. Works, feels and functions just like a full size 1911. It is simply scaled down and chambered in the best of all practice rounds: 22 LR. for focus on the fundamentals
Price: **$600.00**

BROWNING HI-POWER

Caliber: 9mm, 13-round magazine. **Barrel:** 4.625 inches. **Weight:** 32 oz. **Length:** 7.75 inches. **Grips:** Checkered walnut (standard model), textured and grooved polymer (Mark III). **Sights:** Fixed low-profile 3-dot (Mark III), fixed or adjustable low profile (standard model). **Features:** Single-action operation with ambidextrous thumb safety, forged steel frame and slide. Made in Belgium.
Price: Mark III...**$1,060.00**
Price: Fixed Sights..**$1,070.00**
Price: Standard, Adjustable sights **$1,150.00**

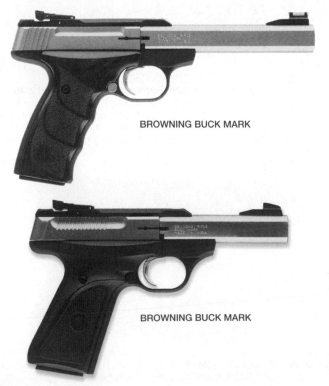

BROWNING BUCK MARK

BROWNING BUCK MARK

BROWNING BUCK MARK

Currently offered in 15 different variations. **Caliber:** .22 LR with 10-shot magazine. Barrel: 4", 5.5" or 7.25". Weight: 28 to 39 oz. Length: 8", 9.5" or 11.3" Overall. Grips: Laminate UDX (black or brown), Rosewood UDX, Composite URX, Cocobolo or Molded Comp, all ambidextrous. URX and UDX have finger grooves. Sights: Pro-Target adjustable rear, TRUGLO fiber-optic or ramp front. Finish: Matte blued, matte green or matte gray; matte stainless.
Price: ....**$380 to $560**

BUSHMASTER CARBON 15 .223

Caliber: 5.56/223, 30-round. **Barrel:** 7.25 stainless steel. **Weight:** 2.88 lbs. **Length:** 20 overall. **Grips:** Pistol grip, Hogue overmolded unit for ergonomic comfort. **Sights:** A2-type front with dual-aperture slip-up rear. **Features:** AR-style semi-auto pistol with carbon composite receiver, shortenend handguard, full-length optics rail.
Price: .... **N/A**
Price: Type 97 pistol, without handguard .. **$1,055.00**

CHIAPPA 1911-22

A faithful replica of the famous John Browning 1911A1 pistol. **Caliber:** .22 LR. **Barrel:** 5". **Weight:** 33.5 oz. **Length:** 8.5". **Grips:** Two-piece wood. **Sights:** Fixed. **Features:** Fixed barrel design, 10-shot magazine. Available in black, OD green or tan finish. Target and Tactical models have adjustable sights.
Price: ....**$300 to $419**

CHIAPPA M9-22 STANDARD

Caliber: .22 LR. **Barrel:** 5 **Weight:** 2.3 lbs. **Length:** 8.5. **Grips:** Black

Prices given are believed to be accurate at time of publication however, many factors affect retail pricing so exact prices are not possible.

molded plastic or walnut. **Sights:** Fixed front sight and windage adjustable rear sight. **Features:** The M9-9mm has been a U.S. standard-issue service pistol since 1990. Chiappa's M9-22 is a replica of this pistol in 22 LR. The M9-22 has the same weight and feel as its 9mm counterpart but has an affordable 10 shot magazine for the 22 long rifle cartridge which makes it a true rimfire reproduction. Comes standard with steel trigger, hammer assembly and a 1/2-28 threaded barrel.
Price: .... (available soon) $369.00

CHIAPPA M9-22 TACTICAL
Caliber: .22 LR. **Barrel:** 5 **Weight:** 2.3 lbs. **Length:** 8.5. **Grips:** Black molded plastic. **Sights:** Fixed front sight and Novak style rear sites. **Features:** The M9-22 Tactical model has Novak style rear sites and comes with a fake suppressor (this ups the "cool factor" on the range and extends the barrel to make it even more accurate). It also has a 1/2 x 28 thread adaptor which can be used by those with a legal suppressor.
Price: .... (available soon) $419.00

CHRISTENSEN ARMS 1911 SERIES
Caliber: .45 ACP, .40 S&W, 9mm. **Barrel:** 3.7", 4.3", 5.5". **Features:** All models are built on a titanium frame with hand-fitted slide, match-grade barrel, tritium night sights, G10 Operator grip panels.
Price: $3,195

COBRA ENTERPRISES FS32, FS380
Caliber: 32 ACP, 380 ACP, 7-shot magazine. **Barrel:** 3.5. **Weight:** 2.1 lbs. **Length:** 6-3/8 overall. **Grips:** Black composition. **Sights:** Fixed. **Features:** Choice of bright chrome, satin nickel or black finish. Introduced 2002. Made in U.S.A. by Cobra Enterprises of Utah, Inc.
Price: $165.00

COBRA ENTERPRISES PATRIOT 45
Caliber: 45 ACP, 6, 7, or 10-shot magazine. **Barrel:** 3.3. **Weight:** 20 oz. **Length:** 6 overall. **Grips:** Black polymer. **Sights:** Rear adjustable. **Features:** Stainless steel or black melonite slide with load indicator; Semi-auto locked breech, DAO. Made in U.S.A. by Cobra Enterprises of Utah, Inc.
Price: $380.00

COBRA ENTERPRISES CA32, CA380
Caliber: 32 ACP, 380 ACP. **Barrel:** 2.8. **Weight:** 22 oz. **Length:** 5.4. **Grips:** Black molded synthetic. **Sights:** Fixed. **Features:** Choice of black, satin nickel, or chrome finish. Made in U.S.A. by Cobra Enterprises of Utah, Inc.
Price: $157.00

COLT MODEL 1991 MODEL O
Caliber: 45 ACP, 7-shot magazine. **Barrel:** 5. **Weight:** 38 oz. **Length:** 8.5 overall. **Grips:** Checkered black composition. **Sights:** Ramped blade front, fixed square notch rear, high profile. **Features:** Matte finish. Continuation of serial number range used on original G.I. 1911A1 guns. Comes with one magazine and molded carrying case. Introduced 1991.
Price: Blue $928.00
Price: Stainless $989.00

COLT XSE SERIES MODEL O
Caliber: 45 ACP, 8-shot magazine. **Barrel:** 5. **Grips:** Checkered, double diamond rosewood. **Sights:** Drift-adjustable 3-dot combat. **Features:** Brushed stainless finish; adjustable, two-cut aluminum trigger; extended ambidextrous thumb safety; upswept beavertail with palm swell; elongated slot hammer. Introduced 1999. From Colt's Mfg. Co., Inc.
Price: XSE Government (5 bbl.) $1,072.00

COLT XSE LIGHTWEIGHT COMMANDER
Caliber: 45 ACP, 8-shot. **Barrel:** 4.25. **Weight:** 26 oz. **Length:** 7.75" overall. **Grips:** Double diamond checkered rosewood. **Sights:** Fixed, glare-proofed blade front, square notch rear; 3-dot system. **Features:** Brushed stainless slide, nickeled aluminum frame; McCormick elongated slot enhanced hammer, McCormick two-cut adjustable aluminum hammer. Made in U.S.A. by Colt's Mfg. Co., Inc.
Price: $1,072.00

COLT DEFENDER
Caliber: .45 ACP (7-round magazine), 9mm (8-round). **Barrel:** 3. **Weight:** 22-1/2 oz. **Length:** 6.75 overall. **Grips:** Pebble-finish rubber

Prices given are believed to be accurate at time of publication however, many factors affect retail pricing so exact prices are not possible.

68TH EDITION, 2014 ✦ **389**

wraparound with finger grooves. **Sights:** White dot front, snag-free Colt competition rear. **Features:** Stainless finish; aluminum frame; combat-style hammer; Hi Ride grip safety, extended manual safety, disconnect safety. Introduced 1998. Made in U.S.A. by Colt's Mfg. Co., Inc.

Price: 07000D, stainless $1,046.00

COLT SERIES 70

Caliber: 45 ACP. **Barrel:** 5. **Weight:** 37.5 oz. **Length:** 8.5". **Grips:** Rosewood with double diamond checkering pattern. **Sights:** Fixed. **Features:** Custom replica of the Original Series 70 pistol with a Series 70 firing system, original rollmarks. Introduced 2002. Made in U.S.A. by Colt's Mfg. Co., Inc.

Price: Blued $1,043.00
Price: Stainless $1,078.00

COLT 38 SUPER

Caliber: 38 Super. **Barrel:** 5. **Weight:** 36.5 oz. **Length:** 8.5 **Grips:** Checkered rubber (stainless and blue models); wood with double diamond checkering pattern (bright stainless model). **Sights:** 3-dot. **Features:** Beveled magazine well, standard thumb safety and service-style grip safety. Introduced 2003. Made in U.S.A. by Colt's Mfg. Co., Inc.

Price: Blued $951.00
Price: Stainless $1,311.00

COLT MUSTANG POCKETLITE

Caliber: .380 ACP. Six-shot magazine. **Barrel:** 2.75". **Weight:** 12.5 oz. **Length:** 5.5". **Grips:** Black composite. **Finish:** Brushed stainless. **Features:** Thumb safety, firing-pin safety block.

Price: $599.00

COLT NEW AGENT

Caliber: 45 ACP (7+1), "9mm (8+1)". **Barrel:** 3. **Weight:** 25 oz. **Length:** 6.75 overall. **Grips:** Double diamond slim fit. **Sights:** Snag free trench style. **Features:** Semi-auto pistol with blued finish and enhanced black anodized aluminum receiver. Skeletonized aluminum trigger, series 80 firing system, front strap serrations, beveled magazine well. Also available in a double-action-only version (shown), in .45 ACP only.

Price: $1,046.00

COLT RAIL GUN

Caliber: 45 ACP (8+1). **Barrel:** NA. **Weight:** NA. **Length:** NA. **Grips:** Rosewood double diamond. **Sights:** White dot front and Novak rear. **Features:** 1911-style semi-auto. Stainless steel frame and slide, front and rear slide serrations, skeletonized trigger, integral; accessory rail, Smith & Alexander upswept beavertail grip palm swell safety, tactical thumb safety, National Match barrel.

Price: .... $1,141.00 to $1,223.00

COLT SPECIAL COMBAT GOVERNMENT CARRY MODEL

Caliber: 45 ACP (8+1), 38 Super (9+1). **Barrel:** 5. **Weight:** NA. **Length:** NA. **Grips:** Black/silver synthetic. **Sights:** Novak front and rear night. **Features:** 1911-style semi-auto. Skeletonized three-hole trigger, slotted hammer, Smith & Alexander upswept beavertail grip palm swell safety and extended magazine well, Wilson tactical ambidextrous safety. Available in blued, hard chrome, or blue/satin nickel finish, depending on chambering. Marine Pistol has Desert Tan Cerakoted stainless steel finish, lanyard loop.

Price: $2,095.00
Price: Marine Pistol...$1,995.00

CZ 75 B

Caliber: 9mm Para., 40 S&W, 10-shot magazine. **Barrel:** 4.7. **Weight:** 34.3 oz. **Length:** 8.1 overall. **Grips:** High impact checkered plastic. **Sights:** Square post front, rear adjustable for windage; 3-dot system. **Features:** Single action/double action design; firing pin block safety; choice of black polymer, matte or high-polish blue finishes. All-steel frame. B-SA is a single action with a drop-free magazine. Imported from the Czech Republic by CZ-USA.

Price: 75 B, black polymer, 16-shot magazine $597.00
Price: 75 B, dual-tone or satin nickel $617.00
Price: 40 S&W, black polymer, 12-shot magazine $615.00
Price: 40 S&W, glossy blue, dual-tone, satin nickel $669.00
Price: 75 B-SA, 9mm Para./40 S&W, single action $609.00

Prices given are believed to be accurate at time of publication however, many factors affect retail pricing so exact prices are not possible.

CZ 75 BD DECOCKER

Similar to the CZ 75B except has a decocking lever in place of the safety lever. All other specifications are the same. Introduced 1999. Imported from the Czech Republic by CZ-USA.
Price: 9mm Para., black polymer **$609.00**

CZ 75 B COMPACT

Similar to the CZ 75 B except has 14-shot magazine in 9mm Para., 3.9 barrel and weighs 32 oz. Has removable front sight, non-glare ribbed slide top. Trigger guard is squared and serrated; combat hammer. Introduced 1993. Imported from the Czech Republic by CZ-USA.
Price: 9mm Para., black polymer **$631.00**
Price: 9mm Para., dual tone or satin nickel **$651.00**
Price: 9mm Para. D PCR Compact, alloy frame **$651.00**

CZ P-07 DUTY

Caliber: 40 S&W, 9mm Luger (16+1). **Barrel:** 3.8. **Weight:** 27.2 oz. **Length:** 7.3 overall. **Grips:** Polymer black polycoat. **Sights:** Blade front, fixed groove rear. **Features:** The ergonomics and accuracy of the CZ 75 with a totally new trigger system. The new Omega trigger system simplifies the CZ 75 trigger system, uses fewer parts and improves the trigger pull. In addition, it allows users to choose between using the handgun with a decocking lever (installed) or a manual safety (included) by a simple parts change. The polymer frame design of the Duty and a new sleek slide profile (fully machined from bar stock) reduce weight, making the P-07 Duty a great choice for concealed carry.
Price: **$487.00**

CZ P-09 DUTY

High-capacity version of P-07. **Caliber:** 9mm, .40 S&W. **Magazine capacity:** 19 rounds (9mm), 15 (.40). **Features:** Accessory rail,

interchangeable grip backstraps, ambidextrous decocker can be converted to manual safety.
Price: **$514.00**

CZ 75 TACTICAL SPORT

Similar to the CZ 75 B except the CZ 75 TS is a competition ready pistol designed for IPSC standard division (USPSA limited division). Fixed target sights, tuned single-action operation, lightweight polymer match trigger with adjustments for take-up and overtravel, competition hammer, extended magazine catch, ambidextrous manual safety, checkered walnut grips, polymer magazine well, two tone finish. Introduced 2005. Imported from the Czech Republic by CZ-USA
Price: 9mm Para., 20-shot mag. **$1,338.00**
Price: 40 S&W, 16-shot mag. **$1,338.00**

CZ 75 SP-01

Similar to NATO-approved CZ 75 Compact P-01 model. Features an integral 1913 accessory rail on the dust cover, rubber grip panels, black polycoat finish, extended beavertail, new grip geometry with checkering on front and back straps, and double or single action operation. Introduced 2005. The Shadow variant designed as an IPSC "production" division competition firearm. Includes competition hammer, competition rear sight and fiber-optic front sight, modified slide release, lighter recoil and main spring for use with "minor power factor" competition ammunition. Includes polycoat finish and slim walnut grips. Finished by CZ Custom Shop. Imported from the Czech Republic by CZ-USA.
Price: SP-01 9mm Para., black polymer, 19+1........**$850.00**

CZ 75 SP-01 PHANTOM

Similar to the CZ 75 B. 9mm Luger, 19-round magazine, weighs 26 oz. and features a polymer frame with accessory rail, and a forged steel slide with a weight-saving scalloped profile. Two interchangeable grip inserts are included to accommodate users with different-sized hands.
Price: **$695.00**

CZ 85 B/85 COMBAT

Same gun as the CZ 75 except has ambidextrous slide release and safety levers; non-glare, ribbed slide top; squared, serrated trigger guard; trigger stop to prevent overtravel. Introduced 1986. The CZ 85 Combat features a fully adjustable rear sight, extended magazine release, ambidextrous slide stop and safety catch, drop free magazine and overtravel adjustment. Imported from the Czech Republic by CZ-USA.
Price: 9mm Para., black polymer **$628.00**
Price: Combat, black polymer **$702.00**
Price: Combat, dual-tone, satin nickel **$732.00**

CZ 75 KADET

Caliber: 22 LR, 10-shot magazine. **Barrel:** 4.88. **Weight:** 36 oz. **Grips:** High impact checkered plastic. **Sights:** Blade front, fully adjustable rear. **Features:** Single action/double action mechanism; all-steel construction. Introduced 1999. Kadet conversion kit consists of barrel, slide, adjustable sights, and magazine to convert the centerfire 75 to rimfire. Imported from the Czech Republic by CZ-USA.
Price: Black polymer **$689.00**
Price: Kadet conversion kit **$412.00**

CZ 75 KADET

CZ 97 B

DAN WESSON DW RZ-10
Caliber: 10mm, 9-shot. **Barrel:** 5.
Grips: Diamond checkered cocobolo. **Sights:** Bo-Mar style adjustable target sight. **Weight:** 38.3 oz. **Length:** 8.8 overall.
Features: Stainless-steel frame and serrated slide. Series 70-style 1911, stainless-steel frame, forged stainless-steel slide. Commander-style match hammer. Reintroduced 2005. Made in U.S.A. by Dan Wesson Firearms, distributed by CZ-USA.
Price: 10mm, 8+1 ....$1,350.00

DAN WESSON DW RZ-45 HERITAGE
Similar to the RZ-10 Auto except in 45 ACP with 7-shot magazine. Weighs 36 oz., length is 8.8" overall.
Price: 10mm, 8+1 ....$1,298.00

CZ 97 B
Caliber: 45 ACP, 10-shot magazine. **Barrel:** 4.85. **Weight:** 40 oz.
Length: 8.34 overall. **Grips:** Checkered walnut. **Sights:** Fixed.
Features: Single action/double action; full-length slide rails; screw-in barrel bushing; linkless barrel; all-steel construction; chamber loaded indicator; dual transfer bars. Introduced 1999. Imported from the Czech Republic by CZ-USA.
Price: Black polymer $779.00
Price: Glossy blue $799.00

CZ 97 BD DECOCKER
Similar to the CZ 97 B except has a decocking lever in place of the safety lever. Tritium night sights. Rubber grips. All other specifications are the same. Introduced 1999. Imported from the Czech Republic by CZ-USA.
Price: 9mm Para., black polymer $874.00

CZ 2075 RAMI/RAMI P
Caliber: 9mm Para., 40 S&W. **Barrel:** 3. **Weight:** 25 oz. **Length:** 6.5 overall. **Grips:** Rubber. **Sights:** Blade front with dot, white outline rear drift adjustable for windage. **Features:** Single-action/double-action; alloy or polymer frame, steel slide; has laser sight mount. Imported from the Czech Republic by CZ-USA.
Price: 9mm Para., alloy frame, 10 and 14-shot magazines $671.00
Price: 40 S&W, alloy frame, 8-shot magazine $671.00
Price: RAMI P, polymer frame, 9mm Para., 40 S&W $612.00

CZ P-01
Caliber: 9mm Para., 14-shot magazine. **Barrel:** 3.85. **Weight:** 27 oz. **Length:** 7.2 overall. **Grips:** Checkered rubber. **Sights:** Blade front with dot, white outline rear drift adjustable for windage.
Features: Based on the CZ 75, except with forged aircraft-grade aluminum alloy frame. Hammer forged barrel, decocker, firing-pin block, M3 rail, dual slide serrations, squared trigger guard, re-contoured trigger, lanyard loop on butt. Serrated front and back strap. Introduced 2006. Imported from the Czech Republic by CZ-USA.
Price: CZ P-01 ....$672.00

DAN WESSON VALOR 1911
Caliber: .45 ACP, 8-shot. **Barrel:** 5. **Grips:** Slim Line G10. **Sights:** Heinie ledge straight eight adjustable night sights. **Weight:** 2.4 lbs. **Length:** 8.8 overall. **Features:** The defensive style Valor, is a base stainless 1911 with our matte black "Duty" finish. This finish is a ceramic base coating that has set the standard for all coating tests. Other features include forged stainless frame and match barrel with 25 LPI checkering and undercut trigger guard, adjustable defensive night sites, and Slim line VZ grips. Made in U.S.A. by Dan Wesson Firearms, distributed by CZ-USA.
Price: $2,012.00

DAN WESSON V-BOB
Caliber: 45 ACP 8-shot magazine. **Barrel:** 4.25". **Weight:** 34 oz.
Length: 8". **Grips:** Slim Line G10. **Sights:** Heinie Ledge Straight-

Prices given are believed to be accurate at time of publication however, many factors affect retail pricing so exact prices are not possible.

Eight Night Sights. **Features:** Black matte or stainless finish. Bobtail forged grip frame with 25 lpi checkering front and rear.
Price: $2077

DESERT EAGLE MARK XIX
Caliber: 357 Mag., 9-shot; 44 Mag., 8-shot; 50 AE, 7-shot. **Barrel:** 6, 10, interchangeable. **Weight:** 357 Mag.-62 oz.; 44 Mag.-69 oz.; 50 AE-72 oz. **Length:** 10.25 overall (6 bbl.). **Grips:** Polymer; rubber available. **Sights:** Blade on ramp front, combat-style rear. Adjustable available. **Features:** Interchangeable barrels; rotating three-lug bolt; ambidextrous safety; adjustable trigger. Military epoxy finish. Satin, bright nickel, chrome, brushed, matte or black-oxide finishes available. 10 barrel extra. Imported from Israel by Magnum Research, Inc.
Price: Black-6, 6 barrel $1,594.00
Price: Black-10, 10 barrel $1,683.00
Price: Component System Package, 3 barrels,
carrying case, from $2,910.00

DESERT BABY MICRO DESERT EAGLE
Caliber: 380 ACP, 6-rounds. **Barrel:** 2.22. **Weight:** 14 oz. **Length:** 4.52 overall. **Grips:** NA. **Sights:** Fixed low-profile. **Features:** Small-frame DAO pocket pistol. Steel slide, aluminum alloy frame, nickel-teflon finish.
Price: $535.00

DESERT BABY EAGLE
Caliber: 9mm Para., 40 S&W, 45 ACP, 10- or 15-round magazines. **Barrel:** 3.64, 3.93, 4.52. **Weight:** 26.8 to 39.8 oz. **Length:** 7.25 to 8.25 overall. **Grips:** Polymer. **Sights:** Drift-adjustable rear, blade front. **Features:** Steel frame and slide; slide safety; decocker. Reintroduced in 1999. Imported from Israel by Magnum Research, Inc.
Price: $619.00

DIAMONDBACK DB380
Caliber: .380, 6+1-shot capacity. **Barrel:** 2.8. **Weight:** 8.8 oz. **Features:** A micro-compact .380 automatic pistol made entirely in the USA. Designed with safety in mind, the DB380 features a "ZERO-Energy" striker firing system (patent pending) with a mechanical firing pin block, a steel magazine catch to secure a sheet metal magaine and real windage-adjustable sights, all in a

lightweight pistol. A steel trigger with dual connecting bars allows for a crisp smooth, five-pound DAO trigger pull. The DB380 features a FEA (Finite Element Analysis) designed slide and barrel that is stronger than any comparable firearm, resulting in durability with less felt recoil, and the absence of removable pins or tools makes field stripping easier than ever. The slide, barrel, and internal parts are coated to resist corrosion.
Price: $340.00

DIAMONDBACK DB9
Caliber: 9mm, 6+1-shot capacity. **Barrel:** 3. **Weight:** 11 oz. **Length:** 5.60. **Features:** A micro-compact 9mm automatic pistol made entirely in the USA. Designed with safety in mind, the DB9 features a "ZERO-Energy" striker firing system (patent pending) with a mechanical firing pin block, a steel magazine catch to secure a sheet metal magazine and real windage-adjustable sights, all in a lightweight pistol. A steel trigger with dual connecting bars allows for a crisp smooth, five-pound DAO trigger pull. The DB9 features a FEA (Finite Element Analysis) designed slide and barrel that is stronger than any comparable firearm, resulting in durability with less felt recoil, and the absence of removable pins or tools makes field stripping easier than over. The slide, barrel, and internal parts are coated to resist corrosion.
Price: $449.00

EAA WITNESS FULL SIZE
Caliber: 9mm Para., 38 Super, 18-shot magazine; 40 S&W, 10mm, 15-shot magazine; 45 ACP, 10-shot magazine. **Barrel:** 4.50. **Weight:** 35.33 oz. **Length:** 8.10 overall. **Grips:** Checkered rubber. **Sights:** Undercut blade front, open rear adjustable for windage. **Features:** Double-action/single-action trigger system; round trigger guard; frame-mounted safety. Introduced 1991. Polymer frame introduced 2005. Imported from Italy by European American Armory.
Price: 9mm Para., 38 Super, 10mm, 40 S&W, 45 ACP, full-size steel frame, Wonder finish $514.00
Price: 45/22 22 LR, full-size steel frame, blued $472.00
Price: 9mm Para., 40 S&W, 45 ACP, full-size polymer frame ..$472.00

EAA WITNESS COMPACT
Caliber: 9mm Para., 40 S&W, 10mm, 12-shot magazine; 45 ACP, 8-shot magazine. **Barrel:** 3.6. **Weight:** 30 oz. **Length:** 7.3 overall.

Otherwise similar to Full Size Witness. Polymer frame introduced 2005. Imported from Italy by European American Armory.
Price: 9mm Para., 10mm, 40 S&W, 45 ACP, steel frame, Wonder finish **$514.00**
Price: 9mm Para., 40 S&W, 45 ACP, polymer frame **$472.00**

EAA WITNESS-P CARRY
Caliber: 10mm, 15-shot magazine; 45 ACP, 10-shot magazine.
Barrel: 3.6. **Weight:** 27 oz. **Length:** 7.5 overall. Otherwise similar to Full Size Witness. Polymer frame introduced 2005. Imported from Italy by European American Armory.
Price: 10mm, 45 ACP, polymer frame, from **$598.00**

EAA ZASTAVA EZ
Caliber: 9mm Para., 15-shot magazine; 40 S&W, 11-shot magazine; 45 ACP, 10-shot magazine. **Barrel:** 3.5 and 4. **Weight:** 30-33 oz.
Length: 7.25 to 7.5 overall. **Features:** Ambidextrous decocker, slide release and magazine release; three dot sight system, aluminum frame, steel slide, accessory rail, full-length claw extractor, loaded chamber indicator. M88 compact has 3.6 barrel, weighs 28 oz. Introduced 2008. Imported by European American Armory.
Price: 9mm Para. or 40 S&W, blued **$547.00**
Price: 9mm Para. or 40 S&W, chromed **$587.00**
Price: 45 ACP, chromed **$587.00**
Price: M88, from **$292.00**

ED BROWN CLASSIC CUSTOM
Caliber: 45 ACP, 7 shot. **Barrel:** 5. **Weight:** 40 oz. **Grips:** Cocobolo wood. **Sights:** Bo-Mar adjustable rear, dovetail front. **Features:** Single-action, M1911 style, custom made to order, stainless frame and slide available. Special mirror-finished slide.
Price: **$3,495.00**

ED BROWN KOBRA AND KOBRA CARRY
Caliber: 45 ACP, 7-shot magazine. **Barrel:** 5 (Kobra); 4.25 (Kobra Carry). **Weight:** 39 oz. (Kobra); 34 oz. (Kobra Carry). **Grips:** Hogue exotic wood. **Sights:** Ramp, front; fixed Novak low-mount night sights, rear. **Features:** Has snakeskin pattern serrations on forestrap and mainspring housing, dehorned edges, beavertail grip safety.
Price: Kobra K-SS **$2,495.00**
Price: Kobra Carry **$2,745.00**

ED BROWN KOBRA CARRY LIGHTWEIGHT
Caliber: 45 ACP, 7-shot magazine. **Barrel:** 4.25 (Commander model slide). **Weight:** 27 oz. **Grips:** Hogue exotic wood. **Sights:** 10-8 Performance U-notch plain black rear sight with .156 notch, for fast aquisition of close targets. Fixed dovetail front night sight with high visibility white outlines. **Features:** Aluminium frame and Bobtail™ housing. Matte finished Gen III coated slide for low glare, with snakeskin on rear of slide only. Snakeskin pattern serrations on forestrap and mainspring housing, dehorned edges, beavertail grip safety. "LW" insignia on slide, which stands for "Lightweight".
Price: Kobra Carry Lightweight **$3,120.00**

ED BROWN EXECUTIVE
Similar to other Ed Brown products, but with 25-lpi checkered frame and mainspring housing.
Price: . . . . **$2,695.00 - $2,945.00**

Prices given are believed to be accurate at time of publication however, many factors affect retail pricing so exact prices are not possible.

ED BROWN SPECIAL FORCES

Similar to other Ed Brown products, but with ChainLink treatment on forestrap and mainspring housing. Entire gun coated with Gen III finish. "Square cut" serrations on rear of slide only. Dehorned. Introduced 2006.

Price: From $2,495.00

ED BROWN SPECIAL FORCES CARRY

Similar to the Special Forces basic models. Features a 4.25" Commander model slide, single stack commander Bobtail frame. Weighs approx. 35 oz. Fixed dovetail 3-dot night sights with high visibility white outlines.

Price: From $2,745.00

EXCEL ARMS ACCELERATOR MP-17/MP-22

Caliber: 17 HMR, 22 WMR, 9-shot magazine. **Barrel:** 8.5 bull barrel. **Weight:** 54 oz. **Length:** 12.875 overall. **Grips:** Textured black composition. **Sights:** Fully adjustable target sights. **Features:** Made from 17-4 stainless steel, comes with aluminum rib, integral Weaver base, internal hammer, firing-pin block. American made, lifetime warranty. Comes with two 9-round stainless steel magazines and a California-approved cable lock. 22 WMR Introduced 2006. Made in U.S.A. by Excel Arms.

Price: $433.00
Price: Camo finishes (2008) $520.00

FN FNS SERIES

Caliber: 9mm, 17-shot magazine, .40 S&W (14-shot magazine). **Barrel:** 4". **Weight:** 25 oz. (9mm), 27.5 oz. (.40). **Length:** 7.25". **Grips:** Integral polymer with two interchangeable backstrap inserts. **Features:** Striker-fired, double action with manual safety, accessory rail, ambidextrous controls, 3-dot Night Sights.

Price: $600

FIRESTORM

Caliber: 22 LR, 32 ACP, 10-shot magazine; 380 ACP, 7-shot magazine; 9mm Para., 40 S&W, 10-shot magazine; 45 ACP, 7-shot magazine. **Barrel:** 3.5. **Weight:** From 23 oz. **Length:** From 6.6 overall. **Grips:** Rubber. **Sights:** 3-dot. **Features:** Double action. Distributed by SGS Importers International.

Price: 22 LR, matte or duotone, from $309.95
Price: 380, matte or duotone, from......................... $311.95
Price: Mini Firestorm 9mm Para., matte, duotone, nickel,
from $395.00
Price: Mini Firestorm 40 S&W, matte, duotone, nickel, from ... $395.00
Price: Mini Firestorm 45 ACP, matte, duotone,
chrome, from $402.00

FN FNX SERIES

Caliber: 9mm, 17-shot magazine, .40 S&W (14-shot), .45 ACP (10 or 14-shot). **Barrel:** 4" (9mm and .40), 4.5" .45. **Weight:** 22 to 32 oz (.45). **Length:** 7.4, 7.9" (.45). **Features:** Double-action/single-action operation with decocking/manual safety lever. Has external extractor with loaded-chamber indicator, front and rear cocking serrations, fixed 3-dot combat sights.

Price: $650

FN FNX .45 TACTICAL

Similar to standard FNX .45 except with 5.3" barrel with threaded muzzle, polished chamber and feed ramp, enhanced high-profile night sights, slide cut and threaded for red-dot sight (not included), MIL-STD 1913 accessory rail, ring-style hammer.

Price: $1100

Prices given are believed to be accurate at time of publication however, many factors affect retail pricing so exact prices are not possible.

68TH EDITION, 2014 395

GIRSAN MC27E
Caliber: 9x19mm Parabellum. 15-shot magazine. **Barrel:** 98.5mm. **Weight:** 650 gr. (without magazine). **Length:** 184.5 mm overall. **Grips:** Black polymer. **Sights:** Fixed. **Features:** Cold forged barrel,polymer frame, short recoil operating system and locked breech. Semi-automatic, double action with a right and left safety sytem latch.
Price: ....**NA**

GLOCK 17/17C
Caliber: 9mm Para., 17/19/33-shot magazines. **Barrel:** 4.49. **Weight:** 22.04 oz. (without magazine). **Length:** 7.32 overall. **Grips:** Black polymer. **Sights:** Dot on front blade, white outline rear adjustable for windage. **Features:** Polymer frame, steel slide; double-action trigger with "Safe Action" system; mechanical firing pin safety, drop safety; simple takedown without tools; locked breech, recoil operated action. ILS designation refers to Internal Locking System. Adopted by Austrian armed forces 1983. NATO approved 1984. Imported from Austria by Glock, Inc.
Price: Fixed sight $690.00

GLOCK GEN4 SERIES
In 2010 a new series of Generation Four pistols was introduced with several improved features. These included a multiple backstrap system offering three different size options, short, medium or large frame; reversible and enlarged magazine release; dual recoil springs; and RTF (Rough Textured Finish) surface. As of 2012, the following models were available in the Gen4 series: Models 17, 19, 21, 22, 23, 26, 27, 31, 32, 34, 35, 37. Price: Same as standard models
Price: .... **N/A**

GLOCK 17 GEN4
25TH ANNIVERSARY LIMITED EDITION
This special gun features an emblem built into the grip signifying the 25 years GLOCK has been in the United States (1986 - 2011). The top of the slide, in front of the rear sight is marked "25 Years of GLOCK Perfection in USA". It comes complete with two magazines, a speed loader, cable lock, cleaning rod and brush, two interchangeable backstraps, a limited edition silver GLOCK case, and a letter of authenticity! Each gun is identified by the

special prefix of 25YUSA. Similar to Model G17 but with multiple backstrap system allowing three options: a short frame version, medium frame or large frame; reversible, enlarged magazine release catch; dual recoil spring assembly; new Rough Textured Frame (RTF) surface designed to enhance grip traction.
Price: $850.00

GLOCK 19/19C
Caliber: 9mm Para., 15/17/19/33-shot magazines. **Barrel:** 4.02. **Weight:** 20.99 oz. (without magazine). **Length:** 6.85 overall. Compact version of Glock 17. Pricing the same as Model 17. Imported from Austria by Glock, Inc.
Price: Fixed sight $699.00
Price: 19C Compensated (fixed sight) $675.00

GLOCK 20/20C 10MM
Caliber: 10mm, 15-shot magazines. **Barrel:** 4.6. **Weight:** 27.68 oz. (without magazine). **Length:** 7.59 overall. **Features:** Otherwise similar to Model 17. Imported from Austria by Glock, Inc. Introduced 1990.
Price: Fixed sight, from $700.00

GLOCK MODEL 20 SF SHORT FRAME
Caliber: 10mm. **Barrel:** 4.61" with hexagonal rifling. **Weight:** 27.51 oz. **Length:** 8.07 overall. **Sights:** Fixed. **Features:** Otherwise similar to Model 20 but with short-frame design, extended sight radius.
Price: $664.00

GLOCK 21/21C
Caliber: 45 ACP, 13-shot magazines. **Barrel:** 4.6. **Weight:** 26.28 oz. (without magazine). **Length:** 7.59 overall. **Features:** Otherwise similar to Model 17. Imported from Austria by Glock, Inc. Introduced 1991. SF version has tactical rail, smaller diameter grip, 10-round magazine capacity. Introduced 2007.
Price: Fixed sight, from $700.00

GLOCK 22/22C
Caliber: 40 S&W, 15/17-shot magazines. **Barrel:** 4.49. **Weight:** 22.92 oz. (without magazine). **Length:** 7.32 overall. **Features:** Otherwise similar to Model 17, including pricing. Imported from Austria by Glock, Inc. Introduced 1990.
Price: Fixed sight, from $641.00

Prices given are believed to be accurate at time of publication however, many factors affect retail pricing so exact prices are not possible.

GLOCK 23/23C
Caliber: 40 S&W, 13/15/17-shot magazines. **Barrel:** 4.02. **Weight:** 21.16 oz. (without magazine). **Length:** 6.85 overall. **Features:** Otherwise similar to Model 22, including pricing. Compact version of Glock 22. Imported from Austria by Glock, Inc. Introduced 1990.
Price: Fixed sight $641.00
Price: 23C Compensated (fixed sight) $694.00

GLOCK 26
Caliber: 9mm Para. 10/12/15/17/19/33-shot magazines. **Barrel:** 3.46. **Weight:** 19.75 oz. **Length:** 6.29 overall. Subcompact version of Glock 17. Pricing the same as Model 17. Imported from Austria by Glock, Inc.
Price: Fixed sight $690.00

GLOCK 27
Caliber: 40 S&W, 9/11/13/15/17-shot magazines. **Barrel:** 3.46. **Weight:** 19.75 oz. (without magazine). **Length:** 6.29 overall. **Features:** Otherwise similar to Model 22, including pricing. Subcompact version of Glock 22. Imported from Austria by Glock, Inc. Introduced 1996.
Price: Fixed sight $750.00

GLOCK 29
Caliber: 10mm, 10/15-shot magazines. **Barrel:** 3.78. **Weight:** 24.69 oz. (without magazine). **Length:** 6.77 overall. **Features:** Otherwise similar to Model 20, including pricing. Subcompact version of Glock 20. Imported from Austria by Glock, Inc. Introduced 1997.
Price: Fixed sight $672.00

GLOCK MODEL 29 SF SHORT FRAME
Caliber: 10mm. **Barrel:** 3.78" with hexagonal rifling. **Weight:** 24.52 oz. **Length:** 6.97 overall. **Sights:** Fixed. **Features:** Otherwise similar to Model 29 but with short-frame design, extended sight radius.
Price: $660.00

GLOCK 30
Caliber: 45 ACP, 9/10/13-shot magazines. **Barrel:** 3.78. **Weight:** 23.99 oz. (without magazine). **Length:** 6.77 overall. **Features:** Otherwise similar to Model 21, including pricing. Subcompact version of Glock 21. Imported from Austria by Glock, Inc. Introduced 1997. SF version has tactical rail, octagonal rifled barrel with a 1:15.75 rate of twist, smaller diameter grip, 10-round magazine capacity. Introduced 2008
Price: Fixed sight $700.00

GLOCK 30S
Variation of Glock 30 with a Model 36 slide on a Model 30SF frame (short frame). **Caliber:** .45 ACP, 10-round magazine. Barrel: 3.78 inches. **Weight:** 20 oz. Length: 7 inches.
Price: $636.00

GLOCK 31/31C
Caliber: 357 Auto, 15/17-shot magazines. **Barrel:** 4.49. **Weight:** 23.28 oz. (without magazine). **Length:** 7.32 overall. **Features:** Otherwise similar to Model 17. Imported from Austria by Glock, Inc.
Price: Fixed sight, from $641.00

GLOCK 32/32C
Caliber: 357 Auto, 13/15/17-shot magazines. **Barrel:** 4.02. **Weight:** 21.52 oz. (without magazine). **Length:** 6.85 overall. **Features:** Otherwise similar to Model 31. Compact. Imported from Austria by Glock, Inc.
Price: Fixed sight $669.00

GLOCK 33
Caliber: 357 Auto, 9/11/13/15/17-shot magazines. **Barrel:** 3.46. **Weight:** 19.75 oz. (without magazine). **Length:** 6.29 overall. **Features:** Otherwise similar to Model 31. Subcompact. Imported from Austria by Glock, Inc.
Price: Fixed sight, from $641.00

GLOCK 34
Caliber: 9mm Para. 17/19/33-shot magazines. **Barrel:** 5.32. **Weight:** 22.9 oz. **Length:** 8.15 overall. Competition version of Glock 17 with extended barrel, slide, and sight radius dimensions. Imported from Austria by Glock, Inc.
Price: Adjustable sight, from $648.00

GLOCK 35
Caliber: 40 S&W, 15/17-shot magazines. **Barrel:** 5.32. **Weight:** 24.52 oz. (without magazine). **Length:** 8.15 overall. **Features:** Otherwise similar to Model 22. Competition version of Glock 22 with extended barrel, slide, and sight radius dimensions. Imported from Austria by Glock, Inc. Introduced 1996.
Price: Adjustable sight...$648.00

GLOCK 36
Caliber: 45 ACP, 6-shot magazines. **Barrel:** 3.78. **Weight:** 20.11 oz. (without magazine). **Length:** 6.77 overall. **Features:** Single-stack magazine, slimmer grip than Glock 21/30. Subcompact. Imported from Austria by Glock, Inc. Introduced 1997.
Price: Adjustable sight $616.00

GLOCK 37
Caliber: 45 GAP, 10-shot magazines. **Barrel:** 4.49. **Weight:** 25.95 oz. (without magazine). **Length:** 7.32 overall. **Features:** Otherwise similar to Model 17. Imported from Austria by Glock, Inc. Introduced 2005.
Price: Fixed sight, from $562.00

GLOCK 38
Caliber: 45 GAP, 8/10-shot magazines. **Barrel:** 4.02. **Weight:** 24.16 oz. (without magazine). **Length:** 6.85 overall. **Features:** Otherwise similar to Model 37. Compact. Imported from Austria by Glock, Inc.
Price: Fixed sight $614.00

GLOCK 39

Caliber: 45 GAP, 6/8/10-shot magazines. **Barrel:** 3.46.
Weight: 19.33 oz. (without magazine). **Length:** 6.3 overall.
Features: Otherwise similar to Model 37. Subcompact. Imported
from Austria by Glock, Inc.
Price: Fixed sight $614.00

GLOCK MODEL G17/G22/G19/G23 RTF

Similar to Models G17, G22, G19 and G23 but with rough textured
frame.
Price: .... **N/A**

HECKLER & KOCH USP

Caliber: 9mm Para., 15-shot magazine; 40 S&W, 13-shot magazine;
45 ACP, 12-shot magazine. **Barrel:** 4.25-4.41. **Weight:** 1.65 lbs.
Length: 7.64-7.87 overall. **Grips:** Non-slip stippled black polymer.
Sights: Blade front, rear adjustable for windage. **Features:** New HK
design with polymer frame, modified Browning action with recoil
reduction system, single control lever. Special "hostile environment"
finish on all metal parts. Available in SA/DA, DAO, left- and right-
hand versions. Introduced 1993. 45 ACP Introduced 1995. Imported
from Germany by Heckler & Koch, Inc.
Price: USP 45 ....$1,033.00
Price: USP 40 and USP 9mm 902.00

HECKLER & KOCH USP COMPACT

Caliber: 9mm Para., 13-shot magazine; 40 S&W and .357 SIG, 12-
shot magazine; 45 ACP, 8-shot magazine. Similar to the USP except
the 9mm Para., 357 SIG, and 40 S&W have 3.58 barrels, measure
6.81 overall, and weigh 1.47 lbs. (9mm Para.). Introduced 1996.
45 ACP measures 7.09 overall. Introduced 1998. Imported from
Germany by Heckler & Koch, Inc.
Price: USP Compact 45 ....$1,086.00
Price: USP Compact 9mm
 Para., 40 S&W $941.00

HECKLER & KOCH USP45 TACTICAL

Caliber: 40 S&W, 13-shot magazine; 45 ACP, 12-shot magazine.
Barrel: 4.90-5.09. **Weight:** 1.9 lbs. **Length:** 8.64 overall. **Grips:**
Non-slip stippled polymer. **Sights:** Blade front, fully adjustable target
rear. **Features:** Has extended threaded barrel with rubber O-ring;
adjustable trigger; extended magazine floorplate; adjustable trigger
stop; polymer frame. Introduced 1998. Imported from Germany by
Heckler & Koch, Inc.
Price: USP Tactical 45 ....$1,325.00
Price: USP Tactical 40 ....$1,168.00

HECKLER & KOCH USP COMPACT TACTICAL

Caliber: 45 ACP, 8-shot magazine. Similar to the USP Tactical except
measures 7.72 overall, weighs 1.72 lbs. Introduced 2006. Imported
from Germany by Heckler & Koch, Inc.
Price: USP Compact Tactical $1,288.00

HECKLER & KOCH MARK 23 SPECIAL OPERATIONS

Caliber: 45 ACP, 12-shot magazine. **Barrel:** 5.87. **Weight:** 2.42 lbs.
Length: 9.65 overall. **Grips:** Integral with frame; black polymer.
Sights: Blade front, rear drift adjustable for windage; 3-dot.
Features: Civilian version of the SOCOM pistol. Polymer frame;
double action; exposed hammer; short recoil, modified Browning
action. Introduced 1996. Imported from Germany by Heckler &
Koch, Inc.
Price: $2,139.00

Prices given are believed to be accurate at time of publication however, many factors affect retail pricing so exact prices are not possible.

HECKLER & KOCH P30L AND P30LS

Caliber: 9mm x 19 and .40 S&W with 15-shot magazines.
Barrel: 4.45. **Weight:** 27.52 oz. **Length:** 7.56 overall. **Grips:** Interchangeable panels. **Sights:** Open rectangular notch rear sight with contrast points (no radioactive). **Features:** Like the P30, the P30L was designed as a modern police and security pistol and combines optimal function and safety. Ergonomic features include a special grip frame with interchangeable backstraps inserts and lateral plates, allowing the pistol to be Individually adapted to any user. Imported from Germany by Heckler & Koch, Inc. Browning type action with modified short recoil operation. Ambidextrous controls include dual slide releases, magazine release levers, and a serrated decocking button located on the rear of the frame (for applicable variants). A Picatinny rail molded into the front of the frame makes mounting lights, laser aimers, or other accessories easy and convenient. The extractor serves as a loaded chamber indicator providing a reminder of a loaded chamber that can be subtly seen and felt. The standard P30L is a 9 mm "Variant 3 (V3)" with a conventional double-action/single action trigger mode with a serrated decocking button on the rear of the slide.

Price: P30L **$1,054.00**
Price: P30L Variant 2 Law Enforcement Modification
(LEM) enhanced DAO **$1,108.00**
Price: P30L Variant 3 Double Action/Single Action
(DA/SA) with Decocker **$1,108.00**
Price: P30LS **$1,054.00**

HECKLER & KOCH P2000

Caliber: 9mm Para., 13-shot magazine; 40 S&W and .357 SIG, 12-shot magazine. **Barrel:** 3.62. **Weight:** 1.5 lbs. **Length:** 7 overall. **Grips:** Interchangeable panels. **Sights:** Fixed Patridge style, drift adjustable for windage, standard 3-dot. **Features:** Incorporates features of HK USP Compact pistol, including Law Enforcement Modification (LEM) trigger, double-action hammer system, ambidextrous magazine release, dual slide-release levers, accessory mounting rails, recurved, hook trigger guard, fiber-reinforced polymer frame, modular grip with exchangeable back straps, nitro-carburized finish, lock-out safety device. Introduced 2003. Imported from Germany by Heckler & Koch, Inc.
Price: **$941.00**
Price: P2000 LEM DAO, 357 SIG, intr. 2006 .... **$941.00**
Price: P2000 SA/DA, 357 SIG, intr. 2006 .... **$941.00**

HECKLER & KOCH P2000 SK

Caliber: 9mm Para., 10-shot magazine; 40 S&W and .357 SIG, 9-shot magazine. **Barrel:** 3.27. **Weight:** 1.3 lbs. **Length:** 6.42 overall. **Sights:** Fixed Patridge style, drift adjustable. **Features:** Standard accessory rails, ambidextrous slide release, polymer frame, polygonal bore profile. Smaller version of P2000. Introduced 2005. Imported from Germany by Heckler & Koch, Inc.
Price: **$983.00**

HELLCAT II

Caliber: .380 ACP, magazine capacity 6 rounds. **Barrel:** 2.75 inches. **Weight:** 9.4 oz. **Length:** 5.16 inches. **Grips:** Integral polymer. **Sights:** Fixed. **Features:** Polymer frame, double-action only. Several

finishes available including black, desert tan, pink, blaze orange. Made in U.S.A. by I.O., Inc.
Price: **$250.00**

HI-POINT FIREARMS MODEL 9MM COMPACT

Caliber: 9mm Para., 8-shot magazine. **Barrel:** 3.5. **Weight:** 25 oz. **Length:** 6.75 overall. **Grips:** Textured plastic. **Sights:** Combat-style adjustable 3-dot system; low profile. **Features:** Single-action design; frame-mounted magazine release; polymer frame. Scratch-resistant matte finish. Introduced 1993. Comps are similar except they have a 4 barrel with muzzle brake/compensator. Compensator is slotted for laser or flashlight mounting. Introduced 1998. Made in U.S.A. by MKS Supply, Inc.
Price: C-9 9mm **$155.00**

HI-POINT FIREARMS MODEL 380 POLYMER

Similar to the 9mm Compact model except chambered for 380 ACP, 8-shot magazine, adjustable 3-dot sights. Weighs 25 oz. Polymer frame. Action locks open after last shot. Includes 10-shot and 8-shot magazine; trigger lock. Introduced 1998. Comps are similar except they have a 4 barrel with muzzle compensator. Introduced 2001. Made in U.S.A. by MKS Supply, Inc.
Price: CF-380 .... **$135.00**

HI-POINT FIREARMS 40 AND 45 SW/POLY

Caliber: 40 S&W, 8-shot magazine; 45 ACP (9-shot). **Barrel:** 4.5. **Weight:** 32 oz. **Length:** 7.72 overall. **Sights:** Adjustable 3-dot. **Features:** Polymer frames, last round lock-open, grip mounted magazine release, magazine disconnect safety, integrated accessory rail, trigger lock. Introduced 2002. Made in U.S.A. by MKS Supply, Inc.
Price: 40SW-B **$186.00**
Price: 45 ACP **$186.00**

HI-POINT 40-45

HIGH STANDARD SPORT KING 22
Caliber: 22 LR. **Barrel:** 4.5" or 6.75" tapered barrel. **Weight:** 40 oz. to 42 oz. **Length:** 8.5" to 10.75". **Features:** Sport version of High Standard Supermatic. Two-tone finish, fixed sights.
Price: **$725.00**

HIGH STANDARD VICTOR 22
Caliber: 22 Long Rifle (10 rounds) or .22 Short (5 rounds). **Barrel:** 4.5"-5.5". **Weight:** 45 oz.-46 oz. **Length:** 8.5"-9.5" overall. **Grips:** Freestyle wood. **Sights:** Frame mounted, adjustable. **Features:** Semi-auto with drilled and tapped barrel, tu-tone or blued finish.
Price: **$845.00**

HIGH STANDARD 10X CUSTOM 22
Similar to the Victor model but with precision fitting, black wood grips, 5.5 barrel only. High Standard Universal Mount, 10-shot magazine, barrel drilled and tapped, certificate of authenticity. Overall length is 9.5. Weighs 44 oz. to 46 oz. From High Standard Custom Shop.
Price: **$1,095.00**

HIGH STANDARD SUPERMATIC TROPHY 22
Caliber: 22 Long Rifle (10 rounds) or .22 Short (5 rounds/Citation version), not interchangable. **Barrel:** 5.5", 7.25". **Weight:** 44 oz., 46 oz. **Length:** 9.5", 11.25" overall. **Grips:** Wood. **Sights:** Adjustable. **Features:** Semi-auto with drilled and tapped barrel, tu-tone or blued finish with gold accents.
Price: 5.5 .... **$845.00**

HIGH STANDARD OLYMPIC MILITARY 22
Similar to the Supermatic Trophy model but in 22 Short only with 5.5 bull barrel, five-round magazine, aluminum alloy frame, adjustable sights. Overall length is 9.5, weighs 42 oz.
Price: **$875.00**

HI-STANDARD SPACE GUN
Semiauto pistol chambered in .22 LR. Recreation of famed competition "Space Gun" from 1960s. Features include 6.75- 8- or 10-inch barrel; 10-round magazine; adjustable sights; barrel weight; adjustable muzzle brake; blue-black finish with gold highlights.
Price: **$1095.00**

HIGH STANDARD SUPERMATIC CITATION SERIES 22
Similar to the Supermatic Trophy model but with heavier trigger pull, 10 barrel, and nickel accents. 22 Short conversion unit available. Overall length 14.5, weighs 52 oz.
Price: **$895.00**

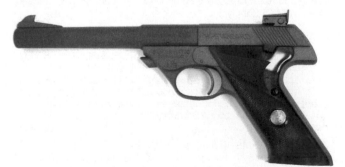

HIGH STANDARD SUPERMATIC TOURNAMENT 22
Caliber: 22 LR. **Barrel:** 5.5" bull barrel. **Weight:** 44 oz. **Length:** 9.5" overall. **Features:** Limited edition; similar to High Standard Victor model but with rear sight mounted directly to slide.
Price: **$835.00**

IVER JOHNSON EAGLE
Series of 1911-style pistols made in typical variations including full-size (Eagle), Commander (Hawk), Officer's (Thrasher) sizes in .45 ACP and 9mm. Many finishes available including Cerakote, polished stainless, pink and several "snakeskin" variations.
Price: .... **$600.00 & UP**

KAHR CM SERIES
Caliber: 9mm (6+1), .40 S&W (6+1).
Barrel: 3. **Weight:** 15.9 oz. **Length:** 5.42 overall. **Grips:** Textured polymer with integral steel rails molded into frame. **Sights:** CM9093 - Pinned in polymer sight; PM9093 - Drift adjustable, white bar-dot combat. **Features:** A conventional rifled barrel instead of the match grade polygonal barrel on Kahr's PM series; the CM slide stop lever is MIM (metal-injection-molded) instead of machined; the CM series slide has fewer machining operations and uses simple engraved markings instead of roll marking and finally the CM series are shipped with one magazine instead of two magazines. The CM9 slide is only .90 inch wide and machined from solid 416

Prices given are believed to be accurate at time of publication however, many factors affect retail pricing so exact prices are not possible.

stainless slide with a matte finish, each gun is shipped with one 6 rd stainless steel magazine with a flush baseplate. Magazines are USA made, plasma welded, tumbled to remove burrs and feature Wolff Gunsprings. The magazine catch in the polymer frame is all metal and will not wear out on the stainless steel magazine after extended use.

Price: CM9093 ....$565.00
Price: PM9093 Match Grade $786.00

KAHR K SERIES

Caliber: K9: 9mm Para., 7-shot; K40: 40 S&W, 6-shot magazine. **Barrel:** 3.5. **Weight:** 25 oz. **Length:** 6 overall. **Grips:** Wraparound textured soft polymer. **Sights:** Blade front, rear drift adjustable for windage; bar-dot combat style. **Features:** Trigger-cocking double-action mechanism with passive firing pin block. Made of 4140 ordnance steel with matte black finish. Contact maker for complete price list. Introduced 1994. Made in U.S.A. by Kahr Arms.

Price: K9093C K9, matte stainless steel $855.00
Price: K9093NC K9, matte stainless steel w/tritium
night sights $985.00
Price: K9094C K9 matte blackened stainless steel $891.00
Price: K9098 K9 Elite 2003, stainless steel $932.00
Price: K4043 K40, matte stainless steel $855.00
Price: K4043N K40, matte stainless steel w/tritium
night sights $985.00
Price: K4044 K40, matte blackened stainless steel $891.00
Price: K4048 K40 Elite 2003, stainless steel $932.00

KAHR MK SERIES MICRO

Similar to the K9/K40 except is 5.35 overall, 4 high, with a 3.08 barrel. Weighs 23.1 oz. Has snag-free bar-dot sights, polished feed ramp, dual recoil spring system, DA-only trigger. Comes with 5-round flush baseplate and 6-shot grip extension magazine. Introduced 1998. Made in U.S.A. by Kahr Arms.

Price: M9093 MK9, matte stainless steel $855.00
Price: M9093N MK9, matte stainless steel, tritium
night sights $958.00
Price: M9098 MK9 Elite 2003, stainless steel $932.00
Price: M4043 MK40, matte stainless steel $855.00
Price: M4043N MK40, matte stainless steel, tritium
night sights $958.00
Price: M4048 MK40 Elite 2003, stainless steel $932.00

KAHR P SERIES

Caliber: 380 ACP, 9x19, 40 S&W, 45 ACP. Similar to K9/K40 steel frame pistol except has polymer frame, matte stainless steel slide. Barrel length 3.5; overall length 5.8; weighs 17 oz. Includes two 7-shot magazines, hard polymer case, trigger lock. Introduced 2000. Made in U.S.A. by Kahr Arms.

Price: KP9093 9mm Para. $739.00
Price: KP4043 40 S&W $739.00
Price: KP4543 45 ACP..$805.00
Price: KP3833 380 ACP (2008)............................$649.00

KAHR PM SERIES

Caliber: 9x19, 40 S&W, 45 ACP. Similar to P-Series pistols except has smaller polymer frame (Polymer Micro). Barrel length 3.08; overall length 5.35; weighs 17 oz. Includes two 7-shot magazines, hard polymer case, trigger lock. Introduced 2000. Made in U.S.A. by Kahr Arms.

Price: PM9093 PM9 ....$786.00
Price: PM4043 PM40 ....$786.00
Price: PM4543 (2007) $855.00

KAHR T SERIES

Caliber: T9: 9mm Para., 8-shot magazine; T40: 40 S&W, 7-shot magazine. **Barrel:** 4. **Weight:** 28.1-29.1 oz. **Length:** 6.5 overall. **Grips:** Checkered Hogue Pau Ferro wood grips. **Sights:** Rear: Novak low profile 2-dot tritium night sight, front tritium night sight. **Features:**

Prices given are believed to be accurate at time of publication however, many factors affect retail pricing so exact prices are not possible.

68TH EDITION, 2014 ✛ **401**

Similar to other Kahr makes, but with longer slide and barrel upper, longer butt. Trigger cocking DAO; lock breech; "Browning-type" recoil lug; passive striker block; no magazine disconnect. Comes with two magazines. Introduced 2004. Made in U.S.A. by Kahr Arms.
Price: KT9093 T9 matte stainless steel **$831.00**
Price: KT9093-NOVAK T9, "Tactical 9," Novak night sight **$968.00**
Price: KT4043 40 S&W **$831.00**

KAHR P380
Very small double action only semiauto pistol chambered in .380 ACP. Features include 2.5-inch Lothar Walther barrel; black polymer frame with stainless steel slide; drift adjustable white bar/dot combat/sights; optional tritium sights; two 6+1 magazines. Overall length 4.9 inches, weight 10 oz. without magazine.
Price: Standard sights **$649.00**

KAHR CW380
Caliber: .380 ACP, six round magazine. **Barrel:** 2.58 inches. **Weight:** 11.5 oz. **Length:** 4.96 inches. **Grips:** Textured integral polymer. **Sights:** Fixed white-bar combat style. **Features:** Double-action only.
Price: **$419.00**

KAHR TP SERIES
Caliber: TP9: 9mm Para., 7-shot magazine; TP40: 40 S&W, 6-shot magazine. **Barrel:** 4. **Weight:** 19.1-20.1 oz. **Length:** 6.5-6.7 overall. **Grips:** Textured polymer. Similar to T-series guns, but with polymer frame, matte stainless slide. Comes with two magazines. TP40s introduced 2006. Made in U.S.A. by Kahr Arms.
Price: TP9093 TP9 .... **$697.00**
Price: TP9093-Novak TP9
  (Novak night sights) **$838.00**
Price: TP4043 TP40 .... **$697.00**
Price: TP4043-Novak (Novak night sights) **$838.00**
Price: TP4543 (2007) **$697.00**
Price: TP4543-Novak (4.04 barrel, Novak night sights) **$838.00**

KEL-TEC P-11
Caliber: 9mm Para., 10-shot magazine. **Barrel:** 3.1. **Weight:** 14 oz. **Length:** 5.6 overall. **Grips:** Checkered black polymer. **Sights:** Blade front, rear adjustable for windage. **Features:** Ordnance steel slide, aluminum frame. Double-action-only trigger mechanism. Introduced 1995. Made in U.S.A. by Kel-Tec CNC Industries, Inc.
Price: From **$333.00**

KEL-TEC PF-9
Caliber: 9mm Para.; 7 rounds. **Weight:** 12.7 oz. **Sights:** Rear sight adjustable for windage and elevation. **Barrel Length:** 3.1. **Length:** 5.85. **Features:** Barrel, locking system, slide stop, assembly pin, front sight, recoil springs and guide rod adapted from P-11. Trigger system with integral hammer block and the extraction system adapted from P-3AT. MIL-STD-1913 Picatinny rail. Made in U.S.A. by Kel-Tec CNC Industries, Inc.
Price: From **$333.00**

KAHR CW SERIES
Caliber: 9mm Para., 7-shot magazine; 40 S&W and 45 ACP, 6-shot magazine. **Barrel:** 3.5-3.64. **Weight:** 17.7-18.7 oz. **Length:** 5.9-6.36 overall. **Grips:** Textured polymer. Similar to P-Series, but CW Series have conventional rifling, metal-injection-molded slide stop lever, no front dovetail cut, one magazine. CW40 introduced 2006. Made in U.S.A. by Kahr Arms.
Price: CW9093 CW9 .... **$549.00**
Price: CW4043 CW40 .... **$549.00**
Price: CW4543 45 ACP (2008) **$606.00**

Prices given are believed to be accurate at time of publication however, many factors affect retail pricing so exact prices are not possible.

KEL-TEC P-32
Caliber: 32 ACP, 7-shot magazine. **Barrel:** 2.68. **Weight:** 6.6 oz. **Length:** 5.07 overall. **Grips:** Checkered composite. **Sights:** Fixed. **Features:** Double-action-only mechanism with 6-lb. pull; internal slide stop. Textured composite grip/frame. Now available in 380 ACP. Made in U.S.A. by Kel-Tec CNC Industries, Inc.
Price: From $318.00

KEL-TEC P-3AT
Caliber: 380 ACP; 7 rounds. **Weight:** 7.2 oz. **Length:** 5.2. **Features:** Lightest 380 ACP made; aluminum frame, steel barrel.
Price: From $324.00

KEL-TEC PLR-16
Caliber: 5.56mm NATO; 10-round magazine. **Weight:** 51 oz. **Sights:** Rear sight adjustable for windage, front sight is M-16 blade. **Barrel Length:** 9.2. **Length:** 18.5. **Features:** Muzzle is threaded 1/2-28 to accept standard attachments such as a muzzle brake. Except for the barrel, bolt, sights, and mechanism, the PLR-16 pistol is made of high-impact glass fiber reinforced polymer. Gas-operated semi-auto. Conventional gas-piston operation with M-16 breech locking system. MIL-STD-1913 Picatinny rail. Made in U.S.A. by Kel-Tec CNC Industries, Inc.
Price: Blued $665.00

KEL-TEC PLR-22
Semi-auto pistol chambered in 22 LR; based on centerfire PLR-16 by same maker. Blowback action, 26-round magazine. Open sights and picatinny rail for mounting accessories; threaded muzzle. Overall length is 18.5", weighs 40 oz.
Price: $390.00

KEL-TEC PMR-30
Caliber: .22 Magnum (.22WMR) 30-rounds. **Barrel:** 4.3. **Weight:** 13.6 oz. **Length:** 7.9 overall. **Grips:** Glass reinforced Nylon (Zytel). **Sights:** Dovetailed aluminum with front & rear fiber optics. **Features:** Operates on a unique hybrid blowback/locked-breech system. It uses a double stack magazine of a new design that holds 30 rounds and fits completely in the grip of the pistol. Dual opposing extractors for reliability, heel magazine release to aid in magazine retention, Picatinny accessory rail under the barrel, Urethane recoil buffer, captive coaxial recoil springs. The barrel is fluted for light weight

and effective heat dissipation. PMR30 disassembles for cleaning by removal of a single pin.
Price: $415.00

KIMBER MICRO CDP
Caliber: .380 ACP (6-shot magazine). **Barrel:** 2.75". **Weight:** 17 oz. **Grips:** Double diamond rosewood. Mini 1911-style single action with no grip safety.
Price: $1,100.00

MICRO CARRY
Caliber: .380 ACP, 6-round magazine. **Barrel:** 2.75 inches. **Weight:** 13.4 oz. **Length:** 5.6 inches **Grips:** Black synthetic, double diamond. **Sights:** Fixed low profile. **Finish:** Blue or stainless. **Features:** Aluminum frame, steel slide, carry-melt treatment, full-length guide rod.
Price: $679.00

KIMBER AEGIS II
Caliber: 9mm (9-shot magazine, 8-shot (Ultra model). **Barrel:** 3", 4" or 5". **Weight:** 25 to 38 oz. **Grips:** Scale-textured zebra wood. **Sights:** Tactical wedge 3-dot green night sights. **Features:** Made in the Kimber Custom Shop. Two-tone satin silver/matte black finish. Service Melt treatment that rounds and blends edges. **Available in three frame sizes:** Custom (shown), Pro and Ultra.
Price: $1299

KIMBER COVERT II

Caliber: .45 ACP (7-shot magazine). **Barrel:** 3", 4" or 5". **Weight:** 25 to 31 oz. **Grips:** Crimson Trace laser with camo finish. **Sights:** Tactical wedge 3-dot night sights. **Features:** Made in the Kimber Custom Shop. Desert tan frame and matte black slide finishes. Available in three frame sizes: Custom, Pro (shown) and Ultra.
Price: $1617

KIMBER CUSTOM II

Caliber: 45 ACP. **Barrel:** 5. **Weight:** 38 oz. **Length:** 8.7 overall. **Grips:** Checkered black rubber, walnut, rosewood. **Sights:** Dovetailed front and rear, Kimber low profile adj. or fixed sights. **Features:** Slide, frame and barrel machined from steel or stainless steel. Match grade barrel, chamber and trigger group. Extended thumb safety, beveled magazine well, beveled front and rear slide serrations, high ride beavertail grip safety, checkered flat mainspring housing, kidney cut under trigger guard, high cut grip, match grade stainless steel barrel bushing, polished breech face, Commander-style hammer, lowered and flared ejection port, Wolff springs, bead blasted black oxide or matte stainless finish. Introduced in 1996. Made in U.S.A. by Kimber Mfg., Inc.
Price: Custom II **$828.00**
Price: Custom II Walnut (double-diamond walnut grips) **$872.00**

KIMBER STAINLESS II

Similar to Custom II except has stainless steel frame. 9mm Para. chambering and 45 ACP with night sights introduced 2008. Also chambered in 38 Super. Target version also chambered in 10mm.
Price: Stainless II 45 ACP **$964.00**
Price: Stainless II 9mm Para. (2008) **$983.00**
Price: Stainless II 45 ACP w/night sights (2008) **$1,092.00**
Price: Stainless II Target 45 ACP (stainless, adj. sight) **$942.00**

KIMBER PRO CARRY II

Similar to Custom II, has aluminum frame, 4 bull barrel fitted directly to the slide without bushing. Introduced 1998. Made in U.S.A. by Kimber Mfg., Inc.
Price: Pro Carry II, 45 ACP **$888.00**
Price: Pro Carry II, 9mm **$929.00**
Price: Pro Carry II
w/night sights **$997.00**

KIMBER RAPTOR II

Caliber: .45 ACP (8-shot magazine, 7-shot (Ultra and Pro models). **Barrel:** 3", 4" or 5". **Weight:** 25 to 31 oz. **Grips:** Thin milled rosewood. **Sights:** Tactical wedge 3-dot night sights. **Features:** Made in the Kimber Custom Shop. Matte black or satin silver finish. Available in three frame sizes: Custom (shown), Pro and Ultra.
Price: .... **$1263 to $1530**

KIMBER SOLO CARRY

Caliber: 9mm, 6-shot magazine. **Barrel:** 2.7. **Weight:** 17 oz. **Length:** 5.5 overall. **Grips:** Black synthetic, Checkered/smooth. **Sights:** Fixed low-profile dovetail-mounted 3-dot system. **Features:** Single action striker-fired trigger that sets a new standard for small pistols. A premium finish that is self-lubricating and resistant to salt and moisture. Ergonomics that ensure comfortable shooting.

Prices given are believed to be accurate at time of publication however, many factors affect retail pricing so exact prices are not possible.

Ambidextrous thumb safety, slide release lever and magazine release button are pure 1911 – positive, intuitive and fast. The thumb safety provides additional security not found on most small pistols. Also available in stainless.

Price: $747.00

KIMBER COMPACT STAINLESS II

Similar to Pro Carry II except has stainless steel frame, 4-inch bbl., grip is .400 shorter than standard, no front serrations. Weighs 34 oz. 45 ACP only. Introduced in 1998. Made in U.S.A. by Kimber Mfg., Inc.

Price: $1,009.00

KIMBER ULTRA CARRY II

Lightweight aluminum frame, 3 match grade bull barrel fitted to slide without bushing. Grips .4 shorter. Low effort recoil. Weighs 25 oz. Introduced in 1999. Made in U.S.A. by Kimber Mfg., Inc.

Price: Stainless Ultra Carry II 45 ACP.....................................**$980.00**
Price: Stainless Ultra Carry II 9mm Para.
(2008) **$1,021.00**
Price: Stainless Ultra Carry II 45 ACP
with night sights (2008) **$1,089.00**

KIMBER GOLD MATCH II

Similar to Custom II models. Includes stainless steel barrel with match grade chamber and barrel bushing, ambidextrous thumb safety, adjustable sight, premium aluminum trigger, hand-checkered double diamond rosewood grips. Barrel hand-fitted for target accuracy. Made in U.S.A. by Kimber Mfg., Inc.

Price: Gold Match II **$1,345.00**
Price: Gold Match Stainless II 45 ACP **$1,519.00**
Price: Gold Match Stainless II
9mm Para. (2008) **$1,563.00**

KIMBER TEAM MATCH II

Similar to Gold Match II. Identical to pistol used by U.S.A. Shooting Rapid Fire Pistol Team, available in 45 ACP and 38 Super. Standard features include 30 lines-per-inch front strap extended and beveled magazine well, red, white and blue Team logo grips. Introduced 2008.

Price: 45 ACP **$1,539.00**
Price: 9mm **$1,546.00**

KIMBER CDP II SERIES

Similar to Custom II, but designed for concealed carry. Aluminum frame. Standard features include stainless steel slide, fixed Meprolight tritium 3-dot (green) dovetail-mounted night sights, match grade barrel and chamber, 30 LPI front strap checkering, two-tone finish, ambidextrous thumb safety, hand-checkered double diamond rosewood grips. Introduced in 2000. Made in U.S.A. by Kimber Mfg., Inc.

Price: Ultra CDP II 9mm Para. (2008) $1,359.00
Price: Ultra CDP II 45 ACP $1,318.00
Price: Compact CDP II 45 ACP $1,318.00
Price: Pro CDP II 45 ACP...$1,318.00
Price: Custom CDP II
(5 barrel, full length grip) $1,318.00

KIMBER ECLIPSE II SERIES

Similar to Custom II and other stainless Kimber pistols. Stainless slide and frame, black oxide, two-tone finish. Gray/black laminated grips. 30 lpi front strap checkering. All models have night sights; Target versions have Meprolight adjustable Bar/Dot version. Made in U.S.A. by Kimber Mfg., Inc.

Price: Eclipse Ultra II (3 barrel, short grip) $1,236.00
Price: Eclipse Pro II (4 barrel, full length grip) $1,236.00
Price: Eclipse Pro Target II (4 barrel, full length grip,
adjustable sight) $1,236.00
Price: Eclipse Custom II 10mm $1,291.00
Price: Eclipse Target II (5 barrel, full length grip,
adjustable sight) $1,345.00

KIMBER TACTICAL ENTRY II

Caliber: 45 ACP, 7-round magazine. **Barrel:** 5". **Weight:** 40 oz.
Length: 8.7" overall. **Features:** 1911-style semi auto with checkered frontstrap, extended magazine well, night sights, heavy

steel frame, tactical rail.
Price: $1,428.00

KIMBER TACTICAL CUSTOM HD II
Caliber: 45 ACP, 7-round magazine. **Barrel:** 5" match-grade. **Weight:** 39 oz. **Length:** 8.7" overall. **Features:** 1911-style semi auto with night sights, heavy steel frame.
Price: $1,333.00

KIMBER SUPER CARRY PRO
1911-syle semiauto pistol chambered in .45 ACP. Features include 8-round magazine; ambidextrous thumb safety; carry melt profiling; full length guide rod; aluminum frame with stainless slide; satin silver finish; super carry serrations; 4-inch barrel; micarta laminated grips; tritium night sights.
Price: $1,530.00

KIMBER SUPER CARRY HD SERIES
Designated as HD (Heavy Duty), each is chambered in .45 ACP and features a stainless steel slide and frame, premium KimPro II™ finish and night sights with cocking shoulder for one-hand operation. Like the original Super Carry pistols, HD models have directional serrations on slide, front strap and mainspring housing for unequaled control under recoil. A round heel frame and Carry Melt treatment make them comfortable to carry and easy to conceal.

SUPER CARRY ULTRA HD™
Caliber: .45 ACP, 7-shot magazine. **Barrel:** 3. **Weight:** 32 oz. **Length:** 6.8 overall. **Grips:** G-10, Checkered with border. **Sights:** Night sights with cocking shoulder radius (inches): 4.8. **Features:** Rugged stainless steel slide and frame with KimPro II finish. Aluminum match grade trigger with a factory setting of approximately 4-5 pounds.
Price: $1,625.00

SUPER CARRY PRO HD™
Caliber: .45 ACP, 8-shot magazine. **Barrel:** 4. **Weight:** 35 oz. **Length:** 7.7 overall. **Grips:** G-10, Checkered with border. **Sights:** Night sights with cocking shoulder radius (inches): 5.7. **Features:** Rugged stainless steel slide and frame with KimPro II finish. Aluminum match grade trigger with a factory setting of approximately 4-5 pounds.
Price: $1,625.00

SUPER CARRY CUSTOM HD™
Caliber: .45 ACP, 8-shot magazine. **Barrel:** 5. **Weight:** 38 oz. **Length:** 8.7 overall. **Grips:** G-10, Checkered with border. **Sights:** Night sights with cocking shoulder radius (inches): 4.8. **Features:** Rugged stainless steel slide and frame with KimPro II finish. Aluminum match grade trigger with a factory setting of approximately 4-5 pounds.
Price: $1,625.00

KIMBER ULTRA CDP II

Compact 1911-syle semiauto pistol chambered in .45 ACP. Features include 7-round magazine; ambidextrous thumb safety; carry melt profiling; full length guide rod; aluminum frame with stainless slide; satin silver finish; checkered frontstrap; 3-inch barrel; rosewood double diamond Crimson Trace lasergrips grips; tritium 3-dot night sights.
Price: $1,603.00

KIMBER STAINLESS ULTRA TLE II

1911-syle semiauto pistol chambered in .45 ACP. Features include 7-round magazine; full length guide rod; aluminum frame with stainless slide; satin silver finish; checkered frontstrap; 3-inch barrel; tactical gray double diamond grips; tritium 3-dot night sights.
Price: $1,210.00

KIMBER ROYAL II

Caliber: .45 ACP, 7-shot magazine. **Barrel:** 5. **Weight:** 38 oz. **Length:** 8.7 overall. **Grips:** Solid bone-smooth. **Sights:** Fixed low profile radius (inches): 6.8. **Features:** A classic full-size pistol wearing a stunning charcoal blue finish complimented with solid bone grip panels. Frint and rear serations. Aluminum match grade trigger with a factory setting of approximately 4-5 pounds.
Price: $1,938.00

KIMBER MASTER CARRY PRO

Caliber: .45 ACP, 8-round magazine. **Barrel:** 4 inches. **Weight:** 28 oz. **Length:** 7.7 inches Grips: Crimson Trace Laser. **Sights:** Fixed low profile. **Features:** Matte black KimPro slide, aluminum round heel frame, full-length guide rod.
Price: $1,568.00

NIGHTHAWK CUSTOM T4

Manufacturer of a wide range of 1911-style pistols In Government Model (full-size), Commander and Officer's frame sizes. **Caliber:** .45 ACP, 7 or 8-round magazine; 9mm, 9 or 10 rounds. **Barrel:** 3.8, 4.25 or 5 inches. **Weight:** 28 to 41 ounces, depending on model. Shown is T4 model, available only in 9mm.
Price: From .... $3,200.00 to $3,500.00

NORTH AMERICAN ARMS GUARDIAN DAO

Prices given are believed to be accurate at time of publication however, many factors affect retail pricing so exact prices are not possible.

68TH EDITION, 2014 ⊕ **407**

NORTH AMERICAN ARMS GUARDIAN DAO

Caliber: 25 NAA, 32 ACP, 380 ACP, 32 NAA, 6-shot magazine. **Barrel:** 2.49. **Weight:** 20.8 oz. **Length:** 4.75 overall. **Grips:** Black polymer. **Sights:** Low profile fixed. **Features:** Double-action only mechanism. All stainless steel construction. Introduced 1998. Made in U.S.A. by North American Arms.
Price: From $402.00

OLYMPIC ARMS MATCHMASTER 5 1911

Caliber: 45 ACP, 7-shot magazine. **Barrel:** 5 stainless steel. **Weight:** 40 oz. **Length:** 8.75 overall. **Grips:** Smooth walnut with laser-etched scorpion icon. **Sights:** Ramped blade, LPA adjustable rear. **Features:** Matched frame and slide, fitted and head-spaced barrel, complete ramp and throat jobs, lowered and widened ejection port, beveled mag well, hand-stoned-to-match hammer and sear, lightweight long-shoe over-travel adjusted trigger, shaped and tensioned extractor, extended thumb safety, wide beavertail grip safety and full-length guide rod. Made in U.S.A. by Olympic Arms, Inc.
Price: $903.00

OLYMPIC ARMS MATCHMASTER 6 1911

Caliber: 45 ACP, 7-shot magazine. **Barrel:** 6 stainless steel. **Weight:** 44 oz. **Length:** 9.75 overall. **Grips:** Smooth walnut with laser-etched scorpion icon. **Sights:** Ramped blade, LPA adjustable rear. **Features:** Matched frame and slide, fitted and head-spaced barrel, complete ramp and throat jobs, lowered and widened ejection port, beveled mag well, hand-stoned-to-match hammer and sear, lightweight long-shoe over-travel adjusted trigger, shaped and tensioned extractor, extended thumb safety, wide beavertail grip safety and full length guide rod. Made in U.S.A. by Olympic Arms, Inc.
Price: $973.00

OLYMPIC ARMS ENFORCER 1911

Caliber: 45 ACP, 6-shot magazine. **Barrel:** 4 bull stainless steel. **Weight:** 35 oz. **Length:** 7.75 overall. **Grips:** Smooth walnut with etched black widow spider icon. **Sights:** Ramped blade front, LPA adjustable rear. **Features:** Compact Enforcer frame. Bushingless bull barrel with triplex counter-wound self-contained recoil system. Matched frame and slide, fitted and head-spaced barrel, complete ramp and throat jobs, lowered and widened ejection port, beveled mag well, hand-stoned-to-match hammer and sear, lightweight longshoe over-travel adjusted trigger, shaped and tensioned extractor, extended thumb safety, wide beavertail grip safety and full length guide rod. Made in U.S.A. by Olympic Arms.
Price: $1,033.50

OLYMPIC ARMS COHORT

Caliber: 45 ACP, 7-shot magazine. **Barrel:** 4 bull stainless steel. **Weight:** 36 oz. **Length:** 7.75 overall. **Grips:** Fully checkered walnut. **Sights:** Ramped blade front, LPA adjustable rear. **Features:** Full size 1911 frame. Bushingless bull barrel with triplex counter-wound self-contained recoil system. Matched frame and slide, fitted and head-spaced barrel, complete ramp and throat jobs, lowered and widened ejection port, beveled mag well, hand-stoned-to-match hammer and sear, lightweight long-shoe over-travel adjusted trigger, shaped and tensioned extractor, extended thumb safety, wide beavertail grip safety and full length guide rod. Made in U.S.A. by Olympic Arms.
Price: $973.70

ejection port, beveled mag well, hand-stoned-to-match hammer and sear, lightweight long-shoe over-travel adjusted trigger, shaped and tensioned extractor, extended thumb safety, wide beavertail grip safety and full length guide rod. Entire pistol is fitted and assembled, then disassembled and subjected to the color case hardening process. Made in U.S.A. by Olympic Arms, Inc.

Price: Constable, 4" barrel, 35 oz. . . . **$1,163.50**
Price: Westerner, 5" barrel, 39 oz. . . . **$1,033.50**
Price: Trail Boss, 6" barrel, 43 oz. . . . **$1,103.70**

OLYMPIC ARMS BIG DEUCE

Caliber: 45 ACP, 7-shot magazine. **Barrel:** 6 stainless steel. **Weight:** 44 oz. **Length:** 9.75 overall. **Grips:** Double diamond checkered exotic cocobolo wood. **Sights:** Ramped blade front, LPA adjustable rear. **Features:** Carbon steel parkerized slide with satin bead blast finish full size frame. Matched frame and slide, fitted and head-spaced barrel, complete ramp and throat jobs, lowered and widened ejection port, beveled mag well, hand-stoned-to-match hammer and sear, lightweight long-shoe over-travel adjusted trigger, shaped and tensioned extractor, extended thumb safety, wide beavertail grip safety and full length guide rod. Made in U.S.A. by Olympic Arms.
Price: $1,033.50

OLYMPIC ARMS SCHUETZEN WORKS 1911

Caliber: 45 ACP, 7-shot magazine. **Barrel:** 4, 5.2, bull stainless steel. **Weight:** 35-38 oz. **Length:** 7.75-8.75 overall. **Grips:** Double diamond checkered exotic cocobolo wood. **Sights:** Ramped blade, LPA adjustable rear. **Features:** Carbon steel parkerized slide with satin bead blast finish full size frame. Matched frame and slide, fitted and head-spaced barrel, complete ramp and throat jobs, lowered and widened ejection port, beveled mag well, hand-stoned-to-match hammer and sear, lightweight long-shoe over-travel adjusted trigger, shaped and tensioned extractor, extended thumb safety, wide beavertail grip safety and full length guide rod. Custom made by Olympic Arms Schuetzen Pistol Works. Parts are hand selected and fitted by expert pistolsmiths. Several no-cost options to choose from. Made in U.S.A. by Olympic Arms Schuetzen Pistol Works.
Price: Journeyman, 4 bull barrel, 35 oz. **$1,293.50**
Price: Street Deuce, 5.2 bull barrel, 38 oz. **$1,293.50**

OLYMPIC OA-93R

OLYMPIC ARMS WESTERNER SERIES 1911

Caliber: 45 ACP, 7-shot magazine. **Barrel:** 4, 5, 6 stainless steel. **Weight:** 35-43 oz. **Length:** 7.75-9.75 overall. **Grips:** Smooth ivory laser-etched Westerner icon. **Sights:** Ramped blade, LPA adjustable rear. **Features:** Matched frame and slide, fitted and head-spaced barrel, complete ramp and throat jobs, lowered and widened

OLYMPIC ARMS OA-93 AR

Caliber: 5.56 NATO. **Barrel:** 6.5 button-rifled stainless steel. **Weight:** 4.46 lbs. **Length:** 17 overall. **Sights:** None. **Features:** Olympic Arms integrated recoil system on the upper receiver eliminates the buttstock, flat top upper, free floating tubular match handguard, threaded muzzle with flash suppressor. Made in U.S.A. by Olympic Arms, Inc.
Price: $1,202.50

OLYMPIC ARMS K23P AR

Caliber: 5.56 NATO. **Barrel:** 6.5 button-rifled chrome-moly steel. **Length:** 22.25 overall.
Weight: 5.12 lbs. **Sights:** Adjustable A2 rear, elevation adjustable front post. **Features:** A2 upper with rear sight, free floating tubular match handguard, threaded muzzle with flash suppressor, receiver extension tube with foam cover, no bayonet lug. Made in U.S.A. by Olympic Arms, Inc. Introduced 2007.
Price: $973.70

OLYMPIC ARMS K23P-A3-TC AR

Caliber: 5.56 NATO. **Barrel:** 6.5 button-rifled chrome-moly steel. **Length:** 22.25 overall. **Weight:** 5.12 lbs. **Sights:** Adjustable A2 rear, elevation adjustable front post. **Features:** Flat-top upper with detachable carry handle, free floating FIRSH rail handguard, threaded muzzle with flash suppressor, receiver extension tube with foam cover, no bayonet lug. Made in U.S.A. by Olympic Arms, Inc. Introduced 2007.
Price: $1,118.20

OLYMPIC ARMS WHITNEY WOLVERINE

Caliber: 22 LR, 10-shot magazine. **Barrel:** 4.625 stainless steel. **Weight:** 19.2 oz. **Length:** 9 overall. **Grips:** Black checkered with fire/safe markings. **Sights:** Ramped blade front, dovetail rear. **Features:** Polymer frame with natural ergonomics and ventilated rib. Barrel with 6-groove 1x16 twist rate. All metal magazine shell. Made in U.S.A. by Olympic Arms.
Price: $291.00

PARA USA BLACK OPS SERIES

Caliber: .45 ACP, single (8 round) or double-stack magazine (14 rounds). **Barrel:** 5 inches. Weight: 39 oz. **Grips:** VZ G10. **Sights:**

Fixed night sights or adjustable. Stainless receiver with IonBond finish.
Price: ....$1,257.00 to $1,325.00

PARA USA EXPERT SERIES

Caliber: .45 ACP, 7+1-round capacity. **Barrel:** 5" stainless. **Weight:** 39 oz. **Length:** 8.5 overall. **Grips:** Checkered Polymer. **Sights:** Dovetail Fixed, 3-White Dot. **Features:** The Para "Expert" is an entry level 1911 pistol that will allow new marksmen to own a pistol with features such as, Lowered and flared ejection port, beveled magazine well, flat mainspring housing, grip safety contoured for spur hammer. Model 1445 has double-stack frame, 14-round magazine.
Price: $663.00
Price: Carry $799.00
Price: Commander...$799.00
Price: 1445 Model...$884.00 to $919.00

PARA USA LDA SERIES

Caliber: 9mm, .45 ACP. **Capacity:** 9 rounds (9mm), 7 rounds (.45) for Officer model; 8 and 6 round capacity for Agent model, which has shorter grip. Double-action only design with PARA's exclusive LDA (Light Double Action) trigger. **Barrel:** 3 inches. **Sights:** Trijicon night sights. **Grips:** VZ Gator.
Price: Officer $1,025.00
Price: Agent $1,025.00

PARA USA WARTHOG

Caliber: .45 ACP, 10-round magazine. **Barrel:** 3 inches. **Sights:** 2-dot rear combat, Green fiber optic front. **Features:** Double-stack aluminum frame, adjustable skeletonized trigger, black nitride or satin stainless finish. Comes with two 10-round magazines.
Price: (black) $884.00
Price: (stainless) $919.00

PARA ELITE SERIES

Caliber: .45 ACP, 9mm (Elite LS Hunter only). **Capacity:** 6, 7 or 8 rounds; 9 rounds (9mm LS Hunter). Barrel: 3, 4 or 5 inches (.45 models), 6 inches (9mm LS Hunter). Pro Model has Ed Brown mag well, HD extractor, checkered front strap and mainspring housing, Trijicon sights.
Price: Elite Standard $949.00
Price: Agent 3.5" $949.00
Price: Officer 4" $949.00
Price: Commander 4.5" $949.00
Price: Target...$949.00
Price: Pro, LS Hunter $1,249.00
Price: Pro Stainless...$1,249.00

PHOENIX ARMS HP22, HP25

Caliber: 22 LR, 10-shot (HP22), 25 ACP, 10-shot (HP25). **Barrel:** 3. **Weight:** 20 oz. **Length:** 5.5 overall. **Grips:** Checkered composition. **Sights:** Blade front, adjustable rear. **Features:** Single action, exposed hammer; manual hold-open; button magazine release. Available in satin nickel, matte blue finish. Introduced 1993. Made in U.S.A. by Phoenix Arms.
Price: With gun lock $130.00
Price: HP Range kit with 5" bbl., locking case
    and accessories (1 Mag) $171.00
Price: HP Deluxe Range kit with 3" and 5" bbls.,
    2 mags, case $210.00

REMINGTON R1

Caliber: .45 (7-shot magazine). **Barrel:** 5". **Weight:** 38.5 oz. **Grips:** Double diamond walnut. **Sights:** Fixed, dovetail front and rear, 3-dot. **Features:** Flared and lowed ejection port. Comes with two magazines.
Price: $729.00
Price: (stainless).....................................$729.00 to $789.00

REMINGTON R1 ENHANCED

Same features as standard R1 except 8-shot magazine, stainless satin black oxide finish, wood laminate grips and adjustable rear sight. Other features include forward slide serrations, fiber optic front sight. Available with threaded barrel.
Price: $940
Price: (threaded barrel) ....$940.00 to $1,140.00

REMINGTON R1 CARRY

Caliber: .45 ACP. **Barrel:** 5 or 4.25 inches (Carry Commander). **Weight:** 35 to 39 oz. **Grips:** Cocobolo. **Sights:** Novak type drift-adjustable rear, tritium-dot front sight. Skeletonized trigger. Comes with one 8-round and one 7-round magazine.
Price: $1,299.00

ROCK RIVER ARMS LAR-15/LAR-9
Caliber: .223/5.56mm NATO chamber 4-shot magazine. **Barrel:** 7, 10.5 Wilson chrome moly, 1:9 twist, A2 flash hider, 1/2-28 thread. **Weight:** 5.1 lbs. (7 barrel), 5.5 lbs. (10.5 barrel). **Length:** 23 overall. Stock: Hogue rubber grip. **Sights:** A2 front. **Features:** Forged A2 or A4 upper, single stage trigger, aluminum free-float tube, one magazine. Similar 9mm Para. LAR-9 also available. From Rock River Arms, Inc.
Price: LAR-15 7 A2 AR2115 ....$955.00
Price: LAR-15 10.5 A4 AR2120 ....$945.00
Price: LAR-9 7 A2 9MM2115..$1,125.00

ROHRBAUGH R9
Caliber: 9mm Parabellum, 380 ACP. **Barrel:** 2.9". **Weight:** 12.8 oz. **Length:** 5.2" overall. **Features:** Very small double-action-only semi-auto pocket pistol. Stainless steel slide with matte black aluminum frame. Available with or without sights. Available with all-black (Stealth) and partial Diamond Black (Stealth Elite) finish.
Price: $1,149.00

RUGER SR9
Caliber: 9mm Para. **Barrel:** 4.14. **Weight:** 26.25, 26.5 oz. **Grips:** Glass-filled nylon in two color options—black or OD Green, w/flat or arched reversible backstrap. **Sights:** Adjustable 3-dot, built-in Picatinny-style rail. **Features:** Semi-DA, 6 configurations, striker-fired, through-hardened stainless steel slide, brushed or blackened stainless slide with black grip frame or blackened stainless slide with OD Green grip frame, ambi manual 1911-style safety, ambi mag release, mag disconnect, loaded chamber indicator, Ruger camblock design to absorb recoil, two 10 or 17-shot mags. Intr. 2008. Made in U.S.A. by Sturm, Ruger & Co.
Price: SR9 (17-Round), SR9-10 (SS) $525.00
Price: KBSR9 (17-Round), KBSR9-10 (Blackened SS).............$565.00
Price: KODBSR9 (17-Round), KODBSR9-10
    (OD Green Grip)..$565.00

RUGER SR9C COMPACT
Compact double action only semiauto pistol chambered in 9mm Parabellum. Features include 1911-style ambidextrous manual safety; internal trigger bar interlock and striker blocker; trigger safety; magazine disconnector; loaded chamber indicator; two magazines, one 10-round and the other 17-round; 3.5-inch barrel;

3-dot sights; accessory rail; brushed stainless or blackened allow finish. Weight 23.40 oz.
Price: $525.00

RUGER SR45
Caliber: .45 ACP, 10-round magazine. **Barrel:** 4.5 inches. **Weight:** 30 oz. **Length:** 8 inches. **Grips:** Glass-filled nylon with reversible flat/arched backstra. **Sights:** Adjustable 3-dot. **Features:** Same features as SR9.
Price: $529.00

RUGER LC9
Caliber: 9mm luger, 7+1 capacity. **Barrel:** 3.12 **Weight:** 17.10 oz. **Grips:** Glass-filled nylon. **Sights:** Adjustable 3-dot. **Features:** double-action-only, hammer-fired, locked-breech pistol with a smooth trigger pull. Control and confident handling of the Ruger LC9 are accomplished through reduced recoil and aggressive frame checkering for a positive grip in all conditions. The Ruger LC9 features smooth "melted" edges for ease of holstering, carrying and drawing. Made in U.S.A. by Sturm, Ruger & Co.
Price: $449.00

RUGER LC380
Caliber: .380 ACP. Other specifications and features identical to LC9.
Price: $449

Prices given are believed to be accurate at time of publication however, many factors affect retail pricing so exact prices are not possible.

RUGER LCP

Caliber: .380 (6-shot magazine). **Barrel:** 2.75". **Weight:** 9.4 oz.
Length: 5.16". **Grips:** Glass-filled nylon. **Sights:** Fixed, LaxerMax or Crimson Trace.
Price: $379
Price: (Laser Max) $449
Price: (Crimson Trace Laserguard)................$559

RUGER P95

Caliber: 9mm, 15-shot magazine. **Barrel:** 3.9. **Weight:** 30 oz. **Length:** 7.25 overall. **Grips:** Grooved; integral with frame. **Sights:** Blade front, rear drift adjustable for windage; 3-dot system. **Features:** Molded polymer grip frame, stainless steel or chrome-moly slide. Suitable for +P+ ammunition. Safety model, decocker. Introduced 1996. Made in U.S.A. by Sturm, Ruger & Co. Comes with lockable plastic case, spare magazine, loader and lock, Picatinny rails.
Price: KP95PR15
safety model, stainless steel..........................$424.00
Price: P95PR15 safety model,
blued finish $395.00
Price: P95PR 10-round model,
blued finish $393.00
Price: KP95PR 10-round model,
stainless steel $424.00

RUGER P345

Caliber: .45 ACP (8-shot magazine). **Barrel:** 4.2". **Weight:** 29 oz. **Length:** 7.5". **Sights:** Adjustable 3-dot. **Features:** Blued alloy/steel or stainless. Comes with two magazines, mag loader and hard plastic case.
Price: ....$599, $639 (stainless)

RUGER 22 CHARGER

Caliber: .22 LR. **Barrel:** 10. **Weight:** 3.5 lbs (w/out bi-pod). **Stock:** Black Laminate. **Sights:** None. **Features:** Rimfire Autoloading, one configuration, 10/22 action, adjustable bi-pod, new mag release for easier removal, precision-rifled barrel, black matte finish, combination Weaver-style and tip-off scope mount, 10-shot mag. Intr. 2008. Made in U.S.A. by Sturm, Ruger & Co.
Price: CHR22-10...$380.00

RUGER MARK III SERIES

Caliber: 22 LR, 10-shot magazine. **Barrel:** 4.5, 4.75, 5.5, 6, or 6-7/8. **Weight:** 33 oz. (4.75 bbl.). **Length:** 9 (4.75 bbl.). **Grips:** Checkered composition grip panels. **Sights:** Fixed, fiber-optic front, fixed rear. **Features:** Updated design of original Standard Auto and Mark II series. Hunter models have lighter barrels. Target models have cocobolo grips; bull, target, competition, and hunter barrels; and adjustable sights. Introduced 2005.
Price: Standard $389.00
Price: Target (blue) $459.00
Price: Target (stainless) ,,$569.00
Price: Hunter $679.00
Price: Competition $659.00

Ruger 22/45 Mark III Pistol

Similar to other 22 Mark III autos except has Zytel grip frame that matches angle and magazine latch of Model 1011 45 ACP pistol. Available in 4 standard, 4.5, 5.5, 6-7/8 bull barrels. Comes with extra magazine, plastic case, lock. Introduced 1992. Hunter introduced 2006.
Price: P4MKIII, 4 bull barrel, adjustable sights $380.00
Price: P45GCMKIII, 4.5 bull barrel, fixed sights $380.00
Price: P512MKIII (5.5 bull blued barrel,
adj. sights) $380.00
Price: KP512MKIII (5.5 stainless bull barrel, adj. sights) $475.00
Price: Hunter KP45HMKIII 4.5 barrel (2007), KP678HMKIII,
6-7/8 stainless fluted bull barrel, adj. sights $562.00

Prices given are believed to be accurate at time of publication however, many factors affect retail pricing so exact prices are not possible.

68TH EDITION, 2014 ✦ **413**

RUGER SR22
Caliber: .22 LR (10-shot magazine). **Barrel:** 3.5". **Weight:** 17.5 oz. **Length:** 6.4". **Sights:** Adjustable 3-dot. **Features:** Ambidextrous manual safety/decocking lever and mag release. Comes with two interchangeable rubberized grips and two magazines. Black or silveranodize finish. Available with threaded barrel.
Price: Black $399.00
Price: Silver $419.00
Price: Threaded barrel $439.00

RUGER SR1911
Caliber: .45 (8-shot magazine). **Barrel:** 5". **Weight:** 39 oz. **Length:** 8.6". **Grips:** Slim checkered hardwood. **Sights:** Novak LoMount Carry rear, standard front. **Features:** Based on Series 70 design. Flared and lowed ejection port. Extended mag release, thumb safety and slide-stop lever, oversized grip safety, checkered backstrap on the flat mainspring housing. Comes with one 7-shot and one 8-shot magazine.
Price: $829.00

RUGER SR1911 CMD
Commander-size version of SR1911. **Caliber:** .45 ACP. **Barrel:** 4.25 inches. **Weight:** 36.4 oz. Other specifications and features are identical to SR1911.
Price: $829.00

SEECAMP LWS 32/380 STAINLESS DA
Caliber: 32 ACP, 380 ACP Win. Silvertip, 6-shot magazine. **Barrel:** 2, integral with frame. **Weight:** 10.5 oz. **Length:** 4-1/8 overall. **Grips:** Glass-filled nylon. **Sights:** Smooth, no-snag, contoured slide and barrel top. **Features:** Aircraft quality 17-4 PH stainless steel. Inertia-operated firing pin. Hammer fired double-action-only. Hammer automatically follows slide down to safety rest position after each shot, no manual safety needed. Magazine safety disconnector. Polished stainless. Introduced 1985. From L.W. Seecamp.
Price: 32 .... $446.25
Price: 380 .... $795.00

SIG SAUER 250 COMPACT
Caliber: 9mm Para. (16-round magazine), 357 SIG, 40 S&W and 45 ACP. **Barrel:** NA. **Weight:** 24.6 oz. **Length:** 7.2 overall. **Grips:** Interchangeable polymer. **Sights:** Siglite night sights. **Features:** Modular design allows for immediate change in caliber and size;

subcompact, compact and full. Six different grip combinations for each size. Introduced 2008. From Sig Sauer, Inc.
Price: P250 .... $750.00

SIG SAUER 1911
Caliber: 45 ACP, 8-10 shot magazine. **Barrel:** 5. **Weight:** 40.3 oz. **Length:** 8.65 overall. **Grips:** Checkered wood grips. **Sights:** Novak night sights. Blade front, drift adjustable rear for windage. **Features:** Single-action 1911. Hand-fitted dehorned stainless-steel frame and slide; match-grade barrel, hammer/sear set and trigger; 25-lpi front strap checkering, 20-lpi mainspring housing checkering. Beavertail grip safety with speed bump, extended thumb safety, firing pin safety and hammer intercept notch. Introduced 2005. XO series has contrast sights, Ergo Grip XT textured polymer grips. Target line features adjustable target night sights, match barrel, custom wood grips, non-railed frame in stainless or Nitron finishes. TTT series is two-tone 1911 with Nitron slide and black controls on stainless frame. Includes burled maple grips, adjustable combat night sights. STX line available from Sig Sauer Custom Shop; two-tone 1911, non-railed, Nitron slide, stainless frame, burled maple grips. Polished cocking serrations, flat-top slide, magwell. Carry line has Novak night sights, lanyard attachment point, gray diamondwood or rosewood grips, 8+1 capacity. Compact series has 6+1 capacity, 7.7 OAL, 4.25" barrel, slim-profile wood grips, weighs 30.3 oz. RCS line (Compact SAS) is Customs Shop version with anti-snag dehorning. Stainless or Nitron finish, Novak night sights, slim-

profile gray diamondwood or rosewood grips. 6+1 capacity. 1911 C3 (2008) is a 6+1 compact .45 ACP, rosewood custom wood grips, two-tone and Nitron finishes. **Weighs about** 30 ounces unloaded, lightweight alloy frame. **Length is** 7.7. Now offered in more than 30 different models with numerous options for frame size, grips, finishes, sight arrangements and other features. From SIG SAUER, Inc.

SIG SAUER P220

Caliber: 45 ACP, (7- or 8-shot magazine). **Barrel:** 4.4. **Weight:** 27.8 oz. **Length:** 7.8 overall. **Grips:** Checkered black plastic. **Sights:** Blade front, drift adjustable rear for windage. Optional Siglite night sights. **Features:** Double action. Stainless-steel slide, Nitron finish, alloy frame, M1913 Picatinny rail; safety system of decocking lever, automatic firing pin safety block, safety intercept notch, and trigger bar disconnector. Squared combat-type trigger guard. Slide stays open after last shot. Introduced 1976. P220 SAS Anti-Snag has dehorned stainless steel slide, front Siglite Night Sight, rounded trigger guard, dust cover, Custom Shop wood grips. Equinox line is Custom Shop product with Nitron stainless-steel slide with a black hard anodized alloy frame, brush-polished flats and nickel accents. Truglo tritium fiber-optic front sight, rear Siglite night sight, gray laminated wood grips with checkering and stippling. From SIG SAUER, Inc.

Price: P220 Two-Tone, matte-stainless slide,
black alloy frame.. **$1,110.00**
Price: P220 Elite Stainless (2008) **$1,350.00**
Price: P220 Two-Tone SAO, single action (2006), from **$1,086.00**
Price: P220 DAK (2006) **$853.00**
Price: P220 Equinox (2006) **$1,200.00**
Price: P220 Elite Dark (2009) **$1,200.00**
Price: P220 Elite Dark, threaded barrel (2009).................... **$1,305.00**

Price: Model 1911-22-B .22 LR
w/custom wood grips **$399.99**
Price: Nitron.. **$1,200.00**
Price: Stainless **$1,170.00**
Price: XO Black **$1,005.00**
Price: Target Nitron (2006) **$1,230.00**
Price: TTT (2006)... **$1,290.00**
Price: STX (2006) **$1,455.00**
Price: Carry Nitron (2006) **$1,200.00**
Price: Compact Nitron **$1,200.00**
Price: RCS Nitron... **$1,305.00**
Price: C3 (2008) **$1,200.00**
Price: Platinum Elite **$1,275.00**
Price: Blackwater (2009) **$1,290.00**
Price: Scorpion **$1,128.00**

SIG SAUER P210

Caliber: 9mm, 8-shot magazine. **Barrel:** 4.7. **Weight:** 37.4 oz. **Length:** 8.5 overall. **Grips:** Custom wood. **Sights:** Post and notch and adjustable target sights. **Features:** The carbon steel slide, machined from solid billet steel, now features a durable Nitron® coating, and the improved beavertail adorns the Nitron coated, heavy-style, carbon steel frame. The P210 Legend also offers an improved manual safety, internal drop safety, side magazine release, and custom wood grips.
Price: P210-9-LEGEND **$2,199.00**
Price: P210-9-LEGEND-TGT
w/adjustable target sights **$2,399.00**

SIG SAUER P220 CARRY

Caliber: 45 ACP, 8-shot magazine. **Barrel:** 3.9. **Weight:** NA. **Length:** 7.1 overall. **Grips:** Checkered black plastic. **Sights:** Blade front, drift adjustable rear for windage. Optional Siglite night sights. **Features:** Similar to full-size P220, except is "Commander" size. Single stack, DA/SA operation, Nitron finish, Picatinny rail, and either post and dot contrast or 3-dot Siglite night sights. Introduced 2005. Many variations availble. From SIG SAUER, Inc.
Price: P220 Carry, from **$975.00;**
w/night sights **$1,050.00**
Price: P220 Carry Elite Stainless (2008) **$1,350.00**

SIG SAUER P224

Caliber: 9mm, .357 SIG, .40 S&W. **Magazine Capacity:** 11 rounds (9mm), 10 rounds (.357 and .40). **Barrel:** 3.5 inches. **Weight:** 25 oz. **Length:** 6.7 inches. **Grips:** Hogue G-10. **Sights:** SIGlite night sights. **Features:** Ultra-compact, double-stack design with features and operating controls of other SIG models. Available in SAS, nickel, Equinox and Extreme variations.
Price: .... **$1,125.00 to $1,218.00**

SIG SAUER P226

Similar to the P220 pistol except has 4.4 barrel, measures 7.7 overall, weighs 34 oz. Chambered in 9mm, 357 SIG, or 40 S&W. X-Five series has factory tuned single-action trigger, 5 slide and barrel, ergonomic wood grips with beavertail, ambidextrous thumb safety and stainless slide and frame with magwell, low-profile adjustable target sights, front cocking serrations and a 25-meter factory test target. Many variations available. Snap-on modular grips. From SIG SAUER, Inc.
Price: From **$993.00**

SIG SAUER P227

Same general specifications and features as P226 except chambered for .45 ACP and has double-stack magazine. **Magazine Capacity:** 10 rounds.
Price: (Night Sights) .... **$993.00 to $1,085.00**

SIG SAUER P229 DA

Similar to the P220 except chambered for 9mm Para. (10- or 15-round magazines), 40 S&W, 357 SIG (10- or 12-round magazines). Has 3.86 barrel, 7.1 overall length and 3.35 height. Weight is 32.4 oz. Introduced 1991. Snap-on modular grips. Frame made in Germany, stainless steel slide assembly made in U.S.; pistol assembled in U.S. Many variations available. From SIG SAUER, Inc.
Price: P229, from **$975.00**
    w/night sights **$1,050.00**
Price: P229 Platinum Elite (2008) **$1,275.00**
Price: P229 Enhanced Elite **$1,175.00**

SIG SAUER SP2022

Caliber: 9mm Para., 357 SIG, 40 S&W, 10-, 12-, or 15-shot magazines. **Barrel:** 3.9. **Weight:** 30.2 oz. **Length:** 7.4 overall. **Grips:** Composite and rubberized one-piece. **Sights:** Blade front, rear adjustable for windage. Optional Siglite night sights. **Features:** Polymer frame, stainless steel slide; integral frame accessory rail; replaceable steel frame rails; left- or right-handed magazine release, two interchangeable grips. From SIG SAUER, Inc.
Price: SP2009, Nitron finish **$613.00**

SIG SAUER P232 PERSONAL SIZE

Caliber: 380 ACP, 7-shot. **Barrel:** 3.6. **Weight:** 17.6-22.4 oz. **Length:** 6.6 overall. **Grips:** Checkered black composite. **Sights:** Blade front, rear adjustable for windage. **Features:** Double action/single action or DAO. Blow-back operation, stationary barrel. Introduced 1997. From SIG SAUER, Inc.
Price: P232, from **$660.00**

SIG SAUER P238

Caliber: .380 ACP (9mm short), 6-7-shot magazine. **Barrel:** 2.7. **Weight:** 15.4 oz. **Length:** 5.5 overall. **Grips:** Hogue® G-10 and Rosewood grips. **Sights:** Contrast / SIGLITE night sights. **Features:** the P238 has redefined the role of a .380 ACP caliber pistol for concealed personal protection, ultimate firepower in an all metal beavertail-style frame.
Price: **$643.00**
Price: P238 Lady w/rosewood grips **$752.00**
Price: P238 Gambler w/rosewood grip **$752.00**
Price: P238 Extreme w/X-Grip extended magazine **$752.00**
Price: P238 Diamond Plate w/diamond plate detailed slide ... **$752.00**

Prices given are believed to be accurate at time of publication however, many factors affect retail pricing so exact prices are not possible.

SIG SAUER P290

Caliber: 9mm, 6/8-shot magazine. **Barrel:** 2.9. **Weight:** 20.5 oz.
Length: 5.5 overall. **Grips:** Polymer. **Sights:** Contrast / SIGLITE
night sights.
Features: Unlike many small pistols, the P290 features drift
adjustable sights in the standard SIG SAUER dovetails. This gives
shooters the option of either standard contrast sights or SIGLITE®
night sights. The slide is machined from a solid billet of stainless
steel and is available in a natural stainless or a durable Nitron®
coating. A reversible magazine catch is left-hand adjustable.
Interchangeable grip panels allow for personalization as well as
a custom fit. In addition to the standard polymer inserts, optional
panels will be available in aluminum, G10 and wood.
Price: Model 290-9-BSS...$758.00
Price: Model 290-9-TSS...$786.00
Price: Model 290-9-BSS-L
with laser sights..$828.00
Price: Model 290-9-TSS with
laser sights...$856.00

SIG SAUER P239

Caliber: 9mm Para., 8-shot, 357 SIG 40 S&W, 7-shot magazine.
Barrel: 3.6. **Weight:** 25.2 oz. **Length:** 6.6 overall. **Grips:** Checkered
black composite. **Sights:** Blade front, rear adjustable for windage.
Optional Siglite night sights. **Features:** SA/DA or DAO; blackened
stainless steel slide, aluminum alloy frame. Introduced 1996.
Made in U.S.A.
by SIG SAUER, Inc.
Price: P239, from $840.00

SIG SAUER MOSQUITO

Caliber: 22 LR, 10-shot magazine. **Barrel:** 3.9. **Weight:** 24.6 oz.
Length: 7.2 overall. **Grips:** Checkered black composite. **Sights:**
Blade front, rear adjustable for windage. **Features:** Blowback
operated, fixed barrel, polymer frame, slide-mounted ambidextrous
safety. Introduced 2005. Made in U.S.A. by SIG SAUER, Inc.
Price: Mosquito, from $375.00

SIG SAUER P522

Semiauto blowback pistol chambered in .22 LR. Pistol version of
SIG522 rifle. Features include a 10-inch barrel; lightweight polymer
lower receiver with pistol grip; ambi mag catch; aluminum upper;
faux gas valve; birdcage; 25-round magazine; quad rail or "clean"
handguard; optics rail.
Price: .... $572.00 to $643.00

SIG SAUER P938

Caliber: 9mm (6-shot magazine). **Barrel:** 3.9". **Weight:** 16 oz. **Length:**
5.9". **Grips:** Rosewood, Blackwood, Hogue Extreme, Hogue
Diamondwood. **Sights:** Siglite night sights or Siglite rear with Tru-Glo
front. **Features:** Slightly larger version of P238 with 9mm chambering.
Price: ....$809.00 to $823.00

SPHINX

Caliber: 9mm Para., 45 ACP., 10-shot magazine. **Barrel:** 4.43.
Weight: 39.15 oz. **Length:** 8.27 overall. **Grips:** Textured polymer.
Sights: Fixed Trijicon Night Sights. **Features:** CNC engineered from
stainless steel billet; grip frame in stainless steel, titanium or high-

strength aluminum. Integrated accessory rail, high-cut beavertail, decocking lever. Made in Switzerland. Imported by Sabre Defence Industries.
Price: 45 ACP (2007) $2,990.00
Price: 9mm Para. Standard, titanium w/decocker $2,700.00

SPHINX SDP
Caliber: 9mm (15-shot magazine). **Barrel:** 3.7". **Weight:** 27.5 oz. **Length:** 7.4". **Sights:** Defiance Day & Night Green fiber/tritium front, tritium 2-dot red rear. **Features:** Double/single action with ambidextrous decocker, integrated slide postion safety, aluminum MIL-STD 1913 Picatinny rail, Blued alloy/steel or stainless. Aluminum and polymer frame, machined steel slide.
Price: ....**NA**

SMITH & WESSON M&P
Caliber: .22 LR, 9mm, .357 Sig, .40 S&W. **Magazine capacity, full-size models:** 12 rounds (.22), 17 rounds (9mm), 15 rounds (.40). **Compact models:** 12 (9mm), 10 (.40). **Barrel:** 4.25, 3.5 inches. **Weight:** 24, 22 oz. **Length:** 7.6, 6.7 inches. **Grips:** Polymer with three interchangeable palmswell grip sizes. **Sights:** 3 white-dot system with low-profile rear. **Features:** Zytel polymer frame with stainless steel slide, barrel and structural components. VTAC (Viking Tactics) model has Flat Dark Earth finish, VTAC Warrior sights. Compact models available with Crimson Trace Lasergrips.
Price: (VTAC) ....**$569.00 to $779.00**
Price: (CT) **$809.00**

SMITH & WESSON PRO SERIES MODEL M&P40
Striker-fired DAO semiauto pistol chambered in .40 S&W. Features include 4.25- or 5-inch barrel, matte black polymer frame and stainless steel slide, tactical rail, Novak front and rear sights or two-dot night sights, polymer grips, 15+1 capacity.
Price: **$830.00**
Price: VTAC® Viking Tactics.................................**$779.00**

SMITH & WESSON M&P 45
M&P model offered in three frame sizes and chambered in .45 ACP. **Magazine capacity:** 8 or 10 rounds. **Barrel length:** 4 or 4.5 inches. **Weight:** 26, 28 or 30 oz. **Finish:** Black or Dark Earth Brown. Available with Crimson Trace Lasergrips.
Price: (CT) **$599.00, $619.00, $829.00**

SMITH & WESSON M&P9 SHIELD
Ultra-compact, single-stack variation of M&P series. **Caliber:** 9mm, .40 S&W. Comes with one 6-round and one 7-round magazine. **Barrel:** 3.1 inches. Length: 6.1 inches. **Weight:** 19 oz. **Sights:** 3 white-dot system with low-profile rear.
Price: **$449.00**

SMITH & WESSON PRO SERIES MODEL M&P9
Similar to M&P40 but chambered in 9mm Parabellum. Capacity 17+1, 4.25-inch barrel, two-dot night sights.
Price: **$830.00**

SMITH & WESSON MODEL SD9
Caliber: .40 S&W and 9mm, 10+1, 14+1 and 16+1 round capacities.
Barrel: 4. **Weight:** 39 oz. **Length:** 8.7. **Grips:** Wood or rubber.
Sights: Front: Tritium Night Sight, Rear: Steel Fixed 2-Dot.
Features: SDT™ - Self Defense Trigger for optimal, consistent pull first round to Last, standard picatinny-style rail, slim ergonomic textured grip, textured finger locator and aggressive front and back strap texturing with front and rear slide serrations.
Price: 9mm Std. Capacity **$459.00**
Price: 9mm Low Capacity **$459.00**
Price: .40 S&W Std. Capacity............................... **$459.00**
Price: .40 S&W Low Capacity.............................. **$459.00**

SMITH & WESSON MODEL SW1911
Caliber: .45 ACP, 9mm. **Magazine capacity:** 8 rounds (.45), 7 rounds (sub compact .45), 10 rounds (9mm). **Barrel:** 3, 4.25, 5 inches. **Weight:** 26.5 to 41.7 oz. **Length:** 6.9 to 8.7 inches. **Grips:** Wood, wood laminate or synthetic. Crimson Trace Lasergrips available. **Sights:** Low profile white dot, tritium night sights or adjustable. **Finish:** Black matte, stainless or two-tone. **Features:** Offered in three different frame sizes. Skeletonized trigger. Accessory rail on some models. Compact models have round butt frame. Pro Series have 30 lpi checkered front strap, oversized external extractor,

extended mag well, full-length guide rod, ambidextrous safety.
Price: Standard model .... **$919.00 to $1,319.00**
Price: Compact SC series .... **$1,369.00 to $1,389.00**
Price: Crimson Trace grips **$1,454.00**
Price: Pro Series .... **$1,159.00 to $1,519.00**

SMITH & WESSON ENHANCED SIGMA SERIES DAO
Caliber: 9mm Para., 40 S&W; 10-, 16-shot magazine. **Barrel:** 4. **Weight:** 24.7 oz. **Length:** 7.25 overall. **Grips:** Integral. **Sights:** White dot front, fixed rear; 3-dot system. Tritium night sights available. **Features:** Ergonomic polymer frame; low barrel centerline; internal striker firing system; corrosion-resistant slide; Teflon-filled, electroless-nickel coated magazine, equipment rail. Introduced 1994. Made in U.S.A. by Smith & Wesson.
Price: From **$482.00**

SMITH & WESSON BODYGUARD® 380
Caliber: .380 Auto, 6+1 round capacity. **Barrel:** 2.75. **Weight:** 11.85 oz. **Length:** 5.25. **Grips:** Polymer. **Sights:** Integrated laser sights with front: stainless steel, rear: drift adjustable. **Features:** The frame of the Bodyguard is made of reinforced polymer, as is the magazine base plate and follower, magazine catch, and the trigger. The slide, sights, and guide rod are made of stainless steel, with the slide and sights having a Melonite hard coating.
Price: **$399.00**

SPRINGFIELD ARMORY EMP ENHANCED MICRO
Caliber: 9mm Para., 40 S&W; 9-round magazine. **Barrel:** 3 stainless steel match grade, fully supported ramp, bull. **Weight:** 26 oz. **Length:** 6.5 overall. **Grips:** Thinline cocobolo hardwood. **Sights:** Fixed low profile combat rear, dovetail front, 3-dot tritium. **Features:** Two 9-round stainless steel magazines with slam pads, long aluminum match-grade trigger adjusted to 5 to 6 lbs., forged aluminum alloy frame, black hardcoat anodized; dual spring full-length guide rod, forged satin-finish stainless steel slide. Introduced 2007. From Springfield Armory.
Price: 9mm Para. Compact Bi-Tone **$1,329.00**
Price: 40 S&W Compact Bi-Tone (2008)............................**$1,329.00**

Prices given are believed to be accurate at time of publication however, many factors affect retail pricing so exact prices are not possible.

68TH EDITION, 2014 ✦ **419**

Price:	Sub-Compact OD Green 9mm Para./40 S&W, fixed sights	$543.00
Price:	Compact 45 ACP, 4 barrel, Bi-Tone finish (2008)	$589.00
Price:	Compact 45 ACP, 4 barrel, OD green frame, stainless slide (2008)	$653.00
Price:	Service Black 9mm Para./40 S&W, fixed sights	$543.00
Price:	Service Dark Earth 45 ACP, fixed sights	$571.00
Price:	Service Black 45 ACP, external thumb safety (2008)	$571.00
Price:	V-10 Ported Black 9mm Para./40 S&W	$573.00
Price:	Tactical Black 45 ACP, fixed sights	$616.00
Price:	Service Bi-Tone 40 S&W, Trijicon night sights (2008)	$695.00

SPRINGFIELD ARMORY XD POLYMER

Caliber: 9mm Para., 40 S&W, 45 ACP. **Barrel:** 3, 4, 5. **Weight:** 20.5-31 oz. **Length:** 6.26-8 overall. **Grips:** Textured polymer. **Sights:** Varies by model; Fixed sights are dovetail front and rear steel 3-dot units. **Features:** Three sizes in X-Treme Duty (XD) line: Sub-Compact (3 barrel), Service (4 barrel), Tactical (5 barrel). Three ported models available. Ergonomic polymer frame, hammer-forged barrel, no-tool disassembly, ambidextrous magazine release, visual/tactile loaded chamber indicator, visual/tactile striker status indicator, grip safety, XD gear system included. Introduced 2004. XD 45 introduced 2006. Compact line introduced 2007. Compacts ship with one extended magazine (13) and one compact magazine (10). From Springfield Armory.

SPRINGFIELD ARMORY XDM SERIES

Calibers: 9mm, .40 S&W, .45 ACP. **Barrel:** 3.8 or 4.5". **Sights:** Fiber optic front with interchangeable red and green filaments, adjustable target rear. **Grips:** Integral polymer with three optional backstrap designs. **Features:** Variation of XD design with improved ergonomics, deeper and longer slide serrations, slightly modified grip contours and texturing. Black polymer frame, forged steel slide. Black and two-tone finish options.
Price: .... **$697.00 to $732.00**

SPRINGFIELD ARMORY XD-S

Caliber: 9mm, .45 ACP. Same features as XDM except has single-stack magazine for thinner profile. **Capacity:** 7 rounds (9mm), 5 rounds (.45). An extra extended-length magazine is included (10 rounds, 9mm; 7 rounds, .45). **Barrel:** 3.3 inches. **Weight:** 21.5 oz. **Features:** Black or two-tone finish.
Price: (two-tone) .... **$599.00 to $669.00**

Prices given are believed to be accurate at time of publication however, many factors affect retail pricing so exact prices are not possible.

SPRINGFIELD ARMORY GI 45 1911A1
Caliber: 45 ACP; 6-, 7-, 13-shot magazines. **Barrel:** 3, 4, 5. **Weight:** 28-36 oz. **Length:** 5.5-8.5 overall. **Grips:** Checkered double-diamond walnut, "U.S" logo. **Sights:** Fixed GI style. **Features:** Similar to WWII GI-issue 45s at hammer, beavertail, mainspring housing. From Springfield Armory.
Price: GI .45 4 Champion Lightweight, 7+1, 28 oz. $619.00
Price: GI .45 5 High Capacity, 13+1, 36 oz. $676.00
Price: GI .45 5 OD Green, 7+1, 36 oz. $619.00
Price: GI .45 3 Micro Compact, 6+1, 32 oz. $667.00

SPRINGFIELD ARMORY MIL-SPEC 1911A1
Caliber: 38 Super, 9-shot magazines; 45 ACP, 7-shot magazines. **Barrel:** 5. **Weight:** 35.6-39 oz. **Length:** 8.5-8.625 overall. **Features:** Similar to GI 45s. From Springfield Armory.
Price: Mil-Spec Parkerized, 7+1, 35.6 oz. $715.00
Price: Mil-Spec Stainless Steel, 7+1, 36 oz. $784.00
Price: Mil-Spec 38 Super, 9+1, 39 oz. $775.00

SPRINGFIELD ARMORY CUSTOM LOADED CHAMPION 1911A1
Similar to standard 1911A1, slide and barrel are 4. 7.5 OAL. Available in 45 ACP only. Novak Night Sights. Delta hammer and coco-bolo grips. Parkerized or stainless. Introduced 1989.
Price: Stainless, 34 oz. $1,031.00
Price: Lightweight, 28 oz. $989.00

SPRINGFIELD ARMORY CUSTOM LOADED ULTRA COMPACT
Similar to 1911A1 Compact, shorter slide, 3.5 barrel, 6+1, 7 OAL. Beavertail grip safety, beveled magazine well, fixed sights. Videki speed trigger, flared ejection port, stainless steel frame, blued slide, match grade barrel, rubber grips. Introduced 1996. From Springfield Armory.
Price: Stainless Steel $1,031.00

SPRINGFIELD ARMORY CUSTOM LOADED MICRO-COMPACT 1911A1
Caliber: 45 ACP, 6+1 capacity. **Barrel:** 3 1:16 LH. **Weight:** 24-32 oz. **Length:** 4.7. **Grips:** Slimline cocobolo. **Sights:** Novak LoMount tritium. Dovetail front. **Features:** Aluminum hard-coat anodized alloy frame, forged steel slide, forged barrel, ambi-thumb safety, Extreme Carry Bevel dehorning. Lockable plastic case, 2 magazines.
Price: Lightweight Bi-Tone $992.00

SPRINGFIELD ARMORY CUSTOM LOADED LONG SLIDE 1911A1
Caliber: 45 ACP, 7+1 capacity. **Barrel:** 6 1:16 LH. **Weight:** 41 oz. **Length:** 9.5. **Grips:** Slimline cocobolo. **Sights:** Dovetail front; fully adjustable target rear. **Features:** Longer sight radius. 7.9.
Price: Bi-Tone Operator w/light rail $1,189.00

SPRINGFIELD ARMORY TACTICAL RESPONSE
Similar to 1911A1 except 45 ACP only, checkered front strap and main-spring housing, Novak Night Sight combat rear sight and matching dove-tailed front sight, tuned, polished extractor, oversize barrel link; lightweight speed trigger and combat action job, match barrel and bushing, extended ambidextrous thumb safety and fitted beavertail grip safety. Checkered cocobolo wood grips, comes with two Wilson 7-shot magazines. Frame is engraved "Tactical" both sides of frame with "TRP." Introduced 1998. TRP-Pro Model meets FBI specifications for SWAT Hostage Rescue Team. From Springfield Armory.
Price: 45 TRP Service Model, black Armory Kote finish, fixed Trijicon night sights $1,741.00

STOEGER COMPACT COUGAR
Caliber: 9mm, 13+1 round capacity. **Barrel:** 3.6. **Weight:** 32 oz. **Length:** 7. **Grips:** Wood or rubber. **Sights:** Quick read 3-dot. **Features:** Double/single action with a Bruniton® Matte black finish. The ambidextrous safety and decocking lever is easily accessible to the thumb of a right-handed or left-handed shooter.
Price: $449.00

STI DUTY ONE
1911-style semiauto pistol chambered in .45 ACP. Features include government size frame with integral tactical rail and 30 lpi checkered frontstrap; milled tactical rail on the dust cover of the frame; ambidextrous thumb safeties; high rise beavertail grip safety; lowered and flared ejection port; fixed rear sight; front and rear cocking serrations; 5-inch fully supported STI International ramped bull barrel.
Price: $1312.00

STI EAGLE
1911-style semiauto pistol chambered in .45 ACP, 9mm, .40 S&W. Features include modular steel frame with polymer grip; high capacity doule-stack magazines; scalloped slide with front and rear cocking serrations; dovetail front sight and STI adjustable rear

sight; stainless steel STI hi-ride grip safety and stainless steel STI ambi-thumb safety; 5- or 6-inch STI stainless steel fully supported, ramped bull barrel or the traditional bushing barrel; blued or stainless finish.
Price: **$1,964.00**

STI TOTAL ECLIPSE
Compact 1911-tyle semiauto pistol chambered in 9x19, .40 S&W, and .45 ACP. Features include 3-inch slide with rear cocking serrations, oversized ejection port; 2-dot tritium night sights recessed into the slide; high-capacity polymer grip; single sided blued thumb safety; bobbed, high-rise, blued, knuckle relief beavertail grip safety; 3-inch barrel.
Price: **$1,843.00**

STI ESCORT
Similar to STI Eclipse but with aluminum allow frame and chambered in .45 ACP only.
Price: **$1,185.00**

TAURUS MODEL 800 SERIES
Caliber: 9mm Para., 40 S&W, 45 ACP. **Barrel:** 4. **Weight:** 32 oz. **Length:** 8.25. **Grips:** Checkered. **Sights:** Novak. **Features:** DA/SA. Blue and Stainless Steel finish. Introduced in 2007. Imported from Brazil by Taurus International.
Price: 809B, 9mm Para., Blue, 17+1 ....**$623.00**

TAURUS MODEL 1911
Caliber: 45 ACP, 8+1 capacity. **Barrel:** 5. **Weight:** 33 oz. **Length:** 8.5. **Grips:** Checkered black. **Sights:** Heinie straight 8. **Features:** SA. Blue, stainless steel, duotone blue, and blue/gray finish. Standard/picatinny rail, standard frame, alloy frame, and alloy/picatinny rail. Introduced in 2007. Imported from Brazil by Taurus International.
Price: 1911B, Blue **$719.00**
Price: 1911SS, Stainless Steel **$816.00**
Price: 1911SS-1, Stainless Steel **$847.00**
Price: 1911 DT, Duotone Blue **$795.00**

TAURUS MODEL PT-22/PT-25
Caliber: 22 LR, 8-shot (PT-22); 25 ACP, 9-shot (PT-25). **Barrel:** 2.75. **Weight:** 12.3 oz. **Length:** 5.25 overall. **Grips:** Smooth rosewood

or mother-of-pearl. **Sights:** Fixed. **Features:** Double action. Tip-up barrel for loading, cleaning. Blue, nickel, duo-tone or blue with gold accents. Introduced 1992. Made in U.S.A. by Taurus International.
Price: PT-22B or PT-25B, checkered wood grips...**$248.00**

TAURUS PT2011 DT
Caliber: 9mm, .40 S&W. **Magazine capacity:** 9mm (13 rounds), .40 S&W (11 rounds). **Barrel:** 3.2 inches. **Weight:** 24 oz. **Features:** Single/double-action with trigger safety.
Price: **$589.00**
Price: (stainless) **$605.00**

TAURUS MODEL 22PLY SMALL POLYMER FRAME
Similar to Taurus Models PT-22 and PT-25 but with lightweight polymer frame. Features include 22 LR (9+1) or 25 ACP (8+1) chambering. 2.33 tip-up barrel, matte black finish, extended magazine with finger lip, manual safety. Overall length is 4.8. Weighs 10.8 oz.
Price: **$273.00**

TAURUS MODEL 24/7
Caliber: 9mm Para., 40 S&W, 45 ACP. **Barrel:** 4. **Weight:** 27.2 oz. **Length:** 7-1/8. **Grips:** "Ribber" rubber-finned overlay on polymer. **Sights:** Adjustable. **Features:** SA/DA; accessory rail, four safeties, blue or stainless finish. One-piece guide rod, flush-fit magazine, flared bushingless barrel, Picatinny accessory rail, manual safety, user changeable sights, loaded chamber indicator, tuned ejector and lowered port, one piece guide rod and flat wound captive spring. Introduced 2003. Long Slide models have 5 barrels, measure 8-1/8" overall, weigh 27.2 oz. Imported from Brazil by Taurus International.
Price: 40BP, 40 S&W, blued, 10+1 or 15+1 ....**$452.00**
Price: 24/7-PRO Standard Series: 4" barrel; stainless, duotone or blued finish **$452.00**
Price: 24/7-PRO Compact Series; 3.2" barrel; stainless, titanium or blued finish **$467.00**
Price: 24/7-PRO Long Slide Series: 5.2" barrel; matte stainless, blued or stainless finish **$506.00**
Price: 24/7PLS, 5" barrel, chambered in 9mm Parabellum, 38 Super and 40 S&W **$506.00**

Prices given are believed to be accurate at time of publication however, many factors affect retail pricing so exact prices are not possible.

TAURUS 24/7 G2

Double/single action semiauto pistol chambered in 9mm Parabellum (15+1), .40 S&W (13+1), and .45 ACP (10+1). Features include blued or stainless finish; "Strike Two" capability; new trigger safety; low-profile adjustable rear sights for windage and elevation; ambidextrous magazine release; 4.2 inch barrel; Picatinny rail; polymer frame; polymer grip with metallic inserts and three interchangeable backstraps. Also offered in compact model with shorter grip frame and 3.5-inch barrel.
Price: **$523.00**

TAURUS MODEL 92

Caliber: 9mm Para., 10- or 17-shot mags. **Barrel:** 5. **Weight:** 34 oz. **Length:** 8.5 overall. **Grips:** Checkered rubber, rosewood, mother-of-pearl. **Sights:** Fixed notch rear. 3-dot sight system. Also offered with micrometer-click adjustable night sights. **Features:** Double action, ambidextrous 3-way hammer drop safety, allows cocked & locked carry. Blue, stainless steel, blue with gold highlights, stainless steel with gold highlights, forged aluminum frame, integral key-lock. .22 LR conversion kit available. Imported from Brazil by Taurus International.
Price: 92B **$542.00**
Price: 92SS **$559.00**

TAURUS MODEL 99

Similar to Model 92, fully adjustable rear sight.
Price: 99B **$559.00**

TAURUS MODEL 90

Similar to Model 92 but with one-piece wraparound grips, automatic disassembly latch, internal recoil buffer, addition slide serrations, picatinny rail with removable cover, 10- and 17-round magazine (9mm) or 10- and 12-round magazines (40 S&W). Overall length is 8.5". Weight is 32.5 oz.
Price: **$725.00**

TAURUS MODEL 100/101

Caliber: 40 S&W, 10- or 11-shot mags. **Barrel:** 5. **Weight:** 34 oz. **Length:** 8.5. **Grips:** Checkered rubber, rosewood, mother-of-pearl. **Sights:** 3-dot fixed or adjustable; night sights available. **Features:** Single/double action with three-position safety/decocker. Reintroduced in 2001. Imported by Taurus International.

Price: 100B **$542.00**

TAURUS MODEL 111 MILLENNIUM PRO

Caliber: 9mm Para., 10- or 12-shot mags. **Barrel:** 3.25. **Weight:** 18.7 oz. **Length:** 6-1/8 overall. **Grips:** Checkered polymer. **Sights:** 3-dot fixed; night sights available. Low profile, 3-dot combat. **Features:** Double action only, polymer frame, matte stainless or blue steel slide, manual safety, integral key-lock. Deluxe models with wood grip inserts.
Price: 111BP, 111BP-12 ....**$419.00**
Price: 111PTi titanium slide **$592.00**

TAURUS 138 MILLENNIUM PRO SERIES

Caliber: 380 ACP, 10- or 12-shot mags. **Barrel:** 3.25. **Weight:** 18.7 oz. **Grips:** Polymer. **Sights:** Fixed 3-dot fixed. **Features:** Double-action-only, polymer frame, matte stainless or blue steel slide, manual safety, integral key-lock.
Price: 138BP **$419.00**

TAURUS 140 MILLENNIUM PRO

Caliber: 40 S&W, 10-shot mag. **Barrel:** 3.25. **Weight:** 18.7 oz. **Grips:** Checkered polymer. **Sights:** 3-dot fixed; night sights available. **Features:** Double action only; matte stainless or blue steel slide, black polymer frame, manual safety, integral key-lock action. From Taurus International.
Price: 140BP..**$436.00**

TAURUS 145 MILLENNIUM PRO

Caliber: 45 ACP, 10-shot mag. **Barrel:** 0.27. **Weight:** 23 oz. **Stock:** Checkered polymer. **Sights:** 3-dot fixed; night sights available. **Features:** Double-action only, matte stainless or blue steel slide, black polymer frame, manual safety, integral key-lock. Compact model is 6+1 with a 3.25 barrel, weighs 20.8 oz. From Taurus International.
Price: 145BP, blued **$436.00**
Price: 145SSP, stainless, ...**$453.00**

TAURUS SLIM 700 SERIES

Compact double/single action semiauto pistol chambered in 9mm Parabellum (7+1), .40 S&W (6+1), and .380 ACP (7+1). Features include polymer frame; blue or stainless slide; single action/double action trigger pull; low-profile fixed sights. Weight 19 oz., length 6.24 inches, width less than an inch.

Price: .... N/A

TAURUS MODEL 709 G2 SLIM

Caliber: 9mm., 9+1-shot magazine. **Barrel:** 3. **Weight:** 19 oz. **Length:** 6.24 overall. **Grips:** Black. **Sights:** Low profile. **Features:** The most heralded concealed carry semi-auto in company history is getting even better with the G2 Slim. Even under the lightest clothing the Slim design reveals nothing. Now with the best in features and performance from the elite G2 series. Also, with the G2 Slim, there are extra rounds with an extended magazine for added confidence.

Price: $376.00

TAURUS MODEL 738 TCP COMPACT

Caliber: 380 ACP, 6+1 (standard magazine) or 8+1 (extended magazine). **Barrel:** 3.3. **Weight:** 9 oz. (titanium slide) to 10.2 oz. **Length:** 5.19". **Sights:** Low-profile fixed. **Features:** Lightweight DAO semi-auto with polymer frame; blued (738B), stainless (738SS) or titanium (738Ti) slide; concealed hammer; ambi safety; loaded chamber indicator.
Price: .... $623.00 to $686.00

TAURUS SLIM 740

Caliber: .380 ACP and .40 cal., 6+1/8+1-shot magazines. **Barrel:** 4. **Weight:** 19 oz. **Length:** 6.24 overall. **Grips:** Polymer Grips. **Features:** Double action with stainless steel finish. Remarkably lean, lightweight design, but it still steps up with big firepower.

Price: $483.00

TAURUS 800 SERIES COMPACT

Compact double/single action semiauto pistol chambered in 9mm (12+1), .357 SIG (10+1) and .40 cal (10+1). Features include 3.5-inch barrel; external hammer; loaded chamber indicator; polymer frame; blued or stainless slide.
Price: ....N/A

TAURUS 809 COMPACT

Caliber: 9mm, .357 SIG and .40 cal. 12+1 round capacity. **Barrel:** 3.5. **Grips:** Checkered Polymer. **Description:** Little brother of the 800 Series, these new pistols were born to perform. They give everything you could want in a 3.5" barrel semi-auto—the best in features, handling, speed and reliability.

Price: $555.00

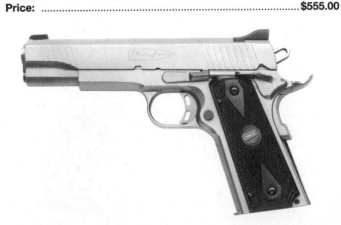

THOMPSON CUSTOM 1911A1

Caliber: 45 ACP, 7-shot magazine. **Barrel:** 4.3. **Weight:** 34 oz. **Length:** 8 overall. **Grips:** Checkered laminate grips with a Thompson bullet logo inlay. **Sights:** Front and rear sights are black with serrations and are dovetailed into the slide. **Features:**

Prices given are believed to be accurate at time of publication however, many factors affect retail pricing so exact prices are not possible.

Machined from 420 stainless steel, matte finish. Thompson bullet logo on slide. Flared ejection port, angled front and rear serrations on slide, 20-lpi checkered mainspring housing and frontstrap. Adjustable trigger, combat hammer, stainless steel full-length recoil guide rod, extended beavertail grip safety; extended magazine release; checkered slide-stop lever. Made in U.S.A. by Kahr Arms.
Price: 1911TC, 5", 39 oz., 8.5" overall, stainless frame **$813.00**

THOMPSON TA5 1927A-1 LIGHTWEIGHT DELUXE
Caliber: 45 ACP, 50-round drum magazine. **Barrel:** 10.5 1:16 right-hand twist. **Weight:** 94.5 oz. **Length:** 23.3 overall. **Grips:** Walnut, horizontal foregrip **Sights:** Blade front, open rear adjustable.
Features: Based on Thompson machine gun design. Introduced 2008. Made in U.S.A. by Kahr Arms.
Price: TA5 (2008).....................................**$1,237.00**

TRISTAR C-100
Caliber: 9mm, .40 S&W. **Magazine capacity:** 15 (9mm), 11 (.40).
Barrel: 3.9 inches. **Weight:** 26 oz. **Grips:** Checkered polymer.
Sights: Fixed. **Finish:** Blue or chrome. **Features:** Single/double action. Similar to CZ-75 design. Imported from Turkey.
Price: **$429.00**

TURNBULL MFG. CO. 1911 CENTENIAL
Features: Forged slide with appropriate shape and style. Proper size and shape of sights. Barrel of correct external contour. Safety lock is the thin style, with a knurled undercut thumb-piece. Short, wide spur hammer with standard checkering. Early style slide stop. Lanyard loop, punch and saw cut magazine, finished in two tone. Pistol is hand-polished in the same manner as an original early production vintage pistol. Period-correct Carbonia Charcoal Blueing on all parts. Stamped United States Property as original. Circled Turnbull trademark on left of slide behind serrations. Early 1913 patent markings and Turnbull Mfg. Co. Bloomfield, NY slide address. Model(s) of 1911 U.S. Army, U.S. Navy and U.S. Marine Corps variations are all available. Inspector's marks are available from Doug Turnbull (TMC Owner, founder) and Keith VanOrman (TMC President).
Price: **$3895.00**

WALTHER P99 AS
Caliber: 9mm, .40 S&W. Offered in two frame sizes, standard and compact. **Magazine capacity:** 15 or 10 rounds (9mm), 10 or 8 rounds (.40). **Barrel:** 3.5 or 4 inches. **Weight:** 21 to 26 oz. **Length:** 6.6 to 7.1 inches. **Grips:** Polymer with interchangeable backstrap inserts. **Sights:** Adjustable rear, blade front with three interchangeable inserts of different heights. **Features:** Double action with trigger safety, decocker, internal striker safety, loaded chamber indicator. Made in Germany.
Price: **$600.00**

WALTHER PK380
Caliber: .380 ACP (8-shot magazine). **Barrel:** 3.66". **Weight:** 19.4 oz. **Length:** 6.5". **Sights:** Three-dot system, drift adjustable rear.
Features: Double action with external hammer, ambidextrous mag release and manual safety. Picatinny rail.
Price: **$389.00**

WALTHER PPK
Caliber: .380 ACP. **Capacity:** 6+1. **Barrel:** 3.3 inches **Weight:** 22 oz. **Length:** 6.1 inches **Grips:** Checkered plastic. **Sights:** Fixed.
Features: Available in blue or stainless finish. Made in the U.S.A.
Price: **$630.00**

WALTHER PPK/S

Prices given are believed to be accurate at time of publication however, many factors affect retail pricing so exact prices are not possible.

68TH EDITION, 2014 ◆ **425**

WALTHER PPK/S

Caliber: .22 LR or .380 ACP. **Capacity:** 10+1 (.22), 7+1 (.380). Made in Germany. **Features:** identical to PPK except for grip length and magazine capacity.
Price: (.380) **$630.00**
Price: (.22 blue) **$400.00**
Price: (.22 stainless) **$430.00**

WALTHER PPQ

Caliber: 9mm, .40 S&W (12-shot magazine). **Barrel:** 4.2". **Weight:** 24.9 oz. **Length:** 7.2". **Sights:** Drift adjustable. **Features:** Quick Defense trigger, firing pin blck, ambidextrous slide lock and mag release, Picatinny rail. Comes with two extra magazines, two interchangeable frame backstraps and hard case.
Price: **$599.00**

WALTHER PPS

Caliber: 9mm Para., 40 S&W. 6-, 7-, 8-shot magazines for 9mm Para.; 5-, 6-, 7-shot magazines for 40 S&W. **Barrel:** 3.2. **Weight:** 19.4 oz. **Length:** 6.3 overall. **Stocks:** Stippled black polymer. **Sights:** Picatinny-style accessory rail, 3-dot low-profile contoured sight. **Features:** PPS-"Polizeipistole Schmal," or Police Pistol Slim. Measures 1.04 inches wide. Ships with 6- and 7-round magazines. Striker-fired action, flat slide stop lever, alternate backstrap sizes. QuickSafe feature decocks striker assembly when backstrap is removed. Loaded chamber indicator. First Edition model, limited to 1,000 units, has anthracite grey finish, aluminum gun case. Introduced 2008.
Price: **$600.00**

WALTHER PPX

Caliber: 9mm, .40 S&W. **Capacity:** 16 rounds (9mm), 14 rounds (.40). **Barrel:** 4 inches. **Weight:** 27.2 oz. **Length:** 7.3 inches. **Grips:** Textured polymer integral with frame. **Sights:** Fixed. **Finish:** Black or black/stainless two-tone. Threaded barrel is optional.
Price: **$449.00**
Price: (threaded barrel) **$499.00**

WALTHER P22

Caliber: 22 LR. **Barrel:** 3.4, 5. **Weight:** 19.6 oz. (3.4), 20.3 oz. (5). **Length:** 6.26, 7.83. **Grips:** NA. **Sights:** Interchangeable white dot, front, 2-dot adjustable, rear. **Features:** A rimfire version of the Walther P99 pistol, available in nickel slide with black frame, or green frame with black slide versions.
Price: From **$362.00**

WILSON COMBAT ELITE PROFESSIONAL

Caliber: 9mm Para., 38 Super, 40 S&W; 45 ACP, 8-shot magazine. **Barrel:** Compensated 4.1 hand-fit, heavy flanged cone match grade. **Weight:** 36.2 oz. **Length:** 7.7 overall. **Grips:** Cocobolo. **Sights:** Combat Tactical yellow rear tritium inserts, brighter green tritium front insert. **Features:** High-cut front strap, 30-lpi checkering on front strap and flat mainspring housing, High-Ride Beavertail grip safety. Dehorned, ambidextrous thumb safety, extended ejector, skeletonized ultralight hammer, ultralight trigger, Armor-Tuff finish on frame and slide. Introduced 1997. Made in U.S.A. by Wilson Combat. This manufacturer offers more than 100 different 1911 models ranging in price from about $2800 to $5000.
Price: From **$3,650.00**

Prices given are believed to be accurate at time of publication however, many factors affect retail pricing so exact prices are not possible.

BAER 1911 ULTIMATE MASTER COMBAT

Caliber: 38 Super, 400 Cor-Bon 45 ACP (others available), 10-shot magazine. **Barrel:** 5, 6; Baer NM. **Weight:** 37 oz. **Length:** 8.5 overall. **Grips:** Checkered cocobolo. **Sights:** Baer dovetail front, low-mount Bo-Mar rear with hidden leaf. **Features:** Full-house competition gun. Baer forged NM blued steel frame and double serrated slide; Baer triple port, tapered cone compensator; fitted slide to frame; lowered, flared ejection port; Baer reverse recoil plug; full-length guide rod; recoil buff; beveled magazine well; Baer Commander hammer, sear; Baer extended ambidextrous safety, extended ejector, checkered slide stop, beavertail grip safety with pad, extended magazine release button; Baer speed trigger. Made in U.S.A. by Les Baer Custom, Inc.
Price: 45 ACP Compensated $2,880.00
Price: 38 Super Compensated $3,140.00

BAER 1911 NATIONAL MATCH HARDBALL

Caliber: 45 ACP, 7-shot magazine. **Barrel:** 5. **Weight:** 37 oz. **Length:** 8.5 overall. **Grips:** Checkered walnut. **Sights:** Baer dovetail front with under-cut post, low-mount Bo-Mar rear with hidden leaf. **Features:** Baer NM forged steel frame, double serrated slide and barrel with stainless bushing; slide fitted to frame; Baer match trigger with 4-lb. pull; polished feed ramp, throated barrel; checkered front strap, arched mainspring housing; Baer beveled magazine well; lowered, flared ejection port; tuned extractor; Baer extended ejector, checkered slide stop; recoil buff. Made in U.S.A. by Les Baer Custom, Inc.
Price: $1,960.00

BAER 1911 PPC OPEN CLASS

Designed for NRA Police Pistol Combat matches. **Caliber:** .45 ACP, 9mm. **Barrel:** 6 inches, fitted to frame. **Sights:** Adjustable PPC rear, dovetail front. **Grips:** Checkered cocobola. **Features:** Lowered and flared ejection port, extended ejector, polished feed ramp, throated barrel, front strap checkered at 30 lpi, flat serrated mainspring housing, Commander hammer, front and rear slide serrations. 9mm has supported chamber.
Price: $2,350.00

BAER 1911 BULLSEYE WADCUTTER

Similar to National Match Hardball except designed for wadcutter loads only. Polished feed ramp and barrel throat; Bo-Mar rib on slide; full length recoil rod; Baer speed trigger with 3-1/2-lb. pull; Baer deluxe hammer and sear; Baer beavertail grip safety with pad; flat mainspring housing checkered 20 lpi. Blue finish; checkered walnut grips. Made in U.S.A. by Les Baer Custom, Inc.
Price: From $2,140.00

COLT GOLD CUP TROPHY

Caliber: 45 ACP, 8-shot + 1 magazine. **Barrel:** 5. **Weight:** NA. **Length:** 8.5. **Grips:** Checkered rubber composite with silver-plated medallion. **Sights:** (O5070X) Dovetail front, Champion rear; (O5870CS) Patridge Target Style front, Champion rear. **Features:** Adjustable aluminum trigger, Beavertail grip safety, full length recoil spring and target recoil spring, available in blued finish and stainless steel.
Price: (blued) $1,158.00
Price: (stainless) $1,180.00

COLT SPECIAL COMBAT GOVERNMENT

Caliber: 45 ACP, 38 Super. **Barrel:** 5. **Weight:** 39 oz. **Length:** 8.5. **Grips:** Rosewood w/double diamond checkering pattern. **Sights:** Clark dovetail, front; Bo-Mar adjustable, rear. **Features:** A competition-ready pistol with enhancements such as skeletonized trigger, upswept grip safety, custom tuned action, polished feed ramp. Blue or satin nickel finish. Introduced 2003. Made in U.S.A. by Colt's Mfg. Co.
Price: $1,995.00

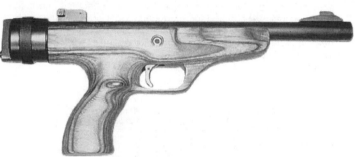

COMPETITOR SINGLE-SHOT

Caliber: 22 LR through 50 Action Express, including belted magnums. **Barrel:** 14 standard; 10.5 silhouette; 16 optional. **Weight:** About 59 oz. (14 bbl.). **Length:** 15.12 overall. **Grips:** Ambidextrous; synthetic (standard) or laminated or natural wood. **Sights:** Ramp front, adjustable rear. **Features:** Rotary cannon-type action cocks on opening; cammed ejector; interchangeable barrels, ejectors. Adjustable single stage trigger, sliding thumb safety and trigger safety. Matte blue finish. Introduced 1988. From Competitor Corp., Inc.
Price: 14, standard calibers, synthetic grip $660.00

CZ 75 TS CZECHMATE

Prices given are believed to be accurate at time of publication however, many factors affect retail pricing so exact prices are not possible.

68TH EDITION, 2014 ⊕ **427**

CZ 75 TS CZECHMATE

Caliber: 9mm Luger, 20-shot magazine. **Barrel:** 130mm.
Weight: 1360 g **Length:** 266 mm overall. **Features:** The handgun is custom-built, therefore the quality of workmanship is fully comparable with race pistols built directly to IPSC shooters wishes. Individual parts and components are excellently match fitted, broke-in and tested. Every handgun is outfitted with a four-port compensator, nut for shooting without a compensator, the slide stop with an extended finger piece, the slide stop without a finger piece, ergonomic grip panels from aluminium with a new type pitting and side mounting provision with the C-More red dot sight. For the shooting without a red dot sight there is included a standard target rear sight of Tactical Sports type, package contains also the front sight.
Price: **$3,000.00**

CZ 75 TACTICAL SPORTS

Caliber: 9mm Luger and .40 S&W, 17-20-shot magazine capacity.
Barrel: 114mm. **Weight:** 1270 g **Length:** 225 mm overall. **Features:** semi-automatic handgun with a locked breech. This pistol model is designed for competition shooting in accordance with world IPSC (International Practical Shooting Confederation) rules and regulations. The pistol allow rapid and accurate shooting within a very short time frame.The CZ 75 TS pistol model design stems from the standard CZ 75 model. However, this model feature number of special modifications, which are usually required for competitive handguns: - single-action trigger mechanism (SA) - match trigger made of plastic featuring option for trigger travel adjustments before discharge (using upper screw), and for overtravel (using bottom screw). The adjusting screws are set by the manufacturer - sporting hammer specially adapted for a reduced trigger pull weight - an extended magazine catch - grip panels made of walnut wood - guiding funnel made of plastic for quick inserting of the magazine into pistol's frame. Glossy blue slide, silver polycoat frame. Packaging includes 3 pcs of magazines.
Price: **$1,272.00**

CZ 85 COMBAT

Caliber: 9mm Luger, 16-shot magazine. **Barrel:** 114mm. **Weight:** 1000 g **Length:** 206 mm overall. **Features:** The CZ 85 Combat modification was created as an extension to the CZ 85 model in its standard configuration with some additional special elements. The rear sight is adjustable for elevation and windage, and the trigger for overtravel regulation. An extended magazine catch, elimination of the magazine brake and ambidextrous controlling elements directly predispose this model for sport shooting competitions. Characteristic features of all versions A universal handgun for both left-handers and right-handers,. The selective SA/DA firing mechanism, a large capacity double-column magazine, a comfortable grip and balance in either hand lead to good results at instinctive shooting (without aiming). Low trigger pull weight and high accuracy of fire. A long service life and outstanding reliability - even when using various types of cartridges. The slide stays open after the last cartridge has been fired, suitable for COMBAT shooting. The sights are fitted with a three-dot illuminating system for better aiming in poor visibility conditions. The COMBAT version features an adjustable rear sight by means of micrometer screws.
Price: **$615.00**

DAN WESSON HAVOC

Caliber: 9mm Luger & .38 Super, 21-shot magazine capacity. **Barrel:** 4.25". **Weight:** 2.20 lbs. **Length:** 8" overall. **Features:** The HAVOC is based on an "All Steel" Hi-capacity version of the 1911 frame. It comes ready to dominate Open IPSC/USPSA division. The C-more mounting system offers the lowest possible mounting configuration possible, enabling extremely fast target acquisition. The barrel and compensator arrangement pairs the highest level of accuracy with the most effective compensator available. The combination of the all steel frame with industry leading parts delivers the most well balanced, softest shooting Open gun on the market.
Price: **$4,299.00**

DAN WESSON MAYHEM

Caliber: .40 S&W, 18-shot magazine capacity. **Barrel:** 6". **Weight:** 2.42 lbs. **Length:** 8.75" overall. **Features:** The MAYHEM is based on an "All Steel" Hi-capacity version of the 1911 frame. It comes ready to dominate Limited IPSC/USPSA division or fulfill the needs of anyone looking for a superbly accurate target grade 1911. Taking weight away from where you don't want it and adding it to where you do want it was the first priority in designing this handgun. The 6" bull barrel and the tactical rail add to the static weight "good weight". We wanted a 6" long slide for the added sight radius and the enhanced pointability, but that would add to the "bad weight" so the 6" slide has been lightened to equal the weight of a 5". The result is a 6" long slide that balances and feels like a 5" but shoots like a 6". The combination of the all steel frame with industry leading parts delivers the most well balanced, softest shooting 6" limited gun on the market.
Price: **$3,899.00**

DAN WESSON TITAN

Caliber: 10mm, 21-shot magazine capacity. **Barrel:** 4.25". **Weight:** 1.62 lbs. **Length:** 8" overall. **Features:** The TITAN is based on an "All Steel" Hi-capacity version of the 1911 frame. Turning the most well known defensive pistol "1911" into a true combat handgun was no easy task. The rugged HD night sights are moved forward and recessed deep in the slide yielding target accuracy and extreme durability. The Snake Scale serrations' aggressive 25 lpi checkering, and the custom competition G-10 grips ensure controllability even in the harshest of conditions. The combination of the all steel frame, bull barrel, and tactical rail enhance the balance and durability of the most formidable target grade Combat handgun on the market.
Price: **$3,829.00**

EAA WITNESS ELITE
GOLD TEAM

Prices given are believed to be accurate at time of publication however, many factors affect retail pricing so exact prices are not possible.

EAA WITNESS ELITE GOLD TEAM

Caliber: 9mm Para., 9x21, 38 Super, 40 S&W, 45 ACP. **Barrel:** 5.1. **Weight:** 44 oz. **Length:** 10.5 overall. **Grips:** Checkered walnut, competition-style. **Sights:** Square post front, fully adjustable rear. **Features:** Triple-chamber cone compensator; competition SA trigger; extended safety and magazine release; competition hammer; beveled magazine well; beavertail grip. Hand-fitted major components. Hard chrome finish. Match-grade barrel. From F.A.A. Custom Shop. Introduced 1992. Limited designed for IPSC Limited Class competition. Features include full-length dust-cover frame, funneled magazine well, interchangeable front sights. Stock (2005) designed for IPSC Production Class competition. Match introduced 2006. Made in Italy, imported by European American Armory.

Price: Gold Team $2,145.00
Price: Limited, 4.5 barrel, 18+1 capacity $1,216.00
Price: Stock, 4.5 barrel, hard-chrome finish $1,013.00
Price: Match, 4.75 barrel, two-tone finish............................... $714.00

FREEDOM ARMS MODEL 83 22 FIELD GRADE SILHOUETTE CLASS

Caliber: 22 LR, 5-shot cylinder. **Barrel:** 10. **Weight:** 63 oz. **Length:** 15.5 overall. **Grips:** Black micarta. **Sights:** Removable Patridge front blade; Iron Sight Gun Works silhouette rear, click adjustable for windage and elevation (optional adj. front sight and hood). **Features:** Stainless steel, matte finish, manual sliding-bar safety system; dual firing pins, lightened hammer for fast lock time, pre-set trigger stop. Introduced 1991. Made in U.S.A. by Freedom Arms.

Price: Silhouette Class $2,376.00

FREEDOM ARMS MODEL 83 CENTERFIRE SILHOUETTE MODELS

Caliber: 357 Mag., 41 Mag., 44 Mag.; 5-shot cylinder. **Barrel:** 10, 9 (357 Mag. only). **Weight:** 63 oz. (41 Mag.). **Length:** 15.5, 14.5 (357 only). **Grips:** Pachmayr Presentation. **Sights:** Iron Sight Gun Works silhouette rear sight, replaceable adjustable front sight blade with hood. **Features:** Stainless steel, matte finish, manual sliding-bar safety system. Made in U.S.A. by Freedom Arms.

Price: Silhouette Models, from $2,091.00

HIGH STANDARD SUPERMATIC TROPHY TARGET

Caliber: 22 LR, 9-shot mag. **Barrel:** 5.5 bull or 7.25 fluted. **Weight:** 44-46 oz. **Length:** 9.5-11.25 overall. **Stock:** Checkered hardwood with thumbrest. **Sights:** Undercut ramp front, frame-mounted micro-click rear adjustable for windage and elevation; drilled and tapped for scope mounting. **Features:** Gold-plated trigger, slide lock, safety-lever and magazine release; stippled front grip and backstrap; adjustable trigger and sear. Barrel weights optional. From High Standard Manufacturing Co., Inc.

Price: 5.5 barrel, adjustable sights $935.00
Price: 7.25, adjustable sights $985.00

HIGH STANDARD VICTOR TARGET

Caliber: 22 LR, 10-shot magazine. **Barrel:** 4.5 or 5.5 polished blue; push-button takedown. **Weight:** 46 oz. **Length:** 9.5 overall. **Stock:** Checkered walnut with thumbrest. **Sights:** Undercut ramp front, micro-click rear adjustable for windage and elevation. Also available with scope mount, rings, no sights. **Features:** Stainless steel frame. Full-length vent rib. Gold-plated trigger, slide lock, safety-lever and magazine release; stippled front grip and backstrap; polished blue slide; adjustable trigger and sear. Comes with barrel weight. From High Standard Manufacturing Co., Inc.

Price: 4.5 or 5.5 barrel, vented sight rib, universal scope base $935.00

KIMBER SUPER MATCH II

Caliber: 45 ACP, 8-shot magazine. **Barrel:** 5. **Weight:** 38 oz. **Length:** 8.7 overall. **Grips:** Rosewood double diamond. **Sights:** Blade front, Kimber fully adjustable rear. **Features:** Guaranteed shoot 1 group at 25 yards. Stainless steel frame, black KimPro slide; two-piece magazine well; premium aluminum match-grade trigger; 30 lpi front strap checkering; stainless match-grade barrel; ambidextrous safety; special Custom Shop markings. Introduced 1999. Made in U.S.A. by Kimber Mfg., Inc.

Price: $2,256.00

KIMBER RIMFIRE TARGET

Caliber: 22 LR, 10-shot magazine. **Barrel:** 5. **Weight:** 23 oz. **Length:** 8.7 overall. **Grips:** Rosewood, Kimber logo, double diamond checkering, or black synthetic double diamond. **Sights:** Blade front, Kimber fully adjustable rear. **Features:** Bumped beavertail grip safety, extended thumb safety, extended magazine release button. Serrated flat top slide with flutes, machined aluminum slide and frame, matte black or satin silver finishes, 30 lines-per-inch checkering on frontstrap and under trigger guard; aluminum trigger, test target, accuracy guarantee. No slide lock-open after firing the last round in the magazine. Introduced 1999. Made in U.S.A. by Kimber Mfg., Inc.

Price: $850.00

Prices given are believed to be accurate at time of publication however, many factors affect retail pricing so exact prices are not possible.

68TH EDITION, 2014 ✦ **429**

RUGER MARK III TARGET

Caliber: 22 LR, 10-shot magazine. **Barrel:** 5.5 to 6-7/8. **Weight:** 41 to 45 oz. **Length:** 9.75 to 11-1/8 overall. **Grips:** Checkered cocobolo/laminate. **Sights:** .125 blade front, micro-click rear, adjustable for windage and elevation, loaded chamber indicator; integral lock, magazine disconnect. Plastic case with lock included. Mark II series introduced 1982, discontinued 2004. Mark III introduced 2005.

Price: MKIII512 (bull barrel, blued) $449.00
Price: KMKIII512 (bull barrel, stainless) $559.00
Price: MKIII678 (blued Target barrel, 6-7/8) $449.00
Price: KMKIII678GC (stainless slabside barrel) $639.00
Price: KMKIII678H (stainless fluted barrel) $659.00

SMITH & WESSON MODEL 41 TARGET

Caliber: 22 LR, 10-shot clip. **Barrel:** 5.5, 7. **Weight:** 41 oz. (5.5 barrel). **Length:** 10.5 overall (5.5 barrel). **Grips:** Checkered walnut with modified thumbrest, usable with either hand. **Sights:** 1/8 Patridge on ramp base; micro-click rear adjustable for windage and elevation. **Features:** 3/8 wide, grooved trigger; adjustable trigger stop drilled and tapped.

Price: S&W Bright Blue, either barrel $1,579.00

SMITH & WESSON MODEL 22A

Caliber: 22 LR, 10-shot magazine. **Barrel:** 4, 5.5 bull. **Weight:** 28-39 oz. **Length:** 9.5 overall. **Grips:** Dymondwood with ambidextrous thumbrests and flared bottom or rubber soft touch with thumbrest. **Sights:** Patridge front, fully adjustable rear. **Features:** Sight bridge with Weaver-style integral optics mount; alloy frame, stainless barrel and slide; blue/black finish. Introduced 1997. The 22S is similar to the Model 22A except has stainless steel frame. Introduced 1997. Made in U.S.A. by Smith & Wesson.

Price: from $308.00
Price: Realtree APG camo finish (2008)...................$356.00

SPRINGFIELD ARMORY LEATHAM LEGEND TGO SERIES

Three models of 5 barrel, 45 ACP 1911 pistols built for serious competition. TGO 1 has deluxe low mount Bo-Mar rear sight, Dawson fiber optics front sight, 3.5 lb. trigger pull.

Price: TGO 1 ....$3,095.00

SPRINGFIELD ARMORY TROPHY MATCH

Similar to Springfield Armory's Full Size model, but designed for bullseye and action shooting competition. Available with a Service Model 5 frame with matching slide and barrel in 5 and 6 lengths. Fully adjustable sights, checkered frame front strap, match barrel and bushing. In 45 ACP only. From Springfield Inc.

Price: $1,573.00

STI APEIRO

1911-style semiauto pistol chambered in 9x19, .40 S&W, and .45 ACP. Features include Schuemann "Island" barrel; patented modular steel frame with polymer grip; high capacity double-stack magazine; stainless steel ambidextrous thumb safeties and knuckle relief high-rise beavertail grip safety; unique sabertooth rear cocking serrations; 5-inch fully ramped, fully supported "island" bull barrel, with the sight milled in to allow faster recovery to point of aim; custom engraving on the polished sides of the (blued) stainless steel slide; stainless steel magwell; STI adjustable rear sight and Dawson fiber optic front sight; blued frame.

Price: $2,805.00

STI EAGLE 5.0, 6.0

Caliber: 9mm Para., 9x21, 38 & 40 Super, 40 S&W, 10mm, 45 ACP, 10-shot magazine. **Barrel:** 5, 6 bull. **Weight:** 34.5 oz. **Length:** 8.62 overall. **Grips:** Checkered polymer. **Sights:** STI front, Novak or Heinie rear. **Features:** Standard frames plus 7 others; adjustable match trigger; skeletonized hammer; extended grip safety with locator pad. Introduced 1994. Made in U.S.A. by STI International.

Price: (5.0 Eagle) $1,985.00
Price: (6.0 Eagle) $2,100.00

STI EXECUTIVE

Caliber: 40 S&W. **Barrel:** 5 bull. **Weight:** 39 oz. **Length:** 8-5/8. **Grips:** Gray polymer. **Sights:** Dawson fiber optic, front; STI adjustable rear. **Features:** Stainless mag. well, front and rear serrations on slide. Made in U.S.A. by STI.

Price: $2,520.00

Prices given are believed to be accurate at time of publication however, many factors affect retail pricing so exact prices are not possible.

STI TROJAN
Caliber: 9mm Para., 38 Super, 40 S&W, 45 ACP. **Barrel:** 5, 6. **Weight:** 36 oz. **Length:** 8.5. **Grips:** Rosewood. **Sights:** STI front with STI adjustable rear.
Features: Stippled front strap, flat top slide, one-piece steel guide rod.
Price: (Trojan 5) $1,135.00
Price: (Trojan 6, not available in 38 Super) $1,455.00

STI TRUBOR
Caliber: 9mm 'Major', 9x23, .38 Super - USPSA, IPSC. **Barrel:** 5" with integrated compensator. **Weight:** 41.3 oz. (including scope and mount) **Length:** 10.5" overall. **Features:** Built on the patented modular steel frame with polymer grip, the STI Trubor utilizes the Trubor compensated barrel which is machined from ONE PIECE of 416, Rifle Grade, Stainless Steel. The Trubor is designed to eliminate misalignment of the barrel and compensator bore or movement of the compensator along the barrel threads, giving the shooter a more consistent performance and reduced muzzle flip. True to 1911 tradition, the Trubor has a classic scalloped slide with front and rear cocking serrations on a forged steel slide (blued) with polished sides, aluminum magwell, stainless steel ambidextrous safetles, stainless steel high rise grip safety, full length guide rod, checkered front strap, and checkered mainspring housing. With mountedC-More Railway sight included with the pistol.
Price: $2,930.00

STI STEELMASTER
Caliber: 9mm minor, comes with one 126mm magazine. **Barrel:** 4.15". **Weight:** 38.9 oz. **Length:** 9.5" overall. **Features:** Based on the renowned STI race pistol design, the SteelMaster is a shorter and lighter pistol that allows for faster target acquisition with reduced muzzle flip and dip. Designed to shoot factory 9mm (minor) ammo, this gun delivers all the advantages of a full size race pistol in a smaller, lighter, faster reacting, and less violent package. The Steelmaster is built on the patented modular steel frame with polymer grip. It has a 4.15" classic slide which has been flat topped. Slide lightening cuts on the front and rear further reduce weight while "Sabertooth" serrations further enhance the aesthtics of this superior pistol. It also uses the innovative Trubor compensated barrel which has been designed to eliminate misalignment of the barrel and compensator bore or movement of the compensator on the barrel. The shorter Trubor barrel system in the SteelMaster gives an even greater reduction in muzzle flip, and the shorter slide decreases overall slide cycle time allowing the shooter to achieve faster follow up shots. The SteelMaster is mounted with a C-More, 6-minute, red-dot scope with blast shield and thumb rest. Additional enhancements include aluminum magwell, stainless steel ambidextrous safetics, stainless steel high rise grip safety, STI's "Spur" hammer, STI's RecoilMaster guide rod system, and checkered front strap and mainspring housing.
Price: $2,930.00

CHARTER ARMS BULLDOG
Caliber: 44 Special. **Barrel:** 2.5. **Weight:** NA. **Sights:** Blade front, notch rear. **Features:** 6-round cylinder, soft-rubber pancake-style grips, shrouded ejector rod, wide trigger and hammer spur. American made by Charter Arms.
Price: Blued **$414.00**
Price: Stainless **$426.00**
Price: Target Bulldog, 4 barrel, 23 oz. **$479.00**
Price: Heller Commemortaive stainless 2.5 .... **$1595.00**

CHARTER ARMS CHIC LADY & CHIC LADY DAO
Caliber: .38 special - 5-round cylinder. **Barrel:** 2". **Weight:** 12 oz. **Grip:** Combat. **Sights:** Fixed. **Features:** 2-tone pink & stainless with aluminum frame. American made by Charter Arms.
Price: Chic Lady **$481.00**
Price: Chic Lady DAO **$492.00**

CHARTER COUGAR UNDERCOVER LITE
Caliber: .38 special +P - 5-round cylinder. **Barrel:** 2". **Weight:** 12 oz. **Grip:** Full. **Sights:** Fixed. **Features:** 2-tone pink & stainless with aluminum frame. Constructed of tough aircraft-grade aluminum and steel, the Undercover Lite offers rugged reliability and comfort. This ultra-lightweight 5-shot .38 Special features a 2" barrel, fixed sights and traditional spurred hammer. American made by Charter Arms.
Price: **$443.00**

CHARTER ARMS CRIMSON UNDERCOVER
Caliber: .38 special +P - 5-round cylinder. **Barrel:** 2". **Weight:** 16 oz. **Grip:** Crimson Trace™. **Sights:** Fixed. **Features:** Stainless finish & frame. American made by Charter Arms.
Price: **$525.00**

CHARTER ARMS OFF DUTY
Caliber: 38 Spec. **Barrel:** 2. **Weight:** 12.5 oz. **Sights:** Blade front, notch rear. **Features:** 5-round cylinder, aluminum casting, DAO. American made by Charter Arms.
Price: Aluminum **$410.00**

CHARTER ARMS MAG PUG
Caliber: 357 Mag. **Barrel:** 2.2. **Weight:** 23 oz. **Sights:** Blade front, notch rear. **Features:** Five-round cylinder. American made by Charter Arms.
Price: Blued or stainless **$400.00**

CHARTER PANTHER BRONZE & BLACK CAMO STANDARD
Caliber: .22 Mag.- 5-round cylinder. **Barrel:** 1-1/8". **Weight:** 6 oz. **Grip:** Compact. **Sights:** Fixed. **Features:** 2-tone bronze & black with aluminum frame. Constructed of tough aircraft-grade aluminum and steel, the Undercover Lite offers rugged reliability and comfort. This ultra-lightweight 5-shot .38 Special features a 2" barrel, fixed sights and traditional spurred hammer. American made by Charter Arms.
Price: **$443.00**

CHARTER ARMS PINK LADY
Caliber: 32 H&R Magnum, 38 Special +P. **Barrel:** 2. **Weight:** 12 oz. **Grips:** Rubber Pachmayr-style. **Sights:** Fixed. **Features:** Snubnose, five-round cylinder. Pink anodized aluminum alloy frame.
Price: **$422.00**
Price: Lavender Lady, lavender frame **$422.00**
Price: Goldfinger, gold anodized frame, matte black barrel and cylinder assembly **$422.00**

Prices given are believed to be accurate at time of publication however, many factors affect retail pricing so exact prices are not possible.

CHARTER ARMS PIT BULL
Caliber: .40 S&W, 5-round cylinder. **Barrel:** 21.3". **Weight:** 20 oz. **Sights:** Fixed rear, ramp front. **Grips:** Rubber. **Features:** Matte stainless steel frame. Five-shot cylinder does not require moon clips.
Price: **$465**

CHARTER ARMS SOUTHPAW
Caliber: 38 Special +P. **Barrel:** 2. **Weight:** 12 oz. **Grips:** Rubber Pachmayr-style. **Sights:** NA. **Features:** Snubnose, five-round cylinder, matte black aluminum alloy frame with stainless steel cylinder. Cylinder latch and crane assembly are on right side of frame for convenience to left-hand shooters.
Price: **$427.00**

CHARTER ARMS TARGET PATHFINDER COMBO
Caliber: .22 LR / .22 Mag. - 6-round cylinder. **Barrel:** 4". **Weight:** 20 oz. **Grip:** Full. **Sights:** Fixed. **Features:** Stainless finish & frame. Charter's Target Pathfinder is a great introductory revolver for the novice shooter. It has the look, feel and weight of a higher-caliber revolver, allowing you to gain proficiency while using relatively inexpensive .22 ammo. Part of the fun of shooting is doing it well, and proficiency requires practice. That's why Charter makes target configurations, with 4" barrels and precision sights. American made by Charter Arms.
Price: **$540.00**

CHARTER ARMS UNDERCOVER
Caliber: Barrel: 2. **Weight:** 12 oz. **Sights:** Blade front, notch rear. **Features:** 6-round cylinder. American made by Charter Arms.
Price: Blued **$352.00**

CHARTER ARMS UNDERCOVER SOUTHPAW
Caliber: 38 Spec. +P. **Barrel:** 2. **Weight:** 12 oz. **Sights:** NA. **Features:** Cylinder release is on the right side and the cylinder opens to the right side. Exposed hammer for both single and double-action firing. 5-round cylinder. American made by Charter Arms.
Price: **$428.00**

CHARTER ARMS UNDERCOVER LITE, RED & BLACK STANDARD
Caliber: .38 special +P - 5-round cylinder. **Barrel:** 2". **Weight:** 12 oz.

Grip: Standard. **Sights:** Fixed. **Features:** 2-tone red & black with aluminum frame. American made by Charter Arms.
Price: **$422.00**

CHIAPPA RHINO
Chambered in .357 Magnum, 9x21, .40 S&W. Features include 2-, 4-, 5- or 6-inch barrel; fixed or adjustable sights; visible hammer or hammerless design. Weight 24 to 33 oz. Walnut or synthetic grips with black frame; hexagonal-shaped cylinder. Unique design fires from bottom chamber of cylinder.
Price: .... **$980.00 to $1,325.00**

COMANCHE I, II, III DA
Caliber: 22 LR, 9 shot. 38 Spec., 6 shot. 357 Mag, 6 shot. **Barrel:** 6, 22 LR; 2 and 4, 38 Spec.; 2 and 3, 357 Mag. **Weight:** 39 oz. **Length:** 10.8 overall. **Grips:** Rubber. **Sights:** Adjustable rear. **Features:** Blued or stainless. Distributed by SGS Importers.
Price: I Blue **$236.95**
Price: I Alloy **$258.95**
Price: II 38 Spec., 3 bbl., 6-shot, stainless, intr. 2006 .... **$236.95**
Price: II 38 Spec., 4 bbl., 6-shot, stainless **$219.95**
Price: III 357 Mag, 3 bbl., 6-shot, blue **$253.95**
Price: III 357 Mag, 4 bbl., 6-shot, blue **$274.95**

EAA WINDICATOR
Caliber: 38 Spec., 6 shot; 357 Mag., 6-shot. **Barrel:** 2, 4. **Weight:** 30 oz. (4). **Length:** 8.5 overall (4 bbl). **Grips:** Rubber with finger grooves. **Sights:** Blade front, fixed or adjustable on rimfires; fixed only on 32, 38. **Features:** Swing-out cylinder; hammer block safety; blue finish. Introduced 1991. Imported from Germany by European American Armory.
Price: 38 Spec. 2 barrel, alloy frame **$308.00**
Price: 38 Spec. 4 barrel, alloy frame **$323.00**
Price: 357 Mag. 2 barrel, steel frame **$324.00**
Price: 357 Mag. 4 barrel, steel frame **$343.00**

KORTH USA
Caliber: 22 LR, 22 WMR, 32 S&W Long, 38 Spec., 357 Mag., 9mm Para. **Barrel:** 3, 4, 5.25, 6. **Weight:** 36-52 oz. Grips, Combat, Sport: Walnut, Palisander, Amboinia, Ivory. Grips, Target: German Walnut, matte with oil finish, adjustable ergonomic competition style. **Sights:** Adjustable Patridge (Sport) or Baughman (Combat),

interchangeable and adjustable rear w/Patridge front (Target) in blue and matte. **Features:** DA/SA, 3 models, over 50 configurations, externally adjustable trigger stop and weight, interchangeable cylinder, removable wide-milled trigger shoe on Target model. Deluxe models are highly engraved editions. Available finishes include high polish blue finish, plasma coated in high polish or matted silver, gold, blue, or charcoal. Many deluxe options available. 6-shot. From Korth USA.
Price: From $8,000.00
Price: Deluxe Editions, from $12,000.00

ROSSI R461/R462
Caliber: .357 Mag. **Barrel:** 2. **Weight:** 26-35 oz. **Grips:** Rubber. **Sights:** Fixed. **Features:** DA/SA, +P rated frame, blue carbon or high polish stainless steel, patented Taurus Security System, 6-shot.
Price: From $389.00

ROSSI MODEL R971/R972
Caliber: 357 Mag. +P, 6-shot. **Barrel:** 4, 6. **Weight:** 32 oz. **Length:** 8.5 or 10.5 overall. **Grips:** Rubber. **Sights:** Blade front, adjustable rear. **Features:** Single/double action. Patented key-lock Taurus Security System; forged steel frame. Introduced 2001. Made in Brazil by Amadeo Rossi. Imported by BrazTech/Taurus.
Price: Model R971 (blued finish,
    4 bbl.) $452.00
Price: Model R972 (stainless steel finish, 6 bbl.) $508.00

ROSSI MODEL 851
Similar to Model R971/R972, chambered for 38 Spec. +P. Blued finish, 4 barrel. Introduced 2001. Made in Brazil by Amadeo Rossi. From BrazTech/Taurus.
Price: $389.00

ROSSI PLINKER
Caliber: .22 LR. **Capacity:** 8 rounds. **Barrel:** 2, 4 or 6 inches. **Sights:** Fully adjustable rear, fiber optic front. **Grips:** Ribber, textured and ribbed rubber with finger grooves. **Features:** Security system with key lock, transfer bar safety, ventilated rib.
Price: $400.00

RUGER GP-100
Caliber: 327 Federal, 38 Spec. +P, 357 Mag., 6-shot, 327 Federal (7-shot cylinder). **Barrel:** 3 full shroud, 4 full shroud, 6 full shroud. **Weight:** 3 full shroud-36 oz., 4 full shroud-38 oz. **Sights:** Fixed; adjustable on 4 full shroud, all 6 barrels. **Grips:** Ruger Santoprene Cushioned Grip with Goncalo Alves inserts. **Features:** Uses action, frame features of both the Security-Six and Redhawk revolvers. Full length, short ejector shroud. Satin blue and stainless steel.
Price: .357 Mag., blued $699.00
Price: .357, satin stainless $759.00
Price: .357, Federal, stainless $759.00

RUGER LCR
Caliber: .22 LR (8-shot cylinder), .22 WMR, .38 Special and .357 Mag., 5-shot cylinder. **Barrel:** 1-7/8. **Weight:** 13.5 oz. –17.10 oz. **Length:** 6-1/2 overall. **Grips:** Hogue® Tamer™ or Crimson Trace® Lasergrips® . **Sights:** Pinned ramp front, U-notch integral rear. **Features:** The Ruger Lightweight Compact Revolver (LCR), a 13.5 ounce, small frame revolver with a smooth, easy-to-control trigger and highly manageable recoil. Packed with the latest technological advances and features required by today's most demanding shooters.

Prices given are believed to be accurate at time of publication however, many factors affect retail pricing so exact prices are not possible.

Price: .22 LR, .22 WMR, iron sights $529.00
Price: .38/.357, iron sights $599.00
Price: .22 LR, Crimson Trace Laser grip $792.00
Price: .38/.357, Crimson Trace Laser grip $869.00

RUGER SP-101
Caliber: 327 Federal, 6-shot; 38 Spec. +P, 357 Mag., 5-shot. **Barrel:** 2.25, 3-1/16. **Weight:** (38 & 357 mag models) 2.25-25 oz.; 3-1/16-27 oz. **Sights:** Adjustable on 327, fixed on others. **Grips:** Ruger Cushioned Grip with inserts. **Features:** Compact, small frame, double-action revolver. Full-length ejector shroud. Stainless steel only. Introduced 1988.
Price: Fixed sights $659.00
Price: Fiber optic sights $699.00

RUGER SUPER REDHAWK
Caliber: 44 Rem. Mag., 45 Colt, 454 Casull, 480 Ruger, 5 or 6-shot. **Barrel:** 2.5, 5.5, 7.5, 9.5. **Weight:** About 54 oz. (7.5 bbl.). **Length:** 13 overall (7.5 barrel). **Grips:** Hogue Tamer Monogrip. **Features:** Similar to standard Redhawk except has heavy extended frame with Ruger Integral Scope Mounting System on wide topstrap. Wide hammer spur lowered for better scope clearance. Incorporates mechanical design features and improvements of GP-100. Ramp front sight base has Redhawk-style Interchangeable Insert sight blades, adjustable rear sight. Satin stainless steel and low-glare stainless finishes. Introduced 1987.
Price: .44 Magnum $1049.00
Price: .454 Casull $1079.00
Price: .454 Alaskan $1079.00
Price: .44 Mag. Alaskan $1079.00

RUGER REDHAWK
Caliber: 44 Rem. Mag., 45 Colt, 6-shot. **Barrel:** 4, 5.5, 7.5. **Weight:** About 54 oz. (7.5 bbl.). **Length:** 13 overall (7.5 barrel). **Grips:** Square butt cushioned grip panels. **Sights:** Interchangeable Patridge-type front, rear adjustable for windage and elevation. **Features:** Stainless steel, brushed satin finish, blued ordnance steel. 9.5 sight radius. Introduced 1979.
Price: KRH-44, stainless, 7.5 barrel $989.00
Price: KRH-44R, stainless 7.5 barrel w/scope mount $989.00
Price: KRH-445, stainless 5.5 barrel $989.00
Price: KRH-444, stainless 4 barrel (2007) $989.00
Price: KRH-45-4, Hogue Monogrip,
   45 Colt (2008) $989.00

SMITH & WESSON GOVERNOR™
Caliber: .410 2 1/2", .45 ACP, .45 Colt; 6 rounds. **Barrel:** 2.75. **Length:** 7.5, (2.5 barrel). **Grip:** Synthetic. **Sights:** Front: Tritium Night Sight (Dovetailed), Rear: fixed. **Grips:** Synthetic. **Finish:** Matte Black. **Weight:** 29.6 oz. **Features:** Capable of chambering a mixture of .45 Colt, .45 ACP and .410 gauge 2 ½-inch shotshells, the Governor is suited for both close and distant encounters, allowing users to customize the load to their preference.
Price: $769.00
Price: with Crimson Trace® Laser Grip $1,019.00

SMITH & WESSON MODEL 14 CLASSIC
Caliber: 38 Spec. +P, 6-shot. **Barrel:** 6". **Weight:** 35 oz. **Length:** 11.5". **Grips:** Wood. **Sights:** Pinned Patridge front, micro adjustable rear. **Features:** Recreation of the vintage Model 14 revolver. Carbon steel frame and cylinder with blued finish.
Price: $995.00
Price: Model 14 150253, nickel finish $1,074.00

SMITH & WESSON NIGHT GUARD
Caliber: 357 Mag., 38 Spec. +P, 5-, 6-, 7-, 8-shot. **Barrel:** 2.5 or 2.75 (45 ACP). **Weight:** 24.2 oz. (2.5 barrel). **Length:** 7.325 overall (2.5 barrel). **Grips:** Pachmayr Compac Custom. **Sights:** XS Sight 24/7 Standard Dot Tritium front, Cylinder & Slide Extreme Duty fixed rear. **Features:** Scandium alloy frame, stainless PVD cylinder, matte black finish. Introduced 2008. Made in U.S.A. by Smith & Wesson.
Price: Model 325, 45 ACP, 2.75 barrel, large-frame
   snubnose $1,049.00

Price: Model 327, 38/357, 2.5 barrel, large-frame
 snubnose **$1,049.00**
Price: Model 329, 44 Magnum/38 Special (interchangeable),
 2.5 barrel, large-frame snubnose **$1,049.00**
Price: Model 386, 357 Magnum/44 Special +P (interchangeable),
 2.5 barrel, medium-frame snubnose **$979.00**

SMITH & WESSON J-FRAME
 The smallest S&W wheelguns come in a variety of chamberings,
barrel lengths, and materials, as noted in the individual model listings.

SMITH & WESSON 60LS/642LS LADYSMITH
Caliber: .38 Spec. +P, 357 Mag., 5-shot. **Barrel:** 1-7/8 (642LS); 2-1/8
(60LS) **Weight:** 14.5 oz. (642LS); 21.5 oz. (60LS); **Length:** 6.6 overall
(60LS); . **Grips:** Wood. **Sights:** Black blade, serrated ramp front,
fixed notch rear. **Features:** 60LS model has a Chiefs Special-style
frame. 642LS has Centennial-style frame, frosted matte finish,
smooth combat wood grips. Introduced 1996. Comes in a fitted
carry/storage case. Introduced 1989. Made in U.S.A. by Smith &
Wesson.
Price: (642LS) **$489.00**
Price: (60LS) **$759.00**

SMITH & WESSON MODEL 63
Caliber: 22 LR, 8-shot. **Barrel:** 5". **Weight:** 28.8 oz. **Length:** 9.5"
overall. **Grips:** Black rubber. **Sights:** Black ramp front sight,
adjustable black blade rear sight. **Features:** Stainless steel
construction throughout. Made in U.S.A. by Smith & Wesson.
Price: **$769.00**

SMITH & WESSON MODEL 442/637/638/642 AIRWEIGHT
Caliber: 38 Spec. +P, 5-shot. **Barrel:** 1-7/8", 2-1/2. **Weight:** 15
oz. (37, 442); 20 oz. (3); 21.5 oz.; **Length:** 6-3/8 overall. **Grips:**
Soft rubber. **Sights:** Fixed, serrated ramp front, square notch rear.
Features: Aluminum-alloy frames. Models 37, 637; Chiefs Special-
style frame with exposed hammer. Introduced 1996. Models
442, 642; Centennial-style frame, enclosed hammer. Model 638,
Bodyguard style, shrouded hammer. Comes in a fitted carry/storage
case. Introduced 1989. Made in U.S.A. by Smith & Wesson.
Price: From **$449.00**

SMITH & WESSON MODELS 637 CT/638 CT/642 CT
 Similar to Models 637, 638 and 642 but with Crimson Trace Laser
Grips.
Price: **$689.00**

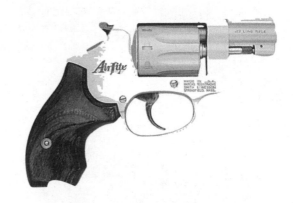

SMITH & WESSON MODEL 317 AIRLITE
Caliber: 22 LR, 8-shot. **Barrel:** 1-7/8. **Weight:** 10.5 oz. **Length:** 6.25
overall (1-7/8 barrel). **Grips:** Rubber. **Sights:** Serrated ramp front,
fixed notch rear. **Features:** Aluminum alloy, carbon and stainless
steels, Chiefs Special-style frame with exposed hammer. Smooth
combat trigger. Clear Cote finish. Introduced 1997. Made in U.S.A.
by Smith & Wesson.
Price: Model 317, 1-7/8 barrel **$699.00**

Prices given are believed to be accurate at time of publication however, many factors affect retail pricing so exact prices are not possible.

SMITH & WESSON MODEL 340/340PD AIRLITE SC CENTENNIAL
Caliber: 357 Mag., 38 Spec. +P, 5-shot. **Barrel:** 1-7/8. **Weight:** 12 oz. **Length:** 6-3/8 overall (1-7/8 barrel). **Grips:** Rounded butt rubber. **Sights:** Black blade front, rear notch **Features:** Centennial-style frame, enclosed hammer. Internal lock. Matte silver finish. Scandium alloy frame, titanium cylinder, stainless steel barrel liner. Made in U.S.A. by Smith & Wesson.
Price: Model 340 .... **$1,019.00**

SMITH & WESSON MODEL 351PD
Caliber: 22 Mag., 7-shot. **Barrel:** 1-7/8. **Weight:** 10.6 oz. **Length:** 6.25" overall (1-7/8 barrel). **Sights:** HiViz front sight, rear notch. **Grips:** Wood. **Features:** Seven-shot, aluminum-alloy frame. Chiefs Special-style frame with exposed hammer. Nonreflective matte-black finish. Internal lock. Made in U.S.A. by Smith & Wesson.
Price: **$759.00**

SMITH & WESSON MODEL 360/360PD AIRLITE CHIEF'S SPECIAL
Caliber: 357 Mag., 38 Spec. +P, 5-shot. **Barrel:** 1-7/8. **Weight:** 12 oz. **Length:** 6-3/8 overall (1-7/8 barrel). **Grips:** Rounded butt rubber. **Sights:** Black blade front, fixed rear notch. **Features:** Chief's Special-style frame with exposed hammer. Internal lock. Scandium alloy frame, titanium cylinder, stainless steel barrel. Made in U.S.A. by Smith & Wesson.
Price: 360PD **$988.00**

SMITH & WESSON MODEL M&P360
Single/double-action J-frame revolver chambered in .357 Magnum. Features include 2-inch barrel, 5-round cylinder, fixed XS tritium sights, scandium frame, stainless steel cylinder, matte black finish, synthetic grips.
Price: $980.00

SMITH & WESSON BODYGUARD® 38
Caliber: .38 S&W Special +P; 5 rounds. **Barrel:** 1.9. **Weight:** 14.3 oz. **Length:** 6.6. **Grip:** Synthetic. **Sights:** Front: Black ramp, Rear: integral. **Grips:** Synthetic. **Finish:** Matte Black. **Features:** The Smith & Wesson BODYGUARD® series is the first in personal protection with integrated lasers. The BODYGUARD® 38 and BODYGUARD® 380 are uniquely engineered as the most state-of-the-art, concealable and accurate personal protection possible. Lightweight,

simple to use and featuring integrated laser sights – nothing protects like a BODYGUARD.
Price: **$509.00**

SMITH & WESSON MODEL 438
Caliber: 38 Spec. +P, 5-shot. **Barrel:** 1-7/8". **Weight:** 15.1 oz. **Length:** 6.31" overall. **Grips:** Synthetic. **Sights:** Fixed front and rear. **Features:** Aluminum alloy frame, stainless steel cylinder. Matte black finish throughout. Made in U.S.A. by Smith & Wesson.
Price: **$449.00**

SMITH & WESSON MODEL 640 CENTENNIAL DA ONLY
Caliber: 357 Mag., 38 Spec. +P, 5-shot. **Barrel:** 2-1/8. **Weight:** 23 oz. **Length:** 6.75 overall. **Grips:** Uncle Mike's Boot grip. **Sights:** Serrated ramp front, fixed notch rear. **Features:** Stainless steel. Fully concealed hammer, snag-proof smooth edges. Internal lock. Introduced 1995 in 357 Mag.
Price: **$729.00**

SMITH & WESSON MODEL 649 BODYGUARD
Caliber: 357 Mag., 38 Spec. +P, 5-shot. **Barrel:** 2-1/8. **Weight:** 23 oz. **Length:** 6-5/8 overall. **Grips:** Uncle Mike's Combat. **Sights:** Black pinned ramp front, fixed notch rear. **Features:** Stainless steel construction, satin finish. Internal lock. Bodyguard style, shrouded hammer. Made in U.S.A. by Smith & Wesson.
Price: **$729.00**

SMITH & WESSON K-FRAME/L-FRAME
These mid-size S&W wheelguns come in a variety of chamberings, barrel lengths, and materials, as noted in individual model listings.

Prices given are believed to be accurate at time of publication however, many factors affect retail pricing so exact prices are not possible.

68TH EDITION, 2014 ◆ **437**

SMITH & WESSON MODEL 10 CLASSIC

Single/double action K frame revolver chambered in .38 Special. Features include bright blue steel frame and cylinder, checkered wood grips, 4-inch barrel, adjustable patridge-style sights.
Price: $719.00

SMITH & WESSON MODEL 17 MASTERPIECE CLASSIC

Caliber: .22 LR. **Capacity:** 6 rounds. **Barrel:** 6 inches. **Weight:** 40 oz. **Grips:** Checkered wood. **Sights:** Pinned Patridge front, Micro Adjustable rear. Updated variation of K-22 Masterpiece.
Price: $959.00

SMITH & WESSON MODEL 48 CLASSIC

Single/double action K frame revolver chambered in .22 Magnum Rimfire (.22 WMR). Features include bright blue steel frame and cylinder, checkered wood grips, 4- or 6-inch barrel, adjustable patridge-style sights.
Price: .... $1,043.00 to $1,082.00

SMITH & WESSON MODEL 64/67

Caliber: 38 Spec. +P, 6-shot. **Barrel:** 3. **Weight:** 33 oz. **Length:** 8-7/8 overall. **Grips:** Soft rubber. **Sights:** Fixed, 1/8 serrated ramp front, square notch rear. Model 67 (**Weight:** 36 oz. **Length:** 8-7/8) similar to Model 64 except for adjustable sights. **Features:** Satin finished stainless steel, square butt.
Price: From .... $689.00 to $749.00

SMITH & WESSON MODEL 617

Caliber: 22 LR, 6- or 10-shot. **Barrel:** 4. **Weight:** 41 oz. (4 barrel). **Length:** 9-1/8 (4 barrel). **Grips:** Soft rubber. **Sights:** Patridge front, adjustable rear. Drilled and tapped for scope mount. **Features:** Stainless steel with satin finish; 4 has .312 smooth trigger, .375 semi-target hammer; 6 has either .312 combat or .400 serrated trigger, .375 semi-target or .500 target hammer; 8-3/8 with .400 serrated trigger, .500 target hammer. Introduced 1990.
Price: From $829.00

SMITH & WESSON MODELS 620

Caliber: 38 Spec. +P; 357 Mag., 7 rounds. **Barrel:** 4. **Weight:** 37.5 oz. **Length:** 9.5. **Grips:** Rubber. **Sights:** Integral front blade, fixed rear notch on the 619; adjustable white-outline target style rear, red ramp front on 620. **Features:** Replaces Models 65 and 66. Two-piece semi-lug barrel. Satin stainless frame and cylinder. Made in U.S.A. by Smith & Wesson.
Price: $893.00

SMITH & WESSON MODEL 386 XL HUNTER

Single/double action L-frame revolver chambered in .357 Magnum. Features include 6-inch full-lug barrel, 7-round cylinder, Hi-Viz fiber optic front sight, adjustable rear sight, scandium frame, stainless steel cylinder, black matte finish, synthetic grips.
Price: $1,019.00

SMITH & WESSON MODEL 686/686 PLUS

Caliber: 357 Mag., 38 S&W Special; 6 rounds. **Barrel:** 2.5, 4, 6. **Weight:** 35 oz. (2.5 barrel). **Length:** 7.5, (2.5 barrel). **Grips:** Rubber. **Sights:** White outline adjustable rear, red ramp front. **Features:** Satin stainless frame and cylinder. Plus series guns have 7-shot cylinders. Introduced 1996. Powerport (PP) has Patridge front, adjustable rear sight. Introduced early 1980s. Stock Service Revolver (SSR) intr. 2007. **Capacity:** 6. **Barrel:** 4. **Sights:** Interchangeable front, adjustable rear. **Grips:** Wood. **Finish:** Satin stainless frame and cylinder. **Weight:** 38.3 oz. **Features:** Chamfered charge holes, custom barrel w/recessed crown, bossed mainspring. High-hold ergonomic grip. Made in U.S.A. by Smith & Wesson.
Price: 686 ....$909.00
Price: Plus, 7 rounds $932.00
Price: PP, 6 barrel, 6 rounds, 11-3/8 OAL $877.00
Price: SSR $1,059.00

SMITH & WESSON MODEL 686 PLUS PRO SERIES

Single/double-action L-frame revolver chambered in .357 Magnum. Features include 5-inch barrel with tapered underlug, 7-round cylinder, satin stainless steel frame and cylinder, synthetic grips, interchangeable and adjustable sights.
Price: $1,059.00

SMITH & WESSON N-FRAME

These large-frame S&W wheelguns come in a variety of chamberings, barrel lengths, and materials, as noted in the individual model listings.

SMITH & WESSON MODEL 25 CLASSIC

Caliber: .45 Colt. **Capacity:** Six rounds. **Barrel:** 6.5 inches. **Weight:** 45 oz. **Grips:** Checkered wood. **Sights:** Pinned Patridge front, Micro Adjustable rear.
Price: $979.00

SMITH & WESSON MODEL 27 CLASSIC

Caliber: .357 Magnum. **Capacity:** Six rounds. **Barrel:** 4 or 6.5 inches.

Weight: 41.2 to 46.6 oz. **Grips:** Checkered wood. **Sights:** Pinned Patridge front, Micro Adjustable rear. Updated variation of the first magnum revolver, the .357 Magnum of 1935.
Price: (6.5") .... **$989.00 to $1,029.00**

SMITH & WESSON MODEL 57 CLASSIC
Caliber: .41 Magnum. Six rounds. **Barrel:** 6 inches. **Weight:** 48 oz. **Grips:** Checkered wood. **Sights:** Pinned red ramp, Micro Adjustable rear.
Price: **$979.00**

SMITH & WESSON MODEL 29 CLASSIC
Caliber: 44 Mag, 6-round. **Barrel:** 6.5. **Weight:** 48.5 oz. **Length:** 12. **Grips:** Altamont service walnut. **Sights:** Adjustable white-outline rear, red ramp front. **Features:** Carbon steel frame, polished-blued or nickel finish. Has integral key lock safety feature to prevent accidental discharges. Alo available with 3" barrel. Original Model 29 made famous by "Dirty Harry" character created in 1971 by Clint Eastwood.
Price: **$1240.00**

SMITH & WESSON MODEL 329PD ALASKA BACKPACKER
Caliber: 44 Spec., 44 Mag., 6-round. **Barrel:** 2.5". **Weight:** 26 oz. **Length:** 9.5. **Grips:** Synthetic. **Sights:** Adj. rear, HiViz orange-dot front. **Features:** Scandium alloy frame, blue/black finish, stainless steel cylinder.
Price: From **$1,159.00**

SMITH & WESSON MODEL 625/625JM
Caliber: 45 ACP, 6-shot. **Barrel:** 4, 5. **Weight:** 43 oz. (4 barrel). **Length:** 9-3/8 overall (4 barrel). **Grips:** Soft rubber; wood optional. **Sights:** Patridge front on ramp, S&W micrometer click rear adjustable for windage and elevation. **Features:** Stainless steel construction with .400 semi-target hammer, .312 smooth combat trigger; full lug barrel. Glass beaded finish. Introduced 1989. "Jerry Miculek" Professional (JM) Series has .265-wide grooved trigger, special wooden Miculek Grip, five full moon clips, gold bead Patridge front sight on interchangeable front sight base, bead blast finish. Unique serial number run. Mountain

---

Gun has 4 tapered barrel, drilled and tapped, Hogue Rubber Monogrip, pinned black ramp front sight, micrometer click-adjustable rear sight, satin stainless frame and barrel, weighs 39.5 oz.
Price: 625JM **$1,074.00**

SMITH & WESSON MODEL 629
Caliber: 44 Magnum, 44 S&W Special, 6-shot. **Barrel:** 4, 5, 6.5. **Weight:** 41.5 oz. (4 bbl.). **Length:** 9-5/8 overall (4 bbl.). **Grips:** Soft rubber; wood optional. **Sights:** 1/8 red ramp front, white outline rear, internal look, adjustable for windage and elevation. Classic similar to standard Model 629, except Classic has full-lug 5 barrel, chamfered front of cylinder, interchangeable red ramp front sight with adjustable white outline rear, Hogue grips with S&W monogram, drilled and tapped for scope mounting. Factory accurizing and endurance packages. Introduced 1990. Classic Power Port has Patridge front sight and adjustable rear sight. Model 629CT has 5 barrel, Crimson Trace Hoghunter Lasergrips, 10.5 OAL, 45.5 oz. weight. Introduced 2006.
Price: From **$949.00**

SMITH & WESSON MODEL 329 XL HUNTER
Similar to Model 386 XL Hunter but built on large N-frame and chambered in .44 Magnum. Other features include 6-round cylinder and 6.5-barrel.
Price: **$1,138.00**

SMITH & WESSON X-FRAME
These extra-large X-frame S&W wheelguns come in a variety of chamberings, barrel lengths, and materials, as noted in individual model listings.

SMITH & WESSON MODEL 500
Caliber: 500 S&W Mag., 5 rounds. **Barrel:** 4, 8-3/8. **Weight:** 72.5 oz. **Length:** 15 (8-3/8 barrel). **Grips:** Hogue Sorbothane Rubber. **Sights:** Interchangeable blade, front, adjustable rear. **Features:** Recoil compensator, ball detent cylinder latch, internal lock. 6.5-barrel model has orange-ramp dovetail Millett front sight, adjustable black rear sight, Hogue Dual Density Monogrip, .312 chrome trigger with over-travel stop, chrome tear-drop hammer, glassbead finish. 10.5-barrel model has red ramp front sight, adjustable rear sight, .312 chrome trigger with overtravel stop, chrome tear drop hammer with pinned sear, hunting sling. Compensated Hunter has .400 orange ramp dovetail front sight, adjustable black blade rear sight, Hogue Dual Density Monogrip, glassbead finish w/black clear coat. Made in U.S.A. by Smith & Wesson.
Price: From **$1,249.00**

Prices given are believed to be accurate at time of publication however, many factors affect retail pricing so exact prices are not possible.

68TH EDITION, 2014 ◆ **439**

SMITH & WESSON MODEL 460V

Caliber: 460 S&W Mag., 5-shot. Also chambers 454 Casull, 45 Colt. **Barrel:** 8-3/8 gain-twist rifling. **Weight:** 62.5 oz. **Length:** 11.25. **Grips:** Rubber. **Sights:** Adj. rear, red ramp front. **Features:** Satin stainless steel frame and cylinder, interchangeable compensator. 460XVR (X-treme Velocity Revolver) has black blade front sight with interchangeable green Hi-Viz tubes, adjustable rear sight. 7.5-barrel version has Lothar-Walther barrel, 360-degree recoil compensator, tuned Performance Center action, pinned sear, integral Weaver base, non-glare surfaces, scope mount accessory kit for mounting full-size scopes, flashed-chromed hammer and trigger, Performance Center gun rug and shoulder sling. Interchangeable Hi-Viz green dot front sight, adjustable black rear sight, Hogue Dual Density Monogrip, matte-black frame and shroud finish with glass-bead cylinder finish, 72 oz. Compensated Hunter has tear drop chrome hammer, .312 chrome trigger, Hogue Dual Density Monogrip, satin/matte stainless finish, HiViz interchangeable front sight, adjustable black rear sight. XVR introduced 2006.
Price: 460V $1,519.00
Price: 460XVR, from $1,519.00

SUPER SIX CLASSIC BISON BULL

Caliber: .45-70 Government, 6-shot. **Barrel:** 10" octagonal with 1:14 twist. **Weight:** 6 lbs. **Length:** 17.5"overall. **Grips:** NA. **Sights:** Ramp front sight with dovetailed blade, click-adjustable rear. **Features:** Manganese bronze frame. Integral scope mount, manual crossbolt safety.
Price: .... **Appx. $1,500.00**

TAURUS MODEL 17 "TRACKER"

Caliber: 17 HMR, 7-shot. **Barrel:** 6.5. **Weight:** 45.8 oz. **Grips:** Rubber. **Sights:** Adjustable. **Features:** Double action, matte stainless, integral key-lock.
Price: From $539.00

TAURUS MODEL 44

Caliber: 44 Mag., 6-shot. **Barrel:** 4, 6.5, 8-3/8. **Weight:** 44-3/4 oz. **Grips:** Rubber. **Sights:** Adjustable. **Features:** Double-action. Integral key-lock. Introduced 1994. New Model 44S12 has 12 vent rib barrel. Imported from Brazil by Taurus International Manufacturing, Inc.
Price: From $742.00

TAURUS MODEL 65

Caliber: 357 Mag., 6-shot. **Barrel:** 4. **Weight:** 38 oz. **Length:** 10.5 overall. **Grips:** Soft rubber. **Sights:** Fixed. **Features:** Double action,

integral key-lock. Seven models for 2006 Imported by Taurus International.
Price: From $419.00

TAURUS MODEL 66

Similar to Model 65, 4 or 6 barrel, 7-shot cylinder, adjustable rear sight. Integral key-lock action. Imported by Taurus International.
Price: From $469.00

TAURUS MODEL 82 HEAVY BARREL

Caliber: 38 Spec., 6-shot. **Barrel:** 4, heavy. **Weight:** 36.5 oz. **Length:** 9-1/4 overall (4 bbl.). **Grips:** Soft black rubber. **Sights:** Serrated ramp front, square notch rear. **Features:** Double action, solid rib, integral key-lock. Imported by Taurus International.
Price: From $403.00

TAURUS MODEL 85

Caliber: 38 Spec., 5-shot. **Barrel:** 2. **Weight:** 17-24.5 oz., titanium 13.5-15.4 oz. **Grips:** Rubber, rosewood or mother-of-pearl. **Sights:** Ramp front, square notch rear. **Features:** Blue, matte stainless, blue with gold accents, stainless with gold accents; rated for +P ammo. Integral keylock. Some models have titantium frame. Introduced 1980. Imported by Taurus International.
Price: From $403.00

TAURUS 380 MINI

Caliber: .380 ACP (5-shot cylinder w/moon clip). **Barrel:** 1.75". **Weight:** 15.5 oz. **Length:** 5.95". **Grips:** Rubber. **Sights:** Adjustable rear, fixed front. **Features:** Double-action-only. Available in blued or stainless finish. Five Star (moon) clips included.
PRICE ....$430 to $461

TAURUS 851 & 651

Small frame SA/DA revolvers similar to Taurus Model 85 but with Centennial-style concealed-hammer frame. Chambered in 38 Special +P (Model 851) or 357 Magnum (Model 651). Features include five-shot cylinder; 2" barrel; fixed sights; blue, matte blue, titanium or stainless finish; Taurus security lock. Overall length is 6.5". Weighs 15.5 oz. (titanium) to 25 oz. (blued and stainless).
Price: From $411.00

TAURUS MODEL 94

Caliber: 22 LR, 9-shot cylinder; 22 Mag, 8-shot cylinder **Barrel:** 2, 4,

Prices given are believed to be accurate at time of publication however, many factors affect retail pricing so exact prices are not possible.

5. **Weight:** 18.5-27.5 oz. **Grips:** Soft black rubber. **Sights:** Serrated ramp front, click-adjustable rear. **Features:** Double action, integral key-lock. Introduced 1989. Imported by Taurus International.
Price: From $369.00

TAURUS MODEL 4510 JUDGE
Caliber: 3 .410/45 LC, 2.5 .410/45 LC. **Barrel:** 3", 6.5" (blued finish). **Weight:** 35.2 oz., 22.4 oz. **Length:** 7.5. **Grips:** Ribber. **Sights:** Fiber Optic. **Features:** DA/SA. Matte Stainless and Ultra-Lite Stainless finish. Introduced in 2007. Imported from Brazil by Taurus International.
Price: 4510T TrackerSS Matte Stainless $569.00
Price: 4510TKR-3B Judge   **$558.00**
Price: 4510TKR-SSR, ported barrel, tactical rail   **$608.00**

TAURUS JUDGE PUBLIC DEFENDER POLYMER
Single/double action revolver chambered in .45 Colt/.410 (2-1/2) Features include 5-round cylinder; polymer frame; Ribber rubber-feel grips; fiber-optic front sight; adjustable rear sight; blued or stainless cylinder; shrouded hammer with cocking spur; blued finish; 2.5-inch barrel. Weight 27 oz.
Price: $459.00

TAURUS JUDGE PUBLIC DEFENDER ULTRA-LITE
Single/double action revolver chambered in .45 Colt/.410 (2-1/2). Features include 5-round cylinder; lightweight aluminum frame; Ribber rubber-feel grips; fiber-optic front sight; adjustable rear sight; blued or stainless cylinder; shrouded hammer with cocking spur; blued finish; 2.5-inch barrel. Weight 20.7 oz.
Price: $668.00

TAURUS RAGING JUDGE MAGNUM
Single/double action revolver chambered for .454 Casull, .45 Colt, 2.5-inch and 3-inch .410. Features include 3- or 6-inch barrel; fixed sights with fiber-optic front; blued or stainless steel finish; vent rib for scope mounting (6-inch only); cushioned Raging Bull grips.
Price: $1,012.00

TAURUS RAGING BULL MODEL 416
Caliber: 41 Magnum, 6-shot. **Barrel:** 6.5. **Weight:** 61.9 oz. **Grips:** Rubber. **Sights:** Adjustable. **Features:** Double-action, ported, ventilated rib, matte stainless, integral key-lock.
Price: $706.00

TAURUS MODEL 425 TRACKER
Caliber: 357 Mag., 7-shot; 41 Mag., 5-shot. **Barrel:** 4 and 6. **Weight:** 28.8-40 oz. (titanium) 24.3-28. (6). **Grips:** Rubber. **Sights:** Fixed front, adjustable rear. **Features:** Double-action stainless steel, Shadow Gray or Total Titanium; vent rib (steel models only); integral key-lock action. Imported by Taurus International.
Price: From $569.00

TAURUS MODEL 444 ULTRA-LIGHT
Caliber: 44 Mag, 5-shot. **Barrel:** 4. **Weight:** 28.3 oz. **Length:** 9.8 overall. **Grips:** Cushioned inset rubber. **Sights:** Fixed red-fiber optic front, adjustable rear. **Features:** UltraLite titanium blue finish, titanium/alloy frame built on Raging Bull design. Smooth trigger shoe, 1.760 wide, 6.280 tall. Barrel rate of twist 1:16, 6 grooves. Introduced 2005. Imported by Taurus International.
Price: $666.00

TAURUS MODEL 416/444/454 RAGING BULL
Caliber: 41 Mag., 44 Mag., 454 Casull. **Barrel:** 2.25" (454 Casull only), 5, 6.5, 8-3/8. **Weight:** 53-63 oz. **Length:** 12 overall (6.5 barrel). **Grips:** Soft black rubber. **Sights:** Patridge front, adjustable rear. **Features:** Double-action, ventilated rib, ported, integral key-lock. Introduced 1997. Imported by Taurus International.
Price: From $641.00

Prices given are believed to be accurate at time of publication however, many factors affect retail pricing so exact prices are not possible.

68TH EDITION, 2014   441

TAURUS MODEL 605 PLY
Caliber: 357 Mag., 5-shot. **Barrel:** 2. **Weight:** 20 oz. **Grips:** Rubber. **Sights:** Fixed. **Features:** Polymer frame steel cylinder. Introduced 1995. Imported by Taurus International.
Price: From $460.00

TAURUS MODEL 608
Caliber: 357 Mag. 38 Spec., 8-shot. **Barrel:** 4, 6.5, 8-3/8. **Weight:** 44-57 oz. **Length:** 9-3/8 overall. **Grips:** Soft black rubber. **Sights:** Adjustable. **Features:** Double-action, integral key-lock action. Available in blue or stainless. Introduced 1995. Imported by Taurus International.
Price: From $584.00

TAURUS MODEL 617
Caliber: 357 Mag., 7-shot. **Barrel:** 2. **Weight:** 28.3 oz. **Length:** 6.75 overall. **Grips:** Soft black rubber. **Sights:** Fixed. **Features:** Double-action, blue, Shadow Gray, bright spectrum blue or matte stainless steel, integral key-lock. Available with porting, concealed hammer. Introduced 1998. Imported by Taurus International.
Price: $436.00

TAURUS MODEL 650 CIA
Caliber: 357 Mag., 5-shot. **Barrel:** 2. **Weight:** 24.5 oz. **Grips:** Rubber. **Sights:** Ramp front, square notch rear. **Features:** Double-action only, blue or matte stainless steel, integral key-lock, internal hammer. Introduced 2001. From Taurus International.
Price: From $411.00

TAURUS MODEL 651 PROTECTOR
Caliber: 357 Mag., 5-shot. **Barrel:** 2. **Weight:** 17-24.5 oz. **Grips:** Rubber. **Sights:** Fixed. **Features:** Concealed single-action/double-action design. Shrouded cockable hammer, blue, matte stainless, Shadow Gray, Total Titanium, integral key-lock. Made in Brazil. Imported by Taurus International Manufacturing, Inc.
Price: From $411.00

TAURUS MODEL 731
Similar to the Taurus Model 605, except in .32 Magnum.
Price: $469.00

TAURUS MODEL 817 ULTRA-LITE
Caliber: 38 Spec., 7-shot. **Barrel:** 2. **Weight:** 21 oz. **Length:** 6.5 overall. **Grips:** Soft rubber. **Sights:** Fixed. **Features:** Double-action, integral key-lock. Rated for +P ammo. Introduced 1999. Imported from Brazil by Taurus International.
Price: From $436.00

TAURUS MODEL 850 CIA
Caliber: 38 Spec., 5-shot. **Barrel:** 2. **Weight:** 17-24.5 oz. **Grips:** Rubber, mother-of-pearl. **Sights:** Ramp front, square notch rear. **Features:** Double-action only, blue or matte stainless steel, rated for +P ammo, integral key-lock, internal hammer. Introduced 2001. From Taurus International.
Price: From $411.00

TAURUS MODEL 941
Caliber: 22 LR (Mod. 94), 22 WMR (Mod. 941), 8-shot. **Barrel:** 2, 4, 5. **Weight:** 27.5 oz. (4 barrel). **Grips:** Soft black rubber. **Sights:** Serrated ramp front, rear adjustable. **Features:** Double-action, integral key-lock. Introduced 1992. Imported by Taurus International.
Price: From $386.00

TAURUS MODEL 970/971 TRACKER
Caliber: 22 LR (Model 970), 22 Magnum (Model 971); 7-shot. **Barrel:** 6. **Weight:** 53.6 oz. **Grips:** Rubber. **Sights:** Adjustable. **Features:** Double barrel, heavy barrel with ventilated rib; matte stainless finish, integral key-lock. Introduced 2001. From Taurus International.
Price: $453.00
Price: Model 17SS6, chambered in 17 HMR $453.00

Prices given are believed to be accurate at time of publication however, many factors affect retail pricing so exact prices are not possible.

BERETTA STAMPEDE SINGLE-ACTION
Caliber: 357 Mag, 45 Colt, 6-shot. **Barrel:** 4.75, 5.5, 7.5, blued. **Weight:** 36.8 oz. (4.75 barrel). **Length:** 9.5 overall (4.75 barrel). **Grips:** Wood, walnut, black polymer. **Sights:** Blade front, notch rear. **Features:** Transfer-bar safety. Introduced 2003. Stampede Inox (2004) is stainless steel with black polymer grips. Compact Stampede Marshall (2004) has birdshead-style walnut grips, 3.5 barrel, color-case-hardened frame, blued barrel and cylinder. Manufactured for Beretta by Uberti.
Price: Nickel, 45 Colt $630.00
Price: Blued, 45 Colt, 357 Mag, 4.75", 5-1/2" $575.00
Price: Deluxe, 45 Colt, 357 Mag. 4.75", 5-1/2" $675.00
Price: Marshall, 45 Colt, 357 Mag. 3.5 ....$575.00
Price: Bisley nickel, 4.75", 5.5" $775.00
Price: Bisley, 4.75", 5.5" $675.00
Price: Stampede Deluxe, 45 Colt 7.5" $775.00
Price: Stampede Blued, 45 Colt 7.5" $575.00
Price: Marshall Old West, 45 Colt 3.5" $650.00

CIMARRON 1872 OPEN TOP
Caliber: 38, 44 Special, 44 Colt, 44 Russian, 45 LC, 45 S&W Schofield. **Barrel:** 5.5 and 7.5. **Grips:** Walnut. **Sights:** Blade front, fixed rear. **Features:** Replica of first cartridge-firing revolver. Blue, charcoal blue, nickel or Original finish; Navy-style brass or steel Army-style frame. Introduced 2001 by Cimarron F.A. Co.
Price: (Navy model)..$493.00
Price: (Army) $519.00

CIMARRON 1875 OUTLAW
Caliber: .357, .38 special, .44 W.C.F., .45 Colt, .45 ACP. **Barrel:** 5-1/2" and 7-1/2". **Weight:** 2.5-2.6 lbs. **Grip:** 1 piece walnut. **Features:** Standard blue finish with color case hardened frame.
Price: $559.94
Price: CA150 Dual Cyl. $665.40

CIMARRON MODEL 1890
Caliber: .357, .38 special, .44 W.C.F., .45 Colt, .45 ACP. **Barrel:** 5-1/2". **Weight:** 2.4-2.5 lbs. **Grip:** 1 piece walnut. **Features:** Standard blue finish with standard blue frame.
Price: $576.28
Price: CA159 Dual Cyl. $681.73

CIMARRON BISLEY MODEL SINGLE-ACTION
Similar to 1873 Model P, special grip frame and trigger guard, knurled wide-spur hammer, curved trigger. Available in 357 Mag., 44 WCF, 44 Spl., 45 Colt. Introduced 1999. Imported by Cimarron F.A. Co.
Price: From $663.00

CIMARRON LIGHTNING SA
Caliber: 22 LR, 32-20, 32 H&R, 38 Colt, **Barrel:** 3.5, 4.75, 5.5. **Grips:** Smooth or checkered walnut. **Sights:** Blade front. **Features:** Replica of the Colt 1877 Lightning DA. Similar to Cimarron Thunderer, except smaller grip frame to fit smaller hands. Standard blue, charcoal blue or nickel finish with forged, old model, or color case hardened frame. Introduced 2001. From Cimarron F.A. Co.
Price: From $555.00

CIMARRON MAN WITH NO NAME
Caliber: .45 LC. **Barrel:** 4-3/4" and 5-1/2". **Weight:** 2.66-2.76 lbs. **Grip:** 1 piece walnut with silver rattle snake inlay in both sides. **Features:** Standard blue finish with case hardened pre-war frame. An accurate copy of the gun used by our nameless hero in the classic Western movies "Fist Full Of Dollars" & "For A Few Dollars More".
Price: $889.71

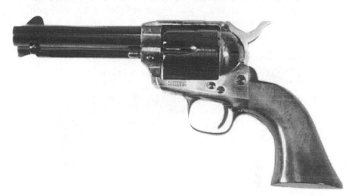

CIMARRON MODEL P
Caliber: 32 WCF, 38 WCF, 357 Mag., 44 WCF, 44 Spec., 45 Colt, 45 LC and 45 ACP. **Barrel:** 4.75, 5.5, 7.5. **Weight:** 39 oz. **Length:** 10 overall (4 barrel). **Grips:** Walnut. **Sights:** Blade front, fixed or adjustable rear. **Features:** Uses "old model" black powder frame with "Bullseye" ejector or New Model frame. Imported by Cimarron F.A. Co.
Price: From $550.00

CIMARRON MODEL "P" JR.
Caliber: 32-20, 32 H&R, **Barrel:** 3.5, 4.75, 5.5. **Grips:** Checkered walnut. **Sights:** Blade front. **Features:** Styled after 1873 Colt Peacemaker, except 20 percent smaller. Blue finish with color case-hardened frame; Cowboy action. Introduced 2001. From Cimarron F.A. Co.
Price: $550.00

CIMARRON ROOSTER SHOOTER
Caliber: .357, .38 special, .45 Colt, and .44 W.C.F. **Barrel:** 4-3/4". **Weight:** 2.49-2.53 lbs. **Grip:** 1 piece orange finger grooved. **Features:** A replica of John Wayne's Colt® Single Action, used in many of his great Westerns, including his Oscar winning performance in "True Grit", where he brings the colorful character Rooster Cogburn to life.
Price: $845.11

CIMARRON THUNDERER
Caliber: 357 Mag., 44 WCF, 45 Colt, 6-shot. **Barrel:** 3.5, 4.75, with ejector. **Weight:** 38 oz. (3.5 barrel). **Grips:** Smooth or checkered walnut. **Sights:** Blade front, notch rear. **Features:** Thunderer grip. Introduced 1993. Imported by Cimarron F.A. Co.
Price: Stainless $534.26

CIMARRON U.S.V. ARTILLERY MODEL SINGLE-ACTION
Caliber: 45 Colt. **Barrel:** 5.5. **Weight:** 39 oz. **Length:** 11.5 overall. **Grips:** Walnut. **Sights:** Fixed. **Features:** U.S. markings and cartouche, case-hardened frame and hammer; 45 Colt only. Imported by Cimarron F.A. Co.
Price: $547.65

COLT NEW FRONTIER
Caliber: .44 Special and .45 Colt. **Barrel:** 4-3/4", 5-1/2",and 7-1/2". **Grip:** Walnut. **Features:** The legend of Colt continues in the New Frontier®, Single Action Army. From 1890 to 1898, Colt manufactured a variation of the venerable Single Action Army with a uniquely different profile. The "Flattop Target Model" was fitted with an adjustable leaf rear sight and blade front sights. Colt has taken this concept several steps further to bring shooters a reintroduction of a Colt classic. The New Frontier has that sleek flattop design with an adjustable rear sight for windage and elevation and a target ready ramp style front sight. The guns are meticulously finished in Colt Royal Blue on both the barrel and cylinder, with a case colored frame.
Price: $1455.00

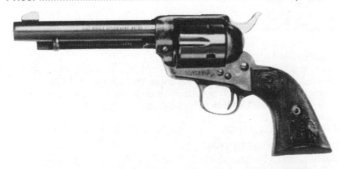

COLT SINGLE-ACTION ARMY
Caliber: 357 Mag., 45 Colt, 6-shot. **Barrel:** 4.75, 5.5, 7.5. **Weight:** 40 oz. (4.75 barrel). **Length:** 10.25 overall (4.75 barrel). **Grips:** Black Eagle composite. **Sights:** Blade front, notch rear. **Features:** Available in full nickel finish with nickel grip medallions, or Royal

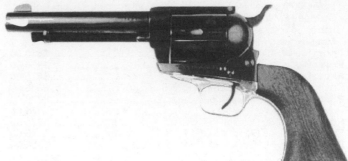

Blue with color case-hardened frame. Reintroduced 1992. Sheriff's Model and Frontier Six introduced 2008, available in nickel in 2010.
Price: (blue)... $1,315.00
Price: (stainless)... $1,518.00

EAA BOUNTY HUNTER SA
Caliber: 22 LR/22 WMR, 357 Mag., 44 Mag., 45 Colt, 6-shot. **Barrel:** 4.5, 7.5. **Weight:** 2.5 lbs. **Length:** 11 overall (4-5/8 barrel). **Grips:** Smooth walnut. **Sights:** Blade front, grooved topstrap rear. **Features:** Transfer bar safety; 3-position hammer; hammer forged barrel. Introduced 1992. Imported by European American Armory.
Price: Blue or case-hardened, from.. $392.00
Price: Nickel $432.00
Price: 22 LR/22 WMR, blue $292.00
Price: As above, nickel $325.00

EMF MODEL 1873 FRONTIER MARSHAL
Caliber: 357 Mag., 45 Colt. **Barrel:** 4.75, 5-1/2, 7.5. **Weight:** 39 oz. **Length:** 10.5 overall. **Grips:** One-piece walnut. **Sights:** Blade front, notch rear. **Features:** Bright brass trigger guard and backstrap, color case-hardened frame, blued barrel and cylinder. Introduced 1998. Imported from Italy.
Price: $485.00

EMF HARTFORD SINGLE-ACTION
Caliber: 357 Mag., 32-20, 38-40, 44-40, 44 Spec., 45 Colt. **Barrel:** 4.75, 5.5, 7.5. **Weight:** 45 oz. **Length:** 13 overall (7.5 barrel). **Grips:** Smooth walnut. **Sights:** Blade front, fixed rear. **Features:** Identical to the original Colts. All major parts serial numbered using original Colt-style lettering, numbering. Bullseye ejector head and color case-hardening on old model frame and hammer. Introduced 1990. Imported by E.M.F. Co.
Price: Old Model $489.90
Price: Case-hardened New Model frame $489.90

EMF GREAT WESTERN II EXPRESS SINGLE-ACTION
Same as the regular model except uses grip of the Colt Lightning revolver. Barrel lengths of 4.75. Introduced 2006. Imported by E.M.F. Co.
Price: Stainless, Ultra Ivory grips $715.00
Price: Walnut grips $690.00

EMF 1875 OUTLAW
Caliber: 357 Mag., 44-40, 45 Colt. **Barrel:** 7.5, 9.5. **Weight:** 46 oz. **Length:** 13.5 overall. **Grips:** Smooth walnut. **Sights:** Blade front, fixed groove rear. **Features:** Authentic copy of 1875 Remington with firing pin in hammer; color case-hardened frame, blue cylinder, barrel, steel backstrap and trigger guard. Also available in nickel, factory engraved. Imported by E.M.F. Co.

Price: All calibers **$479.90**
Price: Laser Engraved **$684.90**

EMF 1890 POLICE
Similar to the 1875 Outlaw except has 5.5 barrel, weighs 40 oz., with 12.5 overall length. Has lanyard ring in butt. No web under barrel. Calibers: 45 Colt. Imported by E.M.F. Co.
Price: **$489.90**

EMF 1873 GREAT WESTERN II
Caliber: .357, 45 LC, 44/40. **Barrel:** 4 3/4, 5.5, 7.5. **Weight:** 36 oz.
Length: 11 (5.5). **Grips:** Walnut. **Sights:** Blade front, notch rear.
Features: Authentic reproduction of the original 2nd generation Colt single-action revolver. Standard and bone case hardening. Coil hammer spring. Hammer-forged barrel.
Price: 1873 Californian **$520.00**
Price: 1873 Custom series, bone or nickel, ivory-like grips ... **$689.90**
Price: 1873 Stainless steel, ivory-like grips **$589.90**

FREEDOM ARMS MODEL 83 PREMIER GRADE
Caliber: 357 Mag., 41 Mag., 44 Mag., 454 Casull, 475 Linebaugh, 500 Wyo. Exp., 5-shot. **Barrel:** 4.75, 6, 7.5, 9 (357 Mag. only), 10 (except 357 Mag. and 500 Wyo. Exp. **Weight:** 53 oz. (7.5 bbl. In 454 Casull). **Length:** 13 (7.5 bbl.). **Grips:** Impregnated hardwood. **Sights:** Adjustable rear with replaceable front sight. Fixed rear notch and front blade. **Features:** Stainless steel construction with brushed finish; manual sliding safety bar. Micarta grips optional. 500 Wyo. Exp. Introduced 2006. Lifetime warranty. Made in U.S.A. by Freedom Arms, Inc.
Price: From **$2,370.00**

FREEDOM ARMS MODEL 83 FIELD GRADE
Caliber: 22 LR, 357 Mag., 41 Mag., 44 Mag., 454 Casull, 475 Linebaugh, 500 Wyo. Exp., 5-shot. **Barrel:** 4.75, 6, 7.5, 9 (357 Mag. only), 10 (except 357 Mag. and 500 Wyo. Exp.) **Weight:** 56 oz.

(7.5 bbl. In 454 Casull). **Length:** 13.1 (7.5 bbl.). **Grips:** Pachmayr standard, impregnated hardwood or Micarta optional. **Sights:** Adjustable rear with replaceable front sight. Model 83 frame. All stainless steel. Introduced 1988. Made in U.S.A. by Freedom Arms Inc.
Price: From **$1,985.00**

FREEDOM ARMS MODEL 97 PREMIER GRADE
Caliber: 17 HMR, 22 LR, 32 H&R, 357 Mag., 6-shot; 41 Mag., 44 Special, 45 Colt, 5-shot. **Barrel:** 4.25, 5.5, 7.5, 10 (17 HMR, 22 LR & 32 H&R). **Weight:** 40 oz. (5.5 357 Mag.). **Length:** 10.75 (5.5 bbl.). **Grips:** Impregnated hardwood; Micarta optional. **Sights:** Adjustable rear, replaceable blade front. Fixed rear notch and front blade. **Features:** Stainless steel construction, brushed finish, automatic transfer bar safety system. Introduced in 1997. Lifetime warranty. Made in U.S.A. by Freedom Arms.
Price: From **$1,995.00**

HERITAGE ROUGH RIDER
Caliber: 17 HMR, 17 LR, 32 H&R, 32 S&W, 32 S&W Long, 357 Mag, 44-40, 45 LC, 22 LR, 22 LR/22 WMR combo, 6-shot. **Barrel:** 2.75, 3.5, 4.75, 5.5, 6.5, 7.5, 9. **Weight:** 31 to 38 oz. **Length:** NA. **Grips:** Exotic cocobolo laminated wood or mother-of-pearl; bird's-head models offered. **Sights:** Blade front, fixed rear. Adjustable sight on 4, 6 and 9 models. **Features:** Hammer block safety. Transfer bar with Big Bores. High polish blue, black satin, silver satin, case-hardened and stainless finish. Introduced 1993. Made in U.S.A. by Heritage Mfg., Inc.
Price: From **$169.95**

LEGACY SPORTS PUMA M-1873

LEGACY SPORTS PUMA M-1873

Caliber: .22 LR / .22 Mag. **Barrel:** 4.75", 5.5", and 7.5". **Weight:** 2.2 lbs. - 2.4 lbs. **Grips:** Wood or plastic. **Features:** With the frame size and weight of a Single Action Army revolver, the M-1873 makes a great practice gun for Cowboy Action or an ideal carry gun for camping, hiking or fishing. The M-1873 loads from a side gate and at the half cock position just like a centerfire "Peacemaker", but is chambered for .22 LR or .22 magnum rounds. The hammer is made to traditional SAA appearance and feel. A key-operated, hammer block safety is standard on the left side of the recoil shield. The M-1873 is offered in matte black or antiqued finish. Construction is of alloy and steel.
Price: .... $178.00 to $320.00

MAGNUM RESEARCH BFR SINGLE ACTION

Caliber: .45/70, .480 Ruger/.475 Linebaugh, .450 Marlin, .500 S&W, .50AE, .444 Marlin, .30/30 Winchester, .45 Long Colt/.410 (not for sale in CA), and the new .460 S&W Magnum - as well as .454 Casull. **Barrel:** 6.5", 7.5", and 10". **Weight:** 3.6 lbs. - 5.3 lbs. **Grips:** Black rubber. **Sights:** Rear sights are the same configuration as the Ruger revolvers. Many after-market rear sights will fit the BFR. Front sights are machined by Magnum in four heights and anodized flat black. The four heights accommodate all shooting styles, barrel lengths and calibers. All sights are interchangeable with each BFR's. **Features:** Crafted in the U.S.A., the BFR single action 5-shot stainless steel revolver frames are CNC machined inside and out from a "pre-heat treated" investment casting. This is done to prevent warping and dimensional changes or shifting that occurs during the heat treat process. The result is a dimensionally perfect-machined frame. Magnum Research designed the frame with large calibers and large recoil in mind, built to close tolerances to handle the pressure of true big-bore calibers. The BFR is equiped with Transfer Bar. This is a safety feature that allows the gun to be carried safely with all five chambers loaded. The transfer bar allows the revolver to fire ONLY after the hammer has been fully cocked and trigger pulled. If the revolver is dropped or the hammer slips while in the process of cocking it the gun will not accidentally discharge.
Price: $1050.00

NAVY ARMS BISLEY MODEL SINGLE-ACTION

Caliber: 44-40 or 45 Colt, 6-shot cylinder. **Barrel:** 4.75, 5.5, 7.5. **Weight:** 40 oz. **Length:** 12.5 overall (7.5 barrel). **Grips:** Smooth walnut. **Sights:** Blade front, notch rear. **Features:** Replica of Colt's Bisley Model. Polished blue finish, color case-hardened frame. Introduced 1997. Imported by Navy Arms.
Price: $503.00

NAVY ARMS 1873 GUNFIGHTER SINGLE-ACTION

Caliber: 357 Mag., 44-40, 45 Colt, 6-shot cylinder. **Barrel:** 4.75, 5.5, 7.5. **Weight:** 37 oz. **Length:** 10.25 overall (4.75 barrel). **Grips:** Checkered black polymer. **Sights:** Blade front, notch rear. **Features:** Blued with color case-hardened receiver, trigger and hammer; German Silver backstrap and triggerguard. American made Wolff trigger and mainsprings installed. Introduced 2005. Imported by Navy Arms.
Price: $545.00

NAVY ARMS 1875 SCHOFIELD

Caliber: 44-40, 45 Colt, 6-shot cylinder. **Barrel:** 3.5, 5, 7. **Weight:** 39 oz. **Length:** 10.75 overall (5 barrel). **Grips:** Smooth walnut. **Sights:** Blade front, notch rear. **Features:** Replica of Smith & Wesson Model 3 Schofield. Single-action, top-break with automatic ejection. Polished blue finish. Introduced 1994. Imported by Navy Arms.
Price: Hideout Model, 3.5 barrel $882.00
Price: Wells Fargo, 5 barrel $882.00
Price: U.S. Cavalry model, 7 barrel, military markings $882.00

NAVY ARMS FOUNDER'S MODEL SCHOFIELD

Caliber: 45 Colt, 38 Spl., 6-shot cylinder. **Barrel:** 7.5. **Weight:** 41 oz. **Length:** 13.75. **Grips:** Deluxe hand-rubbed walnut with cartouching. **Sights:** Blade front, notch rear. **Features:** Charcoal blued with bone color case-hardened receiver, trigger, hammer and backstrap. Limited production "VF" serial number prefix. Introduced 2005. Imported by Navy Arms.
Price: $924.00

Prices given are believed to be accurate at time of publication however, many factors affect retail pricing so exact prices are not possible.

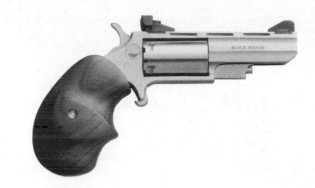

NAVY ARMS NEW MODEL RUSSIAN
Caliber: 44 Russian, 6-shot cylinder. **Barrel:** 6.5. **Weight:** 40 oz. **Length:** 12 overall. **Grips:** Smooth walnut. **Sights:** Blade front, notch rear. **Features:** Replica of the S&W Model 3 Russian Third Model revolver. Spur trigger guard, polished blue finish. Introduced 1999. Imported by Navy Arms.
Price: $924.00

NAVY ARMS SCOUT SMALL FRAME SINGLE-ACTION
Caliber: 38 Spec., 6-shot cylinder. **Barrel:** 4.75, 5.5. **Weight:** 37 oz. **Length:** 10.75 overall (5.5 barrel). **Grips:** Checkered black polymer. **Sights:** Blade front, notch rear. **Features:** Blued with color case-hardened receiver, trigger and hammer; German silver backstrap and triggerguard. Introduced 2005. Imported by Navy Arms.
Price: $545.00

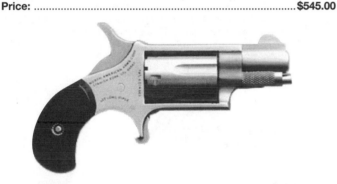

NORTH AMERICAN ARMS MINI
Caliber: 22 Short, 22 LR, 22 WMR, 5-shot. **Barrel:** 1-1/8, 1-5/8. **Weight:** 4 to 6.6 oz. **Length:** 3-5/8 to 6-1/8 overall. **Grips:** Laminated wood. **Sights:** Blade front, notch fixed rear. **Features:** All stainless steel construction. Polished satin and matte finish. Engraved models available. From North American Arms.
Price: 22 Short, 22 LR $229.00

NORTH AMERICAN ARMS MINI-MASTER
Caliber: 22 LR, 22 WMR, 5-shot cylinder. **Barrel:** 4. **Weight:** 10.7 oz. **Length:** 7.75 overall. **Grips:** Checkered hard black rubber. **Sights:** Blade front, white outline rear adjustable for elevation, or fixed. **Features:** Heavy vented barrel; full-size grips. Non-fluted cylinder. Introduced 1989.
Price: Fixed sight $284.00
Price: Adjustable sight $314.00

NORTH AMERICAN ARMS BLACK WIDOW
Similar to Mini-Master, 2 heavy vent barrel. Built on 22 WMR frame. Non-fluted cylinder, black rubber grips. Available with Millett Low Profile fixed sights or Millett sight adjustable for elevation only. Overall length 5-7/8, weighs 8.8 oz. From North American Arms.
Price: Adjustable sight, 22 LR or 22 WMR $299.00
Price: Fixed sight, 22 LR or 22 WMR $269.00

NORTH AMERICAN ARMS "THE EARL" SINGLE-ACTION
Caliber: 22 Magnum with 22 LR accessory cylinder, 5-shot cylinder. **Barrel:** 4" octagonal. **Weight:** 6.8 oz. **Length:** 7-3/4 overall. **Grips:** Wood. **Sights:** Barleycorn front and fixed notch rear. **Features:** Single-action mini-revolver patterned after 1858-style Remington percussion revolver. Includes a spur trigger and a faux loading lever that serves as cylinder pin release.
Price: .... $289.00 (22 Magnum only); $324.00 (convertible)

RUGER NEW MODEL SINGLE SIX SERIES
Caliber: .22 LR, .17 HMR. **Capacity:** Six rounds. Convertible and Hunter models come with extra cylinder for .22 WMR. **Barrel:** 4.62, 5.5, 6.5 or 9.5 inches. **Weight:** 35 to 42 ounces. **Grips:** Black checkered hard rubber, black laminate or hardwood (stainless model only). Single-Six .17 Model available only with 6.5-inch barrel, blue finish, rubber grips. Hunter Model available only with 7.5-inch barrel, black laminate grips.
Price: (stainless) .... $569.00 to $639.00
Price: (Hunter) $799.00

RUGER SINGLE-TEN AND RUGER SINGLE-NINE SERIES
Caliber: .22 LR, .22 WMR. **Capacity:** 10 (.22 LR Single-Ten), 9 (.22 Mag Single-Nine). **Barrel:** 5.5 inches (Single-Ten), 6.5 inches (Single-Nine). **Weight:** 38 to 39 ounces. **Grips:** Hardwood Gunfighter. **Sights:** Williams Adjustable Fiber Optic.
Price: $629.00

RUGER NEW MODEL BLACKHAWK/BLACKHAWK CONVERTIBLE
Caliber: 30 Carbine, 357 Mag./38 Spec., 41 Mag., 44 Special, 45 Colt, 6-shot. **Barrel:** 4-5/8, 5.5, 6.5, 7.5 (30 carbine and 45 Colt). **Weight:** 36 to 45 oz. **Lengths:** 10-3/8 to 13.5. **Grips:** Rosewood or black checkered. **Sights:** 1/8 ramp front, micro-click rear adjustable for windage and elevation. **Features:** Rosewood grips, Ruger transfer bar safety system, independent firing pin, hardened chrome-moly steel frame, music wire springs through-out. Case and lock included. Convertibles come with extra cylinder.

Prices given are believed to be accurate at time of publication however, many factors affect retail pricing so exact prices are not possible.

68TH EDITION, 2014 ◈ **447**

Price:	**$609.00**
Price: (Convertible, .357/9mm)	**$679.00**
Price: (Convertible, .45 Colt/.45 ACP)	**$679.00**
Price: (stainless, .357 only)	**$729.00**

RUGER BISLEY SINGLE-ACTION

Similar to standard Blackhawk, hammer is lower with smoothly curved, deeply checkered wide spur. The trigger is strongly curved with wide smooth surface. Longer grip frame. Adjustable rear sight, ramp-style front. Unfluted cylinder and roll engraving, adjustable sights. Chambered for 44 Mag. and 45 Colt; 7.5 barrel; overall length 13.5; weighs 48-51 oz. Plastic lockable case. Orig. fluted cylinder introduced 1985; discontinued 1991. Unfluted cylinder introduced 1986.
Price: RB-44W (44 Mag), RB45W (45 Colt) **$799.00**

RUGER NEW MODEL SUPER BLACKHAWK

Caliber: 44 Mag., 6-shot. Also fires 44 Spec. **Barrel:** 4-5/8, 5.5, 7.5, 10.5 bull. **Weight:** 45-55 oz. **Length:** 10.5 to 16.5 overall. **Grips:** Rosewood. **Sights:** 1/8 ramp front, micro-click rear adjustable for windage and elevation. **Features:** Ruger transfer bar safety system, fluted or unfluted cylinder, steel grip and cylinder frame, round or square back trigger guard, wide serrated trigger, wide spur hammer. With case and lock.
Price: **$739.00**

RUGER NEW MODEL SUPER BLACKHAWK HUNTER

Caliber: 44 Mag., 6-shot. **Barrel:** 7.5, full-length solid rib, unfluted cylinder. **Weight:** 52 oz. **Length:** 13-5/8. **Grips:** Black laminated wood. **Sights:** Adjustable rear, replaceable front blade. **Features:** Reintroduced Ultimate SA revolver. Includes instruction manual, high-impact case, set 1 medium scope rings, gun lock, ejector rod as standard. Bisley-style frame available.
Price: (Hunter, Bisley Hunter) **$859.00**

RUGER NEW VAQUERO SINGLE-ACTION

Caliber: 357 Mag., 45 Colt, 6-shot. **Barrel:** 4-5/8, 5.5, 7.5. **Weight:** 39-45 oz. **Length:** 10.5 overall (4-5/8 barrel). **Grips:** Rubber with Ruger medallion. **Sights:** Fixed blade front, fixed notch rear. **Features:** Transfer bar safety system and loading gate interlock. Blued model color case-hardened finish on frame, rest polished and blued. Engraved model available. Gloss stainless. Introduced 2005.
Price: **$739.00**

RUGER NEW MODEL BISLEY VAQUERO

Similar to New Vaquero but with Bisley-style hammer and grip frame. Chambered in 357 and 45 Colt. Features include a 5.5 barrel, simulated ivory grips, fixed sights, six-shot cylinder. Overall length is 11.12, weighs 45 oz.
Price: **$809.00**

RUGER NEW BEARCAT SINGLE-ACTION

Caliber: 22 LR, 6-shot. **Barrel:** 4. **Weight:** 24 oz. **Length:** 9 overall. **Grips:** Smooth rosewood with Ruger medallion. **Sights:** Blade front, fixed notch rear. **Features:** Reintroduction of the Ruger Bearcat with slightly lengthened frame, Ruger transfer bar safety system. Available in blue only. Rosewood grips. Introduced 1996 (blued), 2003 (stainless). With case and lock.
Price: SBC-4, blued **$569.00**
Price: KSBC-4, satin stainless **$619.00**

STI TEXICAN SINGLE-ACTION

Caliber: 45 Colt, 6-shot. **Barrel:** 5.5, 4140 chrome-moly steel by Green Mountain Barrels. 1:16 twist, air gauged to .0002. Chamber to bore alignment less than .001. Forcing cone angle, 3 degrees. **Weight:** 36 oz. **Length:** 11. **Grips:** "No crack" polymer. **Sights:** Blade front, fixed notch rear. **Features:** Parts made by ultra-high speed or electron discharge machined processes from chrome-moly steel forgings or bar stock. Competition sights, springs, triggers and hammers. Frames, loading gates, and hammers are color case hardened by Turnbull Restoration. Frame, back strap, loading gate, trigger guard, cylinders made of 4140 re-sulphurized Maxell

3.5 steel. Hammer firing pin (no transfer bar). S.A.S.S. approved. Introduced 2008. Made in U.S.A. by STI International.
Price: 5.5 barrel $1,299.99

UBERTI 1851-1860 CONVERSION
Caliber: 38 Spec., 45 Colt, 6-shot engraved cylinder. **Barrel:** 4.75, 5.5, 7.5, 8 **Weight:** 2.6 lbs. (5.5 bbl.). **Length:** 13 overall (5.5 bbl.). **Grips:** Walnut. **Features:** Brass backstrap, trigger guard; color case hardened frame, blued barrel, cylinder. Introduced 2007. Imported from Italy by Stoeger Industries.
Price: 1851 Navy $549.00
Price: 1860 Army $579.00

UBERTI 1871-1872 OPEN TOP
Caliber: 38 Spec., 45 Colt, 6-shot engraved cylinder. **Barrel:** 4.75, 5.5, 7.5. **Weight:** 2.6 lbs. (5.5 bbl.). **Length:** 13 overall (5.5 bbl.). **Grips:** Walnut. **Features:** Blued backstrap, trigger guard; color case-hardened frame, blued barrel, cylinder. Introduced 2007. Imported from Italy by Stoeger Industries.
Price: .... $529.00 to $549.00

UBERTI 1873 CATTLEMAN SINGLE-ACTION
Caliber: 45 Colt; 6-shot fluted cylinder. **Barrel:** 4.75, 5.5, 7.5. **Weight:** 2.3 lbs. (5.5 bbl.). **Length:** 11 overall (5.5 bbl.). **Grips:** Styles: Frisco

(pearl styled); Desperado (buffalo horn styled); Chisholm (checkered walnut); Gunfighter (black checkered), Cody (ivory styled), one-piece walnut. **Sights:** Blade front, groove rear. **Features:** Steel or brass backstrap, trigger guard; color case-hardened frame, blued barrel, cylinder. NM designates New Model plunger style frame; OM designates Old Model screw cylinder pin retainer. Imported from Italy by Stoeger Industries.
Price: 1873 Cattleman Frisco $809.00
Price: 1873 Cattleman Desperado (2006) $819.00
Price: 1873 Cattleman Chisholm (2006) $549.00
Price: 1873 Cattleman NM, blued 4.75 barrel $619.00
Price: 1873 Cattleman NM, Nickel finish, 7.5 barrel $819.00
Price: 1873 Cattleman Cody $819.00

UBERTI 1873 CATTLEMAN BIRD'S HEAD SINGLE ACTION
Caliber: 357 Mag., 45 Colt; 6-shot fluted cylinder **Barrel:** 3.5, 4, 4.75, 5.5. **Weight:** 2.3 lbs. (5.5 bbl.). **Length:** 10.9 overall (5.5 bbl.). **Grips:** One-piece walnut. **Sights:** Blade front, groove rear. **Features:** Steel or brass backstrap, trigger guard; color case-hardened frame, blued barrel, cylinder. Imported from Italy by Stoeger Industries.
Price: 1873 Cattleman Bird's Head OM 3.5 barrel $569.00

UBERTI CATTLEMAN .22
Caliber: .22 LR. **Capacity:** 6 or 12 rounds. **Barrel:** 5.5 inches **Grips:** One piece walnut. **Sights:** Fixed. **Features:** Blued and case hardened finish, steel or brass backstrap/trigger guard.
Price: (brass backstrap, trigger guard) $509
Price: (steel backstrap, trigger guard).........................$529
Price: (12-shot model, steel backstrap, trigger guard) $559

UBERTI 1873 BISLEY SINGLE-ACTION
Caliber: 357 Mag., 45 Colt (Bisley); 22 LR and 38 Spec. (Stallion), both with 6-shot fluted cylinder. **Barrel:** 4.75, 5.5, 7.5. **Weight:** 2 to 2.5 lbs. **Length:** 12.7 overall (7.5 barrel). **Grips:** Two-piece walnut. **Sights:** Blade front, notch rear. **Features:** Replica of Colt's Bisley Model. Polished blue finish, color case-hardened frame. Introduced 1997. Imported by Stoeger Industries.
Price: 1873 Bisley, 7.5 barrel $599.00

UBERTI 1873 BUNTLINE AND REVOLVER CARBINE SINGLE-ACTION
Caliber: 357 Mag., 44-40, 45 Colt; 6-shot fluted cylinder **Barrel:** 18.

UBERTI 1873 BUNTLINE

Length: 22.9 to 34. **Grips:** Walnut pistol grip or rifle stock. **Sights:** Fixed or adjustable. **Features:** Imported from Italy by Stoeger Industries.
Price: 1873 Revolver Carbine, 18 barrel, 34 OAL **$729.00**
Price: 1873 Catttleman Buntline Target, 18 barrel, 22.9 OAL ..**$639.00**

UBERTI OUTLAW, FRONTIER, AND POLICE
Caliber: 45 Colt, 6-shot fluted cylinder. **Barrel:** 5.5, 7.5. **Weight:** 2.5 to 2.8 lbs. **Length:** 10.8 to 13.6 overall. **Grips:** Two-piece smooth walnut. **Sights:** Blade front, notch rear. **Features:** Cartridge version of 1858 Remington percussion revolver. Nickel and blued finishes. Imported by Stoeger Industries.
Price: 1875 Outlaw nickel finish **$629.00**
Price: 1875 Frontier, blued finish **$539.00**
Price: 1890 Police, blued finish **$549.00**

UBERTI 1870 SCHOFIELD-STYLE TOP BREAK
Caliber: 38, 44 Russian, 44-40, 45 Colt, 6-shot cylinder. **Barrel:** 3.5, 5, 7. **Weight:** 2.4 lbs. (5 barrel) **Length:** 10.8 overall (5 barrel). **Grips:** Two-piece smooth walnut or pearl. **Sights:** Blade front, notch rear. **Features:** Replica of Smith & Wesson Model 3 Schofield. Single-action, top break with automatic ejection. Polished blue finish (first model). Introduced 1994. Imported by Stoeger Industries.
Price: No. 3-2nd Model, nickel finish **$1,369.00**

U.S. FIRE ARMS SINGLE-ACTION
Caliber: 45 Colt (standard); 32 WCF, 38 WCF, 38 Spec., 44 WCF, 44 Special, 6-shot cylinder. **Barrel:** 4.75, 5.5, 7.5. **Weight:** 37 oz. **Length:** NA. **Grips:** Hard rubber. **Sights:** Blade front, notch rear. **Features:** Recreation of original guns; 3 and 4 have no ejector. Available with all-blue, blue with color case-hardening, or full nickel-plate finish. Other models include Custer Battlefield Gun ($1,625, 7.5 barrel), Flattop Target ($1,625), Sheriff's Model ($875, with barrel lengths starting at 2), Snubnose ($1,475, barrel lengths 2, 3, 4), Omni-Potent Six-Shooter and Omni-Target Six-Shooter (from $1,625), Bisley ($1,350, introduced 2006). Made in U.S.A. by United States Fire Arms Mfg. Co.
Price: Blue/cased-colors **$1,150.00**
Price: Nickel **$1,220.00**

U.S. FIRE ARMS U.S. PRE-WAR
Caliber: 45 Colt (standard); 32 WCF, 38 WCF, 38 Spec., 44 WCF, 44 Special. **Barrel:** 4.75, 5.5, 7.5. **Grips:** Hard rubber. **Features:** Armory bone case/Armory blue finish standard, cross-pin or black powder frame. Introduced 2002. Made in U.S.A. by United States Firearms Mfg. Co.
Price: **$1,495.00**

AMERICAN DERRINGER MODEL 1
Caliber: All popular handgun calibers plus .45 Colt/.410 Shotshell. **Capacity:** Two rounds, (.45-70 model is single shot). **Barrel:** 3 inches. **Overall length:** 4.82 inches. **Weight:** 15 oz. **Features:** Manually operated hammer-block safety automatically disengages when hammer is cocked.
Price: .... $600 to $700

AMERICAN DERRINGER MODEL 10
Caliber: .38 Special, .45 ACP, .45 Colt. **Capacity:** Two rounds. **Barrel:** 3 inches.
Price: (.38 Spl.) $625.00
Price: (.45 ACP or Colt) $670.00

AMERICAN DERRINGER DA38
Caliber: .38 Special, .357 Magnum, 9mm Luger, .40 S&W. **Barrel:** 3.3 inches. **Weight:** 14.5 oz. **Features:** Double-action operation with hammer-block thumb safety. Barrel, receiver and all internal parts are made from stainless steel.
Price: .... $655.00 to $705.00

BOND ARMS TEXAS DEFENDER DERRINGER
Caliber: From 22 LR to 45 LC/410 shotshells. **Barrel:** 3. **Weight:** 20 oz. **Length:** 5. **Grips:** Rosewood. **Sights:** Blade front, fixed rear. **Features:** Interchangeable barrels, stainless steel firing pins, cross-bolt safety, automatic extractor for rimmed calibers. Stainless steel construction, brushed finish. Right or left hand.
Price: $399.00
Price: Interchangeable barrels, 22 LR thru 45 LC, 3 ....$139.00
Price: Interchangeable barrels, 45 LC, 3.5 ..... $159.00 to $189.00

BOND ARMS RANGER
Caliber: 45 LC/.410 shotshells. **Barrel:** 4.25. **Weight:** 23.5 oz. **Length:** 6.25. **Features:** Similar to Snake Slayer except no trigger guard. Intr. 2008. From Bond Arms.
Price: $649.00

BOND ARMS CENTURY 2000 DEFENDER
Caliber: 45 LC/.410 shotshells. **Barrel:** 3.5. **Weight:** 21 oz. **Length:** 5.5. **Features:** Similar to Defender series.
Price: $420.00

BOND ARMS COWBOY DEFENDER
Caliber: From 22 LR to 45 LC/.410 shotshells. **Barrel:** 3. **Weight:** 19 oz. **Length:** 5.5. **Features:** Similar to Defender series. No trigger guard.
Price: $399.00

BOND ARMS SNAKE SLAYER
Caliber: 45 LC/.410 shotshell (2.5 or 3). **Barrel:** 3.5. **Weight:** 21 oz. **Length:** 5.5. **Grips:** Extended rosewood. **Sights:** Blade front, fixed rear. **Features:** Single-action; interchangeable barrels; stainless steel firing pin. Introduced 2005.
Price: $469.00

BOND ARMS SNAKE SLAYER IV
Caliber: 45 LC/410 shotshell (2.5 or 3). **Barrel:** 4.25. **Weight:** 22 oz. **Length:** 6.25. **Grips:** Extended rosewood. **Sights:** Blade front, fixed rear. **Features:** Single-action; interchangeable barrels; stainless steel firing pin. Introduced 2006.
Price: $499.00

CHARTER ARMS DIXIE DERRINGERS
Caliber: 22 LR, 22 WMR. **Barrel:** 1.125. **Weight:** 6 oz. **Length:** 4 overall. **Grips:** Black polymer **Sights:** Blade front, fixed notch rear. **Features:** Stainless finish. Introduced 2006. Made in U.S.A. by Charter Arms.
Price: $215.00

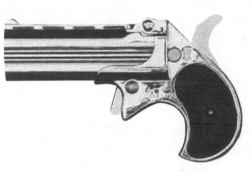

COBRA BIG BORE DERRINGERS
Caliber: 22 WMR, 32 H&R Mag., 38 Spec., 9mm Para., 380 ACP. **Barrel:** 2.75. **Weight:** 14 oz. **Length:** 4.65 overall. **Grips:** Textured black or white synthetic or laminated rosewood. **Sights:** Blade front, fixed notch rear. **Features:** Alloy frame, steel-lined barrels, steel breech block. Plunger-type safety with integral hammer block. Black, chrome or satin finish. Introduced 2002. Made in U.S.A. by Cobra Enterprises of Utah, Inc.
Price: $165.00

COBRA STANDARD SERIES DERRINGERS
Caliber: 22 LR, 22 WMR, 25 ACP, 32 ACP. **Barrel:** 2.4. **Weight:** 9.5 oz. **Length:** 4 overall. **Grips:** Laminated wood or pearl. **Sights:** Blade front, fixed notch rear. **Features:** Choice of black powder

coat, satin nickel or chrome finish. Introduced 2002. Made in U.S.A. by Cobra Enterprises of Utah, Inc.

Price: **$145.00**

COBRA LONG-BORE DERRINGERS

Caliber: 22 WMR, 38 Spec., 9mm Para. **Barrel:** 3.5. **Weight:** 16 oz. **Length:** 5.4 overall. **Grips:** Black or white synthetic or rosewood. **Sights:** Fixed. **Features:** Chrome, satin nickel, or black Teflon finish. Introduced 2002. Made in U.S.A. by Cobra Enterprises of Utah, Inc.

Price: **$165.00**

COBRA TITAN
.45 LC/.410 DERRINGER

Caliber: .45 LC, .410 or 9mm, 2 round capacity. **Barrel:** 3-1/2". **Weight:** 16.4 oz. **Grip:** Rosewood. **Features:** The Titan is a powerhouse derringer designed to shoot a .45 Long Colt or the wide range of personal protection .410 shells with additional calibers to follow soon. Standard finishes include: satin stainless, black stainless, and brushed stainless. Made in U.S.A. by Cobra Enterprises of Utah, Inc.

Price: **$419.00**

COMANCHE SUPER SINGLE-SHOT

Caliber: 45 LC, .410 **Barrel:** 10. **Sights:** Adjustable. **Features:** Blue finish, not available for sale in CA, MA. Distributed by SGS Importers International, Inc.

Price: **$200.00**

MAXIMUM SINGLE-SHOT

Caliber: 22 LR, 22 Hornet, 22 BR, 22 PPC, 223 Rem., 22-250, 6mm BR, 6mm PPC, 243, 250 Savage, 6.5mm-35M, 270 MAX, 270 Win., 7mm TCU, 7mm BR, 7mm-35, 7mm INT-R, 7mm-08, 7mm Rocket, 7mm Super-Mag., 30 Herrett, 30 Carbine, 30-30, 308 Win., 30x39,

32-20, 350 Rem. Mag., 357 Mag., 357 Maximum, 358 Win., 375 H&H, 44 Mag., 454 Casull. **Barrel:** 8.75, 10.5, 14. **Weight:** 61 oz. (10.5 bbl.); 78 oz. (14 bbl.). **Length:** 15, 18.5 overall (with 10.5 and 14 bbl., respectively). **Grips:** Smooth walnut stocks and forend. Also available with 17 finger groove grip. **Sights:** Ramp front, fully adjustable open rear. **Features:** Falling block action; drilled and tapped for M.O.A. scope mounts; integral grip frame/receiver; adjustable trigger; Douglas barrel (interchangeable). Introduced 1983. Made in U.S.A. by M.O.A. Corp.

Price: Stainless receiver, blue barrel **$839.00**
Price: Stainless receiver, stainless barrel **$937.00**

PUMA BOUNTY HUNTER

Caliber: .44/40, .44 Mag. and .45 Colt, 6-shot magazine capacity. **Barrel:** 12. **Weight:** 4.5 lbs. **Length:** 24. **Stock:** Walnut. **Sights:** Fixed sights. **Features:** A piece of 1950's TV nostalgia, the Bounty Hunter is a reproduction of the gun carried by Western character Josh Randall in the series "Wanted: Dead or Alive". The Bounty Hunter is based on a Model 92 rifle, but is considered by Federal Law as a pistol, because it is built from the ground up as a handgun. Manufactured in the U.S.A. by Chiappa Firearms of Dayton, OH, the Bounty Hunter features a 12" barrel and 6 round tubular magazine. At just 24" OAL, the Bounty Hunter makes an ideal pack gun or camp defense pistol. The Bounty Hunter has a teardrop shaped loop lever and is built with the same fit, finish and high grade Italian walnut stocks as our Puma M-92 and M-86 rifles.

Price: .45LC, Case Hardened/Blued **$1,372.00**
Price: .44/40, Case Hardened/Blued **$1,372.00**
Price: .44MAG, Case Hardened/Blued **$1,372.00**

ROSSI MATCHED PAIR , "DUAL THREAT PERFORMER"

Caliber: .22LR, .45 Colt and .410 GA. 2.5" shotshells, single shot. **Sights:** Fiber optic front sights, adjustable rear. **Features:** Two-in-one pistol system with sinle-shot simplicity. Removable choke and cushioned grip with a Taurus Security System.

Price: **$336.00**

ROSSI RANCH HAND

Caliber: .38/.357, .45 Colt or .44 magnum, 6-shot. **eight:** 4 lbs. **Length:** 24 overall. **Stock:** Brazilian hardwood. **Sights:** Adjustable buckhorn. **Features:** Matte blue or case hardened finish with oversized lever loop to accomodate gloved hands. Equipped with classic buckhorn sights for fast target aquisition and a Taurus Security Sytem.

Price: **$676.00**

Prices given are believed to be accurate at time of publication however, many factors affect retail pricing so exact prices are not possible.

THOMPSON/CENTER ENCORE

Calibers: .17 HMR, .22 LR, .204 Ruger, .223, .22-250, .243, .270., 7mm-08, .308, .20-06, .44 Mag., .45 Colt/.410, .45-70 Govt., .460 S&W, .500 S&W. Single shot, break-open design. **Barrel:** 15 inches, 12 inches (.44 Mag., .45 Colt). **Weight:** 4.25 to 4.5 lbs. **Grip:** Walnut on blued models, rubber on stainless. Matching fore-end. **Sights:** Adjustable rear, ramp front. **Features:** Interchangeable barrels, adjustable trigger. Pro Hunter has "Swing Hammer" to allow reaching the hammer when the gun is scoped. Other Pro Hunter features include fluted barrel.
Price: .... $679.00 to $769.00
Price: (Pro Hunter) $1,199.00

ROSSI WIZARD

Caliber: .243 Win. or .22-.250 Rem with other calibers coming soon, single shot. **Barrel:** 11" **Length:** 20.4" **Features:** Offered in blue finish, additional features include pistol grip with custom grooves for fast handling and comfort, manual safety with "S" mark for visual confirmation, hammer extension, scope rail and the unique onboard Taurus Security System. Pistol offers outstanding and reliable performance in a versatile package. Its ingenious break-open barrel system changes quickly by unscrewing the front swivel with no tools needed.
Price: $336.00

THOMPSON/CENTER G2 CONTENDER

A second generation Contender pistol maintaining the same barrel interchangeability with older Contender barrels and their corresponding forends (except Herrett forend). The G2 frame will not accept old-style grips due to the change in grip angle. Incorporates an automatic hammer block safety with built-in interlock. Features include trigger adjustable for overtravel, adjustable rear sight; ramp front sight blade, blued steel finish.
Price: $809.00

Prices given are believed to be accurate at time of publication however, many factors affect retail pricing so exact prices are not possible.

68TH EDITION, 2014 ⊕ **453**

ARMALITE M15A2 CARBINE
Caliber: 223 Rem., 30-round magazine. **Barrel:** 16" heavy chrome lined; 1:9" twist. **Weight:** 7 lbs. **Length:** 35-11/16" overall. **Stock:** Green or black composition. **Sights:** Standard A2. **Features:** Upper and lower receivers have push-type pivot pin; hard coat anodized; A2-style forward assist; M16A2-type raised fence around magazine release button. Made in U.S.A. by ArmaLite, Inc.
Price: Green **$1,174.00**
Price: Black **$1,174.00**

ARMALITE AR-10A4 SPECIAL PURPOSE
Caliber: .243, 308 Win., 10- and 20-round magazine. **Barrel:** 20" chrome-lined, 1:11.25" twist. **Weight:** 9.6 lbs. **Length:** 41" overall. **Stock:** Green or black composition. **Sights:** Detachable handle, front sight, or scope mount available; comes with international style flattop receiver with Picatinny rail. **Features:** Forged upper receiver with case deflector. Receivers are hard-coat anodized. Introduced 1995. Made in U.S.A. by ArmaLite, Inc.
Price: Green **$1,557.00**
Price: Black **$1,557.00**

ArmaLite AR-10A2
Utilizing the same 20" double-lapped, heavy barrel as the ArmaLite AR10A4 Special Purpose Rifle. Offered in 308 Win. only. Made in U.S.A. by ArmaLite, Inc.
Price: AR-10A2 rifle or carbine **$1,561.00**

ARMALITE AR-10B
Caliber: 308 Win. **Barrel:** 20" chrome lined. **Weight:** 9.5 lbs. **Length:** 41". **Stock:** Synthetic. **Sights:** Rear sight adjustable for windage, small and large apertures. **Features:** Early-style AR-10. Lower and upper receivers made of forged aircraft alloy. Brown Sudanese-style furniture, elevation scale window. Charging handle in carry handle. Made in U.S.A. by Armalite.
Price: **$1,699.00**

ARSENAL, INC. SLR-107F
Caliber: 7.62x39mm. **Barrel:** 16.25". **Weight:** 7.3 lbs. **Stock:** Left-side folding polymer stock. **Sights:** Adjustable rear. **Features:** Stamped receiver, 24mm flash hider, bayonet lug, accessory lug, stainless steel heat shield, two-stage trigger. Introduced 2008. Made in U.S.A. by Arsenal, Inc.

Price: SLR-107FR, includes scope rail **$950.00**

ARSENAL, INC. SLR-107CR
Caliber: 7.62x39mm. **Barrel:** 16.25". **Weight:** 6.9 lbs. **Stock:** Left-side folding polymer stock. **Sights:** Adjustable rear. **Features:** Stamped receiver, front sight block/gas block combination, 500-meter rear sight, cleaning rod, stainless steel heat shield, scope rail, and removable muzzle attachment. Introduced 2007. Made in U.S.A. by Arsenal, Inc.
Price: SLR-107CR **$1,200.00**

ARSENAL, INC. SLR-106CR
Caliber: 5.56 NATO. **Barrel:** 16.25", Steyr chrome-lined barrel, 1:7 twist rate. **Weight:** 6.9 lbs. **Stock:** Black polymer folding stock with cutout for scope rail. Stainless-steel heatshield handguard. **Sights:** 500-meter rear sight and rear sight block calibrated for 5.56 NATO.

Warsaw Pact scope rail. **Features:** Uses Arsenal, Bulgaria, Mil-Spec receiver, two-stage trigger, hammer and disconnector. Polymer magazines in 5- and 10-round capacity in black and green, with Arsenal logo. Others are 30-round black waffles, 20- and 30-round versions in clear/smoke waffle, featuring the "10" in a double-circle logo of Arsenal, Bulgaria. Ships with 5-round magazine, sling, cleaning kit in a tube, 16" cleaning rod, oil bottle. Introduced 2007. Made in U.S.A. by Arsenal, Inc.
Price: SLR-106CR **$1,200.00**

AUTO-ORDNANCE 1927A-1 THOMPSON
Caliber: 45 ACP. **Barrel:** 16.5". **Weight:** 13 lbs. **Length:** About 41" overall (Deluxe). **Stock:** Walnut stock and vertical forend. **Sights:** Blade front, open rear adjustable for windage. **Features:** Recreation of Thompson Model 1927. Semi-auto only. Deluxe model has finned barrel, adjustable rear sight and compensator; Standard model has plain barrel and military sight. From Auto-Ordnance Corp.
Price: Deluxe **$1,420.00**
Price: Lightweight model (9.5 lbs.) **$1,145.00**

AUTO-ORDNANCE THOMPSON M1/M1-C
Similar to the 1927 A-1 except is in the M-1 configuration with side cocking knob, horizontal forend, smooth unfinned barrel, sling swivels on butt and forend. Matte-black finish. Introduced 1985.
Price: M1 semi-auto carbine **$1,334.00**
Price: M1-C lightweight semi-auto **$1,065.00**

AUTO-ORDNANCE 1927 A-1 COMMANDO
Similar to the 1927 A-1 except has Parkerized finish, black-finish wood butt, pistol grip, horizontal forend. Comes with black nylon sling. Introduced 1998. Made in U.S.A. by Auto-Ordnance Corp.
Price: T1-C **$1,393.00**

AUTO ORDNANCE M1 CARBINE
Caliber: .30 Carbine (15-shot magazine). **Barrel:** 18". **Weight:** 5.4 to 5.8 lbs. **Length:** 36.5". **Stock:** Wood or polymer. **Sights:** Blade front, flip style rear. A faithful recreation of the military carbine.
Price: $816.00

BARRETT MODEL 82A-1 SEMI-AUTOMATIC
Caliber: .416 Barret, 50 BMG, 10-shot detachable box magazine. **Barrel:** 29". **Weight:** 28.5 lbs. **Length:** 57" overall. **Stock:** Composition with energy-absorbing recoil pad. **Sights:** Scope

Prices given are believed to be accurate at time of publication however, many factors affect retail pricing so exact prices are not possible.

optional. **Features:** Semi-automatic, recoil operated with recoiling barrel. Three-lug locking bolt; muzzle brake. Adjustable bipod. Introduced 1985. Made in U.S.A. by Barrett Firearms.
Price: From $8,900.00

BARRETT M107A1
Caliber: 50 BMG. 10-round detachable magazine. **Barrel:** 20 or 29 inches. **Sights:** 27-inch optics rail with fllp-up iron sights. **Weight:** 30.9 lbs. **Finish:** Flat Dark Earth. Features: Four-port cylindrical muzzle brake. Quick-detachable Barrett QDL Suppressor. Adjustable bipod and monopod.
Price: $12,000.00

BARRETT MODEL REC7
Caliber: 5.56 (.223), 6.8 Rem. SPC. 30-round magazine. **Barrel:** 16 inches. **Sights:** ARMS rear, folding front. Weight: 28.7 lbs. **Features:** AR-style configuration with standard 17-4 stainless piston system, two-position forward venting gas plug, chrome-lined gas block, A2 flash hider, 6-postion MOE stock.
Price: $1,950.00

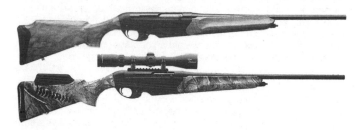

BENELLI R1
Caliber: .30-06 (4+1), .300 Win Mag (3+1), .338 Win Mag (3+1). **Weight:** 7.1 lbs. **Length:** 43.75" to 45.75". **Stock:** Select satin walnut or synthetic. **Sights:** None. **Features:** Auto-regulating gas-operated system, three-lug rotary bolt, interchangeable barrels, optional recoil pads. Introduced 2003. Imported from Italy by Benelli USA.
Price: ....$1,019.00 to $1,249.00

BENELLI MR1
Gas-operated semiauto rifle chambered in 5.56 NATO. Features include 16-inch 1:9 hard chrome-lined barrel, synthetic stock with pistol grip, rotating bolt, military-style aperture sights with picatinny rail. Comes equipped with 5-round detachable magazine but accepts M16 magazines.
Price: $1339.00

BERETTA CX4/PX4 STORM CARBINE
Caliber: 9mm Para., 40 S&W, 45 ACP. **Weight:** 5.75 lbs. **Barrel Length:** 16.6", chrome lined, rate of twist 1:16 (40 S&W) or 1:10 (9mm Para.). **Length:** NA. **Stock:** Black synthetic. **Sights:** NA. **Features:** Introduced 2005. Imported from Italy by Beretta USA.
Price: $900.00

BROWNING BAR SAFARI AND SAFARI W/BOSS SEMI-AUTO
Caliber: Safari: 243 Win., 25-06 Rem., 270 Win., 7mm Rem. Mag., 30-06 Spfl., 308 Win., 300 Win. Mag., 338 Win. Mag. Safari w/ BOSS: 270 Win., 7mm Rem. Mag., 30-06 Spfl., 300 Win. Mag., 338 Win. Mag., plus 270 WSM, 7mm WSM, 300 WSM. **Barrel:** 22-24" round tapered. **Weight:** 7.4-8.2 lbs. **Length:** 43-45" overall. **Stock:** French walnut pistol grip stock and forend, hand checkered. **Sights:** No sights. **Features:** Has new bolt release lever; removable trigger assembly with larger trigger guard; redesigned gas and buffer systems. Detachable 4-round box magazine. Scroll-engraved receiver is tapped for scope mounting. BOSS barrel vibration modulator and muzzle brake system available. Mark II Safari introduced 1993. Imported from Belgium by Browning.
Price: BAR MK II Safari, from $1,300.00
Price: BAR Safari w/BOSS, from $1,500.00

BROWNING BAR SHORTTRAC/LONGTRAC
Caliber: (ShortTrac models) 270 WSM, 7mm WSM, 300 WSM, 243 Win., 308 Win., 325 WSM; (LongTrac models) 270 Win., 30-06 Spfl., 7mm Rem. Mag., 300 Win. Mag. **Barrel:** 23". **Weight:** 6 lbs. 10 oz. to 7 lbs. 4 oz. **Length:** 41.5" to 44". **Stock:** Satin-finish walnut, pistol-grip, fluted forend. **Sights:** Adj. rear, bead front standard, no sights on BOSS models (optional). **Features:** Designed to handle new WSM chamberings. Gas-operated, blued finish, rotary bolt design (LongTrac models).
Price: BAR ShortTrac, 243 Win., 308 Win. from $1,070.00
Price: BAR ShortTrac Left-Hand, intr. 2007, from $1,129.00
Price: BAR ShortTrac Mossy Oak New Break-up
.... $1,249.00 to $1,349.00
Price: BAR LongTrac Left Hand, 270 Win., 30-06 Spfl.,
from $1,129.00
Price: BAR LongTrac, from $1,079.00
Price: BAR LongTrac Mossy Oak Break Up, intr. 2007,
from $1,249.00
Price: Bar LongTrac, Digital Green camo (2009)
.... $1,247.00 to $1,347.00

BROWNING BAR STALKER
Caliber: 243 Win., 308 Win., 270 Win., 30-06 Spfl., 270 WSM, 7mm WSM, 300 WSM, 300 Win. Mag., 338 Win. Mag. **Barrel:** 20-24". **Weight:** 7.1-7.75 LBS. **Length:** 41-45" overall. **Stock:** Black composite stock and forearm. **Sights:** Hooded front and adjustable rear. **Features:** Gas-operated action with seven-lug rotary bolt; dual action bars; 2-, 3- or 4-shot magazine (depending on cartridge). Introduced 2001. Imported by Browning.
Price: BAR ShortTrac or LongTrac Stalker, from...................$1,340.00
Price: BAR Lightweight Stalker, from...............................$1,230.00

BUSHMASTER 300 AAC BLACKOUT
Caliber: .300 AAC. New cartridge for AR platform that matches 7.62x39 ballistics. **Features:** Utilizes regular AR magazines at full capacity. Muzzle brake. Magpul stock and grip.
Price: $1471

BUSHMASTER 308 HUNTER
Caliber: .308 Win / 7.62 NATO., 5-round magazine. **Barrel:** 20". **Weight:** 8-1/2 lbs. **Length:** 38-1/4" overall. **Stock:** Standard A2 stock with Hogue® rubberized pistol grip. **Sights:** Two ¾" mini-risers for optics mounting. **Features:** These top quality Bushmaster .308 Rifles were developed for the Hunter who intends to immediately add optics (scope, red dot or holographic sight) to the rifle. The premium 20" heavy fluted profile barrel is chrome lined in both bore and chamber to provide Bushmaster accuracy, durability and maintenance ease.
Price: 308 Hunter. $1,685.00

BUSHMASTER ACR
Caliber: 5.56mm, 6.5mm, 6.8mm., 30-round polymer magazine. **Barrel:** All three calibers are availaible with 10-1/2", 14-1/2", 16-1/2" and 18" barrels. **Weight:** 14-1/2" bbl 7 lbs.. **Length:** 14-1/5" bbl with stock folded: 25-3/4", with stock deployed (mid) 32-5/8", 10.5" bbl with stock folded: 21-5/16", with stock deployed (mid): 27-7/8", with stock deployed and extended: 31-3/4". Folding Stock Length of Pull - 3". **Stock:** Fixed high-impact composite A-frame stock with rubber butt pad and sling mounts (ORC & A-TACS®) **Features:** Cold hammer-forged barrels with melonite coating for extreme long life. A2 birdcage-type hider to control muzzle flash and adjustable, two-position, gas piston-driven system for firing suppressed or unsuppressed, supported by hardened internal bearing rails. Tool-less, quick-change barrel system available in 10.5", 14.5" and 16.5" and in multiple calibers. Multi-caliber bolt carrier assembly quickly and easily changes from 223/5.56mm NATO to 6.8mm Rem SPC (spec II chamber) Free-floating MIL-STD 1913 monolithic top rail for optic mounting. Fully ambidextrous controls including magazine release, bolt catch and release, fire selector and non reciprocating charging handle. High-impact composite hand guard with heat shield – accepts rail inserts. High-impact composite lower receiver with textured magazine well and modular grip storage. Fire Control – Semi and Full Auto two-stage standard AR capable of accepting drop-in upgrade. Magazine – Optimized for MagPul PMAG Accepts standard NATO/M-16 magazines.
Price: Basic ORC Configuration $2,343.00
Price: A-TACS Basic Configuration $2,540.00
Price: Basic Folder Configuration.........................$2,490.00
Price: Basic State Compliant Configuration $2,343.00

BUSHMASTER VARMINTER
Caliber: 223 Rem., 5-shot. **Barrel:** 24", 1:9" twist, fluted, heavy, stainless. **Weight:** 8.75 lbs. **Length:** 42.25". **Stock:** Rubberized pistol grip. **Sights:** 1/2" scope risers. **Features:** Gas-operated, semi-auto, two-stage trigger, slotted free floater forend, lockable hard case.
Price: $1,430.00

BUSHMASTER 6.8 SPC/7.62X39 PATROLMAN'S CARBINE
Caliber: 6.8 SPC, 26-shot mag. **Barrel:** 16" M4 profile. **Weight:** 6.57 lbs. **Length:** 32.75" overall. **Features:** Semi-auto AR-style with Izzy muzzle brake, six-position telestock. Available in A2 (fixed carry handle) or A3 (removable carry handle) configuration.
Price: $1,368.00

BUSHMASTER ORC CARBINE
Caliber: 5.56/223. **Barrel:** 16" M4 profile. **Weight:** 6 lbs. **Length:** 32.5" overall. **Features:** AR-style carbine with chrome-lined barrel, fixed carry handle, receiver-length picatinny optics rail, heavy oval M4-style handguards.
Price: $1,391.00

BUSHMASTER 11.5" BARREL CARBINE
Caliber: 5.56/223, 30-shot mag. **Barrel:** 11.5". **Weight:** 6.46 lbs. or 6.81 lbs. **Length:** 31.625" overall. **Features:** AR-style carbine with chrome-lined barrel with permanently attached BATF-approved 5.5" flash suppressor, fixed or removable carry handle, optional optics rail.
Price: $1,215.00

BUSHMASTER HEAVY-BARRELED CARBINE
Caliber: 5.56/223. **Barrel:** 16". **Weight:** 6.93 lbs. to 7.28 lbs. **Length:** 32.5" overall. **Features:** AR-style carbine with chrome-lined heavy profile vanadium steel barrel, fixed or removable carry handle, six-position telestock.
Price: $1,215.00

BUSHMASTER MODULAR CARBINE
Caliber: 5.56/223, 30-shot mag. **Barrel:** 16". **Weight:** 7.3 lbs. **Length:** 36.25" overall. **Features:** AR-style carbine with chrome-lined chrome-moly vanadium steel barrel, skeleton stock or six-position telestock, clamp-on front sight and detachable flip-up dual aperature rear.
Price: $1,745.00

BUSHMASTER CARBON 15 TOP LOADER
Caliber: 5.56/223, internal 10-shot mag. **Barrel:** 16" chrome-lined M4 profile. **Weight:** 5.8 lbs. **Length:** 32.75" overall. **Features:** AR-style carbine with standard A2 front sight, dual aperture rear sight, receiver-length optics rail, lightweight carbon fiber receiver, six-position telestock. Will not accept detachable box magazines.
Price: $1,070.00

BUSHMASTER CARBON 15 FLAT-TOP CARBINE
Caliber: 5.56/223, 30-shot mag. **Barrel:** 16" M4 profile. **Weight:** 5.77 lbs. **Length:** 32.75" overall. **Features:** AR-style carbine Izzy flash suppressor, AR-type front sight, dual aperture flip, lightweight carbon composite receiver with receiver-length optics rail.
Price: $1,155.00
Price: Carbon 15 9mm, chambered in 9mm Parabellum $1,025.00

BUSHMASTER 450 RIFLE AND CARBINE
Caliber: 450 Bushmaster. **Barrel:** 20" (rifle), 16" (carbine), five-round mag. **Weight:** 8.3 lbs. (rifle), 8.1 lbs. (carbine). **Length:** 39.5" overall (rifle), 35.25" overall (carbine). **Features:** AR-style with chrome-lined chrome-moly barrel, synthetic stock, Izzy muzzle brake.
Price: $1,350.00

BUSHMASTER GAS PISTON
Caliber: 223, 30-shot mag. **Barrel:** 16". **Weight:** 7.46 lbs. **Length:** 32.5" overall. **Features:** Semi-auto AR-style with telescoping stock, carry handle, piston assembly rather than direct gas impingement.
Price: $1,795.00

BUSHMASTER TARGET
Caliber: 5.56/223, 30-shot mag. **Barrel:** 20" or 24» heavy or standard. **Weight:** 8.43 lbs. to 9.29 lbs. **Length:** 39.5" or 43.5" overall. **Features:** Semi-auto AR-style with chrome-lined or stainless steel 1:9 barrel, fixed or removable carry handle, manganese phosphate finish.
Price: $1,195.00

BUSHMASTER M4A3 TYPE CARBINE
Caliber: 5.56/223, 30-shot mag. **Barrel:** 16". **Weight:** 6.22 to 6.7 lbs. **Length:** 31" to 32.5» overall. **Features:** AR-style carbine with chrome-moly vanadium steel barrel, Izzy-type flash-hider, six-position telestock, various sight options, standard or multi-rail handguard, fixed or removable carry handle.
Price: $1,270.00
Price: Patrolman's Carbine: Standard mil-style sights $1,270.00
Price: State Compliance Carbine: Compliant with various state regulations $1,270.00

CENTURY INTERNATIONAL AES-10 HI-CAP
Caliber: 7.62x39mm. 30-shot magazine. **Barrel:** 23.2". **Weight:** NA. **Length:** 41.5" overall. **Stock:** Wood grip, forend. **Sights:** Fixed-notch rear, windage-adjustable post front. **Features:** RPK-style, accepts

Prices given are believed to be accurate at time of publication however, many factors affect retail pricing so exact prices are not possible.

standard double-stack AK-type mags. Side-mounted scope mount, integral carry handle, bipod. Imported by Century Arms Int'l.
Price: AES-10, from $450.00

CENTURY INTERNATIONAL GP WASR-10 HI-CAP
Caliber: 7.62x39mm. 30-shot magazine. **Barrel:** 16.25", 1:10 right-hand twist. **Weight:** 7.2 lbs. **Length:** 34.25" overall. **Stock:** Wood laminate or composite, grip, forend. **Sights:** Fixed-notch rear, windage-adjustable post front. **Features:** Two 30-rd. detachable box magazines, cleaning kit, bayonet. Version of AKM rifle; U.S.-parts added for BATFE compliance. Threaded muzzle, folding stock, bayonet lug, compensator, Dragunov stock available. Made in Romania by Cugir Arsenal. Imported by Century Arms Int'l.
Price: GP WASR-10, from..$350.00

CENTURY INTERNATIONAL WASR-2 HI-CAP
Caliber: 5.45x39mm. 30-shot magazine. **Barrel:** 16.25". **Weight:** 7.5 lbs. **Length:** 34.25" overall. **Stocks:** Wood laminate. **Sights:** Fixed-notch rear, windage-adjustable post front. **Features:** 1 30-rd. detachable box magazine, cleaning kit, sling. WASR-3 HI-CAP chambered in 223 Rem. Imported by Century Arms Int'l.
Price: GP WASR-2/3, from $250.00

CENTURY INTERNATIONAL M70AB2 SPORTER
Caliber: 7.62x39mm. 30-shot magazine. **Barrel:** 16.25". **Weight:** 7.5 lbs. **Length:** 34.25" overall. **Stocks:** Metal grip, wood forend. **Sights:** Fixed-notch rear, windage-adjustable post front. **Features:** 2 30-rd. double-stack magazine, cleaning kit, compensator, bayonet lug and bayonet. Paratrooper-style Kalashnikov with under-folding stock. Imported by Century Arms Int'l.
Price: M70AB2, from $480.00

COLT MATCH TARGET MODEL
Caliber: 223 Rem., 5-shot magazine. **Barrel:** 16.1", 20" or 24". **Weight:** 7.1 to 8.5 lbs. **Length:** 34.5" to 39" overall. **Stock:** Composition stock, grip, forend. **Sights:** Post front, rear adjustable for windage and elevation. **Features:** 5-round detachable box magazine, flash suppressor, sling swivels. Forward bolt assist included. Introduced 1991.

Made in U.S.A. by Colt's Mfg. Co., Inc.
Price: Match Target HBAR MT6601.................................$1,230.00

COLT CARBINE
Caliber: .223, 9mm, .308. Capacity 9, 10, 20 or 30 rounds. **Barrel:** 16.1 or 20 inches. Offered in a wide range of AR configurations and finishes.
Price: ....$899 to $2129

DPMS PANTHER ARMS AR-15
Caliber: .204 Ruger, 6.8x43mm SPC. **Barrel:** 16" to 24". **Weight:** 7.75 to 11.75 lbs. **Length:** 34.5" to 42.25" overall. **Stock:** Black Zytel composite. **Sights:** Square front post, adjustable A2 rear. **Features:** Steel or stainless steel heavy or bull barrel; hardcoat anodized receiver; aluminum free-float tube handguard; many options. From DPMS Panther Arms.
Price: ....$939.00 to $1,269.00

DPMS PANTHER ARMS PRAIRIE PANTHER
Semiauto AR-style rifle chambered in 5.56 NATO. Features include 20-inch 416 stainless fluted heavy 1:8 barrel; phosphated steel bolt; free-floated carbon fiber handguard; flattop upper with Picatinny rail; aluminum lower; two 30-round magazines; skeletonized Zytel stock; Choice of matte black or one of several camo finishes.
Price: ....$1,269.00 to $1,289.00

DPMS PANTHER ARMS PANTHER REPR
Semiauto AR-style rifle chambered in .308 Win./7.62 NATO. Features include 18-inch 416 stainless steel 1:10 barrel; phosphated steel bolt; 4-rail free-floated handguard; no sights; aluminum lower; two 19-round magazines; Coyote Brown camo finish overall.
Price: $2,549.00

DPMS PANTHER ARMS MK12
Caliber: .308 Win./7.62 NATO. **Barrel:** 18 inches. **Weight:** 8.5 lbs. **Sights:** Midwest Industry flip-up. **Features:** 4-rail free floating handguard, flash hider, extruded 7029 T6 A3 Flattop receiver.
Price: $1,759.00

DPMS 3G2
Caliber: .223/5.56. **Barrel:** 16 inches. **Weight:** 7.1 lbs. **Stock:** Magpul STR with Hogue rubber pistol grip. **Sights:** Magpul Gen 2 BUS. **Features:** Miculek Compensator, two-stage fire control. M111 Modular handguard allows placement of sights on top rail or 45-degree angle.
Price: $1,239.00

DPMS LITE HUNTER
Caliber: .243, .260 Rem., .308, .338 Federal. **Barrel:** 20 inches, stainless. **Weight:** 8 pounds. **Stock:** Standard A2. **Features:** Two-stage match trigger. Hogue pistol grip. Optics ready top rail.
Price: $1,499.00

DPMS 300 AAC BLACKOUT
Caliber: .300 AAC Blackout. **Barrel:** 16-inch heavy 4150 chrome-lined. **Weight:** 7 pounds. **Stock:** Adjustable 6-position.
Price: $1,199.00

DPMS ORACLE
Caliber: .223/5.56 or .308/7.62. **Barrel:** 16 inches. **Weight:** 6.2 (.223), 8.3 (308). Standard AR-15 fire control with A3 flattop receiver. **Finish:** Matte black or A-TACS camo.
Price: ....**.223 $739, $849 (A-TACS)**
Price: ....**.308 $1099, $1189 (A-TACS)**

DSA SA58 CONGO, PARA CONGO
Caliber: 308 Win. **Barrel:** 18" w/short Belgian short flash hider. **Weight:** 8.6 lbs. (Congo); 9.85 lbs. (Para Congo). **Length:** 39.75" **Stock:** Synthetic w/military grade furniture (Congo); Synthetic with non-folding steel para stock (Para Congo). **Sights:** Elevation adjustable protected post front sight, windage adjustable rear peep (Congo); Belgian type Para Flip Rear (Para Congo). **Features:** Fully-adjustable gas system, high-grade steel upper receiver with carry handle. Made in U.S.A. by DSA, Inc.
Price: Congo...$1,975.00
Price: Para Congo $2,200.00

DSA SA58 STANDARD
Caliber: 308 Win. **Barrel:** 21" bipod cut w/threaded flash hider. **Weight:** 8.75 lbs. **Length:** 43". **Stock:** Synthetic, X-Series or optional

folding para stock. **Sights:** Elevation-adjustable post front, windage-adjustable rear peep. **Features:** Fully adjustable short gas system, high grade steel or 416 stainless upper receiver. Made in U.S.A. by DSA, Inc.
Price: From $1,700.00

DSA SA58 CARBINE
Caliber: 308 Win. **Barrel:** 16.25" bipod cut w/threaded flash hider. **Weight:** 8.35 lbs. **Length:** 37.5". **Stock:** Synthetic, X-Series or optional folding para stock. **Sights:** Elevation-adjustable post front, windage-adjustable rear peep. **Features:** Fully adjustable short gas system, high grade steel or 416 stainless upper receiver. Made in U.S.A. by DSA, Inc.
Price: $1,700.00

DSA SA58 TACTICAL CARBINE
Caliber: 308 Win. **Barrel:** 16.25" fluted with A2 flash hider. **Weight:** 8.25 lbs. **Length:** 36.5". **Stock:** Synthetic, X-Series or optional folding para stock. **Sights:** Elevation-adjustable post front, windage-adjustable match rear peep. **Features:** Shortened fully adjustable short gas system, high grade steel or 416 stainless upper receiver. Made in U.S.A. by DSA, Inc.
Price: $1,975.00

DSA SA58 MEDIUM CONTOUR
Caliber: 308 Win. **Barrel:** 21" w/threaded flash hider. **Weight:** 9.75 lbs. **Length:** 43". **Stock:** Synthetic military grade. **Sights:** Elevation-adjustable post front, windage-adjustable match rear peep. **Features:** Gas-operated semi-auto with fully adjustable gas system, high grade steel receiver. Made in U.S.A. by DSA, Inc.
Price: $1,700.00

DSA ZM4 AR SERIES
Caliber: .223/5.56 NATO. Standard Flattop rifle features include 20-inch, chrome moly heavy barrel with A2 flash hider. **Weight:** 9 pounds. **Features:** Mil-Spec forged lower receiver, forged flattop or A2 upper. Fixed A2 stock. Carbine variations are also available with 16-inch barrels and many options.
Price: ....From $820

EXCEL ARMS ACCELERATOR
Caliber: 17 HMR, 22 WMR, 17M2, 22 LR, 9-shot magazine. **Barrel:** 18" fluted stainless steel bull barrel. **Weight:** 8 lbs. **Length:** 32.5" overall. **Grips:** Textured black polymer. **Sights:** Fully adjustable target sights. **Features:** Made from 17-4 stainless steel, aluminum shroud w/Weaver rail, manual safety, firing-pin block, last-round bolt-hold-open feature. Four packages with various equipment available.

Prices given are believed to be accurate at time of publication however, many factors affect retail pricing so exact prices are not possible.

American made, lifetime warranty. Comes with one 9-round stainless steel magazine and a California-approved cable lock. Introduced 2006. Made in U.S.A. by Excel Arms.
Price: MR-17 17 HMR **$488.00**
Price: MR-22 22 WMR **$523.00**

EXCEL ARMS X-5.7R/X-30R
Caliber: 5.57x28mm (10 or 25-round), .30 Carbine (10 or 20-round magazine). **Barrel:** 18". **Weight:** 6.25 lbs. **Length:** 34 to 38". Available with or without adjustable iron sights. Blow-back action (5.57x28) or delayed blow-back (.30 Carbine.)
PRICE: ....**$795.00 to $916.00**

HECKLER & KOCH MODEL MR556A1
Caliber: .223 Remington/5.56 NATO, 10+1 capacity. **Barrel:** 16.5". **Weight:** 8.9 lbs. **Length:** 33.9"-37.68". **Stock:** Black Synthetic Adjustable. **Features:** Uses the gas piston system found on the HK 416 and G26, which does not introduce propellant gases and carbon fouling into the rifle's interior.
Price: **$3,295.00**

HECKLER & KOCH MODEL MR762A1
Caliber: Similar to Model MR556A1 except chambered for 7.62x51mm/.308 Win. cartridge. **Weight:** 10 lbs. w/empty magazine. **Length:** 36 to 39.5". Variety of optional sights are available. Stock has five adjustable positions.
Price: **$3,995.00**

HECKLER & KOCH USC CARBINE
Caliber: 45 ACP, 10-shot magazine. **Barrel:** 16". **Weight:** 8.6 lb. **Length:** 35.4" overall. **Stock:** Skeletonized polymer thumbhole. **Sights:** Blade front with integral hood, fully adjustable diopter. **Features:** Based on German UMP submachine gun. Blowback operation; almost entirely constructed of carbon fiber-reinforced polymer. Free-floating heavy target barrel. Introduced 2000. From H&K.
Price: **$1,788.00**

HI-POINT 9MM CARBINE
Caliber: 9mm Para., 40 S&W, 10-shot magazine. **Barrel:** 16.5" (17.5" for 40 S&W). **Weight:** 4.5 lbs. **Length:** 31.5" overall. **Stock:** Black polymer, camouflage. **Sights:** Protected post front, aperture rear. Integral scope mount. **Features:** Grip-mounted magazine release.

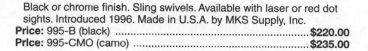

Black or chrome finish. Sling swivels. Available with laser or red dot sights. Introduced 1996. Made in U.S.A. by MKS Supply, Inc.
Price: 995-B (black) **$220.00**
Price: 995-CMO (camo) **$235.00**

LES BAER CUSTOM ULTIMATE AR 223
Caliber: 223. **Barrel:** 18", 20", 22", 24". **Weight:** 7.75 to 9.75 lb. **Length:** NA. **Stock:** Black synthetic. **Sights:** None furnished; Picatinny-style flattop rail for scope mounting. **Features:** Forged receiver; Ultra single-stage trigger (Jewell two-stage trigger optional); titanium firing pin; Versa-Pod bipod; chromed National Match carrier; stainless steel, hand-lapped and cryo-treated barrel; guaranteed to shoot 1/2 or 3/4 MOA, depending on model. Made in U.S.A. by Les Baer Custom Inc.
Price: Super Varmint Model....................................**$2,390.00**
Price: Super Match Model (introduced 2006) **$2,490.00**
Price: M4 Flattop model **$2,360.00**
Price: Police Special 16" (2008) **$1,690.00**
Price: IPSC Action Model **$2,640.00**

LR 300S
Caliber: 5.56 NATO, 30-shot magazine. **Barrel:** 16.5"; 1:9" twist. **Weight:** 7.4-7.8 lbs. **Length:** NA. **Stock:** Folding. **Sights:** YHM flip front and rear. **Features:** Flattop receiver, full length top picatinny rail. Phantom flash hider, multi sling mount points, field strips with no tools. Made in U.S.A. from Z-M Weapons.
Price: AXL, AXLT **$2,139.00**
Price: NXL **$2,208.00**

MERKEL MODEL SR1 SEMI-AUTOMATIC
Caliber: 308 Win., 300 Win Mag. **Features:** Streamlined profile, checkered walnut stock and forend, 19.7- (308) or 20-8" (300 SM) barrel, two- or five-shot detachable box magazine. Adjustable front and rear iron sights with Weaver-style optics rail included. Imported from Germany by Merkel USA.
Price: **$1,595.00**

OLYMPIC ARMS K9, K10, K40, K45 PISTOL-CALIBER AR15 CARBINES
Caliber: 9mm Para., 10mm, 40 S&W, 45 ACP; 32/10-shot modified magazines. **Barrel:** 16" button rifled stainless steel, 1x16 twist rate.

Weight: 6.73 lbs. **Length:** 31.625" overall. **Stock:** A2 grip, M4 6-point collapsible stock. **Features:** A2 upper with adjustable rear sight, elevation adjustable front post, bayonet lug, sling swivel, threaded muzzle, flash suppressor, carbine length handguards. Made in U.S.A. by Olympic Arms, Inc.

Price: K9GL, 9mm Para., Glock lower **$1,092.00**
Price: K10, 10mm, modified 10-round Uzi magazine............ **$1,006.20**
Price: K40, 40 S&W, modified 10-round Uzi magazine **$1,006.20**
Price: K45, 45 ACP, modified 10-round Uzi magazine **$1,006.20**

OLYMPIC ARMS K3B SERIES AR15 CARBINES

Caliber: 5.56 NATO, 30-shot magazines. **Barrel:** 16" button rifled chrome-moly steel, 1x9 twist rate. **Weight:** 5-7 lbs. **Length:** 31.75" overall. **Stock:** A2 grip, M4 6-point collapsible buttstock. **Features:** A2 upper with adjustable rear sight, elevation adjustable front post, bayonet lug, sling swivel, threaded muzzle, flash suppressor, carbine length handguards. Made in U.S.A. by Olympic Arms, Inc.

Price: K3B base model, A2 upper **$815.00**
Price: K3B-M4 M4 contoured barrel & handguards **$1,038.70**
Price: K3B-M4-A3-TC A3 upper, M4 barrel, FIRSH rail handguard **$1,246.70**
Price: K3B-CAR 11.5" barrel with 5.5" permanent flash suppressor.. **$968.50**
Price: K3B-FAR 16" featherweight contoured barrel............. **$1,006.20**

OLYMPIC ARMS PLINKER PLUS AR15 MODELS

Caliber: 5.56 NATO, 30-shot magazine. Barrel 16" or 20" button-rifled chrome-moly steel, 1x9 twist. **Weight:** 7.5-8.5 lbs. **Length:** 35.5"-39.5" overall. **Stock:** A2 grip, A2 buttstock with trapdoor. **Sights:** A1 windage rear, elevation-adjustable front post. **Features:** A1 upper, fiberlite handguards, bayonet lug, threaded muzzle and flash suppressor. Made in U.S.A. by Olympic Arms, Inc.

Price: Plinker Plus.. **$713.70**
Price: Plinker Plus 20... **$843.70**

OLYMPIC ARMS GAMESTALKER

Sporting AR-style rifle chambered in .223, .243 and .25 WSSM and .300 OSSM. Features include forged aluminum upper and lower; flat top receiver with Picatinny rail; gas block front sight; 22-inch stainless steel fluted barrel; free-floating slotted tube handguard; camo finish overall; ACE FX skeleton stock.

Price: **$1,359.00**

REMINGTON MODEL R-15 MODULAR REPEATING

Caliber: 223, 450 Bushmaster **and 30 Rem. AR, five-shot magazine. Barrel:** 18" (carbine), 22", 24". **Weight:** 6.75 to 7.75 lbs. **Length:** 36.25" to 42.25". **Stock:** Camo. **Features:** AR-style with optics rail, aluminum alloy upper and lower.

Price: R-15 Hunter: 30 Rem. AR, 22" barrel, Realtree AP HD camo **$1,225.00**
Price: R-15 VTR Byron South Edition: 223, 18" barrel, Advantage MAX-1 HD camo **$1,772.00**
Price: R-15 VTR SS Varmint: Same as Byron South Edition but with 24" stainless steel barrel **$1,412.00**
Price: R-15 VTR Thumbhole: Similar to R-15 Hunter but with thumbhole stock **$1,412.00**
Price: R-15 VYR Predator: 204 Ruger or .223, 22" barrel ... **$1,225.00**
Price: R-15 Predator Carbine: Similar to above but with 18" barrel **$1,225.00**

REMINGTON MODEL R-25 MODULAR REPEATING

Caliber: 243, 7mm-08, 308 Win., four-shot magazine. **Barrel:** 20" chrome-moly. **Weight:** 7.75 lbs. **Length:** 38.25" overall. **Features:** AR-style semi-auto with single-stage trigger, aluminum alloy upper and lower, Mossy Oak Treestand camo finish overall.

Price: **$1,631.00**

REMINGTON MODEL 750 WOODSMASTER

Caliber: 243 Win., 270 Win., 308 Win., 30-06 Spfl., 35 Whelen. 4-shot magazine. **Barrel:** 22" round tapered. **Weight:** 7.5 lbs. **Length:** 42.6" overall. **Stock:** Restyled American walnut forend and stock with machine-cut checkering. Satin finish. **Sights:** Gold bead front sight on ramp; step rear sight with windage adjustable. **Features:** Replaced wood-stocked Model 7400 line introduced 1981. Gas action, SuperCell recoil pad. Positive cross-bolt safety. Carbine chambered in 308 Win., 30-06 Spfl., 35 Whelen. Receiver tapped for scope mount. Introduced 2006. Made in U.S.A. by Remington Arms Co.

Price: 750 Woodsmaster **$1,004.00**
Price: 750 Woodsmaster Carbine (18.5" bbl.) **$1,004.00**
Price: 750 Synthetic stock (2007)............................. **$884.00**

ROCK RIVER ARMS LAR SERIES

Caliber: .223/5.56, .308/7.62, 6.8 SPC, .458 SOCOM, 9mm and .40 S&W. These AR-15 type rifles and carbines are available with a very wide range of options. Virtually any AR configuration is offered including tactical, hunting and competition models. Some models are available in left-hand versions.

Price: .... **$1010 to $1600**

RUGER SR-556

AR-style semiauto rifle chambered in 5.56 NATO. Feature include two-stage piston; quad rail handguard; Troy Industries sights; black synthetic fixed or telescoping buttstock; 16.12-inch 1:9 steel barrel with birdcage; 10- or 30-round detachable box magazine; black matte finish overall.

Price: **$1,995.00**

RUGER MINI-14 RANCH

Caliber: 223 Rem., 5-shot detachable box magazine. **Barrel:** 18.5". Rifling twist 1:9". **Weight:** 6.75 to 7 lbs. **Length:** 37.25" overall. **Stock:** American hardwood, steel reinforced, or synthetic. **Sights:** Protected blade front, fully adjustable Ghost Ring rear. **Features:** Fixed piston gas-operated, positive primary extraction. New buffer system,

Prices given are believed to be accurate at time of publication however, many factors affect retail pricing so exact prices are not possible.

redesigned ejector system. Ruger S100RM scope rings included on Ranch Rifle. Heavier barrels added in 2008, 20-round magazine added in 1009.

Price: ....$909.00 to $1.069.00
Price: Mini-14/5, Ranch Rifle, blued, scope rings $855.00
Price: K-Mini-14/5, Ranch Rifle, stainless, scope rings ,......... $921.00
Price: K-Mini-6.8/5P, All-Weather Ranch Rifle, stainless, synthetic stock (2008) $921.00
Price: Mini-14 Target Rifle: laminated thumbhole stock, heavy crowned 22" stainless steel barrel, other refinements $1,149.00
Price: Mini-14 ATI Stock: Tactical version of Mini-14 but with six-position collapsible stock or folding stock, grooved pistol grip. multiple picatinny optics/accessory rails $872.00
Price: Mini-14 Tactical Rifle: Similar to Mini-14 but with 16-21" barrel with flash hider, black synthetic stock, adjustable sights $894.00

RUGER MINI THIRTY
Similar to the Mini-14 Ranch Rifle except modified to chamber the 7.62x39 Russian service round. **Weight:** 6.75 lbs. Has 6-groove barrel with 1:10" twist, Ruger Integral Scope Mount bases and protected blade front, fully adjustable Ghost Ring rear. Detachable 5-shot staggered box magazine. 20-round magazines available. Stainless w/ synthetic stock. Introduced 1987.
Price: Stainless, scope rings .... $979.00 to $1,039.00

SIG 556
Caliber: 223 Rem., 30-shot detachable box magazine. **Barrel:** 16". Rifling twist 1:9". **Weight:** 6.8 lbs. **Length:** 36.5" overall. **Stock:** Polymer, folding style. **Sights:** Flip-up front combat sight, adjustable for windage and elevation. **Features:** Based on SG 550 series rifle. Two-position adjustable gas piston operating rod system, accepts standard AR magazines. Polymer forearm, three integrated Picatinny rails, forward mount for right- or left-side sling attachment. Aircraft grade aluminum alloy trigger housing, hard-coat anodized finish; two-stage trigger, ambidextrous safety, 30-round polymer magazine, battery compartments, pistol-grip rubber-padded watertight adjustable butt stock with sling-attachment points. SIG 556 SWAT model has flat-top Picatinny railed receiver, tactical quad rail. SIG 556 HOLO sight options include front combat sight, flip-up rear sight, and red-dot style holographic sighting system with four illuminated reticle patterns. DMR features a 24" military grade cold hammer-forged heavy contour barrel, 5.56mm NATO, target crown. Imported by Sig Sauer, Inc.
Price: From .... $1,266.00 to $1,272.00

SIG-SAUER SIG516 GAS PISTON
AR-style rifle chambered in 5.56 NATO. Features include 14.5-, 16-, 18- or 20-inch chrome-lined barrel; free-floating, aluminum quad rail fore-end with four M1913 Picatinny rails; threaded muzzle with a standard (0.5x28TPI) pattern; aluminum upper and lower receiver is machined; black anodized finish; 30-round magazine; flattop upper; various configurations available.
Price: .... $1,666.00 to $1,706.00

SIG SAUER M400 VARMINTER/PREDATOR SERIES
Caliber: .223/5.56 NATO. AR Flattop design. **Barrel:** 18 or 22-inch heavy stainless match grade with Hogue free-floated fore-end. **Features:** Two-stage Geissele match trigger, Hogue grip, ambidextrous controls, Magpul MOE stock.
Price: $1,384.00

SIG-SAUER SIG716 TACTICAL PATROL
AR-10 type rifle chambered in 7.62 NATO/.308 Winchester. Features include gas-piston operation with 3 round-position (4-position optional) gas valve; 16-, 18- or 20-inch chrome-lined barrel with threaded muzzle and nitride finish; free-floating aluminum quad rail fore-end with four M1913 Picatinny rails; telescoping buttstock; lower receiver is machined from a 7075-T6 Aircraft grade aluminum forging; upper receiver, machined from 7075-T6 aircraft grade aluminum with integral M1913 Picatinny rail.
Price: .... $2,132.00 to $2,666.00

SMITH & WESSON M&P15
Caliber: 5.56mm NATO/223, 30-shot steel magazine. **Barrel:** 16", 1:9 **Weight:** 6.74 lbs., w/o magazine. **Length:** 32-35" overall. **Stock:** Black synthetic. **Sights:** Adjustable post front sight, adjustable dual aperture rear sight. **Features:** 6-position telescopic stock, thermo-set M4 handguard. 14.75" sight radius. 7-lbs. (approx.) trigger pull. 7075 T6 aluminum upper, 4140 steel barrel. Chromed barrel bore, gas key, bolt carrier. Hard-coat black-anodized receiver and barrel finish. Introduced 2006. Made in U.S.A. by Smith & Wesson.
Price: From .... $839.00 to $1,949.00
Price: Sport Model....................................$739.00

SMITH & WESSON M&P15-22
Caliber: .22 LR. (10-round magazine). **Barrel:** 16". **Weight:** 5.5 lbs. **Length:** 30.5 to 33.75". **Stock:** 6-position adjustable. **Sights:** Adjustable. Offered in several variations.
Price: .... $499.00 to $769.00

SMITH & WESSON M&P15-300
Caliber: .300 Whisper/.300 AAC Blackout. Other specifications the same of 5.56 models.
Price: $1,119.00

SMITH & WESSON MODEL M&P15 VTAC
Caliber: 223 Remington/5.56 NATO, 30-round magazine. **Barrel:** 16". **Weight:** 6.5 lbs. **Length:** 35" extended, 32" collapsed, overall. **Features:** Six-position CAR stock. Surefire flash-hider and G2 light

Prices given are believed to be accurate at time of publication however, many factors affect retail pricing so exact prices are not possible.

68TH EDITION, 2014 ✛ **461**

with VTAC light mount; VTAC/JP handguard; JP single-stage match trigger and speed hammer; three adjustable picatinny rails; VTAC padded two-point adjustable sling.
Price: $1,949.00

SMITH & WESSON M&P15PC CAMO
Caliber: 223 Rem/5.56 NATO, A2 configuration, 10-round mag. **Barrel:** 20" stainless with 1:8 twist. **Weight:** 8.2 lbs. **Length:** 38.5" overall. **Features:** AR-style, no sights but integral front and rear optics rails. Two-stage trigger, aluminum lower. Finished in Realtree Advantage Max-1 camo.
Price: $1,539.00

SMITH & WESSON M&P10
Caliber: .308 Win. Capacity: 10 rounds. Barrel: 18 inches. Weight: 7.7 pounds. Features: 6-position CAR stock, black hard anodized finish. Camo finish hunting model available w/5-round magazine.
Price: $1619
Price: (Camo) $1729

SPRINGFIELD ARMORY M1A
Caliber: 7.62mm NATO (308), 5- or 10-shot box magazine. **Barrel:** 25-1/16" with flash suppressor, 22" without suppressor. **Weight:** 9.75 lbs. **Length:** 44.25" overall. **Stock:** American walnut with walnut-colored heat-resistant fiberglass handguard. Matching walnut handguard available. Also available with fiberglass stock. **Sights:** Military, square blade front, full click-adjustable aperture rear. **Features:** Commercial equivalent of the U.S. M-14 service rifle with no provision for automatic firing. From Springfield Armory
Price: SOCOM 16 ....$1,855.00
Price: SOCOM II, from $2,090.00
Price: Scout Squad, from $1,726.00
Price: Standard M1A, from $1,608.00
Price: Loaded Standard, from $1,759.00
Price: National Match, from $2,249.00
Price: Super Match
    (heavy premium barrel) about $2,818.00
Price: Tactical, from $3,780.00

STAG ARMS MODEL 3
Caliber: 5.56 NATO., 30-shot magazine capacity. **Barrel:** 16". **Stock:** Six position collapsible stock. **Sights:** N/A. **Features:** A short barrel with a chrome lined bore and a 6 position collapsible stock. It uses a gas-operated firing system, so the recoil is delayed until the round exits the barrel. Although it doesn't have any sights, it does have a Diamondhead Versa Rail System, which allows users to add Picatinny rails to the top, bottom and sides. The Picatinny rail allows for easy mounting of optics and accessories. Features the Diamondhead Versa Rail System; and right and left handed models are available. Perfect for modification, the Stag Arms Model 3 AR 15 is made to mil-spec requirements to give you the most authentic experience possible.
Price: $895.00

STONER SR-15 M-5
Caliber: 223. **Barrel:** 20". **Weight:** 7.6 lbs. **Length:** 38" overall. **Stock:** Black synthetic. **Sights:** Post front, fully adjustable rear (300-meter sight). **Features:** Modular weapon system; two-stage trigger. Black finish. Introduced 1998. Made in U.S.A. by Knight's Mfg.
Price: $1,695.00

STONER SR-25 CARBINE
Caliber: 7.62 NATO, 10-shot steel magazine. **Barrel:** 16" free-floating **Weight:** 7.75 lbs. **Length:** 35.75" overall. **Stock:** Black synthetic. **Sights:** Integral Weaver-style rail. Scope rings, iron sights optional. **Features:** Shortened, non-slip handguard; removable carrying handle. Matte black finish. Introduced 1995. Made in U.S.A. by Knight's Mfg. Co.
Price: $3,345.00

TAURUS CT G2 CARBINE
Caliber: .40 S&W, 9 mm and .45 ACP, Capacity is 34+1 for 9mm, 15+1 for .40 S&W and 10+1 for .45 ACP. **Barrel:** 16". **Weight:** 134-148 ozs. **Length:** 35.75" overall. **Stock:** Aluminum & Polymer. **Sights:** Adjustable rear sight and fixed front sight. **Features:** Full length Picatinny rail, ambidextrous slide catch, two-position safety/fire selector (semi-auto only…) Made in U.S.A. by Knight's Mfg. Co.
Price: $639.00

WILSON COMBAT TACTICAL
Caliber: 5.56mm NATO, accepts all M-16/AR-15 Style Magazines, includes one 20-round magazine. **Barrel:** 16.25"; 1:9 twist, match-grade fluted. **Weight:** 6.9 lbs. **Length:** 36.25" overall. **Stock:** Fixed or collapsible. **Features:** Free-float ventilated aluminum quad-rail handguard, Mil-Spec parkerized barrel and steel components, anodized receiver, precision CNC-machined upper and lower receivers, 7075 T6 aluminum forgings. Single stage JP Trigger/Hammer Group, Wilson Combat Tactical Muzzle Brake, nylon tactical rifle case. M-4T version has flat-top receiver for mounting optics, OD green furniture, 16.25" match-grade M-4 style barrel. SS-15 Super Sniper Tactical Rifle has 1-in-8 twist, heavy 20" match-grade fluted stainless steel barrel. Made in U.S.A by Wilson Combat.
Price: .... $2,225.00 to $2,450.00

BIG HORN ARMORY MODEL 89 RIFLE AND CARBINE

Lever action rifle or carbine chambered for .500 S&W Magnum. Features include 22-or 18-inch barrel; walnut or maple stocks with pistol grip; aperture rear and blade front sights; recoil pad; sling swivels; enlarged lever loop; magazine capacity 5 (rifle) or 7 (carbine) rounds.

Price: $2,289.00

BROWNING BLR

Action: Lever action with rotating bolt head, multiple-lug breech bolt with recessed bolt face, side ejection. Rack-and-pinion lever. Flush-mounted detachable magazines, with 4+1 capacity for magnum cartridges, 5+1 for standard rounds. **Barrel:** Button-rifled chrome-moly steel with crowned muzzle. **Stock:** Buttstocks and forends are American walnut with grip and forend checkering. Recoil pad installed. **Trigger:** Wide-groove design, trigger travels with lever. Half-cock hammer safety; fold-down hammer. **Sights:** Gold bead on ramp front; low-profile square-notch adjustable rear. **Features:** Blued barrel and receiver, high-gloss wood finish. Receivers are drilled and tapped for scope mounts, swivel studs included. Action lock provided. Introduced 1996. Imported from Japan by Browning.

BROWNING BLR LIGHTWEIGHT W/PISTOL GRIP, SHORT AND LONG ACTION; LIGHTWEIGHT '81, SHORT AND LONG ACTION

Calibers: Short Action, 20" Barrel: 22 250 Rem., 243 Win., 7mm-08 Rem., 308 Win., 358, 450 Marlin. Calibers: Short Action, 22" Barrel: 270 WSM, 7mm WSM, 300 WSM, 325 WSM. Calibers: Long Action 22" Barrel: 270 Win., 30-06. Calibers: Long Action 24" Barrel: 7mm Rem. Mag., 300 Win. Mag. **Weight:** 6.5-7.75 lbs. **Length:** 40-45" overall. **Stock:** New checkered pistol grip and Schnabel forearm. Lightweight '81 differs from Pistol Grip models with a Western-style straight grip stock and banded forearm. Lightweight w/Pistol Grip Short Action and Long Action introduced 2005. Model '81 Lightning Long Action introduced 1996.

Price: Lightweight w/Pistol Grip Short Action, from $1,020.00
Price: Lightweight w/Pistol Grip Long Action $1,100.00
Price: Lightweight '81 Short Action $960.00
Price: Lightweight '81 Long Action $1,040.00
Price: Lightweight '81 Takedown Short Action, intr. 2007,
    from $1,040.00
Price: Lightweight '81 Takedown Long Action, intr. 2007,
    from $1,120.00

CIMARRON 1860 HENRY CIVIL WAR MODEL

Caliber: 44 WCF, 45 LC; 12-shot magazine. **Barrel:** 24" (rifle). **Weight:** 9.5 lbs. **Length:** 43" overall (rifle). **Stock:** European walnut. **Sights:** Bead front, open adjustable rear. **Features:** Brass receiver and buttplate. Uses original Henry loading system. Copy of the original rifle. Charcoal blue finish optional. Introduced 1991. Imported by Cimarron F.A. Co.

Price: From $1,444.78

CIMARRON 1866 WINCHESTER REPLICAS

Caliber: 38 Spec., 357, 45 LC, 32 WCF, 38 WCF, 44 WCF. **Barrel:** 24" (rifle), 20" (short rifle), 19" (carbine), 16" (trapper). **Weight:** 9 lbs. **Length:** 43" overall (rifle). **Stock:** European walnut. **Sights:** Bead front, open adjustable rear. **Features:** Solid brass receiver, buttplate, forend cap. Octagonal barrel. Copy of the original Winchester '66 rifle. Introduced 1991. Imported by Cimarron F.A. Co.

Price: 1866 Sporting Rifle, 24" barrel, from $1,096.64
Price: 1866 Short Rifle, 20" barrel, from $1,096.64
Price: 1866 Carbine, 19" barrel, from $1,123.42
Price: 1866 Trapper, 16" barrel, from $1,069.86

CIMARRON 1873 SHORT

Caliber: 357 Mag., 38 Spec., 32 WCF, 38 WCF, 44 Spec., 44 WCF, 45 Colt. **Barrel:** 20" tapered octagon. **Weight:** 7.5 lbs. **Length:** 39" overall. **Stock:** Walnut. **Sights:** Bead front, adjustable semi-buckhorn rear. **Features:** Has half "button" magazine. Original-type markings, including caliber, on barrel and elevator and "Kings" patent. From Cimarron F.A. Co.

Price: $1,272.00

CIMARRON 1873 DELUXE SPORTING

Similar to the 1873 Short Rifle except has 24" barrel with half-magazine.

Price: $1,272.00

CIMARRON 1873 LONG RANGE

Caliber: 44 WCF, 45 Colt. **Barrel:** 30", octagonal. **Weight:** 8.5 lbs. **Length:** 48" overall. **Stock:** Walnut. **Sights:** Blade front, semi-buckhorn ramp rear. Tang sight optional. **Features:** Color case-hardened frame; choice of modern blue-black or charcoal blue for other parts. Barrel marked "Kings Improvement." From Cimarron F.A. Co.

Price: $1,284.10

EMF 1860 HENRY

Caliber: 44-40 or 45 Colt. **Barrel:** 24". **Weight:** About 9 lbs. **Length:** About 43.75" overall. **Stock:** Oil-stained American walnut. **Sights:** Blade front, rear adjustable for elevation. **Features:** Reproduction of the original Henry rifle with brass frame and buttplate, rest blued. Imported by EMF.

Price: Brass frame $1,149.90
Price: Casehardened frame $1,229.90

EMF 1866 YELLOWBOY LEVER ACTIONS

Caliber: 38 Spec., 44-40, 45 LC. **Barrel:** 19" (carbine), 24" (rifle). **Weight:** 9 lbs. **Length:** 43" overall (rifle). **Stock:** European walnut. **Sights:** Bead front, open adjustable rear. **Features:** Solid brass frame, blued barrel, lever, hammer, buttplate. Imported from Italy by EMF.

Price: Rifle $1,044.90
Price: Border Rifle, Short $969.90

EMF MODEL 1873 LEVER-ACTION

Caliber: 32/20, 357 Mag., 38/40, 44-40, 45 Colt. **Barrel:** 18", 20", 24", 30". **Weight:** 8 lbs. **Length:** 43.25" overall. **Stock:** European walnut. **Sights:** Bead front, rear adjustable for windage and elevation. **Features:** Color case-hardened frame (blue on carbine). Imported by EMF.

Price: $1,099.90

EMF MODEL 1873 REVOLVER CARBINE

Caliber: 357 Mag., 45 Colt. **Barrel:** 18". **Weight:** 4 lbs., 8 oz. **Length:** 43-3/4" overall. **Stock:** One-piece walnut. **Sights:** Blade front, notch rear. **Features:** Color case-hardened frame, blue barrel, backstrap and trigger guard. Introduced 1998. Imported from Italy by EMF.

Price: Standard .... $979.90 to $1,040.00

HENRY .45-70

Caliber: .45-70 (4-shot magazine). **Barrel:** 18.5". **Weight:** 7 lbs. **Stock:** Pistol grip walnut. **Sights:** XS Ghost Rings with blade front.

PRICE: $800

HENRY BIG BOY LEVER-ACTION CARBINE

Caliber: 357 Magnum, 44 Magnum, 45 Colt, 10-shot tubular magazine. **Barrel:** 20" octagonal, 1:38 right-hand twist. **Weight:** 8.68 lbs. **Length:** 38.5" overall. **Stock:** Straight-grip American walnut, brass buttplate. **Sights:** Marbles full adjustable semi-buckhorn rear, brass bead front. **Features:** Brasslite receiver not tapped for scope mount. Made in U.S.A. by Henry Repeating Arms.

Price: H006 44 Magnum, walnut, blued barrel $899.95
Price: H006DD Deluxe 44 Magnum, engraved receiver $1,995.95

HENRY .30/30 LEVER-ACTION CARBINE

Same as the Big Boy except has straight grip American walnut, 30-30 only, 6-shot. Receivers are drilled and tapped for scope mount. Made in U.S.A. by Henry Repeating Arms.
Price: H009 Blued receiver, round barrel $749.95
Price: H009B Brass receiver, octagonal barrel $969.95

MARLIN MODEL 336C LEVER-ACTION CARBINE

Caliber: 30-30 or 35 Rem., 6-shot tubular magazine. **Barrel:** 20" Micro-Groove. **Weight:** 7 lbs. **Length:** 38.5" overall. **Stock:** Checkered American black walnut, capped pistol grip. Mar-Shield finish; rubber buttpad; swivel studs. **Sights:** Ramp front with Wide-Scan hood, semi-buckhorn folding rear adjustable for windage and elevation. **Features:** Hammer-block safety. Receiver tapped for scope mount, offset hammer spur; top of receiver sandblasted to prevent glare. Includes safety lock.
Price: $592.00

MARLIN MODEL 336SS LEVER-ACTION CARBINE

Same as the 336C except receiver, barrel and other major parts are machined from stainless steel. 30-30 only, 6-shot; receiver tapped for scope. Includes safety lock.
Price: $727.00

MARLIN MODEL 336W LEVER-ACTION

Similar to the Model 336C except has walnut-finished, cut-checkered Maine birch stock; blued steel barrel band has integral sling swivel; no front sight hood; comes with padded nylon sling; hard rubber butt-plate. Introduced 1998. Includes safety lock. Made in U.S.A. by Marlin.
Price: $500.00

MARLIN 336BL

Lever action rifle chambered for .30-30. Features include 6-shot full length tubular magazine; 18-inch blued barrel with Micro-Groove rifling (12 grooves); big-loop finger lever; side ejection; blued steel receiver; hammer block safety; brown laminated hardwood pistol-grip stock with fluted comb; cut checkering; deluxe recoil pad; blued swivel studs.
Price: $622.00

MARLIN MODEL XLR LEVER-ACTION RIFLES

Similar to Model 336C except has an 24" stainless barrel with Ballard-type cut rifling, stainless steel receiver and other parts, laminated hardwood stock with pistol grip, nickel-plated swivel studs. Chambered for 30-30 Win. with Hornady spire-pointed Flex-Tip cartridges. Includes safety lock. Introduced 2006. Similar models chambered for 308 Marlin Express introduced in 2007
Price: Model 336XLR $905.00

MARLIN MODEL 308 MXLR

Caliber: 338 Marlin Express. **Barrel:** 24" stainless steel. **Weight:** 7.5 lbs. **Length:** 42.5" overall. **Features:** Stainless steel receiver, lever and magazine tube. Black/gray laminated checkered stock and forend. Hooded ramp front sight and adjustable semi-buckhorn rear; drilled and tapped for scope mounts. Receiver-mounted crossbolt safety.
Price: $905.00
Price: (MX w/blue finish) $686.00

MARLIN MODEL 1894

Caliber: 44 Spec./44 Mag., 10-shot tubular magazine. **Barrel:** 20" Ballard-type rifling. **Weight:** 6 lbs. **Length:** 37.5" overall. **Stock:** Checkered American black walnut, straight grip and forend. Mar-Shield finish. Rubber rifle buttpad; swivel studs. **Sights:** Wide-Scan

hooded ramp front, semi-buckhorn folding rear adjustable for windage and elevation. **Features:** Hammer-block safety. Receiver tapped for scope mount, offset hammer spur, solid top receiver sand blasted to prevent glare. Includes safety lock.
Price: $708.00

MARLIN MODEL 1894C CARBINE

Similar to the standard Model 1894 except chambered for 38 Spec./357 Mag. with full-length 9-shot magazine, 18.5" barrel, hammer-block safety, hooded front sight. Introduced 1983. Includes safety lock.
Price: $708.00

MARLIN MODEL 1894 COWBOY

Caliber: 357 Mag., 44 Mag., 45 Colt, 10-shot magazine. **Barrel:** 20" tapered octagon, deep cut rifling. **Weight:** 7.5 lbs. **Length:** 41.5" overall. **Stock:** Straight grip American black walnut, hard rubber buttplate, Mar-Shield finish. **Sights:** Marble carbine front, adjustable Marble semi-buckhorn rear. **Features:** Squared finger lever; straight grip stock; blued steel forend tip. Designed for Cowboy Shooting events. Introduced 1996. Includes safety lock. Made in U.S.A. by Marlin.
Price: $1,010.00

MARLIN MODEL 1894SS

Similar to Model 1894 except has stainless steel barrel, receiver, lever, guard plate, magazine tube and loading plate. Nickel-plated swivel studs.
Price: $829.00

MARLIN 1894 DELUXE

Lever action rifle chambered in .44 Magnum/.44 Special. Features include 10-shot tubular magazine; squared finger lever; side ejection; richly polished deep blued metal surfaces; solid top receiver; hammer block safety; #1 grade fancy American black walnut straight-grip stock and forend; cut checkering; rubber rifle butt pad; Mar-Shield finish; blued steel fore-end cap: swivel studs; deep-cut Ballard-type rifling (6 grooves).
Price: $950.00

MARLIN 1894CSS

Lever action rifle chambered in .357 Magnum/.38 Special. Features include 9-shot tubular magazine; stainless steel receiver, barrel, lever, trigger and hammer; squared finger lever; side ejection; solid top receiver; hammer block safety; American black walnut straight-grip stock and forend; cut checkering; rubber rifle butt pad; Mar-Shield finish.
Price: $829.00

MARLIN MODEL 1895 LEVER-ACTION

Caliber: 45-70 Govt., 4-shot tubular magazine. **Barrel:** 22" round. **Weight:** 7.5 lbs. **Length:** 40.5" overall. **Stock:** Checkered American black walnut, full pistol grip. Mar-Shield finish; rubber buttpad; quick detachable swivel studs. **Sights:** Bead front with Wide-Scan hood,

Prices given are believed to be accurate at time of publication however, many factors affect retail pricing so exact prices are not possible.

semi-buckhorn folding rear adjustable for windage and elevation. **Features:** Hammer-block safety. Solid receiver tapped for scope mounts or receiver sights; offset hammer spur. Includes safety lock.
Price: **$675.00**

MARLIN MODEL 1895G GUIDE GUN LEVER-ACTION
Similar to Model 1895 with deep-cut Ballard-type rifling; straight-grip walnut stock. Overall length is 37", weighs 7 lbs. Introduced 1998. Includes safety lock. Made in U.S.A. by Marlin.
Price: **$680.00**

MARLIN MODEL 1895GS GUIDE GUN
Similar to Model 1895G except receiver, barrel and most metal parts are machined from stainless steel. Chambered for 45-70 Govt., 4-shot, 18.5" barrel. Overall length is 37", weighs 7 lbs. Introduced 2001. Includes safety lock. Made in U.S.A. by Marlin.
Price: **$813.00**

MARLIN MODEL 1895 SBLR
Similar to Model 1895GS Guide Gun but with stainless steel barrel (18.5"), receiver, large loop lever and magazine tube. Black/gray laminated buttstock and forend, XS ghost ring rear sight, hooded ramp front sight, receiver/barrel-mounted top rail for mounting accessory optics. Chambered in 45-70 Government. Overall length is 42.5", weighs 7.5 lbs.
Price: **$1,039.00**

MARLIN MODEL 1895 COWBOY LEVER-ACTION
Similar to Model 1895 except has 26" tapered octagon barrel with Ballard-type rifling, Marble carbine front sight and Marble adjustable semi-buckhorn rear sight. Receiver tapped for scope or receiver sight. Overall length is 44.5", weighs about 8 lbs. Introduced 2001. Includes safety lock. Made in U.S.A. by Marlin.
Price: **$785.00**

MARLIN MODEL 1895XLR LEVER-ACTION
Similar to Model 1895 except has an 24" stainless barrel with Ballard-type cut rifling, stainless steel receiver and other parts, laminated hardwood stock with pistol grip, nickel-plated swivel studs. Chambered for 45-70 Govt. Government with Hornady Evolution spire-pointed Flex-Tip cartridges. Includes safety lock. Introduced 2006.
Price: (Model 1895MXLR) **$816.00**

MARLIN 1895GBL
Lever action rifle chambered in .45-70 Government. Features include 6-shot, full-length tubular magazine; 18-1/2-inch barrel with deep-cut Ballard-type rifling (6 grooves); big-loop finger lever; side ejection; solid-top receiver; deeply blued metal surfaces; hammer block safety; pistol-grip two tone brown laminate stock with cut checkering; ventilated recoil pad; Mar-Shield finish, swivel studs.
Price: **$713.00**

MOSSBERG 464 LEVER ACTION
Caliber: 30-30 Win., 6-shot tubular magazine. **Barrel:** 20" round. **Weight:** 6.7 lbs. **Length:** 38.5" overall. **Stock:** Hardwood with straight or pistol grip, quick detachable swivel studs. **Sights:** Folding rear sight, adjustable for windage and elevation. **Features:** Blued receiver and barrel, receiver drilled and tapped, two-position top-tang safety. Available with straight grip or semi-pistol grip. Introduced 2008. From O.F. Mossberg & Sons, Inc.
Price: **$497.00**

NAVY ARMS 1874 SHARPS #2 CREEDMOOR RIFLE
Caliber: .45-70 Govt. **Barrel:** 30" octagon. **Weight:** 10 lbs. **Length:** 48"

overall. **Sights:** Soule target grade rear tang sight, front globe with 12 inserts. **Features:** Highly polished nickel receiver and action, double-set triggers. From Navy Arms.
Price: Model SCR072 (2008) **$1,816.00**

NAVY ARMS MILITARY HENRY RIFLE
Caliber: 44-40 or 45 Colt, 12-shot magazine. **Barrel:** 24.25". **Weight:** 9 lbs., 4 oz. **Stock:** European walnut. **Sights:** Blade front, adjustable ladder-type rear. **Features:** Brass frame, buttplate, rest blued. Replica of the model used by cavalry units in the Civil War. Has full-length magazine tube, sling swivels; no forend. Imported from Italy by Navy Arms.
Price: **$1,199.00**

NAVY ARMS IRON FRAME HENRY
Similar to the Military Henry Rifle except receiver is blued or color case-hardened steel. Imported by Navy Arms.
Price: Blued **$1,247.00**

NAVY ARMS 1866 YELLOW BOY
Caliber: 38 Spec., 44-40, 45 Colt, 12-shot magazine. **Barrel:** 20" or 24", full octagon. **Weight:** 8.5 lbs. **Length:** 42.5" overall. **Stock:** Walnut. **Sights:** Blade front, adjustable ladder-type rear. **Features:** Brass frame, forend tip, buttplate, blued barrel, lever, hammer. Introduced 1991. Imported from Italy by Navy Arms.
Price: Yellow Boy Rifle, 24.25" barrel **$915.00**
Price: Yellow Boy Carbine, 19" barrel **$882.00**

NAVY ARMS 1873 WINCHESTER-STYLE
Caliber: 357 Mag., 44-40, 45 Colt, 12-shot magazine. **Barrel:** 24.25". **Weight:** 8.25 lbs. **Length:** 43" overall. **Stock:** European walnut. **Sights:** Blade front, buckhorn rear. **Features:** Color case-hardened frame, rest blued. Full-octagon barrel. Imported by Navy Arms.
Price: **$1,047.00**
Price: 1873 Carbine, 19" barrel **$1,024.00**
Price: 1873 Sporting Rifle (octagonal bbl., checkered walnut stock and forend) **$1,183.00**
Price: 1873 Border Model, 20" octagon barrel **$1,047.00**
Price: 1873 Deluxe Border Model **$1,183.00**

PUMA BOUNTY HUNTER
Caliber: .44/40, .44 Mag. and .45 Colt, 6-shot magazine capacity. **Barrel:** 12". **Weight:** 4.5 lbs. **Length:** 24". **Stock:** Walnut. **Sights:** Fixed sights. **Features:** A piece of 1950's TV nostalgia, the Bounty Hunter is a reproduction of the gun carried by Western character Josh Randall in the series "Wanted: Dead or Alive". The Bounty Hunter is based on a Model 92 rifle, but is considered by Federal Law as a pistol, because it is built from the ground up as a handgun. Manufactured in the U.S.A. by Chiappa Firearms of Dayton, OH, the Bounty Hunter features a 12" barrel and 6 round tubular magazine. At just 24" OAL, the Bounty Hunter makes an ideal pack gun or camp defense pistol. The Bounty Hunter has a teardrop shaped loop lever and is built with the same fit, finish and high grade Italian walnut stocks as our Puma M-92 and M-86 rifles.
Price: .45LC, Case Hardened/Blued **$1,372.00**
Price: .44/40, Case Hardened/Blued **$1,372.00**
Price: .44MAG, Case Hardened/Blued **$1,372.00**

PUMA MODEL 92S AND CARBINES
Caliber: 17 HMR (XP and Scout models, only; intr. 2008), 38 Spec./357 Mag., 44 Mag., 45 Colt, 454 Casull, 480 Ruger (.44-40 in 20" octagonal barrel). **Barrel:** 16" and 20" round; 20" and 24" octagonal. 1:30" rate of twist (exc. 17 HMR is 1:9"). **Weight:** 7.7

lbs. **Stock:** Walnut stained hardwood. **Sights:** Blade front, V rear, buckhorn sights sold separately. **Features:** Finishes available in blue/blue, blue/case colored and stainless/stainless with matching crescent butt plates. .454 and .480 calibers have rubber recoil pads. Full-length magazines, thumb safety. Large lever loop or HiViz sights available on select models. Magazine capacity is 12 rounds with 24" bbl.; 10 rounds with 20" barrel; 8 rounds in 16" barrel. Introduced in 2002. Scout includes long-eye-relief scope, rail, elevated cheekpiece, intr. 2008. XP chambered in 17 HMR, 38 Spec./357 Mag. and 44 Mag., loads through magazine tube or loading gate, intr. 2008. Imported from Brazil by Legacy Sports International.

Price: From **$959.00**
Price: Scout Model, w/2.5x32 Nikko-Stirling Nighteater
  scope, intr. 2008, from **$739.00**
Price: XP Model, tube feed magazine, intr. 2008, from **$613.00**

REMINGTON MODEL 7600 PUMP ACTION
Caliber: 243 Win., 270 Win., 30-06 Spfl., 308. **Barrel:** 22" round tapered. **Weight:** 7.5 lbs. **Length:** 42.6" overall. **Stock:** Cut-checkered walnut pistol grip and forend, Monte Carlo with full cheekpiece. Satin or high-gloss finish. Also, black synthetic. **Sights:** Gold bead front sight on matted ramp, open step adjustable sporting rear. **Features:** Redesigned and improved version of the Model 760. Detachable 4-shot clip. Cross-bolt safety. Receiver tapped for scope mount. Introduced 1981. Model 7615 Tactical chambered in 223 Rem. **Features:** Knoxx SpecOps NRS (Non Recoil Suppressing) adjustable stock, parkerized finish, 10-round detachable magazine box, sling swivel studs. Introduced 2007.
Price: 7600 Wood **$900.00**
Price: 7600 Synthetic...**$756.00**

ROSSI R92 LEVER-ACTION CARBINE
Caliber: 38 Special/357 Mag, 44 Mag., 44-40 Win., 45 Colt, 454 Casull. **Barrel:** 16" or 20" with round barrel, 20" or 24" with octagon barrel. **Weight:** 4.8 lbs. to 7 lbs. **Length:** 34» to 41.5». **Features:** Blued or stainless finish. Various options available in selected chamberings (large lever loop, fiber optic sights, cheekpiece, etc.).
Price: From **$559.00**

ROSSI RIO GRANDE
Caliber: .30-30 or .45-70. **Barrel:** 20". Weight. 7 lbs. **Sights:** Adjustable rear, post front. **Stock:** Hardwood or camo.
PRICE: .... **$545, $559 (.45-70)**

TRISTAR SHARPS 1874 SPORTING
Caliber: 45-70 Govt. **Barrel:** 28", 32", 34" octagonal. **Weight:** 9.75 lbs. **Length:** 44.5" overall. **Stock:** Walnut. **Sights:** Dovetail front, adjustable rear. **Features:** Cut checkering, case colored frame finish.
Price: **$1,099.00**

UBERTI 1873 SPORTING RIFLE
Caliber: 357 Mag., 44-40, 45 Colt. **Barrel:** 19" to 24.25". **Weight:** Up to 8.2 lbs. **Length:** Up to 43.3" overall. **Stock:** Walnut, straight grip and pistol grip. **Sights:** Blade front adjustable for windage, open rear adjustable for elevation. **Features:** Color case-hardened frame, blued barrel, hammer, lever, buttplate, brass elevator. Imported by Stoeger Industries.

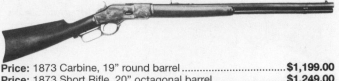

Price: 1873 Carbine, 19" round barrel **$1,199.00**
Price: 1873 Short Rifle, 20" octagonal barrel **$1,249.00**
Price: 1873 Special Sporting Rifle, 24.25" octagonal barrel **$1,379.00**

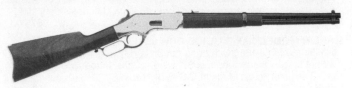

UBERTI 1866 YELLOWBOY CARBINE, SHORT, RIFLE
Caliber: 38 Spec., 44-40, 45 Colt. **Barrel:** 24.25", octagonal. **Weight:** 8.2 lbs. **Length:** 43.25" overall. **Stock:** Walnut. **Sights:** Blade front adjustable for windage, rear adjustable for elevation. **Features:** Frame, buttplate, forend cap of polished brass, balance charcoal blued. Imported by Stoeger Industries.
Price: 1866 Yellowboy Carbine, 19" round barrel.................**$1,079.00**
Price: 1866 Yellowboy Short Rifle, 20" octagonal barrel **$1,129.00**
Price: 1866 Yellowboy Rifle, 24.25" octagonal barrel **$1,129.00**

UBERTI 1860 HENRY
Caliber: 44-40, 45 Colt. **Barrel:** 24.25", half-octagon. **Weight:** 9.2 lbs. **Length:** 43.75" overall. **Stock:** American walnut. **Sights:** Blade front, rear adjustable for elevation. Imported by Stoeger Industries.
Price: 1860 Henry Trapper, 18.5" barrel, brass frame...........**$1,329.00**
Price: 1860 Henry Rifle Iron Frame, 24.25" barrel **$1,419.00**

UBERTI LIGHTNING
Caliber: 357 Mag., 45 Colt, 10+1. **Barrel:** 20" to 24.25". **Stock:** Walnut. Finish: Blue or case-hardened. Introduced 2006. Imported by Stoeger Industries.
Price: 1875 Lightning Rifle, 24.25" barrel **$1,259.00**
Price: 1875 Lightning Short Rifle, 20" barrel **$1,259.00**
Price: 1875 Lightning Carbine, 20" barrel **$1,179.00**

UBERTI SPRINGFIELD TRAPDOOR
Caliber: 4-70, single shot. **Barrel:** 22" or 32.5". **Stock:** Walnut. Finish: Blue and case-hardened. Introduced 2006. Imported by Stoeger Industries.
Price: Springfield Trapdoor Carbine, 22" barrel.....................**$1,429.00**
Price: Springfield Trapdoor Army, 32.5" barrel **$1,669.00**

WINCHESTER MODEL 94 SHORT RIFLE
Caliber: .30-30, .38-55. **Barrel:** 20". Weight: 6.75 lbs. **Sights:** Semi-buckhorn rear, gold bead front. **Stock:** Walnut with straight grip. Fore-end has black grip cap. Also available in takedown design in .450 Marlin or .30-30.
Price: (Takedown)............................ **$1,230.00 to $1,460.00**

Prices given are believed to be accurate at time of publication however, many factors affect retail pricing so exact prices are not possible.

WINCHESTER MODEL 94 CARBINE
Same general specifications as M94 Short Rifle except for curved buttplate and fore-end barrel band.
Price: $1,200.00

WINCHESTER MODEL 94 SPORTER
Caliber: .30-30, .38-55. **Barrel:** 24". **Weight:** 7.5 lbs. Same features of Model 94 Short Rifle except for crescent butt and steel buttplate, 24" half-round, half-octagon barrel, checkered stock.
Price: $1400

WINCHESTER 1873 SHORT RIFLE
Caliber: .357 Magnum. Tubular magazine holds 10 rounds (.357), 11 rounds .38 Special. **Barrel:** 20 inches. **Weight:** 7.25 lbs.

Sights: Marble semi-buckhorn rear, gold bead front. Tang is drilled and tapped for optional peep sight. **Stock:** Satin finished, straight-grip walnut with steel crescent buttplate and steel fore-end cap. Tang safety. A modern version of the "Gun That Won the West."
Price: $1,300.00

WINCHESTER MODEL 1886 EXTRA LIGHT
Caliber: .45-70. **Barrel:** 22". **Weight:** 7.25 lbs. **Sights:** Adjustable buckhorn rear, blade front. Also offered in Short Rifle model in .45-70 or .45-90 with crescent butt.
Price (Short Rifle) ....**$1,269.00 to $1,340.00**

WINCHESTER MODEL 1892 CARBINE
Caliber: . 357 Mag., .44 Mag., .44-40, .45 Colt. **Barrel:** 20 inches. **Weight:** 6 lbs. **Stock:** Satin finished walnut with straight grip, steel fore-end strap. **Sights:** Marble semi-buckhorn rear, gold bead front. Other features include saddle ring and tang safety.

Price: $1,160.00

ARMALITE AR-30A1

Caliber: .300 Win. Mag., .338 Lapua. Bolt-action with five-round capacity. **Barrel:** 24 inches (.300 Win.), 26 inches (.338 Lapua), competition grade. **Weight:** 12.8 lbs. **Length:** 46 inches. **Stock:** Standard fixed. **Sights:** None. Accessory top rail included. **Features:** Muzzle brake, ambidextrous magazine release, large ejection port makes single loading easy, V-block patented bedding system, bolt-mounted safety locks firing pin. Target versions have adjustable stock.
Price: .... $3,264.00 to $3,599.00

ARMALITE AR-50A1

Caliber: .50 BMG, .416 Barrett. Bolt action single shot. **Barrel:** 30 inches with muzzle brake. National Match model (shown) has 33-inch fluted barrel. **Weight:** 34.I lbs. **Stock:** Three-section. Extruded fore-end, machined vertical grip, forged and machined buttstock that is vertically adjustable. National Match model (.50 BMG only) has V-block patented bedding system, Armalite Skid System to ensure straight-back recoil.
Price: $3,359.00
Price: National Match $4,230.00

BARRETT MODEL 95 BOLT-ACTION

Caliber: 50 BMG, 5-shot magazine. **Barrel:** 29". **Weight:** 23.5 lbs. **Length:** 45" overall. **Stock:** Energy-absorbing recoil pad. **Sights:** Scope optional. **Features:** Bolt-action, bullpup design. Disassembles without tools; extendable bipod legs; match-grade barrel; muzzle brake. Introduced 1995. Made in U.S.A. by Barrett Firearms Mfg., Inc.
Price: From $6,500.00

BARRETT MODEL 98B

Caliber: .338 Lapua Magnum (10-shot magazine). **Barrel:** 27" fluted or 20". **Weight:** 13.5 lbs. **Length:** 49.8". Comes with two magazines, bipod, monopod, side accessory rail, hard case.
PRICE: $4,850.00

BARRETT MRAD

Caliber: .338 Lapua Magnum. **Magazine capacity:** 10 rounds. **Barrel:** 20, 24 or 26 inches, fluted or heavy. **Features:** User interchangeable barrel system, folding stock, adjustable cheek piece, 5-position length of pull adjustment button, match grade trigger, 22-inch optics rail.
Price: .... $5,850.00 to $6,000.00

BLASER R93 BOLT-ACTION

Caliber: 22-250 Rem., 243 Win., 6.5x55, 270 Win., 7x57, 7mm-08 Rem., 308 Win., 30-06 Spfl., 257 Wby. Mag., 7mm Rem. Mag., 300

Win. Mag., 300 Wby. Mag., 338 Win. Mag., 375 H&H, 416 Rem. Mag. **Barrel:** 22" (standard calibers), 26" (magnum). **Weight:** 7 lbs. **Length:** 40" overall (22" barrel). **Stock:** Two-piece European walnut. **Sights:** None furnished; drilled and tapped for scope mounting. **Features:** Straight pull-back bolt action with thumb-activated safety slide/cocking mechanism; interchangeable barrels and bolt heads. Introduced 1994.

Imported from Germany by Blaser USA.
Price: From $2,995.00

BROWNING A-BOLT

Common Features: Short-throw (60") fluted bolt, three locking lugs, plunger-type ejector; adjustable trigger is grooved. Chrome-plated trigger sear. Hinged floorplate, detachable box magazine. Slide tang safety. Receivers are drilled and tapped for scope mounts, swivel studs included. Barrel is free-floating and glass-bedded, recessed muzzle. Safety is top-tang sliding button. Engraving available for bolt sleeve or rifle body. Introduced 1985. Imported from Japan by Browning.

BROWNING A-BOLT HUNTER FLD

Caliber: 23" **Barrel:** 270 WSM, 325 WSM (intr. 2005). **Weight:** 6.6 lbs. **Length:** 42.75" overall. **Features:** FLD has low-luster blueing and select Monte Carlo stock with right-hand palm swell, double-border checkering. Available only at Browning Full Line Dealers.
Price: FLD $1,039.00

BROWNING A-BOLT TARGET

Similar to A-Bolt Hunter but with 28" heavy bull blued barrel, blued receiver, satin finish gray laminated stock with adjustable comb and semi-beavertail forend. Chambered in 223, 308 Winchester and 300 WSM. Available also with stainless receiver and barrel.
Price: From $1,480.00
Price: Stainless, from $1,740.00

BROWNING A-BOLT MICRO HUNTER

Calibers: .22 Hornet **Barrel:** 20" **Barrel:** 22-250 Rem., 243 Win., 308 Win., 7mm-08. 22" **Weight:** 6.25-6.4 lbs. **Length:** 39.5-41.5" overall. **Features:** Classic walnut stock with 13.3" LOP. Otherwise similar to A-Bolt Hunter.
Price: Micro Hunter, from $870.00
Price: Micro Hunter left-hand, from $900.00

BROWNING A-BOLT MEDALLION

Calibers: 22" **Barrel:** 223 Rem., 22-250 Rem., 243 Win., 308 Win., 270 Win., 280 Rem., 30-06.; 23" **Barrel:** 270 WSM, 7mm WSM, 300 WSM, 325 WSM (intr. 2005); 24" **Barrel:** 25-06 Rem.; 26" **Barrel:** 7mm Rem. Mag., 300 Win. Mag., 338 Win. Mag., 375 H&H. **Weight:** 6.25-7.1 lbs. **Length:** 41.25-46.5" overall. **Stock:** Select walnut stock, glossy finish, rosewood grip and forend caps, checkered grip and forend. **Metal Finish:** Engraved high-polish blued receiver.

Price: $1,120.00

BROWNING A-BOLT STAINLESS STALKER

Calibers: 22" Barrel: 223 Rem., 243 Win., 270 Win., 280 Rem., 7mm-08 Rem., 30-06 Spfl., 308 Win. Calibers: 23" Barrel: 270 WSM, 7mm WSM, 300 WSM, 325 WSM (intr. 2005). Calibers: 24" Barrel: 25-06 Rem. Calibers: 26" Barrel: 7mm Rem. Mag., 300 Win. Mag., 338 Win. Mag., 375 H&H. **Weight:** 6.1-7.2 lbs. **Length:** 40.9-46.5" overall. **Features:** Similar to the A-Bolt Hunter model except receiver and barrel are made of stainless steel; other exposed metal surfaces are finished silver-gray matte. Graphite-fiberglass composite textured stock. No sights are furnished, except on 375 H&H, which comes with open sights. Introduced 1987.

Price: w/Boss, from $1,240.00
Price: w/Boss (magnum calibers), from................$1,270.00

BROWNING A-BOLT COMPOSITE STALKER

Calibers: 22 Barrel: 270 Win., 30-06 Sprg.; 23» Barrel: 270 WSM, 7mm WSM, 300 WSM, 325 WSM; 24» Barrel: 25-06 Rem.; 26» Barrel: 7mm Rem. Mag., 300 Win. Mag., 338 Win. Mag. **Weight:** 6.6-7.3 lbs. **Length:** 42.5-46.5» overall. **Features:** Similar to the A-Bolt Stainless Stalker except has black composite stock with textured finish and matte-blued finish on all exposed metal surfaces except bolt sleeve. No sights are furnished.

Price: w/Boss, from $1,000.00
Price: w/Boss (magnum calibers), from................$1,030.00

BROWNING A-BOLT III

Caliber: .270 Win., 7mm Rem. Mag., .30-06, .300 Win. Mag. **Barrel:** 22 inches, 26 for magnums. **Weight:** 6.7 to 7.2 pounds. Economy priced A-Bolt model with new detachable box magazine, integrated trigger system, composite stock designs, premium Influx Technology recoil pad.

Price: $600

BROWNING A-BOLT ECLIPSE HUNTER W/BOSS, M-1000 ECLIPSE W/BOSS, M-1000 ECLIPSE WSM, STAINLESS M-1000 ECLIPSE WSM

Calibers: 22" Barrel: 270 Win., 30-06. **Calibers:** 26" Barrel: 7mm Rem. Mag., 300 Win. Mag., 270 WSM, 7mm WSM, 300 WSM. **Weight:** 7.5-9.9 lbs. **Length:** 42.75-46.5" overall. **Features:** All models have gray/black laminated thumbhole stock. Introduced 1996. Two versions have BOSS barrel vibration modulator and muzzle brake. Hunter has sporter-weight barrel. M-1000 Eclipses have long actions and heavy target barrels, adjustable triggers, bench-style forends, 3-shot magazines. Introduced 1997.

Price: Eclipse Hunter w/BOSS, from $1,430.00
Price: M-1000 Eclipse, from $1,340.00
Price: M-1000 Eclipse w/BOSS, from $1,440.00
Price: Stainless M-1000 Eclipse WSM, from $1,640.00
Price: Stainless M-1000 Eclipse w/BOSS, from $1,740.00

BROWNING X-BOLT HOG STALKER

Caliber: .223 or .308 Win. **Barrel:** 20 inches, medium heavy. **Weight:** 6.8 to 7 pounds. **Stock:** Composite black or Realtree Max-1 camo.

Sights: None. Picatinny rail scope mount included.
Price: $1,200.00

BROWNING X-BOLT HUNTER

Calibers: 223, 22-250, 243 Win., 25-06 Rem., 270 Win., 270 WSM, 280 Rem., 30-06 Spfl., 300 Win. Mag., 300 WSM, 308 Win., 325 WSM, 338 Win. Mag., 375 H&H Mag., 7mm Rem. Mag., 7mm WSM, 7mm-08 Rem. **Barrels:** 22", 23", 24", 26", varies by model. Matte blued or stainless free-floated barrel, recessed muzzle crown. **Weight:** 6.3-7 lbs. **Stock:** Hunter and Medallion models have wood stocks; Composite Stalker and Stainless Stalker models have composite stocks. Inflex Technology recoil pad. **Sights:** None, drilled and tapped receiver, X-Lock scope mounts. **Features:** Adjustable three-lever Feather Trigger system, polished hard-chromed steel components, factory pre-set at 3.5 lbs., alloy trigger housing. Bolt unlock button, detachable rotary magazine, 60-degree bolt lift, three locking lugs, top-tang safety, sling swivel studs. Medallion has metal engraving, gloss finish walnut stock, rosewood fore-end grip and pistol grip cap. Introduced 2008. From Browning.

Price: From $900.00

BROWNING X-BOLT MICRO HUNTER

Similar to Browning X-Bolt Hunter but with compact dimensions (13-15/16 length of pull, 41-1/4 overall length).

Price: Standard chamberings $900.00
Price: Magnum $940.00

BROWNING X-BOLT MICRO MIDAS

Caliber: 243 Win., 7mm-08 Rem., 308 Win., 22-250 Rem. **Barrel:** 20". **Weight:** 6 lbs.1 oz. **Length:** 37-5/8" to 38-1/8" overall. **Stock:** Satin finish checkered walnut stock. **Sights:** Hooded front and adjustable rear. **Features:** Steel receiver with low-luster blued finish. Glass bedded, drilled and tapped for scope mounts. Barrel is free-floating and hand chambered with target crown. Bolt-action with adjustable Feather Trigger™ and detachable rotary magazine. Compact 12-1/2" length of pull for smaller shooters, designed to fit smaller-framed shooters like youth and women. This model has all the same features as the full-size model with sling swivel studs installed and Inflex Technology recoil pad. (Scope and mounts not included).

Price: $840.00

BROWNING X-BOLT VARMINT STALKER

Similar to Browning X-Bolt Stalker but with medium-heavy free-floated barrel, target crown, composite stock. Chamberings available: .223, .22-250, .243 Winchester and .308 Winchester only. Varmint Special model has Altamont Paladin laminated thumb-hole stock designed for prone shooting.

Price: Varmint Stalker $1,120.00
Price: Varmint Special $840.00

BUSHMASTER BA50 BOLT-ACTION

Caliber: 50 Browning BMG. **Barrel:** 30" (rifle), 22" (carbine), 10-round mag. **Weight:** 30 lbs. (rifle), 27 lbs. (carbine). **Length:** 58" overall

Prices given are believed to be accurate at time of publication however, many factors affect retail pricing so exact prices are not possible.

68TH EDITION, 2014 ✛ **469**

(rifle), 50" overall (carbine). **Features:** Free-floated Lother Walther barrel with muzzle brake, Magpul PRS adjustable stock.
Price: **$5,300.00**

CARBON ONE BOLT-ACTION
Caliber: 22-250 to 375 H&H. **Barrel:** Up to 28". **Weight:** 5.5 to 7.25 lbs. **Length:** Varies. **Stock:** Synthetic or wood. **Sights:** None furnished. **Features:** Choice of Remington, Browning or Winchester action with free-floated Christensen graphite/epoxy/steel barrel, trigger pull tuned to 3 to 3.5 lbs. Made in U.S.A. by Christensen Arms.
Price: Carbon One Hunter Rifle, 6.5 to 7 lbs. **$1,775.00**
Price: Carbon One Custom, 5.5 to 6.5 lbs., Shilen trigger ... **$3,900.00**
Price: Carbon Extreme **$2,450.00**

CENTURY INTERNATIONAL M70 SPORTER DOUBLE-TRIGGER BOLT ACTION
Caliber: 22-250 Rem., 270 Win., 300 Win. Mag, 308 Win., 24" barrel. **Weight:** 7.95 lbs. **Length:** 44.5". **Sights:** Flip-up U-notch rear sight, hooded blade front sight. **Features:** Mauser M98-type action; 5-rd fixed box magazine. 22-250 has hinged floorplate. Monte Carlo stock, oil finish. Adjustable trigger on double-trigger models. 300 Win. Mag. Has 3-rd. fixed box magazine. 308 Win. holds 5 rounds. 300 and 308 have buttpads. Manufactured by Zastava in Yugoslavia, imported by Century International.
Price: M70 Sporter Double-Trigger........................ **$500.00**
Price: M70 Sporter Double-Trigger 22-250 .... **$475.00**
Price: M70 Sporter Single-Trigger .300 Win. Mag. **$475.00**
Price: M70 Sporter Single/Double Trigger 308 Win. **$500.00**

CHEYTAC M-200
Caliber: 408 CheyTac, 7-round magazine. **Barrel:** 30". **Length:** 55", stock extended. **Weight:** 27 lbs. (steel barrel); 24 lbs. (carbon fiber barrel). **Stock:** Retractable. **Sights:** None, scope rail provided. **Features:** CNC-machined receiver, attachable Picatinny rail M-1913, detachable barrel, integral bipod, 3.5-lb. trigger pull, muzzle brake. Made in U.S. by CheyTac, LLC.
Price: **$13,795.00**

COOPER MODEL 21 BOLT-ACTION
Caliber: 17 Rem., 19-223, Tactical 20, .204 Ruger, 222 Rem, 222 Rem. Mag., 223 Rem, 223 Rem A.I., 6x45, 6x47. **Barrel:** 22" or 24" in Classic configurations, 24"-26" in Varminter configurations. **Weight:** 6.5-8.0 lbs., depending on type. **Stock:** AA-AAA select claro walnut, 20 lpi checkering. **Sights:** None furnished. **Features:** Three front locking-lug bolt-action single shot. Action: 7.75" long, Sako extractor. Button ejector. Fully adjustable single-stage trigger. Options include wood upgrades, case-color metalwork, barrel fluting, custom LOP, and many others.
Price: From **$1,695.00**

COOPER MODEL 22 BOLT-ACTION
Caliber: 22-250 Rem., 22-250 Rem. AI, 25-06 Rem., 25-06 Rem. AI, 243 Win., 243 Win. AI, 220 Swift, 250/3000 AI, 257 Roberts, 257 Roberts AI, 7mm-08 Rem., 6mm Rem., 260 Rem., 6 x 284, 6.5 x 284, 22 BR, 6mm BR, 308 Win. **Barrel:** 24" or 26" stainless match in Classic configurations. 24" or 26" in Varminter configurations. **Weight:** 7.5 to 8.0 lbs. depending on type. **Stock:** AA-AAA select claro walnut, 20 lpi checkering. **Sights:** None furnished. **Features:** Three front locking-lug bolt-action single shot. Action: 8.25" long, Sako style extractor. Button ejector. Fully adjustable single-stage trigger. Options include wood upgrades, case-color metalwork, barrel fluting, custom LOP, and many others.
Price: From **$1,695.00**

COOPER MODEL 38 BOLT-ACTION
Caliber: 17 Squirrel, 17 He Bee, 17 Ackley Hornet, 17 Mach IV, 19 Calhoon, 20 VarTarg, 221 Fireball, 22 Hornet, 22 K-Hornet, 22 Squirrel, 218 Bee, 218 Mashburn Bee. **Barrel:** 22" or 24" in Classic configurations, 24" or 26" in Varminter configurations. **Weight:** 6.5-8.0 lbs. depending on type. **Stock:** AA-AAA select claro walnut, 20 lpi checkering. **Sights:** None furnished. **Features:** Three front locking-lug bolt-action single shot. Action: 7" long, Sako style extractor. Button ejector. Fully adjustable single-stage trigger. Options include wood upgrades, case-color metalwork, barrel fluting, custom LOP, and many others.
Price: From **$1,695.00**

COOPER MODEL 56 BOLT-ACTION
Caliber: .257 Weatherby Mag., .264 Win. Mag., .270 Weatherby Mag., 7mm Remington Mag., 7mm Weatherby Mag., 7mm Shooting Times Westerner, .300 Holland & Holland, .300 Winchester Mag., .300 Weatherby Mag., .308 Norma Mag., 8mm Rem. Mag., .338 Win. Mag., .340 Weatherby V. **Barrel:** 22" or 24" in Classic configurations, 24" or 26" in Varminter configurations. **Weight:** 7.75 - 8 lbs. depending on type. **Stock:** AA-AAA select claro walnut, 20 lpi checkering. **Sights:** None furnished. **Features:** Three front locking-lug bolt-action single shot. Action: 7" long, Sako style extractor. Button ejector. Fully adjustable single-stage trigger. Options include wood upgrades, case-color metalwork, barrel fluting, custom LOP, and many others.
Price: Classic. **$1518.00**
Price: Custom Classic. **$1,618.00**
Price: Western Classic. **$1518.00**
Price: Jackson Game... **$1,618.00**
Price: Jackson Hunter... **$1518.00**
Price: Excalibur. **$1,618.00**

CZ 527 LUX BOLT-ACTION
Caliber: .17 Hornet, .204 Ruger, .22 Hornet, .222 Rem., .223 Rem., detachable 5-shot magazine. **Barrel:** 23.5"; standard or heavy barrel. **Weight:** 6 lbs., 1 oz. **Length:** 42.5" overall. **Stock:** European walnut with Monte Carlo. **Sights:** Hooded front, open adjustable rear. **Features:** Improved mini-Mauser action with non-rotating claw extractor; single set trigger; grooved receiver. Imported from the Czech Republic by CZ-USA.
Price: Brown laminate stock... **$718.00**
Price: Model FS, full-length stock, cheekpiece **$827.00**

CZ 527 AMERICAN BOLT-ACTION
Similar to the CZ 527 Lux except has classic-style stock with 18 lpi checkering; free-floating barrel; recessed target crown on barrel. No sights furnished. Introduced 1999. Imported from the Czech Republic by CZUSA.
Price: From **$751.00**

CZ 550 AMERICAN CLASSIC BOLT-ACTION
Caliber: 22-250 Rem., 243 Win., 6.5x55, 7x57, 7x64, 308 Win., 9.3x62, 270 Win., 30-06. **Barrel:** free-floating barrel; recessed target crown. **Weight:** 7.48 lbs. **Length:** 44.68" overall. **Stock:** American classic-style stock with 18 lpi checkering or FS (Mannlicher). **Sights:** No sights furnished. **Features:** Improved Mauser-style action with claw extractor, fixed ejector, square bridge dovetailed receiver; single set trigger. Introduced 1999. Imported from the Czech Republic by CZ-USA.
Price: FS (full stock) **$894.00**
Price: American, from **$827.00**

Prices given are believed to be accurate at time of publication however, many factors affect retail pricing so exact prices are not possible.

CZ 550 SAFARI MAGNUM/AMERICAN SAFARI MAGNUM BOLT-ACTION

Similar to CZ 550 American Classic. Chambered for 375 H&H Mag., 416 Rigby, 458 Win. Mag., 458 Lott. Overall length is 46.5"; barrel length 25"; weighs 9.4 lbs., 9.9 lbs (American). Hooded front sight, express rear with one standing, two folding leaves. Imported from the Czech Republic by CZ-USA.
Price: $1,179.00
Price: American $1,261.00
Price: American Kevlar $1,714.00

CZ 550 VARMINT BOLT-ACTION

Similar to CZ 550 American Classic. Chambered for 308 Win. and 22-250. Kevlar, laminated stocks. Overall length is 46.7"; barrel length 25.6"; weighs 9.1 lbs. Imported from the Czech Republic by CZ-USA.
Price: $841.00
Price: Kevlar $1,037.00
Price: Laminated $966.00

CZ 550 MAGNUM H.E.T. BOLT-ACTION

Similar to CZ 550 American Classic. Chambered for 338 Lapua, 300 Win. Mag., 300 RUM. Overall length is 52"; barrel length 28"; weighs 14 lbs. Adjustable sights, satin blued barrel. Imported from the Czech Republic by CZ-USA.
Price: $3,673.00

CZ 550 ULTIMATE HUNTING BOLT-ACTION

Similar to CZ 550 American Classic. Chambered for 300 Win Mag. Overall length is 44.7"; barrel length 23.6"; weighs 7.7 lbs. Imported from the Czech Republic by CZ-USA.
Price: $4,242.00

CZ 750 SNIPER

Caliber: 308 Winchester, 10-shot magazine. **Barrel:** 26". **Weight:** 11.9 lbs. **Length:** 48" overall. **Stock:** Polymer thumbhole. **Sights:** None furnished; permanently attached Weaver rail for scope mounting. **Features:** 60-degree bolt throw; oversized trigger guard and bolt handle for use with gloves; full-length equipment rail on forend; fully adjustable trigger. Introduced 2001. Imported from the Czech Republic by CZ-USA.
Price: $2,404.00

DAKOTA 76 TRAVELER TAKEDOWN

Caliber: 257 Roberts, 25-06 Rem., 7x57, 270 Win., 280 Rem., 30-06 Spfl., 338-06, 35 Whelen (standard length); 7mm Rem. Mag., 300 Win. Mag., 338 Win. Mag., 416 Taylor, 458 Win. Mag. (short magnums); 7mm, 300, 330, 375 Dakota Magnums. **Barrel:** 23". **Weight:** 7.5 lbs. **Length:** 43.5" overall. **Stock:** Medium fancy-grade walnut in classic style. Checkered grip and forend; solid buttpad. **Sights:** None furnished; drilled and tapped for scope mounts. **Features:** Threadless disassembly. Uses modified Model 76 design with many features of the Model 70 Winchester. Left-hand model also available. Introduced 1989. African chambered for 338 Lapua Mag., 404 Jeffery, 416 Rigby, 416 Dakota, 450 Dakota, 4-round magazine, select wood, two stock cross-bolts. 24" barrel, weighs 9-10 lbs. Ramp front sight, standing leaf rear. Introduced 1989. Made in U.S.A. by Dakota Arms, Inc.
Price: Classic $6,495.00
Price: Safari $8,395.00
Price: African $9,495.00

DAKOTA 76 CLASSIC BOLT-ACTION

Caliber: 257 Roberts, 270 Win., 280 Rem., 30-06 Spfl., 7mm Rem. Mag., 338 Win. Mag., 300 Win. Mag., 375 H&H, 458 Win. Mag. **Barrel:**

23". **Weight:** 7.5 lbs. **Length:** 43.5" overall. **Stock:** Medium fancy grade walnut in classic style. Checkered pistol grip and forend; solid buttpad. **Sights:** None furnished; drilled and tapped for scope mounts. **Features:** Has many features of the original Winchester Model 70. One-piece rail trigger guard assembly; steel gripcap. Model 70-style trigger. Many options available. Left-hand rifle available at same price. Introduced 1988. From Dakota Arms, Inc.
Price: From $5,395.00

DAKOTA MODEL 97 BOLT-ACTION

Caliber: 22-250 to 330. **Barrel:** 22" to 24". **Weight:** 6.1 to 6.5 lbs. **Length:** 43" overall. **Stock:** Fiberglass. **Sights:** Optional. **Features:** Matte blue finish, black stock. Right-hand action only. Introduced 1998. Made in U.S.A. by Dakota Arms, Inc.
Price: From $3,395.00

DSA DS-MP1

Caliber: 308 Win. match chamber. **Barrel:** 22", 1:10 twist, hand-lapped stainless-steel match-grade Badger Barrel with recessed target crown. **Weight:** 11.5 lbs. **Length:** 41.75". **Stock:** Black McMillan A5 pillar bedded in Marine-Tex with 13.5" length of pull. **Sights:** Tactical Picatinny rail. **Features:** Action, action threads and action bolt locking shoulder completely trued, Badger Ordnance precision ground heavy recoil lug, machined steel Picatinny rail sight mount, trued action threads, action bolt locking shoulder, bolt face and lugs, 2.5-lb. trigger pull, barrel and action finished in Black DuraCoat, guaranteed to shoot 1/2 MOA at 100 yards with match-grade ammo. Introduced 2006. Made in U.S.A. by DSA, Inc.
Price: $2,800.00

EAA/ZASTAVA M-93 BLACK ARROW

Caliber: 50 BMG. **Barrel:** 36". **Weight:** 7 to 8.5 lbs. **Length:** 60". **Stock:** Synthetic. **Sights:** Scope rail and iron sights. **Features:** Mauser action, developed in early 1990s by Zastava Arms Factory. Fluted heavy barrel with recoil reducing muzzle brake, self-leveling and adjustable folding integral bipod, back up iron sights, heavy duty carry handle, detachable 5 round box magazine, and quick detachable scope mount. Imported by EAA. Imported from Russia by EAA Corp.
Price: $6,986.25

HOWA M-1500 RANCHLAND COMPACT

Caliber: 223 Rem., 22-250 Rem., 243 Win., 308 Win. and 7mm-08. **Barrel:** 20" #1 contour, blued finish. **Weight:** 7 lbs. **Stock:** Hogue Overmolded in black, OD green, Coyote Sand colors. 13.87" LOP. **Sights:** None furnished; drilled and tapped for scope mounting. **Features:** Three-position safety, hinged floor plate, adjustable trigger, forged one-piece bolt, M-16 style extractor, forged flat-bottom receiver. Also available with Nikko-Stirling Nighteater 3-9x42 riflescope. Introduced in 2008. Imported from Japan by Legacy Sports International.
Price: Rifle Only, (2008) $479.00
Price: Rifle with 3-9x42 Nighteater scope (2008) $599.00

HOWA M-1500 THUMBHOLE SPORTER

Caliber: 204, 223 Rem., 22-250 Rem., 243 Win., 6.5x55 (2008) 25-06 Rem., 270 Win., 7mm Rem. Mag., 308 Win., 30-06 Spfl., 300 Win. Mag., 338 Win. Mag., 375 Ruger. Similar to Camo Lightning except stock. **Weight:** 7.6 to 7.7 lbs. **Stock:** S&K laminated wood in nutmeg (brown/black) or pepper (grey/black) colors, raised comb with forward taper, flared pistol grip and scalloped thumbhole. **Sights:** None furnished; drilled and tapped for scope mounting. **Features:** Three-position safety, hinged floor plate, adjustable trigger, forged one-piece bolt, M-16 style extractor, forged flat-bottom receiver. Introduced in 2001. Imported from Japan by Legacy Sports International.
Price: Blue/Nutmeg, standard calibers ....$649.00 to $669.00
Price: Stainless/Pepper, standard calibers ....$749.00 to $769.00

HOWA M-1500 VARMINTER SUPREME AND THUMBHOLE VARMINTER SUPREME

Caliber: 204, 223 Rem., 22-250 Rem., 243 Win., 308 Win. **Stock:**

Varminter Supreme: Laminated wood in nutmeg (brown), pepper (grey) colors, raised comb and rollover cheekpiece, full pistol grip with palm-filling swell and broad beavertail forend with six vents for barrel cooling. Thumbhole Varminter Supreme similar, adds a high, straight comb, more vertical pistol grip. **Sights:** None furnished; drilled and tapped for scope mounting. **Features:** Three-position safety, hinged floor plate, adjustable trigger, forged one-piece bolt, M-16 style extractor, forged flat-bottom receiver, hammer forged bull barrel and recessed muzzle crown; overall length, 43.75", 9.7 lbs. Introduced 2001. Barreled actions imported by Legacy Sports International; stocks by S&K Gunstocks.

Price: Varminter Supreme, Blue/Nutmeg.....................$679.00
Price: Varminter Supreme, Stainless/Pepper...........................$779.00
Price: Thumbhole Varminter Supreme, Blue/Nutmeg...............$679.00
Price: Thumbhole Varminter Supreme, Stainless/Pepper $779.00

HOWA CAMO LIGHTNING M-1500

Caliber: 204, 223 Rem., 22-250 Rem., 243 Win., 25-06 Rem., 270 Win., 308 Win., 30-06 Spfl., 300 Win. Mag., 338 Win. Mag., 7mm Rem. Mag. **Barrel:** 22" standard calibers; 24" magnum calibers; #2 and #6 contour; blue and stainless. **Weight:** 7.6 to 9.3 lbs. **Length:** 42" to 44.5" overall. **Stock:** Synthetic with molded cheek piece, checkered grip and forend. **Sights:** None furnished; drilled and tapped for scope mounting. **Features:** Three-position safety, hinged floor plate, adjustable trigger, forged one-piece bolt, M-16 style extractor, forged flat bottom receiver. Introduced in 1993. Barreled actions imported by Legacy Sports International.

Price: Blue, #2 barrel, standard calibers..................................$377.00
Price: Stainless, #2 barrel, standard calibers $479.00
Price: Blue, #2 barrel, magnum calibers...................................$390.00
Price: Stainless, #2 barrel, magnum calibers $498.00
Price: Blue, #6 barrel, standard calibers..................................$425.00
Price: Stainless, #6 barrel, standard calibers $498.00

HOWA/HOGUE M-1500

Caliber: 204, 223 Rem., 22-250 Rem., 243 Win., 6.5x5 (2008), 25-06 Rem., 270 Win., 308 Win., 30-06 Spfl., 300 Win. Mag., 338 Win. Mag., 7mm Rem. Mag., 375 Ruger (2008). **Barrel:** Howa barreled action; stainless or blued, 22" #2 contour. **Weight:** 7.4 to 7.6 lbs. **Stock:** Hogue Overmolded, black, or OD green; ambidextrous palm swells. **Sights:** None furnished; drilled and tapped for scope mounting. **Length:** 42" to 44.5" overall. **Features:** Three-position safety, hinged floor plate, adjustable trigger, forged one-piece bolt, M-16 style extractor, forged flat bottom receiver, aluminum pillar bedding and free-floated barrels. Introduced in 2006. Available w/3-10x42 Nikko-Stirling Nighteater scope, rings, bases (2008). from Imported from Japan by Legacy Sports International.

Price: Blued, rifle only .... $479.00 to $499.00
Price: Blue, rifle with scope package (2008).......... $599.00 to $619.00
Price: Stainless, rifle only...................................... $625.00 to $675.00

HOWA/HOGUE M-1500 COMPACT HEAVY BARREL VARMINTER

Chambered in 223 Rem., 308 Win., has 20" #6 contour heavy barrel, recessed muzzle crown. **Stock:** Hogue Overmolded, black, or OD green; ambidextrous palm swells. **Sights:** None furnished; drilled and tapped for scope mounting. **Length:** 44.0" overall. **Features:** Three-position safety, hinged floor plate, adjustable trigger, forged one-piece bolt, M-16 style extractor, forged flat bottom receiver, aluminum pillar bedding and free-floated barrels. **Weight:** 9.3 lbs. Introduced 2008. Imported from Japan by Legacy Sports International.

Price: From $559.00

HOWA/AXIOM M-1500

Caliber: 204, 223 Rem., 22-250 Rem., 243 Win., 6.5x55 (2008), 25-06 Rem. (2008), 270 Win., 308 Win., 30-06 Spfl., 7mm Rem, 300 Win. Mag., 338 Win. Mag., 375 Ruger standard barrel; 204, 223 Rem., 243 Win. and 308 Win. heavy barrel. **Barrel:** Howa barreled action, 22" contour standard barrel, 20" #6 contour heavy barrel, and 24" #6 contour heavy barrel. **Weight:** 8.6-10 lbs. **Stock:** Knoxx Industries Axiom V/S synthetic, black or camo. Adjustable length of pull from

11.5" to 15.5". **Sights:** None furnished; drilled and tapped for scope mounting. **Features:** Three-position safety, adjustable trigger, hinged floor plate, forged receiver with large recoil lug, forged one-piece bolt with dual locking lugs Introduced in 2007. Standard-barrel scope packages come with 3-10x42 Nikko-Stirling Nighteater scope, rings, bases (2008). Heavy barrels come with 4-16x44 Nikko-Stirling scope. Imported from Japan by Legacy Sports International.

Price: Axiom Standard Barrel, black stock, from......................$699.00
Price: Axiom 20" and 24" Varminter, black or
camo stock, from $799.00
Price: Axiom 20" and 24" Varminter, camo stock
w/scope (2008), from..$819.00

HOWA M-1500 ULTRALIGHT 2-N-1 YOUTH

Caliber: 223 Rem., 22-250 Rem., 243 Win., 308 Win., 7mm-08. **Barrel:** 20" #1 contour, blued. **Weight:** 6.8 lbs. **Length:** 39.25" overall. **Stock:** Hogue Overmolded in black, 12.5" LOP. Also includes adult-size Hogue Overmolded in OD green. **Sights:** None furnished; drilled and tapped for scope mounting. **Features:** Bolt and receiver milled to reduce weight, three-position safety, hinged floor plate, adjustable trigger, forged one-piece bolt, M-16 style extractor, forged flat-bottom receiver. Scope package includes 3-9x42 Nikko-Stirling riflescope with bases and rings. Imported from Japan by Legacy Sports International.

Price: Blue, Youth Rifle $539.00
Price: w/Scope package (2008)..$589.00

H-S PRECISION PRO-SERIES BOLT-ACTION

Caliber: 30 chamberings, 3- or 4-round magazine. **Barrel:** 20", 22", 24" or 26", sporter contour Pro-Series 10X match-grade stainless steel barrel. Optional muzzle brake on 30 cal. or smaller. **Weight:** 7.5 lbs. **Length:** NA. **Stock:** Pro-Series synthetic stock with full-length bedding block chassis system, sporter style. **Sights:** None; drilled and tapped for bases. **Features:** Accuracy guarantee: up to 30 caliber, 1/2 minute of angle (3 shots at 100 yards), test target supplied. Stainless steel action, stainless steel floorplate with detachable magazine, matte black Teflon finish. Made in U.S.A. by H-S Precision, Inc.

Price: SPR...$2,680.00
Price: SPL Lightweight (2008) $2,825.00

KEL-TEC RFB

Caliber: 7.62 NATO (308 Win.). **Barrels:** 18" to 32". **Weight:** 11.3 lbs. (unloaded). **Length:** 40» overall. **Features:** Gas-operated semi-auto bullpup-style, forward-ejecting. Fully ambidextrous controls, adjustable trigger mechanism, no open sights, four-sided picatinny forend. Accepts standard FAL-type magazines. Production of the RFB has been delayed due to redesign but was expected to begin first quarter 2009.

Price: $1,800.00

KENNY JARRETT BOLT-ACTION

Caliber: 223 Rem., 243 Improved, 243 Catbird, 7mm-08 Improved, 280 Remington, .280 Ackley Improved, 7mm Rem. Mag., 284 Jarrett, 30-06 Springfield, 300 Win. Mag., .300 Jarrett, 323 Jarrett, 338 Jarrett, 375 H&H, 416 Rem., 450 Rigby., other modern cartridges. **Barrel:** NA. **Weight:** NA. **Length:** NA. **Stock:** NA. **Features:** Tri-Lock receiver. Talley rings and bases. Accuracy guarantees and custom loaded ammunition.

Price: Signature Series $7,640.00
Price: Wind Walker $7,380.00
Price: Original Beanfield (customer's receiver) $5,380.00
Price: Professional Hunter $10,400.00
Price: SA/Custom $6,630.00

KIMBER MODEL 8400 BOLT-ACTION

Caliber: 25-06 Rem., 270 Win., 7mm, 30-06 Spfl., 300 Win. Mag., 338 Win. Mag., or 325 WSM, 4 shot. **Barrel:** 24". **Weight:** 6 lbs. 3 oz. to 6 lbs 10 oz. **Length:** 43.25". **Stock:** Claro walnut or Kevlar-reinforced fiberglass. **Sights:** None; drilled and tapped for bases. **Features:** Mauser claw extractor, two-position wing safety, action

Prices given are believed to be accurate at time of publication however, many factors affect retail pricing so exact prices are not possible.

bedded on aluminum pillars and fiberglass, free-floated barrel, match grade adjustable trigger set at 4 lbs., matte or polished blue or matte stainless finish. Introduced 2003. Sonora model (2008) has brown laminated stock, hand-rubbed oil finish, chambered in 25-06 Rem., 30-06 Spfl., and 300 Win. Mag. Weighs 8.5 lbs., measures 44.50" overall length. Front swivel stud only for bipod. Stainless steel bull barrel, 24" satin stainless steel finish. Made in U.S.A. by Kimber Mfg. Inc.

Price: Classic **$1,223.00**
Price: Classic Select Grade, French walnut stock (2008)...... **$1,427.00**
Price: SuperAmerica, AAA walnut stock............................ **$2,240.00**
Price: Police Tactical, synthetic stock, fluted barrel
    (300 Win. Mag only) .... **$1,495.00 to $2,650.00**

KIMBER MODEL 8400 CAPRIVI BOLT-ACTION

Similar to 8400 bolt rifle, but chambered for .375 H&H, .416 Remington and 458 Lott, 4-shot magazine. Stock is Claro walnut or Kevlar-reinforced fiberglass. Features twin steel crossbolts in stock, AA French walnut, pancake cheekpiece, 24 lines-per-inch wrap-around checkering, ebony forend tip, hand-rubbed oil finish, barrel-mounted sling swivel stud, 3-leaf express sights, Howell-type rear sling swivel stud and a Pachmayr Decelerator recoil pad in traditional orange color. Introduced 2008. Made in U.S.A. by Kimber Mfg. Inc.

Price: From **$3,263.00**
Price: Special Edition from **$5,031.00**

KIMBER MODEL 8400 TALKEETNA BOLT-ACTION

Similar to 8400 bolt rifle, but chambered for .375 H&H , 4-shot magazine. Weighs 8 lbs, overall length is 44.5". Stock is synthetic. Features free-floating match grade barrel with tapered match grade chamber and target crown, three-position wing safety acts directly on the cocking piece for greatest security, and Pacmayr Decelerator. Made in U.S.A. by Kimber Mfg. Inc.

Price: **$2,175.00**

KIMBER MODEL 84M BOLT-ACTION

Caliber: .22-250 Rem., .204 Ruger, .223 Rem., .243 Win., .257 Robts., .260 Rem., 7mm-08 Rem., .308 Win., 5-shot. **Barrel:** 22", 24", 26". **Weight:** 5 lbs., 10 oz. to 10 lbs. **Length:** 41" to 45". **Stock:** Claro walnut, checkered with steel gripcap; synthetic or gray laminate. **Sights:** None; drilled and tapped for bases. **Features:** Mauser claw extractor, three-position wing safety, action bedded on aluminum pillars, free-floated barrel, match-grade trigger set at 4 lbs., matte blue finish. Includes cable lock. Introduced 2001. Montana (2008) has synthetic stock, Pachmayr Decelerator recoil pad, stainless steel 22" sporter barrel. Made in U.S.A. by Kimber Mfg. Inc.

Price: Classic **$1,223.00**
Price: Varmint **$1,291.00**
Price: Montana **$1,359.00**
Price: Classic Stainless, matte stainless steel receiver
    and barrel **$1,495.00**

KIMBER MODEL 84L CLASSIC

Bolt action rifle chambered in .270 Win. and .30-06. Features include 24-inch sightless matte blue sporter barrel; hand-rubbed A-grade walnut stock with 20 lpi panel checkering; pillar and glass bedding; Mauser claw extractor; 3-position M70-style safety; 5-round magazine; adjustable trigger.

Price: **$1,172.00**

KIMBER MODEL 8400 PATROL

Bolt action tactical rifle chambered in .308 Win. Features include 20-inch 1:12 fluted sightless matte blue heavy barrel; black epoxy-coated laminated wood stock with 20 lpi panel checkering; pillar and glass bedding; Mauser claw extractor; 3-position M70-style safety; 5-round magazine; adjustable trigger.

Price: **$1,476.00**

L.A.R. GRIZZLY 50 BIG BOAR

Caliber: 50 BMG, single shot. **Barrel:** 36". **Weight:** 30.4 lbs. **Length:** 45.5" overall. **Stock:** Integral. Ventilated rubber recoil pad. **Sights:** None furnished; scope mount. **Features:** Bolt-action bullpup design, thumb and bolt stop safety. All-steel construction. Introduced 1994. Made in U.S.A. by L.A.R. Mfg., Inc.

Price: From **$2,350.00**

MAGNUM RESEARCH MOUNTAIN EAGLE MAGNUMLITE

Caliber: .22-250, .223, .224, .243, .257, 7mm Rem. Mag., 7mm WSM, .280, .300 Win. Mag., .300 WSM, .30-06, 3-shot magazine. **Barrel:** 24" sport taper graphite; 26" bull barrel graphite. **Weight:** 7.1-9.2 lbs. **Length:** 44.5-48.25" overall (adjustable on Tactical model). **Stock:** Hogue OverMolded synthetic, H-S Precision Tactical synthetic, H-S Precision Varmint synthetic. **Sights:** None. **Features:** Remington Model 700 receiver. Introduced in 2001. From Magnum Research, Inc.

Price: MLR3006ST24 Hogue stock **$2,295.00**
Price: MLR7MMBST24 Hogue stock **$2,295.00**
Price: MLRT22250 H-S Tactical stock, 26" bull barrel **$2,400.00**
Price: MLRT300WI Tactical **$2,400.00**

MARLIN XL7 BOLT ACTION

Caliber: 25-06 Rem. 270 Win., 30-06 Spfl., 4-shot magazine. **Barrel:** 22" 1:10" right-hand twist, recessed barrel crown. **Weight:** 6.5 lbs. **Length:** 42.5" overall. **Stock:** Black synthetic or Realtree APG-HD camo, Soft-Tech recoil pad, pillar bedded. **Sights:** None. **Features:** Pro-Fire trigger is user adjustable down to 2.5 lbs. Fluted bolt, steel sling swivel studs, high polished blued steel, checkered bolt handle, molded checkering, one-piece scope base. Introduced in 2008. From Marlin Firearms, Inc.

Price: Black Synthetic.. **$391.00**
Price: Camouflaged **$426.00**

MARLIN XS7 SHORT-ACTION BOLT-ACTION

Similar to Model XL7 but chambered in 7mm-08, 243 Winchester and 308 Winchester.

Price: **$391.00**
Price: XS7Y Youth **$391.00**
Price: XS7C Camo, Realtree APG HD camo stock **$426.00**
Price: XS7S Stainless **$500.00**

MERKEL KR1 BOLT-ACTION

Caliber: 223 Rem., 243 Rem., 6.5x55, 7mm-08, 308 Win., 270 Win., 30-06, 9.3x62, 7mm Rem. Mag., 300 Win. Mag., 270 WSM, 300 WSM, 338 Win. Mag. **Features:** Short lock, short bolt movement, take-down design with interchangeable barrel assemblies, three-position safety, detachable box magazine, fine trigger with set feature, checkered walnut pistol-grip semi-schnable stock. Adjustable iron sights with quick release mounts. Imported from Germany by Merkel USA.

CENTERFIRE RIFLES Bolt-Action

Price: **$1,995.00**
Price: Model KR1 Stutzen Antique: 20.8" barrel, case-colored
receiver, Mannlicher-style stock **$3,395.00**

MOSSBERG 100 ATR BOLT-ACTION
Caliber: 243 Win. (2006), 270 Win., 308 Win. (2006), 30-06 Spfl.,
4-round magazine. **Barrel:** 22", 1:10 twist, free-floating, button-rifled,
recessed muzzle crown. **Weight:** 6.7 to 7.75 lbs. **Length:** 42"-42.75"
overall. **Stock:** Black synthetic, walnut, Mossy Oak New Break
Up camo, Realtree AP camo. **Sights:** Factory-installed Weaver-
style scope bases; scoped combos include 3x9 factory-mounted,
bore-sighted scopes. **Features:** Marinecote and matte blue
metal finishes, free gun lock, side lever safety. Introduced 2005.
Night Train (2008)comes with Picatinny rail and factory-mounted
4-16x50mm variable scope. From O.F. Mossberg & Sons, Inc.
Price: From .... **$437.00 to $567.00**

MOSSBERG MVP SERIES
Caliber: .223/5.56 NATO. 10-round capacity. Uses AR-style
magazines. **Barrel:** 16.25 inches medium bull, 20-inch fluted sporter.
Weight: 6.5 to 7 lbs. **Stock:** Classic black textured polymer. **Sights:**
Adjustable folding rear, adjustable blade front. FLEX model has 20-
inch fluted sporter barrel, FLEX AR-style 6-position adjustable stock.
Varmint model has laminated stock, 24-inch barrel.
Price: .... **$681.00 to $928.00**

MOSSBERG 4X4
Caliber: Most popular calibers from .22-250 to .338 Win. Mag.
Barrel: 24" free floating with muzzle brake. **Stock:** Gray laminate
or American black walnut, with Monte Carlo cheek piece, fore-end
vents, recoil pad. Matte blue finish, adjustable trigger.
Price: From **$471.00**

NOSLER MODEL 48 LEGACY AND TROPHY
Caliber: Offered in most popular calibers including .280 Ackley
Improved wildcat. **Barrel:** 24". **Weight:** 7.25 to 8 lbs. **Stock:** Walnut or
composite.
Price: Legacy **$2495**
Price: Trophy.. **$1995**

NOSLER MODEL 48 VARMINT
Caliber: 204 Ruger, .223 Rem., 22-250 Rem., Heavy barrel, 4-shot
capacity. **Barrel:** 24". **Weight:** 7.25 lbs. **Stock:** Coyote tan or Onyx
black Kevlar® and carbon fiber. **Sights:** Fixed sights. **Features:**
The NoslerCustom® Model 48 is built on the same action as our
Custom rifles. Nosler's proprietary push-feed action features a
2-position safety and an adjustable trigger set to a crisp, 3 lb.
let-off. The action features a classic one-piece bottom metal and
trigger guard. To achieve the highest level of accuracy, the Model
48 integrates the unique MicroSlick™ Coating on interior metal
surfaces, including inside the bolt body, and on the firing pin and
firing pin spring, for maximum corrosion and wear-resistance, even
with extensive dry firing.
Price: 204 Ruger **$2,995.00**
Price: .223 Rem., (Black) **$2,995.00**

Price: 22-250, (Black) **$2,995.00**
Price: 22-250, (Grey) **$2,995.00**

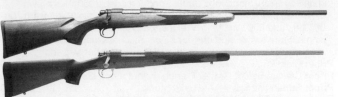

REMINGTON MODEL 700 CDL CLASSIC DELUXE
Caliber: 223 Rem., 243 Win., 25-06 Rem., 270 Win., 7mm-08 Rem.,
280 Remington, 7mm Rem. Mag., 7mm Rem. Ultra Mag., 30-06 Spfl.,
300 Rem. Ultra Mag., 300 Win. Mag., 35 Whelen. **Barrel:** 24" or 26"
round tapered. **Weight:** 7.4 to 7.6 lbs. **Length:** 43.6" to 46.5" overall.
Stock: Straight-comb American walnut stock, satin finish, checkering,
right-handed cheek piece, black fore-end tip and grip cap, sling swivel
studs. **Sights:** None. **Features:** Satin blued finish, jeweled bolt body,
drilled and tapped for scope mounts. Hinged-floorplate magazine
capacity: 4, standard calibers; 3, magnum calibers. SuperCell recoil
pad, cylindrical receiver, integral extractor. Introduced 2004. CDL SF
(stainless fluted) chambered for 260 Rem., 257 Wby. Mag., 270 Win.,
270 WSM, 7mm-08 Rem., 7mm Rem. Mag., 30-06 Spfl., 300 WSM.
Left-hand versions introduced 2008 in six calibers. Made in U.S. by
Remington Arms Co., Inc.
Price: Standard Calibers from .... **$1,019.00 to $1,077.00**
Price: CDL SF from .... **$1,197.00 to $1,259.00**

REMINGTON MODEL 700 BDL
Caliber: 243 Win., 270 Win., 7mm Rem. Mag. 30-06 Spfl., 300 Rem
Ultra Mag. **Barrel:** 22, 24, 26" round tapered. **Weight:** 7.25-7.4 lbs.
Length: 41.6-46.5" overall. **Stock:** Walnut. Gloss-finish pistol grip
stock with skip-line checkering, black forend tip and gripcap with white
line spacers. Quick-release floorplate. **Sights:** Gold bead ramp front;
hooded ramp, removable step-adjustable rear with windage screw.
Features: Side safety, receiver tapped for scope mounts, matte
receiver top, quick detachable swivels.
Price: Standard Calibers **$985.00**
Price: Magnum Calibers **$1,014.00**

REMINGTON MODEL 700 SPS
Caliber: 17 Rem. Fireball, 204 Ruger, 22-250 Rem., 6.8 Rem SPC,
223 Rem., 243 Win., 270 Win. 270 WSM, 7mm-08 Rem., 7mm
Rem. Mag., 7mm Rem. Ultra Mag., 30-06 Spfl., 308 Win., 300
WSM, 300 Win. Mag., 300 Rem. Ultra Mag. **Barrel:** 20", 24" or 26"
carbon steel. **Weight:** 7 to 7.6 lbs. **Length:** 39.6" to 46.5" overall.
Stock: Black synthetic, sling swivel studs, SuperCell recoil pad.
Sights: None. Introduced 2005. SPS Stainless replaces Model
700 BDL Stainless Synthetic. **Barrel:** Bead-blasted 416 stainless
steel. **Features:** Plated internal fire control component. SPS DM
features detachable box magazine. Buckmaster Edition versions
feature Realtree Hardwoods HD camouflage and Buckmasters
logo engraved on floorplate. SPS Varmint includes X-Mark Pro
trigger, 26" heavy contour barrel, vented beavertail forend, dual
front sling swivel studs. Made in U.S. by Remington Arms Co., Inc.
Price: From .... **$709.00 to $813.00**

REMINGTON 700 SPS TACTICAL
Bolt action rifle chambered in .223 and .308 Win. Features include
20-inch heavy-contour tactical-style barrel; dual-point pillar bedding;
black synthetic stock with Hogue overmoldings; semi-beavertail fore-
end; X-Mark Pro adjustable trigger system; satin black oxide metal
finish; hinged floorplate magazine; SuperCell recoil pad.

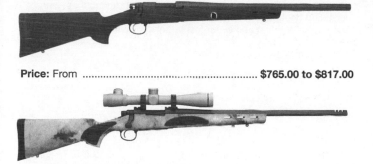

Price: From .... **$765.00 to $817.00**

REMINGTON 700 VTR A-TACS CAMO

Bolt action rifle chambered in .223 and .308 Win. Features include ATACS camo finish overall; triangular contour 22-inch barrel has an integral muzzle brake; black overmold grips; 1:9 (.223 caliber) Or 1:12 (.308) twist.

Price: **$959.00**

REMINGTON MODEL 700 VLS

Caliber: 204 Ruger, 223 Rem., 22-250 Rem., 243 Win., 308 Win. **Barrel:** 26" heavy contour barrel (0.820" muzzle O.D.), concave target-style barrel crown **Weight:** 9 4 lbs. **Length:** 45.75" overall. **Stock:** Brown laminated stock, satin finish, with beavertail forend, gripcap, rubber buttpad. **Sights:** None. **Features:** Introduced 1995. VLSS TH (varmint laminate stock stainless) thumbhole model introduced 2007. Made in U.S. by Remington Arms Co., Inc.

Price: **$1,045.00**

REMINGTON MODEL 700 VSSF-II/SENDERO SF II

Caliber: 17 Rem. Fireball, 204 Ruger, 220 Swift, 223 Rem., 22-250 Rem., 308 Win. **Barrel:** satin blued 26" heavy contour (0.820" muzzle O.D.). VSSF has satin-finish stainless barreled action with 26" fluted barrel. **Weight:** 8 5 lbs. **Length:** 45.75" overall. **Stock:** H.S. Precision composite reinforced with aramid fibers, black (VSSF-II) Contoured beavertail fore-end with ambidextrous finger grooves, palm swell, and twin front tactical-style swivel studs. **Sights:** None. **Features:** Aluminum bedding block, drilled and tapped for scope mounts, hinged floorplate magazines. Introduced 1994. Sendero model is similar to VSSF-II except chambered for 264 Win. Mag, 7mm Rem. Mag., 7mm Rem. Ultra Mag., 300 Win. Mag., 300 Rem. Ultra Mag. Polished stainless barrel. Introduced 1996. Made in U.S. by Remington Arms Co., Inc.

Price: VSSF-II **$1,450.00**
Price: Sendero SF II **$1,450.00**

REMINGTON MODEL 700 XCR CAMO RMEF

Similar to Model 700 XCR but with stainless barrel and receiver, AP HD camo stock, TriNyte coating overall, 7mm Remington Ultra Mag chambering.

Price: **$1,199.00**

REMINGTON MODEL 700 TARGET TACTICAL

Caliber: 308 Win. **Barrel:** 26" triangular counterbored, 1:11-1/2 rifling **Weight:** 11.75 lbs. **Length:** 45-3/4" overall. **Features:** Textured green Bell & Carlson varmint/tactical stock with adjustable comb and length of pull, adjustable trigger, satin black oxide finish on exposed metal surfaces, hinged floorplate, SuperCell recoil pad, matte blue on exposed metal surfaces.

Price: **$2,117.00**

REMINGTON MODEL 700 VTR VARMINT/TACTICAL

Caliber: .22-250, 223 Rem., 243 Win., 308 Win. **Barrel:** 22" triangular

---

counterbored. **Weight:** 7.5 lbs. **Length:** 41-5/8" overall. **Features:** Olive drab overmolded or Digital Tiger TSP Desert Camo stock with vented semi-beavertail forend, tactical-style dual swivel mounts for bipod, matte blue on exposed metal surfaces.

Price: From .... **$908.00 to $959.00**

REMINGTON MODEL 700 VARMINT SF

Caliber: 17 Rem. Fireball, 204 Ruger, 22-250, 223, 220 Swift. **Barrel:** 26" stainless steel fluted. **Weight:** 8.5 lbs. **Length:** 45.75». **Features:** Synthetic stock with ventilated forend, stainless steel/triggerguard/floorplate, dual tactical swivels for bipod attachment.

Price: **$981.00**

REMINGTON MODEL 700 MOUNTAIN SS

Calibers: .25-06, .270 Win., .280 Rem., 7mm-08, .308 Win., .30-06. **Barrel:** 22". **Length:** 40.6". **Weight:** 6.5 lbs. Satin stainless finish, Bell & Carlson Aramid Fiber stock.

Price: **$1,123.00**

REMINGTON MODEL 770 BOLT-ACTION

Caliber: 243 Win., 270 Win., 7mm Rem. Mag., 7mm-08 Rem., 308 Win., 30-06 Spfl., 300 Win. Mag. **Barrel:** 22" or 24", button rifled. **Weight:** 8.5 lbs. **Length:** 42.5" to 44.5" overall. **Stock:** Black synthetic. **Sights:** Bushnell Sharpshooter 3-9x scope mounted and bore-sighted. **Features:** Upgrade of Model 710 introduced 2001. Unique action locks bolt directly into barrel; 60-degree bolt throw; 4-shot dual-stack magazine; all-steel receiver. Introduced 2007. Made in U.S.A. by Remington Arms Co.

Price: **$375.00**
Price: Youth, 243 Win. **$375.00**
Price: Stainless Camo (2008), stainless barrel, nickel-plated bolt, Realtree camo stock **$458.00**

REMINGTON MODEL 783

Calibers: .270 Win., 7mm Rem. Mag., .308 Win., .30-06 Sprg. **Barrel:** 22 inches. **Stock:** Synthetic. **Weight:** 7 to 7.25 lbs. **Finish:** Matte black. **Features:** Adjustable trigger with two-position trigger-block safety, magnum contour button-rifle barrel, Cylindrical receiver with minimum size ejection port, Pillar bedded stock, detachable box magazine, 90-degree bolt throw.

Price: **$451**

REMINGTON MODEL SEVEN CDL

Calibers: .243, .260 Rem., 7mm-08, .308 Win. **Barrel:** 20". **Weight:** 6.5 lbs. **Length:** 39.25". **Stock:** Walnut with black fore-end tip, satin finish. Predator model in .223, .22-250 and .243 has Mossy Oak Brush camo stock, 22" barrel.

Price: **$1,029.00**
Price: Predator **$886.00**

REMINGTON 40-XB TACTICAL

Bolt action rifle chambered in .308 Winchester. Features include stainless steel bolt with Teflon coating; hinged floorplate; adjustable trigger; 27-1/4-inch tri-fluted 1:14 barrel; H-S precision pro series

Prices given are believed to be accurate at time of publication however, many factors affect retail pricing so exact prices are not possible.

68TH EDITION, 2014 ⊕ **475**

tactical stock, black color with dark green spiderweb; two front swivel studs; one rear swivel stud; vertical pistol grip.
Price: From the Remington Custom Shop.................................... **POR**

REMINGTON 40-XS TACTICAL - 338LM SYSTEM

Bolt action rifle chambered in .338 Lapua Magnum. Features include 416 stainless steel Model 40-X 24-inch 1:12 barreled action; black polymer coating; McMillan A3 series stock with adjustable length of pull and adjustable comb; adjustable trigger and Sunny Hill heavy duty, all-steel trigger guard; Harris bi-pod with quick adjust swivel lock Leupold Mark IV 3.5-10x40mm long range M1 scope with Mil Dot reticle; Badger Ordnance all-steel Picatinny scope rail and rings.
Price: .... **NA**

ROCK ISLAND ARMORY TCM

Caliber: .22 TCM. 5-round capacity magazine, interchangeable with .22 TCM 17-round pistol magazine. **Barrel:** 22.75 inches. **Weight:** 6 pounds. Chambered for .22 TCM cartridge introduced in 2013.
Price: **$450**

RUGER AMERICAN RIFLE

Caliber: .22-250, .243, 7mm-08, .308, .270 Win., .30-06 (4-shot rotary magazine). **Barrel:** 22". **Length:** 42.5". **Weight:** 6.25 lbs. **Stock:** Black composite. **Finish:** Matte black. **Features:** Tang safety, hammer-forged free floating barrel.
Price: **$449.00**

RUGER COMPACT MAGNUM

Caliber: .338 RCM, .300 RCM; 3-shot magazine. **Barrel:** 20". **Weight:** 6.75 lbs. **Length:** 39.5-40" overall. **Stock:** American walnut and black synthetic; stainless steel and Hawkeye Matte blued finishes. **Sights:** Adjustable Williams "U" notch rear sight and brass bead front sight. **Features:** Based on a shortened .375 Ruger case, the .300 and .338 RCMs match the .300 and .338 Win. Mag. in performance; RCM stock is 1/2 inch shorter than standard M77 Hawkeye stock; LC6 trigger; steel floor plate engraved with Ruger logo and "Ruger Compact Magnum"; Red Eagle recoil pad; Mauser-type controlled feeding; claw extractor; 3-position safety; hammer-forged steel barrels; Ruger scope rings. Walnut stock includes extensive cut-checkering and rounded profiles. Intr. 2008. Made in U.S.A. by Sturm, Ruger & Co.
Price: **$929.00**

RUGER GUNSITE SCOUT RIFLE

Caliber: .308 WIN., 10-shot magazine capacity. **Barrel:** 16.5". **Weight:** 7 lbs. **Length:** 38-39.5". **Stock:** Black laminate. **Sights:** Front post sight and rear adjustable. **Features:** Gunsite Scout Rifle is a credible rendition of Col. Jeff Cooper's "fighting carbine" Scout Rifle. The Ruger Gunsite Scout Rifle is a new platform in the Ruger M77 family. While the Scout Rifle has M77 features such as controlled round feed and integral scope mounts (scope rings included), the 10-round detachable box magazine is the first clue this isn't your grandfather's Ruger rifle. The Ruger Gunsite Scout Rifle has a 16.5 medium contour, cold hammer-forged, alloy steel barrel with a Mini-14 protected non-glare post front sight and receiver mounted, adjustable

ghost ring rear sight for out-of-the-box usability. A forward mounted Picatinny rail offers options in mounting an assortment of optics – including Scout Scopes available from Burris and Leupold, for "both eyes open" sighting and super-fast target acquisition.
Price: **$1,039.00**
Price: (stainless) **$1,099.00**

RUGER ROTARY MAGAZINE RIFLE

Caliber: .17 Hornet, .22 Hornet, .357 Magnum, . 44 Magnum (capacity 4 to 6 rounds). **Barrel:** 20", .22 Hornet, 18.5" .357 & .44 Magnums). **Weight:** 5.5 to 7.5 lbs. **Stock:** American walnut, black synthetic, camo or brown laminate.
Price: From.. **$899.00 to $969.00**

RUGER M77 GUIDE GUN

Calibers: .30-06, .300 Ruger Compact Mag., .300 Win. Mag., .338 RCM, .338 Win. Mag., .375 Ruger. **Capacity:** 3 or 4 rounds. **Barrel:** 20 inches with barrel-band sling swivel and removable muzzle brake. **Weight:** 8 to 8.12 pounds. **Stock:** Green Mountain Laminate. **Finish:** Hawkeye matte stainless. **Sights:** Adjustable rear, bead front. Newest addition to Model 77 Hawkeye series (2013).
Price: **$1199**

RUGER M77 HAWKEYE

Caliber: 204 Ruger, 223 Rem., 22-250 Rem., 243 Win., 257 Roberts, 25-06 Rem., 270 Win., 280 Rem., 6.5 Creedmoor, 7mm/08, 7mm Rem. Mag., 308 Win., 30-06 Spfl., 300 Win. Mag., 338 Win. Mag., 338 Federal, 358 Win. Mag., 416 Ruger, 375 Ruger, 300 Ruger Compact Magnum, 338 Ruger Compact Magnum; 4-shot magazine, except 3-shot magazine for magnums; 5-shot magazine for 204 Ruger and 223 Rem. **Barrel:** 22", 24". **Weight:** 6.75 to 8.25 lbs. **Length:** 42-44.4" overall. **Stock:** American walnut. **Sights:** None furnished. Receiver has Ruger integral scope mount base, Ruger 1" rings. **Features:** Includes Ruger LC6 trigger, new red rubber recoil pad, Mauser-type controlled feeding, claw extractor, 3-position safety, hammer-forged

Prices given are believed to be accurate at time of publication however, many factors affect retail pricing so exact prices are not possible.

steel barrels, Ruger scope rings. Walnut stock includes wrap-around cut checkering on the forearm and, more rounded contours on stock and top of pistol grips. Matte stainless version features synthetic stock. Hawkeye Alaskan and African chambered in 375 Ruger. Alaskan features matte-black finish, 20" barrel, Hogue OverMolded synthetic stock. African has 23" blued barrel, checkered walnut stock, left-handed model. 375's have windage-adjustable shallow "V" notch rear sight, white bead front sights. Introduced 2007. Left-hand models available 2008.

Price: Standard, right- and left-hand $859.00
Price: All-Weather $859.00
Price: Compact $859.00
Price: Laminate Compact $929.00
Price: Compact Magnum $929.00
Price: African $1,099.00
Price: Alaskan $1,099.00
Price: Sporter $929.00
Price: Tactical $1,199.00
Price: Predator $999.00

RUGER M77VT TARGET

Caliber: 22-250 Rem., 223 Rem., 204 Ruger, 243 Win., 25-06 Rem., 308 Win., 6.5 Creedmoor **Barrel:** 26" heavy stainless steel with target grey finish. **Weight:** 9 to 9.75 lbs. **Length:** Approx. 45.75" to 46.75" overall. **Stock:** Laminated American hardwood with beavertail forend, steel swivel studs; no checkering or gripcap. **Sights:** Integral scope mount bases in receiver. **Features:** Ruger diagonal bedding system. Ruger steel 1" scope rings supplied. Fully adjustable trigger. Steel floorplate and trigger guard. New version introduced 1992.
Price: KM77VT MKII $935.00

SAKO A7 AMERICAN BOLT-ACTION

Caliber: 270 Win., 300 WSM. **Barrel:** 22-7/16" standard, 24 3/8" magnum. **Weight:** 6 lbs. 3 oz. to 6 lbs. 13 oz. **Length:** 42-5/16" to 44-5/16" overall. **Features:** Blued or stainless barrel and receiver, black composite stock with sling swivels and recoil pad, two-position safety, adjustable trigger, detachable 3+1 box magazine.
Price: From $1,375.00

SAKO TRG-22 TACTICAL RIFLE

Bolt action rifles chambered in .308 Winchester (TRG-22). Features include target grade Cr-Mo or stainless barrels with muzzle brake; three locking lugs; 60° bolt throw; adjustable two-stage target trigger; adjustable or folding synthetic stock; receiver-mounted integral 17mm axial optics rails with recoil stop-slots; tactical scope mount for modern three turret tactical scopes (30 and 34 mm tube diameter); optional bipod.
Price: $3,450.00

SAKO MODEL 85 BOLT-ACTION

Caliber: 22-250 Rem., 243 Win., 25-06 Rem., 260, 6.5x55mm, 270 Win., 270 WSM, 7mm-08 Rem., 308 Win., 30-06; 7mm WSM, 300 WSM, 338 Federal. **Barrel:** 22.4", 22.9", 24.4". **Weight:** 7.75 lbs. **Length:** NA. **Stock:** Polymer, laminated or high-grade walnut, straight comb, shadow-line cheekpiece. **Sights:** None furnished. **Features:** Controlled-round feeding, adjustable trigger, matte stainless or nonreflective satin blue. Offered in a wide range of variations and models. Introduced 2006. Imported from Finland by Beretta USA.

Price: Grey Wolf..$1,600.00
Price: Black Bear $1,600.00
Price: Kodiak $1,925.00
Price: Varmint Laminated $2,000.00
Price: Classic $2,200.00
Price: Bavarian ....$2,200.00 - $2,300.00
Price: Bavarian carbine, Full-length stock $925.00
Price: Brown Bear $2,175.00

SAKO 85 FINNLIGHT

Similar to Model 85 but chambered in 243 Win., 25-06, 260 Rem., 270 Win., 270 WSM, 300 WSM, 30-06, 300 WM, 308 Win., 6.5x55mm, 7mm Rem Mag., 7mm-08. Weighs 6 lbs., 3 oz. to 6 lbs.

13 oz. Stainless steel barrel and receiver, black synthetic stock.
Price: $1,600.00

SAVAGE AXIS SERIES BOLT ACTION

Caliber: .243 WIN., 7mm-08 REM., .308 WIN., .25-06 REM., .270 WIN, .30-06 SPFLD., .223 REM., 22-250 REM. **Barrel:** 22". **Weight:** 6.5 lbs. **Length:** 43.875". **Stock:** Black synthetic. **Sights:** Drilled and tapped for scope mounts. **Features:** The AXIS Stainless has a very sleek and modern design plus a silky-smooth operation. It benefits from a very handy detachable box magazine and is available only as a rifle and in a scoped package. It sports a stainless steel barrel with a high luster finish. The stock is synthetic and has a black matte finish. It is one of the most affordable rifles in the 2011 Savage lineup of hunting guns.
Price: From ....$363.00 to $485.00

SAVAGE MODEL 25 BOLT ACTION

Caliber: .17 Hornet, .22 Hornet, .222 Rem., 204 Ruger, 223 Rem., 4-shot magazine. **Barrel:** 24", medium-contour fluted barrel with recessed target crown, free-floating sleeved barrel, dual pillar bedding. **Weight:** 8.25 lbs. **Length:** 43.75" overall. **Stock:** Brown laminate with beavertail-style forend. **Sights:** Weaver-style bases installed. **Features:** Diameter-specific action built around the 223 Rem. bolthead dimension. Three locking lugs, 60-degree bolt lift, AccuTrigger adjustable from 2.5 to 3.25 lbs. Model 25 Classic Sporter has satin lacquer American walnut with contrasting forend tip, wraparound checkering, 22" blued barrel. **Weight:** 7.15 lbs. **Length:** 41.75". Introduced 2008. Made in U.S.A. by Savage Arms, Inc.
Price: From ....$707.00 to $754.00

SAVAGE CLASSIC SERIES MODEL 14/114

Caliber: 204 Ruger, 223 Rem., 22-250 Rem., 243 Win., .250 Savage, 7mm-08 Rem., 308 Win., 2- or 4-shot magazine; 270 Win., 7mm Rem. Mag., 30-06 Spfl., 300 Win. Mag. (long action Model 114), 3- or 4-shot magazine. **Barrel:** 22" or 24". **Weight:** 7 to 7.5 lbs. **Length:** 41.75" to 43.75" overall (Model 14); 43.25" to 45.25" overall (Model 114). **Stock:** Satin lacquer American walnut with ebony forend, wraparound checkering, Monte Carlo Comb and cheekpiece. **Sights:** None furnished. Receiver drilled and tapped for scope mounting. **Features:** AccuTrigger, high luster blued barreled action, hinged floorplate. From Savage Arms, Inc.
Price: $850.00
Price: Stainless $995.00

SAVAGE MODEL 12 SERIES VARMINT

Caliber: 204 Ruger, 223 Rem., 22-250 Rem. 4-shot magazine. **Barrel:** 26" stainless barreled action, heavy fluted, free-floating and button-rifled barrel. **Weight:** 10 lbs. **Length:** 46.25" overall. **Stock:** Dual pillar bedded, low profile, laminated stock with extra-wide beavertail forend. **Sights:** None furnished; drilled and tapped for scope mounting. **Features:** Recessed target-style muzzle. AccuTrigger, oversized bolt handle, detachable box magazine, swivel studs. Model 112BVSS has heavy target-style prone laminated stock with high comb, Wundhammer palm swell, internal box magazine. Model 12FVSS has black synthetic stock, additional chamberings in 308 Win., 270 WSM, 300 WSM. Model 12FV has blued receiver. Model 12BTCSS has brown laminate vented thumbhole stock. Made in U.S.A. by Savage Arms, Inc.
Price: From ....$698.00 to $1,355.00

SAVAGE MODEL 16/116 WEATHER WARRIORS

Caliber: 204 Ruger, 223 Rem., 22-250 Rem., 243 Win., 7mm-08 Rem., 308 Win., 270 WSM, 7mm WSM, 300 WSM (short action Model 16), 2- or 4-shot magazine; 270 Win., 7mm Rem. Mag., 30-06 Spfl., 300 Win. Mag., 338 Win. Mag. (long action Model 114), 3- or 4-shot magazine. **Barrel:** 22", 24"; stainless steel with matte finish, free-floated barrel. **Weight:** 6.5 to 6.75 lbs. **Length:** 41.75" to 43.75" overall (Model 16);

42.5" to 44.5" overall (Model 116). **Stock:** Graphite/fiberglass filled composite. **Sights:** None furnished; drilled and tapped for scope mounting. **Features:** Quick-detachable swivel studs; laser-etched bolt. Left-hand models available. Model 116FSS introduced 1991; 116FSAK introduced 1994. Made in U.S.A. by Savage Arms, Inc.
Price: From .... **$825.00 to $966.00**

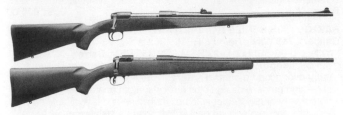

SAVAGE MODEL 11/111 HUNTER SERIES BOLT ACTIONS
Caliber: 223 Rem., 22-250 Rem., 243 Win., 6.5 Creedmoor, .260 Rem., 6.5x284 Norma, .338 Lapua, 7mm-08 Rem., 308 Win., 2- or 4-shot magazine; 25-06 Rem., 270 Win., 7mm Rem. Mag., 30-06 Spfl., 300 Win. Mag., (long action Model 111), 3- or 4-shot magazine. **Barrel:** 22" or 24"; blued free-floated barrel. **Weight:** 6.5 to 6.75 lbs. **Length:** 41.75" to 43.75" overall (Model 11); 42.5" to 44.5" overall (Model 111). **Stock:** Graphite/fiberglass filled composite or hardwood. **Sights:** Ramp front, open fully adjustable rear; drilled and tapped for scope mounting. **Features:** Three-position top tang safety, double front locking lugs. Introduced 1994. Made in U.S.A. by Savage Arms, Inc.
Price: From .... **$899.00 to $1,029.00**
Price: .338 Lapua... **$1,239.00**

SAVAGE MODEL 10 BAS LAW ENFORCEMENT BOLT-ACTION RIFLE
Caliber: .308 Win., .300 Win., .338 Lapua. **Barrel:** 24" fluted heavy with muzzle brake. **Weight:** 13.4 lbs. **Length:** NA. **Features:** Bolt-action repeater based on Model 10 action but with M4-style collapsible buttstock, pistolgrip with palm swell, all-aluminum Accustock, picatinny rail for mounting optics.
Price: .... **$2,218.00 to $2,394.00**

SAVAGE MODEL 10FP/110FP LAW ENFORCEMENT SERIES
Caliber: 223 Rem., 308 Win. (Model 10), 4-shot magazine; 25-06 Rem., 300 Win. Mag., (Model 110), 3- or 4-shot magazine. **Barrel:** 24"; matte blued free-floated heavy barrel and action. **Weight:** 6.5 to 6.75 lbs. **Length:** 41.75" to 43.75" overall (Model 10); 42.5" to 44.5" overall (Model 110). **Stock:** Black graphite/fiberglass composition, pillar-bedded, positive checkering. **Sights:** None furnished. Receiver drilled and tapped for scope mounting. **Features:** Black matte finish on all metal parts. Double swivel studs on the forend for sling and/ or bipod mount. Right- or left-hand. Model 110FP introduced 1990.

Model 10FP introduced 1998. Model 10FCPXP has HS Precision black synthetic tactical stock with molded alloy bedding system, Leupold 3.5-10x40mm black matte scope with Mil Dot reticle, Farrell Picatinny Rail Base, flip-open lens covers, 1.25" sling with QD swivels, Harris bipod, Storm heavy duty case. Made in U.S.A. by Savage Arms, Inc.

Price: Model 10FP, 10FLP (left hand), 110FP **$649.00**
Price: Model 10FP folding Choate stock.................................. **$896.00**
Price: Model 10FCP McMillan, McMillan fiberglass tactical
    stock **$1,178.00**
Price: Model 10FCP-HS HS Precision, HS Precision tactical
    stock **$984.00**
Price: Model 10FPXP-HS Precision.............................**$2,715.00**
Price: Model 10FCP **$866.00**
Price: Model 10FLCP, left-hand model, standard stock
    or Accu-Stock **$866.00**
Price: Model 110FCP **$866.00**
Price: Model 10 Precision Carbine, 20" medium contour barrel,
    synthetic camo Accu-Stock, 223/308 ....**$829.00**
Price: Model 10 FCM Scout **$646.00**

SAVAGE MODEL 10 PREDATOR SERIES
Caliber: 223, 22-250, 243, 204 Ruger, 6.5 Creedmoor, 6.5x284 Norma. **Barrel:** 22"; medium-contour. **Weight:** 7.25 lbs. **Length:** 43"overall. **Stock:** Synthetic with rounded forend and oversized bolt handle. **Features:** Entirely covered in either Mossy Oak Brush or Realtree Hardwoods Snow pattern camo. Also features AccuTrigger, AccuStock, detachable box magazine.
Price: .... **$880.00 to $915.00**

SAVAGE MODEL 12 PRECISION TARGET SERIES BENCHREST
Caliber: 308 Win, 6.5x284 Norma, 6mm Norma BR. **Barrel:** 29" ultra-heavy. **Weight:** 12.75 lbs. **Length:** 50" overall. **Stock:** Gray laminate. Features: New Left-Load, Right-Eject target action, Target AccuTrigger adjustable from approx 6 oz to 2.5 lbs, oversized bolt handle, stainless extra-heavy free-floating and button-rifled barrel.
Price: **$1,505.00**

SAVAGE MODEL 12 PRECISION TARGET PALMA
Similar to Model 12 Benchrest but in .308 Win. only, 30" barrel, multi-adjustable stock, weighs 13.3 lbs.
Price: **$1,927.00**

SAVAGE MODEL 12 F CLASS TARGET RIFLE
Similar to Model 12 Benchrest but in 6.5x284 Norma, 6 Norma BR, 30" barrel, weighs 11.5 lbs.
Price: **$1,480.00**

SAVAGE MODEL 12 F/TR TARGET RIFLE
Similar to Model 12 Benchrest but in 308 Win. only, 30" barrel, weighs 12.65 lbs.
Price: **$1,381.00**

STEVENS MODEL 200 BOLT-ACTION
Caliber: 223, 22-250, 243, 7mm-08, 308 Win. (short action) or 25-06, 270 Win., 30-06, 7mm Rem. Mag., 300 Win Mag. **Barrel:** 22" (short action) or 24" (long action blued). **Weight:** 6.5 lbs. **Length:** 41.75" overall. **Stock:** Black synthetic or camo. **Sights:** None. **Features:** Free-floating and button-rifled barrel, top loading internal box magazine, swivel studs.

Prices given are believed to be accurate at time of publication however, many factors affect retail pricing so exact prices are not possible.

Price: (standard) $399.00
Price: (camo) $439.00
Price: Model 200XP Long or Short Action
Package Rifle with 4x12 scope $449.00
Price: Model 200XP Camo, camo stock $499.00

STEYR MANNLICHER CLASSIC
Caliber: 222 Rem., 223 Rem., 243 Win., 25-06 Rem., 308 Win., 6.5x55, 6.5x57, 270 Win., 270 WSM, 7x64 Brenneke, 7mm-08 Rem., 7.5x55, 30-06 Spfl., 9.3x62, 6.5x68, 7mm Rem. Mag., 300 WSM, 300 Win. Mag., 8x68S, 4-shot magazine. **Barrel:** 23.6" standard; 26" magnum; 20" full stock standard calibers. **Weight:** 7 lbs. **Length:** 40.1" overall. **Stock:** Hand-checkered fancy European oiled walnut with standard forend. **Sights:** Ramp front adjustable for elevation, V-notch rear adjustable for windage. **Features:** Single adjustable trigger; 3-position roller safety with "safe-bolt" setting; drilled and tapped for Steyr factory scope mounts. Introduced 1997. Imported from Austria by Steyr Arms, Inc.
Price: Half stock, standard calibers $3,799.00
Price: Full stock, standard calibers $4,199.00

STEYR PRO HUNTER
Similar to the Classic Rifle except has ABS synthetic stock with adjustable butt spacers, straight comb without cheekpiece, palm swell, Pachmayr 1" swivels. Special 10-round magazine conversion kit available. Introduced 1997. Imported from Austria by Steyr Arms, Inc.
Price: From $1,500.00

STEYR SCOUT BOLT-ACTION
Caliber: 308 Win., 5-shot magazine. **Barrel:** 19", fluted. **Weight:** NA. **Length:** NA. **Stock:** Gray Zytel. **Sights:** Pop-up front & rear, Leupold M8 2.5x28 IER scope on Picatinny optic rail with Steyr mounts. **Features:** luggage case, scout sling, two stock spacers, two magazines. Introduced 1998. Imported from Austria by Steyr Arms, Inc.
Price: From $2,199.00

STEYR SSG08 BOLT-ACTION
Caliber: 7.62x51mmNATO (.308Win) or 7.62x63B (.300 Win Mag)., 10-shot magazine capacity. **Barrel:** 508mm or 600mm. **Weight:** 5.5 kg - 5.7 kg. **Length:** 1090mm - 1182mm. **Stock:** Dural aluminium foldingstock black with 280 mm long UIT-rail and various Picatinny-rails. **Sights:** Front post sight and rear adjustable. **Features:** The STEYR SSG 08 features high grade alumnium folding stock, adjustable cheek piece and butt plate with height marking, and an ergonomical exchangeable pistol grip. The STEYR SSG 08 also features a Versa-Pod, a muzzle brake, a Picatinny rail, a UIT rail on stock and various Picatinny rails on fore end, and a 10-round HC-magazine. SBSrotary bolt action with four frontal locking lugs, arranged in pairs.Coldhammer-forged barrels are available in standard or compact lengths.
Price: $4,915.00

STEYR SSG 69 PII BOLT-ACTION
Caliber: 22-250 Rem., 243 Win., 308 Win., detachable 5-shot rotary magazine. **Barrel:** 26". **Weight:** 8.5 lbs. **Length:** 44.5" overall. **Stock:** Black ABS Cycolac with spacers for length of pull adjustment.

Sights: Hooded ramp front adjustable for elevation, V-notch rear adjustable for windage. **Features:** Sliding safety; NATO rail for bipod; 1" swivels; Parkerized finish; single or double-set triggers. Imported from Austria by Steyr Arms, Inc.
Price: $1,889.00

THOMPSON/CENTER ICON BOLT-ACTION
Caliber: 22-250 Rem., 243 Win., 308 Win., 6.5 Creedmoor, 30TC, 3-round box magazine. **Barrel:** 24", button rifled. **Weight:** 7.5 lbs. **Length:** 44.5" overall. **Stock:** Walnut, 20-lpi grip and forend cut checkering with ribbon detail. **Sights:** None; integral Weaver style scope mounts. **Features:** Interchangeable bolt handle, 60-degree bolt lift, Interlok Bedding System, 3-lug bolt with T-Slot extractor, cocking indicator, adjustable trigger, preset to 3 to 3.5 lbs of pull. Introduced 2007. From Thompson/Center Arms.
Price: $899.00

THOMPSON/CENTER ICON PRECISION HUNTER
Similar to the basic ICON model. Available in 204 Ruger, 223 Rem., 22-250 Rem., 243 Win. and 308 Win., 6.5 Creedmoor, 22" heavy barrel, blued finish, varminter-style stock. Introduced 2009.
Price: $1,019.00

THOMPSON/CENTER VENTURE BOLT-ACTION
Caliber: 270 Win., 7mm Rem. Mag., 30-06 Springfield, 300 Win. Mag., 3-round magazine. **Barrel:** 24". **Weight:** NA. **Length:** NA. **Stock:** Composite. **Sights:** NA. **Features:** Nitride fat bolt design, externally adjustable trigger, two-position safety, textured grip. Introduced 2009.
Price: $529.00

THOMPSON/CENTER VENTURE MEDIUM ACTION
Bolt action rifle chambered in .204, .22-250, .223, .243, 7mm-08, .308 and 30TC. Features include a 24-inch crowned medium weight barrel, classic styled composite stock with inlaid traction grip panels, adjustable 3.5 to 5 pound trigger along with a drilled and tapped receiver (bases included). 3+1 detachable nylon box magazine. **Weight:** 7 lbs. **Length:** 43.5 inches.
Price: $529.00

THOMPSON/CENTER VENTURE PREDATOR PDX
Bolt action rifle chambered in .204, .22-250, .223, .243, .308. Similar to Venture Medium action but with heavy, deep-fluted 22-inch barrel and Max-1 camo finish overall. **Weight:** 8 lbs. **Length:** 41.5 inches.
Price: From $629.00

TIKKA T3 HUNTER
Caliber: 223 Rem., 22-250 Rem., 243 Win., 308 Win., 25-06 Rem., 270 Win., 30-06 Spfl., 300 Win. Mag., 338 Win. Mag., 270 WSM, 300 WSM, 6.5x55 Swedish Mauser, 7mm Rem. Mag. **Stock:** Walnut. **Sights:** None furnished. **Barrel:** 22-7/16"; 24-3/8". **Features:** Detachable magazine, aluminum scope rings. Introduced 2005. Imported from Finland by Beretta USA.
Price: $675.00

Prices given are believed to be accurate at time of publication however, many factors affect retail pricing so exact prices are not possible.

68TH EDITION, 2014 · 479

TIKKA T3 STAINLESS SYNTHETIC

Similar to the T3 Hunter except stainless steel, synthetic stock. Available in 243 Win., 2506, 270 Win., 308 Win., 30-06 Spfl., 270 WSM, 300 WSM, 7mm Rem. Mag., 300 Win. Mag., 338 Win. Mag. Introduced 2005. Imported from Finland by Beretta USA.

Price: $700.00

TIKKA T3 LITE BOLT-ACTION

Similar to the T3 Hunter, available in 223 Rem., 22-250 Rem., 308 Win., 243 Win., 25-06 Rem., 270 Win., 270 WSM, 30-06 Sprg., 300 Win Mag., 300 WSM, 338 Federal, 338 Win Mag., 7mm Rem. Mag., 7mm-08 Rem. Barrel lengths vary from 22-7/16" to 24-3/8". Made in Finland by Sako. Imported by Beretta USA.

Price: $695.00
Price: Stainless steel synthetic $600.00
Price: Stainless steel synthetic, left-hand $700.00

TIKKA T3 VARMINT/SUPER VARMINT

Similar to the T3 Hunter, available in 223 Rem., 22-250 Rem., 308 Win. Length is 23-3/8" (Super Varmint). Made in Finland by Sako. Imported by Beretta USA.

Price: $900.00
Price: Super Varmint $1,425.00

ULTRA LIGHT ARMS BOLT-ACTION

Caliber: 17 Rem. to 416 Rigby. **Barrel:** Douglas, length to order. **Weight:** 4.75 to 7.5 lbs. **Length:** Varies. **Stock:** Kevlar graphite composite, variety of finishes. **Sights:** None furnished; drilled and tapped for scope mounts. **Features:** Timney trigger, hand-lapped action, button-rifled barrel, hand-bedded action, recoil pad, sling-swivel studs, optional Jewell trigger. Made in U.S.A. by New Ultra Light Arms.

Price: Model 20 (short action)................................$3,000.00
Price: Model 24 (long action) $3,100.00
Price: Model 28 (magnum action) $3,400.00
Price: Model 40 (300 Wby. Mag., 416 Rigby) $3,400.00
Price: Left-hand models, add $100.00

WEATHERBY MARK V BOLT-ACTION

Caliber: Deluxe version comes in all Weatherby calibers plus 243 Win., 270 Win., 7mm-08 Rem., 30-06 Spfl., 308 Win. **Barrel:** 24", 26", 28". **Weight:** 6.75 to 10 lbs. **Length:** 44" to 48.75" overall. **Stock:** Walnut, Monte Carlo with cheekpiece; high luster finish; checkered pistol grip and forend; recoil pad. **Sights:** None furnished. **Features:** 4 models with Mark V action and wood stocks; other common elements include cocking indicator; adjustable trigger; hinged floorplate, thumb safety; quick detachable sling swivels. Ultramark has hand-selected exhibition-grade walnut stock, maplewood/ebony spacers, 20-lpi checkering. Chambered for 257 and 300 Wby Mags. Lazermark same as Mark V Deluxe except stock has extensive oak leaf pattern laser carving on pistol grip and forend; chambered in Wby. Magnums—257, 270 Win., 7mm., 300, 340, with 26" barrel. Introduced 1981. Sporter is same as the Mark V Deluxe without the embellishments. Metal has low-luster blue, stock is Claro walnut with matte finish, Monte Carlo comb, recoil pad. Chambered for these Wby. Mags: 257, 270 Win., 7mm, 300, 340. Other chamberings: 7mm Rem. Mag., 300 Win. Introduced 1993. Six Mark V models come with synthetic stocks. Ultra Lightweight rifles weigh 5.75 to 6.75 lbs.; 24", 26" fluted stainless barrels with recessed target crown; Bell & Carlson stock with CNC-machined aluminum bedding plate and tan "spider web" finish, skeletonized handle and sleeve. Available in 243 Win., Wby. Mag., 25-06 Rem., 270 Win., 7mm-08 Rem., 7mm Rem. Mag., 280 Rem, 308 Win., 30-06 Spfl., 300 Win. Mag. Wby. Mag chamberings: 240, 257, 270 Win., 7mm, 300. Introduced 1998. Accumark uses Mark V action with heavy-contour 26" and 28" stainless barrels with black oxidized flutes, muzzle diameter of .705".

No sights, drilled and tapped for scope mounting. Stock is composite with matte gel-coat finish, full length aluminum bedding Hasblock. Weighs 8.5 lbs. Chambered for these Wby. Mags: 240 (2007), 257, 270, 7mm, 300, 340, 338-378, 30-378. Other chamberings: 22-250 (2007), 243 Win. (2007), 25-06 Rem. (2007), 270 Win. (2007), 308 Win. (2007), 7mm Rem. Mag., 300 Win. Mag. Introduced 1996. SVM (Super VarmintMaster) has 26" fluted stainless barrel, spiderweb-pattern tan laminated synthetic stock, fully adjustable trigger. Chambered for 223 Rem., 22-250 Rem., 243. Mark V Synthetic has lightweight injection-molded synthetic stock with raised Monte Carlo comb, checkered grip and forend, custom floorplate release. Weighs 6.5-8.5 lbs., 24-28" barrels. Available in 22-250 Rem., 243 Win., 25-06 Rem., 270 Win., 7mm-08 Rem., 7mm Rem., Mag, 280 Rem., 308 Win., 30-06 Spfl., 308 Win., 300 Win. Mag., 375 H&H Mag, and these Wby. Magnums: 240, 257, 270 Win., 7mm, 300, 30-378, 338-378, 340. Introduced 1997. Fibermark composites are similar to other Mark V models except has black Kevlar and fiberglass composite stock and bead-bead-blast blue or stainless finish. Chambered for 9 standard and magnum calibers. Introduced 1983; reintroduced 2001. SVR comes with 22" button-rifled chrome-moly barrel, .739 muzzle diameter. Composite stock w/bedding block, gray spiderweb pattern. Made in U.S.A. From Weatherby.

Price: Mark V Deluxe $2,300.00
Price: Mark V Ultramark..$3,100.00
Price: Mark V Lazermark $2,600.00
Price: Mark V Sporter $1,600.00
Price: Mark V Ultra Lightweight .... $1,900.00 to $2,100.00
Price: Mark V Accumark $2,300.00
Price: Mark V Synthetic .... $1,300.00 to $1,600.00

WEATHERBY VANGUARD BOLT-ACTION

Caliber: .240, .257, and .300 Wby Mag. **Barrel:** 24" barreled action, matte black. **Weight:** 7.5 to 8.75 lbs. **Length:** 44" to 46-3/4" overall. **Stock:** Raised comb, Monte Carlo, injection-molded composite stock. **Sights:** None furnished. **Features:** One-piece forged, fluted bolt body with three gas ports, forged and machined receiver, adjustable trigger, factory accuracy guarantee. Vanguard Stainless has 410-Series stainless steel barrel and action, bead blasted matte metal finish. Vanguard Deluxe has raised comb, semi-fancy grade Monte Carlo walnut stock with maplewood spacers, rosewood forend and grip cap, polished action with high-gloss-blued metalwork. Vanguard Synthetic Package includes Vanguard Synthetic rifle with Bushnell Banner 3-9x40mm scope mounted and boresighted, Leupold Rifleman rings and bases, Uncle Mikes nylon sling, and Plano PRO-MAX injection-molded case. Sporter has Monte Carlo walnut stock with satin urethane finish, fineline diamond point checkering, contrasting rosewood forend tip, matte-blued metalwork. Sporter SS metalwork is 410 Series bead-blasted stainless steel. Vanguard Youth/Compact has 20" No. 1 contour barrel, short action, scaled-down non-reflective matte black hardwood stock with 12.5" length of pull and full-size, injection-molded composite stock. Chambered for 223 Rem., 22-250 Rem., 243 Win., 7mm-08 Rem., 308 Win. Weighs 6.75 lbs.; OAL 38.9." Sub-MOA Matte and Sub-MOA Stainless models have pillar-bedded Fiberguard composite stock (Aramid, graphite unidirectional fibers and fiberglass) with 24" barreled action; matte black metalwork, Pachmayr Decelerator recoil pad. Sub-MOA Stainless metalwork is 410 Series bead-blasted stainless steel. Sub-MOA Varmint guaranteed to shoot 3-shot group of .99" or less when used with specified Weatherby factory or premium (non-Weatherby calibers) ammunition. Hand-laminated, tan Monte Carlo composite stock with black spiderwebbing; CNC-machined aluminum bedding block, 22" No. 3 contour barrel, recessed target crown. Varmint Special has tan injection-molded Monte Carlo composite stock, pebble grain finish, black spiderwebbing. 22" No. 3 contour barrel (.740 muzzle dia.), bead blasted matte black finish, recessed target crown. Back Country has two-stage trigger, pillar-bedded Bell & Carlson stock, 24-in. fluted barrel, three-position safety. WBY-X Series comes with choice of several contemporary camo finishes (Bonz, Black Reaper, Kryptek) and is primarily targeted to younger shooters. Made in U.S.A. From Weatherby.

Price: Vanguard Synthetic $599.00
Price: Vanguard Stainless $749.00
Price: Vanguard Deluxe, 7mm Rem. Mag., 300 Win. Mag. (2007)...$1,049.00
Price: Vanguard Synthetic Package, 25-06 Rem. (2007).........$799.00
Price: Vanguard Sporter $749.00
Price: Vanguard Youth/Compact $549.00

Prices given are believed to be accurate at time of publication however, many factors affect retail pricing so exact prices are not possible.

Price: Vanguard S2 Back Country $1,399.00
Price: Vanguard WBY-X Series $749.00

WINCHESTER MODEL 70 BOLT-ACTION

Caliber: Varies by model. **Barrel:** Blued, or free-floating, fluted stainless hammer-forged barrel, 22", 24", 26". Recessed target crown. **Weight:** 6.75 to 7.25 lbs. **Length:** 41 to 45.75 " overall. **Stock:** Walnut (three models) or Bell and Carlson composite; textured charcoal-grey matte finish, Pachmayr Decelerator recoil pad. **Sights:** None. **Features:** Claw extractor, three-position safety, M.O.A. three-lever trigger system, factory-set at 3.75 lbs. Super Grade features fancy grade walnut stock, contrasting black fore-end tip and pistol grip cap, and sculpted shadowline cheekpiece. Featherweight Deluxe has angled-comb walnut stock, Schnabel fore-end, satin finish, cut checkering. Sporter Deluxe has satin-finished walnut stock, cut checkering, sculpted cheekpiece. Extreme Weather SS has composite stock, drop @ comb, 0.5"; drop @ heel, 0.5". Introduced 2008. Made in U.SA. from Winchester Repeating Arms.
Price: Extreme Weather SS, 264 Win. Mag., 270 Win., 270 WSM, 30-06 Spfl., 300 Win. Mag., 300 WSM, 308 Win., 325 WSM, 243 Winchester, 7mm WSM, from $1,200.00
Price: Super Grade, 30-06 Sprg., 300 Win. Mag., 270 WSM, 300 WSM, 270 Winchester, from $1,300.00

WINCHESTER MODEL 70 COYOTE LIGHT

Caliber: 22-250, 243 Winchester, 308 Winchester, 270 WSM, 300 WSM and 325 WSM, five-shot magazine (3-shot in 270 WSM, 300 WSM and 325 WSM). **Barrel:** 22" fluted stainless barrel (24" in 270 WSM, 300 WSM and 325 WSM). **Weight:** 7.5 lbs. **Length:** NA. **Features:** Composite Bell and Carlson stock, Pachmayr Decelerator pad. Controlled round feeding. No sights but drilled and tapped for mounts.
Price: $1,099.00

WINCHESTER MODEL 70 FEATHERWEIGHT

Caliber: 22-250, 243, 7mm-08, 308, 270 WSM, 7mm WSM, 300 WSM, 325 WSM, 25-06, 270, 30-06, 7mm Rem. Mag., 300 Win. Mag., 338 Win. Mag. Capacity 5 rounds (short action) or 3 rounds (long action). **Barrel:** 22" blued barrel (24" in magnum chamberings). **Weight:** 6-1/2 to 7-1/4 lbs. **Length:** NA. **Features:** Satin-finished checkered Grade I walnut stock, controlled round feeding. Pachmayr Decelerator pad. No sights but drilled and tapped for scope mounts.
Price: $880.00

WINCHESTER MODEL 70 SPORTER

Caliber: 270 WSM, 7mm WSM, 300 WSM, 325 WSM, 25-06, 270, 30-06, 7mm Rem. Mag., 300 Win. Mag., 338 Win. Mag. Capacity 5 rounds (short action) or 3 rounds (long action). **Barrel:** 22", 24" or 26" blued. **Weight:** 6-1/2 to 7-1/4 lbs. **Length:** NA. **Features:** Satin-finished checkered Grade I walnut stock with sculpted cheekpiece, controlled round feeding. Pachmayr Decelerator pad. No sights but drilled and tapped for scope mounts.
Price: $920.00

WINCHESTER MODEL 70 ULTIMATE SHADOW

Caliber: 243, 308, 270 WSM, 7mm WSM, 300 WSM, 325 WSM, 270, 30-06, 7mm Rem. Mag., 300 Win. Mag. Capacity 5 rounds (short action) or 3 rounds (long action). **Barrel:** 22" matte stainless (24" or 26" in magnum chamberings). **Weight:** 6-1/2 to 7-1/4 lbs. **Length:** NA. **Features:** Synthetic stock with WinSorb recoil pad, controlled round feeding. Pachmayr Decelerator pad. No sights but drilled and tapped for scope mounts.
Price: .... $760.00 to $970.00

ARMALITE AR-50
Caliber: 50 BMG **Barrel:** 31". **Weight:** 33.2 lbs. **Length:** 59.5" **Stock:** Synthetic. **Sights:** None furnished. **Features:** A single-shot bolt-action rifle designed for long-range shooting. Available in left-hand model. Made in U.S.A. by Armalite.
Price: **$3,359.00**

BALLARD 1875 1 1/2 HUNTER
Caliber: NA. **Barrel:** 26-30". **Weight:** NA **Length:** NA. **Stock:** Hand-selected classic American walnut. **Sights:** Blade front, Rocky Mountain rear. **Features:** Color case-hardened receiver, breechblock and lever. Many options available. Made in U.S.A. by Ballard Rifle & Cartridge Co.
Price: **$3,250.00**

BALLARD 1875 #3 GALLERY SINGLE SHOT
Caliber: NA. **Barrel:** 24-28" octagonal with tulip. **Weight:** NA. **Length:** NA. **Stock:** Hand-selected classic American walnut. **Sights:** Blade front, Rocky Mountain rear. **Features:** Color case-hardened receiver, breechblock and lever. Many options available. Made in U.S.A. by Ballard Rifle & Cartridge Co.
Price: **$3,300.00**

BALLARD 1875 #4 PERFECTION
Caliber: 22 LR, 32-40, 38-55, 40-65, 40-70, 45-70 Govt., 45-90, 45-110, 50-70, 50-90. **Barrel:** 30" or 32" octagon, standard or heavyweight. **Weight:** 10.5 lbs. (standard) or 11.75 lbs. (heavyweight bbl.). **Length:** NA. **Stock:** Smooth walnut. **Sights:** Blade front, Rocky Mountain rear. **Features:** Rifle or shotgun-style buttstock, straight grip action, single or double-set trigger, "S" or right lever, hand polished and lapped Badger barrel. Made in U.S.A. by Ballard Rifle & Cartridge Co.
Price: **$3,950.00**

BALLARD 1875 #7 LONG RANGE
Caliber: 32-40, 38-55, 40-65, 40-70 SS, 45-70 Govt., 45-90, 45-110. **Barrel:** 32", 34" half-octagon. **Weight:** 11.75 lbs. **Length:** NA. **Stock:** Walnut; checkered pistol grip shotgun butt, ebony forend cap. **Sights:** Globe front. **Features:** Designed for shooting up to 1000 yards. Standard or heavy barrel; single or double-set trigger; hard rubber or steel buttplate. Introduced 1999. Made in U.S.A. by Ballard Rifle & Cartridge Co.
Price: From **$3,600.00**

BALLARD 1875 #8 UNION HILL
Caliber: 22 LR, 32-40, 38-55, 40-65 Win., 40-70 SS. **Barrel:** 30" half-octagon. **Weight:** About 10.5 lbs. **Length:** NA. **Stock:** Walnut; pistol grip butt with cheekpiece. **Sights:** Globe front. **Features:** Designed for 200-yard offhand shooting. Standard or heavy barrel; double-set triggers; full loop lever; hook Schuetzen buttplate. Introduced 1999. Made in U.S.A. by Ballard Rifle & Cartridge Co.
Price: From **$4,175.00**

BALLARD MODEL 1885 LOW WALL SINGLE SHOT RIFLE
Caliber: NA. **Barrel:** 24-28". **Weight:** NA. **Length:** NA. **Stock:** Hand-selected classic American walnut. **Sights:** Blade front, sporting rear. **Features:** Color case hardened receiver, breech block and lever. Many options available. Made in U.S.A. by Ballard Rifle & Cartridge Co.
Price: **$3,300.00**

BALLARD MODEL 1885 HIGH WALL STANDARD SPORTING SINGLE SHOT
Caliber: 17 Bee, 22 Hornet, 218 Bee, 219 Don Wasp, 219 Zipper, 22 Hi-Power, 225 Win., 25-20 WCF, 25-35 WCF, 25 Krag, 7mmx57R, 30-30, 30-40 Krag, 303 British, 33 WCF, 348 WCF, 35 WCF, 35-30/30, 9.3x74R, 405 WCF, 50-110 WCF, 500 Express, 577 Express. **Barrel:** Lengths to 34". **Weight:** NA. **Length:** NA. **Stock:** Straight-grain American walnut. **Sights:** Buckhorn or flattop rear, blade front. **Features:** Faithful copy of original Model 1885 High Wall; parts

interchange with original rifles; variety of options available. Introduced 2000. Made in U.S.A. by Ballard Rifle & Cartridge Co.
Price: **$3,300.00**

BALLARD MODEL 1885 HIGH WALL SPECIAL SPORTING SINGLE SHOT
Caliber: NA. **Barrel:** 28-30" octagonal. **Weight:** NA. **Length:** NA. **Stock:** Hand-selected classic American walnut. **Sights:** Blade front, sporting rear. **Features:** Color case hardened receiver, breech block and lever. Many options available. Made in U.S.A. by Ballard Rifle & Cartridge Co.
Price: **$3,600.00**

BARRETT MODEL 99 SINGLE SHOT
Caliber: 50 BMG. **Barrel:** 33". **Weight:** 25 lbs. **Length:** 50.4" overall. **Stock:** Anodized aluminum with energy-absorbing recoil pad. **Sights:** None furnished; integral M1913 scope rail. **Features:** Bolt action; detachable bipod; match-grade barrel with high-efficiency muzzle brake. Introduced 1999. Made in U.S.A. by Barrett Firearms.
Price: From **$4,000.00**

BROWN MODEL 97D SINGLE SHOT
Caliber: 17 Ackley Hornet through 45-70 Govt. **Barrel:** Up to 26", air gauged match grade. **Weight:** About 5 lbs., 11 oz. **Stock:** Sporter style with pistol grip, cheekpiece and Schnabel forend. **Sights:** None furnished; drilled and tapped for scope mounting. **Features:** Falling block action gives rigid barrel-receiver matting; polished blue/black finish. Hand-fitted action. Many options. Made in U.S.A. by E. Arthur Brown Co., Inc.
Price: From **$999.00**

C. SHARPS ARMS MODEL 1875 TARGET & SPORTING RIFLE
Caliber: 38-55, 40-65, 40-70 Straight or Bottlenecks, 45-70, 45-90. **Barrel:** 30" heavy tapered round. **Weight:** 11 lbs. **Length:** NA. **Stock:** American walnut. **Sights:** Globe with post front sight. **Features:** Long Range Vernier tang sight with windage adjustments. Pistol grip stock with cheek rest; checkered steel buttplate. Introduced 1991. From C. Sharps Arms Co.
Price: Without sights.. **$1,325.00**
Price: With blade front & Buckhorn rear barrel sights **$1,420.00**
Price: With standard Tang & Globe w/post & ball front sights **$1,615.00**
Price: With deluxe vernier Tang & Globe w/spirit level & aperture sights **$1,730.00**
Price: With single set trigger, add **$125.00**

C. Sharps Arms 1875 Classic Sharps
Similar to New Model 1875 Sporting Rifle except 26", 28" or 30" full octagon barrel, crescent buttplate with toe plate, Hartford-style forend with cast German silver nose cap. Blade front sight, Rocky Mountain buckhorn rear. Weighs 10 lbs. Introduced 1987. From C. Sharps Arms Co.
Price: **$1,670.00**

C. SHARPS ARMS 1874 BRIDGEPORT SPORTING
Caliber: 38-55 TO 50-3.25. **Barrel:** 26", 28", 30" tapered octagon. **Weight:** 10.5 lbs. **Length:** 47". **Stock:** American black walnut; shotgun butt with checkered steel buttplate; straight grip, heavy forend with Schnabel tip. **Sights:** Blade front, buckhorn rear. Drilled and tapped for tang sight. **Features:** Double-set triggers. Made in U.S.A. by C. Sharps Arms.
Price: **$1,895.00**

C. SHARPS ARMS NEW MODEL 1885 HIGHWALL
Caliber: 22 LR, 22 Hornet, 219 Zipper, 25-35 WCF, 32-40 WCF, 38-55 WCF, 40-65, 30-40 Krag, 40-50 ST or BN, 40-70 ST or BN, 40-90 ST or BN, 45-70 Govt. 2-1/10" ST, 45-90 2-4/10" ST, 45-100 2-6/10" ST, 45-110 2-7/8" ST, 45-120 3-1/4" ST. **Barrel:** 26", 28", 30", tapered full octagon. **Weight:** About 9 lbs., 4 oz. **Length:** 47" overall. **Stock:** Oil-finished American walnut; Schnabel-style forend. **Sights:** Blade front, buckhorn rear. Drilled and tapped for optional tang sight. **Features:** Single trigger; octagonal receiver top; checkered steel buttplate; color case-hardened receiver and buttplate, blued barrel. Many options available. Made in U.S.A. by C. Sharps Arms Co.
Price: From **$1,750.00**

C. SHARPS ARMS CUSTOM NEW MODEL 1877 LONG RANGE TARGET
Caliber: 44-90 Sharps/Rem., 45-70 Govt., 45-90, 45-100 Sharps. **Barrel:** 32", 34" tapered round with Rigby flat. **Weight:** About 10 lbs. **Stock:** Walnut checkered. Pistol grip/forend. **Sights:** Classic long

Prices given are believed to be accurate at time of publication however, many factors affect retail pricing so exact prices are not possible.

range with windage. **Features:** Custom production only.
Price: From **$7,250.00**

CABELA'S 1874 SHARPS SPORTING
Caliber: 45-70. **Barrel:** 32", tapered octabon. **Weight:** 10.5 lbs. **Length:** 49.25" overall. **Stock:** Checkered walnut. **Sights:** Blade front, open adjustable rear. **Features:** Color case-hardened receiver and hammer, rest blued. Introduced 1995. Imported by Cabela's.
Price: 45-70 .... **$1,399.99**
Price: Quigley Sharps, 45-70 Govt., 45-120, 45-110 .... **$1,699.99**

CIMARRON BILLY DIXON 1874 SHARPS SPORTING
Caliber: 40-40, 50-90, 50-70, 45-70 Govt. **Barrel:** 32" tapered octagonal. **Weight:** NA. **Length:** NA. **Stock:** European walnut. **Sights:** Blade front, Creedmoor rear. **Features:** Color case-hardened frame, blued barrel. Hand-checkered grip and forend; hand-rubbed oil finish. Introduced 1999. Imported by Cimarron F.A. Co.
Price: From **$1,987.70**

CIMARRON QUIGLEY MODEL 1874 SHARPS SPORTING
Caliber: 45-110, 50-70, 50-40, 45-70 Govt., 45-90, 45-120. **Barrel:** 34" octagonal. **Weight:** NA. **Length:** NA. **Stock:** Checkered walnut. **Sights:** Blade front, adjustable rear. **Features:** Blued finish; double-set triggers. From Cimarron F.A. Co.
Price: From **$2,156.70**

CIMARRON SILHOUETTE MODEL 1874 SHARPS SPORTING
Caliber: 45-70 Govt. **Barrel:** 32" octagonal. **Weight:** NA. **Length:** NA. **Stock:** Walnut. **Sights:** Blade front, adjustable rear. **Features:** Pistol-grip stock with shotgun-style buttplate; cut-rifled barrel. From Cimarron F.A. Co.
Price: **$1,597.70**

CIMARRON MODEL 1885 HIGH WALL
Caliber: 38-55, 40-65, 45-70 Govt., 45-90, 45-120, 30-40 Krag, 348 Winchester. **Barrel:** 30" octagonal. **Weight:** NA. **Length:** NA. **Stock:** European walnut. **Sights:** Bead front, semi-buckhorn rear. **Features:** Replica of the Winchester 1885 High Wall rifle. Color case-hardened receiver and lever, blued barrel. Curved buttplate. Optional double-set triggers. Introduced 1999. Imported by Cimarron F.A. Co.
Price: From **$1,002.91**
Price: With pistol grip, from **$1,136.81**

DAKOTA MODEL 10 SINGLE SHOT
Caliber: Most rimmed and rimless commercial calibers. **Barrel:** 23". **Weight:** 6 lbs. **Length:** 39.5" overall. **Stock:** Medium fancy grade walnut in classic style. Checkered grip and forend. **Sights:** None furnished. Drilled and tapped for scope mounting. **Features:** Falling block action with underlever. Top tang safety. Removable trigger plate for conversion to single set trigger. Introduced 1990. Made in U.S.A. by Dakota Arms.

Price: From **$4,695.00**
Price: Action only **$1,875.00**
Price: Magnum action only **$1,875.00**

DAKOTA SHARPS
Calibers: Virtually any caliber from .17 Ackley Hornet to .30-40 Krag. Features include a 26" octagon barrel, XX-grade walnut stock with straight grip and tang sight. Many options and upgrades are available.
Price: From **$3,995.00**

EMF PREMIER 1874 SHARPS
Caliber: 45/70, 45/110, 45/120. **Barrel:** 32", 34". **Weight:** 11-13 lbs. **Length:** 49", 51" overall. **Stock:** Pistol grip, European walnut. **Sights:** Blade front, adjustable rear. **Features:** Superb quality reproductions of the 1874 Sharps Sporting Rifles; casehardened locks; double-set triggers; blue barrels. Imported from Pedersoli by EMF.
Price: Business Rifle **$1,199.90**
Price: "Quigley", Patchbox, heavy barrel **$1,799.90**
Price: Silhouette, pistol-grip **$1,499.90**
Price: Super Deluxe Hand Engraved **$3,500.00**

HARRINGTON & RICHARDSON ULTRA VARMINT/ULTRA HUNTER
Caliber: 204 Ruger, 22 WMR, 22-250 Rem., 223 Rem., 243 Win., 25-06 Rem., 30-06. **Barrel:** 22" to 26" heavy taper. **Weight:** About 7.5 lbs. **Stock:** Laminated birch with Monte Carlo comb or skeletonized polymer. **Sights:** None furnished. Drilled and tapped for scope mounting. **Features:** Break-open action with side-lever release, positive ejection. Scope mount. Blued receiver and barrel. Swivel studs. Introduced 1993. Ultra Hunter introduced 1995. From H&R 1871, Inc.
Price: Ultra Varmint Fluted, 24" bull barrel, polymer stock....... **$406.00**
Price: Ultra Hunter Rifle, 26" bull barrel in 25-06 Rem., laminated stock **$357.00**
Price: Ultra Varmint Rifle, 22" bull barrel in 223 Rem., laminated stock **$357.00**

HARRINGTON & RICHARDSON/NEW ENGLAND FIREARMS STAINLESS ULTRA HUNTER WITH THUMBHOLE STOCK
Caliber: 45-70 Govt. **Barrel:** 24". **Weight:** 8 lbs. **Length:** 40". **Features:** Stainless steel barrel and receiver with scope mount rail, hammer extension, cinnamon laminate thumbhole stock.
Price: **$439.00**

HARRINGTON & RICHARDSON/NEW ENGLAND FIREARMS HANDI-RIFLE/SLUG GUN COMBOS
Chamber: 44 Mag./12-ga. rifled slug and 357 Mag./20-ga. rifled slug. **Barrel:** Rifle barrel 22" for both calibers; shotgun barrels 28" (12 ga.) and 40" (20 ga.) fully rifled. **Weight:** 7-8 lbs. **Length:** 38" overall (both rifle chamberings). **Features:** Single-shot break-open rifle/shotgun combos (one rifle barrel, one shotgun barrel per combo). Rifle barrels are not interchangeable; shotgun barrels are interchangeable. Stock is black matte high-density polymer with sling swivel studs, molded checkering and recoil pad. No iron sights; scope rail included.
Price: **$362.00**

HARRINGTON & RICHARDSON CR-45LC
Caliber: 45 Colt. **Barrel:** 20". **Weight:** 6.25 lbs. **Length:** 34" overall. **Features:** Single-shot break-open carbine. Cut-checkered American black walnut with case-colored crescent steel buttplate, open sights,

Prices given are believed to be accurate at time of publication however, many factors affect retail pricing so exact prices are not possible.

68TH EDITION, 2014 ✛ **483**

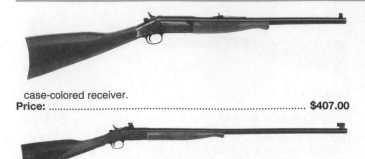

case-colored receiver.
Price: **$407.00**

HARRINGTON & RICHARDSON BUFFALO CLASSIC
Caliber: 45-70 Govt. **Barrel:** 32" heavy. **Weight:** 8 lbs. **Length:** 46"
overall. **Stock:** Cut-checkered American black walnut. **Sights:**
Williams receiver sight; Lyman target front sight with 8 aperture
inserts. **Features:** Color case-hardened Handi-Rifle action with
exposed hammer; color case-hardened crescent buttplate; 19th
century checkering pattern. Introduced 1995. Made in U.S.A. by H&R
1871, Inc.
Price: Buffalo Classic Rifle..**$449.00**

KRIEGHOFF HUBERTUS SINGLE-SHOT
Caliber: 222, 243 Win., 270 Win., 308 Win., 30-06 Spfl., 5.6x50R Mag.,
5.6x52R, 6x62R Freres, 6.5x57R, 6.5x65R, 7x57R, 7x65R, 8x57JRS,
8x75RS, 9.3x74R, 7mm Rem. Mag., 300 Win. Mag. **Barrel:** 23.5".
Weight: 6.5 lbs. **Length:** 40.5. **Stock:** High-grade walnut. **Sights:**
Blade front, open rear. **Features:** Break-open loading with manual
cocking lever on top tang; takedown; extractor; Schnabel forearm;
many options. Imported from Germany by Krieghoff International Inc.
Price: Hubertus single shot, from **$5,995.00**
Price: Hubertus, magnum calibers **$6,995.00**

MEACHAM HIGHWALL SILHOUETTE OR SCHUETZEN
Caliber: any rimmed cartridge. **Barrel:** 26-34". **Weight:** 8-15 lbs.
Sights: none. Tang drilled for Win. base, 3/8 dovetail slot front.
Stock: Fancy eastern walnut with cheekpiece; ebony insert in
forearm tip. **Features:** Exact copy of 1885 Winchester. With most
Winchester factory options available, including double set triggers.
Introduced 1994. Made in U.S.A. by Meacham T&H Inc.
Price: From **$4,999.00**

MERKEL K1 MODEL LIGHTWEIGHT STALKING
Caliber: 243 Win., 270 Win., 7x57R, 308 Win., 30-06 Spfl., 7mm
Rem. Mag., 300 Win. Mag., 9.3x74R. **Barrel:** 23.6". **Weight:** 5.6
lbs. unscoped. **Stock:** Satin-finished walnut, fluted and checkered;
sling-swivel studs. **Sights:** None (scope base furnished). **Features:**
Franz Jager single-shot break-open action, cocking/uncocking slide-
type safety, matte silver receiver, selectable trigger pull weights,
integrated, quick detach 1" or 30mm optic mounts (optic not
included). Imported from Germany by Merkel USA.
Price: Jagd Stutzen Carbine **$3,795.00**

MERKEL K-2 CUSTOM SINGLE-SHOT "WEIMAR" STALKING
Caliber: 308 Win., 30-06 Spfl., 7mm Rem. Mag., 300 Win. Mag.
Features: Franz Jager single-shot break-open action, cocking.
uncocking slide safety, deep relief engraved hunting scenes on
silvered receiver, octagin barrel, deluxe walnut stock. Includes front
and reare adjustable iron sights, scope rings. Imported from Germany
by Merkel USA.
Price: Jagd Stutzen Carbine **$15,595.00**

MILLER ARMS
Calibers: Virtually any caliber from .17 Ackley Hornet to .416
Remington. Falling block design with 24" premium match-grade
barrel, express sights, XXX-grade walnut stock and fore-end with 24
lpi checkering. Made in several styles including Classic, Target and
Varmint. Many options and upgrades are available. From Dakota Arms.
Price: From **$4995**

NAVY ARMS 1874 SHARPS "QUIGLEY"
Caliber: .45-70 Govt. **Barrel:** 34" octagon. **Weight:** 10 lbs. **Length:**
50" overall. **Grips:** Walnut checkered at wrist and forend. **Sights:**
High blade front, full buckhorn rear. **Features:** Color case-hardened
receiver, trigger, military patchbox, hammer and lever. Double-set

triggers, German silver gripcap. Reproduction of rifle from "Quigley
Down Under" movie.
Price: Model SQR045 (20087) **$2,026.00**

NAVY ARMS 1874 SHARPS #2 CREEDMOOR
Caliber: 45/70. **Barrel:** 30" tapered round. **Stock:** Walnut. **Sights:**
Front globe, "soule" tang rear. **Features:** Nickel receiver and action.
Lightweight sporting rifle.
Price: **$1,816.00**

NAVY ARMS SHARPS SPORTING RIFLE
Same as the Navy Arms Sharps Plains Rifle except has pistol grip
stock. Introduced 1997. Imported by Navy Arms.
Price: 45-70 Govt. only....................................**$1,711.00**
Price: #2 Sporting with case-hardened receiver **$1,739.00**
Price: #2 Silhouette with full octagonal barrel **$1,739.00**

NAVY ARMS 1885 HIGH WALL
Caliber: 45-70 Govt.; others available on special order. **Barrel:** 28"
round, 30" octagonal. **Weight:** 9.5 lbs. **Length:** 45.5" overall (30"
barrel). **Stock:** Walnut. **Sights:** Blade front, vernier tang-mounted
peep rear. **Features:** Replica of Winchester's High Wall designed by
Browning. Color case-hardened receiver, blued barrel. Introduced
1998. Imported by Navy Arms.
Price: 28", round barrel, target sights...................**$1,120.00**
Price: 30" octagonal barrel, target sights **$1,212.00**

NAVY ARMS 1873 SPRINGFIELD CAVALRY CARBINE
Caliber: 45-70 Govt. **Barrel:** 22". **Weight:** 7 lbs. **Length:** 40.5" overall.
Stock: Walnut. **Sights:** Blade front, military ladder rear. **Features:**
Blued lockplate and barrel; color case-hardened breechblock; saddle
ring with bar. Replica of 7th Cavalry gun. Officer's Model Trapdoor
has single-set trigger, bone case-hardened buttplate, trigger guard
and breechblock. Deluxe walnut stock hand-checkered at the wrist
and forend. German silver forend cap and rod tip. Adjustable rear
peep target sight. Authentic flip-up 'Beech' front target sight. Imported
by Navy Arms.
Price: Model STC073...**$1,261.00**
Price: Officer's Model Trapdoor (2008) **$1,648.00**

NAVY ARMS "JOHN BODINE" ROLLING BLOCK
Caliber: 45-70 Govt. **Barrel:** 30" heavy octagonal. **Stock:** Walnut.
Sights: Globe front, "soule" tang rear. **Features:** Double-set triggers.
Price: **$1,928.00**
Price: (#2 with deluxe nickel finished receiver) **$1,928.00**

NAVY ARMS 1874 SHARPS NO. 3 LONG RANGE
Caliber: 45-70 Govt. **Barrel:** 34" octagon. **Weight:** 10 lbs., 14 oz.
Length: 51.2". **Stock:** Deluxe walnut. **Sights:** Globe target front and
match grade rear tang. **Features:** Shotgun buttplate, German silver

forend cap, color case hardened receiver. Imported by Navy Arms.
Price: $2,432.00

NEW ENGLAND FIREARMS HANDI-RIFLE
Caliber: 204 Ruger, 22 Hornet, 223 Rem., 243 Win., 30-30, 270 Win., 280 Rem., 7mm-08 Rem., 308 Win., 7.62x39 Russian, 30-06 Spfl., 357 Mag., 35 Whelen, 44 Mag., 45-70 Govt., 500 S&W. **Barrel:** From 20" to 26", blued or stainless. **Weight:** 5.5 to 7 lbs. **Stock:** Walnut-finished hardwood or synthetic. **Sights:** Vary by model, but most have ramp front, folding rear, or are drilled and tapped for scope mount. **Features:** Break-open action with side-lever release. Swivel studs on all models. Blue finish. Introduced 1989. From H&R 1871, Inc.
Price: Various cartridges...$292.00
Price: 7.62x39 Russian, 35 Whelen, intr. 2006 ....$292.00
Price: Youth, 37" OAL, 11.75" LOP, 6.75 lbs. $292.00
Price: Handi-Rifle/Pardner combo, 20 ga. synthetic, intr. 2006 ....$325.00
Price: Handi-Rifle/Pardner Superlight, 20 ga., 5.5 lbs., intr. 2006 ....$325.00
Price: Synthetic $302.00
Price: Stainless $364.00
Price: Superlight, 20" barrel, 35.25" OAL, 5.5 lbs. ...$302.00

NEW ENGLAND FIREARMS SURVIVOR
Caliber: 223 Rem., 308 Win., .410 shotgun, 45 Colt, single shot. **Barrel:** 20" to 22". **Weight:** 6 lbs. **Length:** 34.5" to 36" overall. **Stock:** Black polymer, thumbhole design. **Sights:** None furnished; scope mount provided. **Features:** Receiver drilled and tapped for scope mounting. Stock and forend have storage compartments for ammo, etc.; comes with integral swivels and black nylon sling. Introduced 1996. Made in U.S.A. by H&R 1871, Inc.
Price: Blue or nickel finish $304.00

NEW ENGLAND FIREARMS SPORTSTER/VERSA PACK
Caliber: 17M2, 17 HMR, 22 LR, 22 WMR, .410 bore single shot. **Barrel:** 20" to 22". **Weight:** 5.4 to 7 lbs. **Length:** 33" to 38.25" overall. **Stock:** Black polymer. **Sights:** Adjustable rear, ramp front. **Features:** Receiver drilled and tapped for scope mounting. Made in U.S.A. by H&R 1871, Inc.
Price: Sportster 17M2, 17 HMR $193.00
Price: Sportster $101.00
Price: Sportster Youth $161.00

REMINGTON MODEL SPR18 SINGLE SHOT
Caliber: 223 Rem., 243 Win., 270 Win., .30-06 Spfl., 308 Win., 7.62x39mm. **Barrel:** 23.5" chromo-lined hammer forged, all steel receiver, spiral-cut fluting. **Weight:** 6.75 lbs. **Stock:** Walnut stock and fore-end, swivel studs. **Sights:** adjustable, with 11mm scope rail. **Length:** 39.75" overall. **Features:** Made in U.S. by Remington Arms Co., Inc.
Price: Blued/walnut (2008).................................$277.00
Price: Nickel/walnut (2008) $326.00

REMINGTON NO. 1 ROLLING BLOCK MID-RANGE SPORTER
Caliber: 45-70 Govt. **Barrel:** 30" round. **Weight:** 8.75 lbs. **Length:** 46.5" overall. **Stock:** American walnut with checkered pistol grip and forend. **Sights:** Beaded blade front, adjustable center-notch buckhorn rear. **Features:** Recreation of the original. Polished blue metal finish. Many options available. Introduced 1998. Made in U.S.A. by Remington.
Price: $2,927.00
Price: Silhouette model with single-set trigger, heavy barrel $3,366.00

ROSSI SINGLE-SHOT
Caliber: 17, 223 Rem., 243 Win., 270 Win., .30-06, 308 Win., 7.62x39, 22-250. **Barrel:** 22" (Youth), 23". **Weight:** 6.25-7 lbs. **Stocks:** Wood, Black Synthetic (Youth). **Sights:** Adjustable sights, drilled and tapped for scope. **Features:** Single-shot break open, 13 models available, positive ejection, internal transfer bar mechanism, manual external safety, trigger block system, Taurus Security System, Matte blue finish, youth models available.
Price: $238.00

ROSSI MATCHED PAIRS
Gauge/Caliber: 12, 20, .410, 22 Mag, 22 LR, 17 HMR, 223 Rem, 243 Win., 270 Win., .30-06, 308Win., .50 (black powder). **Barrel:** 23", 28". **Weight:** 5-6.3 lbs. **Stocks:** Wood or black synthetic. **Sights:** Bead front on shotgun barrel, fully adjustable front and rear on rifle barrel, drilled and tapped for scope, fully adjustable fiber optic sights (black powder). **Features:** Single-shot break open, 27 models available, internal transfer bar mechanism, manual external safety, blue finish, trigger block system, Taurus Security System, youth models available.
Price: Rimfire/Shotgun, from $178.00
Price: Centerfire/Shotgun $299.00
Price: Black Powder Matched Pair, from...............$262.00

ROSSI WIZARD
Single shot rifle chambered in 18 different rimfire/centerfire/shotshell/muzzleloading configurations. Featured include drop-barrel action; quick, toolless barrel interchangeability; fiber optic front sight; adjustable rear sight with barrel-mounted optics rail; hardwood or camo Monte Carlo stock.
Price: ....$369.00 to $410.00

RUGER NO. 1-A LIGHT SPORTER
Caliber: .243, 6.5 Creedmoor, .270 Win., .303 British, .308 Win., .300 RCM, .30-06. **Barrel:** 22". **Weight:** 7.25 lbs. **Length:** 38.5". **Stock:**

Prices given are believed to be accurate at time of publication however, many factors affect retail pricing so exact prices are not possible.

68TH EDITION, 2014 ⊕ **485**

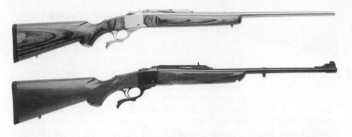

Two-piece American walnut. **Sights:** Adjustable rear, bead front.
Features: Under-lever falling-block design with automatic ejector, top tang safety.
Price: **$1299**

RUGER NO. 1-V VARMINTER

Similar to the No. 1-B Standard Rifle except has 24" heavy barrel. Semi-beavertail forend, barrel ribbed for target scope block, with 1" Ruger scope rings. Calibers 204 Ruger (26" barrel), 22-250 Rem., 223 Rem., 25-06 Rem., 6.5 Creedmoor. Weight about 9 lbs.
Price: No. 1-V **$1,147.00**

RUGER NO. 1 INTERNATIONAL

Similar to the No. 1-B Standard Rifle except has lightweight 20" barrel, full-length International-style forend with loop sling swivel, adjustable folding leaf rear sight on quarter-rib, ramp front with gold bead. Calibers 30-06 Spfl., 270 and 7x57. Weight is about 7.25 lbs.
Price: No. 1 RSI **$1,349.00**

RUGER NO. 1-H TROPICAL RIFLE

Similar to the No. 1-B Standard Rifle except has Alexander Henry forend, adjustable folding leaf rear sight on quarter-rib, ramp front with dovetail gold bead, 24" heavy barrel. Calibers .375 H&H, .450/400 Nitro Express, .458 Lott., 3" (weighs about 9 lbs.).
Price: No. 1H **$1,299.00**

RUGER NO. 1-S MEDIUM SPORTER

Similar to the No. 1-B Standard Rifle except has Alexander Henry-style forend, adjustable folding leaf rear sight on quarter-rib, ramp front sight base and dovetail-type gold bead front sight. Calibers include 9.3x74R, 45-70 Govt. with 22" barrel, .300 H&H, .300 Mag., .45-70 Gov't., .460 S&W Mag., .475 Linebaugh, .480 Ruger. Weighs about 7.25 lbs.
Price: **$1,299.00**

SHILOH CO. SHARPS 1874 LONG RANGE EXPRESS

Caliber: 40-50 BN, 40-70 BN, 40-90 BN, 45-70 Govt. ST, 45-90 ST,

45-110 ST, 50-70 ST, 50-90 ST, 38-55, 40-70 ST, 40-90 ST. **Barrel:** 34" tapered octagon. **Weight:** 10.5 lbs. **Length:** 51" overall. **Stock:** Oil-finished walnut (upgrades available) with pistol grip, shotgun-style butt, traditional cheek rest, Schnabel forend. **Sights:** Customer's choice. **Features:** Re-creation of the Model 1874 Sharps rifle. Double-set triggers. Made in U.S.A. by Shiloh Rifle Mfg. Co.
Price: **$1,902.00**
Price: Sporter Rifle No. 1 (similar to above except with 30" barrel, blade front, buckhorn rear sight) **$1,902.00**
Price: Sporter Rifle No. 3 (similar to No. 1 except straight-grip stock, standard wood) **$1,800.00**

SHILOH CO. SHARPS 1874 QUIGLEY

Caliber: 45-70 Govt., 45-110. **Barrel:** 34" heavy octagon. **Stock:** Military-style with patch box, standard grade American walnut. **Sights:** Semi buckhorn, interchangeable front and midrange vernier tang sight with windage. **Features:** Gold inlay initials, pewter tip, Hartford collar, case color or antique finish. Double-set triggers.
Price: **$3,298.00**

SHILOH CO. SHARPS 1874 SADDLE

Caliber: 38-55, 40-50 BN, 40-65 Win., 40-70 BN, 40-70 ST, 40-90 BN, 40-90 ST, 44-77 BN, 44-90 BN, 45-70 Govt., 45-90 ST, 45-100 ST, 45-110 ST, 45-120 ST, 50-70 ST, 50-90 ST. **Barrel:** 26" full or half octagon. **Stock:** Semi fancy American walnut. Shotgun style with cheekrest. **Sights:** Buckhorn and blade. **Features:** Double-set trigger, numerous custom features can be added.
Price: **$1,852.00**

SHILOH CO. SHARPS 1874 MONTANA ROUGHRIDER

Caliber: 38-55, 40-50 BN, 40-65 Win., 40-70 BN, 40-70 ST, 40-90 BN, 40-90 ST, 44-77 BN, 44-90 BN, 45-70 Govt. ST, 45-90 ST, 45-100 ST, 45-110 ST, 45-120 ST, 50-70 ST, 50-90 ST. **Barrel:** 30" full or half octagon. **Stock:** American walnut in shotgun or military style. **Sights:** Buckhorn and blade. **Features:** Double-set triggers, numerous custom features can be added.
Price: **$1,902.00**

SHILOH CO. SHARPS CREEDMOOR TARGET

Caliber: 38-55, 40-50 BN, 40-65 Win., 40-70 BN, 40-70 ST, 40-90 BN, 40-90 ST, 44-77 BN, 44-90 BN, 45-70 Govt. ST, 45-90 ST, 45-100 ST, 45-110 ST, 45-120 ST, 50-70 ST, 50-90 ST. **Barrel:** 32", half round-half octagon. **Stock:** Extra fancy American walnut. Shotgun style with pistol grip. **Sights:** Customer's choice. **Features:** Single trigger, AA finish on stock, polished barrel and screws, pewter tip.
Price: **$2,743.00**

THOMPSON/CENTER ENCORE

Caliber: 22-250 Rem., 223 Rem., 243 Win., 204 Rem. Spec., 25-06 Rem., 270 Win., 7mm-08 Rem., 308 Win., 30-06 Spfl., 7mm Rem. Mag., 300 Win. Mag. **Barrel:** 24", 26". **Weight:** 6 lbs., 12

Prices given are believed to be accurate at time of publication however, many factors affect retail pricing so exact prices are not possible.

oz. (24" barrel). **Length:** 38.5" (24" barrel). **Stock:** American walnut. Monte Carlo style; Schnabel forend or black composite. **Sights:** Ramp-style white bead front, fully adjustable leaf-type rear. **Features:** Interchangeable barrels; action opens by squeezing trigger guard; drilled and tapped for T/C scope mounts; polished blue finish. Introduced 1996. Made in U.S.A. by Thompson/Center Arms.

Price: $817.00
Price: Extra barrels $328.00

THOMPSON/CENTER STAINLESS ENCORE RIFLE
Similar to blued Encore except stainless steel with blued sights, black composite stock and forend. Available in 22-250 Rem., 223 Rem., 7mm-08 Rem., 30-06 Spfl., 308 Win. Introduced 1999. Made in U.S.A. by Thompson/Center Arms.

Price: .... $680.00 to $738.00

THOMPSON/CENTER G2 CONTENDER RIFLE
Similar to the G2 Contender pistol, but in a compact rifle format. Weighs 5.5 lbs. Features interchangeable 23" barrels, chambered for 17 HMR, 22 LR, 223 Rem., 30/30 Win. and 45/70 Govt.; plus a 45 cal. muzzleloading barrel. All of the 16.25" and 21" barrels made for the old-style Contender will fit. Introduced 2003. Made in U.S.A. by Thompson/Center Arms.

Price: .... $840.00 to $872.00

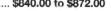

THOMPSON/CENTER ENCORE PROHUNTER PREDATOR RIFLE
Contender-style break-action single shot rifle chambered in .204 Ruger, .223 Remington, .22-250 and .308 Winchester. Features include 28-inch deep-fluted interchangeable barrel, composite buttstock and forend with non-slip inserts in cheekpiece, pistol grip and forend. Max 1 camo finish overall. Overall length: 42.5 inches. Weight: 7-3/4 lbs.

Price: $965.00

TRADITIONS 1874 SHARPS DELUXE
Caliber: 45-70 Govt. **Barrel:** 32" octagonal; 1:18" twist. **Weight:** 11.67 lbs. **Length:** 48.8" overall. **Stock:** Checkered walnut with German silver nose cap and steel buttplate. **Sights:** Globe front, adjustable Creedmore rear with 12 inserts. **Features:** Color case-hardened receiver; double-set triggers. Introduced 2001. Imported from Pedersoli by Traditions.

Price: $1,545.00

TRADITIONS 1874 SHARPS SPORTING DELUXE RIFLE
Similar to Sharps Deluxe but custom silver engraved receiver, European walnut stock and forend, satin finish, set trigger, fully adjustable.

Price: $2,796.00

TRADITIONS 1874 SHARPS STANDARD RIFLE
Similar to 1874 Sharps Deluxe except has blade front and adjustable buckhorn-style rear sight. Weighs 10.67 pounds. Introduced 2001. Imported from Pedersoli by Traditions.

Price: $1,324.00

TRADITIONS ROLLING BLOCK SPORTING
Caliber: 45-70 Govt. **Barrel:** 30" octagonal; 1:18" twist. **Weight:** 11.67 lbs. **Length:** 46.7" overall. **Stock:** Walnut. **Sights:** Blade front, adjustable rear. **Features:** Antique silver, color case-hardened receiver, drilled and tapped for tang/globe sights; brass buttplate and trigger guard. Introduced 2001. Imported from Pedersoli by Traditions.

Price: $1,029.00

UBERTI 1874 SHARPS SPORTING
Caliber: 45-70 Govt. **Barrel:** 30", 32", 34" octagonal. **Weight:** 10.57 lbs. with 32" barrel. **Length:** 48.9" with 32" barrel. **Stock:** Walnut. **Sights:** Dovetail front, Vernier tang rear. **Features:** Cut checkering, case-colored finish on frame, buttplate, and lever. Imported by Stoeger Industries.

Price: Standard Sharps	$1639
Price: Special Sharps	$1949
Price: Deluxe Sharps	$3059
Price: Down Under Sharps	$2509
Price: Long Range Sharps	$2579
Price: Buffalo Hunter Sharps	$2469
Price: Sharps Cavalry Carbine	$1739
Price: Sharps Extra Deluxe	$4869
Price: Sharps Hunter	$1639

UBERTI 1885 HIGH-WALL SINGLE-SHOT
Caliber: 45-70 Govt., 45-90, 45-120 single shot. **Barrel:** 28" to 23". **Weight:** 9.3 to 9.9 lbs. **Length:** 44.5" to 47" overall. **Stock:** Walnut stock and forend. **Sights:** Blade front, fully adjustable open rear. **Features:** Based on Winchester High-Wall design by John Browning. Color case-hardened frame and lever, blued barrel and buttplate. Imported by Stoeger Industries.

Price: From .... $1,009.00 to $1,279.00

UBERTI SPRINGFIELD TRAPDOOR RIFLE/CARBINE
Caliber: .45-70 Govt. **Barrel:** 22 or 32.5 inches. Blue steel receiver and barrel, case-hardened breechblock and buttplate. **Sights:** Creedmore style.

Price: (.32.5" bbl.) .... $1599 to $1879

Prices given are believed to be accurate at time of publication however, many factors affect retail pricing so exact prices are not possible.

68TH EDITION, 2014 ✦ **487**

BERETTA S686/S689 O/U RIFLE SERIES
Calibers: .30-06, 9.3x74R, .444 Marlin. **Barrels:** 23 inches. O/U boxlock action. Single or double triggers. EELL Grade has better wood, moderate engraving.
Price: .... **$4200 to $9000**
Price: EELL Diamond Sable grade, from **$12,750**

BRNO MODEL 802 COMBO GUN
Caliber/Gauge: .243 Win./12 ga. Over/under. **Barrels:** 23.6". **Weight:** 7.5 lbs. **Length:** 41". **Stock:** Walnut. **Features:** Double trigger, shotgun barrel is improved-modified chokes. Imported by CZ USA.
Price: **$2,181.00**

HOENIG ROTARY ROUND ACTION DOUBLE
Caliber: Most popular calibers. Over/under design. **Barrel:** 22" to 26". **Stock:** English Walnut; to customer specs. **Sights:** Swivel hood front with button release (extra bead stored in trap door gripcap), express-style rear on quarter-rib adjustable for windage and elevation; scope mount. **Features:** Round action opens by rotating barrels, pulling forward. Inertia extractor system, rotary safety blocks strikers. Single lever quick-detachable scope mount. Simple takedown without removing forend. Introduced 1997. Made in U.S.A. by George Hoenig.
Price: From **$22,500.00**

HOENIG ROTARY ROUND ACTION COMBINATION
Caliber: Most popular calibers and shotgun gauges. Over/under design with rifle barrel atop shotgun barrel. **Barrel:** 26". **Weight:** 7 lbs. **Stock:** English Walnut to customer specs. **Sights:** Front ramp with button release blades. Foldable aperture tang sight windage and elevation adjustable. Quarter-rib with scope mount. **Features:** Round action opens by rotating barrels, pulling forward. Inertia extractor; rotary safety blocks strikers. Simple takedown without removing forend. Made in U.S.A. by George Hoenig.
Price: **$27,500.00**

HOENIG VIERLING FOUR-BARREL COMBINATION
Caliber/gauge: Two 20-gauge shotgun barrels with one rifle barrel chambered for .22 Long Rifle and another for .223 Remington.
Price: **$50,000.00**

KRIEGHOFF CLASSIC DOUBLE
Caliber: 7x57R, 7x65R, 308 Win., 30-06 Spfl., 8x57 JRS, 8x75RS, 9.3x74R, 375NE, 500/416NE, 470NE, 500NE. **Barrel:** 23.5". **Weight:** 7.3 to 8 lbs; 10-11 lbs. Big 5. **Stock:** High grade European walnut. Standard model has conventional rounded cheekpiece, Bavaria model has Bavarian-style cheekpiece. **Sights:** Bead front with removable, adjustable wedge (375 H&H and below), standing leaf rear on quarter-rib. **Features:** Boxlock action; double triggers; short opening angle for fast loading; quiet extractors; sliding, self-adjusting wedge for secure bolting; Purdey-style barrel extension; horizontal firing pin placement. Many options available. Introduced 1997. Imported from Germany by Krieghoff International.
Price: **$9,995.00**
Price: Engraved sideplates, add **$4,000.00**
Price: Extra set of rifle barrels, add **$6,150.00**
Price: Extra set of 20-ga., 28" shotshell barrels, add **$4,400.00**

KRIEGHOFF CLASSIC BIG FIVE DOUBLE RIFLE
Similar to the standard Classic except available in 375 Flanged Mag. N.E., 500/416 NE, 470 NE, 500 NE. Has hinged front trigger, non-removable muzzle wedge (models larger than 375 caliber), Universal Trigger System, Combi Cocking Device, steel trigger guard, specially weighted stock bolt for weight and balance. Many options available. Introduced 1997. Imported from Germany by Krieghoff International. Imperial Model introduced 2006.
Price: **$12,995.00**
Price: Engraved sideplates, add **$4,000.00**

LEBEAU-COURALLY EXPRESS SXS
Caliber: 7x65R, 8x57JRS, 9.3x74R, 375 H&H, 470 N.E. **Barrel:** 24" to 26". **Weight:** 7.75 to 10.5 lbs. **Stock:** Fancy French walnut with cheekpiece. **Sights:** Bead on ramp front, standing left express rear on quarter-rib. **Features:** Holland & Holland-type sidelock with automatic ejectors; double triggers. Built to order only. Imported from Belgium by Wm. Larkin Moore.
Price: **$50,000.00**

MERKEL DRILLINGS
Caliber/Gauge: 12, 20, 3" chambers, 16, 2-3/4" chambers; 22 Hornet, 5.6x50R Mag., 5.6x52R, 222 Rem., 243 Win., 6.5x55, 6.5x57R, 7x57R, 7x65R, 308 Win., 30-06 Spfl., 8x57JRS, 9.3x74R, 375 H&H. **Barrel:** 25.6". **Weight:** 7.9 to 8.4 lbs. **Stock:** Oil-finished walnut with pistol grip; cheekpiece on 12-, 16-gauge. **Sights:** Blade front, fixed rear. **Features:** Double barrel locking lug with Greener cross bolt; scroll-engraved, case-hardened receiver; automatic trigger safety; Blitz action; double triggers. Imported from Germany by Merkel USA.
Price: Model 96K
(manually cocked rifle system), from **$8,495.00**
Price: Model 96K engraved
(hunting series on receiver) **$9,795.00**

MERKEL BOXLOCK DOUBLE
Caliber: 5.6x52R, 243 Winchester, 6.5x55, 6.5x57R, 7x57R, 7x65R, 308 Win., 30-06 Springfield, 8x57 IRS, 9.3x74R. **Barrel:** 23.6". **Weight:** 7.7 oz. **Length:** NA. **Stock:** Walnut, oil finished, pistol grip. **Sights:** Fixed 100 meter. **Features:** Anson & Deely boxlock action with cocking indicators, double triggers, engraved color case-hardened receiver. Introduced 1995. Imported from Germany by Merkel USA.
Price: Model 140-2, from **$11,995.00**
Price: Model 141 Small Frame SXS Rifle; built on smaller
frame, chambered for 7mm Mauser, 30-06, or
9.3x74R **$8,195.00**
Price: Model 141 Engraved; fine hand-engraved hunting
scenes on silvered receiver **$9,495.00**

RIZZINI EXPRESS 90L DOUBLE
Caliber: 30-06 Spfl., 7x65R, 9.3x74R. **Barrel:** 24". **Weight:** 7.5 lbs. **Length:** 40" overall. **Stock:** Select European walnut with satin oil finish; English-style cheekpiece. **Sights:** Ramp front, quarter-rib with express sight. **Features:** Color case-hardened boxlock action; automatic ejectors; single selective trigger; polished blue barrels. Extra 20 gauge shotgun barrels available. Imported from Italy by Connecticut Shotgun Co.
Price: With case **$5,355.00**

Prices given are believed to be accurate at time of publication however, many factors affect retail pricing so exact prices are not possible.

AMERICAN TACTICAL IMPORTS GSG-522

Semiauto tactical rifle chambered in .22 LR. Features include 16.25-inch barrel; black finish overall; polymer forend and buttstock; backup iron sights; receiver-mounted Picaatinny rail; 10-round magazine. Several other rifle and carbine versions available.

Price: $475.00

BROWNING BUCK MARK SEMI-AUTO

Caliber: 22 LR, 10+1. **Action:** A rifle version of the Buck Mark Pistol; straight blowback action; machined aluminum receiver with integral rail scope mount; manual thumb safety. **Barrel:** Recessed crowns. **Stock:** Stock and forearm with full pistol grip. **Features:** Action lock provided. Introduced 2001. Four model name variations for 2006, as noted below. **Sights:** FLD Target, FLD Carbon, and Target models have integrated scope rails. Sporter has Truglo/Marble fiber optic sights. Imported from Japan by Browning.

Price: FLD Target, 5.5 lbs., bull barrel, laminated stock $700.00
Price: Target, 5.4 lbs., blued bull barrel, wood stock $670.00
Price: Sporter, 4.4 lbs., blued sporter barrel w/sights $670.00

BROWNING SA-22 SEMI-AUTO 22

Caliber: 22 LR, 11+1. **Barrel:** 16.25". **Weight:** 5.2 lbs. **Length:** 37" overall. **Stock:** Checkered select walnut with pistol grip and semi-beavertail forend. **Sights:** Gold bead front, folding leaf rear. **Features:** Engraved receiver with polished blue finish; cross-bolt safety; tubular magazine in buttstock; easy takedown for carrying or storage. The Grade VI is available in either grayed or blued receiver with extensive engraving with gold-plated animals: right side pictures a fox and squirrel in a woodland scene; left side shows a beagle chasing a rabbit. On top is a portrait of the beagle. Stock and forend are of high-grade walnut with a double-bordered cut checkering design. Introduced 1987. Imported from Japan by Browning.

Price: Grade I, scroll-engraved blued receiver $700.00
Price: Grade VI BL, gold-plated engraved blued receiver $1,580.00

CITADEL M-1 CARBINE

Caliber: .22LR., 10-round magazines. **Barrel:** 18" **Weight:** 4.8 lbs. **Length:** 35". **Features:** Straight from the pages of history ... the greatest conflict of modern times, World War II ... comes the new Citadel M-1 carbine. Built to the exacting specifications of the G.I. model used by U.S. infantrymen in both WWII theaters of battle and in Korea, this reproduction rifle comes to you chambered in the fun and economical .22 LR cartridge. Used by officers as well as tankers, drivers, artillery crews, mortar crews, and other personnel in lieu of the larger, heavier M1 Garand rifle, the M-1 carbine weighed only 4.5 to 4.75 pounds. The Citadel M-1, made by Chiappa in Italy, weighs in at 4.8 lbs. – nearly the exact weight of the original. Barrel length and OAL are also the same as the "United States Carbine, Caliber .30, M1", its official military designation.

Price: synthetic stock. $399.00
Price: wood stock. $399.00

CZ MODEL 512

Caliber: .22 LR/.22 WMR, 5-round magazines. **Barrel:** 20.6". **Weight:** 5.9 lbs. **Length:** 39.3". **Stock:** Beech. **Sights:** Fixed adjustable.

Features: The CZ 512 is an entirely new semi-auto rimfire rifle from CZ. The modular design is easily maintained, requiring only a coin as a tool for field stripping. The action of the 512 is composed of an aluminum alloy upper receiver that secures the barrel and bolt assembly and a fiberglass reinforced polymer lower half that houses the trigger mechanism and detachable magazine. The 512 shares the same magazines and scope rings with the CZ 455 making it the perfect companion to your bolt-action rifle

Price: $449.00

HENRY U.S. SURVIVAL AR-7 22

Caliber: 22 LR, 8-shot magazine. **Barrel:** 16" steel lined. **Weight:** 2.25 lbs. **Stock:** ABS plastic. **Sights:** Blade front on ramp, aperture rear. **Features:** Takedown design stores barrel and action in hollow stock. Light enough to float. Silver, black or camo finish. Comes with two magazines. Introduced 1998. From Henry Repeating Arms Co.

Price: H002S Silver finish $245.00
Price: H002B Black finish $280.00
Price: H002C Camo finish $345.00

KEL-TEC SU-22CA

Caliber: 22 LR. **Features:** Blowback action, cross bolt safety, adjustable front and rear sights with integral picatinny rail. Threaded muzzle, 26-round magazine.

Price: ....Appx. $400.00

MAGNUM RESEARCH MAGNUMLITE

Caliber: 22 WMR, 22 LR, 10-shot magazine. **Barrel:** 17" graphite. **Weight:** 4.45 lbs. **Length:** 35.5" overall. **Stock:** Hogue OverMolded synthetic or walnut. **Sights:** Integral scope base. **Features:** Magnum Lite graphite barrel, French grey anodizing, match bolt, target trigger. 22 LR/17M2 rifles use factory Ruger 10/22 magazines. 4-5 lbs. average trigger pull. Graphite carbon-fiber barrel weighs approx. 13.04 ounces in 22 LR, 1:16 twist. Introduced: 2007. From Magnum Research, Inc.

Price: 22 LR $665.00
Price: 22 WMR..$780.00

MARLIN MODEL 60

Caliber: 22 LR, 14-shot tubular magazine. **Barrel:** 19" round tapered. **Weight:** About 5.5 lbs. **Length:** 37.5" overall. **Stock:** Press-checkered, walnut-finished Maine birch with Monte Carlo, full pistol grip; Mar-Shield finish. **Sights:** Ramp front, open adjustable rear. **Features:** Matted receiver is grooved for scope mount. Manual bolt hold-open; automatic last-shot bolt hold open. Model 60C is similar except has hardwood Monte Carlo stock with Mossy Oak Break-Up camouflage pattern. From Marlin.

Price: $197.00
Price: Model 60C camo $232.00

MARLIN MODEL 60SS SELF-LOADING RIFLE

Same as the Model 60 except breech bolt, barrel and outer magazine tube are made of stainless steel; most other parts are either nickel-plated or coated to match the stainless finish. Monte Carlo stock is of black/gray Maine birch laminate, and has nickel-plated swivel studs,

---

rubber buttpad. Introduced 1993. From Marlin.
Price: $298.00

MARLIN 60DLX

Semiauto rifle chambered for .22 LR. Features include 14-shot tubular magazine; side ejection; manual and automatic last-shot bolt hold-opens; receiver top with serrated, non-glare finish; cross-bolt safety; steel charging handle; Monte Carlo American walnut-finished hardwood; full pistol grip; tough Mar-Shield finish; 19-inch barrel with Micro-Groove® rifling. Limited availability.
Price: $261.00

MARLIN 70PSS PAPOOSE STAINLESS

Caliber: 22 LR, 7-shot magazine. **Barrel:** 16.25" stainless steel, Micro-Groove rifling. **Weight:** 3.25 lbs. **Length:** 35.25" overall. **Stock:** Black fiberglass-filled synthetic with abbreviated forend, nickel-plated swivel studs, molded-in checkering. **Sights:** Ramp front with orange post, cut-away Wide Scan hood; adjustable open rear. Receiver grooved for scope mounting. **Features:** Takedown barrel; cross-bolt safety; manual bolt hold-open; last shot bolt hold-open; comes with padded carrying case. Introduced 1986. Made in U.S.A. by Marlin.
Price: $329.00

MARLIN MODEL 795

Caliber: 22. **Barrel:** 18" with 16-groove Micro-Groove rifling. Ramp front sight, adjustable rear. Receiver grooved for scope mount. **Stock:** Black synthetic, hardwood, synthetic thumbhole, solid pink, pink camo, or Mossy Oak New Break-up camo finish. **Features:** 10-round magazine, last shot hold-open feature. Introduced 1997. SS is similar to Model 795 except stainless steel barrel. Most other parts nickel-plated. Adjustable folding semi-buckhorn rear sights, ramp front high-visibility post and removable cutaway wide scan hood. Made in U.S.A. by Marlin Firearms Co.
Price: $181.00
Price: (Stainless) $259.00

MOSSBERG MODEL 702 PLINKSTER

Caliber: 22 LR, 10-round detachable magazine. **Barrel:** 18" free-floating. **Weight:** 4.1 to 4.6 lbs. **Sights:** Adjustable rifle. Receiver grooved for scope mount. **Stock:** Solid pink or pink marble finish synthetic. **Features:** Ergonomically placed magazine release and safety buttons, crossbolt safety, free gun lock. Made in U.S.A. by O.F. Mossberg & Sons, Inc.
Price: $209.00

MOSSBERG MODEL 702 PLINKSTER AUTOLOADING RIFLE WITH MUZZLE BRAKE

Semiauto rifle chambered in .22 LR. Features include a black synthetic stock with Schnabel, 10-round detachable box magazine, 21-inch matte blue barrel with muzzle brake, receiver grooved for scope mount.
Price: $271.00

REMINGTON MODEL 552 BDL DELUXE SPEEDMASTER

Caliber: 22 S (20), L (17) or LR (15) tubular magazine. **Barrel:** 21" round tapered. **Weight:** 5.75 lbs. **Length:** 40" overall. **Stock:** Walnut. Checkered grip and forend. **Sights:** Big game. **Features:** Positive

---

cross-bolt safety, receiver grooved for tip-off mount.
Price: $667.00

REMINGTON 597

Caliber: 22 LR, 10-shot clip; 22 WMR, 8-shot clip. **Barrel:** 20". **Weight:** 5.5 lbs. **Length:** 40" overall. **Stock:** Black synthetic. **Sights:** Big game. **Features:** Matte black finish, nickel-plated bolt. Receiver is grooved and drilled and tapped for scope mounts. Introduced 1997. Made in U.S.A. by Remington.
Price: Synthetic w/Scope $252
Price: M597 Magnum From $597
Price: M597 Camo From... $300
Price: M597 Stainless TVP From $595

RUGER 10/22 AUTOLOADING CARBINE

Caliber: 22 LR, 10-shot rotary magazine. **Barrel:** 18.5" round tapered. **Weight:** 5 lbs. **Length:** 37.25" overall. **Stock:** American hardwood with pistol grip and barrel band or synthetic. **Sights:** Brass bead front, folding leaf rear adjustable for elevation. **Features:** Detachable rotary magazine fits flush into stock, cross-bolt safety, receiver tapped and grooved for scope blocks or tip-off mount. Scope base adaptor furnished with each rifle.
Price: (Stainless) .... $279.00 to $309.00
Price: (LaserMax laser sight) $399.00

RUGER 10/22 DELUXE SPORTER

Same as 10/22 Carbine except walnut stock with hand checkered pistol grip and forend; straight buttplate, no barrel band, has sling swivels.
Price: Model 10/22-DSP..$379.00

RUGER 10/22-T TARGET RIFLE

Similar to the 10/22 except has 20" heavy, hammer-forged barrel with tight chamber dimensions, improved trigger pull, laminated hardwood stock dimensioned for optical sights. No iron sights supplied. Introduced 1996. Made in U.S.A. by Sturm, Ruger & Co.
Price: From $529.00
Price: Stainless from...$569.00

RUGER 10/22VLEH TARGET TACTICAL RIFLE

Semiauto rimfire rifle chambered in .22 LR. Features include precision-rifled, cold hammer-forged, spiral-finished 16-1/8-inch crowned match barrel; Hogue® OverMolded® stock; 10/22T target trigger; precision-adjustable bipod for steady shooting from the bench; 10-round rotary magazine. Weight: 6-7/8 lbs.
Price: $579.00

RUGER RUGER SR-22 RIFLE

AR-style semiauto rifle chambered in .22 LR, based on 0/22 action. Features include all-aluminum chassis replicating the AR-platform dimensions between the sighting plane, buttstock height, and grip; Picatinny rail optic mount includes a six-position, telescoping M4-style buttstock (on a Mil-Spec diameter tube); Hogue Monogrip

Prices given are believed to be accurate at time of publication however, many factors affect retail pricing so exact prices are not possible.

pistol grlp; buttstocks and grips interchangeable with any AR-style compatible option; round, mid-length handguard mounted on a standard-thread AR-style barrel nut; precision-rifled, cold hammer forged 16-1/8-inch alloy steel barrel capped with an SR-556/Mini-14 flash suppressor.
Price: $649.00

SAVAGE MODEL 64G
Caliber: 22 LR, 10-shot magazine. **Barrel:** 20", 21". **Weight:** 5.5 lbs.
Length: 40", 41". **Stock:** Walnut-finished hardwood with Monte Carlo-type comb, checkered grlp and forend. **Sights:** Bead front, open adjustable rear. Receiver grooved for scope mounting. **Features:** Thumb-operated rotating safety. Blue finish. Side ejection, bolt hold-open device. Introduced 1990. Made in Canada, from Savage Arms.
Price: ....**From $187.00**

SAVAGE BRJ SERIES SEMIAUTO RIMFIRE RIFLES
Similar to Mark II, Model 93 and Model 93R17 semiauto rlfles but feature spiral fluting pattern on a heavy barrel, blued finish and Royal Jacaranda wood laminate stock.
Price: Mark II BRJ – .22 LR) **$456.00**
Price: Model 93 BRJ – .22 Mag. **$464.00**
Price: Model 93 R17 BRJ – .17 HMR $464 .... **$464.00**

SAVAGE TACTICAL SEMIAUTO RIMFIRE RIFLES
Similar to Savage Model BRJ series semiauto rifles but feature heavy barrel, matte finish and a tactical-style wood stock.
Price: Mark II TR – .22 LR) **$469.00**
Price: Mark II TRR – .22 LR with three-way accessory rail) .. **$539.00**
Price: Model 93R17 TR – .17 HMR.................... **$477.00**
Price: Model 93R17 TRR – .17 HMR
    with three-way accessory rail) **$536.00**

SMITH & WESSON M&P15-22
.22 LR rimfire verson of AR-derived M&P tactical autoloader. Features include blowback action, 15.5- or 16-inch barrel, 6-position telescoping or fixed stock, quad mount picatinny rails, plain barrel or compensator, alloy upper and lower, matte black finish, 10- or 25-round magazine.
Price: $589.00

THOMPSON/CENTER 22 LR CLASSIC
Caliber: 22 LR, 8-shot magazine. **Barrel:** 22" match-grade. **Weight:** 5.5 pounds. **Length:** 39.5" overall. **Stock:** Satin-finished American walnut with Monte Carlo-type comb and pistol gripcap, swivel studs. **Sights:** Ramp-style front and fully adjustable rear, both with fiber optics. **Features;** All-steel receiver drilled and tapped for scope mounting;

barrel threaded to receiver; thumb-operated safety; trigger guard safety lock included. New 22 Classic Benchmark TGT target rifle variant has 18" heavy barrel, brown laminated target stock, blued with matte finish, 10-shot magazine and no sights; drilled and tapped.
Price: T/C 22 LR Classic (blue)................................**$396.00**
Price: T/C 22 LR Classic Benchmark **$505.00**

UMAREX COLT TACTICAL RIMFIRE M4 OPS CARBINE
Blowback semiauto rife chambered in .22 LR, styled to resemble Colt M16. Features include 16.2.2-inch barrel; front sight adjustable for elevation; adjustable rear sight; alloy lower; adjustable telestock; flattop receiver with removable carry handle; 10- or 30-round detachable magazine.
Price: $599.00

UMAREX COLT TACTICAL RIMFIRE M4 CARBINE
Blowback semiauto rifle chambered in .22 LR, styled to resemble Colt M4. Features include 16.2-inch barrel; front sight adjustable for elevation; adjustable rear sight; alloy lower; adjustable telestock; flattop receiver with optics rail; 10- or 30-round detachable magazine.
Price: $640.00

UMAREX COLT TACTICAL RIMFIRE M16 RIFLE
Blowback semiauto rifle chambered in .22 LR, styled to resemble Colt M16. Features include 21.2-inch barrel; front sight adjustable for elevation; adjustable rear sight; alloy lower; fixed stock; flattop receiver; removable carry handle; 10- or 30-round detachable magazine.
Price: $599.00

UMAREX COLT TACTICAL RIMFIRE M16 SPR RIFLE
Blowback semiauto rifle chambered in .22 LR, styled to resemble Colt M16 SPR. Features include 21.2-inch barrel; front sight adjustable for elevation; adjustable rear sight; alloy lower; fixed stock; flattop receiver with optics rail; removable carry handle; 10- or 30-round detachable magazine.
Price: $670.00

UMAREX H&K 416-22
Blowback semiauto rife chambered in .22 LR, styled to resemble H&K 416. Features include metal upper and lower receivers; RIS – rail interface system; retractable stock; pistol grip wlth storage compartment; on-rail sights; rear sight adjustable for wind and elevation; 16.1-inch barrel; 10- or 20-round magazine. Also available in pistol version with 9-inch barrel.
Price: $675.00

UMAREX H&K MP5 A5
Blowback semiauto rifle chambered in .22 LR, styled to resemble H&K MP5. Features include metal receiver; compensator; bolt catch; NAVY pistol grip; on-rail sights; rear sight adjustable for wind and elevation; 16.1-inch barrel; 10- or 25-round magazine. Also available in pistol version with 9-inch barrel. Also available with SD-type forend.
Price: $525.00

Prices given are believed to be accurate at time of publication however, many factors affect retail pricing so exact prices are not possible.

68TH EDITION, 2014 ⊕ **491**

BROWNING BL-22

Action: Short-throw lever action, side ejection. Rack-and-pinion lever. Tubular magazines, with 15+1 capacity for 22 LR. **Barrel:** Recessed muzzle. **Stock:** Walnut, two-piece straight grip Western style. **Trigger:** Half-cock hammer safety; fold-down hammer. **Sights:** Bead post front, folding-leaf rear. Steel receiver grooved for scope mount. **Weight:** 5-5.4 lbs. **Length:** 36.75-40.75" overall. **Features:** Action lock provided. Introduced 1996. FLD Grade II Octagon has octagonal 24" barrel, silver nitride receiver with scroll engraving, gold-colored trigger. FLD Grade I has satin-nickel receiver, blued trigger, no stock checkering. FLD Grade II has satin-nickel receivers with scroll engraving; gold-colored trigger, cut checkering. Both introduced 2005. Grade I has blued receiver and trigger, no stock checkering. Grade II has gold-colored trigger, cut checkering, blued receiver with scroll engraving. Imported from Japan by Browning.

Price: BL-22 Grade I/II, from...$620.00
Price: BL-22 FLD Grade I/II, from ....$660.00 to $750.00
Price: BL-22 FLD, Grade II Octagon $980.00
Price: Grade II Maple stock $780.00

HENRY LEVER-ACTION RIFLES

Caliber: 22 Long Rifle (15 shot), 22 Magnum (11 shots), 17 HMR (11 shots). **Barrel:** 18.25" round. **Weight:** 5.5 to 5.75 lbs. **Length:** 34" overall (22 LR). **Stock:** Walnut. **Sights:** Hooded blade front, open adjustable rear. **Features:** Polished blue finish; full-length tubular magazine; side ejection; receiver grooved for scope mounting. Introduced 1997. Made in U.S.A. by Henry Repeating Arms Co.

Price: H001 Carbine 22 LR...$325.00
Price: H001L Carbine 22 LR, Large Loop Lever......................$340.00
Price: H001Y Youth model (33" overall, 11-round 22 LR) $325.00
Price: H001M 22 Magnum, 19.25" octagonal barrel, deluxe
walnut stock $475.00
Price: H001V 17 HMR, 20" octagonal barrel, Williams Fire
Sights...$549.95

Henry Lever Octagon Frontier Model

Same as Lever rifles except chambered in 17 HMR, 22 Short/22 Long/22 LR, 22 Magnum; 20" octagonal barrel **Sights:** Marbles full adjustable semi-buckhorn rear, brass bead front. Weighs 6.25 lbs. Made in U.S.A. by Henry Repeating Arms Co.

Price: H001T Lever Octagon $425.00
Price: H001TM Lever Octagon 22 Magnum............................$539.95

HENRY GOLDEN BOY 22 LEVER-ACTION

Caliber: 17 HMR, 22 LR (16-shot), 22 Magnum. **Barrel:** 20" octagonal. **Weight:** 6.25 lbs. **Length:** 38" overall. **Stock:** American walnut.

Sights: Blade front, open rear. **Features:** Brasslite receiver, brass buttplate, blued barrel and lever. Introduced 1998. Made in U.S.A. from Henry Repeating Arms Co.

Price: H004 22 LR...$515.00
Price: H004M 22 Magnum $595.00
Price: H004V 17 HMR $615.00
Price: H004DD 22 LR Deluxe, engraved receiver.................$1,200.00

HENRY PUMP-ACTION 22 PUMP

Caliber: 22 LR, 15-shot. **Barrel:** 18.25". **Weight:** 5.5 lbs. **Length:** NA. **Stock:** American walnut. **Sights:** Bead on ramp front, open adjustable rear. **Features:** Polished blue finish; receiver grooved for scope mount; grooved slide handle; two barrel bands. Introduced 1998. Made in U.S.A. from Henry Repeating Arms Co.

Price: H003T 22 LR..$515.00
Price: H003TM 22 Magnum...$595.00

MARLIN MODEL 39A GOLDEN LEVER-ACTION

Caliber: 22, S (26), L (21), LR (19), tubular magazine. **Barrel:** 24" Micro-Groove. **Weight:** 6.5 lbs. **Length:** 40" overall. **Stock:** Checkered American black walnut; Mar-Shield finish. Swivel studs; rubber buttpad. **Sights:** Bead ramp front with detachable Wide-Scan hood, folding rear semi-buckhorn adjustable for windage and elevation. **Features:** Hammer block safety; rebounding hammer. Takedown action, receiver tapped for scope mount (supplied), offset hammer spur, gold-colored steel trigger. From Marlin Firearms.

Price: $700.00

MOSSBERG MODEL 464 RIMFIRE LEVER-ACTION

Caliber: 22 LR. **Barrel:** 20" round blued. **Weight:** 5.6 lbs. **Length:** 35-3/4" overall. **Features:** Adjustable sights, straight grip stock, 124-shot tubular magazine, plain hardwood straight stock and forend.

Price: $512.00

REMINGTON 572 BDL DELUXE FIELDMASTER PUMP

Caliber: 22 S (20), L (17) or LR (15), tubular magazine. **Barrel:** 21" round tapered. **Weight:** 5.5 lbs. **Length:** 40" overall. **Stock:** Walnut with checkered pistol grip and slide handle. **Sights:** Big game. **Features:** Cross-bolt safety; removing inner magazine tube converts rifle to single shot; receiver grooved for tip-off scope mount.

Price: $682.00

ANSCHUTZ MODEL 64 MP

Caliber: .22 LR. Magazine capacity: 5 rounds. **Barrel:** 25.6 inches. **Weight:** 6.6 pounds. **Stock:** Multipurpose hardwood with beavertail fore-end. **Sights:** None. Drilled and tapped for scope or receiver sights.
Price: $1175

ANSCHUTZ 1416D/1516D CLASSIC

Caliber: 22 LR (1416D888), 22 WMR (1516D), 5-shot clip. **Barrel:** 22.5". **Weight:** 6 lbs. **Length:** 41" overall. **Stock:** European hardwood with walnut finish; classic style with straight comb, checkered pistol grip and forend. **Sights:** Hooded ramp front, folding leaf rear. **Features:** Uses Match 64 action. Adjustable single-stage trigger. Receiver grooved for scope mounting. Imported from Germany by Merkel USA.
Price: 1416D KL, 22 LR $899.00
Price: 1416D KL Classic left-hand $949.00
Price: 1516D KL, 22 WMR..........................$919.00

ANSCHUTZ 1710D CUSTOM

Caliber: 22 LR, 5-shot clip. **Barrel:** 24.25". **Weight:** 7-3/8 lbs. **Length:** 42.5" overall. **Stock:** Select European walnut. **Sights:** Hooded ramp front, folding leaf rear; drilled and tapped for scope mounting. **Features:** Match 54 action with adjustable single-stage trigger; roll-over Monte Carlo cheekpiece, slim forend with Schnabel tip, Wundhammer palm swell on pistol grip, rosewood gripcap with white diamond insert; skip-line checkering on grip and forend. Introduced 1988. Imported from Germany by Merkel USA.
Price: $1,649.00

BROWNING T-BOLT RIMFIRE

Caliber: 22 LR, 17 HMR, .22 WMR, 10-round rotary box Double Helix magazine. **Barrel:** 22", free-floating, semi-match chamber, target muzzle crown. **Weight:** 4.8 lbs. **Length:** 40.1" overall. **Stock:** Walnut, maple or composite. **Sights:** None. **Features:** Straight-pull bolt-action, three-lever trigger adjustable for pull weight, dual action screws, sling swivel studs. Crossbolt lockup, enlarged bolt handle, one-piece dual extractor with integral spring and red cocking indicator band, gold-tone trigger. Top-tang, thumb-operated two-position safety, drilled and tapped for scope mounts. Varmint model has raised Monte Carlo comb, heavy barrel, wide forearm. Introduced 2006. Imported from Japan by Browning. Left-hand models added in 2009.
Price: .22 LR, from....................... $750.00 to $780.00
Price: .17 HMR/.22 WMR, from .... $790.00 to $830.00

BUSHMASTER DCM-XR COMPETITION

Caliber: 223 Rem, 10-shot mag. (2). **Barrel:** Heavy 1"-diameter free-floating match. **Weight:** 13.5 lbs. **Length:** 38.5" overall. **Features:** Fitted bolt, aperture rear sight that accepts four different inserts, choice of two front sight blades, two-stage competition trigger, weighted buttstock. Available in pre-and post-ban configurations.
Price: From .... NA

BUSHMASTER PIT VIPER 3-GUN COMPETITION

Caliber: 5.56/223 Rem, 20-shot mag. (2). **Barrel:** Lapped/crowned

18" A2-profile 1:8. **Weight:** 7.5 lbs. **Length:** 38" overall. **Features:** AR-style semi-auto rifle designed for three-gun competition. Hybrid chambering to accept mil-spec ammunition, titanium nitride-coated bolt, free-floating handguard with two 3" rails and two 4" rails, JR tactical sight.
Price: From .... NA

COOPER MODEL 57-M BOLT-ACTION

Caliber: 22 LR, 22 WMR, 17 HMR, 17 Mach 2. **Barrel:** 22" or 24" stainless steel or 4140 match grade. **Weight:** 6.5-7.5 lbs. **Stock:** AA-AAA select Claro walnut, 22 lpi hand checkering. **Sights:** None furnished. **Features:** Three rear locking lug, repeating bolt-action with 5-shot magazine. for 22 LR and 17M2; 4-shot magazine for 22 WMR and 17 HMR. Fully adjustable trigger. Left-hand models add $150 to base rifle price. 1/4"-group rimfire accuracy guarantee at 50 yards; 0.5"-group centerfire accuracy guarantee at 100 yards. Options include wood upgrades, case-color metalwork, barrel fluting, custom LOP, and many others.
Price: Classic $1,400.00
Price: LVT $1,595.00
Price: Custom Classic $2,395.00
Price: Western Classic $3,295.00
Price: TRP-3 (22 LR only, benchrest style) $1,395.00
Price: Jackson Squirrel Rifle $1,595.00
Price: Jackson Hunter (synthetic) $1,495.00

CZ 452 LUX BOLT-ACTION

Caliber: 22 LR, 22 WMR, 5-shot detachable magazine. **Barrel:** 24.8". **Weight:** 6.6 lbs. **Length:** 42.63" overall. **Stock:** Walnut with checkered pistol grip. **Sights:** Hooded front, fully adjustable tangent rear. **Features:** All-steel construction, adjustable trigger, polished blue finish. Imported from the Czech Republic by CZ-USA.
Price: 22 LR, 22 WMR $427.00

CZ 452 VARMINT RIFLE

Similar to the Lux model except has heavy 20.8" barrel; stock has beavertail forend; weighs 7 lbs.; no sights furnished. Available in 22 LR, 22 WMR, 17HMR, 17M2. Imported from the Czech Republic by CZ-USA.
Price: From $497.00

CZ 452 AMERICAN BOLT-ACTION RIFLE

Similar to the CZ 452 M 2E Lux except has classic-style stock of Circassian walnut; 22.5" free-floating barrel with recessed target crown; receiver dovetail for scope mounting. No open sights furnished. Introduced 1999. Imported from the Czech Republic by CZ-USA.
Price: 22 LR, 22 WMR $463.00

CZ 455 AMERICAN

Caliber: .17 HMR, .22 LR, .22 WMR (5-round magazine). **Barrel:** 20.5". **Weight:** 6.1 lbs. **Length:** 38.2". **Stock:** walnut. **Sights:** None. Intergral 11mm dovetail scope base. **Features:** Adjustable trigger. Six versions available including blue laminate with thumbhole stock, Varmint model with .866" heavy barrel, full-length Mannlicher walnut stock, and others. American Combo Package includes interchangeable barrel to switch calibers.
Price: from .... $424.00 to $615.00

DAVEY CRICKETT SINGLE SHOT
Caliber: 22 LR, 22 WMR, single shot. **Barrel:** 16-1/8". **Weight:** About 2.5 lbs. **Length:** 30" overall. **Stock:** American walnut. **Sights:** Post on ramp front, peep rear adjustable for windage and elevation. **Features:** Drilled and tapped for scope mounting using special Chipmunk base ($13.95). Engraved model also available. Made in U.S.A. Introduced 1982. Formerly Chipmunk model. From Keystone Sporting Arms.
Price: From $220.00

HENRY ACU-BOLT
Caliber: 22, 22 Mag., 17 HMR; single shot. **Barrel:** 20". **Weight:** 4.15 lbs. **Length:** 36". **Stock:** One-piece fiberglass synthetic. **Sights:** Scope mount and 4x scope included. **Features:** Stainless barrel and receiver, bolt-action.
Price: H007 22 LR $399.95

HENRY "MINI" BOLT ACTION 22
Caliber: 22 LR, single shot youth gun. **Barrel:** 16" stainless, 8-groove rifling. **Weight:** 3.25 lbs. **Length:** 30", LOP 11.5". **Stock:** Synthetic, pistol grip, wraparound checkering and beavertail forearm. **Sights:** William Fire sights. **Features:** One-piece bolt configuration manually operated safety.
Price: H005 22 LR, black fiberglass stock................$249.95
Price: H005S 22 LR, orange fiberglass stock..............$249.95

MARLIN MODEL XT-17 SERIES BOLT ACTION
Caliber. 17 HRM. **Magazine capacity:** 4 and 7-shot, included. **Barrel:** 22 inches. **Weight:** 6 pounds. **Stock:** Black synthetic with palm swell, stippled grip areas, or walnut-finished hardwood with Monte Carlo comb. Thumbhole laminate or synthetic available. **Sights:** None, drilled and tapped for scope. Adjustable trigger. Blue or stainless finish.
Price: ....$253.00 to $300.00
Price: (thumbhole stocks) ....$400.00 to $450.00

MARLIN MODEL XT-22 SERIES BOLT ACTION
Features: This is the new line of 22 caliber rimfire rifles from Marlin. Perfect for target practice and small game, these bolt-action 22s are reliable, accurate and fun to shoot. They come in several different models, with 4 or 7-shot clip magazines or 12-shot tube magazines; synthetic, hardwood or laminated stocks; ramp sights, hood sights or fiber-optic sights. All of them have Marlin innovations such as the Pro-Fire™ Adjustable Trigger and Micro-Groove® rifling. The XT-22 series comes chambered in 22 Short, 22 Long, 22 Long Rifle or 22 Winchester Magnum Rifle (WMR). Made in U.S.A. by Marlin Firearms Co.
Price: ....$221.00 to $355.00

MARLIN MODEL XT-22 YOUTH SERIES BOLT ACTION
Features: the first series of rifles designed exclusively for young shooters. It features a shorter stock, shorter trigger reach, smaller grip and a raised comb; making it easier for a youth to acquire and hold the proper sight picture. These guns also feature a reduced bolt

release force, for smoother loading and to prevent jams. Our Pro-Fire™ Adjustable Trigger adjusts the trigger pull, too.
Price: ....$219.00 to $247.00

MEACHAM LOW-WALL
Caliber: Any rimfire cartridge. **Barrel:** 26-34". **Weight:** 7-15 lbs. **Sights:** none. Tang drilled for Win. base, 3/8" dovetail slot front. **Stock:** Fancy eastern walnut with cheekpiece; ebony insert in forearm tip. **Features:** Exact copy of 1885 Winchester. With most Winchester factory options available including double set triggers. Introduced 1994. Made in U.S.A. by Meacham T&H Inc.
Price: From $4,999.00

MOSSBERG MODEL 817 VARMINT BOLT-ACTION
Caliber: 17 HMR, 5-round magazine. **Barrel:** 21"; free-floating bull barrel, recessed muzzle crown. **Weight:** 4.9 lbs. (black synthetic), 5.2 lbs. (wood). **Stock:** Black synthetic or wood; length of pull, 14.25". **Sights:** Factory-installed Weaver-style scope bases. **Features:** Blued or brushed chrome metal finishes, crossbolt safety, gun lock. Introduced 2008. Made in U.S.A. by O.F. Mossberg & Sons, Inc.
Price: Black synthetic stock, chrome finish (2008)..................$279.00

MOSSBERG MODEL 801/802 BOLT
Caliber: 22 LR, 10-round detachable magazine. **Barrel:** 18" free-floating. **Weight:** 4.1 to 4.6 lbs. **Sights:** Adjustable rifle. Receiver grooved for scope mount. **Stock:** Solid pink or pink marble finish synthetic. **Features:** Ergonomically placed magazine release and safety buttons, crossbolt safety, free gun lock. 801 Half Pint has 12.25" length of pull, 16" barrel, and weighs 4 lbs. Hardwood stock; removable magazine plug. Made in U.S.A. by O.F. Mossberg & Sons, Inc.
Price: Pink Plinkster (2008) $199.00
Price: Half Pint (2008) $199.00

NEW ENGLAND FIREARMS SPORTSTER SINGLE-SHOT
Caliber: 22 LR, 22 WMR, 17 HMR; single-shot. **Barrel:** 20". **Weight:** 5.5 lbs. **Length:** 36.25" overall. **Stock:** Black polymer. **Sights:** None furnished; scope mount included. **Features:** Break open, side-lever release; automatic ejection; recoil pad; sling swivel studs; trigger locking system. Introduced 2001. Made in U.S.A. by New England Firearms.
Price: $149.00
Price: Youth model (20" barrel, 33" overall, weighs 5-1/3 lbs.) $149.00
Price: Sportster 17 HMR $180.00

NEW ULTRA LIGHT ARMS 20RF BOLT-ACTION
Caliber: 22 LR, single shot or repeater. **Barrel:** Douglas, length to order. **Weight:** 5.25 lbs. **Length:** Varies. **Stock:** Kevlar/graphite composite, variety of finishes. **Sights:** None furnished; drilled and tapped for scope mount. **Features:** Timney trigger, hand-lapped action, button-rifled barrel, hand-bedded action, recoil pad, sling-swivel studs, optional Jewell trigger. Made in U.S.A. by New Ultra Light Arms.
Price: 20 RF single shot...............................$1,800.00
Price: 20 RF repeater $1,850.00

SAVAGE B-MAG
Caliber: .17 Winchester Super Magnum. Rotary magazine holds 8 rounds. **Stock:** synthetic. **Weight:** 4.5 pounds. Chambered for new Winchester .17 Super Magnum rimfire cartridge that propels a 20-grain bullet at approximately 3,000 fps. **Features:** Adjustable AccuTrigger, rear locking lugs, new and different bolt-action rimfire design that cocks on close of bolt. New in 2013.
Price: $349

ROSSI MATCHED PAIR SINGLE-SHOT/SHOTGUN
Caliber: 17 HMR, 22 LR, 22 Mag. **Barrel:** 18.5" or 23". **Weight:** 6 lbs. **Stock:** Hardwood (brown or black finish). **Sights:** Fully adjustable

Prices given are believed to be accurate at time of publication however, many factors affect retail pricing so exact prices are not possible.

front and rear. **Features:** Break-open breech, transfer-bar manual safety, includes matched 410-, 20 or 12 gauge shotgun barrel with bead front sight. Introduced 2001. Imported by BrazTech/Taurus.
Price: S121280RS...$160.00
Price: S121780RS $200.00
Price: S122280RS...$160.00
Price: S201780RS $200.00

RUGER 77/22 RIMFIRE BOLT-ACTION
Caliber: 22 LR, 10-shot rotary magazine; 22 WMR, 9-shot rotary magazine. **Barrel:** 20". **Weight:** About 6 lbs. **Length:** 39.25" overall. **Stock:** Checkered American walnut, laminated hardwood, or synthetic stocks, stainless sling swivels. **Sights:** Plain barrel with 1" Ruger rings. **Features:** Mauser-type action uses Ruger's rotary magazine. Three-position safety, simplified bolt stop, patented bolt locking system. Uses the dual-screw barrel attachment system of the 10/22 rifle. Integral scope mounting system with 1" Ruger rings. Blued model introduced 1983. Stainless steel and blued with synthetic stock introduced 1989.
Price: walnut stock $829.00
Price: laminated stock $929.00

RUGER 77/17 RIMFIRE BOLT-ACTION
Caliber: 17 HMR (9-shot rotary magazine. **Barrel:** 22" to 24". **Weight:** 6.5-7.5 lbs. **Length:** 41.25-43.25" overall. **Stock:** Checkered American walnut, laminated hardwood; stainless sling swivels. **Sights:** Plain barrel with 1" Ruger rings. **Features:** Mauser-type action uses Ruger's rotary magazine. Three-position safety, simplified bolt stop, patented bolt locking system. Uses the dual-screw barrel attachment system of the 10/22 rifle. Integral scope mounting system with 1" Ruger rings. Introduced 2002.
Price: walnut stock $829.00
Price: laminated stock $929.00

SAVAGE MARK I-G BOLT-ACTION
Caliber: 22 LR, single shot. **Barrel:** 20.75". **Weight:** 5.5 lbs. **Length:** 39.5" overall. **Stock:** Walnut-finished hardwood with Monte Carlo-type comb, checkered grip and forend. **Sights:** Bead front, open adjustable rear. Receiver grooved for scope mounting. **Features:** Thumb-operated rotating safety. Blue finish. Rifled or smooth bore. Introduced 1990. Made in Canada, from Savage Arms Inc.
Price: $246.00

SAVAGE MARK II BOLT-ACTION
Caliber: 22 LR, .17 HMR, 10-shot magazine. **Barrel:** 20.5". **Weight:** 5.5 lbs. **Length:** 39.5" overall. **Stock:** Walnut-finished hardwood with Monte Carlo-type comb, checkered grip and forend. **Sights:** Bead front, open adjustable rear. Receiver grooved for scope mounting. **Features:** Thumb-operated rotating safety. Blue finish. Introduced 1990. Made in Canada, from Savage Arms, Inc.
Price: .... $214.00 to $374.00

SAVAGE MARK II FSS STAINLESS RIFLE
Similar to the Mark II except has stainless steel barreled action and black synthetic stock with positive checkering, swivel studs, and 20.75" free-floating and button-rifled barrel with detachable magazine. Weighs 5.5 lbs. Introduced 1997. Imported from Canada by Savage Arms, Inc.
Price: $273.00

SAVAGE MODEL 93G MAGNUM BOLT-ACTION
Caliber: 22 WMR, 5-shot magazine. **Barrel:** 20.75". **Weight:** 5.75 lbs. **Length:** 39.5" overall. **Stock:** Walnut-finished hardwood with Monte Carlo-type comb, checkered grip and forend. **Sights:** Bead front, adjustable open rear. Receiver grooved for scope mount. **Features:**

Thumb-operated rotary safety. Blue finish. Introduced 1994. Made in Canada, from Savage Arms.
Price: Model 93G..$260.00
Price: Model 93F (as above with black graphite/fiberglass stock) $241.00
Price: Model 93 Classic, American walnut stock (2008)..........$566.00
Price: Model 93 Classic T, American walnut thumbhole stock (2008) $604.00

SAVAGE MODEL 93FSS MAGNUM RIFLE
Similar to Model 93G except stainless steel barreled action and black synthetic stock with positive checkering. Weighs 5.5 lbs. Introduced 1997. Imported from Canada by Savage Arms, Inc.
Price: $306.00

SAVAGE MODEL 93FVSS MAGNUM
Similar to Model 93FSS Magnum except 21" heavy barrel with recessed target-style crown, satin-finished stainless barreled action, black graphite/fiberglass stock. Drilled and tapped for scope mounting; comes with Weaver-style bases. Introduced 1998. Imported from Canada by Savage Arms, Inc.
Price: $347.00

SAVAGE MODEL 30G STEVENS "FAVORITE"
Caliber: 22 LR, 22 WMR Model 30GM, 17 HMR Model 30R17. **Barrel:** 21". **Weight:** 4.25 lbs. **Length:** 36.75". **Stock:** Walnut, straight grip, Schnabel forend. **Sights:** Adjustable rear, bead post front. **Features:** Lever action falling block, inertia firing pin system, Model 30G half octagonal barrel, Model 30GM full octagonal barrel.
Price: Model 30G..$344.00
Price: Model 30 Takedown $360.00

SAVAGE CUB T MINI YOUTH
Caliber: 22 S, L, LR; 17 Mach 2. **Barrel:** 16". **Weight:** 3.5 lbs. **Length:** 33". **Stock:** Walnut finished hardwood thumbhole stock. **Sights:** Bead post, front; peep, rear. **Features:** Mini single-shot bolt action, free-floating button-rifled barrel, blued finish. From Savage Arms.
Price: Cub T Thumbhole, walnut stained laminated.................$266.00
Price: Cub T Pink Thumbhole (2008) $280.00

THOMPSON/CENTER HOTSHOT YOUTH
Single-shot dropping-barrel rifle chambered in .22 Long Rifle. Features include a crowned 19-inch steel barrel, exposed hammer, synthetic forend and buttstock, peep sight (receiver drilled and tapped for optics), three stock pattern options (black, Realtree AP and pink AP). Overall weight 3 lbs., 11.5-inch length of pull.
Price: .... $229.00 to $249.00

WINCHESTER MODEL 1885 LOW WALL .17 SUPER MAG
Caliber: .17 Winchester Super Magnum. Single-shot lever-action recreation of classic Model 1885 design. **Barrel:** 24-inch octagon. **Weight:** 7.5 pounds. **Stock:** Oil finished Grade I walnut, checkered with Schnabel fore-end. **Finish:** Gloss blue.
Price: $1,470.00

Prices given are believed to be accurate at time of publication however, many factors affect retail pricing so exact prices are not possible.

68TH EDITION, 2014 ✛ **495**

ANSCHUTZ 1903 MATCH

Caliber: 22 LR, single shot. **Barrel:** 21.25". **Weight:** 8 lbs. **Length:** 43.75" overall. **Stock:** Walnut-finished hardwood with adjustable cheekpiece; stippled grip and forend. **Sights:** None furnished. **Features:** Uses Anschutz Match 64 action. A medium weight rifle for intermediate and advanced Junior Match competition. Available from Champion's Choice.
Price: Right-hand...$1,195.00

ANSCHUTZ 64-MP R SILHOUETTE

Caliber: 22 LR, 5-shot magazine. **Barrel:** 21.5", medium heavy; 7/8" diameter. **Weight:** 8 lbs. **Length:** 39.5" overall. **Stock:** Walnut-finished hardwood, silhouette-type. **Sights:** None furnished. **Features:** Uses Match 64 action. Designed for metallic silhouette competition. Stock has stippled checkering, contoured thumb groove with Wundhammer swell. Two-stage #5098 trigger. Slide safety locks sear and bolt. Introduced 1980. Available from Champion's Choice.
Price: 64-MP R $950.00
Price: 64-S BR Benchrest (2008)..$1,175.00

ANSCHUTZ 2007 MATCH RIFLE

Uses same action as the Model 2013, but has a lighter barrel. European walnut stock in right-hand, true left-hand or extra-short models. Sights optional. Available with 19.6" barrel with extension tube, or 26", both in stainless or blue. Introduced 1998. Available from Champion's Choice.
Price: Right-hand, blue, no sights $2,595.00

ANSCHUTZ 1827BT FORTNER BIATHLON

Caliber: 22 LR, 5-shot magazine. **Barrel:** 21.7". **Weight:** 8.8 lbs. with sights. **Length:** 40.9" overall. **Stock:** European walnut with cheekpiece, stippled pistol grip and forend. **Sights:** Optional globe front specially designed for Biathlon shooting, micrometer rear with hinged snow cap. **Features:** Uses Super Match 54 action and nine-way adjustable trigger; adjustable wooden buttplate, biathlon butthook, adjustable hand-stop rail. Uses Anschutz/Fortner system straight-pull bolt action, blued or stainless steel barrel. Introduced 1982. Available from Champion's Choice.
Price: Nitride finish with sights, about $3,035.00

ANSCHUTZ SUPER MATCH SPECIAL MODEL 2013

Caliber: 22 LR, single shot. **Barrel:** 25.9". **Weight:** 13 lbs. **Length:** 41.7" to 42.9". **Stock:** Adjustable aluminum. **Sights:** None furnished. **Features:** 2313 aluminum-silver/blue stock, 500mm barrel, fast lock time, adjustable cheek piece, heavy action and muzzle tube, w/ handstop and standing riser block. Introduced in 1997. Available from Champion's Choice.
Price: Right-hand...$3,595.00

ANSCHUTZ 1912 SPORT

Caliber: 22 LR. **Barrel:** 26" match. **Weight:** 11.4 lbs. **Length:** 41.7" overall. **Stock:** Non-stained thumbhole stock adjustable in length with adjustable butt plate and cheek piece adjustment. Flat forend raiser block 4856 adjustable in height. Hook butt plate. **Sights:** None furnished. **Features:** "Free rifle" for women. Smallbore model 1907 with 1912 **stock:** Match 54 action. Delivered with: Hand stop 6226, forend raiser block 4856, screw driver, instruction leaflet with test target. Available from Champion's Choice.
Price: $2,795.00

ANSCHUTZ 1913 SUPER MATCH RIFLE

Same as the Model 1911 except European walnut International-type stock with adjustable cheekpiece, or color laminate, both available with straight or lowered forend, adjustable aluminum hook buttplate, adjustable hand stop, weighs 13 lbs., 46" overall. Stainless or blue barrel. Available from Champion's Choice.
Price: Right-hand, blue, no sights, walnut stock...................$2,895.00

ANSCHUTZ 1907 STANDARD MATCH RIFLE

Same action as Model 1913 but with 7/8" diameter 26" barrel (stainless or blue). Length is 44.5" overall, weighs 10.5 lbs. Choice of stock configurations. Vented forend. Designed for prone and position shooting ISU requirements; suitable for NRA matches. Also available with walnut flat-forend stock for benchrest shooting. Available from Champion's Choice.
Price: Right-hand, blue, no sights $2,089.00

ARMALITE AR-10(T)

Caliber: 308 Win., 10-shot magazine. **Barrel:** 24" target-weight Rock 5R custom. **Weight:** 10.4 lbs. **Length:** 43.5" overall. **Stock:** Green or black composition; N.M. fiberglass handguard tube. **Sights:** Detachable handle, front sight, or scope mount available. Comes with international-style flattop receiver with Picatinny rail. **Features:** National Match two-stage trigger. Forged upper receiver. Receivers hard-coat anodized. Introduced 1995. Made in U.S.A. by ArmaLite, Inc.
Price: Black $1,912.00
Price: AR-10, 338 Federal $1,912.00

ARMALITE AR-10 NATIONAL MATCH

Caliber: .308/7.62 NATO. **Barrel:** 20", triple lapped Match barrel, 1:10" twist rifling. **Weight:** 11.5 lbs. **Length:** 41". **Features:** Stainless steel flash suppressor, two-stage National Match trigger. Forged flat top receiver with Picatinny rail and forward assist.
Price: $2,365.00

ARMALITE M15A4(T) EAGLE EYE

Caliber: 223 Rem., 10-round magazine. **Barrel:** 24" heavy stainless; 1:8" twist. **Weight:** 9.2 lbs. **Length:** 42-3/8" overall. **Stock:** Green or black butt, N.M. fiberglass handguard tube. **Sights:** One-piece international-style flattop receiver with Weaver-type rail, including case deflector. **Features:** Detachable carry handle, front sight and scope mount (30mm or 1") available. Upper and lower receivers have push-type pivot pin, hard coat anodized. Made in U.S.A. by ArmaLite, Inc.
Price: Green or black furniture..$1,296.00

ARMALITE M15 A4 CARBINE 6.8 & 7.62X39

Caliber: 6.8 Rem, 7.62x39. **Barrel:** 16" chrome-lined with flash suppressor. **Weight:** 7 lbs. **Length:** 26.6". **Features:** Front and rear picatinny rails for mounting optics, two-stage tactical trigger, anodized aluminum/phosphate finish.
Price: $1,107.00

BLASER R93 LONG RANGE SPORTER 2

Caliber: 308 Win., 10-shot detachable box magazine. **Barrel:** 24". **Weight:** 10.4 lbs. **Length:** 44" overall. **Stock:** Aluminum with synthetic lining. **Sights:** None furnished; accepts detachable scope mount. **Features:** Straight-pull bolt action with adjustable trigger; fully adjustable stock; quick takedown; corrosion resistant finish. Introduced 1998. Imported from Germany by Blaser USA.
Price: $3,848.00

Prices given are believed to be accurate at time of publication however, many factors affect retail pricing so exact prices are not possible.

BUSHMASTER A2/A3 TARGET
Caliber: 5.56mm, 223 Rem., 30-round magazine **Barrel:** 20", 24". **Weight:** 8.43 lbs. (A2); 8.78 lbs. (A3). **Length:** 39.5" overall (20" barrel). **Stock:** Black composition; A2 type. **Sights:** Adjustable post front, adjustable aperture rear. **Features:** Patterned after Colt M-16A2. Chrome-lined barrel with manganese phosphate exterior. Available in stainless barrel. Made in U.S.A. by Bushmaster Firearms Co.
Price: (A3 type) $1,135.00

BUSHMASTER DCM-XR COMPETITION
Caliber: 5.56mm, 223 Rem., 10-round magazine. **Barrel:** 20" extra-heavy (1" diameter) barrel with 1.8" twist for heavier competition bullets. **Weight:** About 12 lbs. with balance weights. **Length:** 38.5". **Stock:** NA. **Sights:** A2 rear sight. **Features:** Has special competition rear sight with interchangeable apertures, extra-fine 1/2- or 1/4-MOA windage and elevation adjustments; specially ground front sight post in choice of three widths. Full-length handguards over free-floater barrel tube. Introduced 1998. Made in U.S.A. by Bushmaster Firearms, Inc.
Price: A2 .... $1,150.00
Price: A3 .... $1,250.00

BUSHMASTER VARMINTER
Caliber: 5.56mm. **Barrel:** 24", fluted. **Weight:** 8.4 lbs. **Length:** 42.25" overall. **Stock:** Black composition, A2 type. **Sights:** None furnished; upper receiver has integral scope mount base. **Features:** Chrome-lined .950" extra heavy barrel with counter-bored crown, manganese phosphate finish, free-floating aluminum handguard, forged aluminum receivers with push-pin takedown, hard anodized mil-spec finish. Competition trigger optional. Made in U.S.A. by Bushmaster Firearms, Inc.
Price: $1,360.00

COLT MATCH TARGET COMPETITION HBAR RIFLE
Similar to the Match Target except has removable carry handle for scope mounting, 1:9" rifling twist, 9-round magazine. Weighs 8.5 lbs. Introduced 1991.
Price: Model MT6700C $1,250.00

COLT MATCH TARGET COMPETITION HBAR II RIFLE
Similar to the Match Target Competition HBAR except has 16:1" barrel, overall length 34.5" and weighs 7.1 lbs. Introduced 1995.
Price: Model MT6731 .... $1,172.00

COLT ACCURIZED RIFLE
Similar to the Match Target Model except has 24" barrel. Features flat-top receiver for scope mounting, stainless steel heavy barrel, tubular handguard, and free-floating barrel. Matte black finish. Weighs 9.25 lbs. Made in U.S.A. by Colt's Mfg. Co., Inc.
Price: Model CR6724 .... $1,403.00 to $1,653.00

EAA/HW 660 MATCH
Caliber: 22 LR. **Barrel:** 26". **Weight:** 10.7 lbs. **Length:** 45.3" overall. **Stock:** Match-type walnut with adjustable cheekpiece and buttplate. **Sights:** Globe front, match aperture rear. **Features:** Adjustable match trigger; stippled pistol grip and forend; forend accessory rail. Introduced 1991. Imported from Germany by European American Armory.
Price: About $999.00
Price: With laminate stock $1,159.00

OLYMPIC ARMS SM SERVICEMATCH AR15
Caliber: 223 Rem. minimum SAAMI spec, 30-shot magazine. **Barrel:** 20" broach-cut Ultramatch stainless steel 1x8 twist rate. **Weight:** 10 lbs. **Length:** 39.5" overall. **Stock:** A2 grip, A2 buttstock with trapdoor. **Sights:** A2 NM rear, elevation adjustable front post. **Features:** DCM-ready AR15, free-floating handguard looks standard, A2 upper, threaded muzzle, flash suppressor. Premium model adds pneumatic recoil buffer, Bob Jones interchangeable sights, two-stage trigger and Turner Saddlery sling. Made in U.S.A. by Olympic Arms, Inc.
Price: SM-1, 20" DCM ready $1,272.70
Price: SM-1P, Premium 20" DCM ready $1,727.70

OLYMPIC ARMS UM ULTRAMATCH AR15
Caliber: 223 Rem. minimum SAAMI spec, 30-shot magazine. **Barrel:** 20" or 24" bull broach-cut Ultramatch stainless steel 1x10 twist rate. **Weight:** 8-10 lbs. **Length:** 38.25" overall. **Stock:** A2 grip, A2 buttstock with trapdoor. **Sights:** None, flat-top upper and gas block with rails. **Features:** Flat top upper, free floating tubular match handguard, Picatinny gas block, crowned muzzle, factory trigger job and "Ultramatch" pantograph. Premium model adds pneumatic recoil buffer, Harris S-series bipod, hand selected premium receivers and William Set Trigger. Made in U.S.A. by Olympic Arms, Inc.
Price: UM-1, 20" Ultramatch $1,332.50
Price: UM-1P $1,805.70

OLYMPIC ARMS ML-1/ML-2 MULTIMATCH AR15 CARBINES
Caliber: 223 Rem. minimum SAAMI spec, 30-shot magazine. **Barrel:** 16" broach-cut Ultramatch stainless steel 1x10 twist rate. **Weight:** 7-8 lbs. **Length:** 34-36" overall. **Stock:** A2 grip and varying buttstock. **Sights:** None. **Features:** The ML-1 includes A2 upper with adjustable rear sight, elevation adjustable front post, free floating tubular match handguard, bayonet lug, threaded muzzle, flash suppressor and M4 6-point collapsible buttstock. The ML-2 includes bull diameter barrel, flat top upper, free floating tubular match handguard, Picatinny gas block, crowned muzzle and A2 buttstock with trapdoor. Made in U.S.A. by Olympic Arms, Inc.
Price: ML-1 or ML-2 .... $1,188.20

OLYMPIC ARMS K8 TARGETMATCH AR15
Caliber: 5.56 NATO, 223 WSSM, 243 WSSM, .25 WSSM 30/7-shot magazine. **Barrel:** 20", 24" bull button-rifled stainless/chrome-

moly steel 1x9/1x10 twist rate. **Weight:** 8-10 lbs. **Length:** 38"-42" overall. **Stock:** A2 grip, A2 buttstock with trapdoor. **Sights:** None. **Features:** Barrel has satin bead-blast finish; flat-top upper, free-floating tubular match handguard, Picatinny gas block, crowned muzzle and "Targetmatch" pantograph on lower receiver. K8-MAG model uses Winchester Super Short Magnum cartridges. Includes 24" bull chrome-moly barrel, flat-top upper, free-floating tubular match handguard, Picatinny gas block, crowned muzzle and 7-shot magazine. Made in U.S.A. by Olympic Arms, Inc.

Price: K8 ....$908.70
Price: K8-MAG..$1,363.70

REMINGTON 40-XB RANGEMASTER TARGET

Caliber: 15 calibers from 220 Swift to 300 Win. Mag. **Barrel:** 27.25". **Weight:** 11.25 lbs. **Length:** 47" overall. **Stock:** American walnut, laminated thumbhole or Kevlar with high comb and beavertail forend stop. Rubber non-slip buttplate. **Sights:** None. Scope blocks installed. **Features:** Adjustable trigger. Stainless barrel and action. Receiver drilled and tapped for sights. Model 40-XB Tactical (2008) chambered in 308 Win., comes with guarantee of 0.75-inch maximum 5-shot groups at 100 yards. **Weight:** 10.25 lbs. Includes Teflon-coated stainless button-rifled barrel, 1:14 twist, 27.25 inch long, three longitudinal flutes. Bolt-action repeater, adjustable 40-X trigger and precision machined aluminum bedding block. Stock is H-S Precision Pro Series synthetic tactical stock, black with green web finish, vertical pistol grip. From Remington Custom Shop.

Price: 40-XB KS, aramid fiber stock, single shot $2,780.00
Price: 40-XB KS, aramid fiber stock, repeater $2,634.00
Price: 40-XB Tactical 308 Win. (2008) $2,927.00
Price: 40-XB Thumbhole Repeater..................................$2,927.00

REMINGTON 40-XBBR KS

Caliber: Five calibers from 22 BR to 308 Win. **Barrel:** 20" (light varmint class), 24" (heavy varmint class). **Weight:** 7.25 lbs. (light varmint class); 12 lbs. (heavy varmint class). **Length:** 38" (20" bbl.), 42" (24"bbl.). **Stock:** Aramid fiber. **Sights:** None. Supplied with scope blocks. **Features:** Unblued benchrest with stainless steel barrel, trigger adjustable from 1-1/2 lbs. to 3.5 lbs. Special two-oz. trigger extra cost. Scope and mounts extra.

Price: Single shot...$3,950.00

REMINGTON 40-XC KS TARGET

Caliber: 7.62 NATO, 5-shot. **Barrel:** 24", stainless steel. **Weight:** 11 lbs. without sights. **Length:** 43.5" overall. **Stock:** Aramid fiber. **Sights:** None furnished. **Features:** Designed to meet the needs of competitive shooters. Stainless steel barrel and action.

Price: $3,000.00

REMINGTON 40-XR CUSTOM SPORTER

Caliber: 22 LR, 22 WM. **Barrel:** 24" stainless steel, no sights. **Weight:** 9.75 lbs. **Length:** 40". **Features:** Model XR-40 Target rifle action. Many options available in stock, decoration or finish.

Price: Single shot...$4,500.00

SAKO TRG-22 BOLT-ACTION

Caliber: 308 Win., 10-shot magazine. **Barrel:** 26". **Weight:** 10.25 lbs. **Length:** 45.25" overall. **Stock:** Reinforced polyurethane with fully adjustable cheekpiece and buttplate. **Sights:** None furnished. Optional quick-detachable, one-piece scope mount base, 1" or 30mm rings. **Features:** Resistance-free bolt, free-floating heavy stainless barrel, 60-degree bolt lift. Two-stage trigger is adjustable for length, pull, horizontal or vertical pitch. Introduced 2000. Imported from Finland by Beretta USA.

Price: TRG-22 folding stock $3,540.00

SPRINGFIELD ARMORY M1A SUPER MATCH

Caliber: 308 Win. **Barrel:** 22", heavy Douglas Premium. **Weight:** About 11 lbs. **Length:** 44.31" overall. **Stock:** Heavy walnut competition stock with longer pistol grip, contoured area behind the rear sight, thicker butt and forend, glass bedded. **Sights:** National Match front and rear. **Features:** Has figure-eight-style operating rod guide. Introduced 1987. From Springfield Armory.

Price: About $2,900.00

SPRINGFIELD ARMORY M1A/M-21 TACTICAL MODEL

Similar to M1A Super Match except special sniper stock with adjustable cheekpiece and rubber recoil pad. Weighs 11.6 lbs. From Springfield Armory.

Price: $3,355.00

SPRINGFIELD ARMORY M-1 GARAND AMERICAN COMBAT

Caliber: 30-06 Spfl., 308 Win., 8-shot. **Barrel:** 24". **Weight:** 9.5 lbs. **Length:** 43.6". **Stock:** American walnut. **Sights:** Military square post front, military aperture, MOA adjustable rear. **Features:** Limited production, certificate of authenticity, all new receiver, barrel and stock with remaining parts USGI mil-spec. Two-stage military trigger.

Price: About $2,479.00

STI SPORTING COMPETITION

AR-style semiauto rifle chambered in 5.56 NATO. Features include 16-inch 410 stainless 1:8 barrel; mid-length gas system; Nordic Tactical Compensator and JP Trigger group; custom STI Valkyrie hand guard and gas block; flat-top design with picatinny rail; anodized finish with black Teflon coating. Also available in Tactical configuration.

Price: $1328.53

STONER SR-15 MATCH

Caliber: 223. **Barrel:** 20". **Weight:** 7.9 lbs. **Length:** 38" overall. **Stock:** Black synthetic. **Sights:** None furnished; flattop upper receiver for scope mounting. **Features:** Short Picatinny rail, two-stage match trigger. Introduced 1998. Made in U.S.A. by Knight's Mfg. Co.

Price: $1,650.00

STONER SR-25 MATCH

Caliber: 7.62 NATO, 10-shot steel magazine, 5-shot optional. **Barrel:** 24" heavy match; 1:11.25" twist. **Weight:** 10.75 lbs. **Length:** 44" overall. **Stock:** Black synthetic AR-15A2 design. Full floating forend of mil-spec synthetic attaches to upper receiver at a single point. **Sights:** None furnished. Has integral Weaver-style rail. Rings and iron sights optional. **Features:** Improved AR-15 trigger, AR-15-style seven-lug rotating bolt. Introduced 1993. Made in U.S.A. by Knight's Mfg. Co.

Price: $3,345.00
Price: SR-25 Lightweight Match (20" medium match target contour barrel, 9.5 lbs., 40" overall) $3,345.00

TIME PRECISION 22 RF BENCH REST

Caliber: 22 LR, single shot. **Barrel:** Shilen match-grade stainless. **Weight:** 10 lbs. with scope. **Length:** NA. **Stock:** Fiberglass. Pillar bedded. **Sights:** None furnished. **Features:** Shilen match trigger removable trigger bracket, full-length steel sleeve, aluminum receiver. Introduced 2008. Made in U.S.A. by Time Precision.

Price: $2,200.00

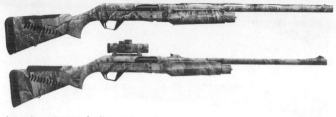

BENELLI LEGACY

Gauge: 12, 20, 2 ¾ and 3" chamber; 28, 2 ¾". **Barrel:** 24", 26", 28" (Full, Mod., Imp. Cyl., Imp. Mod., cylinder choke tubes). Mid-bead sight. **Weight:** 5.8 to 7.4 lbs. **Length:** 49-5/8" overall (28" barrel). **Stock:** Select AA European walnut with satin finish. **Features:** Uses the rotating bolt inertia recoil operating system with a two-piece steel/aluminum etched receiver (bright on lower, blue upper). Drop adjustment kit allows the stock to be custom fitted without modifying the stock. Introduced 1998. Ultralight model has gloss-blued finish receiver. Weight is 6.0 lbs., 24" barrel, 45.5" overall length. WeatherCoat walnut stock. Introduced 2006. Imported from Italy by Benelli USA, Corp.
Price: Legacy (12 and 20 gauge) **$1,799.00**
Price: Legacy (28 gauge) **$2,039.00**
Price: Legacy Sport **$2,439.00**

BENELLI ULTRA LIGHT

Gauge: 28,12, 20, 3" chamber. **Barrel:** 24", 26". Mid-bead sight. **Weight:** 5.2 to 6 lbs. **Features:** Similar to Legacy line. Drop adjustment kit allows the stock to be custom fitted without modifying the stock. WeatherCoat walnut stock. Lightened receiver, shortened magazine tube, carbon-fiber rib and grip cap. Introduced 2008. Imported from Italy by Benelli USA, Corp.
Price: 12 and 20 gauge **$1,699.00**
Price: 28 gauge **$1,799.00**

BENELLI M2 FIELD

Gauge: 20 ga., 12 ga., 3" chamber. **Barrel:** 21", 24", 26", 28". **Weight:** 5.4 to 7.2 lbs. **Length:** 42.5 to 49.5" overall. **Stock:** Synthetic, Advantage Max-4 HD, Advantage Timber HD, APG HD. **Sights:** Red bar. **Features:** Uses the Inertia Driven bolt mechanism. Vent rib. Comes with set of five choke tubes. Imported from Italy by Benelli USA.
Price: Synthetic stock 12 ga. **$1359**
Price: Camo stock 12 ga. **$1469**
Price: Synthetic stock 20 ga. **$1409**
Price: Camo stock 20 ga. **$1519**
Price: Rifled slug .... **$1469 to $1589**
Price: Left-hand 12 ga. **$1409**
Price: Left-hand model 20 ga. **$1519**

BENELLI MONTEFELTRO

Gauge: 12 and 20 ga. Full, Imp. Mod., Mod., Imp. Cyl., Cyl. choke tubes. **Barrel:** 24", 26", 28". **Weight:** 5.3 to 7.1 lbs. **Stock:** Checkered walnut with satin finish. **Length:** 43.6 to 49.5" overall. **Features:** Uses the Inertia Driven rotating bolt system with a simple inertia recoil design. Finish is blue. Introduced 1987.
Price: Standard Model **$1,139.00**
Price: Left Hand Model **$1,229.00**
Price: Silver **$1,779.00**

BENELLI SUPER BLACK EAGLE II

Gauge: 12, 3-1/2" chamber. **Barrel:** 24", 26", 28" (Cyl. Imp. Cyl., Mod., Imp. Mod., Full choke tubes). **Weight:** 7.1 to 7.3 lbs. **Length:** 45.6 to 49.6" overall. **Stock:** European walnut with satin finish, polymer, or camo. Adjustable for drop. **Sights:** Red bar front. **Features:** Uses Benelli inertia recoil bolt system. Vent rib. Advantage Max-4 HD, Advantage Timber HD camo patterns. Features ComforTech stock.

Introduced 1991. Left-hand models available. Imported from Italy by Benelli USA.
Price: Satin walnut **$1,569.00**
Price: Camo stock .... **$1,680.00 to $1,899.00**
Price: Black Comfortech synthetic stock **$1,799.00**
Price: Left hand, camo stock **$1,999.00**
Price: Left hand, Comfortech synthetic **$1,899.00**

BENELLI SUPER BLACK EAGLE II WATERFOWL EDITION

Gauge: 12, (3+1 capacity), chambered for 2 ¾", 3" and 3 ¼" ammunition. **Barrel:** 28". **Weight:** 7.3 lbs. **Length:** 49.6". **Features:** Lengthened and polished forcing cone, Rob Roberts Custom choke tubes, Realtree Max-4 camo finish, Hi Viz front sight, metal middle bead.
Price: **$2,669.00**

BENELLI CORDOBA

Gauge: 20; 12; 3" chamber. **Barrel:** 28" and 30", ported, 10mm sporting rib. **Weight:** 7.2 to 7.3 lbs. **Length:** 49.6 to 51.6". **Features:** Designed for high-volume sporting clays and Argentina dove shooting. Inertia-driven action, Extended Sport CrioChokes, 4+1 capacity. Ported. Imported from Italy by Benelli USA.
Price: Field Models .... **$2,069.00 to $2,099.00**
Price: Performance Shop Model .... **$719.00 to $2,829.00**

BENELLI SUPERSPORT & SPORT II

Gauge: 20; 12; 3" chamber. **Barrel:** 28" and 30", ported, 10mm sporting rib. **Weight:** 7.2 to 7.3 lbs. **Length:** 49.6 to 51.6". **Stock:** Carbon fiber, ComforTech (Supersport) or walnut (Sport II). **Sights:** Red bar front, metal midbead. Sport II is similar to the Legacy model except has nonengraved dual tone blue/silver receiver, ported wide-rib barrel, adjustable buttstock, and functions with all loads. Walnut with satin finish. Introduced 1997. **Features:** Designed for high-volume sporting clays. Inertia-driven action, Extended CrioChokes, 4+1 capacity. Ported. Imported from Italy by Benelli USA.
Price: Supersport **$2,199.00**
Price: Sport II **$1,899.00**

BENELLI VINCI

Gas-operated semiauto shotgun chambered for 2-3/4- and 3-inch 12-gauge. Features include modular disassembly; interchangeable choke tubes; 24- to 28-inch ribbed barrel; black, MAX-4HD or APG HD finish; synthetic contoured stocks; optional Steady-Grip model;. Weight 6.7 to 6.9 lbs.
Price: .... **$1,359.00 to $2,199.00**

BENELLI SUPER VINCI

Gauge: 12 - 2-3/4", 3" and 3-1/2" chamber. **Barrel:** 26" and 28" barrels. **Weight:** 6.9-7 lbs.. **Length:** 48.5"-50.5". **Stock:** Black synthetic, Realtree Max4® and Realtree APG®. **Features:** 3+1 capacity, Crio® Chokes: C,IC,M,IM,F. Length of Pull: 14-3/8". Drop at Heel: 2". Drop at Comb: 1-3/8". Type of Sights: Red bar front sight and metal bead mid-sight. Minimum recommended load: 3-dram, 1-1/8 oz. loads (12-ga.). Receiver drilled and tapped for scope mounting. Imported from Italy by Benelli USA., Corp.
Price: Black Synthetic Comfortech **$1,799.00**

Price: Camo $1,899.00

BENELLI LEGACY SPORT
Gas-operated semiauto shotgun chambered for 12, 20 (2-3/4- and 3-inch) gauge. Features include Inertia Driven system; sculptured lower receiver with classic game scene etchings; highly polished blued upper receiver; AA-Grade walnut stock; gel recoil pad; ported 24- or 26-inch barrel, Crio chokes. Weight 7.4 to 7.5 lbs.

Price: $2,369.00

BERETTA A300 OUTLANDER
Gauge: 12, 3-inch chamber. **Capacity:** 3+1. Operates with 2 ¾" shells. **Barrel:** 28 inches with Mobilechoke system. **Stock:** Synthetic, camo or wood. **Weight:** 7.1 pounds. Based on A400 design at lower price.

Price: .... $725.00 to $825.00

BERETTA A400 XPLOR UNICO
Self-regulation gas-operated shotgun chambered to shoot all 12-ga, loads from 2-3/4 to 3.5 inches. Features include Kick-Off3 hydraulic damper; 26- or 28-inch "Steelium" barrel with interchangeable choke tubes; anodized aluminum receiver; sculpted, checkered walnut buttstock and forend.

Price: $1,755.00

BERETTA A400 XPLOR LIGHT
Gauge: 12-gas operated - 2-3/4" & 3" chamber. **Barrel:** 18" barrel. **Weight:** 6.4 lbs.. **Length:** 39.2". **Stock:** Walnut & polymer. **Features:** The A400 Light combines Beretta's exclusive Blink operating system, self compensating exhaust valve and self cleaning piston, steelium barrel design with 1/4" x 1/4" ventilated rib and Optima-Choke HP, also fitted with the Micro-Core recoil pad. The stock is a wood-oil finish with a mix of walnut and polymer to maximize performance from the forend insert to the trigger guard. Continuing the A400 proprietary family design, the A400 Light is also available with Beretta's improved Kick-Off damper system. Imported from Italy by Benelli USA., Corp.

Price: $1,620.00

BERETTA AL391 URIKA 2
Gauge: 12, 20 gauge; 3" chamber. **Barrel:** 22", 24", 26", 28", 30"; five Mobilchoke choke tubes. **Weight:** 5.95 to 7.28 lbs. **Length:** Varies by model. **Stock:** Walnut, black or camo synthetic; shims, spacers and interchangeable recoil pads allow custom fit. **Features:** Self-compensating gas operation handles full range of loads; recoil reducer in receiver; enlarged trigger guard; reduced-weight receiver, barrel and forend; hard-chromed bore. Introduced 2000. AL391 Urika 2 (2007) has self-cleaning action, X-Tra Grain stock finish. AL391 Urika 2 Gold has higher-grade select oil-finished wood stock, upgraded engraving (gold-filled gamebirds on field models, gold-filled laurel leaf on competition version). Kick-Off recoil reduction system available in Synthetic, Realtree Advantage Max-4 and AP models. Imported from Italy by Beretta USA.

Price: from .... $1,105.00 to $1,755.00

BERETTA A391 EXTREMA 2 CAMOUFLAGE
Gauge: 12 ga. 3.5" chamber. **Barrel:** 24", 26", 28". **Weight:** 7.8 lbs. **Stock:** Synthetic. **Features:** Gas operation system with exhaust valve and self-cleaning gas cylinder and piston that automatically vents the excess gases of the most powerful cartridges. The result is that the shotgun, without any adjustment, fires everything from the weakest 28g (1 ounce, 3 ¾ dram equivalent) game load to the heaviest 64g (2 ¼ ounce) Super Magnum cartridge. The exhaust valve remains attached to the barrel, ensuring easy and quick assembly and disassembly of the shotgun. Semiauto goes with two-lug rotating bolt, extended tang, cross bolt safety, self-cleaning, with case. Also, all steel par ts are now manufactured from stainless steel or are plated with either: nickel, Bruniton, PVD, Aqua Film (receiver & barrel) or chrome (barrel, bore and bolt), making the Xtrema2 a match for even the most extreme environments. All models have camo finish. Choices include Realtree Hardwoods, Advantage Wetlands, Advantage Timber, All Purpose and MAX-4.

Price: From $1,450.00

BREDA GRIZZLY
Gauge: 12, 3.5" chamber. **Barrel:** 28". **Weight:** 7.2 lbs. **Stock:** Black synthetic or Advantage Timber with matching metal parts. **Features:** Chokes tubes are Mod., IC, Full; inertia-type action, four-round magazine. Imported from Italy by Legacy Sports International.

Price: Blued/black (2008)..................$1,826.00
Price: Advantage Timber Camo (2008)..........$2,121.00

BREDA XANTHOS
Gauge: 12, 3" chamber. **Barrel:** 28". **Weight:** 6.5 lbs. **Stock:** High grade walnut. **Features:** Chokes tubes are Mod., IC, Full; inertia-type action, four-round magazine, spark engraving with hand-engraved details and hand-gilding figures on receiver. Blued, Grey or Chrome finishes. Imported from Italy by Legacy Sports International.

Price: Blued (2007) $2,309.00
Price: Grey (2007) $2,451.00
Price: Chrome (2007) $3,406.00

BREDA ECHO
Gauge: 12, 20. 3" chamber. **Barrel:** 28". **Weight:** 6.0-6.5 lbs. **Stock:** Walnut. **Features:** Chokes tubes are Mod., IC, Full; inertia-type action, four-round magazine, blue, grey or nickel finishes, modern engraving, fully checkered pistol grip. Imported from Italy by Legacy Sports International.

Price: Blued, 12 ga. (2008) $1,897.00
Price: Grey, 12 ga. (2008) $1,969.00
Price: Nickel, 12 ga. (2008) $2,214.00
Price: Nickel, 20 ga. (2008) $2,214.00

BREDA ALTAIR
Gauge: 12, 20. 3" chamber. **Barrel:** 28". **Weight:** 5.7-6.1 lbs. **Stock:** Oil-rubbed walnut. **Features:** Chokes tubes are Mod., IC, Full; gas-actuated action, four-round magazine, blued finish, lightweight frame. Imported from Italy by Legacy Sports International.

Price: Blued, 12 ga. (2008) $1,320.00
Price: Grey, 20 ga. (2008) $1,320.00

BROWNING A5
Gauge: 12, 3 or 3.5-inch chamber. **Barrel:** 26, 28 or 30". **Weight:** 6.6 to 7 lbs. **Length:** 47.25 to 51.5". **Stock:** Gloss finish walnut with 22 lpi checkering, black synthetic or camo. Adjustable for cast and drop. **Features:** Operates on Kinematic short-recoil system. Lengthened forcing cone, three choke tubes (IC, M, F), flat ventilated rib, brass bead front sight, ivory middle bead. Available in Mossy Oak Duck Blind or Break-up Infinity camo. Ultimate Model has satin finished aluminum alloy receiver with light engraving of pheasants on left side, mallards on the right. Glossy blue finish, Grade III oil-finished walnut stock,

Price: A5 Hunter $1,560.00
Price: A5 Hunter 3.5" $1,700.00
Price: A5 Stalker (synthetic) $1,400.00
Price: A5 Stalker 3.5" $1,560.00
Price: A5 Ultimate $1,910.00

Prices given are believed to be accurate at time of publication however, many factors affect retail pricing so exact prices are not possible.

BROWING MAXUS HUNTER

Gauge: 12 ga., 3" & 3-1/2" chamber. **Barrel:** 26", 28" & 30" flat ventilated rib with fixed cylinder choke; stainless Steel; Matte finish. **Weight:** 7 lbs. 2 ozs. **Length:** 40.75". **Stock:** Gloss finish walnut stock with close radius pistol grip, sharp 22 lines-per-inch checkering, speed Lock Forearm, shim adjustable for length of pull, cast and drop. **Features:** Vector Pro™ lengthened forcing cone, three Invector-Plus™ choke tubes, Inflex Technology recoil pad, ivory front bead sight, One 1/4" stock spacer. Strong, lightweight aluminum alloy receiver with durable satin nickel finish & laser engraving (pheasant on the right, mallard on the left).
Price: 3" chamber $1,500.00
Price: 3-1/2" chamber $1,640.00

BROWING MAXUS MOSSY OAK BOTTOMLAND

Gauge: 12 ga., 3-1/2" chamber. **Barrel:** 28" flat ventilated rib. **Weight:** 6 lbs. 15 ozs. **Length:** 49.25". **Stock:** Composite stock with close radius pistol grip; Speed Lock forearm; textured gripping surfaces; shim adjustable for length of pull, cast and drop; Mossy Oak® Bottomland™ camo finish; Dura-Touch® Armor Coating. **Features:** Vector Pro™ lengthened forcing cone; three Invector Plus™ choke tubes (F,M,IC), Inflex Technology recoil pad; ivory front bead sight; one 1/4" stock spacer.
Price: $1,539.00

BROWING MAXUS MOSSY OAK DUCK BLIND

Gauge: 12 ga., 3" & 3-1/2" chamber. **Barrel:** 26"& 28" flat ventilated rib with fixed cylinder choke; stainless Steel; Matte finish. **Weight:** 6 lbs. 14 ozs.-6 lbs. 15 ozs. **Length:** 47.25"-49.25". **Stock:** Composite stock with close radius pistol grip, Speed Lock forearm, textured gripping surfaces, Mossy Oak® Duck Blind® camo finish, Dura-Touch® Armor Coating. **Features:** Vector Pro™ lengthened forcing cone, three Invector-Plus™ choke tubes, Inflex Technology recoil pad, ivory front bead sight, One 1/4" stock spacer. Strong, lightweight aluminum alloy receiver. Gas-operated autoloader, new Power Drive Gas System reduces recoil and cycles a wide range of loads.
Price: 3" chamber $1,470.00
Price: 3-1/2" chamber $1,600.00

BROWING MAXUS SPORTING

Gauge: 12 ga., 3" chamber. **Barrel:** 28" & 30" flat ventilated rib. **Weight:** 7 lbs. 2 ozs. **Length:** 49.25"-51.25". **Stock:** Gloss finish high grade walnut stock with close radius pistol grip, Speed Lock forearm, shim adjustable for length of pull, cast and drop. **Features:** This new model is sure to catch the eye, with its laser engraving of game birds transforming into clay birdson the lightweight alloy receiver. Quail are on the right side, and a mallard duck on the left. The Power Drive Gas System reduces recoil and cycles a wide array of loads. It's available in a 28" or 30" barrel length. The high grade walnut stock and forearm are generously checkered, finished with a deep, high gloss. The stock is adjustable and one 1/4" stock spacer is included. For picking up either clay or live birds quickly, the HiViz Tri-Comp fiber-optic front sight with mid-bead ivory sight does a great job, gathering light on the most overcast days. Vector Pro™ lengthened forcing cone, five Invector-Plus™ choke tubes, Inflex Technology recoil pad ,HiViz® Tri-Comp fiber-optic front sight, ivory mid-bead sight, one ¼" stock spacer.
Price: $1,700.00

BROWING MAXUS SPORTING CARBON FIBER

Gauge: 12 ga., 3" chamber. **Barrel:** 28" & 30" flat ventilated rib. **Weight:** 6 lbs. 15 ozs. - 7 lbs. **Length:** 49.25"-51.25". **Stock:**

Composite stock with close radius pistol grip, Speed Lock forearm, textured gripping surfaces, shim adjustable for length of pull, cast and drop, carbon fiber finish, Dura-Touch® Armor Coating. **Features:** Strong, lightweight aluminum alloy, carbon fiber finish on top and bottom The stock is finished with Dura-Touch Armor Coating for a secure, non-slip grip when the gun is wet. It has the Browning exclusive Magazine Cut-Off, a patented Turn-Key Magazine Plug and Speed Load Plus. It will be an impossible task to locate an autoloading shotgun for the field with such shooter-friendly features as the Browning Maxus, especially with this deeply finished look of carbon fiber and the Dura-Touch Armor Coating feel. Vector Pro™ lengthened forcing cone, five Invector-Plus™ choke tubes, Inflex Technology recoil pad, HiViz® Tri-Comp fiber-optic front sight, ivory mid-bead sight, one 1/4" stock spacer.
Price: $1,500.00

BROWING RIFLED DEER STALKER

Gauge: 12 ga., 3" chamber. **Barrel:** 22" thick-walled, fully rifled for slug ammunition only. **Weight:** 7 lbs. 3 ozs. **Length:** 43.25". **Stock:** Composite stock with close radius pistol grip, Speed Lock forearm, textured gripping surfaces, shim adjustable for length of pull, cast and drop, matte black finish Dura-Touch® Armor Coating. **Features:** Stock is adjustable for length of pull, cast and drop. Cantilever scope mount, one 1/4" stock spacer.
Price: $1,400.00

BROWNING SILVER

Gauge: 12, 3" or 3-1/2" chamber; 20, 3" chamber. Barrel: 12 ga.-26", 28", 30", Invector Plus choke tubes. Weight: 7 lbs., 9 oz. (12 ga.), 6 lbs., 7 oz. (20 ga.). Stock: Satin finish walnut. Features: Active Valve gas system, semi-humpback receiver. Invector Plus tube system, three choke tubes. Imported by Browning.
Price: Silver Hunter, 12 ga., 3.5" chamber...........................$1,340.00
Price: Silver Hunter, 20 ga., 3" chamber, intr. 2008 ....$1,180.00
Price: Silver Sporting, 12 ga., 2-3/4" chamber,
intr. 2009 ....$1,300.00
Price: Silver Sporting Micro, 12 ga., 2-3/4" chamber,
intr. 2008 ....$1,300.00
Price: Silver Rifled Deer, Mossy Oak New Break-Up,
12 ga., 3" chamber, intr. 2008...................................$1,419.00
Price: Silver Rifled Deer Stalker, 12 ga., 3" chamber,
intr. 2008 ....$1,280.00
Price: Silver Rifled Deer Satin, satin-finished aluminum
alloy receiver and satin-finished walnut buttstock
and forend $1,340.00
Price: Silver Stalker, black composite buttstock and
forend $1,179.00

CZ MODEL 712/720

Gauge: 12, 20 (4+1 capacity). **Barrel:** 26". **Weight:** 6.3 lbs. **Stock:** Turkish walnut with 14.5" length of pull. **Features:** Chrome-lined barrel with 3-inch chamber, ventilated rib, five choke tubes. Matte

Prices given are believed to be accurate at time of publication however, many factors affect retail pricing so exact prices are not possible.

68TH EDITION, 2014 ✦ **501**

black finish.
Price: $499

ESCORT AVERY WATERFOWL EXTREME SEMIAUTO
Gauge: 12 & 20 ga., 2-3/4" through 3-1/2" chamber, multi 5+1 capacity. **Barrel:** 28". **Weight:** 7.4 lbs. **Length:** 48". **Stock:** Composite stock with close radius pistol grip; Speed Lock forearm; textured gripping surfaces; shim adjustable for length of pull, cast and drop; Mossy Oak® Bottomland™ camo finish; Dura-Touch® Armor Coating. **Features:** The addition of non-slip grip pads on the forend and pistol grip that give you a superior hold in all weather conditions. These grip panels look great and are strategically placed to give you the wet weather grip you need to control your shot. Escort shotguns also have SMART™ Valve gas pistons that regulate gas blowback to cycle every round – from 2.75 inch range loads through 3.5 inch heavy magnums. Escorts also have FAST™ loading systems that allow one-handed round changes without changing aiming position. Next, we've added Avery Outdoors' KW1™ or Buck Brush™ camo patterns to make these shotguns invisible in the field. We are also offering a HiVis MagniSight™ fiber optic, magnetic sight to enhance sight acquisition in low light conditions. Finally, we went to Hevi•Shot and got their mid-range choke tube for waterfowl to round out the perfect hunting machine.

Price: Black/Synthetic	$623.00
Price: Avery BuckBrush Camo	$790.00
Price: Avery KW1 Camo	$790.00
Price: 3.5" Black/Synthetic	$748.00
Price: 3.5" Avery KW1 Camo	$873.00
Price: Left Black/Synthetic	$623.00
Price: Left Avery KW1 Camo	$790.00
Price: Left 3.5" Black Synthetic	$748.00
Price: Left 3.5" Avery KW1 Camo	$873.00
Price: Black/Synthetic 20 gauge	$623.00

ESCORT
Gauge: 12, 20; 3" or 3.5" chambers. **Barrel:** 22" (Youth), 26" and 28". **Weight:** 6.7-7.8 lbs. **Stock:** Polymer in black, Shadow Grass® or Obsession® camo finish, Turkish walnut, select walnut. **Sights:** Optional HiViz Spark front. **Features:** Black-chrome or dipped-camo metal parts, top of receiver dovetailed for sight mounts, gold plated trigger, trigger guard safety, magazine cut-off. Three choke tubes (IC, M, F) except the Waterfowl/Turkey Combo, which adds a .665 turkey choke to the standard three. Waterfowl/Turkey combo is two-barrel set, 24"/26" and 26"/28". Several models have Trio recoil pad. Models are: AS, AS Select, AS Youth, AS Youth Select, PS, PS Spark and Waterfowl/Turkey. Introduced 2002. Camo introduced 2003. Youth, Slug and Obsession camo introduced 2005. Imported from Turkey by Legacy Sports International.
Price: .... $425.00 to $589.00

FABARM XLR5 VELOCITY
Gauge: 12. **Barrel:** 30 or 32". **Weight:** 8.4 to 9.9 lbs. Gas-operated model designed for competition shooting. Features include a unique adjustable rib that allows a more upright shooting position. There is also an adjustable trigger shoe, magazine cap adjustable weight system. Five interchangeable choke tubes. Field grade verstions available.
Price: $2885
Price: Field grade $2200

FRANCHI AFFINITY
Gauge: 12, 20. Three-inch chamber also handles 2 ¾ inch shells. Barrel: 26, 28 inches or 30 inches (12 ga.), 26 inches (20 ga.). 30-inch barrel available only on 12-gauge Sporting model. Weight: 5.6 to 6.8 pounds. Stock: Black synthetic or Realtree Camo.
Price: Synthetic $849.00
Price: Camo $949.00
Price: Sporting $1,149.00

FRANCHI INERTIA I-12
Gauge: 12, 3" chamber. **Barrel:** 24", 26", 28" (Cyl., IC, Mod., IM, F choke tubes). **Weight:** 7.5 to 7.7 lbs. **Length:** 45" to 49". **Stock:** 14-3.8" LOP, satin walnut with checkered grip and forend, synthetic, Advantage Timber HD or Max-4 camo patterns. **Features:** Inertia-Driven action. AA walnut stock. Red bar front sight, metal mid sight. Imported from Italy by Benelli USA.
Price: Synthetic $839.00
Price: Camo $949.00
Price: Satin walnut $949.00

FRANCHI 48AL FIELD AND DELUXE
Gauge: 20 or 28, 2-3/4" chamber. **Barrel:** 24", 26", 28" (Full, Cyl., Mod., choke tubes). **Weight:** 5.4 to 5.7 lbs. **Length:** 42.25" to 48". **Stock:** Walnut with checkered grip and forend. **Features:** Long recoil-operated action. Chrome-lined bore; cross-bolt safety. Imported from Italy by Benelli USA.
Price: Al Field 20 ga. $899.00
Price: Al Field 28 ga. $999.00
Price: Al Field Deluxe 20 ga. $1,149.00
Price: Al Field Deluxe 28 ga. $1,249.00

HARRINGTON & RICHARDSON EXCELL AUTO 5
Gauge: 12, 3" chamber. **Barrel:** 22", 24", 28"; four screw-in choke tubes (IC, M, IM, F). **Weight:** About 7 lbs. **Length:** 42.5" to 48.5" overall, depending on barrel length. **Stock:** American walnut with satin finish; cut checkering; ventilated buttpad. Synthetic stock or camo-finish. **Sights:** Metal bead front or fiber-optic front and rear. **Features:** Ventilated rib on all models except slug gun. Imported by H&R 1871, Inc.
Price: Synthetic, black, 28" barrel, 48.5" OAL $415.00
Price: Walnut, checkered grip/forend, 28" barrel, 48.5" OAL ... $461.00
Price: Waterfowl, camo finish $521.00
Price: Turkey, camo finish, 22" barrel, fiber optic sights $521.00
Price: Combo, synthetic black stock, with slug barrel $583.00

LANBER SEMIAUTOMATIC
Gauge: 12, 3". **Barrel:** 26", 28", chrome-moly alloy steel, welded, ventilated top and side ribs. **Weight:** 6.8 lbs. **Length:** 48-3/8". **Stock:** Walnut, oiled finish, laser checkering, rubber buttplate. **Sights:** Fiber-optic front. **Features:** Extractors or automatic ejectors, control and unblocking button. Rated for steel shot. Lanber Polichokes. Imported by Lanber USA.
Price: Model 2533 .... $635.00

MOSSBERG 930 AUTOLOADER
Gauge: 12, 3" chamber, 4-shot magazine. **Barrel:** 24", 26", 28", over-bored to 10-gauge bore dimensions; factory ported, Accu-Choke tubes. **Weight:** 7.5 lbs. **Length:** 44.5" overall (28" barrel). **Stock:** Walnut or synthetic. Adjustable stock drop and cast spacer system. **Sights:** "Turkey Taker" fiber-optic, adjustable windage and elevation. Front bead fiber-optic front on waterfowl models. **Features:** Self-regulating gas system, dual gas-vent system and piston, EZ-Empty magazine button, cocking indicator. Interchangeable Accu-Choke tube set (IC, Mod, Full) for waterfowl and field models. XX-Full turkey Accu-Choke tube included with turkey models. Ambidextrous thumb-operated safety, Uni-line stock and receiver. Receiver drilled and tapped for scope base attachment, free gun lock. Introduced 2008. From O.F. Mossberg & Sons, Inc.
Price: Turkey, from $736.00
Price: Waterfowl, from $736.00
Price: Combo, from $700.00
Price: Field, from $633.00
Price: Slugster, from $606.00
Price: Turkey Pistolgrip; full pistolgrip stock, matte black or Mossy Oak Obsession camo finish overall $828.00
Price: Tactical; 18.5" tactical barrel, black synthetic stock and matte black finish $683.00
Price: SPX; no muzzle brake, M16-style front sight, ghost ring rear sight, full pistolgrip stock, eight-round extended magazine $787.00

Prices given are believed to be accurate at time of publication however, many factors affect retail pricing so exact prices are not possible.

Price: Home Security/Field Combo; 18.5" Cylinder bore barrel and 28" ported Field barrel; black synthetic stock and matte black finish $604.00

MOSSBERG MODEL 935 MAGNUM AUTOLOADING
Gauge: 12; 3" and 3.5» chamber, interchangeable. **Barrel:** 22", 24», 26», 28». **Weight:** 7.25 to 7.75 lbs. **Length:** 45" to 49" overall. **Stock:** Synthetic. **Features:** Gas-operated semiauto models in blued or camo finish. Fiber optics sights, drilled and tapped receiver, interchangeable Accu-Mag choke tubes.
Price: 935 Magnum Turkey: Realtree Hardwoods, Mossy Oak New Break-up or Mossy Oak Obsession camo overall, 24" barrel $815.00
Price: 935 Magnum Turkey Pistolgrip; full pistolgrip stock $925.00
Price: 935 Magnum Grand Slam: 22" barrel, Realtree Hardwoods or Mossy Oak New Break-up camo overall $832.00
Price: 935 Magnum Flyway: 28" barrel and Advantage Max-4 camo overall $870.00
Price: 935 Magnum Waterfowl: 26"or 28" barrel, matte black, Mossy Oak New Break-up, Advantage Max-4 or Mossy Oak Duck Blind cam overall $682.00
Price: 935 Magnum Turkey/Deer Combo: interchangeable 24" Turkey barrel, Mossy Oak New Break-up camo overall $901.00
Price: 935 Magnum Watorfowl/Turkey Combo: 24" Turkey and 28" Waterfowl barrels, Mossy Oak New Break-up finish overall $901.00

MOSSBERG SA-20
Gauge: 20. 20 (Tactical), 26 or 28". **Weight:** 5.5 to 6 lbs. **Stock:** Black synthetic. Gas operated action, matte blue finish. Tactical model has ghost-ring sight, accessory rail.
Price: From ...... $518.00 to $595.00

REMINGTON MODEL 11-87 SPORTSMAN
Gauge: 12, 20, 3" chamber. **Barrel:** 26", 28", RemChoke tubes. Standard contour, vent rib. **Weight:** About 7.75 to 8.25 lbs. **Length:** 46" to 48" overall. **Stock:** Black synthetic or Mossy Oak Break Up Mossy Oak Duck Blind, and Realtree Hardwoods HD and AP Green HD camo finishes. **Sights:** Single bead front. **Features:** Matte-black metal finish, magazine cap swivel studs. Sportsman Deer gun has 21-inch fully rifled barrel, cantilever scope mount.
Price: ...... $804.00 to $929.00

REMINGTON 11-87 SPORTSMAN SUPER MAG SYNTHETIC
Semiauto shotgun chambered in 12-ga. 3-1/2-inch. Features include black matte synthetic stock and forend; rubber overmolded grip panels on the stock and forend; black padded sling; HiViz sights featuring interchangeable light pipe; 28-inch vent rib barrel; SuperCell recoil pad; RemChoke.
Price: From ...... $859.00 to $998.00

REMINGTON 11-87 SPORTSMAN SUPER MAG SHURSHOT TURKEY
Similar to 11-87 Sportsman Super Mag Synthetic but with ambidextrous ShurShot pistol-grip stock; full Realtree APG HD coverage; 23-inch barrol with fully adjustable TruGlo rifle sights. Wingmaster HD Turkey Choke included.
Price: $972.00

REMINGTON MODEL 1100 50TH ANNIVERSARY EDITION
To celebrate the 50th anniversary of the famous Model 1100 gas-operated autoloading shotgun, Remington announces a Limited

Edition 12-gauge model. Features include a machine-cut engraved receiver with gold-filled retriever, quail and duck images; a high-grade walnut stock with high gloss finish, white diamond grip cap and white-line spacers (features that were popular in 1963); 28-inch light-contour barrel with twin bead sights and Rem Choke. Shipped In a green Romington hard case.
Price: $1999

REMINGTON MODEL 1100 COMPETITION MODELS
Gauge: .410 bore, 28, 20, 12. **Barrel:** 26", 27", 28", 30" light target contoured vent rib barrel with twin bead target sights. **Stock:** Semi-fancy American walnut stock and forend, cut checkering, high gloss finish. **Features:** Classic Trap has 30-inch barrel and weighs approximately 8.25 pounds. Sporting Series is available in all four gauges with 28-inch barrel in 12 and 20 gauge, 27 inch in 28 and .410. Weight: 6.25 to 8 pounds. Competion Synthetic model has synthetic stock with adjustable comb, case and length. Five Briley Target choke tubes. High-gloss blued barrel, Nickel-Teflon finish on receiver and internal parts. Weight: 8.1 pounds.
Price: Classic Trap $1,270.00
Price: Sporting Series, from $1,211.00
Price: Competition Synthetic: $1,242.00

REMINGTON MODEL 1100 TAC-4
Similar to Model 1100 but with 18" or 22" barrel with ventilated rib; 12 gauge 2-3/4"only; standard black synthetic stock or Knoxx SpecOps SpeedFeed IV pistolgrip stock; RemChoke tactical choke tube; matte black finish overall. Length is 42-1/2" and weighs 7-3/4 lbs.
Price: $1,015.00

REMINGTON VERSA MAX™ SERIES
Gauge: 12 ga., 2 3/4", 3", 3 1/2" chamber. **Barrel:** 26" and 28" flat ventilated rib. **Weight:** 7.5 lbs.-7.7 lbs. **Length:** 40.25". **Stock:** Synthetic. **Features:** Reliably cycles 12-gauge rounds from 2 3/4" to 3 1/2" magnum. Versaport™ gas system regulates cycling pressure based on shell length. Reduces recoil to that of a 20-gauge. Self-cleaning - Continuously cycled thousands of rounds in torture test. Synthetic stock and fore-end with grey overmolded grips. Drilled and tapped receiver. Enlarged trigger guard opening and larger safety for easier use with gloves. TriNyte® Barrel and Nickel Teflon plated internal components offer extreme corrosion resistance. Includes 5 Flush Mount Pro Bore™ Chokes (Full, Mod, Imp Mod Light Mod, IC).
Price: Sportsman, from $1,025.00
Price: Synthetic, from $1,399.00
Price: Tactical, from $1,399.00
Price: Waterfowl, from $1,599.00
Price: Camo, from $1,599.00
Price: Zombie Green or Pink, from $1,599.00

STOEGER MODEL 2000
Gauge: 12, 3" chamber, set of five choke tubes (C, IC, M, F, XFT). **Barrel:** 24", 26", 28", 30". **Stock:** Walnut, synthetic, Timber HD, Max-4. **Sights:** Red bar front. **Features:** Inertia-recoil. Minimum recommended load: 3 dram, 1-1/8 oz. Imported by Benelli USA.
Price: Walnut $499.00
Price: Synthetic $499.00
Price: Max-4 ...... $549.00

Prices given are believed to be accurate at time of publication however, many factors affect retail pricing so exact prices are not possible.

68TH EDITION, 2014 ⊕ **503**

Price: Black synthetic pistol grip (2007) $499.00
Price: APG HD camo pistol grip (2007), 18.5" barrel............... $549.00

STOEGER MODEL 3000
Gauge: 12, 2-3/4 and 3-inch loads. Minimum recommended load 3-dram, 1-1/8 ounces. **Magazine capacity:** 4+1. Inertia-driven operating system. **Barrel:** 26 or 28 inches with 3 choke tubes IC, M, XF. Weight: 7.4 to 7.5 pounds. **Finish:** Black synthetic or camo (Realtree APG or Max-4).
Price: Synthetic $529.00
Price: Camo $599.00

STOEGER MODEL 3500
Gauge: 12. 2 3/4, 3 and 3 1/2-inch loads. Minimum recommended load 3-dram, 1-1/8 ounces. **Barrel:** 24, 26 or 28 inches. Other features similar to Model 3000. Choke tubes for IC, M, XF. **Weight:** 7.4 to 7.5 pounds. **Finish:** Black synthetic or camo (Realtree APG or Max-4).
Price: Synthetic $629.00
Price: Camo $719.00

TRISTAR VIPER SEMIAUTOMATIC
Gauge: 12, 20; shoots 2-3/4" or 3" interchangeably. **Barrel:** 26", 28" barrels (carbon fiber only offered in 12-ga. 28" and 20-ga. 26"). **Stock:** Wood, black synthetic, Mossy Oak Duck Blind camouflage, faux carbon fiber finish (2008) with the new Comfort Touch technology. **Features:** Magazine cut-off, vent rib with matted sight plane, brass front bead (camo models have fiber-optic front sight), five round magazine-shot plug included, and 3 Beretta-style choke tubes (IC, M, F). Viper synthetic, Viper camo have swivel studs. Five-year warranty. Viper Youth models have shortened length of pull and 24" barrel. Imported by Tristar Sporting Arms Ltd.
Price: From $469.00
Price: Camo models (2008), from $569.00

WEATHERBY SA-08 SERIES SEMIAUTO
Gauge: 12 ga. & 20 ga., 3" chamber. **Barrel:** 26" and 28" flat ventilated rib. **Weight:** 6.5 lbs. **Stock:** Wood and synthetic. **Features:** The

SA-08 is a reliable workhorse that lets you move from early season dove loads to late fall's heaviest waterfowl loads in no time. Available with wood and synthetic stock options in 12 and 20 gauge models, including a scaled-down youth model to fit 28 ga. Comes with 3 application-specific choke tubes (SK/IC/M). Made in Turkey.
Price: SA-08 Upland $799.00
Price: SA-08 Synthetic (New 2011) $599.00
Price: SA-08 Waterfowler 3.0 .... $749.00
Price: SA-08 Synthetic Youth $599.00
Price: SA-08 Deluxe.. $799.00

WINCHESTER SUPER X3
Gauge: 12, 3" and 3.5" chambers. **Barrel:** 26", 28", .742" back-bored; Invector Plus choke tubes. **Weight:** 7 to 7.25 lbs. **Stock:** Composite, 14.25"x1.75"x2". Mossy Oak New Break-Up camo with Dura-Touch Armor Coating. Pachmayr Decelerator buttpad with hard heel insert, customizable length of pull. **Features:** Alloy magazine tube, gunmetal grey Perma-Cote UT finish, self-adjusting Active Valve gas action, lightweight recoil spring system. Electroless nickel-plated bolt, three choke tubes, two length-of-pull stock spacers, drop and cast adjustment spacers, sling swivel studs. Introduced 2006. Made in Belgium, assembled in Portugal by U.S. Repeating Arms Co.
Price: Field $1,070.00
Price: Black Shadow .... $1,000.00 to $1,070.00 (3.5")
Price: Universal Hunter .... $1,160.00 to $1,230.00 (3.5")
Price: Waterfowl Hunter $1,200.00
Price: Sporting, Adj. comb $1,700.00
Price: Cantilever Buck $1,150.00

BENELLI SUPERNOVA

Gauge: 12; 3.5" chamber. **Barrel:** 24", 26", 28". **Length:** 45.5-49.5". **Stock:** Synthetic; Max-4 , Timber, APG HD (2007). **Sights:** Red bar front, metal midbead. **Features:** 2-3/4", 3" chamber (3-1/2" 12 ga. only). Montefeltro rotating bolt design with dual action bars, magazine cut-off, synthetic trigger assembly, adjustable combs, shim kit, choice of buttstocks. 4-shot magazine. Introduced 2006. Imported from Italy by Benelli USA.
Price: .... $549.00 to $669.00
Price: Rifle slug model .... $829.00 to $929.00

BENELLI NOVA

Gauge: 12, 20. **Barrel:** 24", 26", 28". **Stock:** Black synthetic, Max-4, Timber and APG HD. **Sights:** Red bar. **Features:** 2-3/ 4", 3" chamber (3-1/2" 12 ga. only). Montefeltro rotating bolt design with dual action bars, magazine cut-off, synthetic trigger assembly, 4-shot magazine. Introduced 1999. Field & Slug Combo has 24" barrel and rifled bore; open rifle sights; synthetic stock; weighs 8.1 lbs. Imported from Italy by Benelli USA.
PrPrice: Max-4 HD camo stock $499.00
Price: H₂0 model, black synthetic, matte nickel finish $599.00
Price: APG HD stock , 20 ga. (2007) $529.00
Price: Tactical, 18.5" barrel, Ghost Ring sight $429.00
Price: Black synthetic youth stock, 20 ga. $429.00
Price: APG HD stock (2007), 20 ga.. .... $529.00

BROWNING BPS

Gauge: 10, 12, 3-1/2" chamber; 12, 16, or 20, 3" chamber (2-3/4" in target guns), 28, 2-3/4" chamber, 5-shot magazine, .410, 3" chamber. **Barrel:** 10 ga.-24" Buck Special, 28", 30", 32" Invector; 12, 20 ga.-22", 24", 26", 28", 30", 32" (Imp. Cyl., Mod. or Full), .410-26" barrel. (Imp. Cyl., Mod. and Full choke tubes.) Also available with Invector choke tubes, 12 or 20 ga.; Upland Special has 22" barrel with Invector tubes. BPS 3" and 3-1/2" have back-bored barrel. **Weight:** 7 lbs., 8 oz. (28" barrel). **Length:** 48.75" overall (28" barrel). **Stock:** 14.25"x1.5"x2.5". Select walnut, semi-beavertail forend, full pistol grip stock. **Features:** All 12 gauge 3" guns except Buck Special and game guns have back-bored barrels with Invector Plus choke tubes. Bottom feeding and ejection, receiver top safety, high post vent rib. Double action bars eliminate binding. Vent rib barrels only. All 12 and 20 gauge guns with 3" chamber available with fully engraved receiver flats at no extra cost. Each gauge has its own unique game scene. Introduced 1977. Stalker is same gun as the standard BPS except all exposed metal parts have a matte blued finish and the stock has a black finish with a black recoil pad. Available in 10 ga. (3-1/2") and 12 ga. with 3" or 3-1/2" chamber, 22", 28", 30" barrel with Invector choke system. Introduced 1987. Rifled Deer Hunter is similar to the standard BPS except has newly designed receiver/magazine tube/barrel mounting system to eliminate play, heavy 20.5" barrel with rifle-type sights with adjustable rear, solid receiver scope mount, "rifle" stock dimensions for scope or open sights, sling swivel studs. Gloss or matte finished wood with checkering, polished blue metal. Introduced 1992.

Imported from Japan by Browning.
Price: .... $900.00 to $980.00 (3.5")

BROWNING BPS 10 GAUGE SERIES

Similar to the standard BPS except completely covered with Mossy Oak Shadow Grass camouflage. Available with 26" and 28" barrel. Introduced 1999. Imported by Browning
Price: Mossy Oak camo .... $900.00 to $980.00
Price: Synthetic stock, Stalker $760.00

BROWNING BPS NWTF TURKEY SERIES PUMP SHOTGUN

Similar to the standard BPS except has full coverage Mossy Oak Break-Up camo finish on synthetic stock, forearm and exposed metal parts. Offered in 12 gauge, 3" or 3-1/2" chamber; 24" bbl. has extra-full choke tube and HiViz fiber-optic sights. Introduced 2001. From Browning.
Price: $900.00
Price: 3.5" $980.00

BROWNING BPS MICRO PUMP

Similar to the BPS Stalker except 20 ga. only, 22" Invector barrel, stock has pistol grip with recoil pad. Length of pull is 13.25"; weighs 6 lbs., 12 oz. Introduced 1986.
Price: $600.00

BROWING BPS HIGH CAPACITY PUMP

Gauge: .410 bore. 3" chamber. **Barrel:** 20" fixed Cylinder choke; stainless Steel; Matte finish. **Weight:** 6 lbs. **Length:** 40.75". **Stock:** Black composite on All Weather with matte finish. **Features:** Forged and machined steel; satin nickel finish. Bottom ejection; dual steel action bars; top tang safety. HiViz Tactical fiber-optic front sight; stainless internal mechanism; swivel studs installed. 5 total magazine capacity.
Price: Synthetic $800.00
Price: Wood $730.00

CZ 612

Gauge: 12. Chambered for all shells up to 3 ½ inches. **Capacity:** 5 I 1, magazine plug included with Wildfowl Magnum. **Barrel length:** 18.5 inches (Home Defense), 20 (HC-P), 26 inches (Wildfowl Mag). **Weight:** 6 to 6.8 pounds. **Stock:** Polymer. **Finish:** Matte black or full camo (Wildfowl Mag.) HC-P model has pistol grip stock, fiber optic front sight and ghost-ring rear.
Price: Wildfowl Magnum $409.00
Price: Home Defense .... $290.00 to $350.00 (HC-P)

EMF OLD WEST (SLIDE ACTION)

Gauge: 12. **Barrel:** 20". **Weight:** 7 lbs. **Length:** 39-1/2" overall. **Stock:** Smooth walnut with cushioned pad. **Sights:** Front bead. **Features:** Authentic reproduction of Winchester 1897 pump shotgun; blue receiver and barrel; standard modified choke. Introduced 2006. Imported from China for EMF by TTN.
Price: $449.90

ESCORT

Gauge: 12, 20; 3" chamber. **Barrel:** 18" (AimGuard and MarineGuard), 22" (Youth Pump), 26", and 28" lengths. **Weight:** 6.7-7.0 lbs. **Stock:** Polymer in black, Shadow Grass® camo or Obsession® camo finish. Two adjusting spacers included. Youth model has Trio recoil pad. **Sights:** Bead or Spark front sights, depending on model. AimGuard and MarineGuard models have blade front sights. **Features:** Black-

Prices given are believed to be accurate at time of publication however, many factors affect retail pricing so exact prices are not possible.

68TH EDITION, 2014 ✦ **505**

chrome or dipped camo metal parts, top of receiver dovetailed for sight mounts, gold plated trigger, trigger guard safety, magazine cut-off. Three choke tubes (IC, M, F) except AimGuard/MarineGuard which are cylinder bore. Models include: FH, FH Youth, AimGuard and Marine Guard. Introduced in 2003. Imported from Turkey by Legacy Sports International.

Price: .... **$389.00 to $469.00**

HARRINGTON & RICHARDSON PARDNER PUMP FIELD GUN FULL-DIP CAMO
Gauge: 12, 20; 3" chamber. **Barrel:** 28" fully rifled. **Weight:** 7.5 lbs. **Length:** 48-1/8" overall. **Stock:** Synthetic or hardwood. **Sights:** NA. **Features:** Steel receiver, double action bars, cross-bolt safety, easy takedown, vent rib, screw-in Modified choke tube. Ventilated recoil pad and grooved forend with Realtree APG-HDTM full camo dip finish.

Price: Full camo version **$278.00**

IAC MODEL 87W-1 LEVER-ACTION
Gauge: 12; 2-3/4" chamber only. **Barrel:** 20" with fixed Cylinder choke. **Weight:** NA. **Length:** NA. **Stock:** American walnut. **Sights:** Bead front. **Features:** Modern replica of Winchester Model 1887 lever-action shotgun. Includes five-shot tubular magazine, pivoting split-lever design to meet modern safety requirements. Imported by Interstate Arms Corporation.

Price: **$429.95**

ITHACA MODEL 37 FEATHERWEIGHT
Gauge: 12, 20, 16, 28 (4+1 capacity). Barrel: 26, 28 or 30" with 3" chambers (12 and 20 ga.), plain or ventiltate rib. Weight: 6.1 to 7.6 lbs. Stock: Fancy grade black walnut with Pachmayr Decelerator recoil pad. Checkered fore-end made of matching walnut. Features: Receiver machined from a single block of steel or aluminum. Barrel is steel shot compatible. Three Briley choke tubes provided. Available in several variations including turkey, home defense, tactical and high-grade.

Price: 12, 16 or 20 ga. from ...**$759.00** (plain barrel) **$859.00 (vent rib)**
Price: 28 ga. from **$999.00**

ITHACA DEERSLAYER III SLUG
Gauge: 12, 20; 3» chamber. **Barrel:** 26" fully rifled, heavy fluted with 1:28 twist for 12 ga.; 1:24 for 20 ga. **Weight:** 8.14 lbs. to 9.5 lbs. with scope mounted. **Length:** 45.625" overall. **Stock:** Fancy black walnut stock and forend. **Sights:** NA. **Features:** Updated, slug-only version of the classic Model 37. Bottom ejection, blued barrel and receiver.

Price: **$1,189.00**

MOSSBERG MODEL 835 ULTI-MAG
Gauge: 12, 3-1/2" chamber. **Barrel:** Ported 24" rifled bore, 24", 28", Accu-Mag choke tubes for steel or lead shot. **Weight:** 7.75 lbs. **Length:** 48.5" overall. **Stock:** 14"x1.5"x2.5". Dual Comb. Cut-checkered hardwood or camo synthetic; both have recoil pad. **Sights:** White bead front, brass mid-bead; fiber-optic rear. **Features:** Shoots 2-3/4", 3" or 3-1/2" shells. Back-bored and ported barrel to reduce recoil, improve patterns. Ambidextrous thumb safety, twin extractors, dual slide bars. Mossberg Cablelock included. Introduced 1988.

Price: Thumbhole Turkey ....**$559.00 to $600.00**
Price: Turkey Thug **$687.00**
Price: Waterfowl **$497.00**
Price: Combo **$636.00**

MOSSBERG MODEL 500 SPORTING
Gauge: 12, 20, .410, 3" chamber. **Barrel:** 18.5" to 28" with fixed or Accu-Choke, plain or vent rib. **Weight:** 6-1/4 lbs. (.410), 7-1/4 lbs. (12). **Length:** 48" overall (28" barrel). **Stock:** 14"x1.5"x2.5". Walnut-stained hardwood, black synthetic, Mossy Oak Advantage camouflage. Cut-checkered grip and forend. **Sights:** White bead

front, brass mid-bead; fiber-optic. **Features:** Ambidextrous thumb safety, twin extractors, disconnecting safety, dual action bars. Quiet Carry forend. Many barrels are ported. From Mossberg.

Price: Turkey, from **$466.00**
Price: Waterfowl, from **$537.00**
Price: Combo, from **$593.00**
Price: Field, from **$401.00**
Price: Slugster, from **$434.00**

MOSSBERG 510 MINI BANTAM PUMP
Gauge: 20 & .410 ga., 3" chamber. **Barrel:** 18 1/2 " vent-rib. **Weight:** 5 lbs. **Length:** 34 3/4". **Stock:** Synthetic withoption Mossy Oak Break-Up Infinity **Features:** Available in either 20 gauge or .410 bore, the Mini features an 18 1/2 " vent-rib barrel with dual-bead sights. Parents don't have to worry about their young shooter growing out of this gun too quick, the adjustable classic stock can be adjusted from 10 1/2" to 11 1/2" length of pull so the Mini can grow with your child. This adjustability also helps provide a proper fit for young shooters and allowing for a more safe and enjoyable shooting experience. Weighing in at 5 pounds and only 34 3/4" long, the 510 Mini proves that big things do come in small packages.

Price: From ....**$451.00 to $484.00**

MOSSBERG MODEL 500 BANTAM PUMP
Same as the Model 500 Sporting Pump except 12 or 20 gauge, 22" vent rib Accu-Choke barrel with choke tube set; has 1" shorter stock, reduced length from pistol grip to trigger, reduced forend reach. Introduced 1992.

Price: **$401.00**
Price: Combo with extra slug barrel **$456.00**

NEW ENGLAND PARDNER
Gauge: 12 ga., 3". **Barrel:** 28" vent rib, screw-in Modified choke tube. **Weight:** 7.5 lbs. **Length:** 48.5". **Stock:** American walnut, grooved forend, ventilated recoil pad. **Sights:** Bead front. **Features:** Machined steel receiver, double action bars, five-shot magazine.

Price: **$265.00**

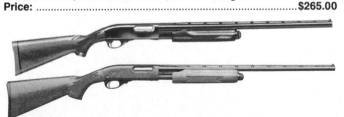

REMINGTON MODEL 870 WINGMASTER
Gauge: 12, 20, 28 ga., .410 bore. **Barrel:** 25", 26", 28", 30" (RemChokes). **Weight:** 7-1/4 lbs. **Length:** 46", 48". **Stock:** Walnut, hardwood. **Sights:** Single bead (Twin bead Wingmaster). **Features:** Light contour barrel. Double action bars, cross-bolt safety, blue finish. LW is 28 gauge and .410-bore only, 25" vent rib barrel with RemChoke tubes, high-gloss wood finish. Gold-plated trigger, American B Grade walnut stock and forend, high-gloss finish, fleur-de-lis checkering.

Price: .... **$818.00 to $929.00**

REMINGTON MODEL 870 MARINE MAGNUM
Similar to 870 Wingmaster except all metal plated with electroless nickel, black synthetic stock and forend. Has 18" plain barrel (cyl.), bead front sight, 7-shot magazine. Introduced 1992. XCS version with

Prices given are believed to be accurate at time of publication however, many factors affect retail pricing so exact prices are not possible.

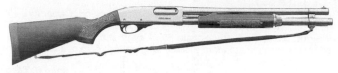

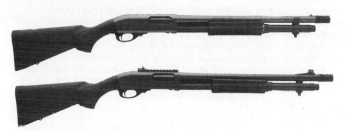

TriNyte corrosion control introduced 2007.
Price: **$829.00**

REMINGTON MODEL 870 CLASSIC TRAP
Similar to Model 870 Wingmaster except has 30" vent rib, light contour barrel, singles, mid- and long-handicap choke tubes, semi-fancy American walnut stock, high-polish blued receiver with engraving. Chamber 2.75". From Remington Arms Co.
Price: **$1,039.00**

REMINGTON MODEL 870 EXPRESS
Similar to Model 870 Wingmaster except laminate, synthetic black, or camo stock with solid, black recoil pad and pressed checkering on grip and forend. Outside metal surfaces have black oxide finish. Comes with 26" or 28" vent rib barrel with mod. RemChoke tube. ShurShot Turkey (2008) has ShurShot synthetic pistol-grip thumbhole design, extended forend, Mossy Oak Obsession camouflage, matte black metal finish, 21" vent rib barrel, twin beads, Turkey Extra Full Rem Choke tube. Receiver drilled and tapped for mounting optics. ShurShot FR CL (Fully Rifled Cantilever, 2008) includes compact 23" fully-rifled barrel with integrated cantilever scope mount.
Price: ....**$411.00 to $571.00**

REMINGTON MODEL 870 EXPRESS SUPER MAGNUM
Similar to Model 870 Express except 28" vent rib barrel with 3-1/2" chamber, vented recoil pad. Introduced 1998. Model 870 Express Super Magnum Waterfowl (2008) is fully camouflaged with Mossy Oak Duck Blind pattern, 28-inch vent rib Rem Choke barrel, "Over Decoys" Choke tube (.007") fiber-optic HiViz single bead front sight; front and rear sling swivel studs, padded black sling.
Price: ....**$462.00 to $620.00**

REMINGTON MODEL 870 SPECIAL PURPOSE (SPS)
Similar to the Model 870 Express synthetic, chambered for 12 ga. 3" and 3-1/2" shells, has Realtree Hardwoods HD or APG HD camo-synthetic stock and metal treatment, TruGlo fiber-optic sights. Introduced 2001. SPS Max Gobbler introduced 2007. Knoxx SpecOps adjustable stock, Williams Fire Sights fiber-optic sights, R3 recoil pad, Realtree APG HD camo. Drilled and tapped for Weaver-style rail
Price: SPS 12 ga. 3" $671.00
Price: SPS Super Mag Max Gobbler (2007) $819.00
Price: SPS Super Mag Max Turkey
ShurShot 3-1/2" (2008).................................$644.00
Price: SPS Synthetic ShurShot FR Cantilever 3" (2008)...........$671.00

REMINGTON MODEL 870 EXPRESS TACTICAL
Similar to Model 870 but in 12 gauge only (2-2/4" and 3" interchangeably) with 18.5" barrel, Tactical RemChoke extended/ported choke tube, black synthetic buttstock and forend, extended magazine tube, gray powdercoat finish overall. 38.5" overall length, weighs 7.5 lbs.
Price: **$372.00**
Price: Model 870 TAC Desert Recon; desert camo stock
and sand-toned metal surfaces **$692.00**
Price: Model 870 Express Tactical with Ghost Ring Sights;
Top-mounted accessories rail and XS ghost ring
rear sight **$505.00**

REMINGTON MODEL 870 SPS SHURSHOT SYNTHETIC SUPER SLUG
Gauge: 12; 2-3/4" and 3" chamber, interchangeable. **Barrel:** 25.5" extra-heavy, fully rifled pinned to receiver. **Weight:** 7-7/8 lbs **Length:** 47" overall. **Features:** Pump-action model based on 870 platform. SuperCell recoil pad. Drilled and tapped for scope mounts with Weaver rail included. Matte black metal surfaces, Mossy Oak Treestand Shurshot buttstock and forend.
Price: **$829.00**
Price: 870 SPS ShurShot Synthetic Cantilever; cantilever
scope mount and Realtree Hardwoods camo
buttstock and forend **$532.00**
Price: 870 SPS ShurShot Synthetic Turkey; adjustable
sights and APG HD camo buttstock and forend **$532.00**

REMINGTON 870 EXPRESS SYNTHETIC SUPER MAG TURKEY-WATERFOWL CAMO
Pump action shotgun chambered in 12-ga., 2-3/4 to 3-1/2 inch. Features include full Mossy Oak Bottomland camo coverage; 26-inch barrel with HiViz fiber-optics sights; Wingmaster HD Waterfowl and Turkey Extra Full RemChokes; SuperCell recoil pad; drilled and tapped receiver.
Price: **$601.00**

REMINGTON 870 EXPRESS SYNTHETIC TURKEY CAMO
Pump action shotgun chambered for 2-3/4 and 3-inch 12-ga. Features include 21-inch vent rib bead-sighted barrel; standard Express finish on barrel and receiver; Turkey Extra Full RemChoke; synthetic stock with integrated sling swivel attachment.
Price: **$445.00**

Prices given are believed to be accurate at time of publication however, many factors affect retail pricing so exact prices are not possible.

68TH EDITION, 2014 ⊕ **507**

REMINGTON 870 SUPER MAG TURKEY-PREDATOR CAMO WITH SCOPE

Pump action shotgun chambered in 12-ga., 2-3/4 to 3-1/2 inch. Features include 20-inch barrel; TruGlo red/green selectable illuminated sight mounted on pre-installed Weaver-style rail; black padded sling; Wingmaster HD™ Turkey/Predator RemChoke; full Mossy Oak Obsession camo coverage; ShurShot pistol grip stock with black overmolded grip panels; TruGlo 30mm Red/Green Dot Scope pre-mounted.

Price: **$679.00**

REMINGTON MODEL 887 NITRO MAG

Gauge: 12; 3.5", 3", and 2-3/4" chambers. **Barrel:** 28". **Features:** Pump-action model based on the Model 870. Interchangeable shells, black matte ArmoLokt rustproof coating throughout. SuperCell recoil pad. Solid rib and Hi-Viz front sight with interchangeable light tubes. Black synthetic stock with contoured grip panels.

Price: **$436.00**
Price: Model 887 Nitro Mag Waterfowl, camo **$532.00**

REMINGTON 887 NITRO MAG CAMO COMBO

Pump action shotgun chambered in 12-ga., 2-3/4 to 3-1/2 inch. Features include 22-inch turkey barrel with HiViz fiber-optic rifle sights and 28-inch waterfowl with a HiViz sight; extended Waterfowl and Super Full Turkey RemChokes are included; SuperCell recoil pad; synthetic stock and forend with specially contoured grip panels; full camo coverage.

Price: **$728.00**

STEVENS MODEL 350

Pump-action shotgun chambered for 2.5- and 3-inch 12-ga. Features include all-steel barrel and receiver; bottom-load and -eject design; black synthetic stock; 5+1 capacity.

Price: Field Model with 28-inch barrel, screw-in choke **$267.00**
Price: Security Model with 18-inch barrel, fixed choke **$241.00**
Price: Combo Model with Field and Security barrels **$307.00**
Price: Security Model with 18.25-inch barrel w/ghost ring
rear sight **$254.00**

STOEGER P-350

Gauge: 12. Designed to fire any 12-gauge ammunition. **Capacity:** 4+1. **Barrel:** 18.5, 20, 24, 26 or 28 inches, with ventilated rib. **Weight:** 6.6 to 7 pounds. **Stock:** Black synthetic, or Realtree APG or Max-4 camo in standard stock configuration. Also available with vertical pistol-style handgrip.

Price: .... **$349 to $479**

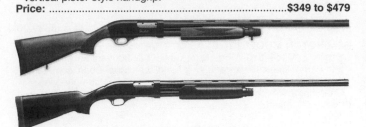

WEATHERBY PA-08 SERIES

Gauge: 12 ga. chamber. **Barrel:** 26" and 28" flat ventilated rib. **Weight:** 6.5 lbs. -7 lbs. **Stock:** Walnut. **Features:** The PA-08 # Walnut stock with gloss finish, all metalwork is gloss black for a distinctive look, vented top rib dissipates heat and aids in target acquisition. Comes with 3 application-specific choke tubes (IC/M/F). Made in Turkey.

Price: PA-08 Upland **$449.00**
Price: PA-08 Synthetic (New 2011) **$399.00**

WEATHERBY PA-459 TURKEY

Gauge: 12, 3-inch chamber. **Barrel:** 21.25 inches. **Stock:** Synthetic with Mothwing Spring Mimicry camo, rubber texturized grip areas. **Features:** Vertical pistol grip, Mil-Spec Picatinny accessory rail with adjustable rear ghost-ring sight, AR type front sight.

Price: **$549.00**

WINCHESTER SUPER X

Gauge: 12, 3" or 3.5" chambers. **Barrel:** 18"; 26" and 28" barrels are .742" back-bored, chrome plated; Invector Plus choke tubes. **Weight:** 7 lbs. **Stock:** Walnut or composite. **Features:** Rotary bolt, four lugs, dual steel action bars. Walnut Field has gloss-finished walnut stock and forearm, cut checkering. Black Shadow Field has composite stock and forearm, non-glare matte finish barrel and receiver. Speed Pump Defender has composite stock and forearm, chromed plated, 18" cylinder choked barrel, non-glare metal surfaces, five-shot magazine, grooved forearm. Weight, 6.5 lbs. Reintroduced 2008. Made in U.S.A. from Winchester Repeating Arms Co.

Price: Black Shadow Field, 3" **$380.00**
Price: Black Shadow Field, 3.5" **$430.00**
Price: Defender $350 to **$370.00**
Price: Waterfowl Hunter 3" **$460.00**
Price: Waterfowl Hunter 3.5" **$500.00**
Price: Turkey Hunter 3.5" **$520.00**
Price: Field **$400.00**
Price: Deer **$520.00**

Prices given are believed to be accurate at time of publication however, many factors affect retail pricing so exact prices are not possible.

BERETTA DT10 TRIDENT
Gauge: 12, 2-3/4", 3" chambers. **Barrel:** 28", 30", 34"; competition-style vent rib; fixed or Optima choke tubes. **Weight:** 8 lbs. **Stock:** High-grade walnut stock with oil finish; hand-checkered grip and forend, adjustable stocks available. **Features:** Detachable, adjustable trigger group, raised and thickened receiver, forend iron has adjustment nut to guarantee wood-to-metal fit. Introduced 2000. Imported from Italy by Beretta USA.
Price: DT10 Trident Trap, adjustable stock............................$8,650.00
Price: DT10 Trident Skeet..$8,050.00
Price: DT10 Trident Sporting, from $7,500.00

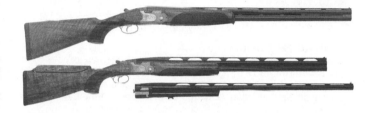

BERETTA SERIES 682 GOLD E SKEET, TRAP, SPORTING O/U
Gauge: 12, 2-3/4" chambers. **Barrel:** skeet-28"; trap-30" and 32", Imp. Mod. & Full and Mobilchoke; trap mono shotguns-32" and 34" Mobilchoke; trap top single guns-32" and 34" Full and Mobilchoke; trap combo sets-from 30" O/U, to 32" O/U, 34" top single. **Stock:** Close-grained walnut, hand checkered. **Sights:** White Bradley bead front sight and center bead. **Features:** Receiver has Greystone gunmetal gray finish with gold accents. Trap Monte Carlo stock has deluxe trap recoil pad. Various grades available. Imported from Italy by Beretta USA.
Price: 682 Gold E Trap with adjustable stock.........................$4,800.00
Price: 682 Gold E Sporting $4,600.00
Price: 682 Gold E Skeet, adjustable stock $4,800.00

BERETTA 686 ONYX O/U
Gauge: 12, 20, 28; 3", 3.5" chambers. **Barrel:** 26", 28" (Mobilchoke tubes). **Weight:** 6.8-6.9 lbs. **Stock:** Checkered American walnut. **Features:** Intended for the beginning sporting clays shooter. Has wide, vented target rib, radiused recoil pad. Polished black finish on receiver and barrels. Introduced 1993. Imported from Italy by Beretta U.S.A.
Price: White Onyx $2,240.00
PPrice: White Onyx Sporting..$2,460.00

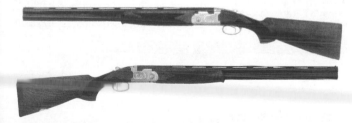

BERETTA 686/687 SILVER PIGEON SERIES O/U
Gauge: 12, 20, 28, 3" chambers (2-3/4" 28 ga.). .410 bore, 3" chamber. **Barrel:** 26", 28". **Weight:** 6.8 lbs. **Stock:** Checkered walnut. **Features:** Interchangeable barrels (20 and 28 ga.), single selective gold-plated trigger, boxlock action, auto safety, Schnabel forend.
Price: 686 Silver Pigeon Grade I...$2,240.00
Price: 687 Grade III..$3,430.00
Price: 687 Grade V...$4,075.00

BERETTA MODEL 692 SPORTING
Gauge: 12, 3-inch chamber. **Barrels:** 30 inches with long forcing cones of approximately 14 inches. Receiver is ½-inch wider than 682 model for improved handling. **Stock:** Hand rubbed oil finished select walnut with Schnabel fore-end. Features include selective single adjustable trigger, manual safety, tapered 8mm to 10mm rib.
Price: .... $4,755.00 to $5,225.00

BERETTA DT11
Gauge: 12. 3-inch chambers. Competition model offered in Sporting, Skeet and Trap models. **Barrels:** 30, 32, 34 inches. Top rib has hollowed bridges. **Stock:** Hand-checkered buttstock and fore-end. Hand-rubbed oil, Tru-Oil or wax finish. Adjustable comb on skeet and trap models. Newly designed receiver, top lever, safety/selector button.
Price: From $8,999

BERETTA SV10 PERENNIA
Gauge: 12, 20. 3-inch chambers. **Barrels:** 26 or 28 inches. **Weight:** 6.5 to 7.3 pounds. **Stock:** Oil-finished walnut with semi-beavertail fore-end, newly designed fore-end latching system. Kick-Off recoil reduction system is optional. Ejection system can be set to automatic or extractors only. Floral engraving. Perennia III model has higher-grade wood, removable trigger group, and more engraving. Also available in SV10 Prevail Sporting and Trap models.
Price: Perennia I $2,890.00
Price: Perennia III $3,620.00
Price: Prevail Sporting ....$2,900.00 to $3,300.00
Price: Prevail Trap $3,000.00

BERETTA ULTRALIGHT O/U
Gauge: 12, 2-3/4" chambers. **Barrel:** 26", 28", Mobilchoke tubes. **Weight:** About 5 lbs., 13 oz. **Stock:** Select American walnut with checkered grip and forend. **Features:** Low-profile aluminum alloy receiver with titanium breech face insert. Electroless nickel receiver with game scene engraving. Single selective trigger; automatic safety. Introduced 1992. Ultralight Deluxe except has matte electroless nickel finish receiver with gold game scene engraving; matte oil-finished, select walnut stock and forend. Imported from Italy by Beretta U.S.A.
Price: $2,075.00
Price: Ultralight Deluxe $2,450.00

BLASER F3 SUPERSPORT O/U
Gauge: 12 ga., 3" chamber. **Barrel:** 32". **Weight:** 9 lbs. **Stock:** Adustable semi-custom, turkish walnut wood grade: 4. **Features:** The latest addition to the F3 family is the F3 SuperSport. The perfect blend of overall weight, balance and weight distribution make the F3 SuperSport the ideal competitor. Briley Spectrum-5 chokes, free floating barrels, adjustable barrel hanger system on o/u, chrome plated barrels full length, revolutionary ejector ball system, barrels finished in a powder coated nitride, selectable competition trigger.
Price: From $7,250.00

BROWNING CYNERGY O/U
Gauge: .410, 12, 20, 28. **Barrel:** 26", 28", 30", 32". **Stock:** Walnut or composite. **Sights:** White bead front most models; HiViz Pro-Comp sight on some models; mid bead. **Features:** Mono-Lock hinge, recoil-reducing interchangeable Inflex recoil pad, silver nitride

---

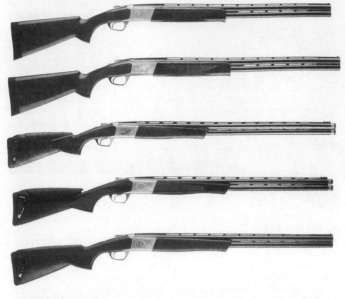

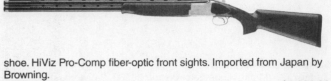

receiver; striker-based trigger, ported barrel option. Models include: Cynergy Sporting, Adjustable Comb; Cynergy Sporting Composite CF; Cynergy Field, Composite; Cynergy Classic Sporting; Cynergy Classic Field; Cynergy Camo Mossy Oak New Shadow Grass; Cynergy Camo Mossy Oak New Break-Up; and Cynergy Camo Mossy Oak Brush. Imported from Japan by Browning.

Price: Field Grade Model, 12 ga. $2,800.00
Price: Field, small gauges......................................$2,860.00
Price: Feather model, from $2,900.00
Price: Sporting, from...$4,020.00
Price: Sporting w/adjustable comb $4,500.00
Price: Sporting composite w/adjustable comb $3,870.00
Price: Classic Field, Sporting from .... $2,540.00 to $3,640.00
Price: Classic Field Grade III, from.......................$4,000.00
Price: Classic Field Grade VI, from........................$6,100.00

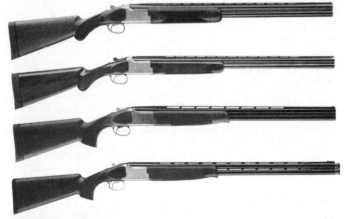

BROWNING CITORI O/U

Gauge: 12, 20, 28 and .410. **Barrel:** 26", 28" in 28 and .410. Offered with Invector choke tubes. All 12 and 20 gauge models have back-bored barrels and Invector Plus choke system. **Weight:** 6 lbs., 8 oz. (26" .410) to 7 lbs., 13 oz. (30" 12 ga.). **Length:** 43" overall (26" bbl.). **Stock:** Dense walnut, hand checkered, full pistol grip, beavertail forend. Field-type recoil pad on 12 ga. field guns and trap and skeet models. **Sights:** Medium raised beads, German nickel silver. **Features:** Barrel selector integral with safety, automatic ejectors, three-piece takedown. Citori 625 Field (intr. 2008) includes Vector Pro extended forcing cones, new wood checkering patterns, silver-nitride finish with high-relief engraving, gloss oil finish with Grade II/III walnut with radius pistol grip, Schnabel forearm, 12 gauge, three Invector Plus choke tubes. Citori 625 Sporting (intr. 2008) includes standard and adjustable combs, 32", 30", and 28" barrels, five Diamond Grade extended Invector Plus choke tubes. Triple Trigger System allows adjusting length of pull and choice of wide checkered, narrow smooth, and wide smooth canted trigger

shoe. HiViz Pro-Comp fiber-optic front sights. Imported from Japan by Browning.

Price: Lightning, from **$1,990.00**
Price: White Lightning, from **$2,070.00**
Price: Superlight Feather **$2,390.00**
Price: Lightning Feather, combo 20 and 28 ga. **$3,580.00**
Price: 625 Field, 12, 20 or 28 ga. and 410. Weighs
6 lbs. 12 oz. to 7 lbs. 14 oz. **$2,630.00**
Price: 625 Sporting, 12, 20 or 28 ga. and 410,
standard comb, intr. 2008...........................**$3,550.00**

BROWNING 725 CITORI

Gauge: 12, 3" chambers. **Barrel:** 26, 28, 30". **Weight:** 7.25 to 7.6 lbs. **Length:** 43.75 to 50". **Stock:** Gloss oil finish grade II/III walnut. Features include a new receiver that is significantly lower in profile than other 12-gauge Citori models. Other features include a mechanical trigger, Vector Pro lengthened forcing cones, three Invector-DS choke tubes, silver nitride finish with high relief engraving.

Price: 725 Field...**$2,470.00**
Price: 725 Sporting.......................................**$3,140.00**

BROWNING CITORI HIGH GRADE

Similar to standard Citori except has engraved hunting scenes and gold inlays, high-grade, hand-oiled walnut stock and forearm. Introduced 2000. From Browning.

Price: Grade IV Lightning, engraved gray receiver,
introduced 2005, from **$3,500.00**
Price: Grade VII Lightning, engraved gray or blue receiver,
introduced 2005, from **$5,560.00**

BROWNING CITORI XT TRAP O/U

Similar to the Citori XS Special except has engraved silver nitride receiver with gold highlights, vented side barrel rib. Available in 12 gauge with 30" or 32" barrels, Invector-Plus choke tubes, adjustable comb and buttplate. Introduced 1999. Imported by Browning.

Price: XT Trap **$2,960.00**
Price: XT Trap w/adjustable comb.......................**$3,390.00**
Price: XT Trap Gold w/adjustable comb, introduced 2005....**$5,720.00**

CAESAR GUERINI ELLIPSE O/U

Gauge: 12, 20, 28 gauge, also 20/28 gauge combo. **Barrel:** 28". **Weight:** 6.5 lbs. **Length:** 49.25". **Stock:** High grade walnut. **Features:** Fast as a grouse's wing tip, sleek as a pheasant's tail feather - The new Caesar Guerini Ellipse EVO represents the next generation of upland game gun. With graceful rounded action and streamlined stock it handles, feels and looks like the world's best handmade round body shotguns. We obsessed over every detail from the engraving created to accentuate the curve of the action to something

Prices given are believed to be accurate at time of publication however, many factors affect retail pricing so exact prices are not possible.

as obscure as the shape of the trigger. This is not a quick makeover of our existing models; the barrels, action and stock are all different. The Ellipse is simply the evolution of the fine over-and-under hunting gun. The Ellipse comes in a fitted case with five choke tube. The EVO is the more expensive of the two Ellipse models and as such boasts more elaborate engraving, a higher grade of walnut in the stock, and a few other aesthetic touches. Otherwise, the two are identical. $205 Additional Charge for Left Hand Stock.

Price: Upland $3,250.00
Price: Ellipse .... $4,195.00 to $5995.00
Price: EVO .... $5,950.00 to $7,975.00

CZ SPORTER
Gauge: 12, 3" chambers. **Barrel:** 30", 32" chrome-lined, back-bored with extended forcing cones. **Weight:** 9 lbs. **Length:** NA. **Stock:** Neutral cast stock with an adjustable comb, trap style forend, pistol grip and ambidextrous palm swells. #3 grade Circassian walnut. At lowest position, drop at comb: 1-5/8"; drop at heel: 2-3/8"; length of pull: 14-1/2". **Features:** Designed for Sporting Clays and FITASC competition. Hand engraving, satin black-finished receiver. Tapered rib with center bead and a red fiber-optic front bead, 10 choke tubes with wrench, single selective trigger, automatic ejectors, thin rubber pad with slick plastic top. Introduced 2008. From CZ-USA.
Price: $2509
Price: (standard grade) $1799

CZ CANVASBACK
Gauge: 12, 20, 3" chambers. **Barrel:** 26", 28". **Weight:** 7.3 lbs. **Length:** NA. **Stock:** Round-knob pistol grip, Schnabel forend, Turkish walnut. **Features:** Single selective trigger, set of 5 screw-in chokes, black chrome finished receiver. From CZ-USA.
Price: $819.00

CZ MALLARD
Gauge: 12, 20, 28, .410, 3" chambers. **Barrel:** 26". **Weight:** 7.7 lbs. **Length:** NA. **Stock:** Round-knob pistol grip, Schnabel forend, Turkish walnut. **Features:** Double triggers and extractors, coin finished receiver, multi chokes. From CZ-USA.
Price: $562.00

CZ REDHEAD
Gauge: 12, 20, .410 (3" chambers), 28 (2 3/4"). **Barrel:** 28". **Weight:** 7.4 lbs. **Length:** NA. **Stock:** Round-knob pistol grip, Schnabel forend, Turkish walnut. **Features:** Single selective triggers and extractors (12 & 20 ga.), screw-in chokes (12, 20, 28 ga.) choked IC and Mod (.410), coin finished receiver, multi chokes. From CZ-USA.
Price: Deluxe $926.00
Price: Mini (28, .410) $960.00
Price: Target $1,348.00

CZ SUPER SCROLL COMBO
Gauge: 20 and 28 combo. **Barrels:** 30 inches for both gauges with five choke tubes for each set. **Stock:** Grave V Turkish walnut with Schnabel fore-end, rounded grip. **Weight:** 6.7 pounds. **Features:** Ornate hand-engraved scrollwork on receiver, faux sideplates, triggerguard and mono-block. Comes in a custom-fitted aluminum case.
Price: $3,899.00

CZ UPLAND STERLING
Gauge: 12, 3-inch chambers. **Barrels:** 28 inches with ventilated rib, fiber optic sight, five choke tubes. **Stock:** Turkish walnut with stippled gripping surfaces. Weight: 7.5 pounds.
Price: $979.00

CZ WINGSHOOTER O/U
Gauge: 12, 20, 28 & .410 ga., 2-3/4" chamber. **Barrel:** 28" flat ventilated rib. **Weight:** 6.3 lbs. **Length:** 45.5". **Stock:** Turkish walnut. **Features:** This colorful Over and Under shotgun has the same old world craftsmanship as all of our shotguns but with a new stylish look. This elegant hand engraved work of art is available in four gauges and its eye-catching engraving will stand alone in the field or range. 12 and 20 gauge models have auto ejectors, while the 28

gauge and .410 have extractors only. Heavily engraved scroll work with special side plate design, mechanical selective triggers, box Lock frame design, 18 LPI checkering, coil spring operated hammers, chrome lined, 5 interchangeable choke tubes and special engraved skeleton butt plate.
Price: $1,040.00

ESCORT OVER/UNDER
Gauge: 12, 3" chamber. **Barrel:** 28". **Weight:** 7.4 lbs. **Stock:** Walnut or select walnut with Trio recoil pad; synthetic stock with adjustable comb. Three adjustment spacers. **Sights:** Bronze front bead. **Features:** Blued barrels, blued or nickel receiver. Trio recoil pad. Five interchangeable chokes (SK, IC, M, IM, F); extractors or ejectors (new, 2008), barrel selector. Hard case available. Introduced 2007. Imported from Turkey by Legacy Sports International.
Price: $599.00

FAUSTI CLASSIC ROUND BODY
Gauge: 16, 20, 28. **Barrels:** 28 or 30". **Weight:** 5.8 to 6.3 lbs. **Length:** 45.5 to 47.5". **Stock:** Turkish walnut Prince of Wales style with oil finish. Features include automatic ejectors, single selective trigger, laser-engraved receiver.
Price: 20 gauge...$4,199.00
Price: 16 gauge...$4,299.00
Price: 28 gauge...$4,599.00

FN SC-1
Gauge: 12. 2-3/4" chamber. **Barrels:** 28 or 30 inches, ported with ventilated rib, Invector-Plus extended choke tubes. **Stock:** Laminated black or blue with adjustable comb and length-of-pull. Weight: 8 pounds.
Price: $2,499.00

FRANCHI ASPIRE
Gauge: 28 or .410. **Barrels:** 28 inches with ventilated rib and fiber optic front sight. **Stock:** Oil-finished checkered walnut with rounded pistol grip. **Weight:** 5.8 pounds. **Features:** Slim, round-action receiver with case-colored finish.
Price: $2,299.00

FRANCHI INSTINCT SERIES
Gauge: 12, 20 with 3" chambers. **Barrels:** 26 or 28". **Weight:** 5.3 to 6.4 lbs. **Length:** 42.5 to 44.5". **Stock:** AA-grade satin walnut (LS), A-grade (L) with rounded pistol grip and recoil pad. Single trigger, automatic ejectors, tang safety, choke tubes. LS model has aluminum alloy receiver, L model has steel receiver.
Price: (Instinct L)..$1149
Price: (Instinct LS) $1349

KOLAR SPORTING CLAYS O/U
Gauge: 12, 2 3/4" chambers. **Barrel:** 30", 32", 34"; extended choke tubes. **Stock:** 14-5/8"x2.5"x1-7/8"x1-3/8". French walnut. Four stock versions available. **Features:** Single selective trigger, detachable, adjustable for length; overbored barrels with long forcing cones; flat tramline rib; matte blue finish. Made in U.S. by Kolar.
Price: Standard...$9,595.00
Price: Prestige..$14,190.00
Price: Elite Gold..$16,590.00
Price: Legend..$17,090.00
Price: Select..$22,590.00
Price: Custom ....Price on request

Prices given are believed to be accurate at time of publication however, many factors affect retail pricing so exact prices are not possible.

KOLAR AAA COMPETITION TRAP O/U

Similar to the Sporting Clays gun except has 32" O/U /34" Unsingle or 30" O/U /34" Unsingle barrels as an over/under, unsingle, or combination set. Stock dimensions are 14.5"x2.5"x1.5"; American or French walnut; step parallel rib standard. Contact maker for full listings. Made in U.S.A. by Kolar.
Price: from $10,995.00

KOLAR AAA COMPETITION SKEET O/U

Similar to the Sporting Clays gun except has 28" or 30" barrels with Kolarite AAA sub gauge tubes; stock of American or French walnut with matte finish; flat tramline rib; under barrel adjustable for point of impact. Many options available. Contact maker for complete listing. Made in U.S.A. by Kolar.
Price: $12,395.00

KRIEGHOFF K-80 SPORTING CLAYS O/U

Gauge: 12. **Barrel:** 28", 30", 32", 34" with choke tubes. **Weight:** About 8 lbs. **Stock:** #3 Sporting stock designed for gun-down shooting. **Features:** Standard receiver with satin nickel finish and classic scroll engraving. Selective mechanical trigger adjustable for position. Choice of tapered flat or 8mm parallel flat barrel rib. Free-floating barrels. Aluminum case. Imported from Germany by Krieghoff International, Inc.
Price: Standard grade with five choke tubes, from $9,395.00

KRIEGHOFF K-80 SKEET O/U

Gauge: 12, 2-3/4" chambers. **Barrel:** 28", 30", 32", (skeet & skeet), optional choke tubes). **Weight:** About 7.75 lbs. **Stock:** American skeet or straight skeet stocks, with palm-swell grips. Walnut. **Features:** Satin gray receiver finish. Selective mechanical trigger adjustable for position. Choice of ventilated 8mm parallel flat rib or ventilated 8-12mm tapered flat rib. Introduced 1980. Imported from Germany by Krieghoff International, Inc.
Price: Standard, skeet chokes...$8,375.00
Price: Skeet Special (28", 30", 32" tapered flat rib, skeet & skeet choke tubes) $9,100.00

KRIEGHOFF K-80 TRAP O/U

Gauge: 12, 2-3/4" chambers. **Barrel:** 30", 32" (Imp. Mod. & Full or choke tubes). **Weight:** About 8.5 lbs. **Stock:** Four stock dimensions or adjustable stock available; all have palm-swell grips. Checkered European walnut. **Features:** Satin nickel receiver. Selective mechanical trigger, adjustable for position. Ventilated step rib. Introduced 1980. Imported from Germany by Krieghoff International, Inc.
Price: K-80 O/U (30", 32", Imp. Mod. & Full), from................$8,850.00
Price: K-80 Unsingle (32", 34", Full), standard, from...........$10,080.00
Price: K-80 Combo (two-barrel set), standard, from $13,275.00

KRIEGHOFF K-20 O/U

Similar to the K-80 except built on a 20-gauge frame. Designed for skeet, sporting clays and field use. Offered in 20, 28 and .410; 28", 30" and 32" barrels. Imported from Germany by Krieghoff International Inc.
Price: K-20, 20 gauge, from..$9,575.00
Price: K-20, 28 gauge, from..$9,725.00
Price: K-20, .410, from..$9,725.00

LEBEAU-COURALLY BOSS-VEREES O/U

Gauge: 12, 20, 2-3/4" chambers. **Barrel:** 25" to 32". **Weight:** To customer specifications. **Stock:** Exhibition-quality French walnut. **Features:** Boss-type sidelock with automatic ejectors; single or double triggers; chopper lump barrels. A custom gun built to customer specifications. Imported from Belgium by Wm. Larkin Moore.
Price: From $96,000.00

LJUTIC LM-6 SUPER DELUXE O/U

Gauge: 12. **Barrel:** 28" to 34"; choked to customer specs for live birds, trap, international trap. **Weight:** To customer specs. **Stock:** To customer specs. Oil finish, hand checkered. **Features:** Custom-made gun. Hollow-milled rib, pull or release trigger, push-button opener in front of trigger guard. From Ljutic Industries.
Price: Super Deluxe LM-6 O/U...$19,995.00
Price: Over/Under combo (interchangeable single barrel, two trigger guards, one for single trigger, one for doubles)..$27,995.00
Price: Extra over/under barrel sets, 29"-32".........................$6,995.00

MERKEL MODEL 2001EL O/U

Gauge: 12, 20, 3" chambers, 28, 2-3/4" chambers. **Barrel:** 12-28"; 20, 28 ga.-26.75". **Weight:** About 7 lbs. (12 ga.). **Stock:** Oil-finished walnut; English or pistol grip. **Features:** Self-cocking Blitz boxlock action with cocking indicators; Kersten double cross-bolt lock; silver-grayed receiver with engraved hunting scenes; coil spring ejectors; single selective or double triggers. Imported from Germany by Merkel USA.
Price: $9,995.00
Price: Model 2001EL Sporter; full pistol grip stock $9,995.00

MERKEL MODEL 2000CL O/U

Similar to Model 2001EL except scroll-engraved case-hardened receiver; 12, 20, 28 gauge. Imported from Germany by Merkel USA.
Price: $8,495.00
Price: Model 2016 CL; 16 gauge $8,495.00

MOSSBERG SILVER RESERVE II O/U

Gauge: 12, 3-inch chambers. **Barrels:** 28 inches with ventilated rib, choke tubes. **Stock:** Select black walnut with satin finish. **Sights:** Metal bead. Available with extractors or automatic ejectors. Also offered in Sporting model with adjustable comb, 30-inch barrels with wide rib, fiber optic front and middle bead sights.
Price: Field ....$693 to $776 (ejectors)
Price: Sporting $1180

PERAZZI MX8/MX8 TRAP/SKEET O/U

Gauge: 12, 20 2 ¾" chambers. **Barrel:** Trap: 29.5" (Imp. Mod. & Extra Full), 31.5" (Full & Extra Full). Choke tubes optional. Skeet: 27-5/8" (skeet & skeet). **Weight:** About 8.5 lbs. (trap); 7 lbs., 15 oz. (skeet). **Stock:** Interchangeable and custom made to customer specs. **Features:** Has detachable and interchangeable trigger group with flat V springs. Flat 7/16" vent rib. Many options available. Imported from Italy by Perazzi U.S.A., Inc.
Price: Trap from $17,370.00
Price: Skeet from $14,221.00

PERAZZI MX8 O/U

Gauge: 12, 20 2 ¾" chambers. **Barrel:** 28-3/8" (Imp. Mod. & Extra Full), 29.5" (choke tubes). **Weight:** 7 lbs., 12 oz. **Stock:** Special specifications. **Features:** Has single selective trigger; flat 7/16" x 5/16" vent rib. Many options available. Imported from Italy by Perazzi U.S.A., Inc.
Price: Standard, from $9,860.00
Price: Sporting, from $12,204.00
Price: SC3 Grade (variety of engraving patterns) from $21,000.00
Price: SCO Grade (more intricate engraving/inlays) from ...$36,000.00

PERAZZI MX8/20 O/U

Similar to the MX8 except has smaller frame and has a removable trigger mechanism. Available in trap, skeet, sporting or game models with fixed chokes or choke tubes. Stock is made to customer specifications. Introduced 1993. Imported from Italy by Perazzi U.S.A., Inc.
Price: From $12,204.00

Prices given are believed to be accurate at time of publication however, many factors affect retail pricing so exact prices are not possible.

PERAZZI MX12 HUNTING O/U
Gauge: 12, 2-3/4" chambers. **Barrel:** 26.75", 27.5", 28-3/8", 29.5" (Mod. & Full); choke tubes available in 27-5/8", 29.5" only (MX12C). **Weight:** 7 lbs., 4 oz. **Stock:** To customer specs; interchangeable. **Features:** Single selective trigger; coil springs used in action; Schnabel forend tip. Imported from Italy by Perazzi U.S.A., Inc.
Price: From $12,698.00
Price: MX12C (with choke tubes) from $13,316.00

PERAZZI MX20 HUNTING O/U
Similar to the MX12 except 20 ga. frame size. Non-removable trigger group. Available in 20, 28, .410 with 2-3/4" or 3" chambers. 26" standard, and choked Mod. & Full. Weight is 6 lbs., 6 oz. Imported from Italy by Perazzi U.S.A., Inc.
Price: From $12,698.00
Price: MX20C (with choke tubes) from $13,316.00

PERAZZI MX10 O/U
Gauge: 12, 2-3/4" chambers. **Barrel:** 29.5", 31.5" (fixed chokes). **Weight:** NA. **Stock:** Walnut; cheekpiece adjustable for elevation and cast. **Features:** Adjustable rib; vent side rib. Externally selective trigger. Available in single barrel, combo, over/under trap, skeet, pigeon and sporting models. Introduced 1993. Imported from Italy by Perazzi U.S.A., Inc.
Price: MX200410 ....$13,500.00

PERAZZI MX2000S
Gauge: 12, 20 **Barrels:** 29.5, 30.75, 31.5 inches with fixed I/M and Full chokes, or interchangeable. Competition model with features similar to MX8.
Price: $13,700.00

PIOTTI BOSS O/U
Gauge: 12, 20, **Barrel:** 26" to 32", chokes as specified. **Weight:** 6.5 to 8 lbs. **Stock:** Dimensions to customer specs. Best quality figured walnut. **Features:** Essentially a custom-made gun with many options. Introduced 1993. Imported from Italy by Wm. Larkin Moore.
Price: From $69,000.00

RIZZINI S790 EMEL O/U
Gauge: 20, 28, .410. **Barrel:** 26", 27.5" (Imp. Cyl. & Imp. Mod.). **Weight:** About 6 lbs. **Stock:** 14"x1.5"x2-1/8". Extra fancy select walnut. **Features:** Boxlock action with profuse engraving; automatic ejectors; single selective trigger; silvered receiver. Comes with Nizzoli leather case. Introduced 1996. Imported from Italy by Wm. Larkin Moore & Co.
Price: From $14,600.00

RIZZINI S792 EMEL O/U
Similar to S790 EMEL except dummy sideplates with extensive engraving coverage. Nizzoli leather case. Introduced 1996. Imported from Italy by Wm. Larkin Moore & Co.
Price: From $15,500.00

RIZZINI UPLAND EL O/U
Gauge: 12, 16, 20, 28, .410. **Barrel:** 26", 27.5", Mod. & Full, Imp. Cyl. & Imp. Mod. choke tubes. **Weight:** About 6.6 lbs. **Stock:** 14.5"x1-1/2"x2.25". **Features:** Boxlock action; single selective trigger; ejectors; profuse engraving on silvered receiver. Comes with fitted case. Introduced 1996. Imported from Italy by Wm. Larkin Moore & Co.
Price: From $5,200.00

RIZZINI ARTEMIS O/U
Same as Upland EL model except dummy sideplates with extensive game scene engraving. Fancy European walnut stock. Fitted case. Introduced 1996. Imported from Italy by Wm. Larkin Moore & Co.
Price: From $3,260.00

RIZZINI S782 EMEL O/U
Gauge: 12, 2-3/4" chambers. **Barrel:** 26", 27.5" (Imp. Cyl. & Imp. Mod.). **Weight:** About 6.75 lbs. **Stock:** 14.5"x1.5"x2.25". Extra fancy select walnut. **Features:** Boxlock action with dummy sideplates, extensive engraving with gold inlaid game birds, silvered receiver, automatic ejectors, single selective trigger. Nizzoli leather case. Introduced 1996. Imported from Italy by Wm. Larkin Moore & Co.
Price: From $18,800.00

STEVENS MODEL 512 GOLD WING
Gauge: 12, 20, 28, .410; 2-3/4" and 3" chambers. **Barrel:** 26", 28". **Weight:** 6 to 8 lbs. **Sights:** NA. **Features:** Five screw-in choke tubes with 12, 20, and 28 gauge; .410 has fixed M/IC chokes. Black chrome, sculpted receiver with a raised gold pheasant, laser engraved trigger guard and forend latch. Turkish walnut stock finished in satin lacquer and beautifully laser engraved with fleur-de-lis checkering on the side panels, wrist and Schnabel forearm.
Price: $649.00

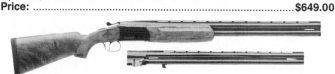

STOEGER CONDOR O/U
Gauge: 12, 20, 2-3/4" 3" chambers; 16, .410. **Barrel:** 22", 24", 26", 28", 30". **Weight:** 5.5 to 7.8 lbs. **Sights:** Brass bead. **Features:** IC, M, or F screw-in choke tubes with each gun. Oil finished hardwood with pistol grip and forend. Auto safety, single trigger, automatic extractors.
Price: from .... $449.00 to $789.00

TRISTAR FIELD HUNTER
Gauge: 12. **Barrels:** 26 or 28 inches. **Weight:** 7.2 to 7.4 pounds. Features similar to Setter series plus automatic ejectors, higher-grade wood, chrome-lined barrels, fiber-optic front sight, five choke tubes.
Price: $729.00

TRISTAR HUNTER EX O/U
Gauge: 12, 20, 28, .410. **Barrel:** 26", 28". **Weight:** 5.7 lbs. (.410); 6.0 lbs. (20, 28), 7.2-7.4 lbs, (12). Chrome-lined steel mono-block barrel, five Beretta-style choke tubes (SK, IC, M, IM, F). **Length:** NA. **Stock:** Walnut, cut checkering. 14.25"x1.5"x2-3/8". **Sights:** Brass front sight. **Features:** All have extractors, engraved receiver, sealed actions, self-adjusting locking bolts, single selective trigger, ventilated rib. 28 ga. and .410 built on true frames. Five-year warranty. Imported from Italy by Tristar Sporting Arms Ltd.
Price: From $619.00

TRISTAR SETTER
Gauge: 12, 20 with 3-inch chambers. **Barrels:** 28" (12 ga.), 26" (20 ga.) with ventilated rib, three Beretta-style choke tubes. **Weight:** 6.3 to 7.2 pounds. **Stock:** High gloss wood. Single selective trigger, extractors.
Price: $549.00

WINCHESTER MODEL 101 O/U
Gauge: 12, 2-3/4", 3" chambers. **Barrel:** 28", 30", 32", ported, Invector Plus choke system. **Weight:** 7 lbs. 6 oz. to 7 lbs. 12. oz. **Stock:** Checkered high-gloss grade II/III walnut stock, Pachmayr Decelerator sporting pad. **Features:** Chrome-plated chambers; back-bored barrels; tang barrel selector/safety; Signature extended choke tubes. Model 101 Field comes with solid brass bead front sight, three tubes, engraved receiver. Model 101 Sporting has adjustable trigger, 10mm runway rib, white mid-bead, Tru Glo front sight, 30" and 32" barrels. Camo version of Model 101 Field comes with full-coverage Mossy Oak Duck Blind pattern. Model 101 Pigeon Grade Trap has 10mm steel runway rib, mid-bead sight, interchangeable fiber-optic front sight, porting and vented side ribs, adjustable trigger shoe, fixed raised comb or adjustable comb, Grade III/IV walnut, 30" or 32" barrels, molded ABS hard case. Reintroduced 2008. From Winchester Repeating Arms. Co.
Price: Field $1,870.00
Price: Sporting $2,320.00
Price: Pigeon Grade Trap, intr. 2008.................$2,470.00
Price: Pigeon Grade Trap w/adj. comb, intr. 2008...............$2,630.00

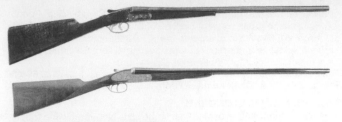

ARRIETA SIDELOCK DOUBLE

Gauge: 12, 16, 20, 28, .410. **Barrel:** Length and chokes to customer specs. **Weight:** To customer specs. **Stock:** To customer specs. Straight English with checkered butt (standard), or pistol grip. Select European walnut with oil finish. **Features:** Essentially custom gun with myriad options. H&H pattern hand-detachable sidelocks, selective automatic ejectors, double triggers (hinged front) standard. Some have selfopening action. Finish and engraving to customer specs. Imported from Spain by Quality Arms, Inc.

Price: Model		
Price: Model 557		$4,500.00
Price: Model 570		$5,350.00
Price: Model 578		$5,880.00
Price: Model 600 Imperial		$7,995.00
Price: Model 601 Imperial Tiro		$9,160.00
Price: Model 801		$14,275.00
Price: Model 802		$14,275.00
Price: Model 803		$9,550.00
Price: Model 871		$6,670.00
Price: Model 872		$17,850.00
Price: Model 873		$16,275.00
Price: Model 874		$13,125.00
Price: Model 875		$19,850.00
Price: Model 931		$20,895.00

AYA MODEL 4/53

Gauge: 12, 16, 20, 28, 410. **Barrel:** 26", 27", 28", 30". **Weight:** To customer specifications. **Length:** To customer specifications. **Features:** Hammerless boxlock action; double triggers; light scroll engraving; automatic safety; straight grip oil finish walnut stock; checkered butt. Made in Spain. Imported by New England Custom Gun Service, Lt.

Price: $2,999.00
Price: No. 2 ....$4,799.00
Price: No. 2 Rounded Action $5,199.00

BERETTA 471 SIDE-BY-SIDE

Gauge: 12, 20; 3" chamber. **Barrel:** 24", 26", 28"; 6mm rib. **Weight:** 6.5 lbs. **Stock:** English or pistol stock, straight butt for various types of recoil pads. Beavertail forend. English stock with recoil pad in red or black rubber, or in walnut and splinter forend. Select European walnut, checkered, oil finish. **Features:** Optima-Choke Extended Choke Tubes. Automatic ejection or mechanical extraction. Firing-pin block safety, manual or automatic, open top-lever safety. Introduced 2007. Imported from Italy by Beretta U.S.A.

Price: Silver Hawk..$3,850.00

CIMARRON 1878 COACH GUN

Gauge: 12. 3-inch chambers. **Barrels:** 20 or 26 inches. **Weight:** 8 to 9 pounds. **Stock:** Hardwood. External hammers, double triggers. **Finish:** Blue, Cimarron "USA", Cimarron "Original."

Price: Blue, ... $575.00 (20") to $594.00 (26")
Price: Original, ... $675.00 to $694.00
Price: USA, ...$832.00 to $851.00

CIMARRON 1881 HAMMERLESS

Gauge: 12. 3-inch chambers. **Barrels:** 20, 22, 26, 28 or 30 inches. **Stock:** Standard or Deluxe wood with rounded pistol grip. Single trigger, extractors, bead front sight.

Price: .... $722.00 to $761.00 (Deluxe)

CONNECTICUT MANUFACTURING COMPANY RBL SIDE-BY-SIDE

Gauge: 12, 16, 20, 28. **Barrel:** 26", 28", 30", 32". **Weight:** NA. **Length:** NA. **Stock:** NA. **Features:** Round-action SXS shotguns made in the USA. Scaled frames, five TruLock choke tubes. Deluxe fancy grade walnut buttstock and forend. Quick Change recoil pad in two lengths. Various dimensions and options available depending on gauge.

Price: 12 gauge $2,850.00
Price: 16 gauge ....POR
Price: 20 gauge $3,995.00
Price: 28 gauge $5,450.00

CZ BOBWHITE AND RINGNECK

Gauge: 12, 20, 28, .410. (5 screw-in chokes in 12 and 20 ga. and fixed chokes in IC and Mod in .410). **Barrel:** 20". **Weight:** 6.5 lbs. **Length:** NA. **Stock:** Sculptured Turkish walnut with straight English-style grip and double triggers (Bobwhite) or conventional American pistol grip with a single trigger (Ringneck). Both are hand checkered 20 lpi. **Features:** Both color case-hardened shotguns are hand engraved.

Price: Bobwhite $789.00
Price: Ringneck...$1,036.00

CZ HAMMER COACH

Gauge: 12, 3" chambers. **Barrel:** 20". **Weight:** 6.7 lbs. **Length:** NA. **Stock:** NA. **Features:** Following in the tradition of the guns used by the stagecoach guards of the 1880's, this cowboy gun features double triggers, 19th century color case-hardening and fully functional external hammers.

Price: $904.00

EMF OLD WEST HAMMER

Gauge: 12. **Barrel:** 20". **Weight:** 8 lbs. **Length:** 37" overall. **Stock:** Smooth walnut with steel butt place. **Sights:** Large brass bead. **Features:** Colt-style exposed hammers rebounding type; blued receiver and barrels; cylinder bore. Introduced 2006. Imported from China for EMF by TTN.

Price: $474.90

FOX, A.H., SIDE-BY-SIDE

Gauge: 16, 20, 28, .410. **Barrel:** Length and chokes to customer specifications. Rust-blued Chromox or Krupp steel. **Weight:** 5-1/2 to 6.75 lbs. **Stock:** Dimensions to customer specifications. Hand-checkered Turkish Circassian walnut with hand-rubbed oil finish. Straight, semi or full pistol grip; splinter, Schnabel or beavertail forend; traditional pad, hard rubber buttplate or skeleton butt. **Features:** Boxlock action with automatic ejectors; double or Fox single selective trigger. Scalloped, rebated and color case-hardened receiver; hand finished and handengraved. Grades differ in engraving, inlays, grade of wood, amount of hand finishing. Introduced 1993. Made in U.S. by Connecticut Shotgun Mfg.

Price: CE Grade...$14,500.00
Price: XE Grade $16,000.00
Price: DE Grade $19,000.00
Price: FE Grade $24,000.00
Price: 28/.410 CE Grade....................................$16,500.00
Price: 28/.410 XE Grade $18,000.00
Price: 28/.410 DE Grade $21,000.00
Price: 28/.410 FE Grade $26,000.00

GARBI MODEL 100 DOUBLE

Gauge: 12, 16, 20, 28. **Barrel:** 26", 28", choked to customer specs. **Weight:** 5-1/2 to 7.5 lbs. **Stock:** 14.5"x2.25"x1.5". European walnut. Straight grip, checkered butt, classic forend. **Features:** Sidelock action, automatic ejectors, double triggers standard. Color case-hardened action, coin finish optional. Single trigger; beavertail forend, etc. optional. Five additional models available. Imported from Spain by Wm. Larkin Moore.

Price: From $4,850.00

GARBI MODEL 101 SIDE-BY-SIDE

Similar to the Garbi Model 100 except hand engraved with scroll engraving; select walnut stock; better overall quality than the Model 100. Imported from Spain by Wm. Larkin Moore.

Price: From $6,250.00

GARBI MODEL 103 A & B SIDE-BY-SIDE

Similar to the Garbi Model 100 except has Purdey-type fine scroll and rosette engraving. Better overall quality than the Model 101. Model 103B has nickel-chrome steel barrels, H&H-type easy opening mechanism; other mechanical details remain the same. Imported from Spain by Wm. Larkin Moore.

Price: Model 103A. From **$14,100.00**
Price: Model 103B. From **$21,600.00**

GARBI MODEL 200 SIDE-BY-SIDE

Similar to the Garbi Model 100 except has heavy-duty locks, magnum proofed. Very fine Continental-style floral and scroll engraving, well figured walnut stock. Other mechanical features remain the same. Imported from Spain by Wm. Larkin Moore.

Price: **$17,100.00**

LEBEAU-COURALLY BOXLOCK SIDE-BY-SIDE

Gauge: 12, 16, 20, 28, .410-bore. **Barrel:** 25" to 32". **Weight:** To customer specifications. **Stock:** French walnut. **Features:** Anson & Deely-type action with automatic ejectors; single or double triggers. Custom gun built to customer specifications. Imported from Belgium by Wm. Larkin Moore.

Price: From **$25,500.00**

LEBEAU-COURALLY SIDELOCK SIDE-BY-SIDE

Gauge: 12, 16, 20, 28, .410-bore. **Barrel:** 25" to 32". **Weight:** To customer specifications. **Stock:** Fancy French walnut. **Features:** Holland & Holland-type action with automatic ejectors; single or double triggers. Custom gun built to customer specifications. Imported from Belgium by Wm. Larkin Moore.

Price: From **$56,000.00**

MERKEL MODEL 47E, 147E SIDE-BY-SIDE

Gauge: 12, 3" chambers, 16, 2.75" chambers, 20, 3" chambers. **Barrel:** 12, 16 ga.-28"; 20 ga.-26.75" (Imp. Cyl. & Mod., Mod. & Full). **Weight:** About 6.75 lbs. (12 ga.). **Stock:** Oil-finished walnut; straight English or pistol grip. **Features:** Anson & Deeley-type boxlock action with single selective or double triggers, automatic safety, cocking indicators. Color case-hardened receiver with standard arabesque engraving. Imported from Germany by Merkel USA.

Price: Model 47E (H&H ejectors) **$4,595.00**
Price: Model 147E (as above with ejectors)......................**$5,795.00**

MERKEL MODEL 47EL, 147EL SIDE-BY-SIDE

Similar to Model 47E except H&H style sidelock action with cocking indicators, ejectors. Silver-grayed receiver and sideplates have arabesque engraving, engraved border and screws (Model 47E), or fine hunting scene engraving (Model 147E). Limited edition. Imported from Germany by Merkel USA.

Price: Model 47EL **$7,195.00**
Price: Model 147EL **$7,695.00**

MERKEL MODEL 280EL, 360EL

Similar to Model 47E except smaller frame. Greener cross bolt with double under-barrel locking lugs, fine engraved hunting scenes on silver-grayed receiver, luxury-grade wood, Anson and Deely boxlock action. H&H ejectors, single-selective or double triggers. Introduced 2000. Imported from Germany by Merkel USA.

Price: Model 280EL (28 gauge, 28" barrel, Imp. Cyl. and
Mod. chokes)..**$7,695.00**
Price: Model 360EL (.410, 28" barrel, Mod. and
Full chokes)..**$7,695.00**
Price: Model 280EL Combo **$11,195.00**

MERKEL MODEL 280SL AND 360SL

Similar to Model 280EL and 360EL except has sidelock action, double triggers, English-style arabesque engraving. Introduced 2000. Imported from Germany by Merkel USA.

Price: Model 280SL (28 gauge, 28" barrel, Imp. Cyl.
and Mod. chokes)..**$10,995.00**
Price: Model 360SL (.410, 28" barrel, Mod. and
Full chokes)..**$10,995.00**

MERKEL MODEL 1620 SIDE-BY-SIDE

Gauge: 16. **Features:** Greener crossbolt with double under-barrel locking lugs, scroll-engraved case-hardened receiver, Anson and Deely boxlock aciton, Holland & Holland ejectors, English-style stock, single selective or double triggers, or pistol grip stock with single selective trgger. Imported from Germany by Merkel USA.

Price: **$4,995.00**

Price: Model 1620E; silvered, engraved receiver **$5,995.00**
Price: Model 1620 Combo; 16- and 20-gauge
two-barrel set **$7,695.00**
Price: Model 1620EL; upgraded wood **$7,695.00**
Price: Model 1620EL Combo; 16- and 20-gauge
two-barrel set **$11,195.00**

MOSSBERG SILVER RESERVE II SXS

Gauge: 12. 3-inch chambers. **Barrels:** 28 inches with front bead sight, five choke tubes. **Stock:** Select black walnut. **Weight:** 7.5 pounds. Side-by-side companion to over/under model with same Silver Reserve name. Blue barrels, silver receiver with scroll engraving. Single non-selective trigger with standard extractors.

Price: **$1,035.00**

PIOTTI KING NO. 1 SIDE-BY-SIDE

Gauge: 12, 16, 20, 28, .410. **Barrel:** 25" to 30" (12 ga.), 25" to 28" (16, 20, 28, .410). To customer specs. Chokes as specified. **Weight:** 6.5 lbs. to 8 lbs. (12 ga. to customer specs.). **Stock:** Dimensions to customer specs. Finely figured walnut; straight grip with checkered butt with classic splinter forend and hand-rubbed oil finish standard. Pistol grip, beavertail forend. **Features:** Holland & Holland pattern sidelock action, automatic ejectors. Double trigger; non-selective single trigger optional. Coin finish standard; color case-hardened optional. Top rib; level, file-cut; concave, ventilated optional. Very fine, full coverage scroll engraving with small floral bouquets. Imported from Italy by Wm. Larkin Moore.

Price: From **$38,300.00**

PIOTTI LUNIK SIDE-BY-SIDE SHOTGUN

Similar to the Piotti King No. 1 in overall quality. Has Renaissance-style large scroll engraving in relief. Best quality Holland & Holland-pattern sidelock ejector double with chopper lump (demi-bloc) barrels. Other mechanical specifications remain the same. Imported from Italy by Wm. Larkin Moore.

Price: From **$39,900.00**

PIOTTI PIUMA SIDE-BY-SIDE

Gauge: 12, 16, 20, 28, .410. **Barrel:** 25" to 30" (12 ga.), 25" to 28" (16, 20, 28, .410). **Weight:** 5-1/2 to 6-1/4 lbs. (20 ga.). **Stock:** Dimensions to customer specs. Straight grip stock with walnut checkered butt, classic splinter forend, hand-rubbed oil finish are standard; pistol grip, beavertail forend, satin luster finish optional. **Features:** Anson & Deeley boxlock ejector double with chopper lump barrels. Level, file-cut rib, light scroll and rosette engraving, scalloped frame. Double triggers; single non-selective optional. Coin finish standard, color case-hardened optional. Imported from Italy by Wm. Larkin Moore.

Price: From **$19,200.00**

RIZZINI SIDELOCK SIDE-BY-SIDE

Gauge: 12, 16, 20, 28, .410. **Barrel:** 25" to 30" (12, 16, 20 ga.), 25" to 28" (28, .410). To customer specs. Chokes as specified. **Weight:** 6.5 lbs. to 8 lbs. (12 ga. to customer specs). **Stock:** Dimensions to customer specs. Finely figured walnut; straight grip with checkered butt with classic splinter forend and hand-rubbed oil finish standard. Pistol grip, beavertail forend. **Features:** Sidelock action, auto ejectors. Double triggers or non-selective single trigger standard. Coin finish standard. Imported from Italy by Wm. Larkin Moore.

Price: 12, 20 ga. From **$106,000.00**
Price: 28, .410 bore. From **$95,000.00**

STOEGER UPLANDER SIDE-BY-SIDE

Gauge: 16, 28, 2-3/4 chambers. 12, 20, .410, 3" chambers. **Barrel:** 22", 24", 26", 28". **Weight:** 7.3 lbs. **Sights:** Brass bead. **Features:** Double trigger, IC & M fixed choke tubes with gun.

Price: **$449.00**
Price: Deluxe (single trigger, AA-grade wood) **$539.00**
Price: Longfowler (12 ga., 30" bbl.) **$449.00**
Price: Home Defense (20 or 12 ga., 20" bbl.,
tactical sights) **$499.00**

STOEGER COACH GUN SIDE-BY-SIDE

Gauge: 12, 20, 2-3/4", 3" chambers. **Barrel:** 20". **Weight:** 6.5 lbs. **Stock:** Brown hardwood, classic beavertail forend. **Sights:** Brass bead. **Features:** IC & M fixed chokes, tang auto safety, auto extractors, black plastic buttplate. Imported by Benelli USA.

Price: ....**$449.00 to $499.00**

BERETTA DT10 TRIDENT TRAP TOP SINGLE
Gauge: 12, 3" chamber. **Barrel:** 34"; five Optima Choke tubes (Full, Full, Imp. Modified, Mod. and Imp. Cyl.). **Weight:** 8.8 lbs. **Stock:** High-grade walnut; adjustable. **Features:** Detachable, adjustable trigger group; Optima Bore for improved shot pattern and reduced recoil; slim Optima Choke tubes; raised and thickened receiver for long life. Introduced 2000. Imported from Italy by Beretta USA.
Price: $8,650.00

BROWNING BT-99 TRAP O/U
Gauge: 12. **Barrel:** 30", 32", 34". **Stock:** Walnut; standard or adjustable. **Weight:** 7 lbs. 11 oz. to 9 lbs. **Features:** Back-bored single barrel; interchangeable chokes; beavertail forearm; extractor only; high rib.
Price: BT-99 w/conventional comb, 32" or 34" barrels $1,430.00
Price: BT-99 w/adjustable comb, 32" or 34" barrels $1,680.00
Price: BT-99 Golden Clays w/adjustable comb, 32" or 34" barrels $4,340.00
Price: BT-99 Grade III .... $2,540.00 to $2,840.00

BROWNING A-BOLT SHOTGUN HUNTER BOLT ACTION
Gauge: 12 ga. 3" chamber. **Barrel:** 22". **Weight:** 7 lbs. 2 ozs. **Length:** 43.75". **Stock:** Satin finish walnut stock and forearm – checkered. **Features:** Drilled and tapped for scope mounts, 60° bolt action lift, detachable two-round magazine, and top-tang safety. Sling swivel studs installed, rrecoil pad, TRUGLO®/Marble's® fiber-optic front sight with rear sight adjustable for windage and elevation.
Price: $1,280.00
Price: Medallion $1,580.00

BROWNING A-BOLT SHOTGUN, MOSSY OAK BREAK-UP INFINITY BOLT ACTION
Gauge: 12 ga. 3" chamber. **Barrel:** 22". **Weight:** 7 lbs. 2 ozs. **Length:** 43.75". **Stock:** Composite stock and forearm, textured gripping surfaces, Mossy Oak® Break-Up® Infinity™ camo finish • Dura-Touch® Armor Coating. **Features:** Drilled and tapped for scope mounts, 60° bolt action lift, detachable two-round magazine, and top-tang safety. Sling swivel studs installed, rrecoil pad, TRUGLO®/Marble's® fiber-optic front sight with rear sight adjustable for windage and elevation.
Price: From $1,300.00

BROWNING A-BOLT SHOTGUN STALKER BOLT ACTION
Gauge: 12 ga. 3" chamber. **Barrel:** 22". **Weight:** 7 lbs. **Length:** 43.75". **Stock:** Composite stock and forearm, textured gripping surfaces, Dura-Touch® Armor Coating. **Features:** Drilled and tapped for scope mounts, 60° bolt action lift, detachable two-round magazine, and top-tang safety. Sling swivel studs installed, rrecoil pad, TRUGLO®/Marble's® fiber-optic front sight with rear sight adjustable for windage and elevation.
Price: From $1,150.00

HARRINGTON & RICHARDSON ULTRA SLUG HUNTER/TAMER
Gauge: 12, 20 ga., 3" chamber, .410. **Barrel:** 20" to 24" rifled. **Weight:** 6 to 9 lbs. **Length:** 34.5" to 40". **Stock:** Hardwood, laminate, or polymer with full pistol grip; semi-beavertail forend. **Sights:** Gold bead front. **Features:** Break-open action with side-lever release,

automatic ejector. Introduced 1994. From H&R 1871, LLC.
Price: Ultra Slug Hunter, blued, hardwood $273.00
Price: Ultra Slug Hunter Youth, blued, hardwood, 13-1/8" LOP...$273.00
Price: Ultra Slug Hunter Deluxe, blued, laminated $273.00
Price: Tamer .410 bore, stainless barrel, black polymer stock $173.00

HARRINGTON & RICHARDSON ULTRA LITE SLUG HUNTER
Gauge: 12, 20 ga., 3" chamber. **Barrel:** 24" rifled. **Weight:** 5.25 lbs. **Length:** 40". **Stock:** Hardwood with walnut finish, full pistol grip, recoil pad, sling swivel studs. **Sights:** None; base included. **Features:** Youth Model, available in 20 ga. has 20" rifled barrel. Deluxe Model has checkered laminated stock and forend. From H&R 1871, LLC.
Price: $194.00

HARRINGTON & RICHARDSON ULTRA SLUG HUNTER THUMBHOLE STOCK
Similar to the Ultra Lite Slug Hunter but with laminated thumbhole stock and weighs 8.5 lbs.
Price: .... NA

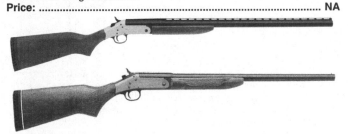

HARRINGTON & RICHARDSON TOPPER MODELS
Gauge: 12, 16, 20, .410, up to 3.5" chamber. **Barrel:** 22 to 28". **Weight:** 5-7 lbs. **Stock:** Polymer, hardwood, or black walnut. **Features:** Satin nickel frame, blued barrel. Reintroduced 1992. From H&R 1871, LLC.
Price: Deluxe Classic, 12/20 ga., 28" barrel w/vent rib $225.00
Price: Topper Deluxe 12 ga., 28" barrel, black hardwood $179.00
Price: Topper 12, 16, 20 ga., .410, 26" to 28", black hardwood..$153.00
Price: Topper Junior 20 ga., .410, 22" barrel, hardwood..........$160.00
Price: Topper Junior Classic, 20 ga., .410, checkered hardwood..$160.00

HARRINGTON & RICHARDSON TOPPER TRAP GUN
Similar to other Topper Models but with select checkered walnut stock and forend wtih fluted comb and full pistol grip; 30" barrel with two white beads and screw-in chokes (Improved Modified Extended included); deluxe Pachmayr trap recoil pad.
Price: $360.00

KRIEGHOFF K-80 SINGLE BARREL TRAP GUN
Gauge: 12, 2-3/4" chamber. **Barrel:** 32" or 34" Unsingle. Fixed Full or choke tubes. **Weight:** About 8-3/4 lbs. **Stock:** Four stock dimensions or adjustable stock available. All hand-checkered European walnut. **Features:** Satin nickel finish. Selective mechanical trigger adjustable for finger position. Tapered step vent rib. Adjustable point of impact.
Price: Standard grade Full Unsingle, from..........................$10,080.00

Prices given are believed to be accurate at time of publication however, many factors affect retail pricing so exact prices are not possible.

KRIEGHOFF KX-5 TRAP GUN

Gauge: 12, 2-3/4" chamber. **Barrel:** 32", 34"; choke tubes. **Weight:** About 8.5 lbs. **Stock:** Factory adjustable stock. European walnut. **Features:** Ventilated tapered step rib. Adjustable position trigger, optional release trigger. Fully adjustable rib. Satin gray electroless nickel receiver. Fitted aluminum case. Imported from Germany by Krieghoff International, Inc.
Price: $5,395.00

LJUTIC MONO GUN SINGLE BARREL

Gauge: 12 only. **Barrel:** 34", choked to customer specs; hollow-milled rib, 35.5" sight plane. **Weight:** Approx. 9 lbs. **Stock:** To customer specs. Oil finish, hand checkered. **Features:** Custom gun. Pull or release trigger; removable trigger guard contains trigger and hammer mechanism; Ljutic pushbutton opener on front of trigger guard. From Ljutic Industries.
Price: Std., med. or Olympic rib, custom bbls.,
    fixed choke. $7,495.00
Price: Stainless steel mono gun $8,495.00

LJUTIC LTX PRO 3 DELUXE MONO GUN

Deluxe, lightweight version of the Mono gun with high quality wood, upgrade checkering, special rib height, screw-in chokes, ported and cased.
Price: $8,995.00
Price: Stainless steel model........................$9,995.00

NEW ENGLAND FIREARMS PARDNER AND TRACKER II

Gauge: 10, 12, 16, 20, 28, .410, up to 3.5" chamber for 10 and 12 ga. 16, 28, 2-3/4" chamber. **Barrel:** 24" to 30". **Weight:** Varies from 5 to 9.5 lbs. **Length:** Varies from 36" to 48". **Stock:** Walnut-finished hardwood with full pistol grip, synthetic, or camo finish. **Sights:** Bead front on most. **Features:** Transfer bar ignition; break-open action with side-lever release. Introduced 1987. From New England Firearms.
Price: Pardner, all gauges, hardwood stock, 26" to 32"
    blued barrel, Mod. or Full choke.....................$140.00
Price: Pardner Youth, hardwood stock, straight grip,
    22" blued barrel $149.00
Price: Pardner Screw-In Choke model,
    intr. 2006 ....$164.00
Price: Turkey model, 10/12 ga., camo finish
    or black...................................$192.00 to $259.00
Price: Youth Turkey, 20 ga., camo finish or black...................$192.00
Price: Waterfowl, 10 ga., camo finish or hardwood.................$227.00
Price: Tracker II slug gun, 12/20 ga., hardwood......................$196.00

ROSSI CIRCUIT JUDGE

Revolving shotgun chambered in .410 (2-1/2- or 3-inch/.45 Colt. Based on Taurus Judge handgun. Features include 18.5-inch barrel; fiber optic front sight; 5-round cylinder; hardwood Monte Carlo stock.
Price: $681.00

ROSSI SINGLE-SHOT

Gauge: 12, 20, .410. **Barrel:** 22" (Youth), 28". **Weight:** 3.75-5.25 lbs. **Stocks:** Wood. **Sights:** Bead front sight, fully adjustable fiber optic sight on Slug and Turkey. **Features:** Single-shot break open, 8 models available, positive ejection, internal transfer bar mechanism, trigger block system, Taurus Security System, blued finish, Rifle Slug has ported barrel.
Price: From $148.00

ROSSI TUFFY

Gauge: .410. **Barrel:** 18-1/2". **Weight:** 3 lbs. **Length:** 29.5" overall. **Features:** Single-shot break-open model with black synthetic thumbhole stock in blued or stainless finish.
Price: .... $164.00-$172.00

ROSSI MATCHED PAIRS

Gauge/Caliber: 12, 20, .410, .22 Mag, .22LR, .17HMR, .223 Rem, .243 Win, .270 Win, .30-06, .308 Win, .50 (black powder). **Barrel:** 23", 28". **Weight:** 5-6.3 lbs. **Stocks:** Wood or black synthetic. **Sights:** Bead front on shotgun barrel, fully adjustable front and rear on rifle barrel, drilled and tapped for scope, fully adjustable fiber optic sights (black powder). **Features:** Single-shot break open, 27 models available, internal transfer bar mechanism, manual external safety, blue finish, trigger block system, Taurus Security System, youth models available.
Price: Rimfire/Shotgun, from $160.00
Price: Centerfire/Shotgun $271.95
Price: Black Powder Matched Pair, from...............$262.00

ROSSI MATCHED SET

Gauge/Caliber: 12, 20, .22 LR, .17 HMR, .243 Win, .270 Win, .50 (black powder). **Barrel:** 33.5". **Weight:** 6.25-6.3 lbs. **Stocks:** Wood. **Sights:** Bead front on shotgun barrel, fully adjustable front and rear on rifle barrel, drilled and tapped for scope, fully adjustable fiber optic sights (black powder). **Features:** Single-shot break open, 4 models available, internal transfer bar mechanism, manual external safety, blue finish, trigger block system, Taurus Security System, youth models available.
Price: From $374.00

TAR-HUNT RSG-12 PROFESSIONAL RIFLED SLUG GUN

Gauge: 12, 2-3/4" or 3" chamber, 1-shot magazine. **Barrel:** 23", fully rifled with muzzle brake. **Weight:** 7.75 lbs. **Length:** 41.5" overall. **Stock:** Matte black McMillan fiberglass with Pachmayr Decelerator pad. **Sights:** None furnished; comes with Leupold windage or Weaver bases. **Features:** Uses rifle-style action with two locking lugs; two-position safety; Shaw barrel; single stage; trigger; muzzle brake. Many options available. All models have area-controlled feed action. Introduced 1991. Made in U.S. by Tar-Hunt Custom Rifles, Inc.
Price: 12 ga. Professional model......................$2,850.00
Price: Left-hand model add..................................$110.00

TAR-HUNT RSG-16 ELITE

Similar to RSG-12 Professional except 16 gauge; right- or left-hand versions.
Price: $2,835.00

TAR-HUNT RSG-20 MOUNTAINEER SLUG GUN

Similar to the RSG-12 Professional except chambered for 20 gauge (2-3/4" and 3" shells); 23" Shaw rifled barrel, with muzzle brake; two-lug bolt; one-shot blind magazine; matte black finish; McMillan fiberglass stock with Pachmayr Decelerator pad; receiver drilled and tapped for Rem. 700 bases. Right- or left-hand versions. Weighs 6.5 lbs. Introduced 1997. Made in U.S. by Tar-Hunt Custom Rifles, Inc.
Price: **$2,585.00**

THOMPSON/CENTER ENCORE RIFLED SLUG GUN

Gauge: 20, 3" chamber. **Barrel:** 26", fully rifled. **Weight:** About 7 lbs. **Length:** 40.5" overall. **Stock:** Walnut with walnut forearm. **Sights:** Steel; click-adjustable rear and ramp-style front, both with fiber optics. **Features:** Encore system features a variety of rifle, shotgun and muzzle-loading rifle barrels interchangeable with the same frame. Break-open design operates by pulling up and back on trigger guard spur. Composite stock and forearm available. Introduced 2000.
Price: **$750.00**

THOMPSON/CENTER ENCORE TURKEY GUN

Gauge: 12 ga. **Barrel:** 24". **Features:** All-camo finish, high definition Realtree Hardwoods HD camo.
Price: **$825.00**

THOMPSON/CENTER ENCORE PROHUNTER TURKEY GUN

Contender-style break-action single shot shotgun chambered in 12 or 20 gauge 3-inch shells. Features include 24-inch barrel with interchangeable choke tubes (Extra Full supplied), composite buttstock and forend with non-slip inserts in cheekpiece, pistol grip and forend. Adjustable fiber optic sights, Sims recoil pad, AP camo finish overall. Overall length: 40.5 inches. Weight: 6-1/2 lbs.
Price: **$899.00**

BENELLI M3 CONVERTIBLE

Gauge: 12, 2-3/4", 3" chambers, 5-shot magazine. **Barrel:** 19.75" (Cyl.). **Weight:** 7 lbs., 4oz. **Length:** 41" overall. **Stock:** High-impact polymer with sling loop in side of butt; rubberized pistol grip on stock. **Sights:** Open rifle, fully adjustable. Ghost ring and rifle type. **Features:** Combination pump/auto action. Alloy receiver with inertia recoil rotating locking lug bolt; matte finish; automatic shell release lever. Introduced 1989. Imported by Benelli USA. Price with pistol grip, open rifle sights.
Price: With ghost ring sights, pistol grip stock **$1,589.00**

BENELLI M2 TACTICAL

Gauge: 12, 2-3/4", 3" chambers, 5-shot magazine. **Barrel:** 18.5" IC, M, F choke tubes. **Weight:** 6.7 lbs. **Length:** 39.75" overall. **Stock:** Black polymer. **Sights:** Rifle type ghost ring system, tritium night sights optional. **Features:** Semiauto intertia recoil action. Cross-bolt safety; bolt release button; matte-finish metal. Introduced 1993. Imported from Italy by Benelli USA.
Price: from .... **$1,239.00 to $1,359.00**

BENELLI M4 TACTICAL

Gauge: 12 ga., 3" chamber. **Barrel:** 18.5". **Weight:** 7.8 lbs. **Length:** 40" overall. **Stock:** Synthetic. **Sights:** Ghost Ring rear, fixed blade front. **Features:** Auto-regulating gas-operated (ARGO) action, choke tube, Picatinny rail, standard and collapsible stocks available, optional LE tactical gun case. Introduced 2006. Imported from Italy by Benelli USA.
Price: Pistol grip stock, black synthetic.................................**$1,699.00**
Price: Desert camo pistol grip (2007) **$1,829.00**

CITADEL LE TACTICAL

Gauge: 12 ga., 3" chamber. **Barrel:** 22". **Weight:** 5.8 lbs -7.15 lbs. **Length:** 49". **Stock:** Composite stock with close radius pistol grip; Speed Lock forearm; textured gripping surfaces; shim adjustable for length of pull, cast and drop; Mossy Oak® Bottomland™ camo finish; Dura-Touch® Armor Coating. **Features:** These shotguns are built in the U.S.A., insuring exacting parts match and a superior fit/finish. Using a common receiver and trigger group, the Citadel LE comes in four models: Spec-Ops, Talon, Pistol Grip with Heat Shield and Standard. All models feature a lightweight receiver, 7 +1 magazine capacity, 20 inch barrel, ergonomic forend, quick feed short stroke pump and rifle style sights. The Spec-Ops model features the BLACKHAWK!® Spec-Ops stock, which is adjustable for 4 inches of LOP, and estimated at absorbing up to 70% of felt recoil. The Spec-Ops gets you on target quickly – and keeps you there shot after shot. The Talon model also offers 70% felt recoil reduction with a skeletonized thumbhole stock from BLACKHAWK! that permits free hand movement with even the heaviest of gloves, and a short, 13.5 inch LOP. Finally, the Pistol Grip and Standard models offer a traditional, synthetic stock with a fixed, 13.5 inch LOP.
Price: Standard Stock **$466.00**
Price: Spec-Ops **$632.00**
Price: Talon **$632.00**
Price: Pistol grip with heat shield **$495.00**

KEL-TEC KSG BULL-PUP TWIN-TUBE

The shotgun bears a stunning resemblance to the South African designed Neostead pump action scattergun. The operator is able to move a switch located near the top of the grip to select the right or left tube, or move the switch to the center to eject a shell without chambering another round. The bull-pup design results in an overall length of only 26" with an 18.5" barrel while the bottom eject design makes the firearm truly ambidextrous. The incredibly short overall length makes it more nimble than a sawed off shotgun, and with a 14+1 capacity with 2 3/4" you don't sacrifice ammunition capacity to get a shotty in a small package. Optional accessories include a factory installed picatinny rail with flip-up sights and a pistol grip.
Price: **$800.00**

MOSSBERG MODEL 500 SPECIAL PURPOSE

Gauge: 12, 20, .410, 3" chamber. **Barrel:** 18.5", 20" (Cyl.). **Weight:** 7 lbs. **Stock:** Walnut-finished hardwood or black synthetic. **Sights:** Metal bead front. **Features:** Available in 6- or 8-shot models. Top-mounted safety, double action slide bars, swivel studs, rubber recoil pad. Blue, Parkerized, Marinecote finishes. Mossberg Cablelock included. From Mossberg. The HS410 Home Security model chambered for .410 with 3" chamber; has pistol grip forend, thick recoil pad, muzzle brake and has special spreader choke on the 18.5" barrel. Overall length is 37.5", weight is 6.25 lbs. Blue finish; synthetic field stock. Mossberg Cablelock and video included. Mariner model has Marinecote metal finish to resist rust and corrosion. Synthetic field stock; pistol grip kit included. 500 Tactical 6-shot has black synthetic tactical stock. Introduced 1990.
Price: Rolling Thunder, 6-shot **$537.00**
Price: HS410 Home Security...**$459.00**
Price: Tactical .... **$583.00 to $630.00**
Price: 500 Blackwater SPX...**$478.00**
Price: 500 Chainsaw pistol grip only; removable top handle ...**$525.00**
Price: JIC **$435.00**
Price: Road Blocker..**$544.00**

MOSSBERG MODEL 590 SPECIAL PURPOSE

Gauge: 12, 20, .410 3" chamber, 9 shot magazine. **Barrel:** 20" (Cyl.). **Weight:** 7.25 lbs. **Stock:** Synthetic field or Speedfeed. **Sights:** Metal bead front or Ghost Ring. **Features:** Top-mounted safety, double slide action bars. Comes with heat shield, bayonet lug, swivel studs, rubber recoil pad. Blue, Parkerized or Marinecote finish. Mossberg Cablelock included. From Mossberg.
Price: Special Purpose 9-shot **$537.00**
Price: Tactical Light Fore-End...**$677.00**
Price: Tactical Tri-Rail **$640.00**

MOSSBERG 930 SPECIAL PURPOSE SERIES

Gauge: 12 ga., 3" chamber. **Barrel:** 28" flat ventilated rib. **Weight:** 7.3 lbs. **Length:** 49". **Stock:** Composite stock with close radius pistol grip; Speed Lock forearm; textured gripping surfaces; shim adjustable for length of pull, cast and drop; Mossy Oak® Bottomland™ camo finish; Dura-Touch® Armor Coating. **Features:**

930 Special Purpose shotguns feature a self-regulating gas system that vents excess gas to aid in recoil reduction and eliminate stress on critical components. All 930 autoloaders chamber both 2 3/4 inch and 3-inch 12-gauge shotshells with ease—from target loads, to non-toxic magnum loads, to the latest sabot slug ammo. Magazine capacity is 7+1 on models with extended magazine tube, 4+1 on models without. To complete the package, each Mossberg 930 includes a set of specially designed spacers for quick adjustment of the horizontal and vertical angle of the stock, bringing a custom-feel fit to every shooter. All 930 Special Purpose models feature a drilled and tapped receiver, factory-ready for Picatinny rail, scope base or optics installation. 930 SPX models conveniently come with a factory-mounted Picatinny rail and LPA/M16-Style Ghost Ring combination sight right out of the box. Other sighting options include a basic front bead, or white-dot front sights. Mossberg 930 Special Purpose shotguns are available in a variety of configurations; 5-shot tactical barrel, 5-shot with muzzle brake, 8-shot pistol-grip, and even a 5-shot security / field combo.

Price: Tactical 5-Shot................$683.00
Price: Blackwater Series................$865.00
Price: Home Security................$612.00
Price: Standard Stock................$787.00
Price: Pistol Grip 8-shot................$883.00
Price: 5-shot Combo w/extra 18.5" barrel................$679.00

REMINGTON MODEL 870 PUMP AND MODEL 1100 AUTOLOADER TACTICAL SHOTGUNS

Gauge: 870: 12, 2-3/4 or 3" chamber; 1100: 2-3/4". **Barrel:** 18", 20", 22" (Cyl or IC). **Weight:** 7.5-7.75 lbs. **Length:** 38.5-42.5" overall. **Stock:** Black synthetic, synthetic Speedfeed IV full pistol-grip stock, or Knoxx Industries SpecOps stock w/recoil-absorbing spring-loaded cam and adjustable length of pull (12" to 16", 870 only). **Sights:** Front post w/ dot only on 870; rib and front dot on 1100. **Features:** R3 recoil pads, LimbSaver technology to reduce felt recoil, 2-, 3- or 4-shot extensions based on barrel length; matte-olive-drab barrels and receivers. Model 1100 Tactical is available with Speedfeed IV pistol grip stock or standard black synthetic stock and forend. Speedfeed IV model has an 18" barrel with two-shot extension. Standard synthetic-stocked version is equipped with 22" barrel and four-shot extension. Introduced 2006. From Remington Arms Co.

Price: 870 Express Tactical................$572.00
Price: 870 Express Magpul................$872.00
Price: 870 Special Purpose Marine (nickel)................$829.00
Price: 870 Express Blackhawk Spec Ops................$638.00
Price: 1100 TAC-4................$1,015.00

REMINGTON 870 EXPRESS TACTICAL A-TACS CAMO

Pump action shotgun chambered for 2-3/4- and 3-inch 12-ga. Features include full A-TACS digitized camo; 18-1/2-inch barrel; extended ported Tactical RemChoke; SpeedFeed IV pistol-grip stock with SuperCell recoil pad; fully adjustable XS® Ghost Ring Sight rail with removable white bead front sight; 7-round capacity with factory-installed 2-shot extension; drilled and tapped receiver; sling swivel stud.
Price: $665.00

REMINGTON 887 NITRO MAG TACTICAL

Pump action shotgun chambered in 12-ga., 2-3/4 to 3-1/2 inch. Features include 18-1/2-inch barrel with ported, extended tactical RemChoke; 2-shot magazine extension; barrel clamp with integral Picatinny rails; ArmorLokt coating; synthetic stock and forend with specially contour grip panels.
Price: $524.00

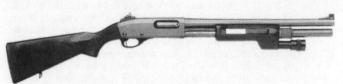

TACTICAL RESPONSE TR-870 STANDARD MODEL

Gauge: 12, 3" chamber, 7-shot magazine. **Barrel:** 18" (Cyl). **Weight:** 9 lbs. **Length:** 38" overall. **Stock:** Fiberglass-filled polypropolene with non-snag recoil absorbing butt pad. Nylon tactical forend houses flashlight. **Sights:** Trak-Lock ghost ring sight system. Front sight has Tritium insert. **Features:** Highly modified Remington 870P with Parkerized finish. Comes with nylon three-way adjustable sling, high visibility non-binding follower, high performance magazine spring, Jumbo Head safety, and Side Saddle extended 6-shot shell carrier on left side of receiver. Introduced 1991. From Scattergun Technologies, Inc.

Price: Standard model, from................$1,540.00
Price: Border Patrol model, from................$1,135.00
Price: Professional model, from................$1,550.00

TRISTAR COBRA

Gauge: 12, 3". **Barrel:** 28". **Weight:** 6.7 lbs. Three Beretta-style choke tubes (IC, M, F). **Length:** NA. **Stock:** Matte black synthetic stock and forearm. **Sights:** Vent rib with matted sight plane. **Features:** Five-year warranty. Cobra Tactical Pump Shotgun magazine holds 7, return spring in forearm, 20" barrel, Cylinder choke. Introduced 2008. Imported by Tristar Sporting Arms Ltd.
Price: Tactical................$304.00 to $361.00

TRISTAR TECH 12 AUTO/PUMP

Gauge: 12. 3-inch chamber. 20-inch ported barrel with fixed cylinder choke. Capable of operating in pump-action or semi-auto model with the turn of a dial. **Stock:** Pistol-grip synthetic with matte black finish. **Weight:** 7.4 lbs. **Sights:** Ghost-ring rear, raised bridge fiber-optic front. Picatinny rail.
Price: $689

WINCHESTER SXP EXTREME DEFENDER

Gauge: 12. 3-inch chamber. Pump action. **Barrel:** 18-inches with chrome-plated chamber and bore, "door breaching" ported choke tube. **Stock:** Adjustable military-style buttstock with vertical pistol grip. **Sights:** Ghost-ring rear integrated with Picatinny rail. Matte black finish.
Price: $520
Price: Marine Model with hard chrome metal finish................$580

Prices given are believed to be accurate at time of publication however, many factors affect retail pricing so exact prices are not possible.

HARPER'S FERRY 1805 PISTOL
Caliber: 58 (.570" round ball). **Barrel:** 10". **Weight:** 39 oz. **Length:** 16" overall. **Stocks:** Walnut. **Sights:** Fixed. **Features:** Case-hardened lock, brass-mounted German silver-colored barrel. Replica of the first U.S. gov't.-made flintlock pistol. Imported by Dixie Gun Works.
Price: Dixie Gun Works RH0225 .... **$550.00**

KENTUCKY FLINTLOCK PISTOL
Caliber: 45, 50. **Barrel:** 10.4". **Weight:** 37-40 oz. **Length:** 15.4" overall. **Stocks:** Walnut. **Sights:** Fixed. **Features:** Specifications, including caliber, weight and length may vary with importer. Case-hardened lock, blued barrel; available also as brass barrel flintlock Model 1821. Imported by EMF.
Price: (.45) **$525.00**
Price: (.50) **$555.00**

KENTUCKY PERCUSSION PISTOL
Caliber: .45, 50. **Barrel:** 10 inch octagonal with 1:20-inch twist. One-piece stock with bird's head grip, case-colored sidelock. Imported by Traditions, Taylor's and others.
Price: ....**$235.00 to $474.00**

LE PAGE PERCUSSION DUELING PISTOL
Caliber: .45. **Barrel:** 10.25" octagon, rifled. **Weight:** 36-41 oz. **Length:** 16.9" overall. **Stocks:** Walnut, fluted butt. **Sights:** Blade front, open style rear. **Features:** Double set trigger. Bright barrel, brass furniture (silver plated). Imported by Dixie Gun Works
Price: PH0310.. **$627.00**

LYMAN PLAINS PISTOL
Caliber: 50 or 54. **Barrel:** 8"; 1:30" twist, both calibers. **Weight:** 50 oz. **Length:** 15" overall. **Stocks:** Walnut half-stock. **Sights:** Blade front, square notch rear adjustable for windage. **Features:** Polished brass trigger guard and ramrod tip, color case-hardened coil spring lock, springloaded trigger, stainless steel nipple, blackened iron furniture. Hooked patent breech, detachable belt hook. Introduced 1981. From Lyman Products.
Price: Finished **$370.00**
Price: Kit **$310.00**

PEDERSOLI MANG TARGET PISTOL
Caliber: 38. **Barrel:** 10.5", octagonal; 1:15" twist, **Weight:** 2.5 lbs. **Length:** 17.25" overall. **Stocks:** Walnut with fluted grip. **Sights:** Blade front, open rear adjustable for windage. **Features:** Browned barrel,

---

polished breech plug, remainder color case-hardened. Imported from Italy by Dixie Gun Works.
Price: PH0503.. **$1,500.00**

QUEEN ANNE FLINTLOCK PISTOL
Caliber: 50 (.490" round ball). **Barrel:** 7.5", smoothbore. **Stocks:** Walnut. **Sights:** None. **Features:** German silver-colored steel barrel, fluted brass trigger guard, brass mask on butt. Lockplate left in the white. Made by Pedersoli in Italy. Introduced 1983. Imported by Dixie Gun Works.
Price: RH0211 .... **$425.00**

TRADITIONS KENTUCKY PISTOL
Caliber: 50. **Barrel:** 10"; octagon with 7/8" flats; 1:20" twist. **Weight:** 40 oz. **Length:** 15" overall. **Stocks:** Stained beech. **Sights:** Blade front, fixed rear. **Features:** Bird's-head grip; brass thimbles; color case-hardened lock. Percussion only. Introduced 1995. From Traditions.
Price: Finished **$209.00**
Price: Kit **$174.00**

TRADITIONS TRAPPER PISTOL
Caliber: 50. **Barrel:** 9.75"; 7/8" flats; 1:20" twist. **Weight:** 2.75 lbs. **Length:** 16" overall. **Stocks:** Beech. **Sights:** Blade front, adjustable rear. **Features:** Double-set triggers; brass buttcap, trigger guard, wedge plate, forend tip, thimble. From Traditions.
Price: Percussion.. **$286.00**
Price: Flintlock **$312.00**
Price: Kit **$149.00**

TRADITIONS VEST-POCKET DERRINGER
Caliber: 01. **Barrel:** 2.25"; brass. **Weight:** 8 oz. **Length:** 4.75" overall. **Stocks:** Simulated ivory. **Sights:** Bead front. **Features:** Replica of riverboat gamblers' derringer; authentic spur trigger. From Traditions.
Price: **$165.00**

TRADITIONS WILLIAM PARKER PISTOL
Caliber: 50. **Barrel:** 10-3/8"; 15/16" flats; polished steel. **Weight:** 37 oz. **Length:** 17.5" overall. **Stocks:** Walnut with checkered grip. **Sights:** Brass blade front, fixed rear. **Features:** Replica dueling pistol with 1:20" twist, hooked breech. Brass wedge plate, trigger guard, cap guard; separate ramrod. Double-set triggers. Polished steel barrel, lock. Imported by Traditions.
Price: **$381.00**

ARMY 1860 PERCUSSION REVOLVER

Caliber: 44, 6-shot. **Barrel:** 8". **Weight:** 40 oz. **Length:** 13-5/8" overall. **Stocks:** Walnut. **Sights:** Fixed. **Features:** Engraved Navy scene on cylinder; brass trigger guard; case-hardened frame, loading lever and hammer. Some importers supply pistol cut for detachable shoulder stock, have accessory stock available. Imported by Cimarron, Dixie Gun Works, Uberti U.S.A. and others.
Price: from .... $350.00 to $400.00

BABY DRAGOON 1848, 1849 POCKET, WELLS FARGO

Caliber: 31. **Barrel:** 3", 4", 5", 6"; seven-groove; RH twist. **Weight:** About 21 oz. **Stocks:** Varnished walnut. **Sights:** Brass pin front, hammer notch rear. **Features:** No loading lever on Baby Dragoon or Wells Fargo models. Unfluted cylinder with stagecoach holdup scene; cupped cylinder pin; no grease grooves; one safety pin on cylinder and slot in hammer face; straight (flat) mainspring. From Armsport, Cimarron F.A. Co., Dixie Gun Works, EMF, Uberti U.S.A. Inc.
Price: from .... $300.00 to $375.00

DIXIE WYATT EARP REVOLVER

Caliber: 44. **Barrel:** 12", octagon. **Weight:** 46 oz. **Length:** 18" overall. **Stocks:** One-piece hardwood. **Sights:** Fixed. **Features:** Highly polished brass frame, backstrap and trigger guard; blued barrel and cylinder; case-hardened hammer, trigger and loading lever. Navy-size shoulder stock requires minor fitting. From Dixie Gun Works.
Price: RH0130... $187.50

LE MAT REVOLVER

Caliber: 44/20 ga. **Barrel:** 6.75" (revolver); 4-7/8" (single shot). **Weight:** 3 lbs., 7 oz. **Length:** 14" overall. **Stocks:** Hand-checkered walnut. **Sights:** Post front, hammer notch rear. **Features:** Exact reproduction with all-steel construction; 44-cal. 9-shot cylinder, 20-gauge single barrel; color case-hardened hammer with selector; spur trigger guard; ring at butt; lever-type barrel release. From Dixie Gun Works.
Price: $850.00

NAVY MODEL 1851 PERCUSSION REVOLVER

Caliber: 36, 44, 6-shot. **Barrel:** 7.5". **Weight:** 44 oz. **Length:** 13" overall. **Stocks:** Walnut finish. **Sights:** Post front, hammer notch rear. **Features:** Brass backstrap and trigger guard; some have 1st Model squareback trigger guard, engraved cylinder with navy battle scene; case-hardened frame, hammer, loading lever. Imported by The Armoury, Cabela's, Cimarron F.A. Co., Navy Arms, EMF, Dixie Gun Works, Euroarms of America, Armsport, CVA (44-cal. only), Traditions (44 only), Uberti U.S.A. Inc., United States Patent Fire-Arms.
Price: Brass frame (Dixie Gun Works RH0100)........................ $275.00
Price: Steel frame (Dixie Gun Works RH0210).......................... $200.00
Price: Engraved model (Dixie Gun Works RH0110) $275.00
Price: Confederate Navy (Cabela's) $139.99
Price: Hartford model, steel frame, German silver trim, cartouche (EMF) $190.00
Price: Man With No Name Conversion (Cimarron, 2006) $480.00

NEW MODEL 1858 ARMY PERCUSSION REVOLVER

Caliber: 36 or 44, 6-shot. **Barrel:** 6.5" or 8". **Weight:** 38 oz. **Length:** 13.5" overall. **Stocks:** Walnut. **Sights:** Blade front, groove-in-frame rear. **Features:** Replica of Remington Model 1858. Also available from some importers as Army Model Belt Revolver in 36-cal., a shortened and lightened version of the 44. Target Model (Uberti U.S.A. Inc., Navy Arms) has fully adjustable target rear sight, target front, 36 or 44. Imported by Cimarron F.A. Co., CVA (as 1858 Army, brass frame, 44 only), Navy Arms, The Armoury, EMF, Euroarms of America (engraved, stainless and plain), Armsport, Traditions (44 only), Uberti U.S.A. Inc.
Price: Steel frame, Dixie RH0220 .... $315.00
Price: Steel frame kit (Euroarms) .... $115.95 to $150.00
Price: Stainless steel Model 1858 (Euroarms, Uberti U.S.A. Inc., Navy Arms, Armsport, Traditions) .... $169.95 to $380.00
Price: Target Model, adjustable rear sight (Cabela's, Euroarms, Uberti U.S.A. Inc., Stone Mountain Arms) .... $95.95 to $399.00
Price: Brass frame (CVA, Cabela's, Traditions, Navy Arms) .... $79.95 to $199.99
Price: Buffalo model, 44-cal. (Cabela's) $119.99
Price: Hartford model, steel frame, cartouche (EMF) $225.00
Price: Improved Conversion (Cimarron) $492.00

NORTH AMERICAN COMPANION PERCUSSION REVOLVER

Caliber: 22. **Barrel:** 1-1/8". **Weight:** 5.1 oz. **Length:** 4.5" overall. **Stocks:** Laminated wood. **Sights:** Blade front, notch fixed rear. **Features:** All stainless steel construction. Uses standard #11 percussion caps. Comes with bullets, powder measure, bullet seater, leather clip holster, gun rag. Long Rifle or Magnum frame size. Introduced 1996. Made in U.S. by North American Arms.
Price: Long Rifle frame $244.00

Prices given are believed to be accurate at time of publication however, many factors affect retail pricing so exact prices are not possible.

BLACKPOWDER REVOLVERS

NORTH AMERICAN SUPER COMPANION PERCUSSION REVOLVER

Similar to the Companion except has larger frame. Weighs 7.2 oz., has 1-5/8" barrel, measures 4" overall. Comes with bullets, powder measure, bullet seater, leather clip holster, gun rag. Introduced 1996. Made in U.S. by North American Arms.

Price: **$360.00**

POCKET POLICE 1862 PERCUSSION REVOLVER

Caliber: 36, 5-shot. **Barrel:** 4.5", 5.5", 6.5", 7.5". **Weight:** 26 oz. **Length:** 12" overall (6.5" bbl.). **Stocks:** Walnut. **Sights:** Fixed. **Features:** Round tapered barrel; half-fluted and rebated cylinder; case-hardened frame, loading lever and hammer; silver or brass trigger guard and backstrap. Imported by Cimarron, Dixie Gun Works, Taylor's, Uberti U.S.A. and others.

Price: Dixie Gun Works RH0422 .... **$315.00**
Price: Hartford model, steel frame, cartouche (EMF) **$300.00**

ROGERS & SPENCER PERCUSSION REVOLVER

Caliber: 44. **Barrel:** 7.5". **Weight:** 47 oz. **Length:** 13.75" overall. **Stocks:** Walnut. **Sights:** Cone front, integral groove in frame for rear. **Features:** Accurate reproduction of a Civil War design. Solid frame; extra large nipple cut-out on rear of cylinder; loading lever and cylinder easily removed for cleaning. From Dixie Gun Works and others.

Price: **$500.00**

SHERIFF MODEL 1851 PERCUSSION REVOLVER

Caliber: 36, 44, 6-shot. **Barrel:** 5". **Weight:** 40 oz. **Length:** 10.5" overall. **Stocks:** Walnut. **Sights:** Fixed. **Features:** Brass backstrap and trigger guard; engraved navy scene; case-hardened frame, hammer, loading lever. Imported by EMF.

Price: Steel frame **$169.95**
Price: Brass frame **$140.00**

SPILLER & BURR REVOLVER

Caliber: 36 (.375" round ball). **Barrel:** 7", octagon. **Weight:** 2.5 lbs. **Length:** 12.5" overall. **Stocks:** Two-piece walnut. **Sights:** Fixed. **Features:** Reproduction of the C.S.A. revolver. Brass frame and trigger

guard. Also available as a kit. From Dixie Gun Works and others.
Price: **$255.00**

UBERTI 1847 WALKER REVOLVERS

Caliber: 44 6-shot engraved cylinder. **Barrel:** 9" 7 grooves. **Weight:** 4.5 lbs. **Length:** 15.7" overall. **Stocks:** One-piece hardwood. **Sights:** Fixed. **Features:** Copy of Sam Colt's first commercially-made revolving pistol, loading lever available, no trigger guard. Case-hardened hammer. Blued finish. Made in Italy by Uberti, imported by Benelli USA.

Price: **$429.00**

UBERTI 1848 DRAGOON AND POCKET REVOLVERS

Caliber: 44 6-shot engraved cylinder. **Barrel:** 7.5" 7 grooves. **Weight:** 4.1 lbs. **Stocks:** One-piece walnut. **Sights:** Fixed. **Features:** Copy of Eli Whitney's design for Colt using Walker parts. Blued barrel, backstrap, and trigger guard. Made in Italy by Uberti, imported by Benelli USA.

Price: 1848 Whitneyville Dragoon, 7.5" barrel ... **$429.00**
Price: 1848 Dragoon, 1st-3rd models, 7.5" barrel . **$409.00**
Price: 1848 Baby Dragoon, 4" barrel **$339.00**

UBERTI 1858 NEW ARMY REVOLVERS

Caliber: 44 6-shot engraved cylinder. **Barrel:** 8" 7 grooves. **Weight:** 2.7 lbs. **Length:** 13.6". **Stocks:** Two-piece walnut. **Sights:** Fixed. **Features:** Blued or stainless barrel, backstrap; brass trigger guard. Made in Italy by Uberti, imported by Benelli USA.

Price: 1858 New Army Stainless 8" barrel............... **$429.00**
Price: 1858 New Army 8" barrel **$349.00**
Price: 1858 Target Carbine 18" barrel **$549.00**
Price: 1862 Pocket Navy 5.5" barrel, 36 caliber **$349.00**
Price: 1862 Police 5.5" barrel, 36 caliber **$349.00**

UBERTI 1861 NAVY PERCUSSION REVOLVER

Caliber: 36, 6-shot. **Barrel:** 7.5", 7-groove, round. **Weight:** 2 lbs., 6 oz. **Length:** 13". **Stocks:** One-piece walnut. **Sights:** German silver blade front sight. **Features:** Rounded trigger guard, "creeping" loading lever, fluted or round cylinder, steel backstrap, trigger guard, cut for stock. Imported by Cimarron F.A. Co., Uberti U.S.A. Inc., Dixie Gun Works.
Price: Dixie RH0420.............................. **$295.00**

1862 POCKET NAVY PERCUSSION REVOLVER

Caliber: 36, 5-shot. **Barrel:** 5.5", 6.5", octagonal, 7-groove, LH twist. **Weight:** 27 oz. (5.5" barrel). **Length:** 10.5" overall (5.5" bbl.). **Stocks:** One-piece varnished walnut. **Sights:** Brass pin front, hammer notch rear. **Features:** Rebated cylinder, hinged loading lever, brass or silver plated backstrap and trigger guard, color-cased frame, hammer, loading lever, plunger and latch, rest blued. Has original-type markings. From Cimarron F.A. Co., Uberti U.S.A. Inc., Dixie Gun Works.
Price: With brass backstrap, trigger guard.............. **$250.00**

WALKER 1847 PERCUSSION REVOLVER

Caliber: 44, 6-shot. **Barrel:** 9". **Weight:** 84 oz. **Length:** 15.5" overall. **Stocks:** Walnut. **Sights:** Fixed. **Features:** Case-hardened frame, loading lever and hammer; iron backstrap; brass trigger guard; engraved cylinder. Imported by Cabela's, Cimarron, Dixie Gun Works, Taylor's, Uberti and others.
Price: **$349.00**
Price: Case hardened frame **$409.00**

CABELA'S BLUE RIDGE RIFLE
Caliber: 32, 36, 45, 50, .54. **Barrel:** 39", octagonal. **Weight:** About 7.75 lbs. **Length:** 55" overall. **Stock:** American black walnut. **Sights:** Blade front, rear drift adjustable for windage. **Features:** Color case-hardened lockplate and cock/hammer, brass trigger guard and buttplate, double set, double-phased triggers. From Cabela's.
Price: Percussion **$569.99**
Price: Flintlock **$599.99**

CABELA'S TRADITIONAL HAWKEN
Caliber: 50, 54. **Barrel:** 29". **Weight:** About 9 lbs. **Stock:** Walnut. **Sights:** Blade front, open adjustable rear. **Features:** Flintlock or percussion. Adjustable double-set triggers. Polished brass furniture, color case-hardened lock. Imported by Cabela's.
Price: Percussion, right-hand or left-hand................................. **$339.99**
Price: Flintlock, right-hand **$399.99**

CABELA'S KODIAK EXPRESS DOUBLE RIFLE
Caliber: 50, 54, 58, 72. **Barrel:** Length NA; 1:48" twist. **Weight:** 9.3 lbs. **Length:** 45.25" overall. **Stock:** European walnut, oil finish. **Sights:** Fully adjustable double folding-leaf rear, ramp front. **Features:** Percussion. Barrels regulated to point of aim at 75 yards; polished and engraved lock, top tang and trigger guard. From Cabela's.
Price: 50, 54, 58 calibers **$929.99**
Price: 72 caliber **$959.99**

COOK & BROTHER CONFEDERATE CARBINE
Caliber: 58. **Barrel:** 24". **Weight:** 7.5 lbs. **Length:** 40.5" overall. **Stock:** Select walnut. **Features:** Re-creation of the 1861 New Orleans-made artillery carbine. Color case-hardened lock, browned barrel. Buttplate, trigger guard, barrel bands, sling swivels and nosecap of polished brass. From Euroarms of America and Cabela's.
Price: **$999.00**

CVA OPTIMA V2 BREAK ACTION RIFLE
Caliber: 45, 50. **Barrel:** 28" fluted. **Weight:** 8.8 lbs. **Stock:** Ambidextrous solid composite in standard or thumbhole. **Sights:** Adj. fiber-optic. **Features:** Break-action, stainless No. 209 breech plug, aluminum loading rod, cocking spur, lifetime warranty.
Price: CR4002 (50-cal., blued/Realtree HD) **$398.95**
Price: CR4002X (50-cal., stainless/Realtree HD) **$456.95**
Price: CR4003X (45-cal., stainless/Realtree HD) **$456.95**
Price: CR4000T (50-cal), blued/black fiber grip thumbhole) .. **$366.95**
Price: CR4000 (50-cal., blued/black fiber grip) **$345.95**
Price: CR4002T (50-cal., blued/Realtree HD thumbhole) **$432.95**
Price: CR4002S (50-cal., stainless/Realtree HD thumbhole) **$422.95**
Price: CR4000X (50-cal., stainless/black fiber grip thumbhole) **$451.95**
Price: CR4000S (50-cal., stainless steel/black fiber grip) **$400.95**

CVA OPTIMA 209 MAGNUM BREAK-ACTION RIFLE
Similar to Optima Elite but with 26" bbl., nickel or blue finish, 50 cal.
Price: .... **$317.00 to $409.00**

CVA WOLF 209 MAGNUM BREAK-ACTION RIFLE
Similar to Optima 209 Mag but with 24 barrel, weighs 7 lbs, and in 50-cal. only.
Price: .... **$247.00 to $329.00**

CVA APEX
Caliber: 45, 50. **Barrel:** 27", 1:28 twist. **Weight:** 8 lbs. **Length:** 42". **Stock:** Synthetic. **Features:** Ambi stock with rubber grip panels in black or Realtree APG camo, crush-zone recoil pad, reversible hammer spur, quake claw sling, lifetime warranty.
Price: CR4010S (50-cal., stainless/black) **$738.00**

CVA ACCURA
Similar to Apex but weighs 7.3 lbs., in stainless steel or matte blue finish, cocking spur.
Price: PR3106S (50-cal, stainless steel/Realtree
APG thumbhole) **$495.95**
Price: PR3107S (45-cal, stainless steel/Realtree
APG thumbhole) **$495.95**
Price: PR 3104S (50-cal., stainless steel/black fibergrip
thumbhole) **$438.95**
Price: PR3100 (50-cal., blued/black fibergrip **$345.95**
Price: PR3100S (50-cal., stainless steel/black fibergrip **$403.95**
Price: PR3102S (50-cal., stainless steel/Realtree APG) **$460.95**

CVA BUCKHORN 209 MAGNUM
Caliber: 50. **Barrel:** 24". **Weight:** 6.3 lbs. **Sights:** Illuminator fiber-optic. **Features:** Grip-dot stock, thumb-actuated safety; drilled and tapped for scope mounts.
Price: Black stock, blue barrel **$177.00**

DIXIE EARLY AMERICAN JAEGER RIFLE
Caliber: 54. **Barrel:** 27.5" octagonal; 1:24" twist. **Weight:** 8.25 lbs. **Length:** 43.5" overall. **Stock:** American walnut; sliding wooden patchbox on butt. **Sights:** Notch rear, blade front. **Features:** Flintlock or percussion. Browned steel furniture. Imported from Italy by Dixie Gun Works.
Price: Flintlock or Percussion **$1,339.00**

DIXIE DELUXE CUB RIFLE
Caliber: 32, 36, 40, 45. **Barrel:** 28" octagon. **Weight:** 6.25 lbs. **Length:** 44" overall. **Stock:** Walnut. **Sights:** Fixed. **Features:** Short rifle for small game and beginning shooters. Brass patchbox and furniture. Flint or percussion, finished or kit. From Dixie Gun Works
Price: Deluxe Cub (45-cal.) **$525.00**
Price: Deluxe Cub (flint) **$530.00**
Price: Super Cub (50-cal) **$530.00**
Price: Deluxe Cub (32-cal. flint) **$725.00**
Price: Deluxe Cub (36-cal. flint) **$725.00**
Price: Deluxe Cub kit (32-cal. percussion) **$550.00**
Price: Deluxe Cub kit (36-cal. percussion) **$550.00**
Price: Deluxe Cub (45-cal. percussion) **$675.00**
Price: Super Cub (percussion) **$450.00**
Price: Deluxe Cub (32-cal. percussion) **$675.00**
Price: Deluxe Cub (36-cal. percussion) **$675.00**

DIXIE PEDERSOLI 1857 MAUSER RIFLE
Caliber: 54. **Barrel:** 39-3/8". **Weight:** 9.5 lbs. **Length:** 54.75" overall. **Stock:** European walnut with oil finish, sling swivels. **Sights:** Fully adjustable rear, lug front. **Features:** Percussion (musket caps). Armory bright finish with color case-hardened lock and barrel tang, engraved lockplate, steel ramrod. Introduced 2000. Imported from Italy by Dixie Gun Works.
Price: PR1330.. **$995.00**

DIXIE SHARPS NEW MODEL 1859 MILITARY RIFLE
Caliber: 54. **Barrel:** 30", 6-groove; 1:48" twist. **Weight:** 9 lbs. **Length:** 45.5" overall. **Stock:** Oiled walnut. **Sights:** Blade front, ladder-style rear. **Features:** Blued barrel, color case-hardened barrel bands, receiver, hammer, nosecap, lever, patchbox cover and buttplate. Introduced 1995. Imported from Italy by Dixie Gun Works.
Price: PR0862.. **$1,100.00**
Price: Carbine (22 barrel, 7-groove, 39-1/4" overall,
weighs 8 lbs.)... **$925.00**

DIXIE U.S. MODEL 1816 FLINTLOCK MUSKET
Caliber: .69. **Barrel:** 42", smoothbore. **Weight:** 9.75 lbs. **Length:** 56 7/8" overall. **Stock:** Walnut w/oil finish. **Sights:** Blade front. **Features:** All

Prices given are believed to be accurate at time of publication however, many factors affect retail pricing so exact prices are not possible.

BLACKPOWDER MUSKETS & RIFLES

metal finished "National Armory Bright," three barrel bands w/springs, steel ramrod w/button-shaped head. Imported by Dixie Gun Works.
Price: FR0305 ....**$1,200.00**
Price: PR0257, Percussion conversion.................................**$995.00**

EMF 1863 SHARPS MILITARY CARBINE
Caliber: 54. **Barrel:** 22", round. **Weight:** 8 lbs. **Length:** 39" overall.
Stock: Oiled walnut. **Sights:** Blade front, military ladder-type rear.
Features: Color case-hardened lock, rest blued. Imported by EMF.
Price: **$759.90**

EUROARMS VOLUNTEER TARGET RIFLE
Caliber: 451. **Barrel:** 33" (two-band), 36" (three-band). **Weight:** 11 lbs. (two-band). **Length:** 48.75" overall (two-band). **Stock:** European walnut with checkered wrist and forend. **Sights:** Hooded bead front, adjustable rear with interchangeable leaves. **Features:** Alexander Henry-type rifling with 1:20" twist. Color case-hardened hammer and lockplate, brass trigger guard and nosecap, remainder blued. Imported by Euroarms of America, Dixie Gun Works.
Price: PR1031 .... **$925.00**

EUROARMS 1861 SPRINGFIELD RIFLE
Caliber: 58. **Barrel:** 40". **Weight:** About 10 lbs. **Length:** 55.5" overall.
Stock: European walnut. **Sights:** Blade front, three-leaf military rear.
Features: Reproduction of the original three-band rifle. Lockplate marked "1861" with eagle and "U.S. Springfield." White metal. Imported by Euroarms of America.
Price: **$730.00**

EUROARMS ZOUAVE RIFLE
Caliber: 54, 58 percussion. **Barrel:** 33". **Weight:** 9.5 lbs. Overall length: 49". **Features:** One-piece solid barrel and bolster. For 54 caliber, .535 R.B., .540 minnie. For 58 caliber, .575 R.B., .577 minnie. 1863 issue. Made in Italy. Imported by Euroarms of America.
Price: **$469.00**

EUROARMS HARPERS FERRY RIFLE
Caliber: 58 flintlock. **Barrel:** 35". **Weight:** 9 lbs. Overall length: 59.5".
Features: Antique browned barrel. Barrel .575 RB. .577 minnie. 1803 issue. Made in Italy. Imported by Euroarms of America.
Price: **$735.00**

HARPER'S FERRY 1803 FLINTLOCK RIFLE
Caliber: 54 or 58. **Barrel:** 35". **Weight:** 9 lbs. **Length:** 59.5" overall.
Stock: Walnut with cheekpiece. **Sights:** Brass blade front, fixed steel rear. **Features:** Brass trigger guard, sideplate, buttplate; steel patchbox. Imported by Dixie Gun Works.
Price: **$995.00**

HAWKEN RIFLE
Caliber: 45, 50, 54 or 58. **Barrel:** 28", blued, 6-groove rifling. **Weight:** 8.75 lbs. **Length:** 44" overall. **Stock:** Walnut with cheekpiece. **Sights:** Blade front, fully adjustable rear. **Features:** Coil mainspring, double-set triggers, polished brass furniture. Imported by Dixie Gun Works.
Price: **$450.00**

J.P. MURRAY 1862-1864 CAVALRY CARBINE
Caliber: 58 (.577" Minie). **Barrel:** 23". **Weight:** 7 lbs., 9 oz. **Length:** 39" overall. **Stock:** Walnut. **Sights:** Blade front, rear drift adjustable for windage. **Features:** Blued barrel, color case-hardened lock, blued swivel and band springs, polished brass buttplate, trigger guard,

---

barrel bands. From Dixie Gun Works.
Price: Dixie Gun Works PR0173 .... **$1,050.00**

KENTUCKY FLINTLOCK AND PERCUSSION RIFLES
Caliber: 44, 45, or 50. **Barrel:** 35". **Weight:** 7 lbs. **Length:** 50" overall. **Stock:** Walnut stained, brass fittings. **Sights:** Fixed.
Features: Available in a wide range of variations and quality from most importers of BP firearms. Kits also available from some importers.
Price: From .... **$500.00 to $1,500.00**

KNIGHT MOUNTAINEER FOREST GREEN
Caliber: .50, .52. **Barrel:** 27" fluted stainless steel, free floated.
Weight: 8 lbs. (thumbhole stock), 8.3 lbs., (straight stock). **Length:** 45.5". **Sights:** Fully adjustable metallic fiber optic. **Features:** Adjustable match-grade trigger, aluminum ramrod with carbon core.
Price: .... **$670.00 to $950.00**

KNIGHT LONG RANGE HUNTER
Caliber: 50. **Barrel:** 27" custom fluted; 1:28" twist. **Weight:** 8 lbs. 6 oz. **Length:** 45.5" overall. **Stock:** Cast-off design thumbhole, checkered, recoil pad, sling swivel studs, in Forest Green or Sandstone. **Sights:** Fully-adjustable, metallic fiber-optic. **Features:** Full plastic jacket ignition system. Made in U.S. by Knight Rifles (Modern Muzzleloading).
Price: SS Forest Green **$769.99**
Price: SS Forest Green Thumbhole **$799.99**

KNIGHT DISC EXTREME
Caliber: 50, 52. **Barrel:** 26", fluted stainless, 1:20" twist. **Weight:** 7 lbs. 14 oz to 8 lbs. **Length:** 45" overall. **Stock:** Stainless steel laminate, blued walnut, black composite thumbhole with blued or SS, Realtree Hardwoods Green HD with thumbhole. **Sights:** Fully adjustable metallic fiber-optics. **Features:** Full plastic jacket ignition system. Made in U.S. by Knight Rifles (Modern Muzzleloading).
Price: From .... **$560.00 to $930.00**

KNIGHT BIGHORN
Caliber: 50. **Barrel:** 26"; 1:28" twist. **Weight:** 7 lbs. 3 oz. **Length:** 44.5" overall. **Stock:** Realtree Advantage MAX-1 HD or black composite thumbhole, checkered with recoil pad, sling swivel studs. **Sights:** Fully adjustable metallic fiber-optic. **Features:** Uses 4 different ignition systems (included): #11 nipple, musket nipple, bare 208 shotgun primer and 209 Extreme shotgun primer system (Extreme weatherproof full plastic jacket system); one-piece removable hammer assembly. Made in U.S. by Knight Rifles (Modern Muzzleloading).
Price: Standard stock **$460.00**
Price: Thumbhole stock **$480.00**

KNIGHT TK-2000 TURKEY SHOTGUN
Gauge: 12. **Ignition:** 209 primer with Full Plastic Jacket. **Barrel:** 26 inches with Mixed Pine camo coverage. **Weight:** 7.7 pounds. **Stock:** Mixed pine camo. Standard grip or thumbhole. **Sights:** Williams fully adjustable rear, fiber optic front.
Price: ....**$410 to $420**

Prices given are believed to be accurate at time of publication however, many factors affect retail pricing so exact prices are not possible.

BLACKPOWDER MUSKETS & RIFLES

KNIGHT ULTRA-LITE
Caliber: .50. **Barrel:** 50 inches. **Ignition:** 209 Primer with Full Plastic Jacket. **Stock:** Oliver green Kevlar. **Weight:** 6 pounds. **Sights:** None, drilled and tapped for scope mounts. **Finish:** Stainless steel
Price: $900

LONDON ARMORY 1861 ENFIELD MUSKETOON
Caliber: 58, Minie ball. **Barrel:** 24", round. **Weight:** 7 to 7.5 lbs. **Length:** 40.5" overall. **Stock:** Walnut, with sling swivels. **Sights:** Blade front, graduated military-leaf rear. **Features:** Brass trigger guard, nosecap, buttplate; blued barrel, bands, lockplate, swivels. Imported by Euroarms of America, Navy Arms.
Price: .... $300.00 to $521.00
Price: Kit .... $365.00 to $402.00

LONDON ARMORY 2-BAND 1858 ENFIELD
Caliber: .577" Minie, .575" round ball. **Barrel:** 33". **Weight:** 10 lbs. **Length:** 49" overall. **Stock:** Walnut. **Sights:** Folding leaf rear adjustable for elevation. **Features:** Blued barrel, color case-hardened lock and hammer, polished brass buttplate, trigger guard, nosecap. From Navy Arms, Euroarms of America, Dixie Gun Works.
Price: PR0330..$650.00

LONDON ARMORY 3-BAND 1853 ENFIELD
Caliber: 58 (.577" Minie, .575" round ball, .580" maxi ball). **Barrel:** 39". **Weight:** 9.5 lbs. **Length:** 54" overall. **Stock:** European walnut. **Sights:** Inverted "V" front, traditional Enfield folding ladder rear. **Features:** Re-creation of the famed London Armory Company Pattern 1853 Enfield Musket. One-piece walnut stock, brass buttplate, trigger guard and nosecap. Lockplate marked "London Armoury Co." and with a British crown. Blued Baddeley barrel bands. From Euroarms of America, Navy Arms.
Price: About .... $350.00 to $606.00

LYMAN TRADE RIFLE
Caliber: 50, 54. **Barrel:** 28" octagon;1:48" twist. **Weight:** 10.8 lbs. **Length:** 45" overall. **Stock:** European walnut. **Sights:** Blade front, open rear adjustable for windage or optional fixed sights. **Features:** Fast twist rifling for conical bullets. Polished brass furniture with blue steel parts, stainless steel nipple. Hook breech, single trigger, coil spring percussion lock. Steel barrel rib and ramrod ferrules. Introduced 1980. From Lyman.
Price: Percussion..$525.00
Price: Flintlock $570.00

LYMAN DEERSTALKER RIFLE
Caliber: 50, 54. **Barrel:** 24", octagonal; 1:48" rifling. **Weight:** 10.4 lbs. **Stock:** Walnut with black rubber buttpad. **Sights:** Lyman #37MA beaded front, fully adjustable fold-down Lyman #16A rear. **Features:** Stock has less drop for quick sighting. All metal parts are blackened, with color case-hardened lock; single trigger. Comes with sling and swivels. Available in flint or percussion. Introduced 1990. From Lyman.

Price: 50 cal. flintlock $560.00
Price: Left-hand flintlock $615.00
Price: 54 ca. flintlock $570.00
Price: Percussion blue $525.00
Price: Percussion stainless $625.00

LYMAN GREAT PLAINS RIFLE
Caliber: 50, 54. **Barrel:** 32"; 1:60" twist. **Weight:** 11.6 lbs. **Stock:** Walnut. **Sights:** Steel blade front, buckhorn rear adjustable for windage and elevation and fixed notch primitive sight included. **Features:** Blued steel furniture. Stainless steel nipple. Coil spring lock, Hawken-style trigger guard and double-set triggers. Round thimbles recessed and sweated into rib. Steel wedge plates and toe plate. Introduced 1979. From Lyman.
Price: Percussion $720.00
Price: Flintlock $770.00
Price: Left-hand percussion $750.00
Price: Left-hand flintlock $785.00

LYMAN GREAT PLAINS HUNTER MODEL
Similar to Great Plains model except 1:32" twist shallow-groove barrel and comes drilled and tapped for Lyman 57GPR peep sight.
Price: Percussion...$720.00
Price: Flintlock $770.00

MISSISSIPPI 1841 PERCUSSION RIFLE
Caliber: 54, 58. **Barrel:** 33". **Weight:** 9.5 lbs. **Length:** 48-5/8" overall. **Stock:** One-piece European walnut full stock with satin finish. **Sights:** Brass blade front, fixed steel rear. **Features:** Case-hardened lockplate marked "U.S." surmounted by American eagle. Two barrel bands, sling swivels. Steel ramrod with brass end, browned barrel. From Navy Arms, Dixie Gun Works, Euroarms of America.
Price: Dixie Gun Works PR0870 .... $825.00

NAVY ARMS 1861 MUSKETOON
Caliber: 58. **Barrel:** 39". **Weight:** NA. **Length:** NA. **Stock:** NA. **Sights:** Front is blued steel base and blade, blued steel lip-up rear adjustable for elevation. **Features:** Brass nosecap, triggerguard, buttplate, blued steel barrel bands, color case-hardened lock with engraved lockplate marked "1861 Enfield" ahead of hammer & crown over "PH" on tail. Barrel is marked "Parker Hale LTD Birmingham England." Imported by Navy Arms.
Price: $900.00

NAVY ARMS PARKER-HALE 1853 THREE-BAND ENFIELD
Caliber: 58. **Barrel:** 39", tapered, round, blued. **Weight:** NA. **Length:** 55-1/4" overall. **Stock:** Walnut. **Sights:** Front is blued steel base and blade, blued steel lip-up rear adjustable for elevation. **Features:** Meticulously reproduced based on original gauges and patterns. Features brass nosecap, triggerguard, buttplate, blued steel barrel bands, color case-hardened lock with engraved lockplate marked "Parker-Hale" ahead of hammer & crown over "PH" on tail. Barrel is marked "Parker Hale LTD Birmingham England." From Navy Arms.
Price: Finished rifle $1,050.00

NAVY ARMS PARKER-HALE 1858 TWO-BAND ENFIELD
Similar to the Three-band Enfield with 33" barrel, 49" overall length. Engraved lockplate marked "1858 Enfield" ahead of hammer & crown over "PH" on tail. Barrel is marked "Parker Hale LTD Birmingham England."
Price: $1,050.00

Prices given are believed to be accurate at time of publication however, many factors affect retail pricing so exact prices are not possible.

BLACKPOWDER MUSKETS & RIFLES

NAVY ARMS PARKER-HALE VOLUNTEER RIFLE
Caliber: 451. **Barrel:** 32", 1:20" twist. **Weight:** 9.5 lbs. **Length:** 49" overall. **Stock:** Walnut, checkered wrist and forend. **Sights:** Globe front, adjustable ladder-type rear. **Features:** Recreation of the type of gun issued to volunteer regiments during the 1860s. Rigby-pattern rifling, patent breech, detented lock. Stock is glass beaded for accuracy. Engraved lockplate marked "Alex Henry" & crown on tail, barrel marked "Parker Hale LTD Birmingham England" and "Alexander Henry Rifling .451" Imported by Navy Arms.
Price: **$1,400.00**

NAVY ARMS PARKER-HALE WHITWORTH MILITARY TARGET RIFLE
Caliber: 45. **Barrel:** 36". **Weight:** 9.25 lbs. **Length:** 52.5" overall. **Stock:** Walnut. Checkered at wrist and forend. **Sights:** Hooded post front, open step-adjustable rear. **Features:** Faithful reproduction of Whitworth rifle. Trigger has detented lock, capable of fine adjustments without risk of the sear nose catching on the half-cock notch and damaging both parts. Engraved lockplate marked "Whitworth" ahead of hammer & crown on tail. Barrel marked "Parker Hale LTD Birmingham England" in one line on front of sight and "Sir Joseph Whitworth's Rifling .451" on left side. Introduced 1978. Imported by Navy Arms.
Price: **$1,550.00**

NAVY ARMS BROWN BESS MUSKET
Caliber: 75, smoothbore. **Barrel:** 41.8". **Weight:** 9 lbs., 5 oz. **Length:** 41.8" overall. **Features:** Brightly polished steel and brass, one-piece walnut stock. Signature of gunsmith William Grice and the date 1762, the crown and alphabetical letters GR (Georgius Rex). Barrel is made of steel, satin finish; the walnut stock is oil finished. From Navy Arms.
Price: **$1,100.00**

NAVY ARMS COUNTRY HUNTER
Caliber: 50. **Barrel:** 28.4", 6-groove, 1:34 twist. **Weight:** 6 lbs. **Length:** 44" overall. **Features:** Matte finished barrel. From Navy Arms.
Price: **$450.00**

NAVY ARMS PENNSYLVANIA RIFLE
Caliber: 32, 45. **Barrel:** 41.6". **Weight:** 7 lbs. 12 oz. to 8 lbs. 6 oz. **Length:** 56.1" overall. **Features:** Extra long rifle finished with rust brown color barrel and one-piece oil finished walnut stock. Adjustable double-set trigger. Vertically adjustable steel front and rear sights. From Navy Arms.
Price: **$675.00**

NEW ENGLAND FIREARMS SIDEKICK
Caliber: 50, 209 primer ignition. **Barrel:** 26" (magnum). **Weight:** 6.5 lbs. **Length:** 41.25". **Stock:** Black matte polymer or hardwood. **Sights:** Adjustable fiber-optic open, tapped for scope mounts. **Features:** Single-shot based on H&R break-open action. Uses No. 209 shotgun primer held in place by special primer carrier. Telescoping brass ramrod. Introduced 2004.
Price: Wood stock, blued frame, black-oxide barrel) **$216.00**
Price: Stainless barrel and frame, synthetic stock) **$310.00**

NEW ENGLAND FIREARMS HUNTSMAN
Caliber: 50, 209 primer ignition. **Barrel:** 22" to 26". **Weight:** 5.25 to 6.5 lbs. **Length:** 40" to 43". **Stock:** Black matte polymer or hardwood. **Sights:** Fiber-optic open sights, tapped for scope mounts. **Features:** Break-open action, transfer-bar safety system, breech plug removable for cleaning. Introduced 2004.
Price: Stainless Huntsman **$306.00**
Price: Huntsman **$212.00**

Price: Pardner Combo 12 ga./50 cal muzzleloader **$259.00**
Price: Tracker II Combo 12 ga. rifled slug barrel /50 cal. **$288.00**
Price: Handi-Rifle Combo 243/50 cal. **$405.00**

NEW ENGLAND FIREARMS STAINLESS HUNTSMAN
Similar to Huntsman, but with matte nickel finish receiver and stainless bbl. Introduced 2003. From New England Firearms.
Price: **$381.00**

PACIFIC RIFLE MODEL 1837 ZEPHYR
Caliber: 62. **Barrel:** 30", tapered octagon. **Weight:** 7.75 lbs. **Length:** NA. **Stock:** Oil-finished fancy walnut. **Sights:** German silver blade front, semi-buckhorn rear. Options available. **Features:** Improved underhammer action. First production rifle to offer Forsyth rifle, with narrow lands and shallow rifling with 1:14" pitch for high-velocity round balls. Metal finish is slow rust brown with nitre blue accents. Optional sights, finishes and integral muzzle brake available. Introduced 1995. Made in U.S. by Pacific Rifle Co.
Price: From **$1,750.00**

RICHMOND, C.S., 1863 MUSKET
Caliber: 58. **Barrel:** 40". **Weight:** 11 lbs. **Length:** 56.25" overall. **Stock:** European walnut with oil finish. **Sights:** Blade front, adjustable folding leaf rear. **Features:** Reproduction of the three-band Civil War musket. Sling swivels attached to trigger guard and middle barrel band. Lockplate marked "1863" and "C.S. Richmond." All white metal. Brass buttplate and forend cap. Imported by Euroarms of America, Navy Arms, and Dixie Gun Works.
Price: **$858.00**

ROCKY MOUNTAIN HAWKEN
Caliber: NA. **Barrel:** 34-11/16". **Weight:** 10 lbs. **Length:** 52" overall. **Stock:** Walnut or maple. **Sights:** Blade front, drift adjustable rear. **Features:** Percussion, double set trigger, casehardened furniture, hook breech, brown barrel. Made by Pedersoli in Italy. Imported by Dixie Gun Works.
Price: **$1,299.00**

SECOND MODEL BROWN BESS MUSKET
Caliber: 75, uses .735" round ball. **Barrel:** 42", smoothbore. **Weight:** 9.5 lbs. **Length:** 59" overall. **Stock:** Walnut (Navy); walnut-stained hardwood (Dixie). **Sights:** Fixed. **Features:** Polished barrel and lock with brass trigger guard and buttplate. Bayonet and scabbard available. From Navy Arms, Dixie Gun Works.
Price: **$1,299.00**

THOMPSON/CENTER TRIUMPH MAGNUM MUZZLELOADER
Caliber: 50. **Barrel:** 28" Weather Shield coated. **Weight:** NA. **Length:** NA. **Stock:** Black composite or Realtree AP HD Camo. **Sights:** NA. **Features:** QLA 209 shotshell primer ignition. Introduced 2007. Made in U.S. by Thompson/Center Arms.
Price: **$457.00**

THOMPSON/CENTER BONE COLLECTOR
Similar to the Triumph Magnum but with added Flex Tech technology and Energy Burners to a shorter stock. Also added is Thompson/Center's premium fluted barrel with Weather Shield and their patented Power Rod.
Price: **$708.00**

THOMPSON/CENTER ENCORE 209X50 MAGNUM
Caliber: 50. **Barrel:** 26"; interchangeable with centerfire calibers. **Weight:** 7 lbs. **Length:** 40.5" overall. **Stock:** American walnut butt and forend, or black composite. **Sights:** TruGlo fiber-optic front and rear. **Features:** Blue or stainless steel. Uses the stock, frame and forend of the Encore centerfire pistol; break-open design using trigger guard spur; stainless steel universal breech plug; uses #209 shotshell primers. Introduced 1998. Made in U.S. by Thompson/Center Arms.

Price: Stainless with camo stock...........................$772.00
Price: Blue, walnut stock and forend $678.00
Price: Blue, composite stock and forend $637.00
Price: Stainless, composite stock and forend $713.00
Price: All camo Realtree Hardwoods $729.00

THOMPSON/CENTER FIRE STORM RIFLE
Caliber: 50. **Barrel:** 26"; 1:28" twist. **Weight:** 7 lbs. **Length:** 41.75" overall. **Stock:** Black synthetic with rubber recoil pad, swivel studs. **Sights:** Click-adjustable steel rear and ramp-style front, both with fiber-optic inserts. **Features:** Side hammer lock is the first designed for up to three 50-grain Pyrodex pellets; patented Pyrodex Pyramid breech directs ignition fire 360 degrees around base of pellet. Quick Load Accurizor Muzzle System; aluminum ramrod. Flintlock only. Introduced 2000. Made in U.S. by Thompson/Center Arms.
Price: Blue finish, flintlock model with 1:48" twist for round balls, conicals $436.00
Price: SST, flintlock $488.00

THOMPSON/CENTER HAWKEN RIFLE
Caliber: 50. **Barrel:** 28" octagon, hooked breech. **Stock:** American walnut. **Sights:** Blade front, rear adjustable for windage and elevation. **Features:** Solid brass furniture, double-set triggers, button rifled barrel, coil-type mainspring. From Thompson/Center Arms.
Price: Percussion model $590.00
Price: Flintlock model $615.00

THOMPSON/CENTER OMEGA
Caliber: 50". **Barrel:** 28", fluted. **Weight:** 7 lbs. **Length:** 42" overall. **Stock:** Composite or laminated. **Sights:** Adjustable metal rear sight with fiber-optics; metal ramp front sight with fiber-optics. **Features:** Drilled and tapped for scope mounts. Thumbhole stock, sling swivel studs. From T/C..
Price: $777.00

THOMPSON/CENTER IMPACT MUZZLELOADING RIFLE
50-caliber single shot rifle. Features include 209 primer ignition, sliding hood to expose removable breechplug, synthetic stock adjustable from 12.5 to 13.5 inches, 26-inch blued 1:28 rifled barrel, adjustable fiber optic sights, aluminum ramrod, camo composite stock, QLA muzzle system. Weight 6.5 lbs.
Price: Impact Camo, Impact Camo / WS Camo, Impact Composite, Impact Weather Shield Black, Impact Weather Shield Camo ....$249.00 to $269.00

THOMPSON/CENTER NORTHWEST EXPLORER MUZZLELOADING RIFLE
50-caliber single shot rifle. Features include dropping block action, #11

---

percussion cap ignition, 28-inch blued or Weathershield 1:48 rifled barrel, adjustable fiber optic sights, aluminum ramrod, black or camo composite stock with recoil pad, QLA muzzle system. Weight 7 lbs.
Price: ....$329.00 to $399.00

TRADITIONS BUCKSKINNER CARBINE
Caliber: 50. **Barrel:** 21"; 15/16" flats, half octagon, half round; 1:20" or 1:66" twist. **Weight:** 6 lbs. **Length:** 37" overall. **Stock:** Beech or black laminated. **Sights:** Beaded blade front, fiber-optic open rear click adjustable for windage and elevation or fiber-optics. **Features:** Uses V-type mainspring, single trigger. Non-glare hardware; sling swivels. From Traditions.
Price: Flintlock $249.00
Price: Flintlock, laminated stock $303.00

TRADITIONS DEERHUNTER RIFLE SERIES
Caliber: 32, 50 or 54. **Barrel:** 24", octagonal; 15/16" flats; 1:48" or 1:66" twist. **Weight:** 6 lbs. **Length:** 40" overall. **Stock:** Stained hardwood or All-Weather composite with rubber buttpad, sling swivels. **Sights:** Lite Optic blade front, adjustable rear fiber-optics. **Features:** Flint or percussion with color case-hardened lock. Hooked breech, oversized trigger guard, blackened furniture, PVC ramrod. All-Weather has composite stock and C-nickel barrel. Drilled and tapped for scope mounting. Imported by Traditions, Inc.
Price: Percussion, 50-cal.; blued barrel; 1:48" twist................$228.00
Price: Flintlock, 50 caliber only; 1:48" twist $278.00
Price: 50-cal., synthetic/blued $224.00
Price: Flintlock, 50-cal., synthetic/blued $256.00
Price: Redi-Pak, 50 cal. flintlock $308.00
Price: Flintlock, left-handed hardwood, 50 cal. $337.00
Price: 50-cal., hardwood/blued $264.00

TRADITIONS PURSUIT ULTRALIGHT MUZZLELOADER
Caliber: .50. **Barrel:** 26", Chromoly Tapered, Fluted Barrel with Premium CeraKote Finish. **Weight:** 5.5 lbs. **Length:** 44" overall. **Stock:** Soft Touch camouflage stocks with thumbhole stocks available. **Sights:** 3-9x40 scope with medium rings and bases mounted and bore sighted by a factory trained technician. **Features:** Williams™ fiber optic metal sights provide a clear sight picture even in low light conditions. The Pursuit™ Ultralight comes equipped with our Accelerator Breech Plug™. This patented and award winning breech plug removes in three full rotations and requires no tools! This full featured gun is rounded out with a corrosion resistant lightweight frame that improves overall handling.
Price: $435.00

TRADITIONS PURSUIT BREAK-OPEN MUZZLELOADER
Caliber: 45, 54 and 12 gauge. **Barrel:** 28", tapered, fluted; blued, stainless or Hardwoods Green camo. **Weight:** 8.25 lbs. **Length:** 44" overall. **Stock:** Synthetic black or Hardwoods Green. **Sights:** Steel fiber-optic rear, bead front. Introduced 2004 by Traditions, Inc.
Price: Steel, blued, 45 or 50 cal., synthetic stock $279.00
Price: Steel, nickel, 45 or 50 cal., synthetic stock $309.00
Price: Steel, nickel w/Hardwoods Green stock $359.00
Price: Matte blued; 12 ga., synthetic stock $369.00
Price: Matte blued; 12 ga. w/Hardwoods Green stock $439.00
Price: Lightweight model, blued, synthetic stock $199.00
Price: Lightweight model, blued, Mossy Oak® Break-Up™ Camo stock $239.00
Price: Lightweight model, nickel, Mossy Oak® Break-Up™ Camo stock $279.00

TRADITIONS EVOLUTION LONG DISTANCE BOLT-ACTION BLACKPOWDER RIFLE
Caliber: 45, 50 percussion. **Barrel:** 26", fluted with porting. **Sights:**

Steel fiber-optic. **Weight:** 7 to 7.25 lbs. **Length:** 45" overall. **Features:** Bolt-action, cocking indicator, thumb safety, aluminum ramrod, sling studs. Wide variety of stocks and metal finishes. Introduced 2004 by Traditions, Inc.
Price: 50-cal. synthetic stock $314.00
Price: 45-cal, synthetic stock $259.00
Price: 50-cal. AW/Adv. Timber HD $370.00
Price: 50-cal. synthetic black/blued $293.00

TRADITIONS PA PELLET FLINTLOCK
Caliber: 50. **Barrel:** 26", blued, nickel. **Weight:** 7 lbs. **Stock:** Hardwood, synthetic and synthetic break-up. **Sights:** Fiber-optic. **Features:** Removeable breech plug, left-hand model with hardwood stock. 1:48" twist.
Price: Hardwood, blued.. $379.00
Price: Hardwood left, blued $469.00

TRADITIONS HAWKEN WOODSMAN RIFLE
Caliber: 50. **Barrel:** 28"; 15/16" flats. **Weight:** 7 lbs., 11 oz. **Length:** 44.5" overall. **Stock:** Walnut-stained hardwood. **Sights:** Beaded blade front, hunting-style open rear adjustable for windage and elevation. **Features:** Percussion only. Brass patchbox and furniture. Double triggers. From Traditions.
Price: percussion $429.00
Price: flintlock $469.00

TRADITIONS KENTUCKY RIFLE
Caliber: 50. **Barrel:** 33.5"; 7/8" flats; 1:66" twist. **Weight:** 7 lbs. **Length:** 49" overall. **Stock:** Beech; inletted toe plate. **Sights:** Blade front, fixed rear. **Features:** Full-length, two-piece stock; brass furniture; color case-hardened lock. From Traditions.
Price: percussion $389.00
Price: flintlock $439.00

TRADITIONS PENNSYLVANIA RIFLE
Caliber: 50. **Barrel:** 40.25"; 7/8" flats, octagon. **Weight:** 9 lbs. **Length:** 57.5" overall. **Stock:** Walnut. **Sights:** Blade front, adjustable rear. **Features:** Brass patchbox and ornamentation. Double-set triggers. From Traditions.
Price: percussion $719.00
Price: flintlock $789.00

TRADITIONS SHENANDOAH RIFLE
Caliber: 36, 50. **Barrel:** 33.5" octagon; 1:66" twist. **Weight:** 7 lbs., 3 oz. **Length:** 49.5" overall. **Stock:** Walnut. **Sights:** Blade front, buckhorn rear. **Features:** V-type mainspring; double-set trigger; solid brass buttplate, patchbox, nosecap, thimbles, trigger guard. Introduced 1996. From Traditions.
Price: percussion $599.00
Price: flintlock $629.00

TRADITIONS TENNESSEE RIFLE
Caliber: 50. **Barrel:** 24", octagon; 15/16" flats; 1:66" twist. **Weight:** 6 lbs. **Length:** 40.5" overall. **Stock:** Stained beech. **Sights:** Blade

front, fixed rear. **Features:** One-piece stock has inletted brass furniture, cheekpiece; double-set trigger; V-type mainspring. Flint or percussion. From Traditions.
Price: percussion $459.00
Price: flintlock $519.00

TRADITIONS TRACKER 209 IN-LINE RIFLES
Caliber: 45, 50. **Barrel:** 22" blued or C-nickel finish; 1:28" twist, 50 cal. 1:20" 45 cal. **Weight:** 6 lbs., 4 oz. **Length:** 41" overall. **Stock:** Black, Advantage Timber® composite, synthetic. **Sights:** Lite Optic blade front, adjustable rear. **Features:** Thumb safety; adjustable trigger; rubber butt pad and sling swivel studs; takes 150 grains of Pyrodex pellets; one-piece breech system takes 209 shotshell primers. Drilled and tapped for scope. From Traditions.
Price: (Black composite or synthetic stock, 22" blued barrel). **$161.00**
Price: (Black composite or synthetic stock, 22" C-nickel barrel) $184.00
Price: (Advantage Timber® stock, 22" C-nickel barrel) $249.00
Price: (Redi-Pak, black stock and blued barrel, powder flask, capper, ball starter, other accessories) $219.00
Price: (Redi-Pak, synthetic stock and blued barrel, with scope) $265.00

TRADITIONS VORTEK ULTRALIGHT SCOPE COMBO
Caliber: .50. **Barrel:** 30 inches fluted. **Weight:** 6.75 pounds. **Finish:** Premium CeraKote and Realtree AP camo. **Features:** Drop-out trigger assembly, Speed Load system, Quick Relief recoil pad. Comes with Leupold Ultimate Slam 3-9x40 muzzleloader scope with Savot Ballistics Reticle (SABR).
Price: $800.00

ULTRA LIGHT ARMS MODEL 209 MUZZLELOADER
Caliber: 45 or 50. **Barrel:** 24" button rifled; 1:32 twist. **Weight:** Under 5 lbs. **Stock:** Kevlar/Graphite. **Features:** Recoil pad, sling swivels included. Some color options available. Adj. Timney trigger, positive primer extraction.
Price: $1,800.00

ZOUAVE PERCUSSION RIFLE
Caliber: 58, 59. **Barrel:** 32.5". **Weight:** 9.5 lbs. **Length:** 48.5" overall. **Stock:** Walnut finish, brass patchbox and buttplate. **Sights:** Fixed front, rear adjustable for elevation. **Features:** Color case-hardened lockplate, blued barrel. Imported by Dixie Gun Works.
Price: $950.00

CABELA'S BLACKPOWDER SHOTGUNS
Gauge: 10, 12, 20. **Barrel:** 10-ga., 30"; 12-ga., 28.5" (Extra-Full, Mod., Imp. Cyl. choke tubes); 20-ga., 27.5" (Imp. Cyl. & Mod. fixed chokes). **Weight:** 6.5 to 7 lbs. **Length:** 45" overall (28.5" barrel). **Stock:** American walnut with checkered grip; 12- and 20-gauge have straight stock, 10-gauge has pistol grip. **Features:** Blued barrels, engraved, color case-hardened locks and hammers, brass ramrod tip. From Cabela's.
Price: 10-gauge **$849.99**
Price: 12-gauge **$719.99**
Price: 20-gauge **$659.99**

DIXIE MAGNUM PERCUSSION SHOTGUN
Gauge: 10, 12, 20. **Barrel:** 30" (Imp. Cyl. & Mod.) in 10-gauge; 28" in 12-gauge. **Weight:** 6.25 lbs. **Length:** 45" overall. **Stock:** Hand-checkered walnut, 14" pull. **Features:** Double triggers; light hand engraving; case-hardened locks in 12-gauge, polished steel in 10-gauge; sling swivels. From Dixie Gun Works.
Price: 12 ga. PS0930 .... **$825.00**
Price: 12-ga. Kit PS0940 .... **$725.00**
Price: 20-ga. PS0334 .... **$825.00**
Price: 10-ga. PS1030 .... **$900.00**
Price: 10-ga. kit PS1040 .... **$725.00**
Price: Coach Gun, 12 ga. 20" bbl PS0914 .... **$800.00**

KNIGHT TK2000 NEXT G-1 CAMO MUZZLELOADING SHOTGUN
Gauge: 12. **Barrel:** 26", extra-full choke tube. **Weight:** 7 lbs., 7 oz. **Length:** 45" overall. **Stock:** Synthetic black or Realtree Hardwoods; recoil pad; swivel studs. **Sights:** Fully adjustable rear, blade front with fiber-optics. **Features:** Receiver drilled and tapped for scope mount; in-line ignition; adjustable trigger; removable breech plug; double safety system; Imp. Cyl. choke tube available. Made in U.S. by Knight Rifles (Modern Muzzleloading)
Price: **$379.99**

BAD BULL X-SERIES MUZZLELOADER RIFLES
Caliber: 45. **Barrel:** 28". **Stock:** Laminated thumbhole stock. **Weight:** 9 lbs., 10 oz. **Length:** 50" overall. **Features:** Remington bolt action, Shilen select stainless steel barrel, Harrell's custom muzzle brake, laminated thumbhole stock, adjustable trigger, pillar bedded, glass bedded, free floated barrel, 1" decelerator pad, Warne rings/weaver, mag-prime 2 stage breech plug.
Price: **$3950.00**

BAD BULL FB SERIES MUZZLELOADER RIFLES
Caliber: 45. **Barrel:** 26". **Stock:** Laminated thumbhole stock. **Weight:** 8 lbs., 1 oz. **Length:** 44" overall. **Features:** Ruger falling block action, Shilen select stainless steel barrel, Harrell's custom muzzle brake, black and gray laminated stock and forearm, mag-prime 2 stage breech plug, 1" decelerator pad, Warne rings, open sights (optional).
Price: **$3950.00**

BAD BULL G SERIES MUZZLELOADER RIFLES
Caliber: 45. **Barrel:** 26". **Stock:** Laminated thumbhole stock. **Weight:** 7 lbs., 14 oz. **Length:** 46.75" overall. **Features:** Remington bolt action, Shilen stainless steel barrel, Harrell's custom muzzle brake, classic laminated stock, trigger adjusted to 2 ½ lbs., Double pillar bedded, 1" recoil pad, mag prime 2 stage breech plug, Warne rings & grand slam bases. The Bad Bull G Series has the short length and lightweight of the FB Series and the extreme accuracy of the X Series. It is a great hunting muzzleloader. The 275 grain Parker/BB Bullet is used with IMR 4350 Powder. With this combination, we are producing MOA or less. If you are a hunter who likes a shorter, lighter muzzleloader with great accuracy capability all the way to 500 yards, this is your muzzleloader.
Price: **$3950.00**

AIRFORCE TALON P

BENJAMIN & SHERIDAN CO2

AIRFORCE TALON P
Caliber: .25, single shot. **Barrel:** 12". **Weight:** 3.5 lbs. **Length:** 24.2".
Quick-detachable air tank with adjustable power. Air tank volume 231
cc.
Price: **$421.00**

ARS HUNTING MASTER AR6 AIR PISTOL
Caliber: .22 (.177 + 20 special order). **Barrel:** 12" rifled. **Weight:** 3
lbs. **Length:** 18.25 overall. **Power:** NA. **Grips:** Indonesian walnut
with checkered grip. **Sights:** Adjustable rear, blade front. **Features:** 6
shot repeater with rotary magazine, single or double action, receiver
grooved for scope, hammer block and trigger block safeties.
Price: **$659.00**

BEEMAN P1 MAGNUM AIR PISTOL
Caliber: .177, 20. **Barrel:** 8.4". **Weight:** 2.5 lbs. **Length:** 11" overall.
Power: Top lever cocking; spring-piston. **Grips:** Checkered walnut.
Sights: Blade front, square notch rear with click micrometer
adjustments for windage and elevation. Grooved for scope mounting.
Features: Dual power for .177 and 20 cal.; low setting gives 350-400
fps; high setting 500-600 fps. All Colt 45 auto grips fit gun. Dry-firing
feature for practice. Optional wood shoulder stock. Imported by
Beeman.
Price: . . . . **$530.00 to $565.00**

BEEMAN P3 PNEUMATIC AIR PISTOL
Caliber: .177. **Barrel:** NA. **Weight:** 1.7 lbs. **Length:** 9.6" overall. **Power:**
Single-stroke pneumatic; overlever barrel cocking. **Grips:** Reinforced
polymer. **Sights:** Front and rear fiber-optic sights. **Features:** Velocity
410 fps. Polymer frame; automatic safety; two-stage trigger; built-in
muzzle brake.
Price: **$290.00**

BEEMAN/FEINWERKBAU P44
Caliber: .177, single shot. **Barrel:** 9.17". **Weight:** 2.10 lbs. **Length:**
16.54" overall. **Power:** Pre-charged pneumatic. **Grips:** Walnut
grip. **Sights:** front and rear sights. **Features:** 500 fps, sighting
line adjustable from 360 to 395mm, adjustable 3-d grip in 3 sizes,
adjustable match trigger, delivered in special transport case.
Price: **$2,575.95**
Price: Left-hand model **$2,655.95**

BEEMAN/FEINWERKBAU P56
Caliber: .177, 5-shot magazine. **Barrel:** 8.81". **Weight:** 2.43 lbs.
Length: 16.54" overall. **Power:** Pre-charged pneumatic. **Grips:**
Walnut Morini grip. **Sights:** front and rear sights. **Features:** 500 fps,
match-adjustable trigger, adjustable rear sight, front sight accepts
interchangeable inserts, delivered in special transport case.
Price: **$2,654.00**

BEEMAN/FWB 103 AIR PISTOL
Caliber: .177. **Barrel:** 10.1", 12-groove rifling. **Weight:** 2.5 lbs. **Length:**
16.5" overall. **Power:** Single-stroke pneumatic, underlever cocking.
Grips: Stippled walnut with adjustable palm shelf. **Sights:** Blade front,
open rear adjustable for windage and elevation. Notch size adjustable
for width. Interchangeable front blades. **Features:** Velocity 510 fps.
Fully adjustable trigger. Cocking effort 2 lbs. Imported by Beeman.
Price: Right-hand **$2,110.00**
Price: Left-hand **$2,350.00**

BEEMAN HW70A AIR PISTOL
Caliber: .177. **Barrel:** 6-1/4", rifled. **Weight:** 38 oz. **Length:** 12-3/4"
overall. **Power:** Spring, barrel cocking. **Grips:** Plastic, with thumbrest.
Sights: Hooded post front, square notch rear adjustable for windage
and elevation. Comes with scope base. **Features:** Adjustable trigger,
31-lb. cocking effort, 440 fps MV; automatic barrel safety. Imported by
Beeman.
Price: **$335.00**

BENJAMIN & SHERIDAN CO2 PISTOLS
Caliber: .22, single shot. **Barrel:** 6-3/8", brass **Weight:** 1 lb, 12 oz.
Length: 9" overall. **Power:** 12-gram CO2 cylinder. **Grips:** American
Hardwood. **Sights:** High ramp front, fully adjustable notched rear.
Features: Velocity to 500 fps. Turnbolt action with cross-bolt safety.
Gives about 40 shots per CO2 cylinder. Black or nickel finish. Made
in U.S. by Crosman Corp.
Price: EB22 (.22) **$118.59**

BENJAMIN & SHERIDAN PNEUMATIC PELLET PISTOLS
Caliber: .177, .22, single shot. **Barrel:** 9-3/8", rifled brass. **Weight:**
2 lbs., 8 oz. **Length:** 12.25" overall. **Power:** Underlever pneumatic,
hand pumped. **Grips:** American Hardwood. **Sights:** High ramp front,
fully adjustable notch rear. **Features:** Velocity to 525 fps (variable).
Bolt action with cross-bolt safety. Choice of black or nickel finish.
Made in U.S. by Crosman Corp.
Price: Black finish, HB17 (.177), HB22 (.22) **$133.59**

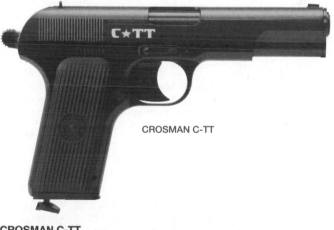

CROSMAN C-TT

CROSMAN C-TT
Caliber: BB, 18-shot magazine. **Length:** 8". Semi-auto CO2-powered
repeater styled after Russian Tarev TT-30. Metal frame and polymer
grip.
Price: **$100.00**

CROSMAN C11
Caliber: .177, 18-shot BB or pellet. **Weight:** 1.4 lbs. **Length:** 8.5".
Power: 12g CO2. **Sights:** Fixed. **Features:** Compact semi-automatic
BB pistol. Velocity up to 480 fps. Under barrel weaver style rail.
Price: **$60.00**

CROSMAN 2240
Caliber: .22. **Barrel:** Rifled steel. **Weight:** 1 lb. 13 oz. **Length:** 11.125".
Power: CO2. **Grips:** NA. **Sights:** Blade front, rear adjustable.
Features: Ergonomically designed ambidextrous grip fits the hand for

perfect balance and comfort with checkering and a thumbrest on both grip panels. From Crosman.

Price: **$69.00**

CROSMAN 3576 REVOLVER

Caliber: .177, pellets. **Barrel:** Rifled steel. **Weight:** 2 lbs. **Length:** 11.38". **Power:** CO2. **Grips:** NA. **Sights:** Blade front, rear adjustable. **Features:** Semi-auto 10-shot with revolver styling and finger-molded grip design, 6" barrel for increased accuracy. From Crosman.

Price: **$80.00**

CROSMAN MODEL 1088

CROSMAN MODEL 1088 REPEATAIR PISTOL

Caliber: .177, 8-shot pellet clip. **Barrel:** Rifled steel. **Weight:** 17 oz. **Length:** 7.75" overall. **Power:** CO2 Powerlet. **Grips:** Checkered black plastic. **Sights:** Fixed blade front, adjustable rear. **Features:** Velocity about 430 fps. Single or double semi-automatic action. From Crosman.

Price: **$75.00**

CROSMAN PRO77

Caliber: .177, 17-shot BB. **Weight:** 1.31 lbs. **Length:** 6.75". **Power:** 12g CO2. **Sights:** Fixed. **Features:** Compact pistol with realistic recoil. Under the barrel weaver style rail. Velocity up to 325 fps.

Price: Pro77CS **$90.00**

CROSMAN T4

Caliber: .177, 8-shot BB or pellet. **Weight:** 1.32 lbs. **Length:** 8.63". **Power:** 12g CO2. **Sights:** Fixed front, windage adjustable rear. **Features:** Shoots BBs or pellets. Easy patent-pending CO2 piercing mechanism. Under the barrel weaver style rail.

Price: T4CS **$85.00**

Price: T4OPS, includes adjustable Red Dot sight, barrel compensator, and pressure operated tactical flashlight. Comes in foam padeed, hard sided protective case **$167.99**

DAISY POWERLINE MODEL 15XT AIR PISTOL

Caliber: .177 BB, 15-shot built-in magazine. **Barrel:** NA. **Weight:** NA. **Length:** 7.21". **Power:** CO2. **Grips:** NA. **Sights:** NA. **Features:** Velocity 425 fps. Made in the U.S.A. by Daisy Mfg. Co.

Price: **$70.00**

Price: With electronic point sight **$84.00**

DAISY MODEL 717

DAISY MODEL 717 AIR PISTOL

Caliber: .177, single shot. **Weight:** 2.25 lbs. **Length:** 13-1/2" overall. **Grips:** Molded checkered woodgrain with contoured thumbrest. **Sights:** Blade and ramp front, open rear with windage and elevation adjustments. **Features:** Single pump pneumatic pistol. Rifled steel barrel. Crossbolt trigger block. Muzzle velocity 360 fps. From Daisy Mfg. Co.

Price: **$200.00**

DAISY MODEL 747 TRIUMPH AIR PISTOL

Caliber: .177, single shot. **Weight:** 2.35 lbs. **Length:** 13-1/2" overall. **Grips:** Molded checkered woodgrain with contoured thumbrest. **Sights:** Blade and ramp front, open rear with windage and elevation adjustments. **Features:** Single pump pneumatic pistol. Lothar Walther rifled high-grade steel barrel; crowned 12 lands and grooves, right-hand twist. Precision bore sized for match pellets. Muzzle velocity 360 fps. From Daisy Mfg. Co.

Price: **$264.99**

DAISY POWERLINE 201

Caliber: .177 BB or pellet. **Weight:** 1 lb. **Length:** 9.25" overall. **Sights:** Blade and ramp front, fixed open rear. **Features:** Spring-air action, trigger-block safety and smooth-bore steel barrel. Muzzle velocity 230 fps. From Daisy Mfg. Co.

Price: **$29.99**

DAISY POWERLINE 693 AIR PISTOL

Caliber: .177, single shot. **Weight:** 1.10 lbs. **Length:** 7.9" overall. **Grips:** Molded checkered. **Sights:** Blade and ramp front, fixed open rear. **Features:** Semi-automoatic BB pistol with a nickel finish and smooth bore steel barrel. Muzzle veocity 400 fps. From Daisy Mfg. Co.

Price: **$76.99**

DAISY POWERLINE 5170

DAISY POWERLINE 5170 CO2 PISTOL

Caliber: .177 BB. **Weight:** 1 lb. **Length:** 9.5" overall. **Sights:** Blade and ramp front, open rear. **Features:** CO2 semi-automatic action, manual trigger-block safety, upper and lower rails for mounting sights and other accessories and a smooth-bore steel barrel. Muzzle velocity 520 fps. From Daisy Mfg. Co.

Price: **$59.99**

DAISY POWERLINE 5501 CO2 BLOWBACK PISTOL

Caliber: .177 BB. **Weight:** 1 lb. **Length:** 9.5" overall. **Sights:** Blade and ramp front, open rear. **Features:** CO2 semi-automatic blow-back action, manual trigger-block safety, and a smooth-bore steel barrel. Muzzle velocity 430 fps. From Daisy Mfg. Co.

Price: **$99.99**

EAA/BAIKAL IZH-46M TARGET AIR PISTOL

Caliber: .177, single shot. **Barrel:** 10". **Weight:** 2.4 lbs. **Length:** 16.8" overall. **Power:** Underlever single-stroke pneumatic. **Grips:** Adjustable wooden target. **Sights:** Micrometer fully adjustable rear, blade front. **Features:** Velocity about 440 fps. Hammer-forged, rifled barrel. Imported from Russia by European American Armory.

Price: **$560.00**

GAMO P-23, P-23 LASER PISTOL

Caliber: .177, 12-shot. **Barrel:** 4.25". **Weight:** 1 lb. **Length:** 7.5". **Power:** CO2 cartridge, semi-automatic, 410 fps. **Grips:** Plastic. **Sights:** NA. **Features:** Walther PPK cartridge pistol copy, optional laser sight. Imported from Spain by Gamo.

Price: . . . . **$89.95**, (with laser) **$139.95**

Prices given are believed to be accurate at time of publication however, many factors affect retail pricing so exact prices are not possible.

GAMO PT-80, PT-80 LASER PISTOL
Caliber: .177, 8-shot. **Barrel:** 4.25". **Weight:** 1.2 lbs. **Length:** 7.2".
Power: CO2 cartridge, semi-automatic, 410 fps. **Grips:** Plastic.
Sights: 3-dot. **Features:** Optional laser sight and walnut grips
available. Imported from Spain by Gamo.
Price: .... $108.95, (with laser) $159.95
Price: (with walnut grip) $119.95

HAMMERLI AP-40

HAMMERLI AP-40 AIR PISTOL
Caliber: .177. **Barrel:** 10". **Weight:** 2.2 lbs. **Length:** 15.5". **Power:** NA.
Grips: Adjustable orthopedic. **Sights:** Fully adjustable micrometer.
Features: Sleek, light, well balanced and accurate.
Price: $1,400.00

MAGNUM RESEARCH DESERT EAGLE
Caliber: .177, 8-shot pellet. 5.7" rifled. **Weight:** 2.5 lbs. 11" overall.
Power: 12g CO2. **Sights:** Fixed front, adjustable rear. Velocity of 425
fps. 8-shot rotary clip. Double or single action. The first .177 caliber
air pistol with BLOWBACK action. Big and weighty, designed in the
likeness of the real Desert Eagle.
Price: $248.00

MAGNUM BABY DESERT
Caliber: .177, 15-shot BB. 4" **Weight:** 1.0 lbs. 8-1/4" overall. **Power:** 12g
CO2. **Sights:** Fixed front and rear. Velocity of 420 fps. Double action
BB repeater. Comes with bonus Picatinny top rail and built-in bottom
rail.
Price: $41.54

MORINI CM 162 EL MATCH AIR PISTOLS
Caliber: .177, single shot. **Barrel:** 9.4". **Weight:** 32 oz. **Length:** 16.1"
overall. **Power:** Scuba air. **Grips:** Adjustable match type. **Sights:**
Interchangeable blade front, fully adjustable match-type rear.
Features: Power mechanism shuts down when pressure drops to a
preset level. Adjustable electronic trigger.
Price: $1,075.00

RUGER MARK I

RUGER MARK I
Caliber: .177. **Barrel:** 6.5". **Weight:** 48 oz. **Sights:** Fiber optic front,
open rear. Spring-piston operated pellet pistol up to 500 fps velocity
with lead pellets, 600 fps with alloy.
Price: $75.00

RWS 9B/9N AIR PISTOLS
Caliber: .177, single shot. **Barrel:** 8". **Weight:** 2.38 lbs. **Length:**
10.4". **Power:** 550 fps. **Grips:** Right hand with thumbrest. **Sights:**
Adjustable. **Features:** Spring-piston powered. Black or nickel finish.
Price: 9B/9N $150.00

SMITH & WESSON 586
Caliber: .177, 10-shot pellet. Rifled. **Power:** 12g CO2. **Sights:** Fixed
front, adjustable rear. 10-shot rotary clip. Double or single action.
Replica revolvers that duplicate both weight and handling.
Price: 4" barrel, 2.5 lbs, 400 fps $215.34
Price: 6" barrel, 2.8 lbs, 425 fps $231.49
Price: 8" barrel, 3.0 lbs, 460 fps $247.65
Price: S&W 686 Nickel, 6" barrel, 2.8 lbs, 425 fps $253.03

STEYR LP10P MATCH AIR PISTOL
Caliber: .177, single shot. **Barrel:** 9". **Weight:** 38.7 oz. **Length:** 15.3"
overall. **Power:** Scuba air. **Grips:** Adjustable Morini match, palm shelf,
stippled walnut. **Sights:** Interchangeable blade in 4mm, 4.5mm or 5mm
widths, adjustable open rear, interchangeable 3.5mm or 4mm leaves.
Features: Velocity about 500 fps. Adjustable trigger, adjustable sight
radius from 12.4" to 13.2". With compensator. Recoil elimination.
Price: $1,400.00

TECH FORCE SS2 OLYMPIC COMPETITION AIR PISTOL
Caliber: .177 pellet, single shot. **Barrel:** 7.4". **Weight:** 2.8 lbs. **Length:**
16.5" overall. **Power:** Spring piston, sidelever **Grips:** Hardwood.
Sights: Extended adjustable rear, blade front accepts inserts.
Features: Velocity 520 fps. Recoilless design; adjustments allow
duplication of a firearm's feel. Match-grade, adjustable trigger;
includes carrying case. Imported from China by Compasseco, Inc.
Price: $295.00

TECH FORCE 35 AIR PISTOL
Caliber: .177 pellet, single shot. **Weight:** 2.86 lbs. **Length:** 14.9"
overall. **Power:** Spring-piston, underlever. **Grips:** Hardwood. **Sights:**
Micrometer adjustable rear, blade front. **Features:** Velocity 400 fps.
Grooved for scope mount; trigger safety. Imported from China by
Compasseco, Inc.
Price: $39.95

TECH FORCE S2-1 AIR PISTOL
Similar to Tech Force 8 except basic grips and sights for plinking.
Price: $29.95

WALTHER LP300 MATCH PISTOL
Caliber: .177. **Barrel:** 236mm. **Weight:** 1.018g. **Length:** NA. **Power:**
NA. **Grips:** NA. **Sights:** Integrated front with three different widths,
adjustable rear. **Features:** Adjustable grip and trigger.
Price: $1,800.00

WALTHER PPK/S
Caliber: .177, 15-shot steel BB. 3-1/2". **Weight:** 1.2 lbs. 6-1/4" overall.
Power: 12g CO2. **Sights:** Fixed front and rear. Velocity of 295 fps.
Lookalike of one of the world's most famous pistols. Realistic recoil.
Heavyweight steel construction.
Price: $71.92
Price: With laser sight $94.23
Price: With BiColor pistol, targets, shooting glasses, BBs $84.62

WALTHER CP99 COMPACT
Caliber: .177, 17-shot steel BB semi-auto. 3". **Weight:** 1.7 lbs. 6-1/2"
overall. **Power:** 12g CO2. **Sights:** Fixed front and rear. Velocity of 345
fps. Realistic recoil, blowback action. Heavyweight steel construction.
Built-in Picatinny mount.
Price: $83.08

WINCHESTER MODEL 11

WINCHESTER MODEL 11
Caliber: BB. CO2-powered pistol with 16-round removable magazine.
Weight: 30 ozs. Can be fired double or single action. Slide stays
open after last shot. Dimensions and operating controls the same as
1911 pistol.
Price: $110.00

AIRFORCE CONDOR RIFLE
Caliber: .177, .22 single shot. **Barrel:** 24" rifled. **Weight:** 6.5 lbs. **Length:** 38.75" overall. **Power:** Pre-charged pneumatic. **Stock:** NA. **Sights:** Intended for scope use, fiber-optic open sights optional. **Features:** Lothar Walther match barrel, adjustable power levels from 600-1,300 fps. 3,000 psi fill pressure. Automatic safety. Air tank volume: 490cc. An integral extended scope rail allows easy mounting of the largest air-gun scopes. Operates on high-pressure air from scuba tank or hand pump. Manufactured in the U.S.A by AirForce Airguns.
Price: **$650.00**
Price: With 4-16x50 scope, Spin-Lock tank, hand pump ... **$1,006.00**

AIRFORCE TALON AIR RIFLE
Caliber: .177, .22, single shot. **Barrel:** 18" rifled. **Weight:** 5.5 lbs. **Length:** 32.6". **Power:** Pre-charged pneumatic. **Stock:** NA. **Sights:** Intended for scope use, fiber-optic open sights optional. **Features:** Lothar Walther match barrel, adjustable power levels from 400-1,000 fps, 3,000 psi fill pressure. Automatic safety. Air tank volume: 490cc. Operates on high-pressure air from scuba tank or hand pump. Manufactured in the U.S.A. by AirForce Airguns.
Price: Gun only (.22 or .177) **$514.25**

AIRFORCE TALON SS AIR RIFLE
Caliber: .177, .22, single shot. **Barrel:** 12" rifled. **Weight:** 5.25 lbs. **Length:** 32.75". **Power:** Pre-charged pneumatic. **Stock:** NA. **Sights:** Intended for scope use, fiber-optic open sights optional. **Features:** Lothar Walther match barrel, adjustable power levels from 400-1,000 fps. 3,000 psi fill pressure. Automatic safety. Chamber in front of barrel strips away air turbulence, protects muzzle and reduces firing report. Air tank volume: 490cc. Operates on high-pressure air from scuba tank or hand pump. Manufactured in the U.S.A. by AirForce Airguns.
Price: Gun only (.22 or .177) **$535.50**

AIRROW MODEL A-8SRB STEALTH AIR RIFLE
Caliber: .177, .22, .25, 9-shot. **Barrel:** 20"; rifled. **Weight:** 6 lbs. **Length:** 34" overall. **Power:** CO2 or compressed air; variable power. **Stock:** Telescoping CAR-15-type. **Sights:** Variable 3.5-10x scope. **Features:** Velocity 1100 fps in all calibers. Pneumatic air trigger. All aircraft aluminum and stainless steel construction. Mil-spec materials and finishes. From Swivel Machine Works, Inc.
Price: About **$2,299.00**

AIRROW MODEL A-8S1P STEALTH AIR RIFLE
Caliber: #2512 16" arrow. **Barrel:** 16". **Weight:** 4.4 lbs. **Length:** 30.1" overall. **Power:** CO2 or compressed air; variable power. **Stock:** Telescoping CAR-15-type. **Sights:** Scope rings only. 7 oz. rechargeable cylinder and valve. **Features:** Velocity to 650 fps with 260-grain arrow. Pneumatic air trigger. Broadhead guard. All aircraft aluminum and stainless steel construction. Mil-spec materials and finishes. A-8S Models perform to 2,000 PSIG above or below water levels. Waterproof case. From Swivel Machine Works, Inc.
Price: **$1,699.00**

BEEMAN HW100
Caliber: .177 or .22, 14-shot magazine. **Barrel:** 21-1/2". **Weight:** 9 lbs. **Length:** 42.13" overall. **Power:** Pre-charged. **Stock:** Walnut Sporter checkering on the pistol grip & forend; walnut thumbhose with lateral finger grooves on the forend & stippling on the pistol grip. **Sights:** None. Grooved for scope mounting. **Features:** 1140 fps .177 caliber; 945 fps .22 caliber. 14-shot magazine, quick-fill cylinder. Two-stage adjustable match trigger and manual safety.
Price: From **$1,470.00**

BEEMAN R1 AIR RIFLE
Caliber: .177, .20 or .22, single shot. **Barrel:** 19.6", 12-groove rifling. **Weight:** 8.5 lbs. **Length:** 45.2" overall. **Power:** Spring-piston, barrel cocking. **Stock:** Walnut-stained beech; cut-checkered pistol grip; Monte Carlo comb and cheekpiece; rubber buttpad. **Sights:** Tunnel front with interchangeable inserts, open rear click-adjustable for windage and elevation. Grooved for scope mounting. **Features:** Velocity 940-1000 fps (.177), 860 fps (20), 800 fps (.22). Non-drying nylon piston and breech seals. Adjustable metal trigger. Milled steel safety. Right- or left-hand stock. Adjustable cheekpiece and buttplate at extra cost. Custom and Super Laser versions available. Imported by Beeman.
Price: Right-hand **$729.95**
Price: Left-hand **$789.95**

BEEMAN R7 AIR RIFLE
Caliber: .177, .20, single shot. **Barrel:** 17". **Weight:** 6.1 lbs. **Length:** 40.2" overall. **Power:** Spring-piston. **Stock:** Stained beech. **Sights:** Hooded front, fully adjustable micrometer click open rear. **Features:** Velocity to 700 fps (.177), 620 fps (20). Receiver grooved for scope mounting; double-jointed cocking lever; fully adjustable trigger; checkered grip. Imported by Beeman.
Price: .177 .... **$470.00**
Price: .20 .... **$500.00**

BEEMAN R9 AIR RIFLE
Caliber: .177, .20, single shot. **Barrel:** NA. **Weight:** 7.3 lbs. **Length:** 43" overall. **Power:** Spring-piston, barrel cocking. **Stock:** Stained hardwood. **Sights:** Tunnel post front, fully adjustable open rear. **Features:** Velocity to 1000 fps (.177), 800 fps (20). Adjustable Rekord trigger; automatic safety; receiver dovetailed for scope mounting. Imported from Germany by Beeman Precision Airguns.
Price: **$470.00**

BEEMAN R11 MKII AIR RIFLE
Caliber: .177, single shot. **Barrel:** 19.6". **Weight:** 8.6 lbs. **Length:** 43.5" overall. **Power:** Spring-piston, barrel cocking. **Stock:** Walnut-stained beech; adjustable buttplate and cheekpiece. **Sights:** None furnished. Has dovetail for scope mounting. **Features:** Velocity 910-940 fps. All-steel barrel sleeve. Imported by Beeman.
Price: **$700.00**

BEEMAN RX-2 GAS-SPRING MAGNUM AIR RIFLE
Caliber: .177, .20, .22, .25, single shot. **Barrel:** 19.6", 12-groove rifling. **Weight:** 8.8 lbs. **Power:** Gas-spring piston air; single stroke barrel cocking. **Stock:** Laminated wood stock. **Sights:** Tunnel front, click-adjustable rear. **Features:** Velocity adjustable to about 1200 fps. Imported by Beeman.
Price: .177, right-hand **$889.95**
Price: .20, right-hand **$909.95**
Price: .22, right-hand **$889.95**
Price: .25, right-hand **$909.95**

BEEMAN R1 CARBINE
Caliber: .177,. 20, .22 single shot. **Barrel:** 16.1". **Weight:** 8.6 lbs. **Length:** 41.7" overall. **Power:** Spring-piston, barrel cocking. **Stock:** Stained beech; Monte Carlo comb and checkpiece; cut checkered pistol grip; rubber buttpad. **Sights:** Tunnel front with interchangeable inserts, open adjustable rear; receiver grooved for scope mounting. **Features:** Velocity up to 1000 fps (.177). Non-drying nylon piston and breech seals. Adjustable metal trigger. Machined steel receiver end cap and safety. Right- or left-hand stock. Imported by Beeman.
Price: .177, 20, .22, right-hand **$749.95**

BEEMAN/FEINWERKBAU 700 P ALUMINUM OR WOOD STOCK
Caliber: .177, single shot. **Barrel:** 16.6". **Weight:** 10.8 lbs. Aluminum; 9.9 lbs. Wood. **Length:** 43.3-46.25" Aluminum; 43.7" Wood. **Power:** Pre-charged pneumatic. **Stock:** Aluminum stock P laminated hardwood. **Sights:** Tunnel front sight with interchangeable inserts, click micrometer match aperture rear sight. **Features:** Velocity 570 fps. Recoilless action. Anatomical grips can be tilted and pivoted to the barrel axis. Adjustable buttplate and cheekpiece.
Price: Aluminum 700, right, blue or silver **$3,934.95**
Price: Aluminum 700, universal...................... **$3,069.95**

Prices given are believed to be accurate at time of publication however, many factors affect retail pricing so exact prices are not possible.

BEEMAN/FEINWERKBAU P70 FIELD TARGET
Caliber: .177, single shot. Barrel: 24.6". Weight: 10.6 lbs. Length: 43.3" overall. Power: Pre-charged pneumatic. Stock: Aluminum stock (red or blue) anatomical grips, buttplate & cheekpiece. Sights: None, receiver grooved for scope mounting. Features: 870 fps velocity. At 50 yards, this air rifle is capable of achieving 1/2-inch groups. Match adjustable trigger. 2001 US Field Target National Champion.
Price: P70FT, precharged, right (red or blue) **$3,819.95**
Price: P70FT, precharged, left (red or blue) **$3,964.95**

BEEMAN/HW97 AIR RIFLE
Caliber: .177, .20, .22, single shot. Barrel: 17.75". Weight: 9.2 lbs. Length: 44.1" overall. Power: Spring-piston, underlever cocking. Stock: Walnut-stained beech; rubber buttpad. Sights: None. Receiver grooved for scope mounting. Features: Velocity 830 fps (.177). Fixed barrel with fully opening, direct loading breech. Adjustable trigger. Imported by Beeman Precision Airguns.
Price: .177 . . . . **$725.00**
Price: .20, .22 . . . . **$750.00**

BENJAMIN & SHERIDAN PNEUMATIC (PUMP-UP) AIR RIFLE
Caliber: .177 or .22, single shot. Barrel: 19-3/8", rifled brass. Weight: 5-1/2 lbs. Length: 36-1/4" overall. Power: Underlever pneumatic, hand pumped. Stock: American walnut stock and forend. Sights: High ramp front, fully adjustable notched rear. Features: Variable velocity to 800 fps. Bolt action with ambidextrous push-pull safety. Black or nickel finish. Made in the U.S.A. by Benjamin. Also manufactured under the Sheridan brand.
Price: Model 397 (.177) **$180**
Price: Model 392 (.20) **$190**
Price: Sheridan CB9 (.22) **$200**

BENJAMIN ROGUE .357 CALIBER MULTI-SHOT AIR RIFLE
Caliber: .357, 6-shot mag (optional single-shot tray). Features: Electronic precharged pneumatic (ePCP), Bolt-action, 2-stage adjustable electronic trigger with dual electronic switches, Ambidextrous synthetic stock w/adjustable buttstock & sling swivel studs, 11mm, Adjustable power, Up to 900 fps (250 ft-lbs. max), 3000 psi (206 bar) max fill pressure (delivers full-power shots with as little as 1000 psi), Shrouded for stealthy hunting, Up to 20 shots at 100 ft-lbs. when filled to 3000 psi, Built-in manometer (air pressure gauge), Weaver bipod rail, LCD screen for EPiC controls on left side of gun, includes fill adapter. Made in the U.S. by Benjamin Sheridan Co.
Price: **$1,349.00**

BERETTA CX4 STORM
Caliber: .177, 30-shot semi-auto. 17-1/2", rifled. Weight: 5.25 lbs. Length: 30.75" overall. Power: 88g CO2. Stock: Replica style. Sights: Adjustable front and rear. Blowback action. Velocity of 600 fps. Accessory ralls.
Price: **$375.00**

BSA SUPERTEN MK3 AIR RIFLE
Caliber: .177, .22 10-shot repeater. Barrel: 17-1/2". Weight: 7 lbs., 8 oz. Length: 37" overall. Power: Precharged pneumatic via buddy bottle. Stock: Oil-finished hardwood; Monte Carlo with cheekpiece, cut checkered grip; adjustable recoil pad. Sights: No sights; intended for scope use. Features: Velocity 1000+ fps (.177), 1000+ fps (.22). Patented 10-shot indexing magazine, bolt-action loading. Left-hand version also available. Imported from U.K.
Price: **$800.00**

BSA SUPERTEN MK3 BULLBARREL
Caliber: .177, .22, .25, single shot. Barrel: 18-1/2". Weight: 8 lbs., 8 oz. Length: 43" overall. Power: Spring-air, underlever cocking. Stock: Oil-finished hardwood; Monte Carlo with cheekpiece, checkered at grip; recoil pad. Sights: Ramp front, micrometer adjustable rear. Maxi-Grip scope rail. Features: Velocity 950 fps (.177), 750 fps (.22), 600 fps (25). Patented rotating breech design. Maxi-Grip scope rail protects optics from recoil; automatic anti-beartrap plus manual safety. Imported from U.K.
Price: Rifle, MKII Carbine (14" barrel, 39-1/2" overall) **$349.95**

BSA MAGNUM SUPERSPORT AIR RIFLE, CARBINE
Caliber: .177, .22, .25, single shot. Barrel: 18-1/2". Weight: 6 lbs., 8 oz. Length: 41" overall. Power: Spring-air, barrel cocking. Stock: Oil-finished hardwood; Monte Carlo with cheekpiece, recoil pad. Sights: Ramp front, micrometer adjustable rear. Maxi-Grip scope rail. Features: Velocity 950 fps (.177), 750 fps (.22), 600 fps (25). Patented Maxi-Grip scope rail protects optics from recoil; automatic anti-beartrap plus manual tang safety. Muzzle brake standard. Imported for U.K.
Price: **$194.95**
Price: Carbine, 14" barrel, muzzle brake **$214.95**

BSA METEOR AIR RIFLE
Caliber: .177, .22, single shot. Barrel: 18-1/2". Weight: 6 lbs. Length: 41" overall. Power: Spring-air, barrel cocking. Stock: Oil-finished hardwood. Sights: Ramp front, micrometer adjustable rear. Features: Velocity 650 fps (.177), 500 fps (.22). Automatic anti-beartrap; manual tang safety. Receiver grooved for scope mounting. Imported from U.K.
Price: Rifle **$144.95**
Price: Carbine **$164.95**

CROSMAN M4-177
Caliber: .177 pellet or BB. Removable 5-shot magazine. Weight: 3.5 lbs. Length: 34". Sights: Windage-adjustable flip-up rear, elevation-adjustable front. Features: Rifled barrel, adjustable stock, pneumatic multi-pump operation gives up to 660 fps muzzle velocity. Bolt-action variation of AR-style rifle. Also available in kit form.
Price: **$94.00**

CROSMAN MODEL POWERMASTER 664SB AIR RIFLES
Caliber: .177 (single shot pellet) or BB, 200-shot reservoir. Barrel: 20", rifled steel. Weight: 2 lbs. 15 oz. Length: 38-1/2" overall. Power: Pneumatic; hand-pumped. Stock: Wood-grained ABS plastic; checkered pistol grip and forend. Sights: Fiber-optic front, fully adjustable open rear. Features: Velocity about 645 fps. Bolt action, cross-bolt safety. From Crosman.
Price: **$105.50**

CROSMAN MODEL PUMPMASTER 760 AIR RIFLES
Caliber: .177 pellets (single shot) or BB (200-shot reservoir). Barrel: 19-1/2", rifled steel. Weight: 2 lbs., 12 oz. Length: 33.5" overall. Power: Pneumatic, hand-pump. Stock: Walnut-finished ABS plastic stock and forend. Features: Velocity to 590 fps (BBs, 10 pumps). Short stroke, power determined by number of strokes. Fiber-optic front sight and adjustable rear sight. Cross-bolt safety. From Crosman.
Price: Model 760 . . . . **$40.59**

CROSMAN MODEL REPEATAIR 1077 RIFLES
Caliber: .177 pellets, 12-shot clip. Barrel: 20.3", rifled steel. Weight:

3 lbs., 11 oz. **Length:** 38.8" overall. **Power:** CO2 Powerlet. **Stock:** Textured synthetic or hardwood. **Sights:** Blade front, fully adjustable rear. **Features:** Velocity 590 fps. Removable 12-shot clip. True semi-automatic action. From Crosman.
Price: **$90.00**

CROSMAN MODEL .2260 AIR RIFLE
Caliber: .22, single shot. **Barrel:** 24". **Weight:** 4 lbs., 12 oz. **Length:** 39.75" overall. **Power:** CO2 Powerlet. **Stock:** Hardwood. **Sights:** Blade front, adjustable rear open or peep. **Features:** Variable pump power; three pumps give 395 fps, six pumps 530 fps, 10 pumps 600 fps (average). Full-size adult air rifle. From Crosman.
Price: **$83.84**

CROSMAN MODEL CLASSIC 2100 AIR RIFLE
Caliber: .177 pellets (single shot), or BB (200-shot BB reservoir). **Barrel:** 21", rifled. **Weight:** 4 lbs., 13 oz. **Length:** 39-3/4" overall. **Power:** Pump-up, pneumatic. **Stock:** Wood-grained checkered ABS plastic. **Features:** Three pumps give about 450 fps, 10 pumps about 755 fps (BBs). Cross-bolt safety; concealed reservoir holds over 200 BBs. From Crosman.
Price: Model 2100B **$62.99**

CROSMAN MODEL NITRO VENOM AIR RIFLE
Caliber: .177 & .22. **Features:** Nitro Venom air rifle feature precision, rifled barrel with fluted muzzle brake and sculpted rubber recoil pad. The rifle is equipped with a CenterPoint 3-9x32mm precision scope and a quick-lock mounting system for quick and easy optic mounting. The ambidextrous hardwood stock with raised cheek piece and modified, beavertail forearm. Crosman Nitro Venom air rifle delivers serious hunting power with muzzle energy up to 21 fpe and up to 1200 fps. Take one on a hunt to experience the power, stability and stealth of Nitro Piston® technology.
Price: .177 .... **$209.99**
Price: .22 .... **N/A**

CROSMAN MODEL NITRO VENOM DUSK AIR RIFLE
Caliber: .177 & .22. **Features:** Nitro Venom air rifle feature precision, rifled barrel with fluted muzzle brake and sculpted rubber recoil pad. The rifle is equipped with a CenterPoint 3-9x32mm precision scope and a quick-lock mounting system for quick and easy optic mounting. The ambidextrous hardwood stock with raised cheek piece and modified, beavertail forearm. Crosman Nitro Venom air rifle delivers serious hunting power with muzzle energy up to 21 fpe and up to 1200 fps. Take one on a hunt to experience the power, stability and stealth of Nitro Piston® technology.
Price: .177 .... **$209.99**
Price: .22 .... **N/A**

CROSMAN MODEL TRAIL NP ALL WEATHER & LAMINATED HARDWOOD AIR RIFLES
Caliber: .177, .22 & .25, up to 1200 fps (.177), 950 fps (.22) & 900 fps (.25). **Weight:** 6.65 lbs. - 8 lbs. **Length:** 43" overall. **Features:** The Nitro Venom Dusk air rifle features a precision, rifled barrel with fluted muzzle break and sculpted rubber recoil pad. The rifle is equipped with a CenterPoint 3-9x32mm precision scope and a

quick-lock mounting system for quick and easy optic mounting. The ambidextrous synthetic stock has a raised cheek piece and modified, beavertail forearm. Crosman Nitro Venom air rifles delivers serious hunting power with muzzle energy up to 18 fpe and up to 1200 fps.. Take one on a hunt to experience the power, stability and stealth of Nitro Piston® technology. The .22 caliber series is equiped with various harwood and laminated thumbhole and standard stocks and also models with bull barrels, imposing 23 ft-lbs of muzzle energy provides 16% more downrange energy than .177 cal. The new XL725 provides 24% more downrange energy than a .177 caliber offers. This is the most powerful Nitro Piston® break barrel available.

Price: .177 Trail NP	**$247.00**
Price: .177 Trail NP XL 1500	**$247.00**
Price: .22 Trail NP All Weather	**$247.00**
Price: .22 Trail NP Hardwood	**$299.00**
Price: .22 Trail NP All Weather with Realtree APG	**$279.95**
Price: .22 Trail NP All Weather 495fps	**$299.00**
Price: .22 Trail NP Laminated Hardwood	**N/A**
Price: .22 Trail NP XL 1100	**$359.00**
Price: .25 Trail NP XL 725	**$329.00**

DAISY 1938 RED RYDER AIR RIFLE
Caliber: BB, 650-shot repeating action. **Barrel:** Smoothbore steel with shroud. **Weight:** 2.2 lbs. **Length:** 35.4" overall. **Stock:** Wood stock burned with Red Ryder lariat signature. **Sights:** Post front, adjustable open rear. **Features:** Walnut forend. Saddle ring with leather thong. Lever cocking. Gravity feed. Controlled velocity. From Daisy Mfg. Co.
Price: **$55.99**

DAISY MODEL 840B GRIZZLY AIR RIFLE
Caliber: .177 pellet single shot; or BB 350-shot. **Barrel:** 19", smoothbore, steel. **Weight:** 2.25 lbs. **Length:** 36.8" overall. **Power:** Single pump pneumatic. **Stock:** Molded wood-grain stock and forend. **Sights:** Ramp front, open, adjustable rear. **Features:** Muzzle velocity 320 fps (BB), 300 fps (pellet). Steel buttplate; straight pull bolt action; cross-bolt safety. Forend forms pump lever. From Daisy Mfg. Co.
Price: **$60.99**
Price: (840C in Mossy Oak Breakup Camo) **$64.99**

DAISY MODEL 4841 GRIZZLY
Caliber: .177 pellet single shot. **Barrel:** NA. **Weight:** NA. **Length:** 36.8" overall. **Power:** Single pump pneumatic. **Stock:** Composite camo. **Sights:** Blade and ramp front. **Features:** Muzzle velocity 350 fps. Fixed Daisy Model 808 scope. From Daisy Mfg. Co.
Price: **$69.99**

DAISY MODEL 105 BUCK AIR RIFLE
Caliber: .177 or BB. **Barrel:** Smoothbore steel. **Weight:** 1.6 lbs. **Length:** 29.8" overall. **Power:** Lever cocking, spring air. **Stock:** Stained solid wood. **Sights:** TruGlo fiber-optic, open fixed rear. **Features:** Velocity to 275. Crossbolt trigger block safety. From Daisy Mfg. Co.
Price: **$39.99**

DAISY AVANTI MODEL 888 MEDALIST
Caliber: .177, pellet. **Barrel:** Lothar Walther rifled high-grade steel, crowned, 12 lands and grooves, right-hand twist. Precision bore sized for match pellets. **Weight:** 6.9 lbs. **Length:** 38.5" overall. **Power:** CO2 single shot bolt. **Stock:** Sporter-style multicolored laminated hardwood. **Sights:** Hooded front with interchangeable aperture inserts; micrometer adjustable rear peep sight. **Features:** Velocity to 500. Crossbolt trigger block safety. From Daisy Mfg. Co.
Price: **$470.00**

DAISY AVANTI MODEL 887 GOLD MEDALIST
Caliber: 177, pellet. **Barrel:** Lothar Walther rifled high-grade steel, crowned, 12 lands and grooves, right hand twist. Precision bore sized for match pellets. **Weight:** 7.3 lbs. **Length:** 39.5" overall. **Power:** CO2 power single shot bolt. **Stock:** Laminated hardwood. **Sights:** Front globe sight with changeable aperture inserts: rear diopter sight with micrometer click adjustment for windage and elevation. **Features:** Velocity to 500. Crossbolt trigger block safety. Includes rail adapter. From Daisy Mfg. Co.
Price: **$500.00**

DAISY MODEL 853 LEGEND
Caliber: .177, pellet. **Barrel:** Lothar Walther rifled high-grade steel barrel, crowned, 12 lands and grooves, right-hand twist. Precision bore sized for match pellets. **Weight:** 5.5 lbs. **Length:** 38.5" overall. **Power:** Single-pump pneumatic, straight pull-bolt. **Stock:** Full-length,

Prices given are believed to be accurate at time of publication however, many factors affect retail pricing so exact prices are not possible.

sporter-style hardwood with adjustable length. **Sights:** Hooded front with interchangeable aperture inserts; micrometer adjustable rear. **Features:** Velocity to 510. Crossbolt trigger block safety with red indicator. From Daisy Mfg. Co.
Price: **$400.00**

DAISY MODEL 753 ELITE
Caliber: .177, pellet. **Barrel:** Lothar Walther rifled high-grade steel barrel, crowned, 12 lands and grooves, right-hand twist. Precision bore sized for match pellets. **Weight:** 6.4 lbs. **Length:** 39.75" overall. **Power:** Recoilless single pump pneumatic, straight pull bolt. **Stock:** Full length match-style hardwood stock with raised cheek piece and adjustable length. **Sights:** Front globe sight with changeable aperture inserts, diopter rear sight with micrometer adjustable rear. **Features:** Velocity to 510. Crossbolt trigger block safety with red indicator. From Daisy Mfg. Co.
Price: **$450.00**

DAISY MODEL 105 BUCK AIR RIFLE
Caliber: .177 or BB. **Barrel:** Smoothbore steel. **Weight:** 1.6 lbs. **Length:** 29.8" overall. **Power:** Lever cocking, spring air. **Stock:** Stained solid wood. **Sights:** TruGlo fiber-optic, open fixed rear. **Features:** Velocity to 275. Cross-bolt trigger block safety. From Daisy Mfg. Co.
Price: **$39.99**

DAISY POWERLINE® TARGETPRO 953 AIR RIFLE
Caliber: .177 pellets, single shot. **Weight:** 6.40 lbs. **Length:** 39.75" overall. **Power:** Pneumatic single-pump cocking lever; straight-pull bolt. **Stock:** Full-length, match-style black composite. **Sights:** Front and rear fiber optic. **Features:** Rifled high-grade steel barrel with 1:15 twist. Max. Muzzle Velocity of 560 fps. From Daisy Mfg. Co.
Price: **$29.99**

DAISY POWERLINE® 500 BREAK BARREL
Caliber: .177 pellet, single shot. **Barrel:** Rifled steel. **Weight:** 6.6 lbs. **Length:** 45.7" overall. **Stock:** Stained solid wood. **Sights:** Truglo® fiber-optic front, micro-adjustable open rear, adjustable 4x32 riflescope. **Features:** Auto rear-button safety. Velocity to 490 fps. Made in U.S.A. by Daisy Mfg. Co.
Price: **$120.99**

DAISY POWERLINE® 800 BREAK BARREL
Caliber: .177 pellet, single shot. **Barrel:** Rifled steel. **Weight:** 6.6 lbs. **Length:** 46.7" overall. **Stock:** Black composite. **Sights:** Truglo fiber-optic front, micro-adjustable open rear, adjustable 4x32 riflescope. **Features:** Auto rear-button safety. Velocity to 800 fps. Made in U.S.A. by Daisy Mfg. Co.
Price: **$120.99**

DAISY POWERLINE® 880 AIR RIFLE
Caliber: .177 pellet or BB, 50-shot BB magazine, single shot for pellets. **Barrel:** Rifled steel. **Weight:** 3.7 lbs. **Length:** 37.6" overall. **Power:** Multi-pump pneumatic. **Stock:** Molded wood grain; Monte Carlo comb. **Sights:** Hooded front, adjustable rear. **Features:** Velocity to 685 fps. (BB). Variable power (velocity, range) increase with pump strokes; resin receiver with dovetailed scope mount. Made in U.S.A. by Daisy Mfg. Co.
Price: **$71.99**

DAISY POWERLINE® 901 AIR RIFLE
Caliber: .177. **Barrel:** Rifled steel. **Weight:** 3.7 lbs. **Length:** 37.5" overall. **Power:** Multi-pump pneumatic. **Stock:** Advanced composite. **Sights:** Fiber-optic front, adjustable rear. **Features:** Velocity to 750 fps. (BB); advanced composite receiver with dovetailed mounts for optics. Made in U.S.A. by Daisy Mfg. Co.
Price: **$83.99**

DAISY POWERLINE® 1000 BREAK BARREL
Caliber: .177 pellet, single shot. **Barrel:** Rifled steel. **Weight:** 6.6 lbs. **Length:** 46.7" overall. **Stock:** Black composite. **Sights:** Truglo® fiber-optic front, micro-adjustable open rear, adjustable 4x32 riflescope. **Features:** Auto rear-button safety. Velocity to 750 fps (BB). Made in U.S.A. by Daisy Mfg. Co.
Price: **$231.99**

EAA/BAIKAL IZH61 AIR RIFLE
Caliber: .177 pellet, 5-shot magazine. **Barrel:** 17.8". **Weight:** 6.4 lbs.

Length: 31" overall. **Power:** Spring-piston, side-cocking lever. **Stock:** Black plastic. **Sights:** Adjustable rear, fully hooded front. **Features:** Velocity 490 fps. Futuristic design with adjustable stock. Imported from Russia by European American Armory.
Price: **$122.65**

GAMO SHADOW AIR RIFLES
Caliber: .177. **Barrel:** 18", fluted polymer bull. **Weight:** 6.1 to 7.15 lbs. **Length:** 43" to 43.3". **Power:** Single-stroke pneumatic, 850-1,000 fps. **Stock:** Tough all-weather molded synthetic. **Sights:** NA. **Features:** Single shot, manual safety.
Price: Sport **$219.95**
Price: Hunter **$219.95**
Price: Big Cat 1200 .... **$169.95**
Price: Fox **$279.95**

GAMO HUNTER AIR RIFLES
Caliber: .177. **Barrel:** NA. **Weight:** 6.5 to 10.5 lbs. **Length:** 43.5-48.5". **Power:** Single-stroke pneumatic, 850-1,000 fps. **Stock:** Wood. **Sights:** Varies by model. **Features:** Adjustable two-stage trigger, rifled barrel, raised scope ramp on receiver. Realtree camo model available.
Price: Sport **$250.00**
Price: Pro **$300.00**

GAMO SILENT STALKER WHISPER
Caliber: .177. Single shot, break-barrel cocking system. **Weight:** 7.15 lbs. **Length:** 43". **Stock:** Molded synthetic with cheekpiece, non-slip texture design on grip and fore-end. Adjustable trigger. Manual safety. 3-9x40 scope included.
Price: **$300.00**

GAMO WHISPER AIR RIFLES
Caliber: .177, .22. **Barrel:** 18", fluted polymer bull. **Weight:** 5.28 to 7.4 lbs. **Length:** 45.7" to 46". **Stock:** Tough all-weather molded synthetic. **Sights:** Fiber-optic front with sight guard, adjustable rear. **Features:** Single shot, manual trigger safety. Non-removable noise dampener (with up to 52 percent reduction).
Price: Whisper **$279.95**
Price: Whisper Deluxe **$319.95**
Price: Whisper VH (Varmint Hunter/Whisper in one rifle) **$329.95**
Price: Whisper .22 .... **$299.95**
Price: CSI Camo (.177) **$329.95**
Price: CSI Camo (.22) **$329.95**

HAMMERLI 850 AIR MAGNUM
Caliber: .177, .22, 8-shot repeater. 23-1/2", rifled. **Weight:** 5.8 lbs. 41" overall. **Power:** 88g CO2. **Stock:** All-weather polymer, Monte Carlo, textured grip and forearm. **Sights:** Hooded fiber optic front, fiber optic adjustable rear. Velocity of 760 fps (.177), 655 (.22). Blue finish. Rubber buttpad. Bolt-action. Scope compatible.
Price: .177, .22 .... **$370.00**

RWS 460 MAGNUM
Caliber: .177, .22, single shot. 18-7/16", rifled. **Weight:** 8.3 lbs. 45" overall. **Power:** Spring-air, underlever cocking. **Stock:** American Sporter, checkered grip and forearm. **Sights:** Ramp front,

adjustable rear. Velocity of 1350 fps (.177), 1150 (.22). 36 lbs. cocking effort. Blue finish. Rubber buttpad. Top-side loading port. Scope compatible.

Price: .177, .22 . . . . **$630.99**

RWS/DIANA MODEL 34
Caliber: .177, .22, single shot. **Barrel:** 19-1/2", rifled. **Weight:** 7.3 lbs. **Length:** 45" overall. **Power:** Spring-air, break-barrel cocking. **Stock:** Wood. **Sights:** Hooded front, adjustable rear. **Features:** Velocity of 1000 fps (.177), 800 (.22). 33 lbs. cocking effort. Blued finish. Scope compatible.

Price: **$259.00**

RWS/DIANA MODEL 34P
Caliber: .177, .22, single shot. 19-3/4", rifled. **Weight:** 7.7 lbs. 46" overall. **Power:** Spring-air, break-barrel cocking. **Stock:** Synthetic black. **Sights:** Ramp fiber optic front, adjustable fiber optic rear. Velocity of 1000 fps (.177), 800 (.22). 33 lbs. cocking effort. Blued finish. Scope compatible. Automatic safety.

Price: .177, .22 . . . . **$243.00**

RWS/DIANA MODEL 48
Caliber: .177, .22, single shot. 17", rifled, fixed. **Weight:** 9.0 lbs. 42-1/2" overall. **Power:** Spring-air, side-lever cocking. **Stock:** Wood stock. **Sights:** Adjustable front, adjustable rear. Velocity of 1100 fps (.177), 900 (.22). 39 lbs. cocking effort. Blued finish. Scope compatible. Automatic safety.

Price: .177, .22 . . . . **$500.00**

TECH FORCE 6 AIR RIFLE
Caliber: .177 pellet, single shot. **Barrel:** 14". **Weight:** 6 lbs. **Length:** 35.5" overall. **Power:** Spring-piston, sidelever action. **Stock:** Paratrooper-style folding, full pistol grip. **Sights:** Adjustable rear, hooded front. **Features:** Velocity 800 fps. All-metal construction; grooved for scope mounting. Imported from China by Compasseco, Inc.

Price: **$69.95**

TECH FORCE 99 AIR RIFLE
Caliber: .177, .22, single shot. **Barrel:** 18", rifled. **Weight:** 8 lbs. **Length:** 44.5" overall. **Power:** Spring piston. **Stock:** Beech wood; raised cheek piece and checkering on pistol grip and forearm, plus soft rubber recoil pad. **Sights:** Insert type front. **Features:** Velocity 1,100 fps (.177; 900 fps: .22); fixed barrel design has an underlever cocking mechanism with an anti-beartrap lock and automatic safety. Imported from China by Compasseco, Inc.

Price: 177 or .22 caliber **$152.96**

WALTHER LEVER ACTION
Caliber: .177, 8-shot lever action. **Barrel:** 19", rifled. **Weight:** 7.5 lbs. **Length:** 38" overall. **Power:** Two 12g CO2. **Stock:** Wood. **Sights:** Fixed front, adjustable rear. **Features:** Classic design. Velocity of 630 fps. Scope compatible.

Price: **$500.00**
Price: Nickel finish. **$600.00**

WINCHESTER MODEL 1029S
Caliber: .177 pellet. Single shot. **Weight:** 6.6 lbs. **Length:** 46.7". Rifled steel barrel. Composite stock with thumbhole grip. Thumb safety. Comes with 3-9x32 scope. Distributed by Daisy.

Price: **$250.00**

WINCHESTER MODEL M14
Caliber: .177. CO2 semi-automatic. 16-round capacity. Maximum velocity 700 fps. **Weight:** 4.4 pounds. **Sights:** Adjustable rear, blade front. Rifled steel barrel, brown composite stock.

Price: **$220**

Prices given are believed to be accurate at time of publication however, many factors affect retail pricing so exact prices are not possible.

THE 2014 GUN DIGEST
web directory

BY **HOLT BODINSON**

The *Gun Digest* Web Directory is now in its fifteenth year of publication and grows with every edition. The firearms industry is doing a remarkably good job of adapting to e-commerce. Most major sites now include Facebook, Twitter, and industry blog options for the informed consumer.

One of the most interesting developments has been the widespread adoption of mobile data applications, or "apps." It wasn't long ago that there wasn't an "apps" culture. Now, more often than not, Americans are carrying cell phones loaded with all sorts of software applications. Fortunately, the firearms industry has been actively engaged in the development of useful applications for use with mobile computing devices, so our sport is staying current.

The world has become a mobile, Internet culture, and that's why web directories like our own have become such essential references. The focus of our directory is on companies that have a proven track record of product success and have been in business for several years.

The following index of web addresses is offered to our readers as a convenient jumping-off point. Half the fun is just exploring what's out there. Considering that most of the web pages have hot links to other firearms-related web pages, the Internet trail just goes on and on once you've taken the initial step to go online. So welcome to the digital world of firearms, where a journey of a thousand sites begins with a single click. Here are a few pointers:

- If the website you desire is not listed, try using the full name of the company or product, typed without spaces, between www.- and-.com, for example, www.krause.com. Probably 95-percent of current websites are based on this simple, self-explanatory format.

- The other option is to go directly to the dominate search engines, www.google.com and www.bing.com, and enter the name of the company or product for which you are searching. This is also an invaluable method of finding companies that have recently changed their web addresses.

- Finally, make it a point to access www.YouTube.com for short videos on the subjects you are pursuing. Firearms enthusiasts and companies have posted literally thousands of firearms-related videos—some good, some bad—but always interesting. Many of the how-to gunsmithing videos, in particular, are excellent. Just be very specific when you type in the subject to be searched.

—Holt Bodinson

A-Square Co. www.asquarecompany.com
3-D Ammunition www.3dammo.com
Accurate Arms Co. Inc www.accuratepowder.com
ADCO/Nobel Sport Powder www.adcosales.com
Advanced Armament Corp. www.300aacblackout.com
Aguila Ammunition www.aguilaammo.com
Alexander Arms www.alexanderarms.com
Alliant Powder www.alliantpowder.com
American Ammunition www.a-merc.com
American Derringer Co. www.amderringer.com
American Pioneer Powder www.americanpioneerpowder.com
American Specialty Ammunition
   www.americanspecialityammo.com
Ammo Depot www.ammodepot.com
Ammo Guide www.ammoguide.com
Arizona Ammunition, Inc. www.arizonaammunition.com
Armscor www.us.armscor.com
Ballistic Products Inc. www.ballisticproducts.com
Barnaul Cartridge Plant www.ab.ru/~stanok
Barnes Bullets www.barnesbullets.com
Baschieri & Pellagri www.baschieri-pellagri.com
Beartooth Bullets www.beartoothbullets.com
Bell Brass www.bellbrass.com
Berger Bullets, Ltd. www.bergerbullets.com
Berry's Mfg., Inc. www.berrysmfg.com
Big Bore Bullets of Alaska www.awloo.com/bbb/index.htm
Big Bore Express www.powerbeltbullets.com
Bismuth Cartridge Co. www.bismuth-notox.com
Black Dawge Cartridge www.blackdawgecartridge.com
Black Hills Ammunition, Inc. www.black-hills.com
Black Hills Shooters Supply www.bhshooters.com
BlackHorn209 www.blackhorn209.com
Brenneke of America Ltd. www.brennekeusa.com
Buffalo Arms www.buffaloarms.com
Buffalo Bore Ammunition www.buffalobore.com
Calhoon, James, Bullets www.jamescalhoon.com
Cartuchos Saga www.saga.es
Cast Performance Bullet www.castperformance.com
CBC www.cbc.com.br
CCI www.cci-ammunition.com
Centurion Ordnance www.aguilaammo.com
Century International Arms www.centuryarms.com
Cheaper Than Dirt www.cheaperthandirt.com
Cheddite France www.cheddite.com
Claybuster Wads www.claybusterwads.com
Clean Shot Powder www.cleanshot.com
Cole Distributing www.cole-distributing.com
Combined Tactical Systems www.less-lethal.com
Cor-Bon/Glaser www.cor-bon.com
Cowboy Bullets www.cowboybullets.com
Cutting Edge Bullets www.cuttingedgebullets.com

D.Dupleks, Ltd. www.ddupleks.lv
Defense Technology Corp. www.defense-technology.com
Denver Bullet Co. denbullets@aol.com
Dillon Precision www.dillonprecision.com
Dionisi Cartridge www.dionisi.com
DKT, Inc. www.dktinc.com
D.L. Unmussig Bullets .14,.17 &.20 cal (804)320-1165
Double Tap Ammunition www.doubletapammo.com
Down Range Mfg. www.downrangemfg.com
Dynamic Research Technologies www.drtammo.com
Dynamit Nobel RWS Inc. www.dnrws.com
E. Arthus Brown Co. wwweabco.com
EcoSlug www.eco-slug.com
Elephant/Swiss Black Powder www.elephantblackpowder.com
Eley Ammunition www.eleyusa.com
Eley Hawk Ltd. www.eleyhawk.com
Environ-Metal www.hevishot.com
Estate Cartridge www.estatecartridge.com
Extreme Shock Munitions www.extremeshockusa.com
Federal Cartridge Co. www.federalpremium.com
Fiocchi of America www.fiocchiusa.com
Fowler Bullets www.benchrest.com/fowler
Gamebore Cartridge www.gamebore.com
GaugeMate www.gaugemate.com
Garrett Cartridges hammerhead.creator@gmail.com
Gentner Bullets www.benchrest.com/gentner/
Glaser Safety Slug, Inc. www.corbon.com
GOEX Inc. www.goexpowder.com
GPA www.cartouchegpa.com
Graf & Sons www.grafs.com
Grizzly Cartridge Co. www.grizzlycartridge.com
H&K Associates www.6mmhagar.com
Haendler & Natermann www.hn-sport.de
Hawk Bullets www.hawkbullets.com
Herter's Ammuniition www.cabelas.com
Hevi.Shot www.hevishot.com
High Precision Down Range www.hprammo.com
Hi-Tech Ammunition www.iidbs.com/hitech
Hodgdon Powder www.hodgdon.com
Hornady www.hornady.com
HSM Ammunition www.thehuntingshack.com
Hull Cartridge www.hullcartridge.com
Huntington Reloading Products www.huntingtons.com
Impact Bullets www.impactbullets.com
IMR Smokeless Powders www.imrpowder.com
International Cartridge Corp www.iccammo.com
Israel Military Industries www.imisammo.co.il
ITD Enterprise www.itdenterpriseinc.com
Jagemann Technologies www.jagemanntech.com
James Calhoon www.jamescalhoon.com
Kent Cartridge America www.kentgamebore.com
Knight Bullets www.benchrest.com/knight/

Kynoch Ammunition **www.kynochammunition.com**
Lapua **www.lapua.com**
Lawrence Brand Shot **www.metalico.com**
Lazzeroni Arms Co. **www.lazzeroni.com**
Leadheads Bullets **www.proshootpro.com**
Leigh Defense **www.leighdefense.com**
Lightfield Ammunition Corp **www.lightfieldslugs.com**
Lomont Precision Bullets **www.klomont.com/kent**
Lost River Ballistic Technologies, Inc.
   www.lostriverballistic.com
Lyman **www.lymanproducts.com**
Magkor Industries. **www.magkor.com**
Magnum Muzzleloading Products **www.mmpsabots.com**
Magnus Bullets **www.magnusbullets.com**
MagSafe Ammunition **www.realpages.com/magsafeammo**
Magtech **www.magtechammunition.com**
Masterclass Bullet Co. **www.mastercast.com**
Maxam **www.maxam-outdoors.com**
Meister Bullets **www.meisterbullets.com**
MEN **www.men-defencetec.de**
Midway USA **www.midwayusa.com**
Miltex, Inc. **www.miltexusa.com**
Mitchell Mfg. Co. **www.mitchellsales.com**
MK Ballistic Systems **www.mkballistics.com**
Mullins Ammunition **www.mullinsammunition.com**
National Bullet Co. **www.nationalbullet.com**
Navy Arms **www.navyarms.com**
Nobel Sport **www.nobelsportammo.com**
Norma **www.norma.cc**
North Fork Technologies **www.northforkbullets.com**
Nosler Bullets, Inc. **www.nosler.com**
Old Western Scrounger **www.ows-ammunition.com**
One Shot, Inc. **www.oneshotmunitions.com**
Oregon Trail/Trueshot Bullets **www.trueshotbullets.com**
Pattern Control **www.patterncontrol.com**
PCP Ammunition **www.pcpammo.com**
Pierce Munitions **www.piercemunitions.com**
Piney Mountain Ammunition
   www.pineymountainammunitionco.com
PMC **www.pmcammo.com**
PolyCase Ammunition **www.polycaseammo.com**
Polywad **www.polywad.com**
PowerBelt Bullets **www.powerbeltbullets.com**
PPU Ammunition **www.prvipartizan.com**
PR Bullets **www.prbullet.com**
Precision Ammunition **www.precisionammo.com**
Precision Reloading **www.precisionreloading.com**
Pro Grade Ammunition **www.progradeammo.com**
Pro Load Ammunition **www.proload.com**
Prvi Partizan Ammunition **www.prvipartizan.com**
Quality Cartridge **www.qual-cart.com**

Rainier Ballistics **www.rainierballistics.com**
Ram Shot Powder **www.ramshot.com**
Rare Ammunition **www.rareammo.com**
Reloading Specialties Inc. **www.reloadingspecialties.com**
Remington **www.remington.com**
Rio Ammunition **www.rioammo.com**
Rocky Mountain Cartridge **www.rockymountaincartride.com**
RUAG Ammotec **www.ruag.com**
RWS **www.ruag-usa.com**
Samco Global Arms **www.samcoglobal.com**
Sauvestre Ammunition **www.centuryarms.com**
SBR Ammunition **www.sbrammunition.com**
Scharch Mfg. **www.scharch.com**
Schuetzen Powder **www.schuetzenpowder.com**
Sellier & Bellot **www.sellier-bellot.cz**
Shilen **www.shilen.com**
Sierra **www.sierrabullets.com**
Silver State Armory **www.ssarmory.com**
Simunition. **www.simunition.com**
SinterFire, Inc. **www.sinterfire.com**
Spectra Shot **www.spectrashot.com**
Speer Ammunition **www.speer-ammo.com**
Speer Bullets **www.speer-bullets.com**
Sporting Supplies Int'l Inc. **www.ssiintl.com**
Starline **www.starlinebrass.com**
Superior Ballistics **www.superiorballistics.com**
Swift Bullets Co. **www.swiftbullet.com**
Tannerite **www.tannerite.com**
Tascosa Cartridge Co. **www.tascosacartridge.com**
Ted Nugent Ammunition **www.americantactical.us**
Ten-X Ammunition **www.tenxammo.com**
Top Brass **www.topbrass.com**
Triton Cartridge **www.a-merc.com**
Trueshot Bullets **www.trueshotbullets.com**
Tru-Tracer **www.trutracer.com**
TulAmmo **www.tulammousa.com**
Ultramax Ammunition **www.ultramaxammunition.com**
Vihtavuori Lapua **www.vihtavuori-lapua.com**
Weatherby **www.weatherby.com**
West Coast Bullets **www.westcoastbullet.com**
Western Powders Inc. **www.westernpowders.com**
Widener's Reloading & Shooters Supply **www.wideners.com**
Winchester Ammunition **www.winchester.com**
Windjammer Tournament Wads. **www.windjammer-wads.com**
Wolf Ammunition **www.wolfammo.com**
Woodleigh Bullets **www.woodleighbullets.com.au**
Zanders Sporting Goods **www.gzanders.com**

CASES, SAFES, GUN LOCKS, AND CABINETS

Ace Case Co. **www.acecase.com**
AG English Sales Co. **www.agenglish.com**

All Americas' Outdoors www.innernet.net/gunsafe
Alpine Cases www.alpinecases.com
Aluma Sport by Dee Zee www.deezee.com
American Security Products www.amsecusa.com
Americase www.americase.com
Assault Systems www.elitesurvival.com
Avery Outdoors, Inc. www.averyoutdoors.com
Bear Track Cases www.beartrackcases.com
Bore-Stores www.borestores.com
Boyt Harness Co. www.boytharness.com
Bulldog Gun Safe Co. www.gardall.com
Burglar Bomb www.burglarbomb.com
Campbell Industrial Supply www.gun-racks.com
Cannon Safe Co. www.cannonsafe.com
CCL Security Products www.cclsecurity.com
Concept Development Corp. www.saf-t-blok.com
Doskocil Mfg. Co. www.doskocilmfg.com
Fort Knox Safes www.ftknox.com
Franzen Security Products www.securecase.com
Frontier Safe Co. www.frontiersafe.com
Goldenrod Dehumidifiers www.goldenroddehumidifiers.com
Granite Security Products www.granitesafe.com
Gunlocker Phoenix USA Inc. www.gunlocker.com
Gun Storage Solutions www.storemoreguns.com
GunVault www.gunvault.com
Hakuba USA Inc. www.hakubausa.com
Heritage Safe Co. www.heritagesafecompany.com
Hide-A-Gun www.hide-a-gun.com
Homak Safes www.homak.com
Hunter Company www.huntercompany.com
Integrity Gunbags www.integrity-gunbags.com
Kalispel Case Line www.kalispelcaseline.com
Knouff & Knouff, Inc. www.kkair.com
Knoxx Industries www.knoxx,com
Kolpin Mfg. Co. www.kolpin.com
Liberty Safe & Security www.libertysafe.com
LockSfa www.locksfa.com
Morton Enterprises www.uniquecases.com
New Innovative Products www.starlightcases
Noble Security Systems Inc. www.noble.co.ll
Phoenix USA Inc. www.gunlocker.com
Plano Molding Co. www.planomolding.com
Plasticase, Inc. www.nanuk.com
Rhino Gun Cases www.rhinoguns.com
Rhino Safe www.rhinosafe.com
Rotary Gun Racks www.gun-racks.com
Sack-Ups www.sackups.com
Safe Tech, Inc. www.safrgun.com
Saf-T-Hammer www.saf-t-hammer.com
Saf-T-Lok Corp. www.saf-t-lok.com
San Angelo All-Aluminum Products Inc.
sasptuld@x.netcom.com

Secure Firearm Products
www.securefirearmproducts.com
Securecase www.securecase.com
Shot Lock Corp. www.shotlock.com
SKB Cases www.skbcases.com
Smart Lock Technology Inc. www.smartlock.com
Snap Safe www.snapsafe.com
Sportsmans Steel Safe Co. www.sportsmansteelsafes.com
Stack-On Products Co. www.stack-on.com
Starlight Cases www.starlightcases.com
Strong Case www.strongcasebytnb.com
Sun Welding www.sunwelding.com
Technoframes www.technoframes.com
Titan Gun Safes www.titangunsafes.com
T.Z. Case Int'l www.tzcase.com
U.S. Explosive Storage www.usexplosivestorage.com
Versatile Rack Co. www.versatilegunrack.com
V-Line Industries www.vlineind.com
Winchester Safes www.winchestersafes.com
Ziegel Engineering www.ziegeleng.com
Zonetti Armor www.zonettiarmor.com

CHOKE DEVICES, RECOIL REDUCERS, SUPPRESSORS AND ACCURACY DEVICES

Advanced Armament Corp.
www.advanced-armament.com
100 Straight Products www.100straight.com
Answer Products Co. www.answerrifles.com
AWC Systems Technology www.awcsystech.com
Briley Mfg www.briley.com
Carlson's www.choketube.com
Colonial Arms www.colonialarms.com
Comp-N-Choke www.comp-n-choke.com
Elite Iron www.eliteiron.net
Gemtech www.gem-tech.com
KDF, Inc. www.kdfguns.com
Kick's Industries www.kicks-ind.com
LimbSaver www.limbsaver.com
Mag-Na-Port Int'l Inc. www.magnaport.com
Metro Gun www.metrogun.com
Patternmaster Chokes www.patternmaster.com
Poly-Choke www.poly-choke.com
SilencerCo www.silencerco.com
Sims Vibration Laboratory www.limbsaver.com
SRT Arms www.srtarms.com
SureFire www.surefire.com
SWR Mfg. www.swrmfg.com
Teague Precision Chokes www.teague.ca
Truglo www.truglo.com
Trulock Tool www.trulockchokes.com
Vais Arms, Inc. www.muzzlebrakes.com

CHRONOGRAPHS AND BALLISTIC SOFTWARE

Barnes Ballistic Program **www.barnesbullets.com**
Ballisticard Systems **www.ballisticards.com**
Competition Electronics **www.competitionelectronics.com**
Competitive Edge Dynamics **www.cedhk.com**
Hodgdon Shotshell Program **www.hodgdon.com**
Lee Shooter Program **www.leeprecision.com**
Load From A Disk **www.loadammo.com**
NECO **www.neconos.com**
Oehler Research Inc. **www.oehler-research.com**
PACT **www.pact.com**
Pjsa Ballistics **Pejsa@sprintmail.com**
ProChrony **www.competitionelectronics.com**
Quickload **www.neconos.com**
RCBS Load **www.rcbs.com**
Shooting Chrony Inc **www.shootingchrony.com**
Sierra Infinity Ballistics Program **www.sierrabullets.com**
Winchester Ballistics Calculator **www.winchester.com**

CLEANING PRODUCTS

Accupro **www.accupro.com**
Ballistol USA **www.ballistol.com**
Battenfeld Technologies
   www.battenfeldtechnologies.com
Birchwood Casey **www.birchwoodcasey.com**
Blue Wonder **www.bluewonder.com**
Bore Tech **www.boretech.com**
Break-Free, Inc. **www.break-free.com**
Bruno Shooters Supply **www.brunoshooters.com**
Butch's Bore Shine **www.lymanproducts.com**
C.J. Weapons Accessories **www.cjweapons.com**
Clenzoil **www.clenzoil.com**
Corrosion Technologies **www.corrosionx.com**
Dewey Mfg. **www.deweyrods.com**
DuraCoat **www.lauerweaponry.com**
Eezox Inc. **www.xmission.com**
Emby Enterprises **www.alltemptacticallube.com**
Extreme Gun Care **www.extremeguncare.com**
G96 **www.g96.com**
Gun Butter **www.gunbutter.com**
Gun Cleaners **www.guncleaners.com**
Gunslick Gun Care **www.gunslick.com**
Gunzilla **www.topduckproducts.com**
Hollands Shooters Supply **www.hollandgun.com**
Hoppes **www.hoppes.com**
Hydrosorbent Products **www.dehumidify.com**
Inhibitor VCI Products **www.theinhibitor.com**
Iosso Products **www.iosso.com**
Jag Brush **www.jagbrush.com**
KG Industries **www.kgcoatings.com**

Kleen-Bore Inc. **www.kleen-bore.com**
L&R Ultrasonics **www.lrultrasonics.com**
Lyman **www.lymanproducts.com**
Mil-Comm Products **www.mil-comm.com**
Militec-1 **www.militec-1.com**
Montana X-Treme **www.montanaxtreme.com**
MPT Industries **www.mptindustries.com**
Mpro7 Gun Care **www.mp7.com**
Old West Snake Oil **www.oldwestsnakeoil.com**
Otis Technology, Inc. **www.otisgun.com**
Outers **www.outers-guncare.com**
Ox-Yoke Originals Inc. **www.oxyoke.com**
Parker-Hale Ltd. **www.parker-hale.com**
Prolix Lubricant **www.prolixlubricant.com**
ProShot Products **www.proshotproducts.com**
ProTec Lubricants **www.proteclubricants.com**
Rigel Products **www.rigelproducts.com**
Rusteprufe Labs **www.rusteprufe.com**
Sagebrush Products **www.sagebrushproducts.com**
Sentry Solutions Ltd. **www.sentrysolutions.com**
Shooters Choice Gun Care **www.shooters-choice.com**
Silencio **www.silencio.com**
Slip 2000 **www.slip2000.com**
Southern Bloomer Mfg. **www.southernbloomer.com**
Stony Point Products **www.uncle-mikes.com**
Tetra Gun **www.tetraproducts.com**
The TM Solution **thetmsolution@comsast.net**
Top Duck Products **www.topduckproducts.com**
Triangle Patch **www.trianglepatch.com**
Ultra Bore Coat **www.ultracoatingsinc.com**
Wipe-Out **www.sharpshootr.com**
World's Fastest Gun Bore Cleaner
   www.michaels-oregon.com

FIREARM AUCTION SITES

A&S Auction Co. **www.asauction.com**
Alderfer Austion **www.alderferauction.com**
Amoskeag Auction Co. **www.amoskeagauction.com**
Antique Guns **www.antiqueguns.com**
Auction Arms **www.auctionarms.com**
Batterman's Auctions **www.battermans.com**
Bonhams & Butterfields **www.bonhams.com/usarms**
Cowan's **www.cowans.com**
Fontaine's Auction Gallery **www.fontainesauction.net**
Greg Martin Auctions **www.gregmartinauctions.com**
Guns America **www.gunsamerica.com**
Gun Broker **www.gunbroker.com**
Guns4Pennies **www.guns4pennies.com**
Guns International **www.gunsInternational.com**
Heritage Auction Galleries **www.ha.com**
James D. Julia, Inc. **www.jamesdjulia.com**

Little John's Auction Service www.littlejohnsauctionservice.com
Morphy Auctions www.morphyauctions.com
Poulin Auction Co. www.poulinantiques.com
Rock Island Auction Co. www.rockislandauction.com
Wallis & Wallis www.wallisandwallis.org

FIREARM MANUFACTURERS AND IMPORTERS

AAR, Inc. www.iar-arms.com
A-Square www.asquarecompany.com
Accuracy Int'l North America www.accuracyinternational.com
Accuracy Rifle Systems www.mini-14.net
Ace Custom 45s www.acecustom45.com
Adcor Defense www.adcorindustries.com
Advanced Weapons Technology www.AWT-Zastava.com
AIM www.aimsurplus.com
AirForce Airguns www.airforceairguns.com
Air Gun Inc. www.airrifle-china.com
Airguns of Arizona www.airgunsofarizona.com
Airgun Express www.airgunexpress.com
Akkar Sporting Arms www.akkar-usa.com
Alchemy Arms www.alchemyltd.com
Alexander Arms www.alexanderarms.com
America Remembers www.americaremembers.com
American Classic www.americanclassic1911.com
American Derringer Corp. www.amderringer.com
American Rifle Co. www.americanrifleco.com
American Spirit Arms Corp. www.gunkits.com
American Tactical Imports www.americantactical.us
American Western Arms www.awaguns.com
Anics Corp. www.anics.com
Anschutz www.anschutz-sporters.com
Answer Products Co. www.answerrifles.com
AR-7 Industries www.ar-7.com
Ares Defense Systems www.aresdefense.com
Armalite www.armalite.com
Armi Sport www.armisport.com
Armory USA www.globaltraders.com
Armsco www.armsco.net
Armscorp USA Inc. www.armscorpusa.com
Arnold Arms www.arnoldarms.com
Arrieta www.arrietashotguns.com
Arsenal Inc. www.arsenalinc.com
Arthur Brown Co. www.eabco.com
Atlanta Cutlery Corp. www.atlantacutlery.com
ATA Arms www.ataarms.com
Auction Arms www.auctionarms.com
Autauga Arms Inc. www.autaugaarms.com
Auto-Ordnance Corp. www.tommygun.com
AWA Int'l www.awaguns.com
Axtell Rifle Co. www.riflesmith.com

Aya www.aya-fineguns.com
Baikal www.baikalinc.ru/eng/
Badger Ordnance www.badgerordnance.com
Ballard Rifles www.ballardrifles.com
Barrett Firearms Mfg. www.barrettrifles.com
Bat Machine Co. www.batmachine.com
Beeman Precision Airguns www.beeman.com
Benelli USA Corp. www.benelliusa.com
Benjamin Sheridan www.crosman.com
Beretta U.S.A. Corp. www.berettausa.com
Bernardelli www.bernardelli.com
Bersa www.bersa.com
Bighorn Arms www.bighornarms.com
Bill Hanus Birdguns www.billhanusbirdguns.com
Blaser Jagdwaffen Gmbh www.blaser.de
Bleiker www.bleiker.ch
Bluegrass Armory www.bluegrassarmory.com
Bond Arms www.bondarms.com
Borden's Rifles, Inc. www.bordensrifles.com
Boss & Co. www.bossguns.co.uk
Bowen Classic Arms www.bowenclassicarms.com
Briley Mfg www.briley.com
BRNO Arms www.zbrojovka.com
Brown, David McKay www.mckaybrown.com
Brown, Ed Products www.edbrown.com
Browning www.browning.com
BRP Corp. www.brpguns.com
BSA Guns www.bsagunusa.com
BUL Ltd. www.bultransmark.com
Bushmaster Firearms/Quality Parts www.bushmaster.com
BWE Firearms www.bwefirearms.com
Cabot Guns www.cabotguns.com
Caesar Guerini USA www.gueriniusa.com
Carbon 15 www.professional-ordnance.com
Caspian Arms, Ltd. www.caspianarmsltd.8m.com
Casull Arms Corp. www.casullarms.com
Calvary Arms www.calvaryarms.com
CDNN Investments, Inc. www.cdnninvestments.com
Century Arms www.centuryarms.com
Chadick's Ltd. www.chadicks-ltd.com
Champlin Firearms www.champlinarms.com
Chapuis Arms www.doubleguns.com/chapuis.htm
Charles Daly www.charlesdaly.com
Charter Arms www.charterfirearms.com
CheyTac USA www.cheytac.com
Chiappa Firearms www.chiappafirearms.com
Christensen Arms www.christensenarms.com
Cimarron Firearms Co. www.cimarron-firearms.com
Clark Custom Guns www.clarkcustomguns.com
Cobra Enterprises www.cobrapistols.com
Cogswell & Harrison www.cogswell.co.uk/home.htm
Collector's Armory, Ltd. www.collectorsarmory.com

Colt's Mfg Co. **www.colt.com**
Compasseco, Inc. **www.compasseco.com**
Connecticut Shotgun Mfg. Co. **www.connecticutshotgun.com**
Connecticut Valley Arms **www.cva.com**
Coonan, Inc. **www.coonaninc.com**
Cooper Firearms **www.cooperfirearms.com**
Core Rifle Systems **www.core15.com**
Corner Shot **www.cornershot.com**
CPA Rifles **www.singleshotrifles.com**
Crosman **www.crosman.com**
C.Sharp Arms Co. **www.csharparms.com**
CVA **www.cva.com**
Cylinder & Slide Shop **www.cylinder-slide.com**
Czechp Int'l **www.czechpoint-usa.com**
CZ USA **www.cz-usa.com**
Daisy Mfg Co. **www.daisy.com**
Dakota Arms Inc. **www.dakotaarms.com**
Dan Wesson Firearms **www.danwessonfirearms.com**
Daniel Defense, Inc. **www.danieldefense.com**
Davis Industries **www.davisindguns.com**
Detonics USA **www.detonicsusa.com**
Diana **www.diana-airguns.de**
Dixie Gun Works **www.dixiegunworks.com**
Dlask Arms Corp. **www.dlask.com**
DoubleTap **www.heizerdefense.com**
D.P.M.S., Inc. **www.dpmsinc.com**
D.S.Arms, Inc. **www.dsarms.com**
Dumoulin **www.dumoulin-herstal.com**
Dynamit Noble **www.dnrws.com**
CAA Corp. **www.caaoorp.com**
Eagle Imports, Inc. **www.bersa-llama.com**
Ed Brown Products **www.edbrown.com**
EDM Arms **www.edmarms.com**
E.M.F. Co. **www.emf-company.com**
Enterprise Arms **www.enterprise.com**
E R Shaw **www.ershawbarrels.com**
European American Armory Corp. **www.eaacorp.com**
Evans, William **www.williamevans.com**
Excel Arms **www.excelarms.com**
Fabarm **www.fabarm.com**
FAC-Guns-N-Stuff **www.gunsnstuff.com**
Falcon Pneumatic Systems **www.falcon-airguns.com**
Fausti Stefano **www.faustistefanoarms.com**
Firestorm **www.firestorm-sgs.com**
Flodman Guns **www.flodman.com**
FN Herstal **www.fnherstal.com**
FNH USA **www.fnhusa.com**
Franchi **www.franchiusa.com**
Franklin Armory **www.franklinarmory.com**
Freedom Arms **www.freedomarms.com**
Freedom Group, Inc. **www.freedom-group.com**
Galazan **www.connecticutshotgun.com**

Gambo Renato **www.renatogamba.it**
Gamo **www.gamo.com**
Gary Reeder Custom Guns **www.reeder-customguns.com**
Gazelle Arms **www.gazellearms.com**
German Sport Guns **www.germansportguns.com**
Gibbs Rifle Company **www.gibbsrifle.com**
Glock **www.glock.com**
Griffin & Howe **www.griffinhowe.com**
Grizzly Big Boar Rifle **www.largrizzly.com**
GSI Inc. **www.gsifirearms.com**
Gunbroker.Com **www.gunbroker.com**
Gun Room Co. **www.onlylongrange.com**
Hammerli **www.carl-walther.com**
Hatfield Gun Co. **www.hatfield-usa.com**
Hatsan Arms Co. **www.hatsan.com.tr**
Heckler and Koch **www.hk-usa.com**
Henry Repeating Arms Co. **www.henryrepeating.com**
Heritage Mfg. **www.heritagemfg.com**
Heym **www.heym-waffenfabrik.de**
High Standard Mfg. **www.highstandard.com**
Hi-Point Firearms **www.hi-pointfirearms.com**
Holland & Holland **www.hollandandholland.com**
H&R 1871 Firearms **www.hr1871.com**
H-S Precision **www.hsprecision.com**
Hunters Lodge Corp. **www.hunterslodge.com**
IAR Inc. **www.iar-arms.com**
Imperial Miniature Armory **www.1800miniature.com**
Interarms **www.interarms.com**
International Military Antiques, Inc. **www.ima-usa.com**
Inter Ordnance **www.interordnance.com**
Intrac Arms International LLC **www.hsarms.com**
Israel Arms **www.israelarms.com**
ISSC, LLC **www.issc-austria.com**
Iver Johnson Arms **www.iverjohnsonarms.com**
Izhevsky Mekhanichesky Zavod **www.baikalinc.ru**
James River Armory **www.jamesriverarmory.com**
Jarrett Rifles, Inc. **www.jarrettrifles.com**
J&G Sales, Ltd. **www.jgsales.com**
Johannsen Express Rifle **www.johannsen-jagd.de**
Jonathan Arthur Ciener **www.22lrconversions.com**
JP Enterprises, Inc. **www.jprifles.com**
Kahr Arms/Auto-Ordnance **www.kahr.com**
K.B.I. **www.kbi-inc.com**
KDF, Inc. **www.kdfguns.com**
Kelby's **www.kelby.com**
Kel-Tec CNC Ind., Inc. **www.kel-tec.com**
Keystone Sporting Arms **www.keystonesportingarmsllc.com**
Kifaru **www.kifaru.net**
Kimber **www.kimberamerica.com**
Knight's Armament Co. **www.knightsarmco.com**
Knight Rifles **www.knighttrifles.com**
Korth **www.korthwaffen.de**

Krebs Custom Guns **www.krebscustom.com**
Kriss **www.kriss-usa.com**
Krieghoff Int'l **www.krieghoff.com**
KY Imports, Inc. **www.kyimports.com**
K-VAR **www.k-var.com**
Lanber **www.lanber.net**
L.A.R Mfg **www.largrizzly.com**
Lazzeroni Arms Co. **www.lazzeroni.com**
Legacy Sports International **www.legacysports.com**
Les Baer Custom, Inc. **www.lesbaer.com**
Lewis Machine & Tool Co. **www.lewismachine.net**
Linebaugh Custom Sixguns **www.sixgunner.com/linebaugh**
Ljutic **www.ljuticgun.com**
Llama **www.bersa-llama.com**
LMT Defense **www.lmtdefense.com**
LRB Arms **www.lrbarms.com**
Lyman **www.lymanproducts.com**
LWRC Int'l **www.lwrci.com**
Magnum Research **www.magnumresearch.com**
Majestic Arms **www.majesticarms.com**
Markesbery Muzzleloaders **www.markesbery.com**
Marksman Products **www.marksman.com**
Marlin **www.marlinfirearms.com**
MasterPiece Arms **www.masterpiecearms.com**
Mauser **www.mauser.com**
McMillan Bros Rifle Co. **www.mcfamily.com**
MDM **www.mdm-muzzleloaders.com**
Meacham Rifles **www.meachamrifles.com**
Merkel **www.hk-usa.com**
Metrol Arms **www.metroarms.com**
Milkor USA **www.milkorusainc.com**
Miller Arms **www.millerarms.com**
Miltech **www.miltecharms.com**
Miltex, Inc. **www.miltexusa.com**
Mitchell's Mausers **www.mausers.net**
MK Ballistic Systems **www.mkballistics.com**
M-Mag **www.mmag.com**
Model "1" Sales **www.model"1"sales.com**
Montana Rifle Co. **www.montanarifleman.com**
Mossberg **www.mossberg.com**
Navy Arms **www.navyarms.com**
Nesika **www.nesika.com**
New England Arms Corp. **www.newenglandarms.com**
New England Custom Gun Svc, Ltd.
    www.newenglandcustomgun.com
New England Firearms **www.hr1871.com**
New Ultra Light Arms **www.newultralight.com**
Nighthawk Custom **www.nighthawkcustom.com**
North American Arms **www.northamericanarms.com**
Nosler Bullets, Inc. **www.nosler.com**
Nowlin Mfg. Inc. **www.nowlinguns.com**
O.F. Mossberg & Sons **www.mossberg.com**

Ohio Ordnance Works **www.ohioordnanceworks.com**
Olympic Arms **www.olyarms.com**
Osprey Defense **www.gaspiston.com**
Panther Arms **www.dpmsinc.com**
Para-USA **www.para-usa.com**
Pedersoli Davide & Co. **www.davide-pedersoli.com**
Perazzi **www.perazzi.com**
Pietta **www.pietta.it**
Pistol Dynamics **www,pistoldynamics.com**
PKP Knife-Pistol **www.sanjuanenterprise.com**
Power Custom **www.powercustom.com**
Precision Small Arm Inc. **www.precisionsmallarms.com**
Primary Weapons Systems **www.primaryweapons.com**
Professional Arms **www.professional-arms.com**
Proof Research **www.proofresearch.com**
PTR 91,Inc. **www.ptr91.com**
Purdey & Sons **www.purdey.com**
Pyramid Air **www.pyramidair.com**
RAAC **www.raacfirearms.com**
Red Jacket Firearms **www.redjacketfirearms.com**
Remington **www.remington.com**
Republic Arms Inc. **www.republicarmsinc.com**
Rhineland Arms, Inc. **www.rhinelandarms.com**
Rigby **www.johnrigbyandco.com**
Rizzini USA **www.rizziniusa.com**
RM Equipment, Inc. **www.40mm.com**
Robar Companies, Inc. **www.robarguns.com**
Robinson Armament Co. **www.robarm.com**
Rock River Arms, Inc. **www.rockriverarms.com**
Rogue Rifle Co. Inc. **www.chipmunkrifle.com**
Rohrbaugh Firearms **www.rohrbaughfirearms.com**
Rossi Arms **www.rossiusa.com**
RPM **www.rpmxlpistols.com**
Russian American Armory **www.raacfirearms.com**
RUAG Ammotec **www.ruag.com**
Sabatti SPA **www.sabatti.com**
Saco Defense **www.sacoinc.com**
Safari Arms **www.olyarms.com**
Safety Harbor Firerms **www.safetyharborfirearms.com**
Sako **www.berettausa.com**
Samco Global Arms Inc. **www.samcoglobal.com**
Sarco **www.sarcoinc.com**
Sarsilmaz Silah San **www.sarsilmaz.com**
Sauer & Sohn **www.sauer.de**
Savage Arms Inc. **www.savagearms.com**
Scattergun Technologies Inc. **www.wilsoncombat.com**
Schmeisser Gmbh **www.schmeisser-germany.de**
Searcy Enterprises **www.searcyent.com**
Sharps Rifle Companies **www.asquareco.com**
Shaw **www.ershawbarrels.com**
Shiloh Rifle Mfg. **www.shilohrifle.com**
Sig Sauer, Inc. **www.sigsauer.com**

Simpson Ltd. **www.simpsonltd.com**
SKB Shotguns **www.skbshotguns.com**
Smith & Wesson **www.smith-wesson.com**
SOG International, Inc. soginc@go-concepts.com
Sphinx System **www.sphinxarms.com**
Springfield Armory **www.springfield-armory.com**
SSK Industries **www.sskindustries.com**
Stag Arms **www.stagarms.com**
Steyr Arms, Inc. **www.steyrarms.com**
STI International **www.stiguns.com**
Stoeger Industries **www.stoegerindustries.com**
Strayer-Voigt Inc. **www.sviguns.com**
Sturm, Ruger & Company **www.ruger-firearms.com**
Super Six Classic **www.bisonbull.com**
Surgeon Rifles **www.surgeonrifles.com**
Tactical Rifles **www.tacticalrifles.com**
Tactical Solutions **www.tacticalsol.com**
Tar-Hunt Slug Guns, Inc. **www.tar-hunt.com**
Taser Int'l **www.taser.com**
Taurus **www.taurususa.com**
Taylor's & Co., Inc. **www.taylorsfirearms.com**
Tempco Mfg. Co. **www.tempcomfg.com**
Tennessee Guns **www.tennesseeguns.com**
TG Int'l **www.tnguns.com**
The 1877 Sharps Co. **www.1877sharps.com**
Thompson Center Arms **www.tcarms.com**
Tikka **www.berettausa.com**
TNW, Inc. **www.tnwfirearms.com**
Traditions **www.traditionsfirearms.com**
Tristar Sporting Arms **www.tristarsportingarms.com**
Turnbull Mfg. Co. **www.turnbullmfg.com**
Uberti **www.ubertireplicas.com**
Ultralite 50 **www.ultralite50.com**
Ultra Light Arms **www.newultralight.com**
Umarex **www.umarex.com**
U.S. Armament Corp. **www.usarmamentcorp.com**
U.S. Fire Arms Mfg. Co. **www.usfasingleactions.com**
Uselton Arms, Inc. **www.useltonarmsinc.com**
Valkyrie Arms **www.valkyriearms.com**
Vektor Arms **www.vektorarms.com**
Verney-Carron **www.verney-carron.com**
Volquartsen Custom Ltd. **www.volquartsen.com**
Vulcan Armament **www.vulcanarmament.com**
Walther USA **www.waltherarms.com**
Weatherby **www.weatherby.com**
Webley and Scott Ltd. **www.webley.co.uk**
Westley Richards **www.westleyrichards.com**
Widley **www.widleyguns.com**
Wild West Guns **www.wildwestguns.com**
William Larkin Moore & Co. **www.doublegun.com**
Wilson Combat **www.wilsoncombat.com**
Winchester Rifles and Shotguns **www.winchesterguns.com**

GUN PARTS, BARRELS, AFTER-MARKET ACCESSORIES

300 Below **www.300below.com**
Accuracy International of North America
    www.accuracyinternational.org
Accuracy Speaks, Inc. **www.accuracyspeaks.com**
Accuracy Systems **www.accuracysystemsinc.com**
Accurate Airguns **www.accurateairguns.com**
Adam Arms **www.adamarms.net**
Advanced Barrel Systems **www.carbonbarrels.com**
Advantage Arms **www.advantagearms.com**
Aim Surplus **www.aimsurplus.com**
AK-USA **www.ak-103.com**
American Spirit Arms Corp. **www.gunkits.com**
Amhurst-Depot **www.amherst-depot.com**
AMT Gun Parts **www.amt-gunparts.com**
Apex Gun Parts **www.apexgunparts.com**
Armatac Industries **www.armatac.com**
Asia Sourcing Corp. **www.asiasourcing.com**
Badger Barrels, Inc. **www.badgerbarrels.com**
Barnes Precision Machine **www.barnesprecision.com**
Bar-Sto Precision Machine **www.barsto.com**
Battenfeld Technologies
    www.battenfeldtechnologies.com
Bellm TC's **www.bellmtcs.com**
Belt Mountain Enterprises **www.beltmountain.com**
Bergara Barrels **www.bergarabarrels.com**
Beyer Barrels **www.beyerbarrels.com**
Bill Wiseman & Co. **www.wisemanballistics.com**
Bravo Company USA **www.bravocompanyusa.com**
Briley **www.briley.com**
Brownells **www.brownells.com**
B-Square **www.b-square.com**
Buffer Technologies **www.buffertech.com**
Bullberry Barrel Works **www.bullberry.com**
Bulldog Barrels **www.bulldogbarrels.com**
Bushmaster Firearms/Quality Parts
    www.bushmaster.com
Butler Creek Corp **www.butler-creek.com**
Cape Outfitters Inc. **www.capeoutfitters.com**
Caspian Arms Ltd. **www.caspianarms.com**
CDNN Sports **www.cdnnsports.com**
Cheaper Than Dirt **www.cheaperthandirt.com**
Chesnut Ridge **www.chestnutridge.com/**
Chip McCormick Corp **www.chipmccormickcorp.com**
Choate Machine & Tool Co. **www.riflestock.com**
Christie's Products **www.1022cental.com**
Cierner, Jonathan Arthur **www.22lrconversions.com**
CJ Weapons Accessories **www.cjweapons.com**
Colonial Arms **www.colonialarms.com**
Comp-N-Choke **www.comp-n-choke.com**

Cylinder & Slide Shop www.cylinder-slide.com
Daniel Defense www.danieldefense.com
Dave Manson Precision Reamers www.mansonreamers.com
Digi-Twist www.fmtcorp.com
Dixie Gun Works www.dixiegun.com
Douglas Barrels www.benchrest.com/douglas/
DPMS www.dpmsinc.com
D.S.Arms www.dsarms.com
eBay www.ebay.com
E. Arthur Brown Co. www.eabco.com
Ed Brown Products www.edbrown.com
EFK Marketing/Fire Dragon Pistol Accessories www.flmfire.com
E.R. Shaw www.ershawbarrels.com
Fast Fire www.fastfire.com
FJ Fedderson Rifle Barrels www.gunbarrels.net
Forrest, Inc. www.gunmags.com
FTF Industries www.ftfindustries.com
Fulton Armory www.fulton-armory.com
Galazan www.connecticutshotgun.com
Gemtech www.gem-tech.com
Gentry, David www.gentrycustom.com
GG&G www.gggaz.com
Green Mountain Rifle Barrels www.gmriflebarrel.com
Gun Parts Corp. www.e-gunparts.com
Guntec USA www.guntecusa.com
Harris Engineering www.harrisbipods.com
Hart Rifle Barrels www.hartbarrels.com
Hastings Barrels www.hastingsbarrels.com
Heinie Specialty Products www.heinie.com
HKS Products wwwhksspeedloaders.com
Holland Shooters Supply www.hollandgun.com
H-S Precision www.hsprecision.com
100 Straight Products www.100straight.com
I.M.A. www.ima-usa.com
Jack First Gun Shop www.jackfirstgun.com
Jarvis, Inc. www.jarvis-custom.com
J&T Distributing www.jtdistributing.com
John's Guns www.johnsguns.com
John Masen Co. www.johnmasen.com
Jonathan Arthur Ciener, Inc. www.22lrconversions.com
JP Enterprises www.jpar15.com
Keng's Firearms Specialities www.versapod.com
KG Industries www.kgcoatings.com
Kick Eez www.kickeez.com
Kidd Triggers www.coolguyguns.com
King's Gunworks www.kingsgunworks.com
Knoxx Industries www.knoxx.com
Krieger Barrels www.kriegerbarrels.com
K-VAR Corp. www.k-var.com
LaRue Tactical www.laruetactical.com
Les Baer Custom, Inc. www.lesbaer.com
Lilja Barrels www.riflebarrels.com

Lone Wolf Dist. www.lonewolfdist.com
Lothar Walther Precision Tools Inc. www.lothar-walther.de
M&A Parts, Inc. www.m-aparts.com
MAB Barrels www.mab.com.au
Magna-Matic Defense www.magna-matic-defense.com
Magpul Industries Corp. www.magpul.com
Majestic Arms www.majesticarms.com
Marvel Products, Inc. www.marvelprod.com
MEC-GAR USA www.mec-gar.com
Mech Tech Systems www.mechtechsys.com
Mesa Tactical www.mesatactical.com
Michaels of Oregon Co. www.michaels-oregon.com
Midway USA www.midwayusa.com
New England Custom Gun Service
   www.newenglandcustomgun.com
NIC Industries www.nicindustries.com
North Mfg. Co. www.rifle-barrels.com
Numrich Gun Parts Corp. www.e-gunparts.com
Osprey Defense LLC www.gaspiston.com
Pachmayr www.pachmayr.com
Pac-Nor Barrels www.pac-nor.com
Power Custom, Inc. www.powercustom.com
Point Tech Inc. pointec@ibm.net
Precision Reflex www.pri-mounts.com
Promag Industries www.promagindustries.com
RCI-XRAIL www.xrailbyrci.com
Red Star Arms www.redstararms.com
River Bank Armory www.riverbankarmory.com
Rock Creek Barrels www.rockcreekbarrels.com
Rocky Mountain Arms www.rockymountainarms.com
Royal Arms Int'l www.royalarms.com
R.W. Hart www.rwhart.com
Sage Control Ordnance www.sageinternationalltd.com
Sarco Inc. www.sarcoinc.com
Scattergun Technologies Inc. www.wilsoncombat.com
Schuemann Barrels www.schuemann.com
Score High Gunsmithing www.scorehi.com
Seminole Gunworks Chamber Mates
   www.chambermates.com
Shaw Barrels www.ershawbarrels.com
Shilen www.shilen.com
Sims Vibration Laboratory www.limbsaver.com
Slide Fire www.slidefire.com
Smith & Alexander Inc. www.smithandalexander.com
Speed Shooters Int'l www.shooternet.com/ssi
Sprinco USA Inc. sprinco@primenet.com
Springfield Sporters, Inc. www.ssporters.com
STI Int'l www.stiguns.com
S&S Firearms www.ssfirearms.com
SSK Industries www.sskindustries.com
Sun Devil Mfg. www.sundevilmfg.com
Sunny Hill Enterprises www.sunny-hill.com

Tac Star **www.lymanproducts.com**
Tactical Innovations **www.tacticalinc.com**
Tactical Solutions **www.tacticalsol.com**
Tactilite **www.tactilite.com**
Tapco **www.tapco.com**
Trapdoors Galore **www.trapdoors.com**
Triple K Manufacturing Co. Inc. **www.triplek.com**
Ultimak **www.ultimak.com**
U.S.A. Magazines Inc. **www.usa-magazines.com**
Verney-Carron SA **www.verney-carron.com**
Vintage Ordnance **www.vintageordnance.com**
Vltor Weapon Systems **www.vltor.com**
Volquartsen Custom Ltd. **www.volquartsen.com**
W.C. Wolff Co. **www.gunsprings.com**
Waller & Son **www.wallerandson.com**
Weigand Combat Handguns **www.weigandcombat.com**
Western Gun Parts **www.westerngunparts.com**
Wilson Arms **www.wilsonarms.com**
Wilson Combat **www.wilsoncombat.com**
Wisner's Inc. **www.wisnerinc.com**
Z-M Weapons **www.zmweapons.com/home.htm**

GUNSMITHING SUPPLIES AND INSTRUCTION

4-D Products **www.4-dproducts.com**
American Gunsmithing Institute **www.americangunsmith.com**
Baron Technology **www.baronengraving.com**
Battenfeld Technologies **www.battenfeldtechnologies.com**
Bellm TC's **www.bellmtcs.com**
Blue Ridge Machinery & Tools **www.blueridgemachinery.com**
Brownells, Inc. **www.brownells.com**
B-Square Co. **www.b-square.com**
Cerakote Firearm Coatings **www.nciindustries.com**
Clymer Mfg. Co. **www.clymertool.com**
Craftguard Metal Finishing **crftgrd@aol.com**
Dem-Bart **www.dembartco.com**
Doug Turnbull Restoration **www.turnbullrestoration,com**
Du-Lite Corp. **www.dulite.com**
DuraCoat Firearm Finishes **www.lauerweaponry.com**
Dvorak Instruments **www.dvorakinstruments.com**
Gradiant Lens Corp. **www.gradientlens.com**
Grizzly Industrial **www.grizzly.com**
Gunline Tools **www.gunline.com**
Harbor Freight **www.harborfreight.com**
JGS Precision Tool Mfg. LLC **www.jgstools.com**
Mag-Na-Port International **www.magnaport.com**
Manson Precision Reamers **www.mansonreamers.com**
Midway USA **www.midwayusa.com**
Murray State College **www.mscok.edu**
New England Custom Gun Service
   www.newenglandcustomgun.com
Olympus America Inc. **www.olympus.com**

Pacific Tool & Gauge **www.pacifictoolandgauge.com**
Penn Foster Career School **www.pennfoster.edu**
Pennsylvania Gunsmith School **www.pagunsmith.edu**
Piedmont Community College **www.piedmontcc.edu**
Precision Metalsmiths, Inc. **www.precisionmetalsmiths.com**
Rail Vise Technologies **www.railvise.com**
Sonoran Desert Institute **www.sdi.edu**
Trinidad State Junior College **www.trinidadstate.edu**

HANDGUN GRIPS

A&G Supply Co. **www.gripextender.com**
Ajax Custom Grips, Inc. **www.ajaxgrips.com**
Altamont Co. **www.altamontco.com**
Aluma Grips **www.alumagrips.com**
Badger Grips **www.pistolgrips.com**
Barami Corp. **www.hipgrip.com**
Blu Magnum Grips **www.blumagnum.com**
Buffalo Brothers **www.buffalobrothers.com**
Crimson Trace Corp. **www.crimsontrace.com**
Decal Grip **www.decalgrip.com**
Eagle Grips **www.eaglegrips.com**
Falcon Industries **www.crgogrips.net**
Herrett's Stocks **www.herrettstocks.com**
Hogue Grips **www.getgrip.com**
Kirk Ratajesak **www.kgratajesak.com**
Lett Custom Grips **www.lettgrips.com**
N.C. Ordnance **www.gungrip.com**
Nill-Grips USA **www.nill-grips.com**
Pachmayr **www.pachmayr.com**
Pearce Grips **www.pearcegrip.com**
Rio Grande Custom Grips **www.riograndecustomgrips.com**
Trausch Grips Int. Co. **www.trausch.com**
Tyler-T Grips **www.t-grips.com**
Uncle Mike's: **www.uncle-mikes.com**

HOLSTERS AND LEATHER PRODUCTS

Active Pro Gear **www.activeprogear.com**
Akah **www.akah.de**
Aker Leather Products **www.akerleather.com**
Alessi Distributor R&F Inc. **www.alessiholsters.com**
Alfonso's of Hollywood **www.alfonsogunleather.com**
Armor Holdings **www.holsters.com**
Bagmaster **www.bagmaster.com**
Bandara Gunleather **www.bandaragunleather.com**
Bianchi International **www.bianchi-intl.com**
Black Dog Machine **www.blackdogmachinellc.net**
Blackhawk Outdoors **www.blackhawk.com**
Blackhills Leather **www.blackhillsleather.com**
BodyHugger Holsters **www.nikolais.com**
Boyt Harness Co. **www.boytharness.com**

Brigade Gun Leather www.brigadegunleather.com
Center of Mass www.comholsters.com
Chimere www.chimere.com
Clipdraw www.clipdraw.com
Conceal It www.conceal-it.com
Concealment Shop Inc. www.theconcealmentshop.com
Coronado Leather Co. www.coronadoleather.com
Covert Carry www.covertcarry.com
Creedmoor Sports, Inc. www.creedmoorsports.com
Cross Breed Holsters www.crossbreedholsters.com
Custom Leather Wear www.customleatherwear.com
Deep Conceal www.deepconceal.com
Defense Security Products www.thunderwear.com
Dennis Yoder www.yodercustomleather.com
DeSantis Holster www.desantisholster.com
Diamond Custom Leather www.diamondcustomleather.com
Dillon Precision www.dillonprecision.com
Don Hume Leathergoods, Inc. www.donhume.com
Elite Survival www.elitesurvival.com
Ernie Hill International www.erniehill.com
Fist www.fist-inc.com
Fobus USA www.fobusholster.com
Front Line Ltd. frontlin@internet-zahav.net
Frontier Gun Leather www.frontiergunleather.com
Galco www.usgalco.com
Gilmore's Sports Concepts www.gilmoresports.com
Gould & Goodrich www.gouldusa.com
Gunmate Products www.gun-mate.com
Hellweg Ltd. www.hellwegltd.com
Hide-A-Gun www.hide-a-gun.com
High Noon Holsters www.highnoonholsters.com
Holsters.Com www.holsters.com
Horseshoe Leather Products www.horseshoe.co.uk
Hunter Co. www.huntercompany.com
JBP/Master's Holsters www.jbpholsters.com
Kirkpatrick Leather Company www.kirkpatrickleather.com
KJ Leather www.kbarjleather.com
KNJ www.knjmfg.com
Kramer Leather www.kramerleather.com
Law Concealment Systems www.handgunconcealment.com
Levy's Leathers Ltd. www.levysleathers.com
Mernickle Holsters www.mernickleholsters.com
Michaels of Oregon Co. www.michaels-oregon.com
Milt Sparks Leather www.miltsparks.com
Mitch Rosen Extraordinary Gunleather www.mitchrosen.com
N82 Tactical www.n82tactical.com
Old World Leather www.gun-mate.com
Pacific Canvas & Leather Co. paccanadleather@directway.com
Pager Pal www.pagerpal.com
Phalanx Corp. www.smartholster.com
Purdy Gear www.purdygear.com
PWL www.pwlusa.com

Rumanya Inc. www.rumanya.com
S.A. Gunleather www.elpasoleather.com
Safariland Ltd. Inc. www.safariland.com
Shooting Systems Group Inc. www.shootingsystems.com
Skyline Tool Works www.clipdraw.com
Solerial Leather www.solerialleather.com
Stellar Rigs www.stellarrigs.com
Strictly Anything Inc. www.strictlyanything.com
Strong Holster Co. www.strong-holster.com
Tex Shoemaker & Sons www.texshoemaker.com
The Belt Co. www.conceal-it.com
The Leather Factory Inc. lflandry@flash.net
The Outdoor Connection www.outdoorconnection.com
Top-Line USA inc. www.toplineusa.com
Tuff Products www.tuffproducts.com
Triple K Manufacturing Co. www.triplek.com
Wilson Combat www.wilsoncombat.com

MISCELLANEOUS SHOOTING PRODUCTS

10X Products Group www.10Xwear.com
Aero Peltor www.aearo.com
American Body Armor www.americanbodyarmor.com
American Tactical Imports www.americantactical.com
Ammo-Up www.ammoupusa.com
Armor Holdings Products www.armorholdings.com
AutoGun Tracker www.autoguntracker.com
Battenfeld Technologies www.battenfeldtechnologies.com
Beamhit www.beamhit.com
Beartooth www.beartoothproducts.com
Bodyguard by S&W www.yourbodyguard.com
Burnham Brothers www.burnhambrothers.com
Collectors Armory www.collectorsarmory.com
Dalloz Safety www.cdalloz.com
Deben Group Industries Inc. www.deben.com
Decot Hy-Wyd Sport Glasses www.sportyglasses.com
Defense Technology www.safariland.com/lesslethal
E.A.R., Inc. www.earinc.com
First Choice Armor www.firstchoicearmor.com
Gunstands www.gunstands.com
Howard Leight Hearing Protectors www.howardleight.com
Hunters Specialities www.hunterspec.com
Johnny Stewart Wildlife Calls www.hunterspec.com
Joseph Chiarello Gun Insurance www.guninsurance.com
Mec-Gar USA www.mec-gar.com
Merit Corporation www.meritcorporation.com
Michaels of Oregon Co. www.michaels-oregon.com
MPI Outdoors www.mpioutdoors.com
MT2, LLC www.mt2.com
MTM Case-Gard www.mtmcase-gard.com
North Safety Products www.northsafety-brea.com
Oakley, Inc. www.usstandardissue.com

Plano Molding **www.planomolding.com**
Practical Air Rifle Training Systems **www.smallarms.com**
Pro-Ears **www.pro-ears.com**
Second Chance Body Armor Inc. **www.secondchance.com**
Silencio **www.silencio.com**
Smart Lock Technologies **www.smartlock.com**
SportEAR **www.sportear.com**
STRAC, Inc. **www.stractech.com**
Surefire **www.surefire.com**
Taser Int'l **www.taser.com**
Vyse-Gelatin Innovations **www.gelatininnovations.com**
Walker's Game Ear Inc. **www.walkersgameear.com**

MUZZLELOADING FIREARMS AND PRODUCTS

American Pioneer Powder **www.americanpioneerpowder.com**
Armi Sport **www.armisport.com**
Barnes Bullets **www.barnesbullets,com**
Black Powder Products **www.bpiguns.com**
Buckeye Barrels **www.buckeyebarrels.com**
Cabin Creek Muzzleloading **www.cabincreek.net**
CVA **www.cva.com**
Caywood Gunmakers **www.caywoodguns.com**
Davide Perdsoli & co. **www.davide-pedersoli.com**
Dixie Gun Works, Inc. **www.dixiegun.com**
Elephant/Swiss Black Powder **www.elephantblackpowder.com**
Goex Black Powder **www.goexpowder.com**
Green Mountain Rifle Barrel Co. **www.gmriflebarrel.com**
Gunstocks Plus **www.gunstocksplus.com**
Gun Works **www.thegunworks.com**
Harvester Muzzleloading **www.harvestermuuzzleloading.com**
Honorable Company of Horners **www.hornguild.org**
Hornady **www.hornady.com**
Jedediah Starr Trading Co. **www.jedediah-starr.com**
Jim Chambers Flintlocks **www.flintlocks.com**
Kahnke Gunworks **www.powderandbow.com/kahnke/**
Knight Rifles **www.knightrifles.com**
Knob Mountain Muzzleloading
   www.knobmountainmuzzleloading.com
The leatherman **www.blackpowderbags.com**
Log Cabin Shop **www.logcabinshop.com**
L&R Lock Co. **www.lr-rpl.com**
Lyman **www.lymanproducts.com**
Magkor Industries **www.magkor.com**
MDM Muzzleloaders **www.mdm-muzzleloaders.com**
Middlesex Village Trading **www.middlesexvillagetrading.com**
Millennium Designed Muzzleloaders
   www.mdm-muzzleloaders.com
MSM, Inc. **www.msmfg.com**
Muzzleloader Builders Supply
   www.muzzleloadersbuilderssupply.com
Muzzleload Magnum Products **www.mmpsabots.com**

Muzzleloading Shotguns **www.muzzleloadingshotguns.com**
Muzzleloading Technologies, Inc. **www.mtimuzzleloading.com**
Navy Arms **www.navyarms.com**
Northwest Trade Guns **www.northstarwest.com**
Nosler, Inc. **www.nosler.com**
October Country Muzzleloading **www.oct-country.com**
Ox-Yoke Originals Inc. **www.rmcoxyoke.com**
Pacific Rifle Co. **pacificrifle@aol.com**
Palmetto Arms **www.palmetto.it**
Pecatonica River **www.longrifles-pr.com**
Pietta **www.pietta.it**
Powerbelt Bullets **www.powerbeltbullets.com**
PR Bullets **www.prbullets.com**
Precision Rifle Dead Center Bullets **www.prbullet.com**
R.E. Davis Co. **www.redavlscompany.com**
Rightnour Mfg. Co. Inc. **www.rmcsports.com**
The Rifle Shop **trshoppe@aol.com**
Savage Arms, Inc. **www.savagearms.com**
Schuetzen Powder **www.schuetzenpowder.com**
TDC **www.tdcmfg.com**
Tennessee Valley Muzzleloading **www.avsia.com/tvm**
Thompson Center Arms **www.tcarms.com**
Tiger Hunt Stocks **www.gunstockwood.com**
Track of the Wolf **www.trackofthewolf.com**
Traditions Performance Muzzleloading
   www.traditionsfirearms.com
Vernon C. Davis & Co. **www.stonewallcreekoutfitters.com**

PUBLICATIONS, VIDEOS, AND CD'S

Arms and Military Press **www.skennerton.com**
A&J Arms Booksellers **www.ajarmsbooksellers.com**
American Cop **www.americancopmagazine.com**
American Firearms Industry **www.amfire.com**
American Gunsmiting Institute **www.americangunsmith.com**
American Handgunner **www.americanhandgunner.com**
American Hunter **www.nrapublications.org**
American Pioneer Video **www.americanpioneervideo.com**
American Rifleman **www.nrapublications.org**
American Shooting Magazine **www.americanshooting.com**
Backwoodsman **www.backwoodsmanmag.com**
Black Powder Cartridge News **www.blackpowderspg.com**
Blue Book Publications **www.bluebookinc.com**
Combat Handguns **www.combathandguns.com**
Concealed Carry **www.uscca.us**
Cornell Publications **www.cornellpubs.com**
Countrywide Press **www.countrysport.com**
Fouling Shot **www.castbulletassoc.org**
George Shumway Publisher **www.shumwaypublisher.com**
Gun Digest Magazine **www.gundigest.com**
Gun Digest Store **www.gundigeststore.com**
Gun Video **www.gunvideo.com**

GUNS Magazine www.gunsmagazine.com
Guns & Ammo www.gunsandammomag.com
Gun Mag www.thegunmag.com
Gun World www.gunworld.com
Harris Publications www.harrispublications.com
Hendon Publishing Co. www.hendonpub.com
Heritage Gun Books www.gunbooks.com
Krause Publications www.krause.com
Law and Order www.hendonpub.com
Man at Arms www.manatarmsbooks.com
Muzzle Blasts www.nmlra.org
Muzzleloader www.muzzleloadermag.com
On-Target Productions www.ontargetdvds.com
Outdoor Channel www.outdoorchannel.com
Paladin Press www.paladin-press.com
Police and Security News www.policeandsecuritynews.com
Police Magazine www.policemag.com
Precision Shooting www.precisionshooting.com
Primitive Arts Video www.primitiveartsvideo.com
Pursuit Channel www.pursuitchannel.com
Rifle and Handloader Magazines www.riflemagazine.com
Rifle Shooter Magazine www.rifleshootermag.com
Safari Press Inc. www.safaripress.com
Schiffer Publishing www.schifferbooks.com
Scurlock Publishing www.muzzleloadingmag.com
Shoot! Magazine www.shootmagazine.com
Shooting Illustrated www.nrapublications.org
Shooting Industry www.shootingindustry.com
Shooting Times Magazine www.shootingtimes.com
Shooting Sports Retailer www.shootingsportsretailer.com
Shooting Sports USA www.nrapublications.org
Shotgun News www.shotgunnews.com
Shotgun Report www.shotgunreport.com
Shotgun Sports Magazine www.shotgun-sports.com
Single Shot Exchange www.singleshotexchange.com
Single Shot Rifle Journal www.assra.com
Small Arms Review www.smallarmsreview.com
Small Caliber News www.smallcaliber.com
Sporting Clays Web Edition www.sportingclays.net
Sports Afield www.sportsafield.com
Sportsman's Channel www.sportsmanschannel.com
Sportsmen on Film www.sportsmenonfilm.com
SWAT Magazine www.swatmag.com
The Sixgunner www.sskindustries.com
Varmint Hunter www.varminthunter.org
VSP Publications www.gunbooks.com

RELOADING TOOLS

21st Century Shooting www.21stcenturyshooting.com
Ballisti-Cast Mfg. www.ballisti-cast.com
Battenfeld Technologies www.battenfeldtechnologies.com

Bruno Shooters Supply www.brunoshooters.com
Buffalo Arms www.buffaloarms.com
CabineTree www.castingstuff.com
Camdex, Inc. www.camdexloader.com
CH/4D Custom Die www.ch4d.com
Colorado Shooters Supply www.hochmoulds.com
Corbin Mfg & Supply Co. www.corbins.com
Dillon Precision www.dillonprecision.com
Forster Precision Products www.forsterproducts.com
Gracey Trimmer www.matchprep.com
GSI International, Inc. www.gsiinternational.com
Hanned Line www.hanned.com
Harrell's Precision www.harrellsprec.com
Holland's Shooting Supplies www.hollandgun.com
Hornady www.hornady.com
Hunter's Supply, Inc. wwwhunters-supply.com
Huntington Reloading Products www.huntingtons.com
J & J Products Co. www.jandjproducts.com
Lead Bullet Technology www.lbtmoulds.com
Lee Precision, Inc. www.leeprecision.com
Littleton Shotmaker www.leadshotmaker.com
Load Data www.loaddata.com
Lyman www.lymanproducts.com
Magma Engineering www.magmaengr.com
Mayville Engineering Co. (MEC) www.mecreloaders.com
Midway www.midwayusa.com
Moly-Bore www.molybore.com
Montana Bullet Works www.montanabulletworks.com
MTM Case-Guard www.mtmcase-guard.com
NECO www.neconos.com
NEI www.neihandtools.com
Neil Jones Custom Products www.neiljones.com
New Lachaussee SA www.lachaussee.com
Ponsness/Warren www.reloaders.com
Precision Reloading www.precisionreloading.com
Quinetics Corp. www.quineticscorp.com
Ranger Products
   www.pages.prodigy.com/rangerproducts.home.htm
Rapine Bullet Mold Mfg Co. www.bulletmoulds.com
RCBS www.rcbs.com
Redding Reloading Equipment www.redding-reloading.com
Russ Haydon's Shooting Supplies www.shooters-supply.com
Sinclair Int'l Inc. www.sinclairintl.com
Stoney Point Products Inc www.stoneypoint.com
Thompson Bullet Lube Co. www.thompsonbulletlube.com
Vickerman Seating Die www.castingstuff.com
Wilson (L.E. Wilson) www.lewilson.com

RESTS— BENCH, PORTABLE, ATTACHABLE

Accu-Shot www.accu-shot.com
Battenfeld Technolgies www.battenfeldtechnologies.com

Bench Master **www.bench-master.com**
B-Square **www.b-square.com**
Bullshooter **www.bullshooterssightingin.com**
Center Mass, Inc. **www.centermassinc.com**
Desert Mountain Mfg. **www.benchmasterusa.com**
DOA Tactical **www.doatactical.com**
Harris Engineering Inc. **www.harrisbipods**
KFS Industries **www.versapod.com**
Kramer Designs **www.snipepod.com**
L Thomas Rifle Support **www.ltsupport.com**
Level-Lok **www.levellok.com**
Midway **www.midwayusa.com**
Predator Sniper Styx **www.predatorsniperstyx.com**
Ransom International **www.ransom-intl.com**
Rotary Gun Racks **www.gun-racks.com**
R.W. Hart **www.rwhart.com**
Sinclair Intl, Inc. **www.sinclairintl.com**
Shooters Ridge **www.shooterridge.com**
Shooting Bench USA **www.shootingbenchusa.com**
Stoney Point Products **www.stoneypoint.com**
Target Shooting **www.targetshooting.com**
Varmint Masters **www.varmintmasters.com**
Versa-Pod **www.versa-pod.com**

SCOPES, SIGHTS, MOUNTS AND ACCESSORIES

Accumount **www.accumounts.com**
Accusight **www.accusight.com**
ADCO **www.shooters.com/adco/index/htm**
Adirondack Opitcs **www.adkoptics.oom**
Advantage Tactical Sight **www.advantagetactical.com**
Aimpoint **www.aimpoint.com**
Aim Shot, Inc. **www.aimshot.com**
Aimtech Mount Systems **www.aimtech-mounts.com**
Alpec Team, Inc. **www.alpec.com**
Alpen Outdoor Corp. **www.alpenoutdoor.com**
American Technologies Network, Corp. **www.atncorp.com**
AmeriGlo, LLC **www.ameriglo.net**
ArmaLaser **www.armalaser.com**
Armament Technology, Inc. **www.armament.com**
ARMS **www.armsmounts.com**
Aro-Tek, Ltd. **www.arotek.com**
ATN **www.atncorp.com**
Badger Ordnance **www.badgerordnance.com**
Barrett **www.barrettrifles.com**
Beamshot-Quarton **www.beamshot.com**
BKL Technologies, Inc. **www.bkltech.com**
BSA Optics **www.bsaoptics.com**
B-Square Company, Inc. **www.b-square.com**
Burris **www.burrisoptics.com**
Bushnell Performance Optics **www.bushnell.com**
Carl Zeiss Optical Inc. **www.zeiss.com**

Carson Optical **www.carson-optical.com**
CenterPoint Precision Optics **www.centerpointoptics.com**
Centurion Arms **www.centurionarms.com**
C-More Systems **www.cmore.com**
Conetrol Scope Mounts **www.conetrol.com**
Crimson Trace Corp. **www.crimsontrace.com**
Crossfire L.L.C. **www.amfire.com/hesco/html**
Cylinder & Slide, Inc. **www.cylinderslide.com**
DCG Supply Inc. **www.dcgsupply.com**
D&L Sports **www.dlsports.com**
DuraSight Scope Mounting Systems **www.durasight.com**
EasyHit, Inc. **www.easyhit.com**
EAW **www.eaw.de**
Elcan Optical Technologies
    www.armament.com, www.elcan.com
Electro-Optics Technologies **www.eotechmdc.com/holosight**
EoTech **www.eotech-inc.com**
Europtik Ltd. **www.europtik.com**
Fujinon, Inc. **www.fujinon.com**
GG&G **www.w.gggaz.com**
Gilmore Sports **www.gilmoresports.com**
Gradient Lens Corp. **www.gradientlens.com**
Hakko Co. Ltd. **www.hakko-japan.co.jp**
Hahn Precision **www.hahn-precision.com**
Hesco **www.hescosights.com**
Hi-Lux Optics **www.hi-luxoptics.com**
Hitek Industries **www.nightsight.com**
HIVIZ **www.hivizsights.com**
Hollands Shooters Supply **www.hollandguns.com**
Horus Vision **www.horusvision.com**
Hunter Co. **www.huntercompany.com**
Huskemaw **Optics www.huskemawoptics.com**
Innovative Weaponry, Inc. **www.ptnightsights.com**
Insight **www.insighttechnology.com**
Ironsighter Co. **www.ironsighter.com**
ITT Night Vision **www.ittnightvision.com**
Kahles **www.kahlesoptik.com**
KenSight **www.kensight.com**
Knight's Armament **www.knightarmco.com**
Kowa Optimed Inc. **www.kowascope.com**
Kwik-Site Co. **www.kwiksitecorp.com**
L-3 Communications-Eotech **www.l-3com.com**
LaRue Tactical **www.laruetactical.com**
Laser Bore Sight **www.laserboresight.com**
Laser Devices Inc. **www.laserdevices.com**
Lasergrips **www.crimsontrace.com**
LaserLyte **www.laserlytesights.com**
LaserMax Inc. **www.lasermax.com**
Laser Products **www.surefire.com**
Leapers, Inc. **www.leapers.com**
Leatherwood **www.hi-luxoptics.com**
Legacy Sports **www.legacysports.com**

Leica Camera Inc. **www.leica-camera.com/usa**
Leupold **www.leupold.com**
Lewis Machine & Tool **www.lewismachine.net**
LightForce/NightForce USA **www.nightforcescopes.com**
Lyman **www.lymanproducts.com**
Lynx **www.b-square.com**
Matech **www.adcofirearms.com**
Marble's Gunsights **www.marblearms.com**
MDS, Inc. **www.mdsincorporated.com**
Meopta **www.meopta.com**
Meprolight **www.kimberamerica.com**
Micro Sight Co. **www.microsight.com**
Millett **www.millettsights.com**
Miniature Machine Corp. **www.mmcsight.com**
Mini-Scout-Mount **www.amegaranges.com**
Minox USA **www.minox.com**
Montana Vintage Arms **www.montanavintagearms.com**
Moro Vision **www.morovision.com**
Mounting Solutions Plus **www.mountsplus.com**
NAIT **www.nait.com**
Newcon International Ltd. **www.newcon-optik.com**
Night Force Optics **www.nightforcescopes.com**
Night Optics USA, Inc. **www.nightoptics.com**
Night Owl Optics **www.nightowloptics.com**
Night Vision Systems **www.nightvisionsystems.com**
Nikon Inc. **www.nikonhunting.com**
Nitehog **www.nitehog.com**
North American Integrated Technologies **www.nait.com**
O.K. Weber, Inc. **www.okweber.com**
Optolyth-Optic **www.optolyth.de**
Osprey Optics **www.osprey-optics.com**
Pentax Corp. **www.pentaxlightseeker.com**
Precision Reflex **www.pri-mounts.com**
Pride Fowler, Inc. **www.rapidreticle.com**
Premier Reticles **www.premierreticles.com**
Redfield **www.redfield.com**
Rifle Electronics **www.theriflecam.com**
R&R Int'l Trade **www.nightoptic.com**
Schmidt & Bender **www.schmidt-bender.com**
Scopecoat **www.scopecoat.com**
Scopelevel **www.scopelevel.com**
Scout Scopes **www.scoutscopes.com**
Segway Industries **www.segway-industries.com**
Shepherd Scope Ltd. **www.shepherdscopes.com**
SIG Sauer **www.sigsauer.com**
Sightmark **www.sightmark.com**
Sightron **www.sightron.com**
Simmons **www.simmonsoptics.com**
S&K **www.scopemounts.com**
Springfield Armory **www.springfield-armory.com**
Steiner **www.steiner-binoculars.com**
Sun Optics USA **www.sunopticsusa.com**

Sure-Fire **www.surefire.com**
Swarovski/Kahles **www.swarovskioptik.com**
SWATSCOPE **www.swatscope.com**
Swift Optics **www.swiftoptics.com**
Talley Mfg. Co. **www.talleyrings.com**
Target Scope Blocks-Steve Earl Products
   Steven.m.earle@comcast.net
Tasco **www.tascosales.com**
Tech Sights **www.tech-sights.com**
Trijicon Inc. **www.trijicon.com**
Troy Industries **www.troyind.com**
Truglo Inc. **www.truglo.com**
Ultimak **www.ultimak.com**
UltraDot **www.ultradotusa.com**
Unertl Optical Co. **www.unertlopics.com**
US Night Vision **www.usnightvision.com**
U.S. Optics Technologies Inc. **www.usoptics.com**
Valdada-IOR Optics **www.valdada.com**
Viridian Green Laser Sights **www.viridiangreenlaser.com**
Vortex Optics **www.vortexoptics.com**
Warne **www.warnescopemounts.com**
Weaver Mounts **www.weaver-mounts.com**
Weaver Scopes **www.weaveroptics.com**
Wilcox Industries Corp **www.wilcoxind.com**
Williams Gun Sight Co. **www.williamsgunsight.com**
Wilson Combat **www.wilsoncombat.com**
XS Sight Systems **www.xssights.com**
Zeiss **www.zeiss.com**

SHOOTING ORGANIZATIONS, SCHOOLS AND RANGES

Amateur Trapshooting Assoc. **www.shootata.com**
American Custom Gunmakers Guild **www.acgg.org**
American Gunsmithing Institute **www.americangunsmith.com**
American Pistolsmiths Guild **www.americanpistol.com**
American Shooting Sports Council **www.assc.com**
American Single Shot Rifle Assoc. **www.assra.com**
American Snipers **www.americansnipers.org**
Antique Shooting Tool Collector's Assoc.
   www.oldshootingtools.org
Armed Citizens Alliance **www.armedcitizensalliance.com**
Assoc. of Firearm & Tool Mark Examiners **www.afte.org**
BATFE **www.atf.ustreas.gov**
Blackwater Lodge and Training Center
   www.blackwaterlodge.com
Boone and Crockett Club **www.boone-crockett.org**
Buckmasters, Ltd. **www.buckmasters.com**
Cast Bullet Assoc. **www.castbulletassoc.org**
Citizens Committee for the Right to Keep & Bear Arms **www.ccrkba.org**
Civilian Marksmanship Program **www.odcmp.com**
Colorado School of Trades **www.gunsmith-school.com**

Contemporary Longrifle Assoc. **www.longrifle.com**
Cylinder & Slide Pistolsmithing Schools
   www.cylinder-slide.com
Ducks Unlimited **www.ducks.org**
4-H Shooting Sports Program **www.4-hshootingsports.org**
Fifty Caliber Institute **www.fiftycal.org**
Fifty Caliber Shooters Assoc. **www.fcsa.org**
Firearms Coalition **www.nealknox.com**
Front Sight Firearms Training Institute **www.frontsight.com**
German Gun Collectors Assoc. **www.germanguns.com**
Gun Clubs **www.associatedgunclubs.org**
Gun Owners' Action League **www.goal.org**
Gun Owners of America **www.gunowners.org**
Gun Trade Asssoc. Ltd. **www.brucepub.com/gta**
Gunsite Training Center, Inc. **www.gunsite.com**
Handgun Hunters International **www.sskindustries.com**
Hunting and Shooting Sports Heritage Fund
   www.huntandshoot.org
I.C.E. Training **www.icetraining.com**
IWA **www.iwa.info**
International Defense Pistol Assoc. **www.idpa.com**
International Handgun Metallic Silhouette Assoc.
   www.ihmsa.org
International Hunter Education Assoc. **www.ihea.com**
Int'l Law Enforcement Educators and Trainers Assoc.
   www.ileeta.com
International Single Shot Assoc. **www.issa-schuetzen.org**
Jews for the Preservation of Firearms Ownership **www.jpfo.org**
Mule Deer Foundation **www.muledeer.org**
Muzzle Loaders Assoc. of Great Britain **www.mlagb.com**
National 4-H Shooting Sports **www.4-hshootingsports.org**
National Association of Sporting Goods Wholesalers
   www.nasgw.org
National Benchrest Shooters Assoc. **www.benchrest.com**
National Defense Industrial Assoc. **www.ndia.org**
National Firearms Act Trade & Collectors Assoc. **www.nfatca.org**
National Muzzle Loading Rifle Assoc. **www.nmlra.org**
National Reloading Manufacturers Assoc
   www.reload-nrma.com
National Rifle Assoc. **www.nra.org**
National Rifle Assoc. ILA **www.nraila.org**
National Shooting Sports Foundation **www.nssf.org**
National Skeet Shooters Association **www.nssa-nsca.com**
National Sporting Clays Assoc. **www.nssa-nsca.com**
National Tactial Officers Assoc. **www.ntoa.org**
National Wild Turkey Federation **www.nwtf.com**
NICS/FBI **www.fbi.gov**
North American Hunting Club **www.huntingclub.com**
Order of Edwardian Gunners (Vintagers) **www.vintagers.org**
Outdoor Industry Foundation
   www.outdoorindustryfoundation.org
Pennsylvania Gunsmith School **www.pagunsmith.com**

Piedmont Community College **www.piedmontcc.edu**
Quail Unlimited **www.qu.org**
Remington Society of America **www.remingtonsociety.com**
Right To Keep and Bear Arms **www.rkba.org**
Rocky Mountain Elk Foundation **www.rmef.org**
SAAMI **www.saami.org**
Safari Club International **www.scifirstforhunters.org**
Scholastic Clay Target Program **www.nssf.org/sctp**
Scholastic Shooting Sports Foundation **www.shootsctp.com**
Second Amendment Foundation **www.saf.org**
Second Amendment Sisters **www.2asisters.org**
Shooting for Women Alliance
   www.shootingforwomenalliance.com
Shooting Ranges Int'l **www.shootingranges.com**
Sig Sauer Academy **www.sigsauer.com**
Single Action Shooting Society **www.sassnet.com**
Steel Challenge Pistol Tournament **www.steelchallenge.com**
Students for Second Amendment **www.sf2a.org**
Sturgis Economic Development Corp.
   www.sturgisdevelopment.com
Suarez Training **www.warriortalk.com**
S&W Academy and Nat'l Firearms Trng. Center
   www.sw-academy.com
Tactical Defense Institute **www.tdiohio.com**
Tactical Life **www.tactical-life.com**
Ted Nugent United Sportsmen of America **www.tnugent.com**
Thunder Ranch **www.thunderranchinc.com**
Trapshooters Homepage **www.trapshooters.com**
Trinidad State Junior College **www.trinidadstate.edu**
United Sportsmen's Youth Foundation **www.usyf.com**
Universal Shooting Academy
   www.universalshootingacademy.com
U.S. Concealed Carry Association **www.uscca.us**
U.S. Int'l Clay Target Assoc. **www.usicta.com**
U.S. Fish and Wildlife Service **www.fws.gov**
U.S. Practical Shooting Assoc. **www.uspsa.org**
U.S. Sportsmen's Alliance **www.ussportsmen.org**
USA Shooting **www.usashooting.com**
Varmint Hunter's Assoc. **www.varminthunter.org**
Winchester Arms Collectors Assoc.
   www.winchestercollector.com
Women Hunters **www.womanhunters.com**
Women's Shooting Sports Foundation **www.wssf.org**

STOCKS, GRIPS, FOREARMS

10/22 Fun Gun **www.1022fungun.com**
Ace, Ltd. **www.aceltdusa.com**
Advanced Technology **www.atigunstocks.com**
Battenfeld Technologies **www.battenfeldtechnologies.com**
Bell & Carlson, Inc. **www.bellandcarlson.com**
Boyd's Gunstock Industries, Inc. **www.boydgunstocks.com**

Butler Creek Corp www.butler-creek.com
Cadex www.vikingtactics.com
Calico Hardwoods, Inc. www.calicohardwoods.com
Choate Machine www.riflestock.com
Command Arms www.commandarms.com
C-More Systems www.cmore.com
D&L Sports www.dlsports.com
Duo Stock www.duostock.com
E.Arthur Brown Co. www.eabco.com
Elk Ridge Stocks
    www.reamerrentals.com/elk_ridge.htm
FAB Tactical www.botachtactical.com
Fajen www.battenfeldtechnologies.com
Falcon Ergo Grip www.ergogrips.com
Great American Gunstocks www.gunstocks.com
Grip Pod www.grippod.com
Gun Stock Blanks www.gunstockblanks.com
Herrett's Stocks www.herrettstocks.com
High Tech Specialties www.bansnersrifle.com/hightech
Hogue Grips www.getgrip.com
Holland's Shooting Supplies www.hollandgun.com
Knight's Mfg. Co. wwwknightarmco.com
Knoxx Industries www.blackhawk.com
KZ Tactical www.kleyzion.com
LaRue Tactical www.laruetactical.com
Laser Stock www.laserstock.com
Lewis Machine & Tool www.lewismachine.net
Lone Wolf www.lonewolfriflestocks.com
Magpul www.magpul.com
Manners Compostie Stocks www.mannerstocks.com
McMillan Fiberglass Stocks www.mcmfamily.com
MPI Stocks www.mpistocks.com
Precision Gun Works www.precisiongunstocks.com
Ram-Line www.outers-guncare.com
Richards Microfit Stocks www.rifle-stocks.com
Rimrock Rifle Stock www.rimrockstocks.com
Royal Arms Gunstocks www.imt.net/~royalarms
S&K Industries www.sandkgunstocks.com
Speedfeed www.safariland.com
TacStar/Pachmayr www.tacstar.com
Tango Down www.tangodown.com
TAPCO www.tapco.com
Slide Fire www.slidefire.com
Stocky's www.newriflestocks.com
Surefire www.surefire.com
Tiger-Hunt Curly Maple Gunstocks
    www.gunstockwood.com
UTG Pro www.leapers.com
Vltor www.vltor.com
Wenig Custom Gunstocks Inc. www.wenig.com
Wilcox Industries www.wilcoxind.com
Yankee Hill www.yhm.net

TARGETS AND RANGE EQUIPMENT

Action Target Co. www.actiontarget.com
Advanced Interactive Systems www.ais-sim.com
Advanced Training Systems www.atsusa.biz
Alco Target www.alcotarget.com
Arntzen Targets www.arntzentargets.com
Birchwood Casey www.birchwoodcasey.com
Bullet Proof Electronics www.thesnipertarget.com
Caswell Meggitt Defense Systems www.mds-caswell.com
Champion Traps & Targets www.championtarget.com
Custom Metal Products www.custommetalprod.com
Handloader/Victory Targets www.targetshandloader.com
Just Shoot Me Products www.ballistictec.com
Laser Shot www.lasershot.com
MGM Targets www.mgmtargets.com
Mountain Plains Industries www.targetshandloader.com
MTM Products www.mtmcase-gard.com
National Muzzleloading Rifle Assoc. www.nmlra.org
National Target Co. www.nationaltarget.com
Newbold Target Systems www.newboldtargets.com
PJL Targets www.pjltargets.com
Porta Target, Inc. www.portatarget.com
Range Management Services Inc. www.casewellintl.com
Range Systems www.shootingrangeproducts.com
Reactive Target Systems Inc. chrts@primenet.com
Rolling Steel Targets www.rollingsteeltargets.com
Savage Range Systems www.savagerangesystems.com
ShatterBlast Targets www.daisy.com
Super Trap Bullet Containment Systems www.supertrap.com
Thompson Target Technology www.thompsontarget.com
Tombstone Tactical Targets www.tttargets.com
Unique Tek www.uniquetek.com
Visible Impact Targets www.crosman.com
White Flyer www.whiteflyer.com

TRAP AND SKEET SHOOTING EQUIPMENT AND ACCESSORIES

Atlas Trap Co www.atlastraps.com
uto-Sporter Industries www.auto-sporter.com
10X Products Group www.10Xwear.com
Claymaster Traps www.claymaster.com
Do-All Traps, Inc. www.doalloutdoors.com
Laporte USA www.laporte-shooting.com
Outers www.blount.com
Promatic, Inc. www.promatic.biz
Trius Products Inc. www.triustraps.com
White Flyer www.whiteflyer.com

TRIGGERS

American Trigger Corp. www.americantrigger.com

Brownells **www.brownells.com**
Chip McCormick Corp. **www.chipmccormickcorp.com**
E-Z Pull Triggers **www.ezpulltriggerassist.com**
Geissele Automatics, LLC **www.ar15triggers.com**
Huber Concepts **www.huberconcepts.com**
Jard, Inc. **www.jardinc.com**
Jewell Triggers **(512)353-2999**
Kidd Triggers. **www.coolguyguns.com**
Shilen **www.shilen.com**
Spec-Tech Industries, Inc. **www.spec-tech-industries**
Timney Triggers **www.timneytrigger.com**
Williams Trigger Specialties **www.williamstriggers.com**

MAJOR SHOOTING WEB SITES AND LINKS

24 Hour Campfire **www.24hourcampfire.com**
Accurate Shooter **www.6mmbr.com**
Alphabetic Index of Links **www.gunsgunsguns.com**
Ammo Guide **www.ammoguide.com**
Auction Arms **www.auctionarms.com**
Benchrest Central **www.benchrest.com**
Big Game Hunt **www.biggamehunt.net**
Bullseye Pistol **www.bullseyepistol.com**
Firearms History **www.researchpress.co.uk/firearms**
Glock Talk **www.glocktalk.com**
Gun Broker Auctions **www.gunbroker.com**

Gun Industry **www.gunindustry.com**
Gun Blast **www.gunblast.com**
Gun Boards **www.gunboards.com**
GunsAmerica.com **www.gunsamerica.com**
Guns Unified Nationally Endorsing Dignity **www.guned.com**
Gun Shop Finder **www.gunshopfinder.com**
GUNS and Hunting **www.gunsandhunting.com**
Hunt and Shoot (NSSF) **www.huntandshoot.org**
Keep and Bear Arms **www.keepandbeararms.com**
Leverguns **www.leverguns.com**
Load Swap **www.loadswap.com**
Long Range Hunting **www.longrangehunting.com**
Outdoor Press Room **www.outdoorpressroom.com**
Real Guns **www.realguns.com**
Ruger Forum **www.rugerforum.com**
SavageShooters **www.savageshooters.com**
Shooters Forum **www.shootersforum.com**
Shotgun Sports Resource Guide **www.shotgunsports.com**
Shotgun World **www.shotgunworld.com**
Sixgunner **www.sixgunner.com**
Sniper's Hide **www.snipershide.com**
Sportsman's Web **www.sportsmansweb.com**
Surplus Rifles **www.surplusrifle.com**
Tactical-Life **www.tactical-life.com**
The Gun Room **www.doublegun.com**
Wing Shoooting USA **www.wingshootingusa.org**

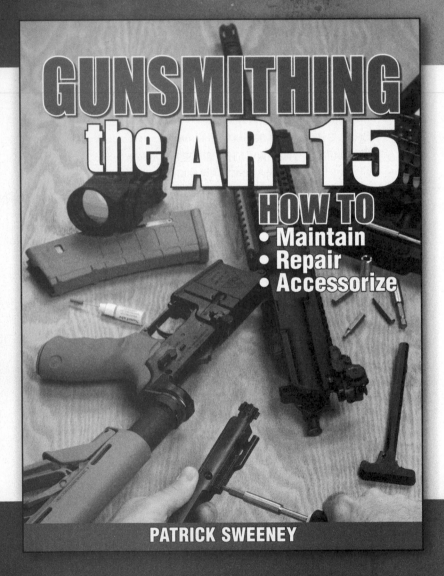

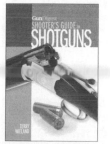

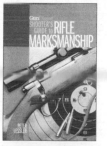

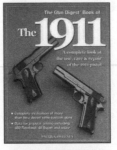
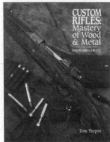
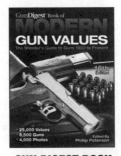
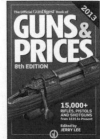

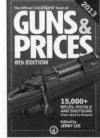

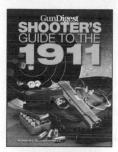
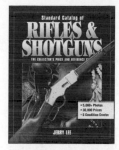

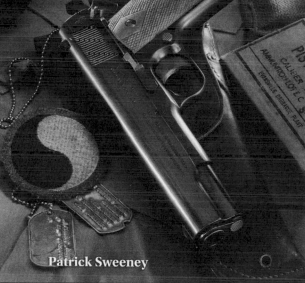

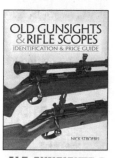
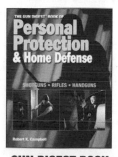

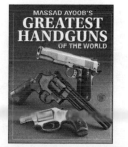
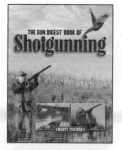

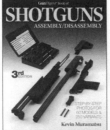
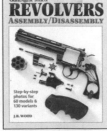

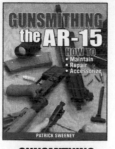

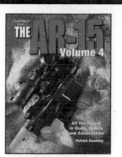

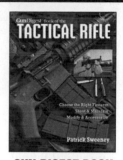
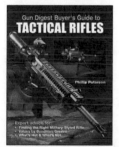
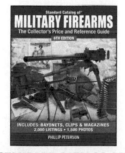

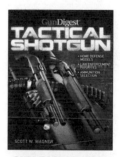
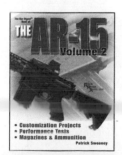

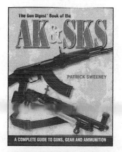

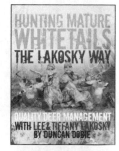

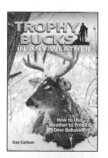

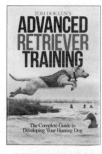

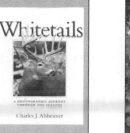

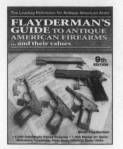

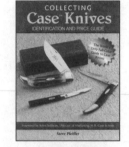
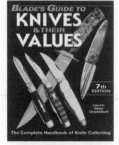

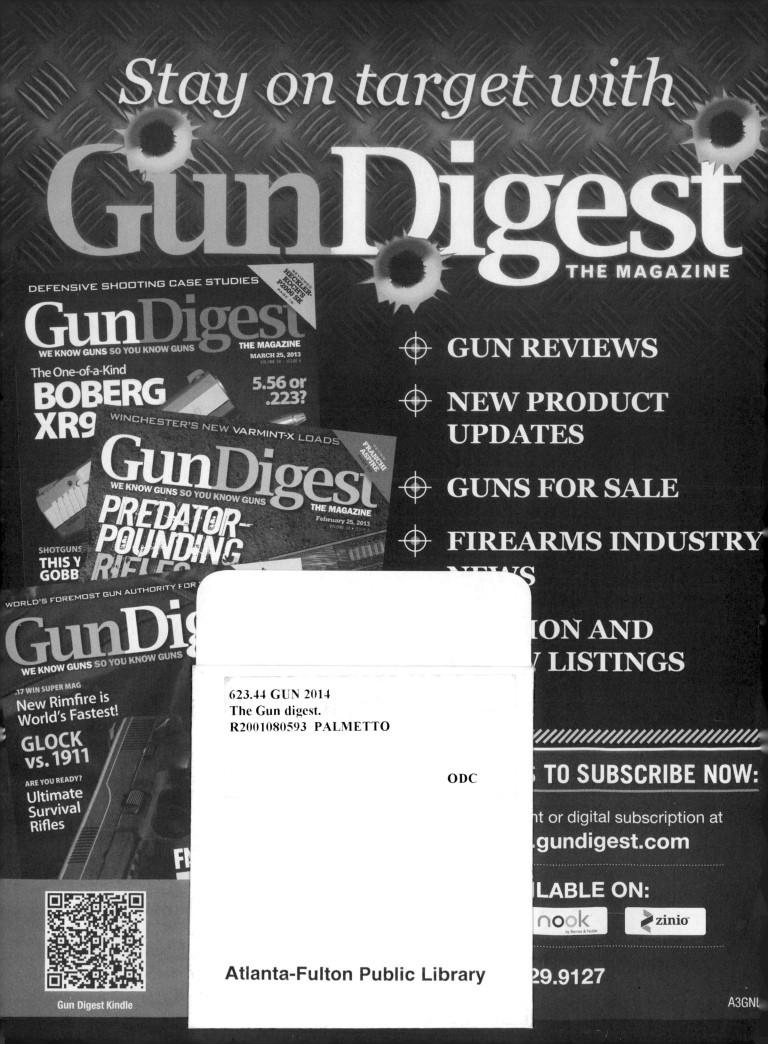